Also by Ron Powers

Tom and Huck Don't Live Here Anymore: Childhood and Murder in the Heart of America

The Man Who Flew the Memphis Belle: Memoir of a WWII Bomber Pilot (with Col. Robert Morgan, USAF, Ret.)

Flags of Our Fathers: Heroes of Iwo Jima (with James Bradley)

Dangerous Water: A Biography of the Boy Who Became Mark Twain

The Cruel Radiance: Notes of a Prosewriter in a Visual Age

Far From Home: Life and Loss in Two American Towns

The Beast, the Eunuch and the Glass-Eyed Child: Television in the Eighties and Beyond

White Town Drowsing: Journeys to Hannibal

Toot-Toot-Tootsie, Good-Bye

Face Value

The Newscasters: The News Business As Show Business

Mark Twain

A Life

Twain

RON POWERS

Free Press

New York London Toronto Sydney

*f*P
FREE PRESS
A Division of Simon & Schuster, Inc.
1230 Avenue of the Americas
New York, NY 10020

FREE PRESS and colophon are trademarks of Simon & Schuster, Inc.

For information about special discounts for bulk purchases,
please contact Simon & Schuster Special Sales at
1-800-456-6798 or business@simonandschuster.com

Designed by C. Linda Dingler

Manufactured in the United States of America

10   9   8   7   6   5   4   3   2   1

Library of Congress Cataloging-in-Publication Data
Powers, Ron.
  Mark Twain : a life / Ron Powers.
      p.   cm.
  Includes bibliographical references (p.   ) and index.
  1. Twain, Mark, 1835–1910.   2. Authors, American—19th century—
Biography.   3. Humorists, American—19th century—Biography.
4. Journalists—United States—Biography.   I. Title.

PS1331 .P69 2005
818'.409—dc22   2005048816
[B]

ISBN-13: 978-0-7432-4899-0
ISBN-10: 0-7432-4899-6

Picture Credits
All photos and illustrations courtesy of The Mark Twain Project, Berkeley, CA, ex-
cept the following: Archives and Special Collections, Vassar College Libraries: 3, 4, 36.
Beinecke Rare Book and Manuscript Library, The Yale Collection of American Litera-
ture: 41. First edition, *A Tramp Abroad,* courtesy of the Mark Twain Papers, The Ban-
croft Library: 34. Houghton Library, Harvard University: 30. Courtesy of the Mark
Twain Archive, Elmira College: 54. The Mark Twain Home Foundation, Hannibal,
MO: 46. The Mark Twain House & Museum, Hartford, CT: 21, 26, 32, 48. Nevada His-
torical Society: 5, 6. The Society of California Pioneers: 10. University of Missouri,
Photograph, 1873–1913, 1937–1954, n.d., Western Historical Manuscript Collection,
Columbia, MO: 47.

To Robert Hirst

The best friend Mark Twain has ever had
And his associate editors, past and present,
At the Mark Twain Project

Contents

Prologue   1

1: "Something at Once Awful and Sublime" (1835–39)   7
2: "The White Town, Drowsing . . ." (1839)   16
3: Of Words and the Word (1840–42)   25
4: The Hannibal Decade (1843–53)   32
5: Apprentice (1848–51)   45
6: Rambler (1852–53)   52
7: "So Far from Home . . ." (1853–56)   62
8: The Language of Water (1856–58)   74
9: Ranger (1858–61)   92
10: Washoe (1861–62)   101
11: A Journalistic Counterculture (1862–63)   110
12: "Mark Twain—More of Him" (1863)   118
13: *Code Duello* (1863–64)   129
14: A Villainous Backwoods Sketch (1864–65)   143
15: ". . . And I Began to Talk" (1865–66)   157
16: On the Road (1866–67)   165
17: Back East (1867)   175
18: "move—move—*Move!*" (1867)   187
19: Pilgrims and Sinners (1867)   197
20: In the Thrall of Mother Bear (October 1867–New Year's Day 1868)   217
21: "A Work *Humorously Inclined* . . ." (February–July 1868)   230
22: The Girl in the Miniature (July 1868–October 1868)   240

23: American Vandal (October–December 1868)   253
24: "Quite Worthy of the Best" (1869)   263
25: Fairyland (1870)   279
26: "My Hated Nom de Plume . . ." (1871)   293
27: Sociable Jimmy (1871–72)   306
28: The Lion of London (1872–73)   319
29: Gilded (1873–74)   335
30: Quarry Farm and Nook Farm (1874–75)   348
31: The Man in the Moon (1875)   366
32: "It Befell Yt One Did Breake Wind . . ." (1876)   382
33: God's Fool (1877)   398
34: Abroad Again (1878–79)   414
35: "A Personal Hatred for Humbug" (1880)   432
36: "A Powerful Good Time" (1881–82)   448
37: "All Right, Then . . ." (1882–83)   464
38: *The* American Novel (1884–85)   481
39: Roll Over, Lord Byron (1886–87)   505
40: "I Have Fed So Full on Sorrows . . ." (1887–90)   518
41: "We Are Skimming Along Like Paupers . . ." (1891–June 1893)   534
42: Savior (1893–94)   552
43: Thunder-Stroke (1895–96)   563
44: Exile and Return (1896–1900)   580
45: Sitting in Darkness (1900–1905)   599
Chapter the Last   618

Notes   629
Bibliography   683
Acknowledgments   691
Index   695

Notice

PERSONS failing to understand why I refer to my subject as "Sammy" in his childhood will be prosecuted; persons failing to understand why I call him "Sam" and "Clemens" in dealing with his personal life thereafter will be banished; persons failing to understand why I use "Mark Twain" when speaking of him as an author will be shot.

BY ORDER OF THE BIOGRAPHER
PER S.L.C.M.T., CHIEF OF ORDNANCE.

Now, trumpeter, for thy close,
Vouchsafe a higher strain than any yet;
Sing to my soul—renew its languishing faith and hope;
Rouse up my slow belief—give me some vision of the future . . .

—Walt Whitman, *Leaves of Grass*

Prologue

On a chilly mid-November afternoon in 1869, a small man with a deranged mop of curly red hair and a wide-swept red mustache sauntered among the pedestrians in the 100 block of Tremont Street in Boston. He was desperately out of place amid these men in their muttonchops and tailored Scottish tweeds, and these women in their jeweled bonnets and brilliant brocade-lined shawls. Tremont bisected the epicenter of American cultural authority and power, announced by the Park Street Church across the thoroughfare and the sweep of the Boston Common behind it; the Georgian residential rooftops lining the far side of the Common; the wrought-iron balconies of Colonnade Row; the great domed neoclassical State House that commanded this elegant realm from the top of nearby Beacon Hill.

It was not just his clothing, black and drably functional, that marked him as an interloper (he owned a smart white collar and swallowtails, but they were reserved for other purposes). It was his gait, a curious rocking, rolling shamble, conspicuously unurbane—the physical equivalent of a hinterland drawl, which he also possessed.

None of this seemed to faze him. At 124 Tremont Street, a dignified little four-story town house recently converted to an office building, he pushed open the door and let himself inside. He stepped past the heavy tome-scented shelves that filled the commercial shop at street level, the bookstore of Ticknor & Fields, and climbed the staircase leading to the second floor.

The stranger was—well, that depended. Born Samuel Langhorne Clemens in "the almost invisible village of Florida, Monroe County, Missouri,"[1] he had taken to calling himself "Mark Twain" as a newspaperman in Nevada and California, after experimenting with such other pen names as Rambler, W. Epaminondas Adrastus Blab, Thomas Jefferson Snodgrass, and Josh. Lately he had been called "The Wild Humorist of the Pacific Slope" and "The Moralist of the Main," tags given him by his friend Charles Henry Webb.

Ambiguous as he was, he was penetrating an enclave quite certain of its

1

own place in the universe. Only Harvard College itself could have fetched him closer to the core of the young nation's most important intellectual forces. Ticknor & Fields comprised not only a bookseller but a prestigious publishing house whose authors, many of whom lived nearby, commanded the first ranks of America's emerging literature: the "Sage of Concord," Ralph Waldo Emerson; the originator of the "Brahmin" aesthetic, Oliver Wendell Holmes; Nathaniel Hawthorne; Henry Wadsworth Longfellow; Harriet Beecher Stowe; Henry David Thoreau.

The visitor's destination was an extension of this authoritative domain: the tiny editorial office of the *Atlantic Monthly,* a literary, cultural, and political magazine whose views, taste, and diction were supplied by the same New England literary aristocracy, and which was distributed to the nation (or at least to some thirty thousand of its citizens) as the highest cultural standard. The *Atlantic* had been founded twelve years earlier by a group of progressive-minded intellectuals, with the support of Emerson, Holmes, Longfellow, Stowe, and others. Harvard professor James Russell Lowell was appointed its first editor.

After knocking on the office door, the red-haired man was greeted by a robust figure enwreathed in flowing curls of hair and beard: the magazine's editor, James T. Fields, publishing partner of William D. Ticknor, and the *Atlantic*'s editor since 1861. Fields was a self-educated businessman from New Hampshire with a genuine love of writers and ideas. He had guided the magazine through the Civil War years as the principled voice of abolitionist sentiment. But perhaps even more importantly, he had retained its emphasis on poetry, criticism, essays, and fiction—an ongoing affirmation of civilization's values in those morbid and despairing times. Now Fields, who had a whimsical taste for eccentrics, swept a pile of handwritten manuscripts from a sofa opposite an open fireplace, and the two men chatted for a few moments.

But it was not Fields for whom Clemens had made this unannounced visit. He had come to meet Fields's young assistant, a moist, bookish fellow by the name of William Dean Howells. Howells had written a favorable, albeit unsigned, notice of Clemens's—make that Mark Twain's—new book for the *Atlantic*'s current issue. The *Atlantic* did not usually deign to review books of this ilk: a humorous travelogue peddled door-to-door by common "subscription" salesmen, titled *The Innocents Abroad, or The New Pilgrim's Progress.* Now, a few days after reading the review, Clemens had arrived in Boston in the course of a lecture tour that, along with the book, was implanting his Western reputation in the formidable circles of the East, and not a moment too soon: he was a few days from turning thirty-four. Clemens knew that no other endorsement was as crucial as the *Atlantic*'s: Howells had handed him an entrée into literary legitimacy. He couldn't help but be curious about who would do such a thing, and why. He'd ascertained the reviewer's identity a few days earlier in Pittsburgh, through a cousin of Howells's whom he'd met there. And now here he was in Boston to look this man in his face and shake his hand.

To the thirty-two-year-old Howells, rising to his height of 5 feet 4 inches from behind his desk, the visitor chatting with his boss was nothing less than— well, what? Graphic? Bold? Shakespearean? ("Or, if his ghost will not suffer me the word," Howells later mused in print with typical fine-tuning, "then he was Baconian."[2]) The fastidious Howells had seldom laid eyes on such a swashbuckler. Discreet dark woolens draped his own plump frame, punctuated by black bow ties. He wore his hair plastered down and parted at midscalp. His own mustache drooped softly over his upper lip, its long, tapering points adding to his aspect of sleepy introspection. His first impulse upon seeing this apparition labeled "Mark Twain," as he later recalled, was of alarm for the proprieties violated. Specifically, he shuddered at what "droll comment" might have been in the mind of his employer Mr. Fields as the two men of letters contemplated the disheveled, blazing-eyed figure in front of them. (And this was one of Clemens's good-grooming days. Others who had encountered him at this stage of his life remembered him as "disreputable-looking," "seedy," even "sinister," and equipped with "an evil-smelling cigar butt.")

The book that Howells had praised was a daring choice for an *Atlantic* review, given that it lampooned much of what the magazine stood for. Exuberantly un-Eastern, impious, and unconcerned with moral improvement, it amounted to a genial pie in the face of the European classicism that still regulated the tone and values of the American intellectuals while they struggled to liberate their nation from it. *The Innocents Abroad* was Mark Twain's eyewitness account of a transatlantic excursion by some sixty-five reverential American tourists, from New York harbor to Old Europe and the Holy Land— the first successful organized "luxury cruise" in U.S. history. The idea for the voyage had been dreamed up by Henry Ward Beecher, the nationally renowned pastor of the Plymouth Congregational Church in Brooklyn. Beecher had conceived it as a way to finance his gathering of material for a biography of Jesus—the idea being, presumably, that the Gospels had preempted the market for such a work quite long enough. Beecher himself soon opted out of the journey, as did eventually a number of highly advertised celebrity-passengers including the Civil War hero William Tecumseh Sherman. Beecher left the expedition and its ship, the paddlewheel steamer *Quaker City,* in the care of a Plymouth Church Sunday-school teacher, one Captain Charles C. Duncan.

No Sunday-school teacher could have been prepared for the alcohol-reeking figure who showed up at the cruise's Wall Street booking office, introduced by his equally disheveled companion Edward H. House as "the Reverend Mark Twain," a Baptist minister who wondered whether Reverend Beecher would allow him to preach Baptist sermons en route to the Holy Land—and who returned the next day, sober, to book the passage under his real name and profession. This voyage was exactly the sort of caper Clemens had been looking for. A veteran of larky, outlandish newspapering exploits in the far West during the Civil War years, he had come back East a prudent year and a half after Appomattox to cash in on the postwar boom in popular journalism and literature—and his own nascent fame as a humorist and platform presence. After securing a berth on the ship, Clemens took steps to adjust his commission from the *Alta California* in San Francisco to pay for his passage in exchange for the letters he would send to the newspaper during the expedition. On his return, he contracted with the Hartford-based American Publishing Company, a subscription house run by Elisha Bliss, to expand the newspaper dispatches into a book.

The result was something previously unseen in the annals of travel literature, in literature of any kind. Fact-laden and reportorial along its narrative spine, heavily illustrated with woodcuts, the book did not hesitate to shift its tone unpredictably. It erupted frequently into playful comic riffs, as when Mark Twain "confessed" to a weeping spell inside the Church of the Holy Sepulchre in Jerusalem, when he came across the tomb of his beloved ancestor, Adam; and it unleashed wicked set-piece send-ups of Italian art, the biblical landscape, and the behavior of Mark Twain's fellow pilgrims aboard the *Quaker City*. As such, it figured to have about as much chance of delighting the dutiful, doubting Howells as an ash dropped into his lap from Clemens's ever-present cigar. But Howells had indeed given his sanction, at least tentatively. "There is an amount of pure human nature in the book that rarely gets into literature," he had written—an insight that bridged the gap between American "high" and popular prose writing. He added: "It is no business of ours to fix his rank among the humorists California has given us, but we think he is, in an entirely different way from all the others, quite worthy of the company of the best."[3]

Mark Twain's career prospects depended on what happened next. Everything in the nation, it then seemed, depended on what happened next. It was a charged moment in American history. At the end of 1869, the national trauma of the Civil War was replaced with new urgencies—competing new visions of the national future. The war's greatest hero sat in the White House, not knowing exactly what to do. The golden spike at Promontory Point in Utah finally linked the East Coast to the West by rail, collapsing distance and time, and erecting unimagined new structures of financial power. The Fifteenth Amendment gave former slaves the right to vote, and the risk of paying for the privilege with their lives. The city of New York was rising on an immigrant tide to challenge Boston as the arbiter of national aspirations.

It was, in short, exactly the sort of moment when a fugitive from one version of America, the nasty and brutish West, could intrude into the settled, exclusionary East and make a pitch for a piece of the action—provided that the fugitive observed the courtesies and deferred to the standards of Brahmin delicacy in manners and language. Sam Clemens was capable of such deference. He had also trampled, at some earlier time, on most of these considerations, and now he was about to lay waste one of the most tender. "When I read that review of yours," Howells recalled Clemens drawling, "I felt like the woman who was so glad her baby had come white." *

This audacious little joke set the animating tenor of the long Clemens-Howells friendship: Clemens goading Howells to imagine something beyond the borders of gentility and to laugh at it even as he squirmed; Howells stretching those borders to give it sanction. Howells must have heard a familiar voice under the surface of that vulgarism, as he had under the horseplay of *The Innocents Abroad*. It was the voice of a boy from Howells's own neck of the West; perhaps the improper boy Howells himself had wished he could be.

So Howells chuckled and let it pass, and the two shook hands and exchanged kind words and the hopes of meeting again. On that note of truant recognition began a symbiotic friendship of forty-one years' duration that would elevate both these men.

Sam Clemens was the greater beneficiary. He was not only reviewed in the *Atlantic;* by 1874 he was contributing to it, to great acclaim. *Life on the Mississippi*, his strange, fabulistic "travel" masterpiece of 1883, began as a series of essay-reminiscences in the magazine, encouraged and edited by this new-found friend. Howells's embrace helped propel the former steamboat pilot to status as *the* representative figure of his nation and his century, and bequeathed America a torrential literary voice more truly, more enduringly its own than any then existing or being conceived by the reigning gods of New England probity and taste.

Howells benefited as well. Mark Twain's rise to critical and popular stardom in his magazine ratified the editor's instincts for finding new, unorthodox writers in America and, later, Europe. Other native-born writers who emerged to prominence under his championing included Emily Dickinson, Sarah Orne Jewett, Frank Norris, and Stephen Crane. He later helped introduce such international figures as Ibsen, Zola, Pérez Galdós, Verga, and Tolstoy. As he moved from editing other people's works to writing his own—he completed more than a hundred books of fiction, poetry, travel essays, biography, reminiscence, criticism, and even dramatic plays—Howells seemed to take inspiration from his fellow Midwesterner. (The novelized memoir of his youth, *A Boy's Town Described*, published in 1890, contained strong echoes of *The Adventures of Tom Sawyer*.) At his best, Howells was considered a novelist on a par with his other great friend, Henry James. Though that level of esteem did not survive the 19th century, Howells finished his long life enjoying the sobriquet, "the Dean of American Letters."

Breaching the ranks of New England literary culture was Clemens's most important achievement (short of his actual works), and a signal liberating event in the country's imaginative history. His audacity, and Howells's accom-

---

* Mark Twain also used this joke in an 1872 letter commenting on Howells's review of *Roughing It*. But Howells delicately suggests in *My Mark Twain* that its first use was in this 1869 interview in Boston.

modation of it, may seem unremarkable to an America long since accustomed to the leveling of hierarchies, the demythifying of great artists and the complexities of their works, the triumph of careerism over apprenticeship to a tradition. In the slipstream of the Clemens-Howells creative bond, American literature ceased its labored imitation of European and Classical high discourse, and became a lean, blunt, vivid chronicle of American self-invention, from the yeasty perspective of the common man. Without Howells's friendship, Mark Twain might have flared for a while, a regional curiosity among many, and then faded, forgotten. On its legitimizing strength, he gained the foundation for international status as America's Shakespeare and struck a template for the nation's voice into the 20th century and beyond.

MARK TWAIN'S great achievement as the man who found a voice for his country has made him a challenge for his biographers. His words are quoted, yet he somehow lies hidden in plain sight—a giant on the historic landscape. He has been so thoroughly rearranged and reconstructed by a long succession of scholarly critics that the contours of an actual, textured human character have been obscured. And his voice, not to mention his humor, has gone missing from many of these analyses.

Twainian critical literature from 1920 onward has been dominated by theory, rather than interpretive portraiture. His biographers have tended to evoke him through the prism of Freudian psychoanalysis. In that way he is seen as an interesting, if not terribly self aware outpatient—a walking casebook of neuroses, unconscious tendencies, masks, and alternate identities. Important questions are inevitably excluded in this approach. What was it that bound Mark Twain and his half of the American 19th century so closely together? In what ways, and by what processes, did this man become, as those who knew him repeatedly claimed, *the* representative figure of his times? What liberating personal magnetism did he possess that moved his contemporaries to forgive him for traits and tendencies that biographers of a later time have found deplorable? What was it about his voice that satisfied American readers in ways that the New England founders of American literature could not? What is it about his writing—nearly all of it problematic, much of it mediocre, a healthy part of it unfinished, some of it simply awful—that continues to exercise the very scholars who expend so much energy trying to reduce him to their pet formulas and crusades?

The answers to these questions lie within Mark Twain as he lived, breathed, and wrote; within the preserved viewpoints of the people who knew him best, and in person; and within the annals of the American 19th century that he helped shape, and that he loved when he could find it in himself to love little else. The answers will remind us of who he was. And of who we are.

I

"Something at Once Awful and Sublime"

(1835–39)

T he prairie in its loneliness and peace: that was what came back to him toward the end of his life, after he had pulled the rug out from under all the literary nabobs, and fired off all his nubs and snappers, and sashayed through all the nations, and collected all his ceremonial gowns and degrees, and tweaked all the grinning presidents, and schmoozed all the newspaper reporters, and stuck it to all his enemies, and shocked all the librarians, and cried out all his midnight blasphemies, and buried most of his family. The prairie was what came back to him as he wrote in 1897—speaking, in his conceit, from the grave, and thus freely. He remembered what had mattered the most, the earliest. He thought not of the Mississippi River, which he encountered most fully later in his life, but of "a level great prairie which was covered with wild strawberry plants, vividly starred with prairie pinks, and walled in on all sides by forests"—a swatch of the great western carpet yet a decade from disfigurement by the grooves of the California gold rushers.[1] There his prodigious noticing had begun. His way of seeing and hearing things that changed America's way of seeing and hearing things.

It was there, as a boy, where his great font of visual images—"the multitudinous photographs one's mind takes," he later called them—began to form. He found enchantment in the way moonlight fell through the rafters of the slanting roof of his uncle's farmhouse into little squares on the floor of the stairway landing. He was struck by the darkness of his bedroom, packed with ghostly stillness. When he woke up by accident in that darkness, his forgotten sins came flocking out of the secret chambers of his memory.

But more powerful than the early images in his memory were the sounds: the crack of a watermelon split open, the rising and falling wail of a spinning wheel, the dismal hoo-hoo of the owl and the howl of the wolf, the crash of summer thunder. It was to the sounds that he had always assigned his deepest fantasies and fears. The spinning wheel "was the mournfulest of all sounds to me . . . and filled my atmosphere with the wandering spirits of the dead." [2] Animal wails were omens of death; the thunderclap was God's wrath over his sinfulness.

Of all the sounds, none had quite the lasting mimetic (or moral) effect on Sam Clemens as the sound of the human voice. And no human voices, save his own mother's, caught his imagination quite like those of the Negro slaves. Those voices spoke in a way different from the people in his family: quick, delicious, throbbing with urgencies half-named, half-encoded. They conjured mind-pictures: lightning bolts, apparitions from the spirit world, chariots swooping down from heaven, skies of blood, animals crying out. Adorned with tonal shifts and repetitions and the counterpointed rhythms of stridency and hush, the slave voices treated language as a cherished creature, to be passed around, partaken of, as well as simply heard. Clear as flowing water, and yet invested with deep currents of meaning that only the fellow speakers could fully understand.

He heard his first slave voices on the prairie before he turned four, and sought them out through the rest of his childhood and beyond. In Mark Twain's manuscript pages half a century later, these voices challenged the genteel paradigm that had sonorously governed the first epoch of indigenous American literature. They ushered in a replacement: gutbucket truth rooted in the solo riffs of the dispossessed—the advent of an American voice derived not from European aesthetics, but entirely from local improvisational sources, black and white. Mark Twain's baton began to mute the Anglican symphony, and strike up the rhythms of American jazz.

His capacity to transform commonplace spoken language into literature, like any artist's gift, remains beyond understanding. A contemporary's remark that "[h]e is the ordinary man—plus genius," probably comes as close as any theory. But his acute attentiveness to language, and some of his other distinguishing traits, can be traced in part to his precarious entry into the world.

Born two months premature, on November 30, 1835, in Florida, Missouri, Sam Clemens narrowly survived childbirth. His labyrinthine personality, subjected to endless analysis by 20th-century Freudians, has never been considered in the context of this difficult birth and his convalescence from it. As a toddler Sammy was sickly and underweight (his adult height reached only 5 feet 8½ inches). He was largely bedridden until his fourth year, and frail for the next three. "When I first saw him I could see no promise in him," his mother Jane admitted. Her frontier fatalism was more than matched by a visitor to the little house. Eyeing the shriveled form, the woman turned to Jane and blandly asked, "You don't expect to raise that babe, do you?" Jane said she would try. [3]

Premature babies are generally unable to sleep deeply and sometimes exist in a kind of dream world that is typical neither of the womb nor of a full-term infant's consciousness—a world of unstable borders between reality and the inner oceans of the mind. The subsuming of reality by dreams was among Mark Twain's signal literary preoccupations, and his writing—whether journalism, travel, memoir, or novel—moved between truth and fantasy with sometimes maddening unconcern.

Sammy grew into a sleepwalker, and his mother felt that he had the gift (or curse) of "second sight." He lived his life on the edges of self-control; he was quick to anger, hounded by guilt and anxiety, and subject to seismic shifts of mood.

Most importantly in terms of his art were the ways in which his senses were affected. The hyperacuity of his ear and his unusual retention of sounds (he never stopped performing the earliest songs and spirituals he heard, and as a mature writer he could reproduce entire blocks of spoken conversation) may have been a vestige of his fitful early months. Hearing develops more quickly in newborns than the sense of sight, especially with premature babies, who are more interested in voices than in other sounds. At any rate, no one expected Sammy to survive the winter. Frontier children routinely died from measles, mumps, smallpox, "bilious fever," malaria, spider bites, cholera, scarlet fever, polio, diphtheria, or teething complications; and, if not from those, then often from the "cures" applied to them. Still, Jane did her best for Sammy. Always alert for omens, Jane may have looked for hopeful signs that he would survive, such as the widely discussed comet named for its British discoverer, Edmund Halley, which neared the earth in its seventy-five-year cycle in the late autumn of his arrival.* The child hung on.

He was in Missouri because his father Marshall's luck had run out more than once. The austere self-educated lawyer, named after John Marshall, had left the Virginia Piedmont first for Kentucky, as a boy, after his father died; then to Tennessee, as a married man, when his farm failed. He began buying up land, amassing deeds to more than seventy thousand acres of virgin yellow-pine acreage, for a total outlay of only a little more than $400. The land was thought to be rich in copper, and Marshall envisioned a day when railroads would haul timber from his forests, building him and his heirs an immense fortune.

But the Tennessee land investment only triggered the Clemens family's decline into poverty. It remained unsold for decades, a financial failure that haunted Marshall Clemens and his children, and fueled Sam Clemens's lifelong anxiety over money.

---

* It has been starchily pointed out that Mark Twain's famous boast that he came in with Halley's Comet and would go out with it must not be taken too literally. The comet's visibility would have peaked in New England for example, on October 16, about six weeks before his birth. The celestial shuttle had not yet peaked by the date of Mark Twain's death (April 21, 1910). Of course Mark Twain never claimed that his birth and death coincided with maximum visibility of the comet, only that he and it came and left together, which they indubitably did. Some folks just don't know how to spot a celestial messenger when they see one.

While waiting for the land-buyers to show up, Marshall opened a general store at Jamestown, which also served as his family's living quarters. Daughter Pamela (sometimes spelled "Pamelia" and always pronounced that way) was born there in 1827. Another arrival, Pleasant Hannibal, followed either one or two years later; he survived only three weeks, although there are no precise records of his life or death even in the family Bible. Margaret came along in 1830. Marshall became overwhelmed by the pressures to provide for his growing family, as the income from his tiny store proved insufficient. His chronic headaches grew more severe, and he began to dull them, or try to, with Cook's pills and other "notions," some of which were 50 percent alcohol. (He seems never to have drunk to excess.) In 1831 he uprooted his family once again, this time to a clearing in the Tennessee woods at the confluence of three mountain streams. He built another cabin, and tried to make a go of it as a farmer/store clerk/postmaster until the financial crash of 1834 wiped out his credit.

Finally, in 1835, he relocated one more time, to Missouri, when his wife's brother-in-law sent a rapturous letter from there. It was a letter whose promised-land spirit Mark Twain would fold in to his great comic character "Colonel" Eschol (later "Beriah" and "Mulberry") Sellers in *The Gilded Age:*

Come right along to Missouri! Don't wait and worry about a good price but sell out for whatever you can get, and come along, or you might be too late . . . It's the grandest country—the loveliest land—the purest atmosphere—I can't describe it; no pen could do it justice . . . I've got the biggest scheme on earth . . . Mum's the word—don't whisper—keep yourself to yourself. You'll see! Come!—rush!—hurry!—don't wait for anything![4]

The model for this letter was written by John Quarles, who had followed his father-in-law, Sam's maternal grandfather, to the flyspeck hamlet of Florida in 1835. (For some reason, the founders of new towns in Missouri indulged a naming whimsy not quite so prominent in other states. As the century went on, Missouri filled up with towns bearing such names as Neck, Torch, Climax Springs, Conception Junction [in Nodaway County], Joy and Romance, Useful, Peculiar, Impo and Ink, Lupus, Zebra, Chloride and Cooter, Advance, Half Way, Fair Play, Pumpkin Center, Nonesuch, Monkey Run, Gerald, and Low Wassie.)

Once arrived, while Sammy hovered between life and death, his father accepted John Quarles's offer to become a co-proprietor of his general store, which allowed him to begin investing for a future powered by the Industrial Revolution. More opportunity for his luck to run out.

Slater mills had long since replaced the household spinning wheel. Coupled with the cotton gin, the mills revived the cotton economy of the South, and reversed a trend toward abolition of slavery in the planter states. Annual cotton production leapt from 3,000 bales in 1790 to 178,000 bales by 1810.

The slave trade reached a higher volume than in any period in its four-hundred-year history, fueled by the avarice of Northern merchants.

Steam suddenly drove just about everything with moving parts. The nation's quiet inland waterways, accustomed to flatboats and scows, were disturbed by paddle wheels: in 1807, a young portrait artist and submarine fantasist named Robert Fulton got his paddle-wheel-driven steamboat the *Clermont* chugging up the Hudson River.

ALMOST BEFORE it began, the steamboat era saw the advent of its vanquisher. The railroad, a horse-powered convenience of the English collieries, was a novelty import in America until Christmas Day of 1830, when a contraption named "The Best Friend of Charleston" chugged six miles along a South Carolina roadbed to launch the era of the steam-powered locomotive. (It later blew up.) By 1850 there would be nine thousand miles of roadbed on the continent, with new construction surging ahead.

A new form of capitalism arose to bring out the economic yield of these new marvels. It ran on frenzied speculation fed by visionary organizers and owners, who structured new national and even international markets for the accelerating flow of goods. These new captains of industry enriched themselves as they increased the national wealth. Their excesses triggered a credit-fueled financial panic in 1837 that damaged the national economy for years.

Marshall Clemens noted and coveted these triumphs of machine-driven wealth as they tumbled westward, paying less heed to the plight of the enslaved subculture on which it all still depended. His son would absorb himself in both ends of this spectrum, and make a different kind of capital of what he saw there.

SAMMY'S HEALTH slowly improved. He grew aware of his appearance, and asked for pure white dresses as soon as he could speak. When he realized that he had no tail, unlike some of his fellow beings around the house, he complained about it: "The dog has a tail bebind, the cat has a tail bebind, and I haven't any tail bebind at all at all."[5] His uncle John made a tail of paper and pinned it onto his dress.

When he gained the strength to leave the small family house on his own, he found himself in a lonely prairie hamlet. Florida comprised fifty-odd low-slung wooden houses and barns, embraced by two forks of a small river, the Salt. In the spring of 1839, John Quarles expanded Sammy's world by opening a 230-acre farm on the prairie land adjoining Florida, and deploying a few slaves to make it run.* It was among these otherwise forgotten tutors who

---

* In 1897 Clemens wrote that the farm had "fifteen or twenty negroes." In an interview with a reporter from the *New York World* in 1891, he had enlarged the farm to a "plantation," and recalled "forty or fifty Negroes." But research by the Hannibal historian Terrell Dempsey has confirmed the smaller number—suggesting that there were, at most, eleven slaves, assuming the records are accurate and complete.

worked the fields and then gathered in their cabins at night that Sam Clemens's self-education as a literary artist began.

The slave cabins were on the far side of an orchard, beyond a stand of hickory and walnut trees that screened the Quarles's double-log farmhouse. Sammy had no inkling of where the black people in the little cabins had come from, or how they had got there. But he knew that they were different, profoundly so. He knew it from their voices. He would remember two of them in particular. One was a bedridden old woman with a bald spot, who was known as Aunt Hannah. Sammy and his cousins had heard from the slave children that Aunt Hannah was a thousand years old. She had known Moses, and Pharaoh, the wicked slave master of Egypt. The horror of watching Pharaoh drown while chasing Moses across the Red Sea had given her a bald spot. Aunt Hannah prayed a lot, and when she wasn't praying she terrified the children with tales of witches.

The other great presence was Uncle Dan'l, "a middle-aged slave whose head was the best one in the negro-quarter," Mark Twain wrote in 1897, "whose sympathies were wide and warm, and whose heart was honest and simple and knew no guile." [6] To the children, black and white, who milled around the premises he was "a faithful and affectionate good friend, ally and adviser." [7] Mark Twain recalled the "privileged nights" as a child when he and an assortment of cousins and slave children clustered at Dan'l's feet in his cabin to hear him tell his thunderous stories.

Uncle Dan, called "Dann" by John Quarles, who emancipated him in 1855, was 6 feet tall, of a black complexion, and still in his early forties when Sammy knew him. [8] He is presumed to be the father of most, or all, of the black children in the quarters, including Mary, one of Sammy's closest playmates and a child of "weird distorted superstitions," as Sammy's cousin Tabitha Quarles recalled in her old age. [9] Only his voice survives him—but what an artifact that is. Uncle Dan'l's voice, amplifying itself in geometric progressions as the American centuries marched on, is the first trumpet note of the first great jazz composition in American literature: the voice of *Huckleberry Finn*'s Jim. As Mark Twain said, late in life:

He has served me well, these many, many years. I have not seen him for more than half a century, and yet spiritually I have had his welcome company a good part of that time, and have staged him in books under his own name and as "Jim," and carted him all around . . . It was on the farm that I got my strong liking for his race and my appreciation of certain of its fine qualities. [10]

He was not the only inspiration for Mark Twain's achievements with black dialect. Many others would lend their distinctive phrasings and points of view: There was the family's slave Jennie. There was a household slave boy named Sandy, whose constant singing got on Sammy's nerves until Jane pointed out to him that singing was probably the child's way of not thinking about the mother taken from him by an owner.[11] There was the young, black servant Mark Twain encountered in 1872 at the Paris House hotel in Paris, Illinois, and whose great burst of rhythmic dialect he recorded and later published as "Sociable Jimmy." There was Mary Ann Cord, a cook for Samuel Clemens's sister-in-law at Elmira, New York, in the 1870s, whose own story of separation burned itself word by word into his brain.[12] There was George Griffin, an ex-slave and beloved family butler during the Clemenses' Hartford years. Finally, the writer had recourse to a storehouse of popular literature that distilled and parodied African-American dialect. (A few of Jim's early speeches in *Adventures of Huckleberry Finn* betray the set-piece archness of blackface minstrel sidemen.)

But something about Uncle Dan'l struck Twain as sole, incomparable. Perhaps it was the way he stirred up Sammy's famous bad nerves with the ghost stories he told in his cabin—stories that Mark Twain would repeat in public and private all his life:

> I can hear Uncle Dan'l telling the immortal tales which Uncle Remus Harris was to . . . charm the world with, by and by; and I can feel again the creepy joy which quivered through me when the time for the ghost story of the "Golden Arm" was reached—and the sense of regret, too, which came over me, for it was always the last story of the evening, and there was nothing between it and the unwelcome bed.[13]

"The Golden Arm" was an old European ghost story that lent itself well to African-American patois. It concerned the "monsus mean" man who robs his wife's grave to steal her prosthetic arm of solid gold. This does not sit well with the dead wife. Her ghost stalks the husband through the snowy night with the harrowing incantation, "Whoooo got my golllllden arrrrm?" Uncle Dan'l always climaxed the tale with a freighted pause, while the children on the floor writhed in juicy anticipation. Then he would thrust his finger at a small victim, evoking a spasm as he roared: *"You've* got it!"

Sammy was addicted to "The Golden Arm." The theme of supernaturally imposed guilt no doubt spoke to him, but his fascination lay mainly in Dan'l's mesmeric style of telling. The timing. The rhythm. The dialect. That *pause.* No other single phrase, gesture, or image better illustrates the impact of his farm companions on his young psyche. As Mark Twain, he built his wildly popular oratorical style largely on the foundation of that pause. As for the story itself, he couldn't stop telling it. He performed it for lecture audiences, houseguests, anyone, every chance he had, for the rest of his life.

While the boy was inspired by the voices in his backyard, his father continued to work at the general store, and dreamed of amassing land. Land was cheap in these years; $1.25 an acre if bought at a certain bulk, as the U.S. government sold off the Louisiana Purchase for settlement and speculation—

some 38 million acres between 1835 and 1837. Nearly every dollar that Marshall earned from the store went toward real estate. He secured a 120-acre tract, then 80 acres, then another 40.

In 1836 Marshall bought a fairly substantial house on the south side of Main Street, from Jane's father, Benjamin Lampton. A year later, he bought a larger house on the tract he'd bought earlier, actually two one-room cabins under a common roof. For the second time in his career he became a judge in fact as well as in title: of the Monroe County Court, in November 1837. As his land holdings increased, he became festooned with chairmanships: the Salt River Navigation Company, the Florida & Paris Railroad commission, the board of trustees of the proposed Florida Academy. On paper, at least, Marshall Clemens was the Jefferson of northeastern Missouri.

Marshall joined other self-invented captains of industry who were arising from one-horse villages throughout the interior. They formed consortiums, printed prospectuses, and overloaded their burgs with grandiloquent names: Herculaneum. Palmyra. Kingdom City. An all-but-nonexistent hamlet on the Mississippi shore, Marion City, was ballyhooed as "the future metropolis of Missouri." Charles Dickens used it as a setting in *Martin Chuzzlewit.* Eventually it sank under floodwaters.

Sammy looked at his father with the same focused intensity that he trained on every object of his fascination. The attention was one-sided. Marshall held himself aloof from his children, except for his oldest son, Orion, whom he recruited at age ten to help out in the general store. He also refused to show any affection for Jane in front of the children, or anyone else. Sammy drew little notice from anyone save Jane. (She may have preferred her children to her husband; she had married him as a spiteful act against another suitor who had infuriated her by a tactless gesture. Jane remained in love with her suitor's memory for the rest of her long life.)

Withdrawn, irascible, given to pranks that could border on the mean-spirited, the thin red-haired Sammy lingered at the borders of activity, escaping notice, but noticing.

Sammy's scrutiny would confer on "the Judge" the renown, in fiction, that eluded him in fact. Mark Twain found many surrogates for John Marshall Clemens in his books. Nearly all were brooding, somewhat gothic misfits haunted by their lost status as Virginia gentlemen. They ranged from roman à clef (the land-burdened Squire Hawkins who dies in Missouri exile in *The Gilded Age*), through indulgent satire (the comically imposing Judge Thatcher in *The Adventures of Tom Sawyer*) through the chilling (the icily honorable duelist, Judge York Driscoll, in *Pudd'nhead Wilson*).

In one of his unfinished fiction manuscripts, "Simon Wheeler, Detective," the writer transports the father of his memory onto the page in iron-plated strokes. "Judge Griswold" is a displaced old-fashioned Virginian. He evokes a whiff of Mary Shelley's Frankenstein: tall, spare, with a long, thin, smooth "intellectual" face, "long, black hair that . . . was kept to the rear by his ears as one keeps curtains back by brackets." He has "an eagle's beak and an eagle's eye." He is emotionless, a churchgoing nonbeliever. Unfortunately for Marshall, none of these characteristics were offset by good fortune.

THE CRACKS in Marshall's grand schemes began to reappear early in 1838. Within two months of his new judgeship he endured the public humiliation of being abandoned by his brother-in-law and business partner, John Quarles. Quarles not only severed his ties in the store ownership with John, he underlined his displeasure by marching across the street and opening up a competing shop.

Later that year, Henry, the last of the Clemens's seven children, was born. Sammy was sixth in line, after Orion, Pamela, Pleasant Hannibal (who died in infancy), Margaret, and Benjamin. After Henry's birth, Marshall watched in despair as hope receded for Florida's date with destiny. His navigation company dissolved under the indifference of the state legislature. The railroad and academy initiatives dangled in limbo. A crushing truth grew ever clearer: Marshall had picked the wrong hamlet, missing the right one by ten miles: a village equipped with the regulation-grandiose name of Paris. Paris was the county seat, and it boasted a racetrack. As Paris's fortunes grew, Florida looked more and more like a backwater. Marshall gradually came to the sickening realization that he would have to sell his house and land, uprooting his family, and start over. Yet again.

2

"The White Town, Drowsing . . ."

(1839)

W hat is an Englishman?" Mark Twain asked himself in an 1883 notebook
entry. "A person who does things because they have been done before."
Then he asked, "What is an American (or difference between 'em)" and
replied, "A person who does things because they *haven't* been done before." [1]
By the close of the 1830s, the new republic was fitfully suspended somewhere
between those two definitions. Politically independent from Great Britain for
nearly sixty years, economically vigorous despite blunders in the banking system, America still lacked an ethos: an inventory of distinctive national ideas in
art, music, literature, religion, or learning comparable to the accumulated
pedagogy of Europe.

Some elements of America's rise to "refinement" were simply acknowledgments of Old World good sense. Full-body bathing, never de rigueur during the Colonial period, finally became commonplace in the cities, and
gained acceptance in the rest of the country. Fashionable families adopted the
European custom of eating food with a fork, instead of balancing it on the tips
of their knives. New England men shaved their faces clean and cropped their
hair close about their skulls, in the virtuous Roman style. On the frontier, they
let their hair grow long and flowing, but still took a razor to their cheeks. Cultivated Americans went wild over phrenology, and sipped on sarsaparilla, and
dined on chicken fricassee. They used ketchup as a medicinal cure.

A jackleg homegrown folk culture had started to emerge, to be sure. The
Fourth of July became the nation's premier holiday. Wild West shows and wild
animal shows toured the land, with Indians hopping around "authentically"

16

and impresarios in gladiator suits shoving their arms into lions' mouths, and beating them with crowbars if they bit. (Accused of cruelty, the showmen invoked the Bible, a document equally in vogue for keeping slaves in line.) White pop entertainment launched its long, slumming flirtation with Negro style and idiom. In the 1830s, the actor Thomas "Daddy" Rice smeared burnt cork on his face and pranced around in various cities, as the addled, ditty-dancing slave/buffoon "Jim Crow." In Rice's crude strut lay the origins of minstrelsy.

The Christian faith as defined by Europe and Scotland came in for a little nativist tweaking. In the '30s, the Second Great Awakening swept the country, melting icy Calvinism with the hot breath of American jump-to-Jesus rapture. Passionate, prophetic, evangelical, and focused on the Second Coming, it ushered the faithful out of their somber Puritan pews and into the head-shaking, talking-in-tongues ecstasies of the camp meeting—or, as it was known in west-central New York, near the fashionable town of Elmira, the "tent revival."

But it was in the development of a native literature that America found itself most whipsawed by the competing pulls of tradition and radical innovation. By 1839, the first great generation of American men of letters had established its authority in New England. Powerful intellectuals whose prowess extended into science, medicine, the law, and social theory, they honored Harvard College's two-hundred-year tradition of moral value achieved through the discipline of scholarship and rhetoric, even as they rebelled against its orthodoxies. Their radical Christian theology was influenced by Eastern philosophy: the Hindu *Vishnu Sarma,* the Persian *Desatir,* the writings of Confucius, and the sayings of Buddha. It rejected chilly Calvinism, calling instead for a sunnier, liberating faith extracted from the divinity within the personal soul. The New England Transcendentalists felt obliged to bestow the soul-enhancing benefits of eloquence, transcendence, and politeness on the new nation, ready or not. They proposed building a perfect society on the scaffolding of golden sentences.

The patron of these new secular saints, Ralph Waldo Emerson, unveiled his groundbreaking Transcendentalist vision in two speeches at Harvard. In 1837, Emerson gave his "American Scholar" lecture to the Phi Beta Kappa Society, calling for the common man to free himself from the orthodoxies of dead books, of colleges and institutions, and discover true knowledge within his own instincts and experiences. "We will walk on our own feet," he famously concluded; "we will work with our own hands; we will speak our own minds . . . A nation of men will for the first time exist, because each believes himself inspired by the Divine Soul which also inspires all men." [2]

A year later, at Harvard's Divinity School, the former clergyman laid out similar contours for a new, deinstitutionalized mode of worship. Rejecting denominational Christianity, he suggested that divinity permeated the daily world, and that man's challenge was to look into himself for the religious impulse that awaited expression. The professors of Harvard expressed their reaction to these sentiments by ostracizing Emerson for thirty years.

No 19TH-CENTURY figure better exemplified the worship of the Eastern Literary Man than a self-made intellectual from the West named William Dean Howells.

Howells would trace his awakening to the night that a Literary Man from the East descended on his Ohio hometown in 1860, when he was twenty-two. The eminence was Bayard Taylor, a poet and adventurer whose books of travel made him one of the best-known authors of his day. Taylor had traveled to Europe in 1844 as a teenager, seeking the sacred ground of Goethe, Byron, Dante, and Milton. He wrote travel letters for the *Saturday Evening Post* and the *United States Gazette* to support himself. The book that resulted from these dispatches, *Views A-Foot,* cemented his reputation. Through the '50s, Taylor turned out books about his sojourns in California, the Holy Land, Asia Minor, Central Africa, India, Sicily, and Spain. A widely circulated illustration depicted him looking fearless in an Arab burnoose and turban. Now here he was in Columbus, Ohio.

Howells crashed Taylor's post-lecture reception. "Heaven knows how I got through the evening," he wrote in his old age. "I do not think I opened my mouth to address him a word; it was as much as I could do to sit and look at him, while he tranquilly smoked, and chatted with our host, and quaffed the beer which we had very good in the West. I longed to tell him how much I liked his poems, which we used to get by heart in those days . . ."[3] A year later, Howells would make his own literary pilgrimage, to Boston. Anticipating Sam Clemens by nine years, Howells planned to drop in on James Russell Lowell at the *Atlantic* and thank him for printing some of his poems. The great man "had even written me a little note about them, which I wore next to my heart in my breast pocket till I almost wore it out."[4]

Lowell received the young visitor graciously in spite of his congenital Puritan frostiness. Howells was mesmerized by Lowell's beautiful eyes and by his general "Christ-look." When the visit ended, Lowell even escorted him "across-lots" toward North Avenue until the pair came to a fence, which Lowell, caught up in the spirit of manly camaraderie, essayed to vault. He succeeded on the third try.

The visit cracked open a brilliant future for Howells. Lowell invited him to dinner a few days later in an upstairs room at the Parker House, a haven for writers, "at the old-fashioned Boston hour of two."[5] Howells was delightedly shocked to discover that the other guests would be Oliver Wendell Holmes and James T. Fields. As coffee and cognac were served at the end of a four-hour feast, Dr. Holmes smiled at the young man, then remarked to Lowell, "Well, James, this is something like the Apostolic succession; this is the laying on of hands." The implication was unmistakable: William Dean Howells, the printer's son late of Martins Ferry and Columbus, Ohio, had been selected as

heir apparent to the editorship of America's premier literary magazine. Howells would join the magazine as an assistant editor in 1866 and succeed Fields
as editor in 1871. His influence over American literature for the remainder of
the 19th century would be unrivaled.

THE NEW England Brahmins may have reigned as the high-Anglo literary
voice of America, but they did not have the field to themselves. A shadow voice
emerged from down in the buckskin-and-cottonfield regions of the country—
the "Southwest," as it was known then, or the South, as it would call itself in a
bloody time yet to come. No lofty bouquets to Soul and Nature here; this
strain was rough, illicit—and funny: the dark twin of the Boston school. Its
purpose was not aesthetic, but political: to defend, by ruthless satire, the interests of the region's monied classes against a rising tide of populism.

The genre originated in newspapers throughout the South. It spread to
books. It took the form of grotesquely comic sketches and tales. The main
characters enacted the Southern gentry's worst nightmare, pollution of the
aristocracy by the backwoods rabble. They were a gothic assortment: violent,
coarse, drunken; they were confidence men, brutish adolescents, addled
Bible-thumpers. Their names gave fair warning: Sut Lovingood, Simon
Suggs, Ransey Sniffle, Flan Sucker. They brawled, boozed, leered, tricked,
lusted, and eye-gouged their way through story after story. Their exploits
fanned the economic and class anxieties that were widening the rift between
North and South in the quarter-century leading up to the Civil War. The authors of the so-called "Southwestern humor" tales were not usually writers by
calling, though many of them proved gifted within the bare-knuckle conceits
of their genre. They were politically engaged newspaper publishers, doctors,
lawyers—men who supported the aristocracy and the reactionary politicians
who kept things nicely stratified.

A pair of stylistic devices—two contrasting "voices"—saved these tales
from being merely disgusting, and allowed readers to be entertained. The
first voice was that of the ruffians themselves. Coarse, ungrammatical, thickly
vernacular, rendered in clunky phonetic spelling, it was the seductively comic
voice of the id. "I jist lent him a slatharin calamity," recalls Sut Lovingood
about a fight he'd once picked for no particular reason,

rite whar his nose commenced a sproutin frum atween his eyes, wif a ruff rock about
the size ove a goose aig. Hit fotch 'im! . . . I jumped hed fust through, atween his belly
an' the pole; my heft broke his holt, an' we cum to the ground a- fitin . . . the fust thing
I did, was tu shut my jaws ontu a mouthful ove his steak, ni ontu the place wher yer foot
itches to go when yu ar in kickin distance ove a fop . . . I thot ove a box ove matches
what I hed in my pocket, so I foch the whole boxful a rake ontu the gravil, an' stuffed
em all a-blazin inter one ove the pockets in his coat-tail . . . I no'd he'd soon show
strong signs ove wantin tu go. So the fust big rare he fotch arter the fire reached his
hide, I jist let my mouth fly open—so—an' *he went!* his hole tail in a blaze![6]

The second voice in these stories was the antithesis of the first. This was the smooth, grammatical, cool, and subtly disdainful voice of the "teller" within the story: the suave gentleman, no doubt a Southern Whig exactly like the reader, who begins the sketch by engaging in conversation with Suggs or Sniffle or Lovingood, and elicits the rough tale that forms the great middle of the piece. This supercilious voice provides the story's indispensable "frame," the point-of-view space that narrator and reader share, in an unspoken but obviously disapproving alliance against the lowlife telling the story. As it gained popularity throughout the Southwest, attracting imitators and recycling itself through the pages of a hundred local weeklies, the "frame story" accomplished its political work of hardening gentrified public opinion against the white-trash underclass. But it accomplished a contradictory and unintended effect as well.

The Suggs/Sniffle/Lovingood "voice" transcended its narrow political agenda. It made people laugh, not just in derision at the grotesques who slouched through the stories, but in recognition of parts of the human condition. It offered a compendium of folk customs—horse races, revivals, shooting matches, courtship rituals, quilting bees. It noted the clothes people wore and the food they ate. And with blithe equal-opportunity malice, it lampooned a whole universe of American types: the preacher, the Yankee peddler, the old wife, the pompous merchant, the rough but morally sensate youth.

What Southwestern frame humor lacked was legitimacy. No one had transplanted its rich vernacular energy or its gleeful grassroots realism into stories of deeper moral complexity. The New England arbiters of enlightenment would not allow these muddy boots inside the foyer. It remained a regional entertainment, its universal power awaiting the maturity of a small boy on the Missouri prairie.

That boy's father, still reeling from the Panic of 1837, saw a notice in the February 27, 1839, edition of a small paper called *Peake's Commercial Advertiser.* Property was available in a larger and growing village, called Hannibal, some forty miles to the northeast, on the banks of a great river. A great river! A town on the rise! Here at last was a can't-miss opportunity! Marshall contacted the seller, one Big Ira Stout, and began trying to scrape together the purchase price. But before the Clemenses left Florida, Jane and Marshall's nine-year-old daughter, Margaret, died on August 17, 1839, after suffering from an attack of "bilious fever."

Jane, who had already lost one baby and was struggling to keep another child alive, went hysterical. Her wailing and invocations of the paranormal world were observed by her children. Orion, then fourteen, swore later that he witnessed an eerie gesture from little Sammy in the early phase of Margaret's illness: as Orion sat beside his sister's bed one evening, Sammy came floating into the room, fast asleep. He placed his hands on Margaret's blanket and fidgeted with it for a few moments, then drifted off again.

Sammy's actions, real or imagined, conformed to a ritual enshrined in Kentucky superstition: a gesture of second sight known as "plucking the coverlet" of someone who was soon to die. After Margaret succumbed several days later, Jane became convinced that Sammy possessed psychic power. For all his later worldliness and rejections of belief in a Christian god, Mark Twain retained similar suspicions. In later years he would experiment in communicating with his dead brother Henry through psychics.

Had the Clemenses understood the actual origins of Margaret's affliction, they would have perceived an omen rooted in human, not paranormal affairs. "Bilious fever"—yellow fever—was a terrifyingly common frontier disease whose sources were murky. A viral infection that attacks the liver, it remains untreatable to this day, although there are now preventive vaccines. A Philadelphia doctor in 1798, groping for explanations for a recent epidemic of the fever in that city, noticed that it had broken out shortly after a ship, transporting slaves to America from the West Indies, docked and released the "foul air" stored up in its hold.

Years later, a fuller understanding emerged. It wasn't the "foul air" itself that transmitted the disease, but what lived in that air: a mosquito, native to the rain forests of central and coastal Africa, the regions in which the slave traders did most of their harvesting. The mosquito was a hardy traveler. Margaret Clemens was likely killed by the same Peculiar Institution that had helped attract her father to Florida.

I n   N o v e m b e r of that year, a couple of weeks before Sammy's fourth birthday, Marshall Clemens completed his plans. He negotiated a land deal with Ira Stout in Hannibal: he would sell Stout, for $3,000, more than 160 acres of his land holdings around Florida. In return, Stout would sell Clemens a 9,000-square-foot city block, for $7,000. Marshall recovered $2,000 of his capital a few days later, when he sold Stout an additional 326 Florida acres.

Hannibal, chartered as a town by the state just that spring, had 1,000 citizens. Marshall and Jane gathered their possessions (including Jenny, the last of their slaves), and their children: Orion, 14; Pamela, 12; Benjamin, 7; Sam; and Henry, aged 16 months.

The family's first lodging in Hannibal was the Virginia House, a rickety wood-frame structure on Marshall's new block of property a few dozen yards from the Mississippi riverbank. The Virginia House was a hotel, technically speaking, and Marshall hoped to draw revenue from its guests. His family occupied the second floor while, on the first, he established yet another grocery and dry-goods store. The problem was that at the time of the Clemenses' arrival, Hannibal was neither a tourist mecca nor a national crossroads. It certainly didn't need another general store. The action lay in sawmilling and hog slaughtering. Three mills processed local timber into boards for building permanent houses to replace log cabins. Hogs jostled dogs for primacy on the dirt streets. The hogs were driven by farmers to the pair of new pork-packing plants in town. Their hides ended up at the nearby tanyard, where they were cured for processing into shoes, boots, and saddles.

While Jane set up housekeeping, Marshall invested $2,000, on credit, toward purchase of foodstuffs and dry goods from a string of wholesalers in St. Louis, 120 miles down the river. He installed Orion behind the counter. If Marshall had overlooked any possible danger of success, his hiring of Orion made things airtight. As he grew more desperate, Marshall borrowed money from his wife's relatives. Still, nothing worked. The new town was shaping up as just another stop on a winding trail of failure.

MEANWHILE, SAMMY took stock of his new surroundings. He saw a different realm entirely. He saw a heavenly place—as he later wrote—for a boy. There was so much, after the torpor of Florida, to excite his mind: the bustle of a town under construction; gable-roofed cottages, shops, and stables taking shape under the whine of sawmill blades and the percussion of hammer on nail. The clanging from the blacksmiths' forges, the pig squeals, and the loud voices of the men in the riverfront bars. All of it was contained in a tidy little square of municipal plotting, with five streets parallel to the river, ending with Main Street nearest to the water's edge. The Virginia House stood at Hill and Main, just yards from the shoreline.

The river meant everything to the town. It carried away tobacco, hemp, pork, and whiskey, and brought back cash. It offered a continuing vaudeville of floating humanity: the solitary canoeists—trappers, Indians—gliding past the town on the tide; the raftsmen and flatboatmen and the keelboatmen. Mark Twain could never stop describing the Mississippi as seen through Sammy's eyes. "The hungry Mississippi . . . astonished the children beyond measure," he wrote in his first long work of fiction. "Its mile-breadth of water seemed an ocean to them . . . and the vague riband of trees on the further shore, the verge of a continent which surely none but they had ever seen before."[7]

Nothing compared to the featured attraction. First the deep coughing of the engines from perhaps a mile distant. Then a series of whistle blasts that echoed off the hillsides. Then the emergence from behind the bluff of the towering white emissary from Somewhere most unmistakably Else: first the prow of the three-tiered superstructure, the thirty-foot smokestacks pumping plumes of soot into the air; the high pilothouse and a figure at the knobbed wheel, staring ahead through the unglassed window; and then the rest of the boat's curving three-hundred-foot length, festooned with fluttering banners, pennants, the American flag; the boat's name written in bright decorative script across the paddle-wheel casing to break the whiteness.

If the steamboat docked at the levee, an expanse of inlaid stones, a land-locked local could glimpse a civilization unimaginable to one bred on the prairie at the nation's far rim: a civilization of chandeliers, brass fittings, draperied windows, and gold-framed mirrors; of red velvet carpets and gilded saloons and skylights of colored glass; a civilization of oil paintings and calliopes and great stacked bales of cotton to be exchanged somewhere for great stacks of money. A civilization inhabited by astounding diverse creatures. Strolling the decks or stepping onto the levee to stretch their legs were Southern planters in striped frock coats and wide-brimmed hats, their wives nearly invisible under deep bonnets, their floor-length silk dresses expanded by petticoat and restrained by corset; immigrants newly arrived from Europe at New Orleans; perfumed French merchants and high-hatted British speculators; expressionless gamblers in their ruffled blouses and jackets with velvet piping; mustachioed military men; assorted divines, actors, whores, circus troupes, politicians, trappers with their sidearms handy.

Sammy Clemens, who lived a block from the river, regularly took in the show. Yet he showed remarkable restraint—he did not try to hitch a ride on a riverboat until he was nine.

LIFE INSIDE the Clemens household was a lot less enchanting. Marshall's hopeless business instincts had sandbagged him again: Stout had inveigled him into some sort of indebtedness that effectively ended any dreams of prosperity. Mark Twain in his autobiographical dictations implied that Stout had bankrupted his father by refusing to repay a loan. This is unprovable in surviving records, but something had happened that deepened Marshall's debt, and the humiliation of penury loomed.

Marshall grew bony, spectral; Sammy later recalled the Judge's "eagle's beak and an eagle's eye." He enforced discipline among his children, mostly by the power of his barely suppressed rage. A deist, he disdained churchgoing, and for a while, the family remained unaffiliated. His idea of a great evening consisted in reading poetry aloud to the family in an inflectionless voice. (Sammy developed a shrewd ear for bad poetry, and parodied it mercilessly later on.)

Outside the household, Marshall spearheaded new committees, tried to practice law, got himself elected justice of the peace in 1844, watched his store slowly strangle, and hoped that his Tennessee land would finally become desirable and make his fortune. Whatever anxieties rattled through the family may have worked their way into Sammy's own consciousness. He was a remote, erratic little boy, with a wicked eye for the ways in which a desperate household betrayed itself—with its shabby décor, for instance; oilcloth window curtains with "pictures on them of castles such as had never been seen anywhere in the world but on window-curtains."[8]

He suffered nightmares. His sleepwalking continued. He was prone to convulsions. Not until he was seven did he enjoy the health of a normal child. Jane and Sammy seemed to feed on each other's hair-trigger nerves. Sammy would slip bats and snakes into her sewing basket; she told him tales of brutal and sadistic Indian attacks on her mother's people. A loathing of Indians, or

at least of Fenimore Cooper's fictitious noble savages, was the one racial prejudice that Mark Twain could never shake off.

He escaped the oppressive household at every opportunity. Out in the
world, he took extravagant physical risks, a lifelong predilection. He ventured
onto the frozen Mississippi in winter and cavorted on its heaving ice floes.
Dangerous water drew him; he dived into the depths of Bear Creek, which
emptied into the Mississippi. The fact that he could not swim did not seem to
matter; he recalls having been rescued from drowning seven or nine times.
One of these episodes prompted Jane's famous wisecrack that "[p]eople born
to be hanged are safe in water."

Sammy discovered another means of escape shortly after his family arrived in Hannibal. He learned to read.

3

Of Words and the Word

(1840–42)

His learning process began well before his fifth birthday, in the spring of 1840, when Jane installed him in a "dame school" in Hannibal. Dame schools, classes taught by women in their homes, were a new phenomenon in the country. Previously, most teachers had been men who, on their way into careers as ministers or lawyers, would spend a year or two as schoolmasters as a way of paying their dues in the community.

Sammy's first dame school convened in a little log structure on the southern flank of town, near Bear Creek. After a year or so Jane moved him on to a "Select School" conducted in a church basement. The teacher, who had known the Clemenses in Florida, boarded for a time in the family's household, where she watched Sammy compulsively steal sugar, and get his knuckles rapped for it, at the dining table. This was Miss Mary Ann Newcomb, who taught Sam Clemens to read. Her granddaughters reported that she always recalled the Clemens household with gentle respect. Jane "was an intellectual woman," whose wit and humor Sammy inherited. Marshall was "a courteous, well-educated gentleman," admittedly not practical, but "a good conversationalist."[1] Overall, she never heard any grumbling in the household despite its straitened circumstances.

Mark Twain graciously returned this esteem years later, by making Miss Newcomb the model for the character Mrs. Bangs in his unfinished manuscript, "Autobiography of a Damned Fool." Here she is "a very thin, tall Yankee person, who came west when she was thirty, taught school nine years in our town, and then married . . . She had ringlets, and a long sharp nose, and thin, colorless lips, and you could not tell her breast from her back if she had her head up a stovepipe hole . . ." [2] He also made her the model for the fussy Miss Watson in *Adventures of Huckleberry Finn*.

Learning to read was by no means an inevitable skill for Sammy. He was a restless child, hated school, spent a lot of his class time daydreaming, and finished his "formal" education by age twelve. Had he been exposed to the standard, Puritan-inspired manner of instruction—rote memorization, as modeled by the New England Primer that appeared in 1686—his edgy attention may well have wandered to the leafy hills outside the schoolhouse window, as it did during other subjects. But a new text for teaching literacy was just being hawked by subscription salesmen across America. Its popularity doomed the Primer to the dustbin in nearly every city and town where it showed up. McGuffey's *Eclectic Readers* would take their place in the pantheon of American brands, along with Coca-Cola and Ford.

The Reader perfectly fit Mark Twain's trope on American style: it did something that hadn't been done before. This was the first schoolbook that conformed to the child's cognitive strengths, rather than the adult's didactic habits.* McGuffey's Reader made literacy available by mass production after two centuries as a special privilege of the elite.

Before the McGuffey's Reader, sons and daughters of the wealthy and the devout were drilled by tutors in a long, slogging metronomic march from letters of the alphabet, to syllables, to words, and finally to phrases. The classic medium for this method was the "horn book"—a sheet of paper with printed alphabet letters, a few short words, and a biblical verse. The paper was fixed to a paddle-shaped wooden board and protected by a sheet of transparent antler horn. The child literally wore the book—attached to his belt by a cord tied to the paddle's handle—to memorize any time the urge hit him. The McGuffey's Reader changed all that. Its methods were practical enough that just about anyone could teach them to a child. McGuffey's drew the child into an active process, as opposed to passive memorization. In its advanced editions, McGuffey's opened up a larger universe of contemporary writing. The Fourth Reader offered Daniel Defoe and Louisa May Alcott, for example; the Fifth, Charles Dickens, James Russell Lowell, James Fenimore Cooper.

The Reader had a further effect on Sammy: it established the primacy of the Bible as a cornerstone of his intellectual edifice—indeed, of his very consciousness. Biblical verses and parables formed the essential texts of the

---

* The author of the Reader, William H. McGuffey, was well-suited to this sensibility. Born in 1800 in Pennsylvania, he taught himself to read, and succeeded well enough that he was teaching in rural Ohio schools by the age of thirteen. In 1826 he joined the faculty of Miami University, Oxford, Ohio, and began to think about public education. He turned his house into a model school for children in his neighborhood, and in observing them, formulated the basic principles of his Reader: that teachers should develop an intimate, "conversational," but demanding relationship with their pupils, and that children's reading skills should be built on a foundation of "wholesome" values: patriotism, charity, honesty, hard work, and a reverence for the Christian God.

McGuffey's earliest editions. As he learned language, Sammy internalized the idioms and metaphors of the Scriptures as well. No reading of Mark Twain's literature can miss the inexhaustible evidence of the Bible as a source.

By the time of the Civil War, the Readers had effected a social transformation. Largely through their use, the first mass-educated and mass-literate generation in the modern world had come of age. Their surviving letters and diaries reveal an intimacy with English rhetoric and its leading avatars, and an assured, unself-conscious grace in deploying it. The prose of ordinary people generated a folk archive of the period unmatched by personal writing in subsequent generations.

For Sammy Clemens, reading became metanoiac, life changing. Words became objects of almost physical beauty to him, tooled and precise and as distinct from one another as snowflakes, each with its unique function and value in the universe.

After a couple of years of tutoring, Sammy moved on to a school for older children organized by an Irish immigrant named Sam Cross. In 1847, at age thirteen, he transferred briefly to John D. Dawson's school, where he spent parts of a couple of years until the family's poverty—Marshall was dead by then—forced him to work full-time. His formal education was finished, but his more formative education was just beginning.

Mark Twain never became a scholar of literature; but he became a passionate amateur scholar of language—his native language and a few others, which he taught himself. An Italian word, he observed while living in Italy, has to be used while it is fresh, "for I find that Italian words do not keep in this climate. They fade towards night, and next morning they are gone."[3] As for German, he advocated eliminating the dative case, requiring it to reorganize the sexes ("in German, a young lady has no sex, while a turnip has"), and, in general, retaining "Zug" and "Schlag" with their pendants "and discard the rest of the vocabulary. This would simplify the language."[4] Hawaiian he had no use for—"there isn't anything in it to swear with."[5]

Mark Twain became a stickler for grammar. Perfect grammar was "the fourth dimension," he said, constantly sought but never found. ("I know grammar by ear only, not by note," he confessed.)[6] He was appalled by the subjunctive: "It brings all our writers to shame."[7] He valued brevity, and indeed his work was seminal in purging American literary English of its heavy Victorian ornamentation. "An average English word is four letters and a half," he observed, adding that he had shaved down his own vocabulary till the average was three and a half. He adored aphorisms and built them throughout his life. Any language, to him, was a form of music. Even the slightest misuse of his native tongue grated on his ears like a false note in a tune—unless it was in dialect, which had its own laws.

Mark Twain would show his appreciation for the Readers in the same way that he paid homage to all the literature that moved him as a child—by lampooning them. He upended McGuffey's pietistic messages in sketches such as

"Story of the Bad Little Boy," whose main character breaks every rule of good conduct with impunity, grows up to attain great wealth by cheating, murders his family with an axe, "and is universally respected, and belongs to the Legislature";[8] and, "The Story of the Good Little Boy," whose insufferably straight-arrow protagonist gets (literally) whacked for his smarmy good-deed doings.[9]

Perhaps the most powerful evidence of his almost biophysical affinity for language, both read and spoken, was his capacity to remember great swaths of it. Even as a small child he could disgorge entire sections of adventure novels to move along the "plot" of some fantasy enactment with his friends. His rote memorization skills at school became legendary. Some of his best sketches— "Sociable Jimmy," "A True Story Just as I Heard It"—are, if not virtual transcriptions of recollected dialogue, masterful approximations of it.

Sammy's other principal source for reading and memorization skills was the Bible. As a boy, he absorbed the Scriptures' verses uncritically; he groped torturously through their implications, with increasing fury and despair, for all of his adult life.

But his attitude toward the Bible, as he navigated the treacherous seas of his adulthood, transmuted itself into a kind of rage. He used it as a literary image, to emphasize the grotesque horror of a shooting, describing how "some thoughtful idiot" had spread it across the chest of a man dying from a gunshot wound.[10] He turned the figure of Satan into an ambiguous hero, and Adam and Eve into characters in a proto–situation comedy. At the height of his fury, he castigated the Good Book as nothing more than a vessel of "blood-drenched history; and some good morals; and a wealth of obscenity; and upwards of a thousand lies."[11] He unleashed similar invective on the works of Fenimore Cooper and Walter Scott, who were other important sources of his enchantment as a boy. This suggested, perhaps, that the sense of romantic estrangement which so deeply haunted him was not so much from the religion and literature he'd cherished as a child, but from childhood itself.

THAT CHILDHOOD was laced with terror and loss. In May 1842 another Clemens child, this time nine-year-old Benjamin, fell suddenly ill and died, seemingly from the same "bilious fever" that had claimed his sister years earlier. Three of Marshall and Jane's seven children were now in their graves. Marshall contained his grief under his well-worn armor of stoicism. Jane, who lived on passion, gave way to helpless keening, as she had after Margaret died. In her throes, she led her surviving children one by one into the bedroom where Benjamin's corpse lay. There, she made each of them kneel beside the body and place a hand on its cheek. No explanation for this gesture survives. It may have been an artifact of mourning ritual learned in her Kentucky girlhood. It may have been a desperate gesture of farewell.

For the high-strung Sammy, already saddled with Jane's belief that he possessed "second sight," the forced touching seems to have carried darkly mystical implications. He never forgot it. Moreover, he linked this ghoulish memory with the conviction that Benjamin's death was somehow his fault. Half a century later, he jotted an entry in his notebook that read: "Dead brother Ben. My treachery to him." In "Villagers of 1840–3," which he composed in 1897, he wrote, speaking unmistakably of himself and his family, but with the veneer of fictional characters,* "The mother made the children feel the cheek of the dead boy, and tried to make them understand the calamity that had befallen. *The case of memorable treachery*" (emphasis added).[12]

"IF CHRIST were here now," reads an entry in Mark Twain's notebook, "There is one thing he would not be—a Christian." The seeds of this contempt for scriptural faith were planted a year into the family's mourning of Benjamin, when Jane Clemens found that she could no longer do without the solace of church attendance. She joined a congregation, leaving Marshall stubbornly ensconced at home with his deist musings. Jane marched to church every Sunday, the four children in tow. Now the "imprinting" of the Bible's influence on Sammy was intensified by the trauma and the torpor of Sunday mornings in the pews.

It was not his first exposure to the faith, strictly speaking. Jane had enrolled him in a Methodist Sunday school almost as soon as the family arrived in town, and soon the boy was blandly memorizing and reciting biblical verses along with the rest of the small inmates in the church basement. But Jane's call to worship gave him his first taste of the ecclesiastical big leagues. In the Presbyterian church his mother chose, a more soul-sobering production of weekly apocalyptic theater probably did not exist.

Presbyterianism was the un-Transcendentalism of the early 19th century. No sunny optimism in its tenets, no cheery vision of liberating faith built on the divinity within the personal soul. Presbyterians derived from an older and chillier strain of worship in the New World, and from a blood-soaked era of Christian rebellion in Europe before that—the Reformation. They refused to believe that sinfulness could be absolved through ceremony and incantation. Far from the Emersonian notion of man's personal divinity, Presbyterians believed in the cold, absolute sovereignty of God's will. Sinners were doomed to Hell. In sum, the Presbyterianism of the dank Scottish moors belonged to nearly every iron-plated spiritual concept that the poet-mystics of Concord and Boston were trying to abolish.†

---

* The Clemenses are the only fictionally named family (the "Carpenters") in "Villagers," which Mark Twain obviously compiled as reference notes for possible future works. It lists and describes more than a hundred citizens of antebellum Hannibal from a perspective of forty-four years.

† Theology aside, Presbyterianism left its mark in the New World in one towering, fundamental way: it formed the model for American representative democratic government. John Knox adapted John Calvin's antipapist scheme of "voluntary associations," organizing his churches as little communities whose elders—"presbyters"—were elected by the laity. These local councils fed into regional bodies, called synods, which in turn sent representatives to national groups, or General Assemblies. This grassroots system of churchly self-government, imported to the colonies in America by the Puritans, became the template for political self-government eventually enshrined in the Constitution of 1789.

Sammy absorbed the bad news every Sunday. He later entertainingly dis-gorged his visual and aural memories of it all—the high pulpit with the red plush pillow for the Bible, the stiff wooden pews, the "melodeon," or primitive organ; the caterwauling choir, the dozing oldsters, and his scattered fellow captives, the other boys, their spitballs at the ready, grateful for the diversion of a dog sitting down on the stinging warhead of a pinch bug—and getting up again.

But the abrasions of what he heard there never healed. Here was a reli-gion seemingly designed in heaven that reinforced all of a nervous child's worst fears. Unless you were one of the "elect," ran the preacher's constant message, there was no hope—you were categorically contaminated by sin. But you should still try to be good and cultivate the Moral Sense, on the off chance that God had elected you. A boy who already felt himself guilty for the death of his brother could conceivably take that kind of message to heart.

SAMMY'S CHURCH attendance also exposed him to the "Bible defense of slavery"—a burgeoning industry in the two decades running up to the Civil War.

The First Presbyterian had not always been a clearinghouse for proslavery propaganda. The church was organized in 1832 by a doctor and minister named David Nelson, a Tennessean who struggled with the moral implica-tions of slaveholding. His temperate views did not, at first, antagonize the local slaveholders, who tolerated the (segregated) presence of slaves in the congregation starting in 1833. All of that changed in 1835, the year of Sammy's birth, when Nelson suddenly declared himself an abolitionist. This was not a shrewd career move in Missouri. Soon his pamphleteering followers were being run out of the state by mobs. In 1836, Nelson himself triggered a riot while preaching abolition in the village of Palmyra, thirteen miles north-west of Hannibal. He narrowly escaped capture and imprisonment—or worse—and fled across the Mississippi River to Illinois. There, he founded an antislavery academy called the Mission School near Quincy.

By the time the Clemenses joined the church, it was solidly proslavery. The new minister, the Rev. Joshua Tucker, was perfectly happy to circulate the growing number of tracts, written and published in the slaveholding South, that explained how the institution of slavery was God's will.

"MAN IS without any doubt the most intriguing fool there is," Mark Twain wrote in 1909. "Also the most eccentric. He hasn't a single written law, in his Bible or out of it, which has any but just one purpose and intention—to *limit* or *defeat* a law of God."

"[Man] concedes that God gives to each man his temperament, his disposition, at birth; he concedes that man cannot by any process change this temperament, but must remain always under its dominion. Yet if it be full of dreadful passions, in one man's case, and barren of them in another man's, it is right and rational to punish the one for his crimes, and reward the other for abstaining from the crime." [13]

In Mark Twain's autobiography, God comes across like an avenging hit man. "I was educated, I was trained, I was a Presbyterian and I knew how these things are done," Mark Twain seethes. "I knew that in Biblical times if a man committed a sin the extermination of the whole surrounding nation—cattle and all—was likely to happen. I knew that Providence was not particular about the rest, so that He got somebody connected with the one He was after." [14] Near the close of his life he still could not put it to rest. To his biographer, he quoted an old minister who declared that "Presbyterianism without infant damnation would be like the dog on the train that couldn't be identified because it had lost its tag." [15]

Yet strong evidence suggests that Mark Twain never could quite outrun the Christian faith. He remained a dutiful Presbyterian believer, at least until 1858 when a cataclysmic holocaust on the Mississippi River took the life of a beloved sibling. In the darkness of his private grieving after that, and even into his hard-drinking and hell-raising days as a wild journalist in the West, he toyed with the notion of becoming a preacher. In the long and grief-laced nights of his later years, even as he fulminated against a pitiless, depraved Christian God; brought Satan forward as a central figure in his tales; and secretly compiled the texts that would fully declare his apostasy after his death, Mark Twain seemed often to behave toward that God less like a coldhearted nonbeliever than like a jilted lover. His torment was Job's torment, the transitory agony of one driven from the comforts of orthodox faith, who seeks a new faith system to fill the void.

4

The Hannibal Decade

(1843–53)

As the dogwood blossomed on the forested hills around Hannibal in 1843, Sammy Clemens began to live the ten most imaginatively fertile years of his life. The "Hannibal Decade," as it has been called, influenced most of his literature.

At age seven, he found a circle of boys his own age and became its animating force, appointing himself scriptwriter and director of all make-believe escapades. His lieutenant was a natural-born sidekick named Will Bowen, a year younger and one of seven children. Their father, a Tennessean named Samuel Bowen, was a fire insurance agent and warehouse owner. The Bowen family lived in a wing of that warehouse a block or so from the Virginia House. Drawing on the tales of Sir Walter Scott, Fenimore Cooper, and the legends of Robin Hood, which he had virtually memorized, Sammy assigned roles and dialogue to everyone. Will usually played the Terror of the Seas to Sammy's Black Avenger of the Spanish Main. Sammy always reserved the star turn for himself. He demanded accuracy, just as Tom Sawyer demanded of "Joe Harper." *

Tom called:

"Hold! Who comes here into Sherwood Forest without my pass?"

"Guy of Guisborne wants no man's pass. Who are thou that—that—"

—"Dares to hold such language," said Tom, prompting—for they talked "by the book," from memory.

---

* Will also inspired "Joe Harper" in *Huckleberry Finn* and *Tom Sawyer's Conspiracy*. He also provides elements of the highly composite "Tom Sawyer," who by tradition is Sammy's alter ego.

"Who are thou that dares to hold such language?"

"I, indeed! I am Robin Hood, as thy caitiff carcase soon shall know."

"Then art thou indeed that famous outlaw? Right gladly will I dispute with thee the passes of the merry wood. Have at thee!" . . .

So they "went it lively," panting and perspiring with the work. By and by Tom shouted:

"Fall! fall! Why don't you fall?"

"I shan't! Why don't you fall yourself? You're getting the worst of it."

"Why that ain't anything. *I* can't fall; that ain't the way it is in the book. The book says 'Then with one back-handed stroke he slew poor Guy of Guisborne.' You're to turn around and let me hit you in the back."

There was no getting around the authorities, so Joe turned, received the whack and fell.[1]

Samuel Clemens kept up his friendship with Will Bowen until Bowen's death in 1893. Clemens greeted him in a famous 1870 letter as "My First, & Oldest & Dearest Friend,"[2] a letter that went on to virtually announce the stirrings of *The Adventures of Tom Sawyer*. This loyalty, even when separated by decades, half a continent, and the oceanic difference in their life fortunes, was deeply characteristic: Clemens held friendship as a value of nearly sacred proportions. The most convincing—if paradoxical—proof of this lay in his well-known rages and vendettas against people who he felt had betrayed his trust. "You could offer Clemens offences that would anger other men and he did not mind," William Dean Howells recalled, ". . . but if he thought you had in any way played him false, you were anathema and maranatha forever."[3]

An edge existed in the Clemens-Bowen friendship, however, in childhood and in later life. Two of Sammy's most dangerous boyhood acts were performed in Will's company. The first could be written off as a prank that nearly went fatally awry. The boys discovered a huge boulder, "about the size of an omnibus" as Mark Twain remembered it,[4] lodged near the peak of Holliday's Hill. One Saturday afternoon, the two boys put their shoulders against the rock, waited until a picnic party had passed on the road below, and gave it a shove. The plummeting rock tore up trees, crushed bushes, pulverized a woodmill—and then bore down on a drayman whose mule had entered the rock's path. At the last instant the boulder struck a hard object and launched itself over the drayman's head and into a frame cooper shop, probably that of Mrs. Horr's husband. "The coopers swarmed out like bees," Mark Twain recalled years later. "Then we said it was perfectly magnificent, and left. Because the coopers were starting up the hill to inquire."*[5]

---

* This version of the story, which Twain recounted in *The Innocents Abroad*, varies significantly from the more cautious version the author told to his biographer Albert Bigelow Paine some thirty-five years later, around 1906. The older Twain now insisted that the boulder had begun moving on its own, and that the incident had occurred on a Sunday, when the cooper's shop was empty.

The second act was far more freighted. A near-suicidal gesture on its surface, it was more likely, by Mark Twain's accounting, a rather brave gesture of his boyhood anxiety about fate—an anxiety almost certainly nourished by the Presbyterian message of predestination that he absorbed at Jane's side every Sunday morning. An epidemic of measles hit Hannibal in the summer of 1845, claimed the lives of several children, and terrified everyone. Funerals occurred almost daily. No mother was more distraught than Jane Clemens, who became obsessively protective of her children. Will Bowen was among the afflicted. Sammy, all but certain that he was next, decided to force the issue. He slipped into the Bowen household and stole his way to the rear bedroom on the second floor, where Will lay. There he was spotted by Mrs. Bowen, who screamed at him and threw him out of the house. He returned, sneaking through the backyard this time, up the rear entrance and into the bed. He lay beside his stricken friend until Mrs. Bowen discovered him again and hauled him all the way home by the back of his collar. The contagion he received nearly killed him. The family gathered around his bed. "I have never enjoyed anything in my life any more than I enjoyed dying that time," he remembered.[6]

TOWARD THE end of 1843, the Clemenses moved out of the Virginia House and into a residence of their own. Marshall had it built on a twenty-foot-wide lot for $330, the money supplied by a cousin in St. Louis, a lawyer named James Clemens Jr. It was an ordinary two-story wood-frame building a few doors up from Marshall's rickety hotel and general store, at 206 Hill Street; but it would one day stand as the most famous frame house in America: the storied Boyhood Home. Pamela and Orion enjoyed separate rooms; Sammy and Henry shared a small bedroom on the second floor, facing the street. Sammy often awakened at night to the soft catcalls of his friends. Easing himself out the window, he would creep along the roof of the ell, drop to the top of a woodshed and then to the ground and his waiting gang, to commence his legendary explorations of the Hannibal night.

Often, a ragged phantom joined Sammy and his friends. "Why, that's Tom Blankenship!" Pamela Clemens cried when she heard someone read the section of *The Adventures of Tom Sawyer* that introduced him.[7] Mark Twain confirmed this four years before his death,[8] yet the figure's identity has been debated. Perhaps he was an amalgam of all the boys, a version of their idealized outlaw selves—including the dreaming child who would one day immortalize him in a timeless river novel.

Huckleberry Finn makes his entrance in *The Adventures of Tom Sawyer* as "the juvenile pariah of the village,"[9] draped in garments cast off by grown men and clutching a dead cat. He is a doorway sleeper and master of profanity, an oracle of superstitions, charms, the ways of witches' incantations, graveyard protocol, the ghosts of murderous men—and he is utterly unconstrained by adult discipline, by schooling or religion. In *Tom Sawyer,* he is a secondary character, the hero's gaudy sidekick. Later, in his own book, Huck Finn liberates himself from Mark Twain's customary boundaries, and takes on a depth and dignity that awed even his author.

By the 1850 census, Tom Blankenship was about four years older than Sammy: the second of eight children in a down-and-out family that had drifted up from South Carolina. His father Woodson was a laborer, and one of the town's leading drunks, along with Jimmy Finn. His mother bore the beautiful name Mahala, a fairly popular name for early 19th-century women who had both Arabic and Native American roots. In their abjectness, the Blankenship family suffered humiliations beyond Woodson's reputation as a drunkard. Mahala's six daughters, as they came into their young womanhood, were accused as prostitutes, a charge never proven.

By the early 1840s Hannibal was shedding its provincial-outpost status, adopting American styles as they arrived from the East. Hoop skirts came into style. Boys and men were strutting around in slouch hats and long cloaks lined with bright plaid. "Worn with a swagger," Mark Twain recalled. "Most rational garment there ever was." [10] Girls plaited their hair into long tails and wore white summer frocks and embroidered pantalettes. People sang to one another. Sheet music, printed in Philadelphia and New York with ornate typefaces under lavish chromolithographic covers, carried popular tunes via stage and steamer into the interior. Twain remembered "Oft in the Stilly Night," "Last Rose of Summer," "Bonny Doon," "Old Dog Tray." Pamela Clemens gave lessons in piano and guitar, and Sammy became proficient in both.

The minstrel show came to town and stayed for a week when he was ten, and featured Thomas "Daddy" Rice himself. Sammy Clemens loved the minstrel show. Samuel Clemens would always love the minstrel show. In the 1870s and '80s, he was fond of entertaining dinner guests at his Hartford estate by jumping from his chair to perform "breakdowns" in an uncanny imitation of Rice—and Jim Crow. He cherished the memory of the minstrel show—only he didn't call it the "minstrel show"—into the last years of his life, even after the founding star's name had mostly slipped his mind ("Where now is Billy Rice?" [11]). His sensory recall of that introductory spectacle remained near-photographic; and the "photographs" offer damning evidence in the one debate that has towered above all others in the ninety-five years since his death: was Samuel Langhorne Clemens, or was he not, a racist?

He was not always the best witness in his own defense—at least judged by the standards of a later time, a time that began with the American civil rights movement. His autobiography affirms his boyish delight in Rice and his performers with their "coal black hands and faces," their coats of curtain calico and their outsized clumsy shoes. "Their lips were thickened and lengthened with bright red paint to such a degree that their mouths resembled slices cut in a ripe watermelon." [12] He never called it the "minstrel show," however, and the word he used in its place serves, for a great many people, as final proof of his racial iniquity. The summit of entertainment for him, he declared in his autobiography, always remained "the real nigger show—the genuine nigger show, the extravagant nigger show—the show which to me had no peer and whose peer has not yet arrived, in my experience."[13]

Certain facts are incontrovertible. Those performers with coal-black hands and faces were white men, not Negroes, and everyone in the tent knew it, including Sammy. Their comedy consisted in shrill, outlandish arguments with one another in an extreme "Negro dialect"—until they were separated from one another by "the aristocrat in the middle," a figure clad in "the white faultless evening costume of the white society gentleman" who spoke in a stilted, artificial, "painfully grammatical form of speech"[14]—the living embodiment, in short, of the disdainful "frame story" narrator. Once "Banjo" and "Bones" were tamed, every blackfaced trouper on stage would do a round or two of shuffle dancing, followed by some sentimental songs in the Stephen Foster vein. Thus the nonpareil entertainment form for Samuel Clemens was a burlesque of slave behavior, created and performed by men of the oppressing race.

But are those the elements on which Clemens's enjoyment of minstrelsy depended? The minstrels' extravagant clothing, Mark Twain was at pains to note, "was a loud and extravagant burlesque of the clothing worn by the plantation slave of the time; *not that the rags of the poor slave were burlesqued, for that would not have been possible; burlesque could have added nothing in the way of extravagance to the sorrowful accumulation of rags and patches which constituted his costume; it was the form and color of his dress that was burlesqued*" (emphasis added).[15] Elsewhere in the reminiscence, he dwells on the hilarity, the delight, the silly punning of the performers; the convulsions and hysterics they evoked; the sweetness of the singing. Without torturing the point, it seems fair to conclude that (a) the young, uncritical Samuel Clemens was tainted by the Original Sin of Negro slavery, and by the assumptions of control and superiority that his slaveholding culture enjoyed; that (b) his enjoyment of the minstrel show derived from the universal absurdities of human strut and vanity that it evoked, and not from its inescapable undertone of cruelty; and to point out that (c) the long trajectory of his life is in many important ways a self-forged path upward and outward from that Original Sin, and toward an egalitarian vision of the races expressed in his best literature and in a range of personal and social gestures. As much as he rejoiced at Bones and Banjo, Sammy was equally distraught as he witnessed the wailing grief expressed by members of slave families when they were separated and sold. Mark Twain wrote about this theme repeatedly: in "A True Story" (1874), in Chapter 21 of *A Connecticut Yankee* (1889), and in Chapter 3 of *Pudd'nhead Wilson* (1894).

No one who knew him, including Frederick Douglass, ever accused him of animosity or condescension to the Negro race. Far from embracing the Bible defense of slavery, he disdained biblical interpretation in general, gravitating as a young man toward egalitarian Enlightenment-derived ideas, such as those of Tom Paine. William Dean Howells, a discerning and progressive man who knew Clemens about as well as anyone, called him "the most serious, the most humane, the most conscientious of men," and added, "I never saw a man more respectful of negroes." [16]

And finally, one must consider (unless one is hopelessly prejudiced against it) the testimony of Mark Twain himself: "I have no race prejudices, and I think I have no color prejudices nor caste prejudices nor creed prejudices . . . I can stand any society. All I care to know is that a man is a human being—that is enough for me; he can't be any worse." [17]

A LITTLE over a year later, Sammy watched a man die from a point-blank gunshot wound to the chest—the first premeditated murder in Hannibal's history. The shooter was William Perry Owsley, a transplanted Kentuckian, town merchant, and the father of two of Sammy's friends. Owsley gunned down a farmer named Sam Smarr after tiring of Smarr's drunken tirades la beling Owsley as a thief and pickpocket. Owsley waited until the farmer returned to town a week later, sober, to sell a side of beef; stepped up behind the man less than a block from the Clemens house; drew a pistol out of his pocket; called, "You, Sam Smarr," and drilled him twice at four paces as the farmer turned. While Marshall Clemens gathered depositions, Sammy watched Smarr be carried into a drugstore on the corner and laid on his back on a table, where it took him half an hour to die.

"[T]here was nothing about the slavery of the Hannibal region to rouse one's dozing humane instincts to activity," Mark Twain wrote.[18] Yet virtually in the next breath, he "vividly" recalled seeing several men and women slaves chained together and sprawled on the levee pavement like sacks of flour, bound for the dreaded Deep South. And not many months after the Smarr shooting, he watched a local slave master lash out at one of his charges for some small mishap. The slave master had a hunk of iron ore in his punching hand. It took the slave an hour to die.

There were further horrors. On a hot August afternoon in 1847, the eleven-year-old Sammy and some friends crossed the Mississippi in a skiff to Sny Island, near the far shore. They tied up the boat and waded the shallow waters of Bird Slough, a sandy stretch between the island and Illinois, idly foraging the bushes for blackberries and pecans. It was an ordinary lark on an ordinary day, until the corpse of a Negro slave abruptly rose up out of the water and stared at them sightlessly. The body was that of Neriam Todd, who had escaped from his Missouri owners, swum the river, and hidden out on the island. Todd had been discovered a few days later by Bence Blankenship, Tom's older brother. Despite the bounty on the slave's head, Bence had looked after him for several weeks, venturing several times across the Mississippi with food that he'd stolen to give to the man. (In *Huckleberry Finn*, Huck comes across the runaway slave Jim hiding out on a Mississippi island, and launches out with him on the immortal raft odyssey downriver.)

Eventually a rumor arose that something suspicious was happening on

Sny Island. A group of woodcutters found Todd and chased him into the slough, where they murdered him, mutilated his body, and left the remains to rot. The corpse had floated feet first with the current until it jammed in the sand. The boys' disruption of the sediment probably set the body in motion again. The children fled the island and paddled madly back to the Hannibal shore, believing in their terror that the corpse was following them.

MARK TWAIN wrote, "when I was a boy everybody was poor but didn't know it; and everybody was comfortable and did know it."[19] Wealth, and prospective wealth, tantalized Samuel Clemens throughout his life. His relations with money, even during his reign as a wealthy prince of literature, were nearly always tortured. He was "never comfortable with money nor satisfied without it," Lewis Leary has accurately written.[20] He alternately ruminated about money's corrupting powers ("Vast wealth, to the person unaccustomed to it, is a bane; it eats into the flesh and bone of his morals") and riffed on its lustrous appeal ("I'm opposed to millionaires, but it would be dangerous to offer me the position"),[21] but neither pose did him much good; he foraged for money throughout his life, and it always got the best of him. He left no doubt as to the origins of money's spell over him. "It is good to begin life poor; it is good to begin life rich," he mused in 1897–98; "—these are wholesome; but to begin it *prospectively* rich! The man who has not experienced it cannot imagine the whole size of the curse of it."[22]

"Curse" was hardly an exaggeration. Despite his strong intellectual gifts, Marshall Clemens could scarcely ever rub two Liberty Cap pennies together while he lived in Hannibal. Nothing worked for him. His tenants at the Virginia House seldom paid their board, while the customers of his general store helped themselves to food and supplies on credit that they never intended to settle. Exasperated, Marshall sent Orion to the town newspaper, the *Journal*, to learn the printing trade—a move that profoundly affected both Orion's and Sam's futures.

MARSHALL'S FAILED ventures soon ate up whatever capital the Clemenses had brought with them from Florida, which did not include five of the six slaves they owned at the time of their marriage. Those had been sold. Marshall advertised his legal services; but, like Pudd'nhead Wilson, he found little demand. He turned to the one remaining fungible asset left over from his days of gentility: Jennie. Jennie had been a part of the Clemens household since Tennessee days. She had helped Jane keep Sammy alive in his sickly early months. In Hannibal she had saved him from drowning in Bear Creek. Marshall sold Jennie toward the end of 1842 or early 1843, to a trader considered wolfish even among owners of blacks in Hannibal. William Beebe was known as "the nigger-trader" because of his unrepentant dealings with the New Orleans slave market.

It is not clear whether the "tall, well formed, nearly black" Jennie was sold against her will or whether she naïvely requested the transaction herself, as Mark Twain maintained.[23] In "Villagers," Mark Twain recalled that "Judge Carpenter" "[h]ad but one slave—she wanted to be sold to Beebe, and was. He [that is, Beebe] sold her down the river. Was seen, years later, ch[ambermaid] on a steamboat. Cried and lamented."[24] Mark Twain describes this woman as being "like one of the family," and suggests that she had been beguiled by Beebe with "all sorts of fine and alluring promises."[25] A fate with strikingly similar components is visited on the nearly white slave Roxana of *The Tragedy of Pudd'nhead Wilson*.

The sale of Jennie did nothing to augment the Clemenses' fortunes. Marshall apparently never collected on her price. He ended up with two promissory notes from Beebe, probably marking the Jennie business and some other transaction, totaling about five hundred dollars. The notes proved roughly as valuable to him as his Tennessee land.

SOON, THE Virginia House slipped out of Marshall's grasp. Marshall naïvely agreed to stand behind some loans to the unscrupulous land speculator Big Ira Stout. When Stout defaulted, the Virginian ponied up. Mark Twain recalled that this honorable action "bankrupted" his father. No records have been found that document this deception, but in 1841 Marshall Clemens surrendered the title of the Virginia House to a St. Louis merchant who had stocked the general store on credit. Even this transaction failed to wipe out Marshall's debt. Although the merchant may have been satisfied, Marshall's code of honor did not allow him to escape with minimal "satisfaction." Sammy and the other children looked on as their parents stripped down their household, offering up their furniture, forks and spoons, and even the family cow in a prideful effort to pay off every cent that they owed. They continued to live in the building as tenants for a while, but eventually quit the house. None of their addresses for about a year are known. Orion, seventeen, sought work in St. Louis as a journeyman printer. He lived on bread and water, read the Bible, and got up before dawn. He was elected president of the St. Louis Apprentices' Association.

Jane saw to it that Sammy remained in school, and sent him each summer to his uncle's farm at Florida. Of his playmates there, he recalled, "All the negroes were friends of ours, and with those of our own age we were in effect comrades. I say, in effect, using the phrase as a modification. We were comrades, and yet not comrades; color and condition interposed a subtle line which both parties were conscious of, and which rendered complete fusion impossible."[26]

DUAL IDENTITY—the divided self, the self transposed, two selves inhabiting the same body—formed a central theme in Mark Twain's literature. To look into his father's life is to confront the fountainhead of this vision. The extraordinary twins conjoined in Marshall Clemens's frame were contradictory almost beyond caricature. One was the Judge: an educated, eloquent, ambitious man, claimant to British peerage; a natural civic leader, apostle of the Southern honor code, a visionary of the America to come. He held the power of life and death over other men: as justice of the peace, he prepared depositions in the trial of William Owsley, the murderer of Sam Smarr. (Owsley was acquitted.) In his Hannibal courtroom, a small space on Bird Street, he once subdued a plaintiff with a mallet blow to the head after the man had fired off a pepper-pot revolver. This version of Marshall Clemens reigned as a titan in Sammy's consciousness.

The Judge's aims were constantly thwarted by Marshall, the proud idealist and frustrated intellectual whose honor code was exploited by lesser, stupider men; who wrecked his health at an early age, married a woman vengefully on the rebound, proved too visionary by a century in his greatest land investment, stood behind bad loans, paid his debts, forgave his creditors, and thus remained poor for most of his life.

The Judge had his moments of intersection with history, however. In 1841 he sat on a jury in a trial that amplified the virulence of Missouri's proslavery passions before the eyes of the nation. Only the United States Supreme Court's Dred Scott ruling in 1857 (which nullified the Missouri Compromise's restrictions on slavery and held that slaves could never become U.S. citizens) surpassed it in the annals of Missouri slave litigation. The trial, held at Palmyra, decided the fates of three Christian abolitionists who had crossed the Mississippi from Illinois in search of slaves to spirit back across the river to freedom. The men, James Burr, George Thompson, and Alanson Work, were captured by vigilantes alerted by the slaves themselves, who thought the strangers might be tricksters trying to get them into trouble. The trial ended with prison sentences of twelve years for each man. The stacked nature of the trial and the harshness of the penalty attracted attention as far away as William Lloyd Garrison's fiery abolitionist paper the *Liberator* in Boston, and the *Observer* in Hartford.

The move into the house at 206 Hill Street in 1843, bankrolled by James Clemens Jr., relieved the family of its anxiety over shelter, for a while. Marshall opened his law office near Hill and Main. He bought a piano for Pamela who by now was giving lessons in piano and guitar. "The Judge" helped organize the Hannibal Library Institute, and provided most of its books. He promoted a Masonic college for Hannibal. Nobody was interested.

Jane's and Sammy's affection for each other deepened in these years, as did her influence on his character. She gamely suffered the red-haired boy's habitual mischief—dosing a cat with a painkiller, fidgeting with pinch bugs in church, tricking her into standing up for Satan as a victim of bad luck. She reinforced Sammy's enchantment with language. Mark Twain marveled at the "unstudied and unconscious pathos" of her native speech. When stirred to indignation "she was the most eloquent person I have heard speak."[27] He added:

It was seldom eloquence of a fiery or violent sort, but gentle, pitying, persuasive, appealing; and so genuine and so nobly and simply worded and so touchingly uttered, that many times I have seen it win the reluctant and splendid applause of tears. . . . [28]

These were the days of the circuses and the mesmerizers; the heyday of Sammy's larking gang. These were the days when Sammy encountered Anna Laura Hawkins, late of Kentucky—or, as she became in her incarnation as "Becky Thatcher," the "lovely little blue-eyed creature with yellow hair plaited into two long tails, white summer frock and embroidered pantalettes." [29] The model for the heroine of *The Adventures of Tom Sawyer* was one of ten children of a prosperous farmer who kept a trim white frame house in town opposite 206 Hill Street. Laura remembered Sammy as a caper-cutting barefoot boy with "fuzzy light curls all over his head that really ought to have belonged to a girl." [30] She also recalled that "Sam and I used to play together like two girls."

In 1846, the Clemens family hit rock bottom. Marshall had sued William Beebe—who now owned a store near the levee—in 1843 over the outstanding notes regarding Jennie. He was awarded damages from them, but (being Marshall) was only able to realize some tin plates, sacks of salt, a screw press, some barrels, and a nine-year-old Negro girl. Marshall got John Quarles to try to collect on a $300 note, which pushed Beebe's nose out of joint. The slave trader got possession of a $290.55 debt claim on Marshall from a local storekeeper and, in August 1846, he gleefully sued Marshall back. Marshall's luck held true, as the judge awarded Beebe not only the amount of the debt, but also $126.50 in damages. A week before Christmas, the trader pressured the court to order the sheriff to sell off the "goods and chattels and real estate" of John Marshall Clemens toward payment of the award. [31]

The sheriff could find nothing to sell. Marshall had foreseen the move and evacuated his family from the little house at 206 Hill Street, surrendering its title back to his cousin James in St. Louis. James rented the house to Dr. Hugh Meredith and his two elderly unmarried sisters. The Clemenses' humiliation was complete. They accepted lodgings offered by the druggist Orville Grant across the street, just downhill from the prosperous Hawkins family. This was the same building—it still stands in Hannibal—where Sam Smarr had died from his gunshot wound. Jane cooked the Grants' meals and washed their clothes. Pamela salvaged the family's weather-beaten piano and continued giving lessons to help keep her family afloat.

Mark Twain found punitive use for William Beebe in his late, unfinished fiction, casting him as slave trader Bat Bradish in *Tom Sawyer's Conspiracy* and alluding to "the nigger-trader" in "Schoolhouse Hill."

In March 1847, Marshall Clemens saddled a horse and made the thirteen-mile trip to Palmyra on court business. On his way home he was overtaken by a sleet storm and contracted pneumonia. He lay abed in Dr. Grant's drugstore for about two weeks. Orion came home from St. Louis. As delirium set in, Marshall's mind returned to the Tennessee land and the hope it had represented. "I am leaving you in cruel poverty," Mark Twain has Judge Hawkins gasp as he dies in *The Gilded Age*. "But courage! A better day is—is coming. Never lose sight of the Tennessee Land! . . . There is wealth for you there—wealth that is boundless!"[32]

In his final moments, on March 24, 1847, Marshall Clemens reached out to Pamela and kissed her ("for the first time, no doubt," Mark Twain notes in "Villagers") and then sank back to die. He was forty-nine. Missouri had not worked out after all.

John Marshall Clemens's personal catastrophes never dimmed his civic visions. In November 1846, in the throes of his collapse at the hands of Beebe, Marshall had chaired a committee of businessmen pushing for a railroad from Hannibal westward to St. Joseph. The Hannibal & St. Joseph Railroad was chartered in 1847 and completed in 1859. It ushered in a boomtown epoch that lasted three-quarters of a century. Fortunes were created as pine logs, harvested in the Northern forests and floated down the Mississippi, were sawed into lumber in one of Hannibal's several mills, stacked onto freight trains and transported west for house building in the newly populous territories.

The railroad that arose posthumously from Marshall Clemens's vision created more wealth in Hannibal than would ever be converted from his son's literary reputation.

A FOUNDATION stone of the Mark Twain myth involves a scene in which Jane leads the eleven-year-old Sammy to the side of his dead father's bed. Paine gives it a hagiographic glow.

"Here by the side of him now,"[33] Jane told Sammy; she needed a promise.

He turned, his eyes streaming with tears, and flung himself into her arms.

"I will promise anything," he sobbed, "if you won't make me go to school. Anything!"

His mother held him for a moment, thinking, then she said:

"No, Sammy; you need not go to school any more. Only promise me to be a better boy. Promise not to break my heart."

So he promised her to be a faithful and industrious man, and upright, like her father. His mother was satisfied with that. The sense of honor and justice was already strong within him. To him a promise was a serious matter at any time; made under conditions like these it would be held sacred.[34]

This account, with its Victorian flourishes, has become suspect in certain critical circles. But in an 1885 interview with the Chicago *Inter-Ocean*, Jane Clemens described a scene that, while different in some respects, confirms the essence of Paine's account. She said in part:

. . . [A]nd when Sam's father died . . . I thought then, if ever, was the proper time
make a lasting impression on the boy and work a change in him, so I took him by the
hand and went with him into the room where the coffin was . . . and with it between
Sam and me I said to him that here in this presence I had some serious requests to
make of him, and I knew his word once given was never broken. For Sam never told a
falsehood. He turned his streaming eyes upon me and cried out, "Oh mother, I will do
anything, anything you ask of me except go to school; I can't do that!" That was the
very request I was going to make. Well, we afterward had a sober talk, and I concluded
to let him go into a printing office to learn the trade, as I couldn't have him running
wild. He did so, and has gradually picked up enough education to enable him to do
about as well as those who were more studious in early life.[35]

To say the least.

Whether or not Sammy's promise changed him, guilt hung like a fog
around Mark Twain's memories of his boyhood. He blamed himself for nearly
every calamity that happened to others. But what *had* he ever done?

A couple of provocative explanations for Mark Twain's guilt arise from the
records. The first is the enigmatic matter of "the autopsy." Twain alluded to
"the autopsy" twice, each time with an obvious self-distancing. In "Villagers,"
he appends the two words to the bottom of his long entry regarding "Judge
Carpenter." In his notebook entry of October 10, 1903, Twain wrote: "*1847.
Witnessed post mortem of my uncle through keyhole.*"

This may be an oblique way of recording that Sammy saw his father's body
cut open with a knife employed by the family physician, Dr. Hugh Meredith.

What was Dr. Meredith looking for? One Twain scholar has surmised that
Dr. Meredith was driven by a professional curiosity similar to that of the
cadaver-storing Dr. McDowell.[36] Meredith may have wanted to assess the effects on Marshall's body of his "lifelong mysterious maladies," the nervous exhaustion and shortness of breath that chronically afflicted the Judge.

More recent scholarship has taken a darker view. One scholar has speculated that Marshall, sexually starved in his passionless marriage, contracted a
venereal disease on that winter trip downriver. Or at least that Jane suspected
as much and ordered the autopsy, a rare procedure after a death of a nonvio-
lent nature.[37]

There was at least one corroborating witness to Marshall's autopsy: Orion,
who wrote of it in an unpublished autobiography, a manuscript he gave to his
brother in the hope of getting it into print. William Dean Howells read this
manuscript, and when he came across the account, he was utterly shocked.*
He pleaded with Mark to suppress it:

But the writer's soul is laid *too* bare; it is shocking . . . if you print it anywhere, I
hope you won't let your love of the naked truth prevent you from striking out some of

---

* Paine read the manuscript as well. In fact, he lost it, either by accident or on purpose,
which is why it remains unpublished.

the most intimate pages. Don't let any one else even see those passages about the autopsy. The light on your father's character is most pathetic.[38]

Judge Clemens was buried in the cemetery that served as the model for the one in *Tom Sawyer,* the hilltop Baptist cemetery north of town, on the same ridgeline that formed Holliday's Hill. Mark Twain never had to look far for his fictional ideas.

5

Apprentice

(1848–51)

Twenty-one-year-old Orion now headed the family, a responsibility essentially beyond him. But there were no other options. Jane Clemens, not yet forty-four, drew inward, wept frequently, became absorbed in omens and dreams. Her flame-colored hair was graying. She took up pipe smoking, played cards, accumulated cats, and grew deeply absorbed in the color red. Pamela was now a pale woman of twenty, kindly disposed, solemn, interested in Eastern spirituality. She gave up her rounds as a traveling music teacher and stayed at home, receiving a few pupils and taking care of Jane. Henry and Sam—he no longer wanted to be called "Sammy"—went to school.

Orion did manage one important act: he prevailed on James Clemens Jr. to let him lease the house at 206 Hill Street, probably for a token sum, and the family moved back there a month after Marshall's death.

At his mother's urging, Sam set out to take whatever work he could find around town. He clerked in a grocery store, but was fired, he later revealed with a wink, for getting into the sugar. He worked in a bookstore, but didn't like it because "the customers bothered me so much I could not read with any comfort."[1] A stint in an apothecary shop ended because "my prescriptions were unlucky, and we appeared to sell more stomach pumps than soda water."[2] He had a paper route for a while, delivering the Hannibal *Gazette;* he delighted in spreading word of the United States Army's victory at Chapultepec Castle in September 1847, which turned the tide of the Mexican War. An officer in that battle—who ordered a howitzer lifted into a church belfry for more effective firing—was Ulysses S. Grant, whom Clemens would get to know rather well.

He worked in a blacksmith's shop. He worked part-time as a printer's devil at the Hannibal *Gazette*, published by one Henry La Cossitt—the first stage of apprenticeship. He claimed that he even spent a week studying the law, but gave it up "because it was so prosy and tiresome."[3] (No offense, Pa!)

This fitful job hopping went on for about a year and a half. Then, around June 1848, Jane apprenticed him to the new twenty-four-year-old publisher of the Hannibal *Gazette*, renamed the *Courier.* Joseph P. Ament took over La Cossitt's shop on the second floor of the L. T. Brittingham drugstore at Hill and Main, Hannibal's hub of commerce.

Sam's workplace was only half a block from the Clemens household, yet it stood directly in history's path. The newspaper age was dawning in America, an age that would effloresce into mass communications and the formation of a transformative popular culture. Sam Clemens, who would come to define that culture, was there from the beginning: he fetched water, swept the floor, and stoked the fireplace in the winter. He was paid nothing, but the arrangement saved Jane a few pennies. Sam wore Ament's hand-me-down clothes and took meals in the Ament household on the edge of the village, returning downtown to sleep on the print-shop floor. Sam loathed the Aments. He considered Joseph a stingy, short-tempered, and generally nasty man—"this diminutive chunk of human meat,"[4] as he would brand him in the Hannibal *Journal* several years later. In his spare moments, however, Sam learned to set type, a valuable skill.

Newspapers proliferated across the nation in the late 1840s. Borne on the rising tide of mass literacy, their page production expanded by steam, their information sources interlinked by the railroad and telegraph, newspapers collapsed time and space between individuals and the events that affected their lives. In the cities, two-cylinder iron printing presses powered by steam replaced the wooden hand-operated ones, some of which had required four days of loading just to print one page. In the hinterlands, smaller and more manageable hand-run presses made start-ups possible in every hamlet. Cities were hotbeds of the press. In Baltimore, a Quaker printer and journalist named Hezekiah Niles created the ancestor of the 20th-century news-magazine: his *Niles' Register,* which he founded in 1811, grew into a national journal of tremendous influence in the pre–Civil War era. Its densely set pages, unrelieved by illustration, were crammed with national and international news, most of which Niles drew (in classic newsweekly fashion) from other publications. Devoted readers included John Adams, Thomas Jefferson, and Andrew Jackson.

America, which claimed only 650 weekly papers and 65 dailies in 1830, boasted double that number in the early 1840s. By the end of the decade the figure would double again. Most of the papers sold for a penny, and took in profits by selling ad space. Newspapering had shifted its raison d'être a few years earlier, from functioning as political-party organs to journals of information aimed at an undifferentiated readership.

The social impact of newspapers reached well beyond information sharing. Collectively, they formed a far-flung archipelago of working writers' workshops: venues where talented young men, and occasionally women, could develop prose writing skills that they might later adapt to the creation of novels, essays, and poems. Most of the nation's best-known writers of the 19th and early 20th centuries made this journey "from fact to fiction," as Shelley Fisher Fishkin has called it.[5] "The poor boy's college," Franklin called the printing shop, and indeed it was the wellspring of America's distinctive literature of personal experience.

The penny-press vogue had reached Hannibal in 1837, with a paper called the *Commercial Advertiser,* later the *Pacific Monitor,* then the *Hannibal Journal and Native American,* and finally the *Journal.* Now, with the quiet *Gazette* transformed, the *Journal* had some real competition. Ament was an ambitious, tight-fisted and shrewd young man who saw ad dollars to be harvested from Hannibal's prospering parasol sellers, cigar and snuff dealers, cookstove merchants, slave traders, and saddle makers. Hannibal was booming. Even a fellow with writing ambitions could get a leg up. The Writing Academy of Messrs. Jennings and Guernsey offered

[c]lasses, day or evening as preferred. A class for ladies only in the afternoons. A chance for Hannibal people who have never had an opportunity to write, to do so now.[6]

The packing plants at Bear Creek now slaughtered thirteen thousand swine a year and the streets were glutted with squealing porkers and their waste. Sam and his friends made balloons out of discarded pig bladders—or at least Tom Sawyer and his friends did. Steam-driven ferries across the Mississippi replaced the ones powered by horses on treadmills. The jostling new steamboats formed a nautical skyline along the levee, replacing the once-a-day packets of Sam's earlier boyhood. The boats took away 110,000 bushels of wheat and other produce; the total value approached $1.25 million.[7] (In the summer of 1845 one of them unknowingly took away the nine-year-old Sammy, who had crept aboard and hidden under a lifeboat. He made it as far as Louisiana, Missouri, thirty-two miles downstream, before a crewman noticed his legs sticking out and he was set ashore.) Almost everyone was making out, it seemed, except the Clemenses.

TYPESETTING WAS arduous, repetitive, exacting work. The steam-driven press had not yet appeared in Hannibal, and many newspapers employed updated versions of the wooden spindle-screw press used by Benjamin Franklin in 1725 London—a device similar to the one invented by Gutenberg almost three hundred years earlier. In 1795, a Scotsman living in Philadelphia named Adam Ramage tossed out the time-consuming spindle screw in favor of a triple-threaded device that allowed for 250 separate impressions an hour. Ramage's lighter model was transportable by steamboats and even horse-drawn carts, and fit into a household-sized room. Even before the advent of steam, the Ramage press brought the age of newspapering across the Mississippi and into the West.

Ament almost certainly owned a Ramage, and this machine became Sam's primer. He and his co-workers learned to put together news pages by picking individual letters (cast backward, of course) from a case of metal typefaces sorted alphabetically. Placing them into the handheld metal tray called a "stick," they formed the letters into words, and the words into lines, which they then placed onto the cast-iron type bed. When the type bed was full, the printers slathered it with viscous ink and covered the inky type with a sheet of paper, usually made of sturdy rag stock. Then they pressed the platen, hinged to the type bed at a right angle, down on the bed via the powerful triple-threaded screw. It was extremely dirty work, if only because of the ink.

Typesetting was not the only source of fascination for Sam in Ament's little newspaper shop. He also delighted in his fellow inmates. Newspapering held a natural attraction for eccentric misfits, whether in a rural outpost or a great city. The *Courier* boasted at least two, not counting the owner: a journeyman printer named T. P. "Pet" McMurry, and Sam's fellow boarder and apprentice, the bear-sized Wales McCormick. Sam rejoiced in McMurry's dandified ways—his plug hat tipped forward almost to the bridge of his nose, his greasy red hair rolled under at the bottom, his red goatee. The part of Pet's hair under the plug hat was so deep and precise that "you could look into it as you would into a tunnel."[8] Sam loved his "mincing, self-conceited gait," which he recalled as "a gait possible nowhere on earth but in our South & in that old day . . ."[9] McMurry, in turn, later remembered Sam as a tiny, curly-haired boy "mounted upon a little box at the case, pulling away at a huge Cigar," wailing the ballad of a drunken man as he worked.[10] McMurry probably mentored the boy in the art of typesetting.

Then there was seventeen-year-old Wales McCormick, who awed Sam with his genial amorality. His bulk bursting through Ament's other cast-off suit, Wales capered through the premises as "a reckless, hilarious, admirable creature; he had no principles, and was delightful company."[11] Among the antics that regaled Sam, who was not yet detached from the racist mores of his time and place, was Wales's pastime of coming on to the daughter of the Aments' elderly slave-woman cook. Mark Twain recounted the casual hazing decades later, still with only a hint of reproach. A "very handsome and bright and well-behaved young mulatto," as Twain remembered her, this hapless figure endured Wales's boisterous bouts of "making love" to her night after night: "It was killingly funny to Ralph [the other apprentice] and me."[12] Mark Twain did not specify what he meant by "making love." In that era the term was often a synonym for "romancing" or "paying court to." But he left it clear that whatever the extent of McCormick's attentions, or intentions, the mother and daughter were helpless: "And, to speak truly," he continued in the passage, "the old mother's distress about it was merely a pretense. She quite well understood that by the customs of slave-holding communities it was Wales's right to make love to that girl if he wanted to." (The fact that the girl was "mulatto" more or less ratified this.) He concluded the anecdote with a moderate acknowledgment of the sordidness of it all: "But the girl's distress was very real. She had a refined nature, and she took all Wales's extravagant love-making in resentful earnest."

McCormick turned his rakehell needling on more formidable targets as well. Not long after Sam joined the *Courier,* an eminence from the booming religious-revival circuit swept into town. In Mark Twain's frequent (and varied) recounting of the story, the figure was Alexander Campbell,* son of Thomas Campbell, the founder of the Campbellites and a co-founder of the Disciples of Christ. The illustrious divine preached a sermon on the town square, and Sam marveled at the turnout. "[T]hat was the first time in my life that I had realized what a mighty population this planet contains when you get them all together." [13] His followers craved a printed version of the homily, and Ament printed five hundred copies for sixteen dollars, a sum exceeding any Sam had ever seen, given that Hannibalians usually settled their debts with sugar, coffee, turnips, and onions.

This visit produced what might be called the Gospel according to Wales. In one version of the story, Twain insisted that when Campbell stopped by Ament's shop with the sermon, he overheard McCormick exclaim, "Great God!" The preacher took the boy aside and admonished him that "Great God!" was blasphemy, and that "Great Scott!" would be one example of an acceptable substitute. McCormick apparently took this to heart: while correcting the proof sheet of the sermon, he dutifully changed Campbell's own pious use of "Great God" to "Great Scott." Taken with the spirit, he amended "Father, Son & Holy Ghost" to "Father, Son & Caesar's Ghost," and then improved even that bit of euphemism—to "Father, Son & Co." [14]

Wales's moment of divine reckoning approached when he removed the full name "Jesus Christ" from a line in the sermon to create more space, and substituted "J. C." For some reason, this infuriated Campbell as he read the proof sheet; he strode back to the print shop and commanded McCormick: "So long as you live, don't you ever diminish the Savior's name again. Put it *all* in." [15] McCormick took this advice to heart: the revised line came out, "Jesus H. Christ."

Typesetting made language more palpable to Sam and he quickly ex-

---

* Mark Twain may have misidentified the churchman. Marc Parsons has pointed out that Campbell's own writings in his *Millennial Harbinger* cite two visits to Hannibal, in 1845 and 1852. The incident in question could have happened only between 1848 and the end of 1850, the span of Sam Clemens's time in Joseph Ament's shop. It remains possible that Campbell, who traveled almost constantly, neglected to record this particular visit.

celled at it. The process of putting his fingers on molded metal letters, feeling their weight, and sliding them along precise rows into words and sentences as he smoked his outsize "Cigar" seems to have annealed him to language as a tactile presence in his hands. The paradigm of typesetting governed his prose writing and his handwriting, resonating with his speaking style. Even as torrentially fast as he worked, twenty manuscript pages a day in the throes of inspiration or need, his sentences were always *constructed,* never dashed off: ". . . [T]he difference between the *almost*-right word and the *right* word is really a large matter—it's the difference between the lightning-bug and the lightning." [16] He loved the last words of the ex-printer, Benjamin Franklin, and the process of their careful composition: "He pondered over his last words for as much as two weeks, and then when the time came he said 'None but the brave deserve the fair,' and died happy. He could not have said a sweeter thing if he had lived till he was an idiot." [17] His handwriting remained exceptionally clear, almost geometrically shaped on the page, throughout his life, and he frequently filled his margins with typesetter's instructions to the printer. His speaking style, famous for its "long talk" and its effective pauses, was virtually an aural analog of typography's orderly flow.

IN 1849, Sam and his cohorts had plenty of news to set in type.

In April, a new stream of transients joined the hogs and dogs jostling for space on Hannibal's streets: fortune hunters from the East, disembarking by ferry and steamboat to commence the two-thousand-mile overland trek to California following the discovery of gold on the American River in the California Territory. Here was the hotel clientele that the late Marshall Clemens had dreamed about. The Gold Rushers galvanized the town and swept eighty of its citizens along with them that year. Three hundred Hannibalians would eventually join the worldwide frenzy—including Dr. Meredith and his son and, in a roundabout way, the small cigar smoker in Ament's printing shop.

Two months later, a darker stream infested the town: cholera. An epidemic broke out in New Orleans at the year's turn, traveled by steamboat up the Mississippi River, left 3,200 dead in St. Louis, and struck Hannibal in June before moving on to Chicago and into Wisconsin. It was the second such attack in three years. The *Courier* toted up the dead—thirty, before the summer was over—and recommended "soap and courage," while the *Journal* advised a flannel or woolen belt around the belly. The Bloomington, Illinois, *Western Whig* theorized that it was a "malignant agent in the atmosphere" that originated somehow in "the decay of vegetable matter about the mouth of the Ganges in Asia." [18]

Cholera was the most dreaded of all the inexplicable diseases to sweep through European and American populations in the 19th century. Like bilious fever, it crossed oceans on westbound ships and then fanned out along inland waterways, borne by a bacterium that lurked in food and drinking water (although science did not figure this out until 1883). It attacked the intestines, causing diarrhea and vomiting, and death resulted within three days. Cholera hitched a ride west with the Gold Rushers. The prospect of it would haunt every ocean voyage that Mark Twain made in his long life, and sometimes it struck the ships on which he sailed.

Later that year, Sam found himself setting type on a gruesome story that spread terror in Hannibal, led to the country's first legal execution, and reinforced the racial tensions that were mounting inexorably toward civil war. This was the rape and murder of a twelve-year-old girl by a young slave known as "Glasscock's Ben." The girl had just brained her ten-year-old brother with a hunk of quarry rock, and Ben responded by cutting the girl's throat. Ament personally covered the slave's trial and death sentence in Palmyra and wrote a long account of it in the December 6 edition of the *Courier.* Ben was reported to have boasted that he would never be hanged because he was worth a thousand dollars. (He was wrong about the first part.) Sam stored the traumatic story in his mind, as he had so many others, and discharged it in the plot of *Pudd'nhead Wilson:* the technically Negroid Tom Driscoll escapes a life sentence for the murder of his uncle because he is revealed to be "the property" of his father's estate.

Mark Twain's prodigious memory often found congenial company with a contrary impulse: the tale teller's impulse to improve memory with fiction. Mark Twain took a democrat's view of fact and fiction; he privileged neither above the other and let them mingle in his work without prejudice, joking famously in later life about being able to remember anything whether it happened or not, and about too much truth as an impediment to good literature. This habit of mind produced good literature indeed, and left biographers over two centuries stumbling into one another as they tried to sort out what actually happened from what actually didn't.

Joseph Ament never drove his rival *Journal* out of business, luckily for the Clemenses. In January 1850, the *Journal*'s publishers and owners, Robert and Joseph Buchanan, hit the trail for California, leaving the paper in the hands of Joe Buchanan's son, Robert, and Samuel R. Raymond. Jane Clemens urged Orion to return to Hannibal with an eye to taking over the paper. In September, he released the first issue of the Hannibal *Western Union.* Not long afterward, he acquired the *Journal,* consolidated the two papers, and hired the as-yet undiscovered Lincoln of American literature.

6

Rambler

(1852–53)

On September 16, 1852, a refined young gentleman named Josiah T. Hinton, the "local" editor for the brand new Hannibal *Tri-Weekly Messenger,* picked up a copy of the rival Hannibal *Journal* and was thunderstruck to find himself wickedly caricatured in a woodcut printed along with a story about him: his head was portrayed as the head of a dog; the Hinton figure was leaning on a cane, carrying a lantern, and advancing toward the moonlit waters of Bear Creek with a liquor bottle suspended in space in front of him. The headline above the drawing announced: " 'Local' Resolves to Commit Suicide." Below the headline, a brief paragraph summed it all up:

> The artist has, you will perceive, Mr. Editor, caught the gentleman's countenance as correctly as the thing could have been done with the real *dog*-gerytype apparatus. Ain't he pretty? and don't he step along through the mud with an air? "Peace to his *re*-manes." [1]

The paragraph was signed, "A DOG-BE-DEVILED CITIZEN." [2]

About three weeks earlier, J. T. Hinton had made the grave, if unsuspecting, mistake of ridiculing Orion Clemens in print. Orion had written a mild complaint about barking dogs at night, in his newly established *Journal.* Hinton, a newcomer, had responded in the *Messenger* with a ponderous bloc of elephantine scorn: "A fierce hater of the canine race pours out his vials of wrath, as if to add a fresh stimulus to our worthy dog-exterminator, whose active exertions have already silenced the plaintive wail and mournful howl of

52

many a pugnacious cur and ferocious mastiff." [3] The response to the response was not from phlegmatic Orion, but from his younger brother. Hinton became the first public victim of the compressed satiric vengeance of the future Mark Twain.

Sam had recently turned fifteen when he joined Henry in Orion's shop in January 1851. Orion needed all the help he could get. Within a few months of his debut as a publisher, he had lost his enthusiasm and had grown depressed. Already, he was turning into his late father: serious, studious, oppressively honest; a young man who, like Marshall, had never really been a boy. Like his father, he was born to failure. Orion lurched and drifted through life from one dreamy impulse to another, never quite surrendering himself to any one thing. Sam once confessed to Howells that he imagined Orion on the stage, a melancholy harlequin, forever shifting his political and religious passions, "& trying to reform the world, always inventing something, & losing a limb by a new kind of explosion at the end of each of the four acts." [4]

Orion served as frequent fodder for Sam's satire. He is the undisguised Secretary in *Roughing It,* and traces of him show up in Washington Hawkins in *The Gilded Age;* he is Oscar Carpenter in the mostly factual "Villagers 1840–3" and in "Hellfire Hotchkiss." He influenced Angelo Capello in *Pudd'nhead Wilson.* He was also the star of a malignant, unfinished story, to which the biographer Paine assigned the title, "Autobiography of a Damned Fool," and which did not see publication until 1967. [5]

Sam's cruelty toward Orion coexisted with a habit of literally giving his older brother the clothes off his back. He pitied, bankrolled, and safeguarded his sibling. In this context, young Sam's counterattack on J. T. Hinton was more than mere adolescent spleen. It was payback for an attack on his flesh and blood. Sam's pen (and knife) treated Hinton to a roasting the likes of which had not been seen in the brief annals of Hannibal journalism. Here were the early glowings of the pen warmed up in Hell.

Sam saw his opportunity when Orion left on a late summer business trip to St. Louis and put him in charge of the paper—or the henhouse, in a manner of looking at it. He "asked me if I thought I could edit one issue of the paper judiciously. Ah, didn't I want to try!" [6]

"Judiciously" was scarcely the point. Sam's fingers must have been snaking toward the typecase before Orion was out the door.

The sixteen-year-old built his payback on an incident that had caused Hinton some embarrassment around town. " 'Local' Resolves to Commit Suicide" referred to Hinton's halfhearted attempt to drown himself in Bear Creek one night after being jilted. Hinton had slogged waist-deep into the water, thought better of the impulse, and sloshed back to shore. In the meantime a friend of his had found his suicide note and made for the creek in time to see Hinton struggling back to safety. "The village was full of it for several days, but Hinton did not suspect it." [7]

Beneath the woodcut—which he had slashed out on the backs of large wooden types, with his jackknife—Sam archly suggested that Hinton's aborted suicide (and his imputed drinking) had to do with a lack of public response to his attack on Orion:

'LOCAL,' disconsolate from receiving no further notice from 'A DOG-BE-DEVILED CITIZEN,' contemplates Suicide. His 'pocket-pistol' (i.e. the *bottle,*) failing in the patriotic work of ridding the country of a nuisance, he resolves to 'extinguish his chunk' by feeding his carcass to the fishes of Bear Creek, while friend and foe are wrapt in sleep. Fearing, however, that he may get out of his depth, he *sounds the stream with his walking-stick.*[8]

Sam and his helpers inked the type, churned the edition out and distributed it, then sat back to wait for the inevitable howl of outrage from down the street. It came with gratifying shrillness and speed later that day. "This newly arisen 'Ned Buntline' [a lurid "dime-novelist" of the period] shall be paid in his own coin," the *Messenger* threatened. But two days after that, Hinton withdrew his threat to retaliate in kind and attempted dignified condescension: "Such controversies are adapted only to those whose ideas are of so obscene and despicable an order as to forever bar them against a gentlemanly or even decent discussion, . . . "[9]

This flotilla of heavily armored prose, so conventional in its midcentury context, was no match for the sleek torpedoes that came foaming back. In the September 23 edition of the *Journal* two more woodcuts appeared. (Sam would be a sketcher and napkin-doodler all his life, and a few of his line drawings, awkward but comically intelligible, would accompany his published work.) The first showed the dog-headed "Local" mincing in excitement over "something interesting in the *Journal.*" The second, metaphorically shrewd, showed the same "Local" being blown away by his own cannon, which he had "chartered" to wage war on the *Journal. "Lead* being scarce," the caption continued, rubbing it in, "he loads his cannon with *Tri-Weekly Messengers.*"

After a little more verbal nose-thumbing, Sam adroitly declared the feud over:

Mr. Editor:

I have now dropped this farce, and all attempts to again call me forth will be useless.

A Dog-be-Deviled Citizen.[10]

Arriving back in Hannibal just as this was going to press, Orion was horrified by Sam's swashbuckling breach of decorum. He rushed an editorial into that very issue, trying to jolly up the *Messenger:* "The jokes of our correspondent have been rather rough; but, originating and perpetrated in a spirit of fun, and without a serious thought, no attention was expected to be paid to them,

beyond a smile at the local editor's expense."[11] Later that day this brought
forth one final, tremendous *harrumph!* from the *Messenger,* and there the
vendetta ended. But Sam Clemens had tapped the lode of invective that
would irradiate his satiric voice forever afterward.

THE FILLETING of J. T. Hinton was not Sam's first identifiable appearance in print. That had occurred eighteen months earlier, on January 16,
1851, within days after Sam had joined Orion's paper, still named the *Western
Union.* The target, unnamed in the item, was a long-suffering apprentice at
the paper named Jim Wolf. The previous week, an early morning fire had broken out in the grocery store next door to the *Western Union* shop. The two boys,
laboring late, had spotted it. Wolf came a little unhinged. Snatching the first
items that caught his eye—a broom, a mallet, a wash-pan and a dirty towel—
he bolted and ran for about half a mile. By the time he made it back, the fire
was out. Sam got it all into a one-paragraph item headlined, "A Gallant Fireman," * which he finished off with a sampling of Wolf's homespun dialect:

He returned in the course of an hour, nearly out of breath, and thinking he had immortalized himself, threw his giant frame in a tragic attitude, and exclaimed, with an
eloquent expression: "If that thar fire hadn't bin put out, thar'd a' bin the greatest *con-
firmation* of the age![12]

So far as is known, Sam didn't write again for Orion's newspaper until just before he ridiculed J. T. Hinton in September 1852. He'd turned his energies toward getting published in the widely circulated papers of the East. His urban
debut was a facetious sketch called "The Dandy Frightening the Squatter,"
published in the May 1 edition of the Boston *Carpet-Bag,* a comic weekly, over
the initials "S. L. C."—his first byline.
    A crude fragment of frontier slapstick, "The Dandy" nonetheless shows
Sam paying attention to the literary conventions of his time. It has some
aspects of the frame story, with young Sam himself in the role of the gentlemanly observer, recounting an incident that happened "About thirteen years
ago, when the now flourishing young city of Hannibal . . . was but a 'wood-
yard,' " that is, a fueling station for steamboats. A brawny woodsman is
leaning against a tree, gazing toward an approaching steamboat. Among
the boat's passengers is a "spruce young dandy, with a killing mustache," who
is keen on impressing the ladies on board. Spotting "our squatter friend" on
the bank, he alerts the ladies that a good laugh is at hand. He sticks a bowie
knife into his belt, takes a horse pistol in each hand, and strides up to the
woodsman.

---

* Some scholars, including Edgar Marquess Branch, an editor of *The Works of Mark Twain:
Early Tales & Sketches,* believe that Sam composed this piece as he stood before the "case," setting
it by hand into type.

"Found you at last, have I? You are the very man I've been looking for these three weeks! Say your prayers!" he continued, presenting his pistols, "you'll make a capital barn door, and I shall drill the key-hole myself!"

The squatter calmly surveyed him a moment, and then, drawing back a step, he planted his huge fist directly between the eyes of his astonished antagonist, who, in a moment, was floundering in the turbid waters of the Mississippi.[13]

He then offers his sputtering accoster a bit of rustic advice: "I say, yeou, next time yeou come around drillin' key-holes, don't forget yer old acquaintances!" The ladies are amused and vote "the knife and pistols to the victor." End of story.

With that surrogate punch in the Dandy's snoot, the sixteen-year-old Missouri truant had shown some bare knuckles to the fancy folks in Boston.

A week after this debut, the boy writer earned another big-city byline. The paper was the Philadelphia *American Courier,* and this time Sam's Huck Finnish outlaw pose had given way to an experiment in Tom Sawyer–like boosterism. His new sketch, also signed "S. L. C.," was a gilt-edged homage to his native town. This was the first published product in a lifetime of Hannibal-conjurings. Encrusted with flourishes that fit him as badly as Joseph Ament's clothes—"Then the wild war-whoop of the Indian resounded where now rise our stately buildings"—the brief piece is flat and unremarkable, except for another hint of Sam's Southwestern edginess regarding the snob culture of the seaboard: "Your Eastern people seem to think this country is a barren, uncultivated region, with a population consisting of heathens."[14]

HIS AMBITION to reach a larger readership was fired by the periodicals that drifted into Orion's humble print shop from around the country. If frontier-era newspapers were a "poor boy's college," they had their texts: other frontier-era newspapers. The Postal Act of 1792 allowed every publisher to send one free copy of his paper to every other publisher in the country, without charge, postal or otherwise, provided only that that publisher did likewise in return. This was the system of the "exchange." No wire services yet existed and the telegraph was limited in its reach; thus small-town papers depended on this exchange, along with "letters" from sojourning friends or relatives, for all their material beyond the strictly local. As Sam sifted through the daily influx in Hannibal, he grew familiar with the names and locales of dozens of dailies, weeklies, and biweeklies around the country, including those in the metropolises east of the Mississippi: Boston, Philadelphia, New York.

He also grew familiar with the kinds of writing that made it into these papers. Besides news stories, they carried topical essays, poetry, and sketches, including the Southwestern frame story.

Yet another branch of dialect humor, rampant through the Southwest, was regularly available in Orion's own paper:

"Julius, is you better dis morning?"

"No. I was better yesterday, but got over it."

"Am der no hopes den ob your discovery?"

"Discovery ob what?"

"Your discovery from de convalescence dat fetch you on yer back?"

"Dat depends, Mr. Snow, altogether on de prognostifications which amplify de disease. Should dey terminate fatally, de doctor tinks Julius am a gone nigger; should dey not terminate fatally, he hopes de colored individual won't die till anoder time. As I said before, it all depends on the prognostics, and till these come to a head, it is hard telling whedder de nigger will discontinue hisself or not." [15]

This darky humor was commonplace in the American press, and blacks rendered by Mark Twain sometimes sounded, on the surface, like these minstrel show end men. Yet the typical darky humor lacked the psychological depth, expressed in cadence, irony, imagery, and declamatory elegance, that issued from Mark Twain's greatest characters. No print models existed for their deeply consummated language. It flowed from Mark Twain's extraordinary auditory memory, and was shaped on the page by his loving respect for its outlaw integrity and its wild improvisational genius.

Orion looked for poetry and essays of the "refined" and the "polite" sort to fill his *Journal.* He sent letters to the New England eminences Emerson and Holmes, offering each the chance to write for the *Journal* at five dollars an essay. Unaccountably, he never heard back. He did manage to print some excerpts from Dickens's new novel *Bleak House,* which he could do in the absence of international copyright laws, and he pressed a copy of the book on Sam as a literary model.

The Clemenses' home life was looking up as the 1850s began. With Orion having finally sold a tiny sliver of the Tennessee land and launching his little newspaper, the Clemenses could feel that some of life's everyday pleasures seemed possible again. Jane had recovered from Marshall's death. Careworn, gentle-eyed Pamela married in October 1851, at the advanced age of twenty-four. The groom was a former neighbor named William Anderson Moffett, eleven years her senior and a partner in the commission-merchant firm of Moffett, Stillwell and Company.

Sam and his younger brother Henry, the Good Boy, worked side by side in Orion's shop during these years. From the sketchy evidence, they behaved toward each other like typical siblings, a little fractiously, each trying to get an edge. They would not fashion a real friendship until the end of their adolescences.

HANNIBAL GREW plump, and brassy, and busy in these last years before the Civil War. It had become Missouri's second-largest city. Orion Clemens did his best to match the new excitement with thundering editorials in his *Journal:* "We notice every day that the side walks, all over the city are obstructed with goods, boxes, &c., &c. This should not be. The streets are so muddy that it is impossible to walk outside the pavement, and the side walks generally are so covered with lumber that there is scarcely room for two to walk abreast of them." [16]

By his own later admission, Sam slipped in a playful paragraph here and there from the very beginning of his stint with Orion.[17] There is no doubting the true identity of "W. Epaminondas Adrastus Perkins," who made his first appearance on September 9, 1852, a week before Sam's strike at J. T. Hinton. This is the first of many pen names that Sam experimented with before he settled on his immortal alias. "A Family Muss" is a rather puerile experiment in Irish-baiting humor, the faux-account of a rampage by the head of a Gaelic family on Holliday's Hill, who, "very much in want of exercise," finds himself a "good stout cudgel" and commences "thumping the heads of his astounded neighbors promiscuously." The short piece ends with an exhibition of boiler-plate Irish dialect—"Och! he's the dreadfulest man I *iver* see. Oh, me, I'se scairt to death, I is, an' I'll niver git over it in the worl'."[18]

W. Epaminondas Adrastus reappears—his last name now changed to "Blab"—in the notorious September 16 edition that ridicules Hinton's abortive suicide. Written with labored grown-up facetiousness and cast as a frame story, "Historical Exhibition—A No. 1 Ruse," begins, "A young friend gives me the following yarn as fact." The sketch deals with a supposed exhibition at a dry-goods store in Hannibal, called "Bonaparte crossing the Rhine"; townsfolk can hear a lecture explaining the "piece" for a dime, children half price. A boy, named Jim C—, plunks down his nickel and demands to see the show. What he sees is the proprietor passing a three-inch piece of hog leg (the "bony part") across a dollar-sized strip of hog skin (the "rind"). "Young man, you have now learned an important historical lesson," the proprietor tells the stricken boy.

As 1 8 5 2 drew to a close, Sam was dealing with a secret but increasingly powerful impulse to indulge a fantasy he'd harbored from early childhood: to hit the river. Now the idea was reinforced by adult considerations. Three weeks after his seventeenth birthday, he could look back on five and a half years of drudgery in various cramped printing offices, and forward to years more of the same. He had become a "swift and clean" journeyman typesetter, in Orion's estimation—not that Orion rewarded this accomplishment with an actual salary. His universe was constricted to the little river town that had held him since the age of four. He could go to the Mississippi levee and watch emissaries from the larger world disembark from the floating palaces up from St. Louis and New Orleans, but then the boats would depart, and the larger world receded from the boy's reach.

He could only ogle the high architecture of the riverboat—"long and sharp and trim and pretty" with its tall, fancy-topped chimneys. He envied the deckhands his own age who strutted on the decks, coils of rope in hand, flaunting their connection to the river life. He gazed upward at the captain lounging by the big bell, calm, "the envy of all." He admired the black smoke rolling out of the chimneys, even though he was shrewd enough to grasp it was "a husbanded grandeur created with a bit of pitch pine just before arriving." He took in the absurdities of his fellow townspeople as a steamer approached: the excitable saddler John W. Stabler ("John Stavely" in *Life on the Mississippi*) tearing down the street and struggling with his fluttering coat at the blast of a whistle—"he liked to seem to himself to be expecting a hundred thousand tons of saddles by this boat, and so he went on all his life, enjoying being faithfully on hand to receive and receipt for those saddles, in case by any miracle they should come." [19]

Other Hannibal men and boys were rushing in the opposite direction, westward, for gold—the California mines would yield $65 million in the ensuing year—but Sam was doomed to climb the same stairs every day to Orion's shop. Outside of Sam's own items, the *Journal* was a desolate, uninviting little sheet, with a readership of about a hundred people, which made almost no money.

BY THE end of 1852 Sam's boyhood had effectively ended. Six months later, in the eternal summer that was the climate for his fictional boyhood adventures, Hannibal would be behind him as well. In March 1853, Orion turned the paper into a daily. The timing was perfect, in an Orionean way of looking at things—people were already paying for their subscriptions in turnips and cordwood instead of cash, and a week earlier someone had spilled several columns of type, delaying publication of the weekly version. He was on a roll.

A new issue every day except Sunday meant more space to fill, which meant more dependence on Sam, and in early May he returned for a final profusion of poetry and madcap pranking in the *Journal*. (Orion was out of town again.) The poems are forgettable. The spree of self-mocking, identity-switching foolery they prompted him to unleash in the paper is less so. Already in a romantically humid (not to say randy) frame of mind, he had been moved by the hearts-and-flowers verse of Robert Burns and others, and on May 5, writing as "Rambler," he disgorged a lovesick ode loaded with "thou's," "wilts," "thines," and "mines" titled "The Heart's Lament," and addressed "TO BETTIE W—E, OF TENNESSEE." The poem was the first of two in that vein. The second, equally sentimental and called "Love Concealed," was addressed "TO MISS KATIE OF H—L."*

The following day, readers of the *Journal* were confronted with a short, waspish letter to the editor expressing outrage at the poem's title: "Now, I've often seen pieces to 'Mary in Heaven,' or 'Lucy in Heaven,' or something of that sort, but 'Katie in *Hell*,' is carrying the matter too far." Sam's letter was

---

* A third poem, titled "Separation" and also signed "Rambler," appeared in the rival *Missouri Courier* on May 12. As the editors of *Early Tales & Sketches* point out, its authorship cannot be conclusively attributed to Clemens; it may have been the work of an imitator.

signed GRUMBLER.[20] Two days after that, RAMBLER shot back at GRUMBLER: "are you so ignorant as not to be able to distinguish 'of' from 'in'? Read again—see if it is not 'of' H—l (Hannibal), instead of 'in' Hell . . ." and recommended a straitjacket.[21]

GRUMBLER was not about to take this lying down. The next day, he attacked again: "Must apologise. I merely glanced at your doggerel, and naturally supposing that you had friends in 'H—l,' (or *Hannibal*, as you are pleased to interpret it,) I . . . considered it my duty, in a friendly way, to tell you that you were going too far."[22]

Two days after that another voice joined the fray—this one the high, reedy know-it-all voice of "PETER PENCILCASE'S SON, JOHN SNOOKS." Snooks offered RAMBLER some high-toned but incoherent advice on lovemaking: "It is really amusing to every intelligent and intellectual mind, to see how consequential some coxcombs are. The parlor is too remote a place, and not conspicuous enough to reveal the overflowing affections of the H-e-a-r-t . . ."[23]

RAMBLER was back in print the next day, getting the last, heavy-handed adolescent word: ". . . I find that I have attracted the notice of a——fool . . . 'Snooks' . . . He calls me a 'Cox-Comb.' I will not say that he belongs to that long eared race of animals that have more head and ears than brains . . ."[24]

This one-man repertory revue was Sam's final boyhood display of his developing gift of "voice"—of tonal and syntactic mimicry.

Orion had returned to Hannibal in time to witness the winding-down stages of Sam's latest romp through his *Journal*. (In addition to the RAMBLER-GRUMBLER put-on, Sam had laced nearly everything in the paper with his screwball wit—proposing in one news item that a newly enacted whiskey tax made it a patriotic duty to drink.) Orion was finally starting to get it: that his younger brother might be the paper's main draw. He gave Sam a showcase for his wit. "Our Assistant's Column," a potpourri of topical items, gossip, feuds, and the general discharge of Sam's rocketing mind, might have become one of the early sensations of Missouri journalism, had it run for more than three editions. Orion's timing, as always, was misbegotten. Sam was bored, broke, and benumbed by the drudge work in his brother's office, and his daily diet at Jane's table of bacon, butter, bread, and coffee.

On May 25, 1853, a notice appeared in the Hannibal *Journal: "Wanted!* An Apprentice of the Printing Business. Apply soon."[25] A few days earlier, Sam had told Jane he was leaving. His destination was St. Louis, where he would put up at the home of Pamela and her husband, possibly get a printing job, and plan his next move. Already Sam had set his sights on destinations far beyond St. Louis, but he was not inclined to add to Jane's anxieties by telling her that.

Mark Twain sculpted the moment of leave-taking from his mother, making it rival the scene at John Marshall's deathbed. Jane holds up a copy of the Testament and demands that Sam take hold of the other end, and extracting a promise from him: "I do solemnly swear that I will not throw a card or drink a drop of liquor while I am gone." Sam repeats the oath and receives his mother's kiss.[26] As with the deathbed scene, this moment seems suspiciously melodramatic. But in a letter to Pamela the following fall, Sam asks her to "tell Ma my promises are faithfully kept."[27]

Sam's departure nearly felled Orion. Shocked, distraught, and immediately self-lacerating, he sank into a depression so paralyzing that he was unable to get an edition of the *Journal* out for an entire month.

One night in the first two weeks of June, Sam boarded a packet and slipped off down the Mississippi. The exact date is lost in the mists; as an old man he simply recalled that "I disappeared one night and fled to St. Louis."[28] There are no accounts of his farewells to anyone besides Jane. His itinerary would take him south, then east, then west, then halfway around the world. Eventually he would circle the globe. He would travel, or reside in some form of exile for most of the rest of his life. He would never again be as integrated with a holy place as he had been with Hannibal. He would return to the town just six more times in his life, and he would never live there again, except in his literature and in his dreams.

7

"So Far from Home . . ."

(1853–56)

It was as though he had launched himself by a slingshot. In the year to come, he would cover more than two thousand miles of American terrain, adapt to life in three Eastern cities, support himself by finding jobs with no benefit of references, and write letters to his family of astonishing perception and eloquence regarding what he saw and heard and did. He would negotiate passage by steamship, stagecoach, train, and omnibus, crossing prairie, inland rivers, lakes, and metropolitan precincts. He would renew and extend his prowess as a newspaper correspondent, commenting suavely on debate in the Senate chamber in Washington, D.C. He would develop a taste for fancy clothing and sit for a portrait outfitted in a high-collared shirt, dark jacket, checked vest, and generously knotted bow tie, slightly scowling just to the right of the camera eye under a magnificent wash of thick groomed hair, his full lips expressionless. If his letters to Jane were at all reliable, he would uphold his promise to behave himself, heading for the library when his work shift ended. Somewhere in the midst of all this, he would turn eighteen.

He stayed in St. Louis for only two months while he bankrolled himself setting type for the *Evening News* and other weekly papers. He almost certainly boarded with Pamela and William Moffett, who had a year-old daughter, Annie, and were themselves living with an aunt while they rented out their Pine Street house. Pamela's husband William, a thickset and jowly fellow, was a rising figure in St. Louis civic life: he had already done a turn on the Committee of Arbitration for the city's chamber of commerce.

No record survives of Sam's first reaction to the urban swirl, and his later recollections were jumbled. St. Louis was a "happy, cheerful, contented old town" in an 1867 correspondence,[1] but a year later he insisted on his "deep hatred" of the city; visiting it, he said, was a "ghastly infliction."[2] As for his feelings about launching out from his lifelong nest, though, Sam was swagger personified. "[N]othing could have convinced me that I would starve as soon as I got a little way from home," he boasted in a letter to Orion.[3] Later in life he joked, "The first time I ever saw St. Louis, I could have bought it for six million dollars, and it was the mistake of my life that I did not do it."[4]

The transition must have been at least a little overwhelming. St. Louis was just then exploding beyond its old borders as a French fur-trading center and headquarters of the Louisiana Territory. River trade and railroad construction had lured a large immigrant workforce—Germans and Irish, principally. The city was swelling from a population of just over 16,000 in 1840 to 160,000 at the eve of the Civil War.

Sam soon received his first taste of big-city condescension. His typesetting skills, so impressive to Orion, didn't cut much ice with his new, tough, older peers. "He always had so many errors marked in his proofs," sneered one of them half a century later, "that it took most of his time correcting them. He could not have set up an advertisement in acceptable form to save his life."[5] This same crusty pressman recalled another contemptible trait: in contrast to the printers' "proud prerogative . . . to be able to drink more red whisky than men of any other trade,"[6] the red-headed kid wouldn't take a drop.

JANE AND the others learned that Sam had ventured beyond St. Louis only when a letter arrived postmarked August 24, 1853, with the return address of New York, N.Y. It is Sam's earliest surviving letter—the earliest of between 50,000 and 100,000 written over his lifetime, by some estimates. Typical of the psychology he always used on Jane, he worked to defuse her likely anger with a joke—in this case, by inverting the reputations of himself and his solemn brothers.

My Dear Mother: you will doubtless be a little surprised, and somewhat angry when you receive this, and find me so far from home; but you must bear a little with me, for you know I was always the best boy you had, and perhaps you remember the people used to say to their children—"Now don't do like Orion and Henry Clemens but take Sam for your guide!"

Well, I was out of work in St. Louis, and didn't fancy loafing in such a dry place, where there is no pleasure to be seen without paying well for it, and so I thought I might as well go to New York. I packed up my "duds" and left for this village, where I arrived, all right, this morning.[7]

The journey might have taxed a veteran traveler. Sam had boarded a steamboat to nearby Alton, Illinois. From there he took a train east to Springfield, the closest he would ever come to Abraham Lincoln. There he boarded a stagecoach headed upstate to Bloomington. To Chicago the next day by rail. A twenty-six-hour layover, and then by rail to Toledo, Ohio, then Monroe, Michigan. A night there, and on Monday morning, across the three hundred-mile length of Lake Erie by the steamer *Southern Michigan* to Buffalo, New York. Onward to Albany on the "Lightning Express," passing close to Saratoga Springs, where a few days earlier a resort chef named George Crum had invented the potato chip. From Albany he boarded the Hudson River steamer *Isaac Newton* into New York City, arriving at about 5 a.m. on August 24. He vowed that he would look out for a "sit," or a printing "situation," after resting up a day or so, tacking on a little bouquet of reassurance to Jane: "for they say there is plenty of work to be had for *sober* compositors." [8]

The letter contained some evidence that while Sam may have breached the New York metropolis, he was still a long way from shedding his received backcountry biases. He tossed off a dismissive reference to "the infernal abolitionists" who had tried to rescue a fugitive slave (from around Hannibal, as it happened) and who had been arrested in Syracuse. He sneered callowly that "I reckon I had better black my face, for in these Eastern States niggers are considerably better than white people." [9]

The missive's longest passage dwelt on a "curiosity" Sam had come upon as he strolled the streets of New York: a pair of dwarfish humanoid brothers, apparently caged, advertised as having been captured years earlier on the island of Borneo. He described them in half-horrified, half-lascivious detail: as small, simian-faced, "with small lips and full breast, with a constant uneasy, fidgety motion, bright, intelligent eyes, that seems as if they would look through you." [10] The creatures may have been the same that P. T. Barnum featured in his circus years later under the billing, "the Wild Men of Borneo." They touched some deep chord in young Sam—the same chord, perhaps, that responded powerfully to themes and images of twinning, and of grotesque beings lifted from their natural habitat to grapple with identity in a hostile, dangerous world.

NEW YORK was hardly a "village" in 1853. Its population, 515,000 and swelling rapidly toward a million at the Civil War's eve, dwarfed that of St. Louis and nearly matched the total of Missouri. The vertical skyline had not risen yet, but the populace was flowing in, and Sam arrived on the tide: Irish fleeing the potato famine, Chinese fortune seekers soured on the Gold Rush and looking for urban labor; Germans; Jews; free blacks; swarms of merchants, financiers, and their employees jostling for a slice of the lucrative import-export trade that funneled Southern cotton and farm products from the interior to European markets, and received British-made machinery and manufactured goods. New York was an expanding poker game played with industry-sized stakes. The mostly Protestant winners built retail palaces of Italian marble, and residential mansions on Fifth Avenue and in Union, Madison, and Washington squares. The mostly Catholic losers fought disease, despair, and one another in some of the worst slums on earth, such as the Five Points that repelled even the slum refugee Dickens.

Sam homed in on Broadway, where he'd spotted the Borneo creatures. He took lodgings in a boardinghouse on Duane Street in lower Manhattan, not far from the future site of the Brooklyn Bridge, a neighborhood that Melville would haunt in his postwar decades as a customs inspector. Sam walked four miles a day, inspecting ornamented fruit salons, libraries, and the Crystal Palace (the venue of New York's first world fair, the Exhibition of the Industry of All Nations). Before long, he was a Broadway swell, commenting suavely on the stagecraft of the actor Edwin Forrest. He attended a performance of *Uncle Tom's Cabin,* by his future neighbor Harriet Beecher Stowe, and recalled years later how "[e]verybody went there in elegant toilettes and cried over Tom's griefs."[11] Young Sam may also have poked his head into some of Broadway's more lurid attractions, such as the wicked girlie show, *The Model Artists.* He apparently stayed long enough to confirm his worst suspicions.[12]

As would Thomas Wolfe a century later, he loved the manswarm on the streets: "I am borne, and rubbed, and crowded along, and need scarcely trouble myself about using my own legs," but disdained "Niggers, mulattoes, quadroons, Chinese" and other inconvenient life forms, including "trundle-bed trash"—children.[13]

WITHIN A week of his arrival, and despite a glut of qualified printers, Sam landed a job. He joined two hundred other employees in the noisy fifth-floor hive of John A. Gray's large job-printing house at 95–97 Cliff Street, preparing type for books and dozens of periodicals. He started at the lowest rate, 23 cents per 1,000 ems, but he satisfied Gray's exacting standards. "[O]ut of all the proofs I saw, without boasting, I can say mine was by far the cleanest," he wrote home. ". . . I believe I *do* set a clean proof."[14] Typesetting, sightseeing, letter writing, haunting the "free printer's library": in the two months that Sam remained in New York, and through all the Eastern urban sojourning that followed until his correspondence abruptly ceased in February 1854, these pursuits defined his life. He strengthened his skills in travel and self-expression. His compunction for noticing, powerful since infancy, fueled letters home that brimmed with detail, easy wit, and acquired information.

Things back home were in flux. Sam complained to Pamela in October that he didn't know where the Hannibal folks were. No one had bothered to inform him that the family had moved from Hannibal to Muscatine, Iowa, where Orion was gearing up to publish the Muscatine *Journal.* By that time Sam was not in New York anymore, either. He was in Philadelphia, as of mid-October, a substitute typesetter at the *Inquirer.*

His petulance didn't last. Sam was in the mood to strut; he had flabbergasted even himself with his blitzkrieg of the East. On October 26 he told his brother: ". . . I like this Phila amazingly, and the people in it." Some of his friends had encouraged him not to get downhearted. " 'Downhearted,' the devil! I have not had a particle of such a feeling since I left Hannibal, more than four months ago."[15] The letter blossomed into a robust travelogue of the city; he'd visited Benjamin Franklin's gravesite at Christ Church and strained to see the inscription on the marker.

HE'D HOPPED a stage for Fairmount Hill, where he inspected the cable bridge above the Schuylkill River, the first suspension bridge in the United States. At the Water Works, he ogled the "[f]at marble Cupids, in big marble vases" as they squirted water. Resuming the letter two days later, Sam described the "old cracked 'Independence Bell' " and how he sat on the same small pine bench where Washington and Franklin had sat: "I would have whittled off a chip, if I had got half a chance."[16] He expressed his awe at standing in the Old State House, where the Declaration of Independence was passed. In a letter written on December 4, he told about a woman billed as "The Largest Lady in the World" who tipped the scales at 764 pounds. He'd been disappointed: "She is a pretty extensive piece of meat, but not much to brag about; however, I suppose she would bring a fair price in the Cannibal Islands."[17]

His voracious cataloguing and disgorging of experience was more than the passing exhilaration of a boy away from home. It was the first rough draft of a writerly instinct in tune with a national literature in chrysalis. (Orion may not have quite grasped that potential, but he did shovel most of these missives from Sam directly into the Hannibal *Journal* and soon also the Muscatine *Journal*.) Here lay the early contours of *The Innocents Abroad* and the other products of Mark Twain's lifelong compulsion to capture life with words. Like Whitman, just then escaping the confines of journalism for the free-verse nonesuch *Leaves of Grass*—but without the older poet's aesthetic self-consciousness—Sam was performing the role of the Poet as redefined by Emerson: a representative man, intoxicated by some divine enhancement of thought, speaking out of his direct experience on behalf of his fellows. "He will tell us how it was with him, and all men will be the richer in his fortune."[18]

"I look in vain for the poet whom I describe," Emerson had lamented in 1844. "We have yet had no genius in America, with tyrannous eye, which knew the value of our incomparable materials, and saw, in the barbarism and materialism of the times, another carnival of the same gods whose picture he so much admires in Homer."[19] Here he came.

Yet he was far from Emersonian on some topics. He wrote to Orion on November 28, of "the eastern people" who were "whisky-swilling, God-despising heathens," adding, perhaps for Jane's eye, "I believe I am the only person in the Inquirer office that does not drink."[20] Referring to the Clemenses' new Iowa address, he concluded with, "How do you like 'free-soil?['] I would like amazingly to see a good, old-fashioned negro."[21]

On Christmas Eve, he wrote the first letter addressed explicitly to the Muscatine *Journal*, indulging a bit of tabloid journalism (a fire fatality's "feet were burned off, his face burnt to a crisp, and his head crushed in").[22] He mixed patriotic travelogue and grumpy preservationism. The Assembly Room in which Congress first met was now occupied by an auction mart. "Alas! that these old buildings, so intimately connected with the principal scenes in the history of our country, should thus be profaned. Why do not those who make such magnificent donations to our colleges and other institutions, give a mite toward their preservation of these monuments of the past?"[23]

His next letter to the *Journal*, written on February 17 and 18, 1854, was from the nation's capital. He arrived in Washington in a snowstorm and immediately set out to inspect the seat of American government. He was not entirely pleased: "The public buildings of Washington are all fine specimens of architecture, and would add greatly to the embellishment of such a city as New York—but here they are sadly out of place looking like so many palaces in a Hottentot village."[24] Sam thawed out inside the Capitol, finding his way to the small, Victorian arena on the second floor of the North Wing. From the visitors' balcony he looked down—in more ways than one—on a huddle of lawmakers as they conducted the nation's business:

I passed into the Senate Chamber to see the men who give the people the benefit of their wisdom and learning for a little glory and eight dollars a day. The Senate is now composed of a different material from what it once was. Its glory hath departed. Its halls no longer echo the words of a Clay, or Webster, or Calhoun . . . the void is felt. The Senators dress very plainly as they should, and . . . do not speak unless they have something to say—and that cannot be said of the Representatives. Mr. Cass [Sen. Lewis Cass, Democrat from Michigan] is a fine looking old man; Mr. Douglas, or "Young America" [Sen. Stephen Douglas, Democrat of Illinois] looks like a lawyer's clerk, and Mr. Seward [Sen. William H. Seward, Whig from New York] is a slim, dark, bony individual, and looks like a respectable wind would blow him out of the country.[25]

The three figures that Sam idly caricatured were just then wrestling with the destiny of the Union. Cass was soon to be secretary of state under President Buchanan. Douglas would make history as Abraham Lincoln's rival for the presidency and in the Lincoln-Douglas debates. Seward would also run for president against Lincoln, then become his wartime secretary of state and, afterward, negotiate the purchase of Alaska. On this snowy day, they were leading the debate on whether to repeal the Missouri Compromise and thus eliminate a powerful bulwark against the extension of slavery westward in the territories. The measure at issue was the Kansas-Nebraska Act, Douglas's vehicle for supplanting the Compromise. This act would allow territorial settlers, and not the federal government, to decide whether to allow slavery on their lands. Douglas steered his brainchild to victory three months after Sam's visit. Its passage created the territories of Kansas and Nebraska and drastically inflamed tensions over the slavery issue. The act prompted opponents of slavery to create the Republican Party and hand Lincoln a coherent political base. It set the stage for bloody border massacres and raids, and accelerated the onset of the Civil War. Sam lacked a sense of context to grasp what the amusing figures down on the floor were gassing on about. He went off to the Smithsonian Institution and to the Patent Office Building, which housed the National Museum, and then to the National Theatre to see Edwin Forrest play Othello.

He would return to Washington a few years later—older, more seasoned, and vastly more plugged in to political nuance, and its uses in fact and fiction.

Only the broad contours of Sam Clemens's next twelve months are known. None of his letters from this period have surfaced. A trail of unclaimed letters to him (listed routinely in newspapers) suggests that he returned to Philadelphia after a few days in Washington, stayed a couple of weeks, and then went back to New York, where he probably struggled through a lean wage-earning period: two publishing houses were gutted by fire, leaving dozens of printers out of work. When he decided to return home to the Mississippi valley, as he probably did in April 1854, financial stress was one of his reasons, or so he said in 1899.[26] He brought with him, no doubt, an awareness of the typesetter's numbing life, its fatiguing demands, and its dim prospects for security.

He rejoined his family, but within a few months, he returned to St. Louis and got himself rehired as a typesetter on the *Evening News*. He arrived in time to get mixed up in a makeshift dress rehearsal for the Civil War. Riots flared around the country like heat lightning in those tense times, many of them stirred up by angry Jacksonians who saw their way of life being swept away by industrialism, abolitionists, and the European Catholic immigrants, who seemed to mock the good Protestant verities, including the "verity" of slavery as divinely ordained. St. Louis was a stronghold of the most virulent dissidents, the Know-Nothings,* who could not abide the flow of German, Italian, and Irish Catholics into the city. A few years later the Know-Nothings would boast a new recruit: the struggling thirty-two-year-old ex-officer Ulysses S. Grant, who joined after a foreign-born opponent beat him out for appointment as county engineer. Grant attended one lodge meeting.

The rioting in St. Louis erupted on August 7, 1854, as Know-Nothings attacked immigrant neighborhoods. Sam, who was living in a boardinghouse, went with a friend to an armory where a militia was being formed to quell the hell-raisers. "We drilled until about 10 o'clock that night," Mark Twain recalled thirty years later; "then news came that the mob were in great force in the lower end of town, and were sweeping everything before them." His column moved out, gripping muskets. As the bloody implications of this adventure clarified themselves in his mind, Sam developed a powerful thirst. "I was behind my friend," Mark Twain remembered; "so, finally, I asked him to hold

* The nickname hung on the nativist American party by Horace Greeley, in reference to members' penchant for saying, "I know nothing," in response to all questions about their organization. Greeley intended the label as an indictment, but party members grew to like it.

my musket while I dropped out and got a drink. Then I branched off and went home."[27] The riot was put down after two days; the Know-Nothings split over the slavery issue in 1856 and eventually faded away. Ulysses S. Grant went on to better things, and so did Samuel L. Clemens.

Orion shut down his *Journal* around the end of March 1855 and, with his brother Henry and his mother, left Muscatine for Keokuk. He had enlivened the paper with occasional dispatches from Sam, still the proud reactionary, in St. Louis—"A new Catholic paper (bad luck to it) is also soon to be established, for the purpose of keeping the Know Nothing organ straight,"[28] he'd groused in one item. But Orion's new wife, Mollie, finally persuaded her husband to move to the city where her family lived. On June 11, Orion set himself up as a job printer, his youngest brother serving as his assistant. Orion soon wrote to Sam and asked him to return to small-town Iowa life, offering him five dollars a week. By mid-June, surprisingly, Sam accepted the offer.[29] He probably accepted on an impulse: the job would get him out of a dangerous city and back on the Mississippi for a while. He had rekindled his boyhood fantasy of being a Mississippi steamboat pilot, and threw himself into making it happen. Once he had established himself in Keokuk, he took a downriver packet to St. Louis, then back to Hannibal, and Paris, Missouri, sometime in July 1855. In St. Louis he pleaded unsuccessfully with his wealthy relative James Clemens Jr. to pull some strings for him. Sam headed for the levee to try the direct approach, but had no luck.

Probably on that downriver trip, he began a practice that would prove incalculably useful to his literary career: he started keeping a notebook, the first of fifty that survive; others, probably dozens, have been lost. Into these, over four decades, he poured "found data": wisps of experience and anecdotes; bursts of indignation, opinion, regret; newly minted aphorisms; maps real and imagined; German vocabulary; timetables and laundry lists; notes on the works of Shakespeare and Matthew Arnold; the listing of facts of all kinds; and, as always, the stunning harvest of his intense noticing ("Sailors walk with hands somewhat spread & palms turned backward") that made his writing burn truer and more mimetic of life-as-lived than anyone else's in America or Europe.

He took a side trip to the Quarles farm in Florida, Missouri, which his uncle John had by now sold—his last glimpse of the prairie in its loneliness and peace—and then traveled to Paris to wrap up some family business. Then he headed back upriver to Keokuk, and the last brief period of a rooted life that he would know for fifteen years.

AS THE nation began to crack, Sam found himself, atypically, far from the center of things. Keokuk, Iowa, was a hotbed of rest. A more insular cocoon could hardly be found than this red-bricked little burg atop the bluffs in southwestern Iowa, where the Des Moines River joins the Mississippi. Keokuk had its rough edges and tough customers, like all steamboat ports of call; but it was being "sivilized." Boosters had attracted a cadre of respectable transplants from New England who were turning the town into a prototype for the new, westward-moving middle class.

Sam floated through this haze of leafy gentility, so far from Bleeding Kansas and the growing polarization in the country. He joined his brothers at Orion's Ben Franklin Book and Job Office: Cards, Circulars, Bill Heads, Bills Lading, Posters, and Colored Work, Printed. It was a mellow time. "I have nothing to write," he informed his mother and sister in St. Louis. (Jane had headed back downriver a few weeks earlier to live with Pamela and William Moffett.) "Everything is going on well . . . I don't like to work on too many things at once."[30] He and Henry shared a bed on the premises, so his board was covered. He read long into the night after Henry had gone to sleep, frowning over Dickens or Poe, and puffing on his Oriental water pipe. One night another boarder, Ed Brownell, asked what he was reading. Sam said that it was a "so-called funny-book," and then muttered that one day he would write a funnier one. Brownell said he doubted this.

To his ever-present notebooks, he added laundry lists, girls' addresses, musical notation, reminders to himself ("Go to Christian Church," "Write to John Shoot"), annotations of chess matches.[31] He sketched out phrenology diagrams that illustrated the regions of the mind ("Moral Sentiments," "Selfish Propensities," "Semi-Intellectual Sentiments").[32] He copied textbook descriptions of the supposed Four Temperaments into which human beings are sorted. He composed detailed appraisals of young women:

Tall, slender, rather regular features medium sized hand, small foot, oblong face, dark hair, pug or turned-up nose, small ears, light, pencilled eyebrows . . . She will go any length to add an admirer to her list, and likes to be complimented on the number of her conquests . . . There is an ocean of passion behind her black eyes which will stop at nothing when lashed to fury.[33]

MOLLIE CLEMENS gave birth to a daughter, Jennie, on September 14, 1855. Orion struggled to match his profits to his household needs and Sam's small salary, but he fell behind. Near the end of the year, Sam blew up over his phantom wages and quit. He took a typesetting job on the far side of the Mississippi, in Warsaw, Illinois.[34] He came back a few weeks later, but his eruption typified his lifelong waspishness toward his older brother. Orion Clemens was an unoffending soul if ever there was one, but something about him drove Sam crazy. Sam remained impatient, condescending, and contemptuous toward Orion, in writing and in life, and his barbs frequently bordered on the cruel. On the other hand, he made sure that Orion and his family were never destitute, and he often exhorted his brother to be better, bolder, more ambitious.

Sam returned to Keokuk just in time to get his first feel of the limelight's hot glow. It happened unexpectedly on the evening of January 17, 1856, at a hotel dinner organized by some printers to celebrate the 150th birthday of the Founding Typesetter, Benjamin Franklin. Orion, who venerated Franklin and fancied himself something of an orator, presided. Nineteenth-century public dinners generally segued into elocution marathons, and this one was no exception: as the plates were cleared, speaker after speaker arose to deliver "remarks." The succession lasted several hours. As the last scheduled orator plumped back down into his chair, some diehard called out for Sam to speak. The twenty-year-old was nonplussed; he hadn't prepared anything. He made his way to the dais and delivered an off-the-cuff performance that alternately convulsed his bleary listeners and moistened their eyes. No one took notes, but the applause rolled on for several minutes. This would happen again.

Sam developed a new, adult friendship with Henry, whom he had hazed through childhood. Now Sam was as solicitous toward his younger brother as he was contrary toward his older one. During his courtship several years later, Sam would remark that only five people had ever known him well, and that of those, he had felt sympathy with only two: his fiancée Livy, and Henry. Sam also brushed up on his piano skills under the tutelage of Oliver C. Isbell, who ran the music studio downstairs from Orion's office; and he dropped in of an evening to sing along and strum his banjo during the singing classes for young ladies. The proper town daughters in their parted ringlets covered their mouths at the way Sam would screw up his face while singing about grasshoppers sittin' on a sweet potato vine, or suddenly leap to his feet to do a shuffle; and they would tease him good-naturedly for being a fool.

He liked the ringlet girls in their long bell-shaped gingham dresses. He flirted with them in a diffident, summer-straw-hat kind of way, and dashed off poems in some of their autograph albums, gentle mock-romantic stanzas in the style of Wordsworth.

Sam met one girl who drove him past doggerel and into heights of giddy wordplay. She was Ann Elizabeth Taylor, daughter of a literary-minded Keokuk alderman, and herself a witty, independent-minded student at Iowa Wesleyan College in Mount Pleasant, just forty-five miles due north. While Henry made shy overtures toward her younger sister Mary Jane, scribbling variations of the French word for "love" on scraps of paper, Sam courted Ann down the locust-lined streets of Keokuk during her trips home from school. His propensity to be inflamed by girls was counterbalanced by a kind of deifying reverence for their chastity. When Ann confessed to him her unfulfilled aspirations toward literature, he responded with self-humbling empathy: "Ah, Annie, I have a slight horror of writing essays myself; and if I were inclined to write one I should be afraid to do it, knowing you could do it so much better if you would only get industrious once and try."[35] When she was away at "Mount *Un*pleasant," he fired off torrents of letters to her, bursts of lovesick silliness:

. . . Bugs! Yes, B-U-G-S! What of the bugs? Why, perdition take the bugs! That is all. Night before last I stood at the little press until nearly 2 o'clock, and the flaring gas light over my head attracted all the varieties of bugs which are to be found in natural history . . . They at first came in little social crowds of a dozen or so, but soon . . . a religious mass meeting of several millions was assembled on the board before me, presided over by a venerable beetle [!], who occupied the most prominent lock of my hair as his chair of state . . .

The big "president" beetle (who, when he frowned, closely resembled Isbell when the pupils are out of time) rose and ducked his head and, crossing his arms over his shoulders, stroked them down to the tip of his nose several times, and after thus disposing of the perspiration, stuck his hands under his wings, propped his back against a lock of hair, and then, bobbing his head at the congregation, remarked, "B-u-z-z!" To which the congregation devoutly responded, "B-u-z-z!" Satisfied with this promptness on the part of his flock, he took a more imposing perpendicular against another lock of hair . . .[36]

Annie saved his letters for sixty years.

THE KEOKUK City Directory rolled off the presses in July 1856, and Orion presented it to the citizenry with a flourish of preemptive defense. "Errors in this Directory," he hedged in his Preface, "apologise for themselves, because the attempt is the first in Keokuk, and it would be a novelty among directories, if there were no mistakes . . . we shall have an opportunity to improve in our next."[37] Perhaps it was the prospect of this sort of tediousness, spun out over a lifetime, that finally got Sam reconnected with his rambling urges. Henry had followed Jane to St. Louis by that time, and though Sam remained enchanted with Annie Taylor, the genteel torpor of Keokuk was too much to bear any longer.

He had been dreaming an exotic destination: Brazil. He'd been reading a book about the Amazon valley, which told of a certain "vegetable product with miraculous powers."[38] He had mentioned this amazing vegetable product to some of the upstanding citizens of Keokuk, including Joseph S. Martin, lecturer on chemistry and toxicology at the local medical college, and a businessman named Ward. The two were sufficiently impressed with the flora's commercial possibilities—"so nourishing and so strength-giving that the native . . . would tramp up-hill and down all day on a pinch . . . and require no other sustenance"[39]—that they initially proposed to accompany him. Sam was "fired with a longing to ascend the Amazon. Also with a longing to open up a trade in [the substance] with all the world. During months I . . . tried to contrive ways to get to Para [Pará, seaport city in Brazil] and spring that splendid enterprise upon an unsuspecting planet."[40]

The idea of Samuel Clemens turning Keokuk, Iowa, into the mid-19th-century cocaine capital of America has its irresistible nutty appeal, but it was not to be. Dr. Martin and Mr. Ward quickly lost their appetites for fortune hunting. Sam, who had no idea exactly where Brazil was or what the Amazon country looked like, decided to forge ahead alone. Yet his boyishness still shone through the grown-up's armor, as did his tug toward Annie. "Between you and I," he wrote to Henry, "I believe that the secret of Ma's willingness to allow me to go to South America lies in the fact that she is afraid I am going to get married! Success to the hallucination."[41] Hallucination, indeed.

"To destiny I bend," Sam had written in a sonorous three-verse poem to Miss Ann Virginia Ruffner in May 1856. Five months later, he departed Keokuk. Mark Twain enshrined the leave-taking with one of the suspiciously "literary" episodes that flavor his life memories. He recalled slogging along Main Street in the midafternoon cold when a piece of paper, plastered against a house by the wind, caught his eye. "It was a fifty-dollar bill . . . the largest assemblage of money I had ever seen in one spot." Sam dutifully advertised the wayward note in the paper, but no one claimed it over four days. "I felt sure that another four could not go by in this safe and secure way. I felt that I must take that money out of danger. So I bought a ticket to Cincinnati and went to that city."[42]

He went first to St. Louis to look in on his family. While in town he took in a production of *Julius Caesar.* He sent a sketch about it up to the Keokuk *Daily Post* under a newly minted persona: Thomas Jefferson Snodgrass. He was riffing again off popular themes in the culture. Snodgrass was a stock-dialect rube off the Simon Suggs/Sut Lovingood template, with maybe a little cornball hick-from-the-sticks shtick that the Grand Ole Opry of seventy years later would recognize.

Snodgrass swaggers into the theater and recognizes that he is a bumpkin in fancy-pants land. He fishes out a pocket comb and plays it in competition with the house orchestra, meaning to take "them one-hoss fiddlers down a peg and bring down the house, too." The audience laughs, which only gets Snodgrass's dander up. He cusses out a man near him and triggers a near riot. When he gets around to summarizing the play's plotline for the Keokuk audience, he reports:

At last it come time to remove Mr. Cesar from office . . . so all the conspirators got around the throne, and directly Cesar come stepping in, putting on as many airs as if he was mayor of Alexandria. Arter he had sot on the house awhile they all jumped on him at once like a batch of Irish on a sick nigger.[43]

Snodgrass shows up in two further dispatches to the *Daily Post.* A trivial creation in himself, he is significant as the first phase of the writer's slow but inexorable reinvention of dialect as a serious literary device.

After about a week in St. Louis, he lurched fitfully around the countryside, eventually making his way to Cincinnati, where he stayed put long enough to earn some money as a printer. Finally, in February 1857, Sam Clemens commenced, more or less by accident, his life on the Mississippi.

8

The Language of Water

(1856–58)

Cincinnati was hardly a tourist mecca. Frances Trollope had been obliged to spend two years there in the 1830s, and found it boring. ("I never saw any people who appeared to live so much without amusement as the Cincinnatians. Billboards are forbidden by law, so are cards.") Nevertheless, Sam spent a few months there, setting type for T. Wrightson and Company. Aside from a couple of Snodgrass letters to the *Post* and a sketch about life in a boardinghouse, he found little to write about. Henry wrote to him from Keokuk on January 23, 1857. The letter is the last of only three letters by him, and our only example of his mature "voice." The diction reveals a literate (he's read *Henry IV*), faintly ironic, and somewhat formal young man of eighteen.

My Dear Brother:

Your letters seem to be very strongly afflicted with a lying-in-the-pocket propensity; for no sooner had I read your last, but one, than it was consigned to one of the pockets of my overcoat, from whose "vasty depths" I have but this moment fished it up, to answer it. But I never did a wrong thing, for which I could not give at least a passable excuse, and this time I have even a better than usual. Several letters were at hand before yours, to which replies were long overdue, that I really feared to delay them longer; and you know enough about my "peculiar writing disposition," as one of my Muscatine correspondents terms it, to know that it is a moral impossibility for me to write more than one letter in one day . . .

You seem to think Keokuk property is so good to speculate in, you'd better invest all your spare change in it, instead of going to South America.

Write soon

Your Brother

Henry.[1]

Sam had let Henry in on his plans the previous August. He had told Jane earlier, but had, as usual, kept Orion in the dark.

About two weeks later, on February 16, Sam resumed his southbound odyssey. He boarded a 353 ton packet, the *Paul Jones,* piloted by one Horace Bixby, and headed south and westward on the Ohio to Cairo, Illinois, and from there down the Mississippi to New Orleans, arriving on February 28.[2] He expected to book passage for Brazil on some vessel leaving the Crescent City.

Just a few days later, on March 4, when Bixby's upriver craft, the *Colonel Crossman,* eased its way off the levee at New Orleans for the return trip to St. Louis, it was steered by a new crew member: Sam Clemens. He had set aside his Amazon dreams and signed on as an apprentice to Bixby.

What is not so certain is exactly how Sam worked this transition. Biographer Albert Bigelow Paine gives it a kind of "creation story" twist that has remained among the most popular of Mark Twain myths: the gruff, grizzled pilot pulling his boat away from Cincinnati, being startled by an unfamiliar drawl, turning around to behold "a rather slender, loose-limbed young fellow with a fair, girlish complexion and a great tangle of auburn hair,"[3] who overcomes the veteran's wary aloofness and charms his way into a "cub-pilot" arrangement: "Do you drink?" "No." "Do you gamble?" "No, sir." "Do you swear?" "Not for amusement; only under pressure." "Do you chew?" "No, sir, never; but I *must smoke.*" "Did you ever do any steering?" "I have steered everything on the river but a steamboat, I guess." "Very well; take the wheel and see what you can do with a steamboat. Keep her as she is—toward that lower cottonwood snag."[4]

Mark Twain recalled that his negotiations with Bixby were gradual—"at the end of three hard days he surrendered"[5]—that his mind was still fixed on getting to the Amazon until reality set in at New Orleans—"I couldn't get to the Amazon . . . I went to Horace Bixby and asked him to make a pilot out of me"[6]—and, lastly, that he didn't think to approach Bixby in the Crescent City until he was broke and a policeman threatened to run him in for vagrancy.[7] What is clear is that he negotiated a two-year apprenticeship with Bixby, on the financial terms the pilot had stipulated: five hundred dollars payable over time, with a down payment of one hundred.

When the *Colonel Crossman* docked at St. Louis on March 15, Sam returned "with an air" to the city where he had labored just two years earlier as a low-rung printer. Along the way, he'd made sure that his silhouette, slouching nonchalantly about the pilothouse up on the third deck, was in clear view of any small boys who might be loitering on any passing levee. Sometime in the next six weeks, he borrowed the hundred dollars for the down payment from William Moffett, who was doing quite well as a commission merchant. Sam and Bixby headed onto the river again, this time on the *Crescent City,* which departed St. Louis on April 29. Sam was now embarked on the second of some 120 professional trips up and down the lower Mississippi River in almost four years, aboard fifteen and perhaps as many as nineteen different steamboats.* He served as a "cub pilot," or steersman, for the first two years. His pilot's license would be signed on April 9, 1859, and on May 4 he would make his inaugural run as a fully licensed pilot. He quit the river only after a Union cannonball whistled into the smokestack of the *Nebraska* (on which he was a passenger), the last boat to enjoy free passage upriver through the Union blockade at Memphis, in May 1861.

During this time Sam Clemens added a new field of information to the growing inventory stored in his mind. He learned the lower Mississippi River, all 1,200 miles of it, quite literally backward and forward. Admonished by his mentor Bixby to "get a little memorandum-book" after it became clear that Sam was not bothering to absorb the various navigation points as they passed,[8] he got a series of them (only two of which survive), and filled them densely with semiencrypted notations that described the river, fathom by fathom, towhead by towhead, hill by hill, sycamore by sycamore, bayou by bayou, snag by snag, from north to south and—a different set of challenges entirely—from south to north. The small boy who had absorbed language like a rushing river had grown into a young man who was learning to absorb the minutiae of river navigation as a kind of language. In an exquisite aria that forever enshrined his passion for the life of a Mississippi steamboat pilot, Mark Twain wedded water and words.

The face of the water, in time, became a wonderful book—a book that was a dead language to the uneducated passenger, but which told its mind to me without reserve, delivering its most cherished secrets as clearly as if it uttered them with a voice. And it was not a book to be read once and thrown aside, for it had a new story to tell every day . . . There never was so wonderful a book written by man; never one whose interest was so absorbing . . .[9]

Sam Clemens's piloting tenure was brief. Yet, as with his small-town newspapering period, he participated in a defining moment of 19th-century America—the Golden Age of riverboating. During these final antebellum years,

---

* The reliability of evidence varies, as Edgar Marquess Branch of the Mark Twain Project has pointed out.

nearly a thousand paddle-wheel steamers, owned by wealthy individuals, small business partnerships, and companies with interlinking interests in the railroads, crowded the Mississippi southward from St. Louis and formed a glittering universe. The steamboat was the first man-made apparatus to radically interrupt the arcadian wilderness, collapse vast distance, and discharge the artifacts of distant cultures into remote places. It was also the most awe-inspiring. "Floating palaces," people called steamboats, and "moving mountains of light and flame." To villagers and backwoods farmers whose daily prospect differed little from that of the aboriginals they had displaced, steamboats cracked through from some brilliant parallel universe: they subjugated the natural world under a spreading curtain of smoke, sparks, sound, and light. Steamboats reshaped much of America, economically and structurally. New Orleans was but the most dramatic creation. On the western rivers alone, steamboat commerce and steamboat-related industry galvanized and connected such outposts as Shreveport, Vicksburg, Natchez, Alton, St. Louis, Hannibal, Quincy, Cincinnati, Paducah, Galena, Nashville, Knoxville, Peoria, Omaha, St. Joseph, and Rock Island.

The steamboat had a strong rival in the steam-driven locomotive. Trains were well on the way toward displacing the paddle wheelers by the time Sam began piloting. But the train lagged behind the boat in its initial impact. Railroad tracks took years to lay down. The steamboat arrived with its roadbed ready-made and open for business—albeit in constant change, which made pilots a necessity. If the river was, as T. S. Eliot later wrote, "a strong brown god," the steamboat was the godhead.

MARK TWAIN'S steamboat years remained the most hallowed period of his life, and formed the epoch most often associated with him in American design and folklore: Mark Twain at the pilot wheel, Mark Twain under the belching twin smokestacks, Mark Twain in a riverman's watch cap. "I supposed—and hoped—that I was going to follow the river the rest of my days," he remembered, "and die at the wheel when my mission was ended." [10] The Mississippi River dominates two of his greatest books and infuses their prose with unforgettable imagery and narrative tension. Steamboats figure in more than half a dozen of his novels. Squire Hawkins takes his family aboard the *Boreas* on their journey to a new life, in *The Gilded Age*. On the first day, Squire Hawkins and his family experience the river's wonders as an "ecstasy of enjoyment":

> When the sun went down it turned all the broad river to a national banner laid in gleaming bars of gold and purple and crimson; and in time these glories faded out in the twilight and left the fairy archipelagoes reflecting their fringing foliage in the steely mirror of the stream. [11]

Later, their boat engages another in a race; a boiler explodes on the rival *Amaranth*, and the conflagration spreads out of control.

Young Sam understood such hazards but, as with most river people, the attractions outweighed them. "A pilot, in those days," Mark Twain wrote, "was the only unfettered and entirely independent human being that lived in the earth . . . a king without a keeper, an absolute monarch who was absolute in sober truth and not by a fiction of words." [12] Two of these titans in particular grabbed his fancy: Horace Bixby and, later on, an eloquent pilot named Isaiah Sellers.

Bixby towered over most of the river personalities of his era. Just thirty-one years old when Sam, aged twenty-one, stepped aboard his boat, he was already a legend in the trade. Born in Geneseo, New York, he'd run away as a boy to Cincinnati, where he worked in a tailor's shop until he could find his way onto a steamboat. At eighteen, he broke into the trade as a lowly "mud clerk" for a packet on the Cincinnati–Kanawha River line. Within a few months he had become its pilot, an unusually rapid rise in status. The packet bore the interesting name *Olivia*.

Bixby was a compact tornado, a born overlord with tremendous willpower and icy courage, whose temper was offset by charm and wit. He was a small, sturdy man with heavy-lidded, appraising eyes set wide apart under bushy brows. He dressed for work in the elegant tradition of the piloting elite, those farmboys and peddlers' sons turned regal on the river, in high starched collars, silk neckties, and stickpins. His piloting days didn't end until two years after Mark Twain's death in 1910.

Sam idolized Bixby. Bixby rousted Sam out of his bunk for midnight shifts; mimicked Sam's drawl when the young man could not identify a point on the river; and once humiliated his apprentice with a hoax designed to test Sam's presence of mind. The veteran pilot arranged with the "leadsman," the deckhand who took constant soundings of the channel depth with a lead-weighted rope, to falsely cry out smaller and smaller depths as Sam manned the pilot wheel across a passage that he *knew* to be safe and deep. Sam gave into panic that overrode his judgment, and begged his engineer: "Oh, Ben, if you love me, *back* her! Quick, Ben! Oh, back the immortal *soul* out of her!" [13] As the deck crew doubled over in laughter, Bixby materialized behind Sam to drive home the point about maintaining confidence in one's knowledge.

Mid-19th-century Mississippi riverboats were dangerous paradoxes: they combined luxurious ornamentation and fragile construction; they offered sumptuous comfort side by side with constant peril. Some were bloated, unwieldy monsters, often more than 300 feet long and weighing more than 350 tons, with the occasional behemoth tipping the scales at twice that. Passengers and crew could number at least two hundred. The boats were designed not for minimal safety but for maximum profit: flat-bottomed, wooden-structured, and usually weighted down with cargo and people. Teaching a youthful ex-typesetter and humorous-sketch writer to maintain control of one was quite unambiguously a matter of life and death.

The Mississippi was not deep. Twenty feet was a good average channel depth, but that could rapidly decrease to four feet or less. Most big boats drew at least nine feet and therefore needed about twelve feet—two fathoms—"mark twain"—to float safely. Any lapse of judgment could ground the boat on a submerged sandbar or rip open the ship's thin hull by a submerged tree branch, rock, or sunken steamboat. Underwater obstructions caused most riverboat disasters, followed by fires, collisions, and exploding boilers. Between 1811 and 1851, before owners began paying (a little) attention to safety measures, nearly a thousand boats snagged, caught fire, exploded, or collided on the western rivers, resulting in hundreds of deaths. The average lifespan of a Mississippi riverboat in the pre–Civil War era was less than five years. Ten of the fifteen riverboats known to be part of Sam Clemens's steersman/piloting career were snagged, burned, destroyed by explosion, or disabled by collision on the river, although none while he was aboard. (Two more were sunk or burned by the Confederate military to prevent their capture during the Civil War.)

"When I find a well-drawn character in fiction or biography," Mark Twain wrote, "I generally take a warm personal interest in him, for the reason that I have known him before—met him on the river." [14] Yet his writing doesn't suggest much interest in life on the lower deck. He mimicked the hauteur of the steamboat ruling class, even as he satirized its members in memoir and fiction. His respectful descriptions of pilots and mates stand as the only authoritative portraiture of these fascinating American archetypes. He pays some attention to the folks who could afford cabin berths and the elegant meals in the brass-and-crystal dining rooms. The paying customers, many of them disreputable, or the menials, predominantly Negro, who served them, are with one exception absent.

Cargo, not passengers, was the profit center of steamboat companies. These boats hauled cotton and tobacco, flour, farm machinery, the U.S. mail, and livestock. The vessels, many of which could carry more than a thousand tons, were routinely loaded to the point where the lower decks were nearly flush with the surface of the river.

Prostitutes swarmed the river and the riverfronts of the 1850s. Prostitution was an inevitable by-product of the society that limited women's careers outside marriage to laundress, domestic servant, or slave; a society in which the preferred approach to the marital act was in the dark, eyes averted; a society that enforced a rigid code of chastity in part by questioning the morals of women who looked into a gentleman's eyes, glanced at themselves in the mirror, fussed with their hair or clothing, laughed immoderately, touched their conversational partner, rolled their eyes, took snuff, beat time with their feet or hands, shrugged, stamped their feet, or, God forbid, folded their shawl carefully upon entering a room "instead of throwing it with graceful negligence upon a table." [15]

If he ever enjoyed the company of any Daughters of Desire on a boat, or along the seamy levees of river towns, Sam kept mum about it. In the chronicle of his middle-aged return to the Mississippi, he noted one of the river's most notorious hellholes, the enclave of vice and violence known as Natchez-Under-the-Hill. He recalled its "desperate reputation" in the steamboating days of his youth—"plenty of drinking, carousing, fisticuffing, and killing there, among the riff-raff of the river, in those days." [16] Not a mention of its main attraction.

On the "texas," where the pilot wheel faced the oncoming river, Sam surrendered himself to the current. The never-ending glide ushered him past cities where whole neighborhoods of steamboats gently knocked against one another in their slips on the levees, and then on into the infinite shoreline that unfolded bend by bend, island by island, the river giving up its literature to him at every turn. He cussed like the older men, smoked his cigars, and put on airs. A community formed around him, and it included members of his old Hannibal boyhood gang, the Bowen brothers. He filled his notebooks with the Mississippi's secrets, writing in precise, encoded pencil notes. He hobnobbed with the freeloading off-duty pilots who often clustered in the pilot house under the pretense of "inspecting the river." He read books, boned up on his French, and probably strummed a guitar.* He bought himself a blue serge jacket and white trousers.

On the first of June, 1857, the day he was to depart New Orleans for his fourth trip under Bixby, aboard the *Crescent City*, he wrote to "My Dear Friend Annie" Taylor with a brimming discharge of his recent experiences. He wrote about a stroll he took around the French market, wishing that he could meet some Keokuk girls, "as I used to meet them at market in the Gate City. But it could not be." [17] He did spot a couple of pretty girls he knew with their beaux, sipping coffee in a "stall," the Starbucks of its day. The plentitude of the market overwhelmed him. "Everything was arranged in such beautiful order, and had such an air of cleanliness and neatness that it was a pleasure to wander among the stalls." [18] He inventoried it for Annie, and one can sense his ardency to make it all real and permanent on the page, as he tried to do with every sight, sound, and episode that fascinated him; to add them to "the multitudinous photographs one's mind takes."

Out on the pavement were groups of Italians, French, Dutch, Irish, Spaniards, Indians, Chinese, Americans, English, and the Lord knows how many more different kinds of people, selling all kinds of articles . . . anything you could possibly want—and keeping up a terrible din with their various cries. [19]

Back on board, Sam read Suetonius, Pepys, Malory, Carlyle, Cervantes, Plutarch, Darwin, Macaulay, and Shakespeare, in addition to the Bible and ceaseless inquiries into history, science, music, languages, biography, astron-

---

* No direct evidence of this exists, but Sam had learned the guitar in Hannibal from his sister Pamela and played the instrument frequently in later years.

omy, geology.[20] One scholar has maintained that "Sam Clemens became a reader and critic of the best in literature by the time he was twenty-five years old."[21] One writer in particular influenced Mark Twain's intellectual development.

Thomas Paine, the British-born American patriot and, later, disputatious French citizen, had helped inspire the American Revolution with the 1776 publication of *Common Sense*. This anticolonial manifesto declared that "[t]he cause of America is, in a great measure, the cause of all mankind," and proceeded to dismantle the hollow godhead of the British monarchy. Fifty-odd years after his death in 1809, however, Paine's critiques of established theology, rather than of government, sustained his claim on the American imagination. In *The Age of Reason,* Paine's icy 1795 deconstruction of the "heathen mythology" that was the Christian faith, Sam was mesmerized by a rebuttal to the terrifying sermons of his Presbyterian boyhood. He "read it with fear and hesitation, but marveling at its fearlessness and wonderful power."[22] The credulous soul who had once cowered under his covers at the sound of thunder, believing it God's terrible judgment on him, could only have cried "Amen!" to Paine's withering judgment that "[p]utting aside everything that might excite laughter by its absurdity, or detestation by its profaneness, and confining ourselves merely to an examination of the parts, it is impossible to conceive a story more derogatory to the Almighty, more inconsistent with his wisdom, more contradictory to his power, than [the Bible] story is."[23]

The Age of Reason stopped short of rejecting the concept of a god—the Anglican Church was Paine's quarry, not faith itself. His countertheology took root in Samuel Clemens, and gave Sam a foundation short of nihilism on which to wage his eventual wars against the Christian God. His mimetic ear absorbed the old radical's sardonic imagery and cadences, and stored them for later use. Toward the end of his life, Mark Twain reread *The Age of Reason* and found it tame. By then, he was privately at work on material that would render tame any previous Christian skepticism.

IN THE 1850s, the nation edged toward a new war, this one a social fratricide. The Kansas-Nebraska Act replaced the Missouri Compromise, restoring popular sovereignty in the developing territories as the standard for settling the slavery question. Kansas became a battleground: militantly abolitionist settlers from New England poured into the state, to preempt potentially destructive backlash against the act's enforcement. Many of them came armed with Sharps rifles, supplied by the Boston minister Henry Ward Beecher. Proslavery Southerners, most of them crossing over from slave-friendly Missouri, mobilized to challenge the interlopers. In the fall, several Southern states threatened to secede if an antislavery Republican were elected president. James Buchanan, a clueless Democrat, won the race. Two days after his inauguration, the Supreme Court announced its long-awaited Dred Scott ruling that legalized slavery in all of the territories, made a martyr of Scott, and further intensified sectional tensions. If Sam had strong opinions about the growing divide, they are lost. In his 1906 autobiographical dictations, Mark Twain recalled his Mississippi River period as halcyon. He reconjured moonlight schottische dances on the decks of a steamer run by lovable country people, "simple-hearted folk and overflowing with good-fellowship and the milk of human kindness." He recalled a romance with a young girl "in the unfaded bloom of her youth, with her plaited tails dangling from her young head and her white summer frock puffing about in the wind of that ancient Mississippi time . . ."[24] The river seemed, in life and in memory, to be a sanctuary for him, as it was for his great characters Huck and Jim, where the sorrows of the world seldom intruded.

Sam was and remained an autodidact, a loner among friends and fans. America is no longer known for its self-taught thinkers (alas), but there were many in the 19th century, and Sam Clemens was one. He would never excel at abstract reasoning. To the twenty-five-year-old Sam, the concepts of "slavery" and "abolition" remained closed fortresses of thought, approachable only by inherited opinions. To some extent, the older man closed these gaps, producing excellent if unorthodox literary criticism. His late-life polemics against United States imperialism showed an engaged, even prophetic consciousness. But even then, when Twain strayed from the flow of his intuitive gifts as a storyteller and struck out into the thickets of deterministic philosophy, he bogged down.

Sam's personal experience gestated over time, not into argumentation but into narrative language, one that produced moral visions of lasting force. His narratives were built on his own joys and sorrows, and the sorrows of the world did not fail to intrude upon the river. Sam soon would be dealt a dream-redolent catastrophe that produced gray hairs on his head, obliterating the last remnants of his boyhood Christian faith, and of his boyhood.

THE YOUNG girl with plaited tails and white frock was named Laura Wright. She floated into Sam's enchanted vision, as he recalled it, on a spring night in 1858 on the New Orleans waterfront, and transported him to a forty-eight-hour tour of heaven that he re-created in his mind, compulsively, for the rest of his life. He paid for this interlude with a session in Hell less than a month afterward, which he also revisited, faithfully. The two episodes resonate eerily with one another. Each involved the same steamboat; a permanent parting; deep love interrupted at the point of its discovery. Each shaped his literature, and his views of mankind, fate, and God. Fourteen-year-old Laura Wright was the daughter of a Warsaw, Missouri, judge who had allowed her to go down to New Orleans on her first trip away from home, accompanied by her uncle, William C. Youngblood, one of the pilots of the sprawling freight steamer *John J. Roe*. Sam knew the *Roe* and all her officers very well, and was delighted to find it in the adjoining slip when, on the evening of May 16, the *Pennsylvania*, the fast packet on which he was then working, put into port at New Orleans. Sam jumped onto the *Roe*'s deck from a rail of this boat, and began shaking hands with old friends. Then, the young girl appeared, almost chimerically. Sam moved toward her and wangled an introduction. She became his "instantly elected sweetheart out of the remotenesses of interior Missouri" for a brief idyll that enlarged itself in his imagination at least until four years before his death.[25]

The notion of a twenty-two-year-old man romancing a girl scarcely out of childhood would trigger suspicion in a later America, but Laura Wright's chastity was safe with Sam. Scandalized by the leg shows in New York and repulsed by the Daughters of Desire who sashayed along every levee of the lower river, he saw Laura as metaphor as much as maiden. She was an emissary from a fast-receding Eden, his boyhood Missouri prairie in its loneliness and peace—"a frank and simple and winsome child who had never been away from home in her life before, and had brought with her to these distant regions the freshness and the fragrance of her own prairies."[26]

He gives few details about what passed between them, but he recalls being not four inches from her elbow ("during waking hours," he stipulates) for the three days that they were together. He invests their farewell with the abruptness of an interrupted dream. On May 20, Zeb Leavenworth, the *Roe*'s captain "came flying aft shouting, 'The *Pennsylvania* is backing out.' I fled at my best speed . . . and just did manage to make the connection, and nothing to spare. My . . . finger-ends hooked themselves upon the guard-rail, and a quartermaster made a snatch for me and hauled me aboard."[27]

He tried to keep the romance alive. He paid a courting visit to her at Warsaw in 1860: a man who claimed to have been introduced to him on that occasion wrote Mark Twain a letter in 1880 reminiscing about their encounter. Sam blamed Laura's mother for "playing the devil" with him on that visit, and putting the kibosh on the romance.[28] He wrote to Laura, and she answered for a while, but Sam grew frustrated as her interest waned, and stopped. Nothing could extinguish Sam's lingering ache. In that same 1861 letter, he recounted how a New Orleans fortune-teller saw the young girl clearly inside his head. This "Madame Caprell" described Laura perfectly, Sam insisted.

THE SECOND fateful event of that summer involved his younger brother, Henry.[29] In February of that year, Sam had found the boy a menial job as "mud-clerk" aboard the *Pennsylvania,* in the hopes of rescuing Henry from the torpor of an aimless life in St. Louis. Those good intentions launched a catastrophic chain of events. Henry Clemens was then nineteen. Whatever dreams he might have had for his own life will never be known. He was living in St. Louis, probably with Jane and Pamela. He read books, sat for a couple of daguerreotypes. In one of them, he appears in the process of vanishing into the background. His face is handsome in the Clemens way, the hair thick and the mouth full, the eyes wide-set and alert.

To Sam, Henry was "the flower of the family."[30] Sam's niece Annie Moffett always thought that his love for his younger brother was one of his outstanding qualities. Orion noted that the thoughtful and quiet Henry was always leaning on Sam for protection. Sam had planned to consolidate their blossoming friendship by expanding Henry's sedate world, drawing him into the dash and glamour of his own new lifestyle.

The two were together for six trips aboard the *Pennsylvania*. Henry labored at the bottom of the boat's labor chain. A mud-clerk got his shoes dirty by hopping off the boat at unscheduled points where the riverbank was unimproved by brick or stone, but where passengers or a few bales of cotton waited to be taken aboard. His pay consisted of meals and a place to sleep.

As an apprentice, or "cub," on loan from Bixby (who had gone to work temporarily on a Missouri packet), Sam was at the center of things, in the pilothouse. Normally this was Sam's idea of heaven, but not on this boat. The *Pennsylvania*'s pilot, William Brown, was a seething and abusive man. His malevolence was enhanced by a powerful memory and an inability to distinguish the significant from the trivial. Brown, unlike Bixby, was not charmed by Clemens. He apparently believed—in wonderful irony—that the cub was the rich son of a slaveholding aristocrat.

> "Here!—You going to set there all day?"
> . . . I said, apologetically:—"I have had no orders, sir."
> "You've had no *orders!* My, what a fine bird we are! We must have *orders!* Our father was a *gentleman*—owned slaves—and *we've* been to *school* . . . ORDERS, is it? ORDERS is what you want! Dod dern my skin, *I'll* learn you to swell yourself up and blow around *here* . . ."[31]

At the end of May 1858, shortly before departing with Henry on their sixth trip aboard the *Pennsylvania,* Sam had an eerily prophetic dream while at the Moffett house, where he stayed between trips. Annie Moffett, who was in the house at the time, maintained years later that Sam told everyone about the dream before leaving, "but the family were not impressed; indeed they were amused that he took it so seriously."[32]

Of this dream, Mark Twain wrote that he

had seen Henry a corpse. He lay in a metallic burial case. He was dressed in a suit of my clothing, and on his breast lay a great bouquet of flowers, mainly white roses, with a red rose in the center. The casket stood upon a couple of chairs.[33]

Sam awoke grief-stricken, believing that Henry's casket lay in the next room. He dressed and approached the door, "but I changed my mind. I thought I could not yet bear to meet my mother. I thought I would wait awhile and make some preparation for that ordeal." He recalled that he actually left the house and walked a block "before it suddenly flashed upon me that there was nothing real about this—it was only a dream." He ran back, charged up the staircase to the second-floor sitting room, "and was made glad again, for there was no casket there." [34]

THE *PENNSYLVANIA* cast off for New Orleans later that day, May 30. The bizarre skein of events on board are recorded by Mark Twain in Chapter 29 of *Life on the Mississippi* and in some letters written at the time. They form the first act of a drama almost operatic in its inexorable progression toward tragedy. Brown continued to make life miserable for Sam. Mid-morning on June 3, a couple of hours above Vicksburg, Brown was at the wheel, and Sam was standing by. Henry appeared outside the pilothouse to relay an order from the boat's captain, John S. Kleinfelter: the *Pennsylvania* was to make an unscheduled stop at a plantation downstream. He shouted it to Brown through a stiff wind; the pilot, a little deaf, did not hear him. The steamboat floated past the stop, and Kleinfelter rushed to the pilothouse yelling for Brown to come about: "Didn't Henry tell you to land here?" Brown denied it. Kleinfelter turned to Sam: "Didn't *you* hear him?" [35]

"Yes, sir," Sam replied, realizing that his answer was fraught with danger: he had contradicted his boss to the ship's captain. Sam braced himself for a vicious retribution.

An hour later, this time with Sam at the wheel, Henry entered the pilothouse, unaware of what was brewing. Brown pounced.

> "Here! Why didn't you tell me we'd got to land at that plantation?"
> "I did tell you, Mr. Brown."
> "It's a lie!"
> I said:—"You lie, yourself. He did tell you." [36]

Brown glowered at Sam, then ordered Henry out of the pilothouse. Before Henry could obey, Brown attacked him. Sam intervened, swinging a heavy stool, knocking Brown to the floor. Sam fell on top of Brown and pummeled him with his fists for several minutes, while the 486-ton steamboat drifted downriver at fifteen miles an hour with no one to control its rudder and paddle wheels. The commotion attracted a crowd on the hurricane deck. Brown eventually struggled free, grabbed the wheel, and got the boat under control. He roared at Sam to leave, but Sam, in Mark Twain's telling, wasn't through.

> I tarried, and criticised his grammar; I reformed his ferocious speeches for him . . . calling his attention to the advantage of pure English over the bastard dialect of the Pennsylvanian collieries whence he was extracted. [37]

Sam's 1883 account of this scene varies slightly from what he said in a letter written soon after it occurred, [38] and the later version might be dismissed as self-mythifying. But what happened next suggests that a confrontation did take place. Captain Kleinfelter was waiting for Sam outside the pilothouse. He hustled the cub pilot to his parlor "in the forward end of the texas" and grilled him about what had led to the brawl. Sam assumed that he would be jailed on arrival at New Orleans. He was astounded when the captain promised not to press charges, and even urged Sam to "lay for" Brown once they were ashore. "Give him a good sound thrashing, do you hear? I'll pay the expenses. Now go—"[39]

Brown bristled for the rest of the downriver trip, Kleinfelter having made it clear that the pilot no longer had his support. After arriving at New Orleans on June 5, the captain tried for three days to replace Brown for the upriver voyage, but the pilots' union thwarted him. Shipboard coexistence between the two was unthinkable, so Kleinfelter secured upriver passage for Sam aboard another boat, the *A. T. Lacey*. The *Pennsylvania* was scheduled to depart on the evening of June 9; the *Lacey*, two days later. On June 8, Sam and Henry spent their last evening together on the lamplit New Orleans riverfront. They hunkered down on a freight pile near the *Pennsylvania*. Dwarfed by the three-tiered silhouettes of docked steamboats falling away in either direction, hulls gently bumping and smokestacks swaying with the current, the brothers talked into the night. As Mark Twain remembered it,

The subject of that chat, mainly, was one which I think we had not exploited before—steamboat disasters. One was then on its way to us, little as we suspected it; the water which was to make the steam which should cause it, was washing past some point fifteen hundred miles up the river while we talked;—but it would arrive at the right time and the right place . . . [W]e decided that if a disaster ever fell within our experience we would at least stick to the boat, and give such minor service as chance might throw in the way. Henry remembered this, afterward, when the disaster came, and acted accordingly.[40]

The *Pennsylvania*, with Brown at the wheel and Henry on the main deck, churned out of port at 5 p.m. the next day, its cargo including barrels of turpentine stored in the hold. The *Lacey* pulled out on June 11, as scheduled. Two days later, Sam Clemens heard a chilling shout from the levee: "The 'Pennsylvania' is blown up at Ship Island, and a hundred fifty lives lost!"[41] Mark Twain is silent on his reaction to this ghastly news. Whatever shock he felt was temporarily allayed at Napoleon, Arkansas: an "extra" edition of a Memphis newspaper, rushed downriver, listed the fates of some of the passengers. Henry's name appeared among the uninjured.

Then the news turned irremediably bad. A later edition reported that Henry Clemens was "hurt beyond help."

A hundred miles downriver from Memphis, the *Lacey* steamed into a watery cemetery: corpses floating in the current, along with fragments of the *Pennsylvania*'s superstructure. At Memphis, Sam Clemens hurried to the makeshift hospital where his brother lay on a mattress among the burned and scalded.

The *Pennsylvania* had been destroyed by a boiler explosion that had occurred at around 6 a.m. Sunday, June 13, about sixty miles below Memphis. A family named Harrison watched from their house as the graceful boat churned upriver. They were preparing for church when, with an ear-shattering blast, the front of *Pennsylvania* erupted in a nebula of fire, steam, and smoke, and human bodies went pinwheeling into the air. A third of the boat, including the pilothouse and the texas and smokestacks, was pulverized into a mass of twisted steel and blackened fragments of wood. It was one of the worst explosions in the history of steamboating. Passengers who moments earlier had been sleeping or gazing at the shoreline, were blown into the river, scalded, decapitated, impaled. Survivors screamed in agony from their burns. William Brown, who had gone off-duty a few hours earlier, was among the dozens whose body was never found. He was propelled into the air on a scalding torrent of steam, and then fell into the river, where a passenger named Reed Young, who had grabbed a life preserver, reached out to him with one hand. Brown "soon slipped away." His last words, Young reported, were "My poor wife and children!" [42]

The ship decks looked like a battlefield. Victims pleaded for water, and for mercy, their bones and bowels exposed. A Catholic priest from Milwaukee was boiled alive. A Tennessee Supreme Court judge and a baritone with the New Orleans French Opera Company were among the fatally scalded. Captain Kleinfelter, freshly shaved, had just left his barber chair when the blast erupted. The force obliterated the chair and left the burned barber stirring his lather in shock for several seconds before he could move. George Ealer, Brown's co-pilot and Sam's good friend, was nearly brained by the heavy, descending pilot wheel. He rummaged for his beloved flute and the scattered pieces of his chess set, and then set about directing the rescue efforts. A French admiral's eighteen-year-old son was hideously scalded and bore it with military stoicism. A plantation owner and his wife found themselves trapped by heavy timbers and, as flames approached them, they offered their acreage, their fortune, and their slaves, to anyone who could save them. Nobody could. Mark Twain later adapted these two vignettes for the steamboat catastrophe scene in *The Gilded Age*.

Among those injured in the opening moments of the first blast was Henry Clemens, who was sleeping above the boilers. The blast drove the youth through the ceiling and into the air on a jet of steam. Instead of landing in the river, he seems to have dropped back onto the heated boilers, where he was bombarded by falling debris. He managed to drag himself off the boat and into the water, probably clutching something that floated. From there, he was pulled into a crowded rescue boat. He and the other occupants waited eight hours for help, many of them with scalded skin peeling, in hundred-degree heat. A southbound rescue boat finally took the injured to the town of Austin, Mississippi, where it waited two hours for an upriver boat to transport them to Memphis. There was another transfer, this time to the *Kate Frisbee*. Henry

Clemens and the others, who had suffered their wounds at dawn on Sunday, arrived at a makeshift hospital, the Memphis Exchange, at 3 a.m. the following day, June 14.

Sam made it to the Exchange a day later. His reaction on seeing his brother was captured by a local newspaper reporter:

We witnessed one of the most affecting scenes at the Exchange yesterday that has ever been seen. The brother of Mr. Henry Clemens, second clerk of the Pennsylvania . . . arrived in the city yesterday afternoon, on the steamer A. T. Lacy. He hurried to the Exchange to see his brother, and on approaching the bedside of the wounded man, his feelings so much overcame him, at the scalded and emaciated form before him, that he sunk to the floor overpowered. There was scarcely a dry eye in the house; the poor sufferers shed tears at the sight. This brother had been pilot on the Pennsylvania, but fortunately for him, had remained in New Orleans when the boat started up.[43]

Three days later, Sam was able to compose a letter to Mollie Clemens, who had stayed in Keokuk during Orion's Kentucky sojourn.

Long before this reaches you, my poor Henry,—my darling, my pride, my glory, my *all*, will have finished his blameless career, and the light of my life will have gone out in utter darkness. O, God! this is hard to bear. Hardened, hopeless,—aye, lost—lost—lost and ruined sinner as I am—I, even *I*, have humbled myself to the ground and prayed as never man prayed before, that the great God might let this cup pass from me [and] spare my brother—that he would pour out the fulness of his just wrath upon my wicked head, but have mercy, mercy, mercy upon that unoffending boy. . . . poor wretched me, that was once so proud, was humbled to the very dust—lower than the dust—for the vilest beggar in the streets of Saint Louis could never conceive of a humiliation like mine. Men take me by the hand and *congratulate* me, and call me **"lucky"** because I was not on the Pennsylvania when she blew up! My God forgive them, for they know not what they say![44]

Henry lingered on for three more days. The scene in the ward was spectral: doctors had covered the surviving patients' skin with a kind of white medical paint (white lead), on which they had pressed raw cotton, so that the victims looked like ghosts of themselves. Henry's body was swathed in this goo, but not his smooth face, which had escaped disfigurement. The doctors and nurses were struck by the dying boy's beauty and by his gracious manner. He became a favorite among them.

On June 21, Sam sent a telegram to William Moffett in St. Louis:

HENRY DIED THIS MORNING LEAVE TOMORROW WITH THE CORPSE

Sam boarded a steamboat for St. Louis along with Henry's body. From St. Louis, family members transported Henry's casket to Hannibal aboard a steamer named the *Hannibal City*. Henry was buried beside his father, John Marshall, in the town's northern Baptist cemetery, the one that appears in the grave-robbing scene in *Tom Sawyer*. In 1876, Mark Twain arranged for the two bodies to be transferred to the new Mount Olivet Cemetery, on a high bluff above the river, south of Hannibal. In time, Marshall and Henry were joined by the remains of Jane, then Orion, then Mollie. The five graves remain there still.

MARK TWAIN relived and rewrote Henry's death for the rest of his life. Henry's survival prospects improve a little with each retelling, until his death comes almost anticlimactically. In his 1858 letter to Mollie, Sam reports that Henry fell back on the hot boilers after the explosion, suffered internal injuries from falling debris, then swam to shore and was pulled into a flatboat with other survivors. In a tribute that Sam published several weeks later, Henry escapes on a "mattrass to a raft or open wood boat," but has suffered brain damage from "the concussion." *Life on the Mississippi* has Henry swimming back to the steamboat after the explosion on a mission to help others, fulfilling the brothers' levee agreement of a few nights earlier. And by the time of Mark Twain's autobiographical dictation (January 13, 1906), Henry is actually pulled back from the brink of death and is on the way to recovery, thanks to a "fine and large-hearted old physician of great reputation,"[45] and probably would have survived, but for a melodramatic irony: an accidental overdosing of morphine administered by inexperienced doctors ("hardly out of medical school") on the night watch. He spoke of the dream repeatedly during his lifetime, and seems to have been unconscious of its permutations. It is as though the dream came at him from differing corners of his mind, and perhaps in his constant retelling, he sought to make peace with it.

HENRY'S DEATH closed a door in Samuel Clemens's heart. Before it happened, he had talked of joining the ministry, a fantasy he had in common with Orion. Now his skepticism regarding the Christian faith hardened into nonbelief, and he embarked on a lifetime of guilt over his role in guiding his brother toward his doom, a guilt compounded by the excruciating luck of his own survival. *"Lucky?"* He beseeched God to strike his "wicked head" and have mercy "upon that unoffending boy."

Death always lurked not far beneath the surface of his writing, even the satire, especially the satire; Mark Twain insisted that the secret source of humor was not joy, but sorrow. G. K. Chesterton was among those who noticed this sometimes subtle dialectic. Mark Twain was "always serious to the point of madness," he observed—"an unfathomably solemn man."[46] At least once, Sam tried to contact his dead brother through a psychic.

And finally, there is the matter that Mark Twain recalled as the prophetic dream. It seems to have been consummated in real life. When Sam Clemens awoke from his stupefied slumber in the Memphis household on June 21 (he claimed in his autobiography), he returned to the "dead-room" at the Exchange. There lay Henry in a metallic burial case, dressed in Sam's clothing. The surrounding coffins were of unpainted pine, but Henry had become a favorite among the Memphis women volunteers, and some of them had made up a purse of sixty dollars and given him this fancier one.

I recognized instantly that my dream of several weeks before was here exactly reproduced, so far as these details went—and I think I missed one detail, but that one was immediately supplied, for just then an elderly lady entered the place with a large bouquet consisting mainly of white roses, and in the center of it was a red rose, and she laid it on his breast.[47]

The losses of these two adored figures—his brother to death, his instantly elected sweetheart, Laura Wright, to the vagaries of fate—were so crushing to Sam Clemens that he could not bear to accept them as losses. He gave Henry a kind of afterlife in three of his books: as "Sid" in *Adventures of Tom Sawyer,* and as himself in *Life on the Mississippi* and in his autobiography. In *A Connecticut Yankee in King Arthur's Court,* Hank Morgan is ordered burned at the stake on June 21, the date of Henry's death; but he is saved from death by the distraction of an eclipse of the sun.

Some scholars have detected traces of Laura Wright moving like an apparition through Mark Twain's literature: one female character, and then another, trailing her long plaited tresses and summer frock, a beautiful eidolon of regret and yearning.[48] And he installed her permanently in the alternate reality of his dream world.

She is perhaps the most indelibly evoked in a little-known Mark Twain essay that describes a hauntingly recurring dream in which a Laura Wright proxy reigned. Like many of Sam Clemens's dreams, this one was so powerful and pervasive as to approach the status of an alternate reality, a theme that gripped him in his late-life writings. He developed the habit of recording his nighttime visions in his notebooks for decades before Sigmund Freud made it a quasi–civic duty. In 1898, living in Vienna, where Freud was then at work on *The Interpretation of Dreams,* Mark Twain chronicled his Laura dreams in "My Platonic Sweetheart."[49] Several magazine editors rejected the piece during his lifetime, bewildered by its hallucinatory strangeness or possibly taken aback by its intimations of sexual desire ("Helen had a summer hat on. She took it off presently and said, 'It was in the way; now you can kiss me better' ").[50] In 1912, it was finally published, minus several censored passages that meditated on the nature of dreams and dream-selves, in *Harper's Monthly Magazine.*

The essay knits together a series of dreams, over a period of several years, in which Sam reencounters a lovely girl, whose name and features vary but whose essence remains intact. Strangers, yet tacitly acquainted, they roam hand in hand, caressing, petting, and kissing across enchanted landscapes. They never consummate their attraction, yet their love is "more clinging, more endearing, more reverent" than romantic or even filial devotion.[51] They speak to each other in an esoteric, but mutually understandable language of dreams: "quite atreous," and "Rax oha tal," and "sufa."[52] In 1866, while sojourning in the Sandwich Islands, Mark Twain dreams that the girl is killed in his arms by an arrow, and the loss persists in the dreamer's heart; and yet she reappears, an always dying yet indestructible muse, "once in two years on the average,"[53] over a span of nearly half a century.

Dreams, reality, fact, fiction—it was all part of a seamless universe to Mark Twain, increasingly so as he aged. "In our dreams—I know it!—we do make the journeys we seem to make; we do see the things we seem to see," he wrote in the 1898 essay. "The people . . . are living spirits, not shadows; and they are immortal and indestructible . . . When we die we shall slough off this cheap intellect, perhaps, and go abroad into Dreamland clothed in our real selves . . ."[54]

As the summer of 1858 faded, only one thing was immediately certain: Sam's boyhood days were at an end. The great wandering epoch of his young manhood was beginning.

9

Ranger

(1858–61)

Less than a month after the *Pennsylvania* catastrophe, Sam was back on the river, where time seemed eternal. This was an illusion. During the three years leading up to the Civil War, Sam Clemens floated on a current that carried him away from the familiar "America" that was his patrimony, and toward the war-tempered nation whose soul he never quite grasped, even as he helped create it. Aboard the *Alfred T. Lacey,* the steamboat that had carried him to his death watch over Henry, Sam served as steersman under two good friends for a brief time: Bart Bowen, Will's older brother, and George Ealer, a hero of the *Pennsylvania* explosion.

In August, twenty-two-year-old Sam said good-bye to these companions and took a two-month steersman assignment aboard the *John H. Dickey,* which plied the St. Louis–Memphis route. Three "correspondence letters" in as many river-town newspapers are attributed to him during this period. The most interesting shows Sam experimenting with a new writerly voice, that of the Insider—the wised-up businessman, hotel connoisseur, and political observer. "The present line of packets between the two cities is nearer what is wanted by shippers than any heretofore established," "C." pronounces in the Missouri *Republican,* "and here let me say to shippers in St. Louis, *stick to the line.* They are all good boats, reliable and prompt . . ."[1] As to politics, "C." recommends the reelection of Stephen Douglas over challenger Abraham Lincoln in the crucial Illinois Senate race. "There assuredly never was a State election to which so many eyes were directed, as the one so soon to come off in Illinois. Will her voters do their duty, and sustain Mr. DOUGLAS? We trust they will."[2] Sam may have been writing under the thrall of attending a Douglas oration in Cairo a month earlier.

Beginning in late October, Sam's letter- and notebook-writing ceases again for a four-month stretch. A few glimpses into his mood and habits in those days survive, thanks to the charming perceptions of his niece Annie Moffett. Annie, six years old in 1858, studied her "Uncle Sam" closely when he boarded with her family between runs on the river. She contributed her memories to a 1946 book published by her son Samuel Charles Webster.[3] Annie recalled that Uncle Sam wore sideburns, and that his "chestnut" hair was curly. He must have enjoyed teasing her: she remembered how she tried to explain the biblical story of Moses to him during one of his visits, but finally fled to her father in frustration: "Papa, Uncle Orion has good sense and Mama has good sense, but I don't think Uncle Sam has good sense. I told him the story of Moses and the bullrushes and he said he knew Moses very well, that he kept a secondhand store on Market Street. I tried very hard to explain that it wasn't the Moses I meant, but he just *couldn't* understand."[4] His rough-and-ready lingo shocked the polite little girl during a family chat in the parlor one evening, and she rushed from the room to formulate a response. Stalking back a few minutes later, she delivered a brief women's-rights manifesto: "Uncle Sam says to dry up. My Mama doesn't want me to dry up. My Papa doesn't want me to dry up. My doll doesn't want me to dry up. Uncle Sam says to dry up. I *won't* dry up!"[5]

In gentler moods, Uncle Sam went into "trances" when Annie practiced her mesmeric powers on him—"he did just what I told him to, and made the most astonishing remarks."[6] He sat at the piano and sang to Annie "by the hour," she recalled, and it was generally the same song, a song many others heard him sing over the years, a silly tune about an old horse whose name was Jerusalem. Or maybe Methusalem (accounts differ). He sang it in the drawling voice that captivated, and sometimes disquieted, nearly everyone who heard it. A friend tried to describe Samuel Clemens's voice years later:

It was not a laughing voice, or a light-hearted voice, but deep and earnest like that of one of the graver musical instruments, rich and solemn, and in emotion vibrant and swelling with its own passionate feeling . . . His way of uttering [words] and his application of them often gave the simplest words which he habitually used a pictorial vividness, a richness of suggestion, a fullness of meaning with which genius alone could endow them.[7]

Uncle Sam flattered Annie by nicknaming her "Old Horse." (He called his various nieces "Trundle-bed trash," until they refused to run errands for him anymore until he stopped.) He sang another song to Annie, whose words she never forgot:

Samuel Clemens! the gray dawn is breaking,
The howl of the housemaid is heard in the hall;
The cow from the back gate her exit is making,—
What, Samuel Clemens? Slumbering still? [8]

IN THE spring of 1859 he was again writing lush, descriptive letters to the homefolk. He described Mardi Gras to Pamela in a way that made him seem to have become one with the crowds in their costumes; the monks and priests and clowns; the " 'free-and-easy' women" whose "costumes and actions were very trying to modest eyes." [9] He saw torches shaped like the spots on a deck of cards; figures whose bodies were vast drums, pitchers, punch bowls; shapes half beast and half human. The dream world, flowing across its boundaries into his waking consciousness.

On April 9, 1859, Sam Clemens fulfilled the most ardent of his boyhood dreams: he received his pilot's license. He was now a fully invested member of the river world's elite lodge, with its $250 monthly salary. He took his ease at the Pilot's Association "Rooms" in New Orleans, and bragged to Orion that when he paid his dues, he enjoyed giving his peers "a glimpse of a hundred dollar bill peeping out from amongst notes of smaller dimensions, whose faces I do *not* exhibit!" [10] He laced his letters with French phrases, and swaggered through the fancy restaurants of New Orleans with Bixby and other pilots, a full equal now, polishing off ten-dollar dinners of sheepshead fish, mushrooms, shrimp and oysters, and coffee with burnt brandy. He bought a pair of twelve-dollar alligator boots for Orion.

Among the great characters on the river was a veteran pilot named Isaiah Sellers, an occasional river correspondent for New Orleans papers. No one knew the river better than Sellers, and no one had stored up more knowledge of its history, and no one was better at delivering long, tedious recitations of his lore. To get a chuckle out of the other pilots, Sam parodied Sellers in a ludicrously detailed "account" of a 1763 river trip on a boat with a Chinese captain and a Choctaw crew. In May 1859, Bart Bowen submitted the piece, which Sam had signed "Sergeant Fathom," to the New Orleans *Crescent*.

Sellers was humiliated, to Sam's distress: "I did not know then, though I do now, that there is no suffering comparable with that which a private person feels when he is for the first time pilloried in print." [11] Years later, perhaps as penance, he claimed that he had taken Sellers's journalistic pen name for his own: Mark Twain.*

Sam's own pride took a bruising in the summer of 1860: at the wheel of the huge *City of Memphis,* Sam crashed it into the New Orleans levee. He had been awaiting orders to "back" from his captain,† whom he thought he could glimpse out of the corner of his eye. The shape turned out to be the captain's

---

* There is no evidence that Sellers ever signed a dispatch that way.
    † The captain retained authority over a boat's movements while it was entering or leaving a port.

coat, draped over the big bell. No serious harm was done and no blame assigned. Less excusable was his grounding of the *A. B. Chambers* and later the *Alonzo Child,* with Bixby and William Bowen as co-pilots. These incidents shook his confidence but they did not harm his reputation. Horace Bixby spoke well of his abilities in later years, and Sam, looking back, rated himself as "a good average St. Louis and New Orleans pilot." [12]

He began to indulge volatile tendencies that would consume him later in life. He picked a shipboard fight with Will Bowen, the closest of his boyhood friends.* Jane Clemens later repeated a rumor that "when Sam and W B were on the Alonzo Child they quarreled and Sam let go the wheel to whip Will for talking secesh [secession] and made Will hush." [13] He was enjoying this new taste for confrontation. "I have disobeyed the Captain's orders over and over again," he boasted to Susan Stotts, Mollie's sister, "and I am ready now to quarrel with anybody in the world that can't whip me." [14]

In May Orion moved to Memphis and tried to set up a law practice; Mollie and Jennie followed a few weeks later. In that same month Lincoln was nominated for the presidency by the Republicans in Chicago. Following the lead of his mentor Edward Bates—himself by now a powerful political figure—Orion at thirty-three launched himself into Lincoln's campaign, bravely speechifying through the hostile territories of northern Missouri for the candidate, a suspected abolitionist.

In St. Louis, William and Pamela Moffett had risen in society. William was founder and president of the Merchants' Exchange. His business was doing better than the real estate and rent collection firm next door, a firm called Boggs & Grant. The company's bored and floundering junior partner, Ulysses S. Grant, killed time by hanging out in Moffett's office.

"YOU MAY not be interested in war," as Leon Trotsky later famously remarked, "but war is interested in you." In November 1860, Lincoln narrowly won the U.S. presidency, gaining only 40 percent of the popular vote. Convinced that Lincoln planned to abolish slavery, South Carolina seceded from the Union fourteen days later. Soon, Mississippi, Florida, Alabama, Georgia, Louisiana, and Texas followed. The Confederate States of America were formed on February 9, 1861, with Jefferson Davis as president.

On June 15 of that year, Ulysses S. Grant found himself a steady job.

Sam Clemens was not interested in war, at least on available evidence. The few letters that survive from these months show no concern over the fact that the Union had dissolved. He stuck doggedly to the river, as if it were exempt from the widening schism. His fantasies of the supernatural muted the disturbing realities of the time. It was as if he'd summoned Uncle Dan'l's storytelling voice as a means of keeping genuine terror at bay. Sometime in that

---

* The dispute involved money Will may have owed Sam, as well as the pair's diverging North-South loyalties, although Sam's loyalties tended to swing back and forth, depending on his mood and surroundings.

spring, in the Moffett parlor, he read aloud a sketch he'd been working on. Annie remembered that it was

a ghost story about a phantom pilot. I was about seven. He was reading the story in his slow, drawling voice that was just like Grandma's, and acting it out as he read it. He was a beautiful reader. The family was gathered in my mother's room. As he read my grandmother touched his arm and said, "Sam, look at Annie." I stood in the middle of the room transfixed with horror, and yet fascinated. I have read the story since, but I have never experienced the same thrill.[15]

This was almost certainly an early draft of "Ghost Life on the Mississippi," a tale about a pilot who tries to run a dangerous channel on a snowy night. As the pilot is blinded at the wheel, the boat is guided by the ghost of an old "King of Pilots" who had run the channel years earlier, in similar conditions, before having fallen to his death.[16]

And then the war grew interested in him. On May 14, 1861, the twenty-five-year-old Sam left New Orleans aboard the *Nebraska*. He was a passenger, looking for a new pilot's assignment: the secessionist captain of his previous boat, the *Alonzo Child*, had decided to keep that craft in Deep Southern waters. Sam's friend from the *John J. Roe*, Zeb Leavenworth, had the *Nebraska*'s wheel, and Sam kept him company.

Just south of St. Louis, the steamer passed the federally held Jefferson Barracks. A day or so earlier, the *Nebraska* had been allowed through the newly formed Union blockade at Memphis—the last nonmilitary boat to cross that line during the war years. No such luck this time. Some artillerymen in the barracks fired a warning shot across the *Nebraska*'s bow. Leavenworth, stunned and confused, continued steering. The next shell hit near the pilothouse, "breaking a lot of glass and destroying a good deal of the upper decoration," according to biographer Paine.

> Zeb Leavenworth fell back into a corner with a yell.
> "Good Lord Almighty! Sam," he said, "what do they mean by that?"
> Clemens stepped to the wheel and brought the boat around. "I guess they want us to wait a minute, Zeb," he said.[17]

Sam's aplomb didn't last long. Once ashore, he hurried to the Moffett household, Annie recalled, "obsessed with the fear that he might be arrested by government agents and forced to act as a pilot on a government gunboat while a man stood by with a pistol ready to shoot him if he showed the least sign of a false move."[18] Eight-year-old Annie now watched her conflicted Uncle Sam struggle with his sympathies, as tens of thousands of his countrymen were also doing during this period before the war's defining carnage began. Watching a group of boys parade down Chestnut Street one day, brandishing a Confederate flag and chanting Jeff Davis's name, Sam sent Annie upstairs to fetch some red-and-white ribbons in his room. He distributed these to the young Confederates. Not long afterward, he watched from a window as a small boy from the neighborhood, innocently waving a Union flag, was overwhelmed by a gang of kids. Sam dashed outside, grabbed the flag back from the attackers and chased them away.

He came in furiously angry; strangely enough not with the hoodlums, but with [the boy] because he did not fight. Grandma said, "But Sam, probably he has been taught that he must not fight." He turned on her and said furiously: "Not fight? He should have guarded that flag with his *life!*"[19]

Years later Annie, perhaps fortified with a shot of Freud, ascribed meaning to Sam's actions: "it was a case of conflicting loyalties. It was not [the boy] that he felt should guard the flag with his life but Sam Clemens." She added, "He loved his country's flag and all that it symbolized . . . I know he would gladly have given his life for his country, but he was a Southerner . . . his sympathies were with the South."[20]

RESOLUTION CAME in mid-June, via a knock on Sam's door. A friend named Smith was enlisting Hannibal-area men to join a Missouri State Guard to resist the Federals, who had occupied Jefferson City, the state capital. Would Sam join up? War had found its way to Sam at last. But if he had to fight, he would fight alongside lifelong comrades, instead of with strangers. Sam left St. Louis for Hannibal accompanied by hometown friends Sam Bowen and Absalom Grimes. A few days later, he was sworn into the Missouri State Guard.

Missouri's political sympathies before and during the Civil War were complex. Most slaveholding Missourians did not favor secession. For one thing, as an isolated northerly catch basin for slave owners, the state would have been virtually surrounded by a hostile nation. Missouri had voted for the pro-Union (and pro-slavery) Stephen Douglas in the 1860 election, and it sent nearly three times as many men to fight for the North as for the South.

Sam Clemens's zigzag march into the military reflected the seriocomic confusion that prevailed during these chaotic days of choosing sides. He and his friends reached Hannibal half-expecting the secession matter to be resolved without combat. These illusions were dissolved one morning when the three young men idly sat near the Hannibal levee, watching the packets go by, and one of the boats docked and discharged some Union troops. A lieutenant cordially offered the trio the "option" of either accompanying him to St. Louis for enlistment as Union pilots, or being clapped in irons.

The stunned boys boarded a downriver packet. But at St. Louis, Sam's fate and perhaps his literary future were spared, by, of all things, the timely appearance of a pair of "stylishly dressed young ladies" who beckoned at the office door of the general about to enlist the trio.[21] The officer excused himself, murmuring about a business matter. The three conscripts-to-be could not have been more understanding. As soon as the door closed, they grabbed luggage, squeezed through a side door, clattered down the stairs and into the street as fast as they could, and hightailed it back north to Hannibal.

Small battles were breaking out all over Missouri. Hannibal teemed with Union troops. The boys melted into the countryside south of town, where new units were forming under the command, more or less, of one General Thomas H. Harris, lately an operator in the Hannibal telegraph office. In the farmhouse of a veteran named John Ralls, Sam and about a dozen other Hannibal boys took an oath of allegiance to the Guard, and formed a training camp. The Green Berets, they were not. No two dressed alike. Weapons ranged from hunting knives to shotguns to squirrel rifles. (A nearby squad bristled with scythes, sickle bars, and its own three-piece orchestra.) They cropped their skulls close with sheep shears, to give them an edge should a battle degenerate, as battles so often do, into a hair-pulling contest.

Grimes recalls that Sam showed up for war on a four-foot-high yellow mule, clutching a valise, a homemade quilt, a frying pan, a squirrel rifle, twenty yards of seagrass rope, and an umbrella. The mule was named Paint Brush. Sam soon developed a painful boil in an area that made mule-sitting an ordeal. The outfit called itself the Ralls County Rangers. Sam was elected second lieutenant, and gave a speech standing on a log. Then they all went haring around the county, cadging meals at farmhouses, sleeping in the rain, and laughing at any passing officer who dared give them an order. In early July, about two weeks before the battle of Bull Run in Virginia, rumor spread that Union troops had broken camp at Hannibal and were marching southward toward the militia groups. The Ralls County Rangers prepared for battle. That night they threw together a picket guard with Sam in charge. The strange nocturnal comedy of errors that ensued likely inspired Mark Twain's 1885 fictionalized magazine memoir of his militia adventure, "The Private History of a Campaign That Failed."

According to Grimes's account, the pickets took cover at the mouth of a country lane, their horses tied in a nearby grove. At around 1 a.m., Grimes thought he heard hostile troops approaching. He woke the others and they took up firing positions. He spotted some moving shapes, stood, leveled his shotgun, and fired both barrels at them. Then everybody turned and ran like hell for their horses.

To our horror we saw our lieutenant more than a hundred yards off and still going. We called to him to halt, and finally Bowen leveled his shotgun and yelled, "Damn you, Sam, if you don't stop I'll let her go!" Clemens halted, and when we caught up with him (Bowen still swearing) he said, " 'Paint Brush' got so excited I could not hold him." We mounted and rode away at full speed for our camp, leaving our lieutenant and "Paint Brush" far in the rear. The last we heard of him he was saying, "Damn you, you want the Yanks to capture me!" [22]

Back at camp, the Rangers braced for battle. Soon they heard hoofbeats and again raised their weapons. At the last moment, someone recalled that Second Lieutenant Clemens was still at large. They held fire, "And so it was! We drew a sigh of relief as he came into the gangway full tilt. He made no effort to stop 'Paint Brush' until he had reached the rear end of the line and then you may bet his picket guards heard from him. Among other abuse he gave us was a special clause for the loss of his hat." [23] At daybreak Grimes and Sam Bowen returned to the mouth of the lane to view the casualties. A mortifying realization took hold of Grimes. He confessed it to Sam Bowen, swearing his friend to secrecy. He pointed to some wildflower stalks near a hill. "Well, last night the wind probably caused them to wave and I would have sworn they were Federals on horseback." [24] Bowen kept his promise of silence until they had reached camp, and then spilled the beans to everyone.

There was one further eruption of gunfire: a drunken Ranger named Dave Young heard tramping in the night. He called for the password, was ignored, and opened up with his shotgun. He nailed his own horse.

Mark Twain tirelessly inventoried his life to service his fiction (especially when the fiction was presented as nonfiction). "A Campaign That Failed" shows this process consummately at work. The tale, couched as a memoir, displays Mark's knack for knowing exactly when to depart from truth in the service of morally charged literature. The story begins as a comic reminiscence of boy soldiers frolicking and bumbling as they prepare for war. It shifts to horror when an unarmed stranger is shot for a Union soldier by the scared boys in the moonlight, and dies on the ground as he mutters about his wife and child. Then the tale plunges darkly into themes of shame, remorse, and the soul-sickening question of cowardice. Pursued by "a Union colonel . . . sweeping down on us with a whole regiment at his heels," [25] the scared company falls back from camp to camp until they reach the village of the narrator's birth. There, he deserts.

It is easy to imagine Mark Twain fashioning the climactic scene from a combination of Grimes's firing on the wildflowers and Dave Young's bringing down his own horse. But from that point, the narrative escalates into Mark Twain sole and incomparable, a chant of moral anguish that has given it life across three centuries— ". . . And it seemed an epitome of war; that all war must be just that—the killing of strangers against whom you feel no personal animosity; strangers whom, in other circumstances, you would help if you found them in trouble, and who would help you if you needed it . . ." [26]

ONE DETAIL was consistent both in historical fact and in Mark Twain's fiction: the officer at the head of the Union regiment in Missouri was Colonel Ulysses S. Grant. Grant, approaching middle age, had nearly missed the war. After failing at Boggs & Grant in St. Louis, he had accepted a job as a clerk in his father's Galena, Illinois, leather-goods store. In April 1861 he had offered his experience as a military academy graduate and veteran to the Illinois governor, who brushed him off with menial duties: clerk, mustering officer. Back home in Galena, he wrote to Washington offering to command a regiment. Nobody answered. He traveled to Cincinnati to seek a staff appointment with General George B. McClellan. McClellan didn't receive him.

Grant pried hmself into the army just at the right moment to place him on a potential collision course with the militia irregular Samuel L. Clemens. The Illinois governor finally offered Grant a colonelcy of a regiment, and he accepted. He led his troops across the Mississippi twenty-three miles upstream from Hannibal. Then the force proceeded southward, with orders to move against Thomas Harris's Missouri Guard forces at Florida.

Mark Twain stretched the truth by several miles—and weeks—when he wrote that "I came within a few hours of seeing [Grant]" in Missouri in the spring of 1861.[27] Research has shown that, far from "sweeping down" on the Rangers, Grant's march to Florida was interrupted by several diversions, including a two-week stint guarding some bridge builders on the Salt River twenty-five miles north of Florida. When he finally reached the hamlet, Harris's troops were forty miles away and Sam Clemens was long gone.[28]

Still, the implications of what might have been are too striking, given the later convergence of the two men, to let pass without notice. Ulysses Grant would have fought the first battle of his Civil War career at the site of Mark Twain's birthplace, had not Harris abandoned his encampment there before Grant's regiment arrived. Sam Clemens would have been there to meet him, had he not ridden away from the war.

Sam Clemens did not stop running from the war until he reached Nevada several weeks later. He sat out the conflict there and in California, about as far as one could get from the four-year mass slaughter without leaving the territories. The man who seems to have been eyewitness to so many consequential moments of the 19th century seemed determined to remove himself from the most consequential of them all.

And yet not quite. He lingered just long enough to take the necessary accounting. "The Private History of a Campaign That Failed" stands alongside Stephen Crane's novel, *The Red Badge of Courage,* as one of the most enduring pieces of literature inspired by the Civil War.

10

Washoe

(1861–62)

In late October 1861, Jane Clemens received a letter from her son Sam reporting, among other newsy nuggets, that he and a friend had accidentally set a mountain on fire. The mountain overlooked a lake called Bigler (later Tahoe), and was located in the territory of Nevada, roughly two thousand miles west of the Mississippi River.

Sam was discovering something about Nevada's mountains even more interesting than their flammability: that beneath their surface lay seams and veins of silver ore that shriveled Marshall Clemens's old dreams of wealth from the Tennessee land. Below their surface lay the Comstock Lode.

He had gone out there with Orion, who had just secured the only prestigious appointment of his life. Orion was to be the secretary of the Nevada Territory, and Sam would serve as his unofficial aide. The post was a reward for Orion's dogged campaigning for Lincoln in the unfriendly northern Missouri counties. The newly inaugurated president had named Edward Bates attorney general, and in January 1861, Orion had petitioned his old mentor for an appointment of some kind. Bates recommended him to Secretary of State William Seward for a territorial secretaryship, and Seward assigned him to far-off Nevada. Orion would be the second-ranking official under the territorial governor, James W. Nye. Sam saw Orion's appointment as a timely ticket out of town. Since stealing away from the Rangers, he had lived virtually as a fugitive from justice in the Moffetts' household. Partisans for both South and North were scouring the city for manpower, and experienced riverboat pilots were in demand. A gun to the head was an effective recruiting tool.

So when the chronically cash-poor Orion visited the Moffett house in St. Louis in July to show off his certificate signed by Abraham Lincoln, Sam made him an offer: in return for a sinecure as an unpaid secretary-to-the-Secretary, he would bankroll the trip to Nevada for the two of them, using twelve hundred dollars he had saved during his piloting career. Mollie Clemens and little Jennie, still back in Keokuk, would join them later. Sam saw his exile as lasting no more than three months, by which time the war would be over and he could get back to piloting steamboats. He certainly never imagined that it would be another six years before he saw the Mississippi again; nor could he have conceived the profoundly altered man who would return east, with a national reputation, an alternate name, and a new career.

Orion took his oath of office before a Supreme Court justice in St. Louis on July 11, 1861, and, a week later, the brothers boarded the packet *Sioux City* for passage westward on the Missouri River to St. Joseph. From there they booked seats on an overland stagecoach for Carson City, Nevada. They packed light: warm shirts, pipes, blankets. A bag of coins, Sam's savings. And as hedge against secretarial spelling slips, a six-pound unabridged dictionary.

It was a magnificent ride. They bowled through Kansas at a hundred miles a day. The brothers lounged on the rear passenger seat-board facing stacks of mail bound for people in Brigham and Carson and 'Frisco. They learned to sleep atop the mailbags, although Orion's dictionary kept sliding down and smacking one of them. In Nebraska Territory, they saw their first specimen of the famous "jackass rabbit" and then their first sagebrush, for both of which Mark Twain would fashion great descriptions in *Roughing It*—the preposterous-eared jackass rabbit sitting quietly, thinking about his sins; the sagebrush like a miniature live-oak tree, the author gazing into their foliage like Gulliver.[1] Nights, they donned their heavy woolens and smoked and lay down on mail sacks. It was complete and satisfying happiness. "There was a freshness and breeziness . . . and an exhilarating sense of emancipation from all sorts of cares and responsibilities . . ."[2]

Tall tales and wild characters were part of the West's atmosphere. Sam heard about a buffalo bull that chased a man up a tree. A little later, myth came alive: their stagecoach was overtaken by a rider for the legendary Pony Express that rushed mail from St. Joseph to Sacramento, and Sam drank him in—"The rider's dress was thin, and fitted close; he wore a 'round-about,' and a skull-cap, and tucked his pantaloons into his boot-tops like a race-rider . . . nearer and still nearer, and the flutter of the hoofs comes faintly to the ear—another instant a whoop and a hurrah . . . and man and horse burst past our excited faces, and go winging away like a belated fragment of a storm!"[3] One night, in hostile Indian territory, they awoke to a man's screams for help, then pistol shots, and then the jolt of the coach jerked into motion down a mountain grade. In the morning they picked up hints from the new man at the reins that their former driver had been murdered while off-shift at a way station. Tales of violence filled the air. Slade, the scourge of the Rockies, dominated all. "There was such magic in that name, SLADE!" Mark Twain wrote. "I stood always ready . . . to listen to something new about Slade and his ghastly exploits."[4] He devoted eighteen pages of *Roughing It* to reviewing them. Joseph Alfred Slade was a Mexican War veteran and stagecoach driver-turned-desperado who shot men with sadistic avidity. Mark Twain's unmistakably enchanted précis of Slade's gunslinging (and hanging and stabbing and beating) adventures—the body count reached 26—informed the emerging myth of the Western Bad Guy in dime novels and later in the movies. Sam and Orion ran into the villain at a stopover in southwestern Wyoming. "He was so friendly and so gentle-spoken that I warmed to him in spite of his awful history," Mark Twain writes.[5] In fact, the Clemens brothers never heard of Slade's reputation until after the stage-stop encounter.

Their journey then took them across the Rockies and down into Salt Lake City, where Orion had been instructed to interview Mormon leaders about their allegiances to the Union in light of the South's secession. The Secretary was taken aback to find that the self-exiled churchmen, wary over the hostility shown their sect inside the United States, half-believed that Lincoln would have attacked them but for his distraction vis-à-vis the South. They fantasized that the Civil War would destroy the Union, after which the Mormons would arise to rule the country.

While these weighty matters were being discussed, Sam was trying to get his mind around all those wives. He found that, aside from hearing stories from the Mormons about their persecution,

the next most interesting thing is to sit and listen to these Gentiles talk about polygamy; and how some portly old frog of an elder, or bishop, marries a girl—likes her, marries her sister—likes her, marries another sister—likes her, takes another—likes her, marries her mother—likes her, marries her father, grandfather, great grandfather, and then comes back hungry and asks for more.[6]

On the twentieth day of their journey, August 14, 1861, Sam and Orion reached Carson City, having clattered nearly two thousand miles from St. Louis. The area was called Washoe, after a regional Indian tribe. "The idea of coming to a stand-still . . . was not agreeable, but on the contrary depressing,"[7] wrote the man who would roam over land and water for most of his life. They found themselves in a burg of two thousand people, surrounded by the Sierra Nevada mountain range. Deep beneath the mountains' surface stretched a newfound labyrinth of unimaginable riches.

Carson City was founded in 1858 by rich lawyers connected to the cattle-ranching trade; they named the town after U.S. Army scout Kit Carson. A year later, a couple of prospectors named Pat McLaughlin and Peter O'Reilly were working the dregs of the California Gold Rush about twenty miles northeast of Carson. Needing a hole in the ground to store water, they scraped out a cavity on a steep ravine on the eastern slope of the mountain, unearthing some gold nuggets. The two miners scrabbled further, and found lots more. Others from the camp below rushed to join them, including a dishonest man named Henry Comstock, who convinced McLaughlin and O'Reilly that the land was his. The prospectors found deposits of strange-looking bluish mud beneath the nuggets, and followed the goo to the greatest single cache of precious minerals in human experience. The mud contained silver, and went on for miles, stretching deep underground. Henry Comstock's name entered history.

The Gold Rush to the West that had flared in 1849 reignited. By the time the Clemens brothers arrived in the area, a slapdash, wood-frame metropolis called Virginia City, eighteen miles north of Carson, was erupting up and down the slope of Mount Davidson. Swarms of humanity poured in: prospectors, speculators, merchants, preachers, menials, con artists, saloonkeepers, builders, engineers, killers, prostitutes, even lawyers: seven thousand of them in three years converged from across the plains and from California. That figure would rise to twenty-five thousand within a decade. Comstock mining produced more than $300 million worth of gold and silver in its first twenty years.

Walking toward the governor's "state palace" (actually a one-story white-frame pillbox), Sam and Orion witnessed their first Western gunfight. A notorious stagecoach robber known as Jack Harris had fired from horseback at some antagonist, missed, and took bullets in the chest and leg for his trouble. As Mark Twain improved on the prosaic facts of the incident, Harris passed the brothers on his horse, began a friendly chat with them, only to abruptly excuse himself and cross the street, where he traded the hot lead. After it was over, he chucked his horse past them, nodding politely, and headed on home, perforated in the lung and hip. "I never saw Harris shoot a man after that but it recalled to mind that first day in Carson," was Mark Twain's "snapper." [8]

They found sleeping space in a slapped-together shanty that passed for a boardinghouse on the town plaza, its inner walls made from stitched-together flour sacks. Its beds were occupied mostly by young New York–Irish party pols who had accompanied the new governor. (James Nye had been New York City's police commissioner and William Seward's presidential campaign manager before his appointment.) Orion plunged into the duties of his new post. He was responsible for supervising the procedural arrangements for the first territorial legislature, scheduled for early October. In addition to setting the territorial budget, he had to find a suitable hall for the meeting, and stock it with chairs, desks, and the other necessary accoutrements. In his spare time, he needed to design an official seal.

Orion also discovered the dark side of territorial politics. Nye, a product of the Tammany Hall political machine, was not interested in proper bookkeeping or playing by the rules. To him, money was used to buy access and people.

PROXIMITY TO the Comstock put Sam within reach of a possibility beyond imagining in his threadbare Hannibal days, when he watched the sinking

Marshall Clemens dream vainly of cashing in the Tennessee land. Here was a chance to get rich.

He bought himself some cowboy clothes—big slouch hat, flannel shirt, thick pants stuffed into leather boots. He struck up friendships with the young Nye pols in the boardinghouse, disarming them with his Pike County drawl, and listening to their plans to cash in on the mining bonanza. Since no one really knew where luck would strike next, the trick, he learned, was to buy up shares—called "feet"—for legal ownership of physical space in the various mining claims believed to hold silver or gold, which anyone with or without cash could do, since barter was commonplace.

The West was a dream world, fast, wild, dangerous. Sam's first few letters home reveal both his exuberant embrace of this new landscape and his instinctual habit of couching his observations in comic-epic imagery. The writer in him was setting up shop, even though Sam may not have been fully aware of it yet.

The country, he told Jane,

is fabulously rich in gold, silver, copper, lead, coal, iron, quicksilver, marble, granite, chalk, plaster of Paris, (gypsum,) thieves, murderers, desperadoes, ladies, children, lawyers, Christians, Indians, Chinamen, Spaniards, gamblers, sharpers, cuyotès (pronounced ki-yo-ties,) poets, preachers, and jackass rabbits. . . . The birds that fly over the land carry their provisions with them.[9]

He liked the sound of that passage, and repeated it virtually word for word in another letter to Jane the next day—this one prepared with an eye toward publication in the Keokuk *Gate City*. It created a stir when it appeared in print and Sam published two more. Annie Moffett always believed that its reception back east was not lost on Sam. "It . . . may be said to have been the real beginning of his literary work."[10]

Meanwhile, Sam was hatching a new idea. The Comstock had created its own satellite economy, with money constantly changing hands. A smart fellow could get rich just by catering to the needs of the miners, without getting his own hands dirty in the pickax wars. Sam decided to go into the timber business. Virginia and Carson cities were devouring lumber as their boundaries expanded. He would hike into the Rockies and select a mountainsideful of thick, hundred-foot yellow pine trees for his inventory. In early September, Sam, accompanied by a young Cincinnatian named John D. Kinney, headed into the mountains.

The plan probably would have worked, if they hadn't set the mountain on fire. They spent two or three days cavorting in the wilderness, swimming and fishing in Lake Bigler, cooking trout dinners over campfires and smoking their pipes under the stars. Eventually they cut down the obligatory two or three trees to mark their claim. Sam lit a fire by the lakeshore and walked off to fetch a frying pan. When he came back, flames were racing up the mountainside, from tree to tree.

> Within half an hour all before us was a tossing, blinding tempest of flame! It went surging up adjacent ridges . . . burst into view upon higher and farther ridges, presently—shed a grander illumination abroad, and dove again . . . threw out skirmishing parties of fire here and there, and sent them trailing their crimson spirals away among remote ramparts and ribs and gorges, till . . . the lofty mountain-fronts were webbed as it were with a tangled network of red lava streams. . . .
>
> Every feature of the spectacle was repeated in the glowing mirror of the lake![11]

The Clemenses never had been too successful getting money out of pine-covered land. Sam shifted to speculation in mining "feet." He caught gold and silver fever. Rumors of sudden wealth abounded: widows without the means to buy a crepe bonnet selling ten "feet" for $18,000; common loafers waking up from the gutter to $100,000 fortunes. The nearby Gold Hill, where it had all started, was now the hottest mining spot in the territory.

In October, Sam's letters home were full of wheeling-and-dealing reports: he had laid a timber claim for William Moffett, situated on "Sam Clemens' Bay."[12] He had amassed 1,650 feet of mining ground, and Moffett's name would go on that, too. He had trekked a hundred miles south to the Black Warrior Gold and Silver Mining Company in the Esmeralda district, where he had "been given" (actually was sold, most likely on credit) fifty feet at ten dollars a foot. He waited eagerly for the men there to "strike it rich." Sam also lent a hand to his brother, who had finally organized the legislature's first meeting. Sam was present when, at noon on October 1, 1861, Orion called the two-week session to order and ran the show until the permanent officers were elected.

For once, Sam felt sympathy for Orion, whose official status he seems to have admired. In *Roughing It,* he parodies the legislators' pettiness and rails against the tight restrictions that the U.S. comptroller levied against the Secretary's expense vouchers. "The government of my country snubs honest simplicity but fondles artistic villainy," Mark Twain fumed, "and I think I might have developed into a very capable pickpocket if I had remained in the public service a year or two."[13]

INSTEAD, HE turned to mining, and got his own pockets picked.

By the end of autumn, Sam was bored with Carson City, and the brothers' cash was running low. He'd grown a faceful of whiskers and mustaches; he looked the part; so why wasn't he mining? In December, he rounded up three companions—a friend from Keokuk, Billy Clagett; an old blacksmith named Combury Tillou and his mean little dog; and a young lawyer from Maine named Gus Oliver (Tillou is "Ballou" in *Roughing It,* and Oliver is "Oliphant"). The four struck out on the 175-mile journey north to the rich mineral region of Humboldt County. Fifteen days later, they reached Unionville.

They built a cabin, staked a claim around some good-looking rock, and tried to sink a shaft with their store-bought picks and dynamite. They gave up after twelve feet and turned to speculating with the other dreamers and dilettantes around them. Before long the Carson City quartet had amassed more than thirty thousand feet apiece in "mines" that essentially did not exist. A collective denial of reality had set in. Sam and Tillou headed back to Carson City, determined to get rich by wheeling and dealing their "feet."

Back in Carson City, Sam wrote letters to his mother and to Orion's wife Mollie that cast his misadventures as amusing tall tales—*Roughing It* rough drafts, in a way. Certain passages in each letter revealed how quickly the West was turning Sam from a modest boy into a man. The letters also showed that he still hadn't tamed the silver-dreaming beast within. He mentioned a keg of beer to Jane, the first hint that he no longer felt bound to any pledges of temperance to her. To Mollie, pining for summer to arrive so that she and her daughter could join Orion in Carson City, Sam was confessional to an extent he never would have dared with his female relatives or an unmarried woman.

Well, Mollie, I think July will be soon enough, because I think that by that time some of our claims will be paying handsomely, and you can come in "high-tone" style . . . And we could have a house fit to live in—servants to do your work . . . I am not married yet, and I never *will* marry until I can afford to have servants [for his wife] . . . I don't want to sleep with a three-fold Being who is cook, chambermaid and washerwoman all in one. I don't mind sleeping with female servants as long as I am a bachelor—by *no* means—but *after* I marry, that sort of thing will be "played out," you know. (But Lord bless you, Mollie, don't *hint* this depravity to the girls.)[14]

He also wrote letters, now and throughout his time in the West, to his beautiful eidolon of regret and yearning, Laura Wright.

Sam fidgeted around Carson City for most of February. He tried to get the territorial Secretary to upgrade his lodgings to quarters worthy of his status, but Orion wouldn't budge from his cramped fifty-dollar-a-month office, rented with his own money. As usual, Orion's naïve frugality on behalf of the territory cut no ice with his political associates. They saw him as a prissy chucklehead—mostly getting in the way of things. Governor Nye lolled around in far fancier digs on Carson's main street, stroked his white goatee, and plotted his ascension to the U.S. Senate. When Nye urged Orion to improve the legislature's financial image by cooking a few "special bills and accounts," Orion insisted that he would do no such thing. Soon the Missouri rustic and the wised-up New Yorker were eyeball-to-eyeball, with Orion's future in the balance. When Sam heard about the impasse, he acted with the same outrage that he had shown the pilot Brown in defense of Henry: he called on the governor and gave him about forty kinds of Mississippi-riverboat-pilot hell. Astonishingly, the governor backed down, and even developed a liking for Sam, a liking that would pay off in a few years.

He played cards, drank a little whiskey—well, a lot of whiskey—and lusted to get back down to Esmeralda, to examine the status of the "feet" he had accumulated earlier from that district.

His head was spinning with "feet." He bought and sold "feet" and related interests like latter-day boys would deal in bubblegum baseball cards, and with about as much to show for it. Steeped in mining arcana, he kept careful track of all his transactions and grew conversant in iron pyrites, copper, selenite crystals, mica, water rights, even the effects of underground springs on rheumatism. He also grew familiar with the phrase "played out."

Finally, in early April 1862, he returned south to the Esmeralda mines. He would spend five months at this desolate outpost: five miserable months of shabby quarters, leaking roofs, bad food, too much whiskey, hard work, dashed hopes. At Aurora, in the center of the district, Sam fired off desperate letters to Orion: "Send me $50 or $100, all you can spare . . . we shall need it soon for the tunnel." [15] "Send me $40 or $50—by mail—immediately." [16] "Don't buy *anything* while I am here—but save up some money for me. Don't send any money home. I shall have your next quarter's salary spent before you get it, I think. I mean to make or break here within the next 2 or 3 months." [17] A week or so later: "No, don't buy any ground, anywhere. The pick and shovel are the only claims I have any confidence in now. My back is sore and my hands blistered with handling them to-day. But something must come, you know." [18]

He continued in this vein—as it were—for the next several months, alternately badgering his brother for money and raving of imminent riches. In mid-May he reported an armed confrontation with claim jumpers at the Monitor hole; a friend had been shot dead in a similar incident a few days earlier. By June 2, it was, "Send me all the money you can spare every week or so." [19] By late June, it was, "No—haven't struck anything in the 'Annipolitan." [20] A month after that, "My debts are greater than I thought for . . . I owe about 45 or $50 . . . how in the h—l I am going to live on something over $100 until October or November, is singular." [21] And on, and on, in a descending arc of hope, over the next several months.

In the summer of 1862, he admitted defeat and gave up mining—or so he thought—and took a job as a common laborer at a quartz mill for ten dollars a week. It was nonstop, backbreaking work, and he stayed at it long enough to collect ten dollars. When he asked for a raise to $400,000 a month, his boss fired him, for some reason. He had one more halfhearted fling with mining that ended in a miasma of bureaucratic misunderstandings. Only then, when all else had failed, did Samuel Clemens submit himself to his true mining career.

Storytelling had been the vein open to him all along, and he'd been toying at it since childhood, incurious about its depth or worth. His writing had been recreation, venting, showing off. He had dealt the riches mostly for free. But now, exhausted from the recurring saga of "sure" fortunes vaporizing, and in debt to Orion, twenty-six-year-old Samuel Clemens finally began to seriously take stock of his own lode. A hint of his gathering awareness lay in a June 22, 1862, letter to his brother, in which he tersely instructed: "Put all of Josh's letters in my scrap book. I may have use for them some day." [22]

"Josh's letters" were brief comic sketches that Sam had been occasionally writing since April, without pay, for a little newspaper in Virginia City called the *Territorial Enterprise*. (None of these sketches survive.) Now Sam would write for pay. In July he'd leaned on Orion to make a connection for him with the Sacramento *Union*, 130 miles to the southwest in the capital of California: "As many letters a week as they want, for $10 a week." [23] But Orion had already made the better connection for Sam: within days, a letter from Bill Barstow of the *Territorial Enterprise* arrived at Aurora with a far better offer: twenty-five dollars a week, as a staff reporter.

"Eureka!" he slyly recalls shouting in *Roughing It.* But in fact, he took some time to think it over, during a hiatus at Mono Lake with Calvin Higbie. Then, swallowing his pride and tacitly conceding failure as a miner, he accepted the job. In Washoe, in the autumn of 1862, while ignorant armies clashed back east, Samuel Clemens finally fell into his true calling.

11

A Journalistic Counterculture

(1862–63)

He walked to work. That is to say, he left Aurora and the Humboldt mines on foot in late September 1862, and hiked the 120 miles north to Virginia City with a bundle of blankets on his back. He was on foot because horses cost money, and being a gold and silver miner, he didn't have any. He showed up at the *Territorial Enterprise* offices with the salutation, "Dang my buttons, if I don't believe I'm lousy," and no one who saw him was prone to disagree. He looked less like somebody who'd come to write for the paper than like somebody who'd come to rob it. He later recalled that he was coatless, and wearing a slouch hat and blue woolen shirt; his pantaloons were stuffed into his boots, and he sported a beard that foliated halfway down to his waist. Thrust under his belt was a navy revolver, his lone conventional piece of Virginia City accessorizing.

The *Territorial Enterprise* was easily the liveliest, if not exactly the most reliable newspaper on the American continent. Much of what it printed could be summed up in a two-syllable phrase, had there been enough bulls in the region to anchor the metaphor. In the three years of its existence, it had attracted a coterie of brilliant, adventuring young poets and misfit writers who had found their way to the *Enterprise* generally by accident.

Three years earlier, Virginia City had been a mud-hole on Mount Davidson, a mile and a half above sea level on the moonscape that was Washoe. After the inevitable tent city sprang up around McLaughlin's and O'Reilly's new digs, a miner named James "Ole Virginny" Finney (actually, Fennimore) smashed his whiskey bottle on the ground one night and named the campsite in honor of himself. When the building boom erupted, "Virginny" received its more dignified name, and became a hive of grasping ambition, excess, treachery, vice, dissipation, murder, and lost hopes.

As riches flowed out of the mines, the hive expanded into a throbbing dynamo of tiered streets—A, B, C, and D—slashed across the mountainside. Vertical connecting streets didn't exist, and so anyone wishing to get from A to B had to do something like enter a building, descend a staircase, and exit on the next street down. The mercantile barons lived on A and B streets. C was the commercial thoroughfare—the *Enterprise* offices were there, above a clothing store. D was home to the town's fifty-one bars and its whorehouses. Below D, the alphabet stopped and the soup began: the stew of hovels for Chinese laborers; miners' slums; and, at the mountain's base, the families of Indians who survived on what was left over from the ongoing orgy above.

Sam started his newspaper career in time to witness the greatest eruption of wealth from the Comstock mines. The bonanza yielded $20 million in ore between 1863 and 1867, and triggered a jackleg gentrification, the materials hauled in from San Francisco. Sam was present at the creation.

There were . . . fire companies, brass bands, banks, hotels, theatres, "hurdy-gurdy" houses, wide-open gambling palaces . . . civic processions, street fights, murders . . . a dozen breweries and half a dozen jails and station-houses in full operation, and some talk of building a church.[1]

Even the prostitutes gained civic renown, of various sorts: the scary "Buffalo Joe" Dodge, because she liked to duke it out with her professional rivals on the street; the British-born madam Julie Bulette, because she drove around in a gleaming carriage, prevailed on the city fathers to build clean cabins on D street for her daughters of desire, and decorated her own cottage, "Julie's Castle," with geraniums and roses. (She ultimately experienced a bad day at the office—strangled and shot in her bed for her jewelry.) Day and night, you could find and do just about anything in Virginia City.

SAM STARTED out writing conventional news items. His tutor was William Wright, a brilliant and fragile poet/essayist whose pen name, Dan De Quille, may have been a subtle pen-pun (Dandy Quill). Sam was soon on his own. De Quille left town in December to visit his wife and children in Iowa, whom he seldom saw over a forty-year period, the commute being difficult. The other *Enterprise* veterans did not quite get De Quille's replacement at first. They sensed a reserve beneath his surface jokey charm. His exaggerated drawl and his peculiar movements—that rocking and rolling gait—led people to assume that he was lazy, or drunk. (The *Enterprise* staff knew a thing or two about being drunk.) The paper's suave young editor, Joe Goodman, pegged him as lacking in industry. The portly and mustachioed Rollin Mallory Daggett, who'd made a reputation in San Francisco and now worked part-time for the paper, thought him slothful, even "abnormally lazy."[2] To C. C. Goodwin, an

Enterprise reporter before he became a judge, Sam was unseasoned, and "more or less uncouth."[3]

These sentiments were modified as the fledgling reporter began to prove his worth. Rather than focusing on the facts that any fool could observe and report, Sam reported facts that would have occurred in a better and more interesting world.

A GALE—About 7 o'clock Tuesday evening . . . a sudden blast of wind picked up a shooting gallery, two lodging houses and a drug store from their tall wooden stilts and set them down again some ten or twelve feet from their original location . . . There were many guests in the lodging houses at the time . . . it is pleasant to reflect that they seized their carpet sacks and vacated the premises with an alacrity suited to the occasion.[4]

He didn't need to explain to his readers what "lodging houses" were.

Less than a week after being hired, Sam graduated from exaggerations to outright hoaxes. His deceptively deadpan sketch of October 4, "Petrified Man," gave him his first real West Coast notoriety. A man's body, Sam wrote, had been discovered in a sitting position in the mountains south of Gravelly Ford.

. . . [T]he attitude was pensive, the right thumb resting against the side of the nose; the left thumb partially supported the chin, the fore-finger pressing the inner corner of the left eye and drawing it partly open; the right eye was closed, and the fingers of the right hand spread apart.[5]

What was more, he continued, the local folks attempting to "bury the poor unfortunate" discovered that he had been glued to the bedrock by limestone sediment that had dripped down on him throughout the centuries. The faithful reporter noted that an inquest, performed by "Justice Sewell or Sowell, of Humboldt City," determined that the stone man had died of "protracted exposure," and that the judge had ruled against a suggestion to dynamite him from his limestone confines. Some three hundred people have "visited the hardened creature during the past five or six weeks."

A private purpose lay beneath the public fun—an early manifestation of Samuel Clemens's legendary vindictiveness. The purpose was to drive G. T. Sewall nuts. Sewall had somehow offended Clemens, perhaps in a mining rights dispute, perhaps by his sectional loyalties. Papers all over Washoe reprinted the story, and Sam made sure that his victim received every issue— half a bushel of papers a day for eleven months, as he insisted in print years later.[6] "I hated Sewall in those days," he told his readers, "and these things pacified me and pleased me. I could not have gotten more real comfort out of him without killing him."[7]

This was mildly audacious stuff from a newcomer, though not out of place in the *Enterprise,* which might as well have been named for its reporters' imaginations. Before leaving town, De Quille had turned in a piece about a fellow who invented a suit made of India rubber that would offer protection for the wearer from the desert heat via a battery-controlled "air compressor." The inventor launched out on a hike across Death Valley and was later found on the valley floor, frozen: he'd flicked the compressor on, but had forgotten to flick it off. An eighteen-inch icicle hung from his nose.[8]

After De Quille, Goodwin, and Daggett, the *Enterprise* cast of characters included Steve Gillis, a printer and lethal barroom fighter who weighed ninety-five pounds; Denis McCarthy, a twenty-one-year-old co-owner of the paper and saloon raconteur; William Gillespie, a speculator-politico-newsman whom Sam used as a comic foil; and Joe Goodman.

Goodman was the *Enterprise*'s co-owner and its legitimizing force. As a twenty-two-year-old transplanted New Yorker, Goodman had bought into the newspaper with McCarthy in March 1861. He was a figure apart in the rough-house *Enterprise* offices, slim and elegant, favoring gray vested suits and watch chains, his face wreathed by thick dark hair and a well-shaped mustache. Goodman's youthfulness and good looks belied a shrewd mind (he may have hired Sam for his writing, but it didn't escape him that Sam's brother the territorial Secretary awarded governmental printing contracts to firms that owned presses). Although he accepted the public-service responsibilities of newspapers, he was attuned to the wild energies erupting in this remote enclave in the West. He hired the wild-eyed poets in mufti who drifted his way, and let them interpret and amplify these energies however they might. A journalistic counterculture coalesced at the *Enterprise,* and improvised a new literature-on-deadline that caught the emerging voice of a self-defined America.

The West may have been the only place where this could happen. The dutiful Augustans of Emerson's circle lacked the temperament to infuse their high philosophies with robust diction. Their robust Southwestern shadow images never advanced beyond narrow political resentment. Save for Whitman, the Civil War was casting a chill on the national literature, as partisan polemics replaced aesthetic innovation. Out west, there were no rules, no frowning Calvinist pieties—only energy and freedom. The voice that emerged and eventually swept eastward was iconoclastic, exuberantly outsized, funny, instinctively populist, and intensely observant.

"Western" writing did not spring full-blown in Virginia City with the *Enterprise.* One progenitor of the form was George Horatio Derby, a young military surveyor stationed in California who gained national popularity under the pen name John Phoenix. Writing for the San Diego *Herald* while on military duty in 1853, Phoenix developed a Western-humor signature style: solemn, mock-serious, with piled-on detail that revealed his narrative to be a tall tale. Phoenix made use of animals, smells, irrelevant dialogue, and irreverence toward great men and sacred ideas. In 1870, the Philadelphia *Evening Bulletin* compared Mark Twain's work to that of Phoenix—although to Twain's advantage, calling him "more extravagant and preposterous."[9]

The Pacific Coast had attracted poets and essayists since the early 19th century, though few bothered to develop a style that departed from the classical-sentimental. Bookstores and publishers specializing in Western topics soon flourished in San Francisco, distant ancestors of City Lights. Rollin Daggett founded the literary-minded *Golden Era* in San Francisco in 1852. Seven years later, a twenty-year-old native of Albany, New York, Francis Bret Harte, began working at the journal. By the time Sam arrived in the West, Harte was a rising literary figure with his own circle of admirers and protégés.

The most distinctive gestation, without question, happened in Virginia City, with Sam Clemens at its center.

Sam dove into life at the *Enterprise*. He probably slept at first on the premises, which were redolent of printer's ink and tobacco and sweat and the leftovers of Chinese food, before he found a room at a boardinghouse. He regularly sent ten or twenty dollars to his mother, when he had it.

At first, Goodman kept him on a tight leash, assigning him the dreary "local" beat of freight shipment figures, courthouse items, and mining yields. But Sam soon made himself into a man about town. The newspaper went to press at 2 a.m., so Sam began his day around noon, hitting the hotels, police stations, and the stock exchange, for information—or gossip—about mines or murders. He also hit the bars: Jane's teetotaling boy had discovered liquor. Liquor lubricated his entrée into the moiling town. He became a figure welcomed for his conviviality as much as for his access to the press. Mining people bought his good companionship with a lager beer or two, and bought mention of their mines in the *Enterprise* with gifts of "feet" in those mines. Late afternoons, he would write up what he had learned at a wooden table crowded with other reporters, noshing on noodles as he scribbled.

After sundown, when gaslights lent the tiered mountainside city the outlines of a steamboat, Sam's beat would shift to nocturnal pleasures: the theaters, opera houses, music halls, and billiard tables. He rekindled his fascination with the stage, hung out with actors and showgirls; he wrote adroit capsule reviews of plays based on a few minutes of action he'd watched before moving on down the street to the next hall. (Sadly, none of these survive.) Back to the office for last-minute items and editing the copy, then off for a late dinner or marathon drinking at a bar where patrons could wash down free cheese and mustard with pots of foaming beer. He was never far from the lethal terrors of the boomtown night. "P.S.," he added in a nocturnal letter to Jane and Pamela, "I have just heard five pistol shots down street—as such things are in my line, I will go and see about it.

"P.S. N° 2—5 A.M.—The pistol did its work well—one man—a Jackson County Missourian, shot two of my friends, (police officers,) through the heart—both died within three minutes. Murderer's name is John Campbell." [10] To bed at sunrise. Up again at noon.

Early on, the newsroom staff discovered Sam's edgy underside, and got their kicks coaxing him into a tantrum laced with pure-grade Mississippi

River swearing. Hide his pipe or his favorite writing-table candle; then watch him go crazy in quick, well-grooved increments: the search, the distracted circular pacing in that odd half-capsized gait of his, and finally the screaming, cursing war dance. Many people in Sam Clemens's lifetime were to go slack-jawed at this transformation.

Mollie and seven-year old Jennie soon joined Orion in Carson City. Mollie, with her drab Iowa roots, now entered the brief zenith of her married life. As the wife of the territorial Secretary, she took on civic stature, organizing parties and entertainments in the two-story frame house that Orion had built at Spear and Division streets.

The star of her gatherings was generally the Secretary's younger brother. In November 1862, Sam talked Joe Goodman into letting him travel to Carson City to cover the second assembly of the legislature, to be held over a six-week period at the town's new Great Basin Hotel. He boarded at his brother's house and sparkled at Mollie's social events, dancing a deft quadrille, drawing laughter with his long-drawled stories, warbling songs from his Missouri days. The Mule named Jerusalem or perhaps Methusalem (and possibly it was a Horse), made its Western debut. He cut a figure in a starched shirt and black boots, a wardrobe he sometimes augmented with a dramatic broadcloth cloak. "Great excitement exists," Sam had written as he and other reporters spent a night raising hell on the street with bonfires, speeches, and brass bands. "Half the population is drunk—the balance will be before midnight." [11]

He had lobbied Goodman for the legislature beat even though he didn't know much about parliamentary procedure (which put him on more or less equal footing with the legislature). Winning the assignment brought him into contact with a young rival reporter from the Virginia City *Union* named Clement T. Rice. Sam recruited Rice as a foil in a zany running newspaper joke that made the two of them close friends, not to mention the talk of Washoe.

At first glance, Rice reeked of rectitude. Solemn, heavy-lidded, with shadows under his eyes and a goatee that hung below a downturned mouth, he belied the rampaging comic primate that he was made to appear in Sam's *Enterprise* columns. In addition to his reporting job, Rice served as registrar of the U.S. Land Office in Carson City. He would go on to become secretary of a consolidated gold and silver mining company and later a wealthy businessman in New York City.

But not before he gyred and gimbled for a while in the wake of Sam Clemens. As he had with stolid Will Bowen back in Hannibal, and as he would with a few other fellows of dignity and stature in future years, Sam drew Clement Rice into a charmed sphere of lost, larking boyhood. The sway that Sam held over these otherwise dull men seems to have held a little of the mesmerist's power, or Pan's. His chosen cohorts thrived inside Sam's imagination, transported and enlarged.

Rice and Sam competed head-to-head for scoops. Rice was the more experienced reporter. Sam sought a crash course in legislative procedure from his friend William Gillespie, chief clerk of the Nevada Territory House of Representatives. Billy Clagett, now a territorial representative, also lent him advice. Still, nothing in this legislative period was anything like the coverage of it.

Rice started things off by gleefully pouncing, in print, on some detail that Sam had jumbled up. Sam retaliated by announcing to his readers that Rice was "unreliable." In subsequent dispatches, Rice became "The Unreliable," a hopelessly dissipated liar, glutton, and borderline criminal. Rice happily fired back, branding Sam "The Reliable." The "feud" went on, readers of both papers loved it, and the two print antagonists became close drinking friends, holidaying together in Carson City and San Francisco. As for Sam's reportage, it quickly stabilized to a level that earned him, along with Rice, a resolution of thanks from the lawmakers at the session's conclusion on December 20. Back in Virginia City, Sam found that newspapers all over Washoe were reprinting his more colorful work. By late December 1862, though, he was back to doodling in his notepad as he slouched in courtrooms and meeting rooms, sketching caricatures of the speakers he was supposed to be covering. Joe Goodman had assigned him to report stock quotations, earnings from some of the five hundred mines on the mountain, and public meetings in the town—the kind of rote work that drove Sam up the wall with boredom.

Sam indulged his ennui by turning the column into a spoof of the genre. Announcing that "our stock reporter" had attended a wedding the previous evening (and, by implication, gotten knee-walking drunk), Sam offered the fictitious reporter's "notes": "Stocks brisk, and Ophir has taken this woman for your wedded wife. Some few transactions have occurred in rings and lace veils, and at figures tall, graceful and charming . . ."[12] Then he reported seeing a fearful "blue and yellow phantom" on New Year's Eve. It turned out to be a familiar mannequin advertising a shooting gallery.[13] A week later, after his hat was filched at an Odd Fellows ball in Gold Hill, he announced menacingly in the column that he suffered from the seven years' itch, "probably the most aggravating disease in the world. It is contagious."[14]

His relations with Goodman, despite Sam's volatility, remained warm— Sam was by now, in effect, the paper's city editor—and so when he asked his boss for a day's vacation to Carson City in late January 1863, and that day turned into a week, with Clement Rice in tow, Goodman did not object. He did not object partly because the letters Sam sent back to the *Enterprise* were very good. Sprung from the humdrum, Sam was alive again, and poured his reawakened zest into his writing. Goodman could see that instead of the flashes of brilliance, interrupted by periods of lazy indifference and forced effects, Sam was perfecting a consistent, arresting voice supple enough to embrace the essentials of the classic 19th-century newspaper "letter": personal intimacy, comic flair, and sharply observed journalism. He wrote three on this trip, each displaying a skillful mixture of first-person narrative (his social adventures in Carson), long comic riffs starring "The Unreliable," and enough factual tidbits from the political sphere to satisfy his editor's standards.

The seeds of his literature were germinating in this compost. Mark Twain scholar Edgar Marquess Branch has pointed out how these and other letters of the early 1860s "exhibit[ed] with marvelous nonchalance his native gift of phrase, his talent for assimilating and appreciating slang, and of course his . . . humor." [15] Sam's letters also demonstrated his capacity for exaggeration. His indifference to the boundary between fact and fantasy became a hallmark of his literature, and later, of his consciousness.

The figure of the Unreliable represents the first successful appearance of an elementary Twainian device: the half- or fully fictionalized "Other," through which the narrator can write in a counterpointing voice, conveying temperaments, points of view, even self-criticism, that are not available to the narrator himself. With his roots in the Southwestern frame story, this Other completes a dialectic that deepens the story and allows the reader to collaborate, constantly deciding which voice is the more persuasive. As the years went on, the Unreliable was replaced by such similar figures as "Brown," "Blucher," "Harris," and even, in a somewhat different way, by Huckleberry Finn.

In the first of his letters, Sam had the audacity to include a fictional version of the reticent Goodman, "that incessant talker." Sam then turned the stage over to the Unreliable, through whose antics he gave an id's-eye-view of a party hosted by former California governor J. Neely Johnson.

About nine o'clock the Unreliable came and asked Gov. Johnson to let him stand on the porch. That creature has got more impudence than any person I ever saw in my life. Well, he stood and flattened his nose against the parlor window, and looked hungry and vicious—he always looks that way—until Col. Musser arrived with some ladies, when he actually fell in their wake and came swaggering in . . . He had on my fine kid boots, and my plug hat and my white kid gloves . . . and my heavy gold repeater, which I had been offered thousands and thousands of dollars for, many and many a time . . . After all the modern dances had been danced several times, the people adjourned to the supper-room. I found my wardrobe there, as usual, with the Unreliable in it . . . he was desperately hungry . . . First, he ate a platter of sandwiches; then he ate a handsomely iced poundcake; then he gobbled a dish of chicken salad; after which he ate a roast pig . . . Dishes of brandy-grapes, and jellies, and such things, and pyramids of fruits, melted away before him as shadows fly at the sun's approach . . . [16]

This first Carson City letter, which ran in the *Enterprise* on February 3, 1863, included two other notable features. One was its arresting lead sentence: "I feel very much as if I had just awakened out of a long sleep." [17]

The other was the signature at the bottom of the letter, a signature Sam had never used before, but one that gave especial resonance to the opening sentence: "Mark Twain." [18]

12

"Mark Twain—More of Him"

(1863)

How he came to select his pen name may never be known. Clemens's own explanation and abiding myth have it that he took it from the language of the river. "Mark twain" (literally "mark two"), a depth of twelve feet—a depth readily navigable and safe. In *Life on the Mississippi,* he wrote that he had "confiscated" the handle from Captain Isaiah Sellers, the legendary steamboatman and occasional river correspondent whose reminiscences Sam had lampooned with wicked accuracy in 1859, and then regretted. Archived New Orleans papers of the period have not yet yielded a single use of the signature "Mark Twain."[1]

Whatever its origins, "Mark Twain" is the most recognized alias in world literature, if not the history of aliases, and the most analyzed. It plays beautifully against the ear: short, resonant; that tight knock of hard consonants trailing off into a subtle chime. "Mark Twain" carries the unforced persuasiveness of an actual, everyday name (as opposed to "Trismegistus," or "Peregrine," or "Ensign Stebbings," or "Uncle Remus," or "Panurge," or "Gipsey Girl," or "Thomas Jefferson Snodgrass"). For the hermeneutically inclined, there is the Comstock lode of possible meanings embedded in "Twain"—that undiscovered signifier from whose bourn no post-structuralist Ph.D. candidate returns.

Something about "Mark Twain" has also attracted psychobiographical analysis the way deep water attracts a dowsing rod. Justin Kaplan has pointed out that twinship was one of Twain's favorite subjects, and proposed that Sam took refuge in the "Mark Twain" persona as a conduit to literary indepen-

dence—it helped free him from his temptations toward bourgeois respectability and blandness—and, as bereavements piled up in his life, as a means of
protecting his sanity.

Some 19th-century reviewers recognized a crucial distance between
Samuel Clemens and his literary alter ego. We cannot "fairly hold Mr.
Clemens responsible for 'Mark Twain's' irreverence," wrote Bret Harte in a famous review of *The Innocents Abroad*.[2] In 1868, Clemens himself wrote jocu-
larly of an "independent Double" who had gone around the country
impersonating him and doing things that the respectable Clemens could not
get away with.[3] Late in his life, Clemens had his alias registered as a trademark. But then, the author/narrator distinction was a given for *all* "frame"
writers and those who used pen names. Nor is it uncommon for celebrities,
politicians, and other notables to talk about their public image in the third
person. Somehow, Samuel Clemens has been held to closer account than most
figures for behaving differently toward the world, or within his artistic
medium, than in private. When T. S. Eliot later wrote of preparing "a face to
meet the faces that you meet," he surely had a wider referent in mind than
Clemens/Twain.

IN TRUTH, Sam probably took a pen name (with Joe Goodman's permission) because pen names were fashionable and also because it gave him a thin
veil of anonymity (as had "Josh," which he signed to his *Enterprise* letters in
mid-1862). His barbed writing had started to draw blood here and there; not
everyone was disarmed by his antics. Virginia City was a small world, and
Sam's more edgy items, usually short and shockingly personal under a pretense of joking, lent him an aspect of meanness in some people's eyes, and
caused others to storm the *Enterprise* editorial offices, looking for a fight.

In mid-February he dashed off a prototype of what would become a favorite exercise: the parody of a genre. In "Ye Sentimental Law Student" Sam
imagined a valentine composed for a sweetheart by a pedantic law student
(who turns out to be the shape-shifting Unreliable): "Such sights and scenes as
this ever remind me, the party of the second part, of you, my Mary, the peerless party of the first part. The view from the lonely and segregated mountain
peak, of this portion of what is called and known as the Creation, with all and
singular the hereditaments and appurtenances thereunto appertaining and
belonging . . ."[4]

Days later, his mercurial mood had turned dark again. He brooded to
Jane and Pamela that his escapade in Carson City had been tolerated only because nobody at the *Enterprise* missed him: "they haven't much confidence in
me now."[5] He turned protective of his privacy: "What do you show my letters
for? Can't you let me tell a lie occasionally to keep my hand in for the public,
without exposing me?"[6]

He kept a wary eye on Orion, who was acting as territorial governor during James Nye's frequent getaways to California and the East. In December

1862, Nye had skipped out, not to return until the following July. This meant that Orion, who'd once had trouble managing his father's dry-goods business, was now in charge of 110,000 square miles of wasteland, silver mines, immigrants, desperadoes, and increasingly resentful Indians. It was starting to look as though he had inherited a responsibility unimaginable from behind the counter in Hannibal: armed conflict with California.

A certain ambiguity prevailed at the California-Nevada line, especially along a stretch of northern land in the ore-rich Honey Lake region of the Sierra Madres (including the Esmeralda region). After Nevada aggressively organized a chunk of that disputed land into a county called Roop, a few dozen men from each side took up firing positions against one another in the village of Susanville. The shooting started on February 15, 1863. A few men were winged, nobody was killed, and after three hours, a truce was called and several of the fellows on both sides got together for dinner and war stories at a local hotel. Still, real tensions were mounting, carrying undertones of the war back east: Nevada was controlled by Unionists, but in California, "secesh" sentiment prevailed. Prickly negotiations went on for weeks, with Orion handling things on the Nevada side. "I suppose we are on the verge of war now," Sam idly remarked in an April 11 letter home.[7] It never happened, thanks mainly to Orion's diplomatic maneuverings, which resulted in a surveying of the disputed land by crews from both California and Nevada. The valuable Esmeralda fields stayed on the Nevada side.

By early May, as the Union army licked its wounds after the battle of Chancellorsville and Ulysses S. Grant began to organize his Vicksburg campaign, Sam was in San Francisco, the Unreliable in tow. He had taken a two-month leave from the *Enterprise*. Money was in the air. The whole western slope, it seemed, was awash in it. Sam and Rice bought sixty days of extravagance with their saved-up salaries and hoarded stock cash-ins. They stayed at the posh Occidental Hotel at Montgomery and Bush streets, and then moved down the street to the even pricier Lick House. They dined on beefsteaks and oysters at the fanciest restaurants; drank their way up and down Montgomery Street, hit the opera and concerts at the Bella Union Melodeon, ordered some handmade suits, and sailed on yachts on the sparkling bay.

San Francisco attracted Sam, and with good reason. In 1863 it was a cosmopolitan city with traditions and luxuries that the raw wealth of Virginia City could not match. The site was settled in 1776 by Spanish missionaries, who built a mission overlooking the bay. The city that grew there was called Yerba Buena, "the Good Herb," but was renamed San Francisco in 1847, a hundred twenty years short of the Summer of Love. At that time it had about five hundred inhabitants. After gold was discovered at Sutter's Mill, thirty miles away, in December of that year, the population jumped to two thousand in February 1848; then fifteen thousand several months later. A local historian writing in 1853 remembered them as the motliest people in the world: the men wore everything from slouch hats, to short-waisted frocks, to swallowtailed dress coats, to double-breasted jackets, to surtouts, to bang-ups, to Spanish wrap-pers, to serapes, to bear skins (when women started arriving in number, the men began to tone it up a little). "In those days the humor of the people in-clined them not in the slightest degree toward intellectual pursuits . . . one might infer without sinning violently against the truth, that drinking was a universal habit."[8]

By the time of Sam and Rice's arrival, most of the men had thrown away their slouch hats and were wearing "trim and formal models from Broadway or Chestnut Street."[9] The city would eventually replace Virginia as Sam's Western gravitational center. He seems to have anticipated this on his initial visit. Trading on his rising celebrityhood in Washoe, he visited the offices of the San Francisco *Morning Call,* and struck a deal to send it letters from Vir-ginia City.

In letters back to the *Enterprise,* Mark Twain kept his readers regaled with tales about the Unreliable's usual simian behavior, "jumping" hotel rooms better than his own as one would jump a mining claim, and shouldering his way into private boxes at the theater: "[He] has conducted himself in such a reckless and unprincipled manner that he has brought the whole Territory into disrepute and made its name a reproach . . ."[10]

In a letter to his mother and sister, he practically strutted between the lines: "I suppose I know at least a thousand people here—a great many of them citizens of San Francisco, but the majority belonging in Washoe—& when I go down Montgomery street, shaking hands with Tom, Dick & Harry, it is just like being in Main street in Hannibal & meeting the old familiar faces."[11] He gassed on, "We dine out, & we lunch out, and we eat, drink and are happy—as it were. After breakfast, I don't often see the hotel again until midnight—or after."[12] Perhaps anticipating that this sort of news would appall the good Presbyterian Jane Clemens, he twisted the knife: "I am going to the Dickens mighty fast."[13]

Whichever of his chest-thumping assertions ignited his mother's famous temper first—the social preening, the big-spending allusions, the reference to drink, the general tone of wild and crazy dissipation—she fired off a reply that pinned his ears back a little. He wrote:

Ma, you are slinging insinuations at me again. Such as "where did I get the money?" and "the company I kept" in San Francisco. Why I sold "wildcat" mining ground that was given me, & my credit was always good at the bank . . . I *never* gamble, in any shape or manner, and never drink anything stronger than claret or lager beer, which conduct is regarded as miraculously temperate in this country . . .[14]

Still, even in this hat-in-hand posture, the prodigal son could not restrain himself from bragging in his last paragraph that "it costs me $100 a month to live."[15]

.   .   .

ANOTHER ASPECT of Sam's deportment in San Francisco with Clement Rice, and indeed, of his subsequent intense friendships with other men, has raised questions undreamed of in Jane Clemens's philosophy. This is the question of whether Sam experimented in homosexual behavior.

The question wasn't raised for nearly a century and a half, until it appeared in (and virtually consumed all critical reaction to) a Mark Twain biography published in 1997. This work, which was otherwise graced with praiseworthy research and interpretation, essentially "outed" Sam on the basis of evidence that, while provocative in parts, remains speculative and circumstantial.[16] The author catalogued every suggestive kernel he could uncover to make his case, which he never framed more explicitly than the boundaries of innuendo permitted. He drew on the fact that Sam and Rice lived together in Virginia City, and that Sam later shared a room, perhaps even a bed, with Dan De Quille; he mused over the "romantic" salutation ("My dearest Love,") in a letter from the unabashedly homosexual humorist Artemus Ward; he ruminated on the long history of San Francisco's attraction for homosexual men. He pounced upon a remark by Sam in a letter to Jane from San Francisco: "We fag ourselves out completely every day . . ."[17]

According to the *Oxford English Dictionary, Second Edition,* "faggot," as an allusion to the lighted brand used to torture heretics and homosexuals in the Middle Ages, does not enter American usage as a homosexual slur until 1914, and the shortened form "fag" doesn't show up until 1923. Before then, "fagged" was slang for "fatigued," and "faggot," interestingly, was a term of contempt for women.

European and American men in the 1800s (well, maybe not the British) hugged, linked arms with, leaned against, expressed endearments to, and paired off platonically with one another far more frequently than they did with women, whom they could scarcely touch without inviting a collective nervous breakdown in the vicinity. Surviving letters, photographs,[18] etiquette books, and descriptive narratives make this unimpeachably clear. Unmarried men, especially when away from home, often shared beds. Homosexual attraction was undoubtedly a component in some of these activities, but it could hardly be said to define all of them. Sam Clemens, who from early boyhood went into head-standing paroxysms over pretty girls, who sustained a lifelong dream-affair with Laura Wright, who returned from the West to marry and preside over a close-knit family, and who carried on at least two lifelong, intense male friendships without a hint of erotic complication, was simply a creature of his century. As perhaps, even, was Abraham Lincoln.

Of course, the question remains: as a virile bachelor in his mid-twenties, how and where *was* Sam attending to his libidinous drives?

Here, too, the trail leads virtually nowhere. Sam Clemens was a joyous connoisseur of bawdy jokes and the originator of at least one comic-pornographic masterpiece ("1601"), and his letters to a few trusted friends sometimes revealed his zest for off-color punning. But apart from the passage in a letter to Mollie Clemens that confessed to bedding the household help (unfortunately, not a betrayal of one's honor in Victorian America), and a few references to young women who had turned his head, Sam kept mum about his actual sex life, a custom he shared with nearly every other writer of his century, and one that has since sadly slipped into desuetude.

SAM AND Rice returned from their San Francisco holiday on July 2, 1863. In Pennsylvania, at Gettysburg, it was the day of the Round Tops, Devil's Den, and Cemetery Hill. In Mississippi, Major General Grant was two days from seizing the shattered city of Vicksburg, restoring Sam's "national banner" to federal control, splitting the Confederacy, and leading to Grant's promotion to general-in-chief of the Union armies. In Virginia City, the only explosions were from mine-shaft dynamite: the boomtown was booming as never before. A silver vein below A Street had been struck, and the mine's stock had rocketed to $6,000 a foot. The company, Gould & Curry, started work on a mill two miles outside town that cost $750,000. The Ophir hit a vein worth $2,500 per ton. More prospectors and mining men converged on the mountainside, followed by more fortune seekers. New hotels, rooming houses, and stores sprung up. Strangers gunned down strangers on drunken impulse. General hysteria reigned.

Mark Twain's first dispatch to the *Morning Call* described Virginia's new "turmoil and confusion,"[19] its brass-band parades in preparation for the Fourth of July celebration, and the midnight shooting of a saloon proprietor. He wound it up with characteristic whimsy: "There was a report about town, last night, that Charles Strong, Esq., Superintendent of the Gould & Curry, had been shot and very effectually killed. I asked him about it at church this morning. He said there was no truth to the rumor . . ."[20]

Town life took on a new intensity. In July the *Enterprise* moved into a three-story building and began printing its expanded editions on a steam press. On July 25, a fire raced through the western sections of the tinderbox town. Among the buildings it consumed were the White House and the boarding-house on B street, where Sam lived with Rice and William Gillespie. Sam was inside when the house went up in flames. Blocked from the doorway by smoke, he dived through a window. He lost most of his belongings, including his San Francisco suits. As elsewhere in the country in those days, rival fire companies battled one another as well as the blaze. Afterward, two companies negotiated the territorial issue at Taylor and C streets; one man was killed and fifteen were injured.

Sam moved into the new Collins House, at whose grand opening two weeks earlier he had given what the rival *Evening Bulletin* had described as "[p]erhaps *the* speech of the evening . . . Those not familiar with this young man, do not know the depths of grave tenderness in his nature. He almost brought the house to tears by his touching simple pathos."[21]

Violence hit new levels. Men hit, stabbed, slashed, shot one another daily,

tly. The more refined classes, repelled by this collapse of decorum,
e Southern tradition of dueling. On August 2, Mark Twain wrote
. a thwarted duel that would have pitted Joseph Goodman against
Thomas Fitch, the editor of the rival *Union*. The two had been sparring in
print about factional Union party politics. Policemen broke up the confrontation before any shooting, but two months later the editors snuck out and met
again. Goodman drilled Fitch below the right knee, crippling him.

On August 4, laid up in bed with a cold, Sam was torpedoed in print by his
"nemesis" the Unreliable. Clement Rice had offered to take over Sam's
"Local" column while he recovered. Appropriating Mark Twain's byline, Rice
wrote a fake "Apologetic" to several town citizens whom Sam had maligned.
Sam furiously annulled the apologies the next day, noting that the Unreliable
was "a reptile endowed with no more intellect, . . . no more Christian principle" than a "jackass rabbit of the Sierras." As if this were not sufficient conflict,
Sam received a letter from Orion lecturing him about his "dissipation," and
another from Jane, admonishing him that if he worked hard, he might get a
real job someday. This hurt. "Ma, you have given my vanity a deadly thrust,"
he raged in reply.

Behold, I am prone to boast of having the widest reputation as a local editor, of any
man on the Pacific coast, & you gravely come forward & tell me "if I work hard & attend
closely to my business, I may *aspire* to a place on a big San Francisco daily, some day."
. . . Why, blast it, I was under the impression that I could get such a situation as that any
time I asked for it. But I don't want it. No paper in the United States can afford to pay
me what my place on the "Enterprise" is worth . . . Everybody knows me, & I feel like a
prince wherever I go . . . And I am proud to say I am the most conceited ass in the Territory.[22]

"Conceited" was hardly the word for it. He was flying now; writing and behaving as though accountability were a joke; he was invulnerable; the objective
world was just an extension of the dreamworld within. He blurted into print
whatever was on his mind, heedless of its effect on others, his reputation, his
safety. His mind played dizzying tricks with words; his antic humor brightened some of them, and his spleen coated others with poison. It was as if he'd
been gripped by a kind of typographical Tourette's syndrome. Perhaps he was
caught up in the surreality that had enveloped Virginia City, the sense that
anything could happen, that limits had been abolished, that the sloping
ground underfoot was the Big Rock Candy Mountain. It was a dangerous assumption, and real consequences were on their way. In the meantime, he was
granted a "furlough" to cure his cold: two weeks at Lake Bigler. Without
Goodman's permission, he lounged for another week at a Washoe County
hotel with the interesting name, the Steamboat Springs, and wrote a puff
piece about it that probably covered his room and board. Bigler was coming to
be known by the Indian name of "Tahoe," given that its namesake John Bigler

was a pro-Southern man in Union country. No one had asked Mark Twain's leave to make this change. He handed down his judgment in the *Enterprise:* "I yearn for the scalp of the soft-shell crab—be he injun or white man—who conceived of that spoony, slobbering, summer-complaint of a name. Why, if I had a grudge against a half-price nigger, I wouldn't be mean enough to call him by such an epithet as that . . ."[23]

Dan De Quille returned from his Iowa hegira on September 5, and resumed his "Local" column. Sam, who'd been back at his post for less than two weeks, seized the opportunity to hightail it back to San Francisco for yet another month at the Lick House. "During his absence the moral tone of this column will be much improved," De Quille kindly remarked in his column.[24] While he was in town, the *Golden Era* reprinted another of his madcap genre-burlesques, a form of mimicry tailored for his extraordinary ear. He'd written this one, titled "All About the Fashions," from the Lick House during his spring visit, and probably first published it in the *Enterprise*. The headline above the title proclaimed, "Mark Twain—More of Him." The send-up of overwrought fashion-writing prose anticipates such 20th-century parodists as S. J. Perelman, Woody Allen, and Steve Martin, with perhaps a touch of Lewis Carroll.

Mrs. B. was arrayed in a superb speckled foulard, with the stripes running fore and aft, and with collets and camails to match; also, a rotonde of Chantilly lace, embroidered with blue and yellow dogs, and birds and things, done in cruel . . .

Mrs. J. B. W. wore a heavy rat-colored brocade silk, studded with large silver stars . . . a bournous of black Honiton lace, scalloped, and embroidered in violent colors with a battle piece representing the taking of Holland by the Dutch . . . upon her bosom reposed a gorgeous bouquet of real sage brush, imported from Washoe . . .

Miss A. H. wore a splendid Lucia de Lammermoon . . . also, a cream-colored mantilla-shaped *pardessus,* with a deep gore in the neck . . . garnished with ruches, and radishes and things. Her *coiffure* was a simple wreath of sardines on a string. She was lovely to a fault.[25]

In that same September 27 issue, the editors of *Golden Era*—in keeping with the too-much-ain't-enough temper of the times—ran a similar sketch by Mark Twain titled "The Lick House Ball." This second send-up of an actual social event at the hotel's famous grand ballroom, attended by the new California governor-elect among others, took the parody even further. "[T]he ball was a grand success," Mark Twain reported. "The army was present and also the navy." As for the fashions, "Mrs. Wm. M. S. wore a gorgeous dress of silk bias . . . set off with *bagnettes,* bayonets, clarinets, and one thing or other—beautiful." As for Miss B., she showed up in "an elegant goffered flounce . . . with a frontispiece formed of a single magnificent cauliflower imbedded in mashed potatoes. Thus attired Miss B. looked good enough to eat."[26] Even the chambermaid inspired imagery; she reminded Mark Twain of U.S. Grant, marching to the center of the room with her broom and slop bucket.

But after just one month in town, Sam's hubris took a terrible jolt. The high-flying prankster finally reached too far. The offending piece was titled, "A Bloody Massacre near Carson." It ranks as one of the most graphically repellent notions ever to flow from Mark Twain's pen. It described in blood-soaked, photorealistic detail the murderous rampage of one Philip Hopkins, of Ormsby County, against his family that took the lives of seven of his nine children, his wife, and, ultimately, himself. The piece—reprinted in newspapers from Sacramento to San Francisco—opened with an account, taken from "Abram Curry," of Hopkins's late-night dash into Carson on horseback, "with his throat cut from ear to ear, and bearing in his hand a reeking scalp from which the warm, smoking blood was still dripping." Hopkins died on the spot. The scalp he carried was that of his wife. The sheriff and a group of citizens hurried to the Hopkins house,

where a ghastly scene met their gaze. The scalpless corpse of Mrs. Hopkins lay across the threshold, with her head split open and her right hand almost severed from the wrist . . . In one of the bedrooms six of the children were found, one in bed and the others scattered about the floor. They were all dead. Their brains had evidently been dashed out with a club . . . The children must have struggled hard for their lives . . .[27]

Two of Hopkins's daughters lay in the kitchen, "bruised and insensible, but it is thought their recovery is possible." The eldest daughter was found in the garret, "frightfully mutilated, and the knife with which her wounds had been inflicted still sticking in her side." [28] The Hopkins family did not exist, and the piece was a hoax. The public's horrified revulsion soon turned to anger.

Mark Twain had written it (unsigned) with the aim of exposing what he called the "dividend-cooking system" of certain incorporated companies in Nevada and California—a practice of overvaluing a stock and selling it before the buyers realized they had been tricked. In the piece, "Hopkins" was revealed to have been an affable and polite man until he started to lose his life savings in various crooked schemes: "It is presumed that this misfortune drove him mad and resulted in his killing himself and the greater portion of his family." [29]

Most readers seem never to have made it that far down in the story. The details of the "murders" were too much to stomach. Some of the public's anguish must have reached the *Enterprise* offices the day the piece appeared, October 28, because the next day's editions carried a brief notice over Mark Twain's byline, titled,

I TAKE IT ALL BACK

He tried to laugh off the furor. Didn't people notice the giveaway clues?—who did not know that the "great pine forest" mentioned in the piece was nonexistent? Or that Empire City and Dutch Nicks (also alluded to) were one and

the same town? Anyway, this wasn't just about kidding around. "It was necessary to publish the story," Mark Twain insisted, "in order to get the fact into
the San Francisco papers that the Spring Valley Water company was 'cooking'
dividends by borrowing money to declare them on for its stockholders. The
only way you can get a fact into a San Francisco journal is to smuggle it in
through some great tragedy."[30] That made matters worse. When people
found out that their sensibilities had been violated on false premises, outrage
spread. Several papers denounced Mark Twain. It didn't help that in naming
the Spring Valley Water Company, he had exaggerated its financial plight, or
that his accusations against the San Francisco press were not wholly accurate.

Mark Twain had tapped real-life events for his grisly lead, as he would so
often in his fiction. There had been an ax-murder spree in the region about
five months earlier, and Twain borrowed details from it for his piece. But the
image of the killer brandishing a scalp was his invention, and it may have been
drawn from deep personal wells. Indian-fighting frontiersmen ran through
the maternal side of Sam Clemens's ancestry; massacres by marauding Indians in old Kentucky formed much of the Lampton family folklore; and Jane,
with her storytelling flair, passed several of these bloody tales along to Sammy.

POLITICS BEGAN to absorb both Sam's and Orion's lives. In October
1863, Nevada called a convention in Carson City to draw up a constitution, as
a move toward statehood. Mark Twain was the reigning reportorial star despite his recent "Massacre" misstep. Once again he also starred in the news-
mens' off-hours cavorting, getting himself elected governor of the mock
legislative body, the Third House (a play on "third estate"). He returned to
Carson in January to report on the Union party's political convention that
produced a slate of candidates for the territory's anticipated first election as a
state.

Orion was nominated by acclamation for secretary of state—his reward
for skillfully negotiating a settlement to the California-Nevada border crisis.
It seemed to be the harbinger of a career in public service. In the January 19
election, he was victorious. Once again Mollie Clemens presided over fabulous parties, Sam delighting the guests with his dance steps and wit. Jennie,
nearly eight now, a bright and religious child, marveled at it all from the side-
lines. A golden future seemed at hand. In fact, Orion's and Mollie's days of
power, prominence, and joy had reached an end. The constitution that had
been drafted before the election was ruled null and void because of technical
irregularities. Voided along with it was the January 19 election. Then, on
February 1, Jennie Clemens died of a disease believed to be meningitis. The
loss put out whatever fire remained in Orion. He and Mollie struggled along
in Nevada for two more years, and then headed back east, effectively into
oblivion.

Sam's fortunes were accelerating in the opposite direction. In November
1863, between the two conventions at Carson City, a literary eminence from

the East visited Virginia City, and struck up a riotous friendship with Mark Twain. The encounter between Sam and Charles Farrar Browne, known to the world as Artemus Ward, pointed Mark Twain toward national recognition, while at the same time nearly destroying him in the flames of his inner furies and despair.

13

Code Duello

(1863–64)

Artemus Ward, foppish, merry, tubercular, doomed, hit town on December 18, 1863. He checked in to the International Hotel and immediately sought out the local enclave of maverick writers. In Virginia City, that was the office of the *Territorial Enterprise,* whose inmates welcomed Ward as one of their own. The former Cleveland *Plain Dealer* columnist had risen to transcontinental acclaim in print and on the lecture stage. His dreamy, off-center comic ramblings, punctuated with social barbs, had made him at once a regular among the louche artists who gathered in the cavernous Pfaff's Beer Hall in Greenwich Village, and a favorite of that ultimate square, Lincoln, who read Ward's comic sketches aloud to his cabinet. Artemus Ward was Sam's first celebrity acquaintance, and Ward introduced him to the perspective of the urban bohemian artist. This perspective ratified some of the town-born Missourian's most subversive instincts.

"Bohemians"—creative renegades who flourished at the edges of conventional culture—were a new subset of American society. Such undergrounds had been common in European capitals for centuries. The New World remained innocent of them until New York swelled into a metropolis in the 1830s, and attained the urban mass necessary to camouflage a maverick demimonde. Now, as an even more exotic city blossomed on the other side of the continent, many bohemians left Pfaff's and made the cross-country pilgrimage to its foggy hills and bayside crannies. From the 1860s on, San Francisco and New York would constitute the poles of the American avant-garde, scandalizing and re-energizing the artistic "establishment." Among

129

the first writers to rise both in bohemia and the establishment was Mark Twain.

In truth, when it came to inventing American culture, the New York bohemians and the Boston Transcendentalists were working the same side of the street. For all their transgressive display, the bohemians were referencing the same classic European standards as Emerson and Holmes and Lowell—for instance, the Seven Arts that had stood since medieval times as the standard of higher learning.* Bohemians and Transcendentalists first converged in Walt Whitman, a regular at Pfaff's by way of the Fulton ferry from Brooklyn. It was Whitman's unrhymed, unmetered *Leaves of Grass,* in 1855, which first answered Emerson's call for a new American voice. Whitman worshipped the Sage of Concord—"I was simmering, simmering, simmering. Emerson brought me to a boil"—and cultivated his approval. Emerson responded with great praise—"I greet you at the beginning of a great career." No such greetings issued from the Boston Brahmin James Russell Lowell, who once warned a friend: "Whitman is a rowdy, a New York tough, a loafer, a frequenter of low places, a friend of cab drivers!"[1]

The barnstorming Artemus Ward had arrived in San Francisco on November 8. He'd sashayed through the city like a skeletal Pan, accepting flagons of his trademark brandy-and-water from adoring strangers, dancing jigs in front of cheering crowds, and bowing to brass-band serenades, before convulsing audiences at Platt's Hall and the Metropolitan Theater. Then he'd lectured his way on to Virginia City. Sam well knew Ward's work. In November he'd announced the humorist's visit via a pitch-perfect parody of Ward's anarchic spelling style, in the *Enterprise:*

We understand that Artemus Ward contemplates visiting this region to deliver his lectures, and perhaps make some additions to his big "sho." In his last letter to us he appeared particularly anxious to "sekure a kupple ov horned todes; alsowe, a lizard which it may be persessed of 2 tales, or any komical snaix . . . I was roomination on gittin a bust of mark Twain, but I've kwit kontemplatin the work. They tell me down heer to the Ba that the busts air so kommon it wood ony bee an waist of wax too git un kounterfit presentiment."[2]

Sam and the boys painted the town with Ward, "collecting" dance halls, hurdy-gurdy parlors, and the Chinese district. They escorted him into the depths of a silver mine, and Ward had so much fun that he extended his scheduled stopover on the mountainside to eleven days, making side trips to lecture in nearby towns. Like so many others, Ward found himself drawn to the small, drawling Missourian with his whimsical asides and his implicit invitation to

---

* They were organized as the Trivium—grammar, rhetoric, and logic, and the Quadrivium—arithmetic, geometry, music, and astronomy.

throw off adult decorum. He and Sam became riotously good chums, and Ward gave Sam a glimpse of what his future could hold.

In Ward, Sam Clemens saw a figure very like himself, only much richer and more famous. (It didn't escape him that Ward's projected earnings from this tour were $30,000.) He seems to have immediately grasped the significance of Ward: here was a fellow of Sam's age, playing the same skills that Sam was retailing around the Nevada hills, but on a national and even international level, and getting rich doing it. Sam welded himself to Ward's elbow and scrutinized him intently throughout the visit.

Their similarities were extensive. Only two years older than Sam, Ward had been born in a small town (Waterville, Maine); like Sam, he lost his father in 1847 and had learned typesetting to support himself; like Sam, he gravitated toward newspapering and eventually wrote under an assumed identity that soon supplanted his given name, Charles Farrar Browne. Like Sam, he wrote fondly of his boyhood years, played practical jokes, and loved the circus and the minstrel show. He was youthful in affect, like his new admirer, but genial where Sam was impulsive and combustible; a whimsical wit, yet capable of genuine moral indignation; a drinker subject to unpredictable mood swings. The two may even have discovered that as boys, they had landed sketches in the same humor magazine, the Boston-based *Carpet-Bag*.

"Artemus Ward" was Browne's concoction of a rustic sojourner, unschooled but shrewd, whose gentle whimsy and phonetic misspellings* sheathed a morally grounded common sense—racial bigotry excepted. Ward's humor was similar to Mark Twain's, but less stinging (except in his contempt for Negroes), and more limited than Mark Twain's mature work. It mainly exploited the fascination that the young nation felt for the eccentricities of its own speaking voice: its vernacular, quaint idioms, and utility for pun making, as when Ward wrote on the topic of "women's rites."

Their main difference, other than talent, lay in notoriety. Mark Twain enjoyed a following around Nevada and California—a visiting bohemian from New York, Fitz Hugh Ludlow, had recently hailed him as "that Irresistible Washoe Giant" [3]—but Artemus Ward had made it big in the East. After a quick rise at the *Plain Dealer*, he moved on to edit *Vanity Fair* in New York; and a year later, in 1861, he launched his lecture career. When he arrived in Washoe he was the premier humorist in America. Whether Ward could have equaled Mark Twain in the American memory will never be known: in March 1867 he died of his tuberculosis while on tour in England. Like Oscar Wilde decades later, he maintained his comic stance until the very end. His biographer re-

---

* These misspellings, or "cacographic" variations, were a little different from the phonetic vernacular used by the Southern "frame" writers and Sam Clemens's "Thomas Jefferson Snodgrass," in that they seemed aimed less at mimicking the sounds of a distinct regional dialect than the capricious misspellings of an uneducated man. Ward also used the device for clever word coinage, as when he described his wife as an unequaled "flapjackist."

ports that as Ward lay dying, his friend the playwright T. W. Robertson chided him for refusing his medicine: "Take it, my dear fellow, just for my sake. You know I would do anything for you." "Would you?" asked Artemus. "I would indeed." "Then *you* take it."[4]

Artemus Ward's two lectures at Maguire's Opera House in Virginia City (on December 22 and 25) were a great success. The miners and their women erupted in knee-pounding laughter again and again as the thin young man peered out across the footlights at them in a perplexed sort of way, and murmured, between seemingly mind-drifting pauses, such nonsense observations as, "I once knew a man in New Zealand who hadn't a tooth in his head—" (pause) "—and yet that man could beat a drum better than any man I ever saw."[5]

Well—it is possible that you had to have been there. But that was pretty much the point. Artemus Ward's manner of telling was nearly as important as the content. This was cutting-edge stuff in mid-19th-century America. The country teemed with traveling lecturers, several of them working in the "humorous" vein. But nobody before Ward had dared rely so heavily on theatrical devices to explode the merely amusing into the hilarious. Ward's onstage illusion of continually drifting off the subject or forgetting his train of thought was his performance equivalent of those "quaint" misspellings in his newspaper pieces: in each, he played the lovable, naïve "ordinary feller" whose deep wisdom radiated through the surface miscues.

At Maguire's, Ward performed his reliable "Babes in the Wood" lecture, a subtle lampoon of the lecturing form itself, particularly the "uplifting" or "informative" genre (the babes are never mentioned outside the title). He poked somber-faced fun at such deities as Emerson, whom he'd once slagged in a *Plain Dealer* review as a "perpendicular coffin." It was the antilecture: maudlin and sentimental on its surface, but designed to slip a banana peel in the path of the pompous half of that industry. Sam Clemens sat in the audience, roaring at Ward's every move and pause. He was absorbing what he saw and heard with the same voraciousness that he had trained on Uncle Dan'l in Florida, Missouri.

Ward's rather tepid audacity must have spoken to Sam's own, far less restrained instincts for hoaxing, mocking, and baiting. But it was the humorist's stage devices, in particular that tantalizing, tension-building illusion of a slow drift away from his main point, which activated Sam's powerful mimetic engines. His admiration for Ward was evident in the review he wrote for the *Enterprise:* "The man who is capable of listening to the Babes in the Wood from beginning to end without laughing either inwardly or outwardly must have done murder, or at least meditated it, at some time during his life."[6] In his letters over the following weeks, he virtually caressed his new friend's pen name with each reference. "When Artemus Ward gets to St. Louis, invite him up to the house & treat him well," he instructed Jane, "for behold, he is a good fellow." (Ward fell ill and never made it there.) Some lines later, Sam casually dropped the news, "At his suggestion, I mean to write semi-occasionally for the New York Sunday Mercury. Of his own accord he wrote a flattering letter about 'Mark Twain' to the editors of this paper; & besides, I have promised to go with him to Europe in May or June . . ."[7]

A few paragraphs after that, Sam mentioned Ludlow's recent praise of him and strutted: "Artemus Ward said that when my gorgeous talents were publicly acknowledged by such high authority, I ought to appreciate them my-self—leave sage-brush obscurity, & journey to New York with him, as he wanted me to do." Then he admitted, "I preferred not to burst upon the New York public too suddenly & brilliantly, & so I concluded to remain here."[8]

The best proof of Sam's esteem lay in the competition he engaged in with the visiting eminence. In the late-night drinking bouts around Virginia City, when the others seemed a little tongue-tied, Sam tried to match Ward *mot* for *mot*. At first, he was overmatched. Ward had his shtick finely honed after more than two years on the road, capped by several performances in New York City. He sandbagged the young Clemens at a dinner given him by leading citizens at the International Hotel, after having alerted the rest of the *Enterprise* entourage about the setup. When the plates had been cleared away, Ward turned to Sam, who was seated next to him, and loudly commenced a conversation on "genius." Dan De Quille recorded it.

Mr. Clemens, . . . genuis appears to me to be a sort of luminous quality of the mind, allied to a warm and inflammable constitution, which is inherent in the man, and supersedes in him whatever constitutional tendency he may possess, to permit himself to be influenced by such things as do not coincide with his preconceived notions and established convictions to the contrary. Does not my definition hit the nail squarely on the head, Mr. Clemens?[9]

It was classic Artemus Ward doubletalk, and Sam never saw it coming. He stammered that he hadn't quite grasped Ward's meaning. The table grew quiet. Ward looked incredulous and repeated the thought, tossing in some-thing about ideas darting like meteors across the intellectual firmament. Again, Sam had to admit confusion. Ward began again. Again Sam pleaded no contest, this time invoking illness: he'd been taken drunk. As laughter arose around the table, it dawned on Sam that he'd been had. He reacted to it as he reacted to all practical jokes played on him: by falling into a snit. "Mark was in no amiable mood the remainder of the evening," De Quille recorded. "He said such a thing 'might be thought by some to be smart,' but he failed to see 'where the fun came in.' "[10] By Christmas Eve, Sam was ready for Ward. Joe Goodman and the others witnessed their crowning duel at Chaumond's, after an oyster dinner; a marathon test of wit and liquor-holding endurance that rolled on through the Yuletide night:

. . . Then begun a flow and reflow of humor it would be presumptuous in me to attempt to even outline. It was on that occasion that Mark Twain fully demonstrated his
right to rank above the world's acknowledged foremost humorist . . . Course succeeded course and wine followed wine, until day began to break . . . The first streaks of
dawn were brightening the east when we went into the streets.[11]

At that point, as Goodman remembered, Ward decided that he wanted to walk
in the skies, but settled for walking on the roofs. Sam followed him to the top
of a house as the others watched, and the two began a lurching, plastered
scramble. A watchman materialized, drew his pistol, and aimed. Before
he could fire, someone in Goodman's group shouted that the figures were
Artemus Ward and Mark Twain. The watchman had nearly shot them for
burglars.*

When Ward bade farewell to Washoe and headed east on December 29,
Sam had good reason to feel that his own future lay in the young humorist's
wake. Ward wrote to him from Austin, Nevada, on January 1, addressing him
as "My Dearest Love," and rehashing some of the wild times in Virginia:

Why did you not go with me and save me that night?—I mean the night I left you
drunk at that dinner party. I went and got drunker, beating, I may say, Alexander the
Great, in his most drinkinist days . . . I shall always remember Virginia as a bright spot
in my existence . . .[12]

The letter reaffirmed Ward's pledge to recommend Sam to the editors at the
Mercury. It thanked Clemens for his "notice," which "did me much good here,
as it doubtlessly will elsewhere." It joked about his making advances on Ward's
mother and aunt. And it interestingly asked: "Why would you make a good artillery man? Because you are familiar with Gonorrhea (gun-nery)."[13]

Sam had already sent off his first submission to the New York weekly. "Doings in Nevada" was an adroit sketch telling Easterners about the ins and outs
of constitution writing for a prospective new state. It arrived ahead of Ward's
recommendation, but the *Mercury* ran it in the February 7 edition. Two weeks
later, Sam scored again, with "Those Blasted Children," which appeared on
February 21 above an introduction of the writer as "our unique correspondent, Mark Twain." The piece skewered the raucous children who had distracted the correspondent at the Lick House, and offered some remedies that

---

* Dan De Quille remembered it a little differently. In an 1893 newspaper article, he recalled
that the roof-walking episode had occurred after Sam and he had taken Ward on a tour of "Chi-
natown sights"; that the watchman had aimed a shotgun at them; that Ward had defused things by
handing the man a few tickets to his lecture; that the trio had moved on to the Clemens/De Quille
apartment, where they all piled in to bed together like "three saints," as Ward put it; that their
sleep was interrupted by hurdy-gurdy music erupting from a dance hall; that they all tumbled out
of bed and went there and danced with "three stalwart and capable girls," and that from there
they met up with a bulky, stovepipe-hatted Sonora miner called "Kettle-belly Browne," who stared
down a bartender who had tried to shortchange them and then joined the trio in a new round of
barhopping that ended up at dawn in front of Aaron Hooper's saloon.

foreshadowed Ring Lardner and W. C. Fields: "When you come to fits, take no chances on fits. If the child has them bad, soak it in a barrel of rain-water over night, or a good article of vinegar. If this does not put an end to its troubles, soak it a week." [14]

Back in Carson City to cover the Union party convention and the legislative session, Mark Twain got himself reelected governor of the satirical Third House, and gave a humorous speech that struck some listeners as a little too obviously influenced by Artemus Ward. Coming as it did only weeks after little Jennie's death, Mark Twain's hilarity might also have struck the grieving Orion and Mollie as inexplicably jaunty. But when he wrote to the folks back in St. Louis about the talk, Sam's thoughts were focused on how he stacked up with his new friend and rival. "I can't send you my Message," he declared to his sister Pamela. "It was written to be *spoken*—to write it so that it would *read* well, would be too much trouble." He added: "I got my satisfaction out of it, though—a larger audience than Artemus had." [15]

A SECOND whirlwind blew through Virginia City in February. Adah Isaacs Menken presented Sam with an entirely different prototype of the bohemian subculture: what a later, jazzier age would call the Red-Hot Mama. The "Menken" was a wildly eclectic actress and poet, the spiritual godmother of Marilyn Monroe, Gypsy Rose Lee, and Madonna. She was born in 1835 to a French Creole mother and a free Negro father. She converted to Judaism after her early marriage to a nice musician from Cincinnati named Alexander Isaac Menken, whom she soon left far behind. Brilliant and drop-dead gorgeous, the Menken became an international sexual icon, at once ridiculed, feared, and desired by her mostly male followers. She shocked people by smoking cigarettes while standing up; she cultivated painting skills, wrote free verse; married several men; and was associated with dozens of others in America and Europe, including Whitman, Charles Dickens, Algernon Charles Swinburne, Dante Gabriel Rossetti, and Alexandre Dumas, *père*, until Alexandre *fils* started muttering about a horsewhip.

Nothing seemed too contemptuous of public decorum for her—probably not even folding her shawl carefully upon entering a room. She made her lasting cultural mark as "Mazeppa," the hero of the Lord Byron poem, an act that called for her to traverse the stage on a galloping horse while clad in a skintight body stocking. (A circus fat woman known as Big Bertha attempted an *homage* to Menken by tugging on pink tights and strapping herself to the back of a donkey, but her act foundered when the struggling animal stumbled with his cargo into the orchestra pit.[16]) By the time of her death at thirty-three, Menken had influenced the nascent concept of celebrityhood in America and Europe, and in Mark Twain's imagination.

Sam had caught the Menken's act at Maguire's theater in San Francisco, the city where she had transplanted herself and her entourage, which included her soon-to-be-discarded latest husband, the humorist Orpheus C.

Kerr. Sam saw her perform both in *Mazeppa* and in *The French Spy,* by John Thomas Haines, and affected disdain for what he saw. He may have been invested in his own countercultural spree in Washoe, but like most Victorian men, he was unable to grant the same license to a woman. Mark Twain eviscerated the actress in a dismissive, thousand-word *Enterprise* piece:

They said she was dressed from head to foot in flesh-colored "tights," but I had no opera-glass, and I couldn't see it, to use the language of the inelegant rabble. She appeared to me to have but one garment on—a thin tight white linen one, of unimportant dimensions; I forget the name of the article, but it is indispensable to infants of tender age . . . In the first act, she rushes on the stage, and goes cavorting around after "Olinska"; she bends herself back like a bow; she pitches headforemost at the atmosphere like a battering-ram . . . she carries on like a lunatic from the beginning of the act to the end of it.[17]

As to Menken's signature horseback ride as Mazeppa, Mark Twain wrote:

They strap Mazeppa on [the horse's] back, fore and aft, and face uppermost, and the horse goes cantering up-stairs over the painted mountains . . . with the wretched victim he bears unconsciously digging her heels into his hams . . . to make him go faster . . . The fierce old circus horse carries his prisoner around through the back part of the theatre, behind the scenery . . . he makes his way at last to his dear old home in Tartary down by the footlights, and beholds once more, O, gods! the familiar faces of the fiddlers in the orchestra.[18]

Yet when Menken brought her act to Virginia City on February 27, she sought out Sam for a social get-together. (She apparently sought out a local horse trainer for more intimate purposes, which scarcely could have humored the now-humorless humorist Kerr.) She invited Sam and Dan De Quille to dine with her and a woman friend (Ada Clare) in her hotel room. The evening was less *soirée* than sorry. De Quille recalled that a certain tension prevailed after Menken barred Orpheus Kerr from the room. Kerr's visit really was not going well. Sam recoiled from the nineteen-odd dogs that the Menken kept in her room, his distaste increasing as the beasts got hammered on the brandy-laced sugar cubes that the diva kept tossing them. The nadir was reached when Sam, intending to kick one of the howling dogs into silence, instead nailed the hostess's "pet corn," causing her, in De Quille's telling, "to bound from her seat, throw herself on a lounge and roll and roar in agony."[19] Sam excused himself shortly afterward, claiming a previous engagement. The friendship did not flourish, although Menken later recalled that she'd had a great time in Virginia City.

MARK TWAIN was a newly anointed "Washoe Giant," praised by Ward and Fitz Hugh Ludlow, sought out by the Menken. His work graced the pages of the Eastern papers. He was unrestrained and restless—a dangerous combination for him. He would find his mischief soon enough, and the consequences would threaten his life, mortify his brother and sister-in-law, and lead to self-exile from Nevada Territory itself. So far, Sam had downplayed his Southernness in the pro-Union territory. In fact, he'd done his best to blot out the cataclysm back east. But war passion surrounded him now. In the early months of 1864, the war washed up at his feet, bringing old guilts and terrors on its tide.

One of the most respected and effective charity resources for Union soldiers during the war was the U.S. Sanitary Commission. Started in April 1861 as a volunteer movement of churchwomen and ladies' aid societies throughout New York, the commission soon obtained sanction from the federal government. Frederick Law Olmsted was a board member, and Walt Whitman was among its volunteer nurses. The Sanitary Commission funneled canned food, blankets, clothing, medical supplies, and books from cities and towns to the front lines, and strove to provide surgeons and nurses for battlefield casualties. In 1881, the commission evolved into the American Red Cross.

The aid effort required lots of money—the commission ended up taking more than $7 million into its treasury, in addition to goods valued at more than $15 million—but by 1862 it was in danger of collapse. It was saved by a nationwide series of Sanitary Fairs that generated enough money and goods to sustain its work through the end of the war. Much of that new support came from the Pacific Coast.

In February 1864, some Union sympathizers in the divided city of St. Louis planned a money-raising Sanitary Fair in the spring. Among its backers was the soon-to-be general of Abraham Lincoln's army, Ulysses S. Grant. Pamela Moffett sent fund-raising circulars for the event to Sam in Virginia City, and he wrote some pieces in the *Enterprise* and the San Francisco *Morning Call* boosting the efforts. A circle of prominent women in Carson City, among them Mollie Clemens, organized a charity dress ball for May 5, intending to send the proceeds to the St. Louis fair. At the same time, an Austin, Nevada, grocer named Reuel Colt Gridley—a Hannibal school chum of Sam's—had been lugging a sack of flour to nearby towns, which he "auctioned," at each stop, to benefit the Sanitary cause. Mark Twain followed Gridley for a day in mid-May, and wrote about it in the *Enterprise*. At which time, unfathomably, Sam Clemens's demons broke loose.

On Monday, May 16, with Joe Goodman out of town again, Sam, by his own admission deracinated by liquor, scribbled a fake "news item" and passed it to De Quille, who agreed that it should never see print. Somehow, though, the squib got picked up by the "foreman, prospecting for copy," Sam later supposed.

On Tuesday, *Enterprise* readers were dumbfounded to read that the proceeds from the Carson City Ball were in danger of being diverted from the commission headquarters in St. Louis. Instead, they were to be sent to "aid a

Miscegenation Society somewhere in the East"—a society, in other words, dedicated to the intermarriage of the Negro and Caucasian races. The item cryptically added that the report was "a hoax, but not all a hoax, for an effort is being made to divert those funds from their proper course."[20] The future author of *Huckleberry Finn* could scarcely have thought up a more explosive bit of mischief.

The Emancipation Proclamation was less than two years old in the spring of 1864; the war that produced it still drained lives and wealth from the continent. Sentiment toward Negroes, even on the "emancipating" side, was saturated with animosity, superstition, sexual fears, and resentment: the liberators would soon have to compete with former slaves for work. Union-"secesh" tensions rippled through Washoe; fights erupted, shootings occurred over the question. Even though Union sympathy prevailed, few people accepted the notion that Negroes were equal to whites. Many pro-Union whites still resented black slaves for having made the war inevitable.

Carson City erupted over the *Enterprise*'s fake report. On Wednesday, May 18, four women drafted a denunciatory letter to the *Enterprise*—the president, vice president, treasurer, and secretary of the Sanitary Ball committee. Joe Goodman, back at work, tried to defuse the uproar by ignoring it. Bad judgment: it ran a week later, for three days (May 25, 26, and 27), as a paid, public notice in the rival Virginia *Daily Union* under the heading "The 'Enterprise' Libel of the Ladies of Carson."[21]

The damage would be extensive. Mollie Clemens, still grieving for Jennie, found herself ostracized from Carson City society. Sam wrote an anguished letter to her on May 20, five days before the ladies' letter was published, but not to apologize for the mortification he'd caused, nor to promise that he would assume public responsibility. He was preoccupied with the damage that the committee women's letter could do to *him*.

My Dear Mollie:

I have had nothing but trouble & vexation since the Sanitary trip, & now this letter comes to aggravate me a thousand times worse. If it were from a man, I would answer it with a challenge . . .[22]

He went on to confess that, yes, it was he who had written "the squib," in the midst of a "drunken jest" with several other parties whom he refused to name. He had laid the item before Dan De Quille "when I was not sober (I shall not get drunk again, Mollie,)—and said he, 'Is this a joke?' I told him 'Yes.' He said he would not like such a joke as that to be perpetrated upon him, & that it would wound the feelings of the ladies of Carson. He asked me if I wanted to do that, & I said 'No, of course not.' " Sam's concern for his honor grew from the women's labeling the item as "a *tissue of falsehoods*, made for *malicious* purposes"[23]—in short, a dirty lie, hence the reference to answering their letter "with a challenge." He saw no other options.

Since it has made the ladies angry, I am sorry the thing occurred, & that is all I can do, for you will see yourself that their communication is altogether unanswerable. I cannot publish that, & explain it by saying the affair was a silly joke, & that I & all concerned were drunk. No—I'll die first.[24]

He indulged further self-pity: "Mollie, the Sanitary [affair] has been very disastrous to me. Aside from this trouble, (which I feel deepest,) I have two other quarrels on my hands, engendered on that day, & as yet I cannot tell how either of them is to end."[25]

Mark Twain felt he could not publicly apologize because he was involved with those "other two quarrels," one still unidentified, the other a gratuitous fight he had picked with the Virginia City *Union* over a related event, the Reuel Colt Gridley flour-sack auctioning campaign. On May 18, the day after his miscegenation hoax had appeared, Mark Twain published an item—"How Is It?"—chiding the *Union* for reneging on its hundred-dollar "bid" for Gridley's flour sack. This charge, too, was bogus. The *Union* fired back the next day, with an angry statement about what "Is" is. " 'How Is It?'—How It Is," repudiated Mark Twain's allegation and included a slur virtually begging for violence: "Such an item could only emanate from a person whose employer can find in his services a machine very suitable to his own manliness."[26]

This was apparently what Sam was looking for: an excuse to unleash the defining ritual of southern manhood, the *code duello*.

The protocols of dueling were published in 1595, by an Italian swordfighter living in London named Vincentio Saviolo. Saviolo's ten rules of etiquette and procedure—intended, paradoxically, to *limit* violence by restricting deadly action to the challenger and the accused, as opposed to acres of their broadsword-wielding friends on each side—were further elaborated in Ireland in 1777. By Mark Twain's time, the Code had twenty-five rules, set forth with detached formality suggestive of a deranged etiquette guide: ". . . [T]he parties engage until one is well blooded, disabled, or disarmed; or until, after receiving a wound, and blood being drawn, the aggressor begs pardon." The Code found a new home in the antebellum South, whose planter aristocrats deluded themselves (as Mark Twain himself never tired of pointing out) that they were the knightly inheritors of Sir Walter Scott's chivalric neverland.

On Saturday, May 21, Sam—who had taken to carrying a pistol once again—sent a note over to James Laird, a publisher of the *Union*, that haughtily identified himself as the author of the original offending "editorial," and demanded a public retraction of the *Union*'s "insulting" response. Laird was furious. It wasn't enough that Joe Goodman had already crippled one of his editors (Thomas Fitch); now came the reigning loudmouth of Washoe, still in-famous from the Carson massacre hoax, to assail his newspaper again. On Sat-urday afternoon and into the evening, the two papers exchanged private missives of aggrieved manly dignity, and the grim *politesse* of the challenge. A *Union* printer named J. W. Wilmington sent Sam a note asserting that it was he, not Laird, who'd authored the "manhood" slur. Sam ignored Wilmington and wrote back directly to Laird, his note filled with high-toned *duello* lingo if not perfect grammar: ". . . any farther attempt to make a catspaw of any other individual and thus shirk a responsibility that you had previously assumed will show that *you* are a cowardly sneak. I now *peremptorily* demand of you the satis-faction due to a gentleman—without alternative." [27]

As the day faded into evening, Laird once again goaded Sam to face Wilmington, taking care to mention Sam's groveling disrespect for truth, de-cency, and courtesy. Sam wrote to Laird a third time: ". . . [I]f you do not wish yourself posted as a coward, you will *at once accept my peremptory challenge, which I now reiterate.*" [28]

This was nothing like the jaunty fake feuding between Mark Twain and the Unreliable. This was dark, deadly stuff. There seemed something despair-ing—if not downright suicidal—about Sam's recklessness. Sam seems to have viewed dueling as a kind of hovering fate, onerous but inevitable, an obliga-tion that must sooner or later be met to confirm his manhood. He was twenty-eight in 1864, a man now, but a man with a "soft" calling in a violent, obsessively masculine society. Restless, unsure of his future or his legitimacy in that society, a serious drinker, and a provocateur who had already made ene-mies, he may have decided, in his delirium, that it was time to toe the mark.

BUT HIS heart was never really in it, and the more apparent his lack of re-solve became to him, the more he tried to mask it with belligerent posturing.

As his Tom Sawyerish challenge to gunplay edged toward reality, Sam fi-nally reached out to the women of the Sanitary Ball committee in Carson; and, indirectly, to Mollie Clemens. On May 23 he sent a somewhat self-exculpatory letter to the president of the committee, Mrs. William K. Cutler ("Madam—I address a lady in every sense of the term . . ."). He offered a somewhat circular explanation of why he had not quickly apologized: he'd been distracted by this feud with the *Union.* He thanked Mrs. Cutler for her continued friendship with Mollie "while others are disposed to withdraw theirs on account of a fault for which I alone am responsible." [29] Mr. Cutler is-sued Sam a challenge anyway.

Sam headed off that particular distraction by sending the ninety-five-pound Steve Gillis over to reason with Cutler, who had come up from Carson and was waiting at a hotel. Whatever Gillis's reasoning, Cutler found it per-suasive, and hurried home. The following day—Tuesday, May 24—Sam made a similar halfway-gesture in the *Enterprise:* yes, "we" published a rumor, and yes, it was a hoax, but "we" stated as much, "And it was—we were perfectly right."[30] "We" were sorry for the "misfortune," and "we venture to apologize for it," and so on.

Yet in the same edition, Mark Twain preempted all hope of a peaceful resolution: he published every one of his letters and Laird's replies, and, in an afterword, denounced Laird as an "unmitigated liar," accused him of backing down from a fight, and added that Laird was a fool. The Carson City ladies' unforgiving letter was published over the next three days. Soon newspapers around the territory were reprinting the letters; some mocked the author of the Carson massacre hoax for being about to experience real-life bloodshed. Then, on the following Sunday, May 29, it ended: not with a bang, but with an absquatulation. Along with Steve Gillis, Sam Clemens climbed aboard a stagecoach and lit out from the territory—from Virginia City to San Francisco. The duel never happened.

How close to the brink of gunfire he and Laird actually came is uncertain. In a letter to Orion dashed off the day before departure, Sam struck a macho pose: "Steve & I are going to the States . . . Say nothing about it, of course. We are not afraid of the grand jury, but Washoe has long since grown irksome to us, & we want to leave it anyhow."[31] The letter asked for two hundred dollars, to be sent to San Francisco.*

The affair continued to vex him long afterward, and he treated it with careful levity in his writings. He can barely bring himself to touch on it in *Roughing It*, published only eight years later. He left Nevada, he says in that book, because "I began to get tired of staying in one place so long." He wrote a funny sketch about it for Tom Hood's *Comic Annual for 1873*, called "How I Escaped Being Killed in a Duel." In his autobiography, he treats the whole matter facetiously, as a kind of boys-will-be-boys romp in the Wild West. Dueling was a "fashion," and "by 1864, everybody was anxious to have a chance in the new sport." He personally "had had no desire to fight a duel," but one day, more or less out of boredom, he "woke up Mr. Laird with some courtesies . . . and he came back at me the next day in a most vitriolic way."[32] It was Rollin Daggett, in this telling, who wrote up the acerbic challenges for him, and it was Laird who backed out on the duel after Steve Gillis shot the head off a sparrow and showed it to Laird's seconds, claiming that Mark Twain had made the shot at thirty yards.

The local Gold Hill *Evening News* administered a farewell kick in the Twainian posterior on the day following his leave-taking.

Among the few immortal names of the departed—that is, those who departed yesterday morning per California stage—we notice that of Mark Twain. We don't wonder. Giving way to the . . . eccentricities of an erratic mind, Mark has indulged in the game infernal—in short, "played hell." [In mounting the miscegenation hoax and embar-

---

* The "grand jury" reference gave a little cover to Sam's dignity. Dueling had killed and maimed so many men in Nevada that the legislature in 1861 mandated two-to-ten-year prison sentences on anyone convicted of even issuing or delivering a challenge.

rassing the ladies of the Sanitary Ball]—he slopped. The indignation aroused by his enormities has been too crushing to be borne by living man, though sheathed with the brass and triple cheek of Mark Twain . . . He has *vamosed*, cut stick, absquatulated; and among the pine forests of the Sierras, or amid the purlieus of the city of earthquakes, he will tarry awhile, and the office of the *Enterprise* will become purified . . .[33]

Sam's absquatulation drew the curtain of charity over the wildest, most irresponsible, and dangerous period of his life. As he ascended into literary stardom and elite society over the next three decades, he would struggle to hold in check the version of himself that exploded into being on the slopes of Mount Davidson: the coarse, dissipated, exhibitionistic jokester and provocateur. (He was at his best, at least on paper, to the extent that these efforts at suppression failed.) But this dangerous interval was also the most important gestative period of his writing life. Sam discovered the true essence of his craft amidst the self-invented poets and prose writers who surged through Virginia City and the *Territorial Enterprise* during the Civil War years. This extraordinary cadre of countercultural exiles and wandering bohemians—Goodman, De Quille, Daggett, the Unreliable, Ward, even Menken—awoke him to the ecstasies of an expressive style unthinkable to the saints of literature back east. It was a style unapologetic to traditional aesthetics, but alive to the needs and impulses of the moment: pared-down and vernacular in diction, unterrified of authority or manners, wisecracking, brutally frank (except when it was hoaxing), joyously attuned to terrain, and above all, attuned to the fate and the legitimate viewpoint of the common man. Soon that voice would come bursting back east and sweep everything before it, riding hell-for-leather on the back of a jumping frog.

14

A Villainous Backwoods Sketch

(1864–65)

L ater, Sam would recall a phase of "butterfly idleness" in the bayside city he called "the most cordial and sociable city in the Union."[1] He lived at the best hotel in San Francisco, his beloved Occidental—"Heaven on the half shell"[2]—with his bantam-rooster buddy Steve Gillis. He wore fancy clothes to private parties, "infested" the opera, played billiards in saloons, "simpered and aired my graces like a born beau, and polked and schottisched with a step peculiar to myself—and the kangaroo."[3]

His esteem did not exaggerate the city's charms. By the mid-1860s, San Francisco had soared to prominence among American cities, a garden of delights on the far end of the continent for those willing to risk drowning, freezing, or dying of Panamanian mosquito bites to get there. (Many were willing, including the thousands of young men eager to escape the Civil War.) The gold-digging '49ers who had swelled the population now supported a robust building and mercantile boom. Importers were bringing in gowns from Paris. Women were changing their hairstyles from the ringlets and curls of Jacksonian America to "the waterfall," a bunching of the hair below the neck into an oblong shape, held in place by a net. Mark Twain hated "the waterfall" look, and said so in print: It "reminds you of those nauseating garden spiders . . . that go around dragging a pulpy, grayish bag-full of young spiders slung to them behind."[4]

San Francisco's art, design, and architecture had an international flair. The four-story Occidental, with its Italianate pediments and storefronts of plate glass, occupied the entire block of Montgomery Street from Sutter to

Bush. Salons abounded, and Sam sampled them, probably including the influential literary circle run by the wealthy North Carolina expatriate Martha Hitchcock, a diarist and rumored Confederate spy, who (when not in Paris) stayed at the Occidental with her flamboyant daughter Lillie.

The salons drew upon a thriving counterculture, the progenitor of the Beat and hippie enclaves of a latter-day San Francisco: the bohemians who'd abandoned Pfaff's bar in New York for this even less hidebound cosmopolis. The bohemian aesthetic animated San Francisco theater, music, painting, and literature. The city published more books than any in the country, and rivaled London for the volume of its newspapers and literary journals. The artists themselves tended to be far wilder than their art—running around the city in rough work clothes, firemen's helmets jammed on their heads, cigars between their teeth, holding marathon poker games, indulging in sex and drugs. The male bohemians were equally colorful. Sam mingled with the forebears of Jack Kerouac and Lawrence Ferlinghetti, mellowing out in the sauna in odd moments. He placed some sketches in the artsy weekly *Golden Era,* home away from home to Adah Menken, among others.

Sam was equally drawn to the seedier sides of the city. He gravitated between salon and saloon. He gambled at cards and even more in the stock market, living on credit as his debts mounted. Earthquakes, a San Francisco specialty, fascinated him. The city rattled with nearly a dozen quakes or tremors between his arrival and the end of the year, and he seems to have relished them all. Later on, in 1865, he compiled an "Earthquake Almanac," offering such blithe prognostications as

Oct. 26.—Considerable phenomenal atmospheric foolishness. About this time expect more earthquakes, but do not look out for them, on account of the bricks . . .

Nov. 1.—Terrific earthquake. This is the great earthquake month. More stars fall and more worlds are slathered around carelessly and destroyed in November than in any other month of the twelve.

Nov. 2.—Spasmodic but exhilarating earthquakes, accompanied by occasional showers of rain, and churches and things.[5]

Expecting to glide along on the "Washoe Giant" fame that he'd assured Jane he had earned in the city, and to continue developing his comic-bombastic style, he had, within a week of arriving in San Francisco, got himself hired as a "local" reporter, at $35 a week, for the *Morning Call,* the paper that had earlier bought his freelance letters from Virginia City. Three months later, when he inevitably grew tired of the long hours, he rejiggered the arrangement to $25 a week, with no nighttime duties. He resumed one of his favorite lifetime hobbies, needling his high-strung mother, who he knew liked to read his letters aloud to friends and neighbors. "You have portrayed to me so often & so earnestly the benefit of taking frequent exercise," he solemnly wrote to her in August, carefully setting her up, that I know it will please you to learn that I belong to the San F. Olympic Club, whose gymnasium is one of the largest & best appointed in the United States . . . I think it nothing but right to give you the whole credit of it . . . I feel like a new man. I sleep better, I have a healthier appetite, my intellect is clearer, & I have become so strong & hearty that I fully believe twenty years have been added to my life.

And then the "nub":

I feel as if I ought to be very well satisfied with this result, when I reflect that I never was in that gymnasium but once in my life, & that was over three months ago.[6]

Jane got back at Sam by retailing several of his letters in the St. Louis press, a practice that predictably ticked him off. The same day, August 12, he resumed his old hoaxing ways, this time in a more genial mode: his "What a Sky-Rocket Did" in the *Morning Call* pretended to report the crash of a burned-out rocket into a tenement building on Bush Street—a dilapidated piece of property that was owned, as it happened, by a plutocratic public figure.[7]

Sam sustained his happy-as-a-clam demeanor to Jane and Pamela some weeks later. He sent them a photograph of his barbered and typically unsmiling self—"like a witness under oath," is the way Louis Budd sums up his posing style—and bragged that "I am taking life easy, now, & I mean to keep it up for a while."[8] Gossiping to Orion and Mollie about Steve Gillis's scheduled wedding to a wealthy heiress, he picked up on a conversational thread by writing, "Your head is eminently sound on the subject of marriage. I am resolved on that or suicide—perhaps."[9] It was a jarring word to drop into a light-hearted chat about nuptials and good friends, perhaps an attempt at whistling in the dark.

He and Steve Gillis changed their lodgings constantly. "I need a change, & must move again," he explained to his folks on September 25.[10] He was restless, bored, and probably lonely. A plaintive query in his upbeat letter to Jane and Pamela revealed a torch that still burned: "What has become of that girl of mine that got married?" he wondered. "I mean Laura Wright."[11]

His reporter's job was turning into a bust. The *Call* was nothing like the *Territorial Enterprise*. He tried to liven its pages up, Virginia City–style. He managed to stir up a real feud, sometimes jokey and more often not, with local reporter Albert S. Evans of the *Alta California*. But Sam soon discovered that the editors at the *Morning Call* weren't interested in wild-and-woolly writing. They wanted to strengthen the paper's journalistic stature, and they expected Sam to chase down *facts*. Sam gave it a try, but found it "fearful drudgery, soulless drudgery, and almost destitute of interest," as he could still grouse forty-two years later.[12] The dreary courthouse with its droning lawyers and pitiful downtrodden litigants was his daytime beat, and he'd taken to amusing himself with a kind of word-doodling—writing up the sordid little trials he covered as scenes in theatrical plays. His enthusiasm for the theater kept him from petrifying: he rushed around to San Francisco's six legitimate stage houses every evening, pausing at each just long enough to glean what was happening onstage, for a review. For four decades afterward, he insisted, even the sight of a theater gave him the dry gripes.

Prodded by Orion and others, he began to think about writing on a more literary level. "As soon as this wedding business is over," he told his brother, "I believe I will send to you for the files, & begin my book." [13] The "files" were the scrapbooks into which Orion had been faithfully pasting Mark Twain's newspaper columns and letters over the past three years, clearly with a book project in mind. But money worries soon imposed an agenda of their own.

Sam had intended to stay in the Bay City only a month, to sell off some mining stock in Orion's name. Then he would head back east, where the Confederacy was disintegrating under Union invasion, and resume his Mississippi River piloting career. His native ground was growing safe for his return. The war could not last much longer: Grant, unaffected by the previous June's carnage at Cold Harbor, where in one twenty-minute stretch he'd traded seven thousand Union lives for a reduction in Robert E. Lee's cadaverous remnants, was closing his grip on Richmond. General William Tecumseh Sherman had set Atlanta on fire and was slashing his way toward the sea. But in 1864 and 1865 Sam was never solvent enough to make that return journey. His few remaining mining stocks weren't moving, and they continued to cost him money simply to hold on to them. He'd taken the *Call* job to bankroll himself, but in mid-October, Sam and the *Call* parted ways.

Mentally, he'd been gone for weeks, trying to deal the mining stock, fiddling with his book idea, and carousing. He'd grown further detached after his editors spiked one of the few pieces he'd cared about: a lacerating eyewitness account of some toughs who'd stoned "a Chinaman who was heavily laden with the weekly wash of his Christian customers." [14] (Like his mother, the youthful Sam could be racially callous in the abstract—as in his miscegenation slur—but he could never stand the sight of racial cruelty.) Finally, the *Call*'s editor in chief, George E. Barnes, took him aside and suggested he might be happier elsewhere. Sam accepted the face-saving offer without rancor, but it hurt. "It hurts yet," Mark Twain maintained in 1906.[15]

He salvaged an income by selling nine sketches and essays to the *Californian* over a two-month period late in 1864. They hardly brought in a bonanza—at twelve dollars each, they amounted to about half his reduced *Call* salary ($108 versus $200)—but they helped him stave off destitution. They also brought him into contact with the journal's new young co-editors, Charles Henry Webb, whom he had already met, and Bret Harte, whom he had not. This was the beginning of an unbeautiful friendship between Clemens and Harte, who would one day share (and vie for) the highest esteem of the postwar nation.

Harte, a few months younger than Sam at twenty-eight, was a rising player on the San Francisco literary scene, just three years away from a stunning national debut. His stature in American letters—as a talented portraitist of Western folk, and the author of two or three enduring standards—would outlast De Quille's and even Artemus Ward's. But he was fated to experience his own public life largely as Mark Twain's sponsor, then mentor, then co-star among Western writers returning east, then collaborator, then object of corrosive envy and, finally, as one of Mark Twain's designated whipping boys.

The two probably met in late September 1864, perhaps when Sam paid a call on Harte to pitch a sketch for the *Californian*. Sam didn't have to travel far: Harte was one floor below the *Call*'s city room on Commercial Street, in the San Francisco branch office of the U.S. Mint. Harte was private secretary to the mint's superintendent, R. B. Swain. His duties, as outlined by Swain, were basically to sit around thinking up writing pieces to publish in the *Californian* and the *Golden Era*. Bret Harte supported by the mint—this made quite an impression on Sam. Harte, in turn, could not help being impressed by Sam. The Clemens voice worked its usual magic on him: "He spoke in a slow, rather satirical drawl," Harte later wrote, "which was in itself irresistible." [16] Yet even his fascination carried a condescending edge. "His head," Harte recalled in an often-quoted remark, "was striking. He had the curly hair, the aquiline nose, and even the aquiline eye—an eye so eagle-like that a second lid would not have surprised me—of an unusual and dominant nature. His eyebrows were very thick and bushy. His dress was careless, and his general manner one of supreme indifference to surroundings and circumstances." [17] Sam was not nearly so indifferent as he may have seemed. Sam wanted—needed—to write for the *Californian*. More urgently, he wanted entry into the literary world, and Harte seemed to have his hand on the doorknob.

But Sam's aquiline eye was recording some imperfections of its own. Decades later, he could still disgorge them with merciless clarity. "He was distinctly pretty," Mark Twain conceded in his autobiography, before adding, "in spite of the fact that his face was badly pitted with smallpox." As for Harte's clothes, "He was showy, meretricious, insincere; and he constantly advertised these qualities in his dress." His neckties tended to be either "crimson—a flash of flame under his chin," or maybe "indigo blue, and as hot and vivid as if one of those splendid and luminous Brazilian butterflies had lighted there." [18]

Harte was a more complex character than Sam Clemens cared to notice. The man soon to gain fame with "The Luck of Roaring Camp" and "The Outcasts of Poker Flat" was a refugee of Albany by way of Brooklyn. He'd come to California as an aspiring poet at seventeen and wandered around for a few years, tutoring ranchers' children, riding shotgun on a stagecoach, and catching on as a printer for the *Northern Californian* in Unionville, where he sneaked his own writing onto the page. He did not blend with the local buckaroos. He could be astoundingly pompous. But he was fearless, and he had a passion for social justice. When he wrote up an infamous massacre of Indians in early 1860, his editor fired him. Harte went down to San Francisco and got a job on Rollin Daggett's *Golden Era*. He married an ambitious woman named Anna Griswold. His poetry caught the attention of the San Francisco literati, the Harte household soon became a salon, and Bret was suddenly a broker of bohemian writers in the city.

Sam strutted like a cakewalker in a letter back to the St. Louis folk, about his influential new connection:

> I have engaged to write for the new literary paper—the "Californian" . . . one article a week, fifty dollars a month. I quit the "Era," long ago. It wasn't high-toned enough. I thought that whether I was a literary "jackleg" or not, I wouldn't class myself with that style of people, anyhow. The "Californian" circulates among the highest class of the community, & is the best weekly literary paper in the United States—& I suppose I ought to know.[19]

His work for the *Californian* shows a burst of his old Virginia City panache. Perhaps he was showing off for Harte. He had some fun at the expense of the Fourth Industrial Fair of the Mechanic's Institute, a group of pre–Silicon Valley technological nerds, using notes he had compiled on assignment for the *Call*. He pretended that the fair was a steamy trysting place for lovers, writing with wicked glee that

> [w]hen you see a young lady standing by the sanitary scarecrow which mutely appeals to the public for quarters and swallows them, you may know by the expectant look upon her face that a young man is going to happen along there presently . . .[20]

A few lines later he exploded into pure dizziness, claiming to have found a love note scrawled between the printed lines of a business card:

> John Smith, (My Dearest and Sweetest:) Soap Boiler and Candle Factor; (If you love me, if you love) Bar Soap, Castile Soap and Soft Soap, peculiarly suitable for (your Arabella, fly to the) Pacific coast, because of its non-liability to be affected by the climate . . .[21]

In a later *Californian* sketch, he settled a score with the *Morning Call*. "The Killing of Julius Caesar 'Localized' " drew on Mark Twain's lifelong gift for language parody. The piece imagines Caesar's assassination as written up not by William Shakespeare in the third act of his great tragedy, but by a reporter from the "*Roman Daily Evening Fasces*," an imaginary paper with a style strikingly similar to a certain plodding, fact-obsessed San Francisco sheet.

> Our usually quiet city of Rome was thrown into a state of wild excitement, yesterday, by the occurrence of one of those bloody affrays which sicken the heart and fill the soul with fear, while they inspire all thinking men with forebodings for the future of a

city where human life is held so cheaply, and the gravest laws are so openly set at defiance . . . The affair was an election row, of course . . .[22]

Still another genre send-up, "Lucretia Smith's Soldier," nailed the syrupy prose of the "sentimental" novels popular during the war years. The heroine (middle name "Borgia") has realized her wish: her lover has been colorfully maimed in battle. She poses at his side at the hospital for days until

the surgeon . . . told her that at last her Whittaker had recovered sufficiently to admit of the removal of the bandages from his head, and she was now waiting with feverish impatience for the doctor to come and disclose the loved features to her view . . . One bandage was removed, then another, and another, and lo! the poor wounded face was revealed to the light of day . . .

"O confound my cats if I haven't gone and fooled away three mortal weeks here, snuffling and slobbering over the wrong soldier!" . . .

Such is life, and the trail of the serpent is over us all.[23]

NEVADA JOINED the Union on October 31, 1864, a week before the national elections that returned Abraham Lincoln to the White House. Orion Clemens was regarded as a strong choice to be renominated and elected to the secretarial post. But on the cusp of triumph, the long-bearded dreamer was seized with what Sam called "a spasm of virtue" that sank his hopes. On the day of the nominating caucus, without prompting, he declared that he was opposed to the consumption of alcohol—this in a part of the world where liquor formed one of the basic food groups. He came in second in the balloting—receiving not a single vote—and would never again hold elective office.

Sam might have continued writing bright, frivolous pieces for Bret Harte and his bohemian paper indefinitely, had it not become propitious for him to absquatulate again.

Technically speaking, he seconded the absquatulation of Steve Gillis, whose fiancée had broken their engagement. Late in November, as he passed "the saloon of 'Big Jim' Casey, on Howard Street," Gillis, an enthusiastic barroom fighter, spotted the barkeeper beginning to push another patron around. Gillis thought to equalize the situation. The beer pitcher that Gillis shattered over his skull put the bartender at death's door in a city hospital. The man recovered, but not before Gillis was arrested, posted bail (with Clemens's help), and then decided to avoid a potential manslaughter charge. He left town for Virginia City. There, he got Joe Goodman to rehire him onto the *Enterprise* as a typesetter, and spent most of the rest of his life as a news editor in the mountainside town.

Sam Clemens followed Gillis out of town, arriving at Jackass Hill on December 4, having signed a $500 bond for his friend, which he could not come close to covering. With $300 in his pocket—probably earned from the sale of a share of Hale & Norcross stock—Sam dropped out of sight for twelve weeks. He returned to San Francisco on February 26 with several tall tales in his note-book, one of them about a frog. American literature as it had been understood roughly from the mythmaking age of Washington Irving and James Fenimore Cooper through the great Anglican-influenced flowering of Hawthorne, Emerson, Melville, and Thoreau, was about to be changed, changed utterly.

SAM JOINED Steve's brother Jim Gillis on a hundred-mile trek east to Jim's stone-and-wood mining cabin atop the hill bearing the charming name of Jackass, in Tuolumne County. Jim Gillis lived there with his younger brother, Billy, and their mining partner Dick Stoker, who had built the shack in 1850, when the terrain harbored the southern tip of the Mother Lode. Angel's Camp, center of the excitement, lay about seven miles northwest, in Calaveras County. Now the region was a moor, its soil diluted into mud by winter rains. The few miners who still hung on were gaunt and solitary men, remnants of the three thousand who had swarmed the area in the rush of '49. They mostly scavenged for stray nuggets: They "pocket-mined," homing in by triangula-tion on the source of gold traces washed down the mountain slopes. Sam's mood seems to have been as somber as the terrain and the weather. He had turned twenty-nine just a few days earlier, an age when most men had mar-ried, started families, settled into their life's pursuits. Sam was back where he'd started when he arrived in the West with Orion three years earlier. Yet he was with his kind of people. Sam admired the Gillis men, a clan of trans-planted Mississippians. The patriarch, Angus Gillis, was said to have fought with the adventurer William Walker in Walker's attempt to conquer the Mexi-can state of Sonora in 1853, where he took a bullet through the eye for his trouble, and through the remaining one saw a son fighting next to him killed.* Jim Gillis was a talkative cuss, as witty as Steve was pugnacious. He knew Latin and Greek, and had taken a degree in medicine in Memphis be-fore joining his father in the Gold Rush. What inspired such a cosmopolitan soul to live in a lonely cabin in a spent mining region is not clear. He kept him-self stimulated by hitting San Francisco regularly, and by turning the little hovel into a kind of jackleg salon. Dan De Quille called it "the headquarters of all Bohemians visiting the mountains." Its influence on American literature was almost eerie: one night in 1855, Bret Harte had found his way to Jim Gillis's door. The speaker in Harte's world-famous poem of 1870, "The Hea-then Chinee," was thought to be modeled on Gillis.[24]

There wasn't much to do on Jackass Hill except drink whiskey, subsist on beans and bad coffee, and talk. It rained constantly. Sam, the Gillis brothers, and Stoker amused one another by telling tales. Sam had arrived in a funk, but as the nights went on he paid more and more attention to Jim Gillis and his stories. Mark Twain recalled how, when Gillis had an inspiration, he

* The source of this legend is Mark Twain in his autobiography. Buyer beware.

"would stand up before the great log fire, with his back to it and his hands crossed behind him, and deliver himself of an elaborate impromptu lie . . . with Dick Stoker as the hero of it, as a general thing." [25] Gillis had the makings of genius, Mark Twain believed.

The cabin. The night. The great fire roaring in the fireplace. The listeners rapt as the storyteller, gifted but obscure, builds the tale. Uncle Dan'l, beside the fireplace in his cabin on the Florida farm a quarter-century earlier, had cast a similar spell on Sammy. Now Sam's personal gloom shifted, and the artist's ear grew alert. The others noticed that he had begun to scribble into a notebook. [26] The shack on the godforsaken hill transformed itself into a "dreamy and delicious sylvan paradise"; [27] or rather, it was words that did the transforming.

Gillis told a comic story of a cat named Tom Quartz, who developed a prejudice against quartz mining after he was blown sky-high by a dynamite blast; and another about a profane blue jay dropping acorn after acorn down a knothole in a cabin roof. He told about a man who crawled around naked in front of audiences as the Royal Nonesuch. Sam noted the absolute solemnity of Gillis's delivery, his insistence that he was telling God's truth.

The group escaped the cabin a time or two, because on the first evening of the new year, Sam wrote in his notebook:

New Years night—dream of Jim Townsend—"I could take this *** book & *** every *** in California, from San Francisco to the mountains. [28]

Sam had heard about James W. E. Townsend, known also as "Lying Jim," in some nearby mine diggings. Townsend was a journalist and tale-teller who had worked at the *Enterprise* and the *Golden Era.* In 1853, while at the Sonora *Herald,* he had printed a tale about a frog that was entered in a jumping contest and then covertly weighted down with shot. (The tale had its origins in the mists of American folklore; traces of it turned up in the strangest places. Sammy may have heard a variation on it from John Quarles back in Florida, Missouri.) By January 22, the weather had cleared up enough that the men could free themselves from the cabin and try some prospecting. Sam and Jim Gillis headed up to Angel's Camp. Around January 25, at the Angel's Camp hotel bar, Sam "[m]et Ben Coon, Ill river pilot here." [29] As fellow pilots, Clemens and Coon had something in common. Coon was known as the region's best teller of the frog tale.

Stoker caught up with them after a week or so, and they took their picks and shovels into the fields when the rain stopped. Sam's mining skills had not improved in the two-year hiatus. Over three weeks, he came up with nary a nugget. He later recalled

the one gleam of jollity that shot across our dismal sojourn in the rain & mud of Angel's Camp—I mean that day we sat around the tavern stove & heard that chap tell

about the frog & how they filled him with shot. . . . I jotted the story down in my notebook that day, & would have been glad to get ten or fifteen dollars for it—I was just that
blind. But then we were so hard up.[30]

On February 6, his notebook jotting reads:

Coleman with his jumping frog—bet stranger $50—stranger had no frog, & C got
him one—in the meantime stranger filled C's frog full of shot & he couldn't jump—the
stranger's frog won.[31]

"Coleman" is likely Mark Twain's original name-choice for the backwoods
hero of the story that he was by then working up to publish somewhere. He
loved telling the story as much as he looked forward to writing it. "And you remember how we quoted from the yarn & laughed over it, out there on the hillside while you & dear old Stoker panned & washed,[32] he wrote to Gillis five
years later. After four decades, Mark Twain could still relive his first hearing,
and the natural deadpan of the storyteller. "He was a dull person," Mark
Twain wrote, ". . . he was entirely serious, for he was dealing with what to him
were austere facts . . . he saw no humor in his tale . . . in my time I have not attended a more solemn conference."[33]

An entry in Sam's notebook dated just a week earlier, February 1:

Saw L. Mark ~~Wrigh~~ Write in a dream ce matin-ce [this morning]—in carriage—
said good bye & shook hands.[34]

Laura Wright had made another nighttime visit, which he recorded in a kind
of code.

Sam left Angel's Camp for the cabin on Jackass Hill on February 20, and
while the others picked away at their mining claims, he began writing the
jumping frog tale. Billy Gillis, twenty-three at the time, later recalled Sam's remark that "[i]f I can write that story the way Ben Coon told it, that frog will
jump around the world."[35] Three days later, he started back for San Francisco,
and arrived at the Occidental on the 26th. Charles Henry Webb, briefly taking
over from Bret Harte, welcomed him back as a regular contributor to the *Californian*. But it was a small packet of letters more than three months old that
carried the most tantalizing portent. The letters, held for him at the hotel,
were from Artemus Ward back in New York, inviting Sam to contribute a
sketch for Ward's forthcoming book about the Nevada Territory. Sam pitched
the jumping frog tale. Back came the reply—as Mark Twain recalled it to his
biographer Paine:—"Write it . . . There is still time to get it into my volume of
sketches. Send it to Carleton, my publisher in New York."[36]

Sam didn't send anything right away. He resumed his freelance work with
a new burst of energy and savoir-faire. He churned out robust, inventive
weekly pieces of up to three thousand words for the *Californian*. His submis-

sions to the *Enterprise*, 80 percent of which have not been recovered, must have been of equal weight and intensity: Goodman claimed in December 1900 that they were "the best work he ever did." [37] (He would soon be writing these on a *daily* basis, six days a week.) His wit and range of topics began to distinguish him as a social critic as well as a "phunny phellow"; they were reprinted and praised in San Francisco and many other California and Nevada newspapers. Someone, probably Webb, had given him a new honorific: the Moralist of the Main.

He was out of the *Californian* for the month of April; the paper had run into money problems and could not pay for his submissions. This was an especially newsy period; it included Robert E. Lee's surrender to Ulysses S. Grant at Appomattox, and, five days later, the assassination of Abraham Lincoln, yet nothing in his surviving work of the period alludes to these events. Instead, returning in May, he took up what would become a favorite topic, the hypocrisy and overreaching of powerful church clerics, in this case an Episcopalian minister named Kip, while identifying himself as a "sort of a Presbyterian in a general way." [38] At the helm of the paper's "Answers to Correspondents" column over a summer stretch, he twitted letter writers and played at the boundaries of absurdist response to the terminally earnest in ways that foreshadow James Thurber. (Asked for a description and opinion of the city's Independence Arch by a reader, he replied: "My friend, I have seen arch-traitors and arch-deacons and architects, and archæologists, and archetypes, and arch-bishops, and, in fact, nearly all kinds of arches, but . . . I never saw an arch like this before.") [39]

He found time in June to toss off a couple of pieces for the San Francisco *Youth's Companion*, the second of which ranks among his best-known short sketches: "Advice for Good Little Boys" ("If you unthinkingly set up a tack in another boy's seat, you ought never to laugh when he sits down on it—unless you can't 'hold in' "), and "Advice for Good Little Girls" ("If at any time you find it necessary to correct your brother, do not correct him with mud—never on any account throw mud at him, because it will soil his clothes. It is better to scald him a little . . .").[40] Through all this, the frog story remained unwritten. Mark Twain's initial confidence had given way to doubts and confusion about the story's structure. In the late summer, Artemus Ward sent Mark Twain a letter or two urging him to get it done.

On August 4, 1865, William Moffett died at forty-nine in St. Louis, leaving Pamela a widow at age thirty-eight. What condolences Sam may have sent are unrecovered. Pamela continued living in the rented house on Chestnut Street with Jane and her children Annie, thirteen, and Samuel Erasmus, not yet five. Sam, who had been sending money to Jane intermittently, would now be obliged to help support this household—and, as time went on, the struggling Orion and Mollie Clemens as well.

Mark Twain wrote at least two unsuccessful (and incomplete) jumping frog drafts sometime between early September to mid-October. Each drew on elements of the frame story. He developed the gentlemanly narrator and his backwoods interlocutor. As usual, he riffed easily on their respective voices, but he could not find a plot.

And then, all of a sudden—but let Mark Twain tell it, as he did in conversation late in his life.

Then one dismal afternoon as I lay on my hotel bed, completely nonplussed and about determined to inform Artemus that I had nothing appropriate for his collection, a still small voice began to make itself heard.

"Try me! Try me! Oh, please try me! Please do!"

It was the poor little jumping frog . . . that old Ben Coon had described! Because of the insistence of its pleading and for want of a better subject, I immediately got up and wrote out the tale . . . [I]f it hadn't been for the little fellow's apparition in this strange fashion, I never would have written about him—at least not at that time.[41]

One can spend some entertaining moments imagining the Twainian drawl cranked up into a froggy falsetto. This is the kind of semidivine intervention that Mark Twain loved to ascribe to decisive moments in his life—the scrap of text from the Joan of Arc book he came upon in Hannibal, the fifty-dollar bill that he discovered in Keokuk. Popular Victorian literature is practically founded on such shapely coincidences. The resulting sketch was printed in the November 18 edition of the *Saturday Press* in New York, under the title, "Jim Smiley and His Jumping Frog," launching Mark Twain into the vapor of national fame. He had mailed the piece to Ward, hoping that it would reach New York in time to be included in Ward's Nevada travel book. The book was just reaching the stores by then; but its publisher, George W. Carleton, forwarded Mark Twain's submission to Henry Clapp, bohemian editor of the *Saturday Press*.

The sketch scored a direct hit upon the American postwar funny bone. Its impact, as it got reprinted up and down the East Coast, and then westward into the interior, was rapid, and stunning. It seems to have had everyone who read it doubled over, gasping for breath, pounding fist against leg. All New York was "in a roar," the San Francisco *Alta California* reported. Bret Harte reprinted it in the *Californian*. Suddenly Mark Twain was being toasted as the best of all the California humorists. "To think that . . . those New York people should single out a villainous backwoods sketch to compliment me on!" he wrote to his mother with transparently false modesty.[42]

BUT WHAT, exactly, was so funny about it?

"The Celebrated Jumping Frog of Calaveras County," as he retitled it in the *Californian* reprinting that December, is among the most recognizable of all titles from the pen of Mark Twain. The central story is straightforward: the narrator visits a mining camp looking for information about a Leonidas W. Smiley, and runs into a talkative old man named Simon Wheeler. Wheeler doesn't recall any Leonidas Smiley, but he does know a Jim Smiley who used to live there. His yarn about Smiley fills up the rest of the 2,600-word sketch. He details Smiley's love of gambling, and a frog of his named Dan'l Webster, whom he has taught to jump high and far enough to win bets. Smiley meets a stranger who wants to bet against the frog, but has none of his own. Smiley offers to find one for him. The stranger waits for "a good while," and then "he got the frog out and prizcd his mouth open and took a teaspoon and filled him full of quail shot . . . pretty near up to his chin—and set him on the floor."[43]

At Smiley's command, "One—two—three—jump!" the new frog hops off, but Daniel only "hysted up his shoulders—so—like a Frenchman, but . . . he couldn't budge; he was planted as solid as an anvil." As the stranger leaves with his earnings, he jerks his thumb and utters the line that had them in convulsions from California to Maine: "Well, *I* don't see no p'ints about that frog that's any better'n any other frog."[44]

The humor of "The Jumping Frog" sometimes eludes contemporary readers. Those lucky enough to hear it declaimed by an accomplished reader are more likely to enjoy it in the way of 19th-century Americans, who recognized in it a familiar American archetype: the deadpan vernacular narrator. "The humorous story is told gravely," wrote Mark Twain himself, who considered the form a work of "high and delicate art." "[T]he teller does his best to conceal the fact that he even dimly suspects there is anything funny about it . . ."[45] The vernacular the serenely innocent Simon Wheeler uses is that called "Pike County"—the same evocative Missouri regional dialect that Mark Twain would later put to transcendent use in *Adventures of Huckleberry Finn*. In this story, the dialect speaker is breaking tradition: unlike Simon Suggs, Sut Lovingood, and the rest of that violent prewar cadre, Simon speaks *benignly*. His guileless sincerity invites the hearer's (and reader's) charmed affection, instead of scorn. At the close of the Civil War, Americans were ready for a good cleansing laugh, untethered to bitter political argument. Simon and the frog gave it to them.

Mark Twain's own response to the tale's career-establishing success was always edgy. He seems to have feared being imprisoned in the kind of reputation that was the lot of mere "humorists" in the genteel East, where his scrutinizing in-laws, the Langdons of Elmira, New York, practically defined gentility. He revealed as much in a now-famous letter to Orion and Mollie, written on October 19 and 20, 1865, probably just after he finished the breakthrough draft. Orion was floundering badly, casting about for some new way to make a living; his thoughts had turned toward the pulpit. He had written to Sam, enclosing a sermon of his, and Sam's reply was unusually tender and encouraging. "Orion there was **genius**—true, unmistakeable **genius**—in that sermon of yours," he declared. ". . . You are honest, pious, virtuous—what would you have more? **Go forth & preach.**"

In the same letter, Sam mulled his ambivalence over his own career choices. He acknowledged to his brother that he too had once considered the ministry as a vocation. In the next few lines, he wrote the manifesto for his immortal calling:

I never had but two **powerful** ambitions in my life. One was to be a pilot, & the other a preacher of the gospel. I accomplished the one & failed in the other, **because** I could not supply myself with the necessary stock in trade—*i. e.*, religion . . . But I *have* had a "call" to literature, of a low order—*i. e.* humorous. It is nothing to be proud of, but it is my strongest suit, & if I were to listen to that maxim of stern *duty* which says that to do right you **must** multiply the . . . talents which the Almighty entrusts to your keeping, I would long ago have ceased to meddle with things for which I was by nature unfitted & turned my attention to seriously scribbling to excite the laughter of God's creatures. Poor, pitiful business! . . .[46]

15

"... And I Began to Talk"

(1865–66)

I am taxed on my income! This is perfectly gorgeous! I never felt so important in my life before. To be treated in this splendid way, just like another William B. Astor! Gentlemen, we *must* drink!"[1] Thus Mark Twain's first encounter with the three-year-old U.S. Revenue Office, as he described it in the *Enterprise* in late November 1865. His effervescent irony is typical of the strong comic voice he deployed in his daily letters back to Joe Goodman's paper, which were earning him one hundred dollars a month. (He wrote more than a hundred of these between October 1865 and March 1866.) Some theater reviews for the *Dramatic Chronicle* brought in another forty. Clemens's private mood may not have matched his professional jauntiness—throughout his life, he was usually able to work through periods of anxiety or depression. Destitution, or the fear of it, haunted him. "I am also in debt," he'd written, commiseratingly, to Orion. "But I have gone to work in dead earnest to get out."[2]

When Sam got more sermons on October 20, he added a thought about them on the back of the letter he'd written but not yet sent the day before. He'd read them, but "as unsympathetically as a man of stone. I have a religion—but you will call it blasphemy. It is that there is a God for the rich man but none for the poor." He added: "If I do not get out of debt in 3 months,— pistols or poison for one—exit *me*." Continuing with brutal irony, in brackets: "There's a text for a sermon on Self-Murder—Proceed."[3] It was probably this period he referred to when he wrote in 1909, "I put the pistol to my head but wasn't man enough to pull the trigger. Many times I have been sorry I did not succeed, but I was never ashamed of having tried."[4]

157

DESPITE THESE dark thoughts, Sam seems to have been just then on his way out of a gloomy period—a period that his old friends at the *Call* took cruel delight in publicizing.

> There is now, and has been for a long time past, camping about through town, a melancholy-looking Arab, known as Marque Twein . . . His favorite measure is a pint measure. He is said to be a person of prodigious capacity, and addicted to a great flow of spirits. He moves often . . . These periods occur at the end of his credit . . . He may feel all right, but he don't *look* affectionate. His hat . . . comes too far down over his eyes, and his clothes don't fit as if they were made for him . . . Beware of him.[5]

As he foraged for income, that ancient chimera of Clemens wealth, the Tennessee land, whispered to Sam once more. "I have just made a proposition to an old friend of mine . . . an energetic, untiring business man & a man of capital & large New York business associations & facilities," he wrote to Orion with near-pathetic optimism on December 13.[6] Sam wanted the businessman, Herman Camp, to swing a land deal, after which Sam would give him half the proceeds. The take could be large. Oil had been added to the list of the land's suspected resources. Sam had reason to believe in Camp's business acumen: two years earlier Camp had offered him a 50 percent mining-claim partnership; Sam refused, and saw the assets sell for $270,000 two months later.

Sam urged Orion to send "all necessary memoranda" to acquaint Camp with the land's location and resources: "Now I don't want that Tenn land to go for taxes, & I don't want any 'slouch' to take charge of the sale of it. I am tired being a beggar . . ."[7] He envisioned returning east to help with the land sale, and then perhaps staying on to parlay his "Jumping Frog" fame into steady work as a writer. Orion mailed the materials. Camp traveled east. From New York, he wired Sam with a stunning, revised scheme: he would buy the thirty thousand acres outright from the Clemens family. His offer was $200,000. Camp had learned about a wild grape that grew well on Tennessee soil; his plan was to encourage European immigrants to buy or rent tracts of the land, which they would then cultivate as vineyards. The appropriate contracts were mailed to Orion, who was then thrashing around for any kind of new livelihood. His signature would put everything in motion; the land would at long last pay off; life for the Clemenses would be pie . . .

Orion said no.

No, as long as the land would be used to debauch the country with wine. Having recently wrecked his chances for a rewarding public career by trumpeting abstinence in the wettest part of the world since Atlantis, Orion now invoked the same piety to quarantine the entire Clemens clan from windfall prosperity. John Marshall Clemens himself might have marveled at his eldest son's resourcefulness at sustaining the family's ancient immunity to wealth— especially given that John Marshall Clemens had been the original promoter of the promising wild grapes. "And so," wrote Mark Twain in 1906, "he quashed the whole trade, and there it fell, never to be brought to life again. The land, from being suddenly worth two hundred thousand dollars, became as suddenly worth what it was before—nothing, and taxes to pay."[8]

Nearly giddy with rage, Sam threw himself back into the ball-and-chain routine of newspaper writing. And newspaper drinking. He boozed his way along the violent streets of the Barbary Coast, and when the police jailed him overnight for drunkenness, his nemesis Albert Evans snidely insinuated his misfortune in the *Gold Hill News.* Sam, stung and embarrassed, lashed out recklessly in the *Enterprise* at police brutality and corruption, an invitation for further harassment, and the police obliged.

Even his family members now felt his petulance in print. A sketch of his, published in the New York *Weekly Review,* excoriated the letter-writing styles of "relatives" in general ("How do you . . . write us such . . . poor, bald, uninteresting trash? . . . Why, you drivel and drivel, and drivel along, in your wooden-headed way . . ."). He targeted his mother in particular, stipulating that she was an above-average correspondent. The charge was overinitializing, as in "J. B. is dead," and "W. L. is going to marry T. D . . ."[9]

Forgivable horseplay, perhaps, but it had an edge. The edge was where Sam lived now. But a new project promised to restore his good spirits. He and Bret Harte were going to cobble a book together, he announced to Jane and Pamela in late January: a compilation of their sketches (later abandoned). "My labor will not occupy more than 24 hours, because I will only have to take the scissors & slash my old sketches out of the Enterprise & the Californian— I burned up a small cart-load of them lately—so *they* are forever ruled out of any book—but they were not worth republishing."[10] Harte had resigned from the *Californian* in December, in contemplation of his return east, and Sam had followed suit, in favor of an arrangement with the New York *Weekly Review.*

And Sam had another, far more ambitious book project in mind, the secret contours of which were being gossiped about in the local papers. The January 12 *Examiner* hinted that the book "will treat on an entirely new subject, one that has not been written about heretofore. We predict that it will be a very popular book, and make fame and fortune for its gifted author."[11]

"The book referred to in that paragraph is a pet notion of mine," Sam told the homefolks, "—nobody knows what it is going to be about but just myself."[12] He expected it to run some three hundred pages; the last hundred would have to be written in St. Louis, "because the materials for them can only be got there."[13] Already he was anticipating a long, difficult siege: "If I do not write it to suit me at first I will write it all over again, & so, who knows?—I may be an old man before I finish it."[14] The "new subject" was the Mississippi, as Sam had hinted in this same letter: "I wish I was back there piloting up & down the river again. Verily, all is vanity and little worth—save piloting."[15]

EVEN AS he composed this letter another form of watery adventure had caught Sam's attention. On January 13, the California Steam Navigation

Company had inaugurated a schedule between San Francisco and Honolulu in the Sandwich Islands, 2,500 miles across the Pacific Ocean. Its flagship, the *Ajax,* was capable of cutting two-thirds off the normal three-month round trip. Sam's cachet as a journalist had gotten him invited on the *Ajax*'s maiden voyage, along with fifty-two others, "the cream of the town," he told his mother and sister. Plus a brass band. But he declined, unable to find a stand-in as San Francisco correspondent to the *Enterprise.* He immediately regretted this decision. Sizing up the glittering passenger list with the same satirical eye that he would train on the *Quaker City* pilgrims to the Holy Land nearly two years later, he fairly smacked his lips: "Where could a man catch such another crowd together?"[16]

When the *Ajax* returned to San Francisco on February 22, Mark Twain was at the docks to greet the passengers with a new journalistic form: the interview. Horace Greeley had conducted the first newspaper interview only seven years earlier, recording the verbatim remarks of the Mormon leader Brigham Young in Salt Lake City. Now Mark Twain, who himself would later become one of the most-interviewed figures of his century, was trying his hand at it for the *Enterprise.*

When the *Ajax* sailed again in March 1866, Mark Twain was on board. His long career as a seafaring writer of travel literature had begun. "I only decided to-day to go," he wrote home on March 5. "I am to remain there a month & ransack the islands, . . . & write twenty or thirty letters to the Sacramento *Union*—for which they pay me as much money as I would get if I staid at home."[17] He spent four months in the unvexed isles, met every local political and religious person of any significance, and wrote twenty-five letters for the *Union.* These became the backbone of Chapters 62–78 of *Roughing It.* (Mark Twain had previously organized the newspaper letters into an "islands book" manuscript that he hoped to sell to a New York publisher.)

The letters reveal a seamless extension of the boy who had left Hannibal at seventeen, a man who could even then make himself at home in St. Louis, Washington, Philadelphia, and New York—and later New Orleans, Virginia City, and San Francisco. Here, as in every other lifetime port of call, Mark Twain found his way to the epicenter of an unfamiliar place. He interacted with the influential locals; he sampled their food, liquor, diversions, and culture with aplomb. Yet he maintained a saving distance that allowed him to write about his sojourns with the detached irony of the self-possessed artist.

He soaked up character, incident, anecdote, language, physical terrain, and local myth with the glorious disregard for conventional order or plot that would flavor his greatest works. Disembarking at the islands, he luxuriated in a world-that-is-not-San-Francisco—a world of cream-cut coral, of trees that cast a shadow like a thundercloud; of people in white coats, vests, pantaloons; a world of centipedes, scorpions, porpoises, and dusky maidens; many, many dusky maidens, who bathed nude and rode horseback trailing their long scarves of tavern-tablecloth brilliance; and cats—"multitudes of cats, millions of cats, and all of them sleek, fat, lazy and sound asleep." [18]

He took a horseback tour through the jungle valleys and mountains of Oahu, the big island of Hawaii, and several other islands. "Brown" made his debut in these rambles, to furnish *Union* readers with coarse commentary on the sojourn, and to lend "Mark Twain" a little class by contrast. Sometimes he called Brown "Billings." Paddling around in a canoe with Billings, he happened upon a 19th-century surfin' safari: "a large company of naked natives . . . amusing themselves with the national pastime of surf-bathing," in which

[e]ach heathen would paddle three or four hundred yards out to sea, (taking a short board with him), then face the shore and wait for a particularly prodigious billow to come along . . . and here he would come whizzing by like a bombshell! [19]

Sam tried his luck at hanging ten. His board caught a wave, but it arrived ashore without him.

At noon I observed a bevy of nude native young ladies bathing in the sea, and went and sat down on their clothes to keep them from being stolen. I begged them to come out, for the sea was rising and I was satisfied that they were running some risk. But they were not afraid . . . [20]

He wrote more than a third of his letters in the early weeks of his visit, concentrating on the islands' warrior past, their religious practices, and their current politics and economy. He witnessed a nighttime eruption of the massive Kilauea volcano, and compared its red-glowing shaft of flame to the pillar of fire witnessed by the children of Israel during their biblical march through the desert. The following night he took a dangerous gambol into the volcano's bubbling crater, writing later that he and a stranger named Marlette negotiated the treacherous paths of navigable lava by themselves after the local guides begged out. (His narrative of the Kilauea adventure ranks among the descriptive masterpieces in *Roughing It.*) He dryly noted the restrictions, encouraged by missionaries, on the storied "hula-hula" dance, "save at night, with closed doors," and for an admission fee of "ten dollars." [21] He visited the temples of gods, and "cabbaged" a bulky history book of the islands (James Jarves's 1849 *History of the Hawaiian Islands*)[22] from a Honolulu chaplain, from which he cribbed large factual sections for his *Union* readers and, later, his lecture audiences.

Sam returned to Honolulu from his horseback tour suffering from a severe case of saddle boils. On June 15, as he lay on his back, a stunning and grotesque—and career-enhancing—phenomenon washed into his life out of the Pacific. A lifeboat filled with half-dead seamen had landed on the sands of Laupahoehoe, a village nearly two hundred miles south of Honolulu. They were the sole survivors of the *Hornet,* a clipper gutted by fire en route from

New York to San Francisco via Cape Horn. The ship burnt up off the coast of South America. Three longboats carrying all thirty-one passengers and crew put to sea, but two boats were lost. The occupants of the third boat, the captain and fourteen others, survived a forty-three-day odyssey during which they meandered for four thousand miles on ten days' rations, eventually arriving at Laupahoehoe.

A week later, Sam sent a quick summary of their story to the *Union*. The following day, eleven of the men arrived at a Honolulu hospital. Despite his saddle-boil pain, Sam got himself there and once again assumed the interviewer's role, this time to thunderous effect. He stayed up all night transforming his notes into a long account, and the next morning threw it onto the deck of a departing fast schooner.[23] The *Union* printed the full story on July 19. It was reprinted throughout a nation conditioned by Civil War reportage to expect personal accounts of peril and high drama from the daily papers. Mark Twain had a worldwide scoop.

Sam's pain would have prevented him from reaching the *Hornet* crewmen but for his encounter with a visiting American diplomat, Anson Burlingame, the United States' minister to China. He and Sam met at a state social event on the island. Burlingame supervised Sam's transportation by stretcher to the hospital.

Sam departed the islands in July on the *Smyrniote*, a schooner that also carried three of the *Hornet* survivors. Toward the end of the voyage, he was copying down Hawaiian phrases and their English translations in an obvious effort to learn the language. More productively, he became acquainted with the ship's captain, Josiah A. Mitchell, and two of its passengers—nineteen-year-old Henry Ferguson and his fatally consumptive brother Samuel, who was about twenty-eight. The Fergusons, scholarly and devout young Connecticut men, allowed Sam to copy the contents of their lifeboat journals. It was a courtesy that Henry Ferguson would later regret, but one that led to a pivotal nonfiction narrative of privation and endurance.

BACK HOME, Sam worked at expanding the survivors' saga into a magazine-length essay. He journeyed the ninety miles northeast to Sacramento, where he handed the editors a bill for his Sandwich Island pieces (at twenty dollars per letter), and then audaciously hit them up for a hundred dollars for the shipwreck saga—*per column,* or three hundred dollars total. They agreed. He sold his long narrative to the influential *Harper's Monthly,* which ran it in December under the title, "Forty-Three Days in an Open Boat," slightly dampening the author's triumph by misidentifying him in its annual index as "Mark Swain." Years later he rewrote the story and sold it to the *Century.* Its title, which survives in his collected essays, is "My Début as a Literary Person." The essay's documentary precision (for once, Mark Twain was adhering closely to the facts) wounded the sensibilities of Henry Ferguson, by then an Episcopal clergyman and history professor at Trinity College in Hartford. Fer-

guson was shocked that Mark Twain had used the real names of some survivors, particularly those who had plotted briefly to mutiny against the captain. In later editions, Mark Twain made editorial alterations that satisfied
Ferguson.

Sam further leveraged his fame by turning his Sandwich Islands writings
into a lecture. If the talk was a hit in San Francisco, he would take it on the
road. By now, Sam had stood up before a few audiences, but these were mostly
friends—the printers in Keokuk, the reporter/politico crowd at the Third
House shenanigans in Carson City, a couple of after-dinner turns in Virginia
City. A public lecture—an attempt to play on Artemus Ward's level—was a voyage into uncharted waters. Luckily for posterity, Sam was desperate. He wrote
a presentation in large, easy-to-read block letters on manila paper that was by
turns comic, descriptive, and airily unctuous—something, he clearly hoped,
for every customer. He rented the biggest house in town, Thomas Maguire's
new Academy of Music, which seated between 1,500 and 2,000 people, for the
night of October 2. Maguire let Clemens have the hall at half-price for fifty
dollars, on credit, plus half the receipts. He showed his lecture to some trusted
friends, asking their opinion of it. He spent $750 dollars on handbills and an
ad that ran in every San Francisco newspaper. Its highlights, written by Sam
himself, have become a part of Mark Twain folklore:

A SPLENDID ORCHESTRA

Is in town, but has not been engaged.

ALSO,

A DEN OF FEROCIOUS WILD BEASTS

Will be on exhibition in the next Block.

MAGNIFICENT FIREWORKS

Were in contemplation for this occasion,

but the idea has been abandoned.

A GRAND TORCHLIGHT PROCESSION

May be expected; in fact, the public are privileged

to expect whatever they please.

Dress Circle. . . . . . . $1   Family Circle . . . . .50 cts.

Doors open at 7 o'clock.   The Trouble to begin at 8 o'clock.[24]

The stakes were high. In *Roughing It* and elsewhere, Mark Twain milked the
drama for all it is worth—perhaps a little more than it is worth. Writer Charles
Warren Stoddard and Bret Harte tried to talk him out of going through with
the lecture, insisting that it would hurt his literary reputation.[25] An editor at
the *Call* (probably George Barnes) bucked him up, and even suggested that
Sam charge the stiff price of a dollar a person. As the evening drew near and
he compulsively reread the manuscript, it became less and less funny to him,
until on the day of the event he was drenched in flop-sweat.

Half-starved—he hadn't eaten in three days—he recruited three "stormy-
voiced" friends to sit in the audience and laugh like hell at his dim jokes. And

then a quintessentially Twainish thing occurred: on the street, Sam ran into a conveniently drunken character—named William Slason. As if anticipating the opening lines of *Huckleberry Finn,* Slason blurts (in *Roughing It*), "You don't know me, but that don't matter. I haven't got a cent, but if you knew how bad I wanted to laugh, you'd give me a ticket. Come, now, what do you say?"[26] Mark Twain asks the man for a sample laugh. "My drawling infirmity of speech so affected him that he laughed a specimen or two that struck me as being about the article I wanted, and I gave him a ticket . . ."[27]

ON TUESDAY night, October 2, 1866, Sam Clemens took the Academy of Music stage in San Francisco. Facing his public for the first time as Mark Twain, nearly blinded by the footlights, trembling with terror, frozen in place for a full minute, he finally gained control of himself,

". . . and I began to talk."[28]

That night, a new kind of personage materialized in America. This figure clearly owed a debt to Artemus Ward and others with Ward's mannerisms, but Ward and the others would fade; this figure would endure. Mark Twain would move quickly to a national and then to a world stage, and his words would yield unimaginable global fame and wealth. The nation would share his ecstasies and his heartbreaks. People would point him out on the street, his rocking, rolling gait, and women in his lecture halls would whisper their dismay when his wife gave him children. The world would be there for him, but he would never quite be there for it. He began to talk, peering at the faces before him, and the enraptured audience inside Thomas Maguire's Academy of Music peered back at the nation's first rock star.

16

On the Road

(1866–67)

"S̲ide-splitting," the San Francisco papers reported. "A hit, a great hit." They described the "continued applause" over his "grotesque imagery, and fearfully ludicrous stories."[1] In a measured and thoughtful review, Bret Harte wrote that Mark Twain's "humor surpassed Artemus Ward's," and was perhaps "more thoroughly national and American than even the Yankee delineations of [James Russell] Lowell."[2] But he had his faults, Harte added, among them "crudeness, coarseness, and an occasional Panurge-like* plainness of statement."[3] Mark Twain had a great act, but bad management. He grossed $1,200 at the Academy of Music, but after paying off the shrewd Maguire and other expenses, pocketed only $400. He needed a partner who could help him with the details of this new dodge. A ready volunteer was at hand: young Denis E. McCarthy, former *Enterprise* co-owner, who had sold out to Goodman in September 1865, and who may have acted and been paid as Clemens's agent for this initial lecture. McCarthy was a savvy businessman who loved the world of artists and show business, but who was struggling financially. In no time, the two of them had plotted out an itinerary.

He performed in Sacramento a week later. Then Marysville, by steamer up the Sacramento River. Then Grass Valley, by stagecoach, a lecture fueled by

---

* Panurge is the atavistic rogue-companion of Pantagruel, in François Rabelais's comic novel *Gargantua and Pantagruel* of 1532–34, who speaks and acts from his most primal impulses. Although Harte was suggesting that Mark Twain himself had his Panurge-like moments onstage, the comparison is even more apt for "The Unreliable," "Brown," and other of Twain's fictional doubles in his (relatively) nonfictional works.

gin and capped off with hot whiskey punches at a local oyster parlor. Nevada City. By horseback to the mining burgs of Red Dog and You Bet. These outposts were so starved for variety that, as a Washoe joke had it, the local preachers altered the Lord's Prayer to, "Give us this day our daily stranger." * Sam and his new manager papered the burgs with variations on the San Francisco handbills—"THE CELEBRATED BEARDED WOMAN! Is not with this Circus"[4]—and caroused through the local bars at every stop, owning each joint.

Then a triumphant return to Virginia City, for a Halloween night lecture at Maguire's Opera House. The newspapers trumpeted him home. "The enthusiasm with which his lecture was everywhere greeted is still ringing throughout California, and now, that his foot is on his native heath, we may expect to see the very mountains shake with a tempest of applause," cried the *Territorial Enterprise*,[5] making sure to add that the *Enterprise* was where Sam Clemens had christened the name Mark Twain "and developed that rich and inexhaustible vein of humor which has made the title famous." Joe Goodman contributed an idea of his own: when the curtain opened, Mark would be sitting at a piano, playing and singing the song that had become his "signature" out west, "The Horse (Mule) Whose Name Was Jerusalem (Methusalem)." He would look up, appear startled to see the audience, and then start talking.

Nursing a cold, Mark Twain electrified his old friends in the hillside boomtown. The Opera House crowd was standing room only, eight hundred strong. They wore their fanciest clothes, and cheered, stamped, and hooted before and after he performed. Steve Gillis remembered that "when he appeared on the platform he was greeted with a hurricane of applause." The newspapers bear-hugged him: "immense success," "drollest humor."[6] Mark Twain considered, but eventually turned down, a request for a second performance. His showman's instinct was coalescing: always leave 'em wanting more.

His new celebrityhood swept away a host of the old antagonisms. A letter from Carson City awaited Mark Twain after he left the Opera House stage: an invitation to bring his lecture there, signed by more than a hundred citizens who said they had "none other than the most kindly remembrances of you."[7] (W. K. Cutler was not one of the signers, but H. F. Rice and Samuel D. King, husbands of two of the Sanitary Ball committee ladies, were.) He telegraphed his acceptance on November 1, and on November 3, he rolled into the capital, McCarthy in tow, for a sold-out performance at the Carson Theater. Then, after a few days, back to the one-horse towns: Washoe City on November 7, the next day at Dayton, eleven miles to the northeast of Carson; back west through Silver City and Gold Hill on November 9 and 10. (McCarthy returned to Virginia City at this point.) Mark Twain in Washoe City stayed at the

---

* Mark Twain attributed this line, in *Roughing It,* to the newspaper editor Thomas Fitch (p. 360).

home of Thomas Fitch, the former *Union* editor and bitter rival whom Joe Goodman had crippled in their duel in 1863. Fitch, minus a kneecap, was now the district attorney of Washoe County. No hard feelings: he brought Mark Twain onto the platform at the courthouse with a rousing introduction ("He needs no introduction . . ."[8]) after acting as doorkeeper. His status as the famous humorist's personal friend had Fitch hobbling on air.

En route home with Fitch, Sam was engulfed in another dark mood, which often happened after a triumph. Told by Fitch that he had taken in over $200, Sam replied, "Yes, and I have taken in over 200 people." He added that as a lecturer, he was "a fraud."[9] The darkness still gripped him when, on November 10, his old drinking pals from Virginia City honored him in the rough-and-tumble Washoe way, with an extravagant practical joke. McCarthy, Gillis, and some others decked themselves out like bandits and held up the stagecoach that was carrying Sam along the lonely "Divide" from Gold Hill to Virginia. After leveling pistols, they absconded with more than a hundred dollars in cash, some jackknives and pencils, and a gold watch worth $300—Mark Twain said he valued it for sentimental reasons "above everything else I own."[10] Forty years later, Steve Gillis plaintively insisted that the objective of the good-humored caper was to supply Mark Twain with fresh material for a second lecture for which the local folks were clamoring. But Sam took it as he always took jokes at his expense: he pouted and nursed a grudge. When his goods were returned and he discovered that the incident was a prank, he stormed out of Virginia City on November 12, arriving in San Francisco the next day. Writing *Roughing It* several years later, he was still sore: "The joke of these highwaymen friends of ours was mainly a joke upon themselves; for they had waited for me on the cold hill-top two full hours before I came, and there was very little fun in that." Moreover, he wasn't nearly afraid enough "to make their enjoyment worth the trouble they had taken."[11]

He certainly had the temperament of a rock star.

BUT IN what sense, really, can that label have meaning when applied to an aspiring Victorian gent and semiapostate ex-Presbyterian journalist/humorist who fashioned his craft on clapboard gaslit stages ninety-odd years before the advent of, say, Metallica? Most of the parallels are merely facile: his adoring press, his tours, his promo schemes, his manager, his eruptions of childish petulance, his worship of money.

His proto-rocker mojo kicked in once he took the stage, and was fueled by something nascent in the American air, something only half-anticipated by Emerson, but grasped by Adah Menken, Ward, and some others. It caught a new-blooming audacity of the Self, a Self set loose from old pietistic constraints. Emerson had got that much of it right, with his God-intoxicated Yankee poet launching out into Old Night, and provoking cries of wild creative delight. Emerson's poet remained faithful to his obligation to speak representative truth, in high and sonorous diction. But this was a new night now, a postwar night lit by cities and industry, and the American Self had caught its reflection in the lorgnette of a fashionable woman in the front row.

As the California tour rolled on, Mark Twain grew more acquainted with what worked, what stirred his audiences, made them abandon their reticence in a wash of laughter; what made them abandon themselves, made them one with him, made them his. He noticed the people in the seats, and he noticed how they noticed him. It was an intimate and extra-verbal communion, and Mark Twain was among the first, and surely the most gifted, of those who played with it on the lecture stage. In some ways it was erotic: a process of creating tension and release. He toyed with the libido.

The eroticism was hardly overt—and certainly unstipulated. (There is no record of his female fans heaving their pantaloons onstage.) Yet a current existed; women responded to him in a sensual way. Years later, at an 1871 gig in Brooklyn, he had several ladies alternately cooing and pouting: "My, what a handsome young man to be a lecturer!"; "He isn't a bit funny now he's married"; "He's got a baby and that takes all the humor out of him." [12]

He faced colorful competition. The lucrative post–Civil War American lecture circuit was filling up. Authors, preachers, feminists, temperance shouters, war heroes, divas, phrenologists, paleontologists, out-and-out buffoons—everybody wanted to get in on the act. They declaimed, they hectored, they trilled, they wept, they testified, they did somersaults, they showed off their fancy clothes, they paced and strutted and gulped water from their pitchers. At times, they even lectured. They achieved varying degrees of renown, even star-quality, in the public mind. Yet even the most accomplished performed at a certain remove from the spectators in front of them; a remove as much psychic as physical. An irreducible taboo remained in place, the taboo of sensual intimacy. Droll, righteous, and passionately reformist the lecturers might be, but only from the far side of an unbreachable gulf between the platform and the people.

Mark Twain broke the taboo by breaking the proscenium and making contact with each individual in the hall. ("He . . . seeks to establish a sort of button-hole connection," wrote one reviewer.) His electric intimacy manifested itself from the moment of his debut on the Academy of Music stage. The swank San Franciscans had begun tittering before he'd uttered a word. He'd had a reputation as a funny man, but in print. He seduced his live audience largely through the tension of his mannerisms: his lingering, silent gaze from face to face across the footlights (an effect of stage fright, in that first appearance, but soon quite expertly mediated); his fingers caressing his wild sprawl of auburn hair and tugging at his mustache; his hands wringing each other; the long, hypnotic drawl as he began to speak, lazily and dreamlike— and then the sudden release: the dazzling "snapper" that came from the caged furies inside, electrifying the crowd, making them "jump out of their skins" and erupt into applause and what he called "artillery laughter," complete with "Congreve rockets and bomb-shell explosions."

Mark Twain broke a lot of rules and traditions in these early Western gigs—words like "coarseness" tended to show up in some of the more conservative reviews, including Bret Harte's. He continued to dress flamboyantly sloppily, slouching onstage in the same lumpy suits, retro string ties, and "heavy arctics" on his feet that he wore around town. (He eventually switched to the regulation claw-hammer coat; by the end of his career he was looking almost Beatle-like in his red Oxford gown, or his white suits and red socks. He once expressed the wish that he could wear a multicolored garment that fit the description of a dashiki.)

His drawling voice could take on a raw, distinctly non-"oratorical" rasp; one reporter compared it to a little buzz saw slowly grinding inside a corpse. He understood shock value: he frequently promised to demonstrate what he meant by "cannibalism" by eating a baby onstage, if someone would hand him one. No one ever did.

He had the impulses of a rock star, which is to say, the impulses of a child. An audience member who kept his hat on during a performance got him crazy, and he railed about it to the local press. He screamed at hotel help, slammed his door repeatedly in the middle of the night to get an innkeeper's attention, berated local hosts and chairmen who did not introduce him properly; he sometimes shooed them away and introduced himself. Once he tossed all his silk shirts out of an upstairs window. He occasionally canceled dates at the last minute. He barnstormed the country on a "Twins of Genius" tour with a fellow performer; he feuded with his co-star; smashed a window shutter with his fists over a scheduling problem. At the end of the tour, the other performer referred to him as a bad dream.

As for what Mark Twain had to say on the platform, it wasn't exclusively humorous. Mood shifting was essential to his aura. He came to understand that much of his onstage power derived from his ability to keep the audience on its toes, play with its emotions. He could bring the crowd to a hush with a lyrical aria—for example, his stunning description of the volcanic eruption at Kilauea. In other moments, he would begin what seemed to be a solemn train of thought, then pause, and turn it to the absurd with a quick "snapper," à la Ward. Then he would unleash a succession of comic *mots* and descriptions that ratcheted the hilarity in the house to the point of hysteria. He revised his material constantly, building on experience. He would tweak and experiment for the rest of his lecturing days. He experimented with a kind of pre-electronic reverb: somewhere in the Comstock, he trotted out an old familiar anecdote concerning the famous editor Horace Greeley and a local stagecoach driver, the punch line of which was: " 'Keep your seat, Horace, and I'll get you there on time'—and you bet he did, too, what was left of him." The story's best laugh-getting days were behind it, which was exactly the point. Mark Twain told it straight-faced at the outset of one lecture, and the crowd sat on its hands. He began it again. And then again. And yet again, until the audience grasped that "unfunny" was the heart of the tension, and laughed at *that*.

UPON HIS return to San Francisco, Sam began to plan his long-desired exit from the West. The showman in him wanted to make a grand departure that would buoy his reputation back on the Atlantic seaboard, from where he imagined that he would travel to Europe and then into India and China (where Anson Burlingame would be his host and guide), writing letters to American papers along the way. A more familiar incentive drove him as well: cash. The box office from his California-Washoe tour had mostly been sponged up by his creditors. Financially, he was running in place.

He arranged what he hoped would be his farewell lecture, a reprise of his Sandwich Island triumph, on November 16. This talk, though judged a "decided success" in the papers, didn't compare to his debut in October. Worse, the San Francisco courts attached his receipts to settle the long-standing matter of the bond he'd posted for Steve Gillis's bail in the bartender-bashing incident. He cobbled together a short tour to San Jose, Petaluma, and Oakland. The reception was only fair—perhaps his money anxieties had caught up with him onstage.

His appearances before large audiences must have reconjured his boyish "powerful ambition" to preach. In November he'd encouraged Pamela's six-year-old son, also named Sammy, to "[k]eep up your lick & you will become a great minister of the gospel some day, & then I shall be satisfied." He added, "I wanted to be a minister myself—it was the only genuine ambition I ever had—but somehow I never had any qualification for it *but* the ambition." [13] "I am running on preachers, now, altogether," he informed Jane. "I find them gay . . . Whenever anybody offers me a letter to a preacher now, I snaffle it on the spot. I shall make Rev. Dr Bellows trot out the fast nags of the cloth [the more liberal clergy] for me when I get to New York." [14]

Bellows and perhaps others must have commended Sam Clemens to a "fast nag" clergyman whose oratory and essays and sermons had established him as a national personage on a par with Emerson: the Reverend Henry Ward Beecher, pastor of the Plymouth Church in Brooklyn.

IN MID-DECEMBER, Sam figured out a way to leave California on his own terms. He negotiated a deal with the *Alta California* in San Francisco as a "Travelling Correspondent." The paper announced this in its December 15 edition.

"Mark Twain" goes off on his journey over the world . . . not stinted as to time, place or direction—writing his weekly letters on such subjects as will best suit him . . .

His itinerary, the paper indicated, would be the stuff of dreams:

. . . crossing the ocean to visit the "Universal Expedition" at Paris, through Italy, the Mediterranean, India, China, Japan, and back to San Francisco by the China Mail

Steamship line . . . [w]e feel confident his letters to the ALTA . . . will give him a world-wide reputation.[15]

On that same day, the thirty-one-year-old Sam Clemens sailed out of the Golden Gate into the Pacific Ocean toward Nicaragua aboard the steamship *America*. He strolled the first-class deck in high spirits, despite a lingering illness. He was satisfied that he had ended his Western years on a plane of accomplishment and prestige. The Civil War fugitive, the failed silver miner, the hard-drinking journalist and provocateur, had risen: he'd won the esteem of nationally famous personalities, moved in the highest literary echelons of America's most sophisticated city, and was now advancing toward a global adventure on commission to a premier newspaper.

In a sentimental mood the night before his debarkation, he'd written to his mother of the friends he was leaving behind—more, he boasted, than any other newspaperman who'd departed the Pacific slope: most of *them* just made enemies. At a church fair earlier in the evening, he'd encountered several men and women "of Sandwich Island nativity," who "came forward, without the formality of introductions, & bade me good bye & God speed. Somehow these people touch me mighty close to home with their eloquent eyes & their cordial words & the fervent clasp of their hands."[16] Already, it seemed, the Wild Humorist was beginning to grow tame.

The first portent of what was to be a hellish voyage struck on the first night. A fast-gathering storm lashed the ship with seas that broke high over the prow, carrying away bulwarks and washing cargo up and down the decks. Many among the four hundred passengers prayed on their knees. Lifeboats were readied, though deemed useless against the towering waves. Sam surveyed the roiling scene down below him, the flooding in steerage, and noted the captain's steadfast command of his crew. Then he rode out the night in the relative stability of his upper-deck berth.

A day or two later, the crisis surmounted, the captain invited Sam to view, through a marine glass, a pair of whaling ships at anchor, as their crews hoisted blubber aboard. The sight reminded the captain of a story, and Sam was captivated by the old salt's manner of telling, and the outlines of an iconic character began to form in his imagination, one that would bestride Mark Twain's literature across many decades.

"I had rather travel with that old portly, hearty, jolly, boisterous, good-natured old sailor, Capt Ned Wakeman than with any other man I ever came across," Sam wrote in his notebook a few days afterward.[17] Edgar Wakeman was a dazzling sea god, a bearded, tattooed, barrel-bellied, pious, profane ripsnorter swathed in diamond stickpins and gold chains. He was born on a Connecticut farm in 1818, ran off to sea at age fourteen, sailed the world, memorized much of the Bible, and had plied the Pacific off California. His past rivaled that of any old Black Avenger of the Spanish Main. He once swiped a steamboat and took it on a joyride around Cape Horn. In San Francisco, he'd hanged at least two men. He even intimated that he'd visited Heaven, and met a fellow up there who sneered at it all; nothing suited him. Hell of a place, the chap declared.

Sam Clemens drank in this apparition, and somewhere within him, Sammy did, too. Wakeman cast a spell vastly more powerful than the one cast by Horace Bixby. The spell floated on a kind of holiness. Jilted as he felt himself to be by his Christian God, chilled by his father, Sam was receptive to the figure who gave off a whiff of brimstone. And who could speak a good sentence.

"The rats," Sam records Wakeman as bloviating about some remembered voyage,

were as big as greyhounds & as lean sir! & they bit the buttons off our coats & chawed our toe-nails off while we slept & there was so many of them that in a gale once they all scampered to the starboard side when we were going about & put her down the wrong way so that she missed stays & come monstrous near foundering! But she went through safe, I tell you—becus she had rats aboard.[18]

Sam transferred Wakefield's surging lingo and fantastical stories, seemingly unaltered, into his notebooks. From there, they infused Mark Twain's stories: Wakeman appears variously as himself (and later as "Captain Waxman") in Mark Twain's *Alta California* letters; as Captain Ned Blakely in *Roughing It;* as Captain Hurricane Jones in the 1877 sketch, "Some Rambling Notes of an Idle Excursion"; as characters in four other works;* and, most memorably, as the title character in "Captain Stormfield's Visit to Heaven." By the time Mark Twain was through with him, Wakeman/Stormfield was racing comets to heaven, in a surreal, disjointed work of fantasy that Mark Twain dabbled at intermittently for three decades.

ON DECEMBER 21, Sam idly speculated on "Genius" in his notebook, while the passengers sang and played leapfrog: "Geniuses are people who dash off wierd, wild, incomprehensible poems with astonishing facility, & then go & get booming drunk & sleep in the gutter . . . people who have genius do not pay their board, as a general thing."[19] On Christmas Eve the first death, a child, occurred—a commonplace shipboard tragedy. Sam recorded the conversation of the ship's officers regarding the sea burial. The incident quieted the passengers. They had no inkling what was coming.

The cholera was waiting for them when they reached Nicaragua. The *America* put into port at San Juan del Sur, and the passengers learned of an outbreak among six hundred westbound passengers awaiting the ship. Sam's notebook mentioned reports of thirty-five deaths among these travelers and

* They are Captain Saltmarsh in *The American Claimant,* Captain Davis in *The Great Dark,* Admiral Abner Stormfield in *The Refuge of the Derelicts,* and Judge Sim Robinson in *Those Extraordinary Twins.*

forty more among the natives. The passengers disembarked Wakeman's ship, climbed into carriages and onto horses, and began the beautiful, perilous twelve-mile isthmus crossing. They gaped at wild monkeys and calabash trees, and bought oranges and bananas and coffee in carved cups from pretty native women, while the disease selected its victims. They boarded a steamer for a short lake voyage and then headed down the San Juan River toward the Atlantic Coast aboard another stern-wheel boat. "Paradise itself," Sam jotted, "—the imperial realm of beauty—nothing to wish for to make it perfect."[20] He began to notice an eccentric young barber named Andrew Nolan, whom he nicknamed "Shape," and also a Jew who he felt had grown overfamiliar with the "white" passengers (himself included) to the point where he'd brazenly lounged on the same stateroom sofa with them.

On New Year's Day, 1867, the passengers boarded the steamboat *San Francisco* at Greytown for the voyage to New York. On January 2, Sam recorded: "Two cases of cholera reported in the steerage to-day."[21] The ship experienced its first mechanical breakdown later that night, and the first of the sick passengers died. And then, after midnight, the second.

The next day Sam listed the ingredients for a tropical drink. Then his notes grow allusive, dreamlike.

Folded his hands after his stormy life & slept in serenest repose under the peaceful sighing of the summer wind among the grasses over his grave.

Brown—yes, you're very sea-sick, ain't you?—you better take a little balsam co—What!

He said "Oh, nothing,—don't mind me,"—but I half believed I heard him mutter something about Mrs Winslows Soothing Syrup for sick infants, as he went out.

Still on January 3, Sam recorded the third cholera death—the fourth fatality since the ship left San Francisco.

January 5: "Seven cases sickness yesterday—didn't amount to anything." A few lines later: " 'Shape' is said to be dying of cholera this morning."

Later: " 'Shape' has been walking the deck in stocking feet—getting wet—exposing himself—is going to die."

The disease has got into the second cabin at last—& one case in the first cabin . . .

Jan. 5—Continued—10 AM—The Episcopal clergyman, Rev. Mr. Fackler, is taken—bad diarrhea and griping . . .

12—"Shape" dead—5th death.—

Rev. Fackler has made himself sick with sorrow for the poor fellows that died.

There is no use in disguising it—I really believe the ship is out of medicines—we have a good surgeon but nothing to work with.

Jan 5 . . . Verily, the ship is fast becoming a floating hospital herself . . .

When I think of poor "Shape" & the preacher, both so well when I saw them yesterday evening, I realize that I myself may be dead to-morrow.

. . . all levity has ceased . . .[22]

Later on January 5 he listed the dead—six thus far, including the infant. The latest casualty was the Reverend St. Michael Fackler. The next day the ship docked at Key West, Florida, and twenty-one passengers, many of them stricken, fled the ship. ("I am glad they are gone, d—n them.")[23] Sam went ashore in a disoriented and fractious mood. The cholera aside, he had felt snubbed and even mocked as the voyage had progressed. Captain Wakeman was a man's man of the sort he felt comfortable with; but Wakeman was behind him now, and he was estranged from the more refined passengers and even by the pursers, who looked at his careless clothing and questioned his first-class status ("None but 1st cabin allowed up here—*you* first cabin?").[24] A "double-chinned old hag" had scolded him for his drinking.

Finally, on Saturday, January 12, after twenty-seven and one-half days, two more mechanical breakdowns, and another bout of frigid weather and rough seas, the *San Francisco* steamed past snowy Staten Island and docked at New York Harbor. Sam had survived a seagoing ordeal in which a pestilence of deadly microbes had claimed eight lives, in which two violent oceans had raged up and pitched his vessels about as if they were microscopic droplets. It had all been like a hideous dream. He scribbled a few last sarcasms in his notebook, packed his trunks, and strode down the gangplank into the hard daylight of the gathering Gilded Age.

17

Back East

(1867)

He walked into a clotted low-slung mecca of immigration, trade, street an-archy, slums, and political bossism. San Francisco had been about art; New York was about buying and selling, and the main chance. This had grown even more true in the nearly fourteen years since Sam had been here last. The city's largely postwar immigrant population was surging past a million and a half, a concentrated pool of greenhorn pockets ripe for the picking by Demo-cratic Party boss William Marcy Tweed and his corrupt minions. What green-backs the pols missed, the merchants were scooping up. The Northeastern factories that had churned out munitions, textiles, shoes, wagons, and utensils for the Union troops now needed this burgeoning civilian market for their survival. The skyline did not yet reflect this ascendancy of commerce. Church spires—notably Trinity's at Broadway and Wall Street, and St. Paul's at Broad-way and Fulton—still towered above all else; the first wave of skyscrapers was still eight years away. But a new phenomenon, the department store, repli-cated itself along the great numbered avenues of Manhattan, drawing a huge consumer wave of women in its wake, and adding to the near gridlock in the streets; within a year, the tunneling for the first subways would commence.

All of this hustler energy meant a couple of hopeful things for an ambi-tious young writer-entertainer fresh in from the Wild West. The retooled fac-tories, new stores, and proliferating railroads of the East were forming a template of mass citizenship in the postwar nation. Along with it came a widening hunger for ideas, for public personalities, for news of the consoli-dating "national character." The same generation that had learned to read from the mass-distributed McGuffey's Reader had come of age, endured a war, and was now hungry to participate in the collective America that was emerging. Much of their access was through the printed word.

The late 1860s and 1870s saw an enormous surge of books and periodicals, concentrated among the "gentlemen publishers" of New York, Boston, and Philadelphia. These years also saw a redefinition of the published product. Alongside the familiar leather-bound volumes of European literature and the sparser American canon produced in small numbers for an upper-class clientele were gaudy and exotic new genres: paperback "dime" adventure novels of the "pluck-and-luck" formula; Western tales, and humor; women's romance. (Not to mention women's writing in general. Harriet Beecher Stowe's success with *Uncle Tom's Cabin*—three hundred thousand copies sold in 1852 alone—did not go unnoticed.) Book production was not yet industrialized; publishing still tended to be a small-scale enterprise, often an adjunct of a printing-bookselling family firm. But now, with the decreasing price of paper and printing, with railroads rushing the inventory to every corner of the country and into the hands of local door-to-door "subscription" salesmen, and with public libraries serving immigrants and the strapped working classes, books were suddenly an important and democratizing mass commodity. This trend fed heavily into the second hopeful prospect for an aspirant like Sam Clemens: it signaled that a new writer could break through on talent and powerful publicity, not just via pedigree or conformity to traditional standards of belles lettres and culture. The sting of Eastern snobbery remained a hazard for any outsider; but in Sam Clemens's short career as a writer—a "writer of a low order," but still by God, a *writer*—no one had dismissed his work.

Bracing himself against the January wind, Sam checked in at the commodious Metropolitan Hotel on Broadway and Prince, in what is now SoHo, just below Greenwich Village. The rates were three times what he'd remembered from 1853. But he was back on Broadway, the street he had strutted at seventeen. He knew this town and what it could do for a fellow with moxie. "Make your mark in New York, and you are a made man,"[1] he instructed his *Alta California* readers a few weeks later. Frank Sinatra himself could hardly have put it better.

He had come a long way from being a completely unknown entity in this market. The "Jumping Frog" story in *Saturday Press* had lit the way east for him, along with the sobriquets "Washoe Giant" and "Moralist of the Main." There was the entrée forged by Ward with the *Sunday Mercury*, which had published a couple of Mark Twain's California sketches. The *Weekly Review* had run several of his pieces. *Harper's Monthly* could have had the city welcoming him as a star based on his *Hornet* survivor interview, but for that d—d misprint "Mark Swain." There were also the introductory letters he carried from the San Francisco clergymen, addressed to Henry Ward Beecher. These connections held out the hope of steady work. But within a couple of days of his arrival, Sam found himself encouraged to pursue the most tantalizing goal on his agenda: getting a book published. He had brought along clippings of his Sandwich Islands letters to the Sacramento *Union,* arranged in the sequence of a book manuscript, expecting to find a book publisher without much trouble. The hazily defined "river book" was still in the back of his mind. To his surprise, it was the "villainous backwoods sketch" and some other pieces from the *Californian* and the *Enterprise* that comprised his book pitch.

The instigator of this turn of events was Charles Henry Webb, founder of, and Harte's partner at, the *Californian.* Webb, who had led the bohemian exodus from New York to the West Coast several years earlier, was now back home. His apartment was just a couple of blocks from the Metropolitan—another lucky thing for Sam, given that getting around this congested city was like trying to swim upstream against a firehose. You couldn't "accomplish anything in the way of business, you cannot even pay a friendly call, without devoting a whole day to it," Sam railed, sounding like generations of out-of-towners.

If you live below Twenty-fifth street, you are "down town;" and if you live anywhere between that and Seven Hundred and Seventy-fifth street (I don't know how far they run—have quit trying to find out), you will never *get* down town with out walking the legs off yourself. You cannot ride . . . unless you are willing to go in a packed omnibus that labors, and plunges, and struggles along at the rate of three miles in four hours and a half . . . Or, if you can stomach it, you can ride in a horse-car and stand up for three-quarters of an hour . . . or you can take one of the platforms, if you please, but they are so crowded you will have to hang on by your eye-lashes and your toe-nails.[2]

Sam called on Webb in the midst of a snowstorm. His host thawed him out with several jolts of Washoe-style "reporter's cobbler," and the reunion was cheery. Also present was a New York drama critic named Edward H. (Ned) House, a friend of Artemus Ward's who, the previous June, had escorted the humorist to England, where Ward struggled with his lecturing career in the face of worsening tuberculosis.

Webb persuaded Sam, still focused on the Sandwich Islands project, that the "Jumping Frog" was the hot ticket for him. As the title sketch of a Mark Twain collection, its popularity was practically guaranteed in advance. Webb volunteered to help select and collate the other pieces, which appealed to the lazy streak in Sam. He even arranged an appointment for Sam with George Carleton, the publisher of Ward, Bret Harte, Josh Billings, and other Western humorists, whose list included Webb's own poetry. (It was Carleton who, back in 1865, had forwarded the "Frog" sketch to Henry Clapp Jr., then editor of the *Saturday Press.*) Sam, "charmed and excited," had every reason to believe that a contract would be extended to him as soon as he walked through Carleton's door. So certain was he of this that he dashed off a private letter to his sponsor at the *Alta,* John McComb, in early February, boasting that he was about to "give" Carleton a volume of sketches for publication. The paper printed a brief summary of this letter for Mark Twain's followers in mid-March—nearly a month after Sam had kept his appointment with Carleton, and been given the bum's rush.[3] He never forgot it: his diffident arrival in the publisher's office at 499 Broadway, the brusque statement of the clerk that Mr. Carleton was in his private office; his admission to the great man's quarters after a long wait; Carleton's icily impersonal greeting: "Well, what can I do for you?"

Sam's abashed response—that he was keeping an appointment to offer a book for publication—triggered a temper tantrum from Carleton that lives in the annals of bad editorial judgment. "He began to swell," Mark Twain recalled,[4] "and went on swelling and swelling and swelling until he had reached the dimensions of a god of about the second or third degree. Then the fountains of his great deep were broken up . . ."* Carleton later told a friend that it was Sam's "disreputable" appearance that had put him on edge.[5] (This was in the days when many writers dressed well.) Whatever the impetus, Carleton treated his speechless visitor to a vintage New York–style tongue-lashing. At the end, he swept his arm around the room and delivered the coup de grace that will forever be associated with his name: "Books—look at those shelves. Every one of them is loaded with books that are waiting for publication. Do I want any more? Excuse me, I don't. Good morning."[6]

The apocryphal editor who sneeringly intoned, *"Whales,* Mr. Melville?" could scarcely have shoved his foot deeper into his mouth. To Carleton's credit, he acknowledged the dimensions of his botched opportunity. More than two decades afterward, encountering Mark Twain in Lucerne, Carleton squared himself, shook the now-famous author's hand, and declared (at least in Mark Twain's memory): "I am substantially an obscure person, but I have a couple of such colossal distinctions to my credit that I am entitled to immortality—to wit: I refused a book of yours, and for this I stand without competitor as the prize ass of the nineteenth century."[7]

Mark Twain welcomed this "long delayed revenge" as "sweeter to me than any other that could be devised,"[8] but it didn't quite atone for the second affront that Carleton had perpetrated virtually at the same time he turned down Mark Twain's manuscript: he'd agreed to publish a collection of Western sketches called *Condensed Novels* by Bret Harte. Sam's envious fury over this perceived (but hardly intentional) slight magnified the insult Carleton had dealt him. A few weeks later, writing to a friend in San Francisco, he asked "How is Bret? He is publishing with a Son of a Bitch who will swindle him, & he may print that opinion if he chooses, with my name signed to it. I don't know how his book is coming on—we of Bohemia keep away from Carleton's."[9]

* This phrase, variations of which Twain used several times, and most memorably in a letter to William Bowen a few days after his marriage in February 1870, refers to Genesis 7:11: "the same day were all the fountains of the great deep broken up, and the windows of heaven were opened."

Carleton's rejection was not an isolated incident; it was simply the only documented one. Newspaper clippings and a later remark by Webb indicate that other houses may have turned down the manuscript as well. Ultimately, having persuaded Sam of the collection's salability, Webb offered to publish it himself, handling the production and arranging for distribution. Sam would take royalties of 10 percent of sales. He plunged into a final editing process with Webb, making several handwritten revisions on newspaper clippings of his California sketches that he had collected in a scrapbook. His changes are almost entirely aimed at purging the most extreme of the rough-and-ready words and phrases that had been his natural coinage in the West. He denied this—the editing had been all Webb's work, he told the *Alta*—but scholarship devoted to the scrapbook proves otherwise. The archive shows, for instance, that Sam converted "hell" to the safer "hades" in three instances. Other substitutions included "embrace" for "tackle," "blucher" for "slush buster,"* "muggings" for "hog wash," "fearful" for "rough," "wickedest" for "vilest," "leer" for "slobber," "jolly" for "bully," and "swindle" for "humbug." He also deleted a reference to the inspiration he had derived from "the excellent beer" manufactured in New York.

These edits marked the beginning of an acute self-refining process that would consume him, to a considerable extent, for the rest of his life: a process of tempering his more atavistic impulses to satisfy the decorous tastes of—well, just about everyone: Mary Fairbanks, Howells, his wife, his daughters, the clergy, the East generally, Great Britain . . . The entire English-speaking world, it must have seemed to him sometimes, was preoccupied with making Mark Twain watch his mouth.

When he'd handed his revisions over to Webb, Sam turned his energies to getting some humorous pieces published in New York newspapers. Success came quickly: the *Sunday Mercury* published seven Mark Twain sketches that year, probably at twenty-five dollars each; the *Evening Express* bought one; and Street and Smith's *New York Weekly* contracted for five of his Sandwich Islands letters recycled from the Sacramento *Union*.[10]

Broadway continued to be a lifeline of opportunity. Frank Fuller, another friend from Washoe days who had his offices there, told Sam that he should take that crackerjack Sandwich Islands lecture of his and get it going again in the East. The idea of facing a discerning Eastern audience gave Sam the fantods, but he said yes, and Frank Fuller joined Charles Henry Webb on the Mark Twain multimedia express, as his lecture manager. (For both men, it would be a long and ultimately bumpy ride.) Fuller sought the biggest hall available in New York, and set a date more than three months away. And then Sam fell back into another depression. He wrote candidly of his "blues" in a letter to the *Alta,* and admitted that his "thoughts persistently ran on funerals

---

* In each case, a shoe with the leather sections overlapped and was tightly laced against moisture.

and suicide." Sometime in late January, he moved out of the Metropolitan and into cheaper quarters on East 16th Street. He tried to keep his mind busy. Work, as always, was an antidote; he trudged about the wintry city, compiling vignettes for his California readers. His mood may have been dark, but his observations remain a rare and charming snapshot collection of the city and its people at the dawn of its international might.

He evoked the city's swelling population, particularly its violent dispossessed, "the brown-stone frontier and the rag-picker of the Five Points." He noted that the newly wealthy "upstart princes" of commerce had displaced the "old, genuine, traveled, cultivated, pedigreed aristocracy of New York, [who] stand stunned and helpless under the new order of things." "Everything is high"—thirty dollars a week for rent, sixty cents a pound for butter, sixty cents a dozen for eggs. "Beggars charge two cents now." [11]

He updated California on one of his favorite topics, women's fashion.

The wretched waterfall still remains, of course, but in a modified form . . . now it sticks straight out behind, and looks like a wire muzzle on a greyhound . . . the glory of the costume is the robe—the dress. No furbelows, no flounces, no biases, no ruffles, no gores, no flutterwheels, no hoops to speak of—nothing but a rich, plain, narrow black dress, terminating just below the knees in long saw-teeth, . . . and under it a flaming red skirt, enough to put your eyes out, that reaches down only to the ankle-bone, and exposes the restless little feet. . . . To see a lovely girl of seventeen, with her saddle on her head, and her muzzle on behind, and her veil just covering the end of her nose, come tripping along in her hoopless, red-bottomed dress, like a churn on fire, is enough to set a man wild. I must drop this subject—I can't stand it. [12]

He got himself invited inside the exclusive Century Club, whose membership was limited to authors, artists, and "amateurs of letters and the fine arts." He poked some outsider's fun at the shiny bald heads on the premises, but almost palpably drooled over a sampling of the membership: Edwin Booth, William Cullen Bryant, "Church, the painter," Frederick Law Olmsted, "Putnam, the publisher," Richard Henry Stoddard. "I carried away some of the hats with me for specimens. They average about No. 11." [13]

He revisited the gaslit theaters along Broadway that he'd sampled as a youth; and noted that the girlie show, which had scandalized him when he gazed disapprovingly and at length upon "The Model Artists" in 1853, had been repackaged as "Grand Spectacular Drama." But it was the same old fleshy dodge. "I warn you that when they put beautiful clipper-built girls on the stage in this new fashion, with only just barely clothes enough on to be tantalizing, it is a shrewd invention of the devil. It lays a heavier siege to public morals than all the legitimate model artist shows you can bring into action." [14] Thank goodness someone was speaking out.

He even managed to extend a genial bow to "My Ancient Friends, the Police."

A transcendent American life unfolded between the making of these two photographs. Samuel Langhorne Clemens was an obscure assistant, not yet eighteen, at his brother Orion's Hannibal, Missouri, *Journal* when he sat for this daguerreotype in 1851 or 1852.

The figure known throughout the world as Mark Twain relaxes with his great literary friend and champion William Dean Howells in 1909, a year before his death.

Sam's uneducated but verbally gifted mother Jane Lampton Clemens (right) in 1858 or 1859. She lived to see her son publish his greatest works—some of them featuring fictionalized versions of her, for instance, as Aunt Polly.

Henry Clemens, Sam's beloved younger brother (left), was nineteen when he sat for this photograph in St. Louis. A few weeks later he died a terrible death in a steamboat explosion.

The eldest of the Clemens siblings, Orion (bottom, left), shown here in the early 1860s, shared Sam's propensity for dreaming, but not a shred of his talent.

Mary E. (Mollie) Stotts (bottom, right) married Orion Clemens in 1854, enjoyed fleeting glamour as a society hostess in Carson City when her husband served as Secretary of the Nevada Territory. She followed him back East into obscurity after Orion bungled his promising political career.

7

Laura Wright (left) was only fourteen when she met the young apprentice-pilot Sam Clemens on a docked steamboat in New Orleans in the spring of 1858. Laura floated through his dreams—and his writings—for the rest of Mark Twain's life, reemerging dramatically in his later years.

8

The legendary pilot Horace Bixby (right) succumbed to the entreaties (and the promise of five hundred dollars) from a drawling young passenger aboard his boat the *Paul Jones,* bound for New Orleans in February 1857, and launched Sam Clemens's steamboating career. Mark Twain immortalized Bixby in *Life on the Mississippi.*

"Floating palaces," the big side-wheelers were called; and races between them were frequent spectacles on the river. In this Currier & Ives chromolithograph (below), the *Queen of the West* is taking on the *Morning Star.* Such races could end in fiery tragedy, as Sam Clemens discovered in 1858.

9

A new kind of American cultural figure—the *star*—materialized in Maguire's Opera House in San Francisco (left) on October 2, 1866. Mark Twain, desperate for cash and dazed with stage-fright, edged onstage, and delivered a lecture on the Sandwich Islands that quickly turned into a riotous triumph.

In May, 1922, an aging Billy Gillis poses on hallowed ground (below). The cabin behind Gillis is a restored version of the one that stood on this site atop Jackass Hill in Calaveras County, California,

in the mining heyday of the Comstock Lode. During his stay on Jackass Hill, Sam grew absorbed in a local "tall tale" about a certain jumping frog. He wrote his own version several months later.

Artemus Ward (Charles Farrar Browne) (left) was the reigning American humorist when he met the newspaperman Sam Clemens in Virginia City, Nevada, while touring the West in 1863. Sam struck up a friendship with Ward, who later encouraged him to send the "jumping frog" comic sketch back east.

"Jim Smiley and His Jumping Frog" was published in the New York *Saturday Press* on November 18, 1865, under the by-line "Mark Twain." Rapidly reprinted around the country, it gained lasting renown as "The Celebrated Jumping Frog of Calaveras County." This 1872 caricature is by Frederick Waddy.

These solemn passengers aboard the *Quaker City,* photographed by William E. James, en route from America to the Holy Land in 1867, had no way of imagining that the red-haired raconteur in their midst would enshrine them in literature in his groundbreaking travel book, *The Innocents Abroad.*

14

15

Rough seas lashed at the *Quaker City* (right) on its departure from New York Harbor on June 8. Mark Twain smiled—and took notes—as his elderly fellow voyagers lurched about the decks, hands clasped to stomachs, muttering, "*Oh,* my!"

16

Among the few passengers who recognized the budding genius beneath Sam Clemens's dispatches back to America was Mary Mason Fairbanks (left), the thirty-nine-year-old wife of a Cleveland newspaper publisher. The two became lifelong friends.

This hand-colored ambrotype of Olivia Langdon was probably made in 1867. It is very likely the image that Clemens, in later life, recalled as an "ivory miniature" shown to him by Olivia's brother Charlie in Charlie's's shipboard cabin at the Bay of Smyrna. Previously published only once, and here identified as that historic image for the first time.

17

"I feel so often as if my path is to be lined with graves," Livy Clemens wrote to a friend in 1872. Her face, as shown in this photo taken around that time, would lose its youthful serenity. In June of that year, the first-born Clemens child, Langdon, had died of diphtheria after surviving for eighteen sickly months.

Healthy daughters soon restored joy to the Clemens household: Susy, born in March 1872, and Clara, born in June 1874 (above).

The ever-restless Sam swept his small family through England, Scotland, and Ireland in 1873. Here, (bottom, left) family friend Clara Spaulding holds the baby Susy in her lap, seated next to Livy and Mark. Their Scottish host, John Brown, looks on.

22

23

Mark Twain accumulated addresses throughout the United States and Europe in his lifetime. Among the most significant are these: "Stormfield," in Connecticut (above). Quarry Farm (left), on a hill above Elmira, New York. The home of John and Isabella Hooker (below, left) in Hartford, Con-

25

24

26

necticut. The house at 472 Delaware Avenue, in Buffalo, (above, right) presented to Sam and Livy as a surprise wedding gift from Livy's father, Jervis Langdon, in February 1870. The octagonal gazebo above Quarry Farm, a gift to Sam from Sue Crane in 1874 (bottom, right). Here, during the summer visits to the farm, Mark Twain wrote much of *The Adventures of Tom Sawyer, Adventures of Huckleberry Finn, The Prince and the Pauper, A Tramp Abroad, Life on the Mississippi,* and *A Connecticut Yankee in King Arthur's Court.* The gazebo now sits on the campus of Elmira College.

27

Samuel Clemens sat for this striking portrait (top, left) by Mathew B. Brady, the great Civil War photographer, in Washington in July 1870.

Judging from the two-toned shoes, Mark Twain (right) may have been aware that a photographer was in the vicinity as he scribbled away inside his Quarry Farm gazebo in the summer of 1874.

Bookish William Dean Howells, shown at left as a young consul in Venice during the Civil War, was an unlikely champion of the rough-edged Western humorist Mark Twain. Yet it was Howells's enthusiastic review of *The Innocents Abroad* in the staid *Atlantic Monthly* that launched the author into respectability in the East.

Dec. 31/74.

An inveterate doodler, Mark Twain was forever dashing off sketches on napkins, in his notebooks and on other available surfaces. This self-portrait (bottom, left) was drawn in December 1874.

Elisha Bliss (top, center) published *The Innocents Abroad* over the strong opposition of his American Publishing Company colleagues. The gentle James R. Osgood (top, left), encouraged Clemens to return to the Mississippi River, and even accompanied him on the 1882 odyssey that resulted in *Life on the Mississippi*. Charles L. Webster (top, right), a small-town New York civil engineer, came on board a few years after marrying Clemens's niece, Annie Moffett—but presided over the failure of Mark Twain's own publishing company, and died at thirty-nine after enduring years of "Uncle Sam's" vitriol.

Mark Twain's book illustrators could not resist including his easy-to-capture likeness in many of their drawings, such as this one (left) of Mark Twain leading "Harris" in *A Tramp Abroad*.

Copyright laws were either lax or nonexistent through most of the 19th century, and no American author was more outraged by pirated editions of his books and plays than Mark Twain. His crusade drew the amused attention of his friend Thomas Nast in this 1882 cartoon (right) for *Harper's Weekly*.

A Portrait of the Artist
as a Young Steamboat Pilot: Samuel Clemens
in 1858.

The squire of Nook Farm with his daughters and wife (above, left) at the height of their happiness in Hartford: (from left), Clara, Jean, Livy, and Susy clustered around "Papa" in the summer of 1884, just months before the publication of *Adventures of Huckleberry Finn.*

Sam Clemens was rarely photographed smiling—or naked—but he seems inclined toward both in this whimsical photograph (above, right) made in 1884.

Sam gets a little nutty with his favorite daughter Susy (below) on the porch of the family's mountainside cabin in Onteora, New York, in 1890.

Straitened finances forced the Clemenses to live abroad for nearly a decade. In 1895, Mark Twain (right) embarked on an audacious around-the-world lecture tour by which he intended to repay the creditors of Charles C. Webster & Co. 100 cents on the dollar. Clara and Livy (center) accompanied him through Australia, New Zealand, Ceylon, India, and South Africa,

NOTICE
ALL STOWAWAYS WILL BE PROSECUTED AT HONOLULU AND RETURNED TO THIS PORT.
BY ORDER.

among other ports of call. Lecture receipts and sales of his resulting book, *Following the Equator*, enabled him to meet his $100,000 goal.

The lecturing triumph quickly dissolved into tragedy, though: just as it ended, in 1896, Clemens learned in England that his beloved daughter Susy (bottom) had died of spinal meningitis back in Hartford. He never fully recovered from the loss.

42

The elegant Henry Huttleston Rogers (left) was a feared and ruthless multi-millionaire capitalist of the Gilded Age; but also a man of taste who admired the works of Mark Twain. In 1893, Rogers entered the author's life, staunched the flow of his bad-investment cash, re-organized his finances, and saved the Clemens family's estate and literary copyrights.

An enthusiastic shipboard gamesman all his life, Mark Twain (third from left, below) poses with fellow shuffleboard players (center photo) aboard the *Minneapolis* on June 16 1907, en route to England. There the author would receive the honor he treasured above all others, a degree from Oxford.

43

44

Clara Clemens, shown here in Florence, (bottom, right) became fiercely protective of her father's posthumous reputation, suppressing his darker writings and evidence of his tempestuous moods. But her own book, *My Father, Mark Twain*, includes many unmatchable renderings of his character.

45

48

In the spring of 1902, Samuel Clemens visited his hometown of Hannibal, Missouri, for the last time. He posed for photographs (top) in front of the house at 206 Hill Street and verified that he had lived there as a boy in the 1840s. He then traveled on to Columbia, Missouri, (bottom, left) where he received an honorary degree from the University of Missouri. In 1903, (bottom, right) Clemens reunited with a hero of his younger days: John T. Lewis, who in 1877 had seized the bit of a run-away carriage-horse at Quarry Hill and saved the lives of three people.

Sam Clemens had learned to play the piano and guitar from his sister Pamela back in Hannibal; he played and sang, mostly spirituals, throughout his life. Here (top, left) he plays at Stormfield in 1908.

Billiards (top, right) was another lifelong passion; games at all hours helped slake his loneliness after the deaths of Susy and Livy, and then Jean.

Clara, Livy, and Sam in a revealing photograph made in 1900 (center, right). A spruced-up Sam addresses the camera while Clara gazes down protectively on her mother, who seems worn and dazed by her life of bereavements and illnesses.

51

A second office for Clemens in his later years was the bed (bottom, left) of carved oak that he and Livy had purchased in Venice for their Hartford house. The bed accompanied him to his late-life residences; he grew fond of working and receiving visitors while propped on pillows.

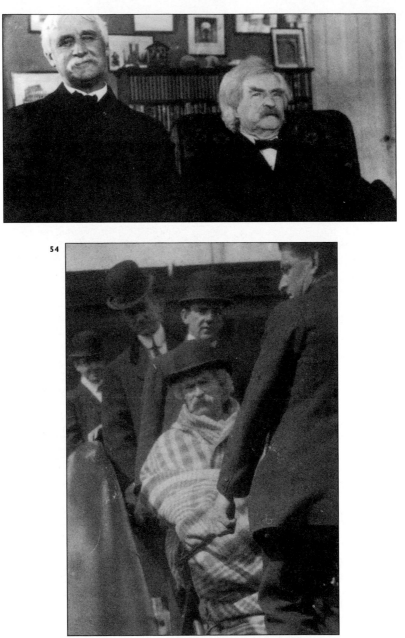

53

54

The Reverand Joseph "Joe" Twichell, shown at left in 1905 (top), was perhaps second only to Howells as an intimate friend of Clemens. Twichell was the sort of "muscular" Christian Clemens admired—but not muscular enough to haul Sam back to the faith.

The final photograph of Mark Twain (bottom), made on April 14, 1910, as he was aided in disembarking at New York Harbor after a hiatus in Bermuda. He died nine days later, in the Stormfield house, at seventy-four, lying in the carved-oak bed.

. . . [H]ow they work!—how they charge through the tangled vehicles, and order this one to go this way, another that way, and a third to stand still or back! . . . They are extremely useful . . . and they earn every cent they get. From one end of town to the other they march to and fro across Broadway with women on their arms . . . The women like it. I stood by for two hours and watched one of them cross seven or eight times on various pretences, and always on the same handsome policeman's arm.[15]

He went to see the fiery twenty-five-year-old feminist Anna Dickinson lecture at the Peter Cooper Institute, noting that she was brought onstage by Peter Cooper and introduced by Horace Greeley. He took a detailed connoisseur's interest in her wild, hectoring performance, which, he was forced to admit to *Alta* readers, was impressive.

She talks fast, uses no notes whatever, never hesitates for a word . . . and has the most perfect confidence in herself. Indeed, her sentences are remarkably smoothly-woven and felicitous. Her vim, her energy, her determined look, her tremendous earnestness, would compel the respect and the attention of an audience, even if she spoke in Chinese—would convince a third of them, too, even though she used arguments that would not stand analysis . . . she hath a certain grim humor that affords an uneasy sort of enjoyment . . .[16]

As for her message, which dealt with "the drudging, unintellectual character of those employments" available to women, he was uncharacteristically sympathetic: "She did her work well. She made a speech worth listening to." Still, he couldn't let her escape without a stiletto thrust: "Her sarcasm bites. I do not know but that it is her best card. She will make a right venomous old maid some day, I am afraid." [17]

On Sunday, February 3, with the thermometer "at 180 degrees below zero, I should judge," [18] Sam boarded a ferryboat that bumped through the ice floes of the East River, and walked stiff-legged into the plump, plain-brick Plymouth Church in Brooklyn, to hear a sermon by the Reverend Mr. Beecher. He made the visit at the urging of his friend Moses Sperry Beach, an owner and editor of the New York *Sun* and a congregant at Plymouth, with close ties to Beecher. Sam pried his way through the packed sanctuary and into a space "about large enough to accommodate a spittoon," [19] and prepared to scrutinize the star attraction. His description of the service endures as the most vivid word-picture on record of Beecher at the pulpit. The great minister

got up and preached one of the liveliest and most sensible sermons I ever listened to. He has a rich, resonant voice, and a distinct enunciation, and makes himself heard all over the church without very apparent effort. His discourse sparkled with felicitous similes and metaphors (it is his strong suit to use the language of the worldly,) . . . poetry, pathos, humor, satire and eloquent declamation were happily blended upon a ground work of earnest exposition of the great truths involved in his text.[20]

Beecher preached that day on the theme of civic duty. His sermon abounded in rhetorical shrewdness, a skill dear to Sam's heart. Beecher invoked the image of an automated loom he'd seen once in Lowell, Massachusetts, a machine that performed "with no apparent intelligence but its own to guide it."[21] Then he sprang his "snapper": given the mental caliber of some "people to whom the elective franchise is accorded in America," it was a shame that the machine "wasn't allowed to vote!" The "congregation let go and laughed like all possessed."[22]

The preacher's physicality struck Mark Twain as well:

Whenever he forsook his notes and went marching up and down his stage, sawing his arms in the air, hurling sarcasms this way and that, discharging rockets of poetry, and exploding mines of eloquence, halting now and then to stamp his foot three times in succession to emphasize a point, I could have started the audience with a single clap of the hands and brought down the house. I had a suffocating desire to do it.

Twain could not resist, of course, a parting snapper of his own:

Mr. Beecher is a remarkably handsome man when he is in the full tide of sermonizing, and his face is lit up with animation, but he is as homely as a singed cat when he isn't doing anything.[23]

Among Samuel Clemens's most singular and least explicable gifts, or recurrences of good luck, was his social radar: his uncanny propensity for finding his way, time and again, into the most consequential circles of American cultural, intellectual, and political life. No constellation of relationships would ever mean more to him than the one centered on the bulky figure prowling the pulpit on this frigid Sunday morning. The adventures and the personal encounters influenced by Henry Ward Beecher would in time lead Sam to his first great book, his wife, his acceptance into the elite social and literary circles of the East, and to the nonesuch neighborhood that encompassed the twenty happiest years of his life. From the vantage point of that neighborhood, Sam would watch at close range as one of the greatest scandals of the American 19th century unfolded, a scandal whose central actor was Beecher.

Henry was only one member of a prodigiously accomplished family, and not even the most famous among his twelve siblings. That distinction belonged to his older half-sister Harriet Beecher Stowe. The patriarch was Lyman Beecher, a Connecticut Congregationalist preacher and theologian who fathered thirteen children by the first two of his three wives. Nine of those offspring attained some public recognition; of those, six would figure in Mark Twain's life. As for Henry, he was a Transcendentalist thunderer in the Emersonian tradition; sweatier, more vernacular, a bit less of a heavyweight; and just now sharing the summit of American notoriety with the Sage himself and Ulysses S. Grant. He had been a somewhat equivocal abolitionist before the war (opposing slavery, but in favor of civil solutions instead of civil war), and now, in the welcome banality of peace, Americans doted on his fortune-cookieish aphorisms: "The mother's heart is the child's schoolroom," "The difference between perseverance and obstinacy is that one often comes from a strong will, and the other from a strong won't." [24]

Within days of his visit to the Brooklyn church, Sam Clemens found himself caught up in a scheme of Beecher's that spoke to every impulse toward travel and adventure that he had nurtured since boyhood. A solicitation prospectus described it: an oceangoing excursion to the Holy Land, Egypt, the Crimea, Greece, and "Intermediate Points of Interest." The excursion was to be sponsored by Plymouth Church, open to as many people as a steamship could accommodate. The excursion would get under way in June, from New York Harbor to Europe, along the Mediterranean Sea, and then across terrain through parts of Lebanon, Syria, and Palestine. The ship would return to New York in November. Beecher, it was hinted (but never explicitly promised), would head the expedition. He planned to research a biography of Jesus. In effect, this would be the first organized luxury cruise in American history.

Sam most likely learned of the grand scheme from Moses Beach. But soon all the Eastern newspapers were trumpeting it. Rumors spread that celebrities from the military and the theater would crown the passenger list: William Tecumseh Sherman, the fearsome Union general who'd burnt his way through Georgia; Robert Henry Hendershot, who as a twelve-year-old had gained pop-cultural fame at Fredericksburg as the "Drummer Boy of the Rappahannock"; a touring actress named Maggie Mitchell, who had wowed Emerson and Lincoln, among many others, with her drop-dead shadow dance in the title role of "Fanchon the Cricket." The celebrity list grew a little diluted a few weeks later with the rumored addition of the Massachusetts congressman Nathaniel Prentiss Banks, who as a Union general had been defeated twice by Stonewall Jackson, and had lost so many supplies in his retreats that the Confederates nicknamed him "Commissary Banks."

The *Quaker City* would in some ways reprise the ambience of Sam Clemens's Mississippi steamboat days. A 1,428-ton side-wheeler with two masts, she had patrolled against blockade runners around the Chesapeake Bay as a Federal gunship during the war. Despite her deep-sea hull, she'd chased a Confederate ramming boat along the lower Mississippi. Afterward, she was refitted for passenger use, with a grand dining hall and fifty-three belowdecks berths. There would be a daily onboard newspaper. As Sam digested the details of this pilgrimage, his depression evaporated, and exhilaration swept in. The prospect of travel always elated him, especially travel over water. Here would be a second chance at the promise offered by the *Ajax* in California: to sign on to a pioneering ocean voyage and observe the behavior of people, famous and ordinary, in a small enclave. Here would be a way to partly fulfill the half-notion he'd entertained since meeting Artemus Ward—

lighting out for Europe and high adventure. More importantly to his creative life, here lay—quite literally—the route to his literature.

Of all the writerly gifts available to Mark Twain, structure was conspicuously not among them. Prolific though he was, he worked most naturally in precise miniature. The exact word mattered to him; he knew and cared about the difference between the lightning bug and the lightning, as he put it. His sentences were typically supple, lean by 19th-century standards, evocative of mood, filled with aural and visual richness. His paragraphs were shrewdly organized to set up and then deliver the required snapper, or irate thunderbolt, or consummating grace note of elegy, as the case required. He had been trained to thematically shape the short sketch, but beyond that, Mark Twain was generally winging it. Formative design, structure, novel-length plot, a sense of the whole, were absent from his newspaper letters, and from most of the books that eventually came—even the masterpieces. Gloriously, in a way, it didn't seem to matter to him. His novels tumbled forth with the serendipity of a wild river—changing channels, overflooding boundaries, trickling along on the force of their own blind weight, seeking a level. His non-novels ("nonfiction" seems a lightning-bug word as it applies to Mark Twain) tended to be sprawling pastiches, grab bags of personal narrative, some of it true, mixed with found art: sections from other books, recollected tales, happenstance memory fragments, self-plagiarized letters and essays, anything to meet the required word count.

This formlessness has provoked strong criticism of Mark Twain, including the persistent opinion that he is at best a "secondary" or a "regional" literary artist—although that line of criticism coalesced mostly in the 20th century, and to some extent reflected aesthetic standards not strictly enforced in the 19th. Perhaps the most sensible way of regarding Mark Twain's tendency toward headlong sprawl is that it removed all impediments from his greatest strength, which was his intuition and his skill at improvisation. There is some reason to believe that he avoided careful plotting or planning, even though he was capable of it, as in *The Prince and the Pauper.* Had he preoccupied himself with solemn formal obligations—had he allowed the Tom Sawyer inside him to become a grown man—the antic content that defined his genius might have died in discarded drafts.

WHILE CHARLES Henry Webb scrambled to arrange publication of the "Jumping Frog" pastiche-book, Mark Twain announced the plan in the *Alta* under the title, "Grand European Pleasure Trip." He began with the facts and figures, and grew progressively giddy. The ship could accommodate 150 passengers, but would carry only 110 to avoid crowding. It would be outfitted to satisfy refined tastes: a library, musical instruments. Fare would be $1,250 in currency, with an additional $500 expense in gold, for land travel from various ports. The voyage would begin the 1st of June and end near the beginning of November, Mark Twain wrote—and then dreaming Sammy took over, exulting in the storybook fantasy of it all.

Isn't it a most attractive scheme? Five months of utter freedom from care and anxiety of every kind, and in company with a set of people who will go only to enjoy themselves, and will never mention a word about business during the whole voyage. It is very pleasant to contemplate.[25]

On the same day, in the same spirit, he fired off a terse telegram to the editors of the *Alta California*. "Send me $1,200 at once," it instructed. "I want to go abroad." [26] No boy in the land could have put it more succinctly. Amazingly, the *Alta* agreed to fork it over.

Sam had found a curious way of demonstrating his reportorial bona fides. He'd showed up at least mildly drunk at the booking office on Wall Street one morning in late February, in the company of the equally buzzed Edward House, the newspaper music critic he had first met in Webb's rooms. Unshaven and sloppily dressed, the two young men tittered and preened before the excursion manager, a devout man named Charles C. Duncan, who had helped plan the expedition and who would be the *Quaker City*'s nominal captain. House introduced Sam as "the Reverend Mark Twain," a Baptist minister just in from the Sandwich Islands and San Francisco, who fretted that he might not be welcome to perform religious ceremonies alongside the Reverend Mr. Beecher, who represented a different denomination. "I had to laugh out strong, here—I could not well help it," Mark Twain confided to his *Alta* readers. "The idea of my preaching . . . with Beecher was so fresh, so entertaining, so delightful." [27]

CAPTAIN DUNCAN came alert. "You don't look like a Baptist minister," he seethed, "and really, Mr. Clemens, you don't smell like one either!" Sam returned sober the following day, owned up to his true occupation, signed his name, and handed Duncan the $125 down payment for a berth aboard the *Quaker City*, the remainder due in mid-April. Clemens and the sanctimonious Duncan were destined to be spirited enemies, feuding frequently through the press after the voyage. After one of Duncan's scoldings fully ten years later, Mark Twain struck back with a devastating wisecrack.

The "captain" says that when I came to engage passage in the Quaker City I "seemed to be full of whiskey, or something," and filled his office with the "fumes of bad whiskey" . . . [F]or a ceaseless, tireless, forty-year public advocate of total abstinence the "captain" is a mighty good judge of whiskey at second-hand.[28]

Wearing a king's robes, feeling solemn and absurd beneath them, Sam attended a Bal d'Opéra at the Academy of Music the first night in March. Instead of dancing, he slunk around the ballroom and, as Justin Kaplan has written, seemed to encounter some of the figures of his accumulating imagination in the crowd: a Joan of Arc pining for a mess of raw oysters; dukes and princes who called one another "Jim" and "Joe" as they debated who would buy the next drink. *Alta* readers must have puzzled over the confessional ending to his description of this glittering event: "I did not feel happy at that ball, but I never felt so particularly unhappy in my life as I do at this moment." [29]

ON MARCH 6, Artemus Ward died in Southampton, defeated by his long battle with tuberculosis. Like Oscar Wilde thirty-three years later—"Either those curtains go, or I do" [30]—he maintained his comic sense until the end. As he lay on his deathbed, his friend the playwright T. W. Robertson chided him for refusing his medicine: "Take it, my dear fellow, just for my sake. You know I would do anything for you." "Would you?" asked Artemus. "Then *you* take it." [31] He was a month short of his thirty-third birthday.

By that time, Sam Clemens was on his way home again, to the river that was his life.

18

"move—move—*Move!*"

(1867)

The evening of March 3, Sam embarked on a fifty-two-hour rail connection to St. Louis, where the homefolks waited to see him for the first time in six years. Jane Clemens was nearly sixty-four now. Pamela was thirty-nine. Annie was an adolescent of fourteen. Sammy was six. Orion very likely was visiting from Keokuk at the time, nearly destitute, having failed again as a lawyer and as seller of the Tennessee land.

The letters he sent to the *Alta* show that his social views had not noticeably moved beyond the conventional bigotries during his years in the West.

The women of Missouri have started a sensation on their own hook. They are petitioning the Legislature to . . . extend to them the privilege of voting (along with us and the nigs., you know) . . . Thirty-nine members of the Legislature have declared in favor . . . Don't you know that such a showing as that is amazing, in view of the colossal dimensions of the proposed innovation? . . . If four or five hen-pecked husbands, or badgered and bully-ragged old bachelors, had been driven into a support of the measure, nobody would have been surprised; but when the list soars up to thirty-nine, it is time for all good men to tremble for their country.[1]

He witnessed the first stirrings of the social-control movement that later would be known as separate but equal: "The Superintendent's Report . . . says of the colored schools ordered by State law, that 'the efforts of the Board to establish schools for colored children have not as yet been successful,' but that a

187

special committee has been ordered to rent proper buildings and open such schools without any delay that can possibly be avoided."[2]

He was alert to changes in popular lingo, and showed off his biblical savvy as he described some of them. St. Louisans had taken to saying they'd been "peeking" through a crack instead of "peeping," and to using "cal'late" for

"reckon," (which latter is a perfectly legitimate word, as the ALTA readers may see by reference to the 18th verse of the 8th chapter of Romans;) and [I] heard them say "I admire to do so and so," (which is barbarous;) and heard them say "bosket" for basket, and "gloss" for glass; and "be you goin' home" for "are you going home;" and heard them say "she is quite pretty" when they meant "she is right pretty"—the one expressing perfection and the other merely a degree of excellence.

He picked up on the lingering sectarian bitterness in the city, a bitterness that would continue to taint American life for the rest of his and all of the next century.

Individual friends and whole families of old tried friends are widely separated yet— don't visit and don't hold any intercourse with each other. If you give a dinner party . . . invite Democrats only or Republicans only. Even Church congregations are organized, not on religious but on political bases; and the Creed begins, "I believe in Abraham Lincoln, the Martyr-President of the United States," or, "I believe in Jefferson Davis, the founder of the Confederate States of America."[3]

Sam's elegiac touch remained graceful: "one of the pleasantest things I noticed was, that those old-fashioned twilights still remain, and enrich all the landscape with a dreamy vagueness for two hours after the sun has gone down. It is such a pity they forgot to put in the twilight when they made the Pacific Coast."[4]

At church with Jane and Pamela, he was delighted when the Sunday-school superintendent approached his pew and asked him if he would say something inspirational to the children. Sam ambled to the altar and unloaded the jumping frog story to a cascade of applause, as the horrified deacon tried in vain to shush everybody up. He liked that. "So I preached twice in the Mercantile Library Hall."[5] The St. Louis *Republican* observed that he "succeeded in doing what we have seen Emerson and other literary magnates fail in attempting—he interested and amused a large and promiscuous audience."[6] He made an impulsive swing upriver for appearances in Hannibal, Quincy, and Keokuk. On April 2, Hannibal gave him the largest turnout in its history.

In St. Louis, one annoyance marred his lecturing triumphs. Before boarding the train back to New York, he noticed that a reporter for the *Missouri-Democrat,* evidently a lightning note-taker, had reproduced one of his Sandwich Islands talks so accurately that Mark Twain felt unable to repeat it in any other city. The reporter was a Welsh-born adventurer and journalist who had fought on both sides in the Civil War. Named Henry Morton Stanley, he was soon to gain worldwide fame for discovering the Scottish missionary David Livingstone, who had disappeared into Tanzania, greeting the object of his search with the words, "Dr. Livingstone, I presume?" Thirty years later, he and Mark Twain would become good friends.

Back in New York, Clemens transferred his residence from the "great caravan hotel" Metropolitan to the pricier Westminster, at 16th and Irving Place, a block east of Union Square. His new digs were "quiet, and genteel and orderly," he assured his *Alta* readers, "—costly, but . . . prodigiously comfortable." [7] The plate-glass windows on the ground floor allowed one to read one's paper, sip one's coffee, and look out at people caught in the rain, "and enjoy it ever so much!" [8]

On April 23, newspapers began to announce the venue for Mark Twain's debut lecture in New York: the two-thousand-seat Great Hall of the Peter Cooper Institute at Astor Place in what is now the East Village. This imposing five-story brownstone, better known as the Cooper Union, was already a city landmark: a pioneering academy for adult education and a leading lyceum. It bore the name of its founder, the self-made polymath with a perfect half-disk of a white beard who had designed the country's first steam engine, whose New York, Newfoundland & London Telegraph Co. had laid the first Atlantic cable in 1850, and who, with his wife Sarah, had invented the mixture that would form the basis of Jell-O.

Rental for the Cooper was five hundred dollars, which Fuller seems to have advanced out of his own pocket. Fuller chipped in another hundred to cover the advance publicity: handbills hung inside omnibuses, pads of paper to be torn off and carried away, newspaper ads, posters, even a pamphlet that inventoried thirty-eight topics to be covered in his talk. The approaching lecture with its make-or-break stakes had Sam nearly as nervous as he'd been in San Francisco before his lyceum debut.

He wanted an introduction from some eminence. His choice was James W. Nye, Orion's former boss as governor of Nevada, now a United States senator in Washington. Sam remembered Nye as an eloquent speaker out West: "His eyes could outtalk his tongue and this is saying a good deal, for he was a very remarkable talker, both in private and on the stump." [9] From the Westminster, filled with "bloated aristocrats"—himself not least among them—he wrote to the homefolks that Webb would publish the "Jumping Frog" on April 25. A few days earlier, looking to the future, he had commanded by postscript: "Scrapbook my letters in Alta." [10] Pamela got busy on it; the scrapbooked collection (which still survives) of printed letters to the *Alta* would provide much of the printer's copy for *The Innocents Abroad*.

Around that time, a New York agent for the *Alta* presented him with a letter that formally, and almost obsequiously, requested his services on the Holy Land excursion.

Your only instructions are that you will continue to write at such times and from such places as you deem proper and in the same style that heretofore secured you the favor of the readers of the Alta California.[11]

As the embarkation date approached, his expectations of the voyage approached the positively Tom Sawyerish. The ship, he told his readers,

is to be furnished with a battery of guns for firing salutes, by order of the Secretary of the Navy, and Mr. Seward has addressed a letter to all foreign powers, requesting that every attention be shown General Sherman and his party. We have got a piano and a parlor organ in the cabin, and a snare drummer, a base drummer and a fifer . . . If they have a choir in that ship I mean to run it. I have got a handsome state room on the upper deck and a regular brick for a room-mate. We have got the pleasantest and jolliest party of passengers that ever sailed out of New York, and among them a good many young ladies and a couple of preachers, but we don't mind them. Young ladies are well enough anywhere, and preachers are always pleasant company when they are off duty.[12]

In the same dispatch, Mark Twain plugged his debut as an author of books. "Webb has gotten up my 'Jumping Frog' book in excellent style, and it is selling rapidly," he told his readers. He was fudging. *The Celebrated Jumping Frog of Calaveras County, and Other Sketches* reached the booksellers at the end of April in less than "excellent style." Its two hundred pages, containing twenty-seven pieces, were littered with typographical errors, spelling inconsistencies, and unauthorized editorial changes—sixteen of those in the title piece alone, by Sam's count.[13] Only a thousand copies were initially bound. An additional 552 were bound on May 20, but in spite of favorable reviews, the book's sales were anemic.

    Cracks were also appearing all along the surface of the grandiose picture he had painted of his forthcoming ocean adventures. The largest crack he had known about for at least a month: the ostensible organizer and star attraction of the Holy Land excursion, Henry Ward Beecher, had elected not to go. For weeks, the New York papers had been referring to the great preacher's leadership role as an established fact, but on April 2, the Brooklyn *Eagle*—Whitman's old paper—broke the story that he and his family would stay behind. Beecher was said to be bowing to pressure from certain congregants who had paid their annual pew fees and objected to the discount implied by his planned five-month absence. His withdrawal threatened the viability of the excursion. Only seventy of the 110 berths were now reserved, at least in part because dozens of Plymouth Church members withdrew on Beecher's announcement. More bad news was to come on the shipboard-celebrity absquatulation front. But for now, Sam was facing a developing disaster at the Cooper Institute. With the Monday, May 6 lecture less than a week away, Senator Nye had not yet committed himself to introducing Sam on the platform. Sam sent

Frank Fuller to Washington to repeat the request in person. Nye signed a letter of assent, but then grew suspiciously quiet.

So had the public. Fuller's promotional efforts seemed to evaporate into the city's maw. The omnibus tearsheets were going unread, as Sam noticed during a few inspection bus rides. As for the small newspaper ads, they disappeared into surrounding columns of gray type. Advance ticket sales were comatose. Sam began to doubt whether anybody would show up. He pounced on Fuller, who was beginning to understand that running a railroad wasn't shucks to running Sam Clemens's career. Fuller dashed around to the papers, carrying copies of the letter that Senator Nye had signed and a list of ninety ex-Californians he'd prevailed on to issue a "call" for attendance by their fellow exiles. The notices ran on Sunday and Monday.

Clemens and Fuller had reason to be concerned about empty seats in the Great Hall. The future Big Apple was to be ablaze with attractions the night of the lecture. *The Black Crook* was on at Niblo's Garden, a ballet extravaganza with splashy stage sets, counts, villagers, star-crossed lovers, and show-stopping lyrics such as, "Hark, hark, hark / Hark the birds with tuneful voices / Vocal for our Lady Fair"—a proto-Broadway musical. A double troupe of "Imperial" Japanese jugglers was booked into the Academy of Music. The internationally acclaimed diva Adelaide Ristori was launching her series of farewell performances at the French Theater. Miss Naomi Porter was steaming things up at Tony Pastor's Opera House in *The Quaker's Temptations*. And the eminent Speaker of the House Schuyler Colfax was slated to deliver his lecture to benefit the Southern Famine Relief Commission at Irving Hall. Luckily, the New York Knickerbockers weren't playing night baseball yet.

"With all this against me I have taken the largest house in New York & cannot back water," he warned Jane and the family on May 1. "Let her slide! If nobody else cares, I don't." To Bret Harte, he asked, simply: "Pray for me."[14]

Fuller's legwork ultimately paid off. Suddenly the New York papers were belching notices that Mark Twain was going to talk about "Kanakadom, or the Sandwich Islands," at the Cooper on Monday night. "The gifted humorist from California," the *Citizen* called him, adding that it hoped he drew a good crowd.[15] The *Times* and the *Dispatch* plugged him, and the *Evening Express* and the *Tribune*. The *Stage,* a show business advertising circular, let on to its ten thousand readers that it spoke from a very deep and very personal relationship with the star in question: "Seth Twain is young, handsome, single and rich, and his future is altogether fair and promising."[16] All of which was gratifying, but not effective: advance sales at the box office remained flat.

A few days before the talk, "Seth" Twain instructed Frank Fuller to paper the house. It was an old trick: print complimentary tickets by the thousands and hand them out to anyone who would take them. Fuller knew that schoolteachers loved cultural events, especially free ones. He soon made sure that comps went out to every schoolteacher within thirty miles of the city.

Sam was in a cursing, frothing rage as he and Fuller left for the Cooper half an hour before curtain time on the night of May 6. His skin crawled inside the new claw-hammer suit and starched collar that Fuller had insisted he wear—the first such getup of his life. Worse, Senator Nye was nowhere to be found. Fuller refused Sam's plea to fill in for Nye with the introduction; he thought Sam should introduce himself.

His mood brightened when their carriage halted a block or so from the Cooper before an astounding swarm of people, horses and coaches. The streets around Astor Place were paralyzed with schoolteacher gridlock. Anyone foolhardy enough to drop a final "g" or misstate the principal export of Portugal within half a mile of the Institute risked being rapped across the knuckles with six thousand rulers.

Sam's spirits transformed once he was inside the hall, watching the house fill up from the wings. Well over two thousand people from the mob outside had managed to shoulder their way through the doors and form a cheek-by-jowl, standing-room throng inside the Great Hall. Perhaps twice that many were turned away. The lucky ones witnessed a drop-dead performance. Sam converted his anxieties into a performer's glee as he awaited the moment to take the stage. It was a stage already consecrated by history. Seven years and three months earlier, Lincoln had stood on these boards and made a last-ditch bid to save the Union with the light of reason. With the precision of a lawyer and the passion of a preacher—his talk was originally scheduled for Beecher's Plymouth Church—the presidential candidate had demolished the Southern Democrats' arguments that the Founding Fathers were indifferent to the expansion of slavery into the territories. Lincoln's Cooper Union address had annealed his support within the Republican Party, probably made the Civil War inevitable, and conferred the damning attention of political genius on the very social atrocity that had drawn Marshall Clemens to Missouri, and thus, indirectly, created the figure who, promptly at 7:30 p.m. Monday, May 7, 1867, slouched onto the Cooper Union stage, a Lincoln of literature in chrysalis.

Dapper in the claw hammer, its ebony fabric counterpointing his bright auburn hair, the stranger from the West began to speak, and the emerging American icon began to announce himself to the world beyond the West. Mark Twain's mastery of moment, material, and audience was complete; nothing could deflect him from triumph on this night. Certainly not the missing Senator Nye, who had ducked his commitment, he explained years later, because he had always privately considered Mark Twain a "damned secessionist." Mark Twain converted this potential humiliation into wicked stagecraft. "There was to have been a piano here, and a senator to introduce me,"[17] he mused aloud, rummaging the stage as the chuckles rippled. He did a few minutes of drawling patter at Nye's expense that drew screams of laughter from the knowing Washoe transplants in the audience. And then he swung into his lecture. For an hour and a quarter, he was in Paradise. "They laughed and shouted to my entire content," he reminisced.[18] The applause cascaded, and the reviews were pie. The *Times* reported that "from the appearance of their mirthful faces leaving the hall . . . few were disappointed . . . seldom has so large an audience been so uniformly pleased as the one that listened to Mark Twain's quaint remarks last evening."[19] "No other lecturer," wrote Ned House in the *Tribune*, "of course excepting Artemus Ward, has so thoroughly succeeded in exciting the mirthful curiosity, and compelling laughter of his hearers."[20]

The performance netted only about thirty-five dollars, at fifty cents apiece from the minority of paying customers. But the artistic success at the Cooper led him to repeat the lecture twice—in Brooklyn on May 10 and in Irving Hall, New York, six nights later. His new fans included the twenty-seven-year-old Thomas Nast, the illiterate German-born illustrator whose legacy would eventually include the images of Santa Claus, Uncle Sam, and Columbia; the Democratic donkey and the Republican elephant; and the political cartoons that led to the downfall and imprisonment of Boss Tweed. Nast wanted to tour the country with Clemens, with Nast drawing pictures as Mark Twain lectured. Clemens didn't have time.

The night after his Irving Hall talk, Sam ran into yet another seminal figure of his century. Lolling in front of the New York Hotel around midnight, talking with a clerk, he glanced up to behold Jefferson Davis, the former president of the Confederacy just recently released from prison, walking toward him in a party of people. "He is tall and spare—that was all I could make of him," Mark Twain told his readers. The spectral figure moved him to thoughts of greatness and oblivion.

He was a fallen Chief, he was an extinguished sun—we all know that—and yet it seemed strange that even an unsuccessful man, with such a limitless celebrity, could drop in our midst in that way, and go out as meekly as a farthing candle . . . The newspapers . . . gave the usual acres of laudation to [Adelaide] Ristori yesterday, and only a dozen meagre lines to Jefferson Davis, head, and heart, and soul of the mightiest rebellion of modern times . . . I am glad I am not Jefferson Davis, and I could show him a hundred good reasons why he ought to be glad he ain't me.[21]

THE FRIGID Eastern winter of 1867 gave way to spring. The promise of postwar Progress floated through the metropolis. The New York legislature approved a controversial plan to build a great suspension bridge over the East River, connecting Manhattan to Brooklyn for the first time. Whitman's *Leaves of Grass* enjoyed a fourth printing; his Self went again to the bank by the wood and became undisguised and naked. Sam was impatient for the *Quaker City* to fire up its boilers. He fretted about the prospects of his Sandwich Islands manuscript, which he had offered to the publishing firm Dick & Fitzgerald. He lined up the New York *Herald* and the *Tribune* for correspondence from the *Quaker City*. Then, somewhere around that time, the debonair toast of the Cooper Institute got himself thrown in jail for brawling on the street. He told his *Alta* readers about it in a letter that veered from bravado, to anger at the police, to acutely observed notes on mid-1860s New York City jailhouse culture. He didn't mind mentioning it, he averred, "because anybody can get into the Station House here without committing an offence of any kind. And so he can anywhere that policemen are allowed to cumber the earth." [22] It was all a mistake, he insisted. He and a friend had tried to break up a fight while heading home around midnight, "and a brace of policemen came up and took us all off to the Station House."

We offered the officers two or three prices to let us go, (policemen generally charge $5 in assault and battery cases, and $25 for murder in the first degree, I believe,) but there were too many witnesses present, and they actually refused.

    . . . I enjoyed the thing considerably for an hour or so, looking through the bars at the dilapidated old hags, and battered and ragged bummers, sorrowing and swearing in the stone-paved halls . . . I fell asleep on my stone bench at 3 o'clock, and was called at dawn and marched to the Police Court with a vile policeman at each elbow, just as if I had been robbing a church, or saying a complimentary word about the police, or doing some other supernaturally mean thing.[23]

He was detained for several more hours with a gaggle of jailbirds that included some psychic casualties from the recent war, all well dressed, but torn inside: a clerk, a college student, and an Indiana merchant. "Two had been soldiers on the Union side, and one on the other, and all had battled at Antietam together. The merchant was arrested for being drunk, and the other two for assault and battery." Also in the lockup was a Negro man, "with his head badly battered and bleeding profusely. He had nothing to say." [24] Sam found himself absorbed by a "bloated old hag," who

sat in the corner, with a wholesome black eye, a drunken leer in the sound one, and nothing in the world on but a dingy calico dress, a shocking shawl, and a pair of slippers that had seen better days . . . She . . . said she lived in the Five Points, and must have been particularly drunk to have wandered so far from home; said she used to have a husband, but he had drifted off somewhere, and so she had taken up with another man; she had had a child, also—a little boy—but it took all her time to get drunk, and keep drunk, and so he starved, one winter's night—or froze, she didn't know which—both, may be, because it snowed in "horrible" through the roof, and he hadn't any bedclothes but a window-shutter . . . and then she chuckled a little, and asked me for a chew of tobacco and a cigar . . . and then she winked a wink of wonderful mystery and drew a flask of gin from under her shawl, and said the police thought they were awful smart when they searched her, but she wasn't born last week . . . She said she was good for ten days, but she guessed she could stand it, because if she had as many dollars as she had been in limbo she could buy a gin-mill.[25]

The judge soon let him go. He continued sending New York dispatches to the *Alta,* while impatiently waiting for his ship to sail. Delays in the embarkation, and further crushing blows to the celebrity passenger list, had driven him to the point of believing that the *Quaker City* was never going to leave port. On May 25, the voyage lost its "lion." Captain Duncan had recruited General Sherman as the replacement star of the excursion after Henry Ward Beecher dropped out. Sherman's abrupt decision to honor his military duty and head west to fight Indians in the territories was seen in the press as a "bombshell" to the hopes of Duncan, who was trying to recover from bankruptcy and who had imagined the red-haired hero filling up the ship's berths and generating worldwide attention at every port of call. Instead, a new wave of cancellations resulted, reducing the complement to half the available space.

But the celebrity attrition had not ended there: the Drummer Boy of the Rappahannock drummed himself out of the lists to elope with his fiancée. On June 5, the exodus was joined by Fanchon the Cricket, along with her mother cricket. The passenger list stood at fewer than eighty-five. A few days earlier, Clemens had written to his mother:

> All I do know or feel, is, that I am wild with impatience to move—move—*Move!* . . . Curse the endless delays! They always kill me—they make me neglect every duty & then I have a conscience that tears me like a wild beast. I wish I never had to stop *any-where* a month. I do more mean things, the moment I get a chance to fold my hands & sit down than ever I can get forgiveness for.[26]

As for that companion in his stateroom,

> I am *fixed*. I have got a splendid, immoral, tobacco-smoking, wine-drinking, god-less room-mate who is as good & true & right-minded a man as ever lived . . . But send on the professional preachers—there are none I like better to converse with—if they ain't narrow minded & bigoted they make good companions.[27]

The roommate was a short, fat customer named Daniel Slote, a fortyish co-owner of a stationery-making firm in New York. Slote was a flamboyant fellow, and a wit. His wisecracks at the expense of tour guides, trinket hustlers, carriage drivers, and relic-touting priests would supply some of the excursion's more memorable quips and aphorisms, amidst a company distinctly lacking in zaniness.

Departure was finally set for Friday, June 7. On the day before, Sam jotted a note to Will Bowen that reflected the curious morbidity Bowen seemed often to activate in Sam.

> We leave tomorrow at 3:00 P.M . . . We have got a crowd of tiptop people, & shall have a jolly, sociable, homelike trip of it for the next five or six months. And then—if we all go to the bottom, I think we shall be fortunate. There is no unhappiness like the misery of sighting land (& work) again after a cheerful, careless voyage. They were

lucky boys that went down in sight of home the other day when the Santiago de Cuba stranded on the New Jersey shore . . . Good bye, my oldest friend.[28]

To Jane and the family in St. Louis, he abandoned his usual flippancy and opened up a more tender, even remorseful side of himself.

> I wish Orion were going on this voyage, for I believe with so many months of freedom from business cares he could not help but be cheerful & jolly . . . My mind is stored full of unworthy conduct toward Orion & toward you all, & accusing conscience gives me peace only in excitement & restless moving from place to place. If I could say I had done any one thing for any of you that entitled me to your good opinions (I say nothing of your love, for I am sure of *that*, no matter how unworthy of it I may make myself . . .) I believe I could go home & stay there—& I *know* I would care little for the world's praise or blame. There is no satisfaction in the world's praise, anyhow . . .[29]

In this last sentiment, he was speaking from limited experience. That was soon to change.

After finishing these letters, Sam Clemens left his hotel room for a night of Washoe-style dining and drinking with friends and newspaper editors—a nine-hour bender. The following afternoon, he made his way, woozily, through heavy rain to the piers at Wall Street, up the gangplank to the decks of the *Quaker City,* and into the company of some sixty-five unsuspecting American pilgrims,[30] whom he was about to immortalize beyond their wildest possible dreams, and fears.

19

Pilgrims and Sinners

(1867)

After a delay of two days in New York Harbor because of high seas, the *Quaker City* steamed off into the Atlantic, and Sam came fully to life again. To move—move—*Move!* reliably fired up his senses, as it had ever since he slipped onto the night packet out of Hannibal for St. Louis fourteen years earlier. The cares and anxieties of New York evaporated into the salt spray, just as the oppressions of San Francisco had lifted when he boarded the *Ajax* for the Sandwich Islands, and later the *America*, at Ned Wakeman's side, for his return from the West. "[T]here is always a cheering influence about the sea," he observed of this latest departure. In his berth, enjoying the rhythmic rocking against the waves, "I soon passed tranquilly out of all consciousness of the dreary experiences of the day and damaging premonitions of the future."[1]

Priding himself on his immunity from seasickness, Sam drank in the gladness in the air, the brightness in the sun, and the distress of one elderly passenger after another who lurched past him, hands clasped to the stomach, muttering, "*Oh, my!*"[2] The steamer pointed itself toward its first port of call, the Azores, off the coast of Spain. Beyond lay Europe and the Holy Land; and beyond those lay the ultimate destination for the captain, crew, and passengers: a niche in America's enduring memory as the Innocents Abroad.

The correspondent for the *Alta California*, who would take them there, found himself filling the "celebrity" vacuum created by the defaulting of Beecher, Sherman, the Drummer Boy, and Fanchon the Cricket. Captain Duncan had tacitly acknowledged this status just before departure, inviting Clemens to occupy the luxury upper-deck cabin originally reserved for General Sherman. Now, Sam quickly emerged as the entourage's most vivid, if not universally beloved, personality. "We have D.D.'s and M.D.'s—we have men of wisdom and men of wit," a genteel *Quaker City* passenger wrote to her husband's Cleveland newspaper after a few days at sea, under the demure pen name "Myra."

There is one table from which is sure to come a peal of contagious laughter, and all eyes are turned toward "Mark Twain," whose face is perfectly mirth provoking. Sitting lazily at the table, scarcely genteel in his appearance, there is nevertheless a something, I know not what, that interests and attracts. I saw today at dinner, venerable divines and sage looking men, convulsed with laughter at his drolleries and quaint original manners.[3]

The writer was the thirty-nine-year-old Mary Mason Fairbanks, former schoolteacher and presently the wife of Abel Fairbanks, owner and publisher of the Cleveland *Herald*. Her Cleveland friend, Emily Severance, agreed; to her, this Mark Twain was "the ruling spirit" of the voyage, "a capital person for ocean life."[4] Another shipboard correspondent, Miss Julia Newell of Janesville, Wisconsin, commented to her hometown *Gazette* on "the only notoriety we have . . . rather a handsome fellow." This fellow, the alert Miss Newell strongly suspected, harbored an intent "to be funny for the amusement of the party," although she judged the effort partly thwarted by his "abominable drawl," which she, for one, found exasperating.[5] A fourth approving female was the seventeen-year-old Emma Beach, daughter of Moses Beach, the New York *Sun* editor who was aboard. Sam and Emma developed an affection for each other that continued after the voyage, which led some in Emma's family to believe that he was courting her.

Mary Fairbanks and Julia Newell were only the latest to notice the "something" that drew people to the small, long-talking young man with the auburn hair and mustache. But they, and the other passengers, could scarcely suspect the power with which he had begun to notice *them*. For literary foils, Sam scarcely needed to aim his gaze. Wherever he glanced, characters wandered innocently into his crosshairs, plentiful as the population of a Dickens novel. He'd inventoried at least two before the ship left New York Harbor. "That Frenchy-looking woman with a dog—small mongrel black & tan brute," he scrawled in his notebook in regard to one passenger, whom he went on to sketch as "a married woman of 30, with dark skin, inclined to hairiness, & a general suggestion all about her of coarseness & vulgarity."[6] Of another: "He says the most witless things & then laughs uproariously at them . . . He laughs dreadfully at *every*thing & swears its good, d—d good, by George. I wish he would f—"[7] After a few days at sea, he homed in on yet another: "Stupid remarks & ? from ? every now & then—make him a character."[8]

He could scarcely get his fill of a bird of plumage who announced himself as the COMMISSIONER OF THE UNITED STATES OF AMERICA TO EUROPE, ASIA,

AND AFRICA. "I fell under that titular avalanche a torn and blighted thing," Mark Twain recalled.

I said that if that potentate *must* go over in our ship, why, I supposed he must—but that to my thinking, when the United States considered it necessary to send a dignitary of that tonnage across the ocean, it would be in better taste, and safer, to take him apart and cart him over in sections, in several ships.[9]

The abundance of these sorts of graying greenhorns and pious fuddy-duddys—so grating against Sam Clemens's temperament and therefore so priceless for Mark Twain's literature—was inevitable, given the *Quaker City*'s revised passenger list. The ship's company, originally conceived by Duncan as an array of the Eastern Protestant social aristocracy, garnished by celebrities from the military and the theater, had transmuted itself, week by downscaling week, into a sampling of the solid, and stolid *nouveau* American middle class. New Yorkers, Brooklynites, and Long Islanders still comprised a demographic majority, but cancellations and lagging sales had obliged Captain Duncan to accept bookings by wayfarers from such outposts as Plaquemine, Louisiana; Circleville, Ohio; Hydeville, Vermont; Aurora, Illinois; and Fulton, Missouri. Also represented were New Orleans, San Francisco, Boston, Pittsburgh, St. Paul, Elmira, and St. Louis. There was even a Hannibal fellow aboard: Dr. George Bright Birch, who joined Sam and his coterie on a trek to the Tomb of St. John in Samaria, where a small boy threw a rock at him. These "pilgrims," as Mark Twain designated them, tended to be pillars of the emerging Main Street community: financially successful, amply upholstered, gray-haired, and itching to prostrate themselves before the storied ruins and sacred shrines that they'd read about in travel books since their childhoods. Medical doctors, clergymen, retired military officers, and "professors" were well represented. Sanctimony ruled among them, flavored with naïveté, boorishness, and a rather un-Christian penchant for swiping relics from those self-same ruins and shrines once the prostrating was over with.

Not all of them, unsurprisingly, were as diverted as Mary Fairbanks by Sam's drolleries. Almost before the American landfall faded away, he had become for many the ship's bad boy: a card-playing, Sabbath-ignoring, horse-billiards-organizing,* tippling scourge whose language could occasionally leave one gasping for fresh air. Miss Newell had taken care to read the *Jumping Frog* book after learning that its author would be among the passengers, and she disclosed to the citizens of Janesville that in one passage, a description of how he cured a cold, "he profanely says: 'That after taking a quart of warm water or salt water . . . he thinks he threw up his immortal soul.' "[10]

This less than enchanted attitude toward the Wild Humorist of the Pacific

---

* In chapter 4 of *The Innocents Abroad*, Mark Twain describes this game as "a mixture of 'hopscotch' and shuffle-board played with a crutch" (p. 39).

Slope was well expressed by Colonel William R. Denny, of Winchester, Virginia, and late of the Confederate army, who opined in his journal that Mark Twain was a worldling and a swearer, and fingered him as a ringleader of the dubious nightly dances on deck. Mrs. Nina Larrowe, smarting several months later from the book that resulted, declared that she'd known right away that this Mark Twain was no good. "Why, why, he drank and he swore . . . When he went on to the Quaker City he was nobody and he resented that no attention was paid to him. Nobody thought he would ever be anything under the sun." [11]

Sam rejoiced from the get-go in their every foible, and noted it down: how they strove to become fluent in shipboard jargon, speaking carelessly of the "for'rard cabin" and the "fo'castle," and replacing "half-past six" with "seven bells"; how nearly half of them began the excursion as self-appointed "correspondents," scribbling away at long dining tables of an evening after prayer meeting (one of them ruefully admitted to him after a few days that he was "as much as four thousand pages behind hand");[12] how, during the nightly dances on the upper deck, "When the ship rolled to starboard the whole platoon of dancers came charging down to starboard with it . . . and when it rolled to port, they went floundering down to port with the same unanimity of sentiment." [13]

Sam insulated himself from the pilgrims inside a small group of younger bloods, whom he called the "Quaker City night-hawks,"[14] and, much later in his book, the "sinners." Their home base was Clemens's smoke-filled cabin, No. 10. Dan Slote, Sam's roommate, paid his dues with constant, inspired wisecracking. Equally droll and irreverent was the deadpan Dr. Abraham Reeves Jackson, the ship's surgeon ("The Doctor, in the narrative"), of Stroudsburg, Pennsylvania, who became a scourge of pesky tour guides. There was also John A. Van Nostrand ("Jack"), of Greenville, New Jersey. "Sinners" on the fringe may have included Frederick H. Greer, one of several models for "Blucher," of Boston, and Julius Moulton ("Moult"). Then there was a slim seventeen-year-old scion of the Elmira social elite, a youth suspended in that magical interlude between callow wonderment and heavy drinking. His name was Charles Jervis Langdon. His parents had nudged him aboard the *Quaker City* in the hope that a European/Middle Eastern voyage would enrich his intellect and spirit, and also, perhaps, to get him out of the house. Charley Langdon may have been the model for the character "Interrogation Point" in the book. More pertinently still, he had a sister.

"Brown" was present, too, for a while. In his first few letters back to the *Alta*, Mark Twain employed the make-believe vulgarian as he always had under the old conventions of the "frame" story: as the common man's ambassador, speaker of sentiments too frankly coarse (and vice versa) for the narrator of polite literature. "Brown" gradually died out of Mark Twain's dispatches, and remains absent from the revised account that became *The Innocents Abroad*. Mark Twain continued to assign pseudonyms to actual shipboard personalities, some of them composites; but in a stroke of intuition with profound results, he absorbed "Brown" into his own voice. For the first time, the author of a travel book spoke frankly as dissenting satirist as well as "responsible narrator." This liberating authorial scope brought Mark Twain to his full maturity as a literary artist, wrote "The End" to America's reflexive subservience toward Old World aesthetics and pieties, and gave *The Innocents* its lasting greatness.

After ten days of stormy seas, evening prayer meetings, nightly Bible study, and constant seasickness, the pilgrims fetched up at their first port of call, the Azores island of Fayal. They were carted ashore by Portuguese boatmen "with brass rings in their ears, and fraud in their hearts." [15] Sam and some friends sashayed down the main street, Mark Twain later noting tactfully how the high, wide hoods of the women resembled circus tents. "Blucher" sprang for dinner for ten, and turned white when he received the bill—twenty-one thousand seven hundred *reis*. He cheered up on finding that this equaled $21.70 in American dollars. Hiring some saddled donkeys, half a dozen of the men found themselves in an uncontrolled stampede. In *Innocents,* Mark Twain reports that Blucher's donkey darts inside a house, scraping Blucher off at the doorway; Blucher remounts, only to instigate a collision that has everyone piled up in a heap. His private notebook account of the episode, which he left unpublished, would have confirmed every dark suspicion of him among the good pilgrims.

The party started at 10 A.M. Dan was on his ass the last time I saw him. At this time Mr. Foster was following, & Mr. Haldeman came next after Foster—Mr. Foster being close to Dan's ass, & his own ass being very near to Mr. Haldeman's ass. After this Capt. Bursley joined the party with *his* ass, & all went well till on turning a corner of the road a most frightful & unexpected noise issued from Capt Bursley's ass, which for a moment threw the party into confusion, & at the same time a portughee boy stuck a nail into Mr. Foster's ass & he ran—ran against Dan, who fell—fell on his ass, & then, like so many bricks they all came down—each & every one of them—& each & every one of them fell on his ass. [16]

Back under way, the voyagers endured another week of gale-force winds and churning seas, and then, on the morning of June 29,

we were fairly within the Straits of Gibraltar, the tall yellow-splotched hills of Africa on our right, with their bases veiled in a blue haze and their summits swathed in clouds . . . On our left were the granite-ribbed domes of old Spain. [17]

Soon the Rock of Gibraltar loomed over the ship. As the passengers scampered ashore to investigate on muleback, Sam fastened his attention on a new object for his off-center reportage, the yammering local guide parroting the same packaged information as the next yammering guide, and the next one after him. After the third repetition of, "That high hill yonder is called the Queen's Chair," [18] and the long explanation why, the narrator-Twain begs for relief as a helpless orphan in a foreign land. He would encounter variations of this stock figure often; and, in lampooning them, further obliterate the proscenium between common reader and rarefied writer.

The Innocents were never far from his noticing eyes, and ears. He began to deepen his portraiture of the more interesting specimens, scarcely bothering to camouflage their real-world personas. The Oracle, in real life the blustery Dr. Edward Andrews of Albany, he presented as "an innocent old ass who eats for four and looks wiser than the whole Academy of France would have any right to look, and never uses a one-syllable word when he can think of a longer one."

. . . He reads a chapter in the guide-books, mixes the facts all up, with his bad memory, and then goes off to inflict the whole mess on somebody as wisdom which has been festering in his brain for years . . .[19]

But Mark Twain rather liked the Oracle, he averred. Less congenial to him were "a poet and a good-natured enterprising idiot on board, and they *do* distress the company." [20] The former tended to inflict his fellow passengers with such verse as "Apostrophe to the Rooster in the Waist of the Ship"; the latter, the selfsame "Interrogation Point," Mark Twain evaluated as "young and green, and not bright, not learned and not wise," [21] a lad capable of accepting uncritically the description of a mountain eight hundred feet high with a two thousand-foot-high tunnel running through it. The model for "Interrogation Point" was not among the many passengers outraged when they saw their foibles revealed to the world in print—fortunately for the sake of Sam Clemens's romantic hopes.

With the ship taking on coal at Gibraltar, Sam and a half-dozen others took a small craft to Tangier, with its 2,200-year-old Roman fountain. This was the first undiluted "foreign" locale Sam had experienced, a city out of the *Arabian Nights* teeming with cloaked Bedouins and turbaned Moors, "no white men visible." [22] Pretty soon Sam and his friends were wearing Moorish garb, too. The exotic atmosphere thrilled him. He seems to have half-imagined himself into antiquity; he stuffed his notebook (and much of a chapter) with straightforward details of the city's history and its ancient stories. He resurfaced long enough to note that "Blucher" jeopardized everyone's life by nearly riding his mule into a mosque. The pilgrims were all back at sea in time to celebrate the Fourth of July with cannon thunder at daylight. "In the afternoon the ship's company assembled aft, on deck, under the awnings; the flute, the asthmatic melodeon, and the consumptive clarinet crippled the Star Spangled Banner, the choir chased it to cover, and George came in with a particularly lacerating screech on the final note and slaughtered it. Nobody mourned." [23] Then, the following evening, the Mediterranean coast of France.

. . .

MARK TWAIN never met a genre he didn't like to lampoon, and travel literature was ripe for it.

Toward nightfall . . . we steamed into the great artificial harbor of this noble city of Marseilles, and saw the dying sunlight gild its clustering spires and ramparts, and flood its leagues of environing verdure with a mellow radiance that touched with an added charm the white villas that flecked the landscape far and near.

He added, in brackets, "[Copyright secured according to law.]"[24]
The positioning and the brio of this particular little spitball suggest that he was by now in charge of his own insurrectionary voice, and aware of its pulverizing potential upon all that had gone before it. He was lighting a dynamite fuse, as he knew, at the foundation of a venerated literary edifice. Since the 16th century, books of travel had found devoted readerships in Europe and then in America. Rich in character, description, and incident, books of travel spoke through their own stiff stylistic conventions to the human hunger for *story*, especially as the emphasis shifted from scientific observation to adventure. Their narrative discharge appealed in particular to Protestant readers, subscribers to a Puritan disapproval for the novel. These books spoke also to a lingering sense of estrangement. Many Americans harbored an instinctual desire, laced with anxiety, to make a reckoning with the Old World of their origins. Envious of Europe's historic continuity from their perspective of flux and change, cowed by European contempt for their still-new society as culturally bereft and a little barbaric, and always avid for tales of exotic lands, Americans loved to embark on these proxy journeys.

Not even the founding fathers of American literature were immune from this tug. Most (save Emerson) had written accounts of their transatlantic ramblings; most of these efforts generated only mild interest. Washington Irving produced his *Spanish Sketchbook* after living for most of 1829 in the crumbling Moorish palace, the Alhambra. The most visible monument to his scrupulous work of history and folklore is the Washington Irving Hotel (three stars, fully equipped bathroom, direct-dial phone), planted right next door to the Alhambra. James Russell Lowell (apartment complex in Kansas City) published a collection of his European travels. Nathaniel Hawthorne (House of Seven Gables in Salem, costumed guides) did not leave New England, but he crafted sketches from the remoter northern terrain in the 1830s; Henry Wadsworth Longfellow (poster available at $5.99 online) and James Fenimore Cooper (poster) were among others who traveled and wrote.

The reigning travel writer before Mark Twain's arrival on the scene was William Dean Howells's old idol, Bayard Taylor. The frustrated poet's popular books about Egypt, Africa, and China, along with his innovative practice of traveling for the purpose of writing about it, established him as America's first professional in the calling. Mark Twain was about to place Taylor, stylistically speaking, on a slow boat to China.

• • •

SAM ALIGHTED on French soil at a dead run, hired a guide, and hit the sightseeing trail, Dan and the Doctor (Jackson) in tow: "we only wanted to glance and go—to move, keep moving!"[25] Marseilles exposed these "travelers" for the tourists they were, and then exposed them to a new tourist phenomenon, the Ugly American. At a restaurant on that first night, the three rolled out their textbook French, only to see their hostess stare at them in bewilderment until one of them blurted something in his native tongue, which triggered the response: "Bless you, why didn't you speak English before?—I don't know anything about your plagued French!"[26] A night or so later, they were embarrassed by a boorish Yank who loudly instructed the restaurant at large in the virtues of drinking wine with meals, and brayed about how he was "free-born sovereign, sir, and American, sir, and I want every body to know it!"[27] His sort would soon be swarming the Continent.

The pilgrims toured the ancient prisons on the island Castle d'If, dank cells mythified by Dumas and the Man in the Iron Mask. Cells and dungeons formed a powerful claim on Sam's attention on this trip. Then Sam and his two sidekicks broke free from the *Quaker City* congregation that had already marginalized them and launched out on a weeklong rail odyssey through the heart of France. Arriving in "magnificent" Paris on July 6, Mark Twain suspended his facetious voice and opened himself to the city that had fired his imagination since his boyhood. Satisfying food in tidy restaurants, polite waiters, music in the air, brilliant streets, dainty trifles in the stores and shops. Even the mustaches on the Frenchmen knocked him out. En route the next morning to the International Exposition, which Sam had dreamed of taking in since Washoe days, the three were taken in by the first of several calculating rascal-guides who surface in *The Innocents Abroad*. The name on his business card was the most un-French "A. Billfinger." The three redubbed the man "Ferguson," a moniker that became the standard nickname for all guides thereafter.

Like his successors, this "Ferguson" became the tail that wagged the dog, enacting some of the scams that would remain familiar with Yank tourists across three centuries. He elbowed his way into their mealtime company and managed to gorge himself or pound down a bottle or two of wine; he ignored instructions to lead them to a given destination, and instead lured them into shops in which his connection to the proprietor appeared suspiciously keen. "I shall visit Paris again some day, and then let the guides beware!" vows Mark Twain in *Innocents*. "I shall go in my war-paint—I shall carry my tomahawk along."[28] Mark Twain plays his "Fergusons" for laughs, but the guides bear symbolic resonance as well. They make apt escorts through the wasteland of fraud, decay, anthill opportunism, and diminished expectations that would comprise Mark Twain's view of Europe at the dawn of modern tourism.

In time, the world headquarters of "modern tourism" would shift to America, with excesses of hucksterism, historic-site hype and souvenirmongering that would put the Old World to shame. Among the most energetically marketed "destination sites" of later centuries would be Hannibal, Missouri, where one could contemplate the house that Mark Twain lived in as a boy, pay admission to tour the cave he once explored, see a lock of his hair and articles of his clothing at the Mark Twain museum, purchase a T-shirt with his likeness, and have a dinner of Mark Twain Fried Chicken at the Mark Twain Dinette after a stirring ride on the Too-Too Twain.

If only he could have lived to skewer it. In his day, the hucksterism still had some class. Inside a "temple" at midnight in the suburb of Asnières, Ferguson, Sam, Dan, and the Doctor found themselves witnessing the dance already synonymous with French high culture.

. . . [T]he music struck up, and then—I placed my hands before my face for very shame. But I looked through my fingers. They were dancing the renowned *"Can-can."* A handsome girl in the set before me . . . grasped her dresses vigorously on both sides with her hands, raised them pretty high, danced an extraordinary jig that had more activity and exposure about it than any jig I ever saw before, and then, drawing her clothes still higher, she advanced gaily to the centre and launched a vicious kick full at her *vis-à-vis* [partner] that must infallibly have removed his nose if he had been seven feet high. It was a mercy he was only six.[29]

He happened upon another convergence with a decisive figure of his century—and in this case, of the next century as well. Standing on a board balanced on two barrels near the Arc de l'Étoile, Sam and his companions took in a parade that featured the crash of military bands, the national colors, file upon file of cavalry and artillery, and, finally, a great carriage bearing the leader of the Second French Empire, Napoleon III. His fellow passenger was Abdul Aziz of Turkey, Lord of the Ottoman Empire. Clemens ogled Napoleon, nephew of *the* Napoleon. Here was the escaped political prisoner, survivor of assassination attempts, president of France, victor in the Crimean War, rebuilder of Paris, and an architect of the 20th century's longest-running conflicts. It was Napoleon III who had violently established a French presence, in 1858, in Vietnam.

AT NOTRE Dame, a de rigueur stop for travel writers, the demands of descriptive prose seemed to weigh on Twain a little. "We had heard of it before," he wrote. ". . . [I]t was like the pictures."[30] He perked up a bit only after a visit to the Morgue—the sight of a purplish, swollen drowned man on a slanting stone reawakened his descriptive brio. Arriving back at the port of Marseilles, Mark Twain was delighted to learn that the *Quaker City*'s crew had waged a three-night dockside brawl with some British sailors, and had ended up kicking some major Britannia butt. "I probably would not have mentioned this war had it ended differently."[31] The excursion sailed on to Genoa, where Mark Twain rated the women the prettiest in Europe. (Frenchwomen, he'd noticed, tended to have large hands and feet, and mustaches, and eat garlic and onions.) At the Cathedral of San Lorenzo, his group was shown a chest that contained the ashes of St. John—the second set of these he'd seen. After being asked by a local cleric to admire a portrait of the Madonna painted by St. Luke ("We could not help admiring the Apostle's modesty in never once mentioning in his writings that he could paint"[32]), he did a little tallying of the relic count: a piece of the true cross in every church they'd gone into; about a keg's worth of the nails; the crown of thorns in three locations; and enough of the bones of St. Denis for them to duplicate him, if necessary.

Having exhausted the wonders of Genoa, Sam and his two "sinner" comrades escaped the *Quaker City* herd again, boarding a train to Milan and points east. They barreled toward a massed inventory of art, cathedrals, landmarks, relics, and curiosities that initially enchanted Sam, then excited his ravenous capacity to absorb minutiae and detail, and finally unleashed the full force of his indignation, which never quite subsided thereafter, and which annealed *The Innocents* as a liberating force in America's self-definition.

Like most of his books, *Innocents* is a grab bag of abrupt digression. A chilling memory, for example, evoked in Milan, became one of the more famous of his personal anecdotes in Chapter 18. His flashback occurred while a cathedral guide was showing the group a piece of sculpture: the anatomically perfect rendering of a man without skin. The figure's exposed veins, muscles, tendons, and tissues horrified Sam, and he knew at once that these would enter his dreams. This awareness propelled him instantly back to Marshall Clemens's law office, and the night when Sammy discovered the stabbed, glassy-eyed corpse in the moonlight. He ends his insertion of this incident with the thought, "I have slept in the same room with him often, since then—in my dreams."[33] The whiplash transition is vintage Mark Twain, an example of his indifference to narrative form or design. William Dean Howells expressed it best: Clemens "was not enslaved to the consecutiveness in writing which the rest of us try to keep chained to. That is, he wrote as he thought, and as all men think, without sequence, without an eye to what went before or should come after. If something beyond or beside what he was saying occurred to him, he invited it into his page, and made it as much at home there as the nature of it would suffer him."[34]

Sam's mood burned off as his entourage slogged through La Scala theater and a Roman amphitheater; and, inevitably, found themselves inside the ruin of a small church (or chapel) that harbored the best-known painting in the world, Leonardo da Vinci's *The Last Supper.* Here, faced with the opportunity to posture again before a treasure of Western culture, Sam turned as contrary as a Missouri mule. He planted his feet and gave it the most withering comeuppance since the Squatter punched the Dandy into the Mississippi. The work was battered and discolored, "and Napoleon's horses kicked the legs off most [of] the disciples when they (the horses, not the disciples,) were stabled there more than half a century ago."[35] He noted the dozen artists in the room, worshipfully copying the original, and said that he liked their work better. "Wherever you find a Raphael, a Rubens, a Michael Angelo, a Caracci, or a Da Vinci (and we see them every day,) you find artists copying them, and the copies are always the handsomest. May be the originals were handsome when they were new, but they are not now." [36]

Babbitt could not have put it better. But Mark Twain seems to have been after something subtler than mere yahoo bloviating. Art criticism wasn't the point; national assertion was. (As was deep-dyed Protestant suspicion of Catholic iconography.) For better or worse, America was a country focused on the future, not on the past; a country of innovation and technology and commerce, not of dead painters and broken-down shrines; a country accelerating toward the perfectibility of man, not one stagnating in ancient glories. Mark Twain saw that it was time for America to be proud of this fact and to face down its sneering European tormentors, like the unflinching gunfighters of Washoe. If there was one thing that got Mark Twain crazier than the Old Masters, it was his fawning countrymen who came to genuflect and to posture before their works.

They stand entranced before it [a da Vinci] with bated breath and parted lips, and when they speak, it is only in the catchy ejaculations of rapture:
   "O, wonderful!"
   "Such expression!"
   "Such grace of attitude!"
   "Such dignity!"
   "Such faultless drawing!"
   "Such matchless coloring!" [37]

He concluded: "I envy them their honest admiration, if it be honest . . . But at the same time the thought *will* intrude . . . How can they see what is not visible?"

When Mark Twain and his cohorts boarded a train for Como, on the shore of the lake that bore its name, his newfound malevolence toward things European intensified with every mile. The Italian women no longer simply had mustaches; they had beards, too. He took a look at storied Lake Como and decreed that Lake Tahoe was *much* finer. As for the rural countryside, "We were in the heart and home of priestcraft—of a happy, cheerful, contented ignorance, superstition, degradation, poverty, indolence, and everlasting unaspiring worthlessness." [38]

Venice, once the Autocrat of Commerce, Mother of Republics, was nothing but deserted piers, empty warehouses, vanished fleets. "She sits among her stagnant lagoons, forlorn and beggared, forgotten of the world." [39] The gondola that carried the trio to the hotel reminded him of a hearse. As for the gondolier, he was "a mangy, barefooted gutter-snipe with a portion of his raiment on exhibition which should have been sacred from public scrutiny" (his shirttail).[40] Mark Twain, Dan, and the Doctor investigated the Bridge of Sighs, where men walked to their incarceration, lunacy, and death under the Doges and the hulking Cathedral of St. Mark.

Amidst these pallid ornaments of a white European past, Sam Clemens encountered a figure who embodied a version of the future nearly unimaginable from Sam's own experience. Guiding the travelers through a trove of Renaissance art was a man who announced himself as the offspring of a South Carolina slave. The son of Missouri slaveholders, who had sneered as a teenager, "I reckon I had better black my face, for in these Eastern States niggers are considerably better than white people,"[41] had for the first time encountered a Negro who knew lofty things he did not—the meaning of the word "Renaissance," for instance. Sam was incredulous.

He is well educated. He reads, writes, and speaks English, Italian, Spanish, and French, with perfect facility; is a worshipper of art and thoroughly conversant with it . . . He dresses better than any of us, I think, and is daintily polite.[42]

In writing about this in *The Innocents*, he gave voice to a transitional opinion in his life and literature: "Negroes are deemed as good as white people, in Venice, and so this man feels no desire to go back to his native land. His judgment is correct."[43] As for Venice itself, the city reminded him of an Arkansas town under floodwaters. After similar cracks about Florence and Pisa, they went to Livorno (Leghorn), on the northwest coast of Italy, on July 25, where they reboarded the awaiting *Quaker City*. Sam felt as though he'd returned home. How jolly, how pleasant the ship was; how good the talk—probably because only about ten of the sixty-five "fossils" were aboard, the rest of them blessedly clattering around overland.

Their onboard stay was brief. The authorities at Leghorn refused to believe that the large steamer from America was merely a pleasure excursion; they prudently theorized that its cohort of Bible-clutching, teetotaling, middle-aged passengers was in fact a cabal of dangerous revolutionaries with ties to the swashbuckling Giuseppe Garibaldi, the scourge of the Papal States and eventually the unifier of modern Italy. Alerted to a possible military quarantine, Sam, Dan, and the Doctor slipped aboard a French steamer bound for Civita Vecchia, from where they hopped a train headed for Rome. Sam arrived in the Eternal City irritated by the obligation of finding something new to say about this most overwritten (and Catholic) of European capitals: "What is there in Rome for me to see that others have not seen before me? . . . What can I discover?—Nothing. Nothing whatsoever."[44] So he turned the point-of-view spotlight 180 degrees around, imagining himself a Roman traveler writing his impressions of America, and produced fifteen hundred words of mockery at Italian deficiencies: "I saw common men and common women who could read . . . [I]f I dared think you would believe it, I would say they could write, also . . . Jews, there, are treated like human beings, instead of dogs . . ."[45] He kept his imagination in high gear as his gaze returned to Rome. In describing the Coliseum in Chapter 26 of *Innocents*, he imagined ancient dry-goods clerks escorting young ladies to the contests and plying them with ice cream while gladiators carved one another up. He pretended to find an old copy of the *"Roman Daily Battle-Ax,"* which covered the carnage in the style of a Washoe drama critic:

He was not thoroughly up in the backhanded stroke [of the broadsword], but it was very gratifying to his numerous friends to know that, in time, practice would have overcome this defect. However, he was killed. His sisters, who were present, expressed considerable regret. His mother left the Coliseum . . . A matinee for the little folks is promised for this afternoon, on which occasion several martyrs will be eaten by the tigers.[46]

The three young men began to amuse themselves by playing dumb with their increasingly predictable guides rattling off their predictable spiels, and their deadpan wickedness made for some of the comic highlights of *The Innocents Abroad*. Their first target was "Michael Angelo," who seemed to be credited for every artistic relic in Italy. ("In Florence, he . . . designed everything, nearly, and what he did not design he used to sit on a favorite stone and look at, and they showed us the stone.")[47] Soon Sam, the Doctor, and Dan were turning it back on their guides: "Statoo brunzo." "By Michael Angelo?" "No—not know who." Then, at the Forum: "Michael Angelo?" A stare from the guide: "No— thousan' year before he is born." An obelisk: "Michael Angelo?" "Oh, *mon dieu,* genteelmen! Zis is *two* thousan' year before he is born!"[48]

Presented with a letter allegedly written by Christopher Columbus, the Doctor shrugs: "Why, I have seen boys in America only fourteen years old that could write better than that."[49] Then they hit upon a bit of shtick that gave them no end of pleasure: the soulful query raised about every personage mentioned to them" "Is—is he dead?" "That conquers the serenest of them," Mark Twain noted with evil satisfaction. "Our Roman Ferguson is the most . . . long-suffering subject we have had yet . . . We have enjoyed his society very much. We trust he has enjoyed ours, but we are harassed with doubts."[50]

This antic mood did not last. In Rome, a city that he found appallingly squalid, Sam beheld a dark dream world where suffering and cruel death had ruled for twenty-five Catholic centuries: a world of graves and tombs and torture chambers; of slaughter as a spectator sport; of the Catacombs where corpses rotted into skeletons; of the Capuchin Convent with its architecture of human bones; a world in which the radiant/terrible Jesus Christ of his Presbyterian boyhood ranked only fifth among holy personages, behind the Virgin Mary, "The Deity," Peter, and twelve or fifteen popes and martyrs.[51] He imagined himself and his friends "moldering away ourselves, and growing defaced and cornerless."[52] Escape from this gloom was at hand: "We will go to Naples."[53] He and his friends headed there by train on August 1, 1867.

• • •

SAM KEPT in touch with Jane Clemens and the family in St. Louis with upbeat letters along the route. He was less faithful to his professional obligations.
Like the amateur "correspondents" he'd privately ridiculed early in the voyage, he fell behind: of the fifty *Alta* letters he had contracted to produce over
the twenty-five-week round trip, he'd managed only five in five weeks, plus
one to the New York *Tribune*. But he had been corresponding on his own behalf. He wrote to Frank Fuller in New York, instructing his agent not to line up
any lecturing dates for him upon his return: "I have got a better thing, in
Washington. Shall spend the winter there." [54] Sam had been offered a position
as private secretary to William M. Stewart, the Republican senator from
Nevada, whom he had known in Washoe. Two days later, Sam accepted
Stewart's offer, and conjectured to his mother that he could secure an office
for Orion as well. Orion was frantic for work; he had begged for a position as
a job-printer in several shops in St. Louis, and had been ignored or turned
down.

The "sinners" made an ascent of Mount Vesuvius and viewed some
volcano-rendered skeletons at Pompeii. The anonymous bones and brief inscriptions led him later to insert a fake historical note "forty centuries into the
future" that revealed the "unsubstantial, unlasting character of fame" as it
touched a certain Civil War hero.

URIAH S. (or Z.) GRAUNT—popular poet of ancient times in the Aztec provinces of
the United States of British America. Some authors say flourished about A.D. 742; but
the learned Ah-ah Foo-foo states that he was a cotemporary of Scharkspyre, the English poet, and flourished about A.D. 1328, some three centuries *after* the Trojan war
instead of before it. He wrote 'Rock me to Sleep, Mother.' [55]

On the morning of August 11, the *Quaker City*—its passengers fully united for
the first time in several weeks, dominoes and prayer meetings rampant—
sailed for Piraeus, the port of Athens. Here the tenor of *The Innocents Abroad*
subtly changes: Sam's distaste for Europe's fetishizing of its Christian history
gives way to awe in the presence of a more ancient, phantasmal past—"the
great Past," Mark Twain called it, the past of Agamemnon and Achilles. He felt
a compulsion to touch it. Quarantined yet again outside the harbor—
another cholera scare—the *Quaker City* passengers could only gaze wistfully
through telescopes at the square-topped Acropolis and the Parthenon that
crowned it. Disembarking was forbidden. Rumors of punishment by prison
sentences swept the ship. "Forbidden" had inflamed Sam as a boy, as it did now.
He enlisted three other daredevils, including William Denny, the same Denny
who had branded Sam a worldling and a swearer in his journal. Sam privately
returned the distaste, but he had begun to cultivate the ex-Confederate
officer's friendship for strategic reasons. Drs. Birch and Jackson were the other
two cohorts. [56] Around midnight, the four paddled ashore in a small boat and
made for the Acropolis. Twice, they were spotted; twice, they went unchal-

lenged. They stole some grapes and were shouted at. Thwarted before a locked gate, they made noises that emptied a garrison of four Greek guards, who accepted a bribe to let them in.

Before us, in the flooding moonlight, rose the noblest ruins we had ever looked upon—the Propylæ; a small Temple of Minerva; the Temple of Hercules, and the grand Parthenon.[57]

But it was not these antiquities that dominated Sam's imagination: it was something else, something suggested by the terrifying profusion of marble statues, many of them fragmented, which confronted him and his friends.

. . . some of them armless, some without legs, others headless—but all looking mournful in the moonlight, and startlingly human! . . . The place seemed alive with ghosts.[58]

Here, amid the oldest remnants he had ever seen, in a place as far as he had yet traveled—5,700 miles from Hannibal, nearly a quarter of the way around the globe—Sam Clemens found himself back in a kind of home. Here was the living dream world, the world inhabited by the Golden Arm; the world where Henry floated, and the essence of Laura Wright, and presences still waiting to reveal themselves. The moonlight melted the present into the past, reality into fantasy: gleaming Athens below them, the Temple of Theseus, Plato, Demosthenes, Mars Hill, Xenophon, Herodotus, the Bema, St. Paul. A biblical passage played at the edges of his mind. Its words eluded him, but later he looked them up. It was St. Paul's reproach to the Athenian men for their worship of idolatry, as recounted in Acts 17.

Then Paul stood in the midst of Mars hill, and said, Ye men of Athens, I perceive that in all things ye are too superstitious;

For as I passed by and beheld your devotions, I found an altar with this inscription: TO THE UNKNOWN GOD. Whom, therefore, ye ignorantly worship, him do I declare unto you.[59]

It was a Twainian moment, a youthful prank, in the service of comic writing that touched deep dreams and fears.

BACK ON board the ship, he headed east through the Dardanelles and into the Hellespont, Turkey's flags visible on the shoreline; into the Golden Horn, and a brief stop at Constantinople—"the very heart and home of cripples and human monsters,"[60] where one could see a three-legged woman and a man with his eye in his cheek. He disapproved of "Mohammedan" morals: "They say the Sultan has eight hundred wives. This almost amounts to bigamy. It makes our cheeks burn with shame to see such a thing permitted here in Turkey. We do not mind it so much in Salt Lake, however."[61] Then, up the

Black Sea to Russia. Brief stops at Sebastapol and Odessa, and then southward again, to Yalta, where they arrived on August 25. Here commenced an unscheduled two-day hobnob with emperors, empresses, dukes, and duchesses that had Sam gushing in his letters home.

The Yalta stop was about business. The *Quaker City*'s owners were looking to unload the vessel, a fact not made prominent in the tour prospectus, and the tour was arranged partly to showcase her. Yalta harbored one of the residences of Aleksandr Nikolaevich Romanov—Czar Aleksandr II, the liberator of the serfs from a lineage of despots. The *Quaker City* money men considered the tsar a likely customer. Sam and the other passengers, just dimly aware of the sale notion, dismissed any thought that an emperor of Russia would take the slightest interest in their presence. To their surprise, the emperor sent an invitation, and the pilgrims elected sinner Sam to draft an acceptance. "The whole tribe turned out to receive our party," an incredulous Sam wrote of the palace visit on August 26.[62] He added later, "[T]he Emperor of Russia and his family conducted us all through their mansion themselves. They made no charge. They seemed to take a real pleasure in it."[63] Abandoning his jaundice, he detailed the royal family's simplicity of dress, their courtesy, their ability to speak English, the charm of the fourteen-year-old Grand Duchess Marie, the tsar's daughter. As for the tsar,

He is very tall and spare, and a determined-looking man . . . It is easy to see that he is kind and affectionate. There is something very noble in his expression when his cap is off.[64]

In his book, Mark Twain detailed his attempts to get his mind around the power of the man whose word could send ships flying through the waves, locomotives speeding across the plains, multitudes to do his bidding.

I had a sort of vague desire to examine his hands and see if they were of flesh and blood, like other men's. Here was a man who could do this wonderful thing, and yet if I chose I could knock him down . . . If I could have stolen his coat, I would have done it. When I meet a man like that, I want something to remember him by.[65]

Sam's notion of the tsar's enchanted rule over a happy kingdom was a bit idealistic—Aleksandr II was assassinated by revolutionaries in 1881, and his grandson Nicholas II was inconvenienced by the Russian Revolution. But at the time he had a rose-colored view: at Yalta he'd danced an astonishing Russian dance for an hour with a pretty girl ("I have never ceased to think of that girl . . . Her dear name haunts me still in my dreams"[66]), and, better still, he got to see some ladies bathing naked near the ship.

ON SEPTEMBER 5, the *Quaker City* pilgrims arrived at Smyrna, their portal into the Holy Land. Just before the passengers disembarked at Smyrna Bay, something had happened to Sam (or so he later claimed): a small moment, but one that would gain force in his imaginative memory until, when he spoke of it thirty-nine years later to the ever-credulous biographer Albert Bigelow Paine, it had taken on the proportions of an omen. He'd wandered into young Charley Langdon's cabin, and Charley had handed him an ivory miniature for a look. On its surface was a tiny portrait of Charley's twenty-two-year-old sister, Olivia. No painting of that description of Samuel Clemens's future wife survives. A famous porcelaintype of Olivia made in 1868—she is looking off across her right shoulder, her hair done up behind, a knotted bow at her neck—is widely accepted as the image Charley handed to Sam, but that is because a Langdon family member later misidentified it to Paine. That and one other porcelaintype image, along with a watercolor miniature of her in 1864, show a young woman more ethereal than beautiful, with rather narrow-set eyes under dark brows; a small, composed mouth; and the sort of ears that might have drawn tugs from her schoolmates.

Mark Twain told Paine that he regarded the image as "something more than a mere human likeness," [67] and asked Charley if he could have it (Charley said no). Perhaps all this is true; perhaps it is the bit of necessary mythologizing—the "Laura Wright moment"—that weaves through Mark Twain's memories of the people whom he loved, or hated, most intensely.

Reconnoitering the city then known as "Beirout" on September 10, the *Quaker City* passengers broke into smaller groups. The most ambitious of these would tackle "the long trip," a trek fifty-five miles southeast to Damascus, then 150 miles south to Jerusalem, across treeless, sun-scorched terrain. The organizer was Colonel Denny, Methodist Sunday-school teacher and the excursion's ranking authority on biblical history. Denny had spent the Atlantic crossing absorbed in his Holy Land guidebooks—books that Sam had grabbed and devoured as soon as Denny set them aside. With his newspaperman's avidity for a good source, Sam began lobbying for a place in the colonel's entourage. Denny put him off: his lifelong wish was about to come true, and he wasn't going to have it ruined by a trashmouth like Sam Clemens.[68] Sam prostrated himself. He promised that he would refrain from uttering one naughty or in-vain word for the duration of the trek. Denny relented, and Sam came aboard, along with Dan Slote, Jack Van Nostrand, and Julius Moulton of St. Louis. They joined "pilgrims" Denny; Dr. George Birch, a plump and somber gentleman from Hannibal; and two others who really pushed Sam's buttons: the well-named William F. Church of Cincinnati, and Joshua William Davis of New York. The group delegated three of its members to procure pack mules, supplies, and guides. Sam passed the time strolling the city, its bright houses and streets yet more than a century away from bombardment. The women "cover their entire faces with dark-colored or black veils . . . and then expose their breasts to the public." [69]

When Sam saw what his cohorts had negotiated, he was staggered. For five dollars a day apiece, in gold, they would be accompanied by nineteen servants tending twenty-six pack mules that bore five circus-sized tents; eight iron bed-steads, each with its own mattress, pillows and sheets; washbasins, pewter pitchers, and towels; carpets; candlesticks; cutlery; and a menu that included roast mutton, chicken, and goose; bread, tea, pudding, and apples, and cof-fee. Camping on Jackass Hill was never like this.

Despite these luxuries, dyspepsia permeates Mark Twain's reportage of the Damascus trek—and the rest of *The Innocents Abroad*. He was infuriated that the pilgrims collapsed an arduous three-day journey into two, so as to avoid travel on the Sabbath. Beside himself at the toll this took on the horses, Mark Twain raged, "It was not the most promising party to travel with and hope to gain a higher veneration for religion through the example of its devo-tees."[70] He plastered the "sinner" label on these hypocrites, "whose idea of the Saviour's religion seems to me distorted."[71] Mark Twain's descriptions of temples and ancient city walls from here on out were offset by bursts of dismay at the poverty he saw everywhere, and the shriveled, sickly, fly-bitten people who were its victims. Gray lizards caught his eye, and yellow, barren desert, and dust, and emptiness. It was as though he had been jilted yet again: the physical Holy Land was as devoid of the numinous as was his spiritual land-scape. Even the grapes were smaller than the Sunday-school books had de-picted them.

Leaving Damascus, the group endured temperatures so hot that Sam thought he could distinguish each ray of sun as it struck his head. The Ameri-cans were wrapped in white, festooned with green sun goggles, clutching white umbrellas. "I thanked fortune that I had one, too, notwithstanding it was packed up with the baggage and was ten miles ahead."[72] At the village of Banias, he brooded on the "incorrigible pilgrims," who

have come in with their pockets full of specimens broken from the ruins. I wish this vandalism could be stopped. They broke off fragments from Noah's tomb; from the ex-quisite sculptures of the temples of Baalbec; from the houses of Judas and Ananias . . . from the worn Greek and Roman inscriptions set in . . . the Castle of Banias; and now they have been hacking and chipping these old arches here that Jesus looked upon in the flesh. Heaven protect the Sepulchre when this tribe invades Jerusalem![73]

This, along with the Sabbath tongue-lashing and other sarcasms directed at the "tribe" through the rest of the book, would arouse outrage among them after *The Innocents Abroad* was published. Which was more or less what Mark Twain intended.

AT TIBERIAS, the pilgrims came alive with excitement. Here lay Galilee, the sea the Apostles sailed, and whose waters Jesus bestrode. "To stand before it in the flesh . . . to sail upon the hallowed sea, and kiss the holy soil that compassed it about," Mark Twain wrote, "these were aspirations they had cherished while a generation . . . left its furrows in their faces and its frosts upon their hair." [74] Mark Twain watched as these middle-aged innocents, frantic to "take shipping" on waters, hailed a passing ship and asked their newest "Ferguson" to find out the price:

"How much? . . . how much to take us all—eight of us, and you—to Bethsaida [i.e., the other side] . . . we want to coast around every where—every where!—all day long!—*I* could sail a year in these waters! . . . ask him how much?—any thing—any thing whatever!—tell him we don't care what the expense is!"

Ferguson told the pilgrims that the boatman wanted two Napoleons, the equivalent of eight dollars. One or two countenances fell. Then a pause.

"Too much!—we'll give him one!"

I never shall know how it was—I shudder yet when I think how the place is given to miracles—but in a single instant of time . . . that ship was twenty paces from the shore, and speeding away like a frightened things! Eight crestfallen creatures stood upon the shore . . .[75]

The pilgrims caved in and offered the two Napoleons, shouting themselves hoarse, but it was too late.

How the pilgrims abused each other! Each said it was the other's fault, and each in turn denied it. No word was spoken by the sinners—even the mildest sarcasm might have been dangerous at such a time.[76]

Well, not exactly. Sam overheard a sarcasm of inspired sacrilege uttered by Jack Van Nostrand, but waited until his late-life biographical interviews with Paine to disclose that as the older men reeled over the two-Napoleon fee, and the boat receded, the young sinner turned to the fuming colonel and asked, "Well, Denny, do you wonder now that Christ walked?" [77]

The "boatman" episode marks a turning point in Mark Twain's reportage. For the first time, he brings his fellow passengers into the narrative for truly critical scrutiny. He draws a distinction between the older "pilgrims" and his group of "sinners." He makes it clear where his sympathies lie—a groundbreaking switch of allegiance in an America that still reflexively lined up on the Puritan side of any good-versus-evil dichotomy. From this point on, the misbehavior of the pilgrims was fair game to Mark Twain.

In Jerusalem, at the tomb of Adam, Mark Twain's satirical voice stirred again.

There is no question that he is actually buried in the grave which is pointed out as his . . . because it has never yet been proven that that grave is not the grave in which he is buried.

In one of the book's best-known passages, Mark Twain erupts in mock grief.

The fountain of my filial affection was stirred to its profoundest depths, and I gave way to tumultuous emotion. I leaned upon a pillar and burst into tears. I deem it no shame to have wept over the grave of my poor dead relative . . . [H]e died before I was born—six thousand brief summers before I was born. But let us try to bear it with fortitude.[78]

At Bethlehem, they paused near the walled olive garden where the shepherds saw the angels on the first Christmas. "[T]he pilgrims took some of the stone wall and hurried on." [79] A visit to the grotto where Christ was born. And then a long downhill trek to the Mediterranean coast. At the end of September, the passengers reassembled on the ship from their various expeditions. The end was drawing near.

After a stop at Alexandria, the *Quaker City* steamed west across the Mediterranean on October 7, the first leg of the voyage back home to an America-that-was-becoming.

It is fair to say that Mark Twain remained unswayed by the charms of the Holy Land. Magdala? "Not a beautiful place," he'd told his readers. "It is thoroughly Syrian, and that is to say that it is thoroughly ugly, and cramped, squalid, uncomfortable and filthy." Galilee? "Dismal and repellant." The Dead Sea? "It is a scorching, arid, repulsive solitude." Palestine? "Desolate and unlovely." Cheops? "A corrugated, unsightly mountain of stone." The region as a whole? "No Second Advent," he scrawled in his notebook—"Christ been here once—will never come again." His judgment was not unremittingly negative. In one of the last thoughts that he entered from Europe in his notebook, he conceded,

Tomb of the Virgin would draw in New York.[80]

20

In the Thrall of Mother Bear

(October 1867–New Year's Day 1868)

Strained civility and moody games of dominoes ruled the shipboard atmosphere during the voyage home. The passengers had been at close quarters for six months, save for overland excursions, and most of them were bored to death with one another. Among the few enthusiasms that united many of them were degrees of disrelish for Sam Clemens. Complaints to Captain Duncan about Sam and his fellow "fast young men" escalated. They had mostly endured Sam's outlaw ways, these gray-haired Christian citizens, during the outward voyage. His card playing, his smoking, his champagne guzzling, his wisecracks, his swearing—these failings could be tolerated as long as Sam and his friends confined their debauchery to cabin No. 10, or at least to the forward deck, which they generally did. Bad publicity about the pilgrims back home—that was something else entirely.

In October, Mark Twain's lampooning of his fellow passengers had completed the loop from the *Quaker City* to American newspapers and back again to the ship. It was during a weeklong stopover at Gibraltar that the passengers got their first inkling of how they were being depicted in print. Sam and the "sinners" were away from the ship when the evidence arrived via mail from America. Amid the letters and newspapers was the September 19 New York *Tribune,* carrying Mark Twain's letter describing the visit to the tsar. It reported in part that the Russians were

able to make themselves pleasant company, whether they speak one's language or not, but our tribe can't think of anything to do or say when they get hold of a subject of the

Czar who knows only his own language . . . However, one of our ladies, from Cleveland, Ohio, is a notable exception to this rule. She escorts Russian ladies about the ship, and talks and laughs with them, and makes them feel at home . . . I wish we had more like her.[1]

Another letter, signed "United States Officer" in the Brooklyn *Eagle*, characterized the *Quaker City* passengers as "a hard, rough-looking set of people; mostly backwoodsmen and country farmers" that included, "as 'Mark Twain' expresses it, 'thirteen women and two ladies,' besides a party of fast young men."[2] The letter was likely written by an American naval officer who'd visited the ship. The passengers would have recognized the source, even if the officer hadn't mentioned it. Sam and his friends boarded the *Quaker City* at Cadiz on the morning of October 25, unaware of the furor on board. Sam was rescued from the passengers' wrath by Charley Langdon, who intercepted the arrivals and gave them a quick summary of what had happened, and of which passengers were mad about it, and how mad. Sam slipped into cabin No. 10 and stayed there for a few days, until certain tempers had cooled down. He began a play that mocked the prissiness of his shipboard critics. One of the characters, no doubt echoing an actual complaint, whined of Sam's crowd:

They drink & drink & drink, in that No. 10 till it is horrible—perfectly *hor*rible! And they smoke there—which is against the ship's rules . . . & they burn safety lanterns there all night (which is against the rule, too) & say they are writing to the newspapers—which is a *lie*, brethren & sisters—they're playing sinful 7-up.[3]

Sam's relations with Captain Duncan had not improved since the day Sam arrived drunk to sign up for the voyage. Sam tallied up his grievances against the captain in his notebook ("No swapping false teeth allowed,"[4] he'd written in parody of the Duncan's tiresome regulations), but held back his public skewering until after the voyage.

When Sam eased back into life on deck, he gravitated toward those eight or so "respectable" travelers who had welcomed his company on the voyage out. He was looking for practical information. He knew that when he arrived back in America, his rough Western manners and speech would not be accepted, even as novelty traits. He had published a book in New York. He had spoken at the Cooper Institute. He was a candidate for inclusion among the Eastern literary men who mattered. It was time that he started figuring out the rules of the lodge.

Solon Long Severance, an elegant banker-intellectual from Cleveland, and his literate and beautiful wife, Emily, were reliably sophisticated, and open to his company. Moses Sperry Beach, the New York *Sun* editor and Plymouth Church stalwart, was companionable—though Mark Twain's slur against the *Quaker City* ladies prompted a letter of rebuttal from him, published in the *Sun*. Young Emeline Beach remained a chess partner and attractive friend. So did three or four others: the witty Dr. Abraham Reeves Jackson, just then launching an adulterous, ultimately successful courtship of Julia Newell, who was also part of this group; the twenty-year-old Van Nostrand; the youthful churchgoer Julius Moulton of St. Louis; and Charley Langdon, the scion of Elmira wealth who had ingratiated himself to Sam in a couple of ways. (Dan Slote, a candidate for this group, had left the ship at Alexandria.) But it was the central figure in this circle who overshadowed all the others in her "sivilizing" influence on Sam, and whose lifelong friendship bore most powerfully on his literary career.

Mary Mason "Mother" Fairbanks was for Sam the anti-Menken, a beacon of Eastern womanhood unsullied by body stockings, or the debauchery of folding her scarf carefully upon entering a room. She was religious without making a big deal about it; an intellectual (fluent in French, at ease with art); a dispenser of good sense; a graceful if somewhat flowery essayist. Ohio-born, a product of the Troy Female Seminary in New York State, she had been a schoolteacher in South Carolina before marrying the Cleveland newspaper owner and publisher Abel Fairbanks. Brooched, braided, and brocaded, plump and tidily "handsome" rather than beautiful at the verge of forty, she had a touch of the Mona Lisa in her gaze, but a Mona Lisa with apple tarts in the oven. Sam adored her. She fed him Egyptian jam when he behaved, and sewed his buttons on.

Ever since the ship headed west from Alexandria, she'd been the young journalist's sounding board. As Sam buckled down to his backlog of newspaper correspondence, he began reading his letters aloud to the small circle of receptive sophisticates. On October 13, Charley Langdon gave his mother an unwitting introduction to her future son-in-law:

> I have been hearing Clemens Holy Land letters. I do wish you could hear them, they are characteristic of him[.] I do not like them as a whole but he says some good things. They are going to the Cal. Alta, so unless you have sent for that paper you wil not see them.[5]

Charley commented more favorably on the *Tribune* letters, and asked his family to save them. But Mary Fairbanks was the only listener whose criticisms mattered to Sam.

For a century, a cloud of conjecture has hovered over the effect of women, "Mother" Fairbanks prominently among them, on Mark Twain's literary development (or the stunting of it). The Cleveland matron is the middle figure of a three-headed hellhag who, under the Freudian template of Mark Twain interpretation, leeched the writer's precious raw Western genius, turning him into a literary girlie-man. (A more recent feminist theory played a variation on this tune: Mark Twain, at once patriarchal and terrified of women, viewed creativity as "illegitimately sexualized, a threateningly uncontrollable power," which was even worse than the usual male pathology of adopting "the model of the pen-penis disseminating its writings on the virgin page.")[6]

The first head is that of the guilt-sorceress Jane Clemens, and the third belongs to the ruthlessly domesticating Olivia Langdon/Clemens.

Did the influence of these women on Mark Twain correspond to this schematic theorizing—theorizing that influenced Mark Twain studies for much of the 20th century? Mrs. Fairbanks certainly would have liked to think so. Playing Margaret Dumont to Sam's Groucho, she did her high-Victorian best, aboard the *Quaker City* and for years afterward, to haul Clemens's voice upward into the high zephyrs of "polite" (read: forgettable) discourse. She enjoyed certain triumphs. In alliance with Olivia, Mother Fairbanks exhorted and applauded Mark Twain through his composition of *The Prince and the Pauper,* the first of his two self-consciously "literary" novels. She showered her blessings on the second—*Personal Recollections of Joan of Arc*—though it was written specifically as a bouquet to his idolized daughter Susy. Her influence was important, and yet the trajectory of Mark Twain's ambitions suggests that reports of his debt are exaggerated. The real objective of his interest in Mrs. Fairbanks's opinions, or Livy's, or those of any man or woman willing to share them, was guidance on how far he could push the boundaries of propriety as defined by the Eastern neo-Calvinists, and still hold on to the views, voice, and vernacular that defined his soul.

Mary Fairbanks's influence on the *Alta* letters was representative of the necessary guidance Mark Twain was seeking. She restrained (and thus added to the powers of) his Washoe-honed impulses toward slang and insolence. When reviews of his books began emanating from Boston and New York, they ratified her moderating instincts, but they also ratified the essential Mark Twain. Puritan standards of "edifying" literature still mattered in the East; but readers were ready for something new—specifically, a truth-teller. Thus Mark Twain's bold comic voice was approved, even celebrated, so long as he could satisfy readers that his humor was not "mean," and so long as he counterbalanced it with passages of eloquence and wisdom, and kept it psychologically accurate. When he stayed within these rather inexact boundaries, he was permitted to demonstrate, as no one had before him, that humor and thematic seriousness were not incompatible. When he stepped over the hazy line, his satire came in for severe scolding.

That audacious new voice rings through these dispatches. His contempt for pietistic art and his eagerness to debunk fraudulent relics survived, or defied, Mrs. Fairbanks's censoring eye; as did his mockery of current standard travel literature; and his de-romanticized appraisals of Holy Land dwellers and terrain; and his chronicling of assorted naked bathing ladies and exposed breasts; and his depictions of hypocrisy and foolishness among the churchly passengers.

True, he succumbed to brief dalliances with "polite" literature in later years, but these hardly defined his life's work. In between them, after all, he wrote *Huckleberry Finn* and the apocalyptic *A Connecticut Yankee in King Arthur's Court.*

One of the first letters Mark Twain wrote after the *Quaker City* left Cadiz, one doubtless not known to Mrs. Fairbanks, was a private letter to Joe Goodman, and it scarcely reached for euphemism regarding the pilgrims.

Between you and I, (I haven't let it out yet, but am going to,) this pleasure party of ours is composed of the d——dest, rustiest, [most] ignorant, vulgar, slimy, psalm-singing cattle that could be scraped up in seventeen States. They wanted Holy Land, and they got it . . . [I]t is an awful trial to a man's religion to waltz it through the Holy Land.[7]

Mark Twain expanded and syntactically enhanced his chronicling of the *Quaker City* voyage from initial drafts to the printer's copy of *Innocents.*[8] But most of this revision occurred after the letters had been published, when he used them as the foundation of his book in progress. For instance, in a coda appended to the celebrated "boatman" scene, he stipulates,

Lest any man think I mean to be ill-natured when I talk about our pilgrims as I have been talking, I wish to say in all sincerity that I do not . . . They are better men than I am . . . they are good friends of mine, too . . . I wish to stir them up and make them healthy; that is all.[9]

This and other revisions, of course, may well have been in keeping with Mrs. Fairbanks's suggestions, which Mark Twain mostly ignored for the published letters but employed to satisfy the higher-toned standards of a book. His postvoyage letters to her are replete with assurances that he has "reformed," yet he is perfectly willing to put her on notice about the hell he intends to raise in his new reporting job for the New York *Herald:* "I just mean to abuse people right & left, in case the humor takes me to do it. There are lots of folks in Washington who need vilifying."[10] As to that use of "Mother" (invented by Charley Langdon, who really did miss Mom): it might have been meant to signal his obsequiousness. Or it might have been meant to suppress an impulse quite the opposite of that. Mary Fairbanks was hardly a toothless crone at age thirty-nine. While photographs of her do not show a woman of mesmerizing beauty, they depict a figure who, enhanced by her urbane self-assurance, her obvious warmth and welcoming nature, might strike a rough-edged young Westerner as sexually attractive. Given the givens of Victorian protocol, what better way to defuse such dangerous feelings than to cast her as a "mother"?

It's just a thought.

THE *QUAKER City* steamed into the port at St. George, Bermuda, at dawn on October 11, and the frazzled passengers enjoyed five restorative days as a storm raged on the Atlantic. Finally, on Tuesday, November 19, the steamer docked at New York Harbor. The first luxury cruise in American history was over. The journalistic core of its narrative had already been written: during the homeward voyage, Mark Twain completed the final third of the fifty letters he would send to the *Alta*. In addition, he had sent six letters to the New York *Tribune* and three to the *Herald*. Sam could not disembark fast enough. Whisking through customs without having to open his bags, he checked in at the Westminster Hotel, and then called on his newspaper friends and editors around the city, testing the market for his work. He had made plans for dinner and the theater that evening with Mary Fairbanks, Charley Langdon, and some other friends. He never kept that engagement. Six p.m. found him scribbling away in an editorial room at James Gordon Bennett's New York *Herald* at 35th and Broadway. The resulting 2,500-word outburst ran in the next day's editions, just in time to be noticed by the pilgrims before they dispersed from the city.

Sam later claimed he hadn't planned this in advance; an editor of Bennett's had "sent for" him as he approached the hotel where his friends were waiting; and, strapped for cash, he'd accepted an offer of fifty dollars to produce the essay. (This was hogwash: he wrote to a *Tribune* editor a few days later that he had stopped there to place the piece, but could find no one he knew, and so turned to the *Herald*.) He worked partly from an earlier draft that had been read by Mary Fairbanks, who'd recoiled at it and later wrote an oblique rebuttal of it in her husband's paper—further evidence that her opinion was not the final arbiter of his impulses. He bandied no words. Branding the ship a "synagogue," and the trip itself "a funeral excursion without a corpse," he churned out a stream of invective worthy of his Washoe rants. He composed a similar letter for the *Alta*. Among the highlights of the two:

> The steamer *Quaker City* arrived yesterday morning and turned her menagerie of pilgrims loose on America . . . Their Pilgrim's Progress is ended, and they . . . can talk [about] it from now till January—most of them are too old to last longer . . .[11]

> The venerable excursionists were not gay and frisky. They played no blind man's bluff; they dealt not in whist; . . . They never romped, they talked but little, they never sang, save in the nightly prayer meeting . . . Such was our daily life on board ship—solemnity, decorum, dinner, dominoes, prayers, slander.[12]

He dilated on their prayer meetings—"I said all along that we hadn't prayer meetings enough; we ought to have them before breakfast, and between meals, and every now and then, and pretty much all the time"—and their fumbling with the French tongue—"We never did succeed in making those idiots understand their own language"—and their mawkish "raptures" in the Holy Land.[13]

> I bear them no malice . . . We didn't amalgamate—that was all. Nothing more than that. I was exceedingly friendly with a good many of them—eight out of the sixty-five—

but I didn't dote on the others, and they didn't dote on me . . . I am tired of hearing about the "mixed" character of our party on the *Quaker City.* It was not mixed enough—there were not blackguards enough on board in proportion to the saints— there was not genuine piety enough to offset the hypocrisy.[14]

Seven months later, Sam still hadn't cooled down. He shoehorned a slightly revised version of the screed into his book manuscript, calling it an "Obituary," and pretended bewilderment that his fellow passengers could have taken offense at it: "I have read it, and read it again; and if there is a sentence in it that is not fulsomely complimentary to captain, ship and passengers, *I* cannot find it." [15]

Sam returned to the Westminster from the *Herald* offices around midnight. He dashed off a note to his (real) mother before he went to bed, assuring her that he had written "a long article that will make the Quakers get up and howl in the morning." [16] The rush of it had left him a little giddy with grandeur: "When Charles Dickens sleeps in this room next week, it will be a gratification to him to know that I have slept in it also."* The *Herald* piece ran unsigned, but an editorial the next day identified the *Quaker City* screed as Mark Twain's, and predicted that a book by him about the pilgrimage "would command an almost unprecedented sale."

There are varieties of genius peculiar to America. Of one of these varieties Mark Twain is a striking specimen. For the development of his peculiar genius he has never had a more fitting opportunity. Besides, there are some things which he knows and which the world ought to know about this last edition of the May Flower.[17]

This last sentence alluded to a thematic point of view that Mark Twain was already developing for the book: a full-bore satirical focus on the passengers themselves, never mind the "travel" paradigm. He backed away from this potentially self-destructive idea as the distress of Mary Fairbanks and other friends sank in with him. Yet he never apologized for his abhorrence of that crowd, nor minimized the pain he felt they'd visited on him. In a letter to Mrs. Fairbanks a couple of weeks later, he declared that "as for those Quakers, I don't want their friendship . . . They can hurt me. Let them. I would rather they should hurt me than help me."

He listed the people he'd considered his shipboard friends, a tight little list indeed: "Yourself; Mr & Mrs. Severance; the cub [Langdon]; Emma Beach; Dan; Moulton; Jack . . ." and concluded:

My opinion of the rest of the ~~gang~~ is so mean, & so vicious, & so outrageous in every way, that I could not collect the terms to express it with out of any less than sixteen or

---

* Dickens had arrived in Boston that same day to begin a five-month lecture tour in America; he was booked at the Westminster during his New York stop.

seventeen different languages. Such another ~~drove of cattle~~ *never* went to sea before. Select party! Well, *I* ~~pass~~.[18]

ON NOVEMBER 22, Sam arrived by overnight train in Washington. He called on Senator Stewart to claim the secretaryship that Stewart had offered him, and boarded with the Nevada Republican at F and 14th streets, taking meals at the nearby Willard's Hotel. Sam did not see this position as a career: before leaving New York, he had negotiated with both the *Herald* and the *Tribune* for "occasional" correspondence; and on November 24, he wrote to Frank Fuller to discuss lecture plans: "If I stay here all winter & keep on . . . getting well acquainted with great dignitaries to introduce me . . . I can lecture next season . . . to 100 houses, & houses that will be readier to accept me without criticism than they are now."[19] He saw the Washington job as a chance to build his Eastern reputation, and to observe and write about legislators in action, much as he had in Carson City. Sam found that the nation's capital had changed significantly during his fourteen-year absence, yet on one question remained frozen in antebellum time. The Kansas-Nebraska Act wrangling had transmuted into the debate over Reconstruction; but two years after the close of the Civil War, sectionalism and race remained a constant as the American dilemma. The low-slung city was bigger, brisker, muddier, more crowded with political parasites, buttonholers from railroad, timber, and mining interests, and other exemplars of the new America. Yet in the Senate, the argument Sam had seen waged by the likes of Stephen Douglas and William H. Seward in 1854 was still going strong. Now Sam Clemens would report on that debate as a seasoned newspaper correspondent.

The issue had become whether a Northern or a Southern version of "citizenship" was to be allotted to a newly emancipated people defined for centuries as slaves. The party of Lincoln favored full federal protection of Negro citizens; but Lincoln, who might have steered the country through the crisis, was dead. His overmatched (and overdrinking) successor, Andrew ("This is a country for white men, and by God, as long as I am President, it shall be a government for white men") Johnson, was bungling the process. The former Tennessee tailor had been antislavery to this extent: he thought that Negroes were more productive when *paid* for their grunt work. He held the Southern view that Negro rights should be limited, and decided not by federal fiat but by individual states. His clumsy attempts to ensure this policy prompted the Radical Republican–led Congress to clamp the South under military supervision in March 1867. Johnson lurched on, vetoing bill after bill drafted to ensure justice for black Americans. Shortly before Sam hit town, the Judiciary Committee recommended Johnson's impeachment. Sam covered Johnson's surly "annual message" to Congress of December 2, writing that it was "making a howl among the Republicans" and that it "has weakened the President. Impeachment was dead, day before yesterday. It would rise up and make a strong fight to-day if it were pushed with energy and tact."[20]

He was right. Johnson's ham-handed attempts to circumvent Congress continued, and in February 1868 the House voted to impeach him. The tippling Tennessean was acquitted the following May by a single vote, but his political career was finished.

Sam's new boss was in the thick of this historic struggle. Stewart had made himself a leading force in the quest for a humane Reconstruction. He was just then drafting what in the following year would become the Fifteenth Amendment, codifying a spectrum of voting rights for American Negroes. Yet it was just as well that Sam hadn't pinned his hopes on Stewart's Washington political career. The relationship between the spade-bearded legislator and the red-haired journalist was edgy from the start. Shortly after arriving, Sam hit Stewart up for a loan. Stewart turned him down. In his memoirs forty years later, William Stewart recalled his first glimpse of Sam in Washington as if it had happened just the previous nightmare.

I was seated at my window one morning when a very disreputable-looking person slouched into the room. He was arrayed in a seedy suit, . . . A sheaf of scraggy black hair leaked out of a battered old slouch hat . . . and an evil-smelling cigar butt, very much frazzled, protruded from the corner of his mouth. He had a very sinister appearance . . .[21]

The author of the Fifteenth Amendment, in short, found himself sharing quarters with Sut Lovingood. It was not an arrangement that held a lot of long-range promise. Sam filled his notebook with shrewd and often pictorial thumbnail sketches of the legislators, sketches that he would draw on for his first excursion into fiction a few years later: "—*very* deep eyes, sunken unshaven cheeks, thin lips . . . whole face sunken & sharp," he observed of the radical, dying Thaddeus Stevens, a leader in the fight against Johnson; "—belongs to another age," he noted of a Maryland representative; "strong, unshaven face hermit—woman-hater—lives up in queer way in mountains alone . . . hair comes washing forward over his forehead in two white converging waves over a bare-worn rock . . ." Of Congressman Ben Butler, the radical Republican known as "the Beast" during his brutal military occupation of New Orleans, Sam accurately wrote: "—forward part of his bald skull looks raised, like a water blister . . . Butler is dismally & drearily homely, & when he smiles it is like the breaking up of a hard winter."[22] His aphorisms crackled: "Whisky taken into Com[mittee] rooms in demijohns & carried out in demagogues." "Sherman—Hunt Indians—hadn't lost any."[23]

One other interesting notation appears in Sam Clemens's notebook for that period: an undated entry, worded with an elaborate carelessness that roars the significance it held for the former Ralls County Ranger.

Acquainted with Gen Grant—said I was glad to see him—he said I had the advantage of him.[24]

It is not clear what date or circumstances produced the first meeting between these two preeminent figures of the 19th century whose lives had orbited each other like charged ions, and would continue to do so, with historic consequences. (Sam, whose letters home had become a veritable Who's Who of dropped names, does not mention the encounter in any extant letter.) It appears possible that Clemens and Grant first laid eyes on each other at a reception in Washington in December 1867.* After shaking the great man's hand, Sam melted back a few paces, leaned against a wall, and trained his prodigious attention on the general for an hour, as the reception line continued.

Poor, modest, bored, unhappy Grant stood smileless . . . nervously seized each hand as it came, and while he gave it a single shake, looked not upon its owner, but threw a quick look-out for the next. And if for a moment his hand was left idle, his arm hung out from his body with a curve that was suggestive of being ready for business at a moment's notice.[25]

Sam was fascinated with Ulysses S. Grant from the start. On the evening of January 19, four days after the reception, he called at the Grants' Washington home, looking for an interview. "He was out at a dinner party," Sam wrote to the homefolks, "but Mrs. Grant said she would keep him at home on a Sunday evening." He continued, no doubt imagining Jane's horror:

I must see him, because he is good for one letter for the Alta, & part of a lecture for San F. Grant's father was there. Swinton [a fellow journalist] & I are going to get [the father] into a private room at Willard's & start his tongue with a whisky punch. He will tell everything he knows & twice as much that he supposes . . .[26]

No such interview appears to have occurred. Either that, or the participants were later unable to remember what had been said.

Grant was in Washington as a key—if inadvertent—player in the Andrew Johnson psychodrama. He had retained his military commission after the Civil War, and Johnson, jealous and fearful of Grant's popularity, had ordered him to Mexico in the fall of 1866. Grant had refused to go. Now, in his dissolution, Johnson had contrived to let Grant humiliate him yet again—by installing him as the replacement secretary of war for Edwin Stanton, the Lincoln holdover whom Johnson had dismissed in a power struggle. One of the new secretary's first actions had been to stand down, a devastating gesture against the president, and Republicans in Congress seized on the "illegal" sacking of Stanton as one of the reasons for impeachment.

Looking into the eyes of the legendary general who had once menaced his Rangers in Missouri was a seminal event for Sam, but by then, he had a

---

* Some scholars, including Robert Hirst, suspect that this meeting may have taken place entirely inside Sam's head, as did the imaginary exchange described in the unpublished manuscript he titled "Interview with Gen. Grant," which he dated "Washington Dec. 6."

separate reason to feel elated. Three weeks earlier, a day after his thirty-second birthday, he'd opened a letter awaiting him at the *Tribune* bureau in Washington. Its author was Elisha Bliss Jr., secretary of the American Publishing Company, and its message thrilled Sam.

We are desirous of obtaining from you a work of some kind, perhaps compiled from your letters from the East &c., with such interesting additions as may be proper . . . If you have any thought of writing a book, or could be induced to do so, we should be pleased to see you . . .[27]

Sam fired back a reply the next day. (*Induced* to do so?) "I could weed [the letters] of their chief faults of construction & inelegancies of expression, & make a volume that would be more acceptable in many respects than any I could now write . . . I could strike out certain letters, & write new ones wherewith to supply their places . . ."[28] He asked for more details on the size and general style of such a book, and an idea of how much money he might make from it. "The latter clause has a degree of importance for me which is almost beyond my own comprehension."[29] Elisha Bliss was not an experienced literary man, but he was an experienced businessman. Balding, middle-aged, his sideburns looping up ferociously to his mustache, he had been a dry-goods and lumbering man before joining American Publishing that year—a house that had opened up only in 1865. His letter to Sam was as portentous as a page from *Joan of Arc* in the face. Suddenly the Washington appointment felt irrelevant. Within a week, Sam was allowing to Frank Fuller that maybe he had made a mistake in deciding not to hit the lecture trail during the winter. His reputation was stronger than he'd reckoned! The ensuing thought was virtually foreordained: "I am already dead tired of being in one place so long."[30]

Dutifully, he looked in on the 40th Congress, then winding up its session, but paid only cursory attention to the issues of nationhood being thrashed out on the floor. He sent off newspaper dispatches about these debates, but his mind was elsewhere.

Back in St. Louis, the homefolks awaited word from Sam about employment prospects for Orion, who was foraging for typesetting jobs to feed and shelter even just himself (Mollie was in Keokuk). They could not have been overjoyed to receive a mid-December letter from him that touched on the topic, then shifted its focus to himself and what a big deal he was getting to be. "I called on the Secretary of the Interior, yesterday, but said nothing about a place for Orion, of course—must get better acquainted first . . . If it were *myself*, I could get a place pretty easily, because I have friends in high places who offer me such things—but it is hard to get them interested in one's relatives."[31] He let it slip that Stephen Johnson Field, a pal from California days and now a Supreme Court justice, wanted to make him postmaster of San Francisco: "I told him *I* didn't want any office. But he said, 'You *must* have an office, with a good salary & nothing to do. *You* are no common scrub of a newspaperman.' "[32] Such esteem for Sam, plus thirty-five cents, would have bought Orion a good lunch in any hotel in the Mississippi Valley.

Everyone was looking to enhance Samuel Clemens's life. To Mary Fairbanks, who hinted that perhaps her "cub" should be scouting around for a young lady bear—"A good wife would be a perpetual incentive to progress"— he allowed that the idea had its points. "I want a good wife—I want a couple of them if they are particularly good—but where is the wherewithal? It costs nearly two letters a week to keep *me*."[33] The cub was pacing his cage again. "I look forward anxiously to my release from Washington," Sam wrote to Emily Severance on Christmas Eve. "I am in a fidget to move."[34] He had ended his employment with Senator Stewart—prompted, as he later wrote, by a subtle hint: "Leave this house! Leave it for ever and for ever, too!"[35]

On Christmas Day, he was back in New York for a boozy reunion with Dan Slote and the other *Quaker City* nighthawks. He stayed at Slote's house, reliving old times in the Holy Land. "I just laughed till my sides ached . . . It was the unholiest gang that ever cavorted through Palestine, but those are the best boys in the world."[36] It was during this hiatus that Sam found an opportunity to unload his pent-up irritation at Captain Duncan. The captain had asked for it. Lecturing on the excursion at Henry Ward Beecher's Plymouth Church on December 3, Duncan claimed that he had observed rampant drunkenness aboard the ship. His charge was refuted by a fellow excursionist and Plymouth congregant, Stephen Griswold, who insisted that the only shipboard drinking was done by a man suffering from "consumption," who had wet his whistle under a doctor's advice. The Brooklyn *Eagle*, spoiling for a public feud, called in print upon the one authority who might give a true accounting: "Mark Twain is the man to settle the point, let us hear from him."[37]

On December 30, writing at Dan Slote's house, he crafted a small masterpiece of satirical inversion that left the captain wiping custard pie from his bald dome and sailor's goatee. Duncan's charge was true but overstated, Mark Twain said, and demonstrated how facts and figures, while stating literal truth, can ruin a reputation when presented the wrong way. He offered some imaginary extracts from his notes.

At sea, August 14—Captain Duncan appeared at breakfast this morning entirely sober. Heaven be praised!

At sea, August 18—Four days of forebodings and uneasiness. But at last Captain Duncan appeared at breakfast again, apparently entirely sober. Cheerfulness sat upon every countenance, and every heart was filled with thankfulness.

At sea, August 24— . . . Capt Duncan has not once been in liquor. Oh, how grateful we ought to be! A movement is on foot to present him a silver dinner service when we shall have arrived in Rome.[38]

And then the "snapper," offered as a P.S.

I am sorry, I am truly sorry to say that in Italy Capt. Duncan bought wine and drank it on board the ship——, and it almost breaks my heart when I reflect that . . . it was his example that seduced the innocent passengers into getting intoxicated . . . Capt. Duncan offered wine to me—he tried to make even *me* fall with his horrid Italian intoxicating bowl—but my virtue was proof against his wiles. I sternly refused to taste it. I preferred the French article. So did Griswold.[39]

The article ran in the *Eagle* the following day. That evening—New Year's Eve—found Sam Clemens out on the town, taking in a reading by the world's most famous living author, with the girl in the ivory miniature on his arm.

He had stopped by the elegant St. Nicholas Hotel on Broadway to call on Charley Langdon, who was staying there with his parents and his sister, down from Elmira. The Langdons were as wealthy and cultured as any people the former printer's devil from Hannibal had yet encountered, short of the tsar's family. Graciously, they included Sam in their dinner party, then invited him along to Steinway Hall at 14th Street in Union Square, to hear Charles Dickens read at 8 p.m. from *David Copperfield*.* Sam later remembered Dickens as a small, slender figure in a black velvet coat with a red flower in the buttonhole, who stood under a bank of strong lights and read "with great force and animation, in the lively passages, and with stirring effect."[40] He was more absorbed with the slim young woman in his company: "sweet and timid and lovely," he later recalled.[41] Yet he was not so distracted that he failed to note, and file away in his mind, a critical bit of Dickensian stagecraft: "[H]e did not merely read but also acted."[42]

The next morning, Sam saw her again, on the first of thirty-four expected New Year's calls on friends in the city. He canceled the remaining thirty-three, having

anchored for the day at the first house I came to—Charlie Langdon's sister was there (beautiful girl,) & Miss Alice Hooker, another beautiful girl, a niece of Henry Ward Beecher's. We sent the old folks home early, with instructions not to send the carriage till midnight, & then I just staid there & deviled the life out of those girls. I am going to spend a few days with the Langdon's, in Elmira, New York, as soon as I get time . . .[43]

First, though, there was a book that needed to be written.

---

* In 1906 Mark Twain stated that he had first met Olivia Langdon on December 27, four days before the Dickens reading, over dinner with the family at the St. Nicholas; but the following year he gave December 31 as the date of the first meeting, and recalled the Dickens reading.

21

"A Work *Humorously Inclined . . .*"

(February–July 1868)

The girl in the miniature may have made a deep impression on Sam, but she disappears from mention in his letters and notes for the ensuing six months. Contrary to the legend created by Mark Twain and maintained by his biographer Paine, she may have disappeared from his thoughts as well. Evidence that Sam continued his bachelor ways after his introduction to Olivia Langdon has surfaced in a letter written to Mollie Clemens on February 21, 1868. Transcribed and then smothered in private files by Paine, it only recently made its way to the archivists at Berkeley.

> I received a dainty little letter from Lou Conrad, yesterday. She* is in Wisconsin. But what worries me is that I have received no letter from my sweetheart in New York for three days. This won't do. I shall have to run up there & see what the mischief is the matter. I will break that girl's back if she breaks my heart. I am getting too venerable now to put up with nonsense from children.[1]

Even as he romanced other young women, including Emma Beach, Sam was working his way into the interlaced community that reached from his world to the Langdons' in Elmira. He wrote to his mother on January 8:

> Henry Ward Beecher sent for me last Sunday to come over & dine (he lives in Brooklyn, you know,) & I went. Harriet Beecher Stowe was there, & Mrs. & Miss

---

* This is the mysterious "Pauline," last name unknown, whom Sam mentions to Charles Henry Webb ("I hunted for her & couldn't find her") in November 1867 (MTL, vol. 2, p. 115).

Beecher, Mrs. Hooker & my old Quaker City favorite, Emma Beach. We had a very gay time, if it *was* Sunday. I expect I told more lies than I have told before in a month.[2]

If Jane Clemens ever needed an index from which to gauge her school-truant son's rise through America's social echelons, this letter provided it. In addition to the famous minister and his even more famous sister, Harriet, there was his sister Catharine, an educator and author; his wife, Eunice; as well as his half-sister, "Mrs. Hooker"—Isabella Beecher Hooker, a leader in the struggle to achieve equal rights for women. She was married to the great lawyer John Hooker, and their daughter Alice was a friend of Olivia Langdon's. Emma Beach was a slightly different proposition. Sam seems to have played at a flirtation with his "old" (as in eighteen) *Quaker City* favorite. He kept up a correspondence with her, frisky in its early weeks ("Shipmate, Ahoy!" "Shipmate, Avast!").

Isabella and John Hooker were the founding residents of Nook Farm, the half-enchanted utopian community at the western edge of Hartford, and which took its name from the forest and fields that encompassed it. Its hundred-acre plat had been a "farm" in name only for decades, as sycamores and sugar maples and chestnut trees reclaimed its hillsides and valleys. The name "Nook" referred to the forty-odd acres embraced by a bend in the Hog River, eventually Victorianized as the Park. John Hooker and a partner bought the estate in 1853 and sold lots to selected friends and relatives. Hooker was a sixth-generation descendant of Thomas Hooker, the Puritan cleric who founded Hartford in 1636. Along with his cerebral wife, John envisioned a city-within-a-city whose subtle borders allowed only kindred spirits: readers and thinkers, yet people impassioned enough to involve themselves in the great issues of the day, the greatest of which was the plight of African-American slaves.

Hooker's partner was Francis Gillette, a Christian abolitionist and United States senator. With his marriage to Hooker's sister Eliza, Gillette forged relational as well as neighborly bonds on the Farm. The Gillettes' son William would become famous for his stage portrayal of Sherlock Holmes (he introduced the deerstalker cap). He used some of his wealth to plant a medieval castle amidst the gabled manors of the Farm.

Sam's own bond to the Hartford area was now assuming its contours. As he hobnobbed in New York, a third letter from Elisha Bliss written on December 24 arrived at the *Tribune* rooms in Washington.

> Now about the book,—we would like to have you get us up one. We can handle it we think, to the advantage of both of us . . . We think we see clearly that the book would sell; a *humorous* work—that is to say, a work *humorously inclined* we believe in . . . The first thing, then, is will you *make* a book?"[3]

For material, Bliss suggested Mark Twain's "Cal. letters, *revamped* & worked over, & all other matter you can command, connected with your Quaker City trip, including all letters written &c., on that trip—or their contents."[4] As for terms, Bliss cited his arrangement with the current star of the American Publishing Company's list, A. D. Richardson, whose *Beyond the Mississippi* had appeared that year: a royalty of 4 percent of his book's sale price, instead of the publisher's alternative deal, an outright purchase.

Clemens was elated, but still in suspense about the terms Bliss would offer. He asked his family to send him any clippings of his newspaper articles that reached them. He'd not made copies of his shipboard letters, and many of these were stacked in the offices of the *Alta California* in San Francisco, awaiting publication. On January 9 he wrote Bliss again, a letter now lost but accessible in part through Bliss's reply to it:

> In regard to what you write about your book, &c., I would say to you that we will make *liberal* terms with you for it, in some shape most satisfactory to you . . . [Y]ou get your letters & overhaul them & be getting the matter in shape. We will manage to get together soon . . . Are you coming to N.Y. again soon? If so perhaps I can meet you there. I think we can make a success of your work & make it pay you well. Please reply to this & let me know that . . . I can in some manner rely upon a book from you in the future.[5]

While he waited for this reply, Clemens wrote late at night in the rooms he shared with Stewart, smoking and singing and whistling as he worked, torturing up memory. He had plenty else to keep him busy and bankrolled: his newspaper commitments, and whatever speaking engagements he could round up. On January 11, at the annual banquet of the Washington Newspaper Correspondents' Club, a quick-fingered reporter recorded his toast and—in brackets—the audience's riotous response to it, as well as Mark Twain's mannerisms as he delivered it: a rare verbal snapshot of him working a crowd. The toast was "Woman: The Pride of the Professions, and the Jewel of Ours."

> Human intelligence cannot estimate what we owe to woman, sir. She sews on our buttons, [laughter,] she mends our clothes, [laughter,] . . . she bears our children—ours as a general thing. . . .
>
> Wheresoever you place woman, sir—in whatsoever position or estate—she is an ornament to that place she occupies, and a treasure to the world. [Here Mr. Twain paused, looked inquiringly at his hearers and remarked that the applause should come in at this point. It came in. Mr. Twain resumed his eulogy.] Look at the noble names of history! Look at Cleopatra!—look at Desdemona!—look at Florence Nightingale!—look at Joan of Arc!—look at Lucretia Borgia! [Disapprobation expressed. "Well," said Mr. Twain, scratching his head doubtfully, "suppose we let Lucretia slide."] . . . look at Mother Eve! [Cries of "Oh!" "Oh!"] You need not look at her unless you want to, but, (said Mr. Twain reflectively, after a pause,) Eve was ornamental, sir—particularly before the fashions changed! . . . look at the Mother of Washington! she raised a boy that could not lie—*could not lie*—[Applause.] But he *never had any chance.* [Oh! Oh!] It might

have been different with him if he had belonged to a newspaper correspondent's club. [Laughter, groans, hisses, cries of "put him out." Mark looked around placidly upon his excited audience and resumed.]

. . . Then let us cherish her—let us protect her—let us give her our support, our encouragement, our sympathy—ourselves, if we get a chance. [Laughter.][6]

Among those present was Schuyler Colfax, the Speaker of the House and a future vice president of the United States. According to Sam, Colfax considered it the best dinner-table speech he had ever heard.

Among those not present was Senator William Stewart. The friction that would separate them had begun to be discernable—Stewart had threatened Sam with a thrashing—and by January 15, Sam was writing from a new address, "356 C [Street] bet. 4½ & 6th." The rift had its poignant aspects. Stewart spoke with pride about the fact that Sam began to rough out *The Innocents Abroad* while sharing quarters with him. "He would work during the day," Stewart recalled, "and in the evening he would read me what he had written, after which he would stroll out about the city for recreation."[7] Unfortunately, it was usually after midnight when Sam returned, and then the cigar smoking would begin. Not to mention the whistling and singing.

IMPATIENT FOR a resolution with the American Publishing Company, Sam replied by telegram to Bliss's last letter, and probably on the same day, January 20, took a train from Washington to New York, where he stayed two days before going on to Hartford. In New York, he sought out Henry Ward Beecher for some negotiating advice, which the worldly preacher was only too happy to give—"Now here—you are one of the talented men of the age—nobody is going to deny that—but in matters of business, I don't suppose you know more than enough to come in when it rains; I'll tell you what to do, & how to do it."[8] Sam arrived in Hartford on January 22, accepting the hospitality of John and Isabella Hooker for three days. (Boarding in that household had its drawbacks—"I hear no swearing here, I see no one chewing tobacco, I have found nobody drunk," he told his *Alta* readers.)[9] Beecher's advice apparently had been good: Sam proved a tough and prescient bargainer. He declined Bliss's offer of a $10,000 purchase, and held out for 5 percent royalty on each book sold—one percentage point higher than the house was paying the established Richardson. In July 1868, he was supposed to deliver a manuscript sufficient for a book of 500 to 600 pages, based on the newspaper letters. The deal made him boastful. "I wasn't going to touch a book unless there was *money* in it, & a good deal of it. I told them so," he told his mother and sister. As for his promise to find an appointment for Orion, why, "I want just one private talk with Andrew Johnson when I get back to Washington, & then I'll know what course to pursue."[10]

As happened so often during transformative moments in his life, he thought to get in touch with Will Bowen.

I have just come down from Hartford, Conn., where I have made a tip-top contract for a 600-page book, & I feel perfectly jolly. It is with the heaviest publishing
house in America, & I get the best terms they have ever offered any man save one . . .
It would take a good deal of money to buy out the undersigned now, old boy.[11]

In the fourth paragraph, Sam got around to commiserating with his childhood friend on the death of his eldest child, seven-year-old daughter Mattie.
A few lines later, his thoughts edged a little closer to the deep dream-trove
that as yet eluded his capacity to reopen it: "I have been thinking of school-
days at Dawson's, & trying to recall the old faces of that ancient time—but I
cannot place them very well—they have faded out from my treacherous memory, for the most part, & passed away."[12] Back in Washington, he worked days
and nights, shifting from newspaper dispatches to the book manuscript after
dark. The pace sapped his stamina, but it may have improved the quality of
his prose. Without a handy mountain of published letters in front of him, in all
their slangy and vitriolic rawness, he was obliged to compose, rather than simply paraphrase; in the process, he took his writing to another level. Metaphor,
clever phrasemaking, and universality replaced the earlier sarcasm and angry
invective, and the controlled satirical vision began to emerge that gave *The Innocents Abroad* the power to resonate far beyond its own time. Yet he knew that
memory alone would not sustain him through the thousand-odd manuscript
pages required to make a 600-page book. He would need the *Alta* letters.

IN STAKING everything on royalty profits from a book that would depend
on door-to-door subscription sales to a largely non-"literary" clientele,
Samuel Clemens revealed a strong intuitive grasp of his natural readership.
The American Publishing Company's products did not darken the doorways
of the Eastern bookstores, whose exalted authors towered over mere "journalists" and "humorists" like Mark Twain. In this fact lay the unique potential of
such books to reinvent American literature. Door-to-door subscription sales,
after all, were the same method that a quarter-century earlier had broadcast
the McGuffey's Reader around America and created mass literacy among
rural children like Sammy Clemens. These children had grown up just in time
for the postwar spread of railroads and industry to group them into new urban
and suburban centers west of the Alleghenies. This new, literate, middle class
viewed reading as a hallmark of gentility, even though it was not altogether
certain what "gentility" entailed. In a way similar to Sam Clemens as he cultivated his circle of wised-up pilgrims aboard the *Quaker City*, these arriviste
Americans hungered to learn the rules of the lodge.

They wanted to know about how to behave and how to speak well. They
wanted to know about science and how to cook and how to make money. They
wanted to learn about family life and how to deal with the suddenly exalted
concept of "childhood." (Advice books about children, and storybooks, enjoyed a huge renaissance during these years.) They wanted to learn the songs

other Americans were singing and what kind of medicine they were taking. They hungered to know about Great Men. (As for Great Women, Queen Victoria pretty much preempted the transatlantic field.) They wanted to know about American adventurers, and how exotic places seemed to American eyes. They wanted to be entertained, inspired, transported, confirmed in their goodness and the goodness of the country. They did not necessarily want to be challenged, or confronted with complexity or erudition. The people who opened their doors to subscription booksellers burdened down with "sample books" for show-and-tell, and order forms, and illustrations and pastedowns and binding samples—these were the Great Emerging American Middlebrow. These were, in effect, the rest of the *Quaker City* pilgrims.

IN EARLY February, still in Washington, Sam fell into bed with exhaustion and remained there four or five days. He had moved again, briefly to 356 C Street and then to 76 Indiana Avenue. When he was stronger, he placed himself on a more routinized work schedule, writing in the daytime and sleeping at night. A visiting fellow journalist was fascinated by the wildness of his working scene: the floor littered with torn-up newspapers from which Sam had slashed out his letters, the "chaotic hovel foul with tobacco smoke," [13] Sam himself stripped down to suspenders and pants, swearing and smoking and ripping up newsprint as he paced the floor. By February 21, he had produced drafts of the first ten chapters.

He could still find time to make mischief for his enemies, and brag about it, especially if he could do it through his influence with the high and mighty. The postmastership in San Francisco retained some appeal for him, and when he found out that another candidate "turned up on the inside track," he prevailed on Justice Field on the Supreme Court to leave a sickbed and pay a visit to President Johnson: "In just no time at all I knocked that complacent idiot's kite so high that it never *will* come down." [14] He canvassed his family for more of his published letters. He groveled a little for Mary Fairbanks about his use of slang in return for clippings of her newspaper correspondence with her husband's Cleveland *Herald*. "I see a good many ideas in your letters that I can steal." [15] He pressed Emma Beach for the names of consuls at Gibraltar and Marseilles. "And please tell me the names of the Murillo pictures that delighted you most—& say all you can about them, too. Remember . . . it is hard to have to write about pictures when I don't know anything about them." [16] He hit up Mary Fairbanks again for more of her work: "Now please hurry them up—there's a good mother." [17] The flop-sweat was starting to flow. Accountable for a 600-page book, he had estimated that his own letters would probably make only about 250 pages. That was probably a bit low.

He had reason to be worried. The temperature out west at the *Alta* had turned arctic. Its editors had picked up on press reports out of New York that Mark Twain was working on a book on the Holy Land expedition. They telegraphed Sam reminding him that his newspaper letters were their property. Sam's reply is lost, but the possibility exists that it might have been cross. ("I expect I have made the Alta people mad," he wrote to Jane and Pamela, "but I don't care.")[18] On January 21, the *Alta* published an explicit claim of copyright ownership, using as pretext the uncredited reprinting of a Mark Twain missive by the Sacramento *Union*.[19]

Anxiety consumed him, and not just about copyright. His newspaper deadlines were an insufferable distraction; yet he needed the money. He hinted that he wouldn't mind an embassy job in a note to Anson Burlingame, the China-America liaison who'd befriended Sam in the Sandwich Islands. He leaned on his family, including Orion, who was still boarding with his mother and sister in St. Louis while Mollie remained stranded in Keokuk, to track down some of his missing letters. (The culprit turned out to be—surprise— Orion, who had wonderfully sent them to his wife instead of to Sam.) He pleaded with Bliss: "If you ever do such a thing as give an author an advance, I wish you would advance me a thousand dollars."[20] Bliss came across with some money.

THE *ALTA* standoff escalated. In late February, word trickled back east that the paper had decided to issue its own book of Mark Twain's letters—clearly a move to preempt Clemens's reprinting them. Appalled, Sam broke his aloof stance. For the first time, he asked permission of the editors that they let him use the letters himself. The reply arrived two weeks later—an infuriating mishmash of legalistic jargon—in any case, not a "yes." One option remained. Sam packed a trunk, and on March 11, the cash from Bliss in his pocket, he boarded the side-wheel steamer *Henry Chauncey* for Panama. He crossed the isthmus and caught the *Sacramento* for the northbound ocean voyage, arriving in San Francisco on April 2. He checked in to his beloved Occidental Hotel and got down to bargaining with the *Alta* editors that same day.

Sam arrived to find his Pacific Slope celebrity still intact—enhanced, even, thanks to his published *Quaker City* adventures. His movements about town were news-item fodder. Perhaps swelled by the attention, he stopped in at the soignée photographic studio of Bradley & Rulofson at Montgomery and Sacramento and had his portrait made. Even the embattled *Alta* editors lightened up enough to report that "the genial and jolly humorist" was back in town and planning a series of lectures on the *Quaker City* tour. He launched his performance, a reheated version of "The Frozen Truth," before a packed house of 1,600, at a dollar a head, at Platt's Hall on April 14. To accommodate those who were "repulsed at the door," he repeated it the following night, and then retailed it around the Bay Area over the next several days, having prevailed on several editors to refrain from printing synopses of the talk and ruining his gate.

The crowds were good, but the press, which had doted on his Sandwich Islands lectures, ranged from cool to vicious. The *Bulletin* wished he had said more about Palestine and "less about the bald-headed, spectacled and sedate old pilgrims." [21] The *Alta* opined that it was not terribly well prepared, save for two bursts of eloquence, one of which was about the ruins of Palestine. The San Rafael *Marin County Journal* scorched him as "this miserable scribbler, whose letters in the *Alta,* sickened everyone who read them"; the *California Weekly Mercury* deplored his "sacrilegious allusions, impotent humor, and malignant distortions of history and the truth." [22] He fared a little better when he returned to Virginia City. Joe Goodman trumpeted him into town with a jolly notice of his speaking dates at the Opera House. Mark Twain revisited Carson City for a pair of talks and then returned to the mountainside town for a few days of renewing old friendships among the Washoe crowd.

For all the savaging his lectures received from the Western newspapers, it was the tongue-lashings from the Western pulpits that stung Clemens the most. Here was a nice irony: the Wild Humorist had departed the Pacific Slope in 1866 fearful that his wild-and-woolly views and language would prove unacceptable in the genteel East. Yet no Yankee minister—not even Henry Ward Beecher, whose brainchild the Holy Land cruise had been— came close to the excoriations unleashed on him by California clergymen. To some of them, he was "this son of the Devil, Mark Twain!" as he reported in a bewildered way to Mary Fairbanks—"What did I ever write about the Holy Land that was so peculiarly lacerating?" [23] Seated up near the pulpit at a Baptist service one Sunday evening, he was nonplussed to hear the pastor, who did not recognize him, hold up his writings as an example of the sin of ridicule, "the weapon of cowards." As worshippers who did recognize Mark Twain shot him embarrassed glances, the preacher excoriated "the letters of this person, Mark Twain, who visits the Holy Land and ridicules sacred scenes and things." The letters were popular "because of his puerile attempts at wit, and miserable puns upon subjects that are dear to every Christian heart." [24] Puns, no less! Was there no bottom to his perfidy?! After the service Clemens introduced himself to the mortified clergyman: "I feel that I deserve everything which you have said about me, and I wish to heartily thank you." [25]

He was delivering a subtly sarcastic message. The hostile reviews, the offended clergy—there were portents here for the prospects of his book, and Clemens, like a politician shoring up his base, was willing to ponder them. The preacher had given him a sense of the limits. A mass reading public was not going to tolerate a book built on self-indulgent retaliations against the pilgrims, certainly not against individually named pilgrims, no matter how cleverly phrased. Nor would it accept a wholesale ridiculing of the sacred. The California reviewers and preachers were carrying out the necessary work of Mary Fairbanks and others to whom Mark Twain turned: the work of alerting him when it was time to turn from nihilism to art.

ON MAY 5, Sam wrote triumphally to Mary Fairbanks: "The *Alta* has given me permission to use the printed letters. It is all right, now." [26] He had stood his ground with the editors and, despite their strong copyright claims, he had prevailed on every point of contention: no, to a compromise that would give him a percentage of the *Alta*'s royalties; and no, to a preface in which he thanked the newspaper for waiving its rights. (He did agree to grant the *Alta* an acknowledgment.) He notified Elisha Bliss of the good news, and predicted he would return east in mid-June with a completed manuscript. Dug in with his manuscript and newspaper letters at the Occidental, breaking for champagne dinners at the Lick House, he launched into another of the marathon writing binges that would propel him through many of his books.

With a little more than a month before his deadline, and with the great bulk of the agreed-on length still ahead of him, Mark Twain became a scavenger-writer. It was the "Jumping Frog" approach all over again, but with better material and higher goals. He'd finished fifteen draft-chapters since he had begun the manuscript in the rooms at 224 F Street, taking the narrative from New York Harbor to the departure from Paris for Versailles. During this stretch he had used the printed letters at his disposal, but these were few and he had largely composed fresh copy. Now, as the time urgency increased, he shifted from original composition to line-edited revisions of the *Alta, Tribune,* and (one) *Herald* dispatches. Many pages from the final manuscript were in fact pasteups of these columns, with his revisions scrawled in the margins. Combined with the undigested data culled from guidebooks and local histories, and passages from the travel books he aimed to lampoon, these pasteups comprised more than half the word count. Sam's slapdash approach worked. Besides providing a convenient structure, the *Alta* and *Tribune* letters were fundamentally strong, and needed mainly the refining elements that Mark Twain now knew were necessary: the elimination of slang and scatology; a more forgiving and generalized portrayal of the pilgrims; and a shift in his satiric aim from sacred art and sacred relics to the parasitic pitchmen and the phony claims surrounding these treasures.

The full revolutionary force of these improvements, sadly, will never engage the 21st-century mind with the same impact as it did the readership of its time. Victorian, pre-electrical America remained largely isolated from direct experience with the world beyond the oceans and reverent toward classical and biblical icons; thus its readers relished the dense exposition of travel books, a genre to which *The Innocents Abroad* inescapably belongs. Mark Twain's work continues to reward a scrupulous reading with bursts of wit and incomparable description; but these tend to be separated by long passages of dutiful reportage, citations from other books, and obvious padding—imperfections noted by some reviewers of the time.

On June 17, Sam reported to Bliss that "the book is finished, & I think it will do. It will make more than 600 pages, but I shall reduce it at sea."[27] He promised to sail for New York within a week, and to deliver the manuscript at Hartford by the end of July.

But it wasn't going to be that easy. The manuscript wasn't finished with *him*—nor would it be for many more months. No one besides himself had read it. He needed another pair of eyes. He needed a benediction pronounced over this terrifying newborn of his. Mother Fairbanks was a continent away. He turned to an old friend and mentor who had been kind to him in Sam's California past.

Bret Harte was now thirty-one, still striving to establish himself among America's important writers. He was just beginning to publish the work that would get him there—the sketches of the California landscape and the miners, gunslingers, golden-hearted prostitutes, and wanderers who populated it. Meanwhile, he edited an ill-starred California poetry journal; he encouraged younger writers and promoted promising ones. At the time of Sam's return, Harte was helping a man named Anton Roman launch a new literary magazine, the *Overland Monthly*, an attempt to match the influence (and the look) of the *Atlantic Monthly* back east. Sam lugged his bundle of verbiage over to the magazine's offices and pleaded with the swamped Harte to read and comment on it. Incredibly, Harte consented. Whatever outrages real or imagined he would visit on Mark Twain in the future, in this moment he was a true friend in need.

A few years later, despite the fractiousness that arose between them, Sam Clemens was able to give Bret Harte his due in the editorial shaping of *The Innocents Abroad*. "Harte read all of the MS," he told Charles Henry Webb in 1870, "& told me what passages, paragraphs & chapters to leave out—& I followed orders strictly."[28] To Thomas Bailey Aldrich, Sam allowed that Harte "trimmed & trained & schooled me patiently until he changed me from an awkward utterer of coarse grotesqueness" into a polished writer.[29] In return, Sam allowed him to publish four chapters from the *Innocents* manuscript in the *Overland Monthly* without charge.

He had planned to set out for New York on June 30, but at the last minute, he succumbed to one final lecturing gig. He addressed an affluent crowd on the night of July 2 on the topic of Venice, drawing almost verbatim on that section of his manuscript. It was a big success: "wit without vulgarity,"[30] no less, and garnished near the end with "all kinds of concealed jokes, drolleries, flashes of humor and sarcasm."[31] It would be his final appearance in California. Four days later he boarded the *Montana* and put the Golden State behind him forever. He reconnected with the *Henry Chauncey* at Panama. He edited the manuscript as he sailed, and disembarked at New York Harbor with the remaining sheaf of papers that would make him permanently and universally famous.

22

The Girl in the Miniature

(July 1868–October 1868)

He checked into the Westminster Hotel on Wednesday, July 29, and, swamped by the greeting of "many friends," anxiously telegraphed Elisha Bliss, "If I do not come until tomorrow will it answer? Answer immediately."[1] He had promised to deliver the manuscript in Hartford by July 28, and, inexperienced in the ways of publishers, thought perhaps Bliss might hold him to his promise. He was thinking of calling his book *The New Pilgrim's Progress,* after John Bunyan's 1678 Puritan allegory of a religious journey through life. Bunyan's book remained second in popularity only to the Bible among Christian believers after nearly two hundred years, and Sam thought to make ironic capital of its universally known title.

Another universally known icon caused him to change his plans. Bliss wired him back suggesting a postponement—the first of many in the book's production—because July 30 was the publication date of another important new book from the American Publishing Company: *A Personal History of Ulysses S. Grant,* by A. D. Richardson. Bliss suggested a meeting in New York the following week, after the Grant book had been launched, and then perhaps a working visit to Hartford after that. With the delay came a journalistic opportunity, and with that came a chance for Sam to express the social conscience that always burned harder in him than ideology.

Arriving at the Westminster on the same day—in one of those coincidences that dotted Mark Twain's life—was his diplomatic friend Anson Burlingame, along with the Chinese delegation. Burlingame had just negotiated a treaty that established consular relations between China and the

United States and recognized China's legitimacy in the community of nations. Burlingame prevailed on Sam to offer the New York *Tribune* an analysis of the treaty; and Sam, remembering his revulsion at the routine brutality dealt by Americans to Chinese laborers in the West, worked up a six-thousand-word piece in only a few hours. Never again, he wrote with "infinite satisfaction," would jealous American workers be able to "beat and bang and set the dogs" on helpless immigrant Chinese.

These pastimes are lost to them forever . . . I have seen Chinamen abused and maltreated in all the mean, cowardly ways possible to the invention of a degraded nature, but I never saw a policeman interfere in the matter and I never saw a Chinaman righted in a court of justice for wrongs thus done to him . . .[2]

He arrived in Hartford on August 4 and spent two weeks there discussing the more delicious elements of making a book: typeface options and illustration ideas. He tightened the manuscript again, until it stood at about 1,100 pages. Things were harmonious enough with Bliss that Sam could turn his thoughts to the ambitious winter lecture tour that he would undertake in a few months. His reputation at the podium had attracted the interest of several booking agents, notably the pioneer of speaker management, James Redpath of the newly founded Boston Lyceum Bureau; G. L. Torbert in Chicago; and representatives of the American Literary Bureau in New York. Here lay an important chance and challenge: to discover how good he really was on the *other* side of the Rockies, by launching out onto a competitive Eastern lecture circuit crowded with established luminaries. Not to mention drawing attention to the book, which he thought was then scheduled for a December publication.

Sam surveyed these prospects in a short letter, written from Bliss's offices, to his former agent, Frank Fuller. Fuller had recently taken on a new career, as co-owner of a company that made products from rubber, including condoms, apparently. It was too much for Sam to resist: "Please forward one dozen Odorless Rubber Cundrums—I don't mind them being odorless—I can supply the odor myself. I would like to have your picture on them."[3] In an *Alta* letter some weeks later, Mark Twain slyly informed his readers that "the ex-Acting Governor of Utah" was "making money hand over fist in the manufacture . . . of a patent odorless India rubber cloth, which is coming greatly into fashion for buggy-tops and such things."[4]

Sam returned to New York on August 17, then several days later caught a train for Elmira on August 21. He had arranged an invitation for himself to spend a few days at the Charley Langdon household—ostensibly to visit Mary Fairbanks's "other cub," but perhaps also to check out the beautiful sister whom he had finally met in New York at New Year's. Afterward, Sam and Charley planned to travel to Cleveland and look in on Mother Bear. Then Sam planned to go on alone to St. Louis for a family visit.

Any hopes that Clemens might have had for a grand entrance into the

Langdon house were bollixed when he mistakenly boarded a local train out of New York. "Express Mail" proved to be more like snail mail; it stopped about every fifteen minutes for stays of nearly an hour, or so it felt to Sam. As the day lurched on into evening, he began to telegraph his spasmodic progress to Charley, finally snapping, "figure out when it will arrive and meet me."[5] The answer was "midnight." By the time Charley responded to this injunction, the train was within fifteen miles of Elmira.

Impeccably tailored, barbered, and mustached in the manner of a young town squire, Charley boarded the train and shrank back at the sight of his highly peccable guest. Sam lounged in the smoking car under a foul-looking yellow duster and the wreckage of a straw hat. Charley blurted: "You've got some other clothes, haven't you?" Luckily for Sam, he did.

LAURA WRIGHT may still have been floating through Sam's dreams, but as he entered the Langdon household, it was the girl in the ivory miniature who now fully entered his waking life. Entering, she changed it utterly. His wild years were over. The great arc of his punishing fame and his majestic sorrows was about to begin.

Her name was of course her mother's name as well. It drew upon the symbol for peace, light, unity, healing, and tradition common to the great religions of the earth: the golden lampstand fueled by the oil from two olive trees in Zecharah's vision; the dove bearing the olive branch in the Noah myth; the blessed olive tree kindling the glass like a glittering star, light upon light, in the Quranic *aya*. Sam, clopping through Palestine on his donkey, probably looked on living olive trees that had taken root in the time of Jesus. In *Twelfth Night*, Shakespeare's Olivia, seeking her true love, is confused by twins with assumed identities. (Olivia, to a disguised twin: "Are you a comedian?")

She was the product of an educated, wealthy, and socially progressive household. Her father's New England line had produced a delegate to the Constitutional Congress who became governor of New Hampshire, and, later, a president of Harvard, but Jervis's fortune was self-made. His grandparents on either side were farmers settled in New York State. When Jervis was sixteen his widowed mother, Eunice Langdon, steered him to a man named Stevens who owned small stores in Vernon and Ithaca, and Jervis learned the mercantile business. By age twenty-three he was running several stores and had married Olivia Lewis (on July 23, 1832). A few years after that, he joined up with a lumber dealer; moved his wife and adopted nine-year-old daughter Susan to Elmira (Mrs. Langdon mistakenly believed she was infertile); witnessed the birth of his daughter Olivia on November 27, 1845, and his son Charles four years later; bought several hundred acres of rich Allegheny County pine-tree land that turned out to be even richer in deposits of coal; shifted into that business just in time to help feed the enormous factory-fuel demand ignited by the Civil War; and ended up owning coal mines from Pennsylvania to Nova Scotia and a railroad transportation system to move the yield. By the war's end he was the wealthiest man in a small prosperous city, a co-founder and benefactor of a Congregational church. Susan made a happy marriage in 1858 with Theodore W. Crane, Jervis's business manager in J. Langdon, Miner & Dealer in Anthracite & Bituminous Coal. In a manner of looking at it, Jervis Langdon was living the life that Marshall Clemens had dreamed of.

Yet Jervis Langdon's personality and social beliefs were as far removed from Marshall's as was possible in this America. A compact man with a square face and mild, quizzical eyes, Jervis liked people, and he liked to laugh, and he liked to sing, and these traits partly tempered an unrelenting reformist zeal. He and his wife shared abolitionist passions so intense that, less than a year after arriving in Elmira, they flaunted them at considerable risk in the town: they joined thirty-nine other congregants in a bolt from the First Presbyterian Church, which, like its sister congregation in Hannibal and many others, held to the "Bible defense of slavery." In January 1846, this group founded the First Independent Congregational Church (soon renamed Park Church), which discriminated, as it were, against slavery sympathizers. Langdon's philanthropy kept the struggling church solvent in its early years.

Riskier still to the Langdons' safety in those years was their link to the Underground Railroad. The Railroad comprised a web of secret way stations in fourteen states, mostly farmhouses and town residences, that received fugitives concealed in wagons under dark of night, sheltered them for a while, and then moved them along to the next stopping point north. Despite the dangers of heavy fines and imprisonment, the operatives along the Railroad liberated some fifty thousand Negroes in the sixty-odd years through the end of the Civil War. Among Jervis Langdon's close comrades in this movement was a former slave whom Langdon and his wife had helped escape from bondage as a Baltimore ship caulker back in 1838. The man had become a self-educated author, international lecturer, and abolitionist symbol; his name was Frederick Douglass.

Langdon and his friends found a dubious but ultimately sympathetic ally in the pastor who arrived in 1854 and steered the church for the ensuing forty-six years: Thomas K. Beecher, the brother of Henry Ward Beecher and Harriet Beecher Stowe.

By autumn 1868, Jervis Langdon was at the peak of his business and civic success. He was also suffering through the early stages of the stomach cancer that in less than two years would kill him. His family lived in a three-story manor decorated with lush carpeting and drapes, and grand chandeliers, whose grounds occupied a full block.

"I SHALL be here a week yet—maybe two," Sam advised Jane and the family from the Langdons' on August 25. "I am most comfortably situated here. This is the pleasantest family I ever knew."[6]

Mark Twain never wrote in detail about these opening moments of his romance with Olivia, but some hints survive, thanks to a cousin of Olivia who was staying at the house and found herself smitten by Sam. Thirty years on, Harriet Lewis Paff wryly recalled her losing battle.

> I really felt that I had one advantage over my cousin . . . She was rich, beautiful and intellectual, but she could not see through a joke, or see anything to laugh at in the wittiest sayings unless explained in detail—I could . . . He said—"How do you do," just as anyone would, except with that lazy drawl which has added much flavor to his wit and humor . . . We rode, walked, talked & sang together, for Mr. C. had a very sweet tenor voice. But alas—I soon discovered that my quickness at seeing the point of a joke and the witty sayings that I had considered almost irresistible were simply nothing in comparison to my cousin's gifts. Mr. C. evidently greatly preferred her sense to my nonsense.[7]

Harriet Lewis sensed well ahead of Livy that some woo was being pitched, and finally left, "thinking the courtship might progress better if I were out of the way."[8] Before leaving, she clued her sheltered friend in on Sam's motives for being there "and said that on my return I should ask a question, in regard to a question I was quite sure would be asked of her, and I wanted a favorable answer to both."[9]

Soon afterward, Sam did ask The Question of Livy that Harriet had predicted. After Livy gave him her answer, she resuscitated him with the only reassuring news she could think of: she would pray for him daily. Suddenly Sam was not so comfortably situated after all.

It is something of a wonder that Sam's welcome at the Langdons' did not expire after that first visit. The family had greeted him warmly and had taken genuine delight in his droll stories in the first few days; but as one week lengthened into two, a kind of frozen cordiality set in, punctuated by the discreet drumming of fingers. (When Livy informed him of this half a year later, Sam was devastated.) Sam's usually trusty bravado was working against him now, as were his normally keen instincts for a situation. He was bloodying his nose against the very fortress of upper-class Eastern manners that he had wished to understand and surmount.

Livy's horrified reaction to Sam's proposal reflected her own acculturation within that fortress. As her biographer Resa Willis has pointed out, Olivia Louise Langdon was Victorian to the core. She lived her childhood in a cloistered garden, all luxury and books and music. Her mother taught her to read, and to explore science, history, mathematics, novels, poetry. She was enrolled at age nine as a day student in the nearby Elmira Ladies' Seminary in 1854. By thirteen, she was a resident there, immersed in Latin and Greek. She was never strong, was frequently ill, and one winter, at age sixteen, she became an invalid. Mark Twain wrote that she'd fallen on ice; no more information than that survives. Willis points out that her prostration was hardly rare: the Beautiful Invalid was a prevalent figure among upper-class women of the time. Neurasthenia, hysteria, melancholia, nervosa—the pre-Freudian names for it were exotic and wonderful. She remained bedridden for two years, resisting treatment—one doctor thought she'd just used up too much mental energy, or electricity, or something—until an eccentric doctor named Newton, offered fifteen hundred dollars by the desperate family, walked into her room, opened the shades, sat her up, coaxed her into hobbling around a little on his shoulder, recommended more of the same, collected his fee, and went home. After a long recovery, she reemerged into the world a small, slight figure, like the man who would marry her, and dark-haired and dark-eyed, and beautiful in a mild sort of way. She tended to tuck her chin into her neck slightly, like her mother, which intensified her gaze. Her characteristic expression was of a young woman considering whether to smile—a frequent dilemma, given her anemic sense of humor.

LIVY WAS getting on in years. To reach twenty-two unmarried in the mid-19th century was to approach spinsterhood and a lifetime of embroidery, good works, and schoolteaching. Livy was a good match for Sam in her love of reading; she copied selections from Whitman and Emerson into the commonplace book that she'd begun just before her eighteenth birthday. So why did she turn Sam Clemens down?

Protocol, for one thing. Politely bred New England ladies, even twenty-two-year-olds, always said "no" the first time a man proposed, especially if he had not obtained the permission of the parents to make such a proposal. For another, she was almost certainly not then attracted to this wild-haired, cigar-smoking, long-drawling, welcome-overstaying creature from the distant west, ten years her senior.* He was a curiosity, not marriage material. The phrasing of her turndown, never recorded, must have pinned his ears back. But Sam had some phrasing of his own to deploy. He began deploying it in the early morning hours of his departure day from the Langdons'. Scribbling away in his guest room, anguished by his romantic desire for Livy and a little unhinged by her rejection, Sam tore from his soul the first of the famous 184† love letters he would write in the course of a courtship conducted largely at long distance, and thus largely by words on a page.

These letters rank among the most compelling documents in Samuel Clemens's literature (he never signed them "Mark Twain"). Lengthy, intense, sonorous, and apologetic at first, then shifting, as their intimacy deepened, into the playful, boastful, needful, and gently seductive, they let us trace the trajectory of Sam's and Livy's convergence. In them, new layers of his personality reveal themselves. Clemens/Twain had built a reputation as a virtuoso of sarcasm and invective and sharply pointed satire, not to say ridicule. From the stage, he could be mesmeric, even sensual; but always at a remove. Up close, he had the capacity to charm his listener and to bring all within earshot into

---

* Ten years almost on the nose. Olivia's birthday fell on November 27, three days before Sam's.

† This is Olivia's own count. Many of the letters have not been recovered.

his force field; but again, the distance never quite closed. In these letters, for Livy, the distance closed.

This first epistle, and several afterward, show the mesmerizer in the throes of self-hypnosis. Here Sam transforms himself with unconscious precision into the sort of lofty, spiritual aspirant he understands Olivia to have been groomed to marry: the perfect Victorian Gentleman undone by his own *faux pas;* the Frame Narrator purging himself of the Sut Lovingood within.

Even getting that far took some fast thinking. Desperate to extricate himself from the crisis posed by Livy's flat turndown, Sam negotiated a compromise with the wary young woman: they would correspond, and continue their friendship, but strictly under the chaste rubric of "brother" and "sister." (His imaginary family was growing by leaps and bounds.) Thus the salutation of the initial letter, written to her while still at Elmira:

> My Honored "Sister"—
>
> The impulse is strong upon me to say to you how grateful I am to you . . . for the patience, the consideration & the unfailing kindness which has been shown me ever since I came within the shadow of this roof . . . I do not regret that I have loved you, still love & shall always love you. I accept the situation, uncomplainingly, hard as it is. Of old I am acquainted with grief, disaster & disappointment, & have borne these troubles as became a man. So, also, I shall bear this last & bitterest, even though it break my heart . . .
>
> And so, henceforward, I claim only that you will let me freight my speeches to you with simply the sacred love a brother bears to a sister . . . If you & mother Fairbanks will only scold me & upbraid me now & then, I shall fight my way through the world, never fear. Write me something from time to time—texts from the New Testament, if nothing else occurs to you . . .[10]

He keeps it up in letters posted over the next several weeks:

> I cannot frame language so that it will express to you how grateful I am for that large charity & thoughtful consideration which prompted you to speak so gently when you could have wounded so deeply . . . You say to me: "I shall pray for you daily." Not any words that ever were spoken to me have touched me like these.[11]

> I am afraid to write any more, because you were just a little severe the other day, you know. Good-bye, & God give you His peace.[12]

He was of a distinctly ecclesiastical frame of mind these days, and managed to let that fact slip in. "And so you . . . are left to say, 'human friendship is impotent to help.' You have read Matt. XXV, 44–45? & XVII, 18–20?"[13] "What was the name of that hymn we fancied so much in church one day? 'Fading, Still Fading' is beautiful—old, but beautiful." [14] He was praying a lot, too. "I pray as one who prays with words, against a firm-set mountain of sin. I pray *too* hopefully, sometimes, & sometimes hopelessly. But I still pray—& shall continue to pray." [15] Most of Livy's responses, unhappily, have not been recovered.

It is tempting, given Mark Twain's mimetic mastery of written and spoken styles, to read these ornate passages in a cynical light, as the stratagem of a worldly pretender, out to ensnare a sheltered rich girl and ride her petticoats to Easy Street. Almost certainly Sam's admitted craving for self-validation—in this case, for acceptance as "authentic" by a girl from the American aristocracy—fueled the intensity of his efforts. But such cynicism withers when viewed against the long and loving arc of Sam's marriage to Olivia. Love, friendship, loyalty—these were values of unconditional importance to Samuel Clemens. Once he bestowed them on someone, his fidelity was unshakable, so long as they were returned in kind; nothing wounded him as deeply as evidence that his faith had been betrayed. The language of these letters may be affected, but their ardency would prove genuine, and permanent. As for the voice, it likely came from that great seamless universe in Clemens's mind where dreams, reality, fact, and fiction conjoined. He likely *was* the perfect Victorian Gentleman as he wrote those lines. As the editors of his letters from this period have observed, "He may well have been working a deception about his own character and beliefs—but it is impossible to read these letters without realizing that if he was, he was not aware of it at the time." [16] Olivia, when she got to know him better, put it more succinctly: she simply called him "Youth."

SAM LEFT the Langdon house on September 8, clinging to what remained of his dignity, and to the permission Livy had given him to keep writing to her. He departed Elmira with Charley Langdon, who was still thankfully in the dark about Sam's romantic aspirations. The two cubs boarded a train for Cleveland, as they'd planned, where Mother Bear awaited them, tapping her paws impatiently. The visit was purely social for young Charley, an innocent reunion with a shipboard friend; but for the other two, it carried some heavy freight. Cleveland was the city Sam had selected for his debut as a professional lecturer. The appearance, set for November 17, would launch a dense winter tour whose schedule was still filling up: requests for bookings had flowed into his agents' offices and to him personally throughout the summer and into the early fall.

By the time he left the Langdons' house, Mark Twain was committed to a staggering itinerary: twenty-six dates (the bookings would eventually approach forty) over nine weeks along a zigzagging trail of cities and towns in Ohio, Pennsylvania, New York, New Jersey, Michigan, Indiana, Illinois, and Iowa. His last scheduled date was in Iowa City on January 9, 1869; but Torbert in Chicago kept nailing down bookings through December and January, and then, after a hiatus, a sort of "curtain call" in Sharon, Pennsylvania, on March

20. He would lecture on Christmas Day, and on all but four of the first fifteen days of January. He would appear in cities as prominent as Cleveland, Pittsburgh, Detroit, Indianapolis, and Chicago, and in towns as obscure as Rondout, New York; Tecumseh, Michigan; and Ottawa, Illinois. (The size of a town was incidental to its importance on the circuit: a full house was a full house, and houses in those days did not differ significantly in size.)

His average fee would be about $100—respectable but not top-of-the-line. The highest-paid speaker in the East at the time was Olive Logan, the women's rights crusader, who commanded $250. Henry Ward Beecher, Anna Dickinson, and Horace Greeley were among those in the $150–$200 range. Sam hoped to make up by sheer volume what he could not amass in per-lecture billing. He needed significant money, the sooner the better. He'd convinced himself that Olivia Langdon would never accept the hand of a vagabond entertainer and freelance journalist of marginal means. But with his Holy Land book on track for a December publication, he had a shot at presenting himself to her as a successful author-lecturer.

To Mary Fairbanks, Sam's tour could establish her protégé as a rising paragon of the lyceum. Or it could anneal his reputation as a clown. Sam had remained suspiciously vague as to the subject of his lecture. He'd indicated that he might dust off his 1866 "Sandwich Islands" success, or possibly unveil a new talk on the subject of California. These topics were mentioned in newspaper advertisements that appeared early in his tour.

Mother Fairbanks was not fooled for a minute. She scented *Quaker City* from the get-go, and she smelled trouble along with it. The Holy Land voyage had taken on semisacred proportions to her and most of her fellow travelers. It was about beautiful, lofty things and pleasant, respectable people. Mark Twain had desecrated this image—and truly presumed on their friendship—with his withering piece in the New York *Herald* the day after the steamship docked. She wasn't overjoyed with what she'd read about his Toast to Woman at the press correspondents' banquet in Washington, for that matter. She saw his visit to Cleveland as a chance for her to gain some control over this lecture, and her cub's moral development along with it.

Sam anticipated all this, and the negotiating it would entail. He knew that Mary Fairbanks had divined the subject matter that he eventually, inevitably, settled on. He knew exactly how she expected him to treat it: with the uplifting (and slang-free) solemnity of the standard-issue Tasteful Victorian Elucidator. This was out of the question; and yet to simply steamroll the Fairbanksean sensibilities with a broadside of ridicule was also unthinkable. He was not so cruel that he would humiliate his adoring mentor in her home city, in the presence of her friends. He needed her goodwill, both professionally and with the Langdons: an admiring review of his talk in her husband's *Herald* would launch his tour on a note of triumph. That was why he had chosen Cleveland as his debut city, and had specifically asked Mrs. Fairbanks to write a review.

Sam spent much of his time in the Mary and Abel Fairbanks household scribbling through preliminary drafts of the lecture. Among his innocuous working titles was "Americans in the Old World." A less bridled theme was taking shape in his mind, but he wasn't yet ready to reveal it. He nodded dutifully at Mary's copious advice for revisions. He and Charley explored the city, and sat for a joint portrait looking world-weary in snazzy evening clothes. Their hosts held a reception for them, at which Charley sparkled, reining in his avidity for alcohol. Sam confided to his "Mother" about his new "sister." (Mary Fairbanks had been after him to find a wife; how she felt about his finding a new sibling remains unclear.) After two weeks of this, Charley returned to Elmira and Sam traveled on for a brief reunion with the homefolks in St. Louis. This time his heart wasn't in the visit. The old Mississippi River city struck him as muddy, smoky, mean, an infection. Perhaps he was making the river a scapegoat for a newfound shame about his non-Eastern origins. He fidgeted under the family's hospitality, impatient to leave. "I am called East." [17]

His prospects had taken an amazing turn out there. Livy had sent a letter to him in Cleveland that contained, miraculously, a photograph of herself. He dashed off a letter of buoyant thanks from Pamela's and Jane's household—"I never dreamt of such a thing" [18]—that was prudently garnished with "mend-my-conduct" language: he even vowed to pray with Livy. Details of timing were left unexamined. He also answered a missive from the Mother Bear, whose advice on the lecture continued to track him through the postal service. "Don't be afraid to write sermons," he assured her gamely. "Your advice about the building of the lecture I shall strictly follow." On the same day, he twitted Frank Fuller about not receiving any "cundrums." "I can get along without them, I suppose. My aunt never uses them." [19] Then in early October he escaped back to the region that felt more and more like home.

He planned to head to New York and then to Hartford to consult on the production of *The New Pilgrim's Progress,* as it was still being called. Rail connections being excellent, it was hardly a problem to detour south through Elmira for an overnight call on the Langdons and Livy. Nursing a bad cold and undoubtedly distracted, he took another pratfall in the maze of elite Eastern manners, and came within another hair of losing the princess he was courting. Yet another pratfall—a real one this time—saved him.

On the afternoon of his planned nighttime departure, Sam took Charley Langdon aside and let him in on his romantic feelings toward Livy. Other family members already had their suspicions—elder sister Susan Crane, who had been around the block a time or two, sensed the current on Sam's first visit, and disapproved. The ever-democratic Jervis Langdon was more forgiving, and more focused on what his daughter wanted. Tormented with the early symptoms of his stomach cancer, he had found relief in sharing laughter with Sam, and seems to have looked kindly on the match from the start. Charley was a different story. As he took on the affectations of his snobbish social circle, the young man's shipboard deference to Sam mutated into condescension. Mark Twain would remember Charley as "conceited, arrogant, and overbearing," hopelessly spoiled by "his worst enemy," his mother. Charley may have accepted the notorious *Quaker City* "sinner" as a traveling companion and a good fellow, but brother-in-law was too much. Livy's brother stunned Sam by his response: an icy suggestion that Clemens might want to board an earlier train; for instance, the one leaving in half an hour. He relented a little; but by evening, he was still only too eager to escort the visitor to the train station.

A split second of slapstick saved Sam's suitor status. The pair climbed into the "democrat wagon" outside the main gate; the horse lurched forward—and Sam and Charley did an involuntary synchronized double-backwards somersault onto the cobblestones. It seemed that the seat had not been locked into place.

Neither was badly hurt. Charley suffered a forehead gash when a seat landed on it, and Sam lay seeing stars for several minutes until the Langdon women rushed outdoors to slosh him with water. They hoisted him inside, tucked him into bed and insisted that he stay an extra day to recuperate, with Livy keeping watch. Sam, who later allowed that he'd faked his injuries a little, let himself be persuaded. Not even catching the measles at Will Bowen's house had been this much fun. He broke his "neck in eleven different places," he gleefully reported to Mother Fairbanks. As for Charley,

> The seat followed Charley out & split his head wide open, so that you could look through it just as if you were looking through a gorge in a mountain. There wasn't anything to intercept the view—which was curious, because his brains hadn't been knocked out.[20]

Sam made good use of his time under Livy's care. "I can't *write* about that matter that is in your mind & mine," he reported to Mrs. Fairbanks, "but suffice it that it bears just a *little* pleasanter aspect than it did when I saw you last . . ."[21] Yet Sam promptly overplayed his hand. Soon after his departure for Hartford, in a fit of "hot-blooded heedlessness," he dropped the brother pose and scorched the young woman with a letter of naked passion—a letter now lost. Clammy regret was not long in forming. "I'll bet I have written a letter that will *finish* me," he moaned to Mother Fairbanks. "I wish I had it back again—I would tone it down some."[22] Livy's reply, also unrecovered, sent Sam hightailing it back to the "Honored Sister" mode on October 18: "You have rebuked me . . . I accept the rebuke, severe as it was, & surely I ought to thank you for the lesson it brings . . . I walk upon the ground again—not in the clouds."[23]

SAM LICKED this wound in leafy Hartford for the rest of October, boarding at the Bliss household and working on the book manuscript and his lecture. Elisha Bliss lived with his second wife, Amelia Crosby Bliss, not far from the American Publishing Company offices at 148 Asylum Avenue, near its conjunction with Farmington Avenue to the south. Farmington and Asylum di-

verged westward in a widening "V" through Asylum Hill, a graceful wooded
swell of 615 acres that had been known as Lord's Hill until 1807, when the
Connecticut Asylum for the Deaf was established there. It was on the southern
slope of Asylum Hill, tucked up against a curved bank of the North Park River,
that Mark Twain was soon to be happy, for a time. There lay Nook Farm.

By 1868, Nook Farm had coalesced into a miniature nonesuch realm: an
intertwined and interrelated Camelot of wealthy artists, social reformers,
thinkers, and writers, who shared a warren of ivy-draped houses in the Victorian, Gothic, and federal styles. It was as much a distillation of high Eastern
culture as Virginia City had been a distillation of the lowdown West. Sam, wandering through this preternaturally small world, had already met some of
Nook Farm's denizens—the Hookers and Harriet Beecher Stowe. Now, he
reentered their paradise—on the wings of Bliss, so to speak.

"SET A white stone—for I have made a friend," he crowed to Livy in that
same you-have-rebuked-me letter. "It is the Rev. J. H. Twichell . . . I could
hardly find words strong enough to tell how much I *do* think of that man." [24]
No doubt Sam would have leapt to claim friendship with just about any clergyman at this point in his relationship with Livy. He made sure to work in the
information that "I met him at a church sociable, (where I made a dozen
pleasant acquaintances, old & young & of both sexes)." But in this case, he
didn't need to exaggerate. Joe Twichell was a spectacular personality—enthusiastic, virile, ridiculously handsome in a boyish, round-faced sort of way—he
even sported an unruly lock of hair that curled over his forehead. He was at
once a bookish grind and a fearless man of action: an honors student in English composition and port-waist on the Yale crew of 1859, just about the time
that the concept of a "muscular Christianity" was beginning to challenge the
pervading concept of an ascetic, rather sad-sack Anglican Jesus. He entered
Union Theological Seminary after his graduation, but left at the outset of the
Civil War to volunteer as a chaplain. At age twenty-two, he asked for a rough
regiment—the more civilized soldiers already had plenty of chaplains, he figured. He was assigned to the ferocious New York Zouaves, who modeled
themselves on the flamboyant and brutal French North African fighters of the
1830s. The Zouaves decked themselves out in turbans, fezzes, embroidered
vests, leggings, and flared scarlet trousers. These outfits drew attention on the
battlefield; the red pants held up well through the smoke and haze, as targets.
The Zouaves didn't seem to mind this, as long as they looked good.

Twichell was shocked at the profanity of these "rough and wicked" men, as
he described them in a letter to his father, but he soon saw worse things. His
corps commander was General Dan Sickles, the former Tammany Hall congressman who in 1858 had gunned down his wife's lover, the son of Francis
Scott Key. Joe Twichell was with Sickles's Third Corps on the second day at
Gettysburg, when Sickles, ignoring orders, advanced his men into the open
field below the Round Tops without protection, where they absorbed a charge

by forty-five thousand of James Longstreet's infantry. The general paid personally for his slaughterhouse mistake when a cannonball mangled his leg. Twichell accompanied the stretcher bearers from the lines to the surgical tent, as Sickles enjoyed a cigar. The two became rather fond of each other.

Comradeships with profane fighting men, and witness to their suffering and deaths, informed Joe Twichell's Christian sensibilities. His theology was less intellectual than emotional. Wagging a finger at commonplace sin mattered less to him than exalting life, and a faith centered on good works—what would come to be known nearly fifty years later as the Social Gospel. He was mustered out of the war in June 1864. After more seminary studies at Andover, he was called to the newly completed Asylum Hill Congregational Church at 814 Asylum Avenue in Hartford, where, during a reception on an October evening in 1868, Twichell overheard a small red-haired guest wisecracking that "this is the 'Church of the Holy Speculators.' " A few minutes later, Amelia Bliss introduced Twichell to Sam Clemens. It was the beginning of a beautiful friendship.

ON THE less satisfying side of the ledger, production on *The New Pilgrim's Progress* languished. Elisha Bliss envisioned many engraved pictures "sandwiched" in the text, and Sam concurred; but rounding up the photographs, and then having these drawn and engraved on wood, was a slow process. Sam supplied many photographs that he had collected during the voyage, and had already solicited Moses Beach and others for any that they could offer. In the end, the book would contain some 230 wood engravings, many taken from the travelers' own collection of prints made by the expedition photographer, William E. James. By mid-October it was clear to Bliss that the book could not appear before March 1869, and he told Clemens of that delay.

The lecture, however, was ready. The finishing surge had kicked in after Mark stopped trying to please others, and homed in on the Holy Land adventure as he had experienced and understood it. In a day or two, he cobbled together a lecture of ninety minutes, taken whole, or lightly edited, from sections of the book manuscript. At the center of this work a gaudy figure preened himself, feet planted apart, green bottle-glasses covering his eyes. He clutched a parasol with one hand and a Bible in the other. His pockets bulged with trinkets and chipped-off specimens from cathedrals, the ruins of statues, the surface of the Sphinx. He was an American, his name was the Vandal, and he was ready to rock.

23

American Vandal

(October–December 1868)

S am broke the news of the lecture's title to Mother Fairbanks as gingerly as he could. As to her latest proposed outline, which even included "heads" for his various transitions—oops! It arrived too late.

> . . . I wrote the *lecture* the day before your letter came . . . I had planned the lecture *just about* as you did, & wrote & wrote & kept writing till I saw that I was never going to weave a web that would suit me. So then I altered the title to "The American Vandal Abroad," & began again.

Mrs. Fairbanks was not to worry, though, because "I treat him gently & good-naturedly . . . To tell the truth there isn't a great deal of Vandal in the lecture." [1]

To tell the truth, there was: but in a form that was inconceivable to Mary Fairbanks's tidy philosophies. This Vandal was not the crude pietistic scavenger that Mark Twain had lampooned in his first newspaper sketches after the *Quaker City* docked. He was a far more complex character than that, and far more original: a new archetype in American culture, eclipsing such provincial icons as Johnny Appleseed, Paul Bunyan, Mike Fink, even Sut Lovingood. This Vandal bestrode the world. Unlike his cowed countrymen who for decades had approached the Old World on bended knee, the Vandal returned the appraising gaze of any European or Arab who dared assert a higher claim on history. If he was boorish and sanctimonious and frequently ignorant of what he surveyed, the Vandal brought a *legitimacy* to his observations, founded on the stubborn American self-invention and good common sense envisioned by Emerson. The Vandal was the ancestor of George F. Babbitt and Alden Pyle; the emerging face of America, as it appeared to the larger world, and also as it appeared in the mirror.

As he marked the days until the unveiling of this new phenomenon, Sam took comfort in the evidence that "Honored Sister's" attitude was thawing a little again. ("Your welcome letter made me entirely *satisfied*.")[2] Clearly, Livy saw promise in Sam's new friendship with Reverend Twichell—his descriptions of the hearty, civic-minded minister probably reminded her a little of her father's temperament. Sam saw this, and began shoehorning in as many Twichell references as he could think of, even if it meant clotting up his usually clean sentence line. "The idea of that party of ministers at his [Twichell's] house the other night thanking me fervently for having written & published certain trash which they said had lit up some gloomy days with a wholesome laugh was a surprise to me."[3] And: "Mr. & Mrs. Twichell and myself . . . drove 10 miles out in the country & back the other day, & in the course of the conversation Mr. T. uttered several things that struck me forcibly."[4] And: "Twichell is splendid. And he has one rare faculty—he is thoughtful & considerate. He lends me his overcoat when I go there without one, lends me his umbrella, lends me his slippers."[5] Not to mention lending him several wagonloads of piety-by-association.

By this time, Sam was feeling bold enough to launch an ongoing prank on his shy and literary inamorata: "deleting" certain passages in his love letters without utterly obscuring them, thus allowing Livy the illusion of reading what he had written, but then decided to take back.* His early dabblings at this were innocuous: "~~I would tease you, only you take everything in such dreadful earnest it hurts my conscience,~~" read part of a barely crossed-out postscript in an October 30 letter. "~~I never could venture farther than to convince you that there was 16 in a cribbage hand that hadn't *anything* in it.~~"[6] As time passed, his "deletions" grew more daring.

Sam's surface playfulness with Livy concealed a growing private despair. He feared that the courtship was futile; he would never prove himself worthy of this *über*–Becky Thatcher, and her parents would never approve the match even if he did. That despair flooded to the surface in one of Samuel Clemens's rare emotional breakdowns, this one in a New York household parlor. Sam had popped down to the city on October 31 for a party at the invitation of a pair of actresses known as the Webb sisters, whom he had met in Virginia City. He was still in town on November 3, the day that Ulysses S. Grant was elected

---

* Scholars at the Mark Twain Project at the University of California, Berkeley, have identified no less than fifteen distinct "crossing-out" styles in Mark Twain's letters. They range from what Robert Hirst has called the "deletions-intended-to-be-read" method he used to twit Mary Fairbanks and Livy, through a range of X's, horizontal slashes that scarcely obscure what he first wrote, to a method of ever-denser loops and false *p*'s and *d*'s written over the original and designed to prevent *anyone* from reading the deleted matter.

the eighteenth president. He paid a call on a family named the Wileys, who lived on East 49th Street near Madison Avenue. The Wileys, by a staggering coincidence, were family friends both of the Clemenses, from Hannibal days, and of Fidele Brooks, a friend of Olivia Langdon's. A young Wiley daughter, Margaret, sat at her desk pretending to do her lessons during Sam's visit, but eavesdropped as Sam sat and talked with her father, George Wiley. She was all ears when the auburn-haired visitor abruptly pleaded for George's advice: "I am DESPERATELY IN LOVE with the most exquisite girl—*so beautiful, unfortunately very rich* . . . I have proposed & been *refused* a dozen times—*what* do YOU think?"[7]

George Wiley replied that he thought Sam was crazy to even think of such a thing. Seventy-six years later, Margaret recounted the moment in prose that has the unself-conscious sweetness of stage melodrama.

"That's what I was afraid you would say. I know I'm too rough—knocking around the world." And the tears came. He took out his handkerchief and wiped them away. Father said: "Sam, are you fooling? Is this one of your blank jokes?" He saw he was terribly serious and hurt. So father jumped up, ran over, took him by the shoulders . . . and said: "Sam you old Galoote, you. You're not rough; you're the most perfect gentleman—the cleanest, most decent man I know today. There is no girl in the world too good for you. Go for her, and get her, and God bless you, Sam."[8]

To which Sam replied, according to Margaret:

"Well, I will go see her again tomorrow, and I'll harass that girl and harass her till she'll *have* to say yes! For George, you know I never had wish or time to bother with women, and I can give that girl the purest, best love any man can ever give her. I can make her well and happy."[9]

Which is what he proceeded to do, more or less. He arrived in Cleveland on Sunday, November 8, to prepare for his premiere lecture. He spent some time cultivating members of the Cleveland press, to whom he was already a celebrity. He chose a cunning way to get his name into the Sunday *Herald* two days before his talk—perhaps a revealing one as well, given his anxieties about acceptance by respectable society.

In a humorous sketch titled "A Mystery," Mark Twain reports that he has been bedeviled by an impostor, a "double" traveling around the country and using the name Mark Twain to borrow money, run up unpaid hotel bills, and get "persistently and eternally drunk." In language that strained the definition of "humor," Mark Twain distanced himself from this disreputable doppelganger.

Now to my mind there is something exceedingly strange about this Double of mine . . . Doubles usually have the same instincts, and act in the same way as their originals—but this one don't. This one . . . does according to its own notions entirely, without stopping to consider whether they are likely to be consistent with mine or not . . . It gets intoxicated—I do not. It steals horses—I do not. It imposes on theatre managers—I never do. It lies—I never do. It swindles landlords—I never get a chance.[10]

On the stormy evening of Tuesday, November 17, Mark Twain ambled onto the third-floor auditorium stage in the newly completed Case Hall in Cleveland—deadpan as usual, one hand in his jacket pocket—to inaugurate the fund-raising lecture series for the planned city library. A crowd of twelve hundred, including Abel and Mary Fairbanks and several *Quaker City* passengers, awaited him in patent-opera chairs. The audience was skeptical. Some of the lyceum regulars doubted this newcomer's ability to divert them. Mark Twain's erstwhile shipmates had their own reasons for apprehension. "I am to speak of the American Vandal this evening," Mark Twain began in his signature drawl, and then he told the audience what he had in mind by that darkly exhilarating term.* The term "Vandal," he said, "best describes the roving, independent, free-and-easy character of that class of traveling Americans who are *not* elaborately educated, cultivated, and refined—and gilded and filagreed with the ineffable graces of the first society."[11]

Pacing around the podium, shifting his shoulders, scarcely consulting the sheaf of notes in his fist, but instead searching out individual pairs of eyes in the crowd—"buttonholing"—Mark Twain embellished the figure he had outlined. As he did so, he melted any Fairbanksean hopes that her protégé would become a gilded and pedigreed darling of high-lyceum pieties, an extension of herself. And he melted the audience's frosty dignity into laughter and applause.

The Vandal was a nosy, pushy cuss, never shy about crossing boundaries: "He attempts to investigate the secrets of the harems; he views the rock where Paul was let down in a basket, and seriously asks where the basket is. He will choke himself to death trying to smoke a Turkish pipe . . ."[12]

The Vandal could be a philistine (but you had to admire his candor).

The Vandal goes to see this picture [Da Vinci's *The Last Supper*], which all the world praises—looks at it with a critical eye and says it's a perfect old nightmare of a picture and he wouldn't give $40 for a million like it—(and I endorse his opinion,) and then he is done with Milan.[13]

---

* No "standard" text of the Vandal lecture exists, although fifty-seven pages of the original manuscript are preserved in the Mark Twain Papers. Mark Twain committed his lectures to memory, and then typically improvised on them from city to city. Useful pastiches of the lecture as reported in newspapers at the time can be found in *The Trouble Begins at Eight: Mark Twain's Lecture Tours,* edited by Fred W. Lorch (Ames: Iowa State University Press, 1968), and in *Mark Twain Speaking,* edited by Paul Fatout (Iowa City: University of Iowa Press, 1976). The excerpts here are drawn from both sources and, where possible, corrected against the manuscript pages.

The Vandal could be vulgar and confrontational. Listen to him telling off a noisy Venetian gondolier.

> Look here, Roderigo Gonzales Michael Angelo—Smith—I'm a pilgrim and I'm a stranger, but I'm not going to stand any such caterwauling as that! If this thing goes on one of us has got [to] take water. It is enough that my cherished dreams of Venice have been blighted forever, without taxing *your* talents to make the matter worse. Another yelp out of you and overboard you go![14]

Most incorrigibly, the Vandal could be . . . well . . . a vandal.

> You could find them breaking specimens from the dilapidated tomb of Romeo and Juliet at Padua—and infesting the picture-galleries of Florence—and risking their necks on the Leaning Tower of Pisa—and snuffing sulphur fumes on the summit of Vesuvius . . . and you might see them with spectacles on and blue cotton umbrellas under their arms benignantly contemplating Rome from the venerable arches of the Coliseum.[15]

Yet the American Vandal was more than the sum of these parts. In his hard-headed, bull-in-a-china-shop way, he was the ambassador of a newly industrialized, populous, and therefore *consequential* America—no longer the familiar apologist for a backwoods culture sneered at by the French and English and Italian aristocracy, but the envy of all these, and damned proud of it.

The lesson of the Excursion was a good one. It taught us that foreign countries are excellent to travel in, but that the best country to live in is America, after all. We found no soap in the hotels of Europe, and they charged us for candles we never burned. We saw no ladies anywhere that were as beautiful as our own ladies here at home and especially in this audience. We saw none anywhere that dressed with such excellent taste as do our ladies at home here.[16]

In fact the Vandal had upended the entire rationale for the American as traveler. Humility, worship, self-abasement before the splendors of antiquity? Forget it.

> If there is a moral to this lecture it is an injunction to all Vandals to *travel*. I am glad the American Vandal *goes* abroad. It does him good . . . for it enlarges his charity and his benevolence, it broadens his views of men and things . . . It *liberalizes* the Vandal to travel. You never saw a bigoted, opinionated, stubborn, narrow-minded, self-conceited, *almighty mean man* in your life but he had stuck in one place ever since he was born and thought God made the world and dyspepsia and bile for *his* especial comfort and satisfaction. So I say, *by all means,* let the American Vandal *go on* traveling, and let no man discourage him.[17]

At the end, the fancy audience on the third floor of Case Hall in Cleveland had been witness to a turning that would be replicated in halls around the nation. The Vandal had taken his rude stance as the new representative American. How they loved it, these Cleveland doctors and businessmen in their soup-and-fish, and their ladies in brocade. How they laughed and applauded this novel good-bad boy as he paced and pivoted onstage. Mark Twain had perfect pitch that night: he reined in the Vandal's coarser proclivities, he steered clear of the Holy Land minefield, and he threw in enough travelogue to establish his authority: the word-pictures of stately palaces; marble miracles of enchanting architecture; great cities with towers and domes and steeples drowsing in a golden mist of sunset; himself wandering the marble-paved lengths of mighty temples as the full moon rides high in the cloudless heavens, and walking on "pavements that had been pressed by Plato, Aristotle, Demosthenes, Socrates, Phocion, Euclid, Xenophon, Herodotus, Diogenes, and a hundred others of deathless fame." [18]

Midway through the lecture, a couple rising to leave the auditorium caught Mark Twain's eye. Thrown off balance, he struggled to regain his train of thought. As he fell silent, the audience started to laugh. Mark Twain's silence and the laughter grew in tandem, until he blurted that he "would be everlastingly obliged if some one in the audience would tell me where I left off." [19] This made the audience laugh even harder. "Finally," Mark Twain recalled years later, "when the suspense had become overpowering, an angel— with a bald head—arose and asked me if I was really in earnest in desiring to know which lie I was telling. I said I was." [20] The gentleman told him. He was Solon Severance, the banker-intellectual from the *Quaker City* voyage.

The evening was a triumph. "Made a *splendid* hit last night & am the 'lion' to-day," he wrote to Jane and Pamela. [21] Among the enchanted was Mary Fairbanks, whose *Herald* review amounted to a gracious acceptance of her friend's persona—although she did emphasize the more uplifting moments.

We expected to be amused, but we were taken by surprise when he carried us on the wings of his redundant fancy, away to the ruins, the cathedrals, and the monuments of the old world. There are some passages of gorgeous word painting which haunt us like a remembered picture.

We congratulate Mr. Twain upon having taken the tide of public favor "at the flood" in the lecture field, and having conclusively proved that a man may be a humorist without being a clown. [22]

The *Plain Dealer* anointed him the "most popular of American humorists since the demise of poor Artemus." [23]

Sam rode to Pittsburgh on this ballast of approbation. Speaking at the Academy of Music during a rainstorm on November 20, he outdrew the great British actress Fanny Kemble, attracting a turnaway crowd of 1,500 to her 200.

The Pittsburgh *Gazette* pronounced him "entitled above all living men to the name of American humorist."[24]

The next stop was Elmira, where a more consequential audience awaited him.

"The calf has returned; may the prodigal have some breakfast?" This was Sam's doorway greeting to the Langdons at their table as famously told by Paine.[25] It was Saturday morning, November 21. He was to lecture in the city two nights later, then rest for a week before heading to Rondout, New York, on December 2. Once again, his jovial affect covered anxieties. A momentous challenge awaited him on this particular podium.

The lecture was a benefit for the city's volunteer fire company. A leading member in that company was young Charley Langdon, who had been so horrified to learn of Sam's intentions toward his sister. On this Monday night, Charley, Jervis, Olivia Lewis Langdon, and Livy Langdon sat facing him from the audience. It was to be Livy's first glimpse of a performance by her suitor.

Sam fumbled the lecture. At least he thought he did. Distracted by Livy, he labored through a subpar performance. At the end, he blurted an apology for his "failure" and slunk from the stage, overcome with humiliation.

The local press saw it differently. The Elmira *Advertiser* judged it pleasing and satisfying; well received, in fact, although the reviewer did note that Mark Twain "was not in good voice."[26]

The next day, Sam began the do-or-die phase of his campaign for Olivia Langdon's hand. He began it with the two of them alone in the Langdon parlor. Livy wore a blue dress, a color that forever afterward symbolized purity to Sam. He then moved on to the formidable Olivia Lewis Langdon and the more genial, cancer-wracked Jervis. When it was over, a day later—or two days, depending on which letter he was writing—he was emotionally spent but triumphant. The girl in the photograph had finally said yes to him. And the parents had given their provisional approval.

His ecstasy radiates from the starburst of letter writing that ensued. To Mary Fairbanks, "It is MY thanksgiving day, above all other days that ever shone on earth. Because, after twenty-four hours of persecution from me, Mr. & Mrs. L. have yielded a *conditional* consent—Livy has said, over & over again, the word which is so hard for a maiden to say, & if there were a church near here with a steeple high enough to make it an object I should go & jump over it."[27]

The deciding element for Livy, he told her, was his lecture—the same lecture for which he had apologized onstage. "[S]ometime in the future she is going to be my wife, & I think we shall live in Cleveland."[28] His dreams of bourgeois domesticity tumbled over one another. Mother Fairbanks would persuade her husband to sell Sam an interest in the *Herald*. "And then we shall live in the house next to yours."[29] He stipulated that the engagement was not yet formal—it was a secret, in fact—and favored her with a gusset of God-belief, the star of Hope breaking through clouds: his vow to be a Christian.

To Joe Twichell two days later, writing from New York, Sam slipped into more of a "guy" mode. "Sound the loud timbrel! . . . for I have fought the good fight & lo! I have won! Refused three times—warned to *quit*, once—accepted at last!"[30] He repeated his willingness to jump over a church steeple.

The conditions of Livy's parents were that if Livy made up her mind "thoroughly & eternally," and if Sam could prove that his past contained nothing shameful or criminal, then would establish a good character and settle down, "I may take the sun out of their domestic firmament, the angel out of their fireside heaven."[31] Jervis had asked him for references during that visit, and Clemens later recalled that he had named "six prominent men," all San Franciscans.[32] Of these, only two are known: the Reverends Horatio Stebbins and Charles Wadsworth. Jervis made some inquiries of his own.

The tone of Sam's letters to Livy changed right away, during his train ride from Elmira to New York. No more "Honored Sister" now; and not as much strained Victorian syntax. In this and the nearly two hundred other letters he would write to her from the lecture trail until their marriage, and in all the letters to her in the thirty-four years afterward, an unself-conscious and undiminished sweetness shines through. It is the sweetness of a jubilant boy who has suffered much, and seen an impossible dream come true.

> My Dear, Dear Livy:
>
> When I found myself comfortably on board the cars last night . . . said to myself: "Now whatever others may think, it is my opinion that I am blessed above all other men that live . . ."

Page upon page of endearment followed, a torrent of consciousness that rushed from thought to thought with no attempt at transition; the ampersands trailed like a steamboat's wake.

> I leave my fate, my weal, my woe, my *life,* in your hands & at your mercy, with a trust, & a confidence & an abiding sense of security which nothing can shake . . .
>
> I do love, love, *love* you, Livy!
>
> You are so pure, so great, so good, so beautiful. *How* can I help loving you? . . . [H]ow can I keep from *worshipping* you, you dear little paragon? . . . I listen for a dear voice, I look for a darling face, I caress the empty air! . . . Good-bye—& I send a thousand kisses—pray send *me* some.

He closed with "Mark" crossed out and "Samuel" inserted, and then:

> P.S.—I do LOVE you, Livy!

Some further thoughts, and then:

> P.P.P.S.—I do *love*, LOVE, LOVE you, Livy, darling.

More thoughts. And:

PPPPP.S—I *do* love you, Livy![33]

OLIVIA AND Jervis Langdon groped for a means to open up the psyche of the mysterious stranger now poised to take their daughter from them. Who was this "Mark Twain"? Where had he come from? What sort of husband might he make for Livy? On December 1, Olivia Lewis Langdon commenced the investigation with a carefully phrased letter to Mary Mason Fairbanks.

> I cannot, & need not, detail to you the utter surprise & almost astonishment with which Mr Langdon & myself listened to Mr Clemens declaration to us, of his love for our precious child, and how at first our parental hearts said no.—to the bare thought of such a stranger, mining in our hearts for the possession of one of the few jewels we have . . . I do not ask as to his standing among men, nor do I need to be assured that he is a man of genius that he possesses a high order of intellectual endowments, nor do I scarcely crave your opinion of his affectional nature, but what I desire is your opinion of him as a *man;* what kind of man he *has been,* and what the man he now is, or is to become.[34]

Mary Fairbanks's answer was positive. But trouble lay ahead. When the responses from Sam's references came back, they were withering. The two clergymen predicted that he would fill a drunkard's grave.[35]

Oblivious to these, Sam lectured across New Jersey and New York State through December, piling up some two thousand miles of railroad travel. He kept up a blizzard of love letters to Livy, who gamely tried to process the sustained pitch of passion unlike any she had experienced. Weak from another of her many spells of illness, she tried to counter the passion by urging "reason." Sam agreed—passionately. Sometimes she simply had to protest Sam's flaming hyperbole—which triggered more of the same: "And you are *not* 'Perfection'—no?" he chided. "And I shan't *say* you are?" Then, lightly scratched out: "There you go, again, you dear little concentration of Literalness!"[36] This particular missive covered twenty-six pages and a two-page postscript, along with evidence that Sam had discarded one whole page and parts of four more. In other responses to her now-lost letters, he declares that his "wild, distempered language" is not deliberate flattery—"But I will curb it, for your sake."[37] He didn't.

He foraged the Bible, already well familiar to him, for pertinent quotations—Corinthians, Psalms, Romans, more Psalms, Matthew. He alluded to Protestant hymns and churches he'd dropped in on. He mentioned prayer sessions with Joe Twichell, and his admission to the young minister that his constant praying had not brought him the "progress" he'd sought, "—& that *now* I began clearly to comprehend that one *must* seek Jesus for himself alone, & uninfluenced by selfish motives."[38] These remarks suggest that Sam was struggling to recapture the Christian faith that had deserted him with the death of Henry; he was not merely trying to fool Olivia Langdon. Fraudulence was never a part of Sam Clemens's makeup. Self-deception perhaps was a different matter.

The tour was depleting him. Travel expenses ate up more than half of his earnings—he later estimated that, from a gross intake of about $9,000, he banked only $3,600. For a while, he accepted the hospitality of citizens, but he learned to avoid the agonies of this luxury. Among its horrors was the obligatory sightseeing tour around the town in which he slumped, scowling, from his carriage seat at the predictable inventory: "the Mayor's house; the ex-mayor's house; the house of a State Senator, . . . the public school with its infernal architecture; the female seminary; paper mill or factory of some kind or other; . . . the place where the park is going to be."[39] "All towns are alike," groused the future bard of American town life, "—all have the same stupid trivialities to show, & all demand an impossible interest at the suffering stranger's hands."[40] The tour was usually followed by the reception, which obliged him to endure hours of "showing off" by local wits and dignitaries; and, finally, the ice-cold guest room with its tacit constraints against smoking cigars and throwing his clothes around. (He did anyway.) Unless he could not avoid it, he put up in hotels.

IN THE midst of it all, Sam found himself obliged to assemble more references. Jervis, having digested the first round, had grown testy in response to the unsuspecting suitor's witticisms, and was rumbling about the need to "make haste slowly." It didn't take Sam long to intuit that his trusted friends had backstabbed him. He put together a more prestigious list: J. Neeley Johnson, a Nevada Supreme Court justice who'd been a governor of California; the current Nevada governor, H. G. Blaisdel; Joe Goodman; and a handful of others. With desperate optimism—"I think all my references can say I never did anything mean, false or criminal,"[41] he assured Livy's father—he waited for the responses to trickle in, traveling and lecturing all the while.

As the year wound down, his esprit flagged a little. "Why *is* it that godliness flies me?" he wrote Livy. "Why is it that prayer seems so unavailing & all my searching & seeking a mockery? I study the Testament every night, I read anything touching upon religion that comes in my way, . . . but sometimes a chilly apathy comes upon me at last."[42] He missed a stop in Fort Wayne. He worried about Livy's health and her misgivings about leaving her family household. Learning, on New Year's Eve, that she had obtained a copy of the *Jumping Frog* book, he felt a new wave of revulsion for "the villainous sketch": "*Don't* read a word in that Jumping Frog book, Livy—*don't*. I hate to hear that infamous volume mentioned. I would be glad to know that every copy of it was burned, & gone forever."[43]

But he could not outrun all sources of infamy. The Langdons' investigation deepened, and as 1869 dawned, Sam Clemens was on trial.

24

"Quite Worthy of the Best"

(1869)

And you had a delightful philosophy lesson, Livy—& wished that we might study it together some day. It is the echo of a wish that speaks in my heart many & many a time." [1]

Philosophy had become only one of her intellectual pursuits. She was tinkering with test tubes as well. Livy had taken up chemistry lessons with her friends the Spaulding sisters, Clara and Allie; visiting Elmira a couple of weeks later, Sam professed fear "because they are always cooking up some new-fangled gas or other & blowing everything endways with their experiments" [2] Livy had been inspired by a meeting of Elmira's Academy of Sciences hosted by her intellectually engaged parents. It was all part of an emerging "science" vogue that fed into America's embrace of Progress and the belief in human perfectibility. This optimistic illusion would radiate through the rest of the 19th century, eventually claiming Mark Twain among its chief adherents, and victims.

Livy's curiosities enhanced their exploration of each other's mind. It was a welcome phase. The first weeks of Sam's courtship bore all the cerebral complexity of a Saint Bernard beating its tail against the floor. But Livy's gravitas and the cerebral cast of her personality must have compelled him from the moment of their first meeting in New York. (Their exchanges after the Charles Dickens lecture, and the subtexts of those remarks, will probably never be known.) By December 1868, discussion of books was a frequent element of their correspondence. They cited sentimental tracts and verse narratives dealing with Christian views of marriage. Soon they were comparing notes on Tennyson, Milton, Elizabeth Barrett Browning, Shakespeare, Swift, Sterne, Victor Hugo, Matthew Arnold, Oliver Wendell Holmes. Sam, unlike Livy, was not an academically trained reader, but he read all the time, his choices as eclectic and humanistic as his narratives would prove to be. What he happened to have with him on the train would often be the topic of their book talk.

They developed an easy way of weaving literary ideas into their correspondence. "Your criticism on the 'Nature & Life' sermons is concentrated excellence," writes Sam, and: "Poor Swift—under the placid surface of this simply-worded book flows the full tide of his venom—the turbid sea of his matchless hate." "It always makes me proud of you when you assault one of her [Elizabeth Barrett Browning's] impenetrable sentences & tear off its shell & bring its sense to light." Even Sam's teasing revealed their mutual immersion in words: remarking on one of her many spectacular spelling gaffes, Sam chides her, " 'Sicisiors' don't spell *scissors*, you funny little orthographist." [3] By January 1869, writing from far-off Illinois, the hot-blooded Casanova of a few months earlier was sounding quite domesticated: "when we are serene & happy old married folk, we will sit together & con other books all the long pleasant evenings, & let the great world toil & struggle & nurse its pet ambition . . ." [4]

Samuel Clemens's immersion in language must have been attractive to Livy, who was otherwise so different from him. The sickly young woman had experienced the world largely at second hand, through books; and now here was this Sam Clemens, back from a part of the globe she never expected to see, with a book about it on the way. Whatever Livy responded to in Sam, it was not the quality that was building his national reputation—his sense of humor. (She wasn't all that thrilled about his drawl, either, for that matter; he worked on cutting it down.) Harriet Lewis's appraisal of her joke-getting limitations was on the money. More disquieting was her conviction, inherited from her family and social strata, that her suitor's calling as a "humor" writer was not a lofty ambition; perhaps not even respectable. Sam himself admitted that "[s]he thinks a humorist is something perfectly awful." [5] It was likely the reason he hoped she wouldn't read the *Jumping Frog* book. Sam found Livy's myopia both amusing and a source of anxiety. In an attack of Respectability, he'd composed a high-blown Christmas epistle in December to Mrs. Fairbanks—that other stranger to the joys of thigh-slappers—and, with Livy in mind as an audience, allowed the Cleveland matron to publish an excerpt in the *Herald* on January 16. It was all about Sam's Yuletide remembrances of Bethlehem during the *Quaker City* expedition, with its now-crumbling wall and venerable olives, back when the stars were shedding a purer luster above the barren hills.[6] Predictably, Livy loved it. "I want to thank you," she wrote to Mrs. Fairbanks. "I want the public, who know him now, only as 'the wild humorist of the Pacific Slope,' to know something of his deeper, larger nature." [7]

As his Vandal tour chugged eastward through Illinois—Rockford and Chicago and Galesburg and El Paso and Ottawa—Sam daydreamed about his forthcoming book. "It will have a great sale in the West—& the East too," he wrote to Elisha Bliss's son Frank, the treasurer of the publishing company, from Chicago. "Why don't you issue prospectuses & startling advertisements now while I am stirring the bowels of these communities?"[8] He didn't know it, but those prospectuses and advertisements were months from seeing the light of day. The book would not be published in March. The book was in danger of not being published at all.

He schemed of other ventures that would establish him as a solid citizen worthy of kinship to Jervis Langdon. He knew that many Elmira friends of the Langdon family viewed him with suspicion if not contempt. Might Mr. Clemens be casting a sidelong glance at the quarter-million-dollar inheritance that awaited young Olivia? Versions of this theory survived Mark Twain's death, but its plausibility seems remote. Sam's own words and behavior revealed an overweening anxiety to hoist himself up to her level—as an Eastern squire and a man of means, but also as an honorable husband. As for Livy, she seemed indifferent to money, in these decades before she saw it taken away from her. She seldom wore the Langdon jewelry, and she delighted in the simple gold engagement ring that Sam obtained through Mrs. Fairbanks.

"I do not wish to marry Miss Langdon for her wealth," Sam had bluntly informed Olivia Lewis Langdon, "& she knows that perfectly well. As far as I am concerned, Mr. Langdon can cut her off with a shilling—or the half of it." He'd assured the matriarch that he had paddled his own canoe since he was thirteen, and was "fully competent to so paddle it the rest of the voyage."[9] Continuing the campaign, he had told Langdon of his interest in buying a share of the Cleveland *Herald*. Shares were going for seven thousand dollars each, and he wanted to buy as many as he could "mortgage my book for, & as many more as I could pay for with labor of hand & brain."[10] He added, "If I *do* buy, I shall retain Horace Greeley on the paper."

His instincts for upgrading his profile to Jervis and Olivia were timelier than he knew. Back in Elmira, the responses to the Langdons' "character" enquiries were starting to trickle in from the West—responses from people Sam himself had suggested. Their general tone indicated that Sam had not improved his ability to read people's attitudes toward him since his duel-dodging Washoe days.

A letter from Livy gave him an inkling of those appraisals. She was shocked by an unnamed respondent, and Sam's attempt to calm her covered more than five hundred words. He didn't mind honest criticism, he told her, "but I *am* ashamed of the friend whose friendship was so weak & so unworthy that he shrank from . . . saying *all* he knew about me, good or bad—for there is nothing generous in his grieving insinuation . . ."[11] He regretted her pain. "Oh, when I knew that your kind heart had suffered for two days for what I had done in past years, it cut me more than if *all* my friends had abused me."[12]

He was speaking a little too soon.

· · ·

AUDIENCES ALONG the circuit were mostly delighted with the Vandal. As long as he salted in "a foundation of good sense," the tidy Main Street critics were prepared to salute his "rich vein of mirth-provoking wit." As long as he gave them a little Athens, looked down upon by bright moonlight from the Acropolis, they could forgive his "native element of quaint humor"—after all, "Cutting wit, unless for the tough hide of vice or bigotry, ought not to be cultivated or indulged in." His "eloquent passages, brilliant in thought and word," gave him license to "tickle" the audiences, even if "they didn't know what they were laughing at half the time."

The travails of touring kept pace with the rewards. Fatigue and frustration began to stimulate the explosive temper that would erupt throughout his life. Lost luggage in Peoria. Then calamity in Ottawa: in a church filling up with well-dressed and eager listeners, Mark Twain seethed as the committee chairman began quacking his introduction while people were still finding their seats. Mark Twain labored a quarter-way through his talk, then exploded at the doorkeeper to shut the doors. His concentration shattered, "angry, wearied to death with travel . . . I just hobbled miserably through, apologized, bade the house good-night, & then gave the President a piece of my mind, without any butter or sugar on it." [13] Another temper tantrum in Iowa City: out of sorts already from a hard fall on the ice and a premature wake-up by the hotelkeeper, Mark Twain reached for the bell cord in his room to order coffee, discovered that no bell existed, and improvised by slamming his door until everyone on his floor was yelling at him. This little preview of American rock-star behavior was covered in all its details in the next day's Iowa City *Republican*, which described the "unearthly screams" of "the veritable animal, with his skin on at least, but not much else." [14] For good measure, the paper panned the animal's lecture as a "humbug . . . it was impossible to know when he was talking in earnest and when in burlesque." [15]

The frustrations, the indignities, the idle time, the fatigue, the loneliness—each of these spelled danger for an emotionally volatile personality such as Sam's. Combined, they produced a pressure for which a good stiff drink or twelve was a tempting antidote, especially for a veteran of Washoe's saloons. But Sam did not compound his lecture tour discontents by drinking. He declared his total abstinence on Christmas Eve, 1868, and a year later was celebrating his first anniversary in a letter to Livy. Sam would resume moderate (and perhaps some immoderate) drinking within a few years; but his days of drunkenness were over—at least until the tormented years near the end of his life.

From Jacksonville, Illinois, Sam embarked on an 860-mile, two-day run to Elmira, where, on February 4, "I was duly & solemnly & irrevocably engaged to be married to Miss Olivia L. Langdon, aged 23½," as he informed Jane and the family in St. Louis. [16] It had not been easy. The day following the conclusion of his exhausting journey, he had been summoned to a private audience with Jervis Langdon to endure his Ordeal by References. Jervis hauled out the testimonials from Sam's old friends and read him their endorsements. Besides the prediction that Sam would fill a drunkard's grave was the suggestion that he was born to be hung, and the declaration that "I would rather bury a daughter of mine than have her marry such a fellow." [17] Nearly seven months afterward, the outrage these letters triggered still burned in Sam Clemens. He vented it in a letter to his old friend Charles Warren Stoddard, placing a special emphasis on the viciousness of a mutual friend, the clergyman Stebbins.

He came within an acc of breaking off my marriage by [relaying his opinion to Jervis Langdon] that "Clemens is a humbug—shallow & superficial . . . a man whose life promised little & has accomplished less—a humbug, Sir, a humbug" . . . It was not calculated to help my case in an old, proud & honored family who are rigidly upright & without reproach themselves.[18]

Stebbins's verdict was far from the exception, Clemens acknowledged.

The friends I had referred to in California said with one accord that I got drunk oftener than was necessary, & that I was wild, & godless, idle, lecherous & a discontented & unsettled rover & they could not recommend any girl of high character & social position to marry me . . .[19]

These defamations did not injure his cause so much, Clemens told Stoddard, "as I had already said all that about myself beforehand." It was the "humbug" that stung. "I had never expected anybody who knew me to say it—& consequently there was a dark & portentious time for a while . . ."

In his dictations of 1906, Mark Twain remembered that as he'd stood shocked and mute, Jervis Langdon had brushed these opinions aside: "What kind of people are these? Haven't you a friend in the world? . . . I'll be your friend myself. Take the girl. I know you better than they do." [20] His letter to Stoddard, only recently recovered in full, offers a more authentic-sounding scenario than that of Jervis's melodramatic recitation. Instead of speaking, the father listened to the opinion of the only person in the world that counted.

"[A]t last the young lady said she had thought it all over deliberately & did not believe it, & would not believe it if an archangel had spoken—& since then there has not been flaw nor ripple upon my course of true love . . ." [21]

THAT WENT well. Sam hurried back to Cleveland to commence another string of eastward whistle-stops. On Valentine's Day, from Ravenna, he sent a cheerful love note to Livy that included some thoughts about his newspaper-affiliation plans. His fancy had shifted from Cleveland to booming, prosperous, prestigious Hartford, postwar America's most resurgent city. Visions of a life with Livy at Nook Farm, swapping lies and theology with his manly new chum Joe Twichell, had cast northern Ohio and the admonishing Mrs. Fair-

banks in a less attractive light. He'd inquired with the co-editor of the Hartford *Courant,* Joseph R. Hawley. Hawley stalled Sam, pleading the need to
consult with his partner Charles Dudley Warner. Sam could not know that his
carousing California reputation had undercut him again. Samuel Bowles, editor of the Springfield, Massachusetts, *Daily Republican,* had run into Clemens
out west; what he'd seen prompted him to secretly steer Hawley away from
Clemens. Hawley regretted following this advice when *The Innocents Abroad*
became a big success. Clemens may have sensed Bowles's animosity; he told
Livy, that "I . . . find myself calling him in my secret heart a born & bred *cur,*
every time."[22]

Stalling of a different sort was emanating from the American Publishing
Company. A letter from Elisha Bliss caught up with Sam in Cleveland. It was
couched in language so carefully jovial that Sam failed to pick up on its true
and troubling message, as Bliss had surely hoped he would. How was Sam's
cold coming along? Had he had a busy trip? Enjoying himself? "Now about
the *Book."* As to the page proofs that Sam had requested—"we have no proofs
as yet to send." Bliss rushed ahead with blandishments. "We are pushing
things now very rapidly however. We are about ready to begin to electrotype.
We are *filling* IT WITH ENGRAVINGS."[23] Translation: the book lagged several
months behind production schedule. No type had been set. The process of
electrotyping the wood engravings for the illustrations, a precondition to the
typesetting, had not begun. The unstated reasons went beyond routine complications, and posed a serious threat to the survival of the book. Sam picked
up on none of this. "[G]lad to hear you are getting along so well," he replied to
Bliss from Ravenna, Ohio. "When I get to Hartford I will read such proofs as
are ready . . ."[24]

He was scheduled to hit Hartford in the first week of March, not a minute
too soon. His exhaustion was deepening, and, with it, frustration. A planned
hiatus of nine days with Livy in Elmira had to be scrapped: new lecture dates.
Indignities mounted. He lectured in Alliance, Ohio, on February 15, stayed
awake at his hotel until 2 a.m. waiting for a train back to Ravenna; arrived
there at 4; slept for an hour and a half and then boarded a train to Titusville,
Pennsylvania; tried to get some shut-eye during a four-hour layover in a town
called Corry; was awakened by a gaggle of businessmen who'd spotted his
name on the register and wanted to talk booking dates. He arrived in Titusville just in time to take the lectern. A drunk in the back of the hall dis-
rupted him; instead of ejecting the man, the policeman on duty tried to
reason with him, and the lout kept up his heckling unrestrained. "[T]he versa-
tile genius of 'Mark Twain' " delivered "rare poetic description," reported the
Titusville *Morning Herald,* "as well as keen and racy bits."[25] He'd slept one
hour in the previous thirty-six.

He clumped into Franklin, Pennsylvania, the following night, and then
(in a rare action) blew off an appearance in Geneseo, New York, pleading impossible rail connections, and detoured to Elmira, eighty-nine miles south, for

a brief rendezvous with his intended. His itinerary, thus far merely backbreaking, accelerated into the near-inhuman. From Stuyvesant, New York, on February 26: "The night is more than half gone, & I take the train at 9 in the morning . . . My stove smokes, & I am enveloped in a fog of it, & my eyes smart, although the doors are open & I am very cold. I am tired, & sleepy, & disappointed, & angry, & yet I am trying to write to *Livy*."[26] It would get no better in a string of upstate New York appearances.

FATIGUE, THOUGHTS of his fiancée, and the sheer dumb exhilaration of getting off the road may have explained his mild reaction to the news that awaited him at 148 Asylum Street in Hartford when he arrived on March 5, the day after Ulysses S. Grant was inaugurated. Elisha Bliss confessed that routine complications with the engraving process were not the reason for the book's scheduling logjam. The real problem involved the company's board of directors, who had finally adjusted their eyeglasses and examined Mark Twain's manuscript. They were staggered by what they read. As Mark Twain recalled in 1906, "the majority of them were of the opinion that there were places in it of a humorous character."[27] Not only that; there was the proposed title. John Bunyan's classic allegory, here in the old cradle of Puritanism, held semisacred status; to employ it ironically was tantamount to blasphemy. The offending work must be rejected.

The board of directors held the advantage in this confrontation with secretary Bliss, the career dry-goods man and publishing neophyte. But Bliss held his ground. His salesman's sense of the public told him that *The New Pilgrim's Progress,* or whatever they decided to call it, was going to be a tremendous success. In a remarkable all-or-nothing stand, Bliss declared that if American Publishing refused the book, he would break from the company and publish it himself.

The board was already in partial retreat when Clemens arrived in town. In a last-ditch attempt to circumvent Bliss, the board chairman, Sidney Drake, invited Sam for a friendly little buggy ride. Drake perhaps overestimated the power of his charm. "He was a pathetic old relic," Mark Twain recalled. "He had a delicate purpose in view and it took him some time to hearten himself [to it] . . . [H]e frankly threw himself and the house upon my mercy and begged me to . . . release the concern from the contract. I said I wouldn't— and so ended the interview and the buggy conversation."[28] The manuscript survived. But now it was hopelessly behind its publishing date.

HIS LETTERS show no signs of anger over this near-miss. He seems more preoccupied with tallying the number of letters he'd received from Livy— which never equaled the total he'd hoped for. "I like the pictures (for the book) ever so much," he wrote to her from Hartford. "They were drawn by a young artist of considerable talent."[29] The artist was True Williams, a dapper, balding, thirty-year-old self-taught illustrator who, like many of his fellow

Civil War veterans, was a loner and flourishing alcoholic. (Marching with Sherman's army through Georgia had given Williams severe varicose veins and many bad nights.) Bliss hired him for *The Innocents* through Williams's employer, the New York syndicate of Fay & Cox. With this assignment, Williams drifted into Mark Twain's penumbra for a decade of work that gave enduring faces and attitudes to Mark Twain's best-known characters, then struggled through two divorces, failing eyesight and dissipation before dying alone in Chicago at age fifty-eight.[30]

Sam visited Joe and Harmony Twichell and admired their two-month-old baby, Julia Curtis Twichell. He attended a lecture by a giant of the circuit, Petroleum V. Nasby (David Ross Locke), who delivered a peculiar, "nigger"-laced précis of the Negro through history that Sam later construed as an argument against slavery.[31] The two talked in Sam's room from 10 p.m. until dawn.

At last Bliss supplied him with an initial thirty pages of proofs of the book. Assured that the rest of them were on the way, he planned a trip to Elmira, where he and Livy together would pore over them as they arrived. "Some proof sheets will doubtless reach Elmira before I do," he alerted her. "Open the package if you choose, little Curiosity, for you have just as much authority to do it as I have . . . you are *part of* me—you are *myself*—& I would no more be troubled by *your* looking over my shoulder than it would embarrass me to look over my *own* shoulder."[32]

Life was suddenly an exciting strut again. On March 14, he sashayed off to Boston with his new chum Petroleum Nasby, where he was introduced to Oliver Wendell Holmes. This was Mark Twain's first encounter with a star of the New England literary establishment whose hegemony his work would render obsolete. Holmes, the physician and poet/essayist who wore his hair combed severely across his head like a Yankee farmer, had sat with the semi-divines of the Saturday Club—Emerson, James Russell Lowell, Richard Henry Dana Jr., and the polymath Louis Agassiz. His *Autocrat of the Breakfast Table,* published serially in the Atlantic in 1857 and later issued in book form, was an effort to exemplify high conversation as an enlivening, morally improving pursuit. His "Autocrat" alter ego assumed contours considered comic by his admirers, and aspiring intellectuals across the country tee-hee'd at such risible aphorisms of his as, "Speak clearly, if you speak at all; carve every word before you let it fall," and "A person is always startled when he hears himself seriously called an old man for the first time."

After two more appearances on Long Island and in Pennsylvania, the season of the Vandal was finally over. The season of the Innocent was about to begin.

"I want a name that is **striking, comprehensive, & out of the common order,**" he'd written to Mary Fairbanks a day before his getaway. "I had chosen 'The New Pilgrims' Progress,' but it is thought that many dull people [meaning Sidney Drake and his board] will shudder at that, as at least taking the name of a consecrated book in vain . . . I have thought of 'The Irruption of the Jonathans—*Or, the Modern Pilgrim's Progress'*—you see the second title can remain, if I only precede it with something that will *let it d o w n e a s y.* Give me a name, please." [33]

Before she could answer, he'd supplied it himself. The Sharon *Herald* reported it in its March 24 editions. Back in Elmira Sam inscribed it in his copy of *The Autocrat of the Breakfast Table,* which he was marking for Livy's edification. Six days later he presented it to Elisha Bliss as one of two choices, the other choice being, *The Exodus of the Innocents.* "I like 'The Innocents Abroad' rather the best," he told the publisher. [34]

By spring, Sam and Livy were shoulder-to-shoulder at her parents' house, editing page proofs as they came in from Bliss. They'd reviewed three hundred pages, yet the Pilgrims were only as far as Rome. Sam had worried that he would have too little material to fill a book; now, with what shaped up to be a thousand-page volume, he faced the prospect of massive cuts in the second half, and fretted that the best parts would be sacrificed.

This concern didn't spoil the delights of pooling his book tasks with Livy—his "serene-&-happy-old-married-folks" fantasy coming true even before the wedding. Besides enjoying the intimacy of the shared work, Sam was eager to hear Livy's criticisms of language and style, and to secure her imprimatur on a book that he hoped would be accepted by people of her social class. Livy entered her corrections in purple ink. The two relaxed with games of cribbage at night.

Livy witnessed her fiancé's debut as a scourge of professional proofreaders who dared tamper with his usage and spelling. To Bliss:

I wish you would have MY revises revised again & look over them *yourself* & see that my marks have been corrected. A proof-reader who *persists* in making *two* words (& sometimes even *compound* words) of "anywhere" and "everything;" & who spells villainy "villiany" & liquefies "liquifies &c, &c, is ~~not three removes from an idiot~~ infernally unreliable . . ." [35]

On May 5, Sam ended his seven-week stay in the Langdon household and entrained with Charley for a brief visit to New York, after which Sam returned to Hartford. Charley's reasons for the trip were medical. Sam's were Victorian. Living under the same roof with the woman he intended to marry had set tongues to wagging—the tongues of Mary Fairbanks, Olivia Lewis Langdon, and his own mother back in St. Louis. Both Sam and Livy were infuriated. "You drove me away from Elmira at last," Sam lectured Mrs. Fairbanks. "You made me feel meaner & meaner, & finally I absolutely couldn't stand it . . . Livy spoke right out, & said that to leave was unnecessary, uncalled-for, absurd, & utterly exasperating & foolish." [36]

By mid-May, Sam believed that publication was imminent, and he turned giddy. He wrote upside-down sentences to Livy. He ticked off for her the delicious statistics: 224 illustrations. Four weeks' time for a mill just to produce the necessary volume of paper—thirty tons' worth. He fidgeted around Hartford, now in grassy springtime bloom; hung with Joe Twichell, read proofs. And he sent nightly romantic epistles to Livy. He poured out his yearning for her in language so feverish as to suggest an underlying inferno of pain, or a loneliness so deeply ingrained that he'd hardly noticed it until its counterforce appeared in his life. "To think that within the last twenty-four hours I should have written fifty mortal pages of manuscript to you," he muses in the second of two long letters one night in March, "& yet am obliged at last to beg further time . . ."[37]

Livy, you are so interwoven with the very fibres of my being that if I were to lose you it seems to me that to lose memory & reason at the same time would be a blessing to me.[38]

Oh, you darling little speller!—you spell "terrible" right, this time. And I won't have it—it is un-Livy-ish. Spell it wrong, next time, for I love everything that is like Livy.[39]

Little sweetheart, I had a scary dream about you last night. I thought you came to me crying, & said "Farewell"—& I knew by some instinct that you meant it for a final farewell. It made me feel as if the world had dropped from under my feet![40]

I wish I could *touch* you. (That word touch is your handwriting—maybe . . . I have unconsciously adopted yours.) Take the pen & write "touch," with your eyes shut.[41]

She did, and the result was indeed strikingly similar.

Livy, Livy, Livy darling, it is such a happiness, such a pleasure, such a luxury, to write you, that I don't know when to stop. Oh, you *must* come down right away with your father & mother [to New York, where he was visiting]. I would be the most delighted man on the whole earth. I would just almost fly away with ecstasy. Please, little woman, little darling, come.[42]

One spring night in Hartford he returned to his rooms from a walk around town and began a letter with a jokey passage about the "ten million frogs" he'd heard croaking. In the midst of that thought, Sam took another of those abrupt plunges into the elegiac darkness that could envelop him at the very summit of joy.

They made good music, to-night, especially when it was very still & lonely & a long-drawn dog-howl swelled up out of the far distance & blended with it. The shadows seemed to grow more sombre, then, & the stillness more solemn, & the whispering foliage more spiritual, & the mysterious murmur of the night-wind more freighted with the moaning of shrouded wanderers from the tombs. The "voices of the night" are always eloquent.[43]

. . .

THE PRESSES did not roll on *The Innocents Abroad* in four weeks, as Sam had believed they would. They did not roll for the rest of June, and they did not roll for half of July. Sam's mood of expectant playfulness deteriorated. His efforts to buy into the Hartford *Courant* were going nowhere. He needed to secure some anchor in the business world. In July he swallowed his scruples and dragged himself to Cleveland to negotiate an interest in Abel Fairbanks's "trimming, time-serving, policy-shifting" *Herald.* He arrived to discover that Fairbanks, a scowling, rimless-glasses fellow with an angry slash of a mouth whom Sam had never liked much anyway, had increased the price.

So Sam, back in Elmira now, was a bombshell waiting to explode when Elisha Bliss sent "Friend Twain" a complacent answer, on July 12, to his latest inquiry as to when the hell *The Innocents* was going to be published. "Unfortunately we have been delayed too long to make a summer Book of it—but *unavoidably.* We propose to make a fall book of it . . ."[44] "Friend Twain" was anything but soothed. Publication was now set at a year beyond the original date. The book had taken a backseat to A. D. Richardson's Ulysses S. Grant biography, and then to his new edition of *Beyond the Mississippi,* and then to *The Great Metropolis,* a book by one Junius Henri Browne. Then there was the idiotic panic of the board of directors. Now this.

"Friend Twain" launched a splenetic letter that spoke for the exasperation of writers in the centuries before his time, and in the centuries since.

"Do not misunderstand," he instructed Bliss,

I am not contending that I am hurt unto death simply because the delay for "Grant" damaged my interests; or because the delay for the "Metropolis" damaged my interests likewise; or because the delay necessary to make me a spring vegetable damaged my interests . . . *No.* All *I* want to know is,—viz:—to wit—as follows:

After it is done being a fall book, upon what argument shall you perceive that it will be best to make a winter book of it? And—

After it is done being a winter book, upon what argument shall you perceive that it will be best to make another spring book of it again? . . .

All I desire is to be informed from time to time . . . so that I can go on informing my friends intelligently—I mean that infatuated baker's dozen of them who faithful unto death, still believe that I *am* going to publish a book.[45]

The secretary wrote back a squeaky little note saying he didn't have time to give a full reply just now. He enclosed three bound volumes, and promised to get review copies out to the newspapers right away.

Through all this, Sam had been vaguely promising his kinfolks that he would soon travel west to visit them. Toward the end of the month a wail issued from Missouri. "I have been waiting, waiting, for you," Jane Clemens wrote.

[S]even years ago all the people I know could not have made me believe that one of my children would not think worth while to come and see me. There is no excuse for a child not to go and see his old mother . . . If a carrige or omnibus comes near the gate we are shure it is Sam. You can immagine the rest.[46]

No doubt he could, and did. He was experienced in that sort of thing.

IN MID-AUGUST, Samuel Clemens finally became a newspaper mogul, of sorts. With the help, not to say prodding, of Jervis Langdon—whose loan of $12,500 carried a subtle settle-down-or-else message—he bought a one-third ownership of the Buffalo *Express*. The *Express* was a plump northern New York state daily of the Republican persuasion. It was published in an old red-brick building on East Swan Street, in which wooden tables, a nailed-up bookshelf, a few smelly coal-burning stoves, and a lot of cobwebs formed the décor. Buffalo was about one hundred railroad miles northwest of Elmira. That was one hundred railroad miles too many for Sam, but he understood that Jervis's was an offer he'd better not refuse. He took over as managing editor on August 15 with the same dang-my-buttons aplomb that had carried him through the door of the Virginia City *Territorial Enterprise* seven years and a lifetime earlier. "Is this the editorial room of The Buffalo Express?" a former editor recalled the auburn-haired stranger asking as he entered the building on East Swan Street. Assured that it was, the questioner ambled on in "and with cold and biting emphasis drawled: 'Well, if this is the editorial room of The Buffalo Express I think that I ought to have a seat, for I am the editor.' "[47] The editorial room was crowded with Republican politicians who liked to hang out with the reporters and editors, an incestuous situation that Mark Twain ended virtually on the moment of his arrival: When several ward heelers jumped up to glad-hand him into their cozy little circle, the ex-editor recalled, "the new editor frowned them down . . . Mark Twain and the politicians never affiliated."[48]

He had learned a thing or two about newspapering from Joe Goodman. He redesigned the paper in the first week. Soon he was ensconced in his personal lounging chair, pipe between his teeth, shoes off, reading copy, and bossing everybody around. He commuted to Elmira on weekends. Before long, his duties evolved from editing other people's work to supplying his own. During his stay at the paper he contributed about sixty feature pieces, including some of his best early sketches. He wrote thirty-one editorials and about as many unsigned items.[49] Among these was an August 26 screed that indexed his progress toward "de-Southernizing" his received racial attitudes. News came from Memphis that a Negro accused of rape and lynched a few years earlier had been exonerated—posthumously—by the confession of another man. The ironic title of Sam's piece was "Only a Nigger."

Ah, well! Too bad, to be sure! A little blunder in the administration of justice by Southern mob-law; but nothing to speak of. Only "a nigger" killed by mistake—that is all . . . mistakes will happen, even if in the conduct of the best regulated and most highly toned mobs . . . What are the lives of a few "niggers" in comparison with the preservation of the impetuous instincts of a proud and fiery race? . . . Keep the lash knotted; keep the brand and the faggots in waiting, for prompt work with the next "nigger" who may be suspected of any damnable crime! . . .[50]

T H E   B I G Eastern journals had received review copies of *The Innocents Abroad* by now. Mark Twain, the scourge of too-chummy politicians in the editorial room, shilled for favorable reviews with several editors. To Whitelaw Reid of the New York *Tribune,* he mock-joshed, "[T]his is to ask you if you won't get your reviewer to praise the bad passages & feeble places in it for me . . . the meritorious parts can get along themselves, of course."[51]

He got his first look at the book on August 11 at the Langdons' house, where Bliss had sent a complimentary copy: a 651-page steamboat encased in a black-cloth cover, the title and subtitle stamped in gold over a montage of images—the Sphinx, a pyramid, the dome of St. Peter's cathedral. "It is the very handsomest book of the season," he wrote gamely to Bliss in the second of two conciliatory letters. "I like the book, I like you & your style & your business vim, & believe the chebang will be a success."[52] Two days later he wrote to James Redpath, asking out of his fall lecture schedule, pleading the distractions of his engagement and his new newspaper responsibilities. To Mary and Abel Fairbanks, he announced that he had decided to "prostitute my talents" to the *Express.*[53]

He bit down on his pipe and waited for reaction to his book.

A little ripple of applause issued from an important quarter. The Elmira *Advertiser* of August 14 declared it written in an "easy and pleasing" style. A week or so of silence. Then, on August 27, Whitelaw Reid's New York *Tribune* rolled out the first review in a metropolitan daily, a measured endorsement that ended, "The greater part of his book is pure fun, and considering how much of it there is, the freshness is wonderfully well sustained."[54] Then the ovation began.

"Very few will be able to read it without laughing at least half the time," declared the Hartford *Courant.* "It may be absurd, but it certainly is funny . . ." "We had no idea so much humor, wit, geniality, fine description and good sense, could be contained within the covers of any one book," trumpeted the *National Standard* of New Jersey. "Mark Twain, always interesting, in this book has outrivaled himself," reported the Meriden (Conn.) *Republican.* "It is instructive, humorous, racy, full of quaint expressions that make you laugh unexpectedly, and before you are quite ready . . . You begin the book and do not want to leave it till the last line is reached . . . No one can read its pages without feeling there is still beauty and sunshine in the world." "The book is a Golconda of wit and a very mine of sparkling entertainment," said the New York *Express.* "The humor is natural, never forced," proclaimed the Newark (N.J.) *Register.* "The narrative is instructive, and the descriptive passages are some of the finest in the English language." On and on the praise flowed, throughout the final months of 1869 and well into March of the following year: "Buy it, and you will bless Mark Twain to the end of your existence . . ." "The book opens richer and richer with every leaf you turn . . ." "One of the most read-able and amusing books of the period . . ." "The book must be taken in inter-rupted doses. There is more fun in it than it is safe to swallow at once . . ."[55]

In San Francisco, Bret Harte, who had helped Mark Twain edit the manu-script, and then published advance excerpts from it in his brand-new *Overland Monthly,* proclaimed it "six hundred and fifty pages of open and declared fun," and added that "Mr. Clemens deserves to rank foremost among Western humorists."[56] From Boston came approbation from the Autocrat himself. Oliver Wendell Holmes, writing in his usual hard-boiled style, began a letter to Sam by averring, "I don't see what excuse you had for sending me such a great big book, which would have cost me ever so many dollars." He went on to rave that "some parts of your travels had a very special interest for me," going even so far as to cite the "frequently quaint and amusing contents," and summing up with the over-the-top declaration that "your book is very enter-taining and will give a great deal of pleasure."[57] Perhaps fearful that his own readers might reach for the smelling salts after digesting such flamboyant rhetoric, Holmes forbade Mark Twain to use the praise in promoting *The In-nocents.*

Genteel Boston had heard from Nevada by way of Missouri, and had ac-knowledged the power behind the barbaric yawp.

Then came the Boston-based review that thrillingly made the Brahmin acceptance public. An essay in the *Atlantic Monthly* declared, "There is an amount of pure human nature in the book that rarely gets into literature . . . among the humorists California has given us . . . we think he is, in an entirely different way from all the others, quite worthy of the company of the best."[58]

Critics found some faults. Most typical was that the book ran on too long, a complaint that conveniently allowed a jab at the "subscription" selling mode. "There is some dead wood in it," declared the *Nation,* "as there has to be in all books which are sold by book-agents . . . The rural-district reader likes to see that he has got his money's worth . . . [N]o man ever saw a book-agent with a small volume in his hand." But the reviewers mostly focused on the book's most wickedly attractive attribute: its permeating, seductive have-an-apple *humor.*

Sam had got it right in his letter to Orion of four years earlier: "Humor" remained literature of a low order in a 19th-century America whose tastes were still legislated by the Boston Transcendentalists, with their neo-Calvinist view that humor was incompatible with the important business of life: elevat-ing the intellect and uniting Man with the Eternal. "Humor" was a curiosity performed by people called "humorists," a specialized skill roughly equiva-lent to sawing one's accomplice in half in a magic show. It was not to be con-fused with Serious Writing. Humorists were "a kind of personages whom no other society has produced," declared one critic, "and who certainly could in no other society attain celebrity . . . [Humor writing is] about as odd a profession, by the bye, as has ever been seen."[59] Especially when that humor reached the Holy Land. Bennett's *Herald* was among the few that met that issue head-on, dismissing the "over-pious and fastidious critics" who condemned Mark Twain's treatment of Jerusalem and its environs.

We cannot find anything so very irreverent in his account . . . After swallowing all the free-thinking and rationalistic emanations of the day, we shall not strain over a few paragraphs, which, if not marked by austere piety, need not, necessarily, be regarded as sacrilege.[60]

Most other reviewers, like Livy, felt obliged to convey something of Mark Twain's deeper, larger nature.

"The author is not straining to be funny; he is not trying to make a joke book; and there is nothing in it of that painfully unnatural sort of wit that is so wearisome." "Its morals are of a high tone . . ." "It is not a book filled with caricature and stale jokes, but a clear, well-written volume . . ." ". . . genuine native humor . . . Not what [is merely] remarkable for its vulgarity and insipidity, but a real, crisp, tangible wit . . ." ". . . aglow with that cheerful, hopeful, wholesome religion which has so much faith that it does not fear to crack a joke or to make one . . ." "The writer sees the humorous side of every thing . . . but is not lacking in power to be sober and wise, and even eloquent . . ." "It is pure in morals . . ." ". . . by no means a mere jest book, but contains more information . . . than would be gathered from many dry books of travel."

America's reviewers were grappling with something that few of them had expected to encounter between book covers, a kind of literary desegregation: humor released from the ghetto and allotted full citizenship; humor and "serious" writing living in the same neighborhood. In its first eighteen months on the subcription market, *The Innocents Abroad* sold 82,524 copies at an average $4 a book (price varied with the choice of binding) for a total royalty of $16,504, or about $217,762 in today's dollars. Sidney Drake was not heard from any further on the subject of its unsuitable humor. Mark Twain would never again, in his lifetime or afterward, be less than a preeminent figure in American culture.

IN SEPTEMBER, under pressure from Redpath to honor some key engagements, notably a November appearance at the Music Hall in Boston, Mark Twain reluctantly resumed his lecture schedule. It was a brutal slog: fifty-one stops over nearly three months, including Christmas Eve (Slatersville, R.I.). He would be away for both Livy's twenty-fourth birthday, on November 28, and his own thirty-fourth, two days later. Sam lectured in Pittsburgh and environs, then spent six weeks in Massachusetts, Rhode Island, Washington,

Maine, and Connecticut, boarding in Boston for most of this time. He suffered another "separation" dream involving Livy, the torment deepened this time by a rival—"He was *always* with you, . . . you put me gently aside, & said you knew you were drifting to certain wreck, but it could not be helped . . . I siezed your hand, & said, 'O, Livy, I loved you with such infinite tenderness!' "[61] Otherwise, this unwanted return to the lecture trail produced some significant rewards. "On the success of [the Boston lecture] depends my future success in New England," he'd written to Pamela. He'd added that he was "twenty-two thousand dollars in debt" (his debt from the *Express* venture), and that he'd had his life insured for ten thousand dollars, taking two hundred dollars out of his pocket "which I was going to send to Ma."[62] Before a full house of 2,600 on November 11, he achieved that success, as adjudged by the daily papers; the *Herald* chortled over its "rich and racy points."

Several days after that he met Frederick Douglass, also on tour. "I certainly was glad to see him," he told Livy, "for I do so admire his 'spunk.' "[63] The exposure to Douglass's gravitas, his absence of reassuring "negritude," registered deeply with Sam, and moved his own intellectual train a little farther down a track that had originated with Uncle Dan'l. Douglass told Sam the story of how in 1848 he had enrolled his daughter Rosetta, then nine, in an all-white female academy in Rochester, New York, only to see her sent home after a parent objected. Douglass had demanded that the principal ask the children to vote on whether they wanted to accept her; their vote in favor was unanimous. "There was pathos in the way he said it," Sam told Livy. "I would like to hear him make a speech. Has a grand face."[64]

Finally on this Boston sojourn, on a chilly afternoon, Mark Twain moved along Tremont Street in his curious rocking, rolling shamble, entered the bookstore Ticknor & Fields, climbed the staircase to the second-floor offices of the *Atlantic Monthly*, inquired for William Dean Howells, and commenced a lifetime of friendship and letters.

25

Fairyland

(1870)

The first rough contours of the super-nation to come were taking shape now. In 1870, a new, uninterrupted railroad line spanned the United States, and John D. Rockefeller founded Standard Oil. Baseball became a professional sport in 1871, and people started going to ball games in large crowds. (Hartford would boast the Dark Blues of the National Association in 1874; Sam was a fan.) The suburb began to assume its own identity, distinct from both city and country town. Howells would become its first chronicler in fiction, anticipating Cheever and O'Hara and Updike. A "middle class" took form, a product of new opportunities in business ownership and management, and it viewed itself as distinctive, certainly from the common rubes and immigrants below it, but also from the conspicuously consuming upper class of the Gilded Age. This new, powerful middle class comprised Victorians, American-style: in a word, "gentry." The upper 10 percent of the prosperous Northeast filled up their "leisure" time by yachting and playing tennis and golf. The Victorians went around on bicycles with extreme wheels—the Dexter and the Shire Boneshaker. (Sam bought a bicycle and fell down several times on it; years later he wrote a novel with lots of bicycles in it, ridden by knights.) Their wives shopped in department stores, buying dresses for fashion as well as durability, and ornamental tchotchkes to put in the parlor, their new household headquarters. Olivia Langdon loved these stores; she assembled much of her wedding trousseau from these stores, and, later, the furnishings of the great house at Nook Farm.

The photographic image, its iconic power unleashed by the ten thousand–

odd battlefield exposures made by Mathew Brady and his associates during the late war, was domesticated; portrait-making studios proliferated. Sam, who'd already had his picture taken several times, had it taken several dozen more, and looked terrific in half-profile every time. (He didn't think any had done him justice, though, until May 1870; he ordered fifteen hundred copies of that one.) Advertising began its historic colonization of the physical world: in the 1870s, product messages were plastered across so many hillsides, boulders, and barn roofs that some states began to restrict outdoor-sign painting. Graphic design accelerated advertising's reach: an 1870 issue of *Harper's Weekly* featured an illustrated pitch for Waltham watches, endorsed by Henry Ward Beecher; by the 1880s, lithographed advertising cards would urge, DON'T FAIL TO SMOKE MARK TWAIN CIGARS.

It was an age of hustle and commerce—and, paradoxically, of the Child. America, by now fatigued with mourning the Union and Confederate dead, turned its sentimental attention to its young, igniting an efflorescence of periodicals and books for children. In 1869 a semiautobiographical novel about a mischievous but ultimately lovable boy was published to widespread acclaim; the boy's name was Tom, but his last name wasn't Sawyer.

THE AUTHOR and newspaper owner Samuel Clemens vaulted into the upper reaches of this new postwar society when he married Olivia Langdon on February 2, 1870, after seventeen months of courtship. He had written an estimated 189 love letters—about half have been recovered, beginning with "My Honored Sister," on September 7, 1868, and concluding with ". . . God bless you, Sam," on January 20, 1870. In that final prenuptial letter, written just before a lecture in Hornellsville, New York, Sam told Livy that it had been "the pleasantest correspondence I ever had a share in. For over two months of the time, we wrote every other day. During the succeeding twelve months we have written *every* day that we have been parted from each other." Her letters "have made one ray of sunlight & created a thrill of pleasure in every one of these long-drawn days," and he promised, "This is the last long correspondence we shall ever have, my Livy—& now on this day it passes forever . . . & becomes a *memory*."[1]

An astonishing self-description of Mark Twain's ability to *own* an audience—his rock idol's instincts and audacity—found its way into Sam's second-to-last known letter of the exchange, written after midnight on January 15, from Bagg's Hotel in Utica. Perhaps his adrenaline was still pumping after the freakish events of his previous night's stop in Cambridge, New York: arriving exhausted in a sleet storm, he was infuriated to find that a local paper, the Troy *Times,* had printed a transcription of his lecture, complete with dashes and hyphens to replicate his famous drawl. As he sat fuming in his hotel, he looked out the window to see the nearby lecture hall site burst into flames from a falling chandelier. ("My spirits came up till I felt that all I needed to be entirely happy was to see the Troy Times editors . . . locked up in that burning building.")² Firemen doused the blaze, to his dismay, and he had to lecture in the soaked, ash-stinking hall.

It was with those events swirling in his mind that Mark Twain ambled on-stage in Utica and surveyed the expectant full house. He decided to mess with their minds a little. They liked pauses? He would give them a pause. Still exhilarated hours after this gambit, he described it to Livy, along with his feelings of conquest.

. . . I stood patient & silent, minute after minute . . . till my roused good-nature passed from my heart & countenance to theirs along a thousand invisible electrical currents & conquered their reserve, swept their self-possession to the winds, & the great house "came down" like an avalanche!³

"No man knows better than I," he continued, "the enormous value of a whole-hearted welcome achieved without a spoken word—and no man will dare more than I to get it. An audience captured in that way, *belongs* to the speaker, body & soul, for the rest of the evening."⁴

THE WEDDING took place inside the Langdon household with at least seventy-five guests present.* Joe Twichell came up from Hartford to assist Thomas K. Beecher in the ceremony. Pamela and Annie Moffett, now seventeen, arrived from St. Louis—the first trip east for either of them. Jane stayed home for reasons that are not clear. Mary and Abel Fairbanks attended with their daughter Alice, as did Harriet Lewis, and Susan Crane, Harmony Twichell, Julia Jones Beecher (Thomas's wife), and several Elmira neighbors and business associates of Jervis, former schoolmates of Livy, some Republican politicians, doctors, lawyers, a former Civil War general and Olivia's eighty-seven-year-old grandmother, Eunice Ford.⁵

Charley Langdon was among the missing. His parents had shooed the twenty-one-year-old out of the house again. Accompanied by the Elmira College professor Darius Ford, a former tutor of Livy's, Charley was on a global "study tour." Chief among his studies was the science of staying sober.

Mary Fairbanks wrote up the affair for the Cleveland *Herald* with admirable tact—no gossip or slang from *this* correspondent! She disclosed that the bride hid her blushes in the folds of her bridal veil, reported that "Mark Twain" "filled the role of bridegroom with charming grace and dignity," and let on that everyone was polite. This was not strictly the case. An Elmira woman (probably Mrs. L. Holden Dent) crashed the party, elbowed her way through the celebrants, and demanded that Sam promenade her around the room. He was furious about it later. As for Livy, Annie Moffett recalled that

* Alma Hutchison Munson, a neighbor of the Langdons, recorded an estimate of the party in her diary. It is not clear whether her first figure is a 7 or a 9.

"[e]ven her sweet disposition was in danger of disintegration."[6] The next day a car supplied by a railroad magnate transported the newlyweds and several guests from Elmira to Buffalo. Sam, for some reason, set aside his new Eastern good manners and spent a good deal of the journey belting out the lyrics of an old song that went frostily unmentioned by Mrs. Fairbanks. Even the spunkier Annie allowed that it did "not seem particularly appropriate for a wedding trip."[7]

> There was an old woman in our town,
> In our town did dwell,
> She loved her husband dearily
> But another man twicet as well,
> Another man twicet as well.

The ditty must have meant something to Sam; he included versions of it in *Adventures of Huckleberry Finn* and *The Prince and the Pauper.*

At Buffalo they were driven to 472 Delaware Avenue, an exquisite two-story brick house with mansard roof, high arching windows, and a small balcony above the entrance. This was nothing like the cheap boardinghouse he'd been led to expect; he could never meet the rent. "Then the battalion of ambushed friends and relatives burst in on us, out of closets and from behind curtains."[8] The house was his and Livy's. Jervis and Olivia had bought it for them as a $40,000 wedding present—horses, stables, coach, furnishings, and servants included. Handed the property deed by Jervis at the doorway, Sam wisecracked that this was "a first class swindle." Within moments, though, he teared up, and croaked out to Jervis Langdon that he was always welcome in the household—"You may stay overnight if you want to. *It shan't cost you a cent.*"[9] The next morning, general uproar ensued.[10] The rest of the twenty or so guests went running around the premises oohing and aahing about the library and the cozy dining room and the shade of blue in the drawing room, while the Reverend Thomas Beecher flopped down on the floor and began rolling over. To his wife's horrified "What are you doing, Mr. Beecher?" he replied, as any gentleman would under the circumstances, "I am trying to take the feather edge off."[11] Then everybody collected in the drawing room, where Mrs. Beecher led them in several verses of "Heaven Is My Home."

ON THE Sunday afternoon following Jervis's staggering bequest, awaiting the dinner bell in his new household, Sam reached for his pen and began a reply to a letter from Will Bowen. "My First, & Oldest & Dearest Friend," was the salutation. Within a few strokes—"Your letter has stirred me to the bottom"—he was deep into an invocational chant, half to Bowen and half to himself, from which the greater part of his literature would issue, including the boy's book forever linked to his name.

"The fountains of my great deep are broken up," it famously began,

& I have rained reminiscences for four & twenty hours. The old life has swept before me like a panorama; the old days have trooped by in their old glory, again; the old faces have looked out of the mists of the past; old footsteps have sounded in my listening ears; old hands have clasped mine, old voices have greeted me, & the songs I loved ages & ages ago have come wailing down the centuries! Heavens what eternities have swung their hoary cycles about us since those days were new!

There followed some five hundred words of impassioned reminiscence that amounted almost to a brief index of the plots and imagery in the works soon to come.

Since we tore down Dick Hardy's stable!; . . . since old General Gaines used to say, "Whoop! Bow your neck & spread;" since Jimmy Finn was the town drunkard . . . since Clint Levering was drowned; . . . since we used to undress & play Robin Hood in our shirt-tails, with lath swords, in the woods on Holliday's Hill on those long summer days; since we used to go in swimming above the still-house branch . . . since I jumped overboard from the ferry boat in the middle of the river that stormy day to get my hat . . . while all the town collected on the wharf & . . . looked out across the angry waste of "white-caps" toward where people said Sam. Clemens was last seen before he went down; . . . since Owsley shot Smar; . . . since Laura Hawkins was my sweetheart . . .[12]

The floodgates of his greatest literature were opened.

Livy expressed her contentment to her parents four days after the arrival. "If I could write you a reem of paper I could not begin to tell you half that I want to tell you—I wish that I could remember some of the funny things that Mr Clemens says and does—and besides these funny things, he is so tender and considerate in every way."[13] Sam began giving the new parlor piano a daily workout, playing and singing his favorite old songs by the hour. Soon, he was coaxing a sense of humor out of his rather sobersided bride, or at least a newfound sense of playfulness. The two took turns scribbling interjections in each other's letters to friends and relatives, often with Livy perched on Sam's lap. Seizing the pen after Sam had accused her of cooking the account book to make the cash flow look balanced, she interjected, "Father it is not true— Samuel slanders me—"[14] And following Sam's assertion to Mary Fairbanks that "I have got her trained so that she tones down & ~~almost~~ stops talking at the word of command," Livy scrawled, "I deny it, I am woman's rights."[15] As proof of her power, she forced Sam to keep his hands out of his pockets and sit up straight. By this time, she was pregnant.

It got to the point that Sam was referring to himself as "Little Sammy in Fairy Land." Livy came up with a more penetrating nickname, one that would virtually replace "Samuel" in her references to him through all the years. After one of his wisecracks in a letter to Olivia Lewis Langdon, Livy began her rebuttal: "Isn't he a funny Youth?"[16]

The Youth was growing fidgety with his new role as newspaper executive.

His byline in the *Express* boosted sales, but the novelty wore off. Schemes, brainstorms, fantasies came and went. The previous November he had thought to capitalize on Charley's and Professor Ford's global travels by rewriting their dispatches into a series in the Saturday paper: "Mark Twain's Voyage Around the World by Proxy." That idea lasted through eight install-ments, and Sam ended up writing mostly about his adventures in the West. He thought about taking Livy to England, thought about hiking the Adirondacks with the Twichells, thought about some inventions, and, in the comfort of his hearth with Livy close by, resolved that his lecturing ordeals were over. "I am not going to lecture any more forever," he notified Redpath in March.[17] And again a couple of months later: "I guess I am out of the field permanently."[18]

He re-redefined his "executive" stance vis-à-vis the *Express* in a way that suited him a little better: near-total detachment. As he told an editor of the *Galaxy*, "I write sketches for it, & occasional squibs & editorials—that is all. I don't go to the office."[19] By the end of 1870, he was boasting that "I never write a line for my paper, I do not see the office oftener than once a week, & do not stay there an hour at any time . . ."[20] His commitment to the paper crum-bled further under a couple of fresh distractions: ongoing encouragement from Isabella Beecher Hooker to sell his interest in the Buffalo paper and move to Hartford; and the chance to get himself back into the Eastern urban spotlight. The latter came via an invitation to write and edit a "humor depart-ment" for the *Galaxy*, the ambitious New York monthly founded in 1866. The magazine's author list included Anthony Trollope, Ivan Turgenev, a new young writer named Henry James, and Sam's new acquaintance William Dean Howells. Its publishers, the brothers William Conant Church and Francis P. Church, had noted the success of *The Innocents* (whose still-ascending sales now averaged more than 7,000 copies a month and $1,300 monthly royalties to Sam[21]), and offered him $2,400. Sam renegotiated for a fee of $2,000 and the rights to everything he wrote, and by late March was pouring his energies into the magazine's ten-page humor section that he called "Memoranda."

The *Galaxy* connection reawakened Mark Twain to the sheer dumb exu-berance of writing. Freed now from the pressures of a long-form manuscript to establish his bona fides with book readers and critics, and playing hooky from his suffocating duties at the *Express,* he dove happily back into the kind of work that he had perfected out in the West: the short, packed, word-slinging serendipity of the sketch. His pieces ranged through pungent social commentary; parodies of the Horatio Alger–style "boy's" book (this time the "good little boy" ends up launched skyward by nitroglycerine, Bugs Bunny–style); fanciful reminiscence; a rather brash anti-appreciation of the godly Benjamin Franklin ("He was twins, being born simultaneously in two different houses in the city of Boston"[22]). One of the first of his efforts, "About Smells," unleashed the democratic indignation in him that would become a hallmark of his popular journalism. He administered a verbal whipping to a popular Presbyterian minister in Brooklyn, Thomas DeWitt Talmage, who had carped in a newspaper essay about the bodily odors of workingmen in his church. "We have reason to believe that there will be laboring men in heaven," Mark Twain observed with dry deadliness; "and also a number of negroes, and Esquimaux . . . and a few Indians, and possibly even some Spaniards and Portuguese. All things are possible with God. We shall have all these sorts of people in heaven; but, alas! in getting them we shall lose the society of Dr. Talmage." [23]

CREATIVELY, FINANCIALLY, and domestically, Little Sammy's Fairyland prospered in the early months of 1870. Jane Clemens conquered her infirmities, and perhaps her nerves, enough to visit the newlyweds; she arrived at Buffalo on April 21, by train and then steamer across Lake Erie, escorted by Pamela and Sammy, now nearly ten. Jane's daughter rented a house at Fredonia, New York, near the steamboat terminus, where she and her son took up residence, Annie joining them at the end of her school year.[24] Later on her arrival day, Jane was hard pressed to recall whether Pamela and Sammy had made the trip with her from St. Louis or not.

Jane's "wool-gathering" state, as Sam called it, was a harbinger of deeper family woes soon to follow. In Elmira, Jervis Langdon's stomach cancer continued to spread; he weakened and endured terrible pain. From his sickbed, Jervis continued to dispatch gifts, and Livy sent back thanks accompanied by false high spirits: "There is no end to surprizes to this young woman, when I opened the check . . . I saw the *one*, I thought it was one hundred, and could scarcely believe my eyes when I saw that it was *one thousand* dollars—I felt as if I had suddenly discovered a fathomless mine . . ." [25]

Back in Missouri, Orion had started to drive Sam crazy—again. The drama was the familiar one: the Tennessee land, with Orion, as Trickster Sibling, notifying Sam that a Pittsburgh entrepreneur had offered $50,000 for the white-elephant property. (To add a little piquance to the plot, Orion— even as he declared himself "penniless," as usual, and said he was reading proof for the St. Louis *Democrat* for $25 a week—had earlier let slip a $30,000 purchase offer from Jervis himself.) Sam, reprising his role of Credulous Brother, replied with the reasonable observation that the figure was more than the land was now worth. *Take* it, he urged: "Providence will not deliver another lunatic into our hands if we slight this present evidence of his beneficent care for us." [26] A few weeks later, that prospect having evaporated, Credulous Brother was still talking as if Trickster Sibling might actually have one oar in the water. "We are offered $15,000 cash for the Tennessee Land," he reported to Jervis; "—Orion is in favor of taking it provided we can reserve 800 acres which he thinks contain an iron mine, & 200 acres of cannel coal . . . I advise Orion to offer them the entire tract . . . at $30,000 . . ." [27]

Months passed, without any action. Then, on August 1, having let this latest opportunity expire, Orion sent Sam a request for a couple of hundred dollars . . . to cover Orion's expenses . . . in trying to sell the Tennessee land. Sam's reply virtually hissed with the sound of steam escaping his ears.

> I have tried for 24 hours to write, but I am too infernally angry & out of patience to write civilly.
>
> You can draw on me for two or three hundred dollars, but only on one condition . . . that you consider yourself under oath to either sell . . . or **give away,** one full half of the Tennessee land within 4 months from date . . . If any stupid fool will give 2,000 for it, do let him have it—shift the curse to his shoulders . . . [T]his is the last time I will ever have anything to do with . . . that doubly & trebly hated & accursed land.[28]

Then, after one more month of Orionian paralysis, the coda: "Leave it in Mellon's hands but *give him 25 per cent*—can you never get that necessity before your face?"[29]

GREATER BURDENS than Orion's bumbling gripped Samuel Clemens. Jervis Langdon lay dying at home, his cancerous stomach a garden of pain. His family kept up an optimistic façade, but the signs were apparent in the spring. On May 30, Jervis summoned Charley home from his global tour. He did not specify to his son that he was dying, but Charley would have had no trouble inferring it: the letter informed him that Jervis's business firm had been reorganized as Langdon & Co., and Charley was to run it.

Sam and a dazed Livy, weakened by her pregnancy, traveled to Elmira on June 7 to commence the death-watch. The idyllic phase of their married life was over after a little less than five months. They would never enjoy such a pitch of untainted happiness again. "It is the saddest, saddest time," Sam wrote to Mary Fairbanks. "There is no sound in the house . . . the sunshine is gone out."[30]

Sam left the household on July 4 for a mission on Jervis's behalf. In the company of some New York congressmen, he took an overnight train to Washington to lobby for a bill that would restructure the Tennessee judicial system. Jervis was suing the city of Memphis to collect half a million dollars due a firm of his for paving its streets. Sam's efforts proved to be in vain, but the trip was productive in other ways. It was on this visit that he paid his second and more storied call on Ulysses S. Grant, now President Grant. Ushered into Grant's office by Senator Bill Stewart, Sam shook the president's hand, and then a heavy silence fell. "I couldn't think of anything to say," Mark Twain later recalled. "So I merely looked into the General's grim, immovable countenance a moment or two . . ." and then Sam blurted, "Mr. President, I am embarrassed—are you?" "He smiled a smile which would have done no discredit to a cast iron image," Mark Twain recalled, "and I got away under the smoke of my own volley."[31]

On July 8, he sat for a photograph by Mathew Brady in his Washington studio. This image is among the most arresting of the many hundreds made of Samuel Clemens. It reveals nothing of the anxieties now pulling at him; rather, it evokes an elegant, somewhat stern figure at a peak of manly vigor, his unlined face in three-quarter profile with the chin raised a little, his eyes narrowed, his mustache swelling over his lower lip, his thick hair piled neatly above his forehead. He is wearing a white waistcoat under a dark formal coat, probably his lecture-hall claw hammer.

Brady's photograph of Mark Twain proved to be among the last successful works for the great Civil War chronicler and portraitist to presidents, whose photograph of Lincoln is still represented on the five-dollar bill. Brady had overinvested in his staff and equipment during the war. The public who, he'd assumed, would buy his prints en masse, had turned its back on all reminders of the nightmarish years. At the time he made his photograph of Mark Twain, Mathew Brady was lapsing into debt, blindness, and the alcoholism that would kill him after twenty-six more years of futility. The image captures the intersection of two artists, one declining and the other rising, who together furnished the preeminent images and language of the American 19th century.

Most usefully for his writing plans, Sam revisited his old haunts, the halls and gallery of the Senate; looked up his old acquaintances, and unleashed his acute noticing: "Oh, I have gathered material enough for a whole book!"[32] Then he entrained back to Elmira to rejoin the death-watch. Livy drew additional support from a former schoolmate of hers, a slim young woman named Emma Nye. Miss Nye was en route from Aiken, South Carolina, where her parents now lived, to Detroit to begin her career as a schoolteacher. She politely extended her Elmira stopover to look after Livy.

JERVIS LANGDON succumbed around 5 p.m. on Saturday, August 6, 1870, after murmuring to his friend and minister, "Beecher, I'm going home."[33] His passing was one of the most-noted events in the history of Elmira. Thomas Beecher offered the memorial tribute at the packed Opera House on August 21. Mark Twain's written eulogy, widely reprinted in northern New York, praised Langdon as a great man who lavished fortunes on the downtrodden and once forgave a recipient of his largesse who had gone on to defraud him. "He was an Abolitionist from the cradle . . . a very pure, & good, & noble Christian gentleman . . . The friendless & the forsaken will miss him."[34]

Langdon's widow, son, and daughter divided his estate of a million dollars. Livy's share was $300,000, a significant sum, but short of a fortune. To his adopted daughter, Susan Crane, and her husband, Theodore, Jervis bequeathed a wooden house on East Hill above the city, overlooking the Chemung River. Jervis had bought the property for family getaways. It was Thomas Beecher who proposed the name for the leafy retreat, making reference to some abandoned slate-mining digs nearby: Quarry Farm.

Mercifully unequipped to imagine the second calamity bearing down on them, Sam and Livy mourned Jervis's death for a few weeks. Sam fell prey to distractions. He noodled around on an idea for a "burlesque autobiography" and daydreamed, like everybody else in this age of better-mousetrap mania, of inventing things and patenting them. (Orion in St. Louis had come up with an idea for a new type of drilling machine.) More solidly, Sam began gearing up for a long narrative of his Western adventures, and for some vehicle that would carry that "whole book's" worth of material he'd gathered in July about the Washington political scene.

On July 15, as sales of *The Innocents* continued to boom, Sam had signed a contract with Elisha Bliss for a second book, due January 1 of the following year. The subject, he confided to Orion on the same day, was a secret, but he more or less let the cat out of the bag in the next line: "Have you a memorandum of the route we took . . . Do you remember any of the scenes, names, incidents or adventures of the coach trip? . . . [F]or I remember next to *nothing* about the matter. Jot down a foolscap page of items for me . . . I suppose I am to get the biggest copyright, this time, ever paid on a subscription book in this country." [35]

Elisha Bliss may have set this project in motion by suggesting a book about Clemens's experiences in the West, as Paine reports; but Sam had been thinking along the same lines since before he left California. Several weeks later, he thanked Orion for what his brother had put together for him, and promised him a thousand dollars from the "secret" book's first earnings. Orion, possibly stunned to receive praise from Sam, got busy and forked over some more.

As for the Washington project, the first indication that Sam saw it as a novel, stocked with vivid and perhaps comic characters, came in a mid-August letter to Pamela.

I wish you would get all the gossip you can out of Mollie about Cousin James Lampton & family, *without her knowing it is I that want it.* I want every little trifling detail, about how they look & dress, & what they say, & how the house is furnished. [36]

James Lampton, of course, was the dinner host who served Sam turnips and water in St. Louis. Sam recalled him as a larger-than-life character, an incorrigible big-talking optimist and dreamer (Lampton was a lawyer and traveling salesman). A fellow born to inhabit a novel if ever there was one.

In early September, Sam, working from Orion's memoranda papers, told Bliss that he had written the first four chapters of the book that would become *Roughing It.* "I tell you the 'Innocents Abroad' will have to get up early to beat it," he boasted, estimating that it would sell ninety thousand copies in its first year. "Now I want it illustrated lavishly." [37] Before long, aided by Orion's material and the misnamed "Around the World" sketches from the *Express,* Sam had completed twenty manuscript chapters.

While all this was going on, a new piece of sketch writing out of the West jolted the nation's funnybone with even more force than "Jim Smiley and His

Jumping Frog" had some five years earlier. The sixty-line bit of doggerel appeared in the September *Overland Monthly* under the title, "Plain Language from Truthful James," by Bret Harte. Reprints swept through the East under the title, "The Heathen Chinee." People couldn't stop reciting it to one another in saloons and on street corners and over the backyard fence. Harte later swore that it was the worst poem he ever wrote, maybe the worst poem anyone ever wrote; and he'd knocked it out only to fill up a corner of empty space in the magazine. But it catapulted him to national fame after sixteen years of obscurity beyond his adopted home state. The poem was about two California fellows cheating each other at euchre with cards hidden in their sleeves. The cheating was equal-opportunity; but one of the two, a Chinese named Ah Sin, overwhelmed the poem and caught the public's fascination, partly via the strangely incantatory cadences of the chorus, echoing—lampooning—those of Swinburne's 1865 verse tragedy, "Atalanta in Calydon,"

> . . . I wish to remark,
> And my language is plain,
> That for ways that are dark
> And for tricks that are vain,
> The heathen Chinee is peculiar . . .[38]

A larger reason for the doggerel's impact was its nudging at a racial stereotype just then troubling the nation's conscience. Americans had never been particularly kind to the hundred-thousand-odd Chinese immigrants attracted to the West by the Gold Rush and later by laboring jobs on farms and in railroad building. Mark Twain's accounts of casual brutality toward Asians in Washoe had illustrated this. The economic downturn of the early 1870s had heightened tensions—and violence—in competition for jobs. Bret Harte had satirized this sort of abuse for years.

The ambiguity of "The Heathen Chinee" gave comfort to both sides of the divide. The narrator seems to argue that Ah Sin's cheating was no worse than that of his Caucasian opponents; yet he alludes to the "Chinee's" dark ways and vain tricks, and to Ah Sin's childlike smile. The phrase "Heathen Chinee" entered the American lexicon. It was used ironically by reformers and straight on by bigots. Its cachet, soon global, did for Harte what the Jumping Frog had done for Mark Twain. Overnight, he was a literary icon. It didn't hurt that James T. Fields, the publisher and *Atlantic* editor, brought out the Californian's *The Luck of Roaring Camp and Other Sketches* at about the same time of the Chinee's sudden sensation. Now Fields offered ten thousand dollars for the rights to anything Harte wrote over the ensuing year in the *Atlantic*, and placed *The Luck of Roaring Camp* at the top of the company's "New Books" listing, ahead of John Greenleaf Whittier, James Russell Lowell, and Charles Dickens.

Sam watched these developments with darkening spirits. He was receding from the public eye as Harte ascended. He had left the lecture trail; his *Galaxy* output had diminished as he concentrated on the Western book; and now, as 1870 drew to an end, that project started to founder as well, as he exhausted Orion's memoranda notes. He had churned out twenty chapters, pushing his pace to fifteen and twenty pages a day, but he wasn't happy with the results, and progress seemed slow to him. "Indeed Harte *does* soar," Sam conceded grudgingly to Charles Henry Webb, "& I am glad of it, notwithstanding he & I are 'off,' these many months."[39] That was a reference to their overblown tiff over a *"daintily contemptuous & insulting letter"*[40]—Sam's words—that arose from a misunderstanding about free copies of *The Innocents*.

SAM WAS at least able to immerse himself in his work during these days of grief and crisis. Livy Clemens could only struggle to cope with the absence of her loving, titanic father. Her limited strength further sapped by the six-month fetus growing inside her, she lay prostrate in the hot late summer ravaged by grief. She had not slept naturally since Jervis's death; Sam forced her unconscious by nightly doses of a "narcotic."

Livy wasn't the only one prostrate. On September 2, Sam advised Mary Fairbanks that "Miss Emma Nye is here & is right sick."[41] Three days after that, he informed a friend that "Poor little Emma Nye lies in our bed-chamber fighting wordy battles with the phantoms of delirium."[42] He and Livy canceled their plans to attend Charley Langdon's wedding. On the morning of September 29, Emma Nye died. Sam and Livy were too depleted to attend her funeral the next day in Elmira.

Yet Mark Twain kept working. On September 15 he wrote to the postmaster of Virginia City in the Montana Territory asking for anecdotes concerning the hanged Slade, the desperado Sam and Orion had met in 1861. A couple of days after that, a specimen of his most madcap inventiveness appeared in the *Express:* an exuberantly crude etching of a fake war map, "Fortifications of Paris." The "map" consisted of several shapes, variously labeled "River Rhine," "Fort," "High Bridge," "Verdun," "Erie Canal," "Omaha," "Farm House," "Fence," etc. The map was printed backward.

In its surface naïveté and underlying shrewdness—readers recognized it as a send-up of the many self-important newspaper maps illustrating the Franco-Prussian War—it anticipated James Thurber. It was reprinted in the Boston *Sun,* the New York *World,* and the November *Galaxy,* which went into three extra editions.

The map's silliness was the polar opposite of the mood in the Clemens household, where Mark Twain carved it out with a penknife on a wooden printer's block. He worked "with a heavy heart, and in a house of lamentation," he recalled.[43] In his old age, he mused that "The . . . periodical and sudden changes of mood in me, from deep melancholy to half insane tempests and cyclones of humor, are among the curiosities of my life."[44] He attacked his *Galaxy* obligations and his new manuscript. He worked on through

Livy's narrow escape from a miscarriage, or premature birthing, a week later. He dashed off letters absently using Emma Nye's stationery. "I am getting along ever so slowly," he informed Mary Fairbanks, adding that "so many things have hindered me."[45] Among them, he noted tersely, was Miss Nye's death. It was not callousness, exactly; more an instinctual resource that he drew on time and again as reversal and bereavement accumulated in his life.

LANGDON CLEMENS was born at 11 a.m. Monday, November 7, a month premature and tiny: thirteen inches, four and one-half pounds. Livy struggled out of bed within a week to look after the infant for as long as she could before giving way to fatigue again. Her milk-giving capacities were anemic; a wet nurse was called in. Sam did not expect the baby to live—just as visitors to the one-room house of his premature birth had not expected him to survive. Yet he announced Langdon's arrival in jolly letters to everyone he could think of, several of them in the infant's voice: "I am not entirely satisfied with my complexion. I am as red as a lobster. I am really ashamed to see company."[46] Mary Fairbanks gamely spoofed herself in her reply: "Evidently . . . you are a stranger in these parts, and are not familiar with my *idiosyncrasies*, else your first greeting would not have been so *familiar* or so *slangey*."[47] He made some adept pencil sketches of the sleeping Langdon, and instructed James Redpath to book the infant on a lyceum tour.

When Livy entered labor in October, Sam had been busy lining up a job in Elisha Bliss's company for Orion. Bliss was starting up a monthly circular, *American Publisher*, to advertise forthcoming books. Sam thought that editing this sheet would be perfect for his forty-five-year-old brother, who had been complaining of bad hours and low wages. He promised Orion a monthly salary of one hundred dollars. Sam's intentions were good, and thus paved a road to Hell. By one of those ironic, or Orionic, twists of fate, the elder brother's proofreading salary had lately crept up to two dollars above the twenty-five dollars a week that he had wailed about earlier. A move east, then, in addition to disrupting his and Mollie's lives, would actually involve an income *reduction*. Orion, nonetheless, slogged eastward, a distinctly reluctant Mollie in tow. Within a few weeks, his life had indeed changed: it was Elisha Bliss who was yelling at him now, not those greasy St. Louis pressmen. "I'll work along here the best I can till I get my machine out," he vowed to Sam.[48] (The contraption was never patented.) He tried to further his writing career by producing a children's story to run serially in Bliss's new circular. After Bliss brushed it aside, Orion took it to Sam, noting that Mollie thought it was pretty good. Sam was characteristically helpful. "You mount a high horse & a dismally *artificial* one," he explained to Orion, "& go frothing in a way that nobody can understand or sympathize with."[49]

Sam, in the meantime, had hatched another "writing-by-proxy" idea, à la the fizzled "Voyage Around the World" gambit involving Dr. Darius Ford. This would be a book about the new bonanza that was just then erupting in a far-off land, one that promised to beggar the riches of the Gold Rush and the Comstock Lode. Children had been picking up pieces of clear, bright, glasslike stones for a couple of years in the fields along the Vaal, Orange, and other rivers in the Cape Colony of South Africa. Soon the grown-ups got interested, and in the spring of 1870, the first diamond strike occurred along the Vaal River, near a town called New Rush. As new "pipes" were discovered, and news accounts spread throughout the world, and ostrich farming paled in comparison, thousands of fortune-seekers rushed into the territory, mining corporations were formed, and New Rush got a name change, to Kimberly.

Sam convinced himself that a book about this "new Golconda," * under his name, would be a Golconda of its own. His choice for a proxy traveler to South Africa was an old reporter friend from California days by the name of John Henry Riley. Riley was now a Washington correspondent for several California papers while he clerked for the House Committee on Mines and Mining. Sam got in touch with Riley and stirred him into a frenzy of excitement over the idea. Then he broke the scheme to Bliss. "I shall write [the book] . . . just as if I had been through it all myself, but will explain in the preface that this is done merely to give it life & reality." [50] Modestly, he scratched out "& sparkle." *"That book will have a perfectly ~~awful~~ beautiful sale."* [51]

Bliss agreed to "go in on that game," [52] and on December 2, Sam handed Riley his marching orders: terminate all other obligations "instantly," get packing for South Africa at Sam's expense and on a salary, and "skirmish, prospect, work, travel, & take pretty minute notes" for three months, [53] after which he would return to America and live at the Clemens house while Sam batted out a manuscript for a 600-page book. As a bonus, Riley could keep all the diamonds he found, up to five thousand dollars worth; after that, Sam got half. As a further bonus, "I can slam you into the lecture field for life & secure you ten thousand dollars a year as long as you live, & all the idle time you want . . ." [54] Sam would even let Riley in on his *"dead sure* tricks of the platform." "This thing is the pet scheme of my life," [55] he assured his prospective alter ego. It all sounded too good to be true, which it was. John Henry Riley sailed for South Africa in January 1871, narrowly escaped death at sea when his steamship got stuck on a sandspit off the African coast, worked the Kimberly fields for the full three months, found no diamonds, stabbed himself with a fork on the return voyage and contracted blood poisoning, and arrived home in the fall with nineteen pages of notes, which Sam never looked at, having lost interest. A year later Riley died of cancer.

---

* The Golconda mines in India generated great wealth from diamonds in the 17th century.

26

"My Hated Nom de Plume . . ."

(1871)

Sam's manuscript for the "big book on California, Nevada & the Plains" was nowhere near finished by January 1871. He was tormented with the fear that his hard-won reputation would dissipate before he could get the new book out, his place in the spotlight usurped by Bret Harte. "Tell you what I'll do, if you say so," he offered to Elisha Bliss in the first month of the new year. "Will write night & day & send you 200 pages of MS. every week . . . & finish it all up the 15th of April if you can without fail *issue* the book on the 15th of May . . . my popularity is booming, now, & we ought to take the very biggest advantage of it."[1] He was kidding himself. He was in no shape to write night and day. His creative interest in the book had stalled,[2] a recurring affliction that Mark Twain eventually came to understand metaphorically as his "tank" running dry. He also came to understand—later—how to deal with the "dry tank": put the manuscript aside and wait, for months or years, until the tank filled up again. That insight was not available to him in early 1871; and so he tried, in effect, to *will* the manuscript to completion—scavenging previously published reminiscences of his time in the West, the notes Orion had sent him—anything that would add bulk to the pastiche in progress.

His anxieties were stoked by the skyrocketing success of his rival out west. Bret Harte was everywhere Sam looked, and sometimes Sam found himself sucked into the Californian's publicity orbit, as a paper villain. In mid-January, Sam was infuriated by an allegation in *Every Saturday,* a Boston weekly of the James Osgood combine, that he had written a "feeble imitation" of "The Heathen Chinee" and published it in the Buffalo *Express,* no less!

"Will you please correct your misstatement . . . ?" he demanded in a scorching letter to the magazine's editor. ". . . I am not in the imitation business."[3] It was all a misunderstanding that might have been prevented had Sam still bothered to show up at the *Express*. A factotum there had innocently run the imitation poem, "The Three Aces," over the byline of "Carl Byng." "Byng" was a frequent contributor who some assumed was Mark Twain wearing another pseudonym. A week later, a cooled-down Sam pleaded with the editor not to publish his angry letter. Too late: 42,000 copies of it were already in print, along with the editor's apology. Now Mark Twain was at least temporarily and enviously joined at the hip with Harte, a reluctant Siamese twin, if ever there was one.

The *Every Saturday* editor, a long-faced fellow who wore his hair parted in the middle and slathered with grease, and who kept his mustache ends twisted into fussy little—well, twists, was Thomas Bailey Aldrich. Aldrich was the author of that mischievous-boy's novel of 1869, *The Story of a Bad Boy*, which chronicled, in mild Victorian-gentleman prose, the mildly naughty exploits of "Thomas Bailey" (a mildly disguised version of the mild Aldrich), a New Hampshire lad given to such depravities as helping push an old stagecoach down a hill (he repents) and absconding without paying for the nine-penny creams at Pettingill's confectionery. Aldrich enlivened his tale with such whiplash prose as, "Great were the bustle and confusion on the Square." Its limitations of audacity notwithstanding (or perhaps because of these limitations), *The Story of a Bad Boy* fed the new market for the boy's adventure book, a genre launched in America two years earlier with the publication of Horatio Alger's *Ragged Dick*. (Louisa May Alcott opened up the girl's domestic book genre in 1869 with *Little Women*.) Mark Twain was familiar with Aldrich's work. "I have read several books, lately, but none worth marking, & so I have not marked any," he wrote to Livy. "I started to mark the Story of a Bad Boy, but for the life of me I could not admire the volume much."[4] He would soon explode the genre.

MEANWHILE, HE was provoked into a creative success of a very different sort. He unleashed, in the February *Galaxy*, a scorching rebuke to a snobbish young Episcopal rector in New York who had refused to officiate at the funeral of an aged comic actor named George Holland. The clergyman, William T. Sabine, had told a friend of Holland's that he "did not care to be mixed up" in the funeral, given that theaters did not teach "moral lessons."[5] Sabine then uttered the condescension that lent him a kind of immortality: "There's a little church around the corner where they do that sort of thing."

Editorialists castigated Sabine. None approached the brimming indignation of Mark Twain, who began on an even-handed note, suggesting that Sabine was a "crawling, slimy, sanctimonious, self-righteous reptile," then revealed his true feelings.

It is almost fair and just to aver . . . that nine-tenths of all the kindness and forbearance and Christian charity and generosity in the hearts of the American people to-day,
got there by being filtered down from their fountain-head, the gospel of Christ, *through
dramas and tragedies and comedies on the stage, and through the despised novel and the Christmas story* . . . and NOT from the drowsy pulpit![6]

The incident became enshrined in the folklore of American theater. When
Holland's friend, Joseph Jefferson, had absorbed Sabine's insolence, he
blurted back: "God bless the little church around the corner!" From that time,
the Church of the Transfiguration, on 29th Street between Fifth and Madison
Avenues—the "Little Church"—attracted people of the theater. And 103
years later, it was designated a United States landmark.

The Sabine essay was a deviation from the dry period. Sam's income was
diminishing along with his published work, and with his interest in publishing
work. Determined not to live off his new wife's wealth, he began to face some
baleful possibilities—such as that he might *not* not lecture anymore forever
after all. "I may talk a little (only in New England) next fall," he wrote to James
Redpath, adding stubbornly that "all the chances are in favor of my not doing
anything of the kind."[7]

On February 2, Francis Bret Harte, accompanied by his wife, Anna, and
their two small sons, Wodie and Frankie, boarded a train in San Francisco and
commenced a magisterial three-week journey across the continent to Boston,
where Harte expected he would claim the national literary peerage toward
which he had struggled for nearly two decades. Behind him, Harte left the
offer of a professorship at the University of California in Berkeley, testaments
to his greatness by the late Charles Dickens—and the peak creative years of his
life. Crowds greeted him at stops along the way. Women went crazy over his
good looks and flowing sideburns (the acne scars were hard to spot at a distance). Newspapers ran telegraphed reports of his eastward progress as if he
were a conquering general. The Hartes arrived at Boston around 11 a.m.* on
Saturday, February 25, to the cheers of a welcoming crowd. Foremost among
the greeters, hunched against the cold, heavy air, was the destined gatekeeper
of American literature, the thirty-three-year-old William Dean Howells, now
the assistant editor of the *Atlantic*.

Watching through the frosty puffs of his own breath as Bret Harte and
family stepped down out of their car onto the crowded platform, Howells
could tell himself (but probably didn't) that the arriving hero's literary fate
was largely in his hands. He was half a year away from the editorship of the *Atlantic*, occasioned by Fields's retirement. But already he had become a powerful, if unbylined arbiter. Many of the forty-odd book reviews he'd written

---

* Eleven a.m. more or less, given that there were then 144 "official" times throughout North
America.

had helped the careers of good young writers; that was the *Atlantic*'s traditional Brahmin role. What surprised readers and terrified his less-than-transcendent targets was the razor cut of his pans. William Rounseville Alger may have considered strangling himself with his own middle name when he opened the magazine in May 1867 and read that he "sometimes produces an effect of grotesqueness and extravagance which might be studied as a model of everything to be avoided in style." [8]

This new sauciness in Howells was borne of liberation. Fields and the Boston crowd could not finally overcome their snobbishness of his "Western" roots, but by God, they needed him anyway, and now that Howells was inside the club, he was going to bring a bit of the West along with him. His awe of the Brahmin brotherhood had begun to crack a little—his recent explorations of Italy and France had shown him that the travel writings of his idols Irving, Cooper, and Taylor were really a little mushy; worse, false. As for Hawthorne, Whittier, Holmes, Lowell, and the others, he now saw how their Puritan instincts had crippled their art—"marred [it] by the intense ethicism that pervaded the New England mind for two hundred years," he wrote many years later,[9] "and that still characterizes it." As a result, "New England yet lacks her novelist, because it was her instinct and her conscience in fiction to be true to an ideal of life rather than to life itself." [10]

Which was exactly why realism now mattered, and why it was time to open the windows of the elite Boston club and let in realism's fresh air. At the Civil War's end, that air was blowing from West to East; it had propelled Bret Harte into Boston, and Mark Twain before him. These writers, with their direct style and skeptical, realist instincts, struck Howells as the future of American literature.

William and his wife Elinor boarded the Hartes in their Berkeley Street house in Cambridge; and on his first day in town, Bret shook the hands of the literary "town team": Henry Wadsworth Longfellow, by now a Jehovah-like presence with his great cyclonic swirl of white mane and beard; James Russell Lowell, Oliver Wendell Holmes, the polymath Louis Agassiz, Richard Henry Dana Jr., and the skipper himself, Emerson. The twenty-six-year-old Henry James canceled a previous engagement the following Monday, "to meet the Bret Hartes at Mrs. Howells's. An opportunity to encounter these marvelous creatures is, I suppose, not lightly to be thrown aside." [11] Harte was indeed worth a detour. He had already criticized as "over-literary" certain verses of Lowell's—to Lowell's face, had made fun of the way Emerson brandished his cigar, and generally had tweaked most of the rest of the Brahmins, with the exception of Longfellow. The Brahmins lapped it up. On March 6, Harte signed that spectacular $10,000 contract with James Osgood & Co. Not long after that, a faint thump emanated from Hartford, as of a redheaded man hitting the ceiling. "I must & will keep shady & quiet till Bret Harte simmers down a little & then I mean to go up head again & *stay* there," Sam seethed to Orion. Several lines later, he added: "I tell you I mean to *go slow*. I will 'top'

Bret Harte again or bust. But I can't do it by dangling eternally in the public view." [12]

This was by way of rejecting a friendly request from Orion, prodded by his new boss Elisha Bliss, that Mark Twain regularly generate material for the *American Publisher.* "There isn't money enough between hell & Hartford to hire me to write once a month for *any* periodical," he raged, furious that Bliss was starting to count on him as the sole *"father & sustainer"* of the new trade sheet. "I lay awake all last night aggravating myself with this prospect of seeing my hated nom de plume (for I do loathe the very sight of it) in print *again* every month." [13]

Harte's celebrityhood was only one assault on Sam's peace of mind. Typhoid fever, the disease that killed Emma Nye, struck Olivia in February. Sam got the news while in Washington, from Susan Crane. He had pushed his manuscript aside for another lobbying trip to the capital in the matter of the late Jervis's monetary claim, and was sitting for his Mathew Brady portrait as Mrs. Crane's letter moved through the mails. He aborted his trip and returned to find his wife prostrate again, delirious and vomiting. Typhoid was fatal in about 12 percent of its cases in those days. Livy survived and was speaking coherently by mid-month. A doctor watched over her at fifty dollars a day. The crisis paralyzed Sam. "In three whole months I have hardly written a page of MS," he told Elisha Bliss. "You do not know what it is to be in a state of absolute frenzy—desperation." [14] With Livy prostrate, the household slipped toward chaos. Sickly little Langdon, cut off from her care, abraided Sam's sensitive ears—"I believe if that baby goes on crying 3 more hours this way I will butt my frantic brains out & try to get some peace," he vented to Elisha Bliss. "I want *rest.*" [15]

The Clemenses had spent nearly eight months now in households teeming with doctors, nurses, and anxious relatives. Buffalo had come to be as loathsome to Sam as the sight of his pen name, and Livy felt the same. Hartford, Nook Farm, the Twichells, the Hookers, tugged at Sam like a recurring dream. He would get his family there, somehow. In stages, he and Livy soon agreed: Elmira first. The future would take care of itself.

On March 2, Sam put Jervis Langdon's $40,000 gift house on the market at a price of $25,000 (the couple elected to keep the $15,000 worth of furniture). The previous day, he had sold his interest in the *Express* to another co-owner, George Selkirk, for $15,000, payable over time. This was a $10,000 discount from the share's $25,000 value, $7,500 of which Sam still owed the previous holder. Two weeks later, Sam wrote to James Redpath, further modifying his vow to not lecture again forever: $150 per appearance in New England, and not a cent less than $250 in Boston. [16]

On March 18, Sam, Livy, and Langdon Clemens left for the Langdon house in Elmira, where Olivia Lewis Langdon welcomed them as temporary guests. Elisha Bliss supervised the Clemens's furniture. Langdon was sickly; Livy was worse. Her doctors saw the move as a health risk for her, and she traveled as an invalid, on a mattress. The doctors were right. So was Livy, for that matter. "I dread very much my first visit at home," she had written to her friend Alice Hooker, now the wife of John C. Day, in January, "—I know that I shall realize more than I possibly can away from there that Father has left us never to return any more—"[17] On arrival, Livy stopped eating. Sam worried for her life. A new wet nurse was brought in for the baby. Livy slowly improved: through early April, she still could not stand. Her convalescence was aided by a new "tonic" that she herself had suggested back in Buffalo, according to Sam; and one that he'd endorsed: ale. "She was as tight as a brick this afternoon," Sam had cheerfully reported to Susan Crane just before the move. "She talks incessantly, anyhow, so the ale hadn't any advantage of her there, but it made her unendurably slangy, & that is what we grieved for."[18]

His preternatural will to work took hold again. He churned out page after page in his almost typographically regular handwriting. Three days after his arrival he sent Bliss and Orion an excerpt from the manuscript for printing in *American Publisher:* the section describing the Pony Express rider on the plains: "by all odds it is the finest piece of writing I ever did," he declared.[19] Not long afterward, he notified the two that he was "to the 570th page & booming along. And what I am writing now is so much better than the opening chapters, or the Innocents Abroad . . ."[20] Two days later he added a postscript to the same letter: "—Am to 610th page, now."[21] But as the weeks went along, it was the work still to be done that overtook his calculations. He figured that he needed 1,800 pages of manuscript to make a 600-page book. The "booming" began to sound more like a dull rumble.

The "farmhouse on top of an Elmira hill" was the epicenter of Quarry Hill Farm, Jervis Langdon's bequest to Susan and Theodore Crane. While Theodore supervised improvements on the old house and acquired acres of adjacent property, Susan, a gentle and thoughtful woman, welcomed Sam to the household as a daytime visitor. He walked from town house to farmhouse, a mile and a half up the mountain, several days each week through the spring and summer of 1871. In the peaceful confines of his first rural residence since the Quarles Farm of his childhood (Jackass Hill perhaps excepted), Mark Twain drove himself through the endless landscape of his Western book. A prominent character from that book materialized at his side on March 24. Joe Goodman, on hiatus from the *Territorial Enterprise,* came back east to spend some time on his poetry and a novel in progress. (Elmira lay less than a hundred miles from Goodman's boyhood hometown of Masonville, New York.) Goodman arrived to find Sam mired in the middle of every writer's nowhere—an unfinished manuscript whose novelty and freshness had worn off, leaving him unable to judge anymore whether it was any good or not. Sam was edging toward the worst symptom of that state: self-loathing. In December, he had coaxed a New York firm to publish *Mark Twain's (Burlesque) Autobiography and First Romance,* a pamphlet he'd thrown together for a quick cash strike; when a Boston periodical panned it for what it was, Sam moped to

Mary Fairbanks that these "slurs" amounted to "a popular author's death rattle."[22]

Joe Goodman, Washoe incarnate, was exactly what Sam needed. As the two men walked and talked along the hilly terrain above the Chemung River, recalling characters, feuds, hoaxes, and roof-walking nights on the town, the fountains of the deep broke up again for Sam. He urged his old friend to hang around a little longer. The Cranes offered their hospitality, and Joe Goodman remained at Quarry Farm into the early summer, writing his own work and helpfully commenting on Sam's. Albert Bigelow Paine, through whose eyes we can glimpse a sweet lost world of stock-company melodrama, reconstructed this interlude with everything but the greasepaint and footlights.

"Joe," [Clemens] said, "I guess I'm done for. I don't appear to be able to get along at all with my work, and what I do write does not seem valuable . . . Here is what I have written, Joe. Read it, and see if that is your opinion."

Goodman took the manuscript and seated himself at a chair . . . Clemens watched him furtively, till he could stand it no longer. Then he threw down his pen, exclaiming:

"I knew it! I knew it! I am writing nothing but rot! You have sat there all this time reading without a smile . . . I am not strong enough to fight against fate . . . Oh, Joe, I wish to God I could die myself!"

"Mark," said Joe, "I was reading critically, not for amusement . . . I have found it perfectly absorbing. You are doing a great book!"[23]

Something like that must have actually happened. Sam sent along a hundred new manuscript pages at end of April, pronouncing his work "pretty readable, after all . . . it will crowd the 'Innocents.' "[24] He let it slip to Orion that he and Goodman were contemplating a 600-page book "which will wake up the nation"[25]—possibly a version of the Washington novel that had been taking shape in his mind. He was writing "with a red-hot interest" now,[26] and over one virtuoso six-day stretch, he accelerated from 23 handwritten pages to 30, then 33, then 35, then 52; and finished the manic sprint with a nearly inconceivable 65.* Two weeks after that, he was two-thirds finished, he said—1,200 manuscript pages. His thoughts tended toward a simultaneous publication in England, to protect his copyright interests there.

---

* Like most writers, Mark Twain was often obsessed with his daily page-count. His pages had only 70–80 words. A newly discovered letter that Mark Twain likely wrote on November 14, 1880, just after he had finished *The Prince and the Pauper*, reads in part: "You see, I write on an average, 400 pages of manuscript per working month—to do this, one must make it a rigid duty to refrain from writing family letters—there isn't any other way. I can't write one before work, for then I should go to work with depleted fuel; I can't write one after work, for that would waste me like sickness (I'm 45 & must go carefully;) when I do write one, I don't do any work that day. You see, I conscientiously put the very best work I possibly can into my books, for I have made an estimate & found that I get 25 cents a word for every word in the 'Tramp,' ('A Tramp Abroad') which is $20 per note-paper page of M.S.—for I usually get 80 words onto a page like this which I am now writing."

As Sam's energy picked up, so did Livy's. By late April she was able to walk three or four steps while holding on to a chair.

He felt sufficiently up to speed for a quick visit to Hartford in early June, bearing another clutch of manuscript for Bliss. He'd been lured there partly by Joe Twichell, who'd merrily summoned him with the mock-heroic "Mark! Mark! dear friend of days gone by, whose delights we tasted in those happy though distant times when thou didst lodge with us . . . where art thou?"[27] He caught a service at Twichell's church, had dinner with the Connecticut governor, and dropped in on Orion and Mollie, making the right appreciative noise about his older brother's newest failed invention, a new kind of riverboat. (Orion had been thinking of this one for years, along with a new kind of wood-sawing machine, a new kind of knife, and an anti-sunstroke hat.)

Back in Elmira, Sam found Livy and Langdon flourishing. He mailed a photograph of Langdon at six and a half months to Bret Harte in Boston, a peace offering after their misunderstanding about the complimentary copies of *The Innocents*.[28] Then Sam faced the dreaded resumption of his damnably lucrative lecturing career.

Sam was determined not to accept the same exhausting conditions he had endured on last year's crazy-quilt tour. He sent a list of "stipulations" to James Redpath, who was already busy booking fall engagements for his growing stable of Boston Lyceum stars. Among Sam's demands: the best price that any given town had ever paid Petroleum Vesuvius Nasby (a Redpath client whose top rate was $400). Main railroad lines only; no "out-of-the way branches." No steamboat trips, or stage or carriage trips longer than two miles. "To simplify it, I don't want *any* engagements OFF the railroads." He would consider nothing "a single rod" west of St. Louis or Davenport, Iowa, nor south of Washington. At least twelve tune-up dates in towns before he hit a major city. No lectures outside New England for less than $125, if Redpath pleased, "because I thereby escape one-horse towns, candle-lighted halls, & execrable hotels."[29]

His "stipulations" preoccupied him more than the tiresome question of the lecture itself. The Vandal was overexposed by now; as for his replacement, "I never liked that stupid Sandwich Islands lecture."[30] What to talk about? An index of his success in answering that question—not to mention of his enlightenment toward women—lay in a lecture he dashed off all in one June day, and advertised his intention to deliver, before ultimately scuttling it. The subject was "An Appeal in Behalf of Extending the Suffrage to Boys."[31] The question of extending the vote to women was enflaming passions in 1871. The previous year had seen the ratification of the Fifteenth Amendment, conferring voting rights on black American men. When the measure had been before Congress two years before that, women had petitioned to be included, but were rebuffed. They lost the support even of Frederick Douglass himself. Women's groups had been at the forefront of the prewar abolitionist crusade, but now Douglass kept silent, out of conviction that Congress would never support the enfranchisement of both Negroes *and* women. Two national suffrage-activist groups surged into prominence that year; the more radical of them with the team of Susan B. Anthony and Elizabeth Cady Stanton as its leaders, the other headed by Sam's friend Henry Ward Beecher. Talk of civil disobedience was in the air, and would soon give way to action. Even the demure Livy Clemens had gone on the record with her "I am woman's rights." [32]

At least ten of Redpath's Boston Lyceum clients had prepared lectures on the subject. They included Susan Anthony (whose talks were sometimes written by Stanton), Anna Dickinson, Mary Livermore, several clergymen—even Petroleum V. Nasby, who proposed to orate on "Struggles of a Conservative with the Woman Question." Olivia Clemens's husband saw himself as the puckish jackanapes of this roster. "Extending the Suffrage to Boys" would have been perfectly familiar to the women of the Nevada Sanitary Ball committee, or to the Menken, or to the Washington journalists who chortled over "She bears our children—ours as a general thing." Or to Livy, whose virginal purity Sam sought to protect in his courtship letters, by discouraging and sometimes "forbidding" her to read *Don Quixote*, parts of Shakespeare, or the racy *Gil Blas*—"It would sadly offend your delicacy," he advised her, "& I prefer not to have that dulled in you. It is a woman's chief ornament." [33] A few days after his brainstorm, Sam learned that Redpath was considering a lecture proposal from a woman who proposed a humorous talk.

> The idea of a *woman* reading a *humorous* lecture is perhaps the ghastliest conception to which the human mind has yet given birth . . . Why, Redpath, the thing is wholly out of the question . . . Tenderness, pathos, tragedy—the earnest, the beautiful, the majestic—all these they can & do succeed in, but they fail in humor, *except in the sparkling, vivacious kind* . . .[34]

Sam's lecture topic got as far as being advertised in Redpath's *Lyceum Magazine* for 1871–72 before he tore it up and wrote a new one on June 27—and, on the same day, put *that* one aside and wrote another. "*It* is the one I am going to deliver," he assured Redpath as soon as he had finished drafting it. "I think I shall call it 'Reminiscences of Some Pleasant Characters whom I have Met.' "[35]

Sam was foraging. The lecture would focus on Mark Twain's encounters with "kings, humorists, lunatics, idiots & all," as he explained to Whitelaw Reid—name-dropping with embellishments, in a phrase. Sam told several people that summer that it was "the best one I ever wrote," but the truth was that he had no real message to bring to the lecture trail that fall. His entire creative focus was on the Western manuscript. In early July, he still lacked 450 pages of his imagined quota. "Some of it is tip-top," he advised Bliss, and offered a possible title:

FLUSH TIMES
in the
SILVER MINES,
& other Matters.
A PERSONAL NARRATIVE [36]

Sam was learning the ball-and-chain element of writing a subscription book. The *Nation* critic was right: it absolutely had to be big and fat, so that it looked like a good bargain to the thrifty rural folk when the salesman knocked on the door. In the throes of mental fatigue and quota panic, Sam swept up his scrapbooks and letters on the land of coconut trees, volcanoes, and hula-hula girls, and hurled them into the maw. The Sandwich Islands were not, strictly speaking, a section of Washoe, but copy was copy. With only three months before the start of his next odyssey by railroad, he scrambled to arrange the material into the final fifteen chapters of the Western book.

Sam was off to Hartford with his fifth clutch of manuscript pages at the beginning of August. Passing through New York, he bought two new coats and five vests for the approaching marathon. ("I didn't need five vests, but sent for them in a spurt of anger when I found I had nothing with me but a lot of those hated old single breasted atrocities that I have thrown away thirteen times, given away six times, & burned up twice . . .")[37] Sam stayed in Hartford nearly three weeks, immersed in cutting and adding copy, and reviewing many of the 304 illustrations that made it into the edition—some of them at the last possible minute.

As to the drawings, Bliss had retained True Williams as the chief artist, backed up by Roswell Shurtleff, whose elegantly detailed landscape portraits complemented Williams's angular but always dynamic cartoonish style. Among Williams's talents was his ability to capture Mark Twain's likeness in a few line strokes: the great bush of dark hair, the severe brow, the strong nose over the thick, compact mustache. Williams had used Mark Twain's features once or twice in *The Innocents Abroad,* but this time, the cartoon-Twain graced nearly every illustration that referred to the narrator. Mark Twain's features were familiar to a great many Americans now, from the lecture platform and advertising handbills. He was perhaps the first American author to thus "star" as a line-drawn image in his own book.

True Williams brought along some familiar liabilities to go with his assets. Chief among these were his drinking binges, which now slowed his output and pushed the illustrations beyond their deadline. Bliss hired a third artist, Edward F. Mullen, and began scavenging for suitable engravings from other books, including those of his own American Publishing Company.

Sam's Hartford trip amounted practically to a family reunion—save for Livy, home with Langdon. Orion and Mollie were now living there, in a second-story room of their boardinghouse on College Street. Downstairs were

Jane Clemens and Annie Moffett, on a visit from Pamela's house in Fredonia. (Pamela and her son, Sammy, were both in Elmira taking a water cure for the nervous disorders that afflicted both of them.) Jane had just turned sixty-eight and was feeling her oats again. She had bought a silk dress for twenty-four dollars "to swell around in." Sam had sent money to his mother over the years, but at times since returning from California, he had regarded his homecoming duties as a nuisance. On this reencounter he recovered his boyhood affection for her, rediscovering the "wonderfully winning woman, with her gentle simplicity & her never-failing goodness of heart & yearning interest in all creatures & their smallest joys & sorrows." [38]

Annie, he found attractive and interesting; Mollie, as attractive as he'd remembered her in her days of social glory in Carson City. As for Orion, he was

as queer & heedless a bird as ever. He met a strange young lady in the hall this evening; mistook her for the landlady's daughter (the resemblance being equal to that between a cameleopard & a kangaroo,) & shouted: "Hello, you're back early!" She took him for a fugitive from the asylum & left without finishing her errand. [39]

Sam gave Orion the single-breasted-atrocity vests.

At work in American Publishing's editorial offices, Sam discovered that not even 1,800 pages were going to be enough. He wrote a new chapter on the spot, possibly Chapter 53, the now-classic "frame" anecdote "about" Jim Blaine's grandfather's old ram, in which the ram disappears from Blaine's story after being mentioned in the second sentence, and Blaine meanders through a dozen digressions before falling asleep drunk. [40] The anecdote, in short, was nothing *but* padding, but padding of a sublime sort. It joined such other tall tales in the book as the one about the bull that chased "Bemis" up a tree in Chapter 7, and the sublime "Buck Fanshaw's Funeral," a compressed encyclopedia of Nevada slang as spewed out by a "stalwart rough" named Scotty, trying to make himself clear to the genteel minister he wants to conduct the service. ("Cheese it, pard; you've banked your ball clean outside the string. What I was a drivin' at, was, that he never *throwed off* on his mother—don't you see?") [41]

Meanwhile, Bliss was moving the business side forward. He'd closed a deal with the English house of George Routledge & Sons for a simultaneous publication in England, thus shoring up rights against "pirated" editions of the book in Great Britain, and now was preparing his door-to-door booksellers for a December canvassing campaign. Missing from the preparation was the book's title. *Flush Times in the Silver Mines* had not captivated Bliss, and the publisher kept ruminating. He and Sam toyed with *The Innocents at Home* for a while, but that one didn't stick, either.

Sam's hiatus in Hartford came to a stop on the last day of August. He rushed home to Elmira, responding to a wire from Livy: sickly little Langdon had weakened again, this time to the point of death. "We have scarcely any hope of the baby's recovery," he notified Orion. "Livy takes neither sleep nor rest." [42]

It is impossible to ignore some curious signs of detachment, or what seems like detachment at the remove of more than 130 years, in Sam's degree of concern about his infant son's crisis. In a letter to a cousin just before he'd left Hartford, Sam reported that Langdon's life "is almost despaired of." [43] But two paragraphs later, he was airily remarking that "[e]very time I am in New York or Boston I try to remember & get some photographs taken, but always fail." And just a few days after his homecoming, he was back in Washington trying to secure a patent for a get-rich invention that had been in his thoughts for the past five years: an elastic waist strap that could be buttoned onto the rear of a pair of pants to keep them from sliding down. (Males wearing trousers that hit well below the navel were thought vulgar in those quaint times.) ". . . I'll have to run, or I'll get no dinner. Am *so* glad to hear you & the cubbie are improving," he wrote Livy on September 8, at the end of a long paragraph of gripes about the annoyances of "the invention business." [44] He had not completely excluded Livy from his affections, however. She was now pregnant with their second child, Susy.

SAM AND Livy had been collaborating on other passionate life plans as well. Getting to Hartford was a predominating aim for both of them, and in his visits there through the hectic summer, Sam had investigated ways to make it happen. Buying or building a house would unavoidably draw upon Livy's inheritance, and Sam, although resigned to this, shared Livy's view that they should be certain that such an investment was the right one. Yet they could not live on indefinitely as Olivia Lewis Langdon's guests in the Elmira household.

An opportunity opened up by way of John and Isabella Hooker, the founding couple of Nook Farm and the parents of Livy's friend Alice Hooker Day. The Hookers offered to lease their house to Sam and Livy for a quarterly rent of three hundred dollars, while they toured Europe and, on returning, lodged in the spacious Francis Gillette house. The Hookers' three-story Victorian Gothic, with its steeply angled roof, arch windows, and multiple gables, had charmed Sam on his first visit in 1868. It was the first of what would become the famous tight cluster of Nook Farm mansions, a cluster just taking form in 1871. The Hookers commissioned the house in 1853 from Octavius Jordan, a British-born architect who lived in Hartford. Jordan was an exponent of the "picturesque" school, with its homage to the timeless English country house enclosed by gardens. Sam and Livy arranged shipping for their furniture in Buffalo in the last days of September, and packed their belongings in Elmira. By October 3, they were ensconced in the Hooker house at Forest and Hawthorne streets, with Livy reeling again under the strain compounded by her pregnancy.

Sam was feeling strains of his own. In two weeks, Mark Twain's lyceum tour was set to begin. The ordeal was going to commence all over again, this time with the additional distractions of a baby son in questionable health and a pregnant wife who was struggling to contain her distress at his long absences. Sam was aware that even America's newest literary darling, Bret Harte, had stumbled badly at Harvard in June. Invited to write and deliver a poem for the Phi Beta Kappa society, Harte had showed up late, his poem unfinished. He had tried to wing it with some other verse he'd brought along; the verse was blatantly irrelevant to the occasion, and the press that had kept track of his great eastward hegira several weeks earlier pronounced him "A Fizzle."

There was also the matter of Sam's lecture, "Reminiscences of Some Pleasant Characters I Have Met."

"The best one I ever wrote, I think," he had assured Orion. Now he could only hope it was the best lecture he wrote on June 27.

27

Sociable Jimmy

(1871–72)

The proportions of the disaster were immediately apparent. Mark Twain unveiled "Reminiscences of Some un-Commonplace Characters I Have Chanced to Meet" (he'd had the good sense to replace "Pleasant") on October 16 at Bethlehem, Pennsylvania, and delivered it again the next night in Allentown. The "chuckle-headed Dutch," as he furiously called them, sat on their hands. The Bethlehem *Times* complained that he was inaudible and had rehashed anecdotes from *The Innocents Abroad,* and that he hadn't been "instructive . . . or entertaining"[1] That was a rave compared to what the Allentown *Chronicle* had to say: "Mark Twain has the reputation of being a funny man, and the greatest joke he ever perpetrated was his 'lecture' last evening."[2]

"This lecture will *never* do," he wailed to Livy after the opening performance. "I *hate* it & won't keep it."[3] He was already scribbling notes for a new talk as he sat swaying in railroad cars; this one was on Artemus Ward, still a cultural icon nearly five years after his death. At Wilkes-Barre, on the third day, he canceled stops in Easton and Reading so he could get something decent together in time for his engagement in Washington five days later. The truth was that he'd never really invested enough care in his fall lecture. The crushing events of the year, combined with the pressure of churning out the long Western manuscript in fast drafts, had fatally distracted him. The *Innocents Abroad* material, which had so enlivened his Vandal tour, was familiar now, and no longer welcome.

Why he did not draw immediately on the new mother lode, the book in production soon to emerge as *Roughing It,* is a mystery. By mid-October he still had not thought to harvest it. In Washington, he worked at the Ward lecture over two days in the newly redecorated Arlington Hotel. Then he ambled out onto the Lincoln Hall stage to face a record audience of 2,000, of whom 150 were crowded around his feet on the stage itself—and bombed again. The *Evening Star* tried to be kind—"pleasant," it proclaimed the talk, in an unwitting irony—but the paper had to admit that the material was basically a confusing mélange of Ward and Mark Twain. "No lecturer has a right to trifle with his audience in that kind of style."[4] The *Morning Chronicle* lambasted Mark Twain's "unfit habits of speech," and drew pointed attention to his faltering stage manner: his "eccentricities of bearing," his "simply *outré*" gestures.[5] In Morristown, New Jersey, he was branded a fraud. In Great Barrington, Massachusetts, the critic called his lecture "plagiaristic" of Ward and blamed it on laziness.[6] The response at Brattleboro was harder to judge; Vermonters rarely changed their expressions for any reason. Then came Boston. Sam knew that the avatars of high American literature would be present, or at least near enough to read the reviews the next day. "Boston must sit up & behave, & do right by me," he'd told Livy. "As Boston goes, so goes New England."[7] Again, he would rely on the Artemus Ward talk. His late-night letter home following his performance was preemptive:

Livy, it was a bad night, but we had a packed house, & if the papers say any disparaging things, don't you believe a single *word* of it, for I never saw a lecture go off so *magnificently* before. I tell you it made me feel like my old self again. I wanted to talk a week. People say Boston audiences ain't responsive. People lie. Boston audiences get perfectly uproarious when they get started. *I* am satisfied with to-night.[8]

The Boston papers gave a different picture. The *Evening Transcript* noted the "pleasure" and "merriment" in the audience, but nothing more.[9] The *Advertiser* panned him, compounding the insult by printing a synopsis of the talk. His disappointment in the reviews evaporated the next day when some of those Boston-based avatars swept him up into a glorious literary luncheon at Louis P. Ober's burnished, masculine Greek Revival restaurant on Winter Place. The organizer was Ralph Keeler, a convivial young bohemian whom Sam had known at the San Francisco *Golden Era*. (Keeler was two years away from his murder aboard a ship off the coast of Cuba.) The other guests were the editor and *Bad Boy* novelist Thomas Bailey Aldrich; the aging James T. Fields, now retired as publisher of the *Atlantic;* Bret Harte; and the *Atlantic*'s new editor, William Dean Howells. Harte (despite his misstep at Harvard) had lately been embraced by the Eastern circle. Fields, in one of his last acts as *Atlantic* editor, had signed Harte to a one-year contract with the magazine for the spectacular retainer of ten thousand dollars. Toward Mark Twain, the Brahmins had been somewhat more skeptical: his authentic Westernness was far less polished, after all, than the variety offered by Harte, which betrayed an Easterner's efforts to sound "Western." But now, with Howells as his sponsor, this luncheon ratified Mark Twain's provisional inclusion among the younger American men of letters.

If Sam recorded any accounts of that luncheon, they are lost. Howells's memory of it remained joyously vivid over the years, though. He described several times "the lurid lunch which the divine Keeler gave us out of his poverty," recalling especially the beefsteak and the shoe-peg mushrooms and the *omelette soufflé,* and the way Harte put his hand on Clemens's "sealskin shoulder" and sputtered out to those present, "This is the dream of his life." [10] The occasion served as the rapprochement between Mark Twain and Harte— for a while, at least. The occasion also marked the first social meeting between Clemens and Howells.* Soon afterward, Sam directed Elisha Bliss to send copies of *The Innocents Abroad* to Howells, Aldrich, and Keeler, marked with his compliments. "We've been having a good many dinners together," [11] he explained. "The Hub of the Solar System," † as Oliver Wendell Holmes liked to call Boston, had become Mark Twain's personal hub for his two weeks of lecturing in the area, just as it had during his previous tour. Aldrich revealed a sharper wit on these evenings than he had shown in *The Story of a Bad Boy.* In later years Mark Twain rated Aldrich in a class by himself as a raconteur: "when he speaks the diamonds flash." [12] Still, the deeper connection was with Howells, and their friendship blossomed even further in the new year.

Mark Twain's affection toward Aldrich developed in spite of Mrs. Aldrich. It was Lilian Aldrich's bad luck to draw suspicious conclusions about Sam Clemens's long drawl and "rocking and rolling gait" on their first meeting, and to behave like a classic Boston bluenose about it. Sam got the message, and tucked the memory into his mental "vengeance due" list. The opera buffa unfolded with Mrs. Aldrich singing the role of Her Offended Ladyship, Thomas Aldrich as the Befuddled Lord, and Sam in the role of the Prince in Disguise. As Act I opens, Aldrich and Mark Twain enter the Aldrich household with a burst of merry laughter, to find Mrs. Aldrich unprepared for a dinner guest. She notices her husband's friend's attire: sealskin coat with the fur outward, cap pulled halfway down over his face, yellowish-brown trousers, and matching stockings. She notices that he is swaying from side to side, and seems to be having trouble with his speech.

Act II finds the trio seated in the library, Her Ladyship rigid with dignity and looking daggers at her husband, who labors to keep the conversational ball rolling until the dinner hour. The dinner hour comes and goes, with no maid making an entrance to announce that the soup was on. Act II is a very strained act.

In Act III, the tragic finale, the mysterious stranger arises sadly and takes his leave. As the strings reach a crescendo, Her Ladyship stands and sings the

---

* Howells almost never spoke or wrote of "Mark" or "Twain" or "Mark Twain" or "Sam." "Clemens" remained his reference of choice throughout the ensuing four decades.
† Bostonians later amended this modestly to "Hub of the Universe."

memorable lament: "How could you have brought a man in that condition to your home / To sit at your table, and to meet your wife? / Why, he was so intoxicated he could not stand straight / He stammered in his speech."[13] To which the anguished Lord responds: "Why, dear, did you not know who he was? / What you thought wine was but his mannerisms and idiosyncrasies, characteristics of himself / And born with Mark Twain."[14] Upon hearing this revelation, Her Ladyship bursts into uncontrollable sobs, and delivers the famous aria: "Mark Twain! / Was that Mark Twain / Oh, go after him, go after him; bring him back and tell him, tell him— / O, what *can* you tell him!"[15] Curtain of charity.

THE ARTEMUS Ward lecture continued to misfire as Mark Twain worked the small cities and towns around Boston. The audience sat staring at him in Worcester, and the chairman with his "owlish mug" perched on the stage behind him, another guaranteed goat-getter for Sam. But the crowds remained large, even on the many rainy evenings; and gradually, thanks to ceaseless tinkering aboard trains and in hotel rooms, Mark Twain pruned the weakest elements from the talk. He replaced its jokey conclusion with a thoughtful meditation on Ward; he recited a sentimental eulogy to the late humorist composed by a British poet. Sam's cheerful letters home to Livy were doubtlessly genuine in their affection, though his ornate lovemaking had long since given way to gossip, anecdotes from the day, and household concerns, such as thanking her for sending him some socks. It is not clear whether Sam appreciated the depths of Livy's loneliness for him, made worse by the growing erosion of her once-ironclad Christian faith. Or it may have been that he already sensed the worst for Langdon, and was steeling himself against the inevitability. A year old, Langdon still could not sit upright without help. He had trouble imitating the sounds Livy made for him each day, and he cried almost constantly. "Kiss cubbie for me" was about the extent of Sam's reference to Langdon in the surviving letters.

Livy kept as mentally and physically active as she could. Her mother came to visit, bringing her quiltwork, through the early phase of the lecture tour, and relieved some of the pressure with Langdon. Livy kept up a dutiful reading schedule, plowing through a tome on the Netherlands and Dickens's *Child's History of England,* and hired tutors for her pursuit of German and French.

Sam managed a weekend detour to Hartford on November 18 and 19. The day afterward, Livy wrote him an affectionate letter that could not conceal an undercurrent of sadness. This is the first in a cluster of four surviving letters from her, written over a two-week span, that afford a rare glimpse into the heart of Olivia Clemens at twenty-six—her concerns, emotional state, and her manner of thought and speech: unadorned at times, but always intelligent, always aimed at the heart of things.

Didn't we have a good visit together? I do hope that this will be the last season that it will be necessary for you to lecture, it is not the way for a husband and wife to live if they can possibly avoid it, is it? Separation comes soon enough— . . .

I am going over to "the club" now in a few minutes I wish you were going with me I rather dread it—I want you along to protect me.

The baby grows so sweet and dear, I know as he grows older you and he will love each other like *every thing* . . .[16]

"I am so sorry to have to leave you with all the weight of housekeeping on your shoulders," he wrote back; and added, a shade patronizingly, "—& at the same time I know that it is a blessing to you—for only wholesome care & work can make lonely people endure existence."[17]

That letter crossed in the mails with

My Dear Heart,

It is too bad to give you the last end of my day when the life and energy are rather gone out of me— . . .

Today I took him [the baby] down town, he rode on the front seat in Margaret's [the nursemaid's] arms . . . Oh Youth he is such a delight to me I am so thankful for him—If anything happens to me you must love him awfully— . . .

I hope that I shall get a letter from you tomorrow morning, I do like to hear from you little man, because you know—well you know all about it— . . .

Do you pray for me Youth? oh we must be a prayerful family—pray for me as you used to do—I am not prayerful as of old but I believe my heart prays— . . .[18]

Her longest and most heartfelt letter of this skein reached him at his lecture stop at Fredonia, New York, where Jane, Pamela, Annie, and Sammy were living. Addressing "My Dear Heart," she opened on an almost accusatory note.

It did me no good to wish for twenty letters, I did not get one—I have rec'd only one letter and one little note from you since you left home, they both came in the same mail—It is Saturday night, and I am homesick for you, not hearing from you makes me feel still more homesick— . . .

She admitted that she was "a little cross, beside wanting you so much and being disappointed about hearing from you . . ." and decided to suspend writing further until

Bed time—

Have been drawing a plan of our house and feel better than at dinner time . . .

Sunday Evening

I tell you I am glad that tomorrow is Monday, because I shall probably get letters— if I do not—well I do not know what I shall do, telegraph you I guess—

Mother and I went to church this morning . . .

It is so long since I have been to church that I was mellowed by the very atmosphere I think, Mr Twichells prayer touched me and made me cry, he prayed particularly for those who had fallen away and were longing to come back to God—Youth I am ashamed to go back, because I have fallen away so many times . . . I hope not to have as delicate a child next time as little Langdon was—

. . . Mrs Warner was speaking this P.M. of lukewarmness toward God . . . I told her if I felt toward God as I did toward my husband I should never be in the least troubled—I did not tell her how almost perfectly cold I am toward God—

She went on to discuss their house-building plans in Hartford. The plan that she had been drawing for the house was serious and sophisticated, well beyond anything Sam was capable of conceiving. She worked at it for nearly two years before submitting it to the architects, and it formed a fairly accurate working blueprint for the finished edifice. Livy had calculated that it would cost them $29,000 to buy acreage, build a house on it, and purchase new furniture—an undercalculation, as things turned out. She was due to receive a settlement when the co-partnership of her father's coal company expired; but that was eight years away and the amount was uncertain. Her inheritance remained mostly tied up in investments. In the meantime, her brother Charley had told her that she could expect an income of three to five hundred dollars a month from the coal enterprise. Sam could expect to earn two thousand dollars from lecturing one month in New England. Livy had concluded that, even discounting the money Sam sent to Jane, and incidental matters, they could live in a cottage with a servant until the co-partnership settlement came in. Mid-paragraph Livy's tone shifted again:

. . . I *can not* and I WILL NOT think about your being away from me this way every year, it is not half living—if in order to sustain our present mode of living you are obliged to do that, then we will change our mode of living— . . .[19]

"AM WRITING a new, tip-top lecture about California & Nevada—been at it all night," Sam reported to Mary Fairbanks from Erie, Pennsylvania. "Have already tried the new lecture in two villages . . . made a tip-top success in one, but was floored by fatigue & exhaustion of body & mind & made a dismal failure in the other . . ."[20] The tip-top lecture's content was the same that had been under his nose all the past summer: anecdotes from *Roughing It,* at last. This new talk saved his lecture tour. Unfortunately, the one village where it flopped was Fredonia, with his mother, sister, niece, and nephew in the audience. He'd arrived there glassy-eyed with fatigue: "so tired out I came near going to sleep on the platform."[21] The local review had been unsparing: a "rather thin diet for an evening's entertainment," decreed the aptly named

Fredonia *Censor,* adding that Mark Twain "does injustice both to himself and to the societies employing him."[22] He retooled the talk en route to Toledo; he pronounced it "perfectly *bully,* now,"[23] the best he'd ever delivered.

A train ride of eleven sleepless hours brought him to the charred remnants of Chicago, in the wake of the Great Fire of October 8. ("There is literally no Chicago *here.* I recognize *nothing* here, that ever I saw before.")[24] Warmed against the frigid Lake Michigan winds by the sealskin coat he'd bought in Buffalo three weeks earlier, he lectured at a hall south of the devastated area on December 18 and 19. He worked from the *Roughing It* stories and scored hits both times. Then a few dates on the outskirts of the city, during which time he composed a Yuletide epistle to his wife, a seasonal set piece of ornamentation, replete with brooding sentiment. He had Christmas weekend off, and spent it back in Chicago, reworking the *Roughing It* material one more time. Livy's reply, written on the last two days of the year, was filled with tender assurances that her loneliness was not a burden. Her thoughts focused on Langdon.

Oh Youth our baby is so sweet and prettie; you will love the little fellow, this morning I would say to him pet, pet-i-pet pet, the motion of my lips seemed to amuse him very much, he laughed until his little shoulders shook—Oh I do *love* the child so tenderly, if anything happens to me in the Spring * you must never let him go away from you, keep him always with you, read and study and play with him, and I believe we should be re united in the other world . . .[25]

MARK TWAIN was in Paris, Illinois, while Livy was penning these words. In this farming village of thirty-three hundred people, 200 miles down the tracks from Chicago and only 225 miles due east of Hannibal, on a drizzly year's-end weekend, Mark Twain experienced a pair of epiphanies that broke up more fountains of the deep, and further alerted his imaginative memory to the literature waiting to be released. The first of these occurred at a church service he dropped in on. The little sanctuary and the people in it filled up his consciousness as he sat in his pew, and sent him hurtling back through time. His letter describing it to Livy is a miniature masterpiece of radiant consciousness, worthy of Thomas Wolfe, Edgar Lee Masters, Thornton Wilder, or Carson McCullers in the annals of lost and holy American place.

It was the West & boyhood brought back again, vividly. It was as if twenty-five years had fallen away from me like a garment & I was a lad of eleven again in my Missouri village church of that ancient time.[26]

He evoked the high pulpit with the red plush pillow for the Bible, the stiff pews, the black contribution purses attached to long poles, "the wheezy

---

* Livy was due to give birth in the spring. Like most expectant mothers of the 19th century, she understood that the process could kill her. Infection and unskilled handling by doctors and midwives caused as many as one in a hundred women to die during or shortly after childbirth.

melodeon in the gallery-front" and the "old maid behind it in severe simplicity of dress," the choir that raved and roared around its "victim" the hymn, "&
pulled & hauled & flayed it." He noticed "the distinguished visiting minister
from the great town a hundred miles away—gray hair pushed up & back in the
stern, intellectual Jacksonian way," indulging his "imperfectly hidden consciousness of being the centre of public gaze & interest."

He became a boy again, fidgeting in his pew:

[T]he three or four old white headed men & women bent forward to listen intently; the
deaf man put his hand up to his ear; a deacon's eye-lids drooped; a young girl near me
stole a furtive look at a photograph between the leaves of her hymn-book; . . . one boy
got out a peanut & contemplated it, as if he had an idea of cracking it under cover of
some consumptive's cough . . . another boy began to catch imaginary flies; the boys in
the gallery began to edge together, with evil in their eyes; & the engaged couple in
front of me began to whisper & laugh behind a hymn-book, & then straighten up &
look steadily at the minister & pinch each other clandestinely . . .

The radiance turned harsh for an instant, as a shaft of the future shed its withering light.

She was a bright, pretty girl of nineteen, & he had his first moustache. These two did
nothing but skylark all through the sermon . . . it was such a pity to think that trouble
must come to that poor child, & her face wither, & her back bend, & the gladness go
out of her eyes. I harbored not a critical thought against her for her un-churchlike behavior. Lord! It was *worship!* It was the tribute of overflowing life, & youth, health, ignorance of care—it was the tribute of free, unscarred, unsmitten *nature* to the good
God that gave it!

The missionary appeal concluded, the sexton & the deacon went around, while
the choir wailed, & collected seventy cents for the carrying of glad tidings of great joy
to the lost souls of Further India.[27]

SAM'S SENSORY absorption in the church built on an encounter of equal
suggestiveness the previous evening. His accounting of this one was published, but not for another three years, in the New York *Times*. It received little
notice and he did not collect or reprint it in his lifetime. It wasn't republished
until 1943, in the *Twainian,* a journal for Mark Twain enthusiasts. It received
no scholarly commentary until 1978.[28] In 1992, Shelley Fisher Fishkin proposed it, controversially, as a seminal moment in Mark Twain's construction of
Huckleberry Finn's narrative voice.*

As he sat in his room at the Paris House Hotel awaiting his dinner, the
door opened and a six- or seven-year-old Negro boy entered, bearing the en-

* A New York *Times* article of that year summarized the argument contained in Fishkin's
1993 book, *Was Huck Black? Mark Twain and African-American Voices* (New York: Oxford University
Press, 1993).

trée, a prairie chicken. Sam learned his name, William Evans—in the sketch, it became "Jimmy"—and invited him to sit down. The ensuing conversation soon had Sam taking notes (in a nice irony) on the flyleaf of *über*-white guy Henry Wadsworth Longfellow's *New England Tragedies*. He worked the notes up into a 1,824-word sketch, of which all but 328 words were dialogue, nearly all of it the small boy's. Mark Twain titled the piece, "Sociable Jimmy."

"Did you have a pleasant Christmas, Jimmy?"

"No, sah—not zackly. I was kind o' sick den. But de res' o' de people *dey* had a good time . . . Dey all got drunk . . ."

" . . . I should think that if you had asked the doctor he might have let you get—get—a *little* drunk—and—"

"Oh, no, Sah—I don' never git drunk—it's de *white* folks—dem's de ones I means . . ."[29]

If first appears that Mark Twain is re-creating the old-fashioned Southwestern "frame" story here, with the educated point-of-view Gentleman eliciting low humor from the comic-stereotype foil. But the cruel conventions of the frame story never play themselves out in "Sociable Jimmy." (It's the white folks who abuse liquor and the black child who abstains, but that is an almost incidental point here.) Instead, the young boy, lounging opposite Sam with his legs draped unobsequiously over the arm of his chair, chats on about common-place things: stray cats and how to get rid of them; the size of the town; the town's big church with its high steeple and how the steeple blew off in the wind one day and killed a cow; the landlord's large family and all their nicknames.

Bill he's de oldest. And he's de bes', too. Dey's fo'teen in dis fam'ly—all boys an' gals. Bill he suppo'ts 'em all—an' he don' never complain—he's *real* good, Bill is. All dem brothers an' sisters o' his'n ain't no 'count—all ceptin' dat little teeny one dat fetched in dat milk. Dat's Kit, Sah. She ain't only nine year ole. But she's de mos' lady-like one in de whole bilin'. You don't never see Kit a-rairin' an' a chargin' around' an' kickin' up her heels like de res' o' de gals in dis fam'ly does gen'ally. Dat was Nan dat you ahearn a-cuttin' dem shines on de pi-anah while ago. An' sometimes ef she don't rastle dat pi-anah when she gits started! . . . Dey's fo'-teen in dis fam'ly 'sides de ole man an' de ole 'ooman—all brothers an' sisters. But some of 'em don't live heah—do' Bill he suppo'ts 'em—lends 'em money, an' pays dey debts an' he'ps 'em along. I tell you Bill he's *real* good. Dey all gits drunk—all 'cep Bill. De ole man he gits drunk, too, same as de res' uv 'em . . . Dey's all married—all de fam'ly's married—cep' some of de gals. Dare's fo'teen.[30]

"Jimmy" is not the butt of any "frame story" joke. There *is* no joke. There is only language. It may or may not have been language that directly animated the voice of Huck Finn—the dialects of Negroes and Caucasians had long since cross-pollinated in much of the American interior—but it was indisputably the voice of a child, conveying the sensibilities of a child: a child speaking contentedly of his town and the people in it: his world and its values, to the limits of his understanding. "I think I could swing my legs over the arms of a chair & that boy's spirit would descend upon me & enter into me,"[31] Sam wrote to Livy no more than ten days after sending her the manuscript of "Sociable Jimmy."

HE SLOGGED on eastward and homeward: Indiana, Ohio, West Virginia, Pennsylvania, then Baltimore and New York City before arriving at Hartford, exhausted and out of sorts, in January. He wasn't finished yet: four days later he dragged himself to Scranton, then Jersey City and Paterson, New Jersey, and Troy, New York. A respite of three weeks, and then the final two stops— Danbury, Connecticut, and Amherst, Massachusetts—in what he called "the most detestable lecture campaign that ever was."[32] It certainly must have ranked high among them. Since leaving Paris, he had picked a fight with a Pittsburgh paper that had printed a transcript of his talk, which retaliated by calling him an overestimated clown, a gross fraud, and a mountebank. He had often spoken six nights a week; he'd boarded trains at 3 a.m.; endured constant rainstorms; seethed at the incomprehension of various "woodenheads" and "leatherheads" in the remoter villages. He had begun the tour with a lecture that didn't work, replaced it with one only a little better, and hacked together a third which he revised at least twice and rememorized each time, working by dim candlelight in railroad cars, yet he still had no reliable success. At Danbury, his penultimate stop, the reviewer remarked not only the failure of the talk, but also the lecturer's "saddening drawl" that contributed to the tedium; he added that "Mr. Twain is not a beautiful man," with his "carroty" hair, shambling gait, and only one (apparently) functioning eye.[33] Mark Twain's final appearance, at Amherst College, drew a sneer from the Amherst *Record:* two hours of nonsense; the audience "had heard enough of him when he was done."[34]

On the other hand, the crowds were generally large to overflowing, and people loved him in the homeward stretch: audiences were reported forced into convulsion, dissolved in almost continuous laughter and applause, held in rapt admiration. The journalists tried to solve the mystery of his mesmeric stage manner by dissecting it as precisely as if he were a creature who had just stepped from a crate packed by Charles Darwin.

Whenever he paused, placed his left arm akimbo and his right elbow in his left hand and began to gesticulate slowly with his right hand, the next word or words he uttered was the funny point toward which all that he had been saying just before tended . . . It is impossible to imitate on paper his gestures and manner of speaking.[35]

[Mark Twain] very much resembles the pictures that are meant to represent him in his great book, "Innocents Abroad," except that he don't wear the check trowsers on the lecture stand that he wore in the holy land [i.e., in the illustrations] . . . He appears to labor under some embarrassment in not knowing just how to dispose of his arms and hands, but this only heightens the drollery of his manner, and may be merely a "stage trick." [36]

The tour was a financial success. Sam estimated that he had earned between ten and twelve thousand dollars; he used most of it to pay off debts, including the $7,500 that he still owed on the *Express* deal. He paid the rent on the Hooker house, settled a debt with James Redpath, sent his mother three hundred dollars and supplied several hundred dollars' worth of household expenses to Livy. Toward the end of his tour, he complained that he scarcely had enough money to return home on.

T H E R E W E R E other, more intimate satisfactions in the tour's closing days. The heavily pregnant Livy, who in December had subjected Sam to some pent-up anger over their long separation, turned tender and subtly erotic as she anticipated his homecoming.

My Youth

You have seemed so near and dear to me . . . [Last evening] I could not help going to the tin box when I went to my room it is never very safe for me to go there, however I did not read any of the oldest love letters, only some that were written since we were married . . . how sweet the memory of all our love life is—often when I get to thinking of you I would like to have a good cry, a happy, thankful cry it would be—but at such times it is hard not to be able to put out my hand and touch you— Last night I had a vivid dream of your return . . . in my sleep I did all the things that I should have done waking if you had returned to me, put my hand in yours, stroked your hair, did every thing that should make me really conscious of your presence—Youth don't you think it is very sweet to love as we love? [37]

He arrived at what he and Livy had nicknamed "The Nook Barn" a few days before their second wedding anniversary, Friday, February 2. There is no record of what Livy thought of his departure the next day by train for an overnight visit to New York, for a private birthday reception for Horace Greeley. The great Abolitionist and founder of the New York *Tribune* had turned sixty-one, and was preparing to oppose Ulysses S. Grant in the 1872 presidential election.* Mark Twain found himself in the midst of several hundred influential people milling through the host's parlors on West 57th Street.

* Greeley ran on the Liberal Republican ticket, endorsed by the Democrats, campaigning against the corruption that had spread through Grant's Republican administration.

They included P. T. Barnum, Bret Harte, Richard Henry Stoddard, and John Hay, with whom he was already on good terms.

Hay, with his high cheekbones and tight little mustache, was among the most accomplished young men in America. He had served, along with John Nicolay, as one of President Lincoln's two private secretaries. He was presently an editorial writer for the New York *Tribune,* but would go on to an outstanding career in diplomacy, helping to create America's "Open Door" policy toward China, and in letters—authoring, along with Nicolay, a ten-volume biography of Lincoln that has stood as a cornerstone of Lincoln scholarship. Hay was already one of Mark Twain's most enthusiastic and perceptive reviewers, and would remain so for the rest of the author's career. A native of the Mississippi river town of Warsaw, Illinois, just north of Hannibal, Hay was a connoisseur of the "Pike County" speech of the region, recognized by writers as the prototypical "Western" dialect. He'd called Mark Twain "the finest living delineator of the true Pike accent" in a January 25 review of the writer's lecture at Steinway Hall.[38]

The Greeley reception was a prototype of the literary soirees that remain among New York's cultural bequests to the world: apartment rooms abuzz with celebrity-intellectuals and with guests craning their necks to spot them. "One of the most remarkable companies of men and women of letters" ever seen in New York, the *World* told its readers.[39] Charles Wingate wrote a pamphlet commemorating the event and said that Mark Twain, along with Harte and Hay, "formed a trinity of wit such as has rarely been found under one roof."[40] This undoubtedly made happy reading for Mark Twain, who was still far from certain about his status in the East.

It may have been on this New York visit, or possibly later in February, in the opinion of editors Lin Salamo and Harriet Elinor Smith, that Sam visited a famous medium named James Vincent Mansfield and ran a pragmatic experiment by trying to see if Mansfield could correctly report how his brother Henry died. He couldn't.[41]

IN ALL, the new year seemed radiant with happy prospects—a new book and a new child foremost among them. The first copies of *Roughing It* arrived at Nook Barn from the binders at about the same time Sam came home for his three-week hiatus. Distribution was to commence around February 19, and Livy expected to give birth within a month after that. Langdon at sixteen months seemed robust, for a change—"very fat & chubby, & always cheerful & happy-hearted," Sam reported to Mary Fairbanks.[42] Sam awaited his new book's publication free from the anxieties that had preceded *The Innocents Abroad.* If any Clemens was afflicted with anxiety this time around, it was Orion in Hartford, who believed that Elisha Bliss had fraudulently cut corners in the production of *Roughing It,* and was thereby cheating Sam out of his fair share of royalties (what Clemens had tried to define as "half profits"). Orion confronted Bliss and was fired. This set the stage for the first in a long series of showdowns for Mark Twain and Elisha Bliss.

On March 18, writing from Elmira, Sam Clemens sent William Dean Howells a most jaunty letter, a note of thanks for the gift of Howells's new novel, *Their Wedding Journey,* and a mock-explanation for why he could not return the favor: "I would like to send you a copy of *my* book, but I can't get a copy myself, yet, because 30,000 people who bought & paid for it have to have preference over the author." [43]

It was true. *Roughing It* had taken off immediately. Twenty thousand orders poured into American Publishing even before distribution began. Within weeks the Chicago *Tribune* was reporting that "[o]wing to the immense rush" for the book "from all parts of the country, the publishers have been unable to manufacture them fast enough to meet the demand . . ." [44] Its sales easily outpaced those of *The Innocents* two years earlier. Sam received his first check from Bliss in May, a handsome $10,562.13. In its first year, the book earned him a little over $20,000. Its sales would fall short of *The Innocents* over the decades; yet it proved a windfall for him and Livy at a moment when their house-building aspirations depended on it.

On the day after Sam's letter to Howells, he issued a raft of even happier ones to friends and relatives throughout the East. At 4:25 on the morning of March 19, Livy gave birth to Olivia Susan Clemens. Like Langdon, she was premature, and tiny at five pounds. But both she and her mother were doing well, Sam assured everyone. Abel and Mary Fairbanks arrived at Elmira within days. There seemed no limit to the joys that 1872 could bring.

28

The Lion of London

(1872–73)

Langdon Clemens died in Livy's arms at nine o'clock on Sunday morning, June 2, 1872, in the Hookers' Nook Farm house at Hartford. He was not quite nineteen months old. The cause was a cold that developed into diphtheria. His chronic coughing had turned severe in the days after Susy's birth, as Livy nursed the infant in the Langdon household at Elmira. Susy was baptized on May 26, and Langdon grew feeble the day afterward, as Susan Crane recalled many years later. Still, a doctor said it was safe for the child to travel, and the Clemenses boarded a train for their journey back to Hartford on May 28. Their route took them through New York City, via a ferry crossing the Hudson from Jersey City. They spent the night at the St. Nicholas Hotel, and arrived back in Hartford on the evening of May 29, with Langdon struggling for breath. He lasted four more days.

The loss plunged Livy into a depression so deep that friends and family feared for her life. She passed out of danger, but melancholy was now her new lifelong companion. "Sue do not think of me as always sad, I am not so I have great comfort in those are left to me, only I feel so often as if my path way was to be from this time forth lined with graves—"[1] she wrote Sue Crane. The woman behind "the sweetest face that ever turned the cares of life into trifles & its ills to blessings" began to brood on the proposition that death was preferable to enduring the bereavements of life. These morbid thoughts anticipated those of her husband.

Sam's reaction to the loss of Langdon was more fatalistic, on the surface. A Nook Farm neighbor wrote to her absent husband that "Mr Clemens was all tenderness but full of rejoicing for the baby—said he kept thinking it was'nt death for him but the beginning of life."[2] Privately, he blamed himself, as he did for every death that touched him. Sam finally confessed this burden in 1906, in his autobiographical dictations, insisting that "I was the cause of the child's illness."[3]

[Langdon's] mother trusted him to my care and I took him for a long drive in an open barouche for an airing. It was a raw, cold morning, but he was well wrapped about with furs and, in the hands of a careful person, no harm would have come to him. But I soon dropped into a reverie and forgot all about my charge.

It was then that the baby's wraps fell away from him, Clemens recalled. When the coachman noticed the child's bare legs,

I hurried home with him. I was aghast at what I had done, and I feared the consequences. I have always felt shame for that treacherous morning's work and have not allowed myself to think of it when I could help it. I doubt if I had the courage to make confession at that time. I think it most likely that I have never confessed until now"[4]

But Sam had been guilty (he thought) of something more sinister than neglect.

I have always felt shame for that treacherous morning's work . . .

"Treacherous," as Sam described his behavior, implies deception, a willful betrayal of trust. This is the second time Clemens used the word in connection with the death of a close relative. Nine years earlier, in composing his detailed series of notes about Hannibal days ("Villagers of 1840–3"), he had written obliquely of the death of his brother Benjamin, and added:

The mother made the children feel the cheek of the dead boy, and tried to make them understand the calamity that had befallen. The case of memorable treachery.[5]

To those who knew him intimately, any notion of Sam's "treachery" toward family members (or anyone else) was absurd. "[W]e never thought of attributing Langdon's death to that drive,"[6] Susan Crane told Paine after Mark Twain's death. "Mr. Clemens was often inclined to blame himself unjustly," she said.

Sam resumed what was, to outward appearances, a normal life within weeks of Langdon's death—just as he had after Henry's, when he quickly returned to piloting. He wrote William Dean Howells a jovial letter on June 15, begging for a copy of a Howells portrait that had appeared in a magazine. "Bret Harte . . . says his family would not be without that portrait for any consideration. His children get up in the night & yell for it,"[7] Sam joked—a peculiar joke, considering. He went on: "There is my uncle. *He* wants a copy. He is lying at the point of death . . ."[8] He played host to Bret Harte, whose career had deteriorated since he reached the East, and loaned him five hundred dollars. He sent autographed copies of *Roughing It* to various people, holidayed down to New York, and quite likely went on to Boston to take in that city's World Peace Jubilee and International Music Festival, with its chorus of twenty thousand voices. In the heat of early July he took his wife, baby daughter, and a nursemaid, Nellie, for a holiday at New Saybrook, Connecticut, on Long Island Sound, where he could be seen playing billiards, bowling, and imitating Charles Dickens characters at the nightly hotel socials. Livy stayed mostly out of sight with her baby—although she did write to Mollie Clemens in July, asking a favor: "Mr Clemens is determined that I shall bathe so I shall *have* to ask you to get me a bathing suit—they advertize them ready made caps & all— . . ."[9]

New Saybrook likely was the setting for an auspicious literary commencement. Isabel Lyon, his secretary in the last decade of his life, repeated to a correspondent in 1934 Mark Twain's memory that it was during this hiatus, with the grief over his son's loss still fresh, that he began work on a novel about the boys he had known as a boy, and the "magic and freedom and careless young life on the river."[10]

ROUGHING IT received generally good reviews along with its sales, though nothing on the scale of *The Innocents Abroad*. This was partly Sam's fault: concerned that the daily press would scorn a book about wild doings in Washoe, and thus undercut his hard-won foothold in the East, he had persuaded Bliss to send out only a handful of review copies to selected reviewers—Howells and Charles Dudley Warner of the *Courant* among them—as opposed to the two thousand that Bliss had distributed for reviews of *The Innocents*. Now, when it became obvious that that misjudgment had severely hampered sales, Sam did the honorable thing: he blamed Bliss for his "frenzy of economy."[11]

The Boston *Evening Transcript* praised the book's eloquence and descriptive passages. Howells and Warner both came through for him. Howells unleashed another rave in the *Atlantic*, calling it "singularly entertaining," applauding its "grotesque exaggeration and broad irony,"[12] which he maintained were "conjecturably the truest colors that could have been used"; and praising its many excursions, digressions, and scattershot anecdotes as being true to the character of the West. "I am as uplifted & reassured by it [the review] as a mother who has given birth to a white baby when she was awfully afraid it was going to be a mulatto,"[13] Sam responded to Howells.*

---

* This bit of naughtiness, of course, amounts roughly to the same wisecrack that Howells remembered hearing from Mark Twain on their first meeting in November 1869: "When I read that review of yours, I felt like the woman who was so glad her baby had come white." Many scholars have concluded from this that Howells confused the date of Mark Twain's quip when he wrote about it in 1910—a conclusion strengthened by the fact that Howells also "remembered" a sealskin coat in the 1869 encounter, a coat that Twain did not purchase until two years later. On the other hand, the two versions of the remark define the difference between written and spoken speech; and it's not inconceivable that Mark Twain used it more than once, with variations.

Other reviews trickled in as the weeks and months went on, but eventually totaled only fourteen. By midsummer, the book's sales had reached 67,395, and by the end of the year, 75,168. Mark Twain's earnings from it in 1872 exceeded $22,000.[14] Among *Roughing It*'s lasting effects on American culture, it provided the single indispensable template for the Old West: indelible word-portraits of terrain; the texture of town and mining camp; the pervading twin obsessions of money and violence; an accounting of social and racial hierarchies; the sharply observed paradoxes of filigreed wealth amid mountainside boulders, and bohemian poet-aesthetes amidst the gunplay; a gift for replicating (and adding to) the sustaining tall tales and myths; and enough stunningly rendered archetypal characters to populate a Dickens novel. Bret Harte and others had supplied elements of this template already. What they lacked, and what gave Mark Twain's book permanence, was the unforgettable presence of the narrator at the center of things: deeply involved in what he described; at risk; suffering from his mistakes and rejoicing in his pleasures; always (unlike, say, the distanced observer Harte, putting his genteel spin on the vulgar subject and its even more vulgar language) on an equal footing with the characters around him; and always attuned to and unapologetic about the new blunt language of the West.

IN SPITE of *Roughing It*'s artistic and financial success, however, Sam found a bone to pick with Elisha Bliss. Orion's accusations against the publisher festered in his mind. What if his brother was right? Bliss had persuaded Sam to accept a royalty agreement of 7½ percent on the list price of the book, assuring the writer that this figure was equal to half the book's profits. The figure in fact represented a third more than Sam had received for *The Innocents,* but he began to brood on the possibility that Bliss was profiting more than he was. In March he had insisted that Bliss go over the bookkeeping with him at Bliss's Hartford house. Bliss obliged him—a risk-free concession, given that Sam knew as much about bookkeeping as he did about marketing an elastic strap for pants. (That particular invention never earned him a penny.) He eventually filed, then dropped, a lawsuit against Bliss. Whether Bliss really cooked the books on Clemens cannot be known, as Harriet Smith points out,[15] because these records are missing. Bliss's perfidy increased in Mark Twain's memory with age, until the publisher had swindled him out of five-sixths of his profits.

By mid-July, James Redpath was trying to cajole Sam into a new fall tour: "Will you? or Wont you? Lecture committees are getting importunate about you. We have $7000 or $8000 of engagements recorded for you—'if he lectures.' "[16] Sam had other plans. He wanted to *move* again, but not along those endless Eastern railroad lines. He was contemplating a getaway in the winter, either in rural England or in Cuba. Cuba interested him because of its ongoing rebellion against the Spanish government. England, with its chivalric legends and titles of nobility, had compelled him since childhood—especially given that some members of his family considered themselves displaced claimants to British royalty.

Either place would no doubt inspire a new literary project, and Mark Twain needed one of those. He contractually owed the American Publishing Company two books. The first, the collaboration with John Henry Riley about the South African diamond mines, had died along with Riley—if it had ever truly lived. The second, a collection of sketches, hung in limbo partly because Mark Twain had cannibalized his own material: using some of those sketches for *Roughing It,* and dumping others into a sketchbook to be published by the British firm George Routledge & Sons. Sam inclined toward Cuba as late as the last week of July; but on August 21, he was aboard the Cunard steamship *Scotia* as it departed New York Harbor for Liverpool. (Mrs. Langdon had come down from Elmira to stay with Livy and Susy, who were still at the seashore.)

Business as well as literary research finally informed his choice. In England he could set about solving an almost insoluble problem, but one that infuriated him more than it did most authors: protecting his work against unauthorized printing and sale by a foreign publisher. Such practice was not against the law—there *were* no laws in this area. In the years before 1886,* no American writer could control, or profit from, the republication of his or her work in England. The same was true in reverse. Regulations did not exist because American publishers had not pushed for regulations. Why should they? The balance of republication profits flowed their way: the enormous U.S. popularity of Dickens and other British writers overwhelmed that of most American authors in Britain.

Clemens found this state of things unacceptable. Publishers' interests be damned; he'd already been shut out of the enormous profits engendered by *The Jumping Frog* and *The Innocents Abroad* in the British market. The idea of being denied reward from his labor, while other people enriched themselves from it, outraged him, and he would pursue the battle for authors' rights throughout the rest of his life. His choices of action were murky, and limited, but going to England was essential, no matter what came next. He would begin with Routledge & Sons. Routledge had published and profiteered from his two previous books. On the other hand, Routledge had shown a sense of fairness: in 1868 it had paid him generously for his "Cannibalism in the Cars" for use in its magazine, the *Broadway.* This was partly self-interest: by including "Cannibalism" in a second edition of *The Jumping Frog,* the firm could claim "authorized" status and thus protection against rival British publishers. Routledge had published *Roughing It* a few days before Bliss brought it out in America, paying Mark Twain about two hundred pounds in return for formal copyright privileges. That was a tiny fraction of what the book earned in the market, but at least it was *something,* and it had led to another modest partner-

---

* When the Berne Convention codified international copyright rules.

ship: Routledge was now preparing an edition of *Innocents* for which Mark Twain had revised the text, again for a modest sum.

The author certainly favored Routledge—which at least flattered him as a coveted "star"—over a less elegant London rival named John Camden Hotten. Hotten had also brought out pirated editions of *The Innocents* and *The Jumping Frog,* and had followed them with two collections of Mark Twain sketches filched from American newspapers and magazines, which he coarsely titled *Eye Openers* and *Screamers,* and which he padded with material that was not Mark Twain's. Faced with inevitability, Clemens decided to throw his weight behind Routledge, and destroy Hotten's plans.

Livy seems not to have resisted the idea of the trip. She believed that Sam would be inspired by England, and she seems also to have desired a period of burrowing in with her new infant daughter. In early August, working from Saybrook, Sam scrambled to put his affairs in order before embarking. He took pity on the deteriorating Bret Harte, who had never fulfilled Howells's hopes, or investment, at the *Atlantic,* and was soon to embark on a disastrous lecturing tour arranged by Redpath. At Harte's pleading, Sam brokered a subscription book deal between Harte and Bliss. Bliss ended up offering Harte a small advance for a novel that took years to produce and, when published, lacked distinction and sales.

Just before departure, Sam tried to dragoon his brother, unemployed since leaving Bliss in March, into traveling around the country promoting Sam's latest brainstorm, *Mark Twain's Self-Pasting Scrapbook.* Anticipating the great American appetite for labor-saving devices, he'd envisioned a book whose leaves were precoated with gum-stickum, to ward off the heartache of brittle, ink-sucking mucilage. Just wet the stickum and put your clippings in place. Orion, usually malleable as a spaniel, wasn't interested. (Typical of his luck, the scrapbook made good money.) His dreams of self-reliance had taken him to Vermont, where he considered buying a country newspaper, with Sam's help. He zeroed in on the Rutland *Herald.* "The best thing I have seen on my whole route." [17] After that deal fell through, he arrived at the Hartford *Evening Post,* guided by Sam's prodding foot at his backside, and took an editor's job there. "Orion is as happy as a martyr when the fire won't burn," Sam reported to Jane in December. [18]

Clemens dined with John Hay in New York on August 20 and boarded the *Scotia* at noon the following day. He had with him a new hat, some books, a sheaf of photographs of himself, a ream of heavy stationery engraved with a tricolor SLC monogram that Sam had designed, and a new journal, which seems not to have survived. Off the Irish city of Queenstown (destined to be the *Titanic*'s last port of call in 1912), he wrote to Livy in a mood reminiscent of his love letters three years and a lifetime earlier.

Livy darling, I have little or nothing to write, except I love you & think of you night & day . . . & how the Muggins [Susy] comes on . . . & whether mother is cheerful

& happy . . . consider, my dear, that I am standing high on the stern of the ship, looking westward, with my hands to my mouth, trumpet fashion, yelling across the tossing
waste of waves, "I LOVE YOU, LIVY DARLING!" [19]

At Liverpool, he boarded a train for London, where he observed a man reading *The Innocents Abroad,* without smiling. This depressed him: no profits, and
no laughs, either. He was still feeling desolate when he awoke the next morning in the magisterial Langham Hotel in Oxford Circus. Overcome with the
desire to shake somebody's hand, or to see somebody smile, he impulsively
took a hansom to his British publishing house at No. 7, the Broadway,
Ludgate, off Fleet Street. The Routledges were a sprawling family, four of
whom were involved in the firm: the father and founder George and his sons
Edmund, William, and Robert. Sam swept in on these Routledges in their upstairs dining room, unannounced, as he had swept into the *Atlantic* offices
three years before.

The Routledges apparently had hearty appetites. "[T]hey had not had a
bite to eat since breakfast. I helped them eat the meal; at eleven I helped them
eat another one; at one o'clock I superintended while they took luncheon;
during the afternoon I assisted inactively at some more meals . . ." [20] They
quickly developed an appetite for the Connecticut Yankee, and by the end of
the day Sam's gloom was gone. A couple of nights later, Edmund Routledge
steered Sam to the Mitre Tavern in Fleet Street for dinner with the Whitefriars
Club, a Friday night salon of artists, writers, and actors. In an atmosphere of
cigar smoke, ale, and wit, and with Ambrose Bierce among the guests, Mark
Twain commenced his long mutual love affair with Great Britain. He responded to a toast with the claim that he, and not Henry M. Stanley, had discovered Dr. Livingstone in Africa. Here as in America, Mark Twain's peculiar
stagecraft worked its magic. The laughter that interrupted him, a journalist
noted, was triggered as much by his "quaint and original manner" as by his
words. [21]

Unlike the British reading public, the British press had not much cared
for *Roughing It.* The papers disapproved of Mark Twain's vulgarity, his slang,
his accounts of brawls and drunken nights. But not even the British press
could resist Mark Twain in person. His visit became an ongoing party: banquets, receptions, guided tours of the city. He took in the statues of Leicester
Square, the "matchless" Hyde Park, the Zoological Gardens, the British Museum ("I would advise you to drop in there some time when you have nothing to do for—five minutes," [22] he advised a roaring audience at the Savage
Club). His thoughts of researching a book about England were swamped
by the merriment. "I accomplish next to nothing," he wrote to Livy. "Too
much company—too much dining—too much sociability." [23] Dickens's former
lecture-tour manager wanted to talk to him. He took lunch with Dickens's favorite comic actor and a member of Parliament. He was written up in the
London *Graphic* alongside an engraving of his face. He had some more pho-

tographic portraits made. He bought a watch for Annie Moffett and a fine new razor for himself. And then he turned his attention to John Camden Hotten. He went after the publisher in a letter published on September 20 in the *Spectator*, three days after the *Graphic* profile, and thus at the peak of his celebrity in the city. He began by conceding that no law prevented Hotten's republishings, and then, noting the extra material shoveled in by the pirate, stuck his verbal cutlass in Hotten's posterior.

My books are bad enough just as they are written; then what must they be after Mr. John Camden Hotten has composed half-a-dozen chapters & added the same to them? . . . If a friend of yours, or even you yourself, were to write a book & set it adrift among the people . . . how would you like to have John Camden Hotten sit down & stimulate his powers, & drool two or three original chapters on to the end of that book? Would not the world seem cold & hollow to you? . . . Let one suppose all this. Let him suppose it with strength enough, & then he will know something about woe. Sometimes when I read one of those additional chapters constructed by John Camden Hotten, I feel as if I wanted to take a broom-straw & go & knock that man's brains out. Not in anger, for I feel none. Oh! not in anger; but only to see, that is all. Mere idle curiosity.[24]

He speculated how Hotten might feel (speaking of padding) if he, Mark Twain, were to call him "John Camden Hottentot," and closed with a plea for fairness on behalf of Routledge & Sons. Hotten responded in crocodile-tear anguish a few days later, insisting incorrectly that the "additional chapters" had in fact been published by Mark Twain under the alias "Carl Byng" in the Buffalo *Express*. Clemens realized that he was helpless to prevent further Hotten depredations. Learning that the opportunist publisher was preparing yet another edition of his sketches, Sam choked down his choler and paid a visit to Hotten, offering to make revisions himself if Hotten would avoid drooling on the texts. Hotten accepted, but Sam was obliged to leave London before he could do the work. Hotten died the following year.

HE NOODLED around London through October and into early November. He wrote to Livy telling her how busy he was, how beautiful the English countryside, and how he wanted to return there with her in the spring. He ventured a bit of friskiness: "I am not going abroad any more without you. It is too dreary when the lights are out & the company gone . . . You may have observed that I do dearly love to go to bed & lie there steeped in the comfort of reading—& I have observed that you will not permit a body to get any satisfaction out of that sort of thing, but you always *interfere*."[25] Yet Sam clearly did not feel the urgency to get back home that he had expressed during his marathon lecture tours in America. It was not until Livy cabled him in the first week of November to insist, "Come home,"[26] that Sam terminated his idyll. Finally, on November 12, Sam boarded the Cunard steamer *Batavia* at Liverpool and sailed home through stormy seas. Among his last errands in London was purchasing a secondhand toy steam engine for his nephew Sammy as a Christmas present. "Sammy must learn how to run it before he blows himself up with it,"[27] he advised Pamela once home in Hartford.

The autumn of 1872 had been a tumultuous one at Nook Farm and in the nation. Ulysses S. Grant won reelection to the presidency over Horace Greeley on November 5, after an ugly campaign laced with charges of corruption from both sides. Greeley was shocked to find himself pilloried by Thomas Nast—by now a friend of Mark Twain's—who savaged the old utopian idealist with a series of drawings for *Harper's Weekly* that showed Greeley conspiring with the loathsome Boss Tweed. Nast's drawings helped Grant win in a landslide. Greeley, devastated by the hateful attacks and by the recent death of his wife, suffered an emotional breakdown and died on November 29, four days after Sam's steamship docked in New York Harbor. Shortly afterward, the erstwhile guest at Greeley's glittery reception congratulated the cartoonist: "Nast you, more than any other man, have won a prodigious victory for Grant—I mean, rather, for Civilization & progress . . ."[28] (In 1872, Samuel Clemens still believed in Civilization and progress; that would change.)

The tumult at Nook Farm struck far closer to home, and was if anything more sordid. Henry Ward Beecher, whose theology radiated with exhortations to all-embracing love, had been publicly accused of taking the concept a bit too literally by having an affair with the wife of one of his parishioners. The woman was a Sunday-school teacher at Beecher's church named Elizabeth Tilton. Her husband Theodore was a religious journalist, also a church member, whose shorthand transcriptions of Beecher's sermons had helped to amplify the cleric's fame. The charge gained national attention and has endured as one of the signature scandals of the American 19th century. Beecher's first accuser, ironically enough, was the most prominent free-love advocate of the times: Victoria Woodhull, a former fortune-teller and stockbroker (backed by Cornelius Vanderbilt), and more recently a close ally of Isabella Beecher Hooker in the women's-rights movement. When Woodhull sprang the charge at a Boston spiritualists' convention on September 25, she was the Equal Rights Party's candidate for president, sharing the ticket with Frederick Douglass, who with inspired timing had rediscovered his deep common cause with the fair sex. It wasn't so much the act of adultery itself that she denounced, Woodhull told her audience, but Beecher's double standard: he condemned free love in his sermons, but practiced it in private. It was probably significant that among those whom Beecher condemned from the pulpit was the party animal Victoria Woodhull who, with her sister, was arrested and jailed (for a month) for sending "obscenity" through the mails.

"How stands Elmira on the Beecher Scandal?" Sam queried Olivia's mother a few days after arriving home.[29] He seemed more bemused than concerned by the developments, opining that Beecher's buttoned lip was mighty suspicious.

I think the silence of the Beechers is a hundred fold more of an *obscene publication* than that of the Woodhulls . . . *Silence has given assent* in all ages of the world—it is a law of *nature,* not ethics—& Henry Ward Beecher is as amenable to it as the humblest of us . . . the general ~~verdict~~ thought of the nation will gradually form itself into the verdict that there is *some* fire somewhere in all this smoke of scandal.[30]

The verdict in the Beecher scandal would not be reached until the famous trial of 1873, when Beecher was acquitted.

With Livy, her hair sensibly braided and piled high on her head, and the tiny Susy beside him at the hearth, Sam settled into a comfortable Yuletide season in the embattled Hookers' Nook Barn. Sam wrote some letters to the editor, and crafted a letter of introduction to Thomas Nast on behalf of Mary Fairbanks's admiring seventeen-year-old son Charlie. In his reply, the cartoonist invited the author to visit him in his Morristown, New Jersey, home, and expressed the hope of soon seeing the book of English travels: "How much I should like to go with you and illustrate it."[31] Mark Twain had lost interest in that project after writing thirty-six draft pages. He put it aside, hoping to rekindle his enthusiasm with a return to England in the spring. A new book idea had begun to consume Mark Twain's imagination. More precisely, it was a new impetus to seize hold of an old idea, one that derived from his fascination with Washington, its political currents and its characters. He had not been exaggerating (for a change) when he told Livy in the summer of 1870, "I have gathered material enough for a whole book!"[32] He had hesitated to develop that material—perhaps because the only form conceivable for it was the novel, and Mark Twain felt unsure of his grasp of the novel's technical requirements. But he was never one to turn down a literary helping hand, and now, in the waning days of 1872, he found one, right in the Nook Farm neighborhood.

The collaboration that produced *The Gilded Age: A Tale of To-Day* seems to have been inspired by an after-dinner conversation one night at Nook Barn during the Christmas season, among Sam and Livy and their guests from the neighborhood, Charles Dudley Warner and his wife Susan. Warner, the co-owner (with the former Connecticut governor Joseph R. Hawley) and editor of the Hartford *Courant,* was a genial, literary sort of fellow who admired Mark Twain's work, and in fact had more or less retraced his *Innocents Abroad* itinerary a few months after the *Quaker City* voyage. A lean, quizzical-looking man whose wavy hair was more silvered than his thick goatee and mustache, Warner was valued for his repartee and erudition; but his prose writing was conventionally polite and stilted, even "dainty" in one reviewer's formulation—Fairbanksian, in other words. His vivacious wife was a skillful pianist who accompanied Sam in his postprandial singing of the spirituals and jubilees of his Missouri youth. On the evening in question (the date is not known), the foursome's talk veered toward books, as it often must have. Mark Twain recalled to Paine that the two husbands had begun abusing "the novels in which their wives were finding entertainment."[33] Susan and Livy challenged them to write one that was better. A newspaper colleague of Warner's, Stephen A. Hubbard, wrote—based on Warner's memory—that the challenge arose from a remark about *The Innocents* success: "Thereupon both Mrs. Clemens and Mrs. Warner began to twit Mark Twain; they made all manner of good-natured fun of his book, called it an accidental hit, and finally ended up by defying him to write another work like it . . ."[34] Warner and Clemens agreed to build a novel together, taking turns writing sections. The two would read their work to the wives each week, and defy them to identify which part was written by which husband. What started out as an extended parlor joke quickly enlarged into a property aimed at the market—a simulacrum of the dynamics now propelling the nation, and the novel that would describe the same.

A NEW, postwar avarice was building in America, a fascination with centralized capital and bureaucratized power, and the exploitative opportunities afforded when the two were combined. Ulysses S. Grant's inattentive administration had opened up a scoundrel's paradise: smart pols and speculators diverted huge reservoirs of public wealth to their private gain, as in the Crédit Mobilier scandal, in which some Union Pacific stockholders rigged shares toward crooked congressmen, who in turn overbudgeted the railroad's construction costs so that all the fat cats made out. Sam's admirer and Grant's vice president, the well-upholstered Schuyler Colfax, was among those who saw their reputations ruined in the ensuing investigation. In New York, the big-bellied Boss Tweed was on trial as the figurehead for that metropolis's teeming graft. The fat Senator Samuel Pomeroy, a hero of the free-soil struggle in Kansas before the Civil War, was exposed for bribery in his own reelection. Cynicism seemed to leak into other spheres of American life: the Beecher scandal, the sensational shooting by Laura Fair of her lover in San Francisco, a sense of expediency everywhere.

Expedience mocked the public trust, for example, at the New York *Tribune* in the wake of Horace Greeley's death. A majority of *Tribune* stockholders with ties to Jay Gould, the railroad speculator who himself was close to Tweed, tried to harness the newspaper to their narrow business interests. They offered Greeley's job of editor in chief to the disgraced Colfax. Whitelaw Reid, the honorable acting editor, resigned in protest of this corrupt power play. John Hay and several others followed suit. Reid's career and the *Tribune*'s integrity were spared only when Colfax himself declined the appointment, perhaps acting under pressure. By Christmas, Reid had regained editorial control of the *Tribune* and declared his intention to keep it a "frank and fearless newspaper."[35] Mark Twain wrote a friendly, mock-heroic poem about the episode for the Hartford *Evening Post*.

Events such as these disgusted the deeply principled Warner. In his newspaper essays, he called for a literature dedicated to a moral examination of the great questions of right and wrong. Mark Twain shared this reformist passion. Here was a chance for the two men to practice what they preached. They chose a thematic universe scarcely visited by novelists until that time, and seldom by serious ones since: Washington politics, as it intertwined with corrupt business speculation and sexual intrigue. Alternately inspiring, rejuvenating, goading, and subtly competing with each other, they attacked their exotic tale full-throttle through the winter and spring of 1873. By April they had completed a curious Siamese twin of a novel, two distinct voices joined at the plot: 161,000 words spread among 63 chapters and 574 book pages when it was issued in December of that year. Mark Twain's and Warner's idle quest for a topic of substance that went beyond mere "entertainment" found its logical target in the American public that already absorbed their intellectual interests.

The Gilded Age ranks among the most combustible works of a tepid time in American letters: a veering, improvised mess of a book that nonetheless contains some of the most memorable characters in all Mark Twain's writing; improbable melodrama coexisting with some of the most trenchant and informed Washington political satire to be found in the fiction of any American era; a social vision equally authoritative in the backwaters of antebellum Missouri and the postwar salons of corrupt cosmopolitan power—and a title at once fanciful and a permanent synonym for the era it described.

The shifting and jam-packed plotline follows a trail of greed and graft that stretches across half a continent, tracing Mark Twain's most obsessive memories. The story begins with the transmigration of an eastern Tennessee family, headed by land-burdened Si "Judge" Hawkins, to Stone's Landing, a small river town in northeastern Missouri in the 1840s. The family survives a steamboat explosion en route, and a minor character named Uncle Dan'l puts in a cameo appearance. The instigator of the move is the flamboyant backwoods dreamer and loudmouth opportunist Beriah ("There's millions in it!") Sellers, a friend of Si's whose get-rich schemes propel him to Washington, accompanied by Hawkins's offspring Washington and Laura. The latter is brilliant and "had the fatal gift of beauty," but is unlucky in love. Laura Hawkins becomes a cynical player in Washington political society, and thus the reader's guide through a rogue's gallery of crooked senators, money-grafting lobbyists, toadying journalists, sinister bosses, and lecherous committee chairmen. By the novel's end she has gunned down her married lover, the ex-Confederate Colonel Shelby; is acquitted at trial; and sinks obligingly into the desuetude and death that is the fate of all fallen Victorian women, no matter how beautiful. Judge Hawkins, after bungling several chances to sell the accursed acreage, dies imploring his family to never lose sight of the Tennessee land. A pair of clean-cut young Eastern land surveyors get involved in a Sellers plot to turn Stone's Landing into a navigation and rail metropolis. Fortunes are won and lost, crooked senators try to purchase their reelections, telegrams are sent, unsuspected identities are discovered, and the novel's reformed malingerer, Philip Sterling, finally gets rich in coal mining. Somewhere along the way, Sellers serves the Judge's son Washington a dinner of turnips and fresh water.

The novel belongs mostly to Mark Twain. Warner supplied a few characters and his knowledge of the surveyor's art, but Samuel Clemens's autobiographical discharge floods the narrative. One can almost feel his elation as he discovers how usable the past is—and, for him, how accessible. His Washington is even, to some extent, a flattened-out Virginia City with a capitol dome: wide-open, muddy, aswarm with arriving opportunists of all stripes, and little garrisons of studied refinement.

Less overtly apparent is Mark Twain's deployment of his great gift for engaging and understanding *process*. One can find in the novel an authoritative depiction of how Washington works—officially, socially, and indictably—as well as the intricacies of finance, the methodology of land-scamming con artists, the décor of salons and parlors, the lore of mines. In many ways, *The Gilded Age* anticipated both the 20th-century "public novel" championed by Tom Wolfe, and the Washington novel of ideas as executed by Gore Vidal.

"We'll . . . so interweave our work that these wives of ours will not be able to say which part has been written by Mark Twain and which by Charles D. Warner," [36] Stephen Hubbard has Mark Twain saying in his reminiscence. If Mark Twain in fact said such a thing, he was being nice. Warner added many valuable elements, but crackling phraseology was not among them. An instructive example is the way in which each man handled the voice of Beriah Sellers. Here is Warner:

"If the people of Napoleon want me to go to Washington, and look after that matter, I might tear myself from my home. It's been suggested to me, but—not a word of it to Mrs. Sellers and the children. Maybe they wouldn't like to think of their father in Washington." [37]

And here is Mark Twain:

"Remarkable clock!" said Sellers, and got up and wound it. "I've been offered—well, I wouldn't expect you to believe what I've been offered for that clock. Old Gov. Hager never sees me but he says, 'Come now, Colonel, name your price—I *must* have that clock!' But my goodness I'd as soon think of selling my wife. As I was saying to—silence in the court, now, she's begun to strike! You can't talk against her—you have to just be patient and hold up till she's had her say. Ah—well, as I was saying, when—she's beginning again! . . . Now just listen at that. She'll strike a hundred and fifty, now, without stopping,—you'll see. There ain't another clock like it in Christendom." [38]

The recovery of voice-memories such as this one exhilarated Mark Twain as if he had struck a vein of ore in Washoe. (He had no idea how inexhaustible this vein would prove to be.) The memories, and the gamelike collaboration with Warner into which he shoveled them, activated his boyish exuberance; the work became a lark, enlivened by his zest for competition. "Have written many chapters twice, & some of them three times," he reported to Mary Fairbanks, and added slyly, "—have thrown away 300 clean pages of MS . . . Warner has been more fortunate—he won't lose 50 pages." [39] Reading the work in progress to the wives each evening sharpened Mark Twain's gleeful sense of the game: "they have done a power of criticising . . . They both pleaded so long & vigorously for Warner's heroine, that yesterday Warner agreed to spare her life & let her marry—he meant to kill her. I killed my heroine as dead as a mackerel yesterday (but Livy don't know it yet)." [40]

A minor feature of *The Gilded Age* is that it contains Mark Twain's first effort to deal with race relations in fictional form. ("Sociable Jimmy" was written, but as yet unpublished, and was more a sketch than a story.) The scenes are of negligible importance to the plot; but they serve as a benchmark of Mark Twain's developing interest in race as a theme, and the mark is not very far advanced down the bench. In Chapter 3, "Uncle Dan'l," the Hawkins's slave, is thrown into terror with his first glimpse of a steamboat on the Mississippi River at nightfall. He thinks the noisy, lighted monster is "de Almighty," and goes into paroxysms of "deah Lord" and "dese po' chil'en" and "De ole niggah's ready, Lord." [41] Later, moments before the steamboat explosion, an exchange between two boatmen offers the reverse image of an enduringly famous ironic passage in Chapter 32 of *Adventures of Huckleberry Finn*. In that one, Huck reports to Aunt Sally that the boat he'd been traveling on had "blowed out a cylinder head."

"Good gracious! anybody hurt?"

"No'm. Killed a nigger."

"Well, it's lucky; because sometimes people do get hurt." [42]

In *The Gilded Age,* Mark Twain has the boatmen engaging in a strikingly similar bit of badinage, but here, three years before he began his fitful composition of his greatest novel, Mark Twain plays it just for laughs:

"How's your draft?"

"Bully! Every time a nigger heaves a stick of wood into the furnace he goes out the chimney with it!" [43]

THE COLLABORATION with Charles Dudley Warner overcame Mark Twain's anxieties about tackling book-length fiction, and the barriers fell quickly. By early January, he regained the confidence to revisit the boy's novel that he'd toyed with the previous summer in Saybrook, perhaps exploring the story on the days when Warner was writing. Worldly matters diverted him as well. "Have just bought the loveliest building-lot in Hartford," he crowed to his friend Whitelaw Reid, "—544 feet front on the Avenue & 300 feet deep . . . the house will be built while we are absent in England." [44]

"The Avenue" was Farmington, in Nook Farm. The house to be built there would one day be celebrated as among the most famous, and most eccentric, in America, and would shelter the Clemens family for the happiest seventeen years of their lives together. The money needed to pay for it had finally come rolling in, on the first year's royalties from *Roughing It*, which by January 1873 had earned Mark Twain more than twenty thousand dollars. That was twice the amount necessary to cover the purchase of the lot offered by a Hartford lawyer named Franklin Chamberlin, who had bought the land from John Hooker in 1864. The property fronted on Farmington—351 was the address—and on the west bordered the Park River. The purchase consummated the dream that Sam and Livy had shared for two years, and whose contours derived from Livy's own sketches. They needed an architect. A recommendation came from Charles Warner's brother George, who was also building a house on Farmington: Edward Tuckerman Potter, known for the churches he had built in the East. Potter, upon being hired (and somehow omitting credit to Livy and the plan she presented to him) announced that the Clemens house would be designed in the style called High Victorian Gothic. Was it ever.

MARK TWAIN and Charles Dudley Warner signed a contract for publication of *The Gilded Age* on May 8, in the American Publishing Company offices of Elisha Bliss in Hartford. This would be the first work of fiction to be sold by subscription. The agreement stipulated a 5 percent royalty for each writer. Then Sam Clemens turned his attention to his dream of the previous autumn, a return visit to England with Livy at his side. He rationalized that he needed to continue his research on the England book, and also to be on British soil when *The Gilded Age* was published there to protect his copyright interests. The more accessible British soil across the border in Quebec was an option he never discussed. Prospects seemed bright not only for Sam but for the extended Clemens family. Orion and Mollie were ensconced in Rutland, Vermont, where Orion had assumed the position of editorial director for the Rutland *Globe*. His younger brother had offered him a typically warmhearted send-off, which Mark Twain recalled many years later.

> I said:
> "You are as weak as water. Those people will find it out right away. They will easily see that you have no backbone; that they can deal with you as they would deal with a slave. You may last six months, but not longer. Then they will . . . fling you out as they would fling out an intruding tramp."[45]

Everything seemed to be pie for Mark Twain as the embarkation date of May 17 neared. Warner had agreed to make any necessary final tweakings of the manuscript before delivering it to Bliss. Little Susy was in robust health at fourteen months, in happy contrast to her late brother. A nurse would accompany her to England. Clemens had enjoyed a respectful gesture from Whitelaw Reid: the *Tribune* editor had been publishing letters on various topics from Mark Twain, and sending along small but respectable checks for each. In January, Reid had invited Mark Twain to submit two long essays on the Sandwich Islands for the newspaper's "Extra Sheet." Reid paid a hundred dollars for the works, which stimulated new interest in the subject and led to three lucrative lecture invitations in February. The two men were enjoying a warm and jovial friendship. "I have a nice putrid anecdote that Hay will like," Mark Twain advised the editor in late March. "Am preserving it in alcohol—in my person." [46]

The Clemens entourage gathered in New York on Thursday, May 15, for a couple of days' quiet companionship before departure for Liverpool and the projected four months in England. Mary Fairbanks accompanied the family from Elmira, and perhaps Charley Langdon as well. Besides the three Clemenses, the party would include Clara Spaulding, Livy's friend from Elmira days who resembled Livy a little; Susy's nurse, Nellie Bermingham; and a twenty-five-year-old man named Samuel C. Thompson, a former *Tribune* reporter and schoolteacher whom Clemens had retained to act as a secretary and auxiliary note-taker in England: Clemens had met Thompson at a lecture in March, and Thompson promised that he would master shorthand if the author would invite him along. Their ship would be the *Batavia,* on which Sam had returned from England the previous November. Its skipper would be the same as well: John Elsey Mouland, who, during the November voyage, directed a daring mid-Atlantic rescue of nine sailors clinging to a disabled barque. Mark Twain and others had recommended him for a medal from the Royal Humane Society of England.

"We feel as happy as possible and as hopeful of a successful voyage," Livy wrote happily to her mother on the day of departure. Sam added, "Good bye, mother dear, we are just backing away from the pier." [47] It was to be Livy's first ocean voyage and her first journey outside the United States. At about the same time, Sam was scrawling out a decidedly less felicitous message on both sides of his calling card, addressed to Charles Warner.

Ask [Edward] House to tell you about Whitelaw Reid. He is a contemptible cur, & I want nothing more to do with him . . .

Yesterday I sued a New York fraud for $20,000 damages for violating my copyright . . .

He signed off: "We are all well, & jolly." [48]

29

Gilded

(1873–74)

The crossing was uneventful, except for some rough seas at the outset. Susy remained serene inside her basket. Livy was charmed by the courtesies of Captain Mouland, who took Clara Spaulding for long walks around the deck, when the seas permitted walking. A lunge of the ship caught Livy in mid-stride toward the dinner table one evening; she grabbed at a curtain and took it with her as she staggered into the adjacent saloon and crashed against a bustle of waiters. "Clara who was coming just behind me was so convulsed with laughter that she was obliged to return to her stateroom and laugh it out," Livy wrote to her mother.[1] They arrived at Liverpool on May 27, spent the night as guests of Captain Mouland and his wife, and then took a train to London. The scenery rushing past the window of the car fulfilled all of Livy's imaginings:

the ride was the most charming that I ever could imagine— . . . So many things that I had read were plain to me as we rode along—the little thatched villages, the foot paths by the side of the road . . .[2]

The Clemenses set up residence in Edwards's Royal Cambridge, a jewel-box hotel in Hanover Square. Its windows offered a view to a little oval green bordered by an iron fence, a cobbled promenade, and a line of red-brick Georgian buildings. Here Mark Twain planned to dictate to Thompson his daily notes for the book about England. The plan soon became impossible: word spread through the old city that the Lion was back in town, and intellectual/artistic/aristocratic London—counts, earls, Benjamin Disraeli—came calling. When the Shah of Persia showed up, Clemens paid Thompson a hundred dollars and sent him back to America.

Mark Twain wrote a series of letters about the Shah's visit to England—for the New York *Herald,* and not for Whitelaw Reid's *Tribune.* His wrathful turn against his friend scarcely seemed to fit with the good fortune that Samuel Clemens was enjoying in the spring of 1873. Given the upswings in his financial fortunes, his international reputation and his influence, not to mention his beachhead at Nook Farm and the new, healthy child, he would hardly seem to have cause for grievance. Yet there it was: an unforeshadowed strike by the serpent that lay coiled just beneath Mark Twain's ingratiating charm, and just above his chronic insecurity.

Reid had done Clemens the shocking injustice of calling a halt to Mark Twain's use of the *Tribune* as his personal publicity organ. A look at the correspondence between Reid and Clemens in the early 1870s shows that beneath his comradely joshing, Clemens was generally angling for mention in the *Tribune* for a book or a lecture of his, or acceptance of an article he wanted to pitch. On April 20 he'd issued a long letter to Reid, thinly disguised as bantering, which chastised the editor for announcing the advent of *The Gilded Age* in a mere one-paragraph "item" (and in mere seven-point type at that!). Noting that recent sales of *Innocents* were still one thousand books a month, he said that it "looks as if it had entered permanently into the literature of the country." Clemens brayed on:

I have a good reliable audience in this country & it is the biggest one in America, too, if I do say it myself. So a novel from me alone would be a good deal in the nature of a literary event, & the Tribune, to be just, should have made it so appear, I think.[3]

Reid, who usually had indulged Mark Twain's self-promotion, was infuriated by this presumption. It almost certainly colored his actions in what happened next.

About a month before the Clemenses left for England, the *Tribune* critic Edward House, a long-standing friend and fan of Mark Twain, read *The Gilded Age* in manuscript at Nook Barn, and—in Mark Twain's version—urged Reid to let him be the first to review the work, in the *Tribune.* Reid refused. The friendship between critic and author tainted House's objectivity, the editor maintained. Mark Twain hit the ceiling: what did *objectivity* have to do with it? House was merely doing him a "favor"![4]

Reid had thrown his body in front of powerful scoundrels intent on corrupting the newspaper; yet now, to Mark Twain, "Friend Reid" became a "cur." He stopped speaking to the editor for more than a decade. That was fine with Reid, who'd had his fill of the author's petulance and special pleading. "There is a nice correspondence on a part of the subject which would make pleasant reading," he remarked to his intended wife, the lecturer and writer Kate Field, "and if Twain gives us trouble, I'm very much tempted to make him a more ridiculous object than he has ever made anybody else."[5] This little war also maimed the relationship between Reid and House. Based on House's advocacy of Mark Twain, Reid decided that the critic was not to be trusted as a disinterested voice. Finally, several years later, to complete the circle of poisoned feelings, Mark Twain broke with Edward House: "Reid had labeled him correctly; he was a blatherskite."[6]

As to the $20,000 lawsuit Mark Twain had mentioned to Warner, it involved the author's displeasure over the publication of some of his sketches by a man named Benjamin J. Such. The suit accomplished its intention of frightening Such into accepting Mark Twain's conditions for publishing the book. Clemens's attorney had been recommended to him by Edward House.

Sam swept Livy into the world of British swank that he'd evoked in his letters to her. Hampton Court Palace. The Brighton Aquarium, among the world's treasures. Stratford-on-Avon, where Livy drank in the environs of her beloved Shakespeare. ("Heavens, where am I!"[7] she exclaimed on glimpsing the Bard's tomb; Clemens and an expatriate American friend named Moncure Conway had brought her there without naming the destination.) Encounters with the philosopher Herbert Spencer and the novelist Anthony Trollope. Invitations to join eight hundred guests at a grand ball at the Mansion House of the Lord Mayor of London. Clemens broke away in mid-June to follow the Shah to Belgium for his *Herald* letters (his competitor for the *Tribune* was Katie Field).

Clemens spent money throughout this trip as though he were a titled lord himself, and no restraints were offered by Livy. He decided that the rooms at the Royal Cambridge were no match for the august stream of visitors seeking an audience. "My wife likes Edwards's Hotel," he told Mrs. Conway, "& so would I if I were dead; I would not desire a more tranquil & satisfactory tomb."[8] Hotels held almost talismanic importance to Mark Twain throughout his sojourning life; his rule of thumb in choosing them seemed to be, the more expensive, the better. On June 25, a day before Clara Spaulding departed for a tour of the Continent, Mark Twain transplanted his party to a suite in the six-story, six-hundred-room Langham Hotel on Regent Street at Oxford Circus, complete with billiard room, where he had stayed during his first visit. The palatial Georgian hostelry, completed in 1865 as the first European "grand" hotel, proclaimed itself the largest building in London. Surely it presented the largest bill. All of this suited Mark Twain, whose callers now included Robert Browning, the self-exiled Russian novelist Ivan Turgenev, and various Cabinet members, playwrights, and authors. Not since Benjamin Franklin was received as a "sage of antiquity" by the French in 1776 had an American enjoyed such veneration in Europe.

Submerged within the frenzy of all this England-gorging was the book on England. Once again—and not for the last time—Clemens put it aside. He and Livy visited Abbotsford, south of Edinburgh on the Tweed River, the final residence of Sir Walter Scott, whom Mark Twain considered responsible for inspiring the American South's lunatic notions of class and chivalry. Toward the end of August they made the famously rough-water crossing to Belfast; headed south to Dublin; recrossed the Irish Sea to Liverpool; and from there toured a succession of English villages, arriving back at London by September 9. Sam shopped: eighty-eight pounds' worth of sealskin coats for Jane, Pamela, and Charley Langdon, "little odds & ends" for the new house in Hartford. Soon the urge to move again grew overpowering; London by now may as well have been Paris, Illinois. On the last day of September, he whisked Livy off to Paris, France.

When they returned to London, Sam and Livy had completed four months of international gadabout partying and holidaying that, but for sobriety, would have reddened the cheeks of Scott and Zelda Fitzgerald. Their cash was about gone: Clemens estimated, perhaps hyperbolically, perhaps not, that he had spent ten thousand dollars since arriving in England. He sent to his New York bank for money, but a financial panic in America, prelude to a six-year depression, caused impediments in receiving it.

Sam may have been a proto–F. Scott, but Livy was no Zelda. For her, the charm of the trip had congealed into fatigue and homesickness. She had been away from America and her mother and sister for four months. The house at Nook Farm was being built in her and Sam's absence. Livy grew blue, and cross. And pregnant.

In a sense, Clemens felt trapped. He couldn't leave England without jeopardizing his interests in *The Gilded Age* there (or so he believed). But when was the book going to be published? As usual, Elisha Bliss hadn't a clue; production was running behind again at Hartford. To fill the time, and rebankroll himself, Mark Twain gave in to a London impresario's entreaties to lecture. "Just now you are the most widely read author in England," George Dolby told him, "and people are eager to see you." [9] Clemens dusted off "Our Fellow Savages of the Sandwich Islands," while the agent quickly arranged six October performances in London. His success was so great that Mark Twain wanted to extend the act for another month, but Livy finally put her foot down. As she had by cable the previous November, she insisted that it was time to go home. In one of the longer courtesy detours in 19th-century travel, Sam agreed to drop her off there.

A farewell lecture in Liverpool on October 20, and the next morning Mark Twain and his entourage boarded the ever-handy *Batavia* for the transatlantic journey to New York. They were met at the dock on November 2 by Olivia's mother and brother Charley. Orion was there, too. He'd washed out of the Rutland *Globe* about four months faster than Sam had predicted, after the paper got into a Washoe-style war of words with the Rutland *Herald*. The *Herald* had called the *Globe* people soreheads and Greeley candidates, which led the *Globe* to call the *Herald* editor a sellout, which led the *Herald* to call the *Globe* the *Globule;* after that, civility grew strained. [10] Orion was trying to find work in New York as an editor or printer or proofreader or something;

tinkering with his latest invention, a flying machine (he'd been reading Jules Verne), and working on a story that struck his brother as rather Verne-like.

Clemens escorted Livy and Susy back to Hartford, arriving November 4. Having seen his wife and daughter safely to the doorstep of Nook Barn, and glancing at his mansion in progress long enough to notice that the roof was in place, Mark Twain turned around and went back to England. He arrived at Liverpool on November 18, made straight for London, resumed his lodging at the Langham, and prepared to push ahead with his lecturing schedule.

A new private secretary had joined him: Charles Warren Stoddard, his poet-friend from California days. The clean-shaven, sad-eyed aesthete was spending a year in the city as a correspondent for the San Francisco *Chronicle*. Clemens was moved by Stoddard's gentleness and high character, and admitted late in life that he valued the younger man more as a companion than as a factotum. Stoddard returned the esteem, kept notes of their days together, and produced some glimpses of a Mark Twain rarely revealed to the world— perhaps even to Livy. Stoddard described their strolls through London parks and picture galleries in the leisurely days before Mark Twain resumed his performances. In the predinner hour, "perhaps the pleasantest in the day,"

[t]here was chat or long intervals of dreamy silence by the fireside, or music at the piano, when to my amazement Mark would sing jubilee songs or "Ben Bowline" with excellent effect, accompanying himself and rolling his vowels in the Italian style.[11]

This languorous routine shifted when Mark Twain resumed lecturing on December 1. Now, his mood began to darken along with the midafternoon London sky; bad nerves and irritation took hold, and Stoddard did his best to humor him, keep him "mentally occupied." Stoddard described a typical lecture night.

A little before eight we would walk over to the Concert Rooms and up the stairs into the tiny room at the back, Mark getting more and more irritable and nervous all the while, looking at his watch, anxious to plunge in and have it over. The moment eight o'clock arrived he invariably said, "It's time now. I'll not wait another moment," and then, as cool and deliberate as could be, he walked on to the platform, "washing his hands in invisible soap and water," slowly saying his first words. The moment he heard his own voice he began to feel better, and I knew he was all right.[12]

It was in the hours *après* lecture, back at the Langham, as church bells tolled the night toward dawn, that Stoddard found his employer at his most revealing. As the two sipped cocktails, he watched Mark Twain's carefully applied public persona melt away to reveal the melancholy creature beneath.

One—two—three in the morning . . . and still we sat by the sea-coal fire and smoked . . . I could have written his biography at the end of the season. I believe I learned much of his life that is unknown even to his closest friends—of his boyhood, his early struggles, his hopes, his aims. I trust that I am betraying no confidence when I state that a good deal of the real boy is blended with the "Story of Tom Sawyer." [13]

Alcohol expedited the removal of the public mask. Clemens had long since fallen away from his courtship vows of temperance to Livy—he had begun to enjoy a drink or three in her presence, and out of it as well, though he seldom gave in to the ravening thirsts of his Washoe days. Stoddard observed Clemens's construction of the cocktails: "Bourbon" * whiskey (for which he had to scour London) Angostura bitters, sugar, lemons. A London Manhattan, so to speak. With the first sip, the drawl of Sam Clemens's voice would begin. Often it would continue until Stoddard was half-asleep, Clemens himself "talking so slowly that the syllables came about every half minute . . ." [14] The thoughts conveyed on those syllables suggest that Samuel Clemens's lifelong concern with making money, even when it meant coarsening his literary gifts or risking what he already had, was fueled by something deeper than mere avarice.

Very, very often these nightly talks became a lament. He was always afraid of dying in the poorhouse. The burden of his woe was that he would grow old and lose the power of interesting an audience, and become unable to write, and then what would become of him? . . . And he'd drink cocktails and grow more and more gloomy and blue until he fairly wept at the misery of his own future. [15]

There were lighter moments. Stoddard invited Clemens with him up to Oxford one evening to watch a company of acrobats perform. Inside the Gothic warren of citadels that spanned eight centuries, Clemens found himself less attentive to the performers than to the students in the audience. His description of them to Livy is a priceless snapshot of young Victorian nobles, prefiguring P. G. Wodehouse.

—& how they do behave, these scions of the bluest aristocratic blood of Great Britain! . . . They wore their hats all through the performance, & they all smoked pipes & cigars . . . every rascal of them brought a bull pup or a terrier pup under his arm, & they would set these creatures up on the broad-topped balustrades, & allow them to amuse themselves by barking at anybody or anything they chose to. [16]

HIS OWN turns onstage worked their usual magic, but he lamented to Livy about his homesickness, made more severe by the oppressive London fog. This yellow stew of vapor and ash from the smokestacks of industrial London coated people's clothing and even crept into the lecture halls, making the eyes

---

* Stoddard may have been mistaken; Clemens later named Scotch as his preference for the cocktail.

burn and rendering his audiences ghostlike. "Livy darling, I am *so* tired of lecturing," he wrote not long before Christmas, adding that the fog had nearly broken his heart.[17] He promised Redpath a couple of days later that he would give a few performances in New York and Boston on his arrival home, and then *"retire permanently* from the platform."[18]

Still, he kept up with his London appearances until December 20, and spent Christmas Day at Salisbury Cathedral and later at Stonehenge. He cancelled a January tour that included Belfast, Dublin, and Cork, and boarded the *Parthia* on January 13 for the voyage home, arriving in Hartford on January 27. "Livy my darling," he had advised his wife eleven days before embarkation, "I want you to be sure & remember to have, in the bath-room, when I arrive, a bottle of Scotch whisky, a lemon, some crushed sugar, & a bottle of *Angostura bitters."* He'd enjoyed this concoction before breakfast, dinner, and bedtime every day, he assured her, and would enjoy it even more in her company.

I love to picture myself ringing the bell, at midnight—then a pause of a second or two—then the turning of the bolt, & "Who is it?"—then ever so many kisses—then you & I in the bath-room, I drinking my cock-tail & undressing, & you standing by—then to bed, and everything happy & jolly as it should be.

And lest Livy go all light-headed and forgetful from this lasciviousness, Clemens refocused her with a postcript: "Nothing but *Angostura* bitters will do."[19]

The Gilded Age was published by Routledge on December 22, 1873, and in the United States by the American Publishing Company the following day. True Williams again had supplied most of the illustrations, along with Henry Louis Stephens and Augustus Hoppin, whose full-page character portraits were daringly based on newspaper photographs of actual Washington insiders (these were all omitted in the Routledge edition).[20] (Mark Twain had lobbied for Thomas Nast, given the book's muckraking and allusions to timely events, but Bliss shied away from the great cartoonist's presumed price tag.) In a subtle satiric poke at the "learned" pretensions of Walter Scott and others, Mark Twain and Warner had commissioned mysterious epigraphs at the beginning of each chapter. These epigraphs, presented in their original Sindhi, Japanese, Latin, Massachusetts Indian, Basque, Guatemalan Quiche, etc., were supplied by James Hammond Trumbull, a Hartford polymath whose store of learning was nearly as imposing as his name. Presented without translation, they offered such ageless profundity as, "Money is very scarce," and "Have you anything to say for her justification?" and, "He who would buy sausage of a dog, must give him bacon in exchange."

The reviewers were not amused—nor impressed with the novel itself. Some of the notices were almost shockingly harsh. The virulence partly reflected the reviewers' lack of preparedness for *The Gilded Age*'s genre: political satire in the novel form had virtually no tradition in America. The New York

Daily Graphic, commenting on the day of publication, excoriated the book as "simply a rather incoherent series of sketches,"[21] and observed that the authors had managed only to suffocate their usually brilliant voices. The Chicago *Tribune* was far worse: "utterly bald," "so puerile," "so vicious even," was the judgment of its unsigned critic, who added, "Thousands will . . . find themselves cheated and robbed."[22] As for Howells, he privately informed Clemens that he would take a pass on reviewing this one: "Up to the time old Hawkins dies your novel is of the greatest promise," the *Atlantic* editor wrote, "—but after that it fails to assimilate the crude material with which it is fed . . ."[23] Considering that "old Hawkins" dies in Chapter 9 of a 63-chapter novel, Howells's remark probably qualifies as faint praise.

Initial sales of the book were strong, especially given the financial crisis that by now had damaged the stock market and clotted the flow of money through banks and finance systems. By February 1874, subscription agents had moved more than 35,000 copies; by the end of the year, more than 50,000 were in print. But only 56,000 copies were sold over the next six years. *The Gilded Age* remained in print through most of the ensuing century, its small but steady sales due more to its sociopolitical witness than its literary value. Mark Twain seems to have detached himself early on from an emotional investment in the novel. "My interest in a book ceases with the printing of it," he declared to Joe Twichell.[24]

BACK WITH his family at the Hooker house in Hartford, Samuel Clemens at thirty-eight now embarked on the most contented stretch of his satisfying years at Nook Farm. John and Isabella Hooker showed amazing patience, remaining at the Gillette mansion as work continued on the Clemens's grand house on Farmington Avenue. Sam smoked his cigars and went to Joe Twichell's church with Livy and kept up with sales of his various books, all of which were nourishing his bank account. His firmly Victorian views on women seemed to be thawing under Livy's influence: he composed a letter to the London *Standard* reporting without sarcasm on the current women's prayerful crusade against "the rumsellers." The crusade was thoroughly justifiable, he maintained:

the women find themselves voiceless in the making of laws & the election of officers to execute them.

Born with brains, born in the country, educated, having large interests at stake, they find their tongues tied & their hands fettered, while every ignorant whisky-drinking foreign-born savage in the land may hold office.

He concluded it with a call to women's suffrage: "this country could lose absolutely nothing & might gain a great deal."[25]

Perhaps the second female in the household was influencing his views as well. Susy was now two; in a photograph of her that he handed out to everyone he could think of, she burns with chubby-cheeked intensity. Her big dark eyes and tiny, bee-stung mouth are fixed in an expression of attention paying, and her head is loaded with curls. Her father claimed that her hairstyle resembled that of the Modoc Indians in northern California, who had captured national attention in a bloody war against American troops. Sam Clemens, whose last unreconstructed bigotries were directed at Indians, but whose distaste for imperialism was equally strong, chose "Modoc" as Susy's nickname.

He took up his England chronicles again. He completed a five-act play "with only one visible character in it," a project he had discussed with the actor Edwin Booth the previous November. The play, never produced, was a revision of *Hamlet*, and the "one visible character" made humorous and modern comments on the unseen action. In concept, if not in quality of execution, Mark Twain anticipated the Theater of the Absurd by about eighty years and Tom Stoppard's *Rosencrantz and Guildenstern Are Dead* by ninety-five. He thought about another play, and worked at organizing some of his sketches for publication. "I am the busiest white man in America," he told Mrs. Fairbanks, "—& much the happiest." [26] He resumed his playful twitting of his easy-target mother. "Kill Susy for me," Jane had requested of him, meaning to write, "Kiss Susy for me." Sam pretended to take her miscue at face value. In the Fredonia household, Annie Moffett watched as Jane read his mock-confessional letter.

He wrote . . . "I said to Livy 'It is a hard thing to ask of loving parents, but Ma is getting old and her slightest whim must be our law'; so I called in Downey [a servant] and Livy and I held the child with the tears streaming down our faces while he sawed her head off." [27]

It worked. "Sawed her head off!" Jane kept exclaiming as she stormed about the house. "*Sawed* her head off!" [28]

Sam even managed some tenderness toward Orion. The older brother lingered in New York, living alone in a rented attic room (Mollie would soon join him from Fredonia), still subsisting on piecework in newspapering—typesetter, proofreader, reporter, whatever. He had tried to land a job at Whitelaw Reid's New York *Tribune* by name-dropping himself as Mark Twain's brother. Reid, with typical humanity, authorized a tryout for Orion; but it didn't work out. Presently he was a substitute proofreader at the *Evening Post*, earning two dollars a day when he worked at all. Sam had given Orion a hundred dollars in November, and then scolded him by way of Jane about the futility of his New York hopes. Touched that Orion could not even afford to buy a copy of *The Gilded Age*, Sam wrote to him on February 4,

God knows yours is hard luck, & one is bound to respect & honor the way in which you bear up under it & refuse to surrender. I thought you were heedless & listless . . . content to drift with the tide & never *try* to do anything. I am glad . . . to know that this is not so. [29]

Then, with surpassing gentleness, alluding to Orion's recent surrender of his latest addled invention project,

I grieve over the laying aside of the flying machine as if it were my own broken idol. But still it must be done . . . It ought to be a savior & a thing to be clung to . . .[30]

From Nook Farm, in the late winter months of 1874, Clemens issued invitations as promiscuously as he had distributed photographs of Susy. "The *best* train leaves the Grand Central Depot, in New York, at 10 AM & comes here in about 3 hours," he informed his old friend Frank Fuller. "You MUST come . . . & we'll have a royal good time telling lies & smoking."[31] "Won't you kindly name a day & hour that I may meet you & yours at the station here & bring you up to our house for a few days' visit?" he coaxed a visiting British clergyman.[32] "We shall look for you & long for you & hunger for you till you come," he told Mary Fairbanks. "We shall have the serenest & happiest time while you are here, & nobody shall know care or fatigue."[33] He tried to coax Will Bowen, recently bereaved, out east for billiards and euchre.

This starburst of bonhomie reached its apogee—and stayed there—in his correspondence to William Dean Howells. He opened up an exuberant, extravagantly facetious volley of correspondence with the terribly earnest *Atlantic* editor in Boston, and before long, humid Howells was answering Clemens in the same giddy manner. "I am in a sweat, and Warner is in another," Clemens happily gabbled to Howells in late February, by way of revealing that Redpath had scheduled his Boston lecture series on the same date that Howells was supposed to visit Nook Farm. "Warner's been in here swearing like a lunatic, & saying he had written you to come on the *4th*—& I said, 'You leatherhead, if I talk in Boston . . . March 5, I'll have to go to Boston the *4th*—& then he just kicked up his heels & went off cursing after a fashion I never heard of before."[34]

Mark Twain performed his *Roughing It* lecture on Thursday, March 5, at Horticultural Hall in Boston. (Among the competing entertainments was a performance of *Our American Cousin,* sans distractions, at the Boston Theatre.) "Why don't you congratulate me," he'd cabled Redpath two days earlier. "Honestly I never expect to stand on a lecture Platform again after Thursday night."[35] He was to honor that expectation for a decade.

Back in Hartford the following day, he and Livy prepared for what amounted to their debut as host and hostess in a legendary series of dinners, soirees, and overnight visits to Nook Farm. They were not yet able to offer the amenities of their (unfinished) house on Farmington Avenue, but they presided with assurance and aplomb as William Dean Howells, the Boston publisher James R. Osgood, and the Aldriches arrived for a three-day visit on Saturday, March 7. The host, braying his welcome in cornball Missouri dialect, boarded the visitors' train at Springfield, Massachusetts, along with Charles Warner, for the final short leg of their trip to Hartford. Lilian Aldrich had glanced out her window as the train slowed, and spotted Clemens's "waving, undulating motion" on the platform. This time, she understood it as part of Mark Twain's "mannerisms and idiosyncrasies." Too late: Lilian Aldrich was on Mark Twain's "vengeance due" list, and this weekend, he would extract his payment. The weaving act may have been a sheathed reminder of her appraisal of him in Boston.

Howells and Osgood lodged with the Warners during the visit; the Aldriches were guests of Sam and Livy, which was the way Sam wanted it. On the morning after the convivial first evening, the Aldriches were startled by a knock on their upstairs bedroom door. Then came Sam's voice: "Aldrich, come out, I want to speak to you." What ensued burned itself into Lilian Aldrich's memory, and eventually into her 1920 memoir. As she wrapped her kimono around her and cupped an ear to the door, she heard Clemens speaking to her husband of something terribly serious. "[His] voice had its usual calmness and slowness of speech, but was lacking in the kindly mellow quality of its accustomed tone."

As Mrs. Aldrich remembered it, Clemens said,

"In Heaven's name, Aldrich, what are you doing? Are you emulating the kangaroos, with hob-nails in your shoes, or trying the jumping-frog business? Our bedroom is directly under yours, and poor 'Livy and her headache—do try to move more quietly, though 'Livy would rather suffer than have you give up your game on her account." [36]

Then he returned downstairs. The Aldriches stood flabbergasted. They looked at their bedroom floor: soft rugs. They finished dressing on tiptoe, speaking in whispers, and crept down to the breakfast room where Livy sat behind a silver coffee urn.

With sorrowful solicitude we asked if her headache was better, and begged forgiveness for adding to her pain. To our amazement she answered, "I have no headache."

Then the Aldriches apologized for the noise they'd made.

"Noise!" Mrs. Clemens replied. "We have not heard a sound. If you had shouted we should not have known it, for our rooms are in another wing of the house." [37]

At the other end of the breakfast table, silently taking this conversation in, sat Mark Twain—looking, Lilian Aldrich noted,

"As guileless as a combination of cherubim and seraphim—never a word, excepting with lengthened drawl, more slow than usual, 'Oh, do come to your breakfast, Aldrich, and don't talk all day.' "

"It was a joyous group that came together at the table that morning, and loud was the laughter, and rapid the talk." [38]

What is touching about Mrs. Aldrich's remembrance of her host's mind game—what softens her earlier moral superiority and lends her a little sympathy—is that she clearly does not grasp the malice beneath Mark Twain's cherubim-seraphim pose, expressed in the sexual innuendo in his complaint to her husband. That Mark Twain harbored the venom necessary for such a veiled insult is obvious from his opinion of Lilian Aldrich, which remained as radioactive thirty-seven years later as on the day he met her. She was "a strange and vanity-devoured, detestable woman! I do not believe I could ever learn to like her except on a raft at sea with no other provisions in sight."[39]

Other than that, it was a most congenial literary weekend. Howells raved about the "charming visit" to a friend, and remarked that Warner and Mark Twain seemed to be living, at Nook Farm, an ideal life.

They live very near each other, in a sort of suburban grove, and their neighbors are the Stowes and Hookers . . . They go in and out of each other's houses without ringing, and nobody gets more than the first syllable of his first name . . . I saw a great deal of Twain, and he's a thoroughly good fellow. His wife is a delicate little beauty, the very flower and perfume of *ladylikeness*, who simply adores him—but this leaves no word to describe his love for her.[40]

Howells was living out a similar stretch of domestic happiness. He and wife Elinor were the parents of three children now: John Mead had followed Winifred in 1868, and Mildred was born in September 1872. The following July, the Howellses moved into a small dream house of their own, at 37 Concord Avenue in Cambridge, designed principally by Elinor.

Aldrich had brought with him a chapter from his forthcoming novel, *Prudence Palfrey*, hoping for advice on a chapter that required a close knowledge of ore mining. (Howells had published the chapter in the March *Atlantic*.) Clemens, who liked Thomas Aldrich, read it closely, and about ten days later sent him several pages of well-considered criticisms. Later still, he agreed to read proofs of the entire novel, and continued to show a diligent editor's eye: "You see (page 109) you've got that *ancient* river-bed in your head, & you've got the modern river-bed in your head too, & you've gone & *mixed the two together*. But they *won't* mix, any more than oil & water."[41] He apologized for the "long delay" in his initial response. Livy had suffered another near-miscarriage, this one a full three months before her delivery date. She endured ten hours of labor pains before the crisis passed.

He enjoyed the idea of literary impresario, and handed out suggestions as freely as he'd assigned fantasy roles to Will Bowen and John Briggs back in Hannibal. "Dialect is your forte, not logic, my boy,"[42] he informed the lecturer William Andrews. He tried to talk both Aldrich and Howells into publishing their work through Bliss and the more lucrative subscription method, but neither of these proper Bostonians could ever quite unbend to that level of commerce. He tried to appoint Orion as editor of a manuscript by the colorful old sea god of the Pacific, Edgar Wakeman, now retired and short of money, who'd pitched the project to Clemens ("I write you this letter to tell you not to take Hold of any other book until you have done with mine, the Public are anxious now about the Island World . . ."[43]) Orion passed, but Wakeman got his book published in 1878, possibly aided by Mark Twain's influence. Carried away with exuberance over his new place in the literary firmament, Sam wrote to Howells with a wonderfully boyish fantasy that he seems to have intended in dead earnest.

> You or Aldrich or both of you must come to Hartford to live. Mr. Hall, who lives in the house next to Mrs. Stowe's, will sell . . . You can do your work just as well here as in Cambridge, can't you? Come, will one of you boys buy that house? Now say yes.[44]

Neither did. The Black Avenger sailed on alone, with folded arms. But his destination, after all these years since the halcyon raft days on the Mississippi, was at last coming into focus. On the tidal fountains of Mark Twain's great deep, he was sailing into literature.

30

Quarry Farm and Nook Farm

(1874–75)

"Y ou want to know *what* I am doing? I am writing two admirable books—I like a good strong adjective—& you shall claw them to pieces & burn the MS when you come," Clemens announced to Mary Fairbanks early in 1874.[1] This agenda was obsolete almost as he declared it. Well before that hectic year was out, the "busiest white man in America" would be even busier. He drastically revised those writing plans. He bailed his brother out of destitution yet again. He finished compiling more than eighty of his sketches and sent the collection off to Elisha Bliss (who selected about sixty of them). In the summer months he removed to a gazebo atop a windswept hill above a river, where, over a series of summers, he would produce much of his best literature. He welcomed a new daughter into the family. He joined the board of an insurance company. He returned to the theater world that had captivated him as a young reporter in Virginia City (and exhausted him in San Francisco)—this time as a playwright and impresario. And he moved his family into their newly finished castlelike house on Farmington Avenue in Nook Farm, where he would commence the happiest—and the last happy—years of his life. Within weeks after his boast to Mrs. Fairbanks, Mark Twain set aside one of those "admirable" books in progress: his fitfully pursued England travel manuscript. By spring, Mark Twain's passion had shifted to the other "admirable" manuscript, the one about "Tom Sawyer," which now called to him with the same power of reverie with which "meadow, grove and stream" had called to Wordsworth seventy years earlier.

The house's exotic contours were already prompting gossip and news items, even though it remained months from completion. "Most of the residents of Hartford know that Mr. Samuel H. Clemens, otherwise known as 'Mark Twain,' is building a residence on Farmington Avenue," purred the Hartford *Daily Times* of March 23, 1874, and then meowed, "Many of the readers of *The Times*, doubtless, have had at least an external view of the structure, which already has acquired something beyond a local fame; and such persons, we think, will agree with us in the opinion that it is one of the oddest looking buildings in the State ever designed for a dwelling, if not in the whole country."[2] At least they almost got his name right.

In mid-April, the Clemenses surrendered Nook Barn back to John and Isabella Hooker. Servants were moving into the new house, but the uproar of dust and hammering still made habitation unthinkable for the family. An attractive alternative beckoned: a summer in Elmira, where Olivia Lewis Langdon and the Cranes offered hospitality. Sam and Livy planned to depart Hartford on April 15, stay at the Church Street house with Olivia Lewis Langdon until the weather warmed up, then accept Susan and Theodore Crane's invitation to live at Quarry Farm on the hill outside of town, where Sam could write, and Livy, eight months pregnant, could enjoy the care of her sister.

Five days before departing Hartford, Sam and Livy welcomed a forlorn guest to Nook Barn: Mollie Clemens, who had splurged on a train trip from New York and the 9th Street hovel she shared with Orion. Mollie's mission was to beg for money. She sought help toward the $2,000 price of a farm that she and Orion wanted to buy in Mollie's hometown of Keokuk, Iowa. The complications surrounding the request were endless, and pathetic: Jane had made it clear that she did not want Sam to help the couple out; she didn't believe the move west would last. Orion, now fifty, weirdly agreed; he considered Mollie's Keokuk idea to be a bad career move. Like Arthur Miller's Willie Loman three-quarters of a century later (and like Marshall Clemens a quarter-century earlier), Orion was obsessed with a muddled American dream that had already failed to come true. Mollie Clemens, the former belle of Carson City, had no dreams left, nor illusions: ". . . *everything* he [Orion] undertakes fails," she wrote to Sam several days after her visit, "and he lives the most dreadful life of *fear* FEAR FEAR."[3] She just wanted to get back to the place she'd started out from; to be near the apple trees of her childhood. And maybe one more small thing.

"I yearn for indipendance."

Sam advanced the couple nine hundred dollars. "I wrote them to furnish their house with the very cheapest stuff they could find," he reported to Jane, "& with no pretentious flummery about it—*be* chicken farmers & not hifalutin fine folks . . ."[4] Orion knuckled under. And then, like Willie Loman, he turned his thoughts to getting some seeds in the ground. "My plan would be to work on the garden and chicken business during the day and refresh my memory in law at night . . ."[5]

Sammy Clemens probably committed no "memorable treachery" against his doomed brother Benjamin, as Mark Twain believed he had. But a few weeks after Mollie's visit, and with no provocation, Sam committed a treachery against Orion that was shameful, if not memorable: he held his hapless brother up to ridicule. The derision was contained in a letter to William Dean Howells (and his wife Elinor) on May 10, 1874: a letter that had little other purpose than to mock Orion's bumbling futility in the world. Clemens compounded the transgression by violating Orion's trust and privacy: he sent Howells the letter from Orion that had reactivated his fraternal contempt. This piece of correspondence does not survive; but its concerns are evident from Sam's post to Howells, which begins,

> I am so strongly tempted to afford you & Mrs. Howells a glimpse of my brother's last, (just received), that I can't resist.
> You observe that he is afraid the interest might fall in arrears, so he pays it some weeks ahead of time.
> You perceive that he is still in some way connected with that infamous Tennessee Land which has been our destruction for 40 years (see opening chapters of Gilded Age—my brother is "Lafayette Hawkins.")

After indulging a few further condescensions, Sam signed off, then added,

> P.S. Do not fail to note the hopeful, glad-hearted, school-boy cheeriness which bubbles out of every pore of this man who has been ALWAYS a failure.[6]

It hardly seems a stretch to imagine that this tawdry impulse was prompted less by meanness than by Sam's own abiding terror of failure. He may have glimpsed a version of himself in Orion's pathos—or feared that others, Howells's circle in particular, might glimpse Orion in him. Not that Sam ran any risk of an identity switch with his brother. By the spring of 1874, some 240,000 copies of Mark Twain's three latest books had been sold, representing a gross intake of nearly a million dollars for the American Publishing Company—an astonishing achievement for that time. While Orion prepared to grapple with the roosters and hens at Keokuk, Sam swept off for a summer of literary work at a farm that was more a country estate. He seemed unconcerned by a budgetary fact that augured serious financial pressures in the years to come: expenses on the Hartford house—land costs, architects' fees, materials for the house and barn—had topped $40,000, more than $10,000 ahead of Livy's projections of 1871. And the end was nowhere in sight.

The family stayed at the Langdon house until May 5 and warmer weather, and then joined Susan and Theodore Crane on the hill at Quarry Farm. Livy's kindhearted sister announced a surprise gift for Sam. She led the couple and Susy along a pathway that wound a hundred yards upward from the main house, through clover fields, and finally to the peak of the hill. On an outcropping that overlooked Elmira, the Chemung River, and the "retreating ranges of distant blue hills" beyond,[7] sat a small wooden octagonal enclosure with a peaked roof, glassed windows, wide doorway, coal grate, writing table, sofa, and chairs.* Susan had had it built as a congenial workspace for Livy's husband, and it proved to be that: Mark Twain would produce some of his most enduring literature within its shelter. It survives on the campus of Elmira College as one of his most popular artifacts. "On hot days I spread the study wide open, anchor my papers down with brickbats," Mark Twain told a friend, "& write in the midst of hurricanes, clothed in the same thin linen we make shirt bosoms of."[8] A photograph shows him there in a white linen suit, with a leg across a knee, sporting those twin badges of the successful salesman, two-toned shoes.

Clemens's affection for Sue Crane was established long before this gesture of hers. In 1872 he had written,

Indeed Susie Crane *is* an angel, & it is such a comfort to me to know that if I *do* chance to wind up in the fiery pit hereafter, she will flutter down there every day, in defiance of law & the customs of the country & bring ice & fans & all sorts of contraband things under her wings . . .[9]

Theodore Crane became a great friend as well, and a quietly important one. A spare-framed lumber-merchant's son, a clerkish businessman with a high hairline and a deferential manner (Clemens once described him as "indestructibly honest," but timid),[10] Crane was usually eclipsed by his wife's vivacity, and has left few traces. But in Elmira folklore, he is credited with ratifying Jervis Langdon's approval of Clemens as Livy's suitor, on the basis of having read and admired his sketches.[11] The Cranes ranked with the Langdons amidst Elmira's progressive and intellectual community, welcoming their Negro servants into the extended family circle for conversations of an evening and including the Clemens girls and other family children at the dinner table. Friends recalled observing Clemens and Crane lying side by side in their portable hammocks on the farmhouse lawn in summer, reading to each other from the Diary of Samuel Pepys and Richard Henry Dana's *Two Years Before the Mast*.[12]

Upon settling into the study on the hill, Clemens absorbed himself in the great memory tale that had begun to reveal itself to him the Sunday afternoon following his wedding, when the old life in Hannibal swept before him like a panorama. He had completed the first five chapters of *The Adventures of Tom Sawyer* by the end of January 1873, when the *Gilded Age* collaboration with Warner began to demand his full attention. He'd covered the introductions of Tom, his Aunt Polly, and half-brother Sid; Tom fast-talking his friends into whitewashing the fence for him, and paying for it; Tom's infatuation with Becky Thatcher; the scene in which Tom bungles his Sunday-school Bible quiz and Judge Thatcher makes his grand appearance; and Tom playing with the

* Susan Crane had hired Alfred Thorp, an associate of the Farmington Avenue's house architect Edward Potter, to design the structure, with small decorative details that referred to Potter's creation.

pinch-beetle in church. He had not yet written his way into the novel's sustaining, interweaving plotlines. But as Tom Sawyer might say, plot ain't shucks to a Mark Twain novel.

HIS WORK on the manuscript endured several interruptions. The most significant of these led to a new work that added greatly to Mark Twain's wealth. In mid-May, word from San Francisco reached Sam that someone had pirated *The Gilded Age* for a stage adaptation. The perpetrator was Gilbert B. Densmore, a drama critic at the *Golden Era,* whom Clemens had known during his time in San Francisco. Densmore had pillaged the novel for its most colorful characters, Silas and Laura Hawkins and Colonel Sellers; then written new material around them, compressing the book's political story lines and pumping up the comedy. (Densmore earlier had run a somewhat similar scam on Bret Harte, lifting several chapters of a Harte story for serialization in the *Golden Era.*) The character actor John T. Raymond had brilliantly captured the larger-than-life essence of Sellers, bringing out the exuberance and appetite that Mark Twain, the lover of Shakespeare, had invested in him—making him a kind of American Falstaff. With Raymond/Sellers stealing the show, the play had been a smash hit in its early performances.

"I know Mr. D. mighty well & he shan't run any play on MY brains," Clemens fumed to Charles Warner in Hartford, and schemed to thwart the swindling playwright: he and Warner would each claim sole copyright for the characters that each of them had created, "& I will buy this play of Densmore, re-write it if it is worth it—or burn it, & write one myself & enjoin D. from playing his."[13] Warner, whose ego could not have been gladdened by the fact that Densmore had jettisoned all of his characters and used only Mark Twain's, agreed. He probably did not cheer up much on discovering that Mark Twain intended to pay him no royalties, on the ground that Warner had no copyright claims on any of its characters. Clemens held his temper in check and negotiated a deal with Densmore, as he had in London with John Camden Hotten. He offered the Californian a hundred dollars for the script of Densmore's play and an agreement to stop producing it—and sent him double that amount. Densmore agreed to the terms. On May 10, Mark Twain set the Tom Sawyer manuscript aside and began his own dramatic adaptation of *The Gilded Age*. Working through three drafts, he completed the five-act play in sixty-odd days. "I don't think much of it, as a drama," he told Howells, "but I suppose it will do to hang Col. Sellers on . . . *He* will play tolerably well, in the hands of a good actor."[14] Clemens had struck a deal with Raymond, who had come east after creating the stage "Sellers" in California. Mark Twain retained most of Densmore's plot—in acknowledgment of which he sent the Californian another two hundred dollars—but created the dialogue essentially from scratch, leaving in only a few lines of Densmore's. The resulting play regathered and heightened the most autobiographical contributions that Clemens had made to the novel: the migration of the Hawkins family to Missouri, the steamboat explosion, the presence of Uncle Dan'l, the delphic influence of the Tennessee land, even that infamous dinner of turnips and water that Sam had choked down at James Lampton's house in 1861. He retained the subplot involving Laura Hawkins and her Confederate lover. But unlike the novel, these elements now served primarily as establishing context for the Colonel. Mulberry Sellers, as he was now called, towered above—obscured, smothered, knocked haywire—all the sociopolitical concerns of the original work. As he had with "Sociable Jimmy"—which finally ran in the New York *Times* in November of that year—Mark Twain tapped into the great catch basin of spoken language contained in his memory. Once again the language, this time that of a small-time white Southern blowhard, flowed easily onto his pages; the character who emerged drew comparisons to the best of Dickens.

LIVY GAVE birth to her second daughter on the morning of June 8, after hours of severe labor pains, in the main Quarry Farm house. She was assisted by one of the pioneering women doctors of the mid-19th century, Rachel Brooks Gleason, an Elmira physician who had treated Livy's progressive-minded parents and some of their friends. Mrs. Gleason was a year older than the first woman to graduate from an American medical school, Elizabeth Blackwell, whose admission to the Geneva (N.Y.) Medical School in 1847 was approved only because everyone there thought it was a practical joke. The infant weighed nearly eight pounds, twice the birth-weight of both Langdon and Susy, leading Sam to describe her as "colossal" and "the great American Giantess." The parents named her Clara, in honor of Clara Spaulding. "It is an admirable child . . . [It] has intellect," Clemens told the Twichells. "It puts its fingers against its brow & thinks." [15] To John Brown, he proclaimed, "I wish the nations of the earth would combine in a baby show & give us a chance to compete." [16]

(Competition would have been stiff. Among the babies of 1874 who would shape the century to come, Guglielmo Marconi entered the world, and Arnold Schoenberg. Winston Churchill was born on Sam's thirty-ninth birthday. Robert Frost emerged wailing, and Gertrude Stein, and Amy Lowell, and Charles Ives, and Harry Houdini, and the computer pioneer Thomas Watson, and the third baseman Honus Wagner.)

LIVY RECOVERED quickly after her delivery. "The Modoc" kindly offered her favorite doll to her new little sister. And Sam Clemens wrote like the wind. He was confident enough of his progress to break away on June 29 for a quick trip to Hartford. He checked in with Bliss at the publisher's office. But the main purpose of his visit was to get in on the ground floor of the new Hartford Accident Insurance Company by buying fifty thousand dollars' worth of stock, paying 25 percent down. (He'd been alerted to the opportunity by Joe Goodman in California, who knew an investor there.) Like nearly all his business investments, this one proved to be a turkey. The well-named Hartford Accident went under in a year and a half, and it took Sam "two or three" years to get back his investment (which was by then up to $23,000).[17] But the company lasted long enough to hold an October banquet at which Mark Twain made one of his best-loved after-dinner speeches. ("Ever since I have been a director in an accident insurance company I have felt that I am a better man. Life has seemed more precious. Accidents have assumed a kindlier aspect . . . I look upon a cripple, now, with affectionate interest . . . to me, now, there is a charm about a railway collision that is unspeakable.")[18] Back in his hilltop studio, he finished up the *Gilded Age* play with one of his typical headlong sprints. "During the past 3 days I have written 157 pages of literature & 25 letters," he informed his mother on July 11.[19] (Normally, he figured, it would take him the ice age of eight days to produce that many pages.) John Raymond organized a supporting cast and rehearsal schedule. He booked a preview performance in Rochester at the end of August before taking it to New York in the fall. Finally, Mark Twain plunged back in to *Tom Sawyer,* his draft pages mounting in his skyborne den. He often reached fifty pages a day. He did not discuss the plot with anyone, nor mention that this was a novel. The reminiscences possessed him. By September, he'd finished more than four hundred pages. And then the fountains closed up.

He'd been displeased with a chapter—seen it as "a failure in conception, moral, truth to nature & execution."[20] So he burned it. Then he set the whole manuscript aside. He went back to playing billiards, and did other things. At least nine months would pass before he touched the work again.

"It was plain that I had worked myself out, pumped myself dry," he wrote almost offhandedly to John Brown, using a metaphor that he came to favor— the inner "tank" draining, and himself helpless to proceed until it filled up again.[21] But what had cut off the flow? The characters and episodes until that point—the end of Chapter 15—had crowded their way onto the pages, now up to the great getaway to Jackson's Island in the Mississippi by Tom, Joe, Huck. He had fed from notes scribbled to himself in the margins of his pages as he wrote. "A ragbag of memories," some scholars have called them[22]— reminders of characters and incidents, most of which eventually found their way into this or other of his books, such as *Adventures of Huckleberry Finn, A Tramp Abroad* and *Life on the Mississippi.* A quite dissimilar note, inscribed on the first manuscript page, may hold the clue to the mystery of his sudden mental dry-pumping.

1, Boyhood & youth; 2, Y & early Manh; 3 the Battle of Life in many lands; 4 (age 37 to 40,) return & meet grown babies & toothless old drivelers who were the grandees of his boyhood. The Adored Unknown a faded old maid & full of rasping, puritanical vinegar piety.[23]

This little self-memo comprises the only outline that has ever been discovered for *Tom Sawyer*—not surprising given Mark Twain's famous indifference to formal structure. The memo shows that structure was not *utterly* beyond his interests, and suggests that a structural quandary was what brought the writer to his skidding halt: namely, one posed by the third item, "The Battle of Life in many lands." Hamlin Hill and others have argued that following this prompt would have taken Tom Sawyer into radically different territory than that bounded by "St. Petersburg" and the Mississippi River: namely, Tom's escape from his hometown and his maturation into a man as he visited corners of the world perhaps similar to those described in *The Innocents Abroad*. Mark Twain pigeonholes the manuscript after Tom, having stolen away from his sleeping comrades on Jackson's Island, slips back into St. Petersburg in the night and stands beside the bed of his sleeping Aunt Polly, pondering whether to leave her a note that he has written. What will the note say? Will it inform her that Tom and his friends are merely "off playing pirates," as is the case with the published version? Or will it announce to his aunt the onset of a worldwide odyssey?—an odyssey that would culminate with Tom's return in old age, to find his boyhood chums now toothless drivelers and the Adored Unknown a rasping old maid? The second option exerted a powerful pull on Mark Twain, in literature and in his life. The archetypal journey of the hero; Percival, Orestes, outward flight, initiation, the conquering of adversaries, the triumphal return. Mark Twain intended to take the myth a little farther than Homer's Odysseus; into age, decay, death, toothless drivelers, and vinegary crones. (Sixteen years on, he was still haunted with the vision of his surrogate selves returning to Hannibal as old men.)

SAM CLEMENS'S manuscript-writing pace seldom diverted him from spraying letters to friends and strangers—often a half dozen or more each day. On July 29, he answered a rambling query from one Mary M. Field, a self-described "Serial" writer who begged him for a hundred dollars to help her through a dry patch in the freelance market. Unconscious of the target she was presenting, she promised him a diamond ring and an Elgin watch as security, and mentioned a few publishing opportunities.

The vituperation of Mark Twain's reply nearly transcends hostility.

Madam: Your distress would move the heart of a statue. Indeed it would move the entire statue if it were on rollers . . . I never have heard of a case so bitter as yours. Nothing in the world between you & starvation but a lucrative literary situation, a few diamonds & things, & three thousand seven hundred dollars worth of town property. How you must suffer. I do not know that there is any relief for misery like this. Suicide has been recommended by some authors . . .

I suppose you will think, now, that I am not a "gentleman." Then I shall be crushed clear into the earth.[24]

And on in that vein for a few smoking pages. It is not clear that Mark Twain actually sent the letter; he retained the draft, and no response from Mary Field has been found. But the exercise of writing it must have cleared his passages wonderfully.

By August the Nook Farm house was so close to completion that Sam and Livy began plans to occupy it. They departed Quarry Farm for a series of visits around August 5, preparatory to the move back to Hartford. They left their daughters with the Cranes, the idea being that this would be a relaxing hiatus for Livy. The "hiatus" became an extravaganza: first, a railroad trip of 180 miles to visit the Fredonia contingent; then on to Buffalo (47 miles) to look up old friends; then Canandaigua, New York (91 miles), to look up more old friends; then, finally, back to Elmira (75 miles) on August 14. All this relaxing had worn Livy out, so instead of departing immediately for Hartford, the family remained at Quarry Farm until September 10.

Mark Twain's version of the play made its road debut as scheduled on August 31 at the Opera House in Rochester, New York. Raymond sent an invitation to Sam, but received a curious telegram on the day of the performance: "We are threatened with scarlet fever, & I fear to leave my family." [25] Given that scholars Michael Frank and Harriet Elinor Smith have found no evidence of scarlet fever in Elmira, it may have been that Sam simply wanted to be near his recuperating wife, or even that Livy insisted that he stay at home. Perhaps it was just as well: one local paper panned the play as "simply an incoherent jumble of scenes and acts, without any sequence or continuity whatever;" [26] another called it "a very clever drama" that still needed some fine-tuning, [27] and a third congratulated Clemens on his success as a dramatist. The critics agreed that Raymond was brilliant in the role of Sellers and predicted great things for him. The company then shuffled off to Buffalo, and the Clemenses returned to Elmira.

"I ENCLOSE also a 'True Story' which has no humor in it," Mark Twain advised Howells on September 2, what would become his first published piece in the *Atlantic,* and endure as one of his finest short sketches. "You can pay as lightly as you choose for that, if you want it, for it is rather out of my line." [28] He misjudged the work's value. "A True Story, Repeated Word for Word as I Heard It" was the "afterthought" in a package of two pieces he was sending Howells, the other being a bit of Mark Twain foolery called "Fable for Old Boys & Girls." Howells recognized the brilliance of "True Story." Though only three magazine pages long, it encapsulated the centuries-long threnody of separation, suffering, and forbearance among African slaves and their children in America. One can hear the voice, and the moral concerns, of Jim developing in it.

"A True Story," like "Sociable Jimmy," replicates the dialect of a Negro with whom Mark Twain has conversed. In this case, the person is Mary Ann "Auntie" Cord, born in 1798, a slave most of her life, and now the Cranes' cook at Quarry Farm. On an evening in late June, in the democratic little circle of household members and servants on the farmhouse porch, she had responded to an inane bit of small talk from Sam—"how is it that you've lived sixty* years and never had any trouble?"—with the story of the forced dispersion of her husband and seven children by slave owners in 1852; her years of yearning for them; and her near-miraculous reencounter with Henry, her youngest, during the Civil War. Henry, a Union soldier, turned up at an encampment where Mary Ann was the cook.

"Dey put chains on us an' put us on a stan' as high as dis po'ch," the cook tells her listeners, telling of her family's forced breakup:

An' all de people stood aroun', crowds an' crowds. An' dey'd come up dah an' look at us all roun', and squeeze our arm, an' make us git up an' walk, an' den say, "Dis one lame," or "Dis one don't 'mount to much . . . an' dey begin to sell my chil'en . . . an' I begin to cry; an' de man say, "Shet up yo' dam blubbedrin'," an' hit me on de mouf wid his han'.[29]

She describes the moment of reconciliation with Henry, thirteen years later.

. . . I jist stopped *right dah,* an' never budged! jist gazed, an' gazed, so; an' de pan [in her hand] begin to tremble, an' all of a sudden I *knowed!* . . . "Boy!" I says, "if you an't my Henry, what is you doin' wid dis welt on yo' wris' an' dat sk-yar on yo' forehead? De Lord God ob heaven be praise', I got my own ag'in!"

Oh, no, Misto C—, *I* hain't had no trouble. An' no *joy!* [30]

As with "Sociable Jimmy," this soliloquy is not so much "word for word" as artful reconstruction, intensely considered and revised. Mark Twain's letter accompanying the submission advised Howells that he didn't alter Cord's story "except to begin it at the beginning, instead of the middle, as she did—& traveled both ways."[31] Three weeks later, offering to make more revisions on the proof sheets, Mark Twain gave Howells a glimpse into his methodology: "I amend dialect stuff by talking & talking & *talking* till it sounds right—& I had difficulty with this negro talk because a negro sometimes (rarely) says 'goin'' & sometimes 'gwyne' . . . & when you come to reproduce them on paper they look as if the variation resulted from the writer's carelessness . . ."[32] More important is the fact that the story *could have* fallen word for word from the lips of an elderly former slave woman. The rhythms and syntax are plausible, and there is not a trace of "stage-darky" dialect that would show up even in the early-chapter conversations between Huck and Jim. The climactic line—*"I* hain't had no trouble. An' no *joy!"*—is not merely a Twainian "snapper"; it is a thunderbolt of accusatory irony. It is almost as though Mark Twain were telling the story to his prewar self, whose idea of a punchy ending to a slave's

---

* Twain fictionalized both her age and her name; in the story she was "Aunt Rachel."

ghost story was "*You've* got it!" and who looked forward to summer weather when "niggers begin to sweat and look greasy."

To Howells, reminiscing in old age, the story was nothing less than "one of those noble pieces of humanity with which the South has atoned chiefly if not solely through him for all its despite to the negro . . ."[33] With the consent of the publisher, Henry O. Houghton, he rewarded the author with the highest purchase rate in the magazine's history, twenty dollars a magazine page (sixty dollars).

Sam was beginning to feel grateful for every dollar he could earn. Around that time, he noted to a friend that his new house was running up three times as much cost as he and Livy had planned for.

THE GILDED AGE enjoyed a successful weeklong tryout in Buffalo, despite equivocal reviews. Mark Twain attended the opening night this time, on September 7. He arose in his private box, by request, at the end of the fourth act, to make a speech, during which he appeared overcome with emotion. He sat down again to an ovation.

Sam, Livy, and Clara Spaulding left Elmira on September 10 for New York and the white-marble Hoffman House at Broadway and 24th Street, two blocks north of the Park Theater, where *The Gilded Age* was to make its New York debut in less than a week. Sam spent the days supervising rehearsals, while Livy, fatigued and menstruating profusely, lay in her room under Clara's care. "Now no doubt 'treatment' is necessary again," Sam wrote delicately to Rachel Gleason. "If so, will you write & tell a reliable lady physician here to come to the hotel, & administer it?"[34] Livy eventually showed an unmistakable sign of recovery: she wanted to go shopping, and did, and selected a ton of carpets and furniture for the new house.

A "brilliant audience of literary people" greeted the retooled play on opening night in New York, September 16.[35] The crowd responded warmly. In a curtain speech after the fourth act, Mark Twain told the audience that he had composed two endings, to be performed in rotation: in one, a jury would convict Laura of murdering her lover; in the other, she would be acquitted. He was unable to decide, he explained, which one was the more effective way of "teaching what ought to be done" given Laura's circumstance—"strict truth" or "satire," the latter being the not-guilty verdict. It was a curious rumination, and Mark Twain made it stranger still by launching what sounded on the surface like an attack on the play's star.

I threw all my strength into the character of *Colonel Sellers*, hoping to make it a very strong tragedy part and pathetic. I think this gentleman [referring to Raymond, as the actor listened from the wings] *tries* hard to play it right and make it majestic and pathetic; but his *face* is against him. And his clothes! . . . He is from one of the Indian reservations. Oh! I can see that he tries hard to make it solemn and awful and heroic, but really sometimes he almost makes me laugh.[36]

Was he kidding? Yes, profoundly so. This was one of Mark Twain's lecture-stage devices, the deadpan reversal of what he actually meant—or of what the audience expected him to say. Colonel Sellers, a tragedy figure?! As the author rambled on, the comic intent slowly grew more hilariously clear.

I meant that turnip dinner to be pathetic, for how more forcibly could you represent poverty and misery and suffering by such a dinner, and of course if anything would bring tears to people's eyes *that* would; but this man eats those turnips as if they were the bread of life, and so of course the pathos is knocked clear out of the thing. But I think he will learn . . .[37]

At least the intent grew clear to some. The New York *World* printed Mark Twain's remarks without comment in the body of a strongly positive review of the play, suggesting that Mark Twain's joke was self-evident. But Margaret Duckett, among other scholars, accepts his sentiments at face value, noting his late-life remarks to Paine that Raymond was a pygmy of an actor and that the turnip-eating scene was intended as piteous.[38] Given that the line between humor and sorrow was thin, tending toward nonexistent, in Samuel Clemens's mind, and given that this scene was drawn directly from a highly fraught moment of his young manhood, he may have been speaking the truth as he felt it.

He eventually accepted that *The Gilded Age* play (which, after all, came to be popularly known as *Colonel Sellers*) was a mediocre "vehicle" with one great role played by one great star, its chief virtue being its box-office appeal. The reviews tended to support this. The most perceptive one came from Andrew Carpenter Wheeler, writing as "Nym Crinkle." Crinkle began his New York *World* column of September 17 with a detailed synopsis of the plot, praising the language and actions of Colonel Sellers throughout. And then he identified a weakness that pervaded Mark Twain's literature:

It is not possible to admire this plot. It bears all the evidences of having been fabricated round *Colonel Sellers* and worked out laboriously under exigent stage demands. What it lacks is the fluent, coherent, and natural growth of interest which alone would give it symmetry and strength.[39]

Noting that "[t]here is no adequate motive until *Laura* kills *Colonel Selby* [two-thirds of the way through the play]," Crinkle remarks,

Previous to that the interest is held mainly, if not altogether, by the play of character and not by the progress of events, which is an aesthetic defect . . .
We do not think that it is from any lack of creative power that the play is thus amenable to criticism. *It is rather the want of constructive art in the writer* . . . [emphasis added][40]

"Constructive art," of course, was the central weakness in question—or was it a weakness? The serendipity in Mark Twain's narratives might be explained by his lack of formal training in rhetoric and composition. Or it might be explained by his intuitive understanding that he didn't need it. The question begged by Crinkle's declaration is: if he *had* been schooled in the formal requirements of literature, would that have suffocated the divine, anarchic spontaneity that provides the greatest pleasures in his work?

Crinkle more or less acknowledges this conundrum with his next thought:

The one remaining impression when the curtain falls has been made by *Colonel Sellers*. We do not connect him with the circumstances that have been narrated; we remember only with a keen sense of delight his personal peculiarities, his sincerity of self-deceit, his gentlemanly poverty, his egregious folly, wrapped about by his amiability and homely courtliness.[41]

The Gilded Age or *Colonel Sellers* ran for 115 nights in New York, and, as Mark Twain pointed out, "as it has no scenic effects & no bare legs, this is extraordinary & was not a thing to be expected."[42] Among its devotees was President Ulysses S. Grant, who attended the September 28 performance, laughed and applauded along with everyone else, and made his way backstage afterward to congratulate Raymond.

Mark Twain never published the play. Already burned by piracy, he had no intention of letting hinterland companies leech its profits. He was right about its value: *Colonel Sellers* netted $10,000 in its first three months. It earned Mark Twain around $70,000 across his lifetime. Its chief liability was that it inspired in him a renewed fascination with the theater, along with the dangerous notion that he was a playwright.

ON SEPTEMBER 21, in the orange-tinted brilliance of a New England autumn, the Clemenses took possession of their Nook Farm house at last. Or perhaps, the Nook Farm house took possession of them. It sat nearly completed in its three-storied splendor, its salmon-hued brick façades outshining the maple trees in sunlight, at the crest of a rise at 351 Farmington Avenue, across the lawn from the house of Harriet Beecher Stowe. Its five balconies and several sharply pitched gables lent it the aspect of a Gothic castle. A two-story tower, its main window overlooking the long canopy that crossed the driveway entrance, put some people in mind of a pilothouse above a deck, and a false myth took hold over the years that Mark Twain had intended the house to resemble a steamboat.

Inside, Edward Potter's handiwork generally fulfilled the vision that Livy had begun sketching out nearly three years earlier. The house boasted nineteen rooms and seven bathrooms, each equipped with the modern wonder of a flush toilet. "Speaking tubes" carried the voice from floor to floor. A coal furnace provided heat, and gas lamps supplied illumination. On the main floor a grand entrance hall displayed ornamentally carved wood. The drawing room, the house's social center, was dominated by a huge mirror that had been a wedding gift to Sam and Livy. In 1881 its walls, like those of other rooms, acquired the stenciling designs of Lockwood de Forest, a partner in the Associated Artists firm founded by Louis Comfort Tiffany. The library (the center of family life), the dining room, and the servants' kitchen commanded the remaining ground-floor space. Bedrooms occupied most of the second floor, with Sam and Livy's set off to itself. In Venice a few years later, Sam purchased what remains the house's most famous furnishing: a heavy bed of carved oak, the posts at its head crowned by sculpted angels. Sam and Livy placed their pillows at the foot of the bed so that they could admire these. Mark Twain was often photographed in this bed in his old age, head propped on a pallet, cigar in mouth, a manuscript tucked against his stomach. It was the bed he died in.

The third floor was dominated by a billiard room: Sam's sanctuary, his refuge for poking his cueball and smoking his cigars and working on his manuscripts.

When the Clemenses moved in, carpenters and plumbers still crowded the downstairs rooms; hammers rang throughout the day, and the family was obliged to decamp on the second floor, sleeping in the guest room, eating in the nursery, and using Sam's hideaway upstairs as a parlor. Life for the rich in those times was not always easy.

The Hartford house was Livy's creation. Sam contributed the Venetian bed, a Scottish-castle mantel for the library, an assortment of gadgets (in addition to the speaking tubes, they included a telephone, a "type-machine," and a home-rigged rubber tube that transferred gas from a chandelier to a bedside lamp for nighttime reading). But as the house filled up with statuary, paintings, carpets, tapestry and fabric, lamps, plants, silver and pewterware, framed portraits, books, piano, travel souvenirs, and—not least—fashionable guests, it perfectly reflected Livy's understanding of Victorian material display as evidence of moral and intellectual worth. Judging by her house, the Clemenses were saints.

OCTOBER FOUND the hammers still rat-a-tatting away in the house; Mark Twain couldn't concentrate on writing. The carpenters were there for eternity, he fumed to Howells. "I kill them when I get opportunities, but the builder goes & gets more." [43] He was responding to a plea from the *Atlantic* editor that most literary men would have killed a carpenter or two for: "Couldn't you send me some such story as that colored one, for our Jan'y number—that is, within a month?" [44] On a hazy Saturday afternoon three weeks later, he was still depleted. "So I give it up." [45] But just a few hours later he excitedly reversed himself: "I shall not stop the letter I wrote 2 hours ago, because it has the suggestion about the play—but I take back the remark that I can't write for the Jan. number." [46]

Inspiration struck during a walk through the fallen leaves in the woods with Joe Twichell.

I got to telling him about old Mississippi days of steamboating glory & grandeur as I saw them . . . *from the pilot house.* He said "What a virgin subject to hurl into a magazine!" I hadn't thought of that before. Would you like a series of papers to run through 3 months or 6 or 9?—or about 4 months, say?[47]

Howells saw the magnitude in the idea at once. Soon Mark Twain had an agreement with the *Atlantic* to submit a series of essays, at the premium rate of twenty dollars the printed page. His boyhood self and chums would have to cool their heels a while longer before their novel could be finished. The Mississippi "river book" that he had begun imagining nearly a decade earlier on the landlocked slopes of Nevada now welled up in him, and suddenly he was writing again. On November 20, he mailed Howells the first of seven essays for the *Atlantic* under the heading, "Old Times on the Mississippi." He proposed an every-other-month schedule, but Howells would have none of that. "The piece about the Mississippi is capital," he notified Clemens, "—it almost made the water in our ice-pitcher muddy as it read it . . . I want the sketches, if you can make them, **every** *month.*"[48] His enthusiasm galvanized Sam. Thirteen days later he had completed three installments. His cover letter reflected his mounting ecstasy. Piloting! That was the perspective from which he, alone among all writers, could evoke the river.

I have spoken of nothing but of piloting *as a science* so far; & I doubt if I ever get beyond that portion of my subject. And I don't care to. Any muggins can write about Old Times on the Miss of 500 different kinds, but I am the only man alive that can scribble about the *piloting* of that day—& no man has ever tried to scribble about it yet. Its *newness* pleases me all the time—& it is about the only new subject I know of.[49]

Thus began Mark Twain's symbolic return, as his thirty-ninth birthday approached, to the river that he had never wanted to leave. The reencounter with this part of his past transformed him. He hardly stopped writing for the ensuing decade, the most prolific and profitable of his life, although his social and ceremonial calendar was unsparing and his travels took him back to England, and a good part of Western Europe, and back to the corporeal river itself, and, briefly, to his hometown again. The river figured in the three greatest of the seven books he published through the beginning of 1885, along with another play and many of his strongest sketches and tales.

SAMUEL CLEMENS capered and backslapped his way through the last months of 1874 like a boy on the last day of school. On a bright frigid Thursday morning two weeks before Thanksgiving, he and his muscular-Christian chum Joe Twichell left Hartford and headed northeast on foot, intending to walk the hundred miles to Boston. Twichell was carrying a small bag of something; Sam had a basket of lunch, and a pocket filled with envelopes Livy had addressed to herself and given him so he could write along the way. "Our jaws have wagged ceaselessly, & every now & then our laughter does wake up the old woods," he reported from Vernon, eleven miles out.[50] They made it to Ashford, Connecticut, twenty-eight miles, an hour after dark, with Sam's knee joints aching enough to give him "the lockjaw,"[51] he said; they found a hotel run by a man who answered every conversational gambit of Twichell's with a stream of unself-conscious profanity; Sam thought it was the funniest scene he'd ever seen. The next morning, with Sam sleepless and limping, the pair managed seven subzero miles to North Ashford, where they said the hell with it and hitched a ride for the nearest railroad line to Boston. Sam telegraphed the trusty Howells that they would be in town around 7; Howells fired back orders for them to report to his Cambridge house "near observatory Party waiting for you."[52] They arrived at 9, and partied hearty with Nathaniel Hawthorne's daughter Rose, one of Longfellow's daughters, and the philosopher John Fiske, among others. Howells described Sam's behavior in much the same way a younger Sam had described the Unreliable: "I never saw a more used-up, hungrier man, than Clemens. It was something fearful to see him eat escalloped oysters."[53]

Back in Hartford, Clemens informed Howells that "Mrs. Clemens gets upon the verge of swearing & goes tearing around in an unseemly fury when I enlarge upon the delightful time we had . . . & she not there to have her share."[54] This was part of an ongoing joke the two men had worked out—the notion that their mild wives were hell-raising harridans.

In a Boston store window, Sam had spotted the new contraption called a "type-machine." He went inside, watched the salesman's "type-girl" demonstrate that she could bang out fifty-seven words a minute, and bought one for $125. Back in Hartford, he practiced typing "The boy stood on the burning deck" until he could make twelve words a minute (all in caps and with a carriage return that worked via a foot pedal), and sent typewritten letters to relatives and friends, most of them on the topic of sending typewritten letters. Howells was so intrigued that he wanted to play with it, too: "when you get tired of the machine, lend it to me," he coaxed Clemens.[55]

Late in life Clemens claimed that he was "the first person in the world to apply the type-machine to literature."[56] He thought he'd written part of *Tom Sawyer* with it, but he misremembered: an assistant typed out his handwritten manuscript of *Life on the Mississippi*. It was likely the first book ever typed before being sent to the printer.

The capstone to his year was a dinner at the Parker House in Boston on the evening of December 15, an event "to be ranked with the most noteworthy gathering of the kind that the Athens of America has seen," panted the Boston *Globe*.[57] The dinner was to celebrate the *Atlantic*'s first year under its new owners, a group that included Henry O. Houghton and George H. Mifflin. "Don't you dare to refuse that invitation," Howells had scolded him a few days earlier.[58] The tables were landscaped with sideburns and mustaches: authors, editors, leading clergymen, academic dons, Oliver Wendell Holmes, architects, Houghton, Mifflin, a former Confederate soldier who was now a memoirist featured in the magazine. Mark Twain spoke—twice—shook hands with everybody, then hosted an all-nighter in his room, along with Howells and Aldrich. He went home feeling good, wrote a third installment of "Old Times on the Mississippi," and launched a practical joke at Aldrich, who had requested a photograph: Clemens sent him one every day for the last week of the year, crowning it on New Year's Eve with an avalanche of forty-five envelopes, "containing an aggregate of near seventy differing pictures of myself, house & family. It loaded the postman down."[59] Included in this mélange was a reasonably good self-portrait sketched in thick strokes of black ink. These were the sorts of things a fellow from the wilds of Missouri could get away with once he'd become the representative voice of America.

But no voice remains representative forever. Seated not far from Mark Twain and Howells at the *Atlantic* dinner was the same suave young writer who four years earlier had canceled an appointment so he could meet Bret Harte at the Howells household in Cambridge. Mark Twain almost certainly shook hands with him, but there was no particular reason for him to have marked the moment. Henry James was still largely unknown at thirty. His first novel, the mildly shocking *Watch and Ward,* had appeared just three years earlier, and more or less disappeared again. *Roderick Hudson* was finished but unpublished, and James's own chronicle of an innocent abroad, *Daisy Miller,* which would establish his international reputation, lay three years in the future. In time, Mark Twain would learn very well who Henry James was: the complementary "other half" of the American literary sensibility.

The younger writer's life comprised a striking antithesis of Mark Twain: he was urban-born (New York) into a wealthy and intellectually powerful family. His father, Henry Sr., was an eccentric heir to a family fortune (after he sued his own father's estate) who drank, gambled, and then became a prominent religious philosopher, European habitué, member of the storied Metaphysical Club, and an edgy friend of Emerson. His older brother, William, was the polar opposite of Orion: a graduate of Harvard Medical School, a visionary psychologist, and the philosophical father of pragmatism. Henry's own life filled the blanks in Sam Clemens's: as a boy in his father's orbit, he was tutored in Geneva, London, Paris, Bologna, and Bonn, and absorbed the classics of international literature. He briefly attended Harvard Law School before settling into a life of letters.

IN THE span of his twenty novels, James pulled American literature in as different a direction from Mark Twain as Mark Twain had pulled it from the pietistic Concord masters. Mark Twain democratized the national voice by availing it of vernacular; rough action that sprawled over waterway and open terrain; comedy, political consciousness, and skepticism toward the very idea of lofty instruction. James, a skeptic of a different sort, introduced techniques and concerns unavailable to an uneducated prodigy such as Mark Twain. His novels were rooted in the urbane subsocieties of Eastern America and of American expatriates in Europe; they viewed human character indoors, as it were, and through the emerging prisms of symbolism and psychological nuance, and they explored the drastic post–Civil War reversals of Christian optimism. Henry James imposed new obligations on the reader, as Howells himself perceived—not least among them a reexamination of one's very motive for reading fiction. "We must take him on his own ground," Howells wrote, "for clearly he will not come to ours . . . [and] find, when we can, a name for this new kind in fiction. Evidently it is the character, not the fate, of his people which occupies him; when he has fully developed their character he leaves them to what destiny the reader pleases . . . It is, after all, what a writer has to say rather than what he has to tell that we care for nowadays."[60]

Mark Twain's own assessment was somewhat less varnished. "I would rather be damned to John Bunyan's heaven," he famously told Howells, than read *The Bostonians*.[61]

Henry James's challenge to Mark Twain at least had the virtue of an aesthetic idea. The seeds of another, blinder, far more destructive menace to his supremacy were sewn within a few days of the *Atlantic* dinner, when an obscure Rochester machinist named James W. Paige was granted a patent for an invention in progress of his, a new kind of typesetting machine.

31

The Man in the Moon

(1875)

As "Old Times on the Mississippi" began running in the *Atlantic* in January 1875, a wave of racial violence swept through the South. Reconstruction was falling apart under a reactionary onslaught against the masses of former Negro slaves who had acquired full citizenship and voting power through the Fourteenth and Fifteenth Amendments. The depredations of 1875 differed only in degree from previous years: Negroes in the old Confederacy had been beaten, burned out of their houses, and lynched since the close of the Civil War. But white paranoia increased as the gulf between "African" and "American" narrowed, and as it dawned on the defeated Southern nation that its ex-slaves formed a majority in the population. As Negroes ascended to the U.S. Senate and House of Representatives, white vengeance coalesced under the robes of the Ku Klux Klan. President Grant sent federal troops to occupy vast regions of the South, and blood-resentment and terror turned the region into a midnight of the spirit. A different set of discontents prevailed north of the Mason-Dixon Line, where new machines, mushrooming cities, proliferating railroads, and astounding new forms of communication were transforming daily life. The mid-1870s witnessed a second industrial revolution, propelled by the chilly acquisitive genius of the new capitalists John D. Rockefeller, Andrew Carnegie, Cornelius Vanderbilt, and others.

With hyper-mechanization, hyper-capitalism, and hyper-urbanization came hyper-anxieties. Alcoholism increased, and divorce, and suicides. Even the Virginia City fathers found it necessary to enact anti-opium laws. The new science of neurology identified a new malady, "American nervousness," and linked it to the accelerating national race for power, money, and status. Sources of "American nervousness" were postulated: the press, steam power, the telegraph, the sciences, and—in particular—"the increased mental activity of women."[1] Perhaps not coincidentally, many male American go-getters began to look upon the affliction as a badge of honor, a kind of masculine war wound. Here in force was the Gilded Age.

Art and literature would soon catch up with these upheavals, thanks in no small part to Howells, whose criticisms continued to legitimize social realism and devalue the "polite" novel. At the same time, the disruptions awakened a more visceral appetite among Americans: for nostalgia and sentimentality, as sanctuary from the violent energies of the nation. Gilded Age longed for Golden Age, and the lost Edenic innocence of the child. These nostalgic yearnings formed the context for the warm reception that awaited Mark Twain's evocations of his antebellum river dreams in the *Atlantic*, and the boy's book that was soon to follow.

No one was as transported by "Old Times on the Mississippi" as the author himself, except possibly Howells, whose own childhood had been privileged yet constricted, and dogged by bullies. The process of writing the series catapulted Sam back into the "river book" idea that had called to him for so many years; he was mentally organizing a grand expedition down the river almost before the leaves were off his boots from that walk in the woods with Twichell. Like his boyhood self in Hannibal spinning adventures out of dreams, the grown man envisioned leading a coterie of comrades on the quest. "I have a notion of going west about May 1, to make a lagging journey down the Mississippi," he told Redpath, "dining pilots & pumping stuff out of them for a book . . . Would like you to do the trip both *for* me & *with* me . . . & talk, & lie, & have a good time."[2] Then he began pestering Howells, who had more or less asked for it. At the *Atlantic* dinner, the portly little editor had blurted to Clemens that the two should travel downriver to New Orleans in the spring with their wives. Clemens pounced on the idea like a bulldog on a flung stick. "We'll leave for N.O., Feb. 15," he declared.[3]

Who would have made a more ideal sidekick for Mark Twain? With his stewardship of "Old Times on the Mississippi," Howells had begun the gorgeous tapestry that would interweave his informed sensibilities with Twain's raw gifts, to the enrichment of the nation and the deep soul-comfort of the two men. Howells understood that Mark Twain's incantatory river reverie spoke to the American ache for its lost arcadian universe, while at the same time offering an unparalleled example of the emerging American realism. He guided the author through the series's conceptual stages. "[S]tick to actual fact and character in the thing, and give all things in **detail**," he encouraged his writer as Mark Twain prepared the second installment. "**All** that belongs to the old river life is novel and is now mostly historical. Don't write *at* any supposed Atlantic audience, but yarn it off as if into my sympathetic ear."[4] A few weeks later: "This number is extraordinarily good. I've just been reading it to my wife, who's delighted with it." [5] By May, when Mark Twain turned in his seventh and last installment, Howells was still cheerleading: "This is capital—I shall hate to have you stop!" [6]

Howells could get starchy on one issue: profanity. He let exactly one "hell" get through in the first installment, then clamped down. Here, of course, he had plenty of backup—his wife Elinor, Olivia Clemens, and just about everybody else in New England, with Mother Fairbanks standing by in Cleveland as a final reinforcement. "I've just been reading [the second installment] to Mrs. Howells . . . and she has enjoyed it every word—but the profane words," Howells wrote to Mark Twain with surpassing tact. "These she thinks could be better taken for granted; and in fact I think the sagacious reader could infer them." [7] This particular query got Sam in hot water with Livy, who had opened the letter. "She lit into the study with danger in her eye & this demand on her tongue," Mark Twain mock-wailed to his editor: " 'Where is this profanity Mr. Howells speaks of?' " [8] Whatever it was, it did not survive. "I have noticed that a little judicious profanity helps out an otherwise ineffectual sketch or poem remarkably," the former Wild Humorist of the Pacific Slope joked to Howells, [9] but, typically, he made no real resistance.

Mark Twain depended on Howells. "Cut it, scarify it, reject it—handle it with entire freedom," he'd invited in the cover letter to the first installment. [10] He proved as deferential as his word: "Your amendment was good. As soon as I saw the watchman in print I perceived that he was lame & artificial. I . . . couldn't get Mrs. Clemens to approve of him at all." [11] In a note with installment No. 2, he was positively giddy: "Say—I am as prompt as a clock, if I only know the *day* a thing is wanted—otherwise I am a natural procrastinaturalist. Tell me what day & date you want Nos. 3 & 4, & I will tackle & revise them & they'll be there to the minute." [12]

Howells cared about "Old Times" for several reasons. He hoped the series would rescue the *Atlantic*'s drooping sales figures. The quasi-official organ of Brahmin discourse was in trouble. Circulation, after a climb to 50,000 copies a month by 1869, had started to plummet: to 35,000 in 1870, then to fewer than 21,000 in 1874, and falling. Smart new illustrated numbers out of New York, such as *Harper's* and *Scribner's*, each selling around 100,000 copies a month, were modernizing the magazine world. The *Atlantic*'s new publisher, the self-made go-getter from Vermont, Henry Oscar Houghton, had begun to mutter about new writers, new topics—and new advertising. (Howells later made his proto-Babbitt Silas Lapham a self-made go-getter from Vermont. Coincidence? Maybe.) Howells, shocked and anxious, saw Mark Twain as a heaven-sent solution: a writer at once popular among the proletarians, and profound.

Mark Twain's renown had reached a pinnacle matched by no other popular culture figure until Will Rogers half a century later. An index of it was the letter he received from Phineas Taylor Barnum, whom Mark Twain had met at the Horace Greeley dinner in 1872. P. T. Barnum had not yet merged with

James A. Bailey to form the mega-circus known as "The Greatest Show on Earth," but already his Hippodrome was the crowning extravagance in an age of extravagant public amusements: magic shows, puppet shows, Wild West shows, "moving panoramas" that unwound from one spool onto another, wax museums, professional baseball games. A hundred twenty-five railroad cars moved his great show around the country: two 800-by-400-foot tents; 1,200 employees; 750 horses; assorted camels, elephants, ostriches, and other beasts; wardrobes totaling $70,000 in value; two concert bands. His many "scenes" included an Indian camp in which scores of braves, squaws and papooses sat in wigwams, danced war dances, hunted real buffalo, raced their ponies, and then were "surprised" by attacking Mexicans, which ignited "such a scene of savage strife and warfare as is never seen except upon our wild western borders." [13] This is not even to mention the elephant races, ostrich races, monkey races, and the other attractions that required a capitalization of nearly a million dollars. As if his day job were not fulfilling enough, Barnum was running for mayor of Bridgeport, Connecticut; he would win the election in April.

Barnum wrote to Mark Twain asking for a little boost, publicitywise. A plug in one of his pieces. "Such an article in Harpers Weekly would be immense . . ." [14] He enclosed some free passes. Mark Twain cordially turned him down.

H E A L S O rejected a highly prestigious invitation from Hurd & Houghton: to contribute the first work in a series of books aimed at elevating the status of American writers to match that of the Europeans. Mark Twain didn't see enough money in it. He may have had status anxiety, but he was no fool.

The Mark Twain magic was not powerful enough to erase Howells's circulation woes. It may have added to them: as soon as each new "Old Times" installment appeared, newspapers around the country reprinted it for their own, far larger readerships, taking advantage of lax copyright laws and enforcement: "the sales of the *Atlantic Monthly* were not advanced one single copy, so far as we could make out," Howells ruefully recalled. [15] Clemens, predictably, was more than rueful. This was but one of several brush fires that were driving him crazy: unauthorized use of his sketches and excerpts from books proliferated in America and England, and he sued or fired off threatening letters with each new discovery. "[I give] you fair warning that if a single line of mine appears in one of your books I will assuredly stop that book with an injunction," he wrote to one aspiring scavenger, who scavenged him anyway. [16] He had a U.S. marshal halt a pirated performance of *The Gilded Age* in Salt Lake City.

M A R K T W A I N ' S Mississippi River reminiscences worked on Howells in a way scarcely expressible in business or editorial terms. They reawakened his own memories of boyhood—or rather, his memories of what that boyhood should have been like, if only somebody like Sammy could have been around to help him live it. At thirty-eight, Howells gave the impression that he'd been born with his droopy mustache and a stiff collar.* Already a fortress of American letters, he was first and foremost a *responsible* man: responsible husband and father, responsible critic, responsible editor, and responsible reader: he elevated the careers of Henry James, Emile Zola, Flaubert, Guy de Maupassant, Frank Norris, Benito Perez Galdos, Sarah Orne Jewett, Edith Wharton, Dostoyevsky, Tolstoy, and Turgenev, besides Mark Twain. Even the hundred-odd volumes he completed, including more than fifty novels, bore the stamp of self-imposed obligation. He assigned himself and his contemporaries the task of discovering the American soul, as it was revealed not through tales of adventure and romance, but within the details of the ordinary life, parsed for its psychological revelations. Two misfortunes debilitated this project: Henry James did it better; and Howells crippled his own legacy with one colossally badly chosen phrase: American writers, he declared in the 1890s, should concern themselves with "the smiling aspects of life." He meant to promote a contrast to the death-obsessed Russian novelists, but his detractors seized on the remark as revealing a fatally insipid sensibility. Instead of the lasting honor he deserved for steering the post–Civil War revitalization of American letters, he was saddled with the legacy of America's pioneering suburban sage.

Like Sammy, Howells was a product of small-town life in the interior: he was born in Martinsville (later Martins Ferry), across the Ohio River from West Virginia, and spent his boyhood in Hamilton, north of Cincinnati. Like Sammy, he was enthralled with steamboating as a lad. Like Sam, Howells married a brainy but physically frail woman who became an invalid. Like Sam, he lost a beloved daughter. Unlike Sam, Howells had a fairly lousy boyhood. He did not "emerge" from it as much as escape from it, by the skin of his teeth, with a bloody nose and rocks whizzing around his head, his eyes smarting from a cloud of pencil shavings blown into them.

Now Howells found himself with the chance to tag along with the author of the greatest boyhood ever lived; to play hooky from his life and escape on a steamboat down to New Orleans with the Black Avenger of the Spanish Main. Sadly for Howells, responsibility intruded, and the dream remained only a dream. He quickly felt the gravitational tug of Planet Elinor, and began a long glum struggle to extricate himself from his proposal. "I don't give it up yet, and don't *you*," he advised Sam a couple of days after the invitation,[17] but he may already have resigned himself. He begged off the trip in mid-January, pleading a prior promise to take Elinor on a visit to Bethlehem, Pennsylvania. "I must be a man for once in my life, and say No, when I'd inexpressibly rather say Yes."[18] "We *mustn't* give up the New Orleans trip," Sam wheedled. "Mrs.

---

* One surviving photo of him as a youth gives the lie to this impression. He is eighteen, clean-shaven, his dark hair cut at page-boy length on the sides and combed into a pompadour on top. Head tilted, gazing into the camera with smoldering eyes, he looks like nothing so much as a pop star from the 1970s.

Clemens would gladly go if her strength would permit, but can't Mrs. Howells go anyway? I think she would find it very pleasant. I *know* she would . . . You just persuade her." [19] He kept at it: "Mind you try *hard,* on the 15th, to say you will go to New Orleans. If Mrs. Howells will consent to go, too, I will make a pleasant young lady neighbor of ours go also, so she can have respectable as well as talented company." [20]

Sam continued foraging for other recruits in case this persuasion failed. "[Howells] is not sure, now, whether he can go or not," he wrote to Osgood, stretching the truth, "but I wish you would go. Think of the gaudy times you & Howells & I would have on such a bender!" [21] Osgood, no sprite himself, begged off. The business part of this letter contained bad news for Sam's old friend. Clemens had led Osgood to hope that he could acquire the newest Mark Twain manuscript, a collection of eighty-one periodical sketches dating to 1863. But Elisha Bliss produced a four-year-old contract guaranteeing his company the rights to such a work. Clemens agreed that the contract was binding, and *Mark Twain's Sketches, New and Old* went into production at the American Publishing Company for publication in July.

Osgood would have his turn.

SAM'S BLIZZARD of personal correspondence scarcely ever abated regardless of his growing authorial obligations. (He once even began a letter, "My Dear Clemens," but that was a mistake.) Letters fascinated him; he seemed to regard them almost as living things, wisps of human character caught on paper. Learning of the "queer letters" that poured in to Barnum, he begged the showman to send him examples, and devoured them on their arrival, and begged for more. Barnum obliged.

> It is an admirable lot of letters. Headless mice, four-legged hens, human-handed sacred bulls, "professional" Gypsies . . . deformed human beings anxious to trade on their horrors, school-teachers who can't spell,—it is a perfect feast of queer literature! Again I beseech you, don't burn a single specimen, but remember that all are wanted & possess value in the eyes of your friend
>
> Saml. L. Clemens [22]

No one knows how many letters he wrote beyond the twelve thousand accounted for at the Mark Twain Project. Many valuable ones have been lost, such as hundreds to Jane that Mark Twain ordered burned in 1904. The letters reveal every shade of emotion. Few of them open a wider window on his antic side than the ones addressed to Howells. Grinding through revisions of *Tom Sawyer* in the upstairs billiard room, Mark Twain in January could find time to riff on a photograph that William and Elinor had sent to him, of themselves.

I can perceive . . . that Mr Howells is feeling as I so often feel, viz: "Well no doubt I *am* in the wrong, though I do not know where or how or why—but anyway it will be safest to look meek, & walk circumspectly for a while, & not *discuss* the thing."

Then Sam aimed a teasing barb at Elinor herself—and in doing so offered a pitch-perfect send-up of Livy's diction.

And you look exactly as Mrs. Clemens does just after she has said, "Indeed, I do not *wonder* that you can frame no reply: for you know only too well that your conduct admits of no excuse, palliation or argument—*none!*"[23]

Clemens soon gave up on his Mississippi fantasy, but only for a few months— or so he hoped. "I've put off the Miss River trip till June, & shall write a new book meantime," he notified Bliss.[24] The "new book" being more than half-written by now, Mark Twain seemed to be gearing up for another of his patented sprints to the final page. The sprint lasted into summer, interrupted by social and family distractions, one of which involved a familiar relative and a familiar issue. "Hoping that the Tennessee Land is now in hell, please pay the enclosed bill," he directed Orion along with a payment for services to the latest agent hired (futilely) to dump the property.[25] A couple of weeks later, he deflected a new land-investment scheme from Orion—purchase of the Stotts family's Keokuk farm—with an explanation that revealed the ongoing drain of the new Nook Farm house: "We are under too heavy an expense to be venturing upon outlays that amount to much . . . We look for the bills, tomorrow, for the furniture of a guest room, our bedroom, the study, & odds & ends in the other rooms. These cannot fall short of $5000; & we are purposing to pay off the $16000 which we still owe on our ground, & thus free ourselves of debt."[26]

Visitors in fact formed a constant stream in and out of the Clemens household, as they would through all the Nook Farm years, from family and friends to P. T. Barnum, minus his circus. Dinner guests usually ended up agog at the improvisational theater Clemens liked to create: he would arise from the table and go pacing about the room, waving a handkerchief and discharging torrents of talk; or he would attack the piano and pound out jubilees, or croon spirituals and the songs of riverboatmen to himself in a far corner as if oblivious of the company; or he would pull on some worn cowskin slippers and hobble around in his "crippled colored uncle" breakdown; or work the edges in some other way that would finally get Livy to cry, "Oh, *Youth!*"

Despite the household hubbub, Mark Twain tore along on the book, filling the billiard room with a blue haze of cigar smoke as he scribbled. "I wrote 4000 words yesterday," he boasted to Howells on March 16.[27] A month later, he reported to Mary Fairbanks that "[w]e have determined to try to sweat it out, here in Hartford, this summer, & not go away at all. That is Livy's idea, not mine; for I can write ten chapters in Elmira where I can write one here. I work *at* work here, but I don't accomplish anything worth speaking of." He added, "I mean to try to go down the Mississippi river in May or June . . ."[28] Yet Sam was already absorbed in a new dream adventure. Another figure from his Virginia City past had reemerged, via a letter: William Wright, the "Dan De Quille" of *Territorial Enterprise* renown. Now Sam was trying to conjure De Quille across the continent and into his present life, as he had conjured Joe Goodman four years earlier.

Life had not been easy for De Quille, who had never quite recovered from the shock of returning to the newspaper from his 1862 vacation in the East to discover that a "Mark Twain" had claimed his pride of place as the writing star of the territory. By the time the Wild Humorist left the Pacific Slope in 1866, the erstwhile literary man was a serious drunk, a barroom fistfighter, a patron of whorehouses, and a hack. Joe Goodman tolerated him until 1869, and then fired him; then rehired him; and for several years, De Quille wavered between a literary comeback and delerium tremens. He pulled himself together at the beginning of 1873 to produce for Goodman a series of pointillist sketches about life in the mines, and began gathering material for a planned "work of merit": a history of the Comstock Lode. This was the project that led De Quille to seek his old adversary's advice in the early spring of 1875. Should he offer the Comstock manuscript as a "pamphlet" to a San Francisco publisher? Or was there any chance that Sam could help him find a better house back east?

"Meddle with no Western publisher," Sam commanded by telegram the day he received De Quille's letter, March 29. "Make bargains of no kind until you get my letters."[29] Then, in a long missive begun later that day and finished nearly a week later, Sam whisked De Quille into one of his favorite realms, the paranormal. He'd *known in advance* the contents of De Quille's incoming letter before even breaking the seal. Why? Because less than five days earlier, *he had written to De Quille suggesting that he write this very book!* "My *mind* suggested it to *his* mind," he'd told Livy.[30] The explanation? *Mesmeric currents.* Having checked the postmarks, Clemens realized he had the direction of influence reversed.

So it was *your* mesmeric current that had flowed across the mountains & deserts three thousand miles & acted upon *me,* instead of mine flowing westward & acting upon *you.* So *you* were the originator of the idea.[31]

These currents had established three things, Sam went on. Namely:

1st Mesmeric sympathies can flash themselves 3000 miles within the space of 12 hours—possibly *instantly* . . .

2d They come clear through, & don't have to be repeated at way stations between, like land telegraphy.

3d They travel from west to east, not from east to west.

However, this point on No. 3 is not well taken, because there isn't any *proof* that they don't travel westwardly upon occasion.[32]

One can fairly imagine Dan De Quille reaching for a good stiff jolt of something as he tried to absorb all this. He'd just wanted a little advice on a book. But Sam wanted metaphysics, and, by the way, had taken it upon himself to run De Quille's business and literary interests, whether De Quille liked it or not. "I want you, about August, to canvas Virginia & Gold Hill *yourself,*"[33] he instructed—"canvas," as in "sign up miners to buy this book that I'm going to teach you how to write." "Reserve *other* Nevada camps for yourself, too—that is, be *General Agent* for the whole State, & sublet to canvassers at 40 per cent off . . ."[34] After several thoughts about retail pricing, Sam shifted to the literary agenda. Dan De Quille was about to become one of the few men ever to experience a writing lesson from Mark Twain.

Dan, there are more ways than one of writing a book; & your way is *not* the right one. You see, the winning card is to nail a man's interest with *Chapter 1,* & never let up on him for an instant . . . That can't be done with detached sketches; but I'll show you how to make a man read every one of those sketches, under the stupid impression that they are mere accidental incidents that have dropped in on you unawares in the course of your *narrative* . . . It isn't any more trouble to write that book than it is to report an inquest.[35]

Oh, and one more thing. *"Drop your reporting & come here, right away.* Whatever money you need, get it off Joe, or telegraph me. *Come right along at once."*[36] It seemed as though Sam were speaking through Colonel Sellers.

Here you shall stop at the best hotel, & every morning I will walk down . . . bring you to my house & we will grind literature all day long in the same room; then I'll escort you half way home again. Sundays we will smoke & lie. When you need money you will know where to get it . . . there's a most noble divan in my study to stretch your bones on when you get tired. Besides, when it comes to building a book I can show you a trick or two which I don't teach to everybody, I can tell you![37]

And in a culminating brainstorm that assumed, boylike, that any passing impulse could be turned into reality: "Bring Joe along with you."[38]

With that off his chest, Sam got back to his own manuscript.

After all the months away from *Tom Sawyer,* returning to it had the effect of mounting a still-unbroken horse. In which direction would it gallop off? Manhood or boyhood? In July, Howells advised him toward the former choice. "I really feel very much interested in your making that your chief work," he urged Mark Twain; "you wont have such another chance; don't waste it on a **boy,** and don't hurry the writing for the sake of making a book."[39] Mark Twain, though, had reached a contrary decision. He would not send Tom out into the world for a Battle of Life in Many Lands. He would conclude the tale while his hero was still an un-driveling boy. Whether this would make *Tom Sawyer* a "boy's book," like Aldrich's had been, or a book for grown-ups—that issue remained murky. Nor did his choice of direction guarantee that the novel was under control. Scholarly analyses of his writing process show that through the rest of the story's construction, Mark Twain continued to struggle with organizing the plotline, shuffling and reshuffling episodes, even revisiting the first half of the manuscript to foreshadow certain plot twists that had come to him. He breezed past any further crippling plot dilemmas. The incidents and voices flowed again: Tom returns to the island, the three friends slip back into town to observe their own funerals from the church gallery and then march down to revel in the villagers' joy that they are still alive; Tom and Becky resume their rocky romance; Tom has his famous stint with the Cadets of Temperance; the boys slip matches and tobacco to the jailed Muff Potter, accused of Dr. Robinson's murder (a faint but unmistakable echo of Sammy's role in the jailhouse burning of the drunken tramp); Tom heroically fingers Injun Joe at Potter's trial; Tom and Huck discover the villain's buried treasure; the great children's picnic scene plays itself out, ending with Tom and Becky lost in the cave where Injun Joe is hiding out; Tom leads Becky to freedom and the townsmen seal the cave with Joe inside; Tom produces the treasure's gold coins, which the grown-ups invest for him and Huck; and the novel ends with Huck warily facing "sivilization" at the Widow Douglas's hands, but still plotting one more midnight rendezvous with Tom.

WHILE CLEMENS smoked and scribbled in his billiard room–study, working toward a November delivery date, Livy worked at holding the vast Nook Farm premises together. This included the challenge of overseeing the revolving and ever-bumptious household staff. That staff now included nurses for both Susy and the baby Clara; a cook, and a coachman. Among the most vivid figures was Mara McLaughlin, the last of the five wet nurses who augmented Livy's thin supply of milk in breast-feeding Clara. Judging from Mark Twain's unpublished late-life sketch, it was a wonder that Mara's nourishment didn't spur Clara to join a railroad crew in later life.

She stood six feet in her stockings . . . she had the martial port & stride of a grenadier . . . She was as independent as the flag . . . she had the appetite of a crocodile, the stomach of a cellar, & the digestion of a quartz-mill . . . she devoured anything & everything she could get her hands on, shoveling into her person fiendish combinations of fresh pork, lemon pie, boiled cabbage, ice cream, green apples, pickled tripe, raw turnips, & washing the whole cargo down with freshets of coffee, tea, brandy, whisky, turpentine, kerosene . . . she smoked pipes, cigars, cigarettes, she whooped like a Pawnee & swore like a demon; & then she would go upstairs loaded as described & perfectly delight the baby with a bouquet which ought to have killed it at thirty yards . . .[40]

In a later reminiscence, Mark Twain was kind enough to add that "[i]n the shortest month of the year she drank two hundred and fifty-eight pints of my beer, without invitation, leaving only forty-two for me. I think it was the dryest month I ever spent since I first became a theoretical teetotaler."[41]

The staffing situation stabilized considerably with the chance arrival, that spring, of a former slave and Union army aide, who remained as the Clemens butler for sixteen years. George Griffin "was an accident," Sam remembered. "He came to wash some windows, & remained half a generation."[42] Griffin was an intelligent and forceful man, politically opinionated but graced with a sense of diplomacy: he softened Clemens's tirades as he relayed the gist of his employer's opinions to others, and served as the peacemaker among the hired help. Clemens deeply admired the man, and probably transported some of his strength of character to the persona of Jim. It was Livy, the daughter of abolitionists, who showed less tolerance for such Griffin habits as speaking man-to-man with dinner guests and probing them about political issues. As Paine tells it, her disapproval of him led her to fire him once—only to find him standing at the breakfast-table the following morning.

"George," she said, "didn't I discharge you yesterday?"

"Yes, Mis' Clemens, but I knew you couldn't get along without me, so I thought I'd better stay awhile."[43]

IN MID-APRIL, Sam and Joe Twichell traveled to Brooklyn to attend a critical session of Henry Ward Beecher's adultery trial. Beecher's scheduled cross-examination by Theodore Tilton's attorney William Fullerton, a moment expected to produce shocking testimony, drew ten times as many spectators as the trial room could hold. A New York *Tribune* editor recognized Clemens, and escorted him and Twichell through the packed premises to the newspaper's reserved seats adjacent to the judge's desk. The *Tribune* reported the event, and even the rival *Sun* noted the great man's privileged access: "Mark Twain shambled in loose of coat and joints and got a seat near the plaintiff's table."[44]

It was Twichell, not Mark Twain, who captured the high pitch of drama in the day's proceedings. In his journal, the clergyman wrote:

The excitement was such as to be painful. It was very trying to me to see Mr. B. subject to such questioning. He appeared well—innocent—unafraid—at ease . . . He was a little as though speaking to an audience.

I was immensely drawn out to him, and wished for his sake that I was a better man—good enough to sit there and pray for him . . .

At the close of the p.m. session when the Court adjourned I saw Mr Beecher shake hands with . . . the opposing counsel, and (being very near) heard him say to him, "Sometime I'll tell you all about it," or that substantially . . .[45]

•   •   •

Dan De Quille, gaunt beneath his trademark wispy goatee, materialized in Hartford on May 27, luggage in hand, as he had been instructed. (He traveled by train rather than mesmeric current, and couldn't quite manage to deliver Joe Goodman.) He took a room at the Union Hall Hotel on Farmington Avenue, and, just as Goodman had done in 1871 at Quarry Farm, spent his days ensconced with Sam, writing. The two old friends shared a makeshift study in the loft over the Clemens's stable, where they could work and smoke in seclusion. "[H]is stable is as fine as most houses," the guest marveled to his sister.[46] A day or so after De Quille arrived, Clemens took him and the writer Joaquin Miller, who'd stopped over after a visit to Europe, to Elisha Bliss's offices. It was probably on this visit that De Quille and Bliss reached a publishing agreement for the book that became famous as *The Big Bonanza.*

DE QUILLE'S presence apparently didn't distract Mark Twain from his sprint to the finish line with *Tom Sawyer.* Neither did Livy's illness; she lay abed through the last week of June. Sam did find time to look after her nutritional needs, in his way. "I have taught Livy at last to drink a bottle of beer every night," he reported to his abstinence-minded sister, "& all in good time I shall teach the children to do the same. If it is wrong, then, (as the Arabs say,) 'On my head be it!' "[47]

Howells received portentous news in a letter dated July 5.

I have finished the story & didn't take the chap beyond boyhood. I believe it would be fatal to do it in any shape but autobiographically—like Gil Blas. I perhaps made a mistake in not writing it in the first person. If I went on, now, & took him into manhood, he would just be like all the one-horse men in literature & the reader would conceive a hearty contempt for him. It is *not* a boy's book, at all. It will only be read by adults. It is only written for adults.[48]

Mark Twain's slightly overwrought insistence on this point possibly arose from the "postpartum" malaise that many authors report on completion of a work. It likely also reflected a shift in his thinking from art to business. He would like to see it serialized in the *Atlantic,* he allowed to Howells—who had been angling hard for just that—"but I doubt if it would pay the publishers to buy the privilege, or me to sell it." This was all about competition with Bret Harte, who had just finished *Gabriel Conroy* and sold serial rights to *Scribner's Monthly* for $6,500—Sam had the figure right at the tip of his fingers.* Clemens doubted he could pull down the same serial fee from the *Atlantic.* By implication, if he couldn't outsell Harte, he would not be humiliated by accepting a lesser fee.

Then, having dashed his friend's acquisition hopes, Sam hit Howells up for a favor. It involved that confounded nagging aesthetic part.

* *Gabriel Conroy* in fact was destined to be a disastrous flop in hardcover sales.

I wish you would promise to read the MS of Tom Sawyer some time, & see if you don't really decide that I am right in closing with him as a boy—& point out the most glaring defects for me. It is a tremendous favor to ask . . . But the thing has been so many months in my mind that it seems a relief to snake it out. I don't know any other person whose judgment I could venture to take fully & entirely.[49]

Just before this request to Howells, Clemens had alluded almost absentmindedly to an idea he'd been mulling for a new boy's book.

By & by I shall take a boy of twelve & run him on through life (in the first person) but not Tom Sawyer—he would not be a good character for it.[50]

Mark Twain continued to revise *The Adventures of Tom Sawyer* through the summer and fall. He found time to knock off a piece for the October *Atlantic*, apparently unironic and wisely unsigned, that modestly proposed a change in the suffrage laws. Titled "The Curious Republic of Gondour," the essay argued, in essence, that universal suffrage was fine—but why not allot bonus voting privileges on an escalating scale based on extent of education and property holding.

At the end of July, as *Mark Twain's Sketches, New and Old* was being published, Sam and his family fled the heat of Hartford for a vacation resort near Newport, Rhode Island. They invited De Quille along for a week. There they promenaded in white linens, heard a lecture by the great naturalist Alexander Agassiz, and took tea with the poet Julia Ward Howe. Sam went bowling by candlelight on a decrepit single alley on the premises, in rarefied company: Thomas Wentworth Higginson, the Unitarian minister, essayist, icon of abolitionists, and a youthful confidant of Emerson and Lowell and Holmes.

Back at Nook Farm, still bedeviled by his household expenses, Sam finally turned loose of the manuscript, shipping it off to Bliss on November 5, with a recommendation that True Williams be assigned the illustrations. Immediately, he began scheming for ways to wring more profit from it. Remembering that the stage version of *The Gilded Age* had been a cash cow, he shipped an "amanuensis" copy of the novel down to Howells in Boston, along with instructions for the *Atlantic* editor, who may or may not have had other obligations to burden him:

[D]ramatize it if you perceive that you can, & take . . . half of the first $6,000 which I receive for its representation on the stage. You could alter the plot entirely, if you chose . . . I have my eye upon two young girls who can play "Tom" & "Huck."* . . . Come—can't you tackle this in the odd hours of your vacation?—or later, if you prefer.[51]

* Casting girls in boys' roles to enhance the image of youthful freshness was a common convention of the 19th-century theater. Stage and screen versions of *Peter Pan* have featured women in the title role for a century—from Nina Boucicault in 1904 through Cathy Rigby in 1999.

Howells stood his ground on this one. It was a very pleasant proposal. "But I couldn't do it, and if I could, it wouldn't be a favor to dramatize your story."[52] Still, shipping Howells the amanuensis copy brought its rewards.

I finished reading Tom Sawyer a week ago, sitting up till one A.M., to get to the end, simply because it was impossible to leave off. It's altogether the best boy's story I ever read. It will be an immense success. But I think you ought to treat it explicitly *as* a boy's story.[53]

And then the great arbiter of American letters blurted his famous confession.

The adventures are enchanting. I wish *I* had been on that island. The treasure-hunting, the loss in the cave—it's all exciting and splendid.[54]

Howells did permit himself one critical thought. "I don't seem to think I liked the last chapter. I believe I would cut that."[55]

Mark Twain agreed on all counts. "Mrs. Clemens decides with you that the book should issue as a book for boys, pure & simple," he wrote back, "—& so do I. It is surely the correct idea."[56] He added: "Something told me that the book was done when I got to that point—& so the strong temptation to put Huck's life at the widow's into detail . . . was resisted."[57]

No copies of that "last chapter" have been recovered; Mark Twain replaced the "last" chapter with the familiar two-paragraph "Conclusion" ("So endeth this chronicle. It being strictly the history of a *boy*, it must stop here . . ."[58]) Some scholars have speculated that it contained the seeds of "Adventures of Huckleberry Finn." More carefully inductive analysis has concluded that Mark Twain had Chapter 35—the present ending—in mind when he spoke of the book being done, and not the omitted chapter. His decision to resist developing Huck's life had already been made. Thus the missing chapter is likely nothing more than further musing on why the narrative "must stop here."[59]

A couple of weeks after receiving Howells's praise for *Tom Sawyer,* Sam "afflicted" the editor with his newfangled toy, the typewriter, as he'd threatened to do for months, sending it by way of Frank Bliss. Howells's internationally respected intellect proved no match for the machine; he was practically devoured by it.

"Of course it doesn't work," he wailed to Clemens.

[I]f I can persuade some of the letters to get up against the ribbon they wont get down again without digital assistance. The treadle refuses to have any part or parcel in the performance; and *I* don't know how to get the roller to turn with the paper. Nevertheless, I have begun several letters to *My d ar lemans,* as it prefers to spell your respected name . . .[60]

. . .

SAMUEL CLEMENS had spent much of 1875, his fortieth year, absorbed in adult concerns. Yet in certain ways, this year had also restored him powerfully to his youthful past. He and Howells had begun to encounter each other as playful boys-in-mufti; and Livy indulged his dinner-table hijinx as the irrepressible "Youth." As the year ended, Sam, nearly disabled with dysentery, found in it some comic relief, as it were. *"Question:"* he scrawled to the Reverend Mr. Twichell, "If a Congress of Presbyterians is a PRESBY*tery,* what is a Congress of dissenters?"[61] This may have been the ancestor of Woody Allen's quip about *Dissent* and *Commentary* magazines. On November 27, her thirtieth birthday, Sam composed a prose poem for Livy that reinvoked the passion of his love letters of seven years earlier. "You are dearer to me today, my child, than you were upon the last anniversary of this birth-day," he wrote;

you were dearer then than you were a year before—you have grown more & more dear from the first of those anniversaries . . . Let us look forward to the coming anniversaries . . . trusting & believing that the love we bear each other will be sufficient to make them blessed.[62]

And then on Christmas morning, he outdid himself, with a fanciful letter to the elder daughter, not yet quite four, whom he already worshipped—a letter that almost unconsciously surrenders to its own childlike conceits as it progresses.

> Palace of St. Nicholas,
> In the Moon,
> Christmas Morning.

My Dear Susie Clemens:

I have received & read all the letters which you & your little sister have written me by the hand of your mother & your nurses; & I have also read those which you little people have written me with your own hands—for although you did not use any characters that are in grown people's alphabets, you used the character which all children, in all lands on earth & in the twinkling stars use . . . [Thus] I can read your & your baby sister's jagged & fantastic marks without any trouble at all.

He continued,

You will find that I made no mistakes about the things which you & the baby ordered . . . I went down your chimney at midnight when you were asleep, & delivered them all, myself—& kissed both of you . . .

He reported that in the case of a couple of orders, he had run out of stock:

Our last lot of kitchen furniture for dolls had just gone to a very poor little child in the North Star, away up in the cold country above the Big Dipper. Your mama can show you that star, & you will say, "Little Snow Flake (for that is the child's name,) I'm glad you got that furniture, for you need it more than I."

He confessed difficulty in deciphering "a word or two in your mama's letter," and promised to stop by the house at 9 a.m. Christmas morning to inquire about it.

But I must not see anybody, & I must not speak to anybody but you. When the kitchen door-bell rings, George must be blindfolded & sent to open the door . . . Then you must go to the nursery & stand on a chair or the nurse's bed, & put your ear to the speaking tube that leads down to the kitchen, & when I whistle through it, you must speak in the tube & say, "Welcome, Santa Claus!" [Then, when I leave] You must say, "Good bye, good old Santa Claus, & thank you very much—& please tell that little Snow Flake I will look at her star to-night & she must look down here . . ."

He added an instruction that hinted of the preoccupation many fathers feel in relation to their children.

If my boot should leave a stain on the marble, George must not holy-stone it away. Leave it there always in memory of my visit . . .

Your loving

Santa Claus,

Whom people sometimes call "The Man in the Moon." [63]

32

"It Befell Yt One Did Breake Wind . . ."

(1876)

America celebrated its Centennial in 1876—banners, polished brass, parades in all the cities and towns, the Eagle rampant, talons filled with thunderbolts—but Samuel Clemens seemed hardly to notice. The national boundaries had shrunk for this onetime wanderer, down to the precincts of New York and Boston and the parlors of Hartford. Clemens was a bill-paying burgher now, a society host, a celebrity. Happy as a husband and father, he seemed suspended between his successful past and an uncertain future. Could he sustain his rise, inconceivable a decade earlier, from obscurity to preeminence in America? Or would he realize the late-night fear he'd confessed to Stoddard?—lose the power of interesting an audience, become unable to write, die in the poorhouse?

A lot depended on the work now inching its way toward publication, this departure from sketch and chronicle into fiction, without the support of a partner. He braced for the final revisions of *Tom Sawyer* in January, motivated by the assumption that Elisha Bliss would have the book on the market right away. Still weakened with dysentery, he regarded the task as "dreary, & hateful."[1] He felt numbed to the novel that had been on his mind for five years. He had worked and reworked it until he could no longer judge its aesthetic worth; it was a property now, and he hungered to see it return some capital. Clemens should have known his publisher better. Bliss was not even close to a production run.

"I want you to take my new book to England," he instructed Moncure Conway, in early January, "& have it published there by some one . . . before it is issued here."[2] Conway, who had helped Sam guide Livy blindfolded to Shakespeare's gravesite two and a half years earlier, was Clemens's informal literary agent in England. A Southern cleric who had dared preach abolitionism before the Civil War, he had taken up residence in London, where he was pastor to a Unitarian church, and also a biographer, novelist, and pamphleteer. In January 1876 he had just finished a lecture tour in America and was about to return to his adopted country. He agreed to take with him the amanuensis copy of the manuscript, to which Clemens had transferred almost all of Howells's suggestions.

Clemens was cheered by the superb gallery of illustrations that arrived from True Williams. "Rattling good" pictures, he told Howells, "—some of them very dainty." He added, "Poor devil, what a genius he has & how he does murder it with rum."[3] Clemens hardly exaggerated. Working from the text and his imagination, the self-taught and self-destructive Williams contributed 159 drawings, from cartoonish thumbnails to the introductory full-page rendering of Tom that presented him in an almost pre-Raphaelite aura: wreathed in curls, with full lips and unfocused upcast eyes. The god-boy half-reclines against the trunk of a brookside tree, a wide-brimmed hat pushed back on his head, feet bare, ankles crossed, a fishing pole lightly depending from his left hand. This image, far more idealized than Mark Twain's own affectionate word-portraits, helped establish Tom Sawyer as the iconic American boy for generations of readers even before they turned to the famous opening one-word sentence, "Tom!"

More portentous in literary terms, Williams struck a visual introduction to a far humbler boy on page 64, this one ragged and half-grinning, his hat brim torn, his patched trousers pulled nearly to his chin, a dead cat dangling from his hand: Huckleberry Finn.

On the day he planned to commence the hated drudgery of revisions, Clemens plucked a package from the usual onslaught of daily mail and unwrapped it to behold salvation: there was the amanuensis copy he'd sent to Howells, now marked throughout with the *Atlantic* editor's own penciled emendations. His work had been done for him! "This was splendid, & swept away all labor," he exulted to his patron. "Instead of *reading* the MS, I simply hunted out the pencil marks & made the emendations which they suggested."[4] These included the reduction of Tom's battle with the new boy in Chapter 1 to a couple of paragraphs interspersed by the famous "I-can-lick-you" / "I'd-like-to-see-you-try-it" routine; the reduction of the Superintendent's smarmy Sunday-school speech to a brief paragraph, and the taming of "various obscenities"—except for one, which had somehow slipped past Howells, Livy, and "her aunt & her mother": Huck Finn's complaint in chapter 35 that at the Widow Douglas's house, "they comb me all to hell." Clemens confessed to Howells that he'd been glad at first that no one had flagged it; but now, given his intention to aim the book toward girls and boys, he wondered at its propriety. Did Howells?

Howells made an immediate stand for literary propriety.

> I'd have that swearing out in an instant. I suppose I didn't notice it because the locution was so familiar to my Western sense, and so exactly the thing that Huck would say.[5]

Mark Twain changed "hell" to "thunder."

Howells made another diving goal-line interception: he persuaded Clemens to radically modify the "Anatomy book" section in Chapter 22. Seizing a chance, Becky riffles through this "mysterious book," which the schoolmaster Dobbins pulls from his desk drawer every day and absorbs himself in. As she stands looking at the frontispiece—"a human figure, stark naked"[6]— Tom startles her from behind, and she tears the page.

At this point in the finished chapter, the focus turns to Tom's chivalry as he takes the blame for the ripped frontispiece, earns a whipping, and saves Becky's reputation. The chapter may have been headed elsewhere before Howells intervened: although Mark Twain gives Dobbins the fig leaf, as it were, of respectability—noting that he'd once aspired to be a doctor— Howells's alarm suggests that his absorption in the Anatomy figure (gender undisclosed) may have exceeded the strictly morphological.

THESE EDITS were also made in the copy Moncure Conway would carry with him. Conway secured an agreement with the British firm of Chatto & Windus to publish an edition of the book in June. They would become Mark Twain's standard English publisher for the rest of his career.

Where was Bliss? In mid-March, Clemens still assumed that his publisher was preparing the presses and the subscription canvassers—but he was sensing trouble. "It is going to rush you too tight to do your canvassing & issue 'Tom' the middle of April, isn't it?" he queried "Friend Bliss" on March 19th. "If so, you better clap on your canvassers at once but not publish till the middle of May. Drop me a line about this at once . . ."[7] As April began, he still held out hope for a May publication. "A week from now the Atlantic will come out with a mighty handsome notice of the book, by Howells," he wrote to Conway on April 9, ". . . but the book won't issue till 2 or even 4 weeks later."[8] His awareness of the lag between Howells's review and the new publication date embarrassed Clemens, and he struggled to ease the impact of the bad news. "Bliss made a failure in the matter of getting Tom Sawyer ready on time," he hedged to the editor in late April, when the issue was in the mail to its subscribers, "—the engravers assisting, as usual."[9] He'd visited the publisher to find out the extent of the delay, Clemens went on, "& found that the man had not even put a canvasser on or issued an advertisement yet—in fact that the *electrotypes* would not all be done for a month! But of course the main trouble was the fact that no canvassing had been done—because a subscription harvest is *before* publication, (not *after,* when people have discovered how bad one's book is)."[10] Then, with artful nonchalance, he spilled most of the rest of the beans: "When I observed that my Sketches [New and Old] had dropped from a sale of 6 or 7000 a month down to 1200 a month, I said '*this* ain't no time to be publishing books; therefore, let Tom lay still till autumn, Mr. Bliss, & make a holiday book of him to beguile the young people withal.' "[11] Nine months would separate the review from the publication.

The delay produced one further bit of misfortune. In June, a Canadian band of brigands, Belford Brothers, snatched a copy of the Chatto & Windus edition and rushed an unauthorized version of the book into print. By summer's end, some hundred thousand copies at seventy-five cents each had crossed the border and reached American bookstores, a devastating drain on the novel's tardy legitimate sales.

HOWELLS'S UNSIGNED, warmhearted review of *Tom Sawyer* was all that Sam could have wished for—except timely. The ever-pragmatic author saw the notice as a preemptive weapon: "It is a splendid notice, & will embolden weak-kneed journalistic admirers to speak out, & will modify or shut up the un-friendly."[12] The rave came at a time when it could only help sales of the Canadian edition. Still, it struck some notes that ratified the novel's place at the forefront of postwar American fiction, and mitigated Howells's compromised stance as Mark Twain's literary advisor, de facto editor, *and* reviewer. Howells began with a bow (and oh-so-subtle dismissal) to his and Mark Twain's friend Thomas Bailey Aldrich: he remarked pleasantly on how the 1869 *Story of a Bad Boy* depicted its New England hero as "more or less part of a settled order of things," hemmed in by "the traditions of an established civilization."[13] Then he shifted to a full-bore celebration of Mark Twain's creation.

> Mr. Clemens, on the contrary, has taken the boy of the Southwest for the hero of his new book, and has presented him with a fidelity to circumstance which loses no charm by being realistic in the highest degree, and which gives incomparably the best picture of life in that region as yet known to fiction.[14]

The review went on to make clear that the "best picture" Howells had in mind was of something even greater: the best picture of *childhood* yet written by an American.

> [T]hroughout there is scrupulous regard for the boy's point of view in reference to his surroundings and himself, which shows how rapidly Mr. Clemens has grown as an artist . . .
>
> The story is a wonderful study of the boy-mind, which inhabits a world quite distinct from that in which he is bodily present with his elders, and in this lies its great charm and its universality, for boy nature, however human nature varies, is the same everywhere.[15]

Howells was announcing to his educated readers two cornerstones of the American realistic aesthetic a-borning: (1) the fresh, bold, colloquial Western voice now taking its rightful place beside "polite," Augustan, Eastern letters, and (2) the use of a new psychological realism that would soon leave all the Aldriches (and the Holmeses and the Longfellows and the Whittiers) in the swirling American dust.

SAM WAS not through scheming. On June 24, he wrote to Bliss in his capacity as a board member of American Publishing Company to propose a shift in management philosophy: the company should sell two-thirds of its copyrights, auction off its newly acquired offices and printing presses, move back into "cheap quarters" again, and limit its publishing output to one or two books at a time. Clemens gave Bliss the benefit of his reasoning. "If the directors will cut the business down two-thirds, & the expenses one half, I think it will be an advantage to all concerned," he wrote, "& I feel persuaded that I shall sell more books."[16] More books *than Bret Harte,* may have been part of the implied subtext.

Two months after his praise of Mark Twain's psychological realism, Howells published an extraordinary experiment by Mark Twain in psychological *surrealism,* of a type that the author would revisit and refine over the rest of his life. ("Please correct it mercilessly," he pleaded, typically, in his cover letter.)[17] Mark Twain had earlier read it to a gathering in the Clemens household of the Monday Evening Club. This group of Hartford intellectuals, writers, and clerics (including Twichell) had been convening fortnightly since its founding in 1869. At each meeting, one member of the club would read from a scholarly, political, or philosophical paper, which would be dissected by the others. The group had elected Mark Twain a member in 1873, even before he moved his family into Nook Farm, and for the next decade he contributed a paper every couple of years or so. This one figured to bring the Victorian gents upright in their horsehair sofas. Mark Twain had given it a carefully ambiguous title: "The Facts Concerning the Recent Carnival of Crime in Connecticut." In fact, the sketch described a dark fantasy encounter between the narrator and a household-invading dwarf. The dwarf turned out to be the narrator's conscience—wrenched into visibility through an inadvertent wish voiced by its owner.

The shocking element in the piece was its self-lacerating autobiographical dimension. The creature's resemblance to its victim, in "mean form," looks, clothes, and attitude, virtually insists that the reader understand it as a Twainian "double." As the dwarf-conscience mimics his owner's bad habits and inventories his bad behavior, it becomes obvious that Mark Twain is holding himself up to a kind of public tribunal. The narrator has turned a tramp away from his door with a cruel lie (tramps were frequent visitors to the great Clemens house); rebuffed a young woman who'd asked him to read her manuscript; raged at his young children. "In truth," the dwarf rails, "you are always consistent, always yourself, always an ass."[18] The narrator bristles at the dwarf's "exasperating drawl," and seethes that "there is nothing I am quite so sensitive about as a mocking imitation of my drawling infirmity of speech." [19]

This public, if partial, purging of Samuel Clemens's guilt, along with the "doubling" device that he used as his cleansing agent, are examples of why psychoanalysis has formed a template for examinations of his life. Perhaps it is moot to point out that the narrator's resolution of the dwarf problem—tearing the little bugger to bits and throwing his remains into the fire, then celebrating his freedom from conscience by murdering thirty-eight people, burning a house, swindling a widow and otherwise ringmastering the "Carnival of Crime in Connecticut"—are all acts of imagination, and did not happen in real life. "Carnival of Crime" seems to have gone over rather well with the Monday Evening Club: one of its clerical members offered Mark Twain his pulpit to deliver it as a sermon. Howells published it in the June *Atlantic*.

With time on his hands, Sam foraged for ways to keep himself amused. He took up with a troupe of amateur Hartford actors, and on April 26 he made his theatrical stage debut in the role of Peter Spyuk in *The Loan of a Lover*. (On the following night, he seems to have given his farewell performance.) He managed to recite every one of his character's written lines—many of them rewritten by him—and spontaneously contributed several more during the performances, free of charge, which had the rest of the cast members groping for their cues; the audience loved it, and Mark Twain had fun. He cooked up another (doomed) nutty literary scheme and dragooned Howells into it—Howells, who had begun writing theatrical farces between serious novels to subsidize his own heavy household bills. This one would be a "skeleton novelette," or perhaps a "blindfold novelette," in which a dozen or so famous writers would each work up a short story based on a plot outline common to all of them—"A Murder a Mystery & a Marriage" being the general idea. The results would be serialized in the *Atlantic*. Mark Twain envisioned Howells, Harte, Aldrich, Holmes—hell, whomever they could coax into the game. In the event, the only contribution ever written was Mark Twain's; it started out well but the ending was jumbled and somehow worked in a swipe at Jules Verne. The *Atlantic* waited a judicious 125 years before publishing it in the fall of 2001.*

---

* In 1906, Howells resurrected Mark Twain's idea and proposed a collaboration under the title, *The Whole Family*, a novel to be serialized in *Harper's Bazaar* by twelve authors, each contributing a chapter about a separate character. Among the authors chosen were Howells, Henry James, and four women named "Mary," who averaged 1.25 middle names apiece. Howells assigned himself to write Chapter 1, a chaste and decorous effort concerning "The Father." He offered Mark Twain the more comical chapter, "The School-Boy," but Twain, who was struggling with his epileptic daughter Jean and brooding over such topics as "What Is Man?", was no longer in the mood. Other complications ensued. As if in answer to the question, "How many authors does it take to screw up a story?" Henry James wrote a chapter twice as long as anyone else's and pouted at the suggestion of cutting it; one of the Marys, Mary E. Wilkins Freeman, read Howells's chapter, grew irritated at its take on women, more or less seized control over the entire manuscript, sexed it up in ways that scandalized Howells, and the editor of *Harper's*, another emancipated woman named Elizabeth Jordan, let Freeman have her way. Plans to publish the novel in book form were put on hold until the Ungar Publishing Company of New York took it on in 1986, after everyone's feelings had cooled somewhat.

"I . . . began another boys' book—more to be at work than anything else," he casually notified Howells in August from the Crane farm. "I have written 400 pages on it—therefore it is very nearly half done. It is Huck Finn's Autobiography. I like it only tolerably well, as far as I have got, & may possibly pigeonhole or burn the MS when it is done." [20]

Quarry Farm worked its soothing spell on the family. Livy, suffering from early rheumatism and a sore throat, relaxed in the cool breezes at her sister's hilltop household. She wrote letters about how Susy and Clara, now four and two, "are grown fat and hearty feeding chickens & ducks twice a day, and are keenly alive to all the farm interests." [21] Susy was already developing her renowned aphoristic skill. When Sam sent into Elmira for "a vast pair of shoes with a most villainous pattern," [22] as he admitted to Howells, Susie gave them an "ew, gross" sort of once-over but wore them anyway. At prayer time that night, when Livy cued her with the usual prompt, "Now Susie—think about God," the child responded, "Mamma, I can't, with these shoes." [23]

The getaway reawakened Mark Twain's lyric voice.

The farm is perfectly delightful, this season. It is as quiet & peaceful as a South-sea island. Some of the sun-sets which we have witnessed from this commanding eminence were marvelous. One evening a rainbow spanned an entire range of hills with its mighty arch, & from a black hub resting upon the hill-top in the exact centre, *black* rays diverged upward in perfect regularity to the rainbow's arch & created a very strongly defined & altogether the most majestic, magnificent, & startling half-sunk wagon wheel you can imagine. [24]

QUARRY FARM offered intellectual as well as sensory pleasures. Theodore and Susan Crane were socially progressive Congregationalists and read widely in literature; their circle of friends echoed the enlightened intensity of Nook Farm. (Just down the steep hill lay the Elmira Water Cure sanitarium, run by the pioneering woman physician Rachel Gleason and her husband.) Household servants were welcomed as equals in the evening conversations on the front porch; children—the Clemens girls and their Langdon cousins—were accepted at the dining table, and ran about the premises free from "seen-but-not-heard" restraints. The Cranes constructed a playhouse for the girls, a scaled-down variation on their father's gazebo.

Clemens's reverie drifted in several directions in the summer of 1876. He'd begun to think of visiting England, but the old fountains of the deep were a-churn as well. Stories from several sources were flowing together: stories, story fragments, elements of stories; or perhaps one meta-story so disparate in its elements that it would have to be dammed off, over the next few years, and channeled into separate books. The Mississippi River was calling him again. The Mississippi coursed through those four hundred pages of that new, imperiled boy's book.

Reveries of boyhood nearly always put him in mind of Will Bowen—which was not always great news for Will Bowen. How Sam happened to feel about his boyhood friend in those moments depended on how he was feeling about himself. This summer, he rounded mercilessly on Bowen, who evidently had made the innocent mistake of sending a nostalgia-leavened letter. Clemens's first draft of a reply was a cannonade from the outset.

> Damnation, (if you will allow the expression,) get up & take a turn around the block & let the sentiment blow off you. Sentiment is for girls . . .
> You are petting & pitying & admiring yourself over your years of patient endeavor . . . & your good fight against misfortune & disaster . . . O, relegate all that to the days of callow adolescence, where it belongs . . .[27]

Responding to another Bowen blunder—a complaint about his finances—Clemens angrily disclosed his own well-shrouded anxieties.

> Have you a monopoly of possible misfortune & beggary? I think not. Every demi-year threatens me—& most of the people that I know. Then why think & talk about it . . . ?
> As to the past, there is one good thing about it, & that is, that it *is* the past, & we don't have to see it again . . . Each day that is added to the past is but an old boot added to a pile of rubbish . . . If you can find valuables in your pile, lucky boy you—that is all.[28]

The tone borders on the brutal, but Clemens's message is heartfelt: "You need a dose of salts, & I am trying to give it to you."[29] In fact he tossed this screed away after finishing it. As he later told his friend Jacob Burrough, "I went to the unheard-of trouble of re-writing the letter & saying the same harsh things softly, so as to sugar-coat the anguish & make it a little more endurable; & I asked him to write & thank me honestly for doing him the best & kindliest favor that any friend ever *had* done him—but he hasn't done it yet."[30] He added, revealingly:

> There is one thing which I can't stand, & *won't* stand, from many people. That is, sham sentimentality . . . the sort that makes up the Original Poetry column of a country newspaper; the rot that deals in 'the happy days of yore,' 'the sweet yet melancholy past,' with its 'blighted hopes' & its 'vanished dreams'—& all that sort of drivel.[31]

This was a far different Sam Clemens than the dreamy bridegroom who in 1870 had serenaded Bowen about those breaking-up fountains, the old faces peering out of the mists. In the six intervening years, Mark Twain had peered deeply back at those old faces and listened to their voices; and what he saw and heard had sharpened his edge. In *Tom Sawyer,* and to a far greater degree in the Huck Finn manuscript now underway, he had abolished sentimentality as a legitimate pet conceit of American literature, and replaced it with what a later writer* called, "The Cruel Radiance of What Is."

HOWELLS WAS the one correspondent who almost never felt the sting of Clemens's bad moods. One of Sam's greatest pleasures throughout that fretful period was exchanging letters with the august Boston editor. The two men wrote constantly through the late 1870s; were always inviting each other for a visit, usually in a mock-wheedling tone ("[W]on't you & Mrs. Howells come down Saturday the 22d, & remain to the Club† on Monday night? We always have a rattling good time at the Club, & we do want you to come, ever so much. Will you? Now say you will"[32]). Sometimes the invitee actually had time to accept ("My dear Clemens . . . Your visit was a perfect ovation for us: we *never* enjoy anything so much as those visits of yours. The smoke and the Scotch and the late hours almost kill us; but we . . . say what a glorious time it was, and air the library . . ."[33]). More often, a glum demurral came back ("I shall not be able to come down to Hartford this Saturday, but I am getting the better of my literary misery, and you may depend upon seeing me very soon"[34]).

They gossiped about other writers—Mark Twain accused Bret Harte of imitating Dickens—they issued literary commands ("Why don't you come out with a letter, or speech, or something, for [Rutherford B.] Hayes?"[35] "Write a drama, Howells."[36]); they inflated their influence on the tides of history ("You know I wrote the Life of Lincoln which elected him."[37]); they kept up the conceit that their demure, cerebral wives were dangerous shrews ("*Con*sound my cats—as Mrs. Clemens says when roused to ferocity"[38]); they mock-scolded each other ("Oh, come, now, I won't stand this!"[39]); they told each other to "Look here," and "See here." Howells, who otherwise bore the weight of Western letters on his small shoulders, adopted an unbuttoned voice for these letters. He sounded like a dignified man doing his best to seem jaunty; to seem less like a Victorian gent than like a Victorian *guy*.

I wrote you a long and affectionate letter just before you left Hartford, and you replied with a postal card; on which instantly forgetting all the past kindnesses between us, I dropped you. You may not have known it but I did. Now I find I can't very well go on without hearing from you, and I wish you would give me your news—what you are doing, thinking, saying.[40]

THE WRAITH that had once been Bret Harte showed up at Nook Farm shortly after the Clemenses returned there from Elmira in early October. He brought with him an idea for a return to glory, and he wanted Mark Twain to be his partner in it. Harte's fabulous clothes were now gone shiny, his early

---

* James Agee, in "Let Us Now Praise Famous Men."
† Inferentially, the Monday Evening Club.

good looks gone haggard. He was badly in debt (he owed Clemens money), often drunk in public, delinquent at scheduled appearances, shunned by the Boston literati who'd welcomed him east a lifetime ago (he never had fulfilled that spectacular $10,000 contract presented him by Fields), groping for the creative magic that had once seemed his birthright. Yet he clung to the remains of the ironic hauteur that so unnerved and irritated Sam. He clung also, in a kind of death grip, to the bit of racially ambiguous doggerel that had skyrocketed him to Eastern fame in 1870: "Plain Language from Truthful James." The doggerel clung to him in return, like a personal demon. Harte regretted the day he had conceived the Heathen Chinee, Ah Sin, and his idiotic verse tale. He regretted it even more as it swelled to a kind of cultural shorthand for Everybigot's view of the grasping "John Chinaman," * the polar opposite of the writer's intention. But now, Harte was desperate, and he needed to haul out the Chinee for one more payday.

Harte had taken the train up from New York, where he had already stripmined his reputation by mounting a problematic melodrama called *Two Men of Sandy Bar*. The play showed flashes of Harte's old skills and passion for brotherhood. Its characters, drawn from Harte's earlier fiction, brought to the stage some of his genius for Western setting and character; but the load of "ideas" they were obliged to carry—Social Justice, Loyalty, Redemption—drained their charm and slowed the action to a four-hour crawl. Things were brightened only by the brief appearance of a chop-chopping Chinese laundryman named Hop Sing, brought shamelessly to life by the popular actor Charles Thomas Parsloe, who convulsed audiences with such flights of language as "Me plentee washee shirtee . . . he no pay washee").[41]

The critics had no likee, and Harte had reacted with helpless fury; but he'd perked up when someone suggested that he write a new play built around Parsloe's "Chinaman." Aware that Sam had seen the play and found it entertaining, Harte proposed a collaboration: the two would insert the Ah Sin brand name into the boilerplate "Chinee" role, give Parsloe license to go chop-chopping around the stage to his heart's content, and throw in some supporting characters from Mark Twain's literary attic, notably the colorful Scotty Briggs from "Buck Fanshaw's Funeral" in *Roughing It*. Sam Clemens, infallible business visionary, saw the genius of this at once. Two famous authors combining two of their best-loved characters: why, as Colonel Sellers himself might say, "there's millions in it!" The two playwrights would "divide the swag," as Sam confidently phrased it to Howells.[42] He signed on to the collaboration. Harte went back to New York to work on an outline, and Mark Twain

---

* A good example of this is the following news item in a December edition of the 1874 Boston *Transcript*, as quoted by Gary Scharnhorst (" 'Ways That Are Dark' "): "Our civilization is not a failure, and the Caucasian is not played out at Ruby Hill, Nevada. A heathen Chinee over there, having been impudent enough to accost Nick Garland, an honest miner, and suggest that it was high time his wash bill was paid, Mr. Garland promptly rose up and slew the heathen. Much sympathy for Mr. Garland is expressed, and there is talk at Ruby of getting up some kind of a testimonial to him. The heathen are not popular in the mines."

threw himself into six days of concentrated work on his own version. In November, Harte returned to the Clemens household at Nook Farm to join Twain in fusing the two drafts into a single script.

As he worked at the new boy's book, and waited for *Tom Sawyer* to appear, and pored through his English history volumes, Mark Twain channeled his edginess into a couple of new hobbies in the election year of 1876: politics and pornography. (As he might have added: "But I repeat myself.") Porn was a flourishing if unacknowledged commodity in those days—the Victorian Secret, the suppressed dark twin to "polite" literature. Venus had been donning her furs and whipping up on poor old Leo Sacher-Masoch since 1870, and *The Marchioness's Amorous Pastimes* was followed intently by many Victorian gents, especially when the little Guardian of Purity was busy flipping through *Godey's Lady's Book*. The sublimely named Lady Pokingham, never far from a convenient keyhole, was another star of the genre. Purveyors with printing presses, especially in Europe, were nudging pornography toward a clandestine mass-market status. Mark Twain's contributions to the genre—a few lewd poems, some dirty jokes in his notebook, the sketch *1601,* and a mock-serious lecture to the Stomach Club in Paris on masturbation—showed a connoisseur's familiarity with the preoccupations and the lingo of porn, what Howells dryly referred to as his "Elizabethan breadth of parlance"; but the playfulness in them obviates any possibility that he was writing for purposes other than a good ribald hoot. In *1601: Conversation As It Was by the Social Fireside, in the Time of the Tudors,* he created a hysterical underground masterpiece.

The sketch was a by-product of Mark Twain's immersion in English history and its linguistic forms—in particular, those of Samuel Pepys, whose 17th-century diary he was reading. It has more in common with his own zany "The Lick House Ball" than with *The Lustful Turk*. Mark Twain wrote it for an audience of one, his man's-man Christian pal Joe Twichell, whose threshold of obscenity was the Civil War. Mark Twain's brainstorm was to portray an imaginary conversation among several deities of the age: Queen Elizabeth, William Shakespeare, Francis Bacon, Lady Alice Dilberry, Ben Jonson, Sir Walter Raleigh, and some others. The twist, as they say in Burbank, is that as we join the conversation, it has turned to farting.

The following excerpt is more intelligible if one converts "ye" to "the," "yt" to "that," and most of the effs to esses. (The speaker is the queen's elderly cupbearer.)

In ye heat of ye talke it befell yt one did breake wind, yielding an exceding mighty & diftrefsfull stink, whereat all did laffe full fore, and the[n]:

Ye Queene. Verily in mine eight and fixty yeeres have I not heard ye fellow to this fart . . . Prithee, lette ye author confeffe ye offfpring. Wil my Lady Alice teftify?

Lady Alice. Good your grace, an' I hadde room for such a thunderguft within mine auncient bowels, 'tis not in reafon I coulde difcharge ye same & live to thanck God for yt Hee did chufe handmayd so humble whereby to shew his power . . .

Ye Queene. O' God's naym, who hath favoured us? Hath it come to pafs yt a fart fhall fart *itfelfe?* . . . What faith ye worfhipful Mafter Shaxpur?

Shaxpur. In ye grete hand of God I ftand, & so proclaim my innocence. Tho'gh ye finlefs hofts of Heav'n hadde foretold ye coming of ys moft defolating breath, . . . yet hadde not I believed it; but hadde sayd ye pit itfelf hath furnifhed forth ye stink & Heav'n's artillery hath shook ye globe in admiration of it.[43]

It goes on like that for a while, until Sir Walter Raleigh 'fesses up and then delivers an encore "of fuch a godleffe & rocke-fhivering blaft yt all were fain to ftop their ears, & following it did come fo denfe & foul a ftink yt that which went before did feeme a poor & trifling thing befide it."[44] The company then proceeds blithely on to matters more explicitly sexual, and from there to Lutheranism and Rubens.

Twichell and Sam would read *1601* aloud to each other during their walks in the woods, and fall on the ground gasping for breath. Twichell found himself too weak in spirit to resist passing the sketch around to everyone whose discretion he could trust. A copy found its way into the hands of John Hay, who had it set in type. It was redone on expensive linen, though not under Mark Twain's name. As its cult status grew through the decades, even the parsonlike Paine was forced to admit that the sketch was a classic, and to hope that standards of decorum in future years would relax enough to give the essay "shelter and setting among the more conventional writings of Mark Twain."[45]

If Paine only knew.

AS FOR politics: in the late autumn of 1876, Mark Twain became one of the first popular-culture celebrities to lend his support to a presidential candidate, helping to launch a tradition that led, over the decades, from Babe Ruth to Whoopi Goldberg. At Howells's urging, he announced himself a supporter of the Republican Rutherford B. Hayes, the former governor of Ohio (and cousin of Elinor Howells) in Hayes's campaign against Samuel J. Tilden to succeed the retiring two-term president Ulysses S. Grant. Tilden was a high-strung lawyer and Democratic Party insider who had opposed radical Reconstruction, but was an enemy of Boss Tweed and other corrupt machine men. Grant was preparing to quit the White House after eight years of political battle as consumptive in its own way as had been the Civil War. He had been prepared for the presidency in the same way he had been prepared for real estate sales in St. Louis: hardly at all. The Hero of the Republic had been tarnished by the factional politics of Reconstruction, and by the treacheries and frauds of the presumed friends he had appointed into his administration. These were the mistakes of an antebellum Northern gentleman who never understood the cold, utilitarian new society birthed in part by his battlefield victories.

The scandals—Crédit Mobilier, Whiskey Ring, Belknap, Black Friday, Delinquent Tax—would draw history's gaze from Grant's social and policy achievements. As Frank Scaturro and other rehabilitative scholars have pointed out, these included the president's firm but humane stewardship of the old Confederacy (he sent federal troops into South Carolina to crush the Ku Klux Klan, triggering a crisis of constitutional authority; but the Amnesty Act of 1872 reinstated citizenship and voting rights to all Southerners except Jefferson Davis and Robert E. Lee); civil rights initiatives including the underenforced Civil Rights Act of 1875 (his initiative to turn American Indians into Methodists and Presbyterians was somewhat less visionary); his reduction of the national debt by $435 million and his cutting of taxes by $300 million; his leadership in establishing principles of international arbitration that anticipated the United Nations; and ironically his pioneering efforts at civil service reform.

A larger irony found Grant's progressive racial policies under attack by insurgents within his own party who called themselves Liberal Republicans. These reformers, focusing more on Reconstruction's corrupt excess than on its aims, and glossing over their own embedded racism, fought to end the system's problematic domination of the South, and turned the administration's scandals into a bludgeon against the president. Confronted with opportunism and greed, and with the rot of exploitation rampant in the capital, Grant found himself, near the end of his presidency, living inside *The Gilded Age*.

HOWELLS, ARDENTLY for Hayes, was rekindling the magic he'd worked on behalf of Lincoln—a campaign biography. (It sold a whopping two thousand copies.) Mark Twain, who'd never been politically active, responded artfully to his friend's first overture: "When a humorist ventures upon the grave concerns of life he must do his job better than another man or he works harm to his cause."[46] A loose translation of that might come out as, *"Alienate half my readership? Do you think I'm nuts?"*

Soon, though, he awoke to the deeper satisfactions of the great stage of public affairs: patronage and the opportunities for mischief. In one of his "Look-here-Howells" letters, Clemens instructed his friend to badger Hayes for a consulship for Charles Warren Stoddard. As for mischief, it took him no time at all to concoct an attack ad: "A miniature volume, with a page the size of a postage stamp, with this title-page: 'What Mr. Tilden Has Done for His Country.' "[47]

His one known campaign speech for Hayes, delivered in Hartford, fell a little short of divine oratory—the Boston *Transcript* later opined that "somebody should have led him from the platform by the ear."[48] Clemens in turn had some harsh words for Tilden's rhetoric in a letter to a friend that was excerpted in the Hartford *Courant*.

> If Mr. Hayes wanted to say "Accidents happen in even the best regulated families," he would *say* "Accidents will happen in even the best regulated families," & you would know what he meant; but Mr. Tilden would probably say:—"It is believed by many honest & right-feeling, but possibly mistaken men—though more or less might be weightily said both for & against the proposition—that infelicitous conjunctions of cause and effect will eventuate even in fireside circles accustomed to the most exact, exhaustive, elaborate, and unsufruct systems of domestic dominion." [49]

The criticism retains an oddly contemporary feel.

Despite Clemens's and Howells's intervention, the initial election returns on November 7 indicated a narrow victory for Tilden. Sam, by now thoroughly Republicanized, received the early returns with escalating anxiety and he took refuge in Christian devotion. He dashed off a telegram to Howells advising that "I love to steal a while away from every cumbering care / and while returns come in today lift up my voice & swear." [50]

If the one-legged, wife's-lover-shooting Civil War hero Daniel Sickles had not gone to the theater on election night, and hobbled past Republican headquarters in New York on the way home, Samuel Tilden would probably have been sworn in as president the following January. Scanning the state-by-state tickers more intently than the traumatized party workers in the office, Joe Twichell's old field commander realized that Hayes, though lagging in the popular tally, still had a chance to win in the Electoral College by one vote if certain states—namely, Florida, Louisiana, and South Carolina—held for the Republicans. He fired off telegrams to party leaders in those states over the signature of Zachariah Chandler, the party's national chairman, who was just then taken drunk. The state operatives mobilized their forces. With both candidates short of the electoral minimum, Republicans in the three critical states did their patriotic duty, sabotaged enough Democratic ballots to tilt the electoral vote to Hayes, and stood fast for several weeks. A commission was appointed to investigate, and ultimately a deal was struck: the Republican candidate would be the victor, but federal troops enforcing Reconstruction would be pulled out of the South. Reconstruction died and the Republican Party continued to thrive. Such an extra-electoral outcome, of course, was an extreme anomaly of the constitutional system, and bore no possibility of ever happening again.

THE ADVENTURES of Tom Sawyer was finally published in December 1876. The reviews were mostly genial; reflective of the culture's preoccupations and norms; clueless as to the novel's prospects for becoming a permanent American classic—and too late to help very much with sales. The reviews typically reprised the plot, inventoried the main character's traits ("Tom is a reckless, daredevil fellow, ready to hazard life for an adventure any time . . ."[51]); speculated as to how much of the story was autobiographical; praised True Williams's illustrations, and gave the novel credit for moving past the moralizing and "morbid sentimentality" of past books in the genre. The New York *Times* endorsed the novel's humor and its departure from the "one monotonous key" that had usually suffocated books for children: "A child was supposed to be a vessel which was to be constantly filled up. Facts and morals had to be taken like bitter droughts or acrid pills."[52] Yet the *Times* had reservations about the downsides of this liberation—timeless reservations, in retrospect. *Exposure to inappropriate content* was one of them: "[I]t is not desirable that in real life we should familiarize our children with those of their age who are lawless or dare-devils."[53] Not to mention all the *gratuitous violence,* such as the graveyard knifing of Muff Potter by Injun Joe, an example of "ugly realism." The *Times* reviewer actually touched on *substance abuse* in his summarizing metaphor: "A sprinkling of salt in mental food is both natural and wholesome; any cravings for the contents of the castors, the cayenne and the mustard, by children, should not be gratified."[54] Just, in other words, Say No to Tom.

Among the more thoughtful commentators was Moncure D. Conway. His unsigned review in the London *Examiner* was among the very few to anticipate the universality of Mark Twain's characters and story, even in a world that had already accelerated well beyond Tom Sawyer's time frame. "With the Eastern Question upon us," Conway wrote, "and crowned heads arrayed on the political stage, it may be with some surprise that we find our interest demanded in . . . humble folk whose complications occur in a St. Petersburg situated on the Missouri [sic] river." He added another thought rarely voiced among critics in Mark Twain's lifetime, Chesterton being a notable exception.

[A] great deal of Mark Twain's humour consists in the serious—or even at times the severe—style in which he narrates his stories and portrays his scenes, as one who feels that the universal laws are playing through the very slightest of them.[55]

The novel sold only 15,000 copies in its opening weeks, and after a year, sales still languished at around 27,000, a third the pace of *Roughing It.* The book would not begin to sell briskly until 1885, when it became linked in the public mind with *Adventures of Huckleberry Finn.* It has never been out of print since first publication. The saturation of the illegitimate Canadian edition was mostly to blame for the poor sales; but Clemens in his bitterness blamed Bret Harte. It was Harte's *Gabriel Conroy* (5,000 in sales) that had clogged up American Publishing's marketing efforts on *Tom Sawyer's* behalf, Clemens made himself believe. He barely tolerated his *Ah Sin* collaborator, who remained boozily underfoot in the Clemens household in the closing weeks of 1876.

.   .   .

" I F I can make a living out of plays, I shall never write another book," he advised Moncure Conway as Christmas approached. He had convinced himself that copyright law would never protect him; and there was no point in emptying out his soul for the profit of Canadian thieves. First he had made *The Gilded Age*. That was for practice. Now he would make *Ah Sin*.

33

God's Fool

(1877)

In 1877, devotees of *The Adventures of Tom Sawyer* who wrote the author asking about a possible sequel received copies of what may have been the first celebrity form letter in the annals of literature. Or perhaps it was the great-great-grandfather of the recorded phone message.

> I HAVE THE HONOR TO REPLY TO YOUR LETTER JUST RECEIVED, THAT IT IS MY PURPOSE TO WRITE A CONTINUATION OF TOM SAWYER'S HISTORY, BUT I AM NOT ABLE AT THIS TIME TO DETERMINE WHEN I SHALL BEGIN THE WORK.
>
> YOU WILL EXCUSE THIS PRINTED FORM, IN CONSIDERATION OF THE FACT THAT THE INQUIRY WHICH YOU HAVE MADE RECURS WITH SUFFICIENT FREQUENCY TO WARRANT THIS METHOD OF REPLYING.[1]

Mark Twain had another boilerplate reply printed up—this one for the folks who were by now sending him *their* manuscripts. It announced

> Dr. Sir or Madam:
>
> Experience has not taught me very much; still it has taught me that it is not wise to criticise a piece of literature, except to an enemy of the person who wrote it; then, if you praise it, that enemy admires you for your honest manliness, & if you dispraise it he admires you for your sound judgment.[2]

This was Mark Twain's firewall against the gathering tribe of dreamers that William Saroyan in the next century would gently damn as "magnificent no-bodies": the clerks and the station agents "just daring to set their feet upon the literary field," as one letter-writer put it, and the Civil War veterans and the foreign stamp dealers who saw themselves as "budding authors in the hu-morous style"; all the ardent bards of the republic who wanted this common-man-made-good to bless their own home-baked novels and memoirs and "views" and "observations," and who wrote to him in their beautiful swirling 19th-century cursive scripts that so often outshone their talent.

"I send you herewith an index of some writings composed by myself, which, I flat-ter myself, if properly edited and put upon the market, will prove remunerative."[3]

"Do you think you could find time to look over say 400 pages M.S.S. written. Something out of the treadmill style of the latter day novels?"[4]

Mark Twain wrote on the envelope: "An absurd request." He later estimated to Mary Fairbanks that over a two-week period in 1879, five separate strangers, from different parts of the country, asked him to read their book manuscripts and use his influence to get them published. "These MS, combined, aggre-gated 11,000 pages."[5] No form letter could answer the full volume and variety of correspondence that flowed into the house on Farmington Avenue. The let-ters came from around the nation and the world. Many were merely addressed "Mark Twain, Hartford, Connecticut"; one envelope arrived with only his sketched silhouette to identify the recipient. "I have a badgered, harassed feeling, a good part of the time," Sam eventually confessed to his mother. "It comes mainly of business responsibilities . . . & the persecution of kindly let-ters from well-meaning strangers—to whom I must be rudely silent or else put in the biggest half of my time bothering over answers."[6]

The National Home for Disabled Volunteer Soldiers wondered if he would send them some of the books he'd written (he did). Most entreaties were individual.

"Gracious Sir;

"You are rich. To lose $10.00 would not make you miserable.
"I am poor. To gain $10.00 would not make me miserable.
"Please send me $10.00 (ten dollars) . . ."[7]

"I thought that you might take pity up on me. The closing exercises of our school comes April 20, and I have a thesis to write—Subject, 'Boys' . . . Will you please write to me, giving your opinion of boys?"[8]

"Please, sir; don't smile scornfully behind your mustache (if you have one), and then toss this into the waste-basket," instructed a "young authoress from

Wisconsin." "You see I want your photograph." And then the floodgates opened.

> . . . I know you will be too kind-hearted to refuse me. How do I know? This way—
> Once you were poor now you are rich. Once you were obscure now you are famous.
> How did you come so? By *working* and *fighting*. Was the world kind to you, did it reach
> out a helping hand when you were down? No! It fought you every step of the way, and
> growls at your feet now, ready to tear you in pieces and devour you the moment you
> show sign of weakness . . .[9]

> Is there the slightest probability of your writing and publishing any other books.
> "Innocents Abroad" ["]Roughing It" & "The Gilded Age" have about up-set our
> youngest brother . . . a youth of seventeen, now six feet two in his stocking-feet . . . If
> you contemplate issuing any more books like these . . . please let us know, in due time
> in order that we may get him out of the way—send him to Patagonia or some other re-
> gion where access to them will be impossible . . . [H]e has since read them [your works]
> forty times, and then re-read them backwards and cross-ways. He has literally read
> them to pieces . . . To cap the climax he has begun writing a book of his own, and takes
> yours for his models . . .[10]

FINALLY, MARK Twain hired a secretary, Miss Fanny Hesse, to allow him to dictate his replies.

The letters flowing to Mark Twain from all these strangers—including the many that he filed away under the brusque scrawl, *"From an ass"*—were perhaps more numinous than he was capable of recognizing under the circumstances. The category that they largely pioneered, fan mail, would not find its name until the movie-star era of the 20th century; but the impulse that prompted them—their almost palpable yearning—was similar. This was a hunger for a kind of faith, or a godhead that represented faith. The mid-1870s saw religious faith, particularly Christian Protestant faith, suffering a crisis of authority and influence. The war and its root causes had fractured the Presbyterian Church and its aura of certitude. Darwin's discoveries were transferring power in the universe from God to nature in ways that beggared Emerson's metaphors of the individual divine. The emerging America of rails and electricity, the America whose densely packed cities were already draining off the old farm-and-village culture and the pieties that sustained it—all these contributed to a kind of psychic loneliness never before experienced on such a scale.

In nearly all precincts beyond the Deep South, "faith" was being redefined by the concerns of the moment: liberal Protestants such as Joe Twichell and the Beechers promoted their programs of social justice. Social Darwinism promoted its fantasies of human perfectibility, oblivious to the attractions such notions might hold for a totalitarian state. Heresy trials traumatized many Northern congregations. Caught in the swirl of this maelstrom, individuals seeking a personal connection with the divine turned their attention from the whipping gales of "theology" and toward more graspable icons. This was the true birth of the celebrity culture. The celebrity that many of them fastened on was the same mesmeric figure who had arisen as a god of the lecture platform in San Francisco in 1866, the same who had often betrayed the wish that he could be a preacher of the Gospel but for a lack of the necessary stock in trade—religion. Now this figure had restored Americans to a vision of their receding Eden, and had given them a fictive boy who seemed to ratify Ralph Waldo Emerson's haunting aphorism, in "Nature," that "[i]nnocence is the perpetual Messiah, which comes into the arms of fallen men, and pleads with them to return to Paradise." [11]

SAM CLEMENS strained against the limitations on his unceasing drive to get things done. Aware of his descent along the "downward slope" from forty, he brimmed with plans and projects, and was not shy about interrupting the lives of others to help him carry them out. As with Whitelaw Reid, his presumption could be breathtaking—a holdover, perhaps, from his riverboat days. "By long habit, pilots came to put all their wishes in the form of commands," he recalled once. "It 'gravels' me, to this day, to put my will in the weak shape of a request, instead of launching it in the crisp language of an order." Not even the great Howells, before whom all literati trembled, was exempt. There was that matter of the consulship lobbying for Charles Warren Stoddard—followed a couple of weeks later by another request for a "favor": "You will have the words 'Ah Sin, a Drama,' printed in the middle of a note-paper page, & send the same to me, with bill." [12] (The printed title page was needed to help Clemens comply with copyright requirements.) Now, in January, he fretted to a friend, "Harte hasn't come yet—so the play isn't licked into shape—consequently I haven't demanded Howells's presence. (He is to come when the play is ready to be read & criticised.)" [13]

He issued orders to Moncure Conway in England to hire a lawyer at his expense to prosecute the Canadian pirate Belford on behalf of Chatto, on the theory that the British copyright for *Tom Sawyer* stood in Chatto's name. To Frank Bliss, he decreed, "You may send me that Bret Harte piece of paper to keep as evidence of his indebtedness to me." [14] He had a command performance in mind for the travel writer whose fame he'd eclipsed, Bayard Taylor: to "entertain" his young girls' Saturday Morning Club with a talk on the morning after Taylor's upcoming lecture in Hartford. "Your N.Y. train doesn't leave here till afternoon. I hope you can & will." [15] And he informed Pamela that he had "found the right school" for Sammy: the St. Paul's School in Concord, New Hampshire, "the best preparatory school for boys in this country." [16] Only one figure dared challenge his will. "Mr Clemens grows more and more determined to go to Germany next Summer," Livy wrote to her mother,

"—I combat it and say the farm next Summer and Germany a year from next Summer if we have money enough—I don't know who will come out ahead but I think I shall."[17]

Harte finally arrived. His visit dealt the final blow to the touchy friendship. In spite of his annoyance at Harte's priggishness and condescension, Clemens had done what he could over the years to arrest his onetime mentor's slide into dissipation and debt. Now, he guarded his household against what he saw as Harte's vulgarizing presence. He kept Harte quarantined up on the third floor during most of the day, where the visitor hunched over a table and attacked the script's broad contours while Sam prowled the billiard table, blue smoke billowing from his cigar, supplying dialogue for the characters as Harte called for it. He sensed the futility of it all. He wrote to Pamela, whose son Sammy had arrived at the house for a visit, that he was no company for Sammy or anybody else because he "was in a smouldering rage, the whole time, over the precious days & weeks of time which Bret Harte was losing for me."[18]

Mealtime brought the monster out of his lair. When Harte and Clemens descended the stairs to join Livy, Sammy and the girls at table, tensions surfaced. Livy was weakened by rheumatism and diphtheria that summer, and was treating Susy's own diphtheria when she was able. Sam, protective of his wife in the calmest circumstances, gritted his teeth as Harte aimed supercilious jibes at the house, its furniture and decorations, and—dangerously—toward Livy herself. The actual degree of Harte's offenses is open to question: Harte repeatedly expressed affection toward Susy and Clara in letters to Sam, giving them pet names and inquiring after them. As for Livy, he seems respectful of her in every bit of independent evidence that survives. On the other hand, Harte was a problem drinker now, and may have trailed whiskey fumes downstairs. And Harte seemed incapable of discarding the epicene, insinuating veneer—the over-the-top dress, gestures, and put-downs—that had always contradicted his essential humanitarian beliefs. Clemens held his temper until the end of the visit, heating it to furnace temperatures. "[F]or Mrs. Clemens's sake I endured it all until the last day," Sam recalled in old age.[19] On that day, over luncheon, Harte uttered what sounded to Sam like an impertinence to Olivia Langdon Clemens. Back in the billiard room, Sam pounced.

[Y]ou are a shabby husband to [Mrs. Harte] and you often speak sarcastically, not to say sneeringly, of her . . . but your privilege ends there; you must spare Mrs. Clemens.

Sam then got a few other things off his chest.

. . . you have made sarcastic remarks about the furniture of the bedroom, and about the tableware, and about the servants, and about the carriage and the sleigh, and the coachman's livery . . . [T]his does not become you; you are barred from these criticisms by your situation and circumstances . . . [Y]ou are a loafer and an idler and you

go clothed in rags . . . You have lived in the Jersey woods and marshes and have supported yourself as do the other tramps; you have confessed it without a blush . . .[20]

How much of that tirade was actually delivered, and how much was added on
in reverie, is unclear. (Some of it may have been delivered via a letter, now
lost.) But the explosion discharged years of pent-up resentments. Sam
Clemens may have at last struck a psychic parity with Bret Harte by delivering
it, but their friendship never recovered. In his reminiscences, Mark Twain savaged Harte as "an invertebrate without a country," bereft of the higher passions; bereft of feeling, in fact, "for the reason that he had no machinery to
feel with."[21] Oh—and no conscience.

THE PLAY that lurched into being out of this dysfunctional alliance scarcely
survived its birth scars. Its brief life traced a downward spiral of popularity. It
pivoted on mistaken identity (one of Mark Twain's favorite devices) and assumed names. It was set in territory that both men knew well, the California
mining camps. The main characters were the rugged champion liar Bill Plun-
ket, and a fussily dressed mining engineer named York. As Margaret Duckett
has pointed out, these two bore interesting resemblances to Mark Twain and
Bret Harte.[22] A malapropistic mother and her practical daughter supplied
heavy-handed comic scenes (neither Livy nor Anna Harte could bear them).
Charles Thomas Parsloe as Ah Sin had all the good lines, spouting Chinese
pidgin English and bamboozling the miners with his Oriental trickery while
he tried to solve a murder. Or something.

Ah Sin was scheduled to open at the National Theater in Washington for a
week's trial run on May 7, 1877. Mark Twain joined the cast in rehearsal at
Ford's Theater in Baltimore, taking a suite in Guy's Hotel on Monument
Square. It was here that he began his campaign to wrest control of the production from his partner—really, to purge the play of his partner's imprint and
identity, to the extent possible. He dominated rehearsals. Prowling the wings
and the proscenium, he peppered the actors with directions. He scribbled off
daily revisions, although Harte disapproved of them, and for good reason:
they were moving the title character ever-farther away from the nuanced Chinese of Harte's humane California sketches, and toward the baser but box-
office-friendly "Heathen Chinee."

In his spare time, he visited the state prison (Heaven for climate, Hell for
society), and was also drawn to the city's famous "automated" house known as
Alexandroffsky, whose owner, the railroad baron Thomas DeKay Winans,*

---

* Winans and his partner, Major George Washington Whistler, had contracted with Czar
Nicholas I of Russia in 1844 for the construction of a railroad line between Moscow and St. Petersburg, a venture that made both of them wealthy—hence the name of the "automated" house.
The major's son was the painter James McNeill Whistler, who worked briefly at the Winans Locomotive Company in Baltimore in 1854. James's half-brother George Whistler married a daughter
of Winans. Mark Twain encountered "two Whistler girls" seated at the (pivoting) dinner table on
his tour of the house.

gave him a tour of the onrushing technological dream world that he worshipped. He saw a gas heating system regulated by a thermostat and a rudi-
mentary air-conditioning system; tables and chairs that revolved at the turn of
a knob; a steam engine that drove machinery fifty yards distant; a skating
rink; a new kind of carriage wheel. He absorbed it all as thoroughly as he absorbed spoken language or the lower Mississippi River, and he poured it all
out again in a thirty-two-page letter to Livy that inventoried nearly every device. What he could not adequately describe, he sketched. "Automatic devil-
tries," [23] he called them.

Mark Twain's coldest ploy in his anti-Harte campaign was to lure Parsloe
into an alliance that excluded Harte—who, after all, had conceived the role
that figured to make the actor famous. Soon Parsloe was echoing Mark's complaints about Harte's intrusiveness and general inconvenience. Despite these
backstage tensions, *Ah Sin: A Drama* delighted audience and critics in its premiere, particularly the Hop Sing-type shenanigans. Harte assumed the play
was a hit, but Mark Twain was still not satisfied. He spent a week re-revising
the script, again without bothering to consult his co-writer. Again, Harte
hated what his partner had done. But now he was outnumbered; Parsloe sided
with Mark Twain.

BY THE end of the Washington tryout, Clemens had worn himself out mentally and physically. He'd anticipated this for weeks. Sometime in April, he
had approached Joe Twichell in Hartford and invited him on an ocean cruise
to Bermuda. Susan Crane journeyed to Hartford to stay with Livy. Clemens
and Twichell left New Haven for the first leg of their ten-day adventure on
May 16; a nighttime boat trip down to New York. They embarked there the
next day for the island in the wide Sargasso Sea. "First actual pleasure trip I
ever took," [24] Sam remarked in his notebook. A primary subject of Sam's notes
was the Reverend Mr. Twichell. The rugged Christian and Civil War veteran
may have been a commanding presence in the pulpit at Hartford, but away
from his habitat, he revealed his naïveté in matters of the world. He yakked on
with strangers like a yokel, and took literally certain unfamiliar terms ("Do
they make arrows of the arrowroot?" [25]). Soon Clemens was identifying
Twichell by a rather uncomradely notebook pseudonym.

Fool Walked to ship, got a bot. of beer, drew cork, but couldn't succeed in carrying
it home. It kept foaming up & had to keep stopping to drink off surplus. Finished &
threw bottle away. [26]

Something in the soup which the fool recognized—ah, it's hellfire. [27]

The friends took a pair of rooms at a boardinghouse in Hamilton. They
strolled the island and admired the shimmering white houses, the brightly
colored birds, the red pomegranate blossoms and the fine calla lilies, a bride

and her bridegroom. Sam ruminated on a stage adaptation for the English-historical novel that was already well advanced in his mind, and which he had already titled: *The Prince and the Pauper.* The two returned home on May 27. A week later Sam swept his wife and children off to Quarry Farm for a respite before *Ah Sin*'s New York opening. Sam used his share of the "respite" to write an account of the Bermuda trip for Howells at the *Atlantic:* "Some Rambling Notes of an Idle Excursion." In the four installments serialized from October 1877 through January 1878, "the fool" modeled on Twichell undergoes another name change. He becomes the Ass. Twichell, apparently, maintained a Christian forbearance. Perhaps he reminded himself that it was an ass who'd carried a certain religious figure into Jerusalem.

The travelogue finished, Mark Twain kept busy in his hilltop study by dashing off a new play: *Cap'n Simon Wheeler, The Amateur Detective.* "Simon Wheeler" was the narrator of the "Jumping Frog" tale, but the two characters were not similar. Clemens was now so deeply theater-struck that he toyed with the idea of giving up book writing to become a playwright. He estimated to Howells that the "Wheeler" play could earn him fifty thousand dollars. After all, he'd spent an entire six and a half days writing it.

He returned to New York on July 15, as *Ah Sin* was moving into rehearsal at Augustin Daly's Fifth Avenue Theater. (Playbills around the city were trumpeting the play, its co-authors, and its cast of internationally acclaimed actors.) Bret Harte was absent: looking for work in Washington, and thoroughly disgusted with his collaborator in any case. Clemens again seized control of "that dreadful play." [28] He whipped the cast through four-hour "coaching" sessions inside the sweltering theater, shaping the production toward his vision. In off-hours he canvassed the theatrical demimonde, trying to sell *Cap'n Simon Wheeler* to some backer or producer. He was unsuccessful; the play was never mounted.

On opening night, July 31, Mark Twain stepped to the footlights after the performance, dressed in the blinding white linen that would become his signature garb a quarter-century later—and delivered another strangely denigrating curtain speech. He attacked the play's "lack of invention" and "didacticism" [29] and even dropped the word "plagiarism"—all daggers aimed at Harte. Then, grotesquely, he went on to suggest that Ah Sin, as enacted by Parsloe, was an "illustration," perfectly portrayed, of the Chinaman, who "is going to become a very frequent spectacle all over America, by and by, and a difficult political problem, too." [30]

Back at Quarry Farm, Livy fretted about her husband and his corrosive temper. (Sam had sensed her anxiety the day of his departure: "Cheer up!" he'd instructed her from the city.)[31] She knew her husband's rage at Harte, and seems to have sensed something like this in the making. In a letter that he probably received on the day of the opening, she had tried to deflect him from it. "Youth I want to caution you about one thing, don't say harsh things about Mr. Harte," she wrote, "don't talk against Mr. Harte to people, it is so much better that you be reticent about him . . . We are so desperately happy . . . and he is so miserable, we can easily afford to be magnanimus toward him . . . be careful my darling . . ."[32] But Mark Twain did not know the meaning of magnanimus.

Clemens's "spectacle/difficult political problem" remark—so at odds with his typical sympathy for any downtrodden class—seems to have emboldened the real bigotry of some critics, who took his remarks as license to savage the character Ah Sin as though he were a living avatar of the Yellow Peril. "Ah Sin is a contemptible thief and an imperturbable liar," fulminated the New York *World*.[33] "[A] typical Chinaman," declared the *Times*.[34] The play's box-office business soon took a downturn from which it never recovered.

Back in Elmira as August began, confident that *Ah Sin* was a success, Sam and the family settled into the dreamy rhythms of life at Quarry Farm. (He'd convinced himself that only Harte's name on the playbill held it back from being a runaway hit.) Many years later Clara retained an elegiac image of two figures

engaged in lively conversation. Aunt Sue was picking flowers, and my father had joined her before starting his day's work. His lovely gray hair was shining in the sunlight and his arms, greatly agitated by his thoughts, made life dangerous for Aunt Sue . . . I am certain now that the subject of their talk was . . . the undying topic of religion.[35]

Aunt Sue had a strong faith in God, Clara recalled, and as "Father" pressed his attack on the Christian faith, "Her lovely, silver laugh tinkled into the air from the flowery path . . ."[36]

Livy, conserving her limited strength, usually stayed on the porch through the day, but always with someone to talk to. Unless one watched her closely during a dark mood, Clara maintained, "one could not discover it."[37] Of an evening, at the farmhouse, Sam would read to the family from his day's work, or play chess with Theodore Crane while Livy read stories to the children. Or everyone would gather on the porch to hear the tales told by Auntie Cord. Barouches came and went during these summer days, bringing women in short-brim hats trimmed with bright ribbons and scalloped day dresses over petticoats; their menfolk more cautious than Sam in their dark frock coats and small bow ties. Near sunset one afternoon a carriage departing with Charley's wife Ida, and their daughter and a nursemaid began speeding uncontrollably. Sam described the scene:

The next moment Livy said, "Ida's driving too fast down hill!" She followed it with a sort of scream: "Her horse is running away!"[38]

The lawn people looked on helplessly as the buggy gathered speed down the two hundred-yard descent, bouncing high in the air when it struck a rock or a tree stump. Sam and Theodore Crane ran after the runaway, but it was hopeless. Sam braced himself for another encounter with the death of loved ones.

> I ran on & on . . . saying to myself "I shall see it at the turn of the road; they never can pass that turn alive." When I came in sight of that turn I saw two wagons there bunched together . . . I said, "Just so—they are staring petrified at the remains." [39]

He was wrong. The carriage had been stopped, the party rescued by a tenant farmer employed by the Cranes, John T. Lewis. Guiding his own two-horse wagon uphill with a load of manure, Lewis had found himself in the path of the onrushing buggy. He'd turned his horses into the path, forming a V-shaped chute with a roadside fence.

> Then Lewis sprang to the ground & stood in this V He gathered his vast strength, & . . . seized the gray horse's bit as he plunged by, & fetched him up standing! [40]

Lewis was about forty-five. Hardworking and honest, a veteran of Gettysburg, a strong Dunkard Baptist, he had indebted himself to the Cranes to the tune of about $700, and his net earnings each year scarcely covered his meals and board. Now, he stood a hero in everyone's eyes. The Cranes forgave him $400 of his debt, and quietly decided never to collect the balance. Everyone showered him with grateful letters, with banknotes attached. Ida gave him a gold Swiss watch. No one was more transported by the rescue than Sam Clemens. Lewis had performed an act appropriate to the pages of an adventure book that Sammy Clemens had read—or that Mark Twain might write. In fact, Mark Twain did write it, in versions that appeared in *Pudd'nhead Wilson* and *Life on the Mississippi*. He formed a friendship with Lewis that lasted until the farmer's death in 1906.

The incident proved another marker in Samuel Clemens's "de-Southernization." A trace of categorical thought toward blacks showed in his letters to Howells and Brown describing the rescue and its aftermath. He reported that when someone asked him whether a watch would be "a wise gift" for the black man, "I said, 'Yes, the very wisest of all; I know the colored race, & I know that in Lewis's eyes this fine toy will throw the other more valuable testimonials far away into the shade.' "[41] But he added, "[&] if any scoffer shall say, 'Behold this thing is out of character,' there is an inscription within, which will silence him; for it will teach him that this wearer aggrandizes the watch, not the watch the wearer."

AT MID-OCTOBER, after a failed tour in the West, and more rewrites, Mark Twain admitted that *Ah Sin* was a lost cause.

Mark Twain and Bret Harte never saw each other again. Harte struggled on against destitution for a while in Washington, writing popular journalism for a pittance and sending money, when he could, to his wife and children back home. Clemens remained actively and permanently vengeful to his former mentor, writing to President Hayes in a futile attempt to block a consular appointment for Harte. When Clemens read about the appointment in a paper, he threw a fit.

"Harte is a liar, a thief, a swindler," he raged to Howells,

a snob, a sot, a sponge, a coward, a Jeremy Diddler,* he is brim full of treachery, & he conceals his Jewish birth† as carefully as if he considered it a disgrace . . . If he had only been made a home official, I think I could stand it; but to send this nasty creature to puke upon the American name in a foreign land is too much.[42]

Clemens's abhorrence had not cooled when Harte died of throat cancer in 1902.

What fueled Samuel Clemens's out-of-scale hatred of former friends such as Harte, Whitelaw Reid, occasionally Will Bowen, and several figures in the years to come? The answer, of course, died with Clemens—if in fact it was ever available even to him. Yet it may be similar to the loathing that Clemens, the fallen boyhood believer, directed toward the Christian faith: the entrenched bitterness and despair of the jilted lover. Howells saw this. "If he thought you had in any way played him false," he later remembered, "you were anathema and maranatha forever." Howells added,

Clemens did not [even] forgive his dead enemies; their death seemed to deepen their crimes, like a base evasion . . . he pursued them to the grave; he would like to dig them up and take vengeance upon their clay.[43]

IN THE fall of 1877, Samuel Clemens grandly installed Hartford's first private telephone in his house, with a line running directly to the *Courant*. At about this time, a letter from his own closest jilted suitor, Orion, arrived, continuing some correspondence about Orion's attempts to write fiction.

Sam, I've been seized with an idea. Can't you take my "Kingdom of Sir John Franklin," use it as a skeleton or as memoranda, expand it (with stories told by the imprisoned crew? &c) into a book, send it out in your name and mine (with some nom de plume if that's best) (or else in your own name, if you prefer that), give me such part of the profits as you please, and enable me to pay you and the government and my other creditors, and leave me something over?[44]

Sam of course brushed aside this unworkable idea. "If I write all the books that lie planned in my head, I shall see the middle of the next century," he told his brother. "But go ahead & write it yourself," he went on, unable to resist adding

---

* A term for a con artist.
    †Harte's paternal grandfather, Bernard Harte, was Jewish. Interestingly, Sam Clemens himself had felt the sting of anti-Semitism as he struggled for acceptance with the Boston Brahmins. James Russell Lowell, for one, strongly suspected that Clemens was a Jew.

the little dig: "—that is, if you can drop other things."[45] He didn't stop there. Unbeknownst to Orion, Sam had begun a manuscript (never finished) that exploited his brother far beyond Orion's own innocent imaginings of riding Sam's coattails: he was writing Orion's biography. In late March, he confided to Howells, "I have started him at 18, printer's apprentice, soft & sappy, full of fine intentions & shifting religions & not aware that he is a shining ass . . . am driving along without plot, plan, or purpose—& enjoying it."[46]

ON THE Tuesday evening of December 17, 1877, in a banquet room of the swank Hotel Brunswick in Boston, under the gaze of New England's most distinguished writers and some founding gods of American literature, Samuel Langhorne Clemens made as shining an ass of himself as at any time over the long course of his life. At least that was how it seemed to him, and Howells, too. This thunderbolt of shame and remorse, traumatic enough to drive him to Europe with his family a few months later, settled into his consciousness, where it joined the incumbent ghosts: Benjamin, Marshall, Henry, Langdon, the burning tramp, the drowned boys of Hannibal.

The occasion was a seventieth-birthday dinner for John Greenleaf Whittier, a silver-bearded Brahmin to the core: protégé of the abolitionist editor William Lloyd Garrison; stalwart patron of the *Atlantic;* essayist; a founder of the Republican Party; sturdy versifier in rhyming tetrameter, his stanzas marching forward through the parlors and the firesides of the new republic like so many fifers and drummers. Crowning the roster of sixty-odd distinguished celebrants at the U-shaped arrangement of tables were some of Whittier's fellow archangels: Ralph Waldo Emerson (himself seventy-four now, and slipping toward senility), Henry Wadsworth Longfellow, Oliver Wendell Holmes. These great "sweet singers" must have seemed, to Mark Twain, a kind of living frieze: the creators of the American literary tradition that he himself was now revising beyond recognition. What to say, given this suffocating augustness, that would rock the joint?

The evening groaned under its self-importance. The Boston *Advertiser* later proclaimed the company the most distinguished ever assembled in America in one room. The celebrants dined for hours as course piled upon course: Oysters, a Puree of Tomato Soup, Smelts *Panne,* Saddles of English Mutton, Squabs *en Compote à la Française,* Stewed Terrapin, Broiled Partridges on Toast, Canvasback Ducks, Dressed Lettuce, and Desserts of *Charlotte Russe, Gelée au Champagne, Gâteaux Variés* and Confections, the successive courses washed down with a succession of wines: a Sauterne, a Sherry, a Chablis; then Mumm's Dry Verzenay or Roederer Imperial champagne with the "removes"; then a claret with the beef; then a Burgundy with the partridges. As the plates were cleared, the literary gentlemen scooted their chairs back to give their full literary bellies some room, and the toasts began. Speaker after mustachioed speaker arose, glass lifted high, to deliver unction upon unction. Sometime in the early mists of Wednesday morning, William Dean Howells called on the speaker most eagerly anticipated. His introduction proved a kind of chilling Greek omen. Mark Twain, Howells assured the assemblage, was "a humorist who never makes you blush to have enjoyed his joke; whose generous wit has no meanness in it, whose fun is never at the cost of anything honestly high or good . . ."[47] It was at this moment, perhaps, that Mark Twain began to feel a certain dryness in the throat.

The small, auburn-haired humorist stood up from his chair halfway down one of the long table rows, acknowledged his fellow guests, and drawled out the first sentences of what had seemed, in conception, an inspired counter-point to all the flowery flattery he'd known would rule the evening's toasts. His remarks took the form of a "frame" tale as impolite, as *Western*, as a spur in the flank of a mule. In the tomblike hush that quickly descended on the room (at least he remembered it that way), Mark Twain realized that he had made a horrible miscalculation.

The tale begins with a younger Mark Twain knocking at a miner's cabin one snowy night in the mining foothills of California. He is received by a bare-foot man of fifty, who looks dejected upon hearing the visitor's *"nom de guerre"* (Mark Twain). "You're the fourth—I'm going to move," the host complains. To Mark Twain's query, "The fourth what?", the miner responds, "The fourth littery man that has been here in twenty-four hours." He names as the others "Mr. Longfellow, Mr. Emerson and Mr. Oliver Wendell Holmes—consound the lot!"[48] In the host's telling—here the assembled dignitaries may have ceased toying with their after-dinner mints—Emerson was seedy, Holmes a three hundred-pound blubberball, Longfellow built like a prizefighter with cropped hair and a pulverized nose. Once inside the cabin, each man gave out with a few lines of his signature poetry. The miner tried to stop the on-slaught—". . . says I, 'Beg your pardon, Mr. Longfellow, if you'll be so kind as to hold your yawp for about five minutes and let me get this grub ready, you'll do me proud' "—but to no avail. The three "littery people" got to drinking, and "swelling" around the cabin, striking attitudes and before long produced a greasy deck of cards and played euchre "at ten cents a corner—on trust."[49] When they spoke, it was always a quotation from each of their more famous poems—Mark Twain's genuflection to their greatness that perhaps escaped the notice it deserved.

When "Mark Twain" suggests to his host that *"these* were not the gracious singers to whom we and the world pay loving reverence and homage; these were imposters," the old miner springs the story's "snapper": "Ah! impostors, were they? Are *you?*"[50] This was intended as the moment of "reversal" into self-satire: the shift of suspicion from the immortal poets to Mark Twain him-self. But by the time he reached it, he sensed horror in the room, and he was speaking (as he recalled it) in a hollow croak. The memory still seared him twenty-eight years later, when he resurrected it for his autobiographical dicta-tions. His reconstruction of the event is fascinating: not for its accuracy, which was almost certainly flawed, but for its employment of his most typical writerly impulse. Here, Mark Twain does what he did with so many of his memories: he improves it, by making a *story* out it. One can almost sense him being struck by idea after idea for embellishment as he goes, much as in his Christmas Eve letter to Susy in 1875. Self-flagellating as the result may be, his memory is also hilarious—one of the most perfect passages of set-piece comedy he ever wrote. He begins by portraying the faces of the deities seated expectantly at the grand table: Emerson, "supernaturally grave, unsmiling"; Whittier, "his beautiful spirit shining out of his face"; Longfellow, with his "silken white hair and his benignant face"; Dr. Holmes, "flashing smiles and affection" for everyone: "I can see those figures with entire distinctness across this abyss of time." He describes his arising and launching into his speech. He describes how, some two hundred words in, he realizes that he is committing an act of secular blasphemy. "The expression of interest in the faces turned to a sort of black frost . . . I went on, but with difficulty . . . always hoping—but with gradually perishing hope—that somebody would laugh, or . . . at least smile, but nobody did." [51]

It gets worse. (And better.) When he pursues the albatross of a joke to its conclusion, the audience and the presiding saints have turned to stone replicas of themselves. He sits down "with a heart which had long ceased to beat," confronted by "an awful silence, a desolating silence." Howells tries to whisper out a comforting word, "but couldn't get beyond a gasp." [52] The next speaker (as he recalls it) is a promising young Wisconsin novelist about to make his first public speech. This fellow arises with "a sort of national expectancy in the air . . ." [53] but in the desolating chill of the moment, the youth can only croak out a few sentences, and then "began to hesitate, and break, and lose his grip, and totter, and wobble, and at last he slumped down in a limp and mushy pile." [54]

There exists no newspaper record of a Wisconsin novelist's meltdown. The Boston *Advertiser* reported the palpable enjoyment of the three subjects of the burlesque. As for the awful, desolating silence, the city's *Daily Globe* remarked on "the most violent bursts of hilarity" that the speech elicited, and the *Evening Transcript* declared, "there was no mistaking the hearty fun elicited by the droll attitude in which these literary lights were represented." [55] Henry Nash Smith, who assembled these records, stipulates that despite this evidence of a noncrisis, there were clearly "misgivings" about the speech: the Chicago *Tribune* reported Whittier with an "odd, quizzical pucker to his lips." [56] And by the third or fourth day after the affair, after newspaper transcripts of Mark Twain's remarks had spread westward from Boston, a backlash in fact set in. Scoldings of "bad taste," opinions that "he ought to have known better," and intimations of "high-flavored Nevada delirium tremens" emanated from such publications as the Cincinnati *Commercial*, the Chicago *Tribune*, and the Springfield (Massachusetts) *Republican*.

Howells of course was devastated. Despite his championing of the realism and psychological acuity that opened the East to the likes of Mark Twain—or maybe because of it—Howells retained his strong reverence for the old masters. As a fellow Westerner and a chief sponsor of Mark Twain, he also retained a kind of phobia about being unveiled as an "imposter" himself, and booted back to Ohio. He, too, recalled a terrible silence—"weighing many tons to the square inch"[57]—a silence broken, in his memory, "only by the hysterical and blood-curdling laughter of a single guest, whose name shall not be handed down to infamy."[58] (Which is just as well, given that this guest probably did not exist.) Howells was afflicted, measleslike, with Mark Twain's "embellishment" contagion.

SOMEWHAT LESS familiar to followers of Mark Twain than his "awful mistake" is the letter of apology he sent to each of his victims, and the sages' responses. He pleaded a purity of intent—"I did it as innocently as I ever did anything . . . But when I perceived what it was that I had done, I . . . suffered as sharp a mortification as if I had done it with a guilty intent."[59] He admitted that "as to my wife's distress, it is not to be measured; for she is of finer stuff than I; and yours were sacred names to her. We do not talk about this misfortune—it *scorches;* so we only think—and think."[60] Holmes and Longfellow wrote gently understanding replies, examples of the civility and forbearance that were natural to the founders of American "polite" literature; qualities that shine all the more brightly against the darker landscape of later times. The letter from Holmes began:

> My Dear Mr. Clemens,
>
> I have just read your letter and it grieves me to see that you are seriously troubled about what seems to me a trifling matter. It never occurred to me for a moment to take offence, or to feel wounded by your playful use of my name . . .
> The world owes you too large a debt for the infinite pleasure and amusement you have furnished to both hemispheres to quarrel with you because your invention has for once led you a little farther than what some would consider the proper limit of its excursions.[61]

Several days later, Longfellow sent his own gentling message.

> Dear Mr. Clemens,
>
> I am a little troubled that you should be so much troubled, about a matter of such slight importance. The newspapers have made all the mischief. A bit of humor at a dinner table is one thing; a report of it in the morning papers is another. One needs the lamp-light, and the scenery. These failing, what was meant in jest, assumes a serious aspect.[62]

Ellen Emerson, writing chastely not to Sam but to Olivia Clemens on behalf of her father, offered the most cryptic of the responses. Her phrasing suggests the Jamesean ambiguity by which polite Boston could eviscerate with a smile.

> Dear Mrs. Clemens,
>
> Today my Father came . . . and brought with him Mr. Clemens's letter, so that I read it to the assembled family, and I have come right up stairs to write to you about it. My sister said "Oh let Father write!" but my Mother said "No, don't wait for him. Go now . . ."
>
> First let me say that no shadow of indignation has ever been in any of our minds . . . But what you will want is to know without any softening [is] how we did feel. We were disappointed. We have liked almost everything we have seen over Mark Twain's signature . . . Therefore when we read this speech it was a real disappointment. I said to my brother that it didn't seem good or funny, and he said, "No it was unfortunate. Still some of those quotations were very good," and he gave them with relish and my Father laughed, though never having seen a [playing] card in his life, he couldn't understand [the reference] like his children.[63]

Some scholars have discerned malice here. Smith quotes a British writer as suggesting that Miss Emerson's "letter of bland forgiveness, gently rubbing it in all the time," was "one of the most subtly irritating documents ever printed."[64]

Whatever else one might make of Mark Twain's Whittier birthday speech, this much seems irrefutably true: he had inaugurated a venerable institution of American popular culture: the celebrity roast.

34

Abroad Again

(1878–79)

I haven't done a stroke of work since the Atlantic dinner; have only moped around," Clemens told Howells a day after writing to his presumed victims.

". . . How could I ever have—

"Ah, well, I am a great & sublime fool. But then, I am God's fool, & all His works must be contemplated with respect."[1]

The oldest, most reliable solution beckoned: *move.* But where? Clemens prodded at Thomas Nast to revive his old idea of a joint tour, with Mark Twain lecturing while the cartoonist sketched out images on a large easel pad. Mark Twain estimated that the "swag" would total $100,000 in one hundred nights, after which the two could "retire from public life."[2] But Nast turned him down; he'd grown to hate the lecturing scene. His mother was the first to learn of his next plan: "Life has come to be a very serious matter with me," Sam informed her in February. "I cannot write a book at home . . . Therefore, I have about made up my mind to take my tribe & fly to some little corner of Europe & budge no more until I have completed one of the half dozen books that lie begun, up stairs . . . We propose to sail the 10th April."[3] He elaborated to Mary Fairbanks that "I want to find a German village where nobody knows my name or speaks any English, & shut myself up in a closet 2 miles from the hotel, & work every day without interruption . . ."[4]

It would almost happen like that, but not on any preexisting project. Among the works that he longed to complete were *The Prince and the Pauper,* the mischievous family memoir "The Autobiography of a Damned Fool" (which Livy eventually made him give up); a draft of "Captain Stormfield's

Visit to Heaven," and a novel, which he never finished, *Simon Wheeler, Detective*. Tacked on to the scaffolding of the unproduced play, *Cap'n Simon Wheeler, The Amateur Detective*, this enigmatic, dream-ridden fantasy involves a young man who travels three days on horseback from Kentucky to a small Missouri town with the intention of shooting to death a cousin, who is described as sappy, sentimental, giddy, and thoughtless, to settle a family feud. Some scholars have seen in it a fictionalized fantasy of Sam Clemens murdering Orion.[5] The unfinished work would take a backseat to a contract he was quietly negotiating for a book about this expedition, which he already imagined as a follow-up success to *The Innocents Abroad:* not with Elisha Bliss—he was fed up with Bliss and the American Publishing Company—but with Bliss's son Frank, who was forming his own enterprise. With the shrewd instinct of the professional writer selecting a narrative foil, Sam arranged for Joe Twichell to join the entourage in August: the two chums would hike the mountains of Germany and Italy together, and Mark Twain would write up their adventures real and imagined in his book.

Clemens reserved two staterooms on the steamship *Holsatia*, set to depart New York for Hamburg, Germany, on April 11. The entourage would include Livy and the girls, Livy's friend Clara Spaulding, and the German nursemaid Rosina Hay. He told some friends and relatives that he expected to be gone between two and three years. Orion reached out to him in the weeks before departure, sending him some hopeful pages of a novel in progress. Sam wasn't impressed. "You make it appear that you are rewriting a portion of Jules Verne's book," Sam chided his brother. "You will have to leave out your gorilla, your disordered compass & your trip to the interior world . . . I think the world has suffered so much from that French idiot that they could enjoy seeing him burlesqued—but I doubt if they want to see him imitated."[6] A month later, he added: "I shall speak [about offering it] to the N.Y. Weekly people. To publish it in that will be to bury it."[7]

In the first week of April Sam dashed off alone to Fredonia for a farewell visit with the Clemens clan. Being again under the same roof with Jane and Pamela, reliving vestiges of the boyhood he had fled, must have merged in his night thoughts with the imminent voyage, and he composed a tone poem of remarkable despair in his notebook: half aphoristic, half syllogistic, all dark.

To go abroad has something of the same sense that death brings—I am no longer of ye—what ye say of me is now of no consequence—but of how much consequence when I am with ye & of ye! I know you will refrain from saying harsh things *because* they can't hurt me, since I am out of reach & cannot hear them. This is why we say no harsh things of the dead.[8]

A good-bye visit to Olivia Lewis Langdon in Elmira, and then the entourage entrained for New York on April 10. They stayed overnight at the Gilsey

House, and the next day they were at sea, leaving the sorrows of the Whittier speech behind. Six weeks later, Ulysses and Julia Grant and one of their sons, Jesse, embarked on their own tour of western Europe, then the Holy Land, and on into the Far East. Jesse, an innocent abroad at nineteen, scandalized Queen Victoria with his bad manners.

The two-week crossing was "almost devilish," Clemens reported: sunlit skies alternating with storms of rain, hail, sleet, and snow. Hamburg proved a restorative port of call. The Clemenses entrained through the German countryside and a string of capacious hotels, and suddenly all dark weather was banished, external and internal. "What a paradise this land is!" Clemens rhapsodized. "What clean clothes, what good faces, what tranquil contentment, what prosperity, what genuine freedom, what superb government! And I am so happy, for I am responsible for none of it." [9] Livy rejoiced in the beauty of the land and the luxury of hotel life. She devoured all available sources of German culture, including the language, more or less. Hearing a woman exclaim, "Wunderschön!" at the sight of some flowers in a hotel dining room, she told her husband, "There—Gott sei dank, I understood THAT, anyway—*window-shade!*" [10] Livy imposed the language on her small daughters. "Poor Susie!" Clemens told Howells. "From the day we reached German soil we have required Rosa to speak German to the children—which they hate with all their souls. The other morning in Hanover, Susie came to me . . . & said, in halting syllables, 'Papa, wie viel Uhr is tes?'—then turned, with pathos in her big eyes, & said, 'Mamma, I wish Rosa was made in English.' " [11]

Their first extended stay was at Heidelberg. The family put up at the Schloss Hotel on the side of a steep, thickly forested mountain overlooking Heidelberg Castle, the town, and the valley beyond. Clemens wired three hundred dollars to Joseph Twichell to cover his August crossing. "We are divinely located," he told Howells, as his ecstasies of description surged to life once more.

Our bed-room has two great glass bird-cages (enclosed balconies) one looking toward the Rhine Valley & sunset, the other looking up the Neckar-cul de sac, & naturally we spend nearly all our time in these . . .

The view from those bird-cages is my despair. The picture changes from one enchanting aspect to another in ceaseless procession . . . To look out upon the Rhine Valley when a thunderstorm is sweeping across it is a thing sublime . . . And then Heidelberg on a dark night! It is massed, away down there, almost right under us . . . Its curved & interlacing streets are a cobweb, beaded thick with lights . . . then the rows of lights on the arched bridges, & their glinting reflections in the water; & away at the far end, the Eisenbahnhof, with its twenty solid acres of glittering gas-jets, a huge garden, one may say, whose every plant is a flame. [12]

These and other notebook entries form the rough drafts of some of the luminous word-pictures in *A Tramp Abroad,* which Clemens began writing on the scene, in May. As is often the case, his transfer of the material from journal to manuscript was marked by an intense distillation, as in this passage from Chapter 2.

> One thinks Heidelberg by day—with its surroundings—is the last possibility of the beautiful; but when he sees Heidelberg by night, a fallen Milky Way, with that glittering railway constellation pinned to the border, he requires time to consider upon the verdict.[13]

Capturing the physical world—terrain, weather, architecture—with words is one of the commonest errands of literature, at least through the modernist era; but the art of it is often a lot more elusive than the passage on the page might make it appear. Mark Twain accomplished this lapidary miracle again and again, from the Mississippi River as "national banner" in *The Gilded Age* through the Acropolis by night in *The Innocents Abroad* through the Rockies as "Sultans of fastness" in *Roughing It* through the interior of a cave in *Tom Sawyer*. Verbal description was among his greatest literary gifts; yet today it ranks among the least remarked, behind his aphorisms and comic tales. Even as Mark Twain was reaching the zenith of this lucidity, technology had begun to devalue visual prose writing as surely as the railroad devalued the steamboat. All those engraved steel-plate illustrations in his big books, working at cross-purposes with the intimate linguistic collaboration he elicited from his readers, were only the beginning. Newspaper rotogravure ushered in the photojournalism age in the 1890s; movies soon followed; and finally television, and typographic language shriveled before each new wave. Iconic images ruled the world's imaginative consciousness. Virtually the first iconic image to saturate the mass media, of course, was the face of Mark Twain.

"I HAVE some good news to tell you . . . *we've quit feeling poor!*" Sam crowed to Howells in June.[14] Livy's inherited interest in her father's company (since renamed McIntyre Coal, with Charley Langdon as president) had remained constricted since the financial panic of 1873. Now, income had begun to flow again as the business recovered. The surge of income would allow the Clemenses "to live in Hartford on a generous scale," Sam exulted, and immediately turned plutocrat: "[O]f course the communists & the asinine government will go to work & smash it all."* Livy computed the family's monthly expenses at $250 a month, a tenth of their household budget back on Farmington Avenue. Europe's remarkable affordability was an amusement to the Clemenses now; in little more than a decade, it would prove a critical necessity.

---

* Later, in his Paris notebook, Clemens expanded his critique: "Communism is idiotcy [sic]. They want to divide up the property. Suppose they did it—it requires brains to keep money as well as make it. In a precious little while the money would be back in the former owner's hands & the Communist would be poor again." (N&J, vol. 2, p. 302.)

The strongest evidence of Sam's psychic revival lay in his renewed appetite for writing: letters, manuscripts, and, strikingly, his journal entries. Wild, eclectic, aphoristic, confessional, experimental, packed with diamond-sharp slivers of sight and sound and *mise-en-scène,* his notebooks from this sojourn show a writerly mind fully regathered and primed for work. Even his chronic kvetching is buoyed with exuberance. "Drat this German tongue,"[15] he wailed gleefully to Howells after two weeks of lessons in which he rapidly fell behind Livy's and the children's progress. His notebook records the early contours of what became a tour de force in Appendix D of *A Tramp Abroad:* "The Awful German Language."

A dog is *der* Hund *the* dog; a woman is *die* Frau the wom[an]; a horse is *das* Pferd, *the* horse; now you put that dog in the Genitive case, & is he the same dog he was before? *No* sir; he is *des* Hundes; put him in the Dative case & what is he? Why, he is *dem* Hund. Now you snatch him into the Accusative case & how is it with him? Why he is *den* Hunden? But suppose he happens to be twins & you have to pluralize him—what then? Why sir they'll swap that twin dog around thro' the four cases till he'll think he's an entire International Dog-Show all in his own person. I don't like dogs, but I wouldn't treat a dog like that. I wouldn't even treat a borrowed dog that way.[16]

Some of the words are so long that they have a perspective. When one casts his glance along down one of these, it gradually tapers to a point like the receding lines of a railway track.[17]

He sketched out a rough draft of what would become one of his most famous aphorisms: "He would rather decline 2 drinks than one German verb."[18]

Another series of entries testifies to the price he paid for his famously sensitive ear. "But the piano is the *special* hell—how it racks one's head!"[19] "The hated Cuckoo-clock."[20] "Heard cuckoo in woods . . . first cuckoo I ever heard outside of a clock. Was surprised to see how closely it imitated the clock . . . The hatefulest thing in the world is a cuckoo clock."[21] "Curse the eternal hotel fashion of noisy pets."[22] "Drat this stupid 'yodling.' "[23] "Church bells are usually hateful things . . ."[24] "Still that ringing goes on. I wish to God that church wd burn down."[25] A special source of acoustical hell was the opera. "Lohengrin . . . accomplished for me what no circumstance . . . has ever been able to do before . . . it gave me the headache."[26] "[The music] so reminds me of the time the orphan asylum burned down."[27] "I hate the very name of opera—partly because of the nights of suffering I have endured in its presence, & partly because I want to love it and I can't."[28] In his resulting book, he devotes an efficient two chapters to a thorough demolition of Wagner, German opera, opera in general, and opera audiences, warming himself up with a two-pronged assault on German theater and German language. Seeing *King Lear* played in German was a mistake, he says; his party "never understood anything but the thunder and lightning; and even that was reversed to suit German ideas, for the thunder came first and the lightning followed after." [29]

The Clemens party moved on to Baden-Baden in July (notebook entry: "See Naples & then die.—but endeavor to die *before* you see B.B." [30]). There, a week later, they greeted Joe Twichell. The arrival of Mark Twain's friend and compliant foil pushed his manuscript-on-the-go to full cruising speed at Chapter 11, and crystallized its design. For the ensuing thirty-five chapters (four short of the conclusion), Twichell co-stars with the narrator as the prim and naïve "Harris." Now the extended joke of the "tramp" sets in: the narrator and his friend are embarked on a planned foot tour of Europe. "I . . . *start* on pedestrian tours," he later explained to Howells, "but mount the first conveyance that offers . . . endeavoring to seem unconscious that this is not legitimate pedestrianizing." [31] An onset of rheumatism in Clemens's legs made the comic conceit all but unavoidable.

Twichell arrived in the nick of time. Clemens's inspired word-portraits at the manuscript's outset had given way to darker preoccupations. Dueling, a normative (if disfiguring) practice among German students, seized his attention, probably on the surge of painful old Washoe memories reawakened. He devoted most of five early chapters to bloody descriptions of student duels and their aftermath, and eventually posited himself as a fictional second in a duel between Frenchmen.

With Livy, the children, and the staff stashed safely in Baden-Baden, Clemens and Twichell stepped off into the Black Forest. The Hartford preacher, still rugged at forty, must have set a challenging pace for the short-legged and now achy-legged author—although in *A Tramp*, it is the dandified "Harris" who huffs and puffs to keep up. They roamed and rambled throughout August and the first month of September, and the book narrative swelled, first in Clemens's overflowing notebooks and then on the draft page.

They run into cuckoos and beer gardens and the Empress of Germany, and then a gigantic French Countess: "—did wish I might venture to ask her for her dimensions." [32] "Harris" twits the narrator about butchering the native tongue during a confidential chat on a train: "Speak in German,—these Germans may understand English." [33]

Mark Twain worked out the rudiments of a running joke.

Guidebook says no tourist should fail to climb the mountain & enjoy the view. Hired boy to climb the Mt & examine (or enjoy?) the view. He felt well repaid for all his trouble. [34]

On August 9, Twichell and Clemens boarded a boat at Heilbronn for an excursion down the Neckar River. They stopped for cold beer and hot chicken along the way, and continued toward Hirschhorn in a smaller craft. Sam maintained his near-preternatural gift for spotting undraped females while traveling: "a dozen naked little girls bathing" just below Jagtfeldt, [35] and, a little later on, a "[s]lender naked girl" who "snatched a leafy bow of a bush across her front & then stood satisfied gazing out upon us as we floated by—a very pretty picture." [36] (In *A Tramp Abroad,* he estimates her age at an eyebrow-raising twelve. Luckily, the illustrator upholds Victorian propriety by giving the protective bush enough foliage to cover the entire Saturday Morning Club.)

This little side trip undergoes a deeply freighted transformation in *A Tramp Abroad.* Mark Twain, writing in Munich in early 1879, spins it into a nonesuch adventure: "*I* am going to Heidelberg on a raft. Will you venture with me?" [37] "Harris" recedes into an amorphous "party," the narrator takes over navigation duties, and a mock-heroic odyssey ensues: At first, "The motion of the raft is . . . gentle, and gliding, and smooth . . . it soothes to sleep all nervous hurry and impatience . . . all the troubles and vexations and sorrows that harass the mind vanish away, and existence becomes a dream . . ." [38] Steamboats pass them by, old tales are told. Then a frightful, if comically miniature storm ("the sea was running inches high" [39]), forces all on board to shore. After some dry-land adventures, the narrator secures another raft for the final leg of the voyage into Heidelberg. A bridge looms; the narrator-navigator realizes a collision is inevitable and "judiciously stepped ashore."

The next moment I had my long coveted desire: I saw a raft wrecked. It hit the pier in the center and went all to smash and scatteration like a box of matches struck by lightning. [40]

This was not the first raft that Mark Twain had "seen" wrecked. He'd wrecked another one in the unfinished boy's novel back home; wrecked it in the final pages before he set the manuscript aside and nearly burned it, out of ideas. Huck Finn and Jim, having unknowingly drifted past Cairo, Illinois, and into slave territory in the night, find their wooden craft suddenly in the path of an upriver Mississippi steamboat. "There was a yell at us, and a jingling of bells to stop the engines, a pow-wow of cussing, and whistling of steam—and as Jim went overboard on one side and I on the other, she come smashing through the raft and tore it to tooth-picks and splinters." [41]

A psychically revived Mark Twain, in Germany, engaged his river saga once more. Justin Kaplan has suggested that in tackling the raft-destruction theme in parody, the writer was defusing old anxieties about the river, and thus ready to pick up his great novel in progress once again. (Kaplan has even gone to the trouble of tracking down the etymology of "Heidelberg," discovering that the name is a telescoping of the German "Heidelbeereberg," which, as Mark Twain presumably discovered as well, means "Huckleberry Mountain.") [42]

Clemens and Twichell continued their excellent "pedestrian" adventure, touring Germany, Switzerland, and their Alpine glaciers and passes by train, steamboat, donkey cart and, occasionally, on foot. Sam marveled at gorges and glaciers and the sun shining on green ice, and clucked in his notes about the reverend's lack of the self-denial spirit after they'd watched a small girl narrowly avoid falling into a rocky chasm: "He continually expresses gratitude that that child was not killed– –never caring a cent for *my* feelings & my loss of such a literary plum hanging ready to fall into my mouth."[43] Twichell was struck by the boyishness of Sam's enthusiasms, especially around running water. "There is nothing that he so delights in as a swift, strong stream," he reported to his wife Harmony. "—To throw in stones and sticks seems to afford him rapture."[44] Twichell himself tossed a piece of driftwood into a river, and beheld Clemens "running down-stream after it as hard as he could go, throwing up his hands and shouting in the wildest ecstasy."[45] Sam detected new signals of "mental telegraphy" between himself and Joe; Twichell remarked on a book's passage moments after Sam had read it; Joe suggested checking for a telegram an instant before Sam was to use the same words; during a mountain hike, Twichell reminisced to Clemens about an old, lost friend—only to encounter the very man as they rounded a turn in the cliff. Sam poured the raw materials of each day's adventures into his notebooks to await transformation in *A Tramp Abroad*.

Mental telegraphy was one thing; the Christian faith was another; and on one of their hikes (as Paine records) Sam was moved to tell his friend what Twichell no doubt suspected all along: he could not accept the divinity of the Bible. The two, says Paine, never spoke of the topic again.

Joseph Twichell said farewell to the Clemenses in Geneva and departed for America on September 9. The Clemens entourage reached Venice, where Mark Twain enjoyed a flurry of recognition from American travelers and expatriate artists, and Livy hit the stores, stocking up on furniture, mirrors, tapestries, Venetian glass, and brass plates for the Hartford house. Then to Florence, and Rome; and finally, back northward and across the border into Germany. In the drizzle and fog of mid-November, they arrived at the dark and chilly hotel on the Karlstrasse in Munich where they would spend the winter while Sam completed *A Tramp Abroad*. Among the hotel's few gestures to conviviality, Sam discovered as he drifted toward sleep on the first night, was a cuckoo clock.

On December 1, 1878, the day after his forty-third birthday, Sam wrote to his mother, "I broke the back of life yesterday & started down-hill toward old age."[46] He signed a letter to Olivia Langdon, "Your now middle-aged son, Saml."[47] Middle age was, to be sure, more freighted in those times. From Geneva a few weeks earlier, Sam had written affectionately to Bayard Taylor, "One of these days I am going to whet up my German again, & take a run to Berlin, & have a talk with you in that fine old tongue."[48] On December 14, concerned by newspaper reports that the literary adventurer-turned-diplomat had been ill, he wrote again: the Clemenses were "heartily glad to hear that you are coming happily out of it," he said, and renewed his promise to "run over to Berlin in the spring."[49] Five days later, the father of American travel literature was dead at fifty-three.

Through the drizzly weather of early 1879, Mark Twain struggled along on *A Tramp Abroad*, a book whose purpose he never quite defined for himself, and to which he never fully surrendered himself, despite a prodigious amount of draft writing. (He had destroyed some four hundred pages of the considerable writing he'd done in Heidelberg—leaving him, as he told Joe Twichell, with only nine hundred pages—half his projected total.) Perhaps he had warmed to Bayard Taylor partly out of a belated respect for the challenges of the genre. This manuscript was not exactly "travel," in the sense of rigorous reportage evoking authentic surrogate experience. Nor did it promise to be what one might comfortably call "literature." Thus it hardly promised to live up to the implication in its title, as a sequel to and co-equal of *The Innocents Abroad*. It was mainly set-piece horsing around, with the "Harris" passages providing a godsend of material. A crazy quilt of dropped-in anecdotes, some of them uproarious, as in the tale that begins Chapter 3, "Baker's Blue-Jay Yarn," and the almost equally clever setup for it at the end of Chapter 2, which introduces the miner-narrator Jim Baker and his point that blue jays are "just as much a human as you be": "A jay hasn't got any more principle than a Congressman," [50] and, "a jay can out-swear any gentleman in the mines. You think a cat can swear. Well, a cat can; but you give a blue-jay a subject that calls for his reserve-powers, and where is your cat?" [51]

Here is a sliver of Mark Twain at his best. Many of his contemporaries, Joel Chandler Harris, for example, found success with animal stories by giving their animals amusing human attributes. As the blue-jay yarn shows, Mark Twain's animal stories rise above the genre partly by virtue of his uncanny ability to make a fictive animal seem simultaneously humanlike (except for its superior sense of humor), and *like the real animal*. Thus,

He cocked his head to one side, shut one eye and put the other one to the hole, like a 'possum looking down a jug; then he glanced up with his bright eyes, gave a wink or two with his wings—which signifies gratification, you understand,—and says, "It looks like a hole, it's located like a hole,—blamed if I don't believe it *is* a hole!" [52]

But such flights of inspiration were the exception to this manuscript, and Mark Twain seemed to understand it. The euphoric energy surge that marked the family's arrival at Heidelberg was long gone. Life began again to weigh on him: middle age, the wetness of the German weather, the endlessness of his writing task, the d—d cuckoo clocks. He found himself looking ahead from the book at hand, pining to get back at Ned Wakeman and his voyage to Heaven. "I *hate* travel, & I *hate* hotels, & I *hate* the opera, & I *hate* the Old Masters," he vented to Howells. [53] ("Hate" had by now become a fairly reflexive usage by Clemens as a gauge of his feelings.) This may have struck his friend as a passing snit, coming as it did from the connoisseur of fine hostelries, the apostle of *move!* but Sam Clemens meant it this time. He made some forty voyages during the rest of his life, he later calculated; and he resented every last one of them.

Through his blackest moods, however—and this one was far from his blackest—Sam Clemens could never conceive of turning his wrath directly upon his closest ally and friend. His reserves of kindliness illuminated his reaction to an installment in the *Atlantic* of Howells's novel in progress, *The Lady of the Aroostook,* which deals with a young American girl's first encounter with Europe.

If your literature has not struck perfection now we are not able to see what is lacking. It is all such truth—truth to the life; everywhere your pen falls it leaves a photograph . . . only you see people & their ways & their insides & outsides as they *are,* & make them talk as they *do* talk. I think you are the very greatest artist in these tremendous mysteries that ever lived.[54]

As if intuiting that the world might think differently—that Howells's embrace of psychological realism would not find acceptance with an American readership—he added:

Possibly you will not be a fully accepted classic until you have been dead a hundred years,—it is the fate of the Shakespeares & of all genuine prophets . . . In that day *I* shall still be in the Cyclopedias, too,—thus: "Mark Twain; history & occupation unknown—but he was personally acquainted with Howells."[55]

A lovely grace note (privately, Mark Twain believed that the explorer Henry M. Stanley was the only living man who would likely be remembered a century later)[56]—but of course, the reverse of history's verdict. In this same year of 1879, the true enduring genius of "these tremendous mysteries" came out with his first masterpiece, which also treated a young American girl's initiation to Europe: Henry James published *Daisy Miller.*

WHEN ALL other subjects in Mark Twain's inventory grew stale—when nothing else could inspire him to creative passion—there was always one standby. "I have just received this letter from Orion," he gloated to Howells in February—"take care of it, for it is worth preserving. I got as far as 9 pages in my answer to it, when Mrs. Clemens shut down on it, & said it was cruel . . . I thought that I was writing a very kind letter."[57] Orion's latest crime against humanity was an imagined lecture series, in which he apparently meant to speak up for the Christian religion against the rising tide of Darwinian scientists and rationalists who were assailing it. (Howells did *not* preserve his offending letter to Sam.) Sam's abusive response to his brother was matched in its unwholesome energy only by his eagerness to let Howells in on his *schadenfreude.* "Did you ever see the grotesquely absurd & the heart-breakingly pathetic more closely joined together?" he asked. "You *must* put him in a book or a play right away . . . You might die at any moment, & your very greatest work would be lost to the world."[58]

Clemens then laid out a ten-point bill of particulars, roasting and damning his brother, variously, for switching his religious denominations, trying to write a burlesque of *Paradise Lost,* failing at agriculture, failing as a lawyer, and other offenses. Seemingly helpless to control his rage, his syntax slackening as he wrote, Sam abruptly switched his vitriol to the unoffending Mollie.

> And then his wife is the only woman who could have so rounded & perfected Orion's character. She was a bald-headed old maid. She was poor & taboo; she wanted position & clothes, oh, so badly; she had the snaffle on this ass before he knew what he was about . . . She is saturated to the marrow with the most malignant form of Presbyterianism . . .[59]

This defamation continued, in a rising pitch of free-associating bile, for some four hundred words. It ranks among the ugliest outbursts of Samuel Clemens's life, especially given its Cain-like onslaught against an overmatched sibling.

THE CLEMENSES gave up dreary Munich for Paris in late February, and discovered that it rained in the City of Light as well. They put up at a drab *pension,* the Normandy Hotel on rue de l'Echelle, where they were soon tracked down by the usual horde of European and American intellectuals. Sam took refuge in a studio in the Montmartre that he'd hired from a painter friend and dug into his writing chores again. "I've been having a dismal time for months over this confounded book," he admitted to Mary Fairbanks in March.[60] He'd had a setback a few weeks earlier: when he'd reached page 900 he'd celebrated the book's halfway mark, on the strength of several 30-page-a-day weeks—only to realize later that he'd been writing only 65 or 70 words a page instead of the hundred he'd assumed. In the next eight days before leaving Munich, he'd cranked it up and churned out 400 pages, "& so brought my work close up to half way."[61] He *had* allowed himself one day off in that spurt, a Sunday, and had used it to write sixty letters.

He reported to Frank Bliss in May that he hoped to have the book finished by the end of July, but his progress in Paris was hindered by rheumatism and dysentery, which kept him in bed for much of five weeks. The "racket and thunder" in the streets drove him crazy until he and Livy moved their beds to the other side of the apartment.

Unwelcome noise was still on his mind in late May when he knocked off a satiric letter to the New York *Evening Post* announcing for the presidency: appalled by the recent muckraking of candidates' lives, "I am going to own up in advance to all the wickedness I have done . . ."[62] For example, "I admit that I treed a rheumatic grandfather of mine in the winter of 1850 . . . I ran him out of the front door in his nightshirt at the point of a shotgun, & caused him to bowl up a maple tree, where he remained all night, while I emptied shot into his legs. I did this because he snored. I will do it again if I ever have another grandfather." [63] His acutely tuned ear, such an asset in his literature, continued to torment him in his daily life. "How rich & strong & musical these voices are," he observed of some peddlers outside his window, "—& how some bore into your head & *through* it—& what long distances they can be heard. What *vast* sounds some of them are!" [64] And, "Dropping the g's—everybody." [65]

In May, Henry rose up again from his dreamy depths. Sam's mind turned once again to the séance with James Vincent Mansfield he had attended in New York in early 1872. His notebook bore the entry

> A Talk with the departed.
>
> To Henry, (through medium Mansfield)—Pray try the other place; it is better to be less comfortable you don't seem to have much intellect left, but even that is worth saving, & a change might help. [66]

At around the same time, Sam Clemens revisited his "Autobiography of a Damned Fool" fantasy, but with an infinitely darker twist. "The Autobiography of a Coward," he wrote in his notebook. "Make him hideously but unconsciously base & pitiful & contemptible." [67]

He reached page 2,041 of the "Tramp" manuscript by the end of that month despite all the distraction, and wishfully hoped to return to America in August, with the book to be published in the fall. He lobbied Frank Bliss on behalf of a young American illustrator named Walter F. Brown, who was in Paris studying painting, and sent the publisher thirty-five drawings by Brown and one by the heretofore obscure illustrator Mark Twain. "(I am making part of the illustrations for it *myself.*)," he'd earlier boasted to Mary Fairbanks. [68] Hartford tugged at him; tugged at them all. "We are mighty hungry," Sam wrote to Twichell, carefully softening the frustration he'd earlier vented to Howells; "—we want to get home & get something to eat." [69] Fried chicken and hot biscuits may have been part of the attraction, but another part was surely economic: Sam totaled their cash and credit-letter outlay in Paris from March through May, and found that it was four thousand dollars. Europe, it seemed, was cheaper than America only if you spent less money there.

IN LATE May, Sam responded to Orion's latest crisis, a certain contretemps with his Presbyterian brethren, with unusual gentleness.

> Never mind the Excommunication. If you made a square deal & told your honest thought in the lecture, I wouldn't care a damn what people say . . . I judge you wrote a good lecture. I am bound to say you showed a deal of moral courage to deliver it. [70]

Orion had been dismissed from his church after delivering a lecture that seemed to support the agnostic views of the pro-Darwinist Robert Green Ingersoll. Orion's talk, titled "Man the Architect of Our Religion," had proved too much for the good churchmen of Keokuk.

Sam closed his letter to his brother with the information, "We leave here in a month." He was optimistic by more than three months.

"FRANCE HAS neither winter nor summer nor morals," he complained,[71] and, "A Frenchman's home is where another man's wife is,"[72] and, "The nation of the filthy-minded"; and to prove it, he copied smutty passages about hands on naked thighs from French matchboxes into his notebook. Before long, he got to feeling a little French himself—at least on paper. In the early summer he reported to Joe Twichell, slyly setting up a bit of pun-filled naughtiness, that a friend of his had recently visited Victor Hugo and the philosopher Ernest Renan,

& had a good time with both of those old cocks, but I didn't go—my French ain't limber enough. I *can* build up pretty stately French sentences, but the producing of an erection of this sort is not my best hold—I make it too hard & stiff—& so tall that only a seaman [sic] could climb it, or a monkey [sic]—but the latter would have to "tend to business" couldn't carry his nuts up in his hands, or any other provender . . .[73]

Sexual self-reliance—a virtue left oddly unexamined by Emerson—seemed much on his mind. He fell in with some American expatriates who'd formed a hale-fellow group called the Stomach Club. At one of their dinners, he unburdened himself on the topic, "Some Thoughts on the Science of Onanism." While not quite up to the aesthetic standards of *1601,* this disquisition had its moments. He mock-quoted a long list of historic figures such as Homer, Caesar, and Queen Elizabeth on the subject, and proceeded to a rather stilted series of witticisms along the lines of, "as an amusement it is too fleeting; as an occupation it is too wearing; as a public exhibition there is no money in it."[74]

THE CLEMENS entourage returned to America on September 3, 1879, aboard the *S.S. Gallia* out of Liverpool. They brought twenty-two freight packages—not counting the crockery, carved furniture, and other goods they'd shipped to America. In light of another financial downturn at McIntyre Coal, this haul began to seem regretfully extravagant. Among Sam's souvenirs was a permanent loathing of all things Gallic (here again, he was an American ahead of his time). "French are the connecting link between man & the monkey," he'd jotted down,[75] and, "Trivial Americans go to Paris when they die,"[76] and, when he couldn't think of anything else, "French women poke your eye with umbrella."[77] They had been away from America for seventeen months. Susy had turned five, and then six on the Continent; Clara, three and then four. Livy had turned pregnant again. Mark Twain's hair had begun to turn gray. His travel manuscript was still unfinished. "I shall finish it here, after the MS comes back to me," he told Frank Bliss from Elmira. "There is nearly matter enough, but I shall probably *strike out* as well as *add.*"[78] He didn't finish it in Elmira. The family spent a week there, then visited Sam's in-laws in Fredonia, before reopening the house on Farmington Avenue in Hartford. (They rehired George, but scaled back on the overall staff because of their new financial anxieties.) And Mark Twain bent over his manuscript yet again.

IN EARLY October, as he was preparing to turn his still-unfinished work over to Bliss, Mark Twain got word of a great ceremonial event scheduled for the following month in Chicago: a reunion of the Army of the Tennessee, at which the honored guest would be its former commander and the former president, Ulysses S. Grant. Grant was hoping to rebuild his tattered political image for another run at the presidency in 1880. Clemens was one of fifteen prominent Americans invited to speak at a banquet for the general that would conclude several days of festivities. He accepted, and then got cold feet. At month's end he notified the committee chairman that he would have to withdraw. Perhaps his stated reason—a book being rushed to production—was the real one. Perhaps the memory of the banquet catastrophe two years earlier played its chilling part. Several days later, Clemens mysteriously reversed himself. An idea had struck him; an idea laden with risk, but too tantalizing to resist. He wired the chairman saying that he would honor the invitation after all—provided that he could decline the toast subject assigned to him in favor of one of his own choosing. He swept *A Tramp Abroad* to one side, and began working on his after-dinner speech.

Sam arrived by train in Chicago on November 10, checked in at the Palmer House, and then walked seventy-nine miles around the lakeside city, by his estimation, taking in the "costly dwellings," the landmarks, and especially the street decorations for the imminent extravaganza. The clean boulevards, the bunting, the streamers, the bronze eagles, the undulating national banners in their purities of red, white, and blue—these were the accoutrements of a city and a Union headed full-thrust toward something powerful, and only half-imaginable. Clemens had seen Chicago a sodden cinder in 1871. Now it was a city resurgent; half a million strong, double that in a decade, a coming prairie empire of skyscrapers and livestock. The warrior awaiting its toasts was the embodiment of American military might and one of the greatest generals in history. At the center of the ceremonies would be this small fugitive from a band of Southern irregulars who but for a weakening of will might have fought against this general in the village of his birth. Samuel Clemens's exuberant letters to Livy amount to a time-capsule preservation of that moment in time. On Tuesday, November 11, he slept through the morning, and then awoke and passed into the living dream world of the great occasion. A parade of eighty thousand Union veterans was forming in the central city, and an equally massive crowd had gathered to view it—in the streets, at windows, and on the roofs of buildings. Clemens joined some dignitaries on the review platform atop two stories of scaffolding; he was studying the vast prairie of humanity, when it suddenly erupted into a volcanic cheer. Another figure had emerged onto the platform behind him.

Gen. Grant bowed to the people two or three times, then approached my side of the platform & the mayor pulled me forward & introduced me . . . The General said a word or so—I replied, & then said, "But I'll step back, General, I don't want to interrupt your speech."

"But I'm not going to make any—stay where you are—I'll get you to make it for me." [79]

Then William Tecumseh Sherman joined the platform dignitaries, and then the parade passed beneath them.

When the head of the procession passed it was grand to see [General Philip] Sheridan, in his military cloak & his plumed chapeau, sitting as erect & rigid as a statue on his immense black horse . . . And the crowd roared again. [80]

At Haverley's Theatre the following night, Mark Twain sat on the stage among thirty or so military demigods—Grant, Sherman, Sheridan, Schofield, Pope, and others—as the Army of the Tennessee received the guest of honor, and Sherman made a speech. As was true at the 1868 reception in Washington, Mark Twain could not take his eyes off Grant. He memorized, and later disgorged to Livy, the details of the general's physical presence—how he sat "facing the house, with his right leg crossed over his left & his right boot-sole tilted up at an angle, & his left hand & arm reposing on the arm of his chair . . ." [81] Clemens found it remarkable that Grant—the same Grant who had superintended the great slaughters at the Wilderness and Cold Harbor—could remain impassive in the face of the applause. Grant

was under a tremendous & ceaseless bombardment of praise & gratulation, but . . . he never moved a muscle of his body for a single instant, during 30 minutes! You could have played him on a stranger for an effigy. Perhaps he never *would* have moved, but at last a speaker made such a particularly ripping & blood-stirring remark about him that the audience rose & roared & yelled & stamped & clapped an entire minute . . . Gen. Sherman stepped to him, laid his hand affectionately on his shoulder, bent respectfully down & whispered in his ear. Then Grant got up & bowed, & the storm of applause swelled into a hurricane. [82]

The reunion's crowning event, the Grand Banquet, took place on Thursday night, November 13, in the bunting-draped Palmer House banquet hall. Five hundred male civic and military leaders, magnificent in their bristling sideburns and polished brass buttons, marched into the hotel through a crowd of onlookers—nearly all of them women. Waiters raced around dispensing food that rivaled the Whittier dinner fare: bluepoint oysters; roast fillet of beef larded with mushrooms; breasts of duck covered with currant jelly; cake; fruits; Roquefort and English cheeses—all accompanied by elegant wines and champagnes. There was even celery.[83] At 10:45 p.m., the cutlery was cleared, the brandy poured, and the toasts began. Mark Twain was to be the last among the fifteen speakers, a tribute to his renown. He had been the last speaker at the Boston affair as well, and for the same reason. The circumstances, in fact, might have been elements from a nightmare: Sam, trapped in a reenactment of his most traumatic humiliation.

As the first toast was announced, Mark Twain rose from his chair and hurried virtually unnoticed toward the rear of the room. A military brass band was assembled there, and he climbed the bandstand steps for a view of the entire panorama. He watched as orator after orator arose to invoke the Defenders of Humanity who received the Sword of Rebellion and rolled the Stone from the Sepulcher of Progress; the Soldiers of the Republic who were grander than the Greek and nobler than the Roman; who shed their Blood until one Flag floated over the Republic without a Master and without a Slave. Somewhere amid the toasts, a battle flag punctured with bullet holes was unfurled. As the old soldiers erupted in applause, General Grant himself stepped into view; the brass band broke into "Marching Through Georgia"; and the banquet hall thundered with shouts and the singing voices of weeping men.

It was getting on past 2 o'clock on Friday morning, the banqueteers into their sixth hour of indigestion, when the penultimate dignitary, General Thomas C. Fletcher, completed his sonorous response "To Woman" ("The fires were kept by them bright upon the Altar of Home . . ."[84]). This was the toast that Mark Twain had shrewdly turned down in favor of his own choice. The general resumed his seat to mild applause, Mark Twain's name was called, and the small Marion Ranger who'd run away from the Civil War shuffled his way toward the front of the room, and captured the Army of the Tennessee, its generals and not least of all, its commander.

"Babies." That was the topic Mark Twain had asked permission to address, instead of "Women." It was an extraordinary leap of intuition, and an even greater act of nerve. If it worked—if its final sentence worked—he would upend the hours of brass-plated solemnity that preceded him with an audacious comic counterpoint. If it didn't, there was always that miner's cabin back in California.

Laughter greeted his first casual sentences; it grew boisterous and swelled into shouts, roars, and convulsive screams as he progressed, never once deviating from his legendary "long talk" and dead pan. "I like that," he began offhandedly, with a nod to the previous remarks. "We have not all had the good fortune to be ladies. We have not all been generals, or poets, or statesmen; but when the toast works down to the babies, we stand on common ground."[85] He draped a figurative arm around the shoulders of the veterans.

"You soldiers all know that when that little fellow arrived at family headquarters, you had to hand in your resignation. He took entire command . . . You had to execute his order whether it was possible or not."[86] He paid homage to their valor, and braided it seamlessly with the domesticity they had yearned for as fighting men. "You could face the death-storm at Donelson and Vicksburg, and give back blow for blow; but when he clawed your whiskers, and pulled your hair, and twisted your nose, you had to take it."[87] (Here a roar erupted.) He slyly flattered the manly young stalwarts they once had been.

If the baby proposed to take a walk at his usual hour, two o'clock in the morning . . . Oh! you were under good discipline . . . you not only prattled undignified baby-talk, but even tuned up your martial voices and tried to *sing!—Rock-a-by Baby in the tree top,* for instance. What a spectacle for an Army of Tennessee![88]

After joshing along in that vein a little longer, Mark Twain began to shift the thrusts of his witticisms toward their ultimate target.

Among the three or four million cradles now rocking in the land are some which this nation would preserve . . . as sacred things, if we could know which ones they are. In one of these cradles the unconscious Farragut of the future is at this moment teething . . .

He enumerated several other imaginary cradles. Then . . .

And in still one more cradle, somewhere under the flag, the future illustrious commander-in-chief of the American armies . . .

Just murmurs of laughter here. The audience was still with him, but it seemed to sense the audacity to come.

. . . is so little burdened with his approaching grandeurs and responsibilities as to be giving his whole strategic mind at this moment to trying to find out some way to get his big toe into his mouth . . .

This drew a surprised laugh—enough to fortify him as he went on to ". . . an achievement which, meaning no disrespect, the illustrious guest of this evening turned *his* entire attention to some fifty-six years ago . . ."

Now all laughter ceased and a "shuddering silence" replaced it, as Mark Twain later recalled, "for this was apparently carrying the matter too far."[89] He boldly risked one of his patented pauses, "to let this silence sink well home,"[90] and then he turned toward the general to unleash his "snapper."

And if the child is but a prophecy of the man, there are mighty few who will doubt that he *succeeded.*[91]

"The house came down with a crash," he scribbled to Livy sometime after 5 a.m., still delirious from two and a half hours of wild congratulation from everyone who could manage to touch him.

> Bless your soul, 'twas immense. I never was so proud in my life. Lots & lots of people—hundreds, I might say—told me my speech was the triumph of the evening . . . even the policemen . . . captured me in the halls & shook hands, & scores of army officers . . . General Pope came to hunt me up . . . Gen. Schofield, & other historic men, paid their compliments.[92]

And there was the matter of the only listener who mattered.

> And do you know, Gen. Grant sat through fourteen speeches like a graven image, but I fetched him! I broke him up, utterly! He told me he laughed till the tears came & every bone in his body ached. (And do you know, the biggest part of the success . . . lay in the fact that the audience *saw* that for once in his life he had been knocked out of his iron serenity.)[93]

35

"A Personal Hatred for Humbug"

(1880)

On the ballast of his triumph at the Grant banquet, Samuel Clemens closed out the 1870s with a flourish of self-redemption. He returned to Boston and faced the same assemblage of literary demigods that had witnessed his fall from grace (as he believed) two years earlier. At an almost identical celebration—a breakfast honoring Oliver Wendell Holmes on his seventieth birthday, with the eyes of Emerson, Longfellow, and Whittier on him once again—Mark Twain delivered a graceful toast that aimed to heal whatever bad feelings might still have existed. Sam insisted that Howells read over his remarks in advance this time, just to be certain that no boozy tramp-sages were lurking between any lines; and at the breakfast on the morning of the 3rd he delivered what amounted to a layered and gently humorous atonement to Holmes. Clemens's toast was an apology of a different sort—for unconsciously plagiarizing Holmes's dedication to *Songs in Many Keys,* in his own dedication of *The Innocents Abroad.** Everyone present understood the deeper message, and Mark Twain left Boston with a renewed sense of acceptance. He returned to a Yuletide season at Nook Farm, a dress rehearsal for the overheated decade that lay just ahead. Livy was frantically completing the restoration of the Farmington Avenue house, uncrating the last of the European furniture, bric-a-brac, and crockery and distributing it among the rooms. At the same time, she was decorating for Christmas and launching her seasonal

---

* Both dedications read, "To My Most Patient Reader and Most Charitable Critic, MY AGED MOTHER, This Volume is Affectionately Inscribed."

charitable rounds. "Christmastide" was to become a major production in the Clemens household, with Livy shouldering most of the duties. Clara remembered the "royal" preparations: the prodigious buying and wrapping of presents for the family, the staff, friends abroad, the poor children of Hartford, "for the sick and insane."[1] On Christmas Eve, Livy would recite " 'Twas the Night Before Christmas" to the girls, and then Sam, in a cotton Santa Claus beard, would burst into the room, gather his daughters, and tell them stories about his experiences on his journey around the world.

Weak, as usual, from exertion and her pregnancy, Livy was headed for another collapse, which she forestalled until the early New Year. On Sam's forty-fourth birthday she wrote to her mother,

I told Mr Clemens the other day, that in this day women must be everything they must keep up with all the current literature, they must know all about art, they must help in one or two benevolent societies—they must be perfect Mothers—they must be perfect housekeepers & graceful gracious hostesses, they must know how to give perfect dinners, they must go and visit all the people in the town where they live, they must always be ready to recieve their acquaintances—they must dress themselves & their children becomingly and above all they must make their houses *"charming"* & so on without end—then if they are not studying something their case is a hopeless one.[2]

Sam acknowledged his wife's overexertion in his inimitable style. "Livy wants Sue & Mother to excuse her from writing, because she is 'gutting the house.' I wish to God she wouldn't use such language."[3]

Livy struggled to maintain her "perfection" as she and Sam waded into a round of swank social display: hosting dinner parties for a succession of famous visitors; joining a thousand guests at a reception given by the widow of Samuel Colt, inventor of the repeating firearm, at Armsmear, the family's mansion on the edge of Hartford. Sam, who'd practically memorized the "automated house" in Baltimore, could not have helped envying Samuel Colt's legacy as he surveyed the mansion and grounds. Colt had produced a world-changing mechanical device that in turn produced fabulous wealth. Writing, as Tom Sawyer might have remarked, wasn't shucks to inventing.

Certainly not these days. He wasn't quite as finished with the d—d *A Tramp Abroad* as he'd told Howells. Elisha Bliss was back in control of Mark Twain's publishing. He'd regained publishing rights to *A Tramp* after Frank conceded that he was over his head in his new venture; both Mark Twain and Frank returned rather gratefully to the old swindler's company. Elisha, far more exacting than his son, imposed a 2,600-page count on his author. Sam filled the Farmington Avenue house with fresh bursts of cigar smoke and profanity with every new page, and drove his exhausted wife a little closer to the edge. He needed 300 pages to make Bliss's quota; wrote 600; tore up 312 of those; and moaned to Howells he'd poured a total of 4,000 pages into the infernal manuscript. He might have been writing through Groundhog Day, had not a Nook Farm neighbor alerted him that his wife was on the verge of collapse. Mary Beecher Perkins, a sister of Henry, burst into the billiard room on January 7, 1880, and scolded Sam that giving lip service to his wife's need for rest was no longer enough: "[I]t is time to use *force;* she *must* have a change; take her home & leave the children here."[4] That very day, Clemens thrust the final 288 pages at Bliss in the American Publishing office (he'd been about to tear *those* up when Mary Perkins interrupted him), and set out for the Hartford train station, the bundled-up Livy leaning on his shoulder. They remained at the Langdon house three weeks, Livy carefully nursed by her mother.

The American Publishing Company, functioning at maximum speed and efficiency for a change, sent *A Tramp Abroad* to its subscription salesmen around the country on March 13, just two months after receiving the final pages from Mark Twain. It sold some 62,000 copies through 1880, respectable but well off the pace of *Roughing It* and *The Gilded Age,* to say nothing of *The Innocents Abroad.* Clemens blamed the Canadians for "working us heavy harm."[5] But he now regarded the press as a nemesis equal to the pirates. "I am glad no big newspaper has had a chance to give it a black eye with a left-handed notice," he told Elisha Bliss, "for . . . I see distinct evidence that if the Gilded Age had been kept away from the newspapers . . . its early sale would not have been 'knocked.' "[6]

Reviews ranged from bad to worse. Howells, predictably, kept his dangerous left hook well away from Mark Twain's eyes in the *Atlantic* in May 1880. His lone power punch was the observation that "Mr. Clemens" went on a little too long about climbing the Riffelberg—"we would rather have another appendix in its place."[7] He conceded, "The appendixes are all admirable . . ."[8] Howells's criticism never lacked profundity, and this critique offered its underappreciated share. Howells found something in the book's "humor" that the other critics had failed to notice, or else misidentified as "studied" or "straining": specifically, a current that flowed just below the surface of Mark Twain's jibes at European manners, languages, bloody folkways, and twittering cuckoo clocks, and his fellow American travelers. It was an undercurrent of rage. Howells made a prophetic link here: it was *precisely* this rage, he argued, that conferred revisionist greatness on Mr. Clemens's humor: separated it categorically from that of the derivative "school" rapidly forming in Mark Twain's wake—forming so rapidly that "sober-minded people are beginning to . . . question whether we are not in danger of degenerating into a nation of wits."[9] Unlike these imitators, Howells asserted, Mark Twain did not simply seek to amuse. (This distinction applied equally to Mr. Holmes and his generation of refined aphorists, though Howells was too polite to say so.) Mark Twain's laughter was a seamless extension of his anger.

It may be claiming more than a humorist could wish to assert that he is always in earnest; but this strikes us as the paradoxical charm of Mr. Clemens's best humor. Its wildest extravagance [springs from] a deep feeling, a wrath with some folly which disquiets him worse than other men, a personal hatred for some humbug or pretension that embitters him beyond anything but laughter . . . At the bottom of his heart he has often the grimness of a reformer; his wit is turned by preference not upon [the trivial] . . . but upon things that are out of joint, that are unfair or . . . ignoble, and cry out to his love of justice or discipline.[10]

These insights, offered by a contemporary who knew both his subject and the received cultural assumptions that his subject was revising, seem at least to hold their own against the counterorthodoxy that took hold after Mark Twain's death: that his humor, and anger, amounted to character deformations, and worked fatally against his higher literary potential. To the contrary, Howells shouted into this approaching wind: these qualities, far from restrictive, were liberating—both to Clemens and to a still-nascent America whose native personality Clemens was helping it to realize.

AMERICA, STRUGGLING toward that personality, shrugged off more layers of its provincial heritage and reached new levels of gentrified sophistication as the 1880s began. "Evolution" had mostly lost its power to shock, and had become a template for all sorts of transforming energy short of "revolution." Infinite progress, infinite wealth, the control of nature, and the perfectibility of man were commonplace aspirations. In 1880, urban industrial workers surpassed farmers for the first time in the American population. The first pay telephone was installed in a New Haven bank. Broadway was lit by electricity and the Great White Way blazed in the night; and Thomas Edison redirected his captured currents from the vacuum bulb to the electric chair. No one relished it more than Mark Twain, the provincial town boy turned Eastern squire. Free at last from the dead weight of the European travel book, he felt reenergized, ready for new exploits; hungry, and in fact anxious, to claim his slice of the American capitalist pie. And with good reason: he had a wife, two children (with a third on the way), a social image, and a growing house to feed.

Inventions? He knew a thing or two about inventions. Did he not hold the patent for the Adjustable and Detachable Garment Strap? (All right; no sales, but a *patent*.) Had his Self-Pasting Scrapbook not captured the fancy of the twenty-five thousand?

"I got up a kind of marvelous invention the other day, & I could make a mighty fortune out of it . . ." he boasted to Pamela in late February.[11] He had purchased four-fifths of a product patent, he told Orion, and had even dreamed up an improving application for it on his own "which I think will utterly annihilate & sweep out of existence one of the minor industries of civilization, & take its place . . ."[12] The invention was Kaolatype, a clay-based method that promised to speed up the production of engraved illustrations, which were increasingly demanded by the book-reading public. Dan Slote, the "sinner" whose larking wisecracks were preserved in *The Innocents Abroad,* owned the patent, and alerted his famous *Quaker City* shipmate to the opportunity. Sam should have been wary: Slote, Woodman & Company, which had published Mark Twain's Self-Pasting Scrapbook, failed in July 1878, shortly after receiving a $5,000 loan from Clemens. It later reorganized as Daniel Slote & Company. Clemens snapped up 800 of his friend's 1,000 shares as soon as Slote contacted him. The cost was $20,000, which Sam paid in cash, buying him the presidency of Kaolatype, the company. Sam proposed to adapt Kaolatype to incorporate brass molds that could stamp out book covers. It was a pretty good idea, and worked—briefly. An even better idea was halftone photoengraving, introduced by Frederic Ives six years later, which made any manual process obsolete, and doomed Kaolatype, and led indirectly to the lithographic dynasty of another Ives, James, and his partner Nathaniel Currier.

Kaolatype was for practice. In a notebook entry for 1881, at the middle of a series of fragmentary musings concerning the Kaola process, Sam jotted:

Get K base & clay & have Page experiment.[13]

"K" obviously refers to Kaola. "Page" is the first known reference by Clemens to the aspiring inventor trying to improve a technology allied to engraving: typesetting. "Page" was just then pocketing the first trickle of the hundreds of thousands of dollars he would receive in investments from Clemens over the next fourteen years—the lifeblood of Mark Twain's fortune. Clemens met the thirty-two-year-old James William Paige (whose name he consistently misspelled, in a kind of Freudian typo) sometime in 1880, through a Hartford jeweler named Dwight Buell. During cigars and conversation in Sam's billiard room one evening, Buell told his host about a fellow right there in Hartford who was working on a machine that could set type as fast as four men working at once—could set entire *words* instead of mere letters—and whose speed was bound to double, perhaps triple, as its inventor perfected the design. Clemens understood the implications instantly: a worldwide revolution in publishing efficiency; the first breakthrough in the technology since Gutenberg; an end to the aggregate centuries, eons, of finger-produced, line-by-line, em-by-em sliding of molded-lead alphabet characters into the composing stick by legions of weary, underpaid men and boys such as Orion and Sammy Clemens, and Will Howells, and Ben Franklin. Millions in it. Millions.

Clemens believed a machine like that was impossible. He bought $2,000 in stock via Buell on the spot anyway. Within days, he visited the inventor in his shop (in the Samuel Colt arms factory, as irony would have it) and watched the skeletal apparatus do a rudimentary version of its stuff. He laid down $3,000 more. "It is here," as he ruefully recalled in 1901, "that the music begins."[14]

James Paige was but one denizen in the crowded Eden of machine-worshipping dreamers for whom the Industrial Age was a kind of Genesis: schoolteachers and shop owners who brainstormed away in thousands of sheds and cellars and attics, frowning over their calipers, marking down the arrows and equation marks along the path to Eureka! Of these, hundreds were tinkering at contraptions similar to Paige's, and several had already secured patents. The marketable automatic typesetter was the yet undiscovered Comstock Lode of gadgetry. A Rochester native, "a small, bright-eyed, alert, smartly dressed man" in Paine's description,[15] Paige had been summoned to Hartford three years earlier by the Farnham Type-Setting Company, which had bought the patent to a promising but flawed machine in North Carolina, and wanted somebody who could fix it. Paige said he could. Of all the people who believed him, no one believed him longer or with more irrational passion than Samuel Clemens, who was helpless before the inventor's mesmeric, poetic blandishments of imminent success and wealth, even as the years bled on and Sam's and Livy's fortunes bled white. Perhaps it was an overwhelming obsession-compulsion; perhaps it was uncontrollable money lust. Or perhaps for the first time in his life, Samuel Clemens had run into someone as dreamy as he was, and as transcendently unconcerned about the boundary where fact ended and fiction began: perhaps, in the end, the Paige typesetting machine was simply the best tall tale he'd ever heard.

At about this same time, Mark Twain rediscovered his zest for writing—a felicitous rediscovery, given that he was otherwise sowing the seeds of his financial ruin. His notebook (Number 19, now, among those preserved) shows him snatching idea fragments out of the air and pinning them like butterflies in amber: he thought of licorice drops and pincushions;[16] the superiority of 29th Street hotels above all others in New York; and "Whoopjamboreehoo" and "Blatherskite" and "Flapdoodle High-daddy."[17] He roughed out some new jokes.

> (In Methodist class-meeting.)
> *He*—What was your first notable Christian experience, after you became reconciled to God?
> *She*—I had a miscarriage.
> (Pretend this happened somewhere.)[18]

In March, he told Howells of a larger game afoot: "I take so much pleasure in my story that I am loth to hurry, not wanting to get it done."[19] He was not referring to the Huckleberry Finn saga, although he had quietly picked it up again that month after more than three years of neglect. No, this one was prettier, more charming, the sort of novel one wrote after reading a lot of other books. A novel with footnotes! (Not even *Holmes* wrote novels with footnotes.) "Did I ever tell you the plot of it? It begins . . . seventeen & a half hours before Henry VIII death, by the swapping of clothes *and places*, between the prince of

Wales & a pauper boy of the same age & countenance . . ." [20] Here it was, the first direct allusion by Mark Twain to his central, and infinitely suggestive cluster of literary obsessions: identities switched and mistaken, twins and twinning, stolen birthrights, impostors, pretenders, false claimants. As America shrugged off its provincial heritage, Mark Twain acted to shrug off his, by essaying a mannered novel about a poor boy of the 16th century who shrugs off *his* low-down status and walks on the royal side, for a while.

Princes and paupers had been opposing one another in Mark Twain's imagination at least since that cryptic remark from wild Washoe in 1864—*"We have lived like paupers that we might give like princes."* While opening his soul to Britain and its heraldic history in 1873, he'd been absorbed by the sensational London trial of a fat eccentric who claimed to be the elegant Roger Charles Tichborne, young heir to a baronetcy who had gone missing at sea two decades earlier. The case bulged with allegations of false identities, false names, and other fantastical perfidies, and the claimant was finally judged to be an Austrian butcher seeking to shrug off *his* proletarian past. Coincidentally, Clemens had been receiving occasional letters from a distant cousin who billed himself "the Rightful Earl of Durham." Finally, Mark Twain's absorption in things British had led him to English history and historical drama: the great meditative tomes of William E. H. Lecky and J. A. Froude; parts of David Hume; Shakespeare, always Shakespeare, whose works he knew nearly as well as he knew the Bible. In 1876 he'd come upon *The Little Duke,* by Charlotte M. Yonge, which covered the boyhood of the Duke of Normandy. The setting was France, but the genteel tone and emphasis on moral education struck him as exactly the sort of thing that a polite fellow from an elite Hartford literary neighborhood would want to publish.

> Imagine *this* fact—I have even fascinated Mrs. Clemens with this yarn for youth. My stuff generally gets considerable damning with faint praise out of her, [but this time] my mill doesn't grind fast enough to suit her. This is no mean triumph, my dear sir. [21]

And not only Mrs. Clemens. The daughters were nine and seven now. Susy, who had inherited her father's acuteness of noticing as well as his temper, was already surpassing him as a creature of elite society. Perhaps it was the buzz at the Saturday Morning Club that her Papa was a "humorist," accompanied by a little refined eye-rolling, that had made her an early lobbyist for the Polite side of Papa (although she couldn't suppress an atavistic thrill at his occasional descent into slang). Reading draft chapters to his pregnant wife and daughters by the fireplace had seldom drawn more gratifying feedback. As he worked, his mail brought more evidence of a high-end desire for uplift from Mark Twain: a Hartford minister requested something with a sober character; and from a lakeside cabin in Ohio, a hideaway that Sam on a visit had dubbed the Lodge of Fair Banks, issued a prescription-request for a new book "that would give you the fresh enjoyment of *surprising* the public . . . The time has come for your *best book* . . . your best contribution to American literature." [22]

IN THE transport of all this bookish romance, Samuel Clemens idly opened a letter from the mail one March day, and was stunned to find himself reconnected with the enduring romantic crush of his young manhood. The inspiration for the "platonic sweetheart" of his dreams, Laura Wright, had reemerged into his waking life—at a remove of sixteen hundred miles. The letter, crafted with sturdily rounded penmanship, was from a twelve-year-old schoolboy in Dallas named David Watt Bowser. "Wattie," as he signed himself, was writing "Dear Mr. Twain" to ask his help in a class assignment. Nothing unusual there; such requests poured in all the time. It was the name of Wattie's teacher that had Sam staring as if he'd seen a ghost.

Wattie opened in a jovial, between-us-men-of-the-world tone.

At school we were required to select some man among the living great ones, (a live dog is better than a dead lion, you know), with whom we would exchange places, and I selected you. My reasons for so doing, you will see in my composition, if you do not throw both articles in the fire, before you have read even this far . . .[23]

Wattie elaborated his "reasons for so doing" in his enclosed composition: "First, because he is so Jolly; I imagine him to be a funny man . . . who always keeps every body laughing and who is happy as the Man in the Moon looks"; second, because "he" is worth millions; third, because "he" has a beautiful wife and children, and "Fourth—Because I have been an agent * for his book, ('A Tramp Abroad') and because he has everything a man could have." [24] The letter continued:

A few of us boys thought it would be a "lark" to send our compositions to our favorites, and ask them if they would be willing to change with us, and if their fame, riches, honors, and glory had made them perfectly happy—in fact to ask them if they would "Be a boy again." [25]

Wattie had some specific questions: "When you were a little boy did you think you would be a great man, or were you like Tom Sawyer? I like Tom splendidly, but his teacher did not make him wish and try to be great as ours does." He added a bit of shrewd buttering up—"I do not think Mr. Longfellow, Mr. Whittier &c. can stand a joke like you, so I feel surer than the other boys, that I will have a line in return." He signed off "With profound Respect"—and then added his thunderclap of a postscript.

* Inferentially, a door-to-door subscription salesboy.

O! I forgot to tell you that our principal used to know you, when you were a little boy and she was a little girl, but I expect you have forgotten her, it was so long ago.[26]

The principal's name was printed on the report card. She doubled as Wattie's teacher. Her name was Laura M. Dake—née Wright.

"A line in return"? Wattie could hardly have been prepared for the out-pouring of calculated soulfulness that came churning back from Hartford to Dallas. Would Mark Twain be a boy again? Well, without any "modifying stip-ulations," no, but . . .

Would I live it over again under certain *conditions?* Certainly I would! The main condition would be, that I should emerge from boyhood as a "cub pilot" on a Missis-sippi boat, & that I should by & by become a pilot, & remain one. The minor condi-tions would be these: Summer always; the magnolias at Rifle Point always in bloom, so that the dreamy twilight should have the added charm of their perfume; the oleanders . . . always in bloom, likewise; the sugar cane always green . . .[27]

And his boat, Mark Twain told Wattie, would be a big and dignified freight boat, never in a hurry, and her crew "should never change, nor ever die . . ."

And in addition, I should require to be notorious among speakers of the English tongue . . . And when strangers were introduced I should have them repeat "Mr. Clemens?" doubtfully, & with the rising inflection—& when they were informed that I was the celebrated "Master Pilot of the Mississippi," & immediately took me by the hand & wrung it with effusion, & exclaimed, "O, I know *that* name very well!" I should feel a pleasurable emotion trickling down my spine & know I had not lived in vain.[28]

It was a bravura, not to say scenery-chewing, performance—intended, almost beyond any doubt, as much for the principal/teacher reading over Wattie's shoulder as for the boy himself. Lest there be any misunderstanding along those lines, Mark Twain added the faux afterthought toward the end,

No indeed, I have not forgotten your principal at all. She was a very little girl, with a very large spirit, a long memory, a wise head, a great appetite for books . . . with grave ways, & inclined to introspection—an unusual girl. How long ago it was! Another flight backward like this, & I shall begin to realize that I am cheating the cemetery.[29]

Mark Twain and Wattie exchanged ten letters over the ensuing months, the boy ardent, the author indulgent and a little distracted. Wattie poured out his kidhood enthusiasms: "I like plucky heroes better than martyrs, don't you?" "I am looking anxiously forward to the next book." "Sometime since, I sent you a horned frog, and hope it went through all right." Mark Twain replied with guarded forbearance: "Many thanks for the photograph & the pretty pictures." "I was very glad you got the gold medal." "My boy, I clear forgot about that frog, because he came when I was in Canada . . . The gardener hunted for him every day or two, & three days ago he found him." [30] But this was only the "surface" correspondence. On a subtler level, two long-ago innocent sweethearts were communing with each other through the innocent medium of a boy. One of Wattie's letters passed along the information that Mrs. Dake was pleased with Mark Twain's renown, "for she remembers you as the best friend of her youth." [31] The schoolteacher may also have influenced Wattie to report that she had cautioned one of her young female students against adopting a "hard-to-get" attitude with boys, because she might suffer the same fate "as a romantic girl *she* once knew did." "This girl had some wild ideas about 'being too lightly won' &c., and when her Prince really came she said 'no.' She thought he would come back and 'take her in a whirlwind'—but he went his way and she never saw him again." [32]

Laura Dake herself did not write to Clemens during the Wattie Bowser correspondence, but she apparently talked up the connection among her friends. In the second week of May, a letter arrived at Nook Farm from a forty-four-year-old man named Thomas H. Murray, who lived in McKinney, Texas, thirty-two miles from Dallas. (Murray was Wattie Bowser's uncle, according to his letter of May 26.) It confirms that young Sam Clemens did indeed pay a courting visit to Laura at her hometown in Missouri after meeting her aboard the *John J. Roe.*

> Dear Sir: I remember a young man, (and often have I thought of him,) bearing your honored name. I met him at Warsaw, Mo., before the war, "fighting for his *Wright's.*" I was then chief clerk of the Missouri Legislature—he, a sailor on the Father of Waters. We met at Judge Wright's: he, courting Laura; I, eating Brandy peaches with the Mother.
>
> "Art thou the man?" If yes, then I rejoice that my boy-hood friend has kept his light burning *on top* of the bushel-measure, and mankind have had pleasure thereat. [33]

Clemens responded promptly:

> I remember you well, & most pleasantly, too. Do you remember the night journey in the stage coach? I ask because last year, in . . . Germany, I came across a particularly seedy old fellow . . . who said *he* was along, that night . . . & that the horses ran away & were making for a precipice when he seized the reins & saved our lives—then he stuck me for ten dollars. I paid him, though I intimated that I thought he charged rather high. The truth is, I did not believe [him] . . . Do you remember that man? . . . [34]

Five years later, Samuel Clemens still had not completely cooled down. He brooded about Laura in a notebook entry: "May 26 '85.—This date, 1858,

parted from L, who said 'We shall meet again 30 years from now.' " *[35] The "L"
was characteristic: the writer always kept Laura's identity deeply camouflaged
during Olivia's lifetime, an indication that he felt guilt over his obsessive
memories.

I T W A S during the bright false spring of 1880, while the Grant testimonial
applause still roared in his reverie, while his investing prospects seemed to
promise endless wealth, and while his ornate book in progress seemed to
point him toward a literary earldom unimaginable even a year earlier—it was
in this season of hope unbounded that Samuel Clemens cast his darkest spell
on his brother Orion. At fifty-five, Orion remained ineffectual, a locus of
Sam's perpetual pity, guilt, scorn, and perhaps dread. He and Mollie depended on Sam's stipends for their livelihood in Keokuk; he begged for Sam's
instructions and approval; he accepted Sam's most lacerating upbraidings
without complaint, and he cheered every new triumph of Sam's with enthusiasm. "Another Ten Strike for the family! Let me shake hands with you across
the continent," he exulted on reading the newspaper reports of Mark Twain's
toast at Chicago.[36] He had been laboring for the weeks following his ex-
communication on a foredoomed book seeking to prove that morality and
religion are independent of each other—largely on the strength of one encouraging letter from Sam. Sam responded to his brother's warmth by inviting Orion and Mollie to Hartford for a February visit, sending them the
money to cover travel expenses. The visit went well. Not long after returning
to Keokuk, Orion opened a letter from Sam that contained one of the stranger
literary suggestions ever to issue from a gentleman writer of the East. Sam was
writing, he told Orion,

to suggest to *you* to write two books which it has long been my purpose to write, but I
judge they are so far down on my docket that I shan't get to them in this life.

I think the subjects are perfectly new. One is "The Autobiography of a Coward," &
the other "Confessions of a Life that was a Failure."

My plan was simple—to take the absolute facts of my own life & tell them simply &
without ornament or flourish, exactly as they occurred, with this difference, that I
would turn every courageous action . . . into a cowardly one, & every success into a failure. You can do this, but only in one way; you must *banish* all idea of an audience—for
few men can straitly & squarely confess shameful things to others—you must tell your
story *to yourself* . . . you must not use your own name, for *that* would keep you from
telling shameful things, too.[37]

Even better, Sam went on,

---

* If, as records show, the *Pennsylvania* docked at New Orleans on May 16, Twain is probably
in error in this dating by a week or so.

would be to tell the story of an abject coward who is *unconscious* that he is a coward; & to tell the story of an unsuccessful man who is blissfully unaware that he was unsuccessful & does not imagine the reader sees he was unsuccessful.

. . . Tackle one of these books, & simply tell your story to *yourself,* laying all hideousness utterly bare, reserving nothing . . . If the book is well done, there's a market for it. There is no market, yet, for the one you are now writing—it should wait.

Then, the bland sign-off—"Love to Molly & all."[38]

Mark Twain had proposed the prototype of the 20th century's defining cash-cow genre, the confessional memoir. He was suggesting that his brother, in the depths of his helpless abasement, abase himself a little further, for cash. "The Autobiography of a Coward," of course, was the idea that Mark Twain had jotted to himself in Paris the previous year. He'd fled to Europe in part to make himself invisible after the Whittier dinner embarrassment—an absquatulation that, like his departure from Virginia City on the eve of that famous near-duel, might qualify as an act of cowardice. Now, having erased his humiliation with the bold strokes in Chicago and Boston, Mark Twain threw the idea at Orion, like a cudgel. And Orion accepted it. As his brother's earnest chapters began arriving at Nook Farm, Sam responded with what seemed respectful encouragement.

I have stolen part of my Sunday holiday & have read your chapters. I like them very much.[39]

And later,

It is a model autobiography.

Continue to develop your own character in the same gradual, inconspicuous & apparently unconscious way. The reader, up to this time, may have his doubts . . . but he can't say decidedly, "This writer is not such a simpleton as he has been letting on to be." Keep him in that state of mind. If, when you shall have finished, the reader shall say, "The man *is* an ass, but I really don't know whether HE knows it or not," your work will be a triumph.[40]

His tone was entirely different as he recounted the project to Howells.

He started in—& I think the result is killingly entertaining; in parts absolutely delicious. I'm going to mail you 100 pages or so of the MS. Read it; keep his secret; & tell me, if, after surplusage has been weeded out . . . you'll buy the stuff for the Atlantic at the ordinary rates for anonymous matter from unknown writers.[41]

Howells never bought "the stuff." This was the manuscript that wrung his heart and left him feeling haggard after he'd finished it—the manuscript that elicited his warning that the writer's soul was laid too bare; and his plea not to let anyone else even see the passages about the autopsy of Marshall Clemens. "The Autobiography of a Coward" (or "Confessions of a Failed Business Man," or whatever Orion chose to call it) was never published in any form. Sam kept the manuscript for several years, and ultimately showed it to Albert Bigelow Paine, who conferred on Orion, by then years dead, the kindness of losing it.

THE YEAR 1880 saw a profusion of European art that would make obsolete the Twainian barbs about petrified reverence for the Old Masters. Vincent Van Gogh took up painting in that year, and Monet painted *Sunset on the Seine in Winter,* and the sculptor Rodin turned out *The Thinker,* and Renoir began his riverscape masterpiece, *Luncheon of the Boating Party.* In America, artistic expression lagged behind postwar industry and capitalism. The ranking literary event was *Ben Hur,* by the former Civil War general Lew Wallace, a novel about the origins of Christianity that ended with a chariot race. In California, the poet Joaquin Miller published *Utopia,* and the British novelist Robert Louis Stevenson arrived with his new wife at an abandoned mining camp above Napa Valley, not far west of Washoe, where he worked on *Treasure Island.*

America's most important transition from past to future was political. At the Republican National Convention in Chicago in June, Ulysses S. Grant lost his bid for a third term, as the nomination went to the log cabin–born Ohio governor James A. Garfield after thirty-five ballots. Garfield had been a congressman and a Civil War general. Chester A. Arthur was nominated for vice president. Grant had toured every former Confederate state in the months leading up to the convention, preaching the virtues of Republicanism as the country's national party, seeking the greatest good for the greatest number; and scoring the Democrats as a sectionalist party, intent only on preserving the "solid South." He was cordially received there, but at Chicago his message of conciliation was muted by memories of the scandals that had diminished his two terms in the 1870s. Grant, who had been treated like a royal emissary during his world tour, being received by Queen Victoria and emperors in Siam and Japan, now retired to private life to face years of business failure, obscurity, and financial anxiety. He had made the principled decision to resign his army commission, and the salary that went with it, when he first ran for president in 1868. He and his wife Julia lived for a while on the income from a quarter-million-dollar fund assembled by his friends; but in time, the securities in which the fund was invested went under and the Grants faced destitution.

On July 26, 1880, at the Langdon house in Elmira, Livy gave birth to Jane Lampton Clemens, the last of the children she and Sam would have. The seven-pound baby was known forever afterward as Jean. Sam stayed anxiously at Livy's bedside during her labor—she had remained thin throughout her pregnancy—but the delivery passed without a crisis, and she began to recover after a few days. Sam wrote a letter "from" Jean to his mother in Fredonia, and reported to Howells a week later that "[t]he new baby is thoroughly satisfactory, as far as it goes; but we did hope it was going to be twins."[42]

At around that time, Clemens opened a letter from a subscription publisher in Philadelphia named George Gebbie and found a book proposal that he liked immediately: an anthology of American humor, to be edited by Mark Twain. He invited Howells to share the editorial work (but not necessarily the authorial credit) with him and Howells accepted with delight, consigning himself to nearly a decade of intermittent distraction.

Grant, campaigning for Garfield, made a stop at Hartford on October 16, and once again Samuel Clemens was waiting to ambush him with laughter. He labored through three drafts of a three-paragraph welcoming speech that he delivered at Bushnell Park before a great crowd of his fellow citizens. Ornate and celebratory until its second-to-last sentence, Twain's humor detonated on the widely known fact that the government had not acted to restore the former president's army commission and pension.

"Your country stands ready from this day forth," Sam concluded, to testify her measureless love and pride and gratitude toward you in every conceivable [pause] inexpensive way.[43]

At the word "inexpensive," the crowd erupted, and the general, Sam declared in a letter to Howells, "came near laughing his entire head off."[44]

ON OCTOBER 24, Sam began a letter to Orion with the curt announcement that "Bliss is dead." His next sentence read, "The aspect of the balance-sheet is enlightening."[45] The man who had recruited the humorist-lecturer Mark Twain into subscription book publishing, issued the titles that elevated him to a pinnacle of American literature and perhaps bilked him of a few thousand dollars, had died of heart failure nearly a month earlier, just as Mark Twain was completing *The Prince and the Pauper.* Frank Bliss, also in poor health, succeeded his father as manager of American Publishing. In that same month Livy Clemens hired a new maid, the twenty-four-year-old Katy Leary, a daughter of Irish immigrants. Leary would remain with the family for thirty years, looking after them, attending their deaths, until Clara remained the only survivor; and then Katy Leary assisted with the birth of Clara's daughter Nina.

Finally finished with a draft of *The Prince and the Pauper,* Sam sent it off to Howells. Howells suggested tightening certain descriptive passages, but his verdict to Clemens was, "marvelously good . . . all the infernal clumsiness and cruelties of the law—are incomparable."[46] This referred to the acutely described scenes in the second half of the novel, as young Prince Edward VI, accidentally cast into a poor boy's identity, roams the English countryside, running afoul of draconian British law. Howells restated to Clemens the perception at the core of his *Tramp Abroad* review: "It is such a book as *I* would expect from you, knowing what a bottom of fury there is to your fun . . ."[47]

Mark Twain revised the text (in proof) generally along Howells's recommendations, and returned it to his publisher. His publisher was no longer American Publishing. Elisha Bliss had swindled him, he believed, and the company would pay the price.

James Osgood had longed to issue Mark Twain's books at least since 1872, when he'd nearly won the rights to *Sketches, New and Old.* (In 1877 he'd managed to get out a small Mark Twain collection that included the masterful title pieces, *A True Story, and the Recent Carnival of Crime.*) A handsome fellow with amused eyes, he was a natural scholar—he'd learned Latin at age three and entered college at twelve—who loved literature, and he venerated literary men, but when it came to the business of literature, his name, for the most part, might as well have been "Clemens." (After a few years of working with Clemens, his name might as well have been "Mud.") A partner at Ticknor & Fields before he turned thirty, Osgood had befriended Charles Dickens during Dickens's American tour of 1867, when Sam Clemens and Olivia Langdon heard him read on their first "date." It was Osgood who brought Dickens's works to American readers, and it was Osgood who made the house a home to Emerson, Holmes, Longfellow, Whittier, and Thoreau, whose works he published in beautifully produced editions.

Marketplace savvy, however, was not his strong suit. He got caught up in the rapid reshuffling of Boston publishing houses in the post–Civil War years when Ticknor & Fields dissolved in 1870, and he joined up with George Ticknor's son Benjamin and renamed the firm James R. Osgood & Co. His big brainstorm there was to hand that $10,000 advance to Bret Harte. Then, when bad luck struck the business, in the form of fires and contagious horse diseases that slowed down book shipment, he overreacted by slashing the prices of his books, which cut the royalties to stars such as Longfellow, which made those stars mad. Then he began selling off the printing plates of some classics by the likes of Dickens and Thackeray. James R. Osgood & Co. dissolved in 1878, but Osgood and Oscar Houghton quickly formed Houghton, Osgood & Co. That firm managed only one profitable book, Howells's *The Lady of the Aroostook.* Osgood and Houghton argued and split up in 1880; Osgood rounded up some other partners including his brother Edward, and started a new James R. Osgood & Co. (Houghton did a little better, founding Houghton, Mifflin.) In the autumn of 1880, the restored magnate found himself on the receiving end of jovial challenges to billiards at the house on Farmington Avenue, and of the much-coveted Twainian folksy invite.

. . . Now look here, Mrs. Clemens & I require that you bide in this shanty while in Hartford . . . [T]elegraph me what train you'll arrive by, & I will waltz down after you with private carriage, & will throw an amount of style around you that will make you say, yourself, that you wouldn't trade places with a stud-horse.[48]

Clemens was trolling Osgood as his new publisher—"a thing which I do not want the Am. Pub. Co. to suspect for some months yet," he confided to Orion; he wanted to retain access to American Publishing's suspect ledgers for as long as possible.[49] By the end of the year, Osgood and Mark Twain reached a quiet contractual agreement: Osgood would publish *The Prince and the Pauper,* but on terms that made Mark Twain more a co-equal investor than a conventional client. Osgood, the genial and beneficent man of letters, was about to learn just how cruel the publishing business could be, even as he learned the definition of the phrase, "vengeful scrutiny."

36

"A Powerful Good Time"

(1881–82)

Now, the business of Mark Twain was business. Within a decade he would come to detest that word and spit it out like a sibilant oath, but he could never conquer his addiction to "business's" narcotic allures. He played the role of publishing mastermind; he brainstormed grandly; he threw money into get-rich schemes and renovations of the great house, and bad money after the good; he went looking for ways to sue the various liars and frauds and swindlers he thought had betrayed his faith in them, much as the Christian God had.

His unorthodox arrangement with James Osgood* presaged an era in which "book" generally was synonymous with "consumer product" in his thinking. He worked up enthusiasm for novelty ideas cooked up by friends in the trade—an encyclopedia of American humor, a spoof on books of etiquette. He combed the ledgers of the American Publishing Company, inventorying discrepancies in assets and liabilities, preparatory to siccing his attorney Charles Perkins on the company. (Perkins eventually talked him out of any litigation.) His speculative investments accelerated, and careered toward their various brick walls. In 1881, by his own accounting, Samuel Clemens threw $14,500 into an engineering company, $10,600 into the Crown Point Iron Co., another $5,000 into Mr. Paige's typesetter, $4,500 in stock investments, and $3,000 into Kaolatype. This was apart from the

---

* Under the terms, Clemens would underwrite production and publication costs for his books with Osgood, and would receive all profits, except for a 7½ percent royalty fee for the publisher. He retained copyright ownership, as he had not been able to do with Bliss.

$10,000 he committed to production costs for *The Prince and the Pauper:* the best paper stock, the most ornate illustrations, the most lavishly produced book cover.[1] The opulence was at least as much his wife's idea as his own. Livy was insisting on elegance in the book that would establish her husband's "polite" bona fides, Sam informed his sister, "even if the elegance of it eats up the publisher's profits and mine too."[2]

The warning signs issuing from Kaolatype would have been apparent to any genuine businessman. The fact that it couldn't do what it was designed to do, for starters. Another involved Dan Slote's shadowy young German metallurgist, a fellow named Sneider, who was in charge of adapting the contraption to the brass-plate cover-stamping idea. Clemens was eager to witness a demonstration of Sneider's progress. But as he later wrote Howells, "the self-styled 'inventor' had a very ingenious way of keeping me see him *apply* his invention":

[T]he first appointment was spoiled by his burning down the man's shop in which it was to be done, the night before; the second was spoiled by his burning down his own shop the night before. He unquestionably did both of these things.[3]

(Fire was a motif for Clemens in those days. Flames erupted three times in the Clemens household in early 1881, each combination threatening a different Clemens daughter. A gust from a window sent the flame from an alcohol lamp spreading across the canopy of Clara's bed one morning; she was saved by Rosina, who entered the room at a lucky moment. A spark escaping through the screen of a fireplace set fire to the lace on the baby Jean's crib the next day; her nursemaid and Rosina came to her rescue. On the third successive day, a fireplace log broke in half and showered sparks onto the mantel in the "schoolroom" where Susy was practicing piano. Clemens's personal barber spotted the danger this time and doused the wood with water from a pitcher.)

The apparent arsons forced Sam to confront the possibility that not only Sneider, but Dan Slote himself might be trying to fleece him, and indeed that proved the case. (It turned out that Slote really was a "sinner.") But instead of walking away from these characters, he moved to enmesh himself deeper in their tentacles. A "handsome" sheaf of sample impressions sent to him by Slote in mid-March spiked his enthusiasm to reckless heights: He'd noticed that a next-door neighbor was beginning an extension to his house, threatening the Clemenses' view to the east. On the strength of Slote's blandishment, Clemens strolled over to the work site and bought the land under development, instantly meeting the man's outlandish price of twelve thousand dollars. Then he and Livy plunged into lavish renovation plans for their own house: library walls and ceiling to be covered with metal leaf designed by Louis C. Tiffany & Co. (for $5,000, replacing Sam's original notion to cover the area in Kaolatype brass plates); a rebuilding and twenty-foot extension of the kitchen ($4,000); an extension of their driveway one hundred feet eastward; black walnut paneling for other rooms; new pipes; new fireplace tiles; one "Irish setter (red)."[4] Sam ordered a new carriage built to his specifications by a New Haven company.

Twelve thousand dollars here, ten thousand there—it was beginning to add up. Clemens's domestic, business, and investment outlays were in fact exceeding $100,000 for the year—or slightly less than $2 million in early 21st-century dollars. But why should he care? *A Tramp Abroad* was selling well and pulling *Tom Sawyer* along in its wake; his earlier books remained in demand; *Colonel Sellers* still generated good box-office revenue;* his occasional lectures paid well. His income for 1880 totaled $250,000, allowing him to laugh at any notion of restraint. For the time being.

On February 2 Howells ended his twelve-year association with the *Atlantic*. Thomas Bailey Aldrich succeeded him as editor. Under terms of the ownership breakup, control of the *Atlantic* went to Houghton, but Howells's loyalties lay with Osgood, and so he signed a contract with Mark Twain's new publisher for an annual sum ($7,500) to produce a novel a year as well as shorter pieces. This was a time of personal crisis and artistic richness for the forty-three-year-old literary man. Howells had written several successful plays, most of them light farces or comedies of manners. He was at work on one of his signature pieces of fiction, *A Modern Instance,* which brought the themes of Euripides' *Medea* under his modernist-realist lens. *The Lady of the Aroostook,* due out soon, would solidify his reputation as a novelist on a par with Henry James. (James published *Portrait of a Lady* that year, starting the trajectory that left Howells behind.) But in the fall of 1880 Winifred Howells, a promising young writer at seventeen, suffered a "nervous breakdown" that resisted treatment. Distraught, Howells sank into his own malaise. "I have grown terribly, miserably tired of editing," he told a friend.[5] "I think my nerves have given way . . . [T]he MSS., the proofs, the books, the letters became insupportable."[6]

Mr. Clemens sympathized, in his fashion. "The news about Winny is too bad, too bad," he remarked—at the tag end of a letter mostly concerned with the problematic Philadelphia publisher Gebbie.[7] His eulogy to Howells's tenure at the *Atlantic,* a career that meant everything to Mark Twain's ascendancy, was contained in a postscript to the same letter: "Mighty glad you are out of that cussed mill, that gilded slavery."[8]

The stream of company continued at the Nook Farm house. Clemens presided over dinners of pheasant, and mutton, and baked oysters, regaling the table with his stories. When Howells visited Nook Farm, he was Clara's favorite guest. "He always brought sunshine and cheer into the house as no one else could . . . To see him and Father enjoy a funny story or joke together was a complete show in itself. Both of them red in the face from laughing, with

---

* Mark Twain recorded in his Notebook 19 that from July 1879 to July 1880, *The Innocents Abroad* had sold 3,182 copies; *Roughing It,* 2,466; *The Gilded Age,* 1,700; *Tom Sawyer,* 3,186, *Sketches, New and Old,* 1,518. From March to July 1880, *A Tramp Abroad* had sold 47,563. N & J, vol. 2, p. 428.

abundant gray hair straggling over their foreheads and restless feet that carried them away from their chairs and back again!"[9] Imperious Elinor was a different proposition. Annie Moffett, who encountered her at the Hartford house, later told her son Samuel that "for some reason Mrs. Howells was treated formally . . . [There were] all kinds of special preparations being made because Mrs. Howells was coming."[10]

As for the hostess, she stage-managed the ongoing pageant without drawing any attention to herself; but she confided to her mother:

> The house has been full of company and I have been "whirled around." . . . Oh, I cannot help sighing for the peace and quiet of the farm. This is my work, and I know that I do very wrong when I feel chafed by it, but how can I be right about it? Sometimes it seems as if the simple sight of people would drive me *mad* . . . I want so much to do other things, to study and do things with the children, and I cannot.[11]

In the evenings when no parties were scheduled, the master of the house would take his favorite chair in the library. As flames blazed in the fireplace under the mantel, firing up the brass fixtures and the porcelain figurines and the walnut arms of the chairs, the womenfolk would arrange themselves around him (with excellent posture) and listen as he read aloud from *The Prince and the Pauper*, in progress. Little Susy and Clara, their laps filled with ambient cats, were charmed by Papa's chaste fable. "I like this tale better than 'Tom Sawyer,' " Mark Twain remarked to a friend that winter, adding, ambiguously, "—because I haven't put any fun in it. I *think* that is why I like it better."[12]

BY THE end of March, Clemens's spending spree may have begun to feel a little premature. Kaolatype still had not generated the "mighty fortune" that he'd predicted to Pamela. He found himself still awaiting "palpable & demonstrable . . . reasons for going on," he warned Slote; "but my hopes are not high."[13] He decided to hire a middleman to monitor the venture. His choice was Charles Webster. Annie Moffett's husband was twenty-nine, a civil engineer turned real estate man in Fredonia. As his son Samuel Charles Webster noted, his father had been born in Connecticut and "was connected with the usual New England families and directly descended from three governors—Winthrop, Bradford, and Endicott." Samuel added, with what may have been a lingering trace of familial bitterness, "The women of his family were advanced for their time, even more advanced than the women of the Clemens family."[14]

Webster had stepped into Mark Twain's world on another matter. He'd called at Farmington Avenue in March as the delegate of the Independent Watch Company of Fredonia, which was rounding up stock investors. (Sam's reputation as a soft touch was by now detectable by main-chance bloodhounds for hundreds of miles.) Sam went in for five thousand dollars and then signed his nephew on as his own representative. Within a week of coming aboard, Webster uncovered evidence of fraud by Slote and Sneider. Clemens, wounded and enraged by this latest betrayal of his faith, directed his attorney Perkins to go after Sneider first, lulling Slote by making him a co-litigant. As Sneider began wailing about suicide, Sam turned his vengeful eye on Slote. He kicked his conniving old friend out of the company and made noises about "tackling" him and "forcing him to terms." After less than a year of Sam's unrelenting harassment, the joyful youth of the Holy Land hijinks disintegrated in health; and, in February 1882, he died. Sam stayed away from the funeral, he informed Mary Fairbanks, and saved his tears. Kaolatype died a few years afterward, along with fifty thousand dollars of Samuel Clemens's money.

The big winner, in the short term at least, was Webster. Sam gave him "complete authority over Kaolatype & its concerns already vested in you. You will take entire control of the property & employes of the Company; you will hire whom you please, discharge whom you please . . ."[15]

Some flashes of his old exuberance surfaced during these hard-edged days. Riding on the same train with the uniformed General Sherman to West Point, where both were scheduled to speak, the author of *Tom Sawyer* persuaded the author of the March to the Sea to swap clothing at alternating whistle stops, delighting crowds.

Reunion with a higher-ranking general awaited him. On July 2, President Garfield was shot and fatally wounded by a deranged lawyer named Charles J. Guiteau in a Washington railway station. Garfield lingered for weeks as doctors tried to locate and remove the bullet embedded in his back. Alexander Graham Bell invented a metal detector to help them out. Garfield died on September 19, from infection caused by the doctors' unsterilized probing fingers. Not long afterward Clemens visited the New York business office of Ulysses Grant, with an awed Howells in tow. Sam was lobbying: Howells's father, W. C. Howells, the consul at Toronto, feared that the new president, Chester Alan Arthur, would replace him, and Clemens wanted a letter from Grant to Arthur telling him not to. Howells, who years earlier had stood paralyzed at the sight of Lincoln, practically swooned at "the soft, rounded, Ohio River accent to which my years were earliest used," and could not get over taking a carry-in luncheon of beans and coffee with the great man: it was like "sitting down to baked beans and coffee with Julius Caesar, or Alexander, or some other great Plutarchan captain."[16] It was at this meeting that Mark Twain first suggested that Grant write his personal memoirs.

THAT NOTION would take a few years to bear fruit. Sam was full of lesser ideas for himself and others in the meantime. He wondered whether a book about mental telegraphy would make a go. He offered Howells five thousand dollars to assume editorial responsibilities for the Cyclopedia of Humor project (so named now). He mulled a new invention. He brainstormed about adding a character to Shakespeare's *Hamlet:* a subscription book agent, actually, named Basil Stockmar, who carries an umbrella and—well, tries to sell subscription books to the other characters, when he's not being scared silly by Hamlet's father's ghost. Howells, remarkably, could see nothing remiss in such a correction of the Bard's oversight. "That is a famous idea," he responded.[17] Encouraged, Mark Twain began talking up a playwriting collaboration with Howells, one that would take Colonel Mulberry Sellers into old age and make him an eccentric scientist.

As the publication date for *The Prince and the Pauper* neared, Clemens directed Osgood to send the proof sheets to Howells for one last vetting. As usual, his busy Boston patron accepted the simultaneous (and ethically questionable) roles of editor and reviewer. Editor, reviewer, and *press agent,* to be completely accurate: the booster of the new realism still had enough of the old Brahmin piety in his soul to be swept away by the novel's high-Victorian pretensions. Howells decided to place his review in a journal that would alert the broadest possible audience that the old *Quaker City* sinner was finally in recovery. The New York *Tribune* would do nicely (luckily, Whitelaw Reid was on a honeymoon vacation in Europe, and the Mark Twain fan John Hay was running things). Howells volunteered a review, unsigned, to Hay, arguing the need to broadcast "that unappreciated serious side of Clemens' curious genius."[18] Hay agreed, and relayed the proposal to Reid—who fulminated against the idea but ultimately decided not to block it.

The press agent having done his work, the editor then scolded Clemens for some passages guaranteed to shock the reviewer. Most offensive was the appearance of the same bawdy "There-was-a-woman-in-our-town" doggerel that Sam had brayed out during his post-wedding train trip to Buffalo. "[S]uch a thing as that . . . I can't cope with."[19] Neither could he cope with such words as "devil," and "hick" (for "person") and "basting" for "beating." A day later, Howells was still rooting out offenses to clean-minded fellows: "I send some passages marked, which I don't think are fit to go into a book for boys."[20] Sam could not have cared less: "Slash away . . . [T]he more you slash, the better I shall like it . . . Alter any and everything you choose—don't hesitate."[21] He kept the bawdy ditty, slightly revised, in the book anyway.

Osgood issued *The Prince and the Pauper* in mid-December—sanitized, plump and glossy as a sofa pillow, and garlanded with Mark Twain's inscription to "those good-mannered and agreeable children, Susie and Clara Clemens." Reviewers were flummoxed, as they had been by *The Innocents Abroad* twelve years earlier. Here, in fact, was the mirror image of *Innocents:* a book without recognizable lineage, but startling for its *propriety* this time. Into a tale set in an England of yore, Mark Twain had pretty much emptied his vast accumulated grab bag of "period" color, language, and documentary Tudor research (operating, perhaps, on the proverbial theory that we cannot have "archaic," and edit, too). The diction and dialogue were relentlessly retrogenteel. ("Thou are right; say no more; thou shalt see that whatsoever the king of England requires a subject to suffer under the law, he will himself suffer while he holdeth the station of a subject," and so on.)

And yet the book stipulated itself for *children*. Its title characters were not manly knights and knaves, but a pair of fourteen-year-olds who, in one doffthy-rags-and-don-these-splendors moment, become trapped in each other's identity and must experience, for a while, each other's fate. The children's fates are governed, as Mark Twain made starkly clear, by the inflexible laws and etiquette of the adult class system. Even Howells's eighteen-year-old daughter, the sensitive Winifred, was taken aback. "I never knew or realized before how in old times the Laws hindered instead of helping justice," she remarked in a letter of thanks for her inscribed copy; "and now they seem to me much worse than if there had been none." [22]

Nothing quite like it had ever appeared before. Certainly nothing from the now-familiar "humorist" Mark Twain. The reviewers cogitated, decided that they liked it—most of them—and struggled to explain why. Nearly everyone pounced on one handy reason: the book was *polite;* and that fact became the consensus launching pad for commentary. H. H. Boyesen, Howells's replacement reviewer in the *Atlantic,* remarked that Mark Twain "has written a book which no reader, not even a critical expert, would think of attributing to him" [23]—that is, a book whose humor departs from the "boisterous and rollicking" and depends on the plot for its impact.

Howells alone, it seemed, possessed the insight necessary to explain the book—he had, after all, noted its "bottom of fury" in his private letter to Clemens—but here he was ensnared by his nonliterary agenda of seeing Clemens consecrated. His unsigned review had run in October, two months ahead of publication, and it set the tone of all that followed. True, he probed deeper than most in pointing out the strong subtext of satire aimed at the British monarchy, and remarking that "this is the sort of manual of republicanism which might fitly be introduced in the schools." There he veered off, into the vapors of conventional sentiment. The book "breathes throughout the spirit of humanity and the reason of democracy." Its "romance" "is imagined with poetic delicacy," and was "touched with the tenderest, sweetest feeling." [24]

Not entirely. *The Prince and the Pauper* contained scenes that hardly seemed aimed at the kiddies. Two Baptist women considered heretical are burned at the stake as their daughters wail for their lives; the victims issue "a volley of heart-piercing shrieks of mortal agony." [25] Decaying heads impaled on iron spikes along London Bridge furnish " 'object lessons' in English history for its children." [26] Farmers are sold into slavery; prison life and its horrors are omnipresent dangers. Royal "etiquette" is continually revealed as absurd, constricting, hollow.

If such scenes do in fact hint at controlled "fury," it appears once again to be the fury of the frustrated believer: Mark Twain, who had grown skeptical of voting rights for the uneducated, had traveled to England and lost his heart to the very sort of grim dowager he'd roasted in *Innocents Abroad:* an old European country hidebound by sovereign rule. But the very process of absorbing British history—the better to know his inamorata—proved fatal to the flame. The "exceeding severity of the laws of that day" shocked him and spurred his desire to make that severity clear to his readers, he told Howells.

The reviews, to him, were devastating—it was as though a vast, polite-wing conspiracy had formed, insisting on depicting a refined Connecticut Yankee businessman, ensconced in his refined Connecticut estate, tossing off refined Connecticut literature for his refined Connecticut readers. Bret Harte himself could not have plotted a more effective assassination of the Vandal. Yet *The Prince and the Pauper* contained some trace elements of Mark Twain's developing vision as an artist. These traces would not have been apparent even to Howells; they become visible only against the relief of his later work. One of them was the elaboration of the twinned- and switched-identity motif, which had first surfaced in the narrator/dwarf of "The Facts Concerning the Recent Carnival of Crime in Connecticut." Mark Twain never offered a specific referent for this shifting, recurring metaphor—if indeed he understood it himself—but it would float through his fiction as persistently as Laura Wright floated through his dreams.

The other, and related, element was the boys. Their very centrality in the novel certified that Mark Twain's creative imagination, however battered by his financial, societal, and domestic distractions, would never shrivel beyond an inextinguishable core. While it is true that the boyish spirits of Tom Canty and young Prince Edward are heavily muffled under the novel's artifices, flashes show through now and again—as when each draws on an instinctual moral decency when prevailing "etiquette" would require a brutal action; or when the rustic Tom confesses that while playing the Prince, he used the Great Seal for cracking nuts. Almost outside the author's awareness, the boys press against the implausible set pieces, the appliqué of Victorian pieties and their own assigned brittle dialogue. Each, in his way, is fighting for survival—not so much against the enemies inside the pages, as against their author's worst instincts.

ON APRIL 17, 1882, Samuel Langhorne Clemens set aside the burdens of a middle-aged Connecticut businessman and headed west to the replenishing river of his youth. With two companions, he boarded a train in New York for Indianapolis, changed there for St. Louis, and arrived at 8 p.m.,* when the Mississippi still was faintly visible in the cloudy twilight. The ensuing thirty-three days and 33,000 miles would comprise the most essential sojourn of his creative life: a tour of his old steamboating circuit from St. Louis to New Or-

---

* In *Life on the Mississippi,* Twain gives the arrival time as ten o'clock at night.

leans, and then upriver, with a three-day stop in Hannibal before arriving at St. Paul, Minnesota, about 235 miles south of the Mississippi's headwaters. Two of his most enduring books would issue from this sojourn.

His companions were James Osgood and a thirty-seven-year-old ex-Hartford schoolteacher named Roswell Phelps. Clemens had signed a contract a week earlier with Osgood to produce a book about the Mississippi—the project he had begun thinking about in San Francisco. Once again, he would invest in the book and function effectively as publisher, with Osgood responsible mainly for distribution. Once again, Clemens ignored warning signs: this arrangement had depressed sales of *The Prince and the Pauper,* owing largely to Osgood's unfamiliarity with the antiquated subscription-sales process, which Sam stubbornly clung to. A fifth of the novel's initial 25,000 copies remained unsold for several years, before it finally emerged as a popular favorite. Phelps would be the author's "stenographic secretary," on constant alert for pithy remarks by Clemens, which he would record in shorthand for use as writing notes. (Phelps had wanted to know whether *"typewriting* is a disideratum"; if so, he "must proceed at once to acquire that occult science.")[27]

The sunny-spirited Osgood had a more immediate function: as a stand-in for the absent William Dean Howells. Clemens's eight-year dream of sweeping Howells along to the realm of his boyhood had finally run aground: Howells lay recovering in Boston from a deathly illness made worse by overwork and anxieties over Winifred's own fragile health. "I am sorry that Osgood is with you on this Mississippi trip," he'd written Clemens with bluff jocularity. "I foresee that it will be a contemptible half-success instead of the illustrious and colossal failure *we* could have made it." And then, all pretenses down: "—*Ah,* how I should like to be with Osgood and you!"[28]

Clemens chose a good moment to step outside the pressurized world he'd been creating for himself. His prevailing anxieties had steamed toward rage since the year began. The new burglar alarm didn't work; or rather, it worked too well. His stocks were floundering. Copyright threats continued to bedevil him. The Fredonia Watch Company turned out to be fraudulent. Through it all, Clemens had managed to gather up an olio of his sketches, stories, and speeches for a quick Osgood book. He sent the title piece, a wild burlesque of detectives and detective fiction called "The Stolen White Elephant," to the publisher in late March. He included the terse instruction: "Submit this to Howells first."[29] Again, the presumption on his old friend beggared belief. Howells, ailing and overextended, now scraped along with his family in a Boston boardinghouse as he struggled to write the final 400 pages of *A Modern Instance,* having just revised the previous 1,466. Yet he read, without complaint and without a fee from his wealthy protégé, not only the title sketch but twenty-seven other pieces, recommending eighteen for the collection—some eighty thousand words.[30] Osgood hustled it all into a June printing.

Clemens's state of mind as 1882 began was illustrated by a new vendetta that consumed him through January. He was glad to share this with Howells, free of charge. He began by complaining that "there are times when swearing cannot meet the emergency." He went on, "About three weeks ago, a sensitive friend [possibly George Warner, Charles's brother[31]] . . . intimated that the N.Y. Tribune was engaged in a kind of crusade against me . . . it made me very angry."[32] What Clemens learned—or thought he learned—was that since Reid's return from Europe, "the Tribune had been flinging sneers & brutalities at me," apparently almost daily over a period of two months. "Angry" hardly covered it. Every vengeful instinct in Mark Twain clicked on to full alert. He spent three weeks filling his notebook with notes for what he intended to be a book-length character assassination of Reid, couched as a "biography." He conceived that Thomas Nast would illustrate it. "Grant calls him Outlaw Reid," ran one entry, and it got worse: "Chased after all the rich girls in California." "I do not begin with his boyhood, which is of no consequence—nor with his manhood, which has never existed." "Reid is Guiteau with the courage left out."[33] And then it reached rock bottom.

He could not lie. He said, "Alas, I have no nuts." Pity but he had made those sweet & simple words his motto, through life—his charm against sin, his protection against all tamperings with the truth. I have no nuts! How many & many a time they might have saved him from evil doing . . . I have no nuts![34]

The polite patrons of *The Prince and the Pauper,* it seemed, were in for a shock.

In the throes of this rage, the diatribe shifted into something else. Mark Twain made a mental conversion of the sort essential to his art, and deeply characteristic of it. His intoxication with words detached his aim from retribution, and built on the act of creation itself, and became its own reward. He described it to Howells:

As my labors grew, so also grew my fascination. Malice & malignity faded out of me—or maybe I *drove* them out of me, knowing that a malignant book would hurt nobody but the fool who wrote it. I got thoroughly in love with this work; for I saw that I was going to write a book which the very devils & angels themselves would delight to read . . .[35]

Devils and angels, maybe, but not Livy. She watched Sam's day-and-night mobilization with silent distress, until she hit on the perfect defusing tactic: she suggested that it might be a good idea to find out whether the rumors of Reid's campaign were true. Clemens hadn't thought of that. He dispatched Charlie Webster to New York to pore through every edition of the paper since the end of October. He himself subscribed to the *Tribune* and ransacked it daily. At the end of January, he sheepishly itemized the results to Howells: one unfriendly criticism of *The Prince and the Pauper* (reprinted from the *Atheneum*) and a couple of other references to him that not even he could construe as malicious. The Reid screed had lost its raison d'être. "Confound it, I could have earned ten thousand dollars with infinitely less trouble."[36] The Whitelaw Reid "biography" never saw the light of day.

He hurried to Boston on April 14 to give a talk on mental telegraphy, and then joined Howells and Aldrich in a visit to the dying Emerson in Concord. There, he somehow managed to disgrace himself one final time (or thought he did) in the Sage's presence. He confessed it to Livy, perhaps embroidering again in his word-intoxicated way. He paid for it via her "measureless scorn & almost measureless vituperation," he wrote to Howells. But then, he deserved it. Or so he thought. His actions (never described) were

Brutalities & stupidities & crimes . . . [I]t makes me wish, in the bottom of my broken heart, that this might be a lesson to me . . . But oh, hell, there is no hope for a person who is built like me; —because there is no cure, no cure.[37]

On that happy note, he lit out for the river.

IN ST. Louis on April 20, he and Osgood and Phelps stepped aboard the *Gold Dust* and felt it slide into the current at five o'clock in the afternoon—sliding, in a sense, into the wish that he had outlined to Wattie Bowser. The following day, he exulted to Livy, "I am in solitary possession of the pilot house." The day after that, he found "steering a steamboat [is] as familiar as if I had never ceased from it." He soon gave the wheel back, and returned to "having a powerful good time & picking up & setting down volumes of literary stuff."[38] Even the meals excited him: "Soup & fish & two kinds of meat and several kinds of *Pie!*"[39]

The oleander was in bloom.

The packet stopped at Cairo, on the southern tip of Illinois, and then crossed into the former Confederacy. The passengers toured Memphis on the 23rd, and on the following day the *Gold Dust* passed the site of Napoleon, Arkansas. Napoleon was the town when he'd received false hope in a newspaper that Henry's life had been spared in the *Pennsylvania* explosion. Now Napoleon no longer existed; the river had consumed it. Ralph Waldo Emerson died on April 28. The next day, the *Gold Dust* docked in New Orleans, where Clemens's party lingered a week.

He grew playful again, and observant. Loafers kept both hands in their pockets at railway stations west of New York, he'd noticed, and goatees were everywhere, a fact that he somehow tied to the belief in biblical inerrancy.[40] St. Louis was now a domed and steepled metropolis, its streets lighted at night by Mr. Edison's electrical bulb. Electric lights necklaced the river now. He found them enchanting at first: "Let artist make picture of boat at country landing with electric light glaring on trees & white houses."[41] He excepted the "government" lights to assist pilots: "This is too much."[42] He tried hiding his imposing identity under a series of aliases, signing himself into hotels as "C. L. Samuel" and "S. L. Samuel," and was always delighted when the ruse failed to work. His pilot-wheel stint had occurred after he "ascended to the hurricane deck and cast a longing glance toward the pilot-house." [43] The pilot, he wrote, sized him up and told him a series of outrageous river lies; and then spoke his true name and offered him the great wheel—"Trying to play yourself for a stranger and an innocent!—why, I knew you before you had spoken seven words." [44] Or so he claimed in *Life on the Mississippi.* He'd started thinking up ways to improve on the reality of the trip well before it began, and jotted down the best ones: "Let pilots tell me all sorts of lies & give me all sorts of taffy, thinking me to be green." [45] He'd planned other elements of this book before departure, preeminent among them the accounting of Henry, and their last days together, and the skein of events that seemed to prefigure his death.

> Tell now in full, the events preceding & following the Pennsylvania's explosion: the fight with Brown; the boat steaming down Bend of 103 with nobody at the wheel—the white-aproned servants & passengers in deck approving the fight—the prophetic talk on the levee between Henry & me that night in N.O. before Pa. sailed on her fatal voyage. [46]

A couple of lines below that entry he jotted an instruction to himself: *"Leave out* that wonderful dream." [47] This referred to the premonitory dream of seeing Henry's corpse in its metal casket, garlanded with white roses. He withheld that detail until his autobiographical dictations, to spare his mother the shock of learning it. Once on the river, he added: "Make exhaustive picture of pilot Brown & his snarling ways & meanness." [48]

TWENTY-ONE YEARS had changed not only the cities, towns, and illumination along the Mississippi; they had changed the Mississippi itself. Hat Island was gone. Goose Island was gone. Two Sisters Island was gone. A whole cluster of islands around Cairo were missing. "The river is so thoroughly changed that I can't bring it back to mind even when the changes have been pointed out to me. It is like a man pointing out to me a place in the sky where a cloud has been." [49] He sadly marked the most dramatic change, the accelerating extinction of the steamboat itself. By the early 1880s, railroads had vitiated steamboat trade. The great stern-wheelers and side-wheelers no longer lay with their noses against the wharf, he observed, like sardines in a box, but end to end. He noticed the name on one survivor as it lay in the mouth of a tributary: *Mark Twain.*

As always, he homed in on the language around him: "The r ignored, South. S. says b'fo' the waw. N.Y.r. says lawr for law." [50] He homed in on Southern culture as well, and his years in the East had sharpened his contempt for its chivalric affectations: "South still in the sophomoric (gush) period. All speech there is flowery & gushy—pulpit, law, literature, it is all so." [51] Sometimes he heard in that speech a ripe hypocrisy: "Was told that South they don't keep negro mistresses as much as befo' the waw." [52] Conversely, he was happy to reencounter the particular music of Southern Negro speech, and he filled several notebook pages with overheard conversations ("What a splendid moon!" "Laws bless you, honey you ought to seen dat moon befo' de waw"[53]). And then there was the speech of the pilots—speech that was fated soon to be a dead language. With Phelps's stenographic help, he harvested a colorful inventory of their yarns, river lore, varieties of swearing, and jargon, all essential to the foundation of the book he would soon write.

TWO DECADES' worth of fraught and freighted exile washed away from him and left him clearheaded again, receptive to wonder. On deck at four o'clock with the early watch at Kentucky Bend on April 25, he took in a spectacle he had too long ignored, the planetary roll from darkness to morning light. He consecrated the tableau in a dictation to Phelps.

> Birds singing here at sunrise, foliage green in the distance . . . walls of forest near at hand paling gradually with the distance and vanishing . . . The first blush of the rising sun out on the overflow, was pink, then purple; and the reflections in the water still beautiful.[54]

Later that day he fleshed the images into sentences, embellishing his dictated thoughts into a letter for Livy.

> It was fascinating to see the day steal gradually upon this vast silent world; & when the edge of the shorn sun pushed itself above the line of forest, the marvels of shifting light & shade & color & dappled reflections, that followed, were bewitching to see . . . & the remote, shadowy, vanishing distances, away down the glistening highway under the horizon! *and* the riot of the singing birds!—it was all worth getting up for, I tell you.[55]

Here was descriptive prose writing that easily eclipsed his rhapsodies from the hill atop Quarry Farm, and his limning of Heidelberg from the bird-cage room of his mountainside hotel. Here was joy of being transfused into words. In 1880, Mark Twain had composed a draft of the famous "sunrise" passage that begins Chapter 19 in *Adventures of Huckleberry Finn*. It was this moment, perhaps, that led him to meticulously revise that draft in 1883 and 1884, adding certain sounds (bullfrogs "cluttering") and aromas (dead fish on the ground); the likely use of a small log cabin on the far side of the river; the elaboration of meaning found in a streak on the water. Harold Bloom has called the finished passage "the most beautiful prose paragraph yet written by an American."[56]

Civilization constricted Mark Twain as badly as it did Huck, and the river liberated him equally. Perhaps he had not been far wrong in his answer to Wattie Bowser. Perhaps he really should have remained a river pilot in summer always, on a freight boat never in a hurry, with a crew that would never die.

·   ·   ·

NEW ORLEANS opened itself to Mark Twain. He was in demand at dinner parties, Sunday-school classes, cockfights, and mule races. He got to know two of the South's most prominent young writers, with whom he'd corresponded from Hartford: the tiny ex-Confederate cavalryman George Washington Cable, whose sympathetic novels of Creole and Negro life had won him a following, and the excruciatingly shy Joel Chandler Harris, creator of "Uncle Remus," who'd traveled from Atlanta to meet Mark Twain, but didn't have much to say. On May 3, Sam enjoyed a reunion with his old mentor Horace Bixby, now the captain of the 300-foot, 2,300-ton *City of Baton Rouge,* a splendid new steamboat for the Anchor Line, with its six bridal chambers and nickel-plated bell pull; and one of the last of its dimensions to be built. The reporters who by now clustered in Mark Twain's wake recorded the moment when he and the old pilot met and embraced. He took a sightseeing tour aboard a tug with Bixby, and when Clemens's party disembarked upriver on May 6, it was aboard the *Baton Rouge.* He would never see the Mississippi south of St. Louis again.

In the domed and steepled metropolis, he tossed off a couple of farewell hot scotches with Bixby and also said good-bye to Osgood, who entrained for the East and the demands of business. And then, with Phelps in tow, Sam Clemens reversed an itinerary that he had followed twenty-nine springs ago: he boarded an overnight packet from St. Louis to Hannibal.

HE HAD thought about reentering his boyhood hometown incognito.* Whether he followed through on that hardly mattered; he arrived on a Sunday morning, when everyone was asleep, and Hannibal had become a town of mysterious strangers anyway: girls with familiar faces who turned out to be the daughters of the girls he knew; clerks and shopkeepers from someplace else. "Many of the people I once knew in Hannibal are now in heaven," he mused while standing on Holliday's Hill.† "Some, I trust, are in the other place."[57] Hannibal had grown to a city of fifteen thousand people, with paved streets and a hundred-thousand-dollar castle of a depot at the convergence of six railroad lines. The railroads struck Sam Clemens as a violation.

> The romance of boating is gone, now. In Hannibal the steamboatman is no longer a god. The youth don't talk river slang any more. Their pride is apparently railways— which they take a peculiar vanity in reducing to initials ("C B & Q")—an affectation which prevails all over the west. They roll these initials as a sweet morsel under the tongue.[58]

It would be several years yet before Clemens comprehended the identity of the man who'd brought the railroads to Hannibal, igniting its prosperity:

* He noted in *Life on the Mississippi* (Chapter 53) that he had glimpsed the town fifteen years earlier, and six years before that, "but both were so brief that they hardly counted."
† He calls it "Holiday's Hill" in *Life on the Mississippi.*

Marshall Clemens, who'd led the drive to charter the first line, the Hannibal & St. Joseph, in 1846, then died before it was built.

"Alas!" he wrote in his notebook,

everything was changed in Hannibal—but when I reached third or fourth sts the tears burst forth, for I recognized the mud. *It*, at least, was the same—the same old mud— the mud that Annie McDonald got stuck in.[59]

His three days there struck a deep chord. He looked down from the hill and visualized the old Hannibal imprinted on the new one, the vanished houses restored. He saw "Lem Hackett" drowned again, and Dutchy, and watched as the tramp burned in the fire started with the match Sammy had given him, and he talked in his sleep again as Henry listened in. The four biographical chapters in the second half of *Life on the Mississippi,* and the similar sections in his autobiographical dictations, are largely the product of this brief stay, in which he imagined for a while that all his life since the Hannibal days had been nothing but a dream.

THE REST of the trip was anticlimactic. Clemens left Hannibal on May 17 on the *Minneapolis* for his first tour of the upper river. He traveled alone, Phelps having headed back for Hartford from Hannibal. He praised "this amazing region, bristling with great towns," and ticked off their names— Muscatine, Winona, Moline, Rock Island, La Crosse, and so on—but it was perfunctory. Osgood rejoined him at Davenport, Iowa. The two arrived at the "Siamese twins" of St. Paul and Minneapolis, Minnesota, to find the weather still wintry. Clemens walked around St. Paul in the cold and reminded himself, "Tell some big yarns about blizzards."[60] And that was how it ended. He and Osgood left St. Paul by train on Monday, May 22, and arrived at New York two days later. Clemens caught a connection to Hartford, and found his world pretty much as he'd left it. Soon after he arrived, the baby Jean fell gravely ill with scarlet fever, and then Susy was stricken. Charles Webster, who had been rooting in the American Publishing Company's records, reported that the company had concealed the news of three stock dividends over nine years; but the amount of the swindle was so low, about $2,000, that Clemens decided against litigation.

He reopened the manuscript of *Life on the Mississippi* in Hartford, and continued writing it inside his hilltop gazebo at Quarry Farm when the family went there in July. He wrote Howells,

I never had such a fight over a book in my life before . . . I started Osgood to editing it before I had finished writing it. As a consequence, large areas of it are condemned here and there and yonder, and I have the burden of these unfilled gaps harassing me and the thought of the broken continuity of the work . . .[61]

The most exhilarating adventure of his life was irrevocably behind him now, as was the joyful state of mind that had accompanied it. Mark Twain was once more enmeshed in the duties and the anxieties of the grown-up that Sam Clemens had become—but with one important difference. The book now assuming its contours, and, even more, the overlapping opus to follow, were to make permanent, revitalizing contributions to American literature, and to the American dream.

37

"All Right, Then . . ."

(1882–83)

In the *Century* magazine of September 1882, William Dean Howells published one of the earliest "appreciations" of Mark Twain's literature. The essay lifted its sights from a particular work and assessed its subject's influence on his culture, aiming to lift one of the persistent dead weights from Mark Twain's reputation: the old Calvinist jeremiad that as a mere "humorist," Mark Twain was categorically second-rate. Howells didn't stint on comparisons. Just as Shakespeare was the first to make poetry all poetical, he argued, "Mark Twain was the first to make humor all humorous . . . There is nothing lost in literary attitude, in labored dictionary funning, in affected quaintness, in dreary dramatization, in artificial 'dialect'; Mark Twain's humor is as simple in form and as direct as the statesmanship of Lincoln or the generalship of Grant." [1]

He pointed out the strain of authentic social criticism that separated Mark Twain from the "merely facetious," such as Josh Billings and the late Artemus Ward: "[T]he innumerable characters sketched by Mark Twain are actualities, however caricatured—and, usually, they are not so very much caricatured . . . there is no drawing from casts." [2] And Howells dwelt once again on the quality that he, alone among all contemporary critics, seemed able to discern: the anger. Or, as he put it in this context, "the indignant sense of right and wrong . . . an ardent hate of meanness and injustice." [3]

Howells put his finger on several key elements. Mark Twain, and his voice, were self-made, direct, and morally fired. Clemens lived life firsthand, and spoke truth as he saw and experienced it. The essay gratified Sam (he read it before publication), and probably worked as a corrective to all the mandates for "polite literature" the writer had been hearing. What it did not convey was the enormous strain of putting words on paper.

Writing his great river adventure proved a good deal more of a strain than living it. Mark Twain returned to Hartford with a skimpier supply of material than he'd expected. His New Orleans gallivanting had cut deeply into the time he'd planned to invest in the memories of riverboat pilots. The "explosion" of his incognito status had deprived him of a useful literary device: a narrator who was a fictionalized version of himself. His celebrityhood had colored his experiences along the river, and this worked against the mock-biographical set pieces of the sort he'd used in *A Tramp Abroad*. Finally, most of the people he'd solicited for informational books and clippings up and down the river did not bother to send him anything. Thus, the composition of *Life on the Mississippi* was going to be a long night of navigation, with limited charts.

He was bogged down, distracted by lumbago and the onset of rheumatism. His narrative lacked a center. He remained outwardly nonchalant: "I will finish the book at no particular date; [and] will not hurry it . . ."[4] he wrote to Howells. Yet his frantic search for supplemental text gives the lie to this pose. He instructed Osgood to hire a "cheap expert to . . . collect local histories of Mississippi towns & a lot of other books relating to the river."[5] Osgood sent him twenty-five volumes. Then he asked for more. The boundaries of "genre" disintegrated as he raided and scavenged. After a while, so did the boundaries between original art and found art. The volume of borrowed material that Mark Twain poured into the second half of *Life on the Mississippi* exposed him to charges, then and afterward, of "padding" his book, or shifting, in Paine's phrase, "from art to industry." There may be truth to this. A related criticism is that Mark Twain's "voice," so strong at the outset, disappears under this generic onslaught. That, too, is true, as far as it goes.

But that is not the whole story. A conversion had occurred. At some point—perhaps at the sight of the steamboat that rebuked him with his pen name—Sam Clemens discarded his old promise to Livy of writing a "standard work" on the Mississippi. Writing again overtook intention, and "standard" no longer answered. Personal reportage, factual citations from other works—these were inadequate to the Homeric urgencies now building in Mark Twain's mind. The Mississippi as he'd known it was disappearing; reduced and violated by the governmental snag boats "pulling the river's teeth";[6] by the West Point engineers straightening its lawless contours with wing dams and dikes and then clear-cutting its shoreline and paving it with stones; and by the leeching effect of the railroads. The "progress" that Samuel Clemens embraced as a businessman-investor was a betrayal of what remained of Sammy's faith. Against the sterilizing tide, Mark Twain needed to build a bulwark: a life on the Mississippi as permanent as words could make it. New Orleans coffins needed to be in this accounting, and Indian myths; the arcana of lost river cities and towns; the confessions of dying men and the intimation of buried treasure; murderous family feuds; hymns to heroic pilots at the wheel of their burning boats; the overheard shoptalk of traveling salesmen; the lingering thunder of the Civil War and the legends of Grant; Sammy a boy again; Henry, alive.

Mark Twain tries to condemn the violations he'd witnessed via a fictional surrogate, the steamboat mate "Uncle Mumford," who alludes to Ecclesiastes 7: 13 ("Consider the work of God: for who can make that straight, which he hath made crooked?"[7]). But even Scripture proves insufficient to the enormity of the violation. In retracing the assemblage of *Life on the Mississippi,* one can sense Mark Twain pounding against the limitations of narrative, and pinning his hopes on an accretion of word-sculptures not too unlike the Constructivist art that would spread through Russia, Germany, and France in the early 20th century. (*Life on the Mississippi* was a big hit in Germany.) He appears to be doing his best, against all hope and reason, to defeat what James Cox has called "the lie that language can't help telling,"[8] and conjure on the page a meta-Mississippi, forever sweeping up the damned human race on its mile-wide tide, its "Life" protean and everlasting. He appears to have succeeded.

HIS WORKADAY temperament, in the midst of all this mythifying, re-mained reliably frazzled with quotidian concerns. In July, the Independent Watch Company proved fraudulent, and Orion tried to persuade his brother that Webster had been a part of the con. The notion wrenched him. He'd en-trusted Annie Moffett's husband with more and more authority in his business affairs—even with managing the Tennessee land. Clemens wrestled with his hair-trigger suspicions, and convinced himself that Webster was honest; and indeed, Webster, with goading from Clemens, pressured his former associates to make good on Sam's and Pamela's investments.

The annual getaways to Sue and Theodore Crane's hilltop Arcadia nearly always restored Clemens, but this summer of 1882, even Quarry Farm had its limits. The multiplying pressures sent him to the guest-room bed each night with a throbbing head and little patience for Livy's conversation. Yet he worked on, adding to the pastiche now with chapters left over from *A Tramp Abroad.* Creative attention to his manuscript alternated with hardheaded strategizing for its commercial success. Osgood had not met Sam's standards with sales of *The Prince and the Pauper* and *The Stolen White Elephant;* and so on this one Clemens would take no chances. Ominously, the author sent Charles Webster to visit Osgood in mid-October: "I would like him to take pretty full charge of the matter of running the book, if this will disadvantage you in no way."[9] Technically, Webster was assigned to run Osgood's subscription opera-tions in New York, supervising the outlying agencies and their salesmen. In fact, as Osgood was slow to grasp, this was the first step toward Webster's re-placement of Osgood as Mark Twain's publisher. The supreme commander, however, remained Mark Twain, who had mastered every detail of the making and selling of books. Or so he thought.

At Nook Farm in October, Mark Twain calculated that he still lacked thirty thousand words of a complete manuscript. Weakened by his ailments, bedridden at times, he nonetheless closed the gap as only he could. "I am going to write all day and two thirds of the night, until the thing is done," he vowed to Howells, "or break down at it." [10] That very day, he reported, he'd worked from 9 a.m. until an hour after midnight, churning out 9,500 words ("mainly stolen from books, tho' credit given" [11]), reducing the load by a third. "I have nothing more to borrow or steal; the rest must all be writing. It is ten days work, and unless something breaks, it will be finished in five." [12] It proved more than ten days' work. Meanwhile, Mark Twain sent Osgood a large section of the unfinished manuscript for editing. This was not a great idea: Osgood's copy-slashes reflected an inability to accept the book's quirky personality. "[L]arge areas of it are condemned here and there and yonder," the author railed, "and I have the burden of these unfilled gaps harassing me and the thought of the broken continuity of the work." [13] Some of the excised matter was disposable, such as two chapters by other travel writers. But Osgood's tin ear caused real damage as well. Overly focused on shaping a safe, conventional book of travel information, the editor slashed out sections that contained—as Everett Emerson has noted—the best of Mark Twain's literary personality: tall tales, vernacular narrators, pungent criticism of decaying Southern culture.*

As Sam struggled through December to finish the manuscript, Orion found a few new ways to drive him crazy. He'd hatched a plan for Sam to invest in the installation of electric lights in Keokuk. Orion would manage the deal, thus guaranteeing its success. Sam responded with restraint—Orion's restraint. He demanded that his brother sign a pledge swearing to abstain from business and literary proposals to Sam through 1884; to stop asking Sam's advice about these things; and also to stop lecturing. Orion, who seems to have been losing his tenuous grip on reality by then, meekly complied.

On January 6, 1883, still writing and revising but nearing the end, Mark Twain informed Osgood that he expected a print run of 50,000 copies. "We must give Webster all the thunder-and-lightning circulars and advertising enginery that is needful. We must sell 100,000 copies of the book in 12 months, and shan't want him complaining that we are parties in the fault if the sale falls short of it." [14] Osgood did not grasp the obsessive importance Clemens attached to canvassing, or signing up subscriptions in advance of publication. He would suffer for this lapse.

A week or so later, *Life on the Mississippi* was finished. Osgood prepared to publish it in May. Mark Twain warned him that once set in type, the book

---

* Most of these survive in archival files, and some have been printed as appendices in later editions.

would still require vetting by the supreme commander's supreme commander. Mrs. Clemens ". . . will not let a line of the proof go from here till she has read it and possibly damned it." [15] He scarcely seemed to notice that his helpmeet, who rarely drew a healthful breath, had fallen victim to diphtheria. "[She] is still proportioned like the tongs," he confided to Howells, "but she is pulling up, now, & by & by will get some cushions on her, I reckon. I hope so, anyway—it's been like sleeping with a bed full of baskets." [16]

Building a dam across this particular *Mississippi* would have probably daunted the entire corps of West Point engineers; its sixty chapters flow off in every which direction. The first 216 of its 593 pages (not counting appendices) consist mainly of Mark Twain's luminous "Old Times on the Mississippi" that Howells had serialized in the *Atlantic* in 1875. For many readers and scholars, this self-contained sentimental masterwork remains the heart and soul of the larger volume. Mark Twain broke each of the seven published essays in two, prefacing them with three newly written chapters. The first two of these, deceptively businesslike in their recitation of fact (and "petrified" fact*), lull the reader into expecting the "standard" tome that Sam had promised to Livy: the river's length in miles, varying depth, propensity to change its channels; Indian lore; historical utility to de Soto, La Salle, Jolliet, and so on.

Chapter 3 bumps things abruptly into Twainland. In a genre shape-shift without known precedent in literature, Mark Twain casually announces that he will leave off the dry recitation "and throw in, in its place, a chapter from a book which I have been working at, by fits and starts, for the past five or six years . . ." [17] What follows is the classic "Raft Chapter" that he'd written for the still-unfinished *Adventures of Huckleberry Finn*. The transplant gives readers a glimpse, through Huck's eyes, of the lusty life of the ex-keelboatmen, deck hands on what replaced keelboats, the large lumber rafts, their brawling, tall tales, and song. (The "song" begins—who'd have guessed it?—"There was a woman in our towdn / In our towdn did dwed'l.") From there on, the narrative pinballs: the "Old Times" section ensues, capped off by three new chapters covering the operatic story of Henry and his fate aboard the *Pennsylvania*. Then comes the famous flash-transition: the single-page chapter that distills in twenty lines "the twenty-one slow-drifting years" [18] between the author's leaving the Mississippi and his 1882 return—a finger-snap of rhetoric that replicates the mood of Sam's joyful reawakening aboard the *Gold Dust*.† Then the great collage unfolds.

LIFE ON the Mississippi was issued on May 17, 1883, and once again, the reviewers were overmatched. Here again, conventional literature had not devel-

---

* James M. Cox has famously identified one of these in his introduction to the Penguin Classics edition of *Life on the Mississippi:* Twain's deadpan claim in the book's first paragraph that the river "drains" the far-off state of Delaware.

† On August 7, the *Gold Dust* had exploded, killing the pilot Lem Gray, a fact that Twain folded into *Life on the Mississippi*.

oped a language to encompass Mark Twain's innovations and complexities. The gentlemen of the press generally liked the book, but most of them chose to comment on it strictly from within the old familiar context of its utilitarian value. The Chicago *Tribune* found that it "imparts a great deal of useful information, and . . . is much more than a mere 'funny' book."[19] It remained, as usual, for Howells to grasp the essence of the matter. Writing many years later, and not referring specifically to *Life on the Mississippi,* Howells identified the cast of mind that alone could make such a book possible.

So far as I know, Mr. Clemens is the first writer to use in extended writing the fashion we all use in thinking, and to set down the thing that comes into his mind without fear or favor of the thing that went before or the thing that may be about to follow . . . He would take whatever offered itself to his hand out of that mystical chaos, that divine ragbag, which we call the mind, and leave the reader to look after relevancies and sequences for himself.[20]

A phrase from the Hartford *Times*'s review, that the book is "by no means all devoted to fun," could be applied to James R. Osgood's life in the summer of 1883. The initial sales of *Life on the Mississippi* languished at 30,000 copies. Agents had stopped going door-to-door and were unloading copies in bookstores. More than 10,000 copies lay printed but unbound. Clemens was enraged. *Innocents Abroad, Roughing It,* and *A Tramp Abroad* each (eventually) climbed past 100,000 copies sold, a figure that Sam had come to regard as nearly an entitlement. He blamed Osgood for having failed to secure the massive prepublication subscriptions necessary for his idea of success. His "big-sale-always-before-issue" theory was cockeyed, as even Charlie Webster had dared suggest. A study of the American Publishing Company's ledgers convinced Webster that Bliss's salesmen had never reached 40,000 in advance sales, as Clemens had assumed. Sam was unpersuaded: he lit into Osgood for having mismanaged the book. The letter, which does not survive, may have hinted at profiteering.

Osgood was stunned by this tongue-lashing. The lifelong lover of words; the scrupulous steward of Emerson, Holmes, Longfellow, Howells, Dickens, and James; the man who had agreed to rescue Mark Twain from Bliss, then submitted to an ancillary role in Mark Twain's business designs, encouraged Mark Twain to revive his river-journey dream, and then accompanied him most of the way, now found himself branded as the cause of Mark Twain's "failure" (if sales of 30,000 could be called a "failure"). The former Ticknor & Fields man strained for the language of literary gentlemen in defense of himself, and wrote a classic publisher's self-defense.

We are deeply conscious of having done everything which anybody could have done for this book. We . . . had more trouble and anxiety in connection with it than any book we ever had to do with. So far from being a source of undue profit to us, we have done the business at an unprecedentedly low commission. If it is a failure it is not due to lack of intelligent, conscientious and energetic effort on our part.[21]

Osgood's response made Clemens regret his outburst—for once. He replied with a rare apology ("I am sorry I made that remark, since it hurts you"[22]), but within a few lines he was railing again, about "the failure of a book which could not have failed if you had listened to me." *The Prince and the Pauper* and *Life on the Mississippi* were the only books of his that had ever failed, he went on, neglecting *The Stolen White Elephant*, "—but this second one is so nearly [unbearable] that it is not a calming subject for me to talk upon."[23] He maintained that Osgood's failures had cost him fifty thousand dollars, given that (in his opinion) the book should have sold 80,000 copies initially instead of the 30,000. He ended the business relationship, committing himself even more deeply to self-publishing, and leaned on Osgood to accept a lesser share of the river book's receipts than the agreed-on 7½ percent. Osgood knuckled under.

Clemens at least spared this affable, well-intentioned man the curse of his lingering vindictiveness. He favored Osgood with that most prized of Twainian invitations: "I have invented a new game of billiards, and I want you to stop over with us, next time you are passing Hartford, and try it on."[24] He even mailed the decorous publisher a copy of *1601* ("if it is for a lady you are to assume the authorship of it yourself"[25]). But Osgood never regained his self-assurance. His firm went bankrupt in 1885; he held various book-related jobs; made a brief comeback by publishing a Thomas Hardy novel in 1891 (*Tess of the D'Urbervilles*) and then died the next year at fifty-six.

There was one ancillary failure that Samuel Clemens could not blame on Osgood: the final failure of Kaolatype. *Life on the Mississippi* contained some 310 illustrations, and the artists who drew them—the prestigious landscape painter Henry Garrett; John J. Harley, who did most of the work; and A. B. Shute—refused to allow their work to be reproduced by the process. Clemens cut his losses on Kaolatype soon afterward.

"I HAVE been an utterly free person for a month or two," Clemens happily informed Howells on March 1, as his finished book was being set in type. "I do not believe I ever so greatly appreciated and enjoyed . . . the absence of the chains of slavery as I do this time. I have nothing to do . . . I belong to nobody." He added, "Of course the highest pleasure to be got out of freedom . . . is labor. Therefore I labor."[26]

His labors sprawled across a wide swath of ideas; his mind, freed from its one great chore, had typically grown voracious again. He dithered in new stock transactions that would cost him several thousand dollars. He sketched out an idea for replacing the forthcoming Statue of Liberty (excavation work was just beginning on Bedloe's Island in New York Harbor) with a statue of Adam: "What have we done for Adam? Nothing. What has Adam done for us?

Everything."[27] He started writing a long burlesque, "1002d Arabian Night," that turned out to be so bad that even Howells eventually had to ward him off. "I don't mean to say that there were not extremely killing things in it; but on the whole it was not your best or your second-best; and . . . it skirts a certain kind of fun which you can't afford to indulge in . . ."[28] The "certain kind of fun" involved getting Scheherazade into bed with King Shahriyar. He and Howells began scheming toward collaboration on a play that would exploit the popularity of Mark Twain's great stage character and the national mania for discovery; its title was *Colonel Sellers as a Scientist.*

Inspired by his efforts to teach history to Susy and Clara, he filled page upon page of his notebook with an idea for a new "history" game, a "Memory-Improver" with 4,000 Historical Facts. Children would advance along a marked outdoor space by correctly naming kings, presidents, battles, plagues, revolutions, "Memorable Earthquakes," and so on. He proposed three "trumps"—Judas Iscariot, Guiteau, and Whitelaw Reid. "[W]ho gets either, loses 3 points. It is called being smirched."[29] He described his brainchild to Joe Twichell, and Twichell thoughtlessly repeated the description in the Hartford *Courant,* a tacit invitation for others to pirate the scheme. Clemens seethed, but spared his old hiking chum the friendship death penalty.

H IS M O S T significant labor was the completion of the other great story that his river journey had reawakened in him. Finally, after seven years of approaching and avoiding Huckleberry Finn, he was fully invested in the fugitive boy and his tale. To Jane, in May, he declared, "I haven't had such booming working-days for many years. I am piling up manuscript in a really astonishing way . . . This summer it is no more trouble to me to write than it is to lie."[30] On July 20 he bragged to Howells from Elmira, "I wrote 4000 words to-day & I touch 3000 & upwards pretty often . . . It's a kind of companion to Tom Sawyer."[31] On September 1, 1883, Mark Twain notified James Osgood and his new British publisher Andrew Chatto in London that he was finished.

His burst of energy—695 handwritten pages in six weeks—was all the more astonishing given the sourness that had dampened the early, interrupted stages of the manuscript; as when he'd told Howells in the summer of 1876 that "I like it only tolerably well . . . & may possibly pigeonhole or burn the MS when it is done."[32] His attitude had changed at some point in the years since he'd conceived the novel's metafictive opening sentences: "You will not know about me, without you have read a book by the name of 'The Adventures of Tom Sawyer,' but that ain't no matter. That book was made by Mr. Mark Twain, & he told the truth, mainly."[33] Now, with the river again fresh in his imagination, and his jilted-lover's anger whetted by the profanation of his childhood Eden, Mark Twain finished the book at near stream-of-consciousness speed. The pace of his output would suggest little time for the meditative pauses that most writers require before producing a section, or even a word. Revision would come later, but the wildly complex grand scheme—the "evasion" chapters—form the conclusion to *Huckleberry Finn* seems never to have produced a moment of doubt.

This flow had required years to gain its momentum. Mark Twain breezed through the first 446 pages inside his gazebo at Quarry Farm before turning away from it in the late summer of 1876. The story to that point betrayed little more ambition than to divert young readers. The urchin Huck, rich on his share of the treasure that he and Tom discovered in the previous book, and in the throes of being "sivilized" in St. Petersburg, is kidnapped by his monstrous "Pap" and spirited to a cabin on the opposite shore of the Mississippi. (In his anti-"guvment" speech and angry-white-guy attitude, Pap is the book's most recognizable character by today's standards.) Huck escapes by faking evidence of his own death and slips off to Jackson's Island, where he encounters Jim, on the run after learning that his owner, Miss Watson, intends to sell him down the river. By Chapter 11 the two are off on their raft, co-fugitives from the brutal order of the world ashore. They're hoping to make it to Cairo, at the tip of Illinois, where the Ohio River merges with the Mississippi, and leave the raft there, heading up the Ohio for safety in the free states or Canada. But they drift past that village in the fog and awaken to find themselves in the South, where Jim faces certain capture, or worse.

That was where Mark Twain suspended the novel: in mid-chapter, with Huck wandering on shore, separated from Jim after the raft is smashed by a steamboat. He is on the verge of witnessing an episode of such gruesome depravity and symbolic power that it will change the novel's fundamental purpose for *being* a novel, abolishing the "boy's adventure" motif and launching the development of a dark national vision.

Huck is welcomed into an imposing household of an aristocratic gentleman, Colonel Grangerford. He worshipfully (and hilariously) records the décor fashioned by the Colonel's wife and daughter. He limns the crockery cats and dogs, the fake oranges and grapes on the table, and the table's "beautiful" oilcloth, with its painted spread eagle and fancy border. "It come all the way from Philadelphia, they said."[34] He drinks in the painting of a young woman "leaning pensive on a tombstone,"[35] over the caption, "Shall I Never See Thee More Alas,"[36] and is moved by the daughter's "very good poetry," an ode to one Stephen Dowling Bots, dead from a fall down a well. ("No whooping-cough did rack his frame, / Nor measles drear, with spots; / Not these impared the sacred name / Of Stephen Dowling Bots . . .")[37] "If Emmeline Grangerford could make poetry like that before she was fourteen, there ain't no telling what she could a done by and by."[38] The merciless chronicler of the Lick House Ball is back, disguised as a credulous rube. It is wonderful set-piece satire. But when Mark Twain returned to the story four years later, the function of this scene deepened, as the same family that surrounded itself with this kitschy Americana emerged as capable of another American pursuit, blood violence.

The other subplot that enlarged and drove the book to immortality—slavery and its enabler, the dehumanization of Negroes—had been introduced, but still hung at the edges of the narrative. Jim, deceptively innocuous, appeared little more than a sympathetic minstrel-darky, bursting with laughable superstitions and speaking a generic blackface dialect.

Mark Twain had suspended the book with Huck's question ("What's a feud?") unanswered at the end of that summer, and returned to Hartford with new projects in mind. The Rutherford Hayes campaign absorbed him. He began outlining his Tudor romance before heading for Europe in 1878. He finished *A Tramp Abroad,* and then worked at *Prince and the Pauper* through the first months of 1880, while the Huck manuscript lay neglected. But not unused. The deep imaginings of boyhood adventure—of boyhood—that Mark Twain had invested in the river tale transmigrated to the court of King Edward VI. The Huck Finn a-borning infused the costume-tale prince and pauper with their essential connection to the human heart.

The two manuscripts were linked in a more explicit way: revealingly, Clemens made a "verbal agreement" with James Osgood in 1880 in which both novels would be published under the same cover.[39] Livy quashed this idea, insisting that *Prince and the Pauper* be issued free from contamination by its rough-edged cousin. But the very fact that Mark Twain envisioned the coupling shows that retooling himself as a polite Victorian was never a serious option of his. He would not be sivilized.

Mark Twain revisited *Huckleberry Finn* for 216 pages in March 1880, while taking a break from *Prince and the Pauper,* and stayed with it through June. His shift from manuscript to manuscript was accompanied by a more important shift: from one writing provenance to another. This shift preserved his literary greatness. Turning away from the artificiality of *Prince,* he opened himself again to the wellspring of personal memory, inseminated by his imagination. He stormed back into what is now Chapter 18 armed with his deep knowledge of violence on the Mississippi River—and, by only the slightest extension, in America. Huck's brief respite amid the domestic torpor of the Grangerford farm is interrupted by gunfire: a reeruption of the family's bloody feud with the equally "high-toned" Shepherdson clan that lives a few miles upstream. Before Huck can escape the premises and rejoin Jim on the raft, he has seen his new friend Buck try to ambush a Shepherdson from behind a bush. A few days later he looks on in disbelief as the two warring families assemble in a common church, fully armed, to hear a sermon about brotherly love. Then he is eyewitness to the slaughter of Buck and his cousin Joe by four Shepherdsons who fire mercilessly into the boys as they try to escape by swimming in the Mississippi. The complacent décor of the Grangerford house, merely funny a few pages earlier, now stands revealed as ghastly evidence of a diseased culture's pretentions to gentility. (Luckily for Samuel Clemens's own pretentions, the Mississippi didn't flow through Hartford.)

This fictional vendetta had authentic origins: the so-called Darnell-

Watson feud in the vicinity of a Kentucky landing named "Compromise" in the late 1850s and '60s. Clemens claimed in later life to have nearly been an eyewitness to one of its episodes. Scholarly research supports the claim, making allowances for "nearly."[40] In August 1859 the young Sam witnessed a "row" at the landing at Compromise from aboard a Memphis packet. A month later, he was a co-pilot on a boat that steamed upriver past the same site, three days after the "row" was reignited with deadly results: a grisly struggle involving pistols, the butt of a shotgun, and bare hands that left one man drowned in the river and his enemy gravely wounded by bullets. This was but the latest face-off in a vendetta that left several men dead over many years. Sam assimilated the details from eyewitnesses, and learned of the feud's larger contours from the father of a fourteen-year-old boy who had been killed. Newspaper accounts added to his understanding. Mark Twain's imagination took over from there, as it always did with vivid real-life events. He tried out a version of it in *Simon Wheeler, Detective,* abandoned in 1878. By 1880, when he returned to *Huckleberry Finn,* he had conflated and shaped these events into story, and invested them with the power of metaphor.

The novel reaches its apogee with the "feud" chapters and their aftermath. Huck, reunited with Jim, admires the greatest sunrise in Western literature a few pages later, the river Eden counterpointing the fallen world onshore. They encounter another set of civilized predators, the fraudulent King and the Duke, who board the raft and direct it to Bricksville, Arkansas. After the comedy of the Duke's sideshow mangling of Shakespeare, a new macabre mood shift follows: the gunning down of addled Boggs by Colonel Sherburn, yet another specimen of Southern gentility. Mark Twain sketches a version of the consequences: "Well, by-and-by somebody said Sherburn ought to be lynched. In about a minute everybody was saying it; so away they went, mad and yelling, and snatching down every clothes-line they come to, to do the hanging with."[41] But "they was too late. Sherburn's friends had got him away, long ago."[42]

Not quite. Beneath that tentative chapter ending, Mark Twain, his contempt for the South apparently ripening by the minute, pencils a note to himself: "No, let them lynch him."[43]

And then Mark Twain returned again to *The Prince and the Pauper.* Soon after that, he became preoccupied with the Paige device, and Kaolatype, and the birth of Jean, and investments in the house. Worldly matters beset him until the spring of 1882, when he walked away from all of it and revisited the great Mississippi of his youth, filling his tank with river water. In June 1883, Mark Twain was ready at last to throw himself into the labyrinthine finale of *Huckleberry Finn.*

The lynch mob storms Sherburn's house, only to be stared down by the Colonel with his double-barrel shotgun. He flays them all as pitiful cowards; the crowd washes back and then bolts in all directions; and then—with Boggs's body still cooling in the drugstore—Huck takes in the circus.

Deep in Arkansas, Jim is captured and held prisoner at the Phelps farm. It is at this point, perhaps, that Mark Twain's despised nights in the opera houses of Heidelberg pay their dividends: Huck, alone inside the wigwam on the raft, begins the Wagnerian aria that many believe to be the moral center of the novel. He debates with himself what to do; rationalizes that his social, even Christian duty requires him to write a letter to Miss Watson telling her of her property's whereabouts; regrets his lifelong apostasy; tries to pray his sins away; finds himself mute because he knows the prayer is false:

I was letting *on* to give up sin, but away inside of me I was holding on to the biggest one of all. I was trying to make my mouth *say* I would do the right thing and the clean thing, and go and write to that nigger's owner and tell where he was; but deep down in me I knowd it was a lie . . . You can't pray a lie—I found that out.[44]

He writes the letter designed to seal Jim's fate, and feels washed clean of sin, until he thinks some more,

And got to thinking over our trip down the river; and I see Jim before me, all the time, in the day, and in the night-time, sometimes moonlight, sometimes storms, and we a-floating along, talking, and singing, and laughing . . . somehow I couldn't seem to strike no places to harden me against him . . . and at last I struck the time I saved him by telling the men we had small-pox aboard, and he was so grateful, and said I was the best friend old Jim ever had in the world . . . and then I happened to look around, and see that paper.[45]

He takes up the letter and studies it a minute—and delivers the purification lyric worthy of Brunhilde's immolation in the *Gotterdammerung:*

" 'All right, then, I'll *go* to hell'—and tore it up." [46]

From the mid-20th century on, the moral majesty of this moment has been almost universally assumed. It forms the novel's abiding claim as an oracle of the American soul. Norman Podhoretz's 1959 declaration that the scene "is one of the supreme moments in all of literature"[47] remains representative. What bedevils the proponents of this view—including those who posit *Huckleberry Finn* as a deliberately antiracist work—is nearly everything that follows.

Mark Twain himself sounded the first warning. Toward the end of his 1880 stint, he thought to write the novel's famous "Notice": "Persons attempting to find a Motive in this narrative will be prosecuted; persons attempting to find a Moral in it will be banished; persons attempting to find a Plot in it will be shot." And sure enough: within a dozen pages of Huck's stirring declaration, Tom Sawyer makes his flagrantly improbable reentry into the story; realism vanishes; measured satire gives way to borderline slapstick, and the shackled Jim endures a prolonged ordeal of pointless tormenting at the hands of his avowed liberators, with Huck a submissive agent of Tom's wild-eyed scenarios. The meaning of Huck's response to his friend's high-spirited depravity, and, indeed, of his complicity in it, has been endlessly debated and never resolved.

Huck favors a quick and simple rescue plan: steal the key to the lock on the cabin, free Jim, and make a run for the raft. Tom, ever book-addled, is dismissive: "I should *hope* we can find a way that's a little more complicated than *that,* Huck Finn."[48] He has been marinating in stories of history's famous escapes, and wants to try some of the methods out on Jim. "When a prisoner of style escapes, it's called an evasion," he later explains,[49] using the word that now embraces the ten chapters explicating his tortuous scheme. Opera now becomes *opera buffa,* with a discomfiting sadistic edge. Tom wants Jim to free his chain from the bed leg, not by simply lifting it off the floor, but by sawing it through. He proposes digging a hole to the cabin floor—with case knives, not spades. He wants to leave "clews." Rope ladders are contemplated for the ground-level caper. Days pass. Absurdity reaches its height when the boys actually free Jim from the cabin so that he can help them lug a huge grindstone into his room, so that he can write inscriptions on it while awaiting his freedom. Then morbidity reaches its depth: for historical accuracy, Tom wants to fill the cabin with spiders, rats, and snakes. (Jim spoils the fun by rejecting Tom's pleas to include a rattlesnake.) Three weeks have now passed, with Jim now in bondage as much to the two boys as to the Phelpses. Tom fakes a letter warning that a gang of abolitionists is in the area, drawing a posse of fifteen armed farmers to the Phelps farm—as he'd hoped. The breakout ensues amid a riot of staged and stagey farce: Huck masking as Tom, Tom masking as his brother Sid, Jim and Tom-Sid in women's clothes, the farmhouse crawling with serpents, melted butter streaming down Huck-Tom's face, bloodhounds baying, bullets flying, a slug of lead in Tom-Sid's calf.

Later—Jim having been recaptured while watching over the wounded Tom, and brought back to the farm—Tom delivers the final pie-in-the-face: Jim is a free man, he announces. The Widow, who died two months earlier, liberated him in her will. Tom knew this all along, but played out the "evasion" charade because "I wanted the *adventure* of it."[50] In case anyone doubts him, Aunt Polly materializes in the doorway, all the way from St. Petersburg, to confirm the facts. The book ends with Tom proposing that the trio head out west for adventure among the Indians, and Huck allowing that he would "light out for the Territory ahead of the rest, because Aunt Sally she's going to adopt me and sivilize me and I can't stand it. I been there before."[51]

Huckleberry Finn endures as a consensus masterpiece despite these final chapters. Its greatness rests on its lapidary portraiture of America as encapsulated in a time and place; on its revelatory use of vernacular American dialect as the vehicle for its story; and for the authentic passion, metaphor, self-expression, and moral reasoning released via this dialect. This departure from high diction is what Ernest Hemingway had in mind in his 1935 pronouncement that "all modern American literature comes from" this novel. As for the "evasion" chapters, early commentators have tended to excuse (or damn) them as a failed attempt to conclude an otherwise great tale whose perpetual-motion narrative defies conclusion. More recent analysis has been more respectful, perceiving a grand design: the chapters are, for instance, an allegory of the torments visited on former slaves during the post-Reconstruction era in which Mark Twain wrote. But nearly everybody agrees that it is one hell of a book.

ITS GREATNESS owes nearly as much to Mark Twain's technical dedication as to his conceptual genius. Mark Twain always revised as he worked, scrawling his emendations in the margins and between the lines of his pages. This was especially true of *Huckleberry Finn*. After announcing from Elmira that he was "finished" with it in September 1883, the author took the great stack of pages home to Hartford and worried over it for six more months, refusing to surrender it until mid-April 1884. His improvements were pointillist: an accretion of small, sharp edits that greatly enhanced the diction and imagery of the novel entire.

In the summer of 1882, Clemens hired a pair of typists from Elmira—among the first professionals in that new skill—to copy his *Life on the Mississippi* manuscript. He liked the results so well that he directed the typists to start in on the first 663 manuscript pages of *Huckleberry Finn*. Typescripts absorbed and eliminated the clutter of an annotated draft manuscript. For the first time, Mark Twain could make a second round of revisions on clean pages, and he used that opportunity to full advantage. The typescripts are presumed lost, but in 1990 the first 665 manuscript pages reemerged in a Hollywood attic.* Now a sentence as Mark Twain first wrote it could be compared to its final version in the book, and the differences between them identified as changes on the typescript or proofs (including changes made inadvertently by the typist).

Certain myths immediately evaporated. Foremost among them was the accepted view that Huckleberry Finn's voice flowed unaltered from Mark Twain's raw imagination onto the book page. Far from it: the author constantly rummaged through Huck's (and Jim's) dialect, weeding out words and phrases that bore any taint of a mature well-read man's syntax. "Always" became "awluz"; "never heard anything" became "didn't hear nothing." In draft, Huck might have remarked that "I had about made up my mind to stay there all night, when I heard horses," but by the time the presses rolled, he'd

---

* The discovery was made by Barbara Gluck Testa, a granddaughter of James Fraser Gluck, a curator of the Young Men's Christian Association in Buffalo, who in 1885 had asked Clemens to donate the manuscript to the library. Clemens consented, but found that he could send only the second half; he'd misplaced the first half and did not find it for some nineteen months. When James Gluck finally received this second bundle, in 1887, he neglected to put it on display alongside the concluding holograph, and died ten years later with it still stored in his personal possessions. It remained unrecovered for 103 years.

corrected himself to ". . . when I hear a *plunkety-plunk, plunkety-plunk,* and says to myself, horses coming."[52]

Mark Twain also fine-tuned Huck's capacity for reasoning, especially moral reasoning. In Chapter 16, Huck suffers a guilty conscience after he fast-talks some slave hunters in a boat out of searching the raft where Jim is hiding, by leading them to think there is smallpox on board. The first draft reads

They went off & I hopped aboard the raft, saying to myself, I've done wrong again, & was trying as hard as I could to do right, too; but when it come right down to telling them it was a nigger on the raft, & I opened my mouth a-purpose to do it, I couldn't. I am a mean, low coward, & it's the fault of them that brung me up. If I had been raised right, I wouldn't said anything about anybody being sick, but the more I try to do it right, the more I can't.[53]

Many novelists would be willing to ransom their agents for a passage of that caliber, but Mark Twain wasn't satisfied. It became:

They went off, and I got aboard the raft, feeling bad and low, because I knowed very well I had done wrong, and I see it warn't no use for me to try to learn to do right; a body that don't get *started* right when he's little, ain't got no show—when the pinch comes there ain't nothing to back him up and keep him to his work, and so he gets beat.[54]

Mark Twain himself expressed the value of this system—and offered a glimpse into the near-tactile relationship between a writer and his words on the page—in a letter of recommendation for one of the typists, Harry M. Clarke. "THE EXPERIENCE WITH THE TYPEWRITER HAS BEEN OF SO HIGH A VALUE TO ME," he wrote,

THAT NOT EVEN THE TYPE-WRITER ITSELF CAN DESCRIBE IT . . . THE PAGES OF THE [typewritten] SHEETS BEGIN TO LOOK AS NATURAL, AND RATIONAL, AND AS VOID OF OF-FENSE TO HIS EYE AS DO HIS OWN WRITTEN PAGES, AND THEREFORE HE CAN ALTER AND AMEND THEM WITH COMFORT . . . [Books copied by pen] HAVE A FOREIGN AND UNSYM-PATHETIC LOOK . . . ONE CANNOT RECOGNIZE HIMSELF IN THEM . . . MY COPYING IS AL-WAYS DONE ON THE TYPE-WRITER, NOW, AND I SHALL NOT BE LIKELY TO EVER USE ANY OTHER SYSTEM.[55]

WILLIAM AND Elinor Howells and their three children returned from Europe in mid-July of 1883, just as Mark Twain was tearing through the homestretch of *Huckleberry Finn.* They took up residence in a rented house on Beacon Hill in Boston. The year abroad had restored Howells from his near-nervous collapse and the rigors of finishing *A Modern Instance,* the rather dar-ing update of *Medea,* with its themes of marital betrayal and jealousy, to contemporary Boston ("daring" partly because the obsessive female protagonist bore unmistakable resemblances to Elinor). The novel had brought him to a new level of popular recognition and literary esteem. Henry James liked it, as did many Europeans. Mark Twain himself, who knew a thing or two about the subject, assured Howells that one particular passage was "the best drunk scene that I ever read . . . How very drunk, & how recently drunk, & how altogether admirably drunk you must have been to . . . contrive that masterpiece."[56]

Back home, Howells lost no time resuming his prodigious literary output. Despite his health failures, family tensions, economic crises, personal correspondence, a writing wrist chronically in pain, and attention to Clemens's frequent whims, Howells had generated nearly a novel in each of the last dozen years—in addition to a stream of plays, poetry, travel essays, and criticism. Now he plunged back to work on three other novels, *A Woman of Reason*, *The Minister's Charge*, and his most enduring work, *The Rise of Silas Lapham*.

And then he plunged out again, because a boy called him away from these grown-up chores. He found himself once again roped into playing Joe Harper to Clemens's Tom. Looking beyond the completion of his own novel, and back on the prowl for a money-making project, Sam revived the idea of co-writing a new Colonel Sellers play, with Howells as his partner. He wanted to build on the theme of Sellers as a mad scientist: why not also make the old blowhard a claimant to a British title—the Earl of Durham? (Sam had daydreamed several possibilities in church one Sunday, as his attention wandered from Joe Twichell's sermon.) The lion of letters in Boston was more than game. Howells swept aside his unfinished manuscripts and prepared to play hooky: "As soon as I mentioned our plan for a play," he gleefully told Clemens, "Mrs. Howells nobly declared that she would do anything for money, and that I might go to you when I liked."[57] Sam signaled his gratitude by mentioning that two-thirds of the royalties should go to himself, given that he was Sellers's creator. No problem! "The terms are good and just," Howells wrote back, "two thirds for you and one for me . . . I've read every bit about Sellers in [*The Gilded Age*]. There's a great play in him yet."[58]

Howells arrived at the Nook Farm house in November to find that Mark Twain had not really developed the play's plot much beyond the vague-idea stage. Again, no matter! The two old friends spent the next several days brainstorming hilariously. Mad scientist? Peerage claimant? Why not give Sellers some *eccentric* traits as well! Make him a spiritualist! A temperance reformer! A drunken temperance reformer! Get him involved in recording profanity, to be pawned off to ships' officers so they wouldn't run out during emergencies! Strap a fire extinguisher on his back! Give him wings! They seem to have laughed themselves silly. "We had loads and loads of fun about it," Howells later told Paine. "We cracked our sides laughing over it as we went along. We thought it was mighty good . . ."[59]

After a few days of this, Clemens and Howells had worked themselves into such a pitch of hysteria that they half-convinced themselves they'd written a comic masterpiece. In the middle of it all, the living monument to British high culture, Matthew Arnold, arrived in Hartford to lecture, and Howells dragged Clemens off to a reception for the poet. In Boston a few days earlier, upon hearing that Howells had gone to visit Mark Twain, Arnold had murmured, "Oh, but he doesn't like *that* sort of thing, does he?"[60] Now, chatting with Howells at the Hartford soiree, Arnold's gaze fell upon a small man with graying red hair across the room. "Who—who in the world is that?" he asked.[61] Introduced, he spent the remainder of the evening in Mark Twain's thrall, and the next night, "as if still under the glamour of that potent presence,"[62] Arnold presented himself at the Clemens house. Clemens never spoke to Howells of what they talked about.

Colonel Sellers as a Scientist was published in 1887, but never performed in New York. Clemens eventually acquired Howells's share of the rights to it and financed a brief tour of one-night stands; and then it was over. Howells believed until his dying day that it could have been a success. What seems more significant, in view of the difficult years bearing down on them but yet unseen, is that in their brief stolen holiday of writing the play, Sam Clemens and William Dean Howells probably laughed as hard and as long together as either man would laugh for the rest of his life.

38

The American Novel

(1884–85)

Even as he raced through final revisions of his unsuspected masterpiece in early 1884, Mark Twain foraged for the next big thing. He finished a stage version of *Tom Sawyer* that he'd somehow found time to begin drafting the previous fall. He searched for a producer to buy *Colonel Sellers as a Scientist*. He brainstormed a comic almanac. He dreamed up new inventions: a glass "hand grenade" filled with extinguishing liquid that could be thrown into the midst of a fire; a bed clamp to keep babies from kicking off their covers. He considered promoting a musical game invented by Susy. He mulled the minutiae of contracts, incentives for sales agents, the comparative cost/benefits of printing paper. He roughed out a discount strategy for selling *Huckleberry Finn* and *Tom Sawyer* as a matched set (which he later abandoned). And he nurtured an idea that had gripped him at least since he and Howells had had their luncheon with Ulysses S. Grant in New York: to encourage Grant to write and publish his memoirs.

He needed professional autonomy and a tireless (and compliant) right-hand man. In May 1884, a new publishing firm announced itself to the world: Charles L. Webster & Company, of New York. The former Fredonia real estate salesman found himself, at thirty-two, in charge of Mark Twain's publishing fortunes. At least that's what the letterhead implied. "Webster & Company" was in fact Mark Twain himself (as he allowed to the New York *Herald* in 1885). From now on he would publish his own books and plays, avoiding the blunders of Bliss and Osgood and keeping their share of the swag. His titular publisher, husband of his niece, would function as his eyes and ears, his business enforcer, his legal researcher, his surrogate in the theater world—as the consummator of every Mark Twain scheme, plan, or whim.

Don Quixote had found his Sancho Panza. Webster was bright, and almost painfully serious-minded. He was willing to immerse himself in every sort of detail—he assimilated the many-layered requirements of the book trade with remarkable speed—and he seemed infinitely obedient. "[Y]our smallest wish shall be gratified no matter how much it discommodes me," he assured his boss.[1] Webster was soon to learn how stressful it could be to lose one's commode.

Clemens started him at a salary of $2,500, a little more than that earned by a St. Louis schoolteacher, plus a share of the company's net profits (a third of the first $20,000, but only a tenth thereafter). Clemens retained the right to approve any business expenses over $1,000, and to complain about the rest (postage, for example). Clemens never quite figured out why Webster needed a starting salary at all; he was, after all, an apprentice in spite of what the letterhead said, and apprentices never received salaries—Sam Clemens certainly hadn't, as an apprentice pilot.

Surmounting his role as Bob Cratchit to Clemens's Ebeneezer Scrooge, Webster performed admirably in the early production stages of *Huckleberry Finn*. He hunted for a printing firm after negotiations with Frank Bliss at American Publishing broke down, and settled on J. J. Little and Company of New York. Bargaining shrewdly with two paper companies, he nailed a favorable contract for printing and binding. It was Webster who persuaded Mark Twain to omit the "raft episode" that he had earlier smouched for *Life on the Mississippi*, to lighten the bulk of *Huck Finn*. Mark Twain miraculously offered no objections.

Mark Twain's temper had to rear its head sooner or later, and it did so sooner, during the search for the novel's illustrators. Illustrations were always of critical importance. The author's first choice probably would have been True Williams. But as Williams's alcoholism grew worse, he became less reliable, and surly—Mark Twain once called him the greatest combination of hog and angel he'd ever seen.[2] He had managed some forty illustrations for *A Tramp Abroad*, and then faded away: he moved to Chicago and eventually worked for Mark Twain's arch-nemesis, the Canadian publishing pirate Alexander Belford.[3] Webster's search for a replacement devolved on Edward Windsor Kemble, a twenty-three-year-old Californian and son of the founder of the *Alta California*. He was drawing cartoons for *Life* magazine and the New York *Graphic* when he came to Webster's attention. Kemble's work was more angular and less embellished than Williams's, but it conveyed movement, character, and raw power. "Kemble will do the work for $1200,00," Webster notified his boss from New York in April, shortly before Webster & Co. was announced, and then headed for Hartford with samples of the artist's work. Sam and Livy accompanied Webster back to New York—Livy needed to shop. Webster had bargained Kemble down to $1,000, but that feat did not excuse him for a serious faux-pas during the train ride. Webster tried to pin Clemens down on a publication date for *Huckleberry Finn,* for Kemble's benefit. The author held his tongue for Livy's sake; but a few days later, a scalding letter arrived at Webster's new office on Broadway:

> Here is a question which has been settled not less than 30 times, & always in the same way . . . This is the answer—& it has never received any other. *The book is to be issued when a big edition has been sold*—& NOT BEFORE.
>
> Now write it up, somewhere, & keep it in mind; & let us consider that question settled, & answered, & done with . . .
>
> Write it up, & don't forget it any more.[4]

A couple of weeks after his chastisement, Charles Webster received another directive from the boss: "Yes, I want Howells to have carte blanche in making corrections."[5] Once again, the congenitally swamped Howells had offered to put his own concerns aside and serve as unpaid, uncredited editor of a Mark Twain manuscript. (Besides his array of novels in progress, he had just sprinted through two weeks of writing a libretto, *A Sea-Change,* to be performed to the music of George Henschel, while also trying to find a manufacturer for some grape shears his father had invented.)

Howells had made an unfortunate word choice in that offer: "proofs." He was referring to the typewritten version of Mark Twain's manuscript, and his intent was to give it his usual editorial once-over for broad issues of usage, tone, and coherence. ("Typescript" had not yet entered the language.) Clemens understood him to mean he would read the printers' *galley* proofs, a far more painstaking chore and one that Sam hated, given that it meant scanning each sentence and each word for typographical errors. Hardly believing this windfall, Sam gushed,

> It took my breath away, & I haven't recovered it yet, entirely . . . Now if you *mean* it, old man—if you are in *earnest*—proceed, in God's name, & be by me forever blest.[6]

Howells serenely replied:

> It is all perfectly true about the generosity . . . [I]t seems as if I were glad of the notion of being of use to you; and I shall have the pleasure of admiring a piece of work I like under a microscope.[7]

Howells corrected Clemens's misunderstanding at a meeting in Boston, and shortly afterward bent to his carte-blanche endeavors. At least he *thought* he'd corrected that misunderstanding.

Clemens reviewed the book illustrations carefully as Webster rushed them up from New York in batches from Kemble's drawing board. He was aware that this new book would take his readers into disturbingly unexpected territory—bloody violence, racial ugliness—and that the drawings could either reinforce or relieve some of the textual tension. He was not pleased with Kemble's early efforts. One of the objectionable pieces was the cover drawing of Huck. Clemens complained that "the boy's mouth is a trifle more Irishy than necessary," [8] a reference to Huck's long upper lip. Kemble redrew it. A more general objection was that Kemble had dashed the drawings off; Clemens found several of them "careless & bad," [9] and sent them back to the artist with instructions to soften the faces; make them less "forbidding & repulsive." [10] In some of his revisions, Kemble may have gone too far in the opposite direction: Jim, especially in the early chapters, has the pop-eyed, slack-mouthed look of a minstrel darky.

Clemens's general complaints about the drawings are quite telling. "Some of the pictures are good, but none of them are very *very* good," he complained to Webster. "The faces are generally ugly, & wrenched into overexpression amounting sometimes to distortion. . . . Reduction will modify them, no doubt, but it can hardly make them pleasant folk to look at. An artist shouldn't follow a book too literally, perhaps? If this is the necessary result. . . . The pictures will *do*—they will just barely do—& that is the best I can say for them. . . . Huck Finn is an exceedingly good-hearted boy, & should carry a good & good-looking face." [11] Webster bore down on the artist, who coughed up thirty-four new drawings in early June. These Clemens pronounced "most rattling good. They please me exceedingly." [12] Working under deadline pressure and sometimes without benefit of a text, Kemble produced 175 drawings for *Huckleberry Finn*.

HOWELLS FINISHED his editorial vetting in the third week of May, and Webster signaled J. J. Little and Company to commence typesetting for an order of 30,000 books. Clemens consented to this, but remained obsessed with his own magic number. "Begin your canvass early, and *drive* it; for if, by the 5th of December, we have 40,000 orders, we will publish on the 15th . . . [L]et's never allow ourselves to *think* of issuing with any *less* than 40,000 while there's the ghost of a show to get them." [13] Money had become an urgent need again, his usual expenditures increased by recent investments in the publishing company. In June, Howells diffidently requested a check for $2,000 to compensate his editorial work on *Mark Twain's Library of Humor;* Clemens, pleading "losses, ill luck, & botched businesses," turned him down. [14] When Howells repeated the request a discrete year and a half later, Clemens again complained that he was strapped, this time because of Grant's book: "do you need & must you require that $2,000 *now?*" [15] He sent the check after six weeks, when his cash flow improved.

In the spring of 1884 he began to dream of a rollicking adventure that was sure to make money for himself, Howells, and some other close friends. The idea tapped into the Gilded Age's taste for grand gesture and the ever-accelerating American fascination with celebrityhood. The scheme was to reintroduce the icon that had materialized on the San Francisco stage in October 1866, and effloresced into the Vandal of the lecture circuit. The Vandal was retired now, but Clemens's brainstorm was to bring him back, in spirit if not in name; round up Howells, Thomas Bailey Aldrich, and George Washington Cable to perform with him; rent a private railroad car; and go "gadding around the country," delivering readings from their work to audiences in sequence each night: a kind of literary proto–rock 'n' roll revue. Howells and Aldrich loved the idea, but soon accepted reality: their careers and families would never permit it. Cable was a different story. The tiny Southerner adored Sam Clemens. He'd signaled his adulation in a whimsical way, organizing a scheme among 150 of Mark Twain's literary friends to send him requests for autographs, the letters to arrive simultaneously on April Fool's Day. Clemens, notoriously thin-skinned about jokes at his expense, elected to be amused, and the friendship solidified. With Cable on board for the fall tour, Clemens scaled back on the rented-train-car idea, but hired a manager and gave the project a flashy marquee name: the Twins of Genius Tour.

He spent a distracted summer waiting for the tour, and the novel, to happen. He writhed through some sessions in the dentist's chair. Along with Joe Twichell, he tried to master the fashionable new high-wheeled bicycle, with bruising results: his German instructor remarked to him that he could fall off a bicycle in more ways than the man who had invented it.[16] Clemens later maintained that he had invented all the new bicycle profanity that had since come into general use.[17]

ON THE morning of June 2, 1884, Ulysses S. Grant wandered into the pantry of his summer oceanside cottage at Long Branch, New Jersey, where his wife Julia was laying out some fruit. Grant picked up a peach, bit into it, and screamed. He had never experienced pain like that which flared in his throat. In a minute things seemed all right again, but as the weeks went on, he felt it again. And again. His wife consulted a doctor.

ENSCONCED AT Quarry Farm with Livy and the children, Clemens sat for a bust sculpted by Karl Gerhardt, a young Hartford mechanic who had studied in Paris under Mark Twain's sponsorship. A photograph of the bust was included as a second frontispiece in *Huckleberry Finn*. He started writing a new Tom and Huck vehicle, *Huck Finn and Tom Sawyer Among the Indians*. He thought up new tasks for Charles Webster: look for someone to fix the Clemens furnace in Hartford, round up some books about the West (for the new book), find a manufacturer for Susy's game, get ready to market yet another Mark Twain invention (a portable calendar), negotiate a contract with a business manager for the reading tour, negotiate production rights with John T. Raymond to get the Sellers play up and running, and organize the sales force for *Huckleberry Finn*.

One matter for which Clemens did *not* have room in his schedule was

Huckleberry Finn, or anything that even looked like it might force him to think about it. Clemens typically wanted his latest literary offspring out of the house and earning a paycheck immediately. It was hardly surprising, then, that when Webster sent a shipment of typeset galleys up to Elmira in August for proofreading—parts of Chapters 26 through 30—Sam made it only as far as opening the package before he flung the whole bundle down to Boston, and Howells.

I have no doubt I am doing a most criminal & outrageous thing—for I am sending you these infernal Huck Finn proofs—but the very last vestige of my patience has gone to the devil, & I cannot bear the sight of another slip of them. My hair turns white with rage, at sight of the mere outside of the package . . .

Blackguard me if you want to—I deserve it.[18]

Well . . . Howells had *offered* to read the proofs. Hadn't he?

To Webster, Clemens explained that "Howells will maybe return it to *you* to be read—in which case you may send it to me again, & I will get my profanity together & tackle it."[19] Howells didn't return it to Webster, of course. He had intended to relax in Kennebunkport, Maine, in August, but he agreed to take the work along with him, gallantly observing, "If I had written half as good a book as Huck Finn, I shouldn't ask anything better than to read the proofs; even as it is I don't."[20] Eventually, Clemens accepted his plight, and burrowed into a stack of proofs himself.

Back in Hartford in September, the Clemens family experienced a horrific foretaste of the emerging American urban life: Susy and Clara, wandering down Farmington Avenue by themselves, were confronted by a drunken thug who drew a gun on them. The man was captured and jailed, but escaped and fled.

At around the same time, Clemens assented to a far happier, more significant connection with modern times: a stylish New York magazine, a forerunner of the sophisticated periodicals that would flourish in the first half of the 20th century, had been pressing Clemens all summer for extensive serialization rights to *Huckleberry Finn.* In September, Clemens said yes to a version of this request. The magazine was the *Century,* in its third year of evolvement from the old *Scribner's Monthly.* Its editor, the forty-year-old Richard Watson Gilder, embodied the national trend away from romantic sentiment toward a worldly sort of cosmopolitan knowledge. (Gilder named the magazine after the Century Club, of which he was a member.) Gunslinger-angular and clean-shaven except for an eagle's-wing mustache, Gilder was a soldier-sonneteer turned broker of cultural opinion. He'd fought against Lee at Gettysburg. After the war he'd stolen away the sweetheart of the painter Winslow Homer, Helena de Kay, with his romantic poems, and married her. Then, at the helm of his new and sophisticated publication, Gilder unfurled his gifts as a visionary editor. The magazine covered science, religion, political trends, and nuance ("The Lack of Earnestness in Today's Politicians"); travel, architecture ("Old Public Buildings in America"); education, and law, and soon built a circulation of 180,000 a month, dwarfing the *Atlantic*'s reach. Its greatest contribution, though, proved to be in the realm of letters. American literature had gone adrift in the immediate postwar years, the Transcendentalists aged or dead, commerce and industry dominating the nation's attention. Britain had recaptured its ancient literary predominance. Gilder almost single-handedly led a resurgence, showcasing the most vital of American writers. In early 1884 the *Century* was serializing two classics-to-be, Howells's *The Rise of Silas Lapham* and Henry James's *The Bostonians*.

Mark Twain had given Gilder proofs of the book in the spring, hoping to sell a short excerpt. Gilder at once recognized the radically new native voice. Diametrically the opposite of Jamesian eloquence, it radiated, in its very homespun ardency, a new sort of American truth. Gilder tried to coax Mark Twain into allowing him to print most of *Huckleberry Finn* before publication. The urbane editor tried a folksy approach: "Take a long pull & a strong pull & a pull altogether & listen to what I have to say, & don't get wrothy till you get through." Webster & Company would need to delay publication for a few months for this to be possible; but Gilder argued strongly that such exposure in the influential magazine would increase book sales. "In naming a price," he wrote to Clemens, "please remember that you have the largest audience of any English writer above ground . . . [D]on't name a price so high" (as to nullify the magazine's profits).[21]

Mark Twain resisted this flattery. Years of seeing his book sales undercut by pirates had hardened his conviction that if most of the novel appeared in print before publication, the market would only dry up. He consented to allow Gilder a single episode. Gilder pressed for more. They reached a compromise: the *Century* published three installments, beginning in December 1884 with the Grangerford-Shepherdson feud section. Gilder himself edited the selections from pages of unbound book type. He edited on the side of caution: though assuring Clemens that "I have a pretty 'robustuous taste,' "[22] he understood that Mark Twain's unprecedented use of vernacular pushed against the limits of public tolerance. Many of his changes were excisions that bowed to prevailing disapproval of bad grammar, slang, and even indirect references to sex.

While negotiating for Mark Twain's literature, Gilder was also spearheading a bold new concept in social journalism. His editors canvassed former Union and Confederate military officers, asking them to contribute essays of personal reminiscence for a series to be called "Battles and Leaders of the Civil War"—the essays later to be collected in a book. So far, the generals had remained aloof and unavailable. Gilder and his gifted associate editor, the poet and future diplomat Robert Underwood Johnson, believed that Union officers, at least, would change their minds if their beloved old commander in chief could be induced to break the ice. Johnson called on Ulysses S. Grant at

Long Branch in June. The former president, his painful throat cancer yet un-diagnosed, admitted to his visitor that he and his family had never recovered from the bankruptcy of Grant & Ward, and that he felt his honor had been fa-tally tarnished. When Johnson offered him the chance to repair both these problems by publishing in the *Century,* Grant demurred at first: he was no writer. Johnson named a fee: $500 for four war-related pieces—a total of $40,000 by today's standards. This was hardly a fortune, but Grant under-stood that he needed every penny he could make. He decided that he might be able to write a little bit after all. Already he was thinking like a writer.

RICHARD GILDER had significant backup in patrolling the pages of *Huck-leberry Finn* for affronts to public taste. Howells of course was on the case, and Livy was giving the book her most acute attention—taking her pen to sections after Clemens had read them aloud at Quarry Farm. Susy, beautiful and pre-cocious at twelve, noted these sessions carefully, and recorded them, with oc-casional spelling innovations her father would later cherish.

Papa read "Huckleberry Finn" to us in manuscript just before it came out, and then he would leave parts of it with mamma to expergate, while he went off up to the study to work, and sometimes Clara and I would be sitting with mamma while she was looking the manuscript over and I remember so well, with what pangs of regret we used to see her turn down leaves of the pages which meant, that some delightfully dreadful part must be scratched out. And I remember one part pertickularly which was perfectly fas-cinating it was dreadful . . . and oh with what dispare we saw mamma turn down the leaf on which it was written, we thought the book would be almost spoiled without it.[23]

Clemens answered this by insisting that the "expergated" passages were ones that he dropped into the text with just that function in mind; he never ex-pected them to survive.

Mark Twain was not the only person interested in smuggling shockworthy material into *Huckleberry Finn.* In November, as presses were starting to roll to-ward a January publication, a workman happened to glance at one of Kemble's picture proofs and spotted a potentially ruinous bit of graffiti. Some slyboots in the printing pressroom had etched a few strokes into the illustration's en-graved plate—the depiction of Uncle Silas braced in front of Huck, his pelvis thrust out in a posture of sternness.[24] The added strokes made it appear as though Uncle Silas's pelvis wasn't the only thing that was out, and they lent an entirely different meaning to the smiling, sidelong glance of Mrs. Phelps. An-other crisis for Charles Webster. Alerted by telegram while making a nation-wide canvass of book agents—probably in San Francisco—Webster acted decisively and on his own: he fired back a telegram ordering the presses stopped and the plate destroyed, and required salesmen to return the offend-ing image by cutting it out of their properties. Webster managed to cauterize the damage at 250 copies, a fraction of the 30,000 set to be printed, saving reprint costs that he estimated at $25,000. Several New York newspapers covered the story. Then it was all promptly forgotten—no big thing.

ADVENTURES OF Huckleberry Finn was published in Canada by Dawson Brothers and in London by Chatto & Windus on the same date, December 10, 1884. Both editions were authorized. Charles Webster & Company published it in America on February 18, 1885. The initial run fell 10,000 short of Clemens's "magical" figure of 40,000, but brisk sales obliged Webster to make up that deficit almost immediately, and he ordered another 10,000 in March. The first edition ran for six years, and the book continued to sell after that—worldwide and into the 20th and 21st centuries, exceeding the 20 million mark in the 1990s. The early reaction was sophisticated and enthusiastic, ratifying Gilder's instincts. William Ernest Henley in the London *Athenaeum*, which had often treated Mark Twain harshly, applauded the writer's turn away from pretentious "fine writing" and toward the "real creations" that were Jim and Huck.[25] "The skill with which the character of Huck Finn is maintained is marvelous," declared the rising American critic Brander Matthews in the London *Saturday Review*, adding that Huck's natural voice erased the need for "scenes which would have afforded the ordinary writer matter for endless moral and political and sociological disquisition . . ."[26] The hometown Hartford *Courant*, probably in the person of Charles Dudley Warner, praised the author's "picture of a people, of a geographical region, of a life that is new in the world."[27]

An intense conversation developed in the press over this transitional American novel. It began slowly, because not many copies had been sent to reviewers. At the end of January Clemens had ordered Webster to hold back: "What we want is a favorable review, by an authority—then immediately distribute the book among the press."[28] Now, indecision gnawed at him. As the publication date bore down, he reversed himself: send copies to the big New York dailies, and if the reviews looked good, *only* if they looked good, "then send out your 300 press copies over the land."[29] In the next breath: "how in *hell* we overlooked that unspeakably important detail [sending copies to magazines], utterly beats my time."[30] An exasperated Webster pointed out that "you told me in the start that press notices *hurt* the last book before it was out & that this year we would send *none* until the book was out."[31]

It was about then that the public conversation over *Huckleberry Finn* took a sharp turn, a turn toward denunciation that has laced debate over the book ever since. The Puritan scowl that Mark Twain seemed to have melted over his fifteen years in the East abruptly hardened again. In an unconscious rebuke to Mark Twain's 1865 embrace of "literature of a low order—*i.e.* humorous," the New York *World*'s headline scolded, " 'Humor' of a Very Low Order—Wit and Literary Ability Wasted on a Pitiable Exhibition of Irreverence and Vulgarity." Below that, the critic ended the suspense as to how he felt about the book:

"—[W]hat can be said of a man of Mr. Clemens's wit, ability and position deliberately imposing upon an unoffending public a piece of careless hack-work in which a few good things are dropped amid a mass of rubbish . . ."[32]

The Boston *Advertiser* sputtered about "coarseness and bad taste."[33] The San Francisco papers were divided. The *Bulletin* took literalism to the extreme, scolding Mark Twain for "telling his juvenile readers that there are some lies in his book—that most people lie, and that it is not very bad after all."[34] The *Chronicle* disagreed, praising the revealing power of the book's dialect: "Mark Twain may be called the Edison of our literature. There is no limit to his inventive genius . . ."[35] Onto this combustible pile, the lighted match was tossed in mid-March 1885: the Concord, Massachusetts, Public Library announced that it would withhold the novel from its patrons because of its coarseness of language and questionable morals. Suddenly the press was fascinated with the book—not so much as literature but rather as a litmus test of civic standards. The library's decision made headlines around the country. The far-off St. Louis *Globe-Democrat*, from Clemens's home state, sent a reporter to interview the board's committee members. One told him,

While I do not wish to state it as my opinion that the book is absolutely immoral in its tone . . . it contains but very little humor, and that little is of a very coarse type . . . I regard it as the veriest trash.

Another committeeman remarked,

It deals with a series of adventures of a very low grade of morality, . . . and all through its pages there is a systematic use of bad grammar and an employment of rough, coarse, inelegant expressions . . . The whole book is of a class that is more profitable for the slums than it is for respectable people, and it is trash of the veriest sort.[36]

Clemens's first reaction was to laugh it off. "[The library committee] have given us a rattling tip-top puff which will go into every paper in the country,"[37] he told Webster, and predicted that the expulsion would be good for 25,000 sales. Even without the "puff," *Huckleberry Finn* was enjoying the best start of any new Mark Twain book in the previous ten years, 39,000 as of March 14, Charles Webster reported. Ten days later the number would climb to 43,500. Sam's financial problems were apparently over. Indeed, there were indications that he was on the verge of a fortune. One set of glad tidings came by way of James Paige. His long-awaited typesetter was perfected, the inventor claimed in April. (He had made similar claims in April 1881 and in February and March of 1883.) It awaited expert testing, the final formality before taking it to the manufacturing level! Paige would sell all rights to the machine to the stockholders for $350,000 and royalties on each machine manufactured. Models in eight sizes would be sold at $5,000 each. Clemens would realize

$250,000 in cash or stock under the complicated terms. Even better: "Three years from now I calculate to have about 1000 of those machines hired out in this country at $2,500,000."[38] It seemed as though Samuel Clemens's long-standing faith in the machine and its godlike powers was at last to be fulfilled. Charles Webster was instructed to summon experts, capitalists, and press to Hartford for a viewing. The viewing proved . . . inconclusive. Paige serenely took the machine apart and started over.

Clemens remained unfazed. A company was needed! With European subsidiaries! Millions in it! In the summer of 1885 he joined into a working partnership with William Hamersley, the Hartford lawyer who was president of Farnham typesetting, and prowled the offices and elite clubs of New York millionaires, including Jay Gould and his son, looking for investors. He had little luck. The businessmen, well aware of all the competing designs out there, had no reason to believe that the Paige was the best of them. A lot of smart money, in fact, was quietly moving toward a workshop in Brooklyn. There, a thirty-one-year-old German-born inventor, Ottmar Mergenthaler, a former watchmaker's apprentice, had formulated a highly rational approach to the setting of type: a machine operated via a keyboard, derived from the new typewriter. It set molds for typefaced characters along a line; hot lead was poured into the molds, and the resulting type was transferred to a galley tray: an early prototype for mass production. (The Paige also had a keyboard, but it was designed ponderously to set type by entire syllables and words—the product of "an analytical study of the language, covering all subjects," as an engineer connected with the project admiringly recalled it in 1916.[39] The Mergenthaler simply summoned molds for individual letters, fast.) Among the enthusiastic backers of this more promising machine was a syndicate headed by Whitclaw Reid.

Samuel Clemens chose to ignore Mergenthaler's device, convincing himself that it was hopelessly flawed, and scribbling down the Paige's tiniest advantages: "This type-setter does not get drunk . . . He does not join the Printer's Union . . ."[40]

THE OTHER happy development touched even deeper chords of Clemens's psychology and personal history, and consummated a dream of three years. It concerned Ulysses Grant. Grant had exceeded Gilder's hopes with the first draft of his Shiloh essay. His untutored prose writing displayed all the cognitive strengths that had made him a great general. Unadorned and rather flat in the early draft stages, it nonetheless surged forward along a terse, logical, comprehensive narrative line. Richard Gilder dispatched Robert Underwood Johnson to Long Branch to guide the ailing former president in revising the effort, hoping to extract from him some traces of anecdote, character development, and personal feeling. Once again, Grant astonished. As Mark Perry has illustrated, the old soldier proved a writer nearly as adept in his factual way as the dreamy writer-to-be he'd once menaced in Missouri. Grant rewrote the article completely, pouring in vignettes of sound and sight: the shock of musketry, a general losing his hat in the confusion of battle, Grant's own sword scabbard shattered by a ball. The great swell of interest in his published articles (the Shiloh issue sold 220,000 copies, Mark Twain remembered) led Gilder and Roswell Smith, the Century Company's president, to quickly open talks with Grant about expanding his memories into a book. Grant, who knew by this time that his days were numbered, found that he enjoyed writing—enjoyed it as much as he could write through his worsening throat pain. By the end of the summer he and the Century had reached a verbal agreement to produce a memoir. All that was lacking was his signature on a contract.[41] Enter Mark Twain.

Clemens looked in on the general several times in October and November of 1884, at the house on 66th Street in New York where the Grant family had repaired after the summer in Long Branch. Grant was deteriorating. He kept his throat wrapped in a shawl and wore a knit cap pulled tightly over his head, but managed to write each day, with research help from his son Fred and editorial suggestions from Adam Badeau, a wartime aide who had written a three-volume account of the general's military career. The pain kept the dying man awake at night. A trusted doctor, George Frederick Schrady, came up with a suggestion for calming him down: "Pretend you are a boy again."[42]

Although he deeply desired to publish Grant's memoirs, Clemens seems to have restrained himself on the topic at first during these visits; it was enough to spend time with the public idol of his life, who had now become an old friend. He dropped his reticence in the first week of November, shortly before he left on his reading tour with Cable. In another of the unlikely coincidences that peppered his life, Clemens was walking toward his hotel after lecturing on a foggy night in New York, when two figures stepped into his path from out of a doorway and fell to talking as they walked ahead of him.

I heard one of them say, "Do you know General Grant has actually determined to write his memoirs and publish them? He has said so today, in so many words."[43]

Mark Twain pretended in his autobiographical dictations that the two figures were strangers, and that this was how he learned of Grant's intentions. This was not so; but the truth was eerie enough: one of the men was Gilder; and over dinner at his house a few nights later, Clemens listened with studied fascination as the editor laid out the details of the proposed contract. Privately, he felt contempt for the miserly terms—as he saw them—that the Century Company (parent to the magazine) offered to Grant: royalties of only 10 percent, and not a penny in advance. Through his indignation, he saw that Century, complacent in its ignorance of book-publishing realities, had made a bad miscalculation: if handled correctly, the memoirs of Ulysses S. Grant were almost certain to be a worldwide bonanza, and Gilder's people had made their lowball offer with no thought that someone else might gladly top it. Clemens was in Grant's library the following morning. As he later told it, the general had taken up his pen to sign the Century contract when Sam intervened. He urged Grant to ink in 20 percent as the royalty rate, and added, "Better still, put seventy-five percent of the net returns in its place."[44] Grant was incredulous: no publisher would pay for a book on that scale, and besides, he had said he'd sign the contract; his honor required that he follow through. Clemens countered that buried in the Century contract was an "offensive detail": part of Grant's 10 percent would be withheld for "clerk hire, house rent, sweeping out the offices, or some such nonsense as that."[45] Grant should have three-fourths of the profits, with no deductions, Clemens declared, adding that Frank Bliss's American Publishing Company would doubtless jump at this chance.

Grant was beginning to understand the scale of what Clemens was talking about. Julia was faced with penury if Grant died in his present financial condition. Clemens extracted Grant's promise to wait twenty-four hours before making a decision. On the following day, Mark Twain took Grant like Grant took Richmond. Switching from his feint toward American Publishing, he suddenly proposed: "Give me the book on the terms which I have already suggested that you make with the Century people"—in other words, either a 20 percent royalty or 75 percent of the profits.[46] (He wrote in a $10,000 advance, but Grant rejected it on principle.) His own profitability was assured, he believed, even on these terms: he would sell Grant's book by subscription, rather than over the counter as Century had intended, and the revenues would be incomparable. Grant pondered for several weeks, but hardly any doubt remained. On February 21, 1885, Mark Twain arrived in New York for his fourth-last performance on the "Twins of Genius" tour. He paid Grant a house call, and the thin and ravaged general confirmed his decision: "I mean you shall have the book—I have about made up my mind to that . . ."[47] Now Mark Twain had topped even his "victory" over Grant at the Chicago reunion banquet ("I shook him up like dynamite . . . I had measured this unconquerable conqueror . . . I knew I could lick him"). This was a victory that not even Robert E. Lee had been able to achieve: soon, the greatest general since Napoleon would pick up a pen and sign an agreement on his—Mark Twain's—terms.

What with the Paige typesetter, *Huckleberry Finn*, and Ulysses S. Grant's memoirs, the former printer's apprentice from Hannibal, Missouri, now bestrode the realms of technology, literature, and history in the legacy of a great general. Mark Twain appeared, at that moment in mid-March, indomitable, a god of his century. He had no way of knowing that his greatest work was now behind him, and that the fortune churning his way would be ground to dust in the Paige machine's malfunctioning parts. In his final quarter-century, life would never again be quite as sweet for Samuel Langhorne Clemens as it was at this moment, as he surveyed the American continent like the pilot of a steamboat looking out on an endless national banner.

· · ·

CRITICAL COMMENTARY about *Huckleberry Finn* continued undiminished, until it became an essential subgenre of American letters. To trace the constantly mutating concerns of the novel's reviewers from the moment of publication onward is to watch the novel itself effloresce in the exact patterns of the nation's shifting ideals and anxieties. *Huckleberry Finn* is the Vandal of American literature: castigated as "trash" of varying categories; banned periodically; yet constantly reemerging to seduce the respectable folk; to break the rules and defy anyone to make something of it; to flaunt its capricious shifts of tone and mood and plot; to blow its outlaw jazz riffs of spoken language; and, finally, to stand immutable as a moral touchstone of the American saga by its simple offer to go to hell.

Concern over its "coarse" language and its antisocial protagonist—a lying, uncouth piece of white trash who couldn't spell—prevailed as a critical norm until the early 20th century. Then, the menace of an armed and destabilized world prompted critics to see in the novel the exaltation of the unconquerable American soul. H. L. Mencken in 1913 declared it "a truly stupendous piece of work, perhaps the greatest novel ever written in English," and its author "the true father of our national literature, the first genuinely American artist of the blood royal."[48] Waldo Frank in 1919 asserted, "Huckleberry Finn is the American epic hero. Greece had Ulysses. [Huck] expresses . . . the movement of the American soul through all the sultry climaxes of the Nineteenth Century."[49]

Hardly anybody seemed to notice the wayward ending for half a century, until Bernard DeVoto declared in 1932 that the final chapters were "far below the accomplishment of what has gone before," theorizing that Mark Twain's lack of formal training made him unable to grasp that they were "a defacement of his purer work."[50] In the same year, Hemingway agreed, in the breath following his "All-modern-literature-comes-from-one-book" declaration: "If you read it you must stop where the Nigger Jim is stolen from the boys. That is the real end. The rest is just cheating."[51]

These objections were recast two decades later under the new intellectual rubric of literary theory. Leo Marx, in a landmark 1953 essay, interrogated the "evasion" chapters in relation to the rest of *Huckleberry Finn*, and concluded that they jeopardized the novel's significance. Rebutting the approval of the ending implicitly conferred by T. S. Eliot ("a masterpiece"[52]) and Lionel Trilling ("one of the world's great books"[53]), Marx held that it was in fact a disaster. Tom Sawyer's grotesque and unnecessary contrivances to free Jim contervene the "coil of meaning" developed up to that point: a quest for freedom and dignity withheld by a corrupted social order. The hard-won stature that Jim has gained during the downriver voyage is discarded: suddenly he is a compliant darky, childishly enduring Tom Sawyer's manic torments. Similarly, Huck loses the moral consciousness that the river crises instilled in him. "The unhappy truth about the ending of *Huckleberry Finn*," Marx wrote, "is that the author, having revealed the tawdry nature of the culture of the great valley, yielded to its essential complacency."[54]

The "evasion chapter" debate has continued, and grown ever more complex. Stephen Railton of the University of Virginia sees unworthy slapstick in much of Jim's behavior, yet maintains that the book presents two Jims: the noble, suffering figure on the raft who illuminates the cruelty of a society that deals in human bondage; and the comic-minstrel Jim at the beginning and end. The latter, Railton suggests, is Mark Twain's concession to the core of racism among his readers.[55]

This theory tends to discount the historical truth that many blacks in the 19th century, and into the 20th, learned to deflect the aggression of racist white people by developing a day-to-day protective layer of comic shuffling and deference. This survival strategy, variants of which are practiced within all enslaved societies, was designed to preserve, rather than cancel out, the nobler human qualities of the individual—such as the impulse to stand beside a valued friend (Tom) at great personal risk.

In 1984, Charles H. Nilon introduced an arresting defense of the ending.[56] The chapters are in fact a masterstroke: a sustained ironic allegory of white America's attempts to circumvent the Reconstruction by devising as many cruel and unnecessary roadblocks to Negro autonomy. Bruce Michelson argued that it was all about identity evasion: Huck was on a quest to avoid "the disaster of becoming," a quest that puts him in perpetual flight "from both the dark angel *and* the white."[57] (Dismissing the significance of "I'll go to hell," Michelson points out a decision by Huck that soon follows, regarding future struggles over right and wrong: "I reckoned I wouldn't bother no more about it, but after this always do whichever come handiest at the time."[58]) While intellectually fascinating, these notions would seem to assume a late 20th-century mode of thought—highly schematic, informed by sophisticated depth-psychology—in the mind of an intuitive 19th-century writer who'd previously shown no interest in allegory or Lacanian symbolism.

In 1957 an explosive new indictment of the novel swept aside the literary critics and established itself as the defining controversy over *Huckleberry Finn*. Amid the gathering force of the civil rights movement, the NAACP condemned the novel as racist—a condemnation that rested in large part on Jim's diction, and on Mark Twain's 211 uses of the word "nigger." Although passionately rebutted by critics and writers of both races—who have maintained ceaselessly that "nigger" did not reflect authorial intention but authentic regional/period dialogue, and that its appearance frequently made a satirical case against the speaker—the "racist" charge has never lost its grip on the novel's reputation. Pressure by antiracist advocacy groups led to new bannings: in Virginia in 1982, Illinois in 1984, and Connecticut in 1995. Teaching of the novel survived challenges by parents and the courts in California, Washington, Arizona, and Oklahoma, and a student boycott in New Jersey.

Many African-American writers and intellectuals, of course, have defended the book. Walter Mosley remarks that "my memory of Huckleberry wasn't one of racism. I remember Jim and Huck as friends out on the river. I could have been either one of them." Toni Morrison, acknowledging her unease at "this amazing, troubling book," whose imperfections include "the disproportionate sadness at the center of Jim's and [Huck's] relationship" and also Huck's "engagement" with a racist society, nevertheless concludes, "the rewards of my efforts to come to terms have been abundant."[59]

The case against the "racist" accusers received its most innovative support in 1996, with the publication of Shelley Fisher Fishkin's audaciously titled *Was Huck Black? Mark Twain and African-American Voices*. Fishkin, who champions the view that *Huckleberry Finn* is an explicitly antiracist novel, drew on a font of characteristics in Huck's speech to argue that Mark Twain had modeled his dialect on that of "Sociable Jimmy." Fishkin's own critics have pointed out certain limitations in this argument—white and black children in the prewar South tended to share many nonstandard speech patterns, for instance—but the book remains a significant reminder that American literature, beginning with *Huckleberry Finn*, was irrevocably changed by African-American influences.

THESE AND many other controversies have left deep imprints on *Adventures of Huckleberry Finn*, encouraging students and general readers to approach the work not so much as literature but as battleground in the American culture wars. Against this century-long tidal flow of overwrought diagnoses, the Mark Twain scholar Thomas Quirk has issued a replenishing call: an invitation to read *Huckleberry Finn* less for what its various claimants would have it be, and more for what it is: an act of imagination, and one so propulsive that it pulled the author himself along into its created verities. "Whether or not Twain the man was a racist," Quirk writes, "his imaginative parts created a character [Jim] who challenged Twain's own moral nature." Imagination, not political courage or piety, is what finally ennobles the book: "We become less and less interested in the anti-Southern, antisentimental, antiaristocratic, anti-everything-under-the-sun elements . . . and more and more concerned with its affirmations, which is to say we become more and more concerned with Jim. Jim not as a representative of the Negro, the oppressed, or the wretched, but as Jim."[60]

Robert Hirst, the editor in chief of the Mark Twain Project at Berkeley, agrees with the "Jim-as-Jim" approach, but with an emphatic difference: no external suppositions of any kind need be raised regarding the writer who created him. Everything that one need understand about Mark Twain's motives may be found in the work itself. Against the most invidious supposition of all—racism—Hirst cites the powerful scolding, in Chapter 15, that Jim administers to Huck for toying with his mind after the two became separated in the fog.[61] (" '. . . En when I wake' up en fine you back agin, all safe en soun', de tears come en I could a got down on my knees en kiss yo' foot I's so thankful. En all you wuz thinkin' 'bout, wuz how you could make a fool of old Jim wid a lie.' "[62]) After this tongue-lashing, Huck "humbles" himself to Jim.

Calling Jim the supreme imaginative character of the whole book, Hirst speaks for more than a few scholars by noting that Jim denounces Huck's racist treatment of him, pointing out that no other American author of the 19th century dedicated his masterpiece to combating postwar racism.

THE STRONG initial sales of the novel, and the soon-to-come revenue from Grant's memoir, were, amazingly, overshadowed by income from yet a third source. The "Twins of Genius" tour proved a financial bonanza, an artistic phenomenon, and a backstage psychodrama, befitting any American all-star road show—what the Brooklyn *Daily Eagle* recognized as "a new form of popular entertainment."[63]

Mark Twain and Cable opened in New Haven, Connecticut, on November 5, 1884, a month before the first excerpt of *Huckleberry Finn* appeared in the *Century*. A hundred and three performances later, after covering eighty cities in the United States and Canada, they wound it up in Washington, D.C., on the last day of February 1885. Before audiences of up to a thousand people, the two men performed some of their greatest hits and tried out new material for about two hours a night. Cable sang a little. They feuded with the press and with each other through the press. They had at least one public confrontation. Exploiting Cable's comparative stiffness onstage—he rattled through his readings in a brisk, polite style—Mark Twain worked the crowds like the Vandal of yore. He memorized the text of each performance and prowled the platform, his eyes searching the faces in front of him, drawling his drawl and timing his snappers to bombastic effect: he had his "Golden Arm" mojo working. He fed on the "long roll of artillery-laughter all down the line, interspersed with Congreve rockets & bomb shell explosions." He exulted when "the old Jumping Frog swept the place like a conflagration."[64] He milked the applause for encore upon encore, and tried to figure out ways to curtail Cable's face time. When it was over, Clemens had netted some $16,000, and Cable, $5,000. It would stand as Mark Twain's last interlude of pure exuberant, prancing showmanship. But what an interlude—filled with marvels to overwhelm a noticing man's senses. Things had changed along the lecture trail since the old days, a decade ago. Clemens noticed that hotels had dry towels now, and electrical buttons had replaced the bell handle for summoning the maid. The telephone had replaced "the petrified messenger boy."[65] Most wondrous of all was the miracle of the new urban nightscape, bathed in electric light. In Detroit,

[I] for the first time saw a city where the night was as beautiful as the day; saw, for the first time, in place of sallow twilight . . . clusters of coruscating electric suns floating in the sky without visible support, & casting a mellow radiance upon the snow covered spires & domes . . . & roofs & far stretching thoroughfares, which . . . reminded one of airy unreal cities caught in the glimpses of a dream.[66]

Clemens had not yet gained complete mastery of all the changes. Arriving at Albany on December 3, he and Cable were greeted by a representative of Governor Cleveland, who had enjoyed Clemens's support in the recent election. The president-elect "had expressed a strong desire to have me call." In the midst of bantering with Cleveland, Clemens "sat down on four electrical bells at once . . . & summoned four pages whom nobody had any use for."[67]

In a Rochester bookstore, Cable handed Clemens a copy of *Le Morte D'Arthur*, the Thomas Malory romance about King Arthur and his knights of the Round Table. Clemens read it, and immediately began to make notes for a strange new story forming in his mind.

> Have a battle between a modern army, with gattling guns—(automatic) 600 shots a minute, torpedos, balloons, 100-ton cannon, ironclad fleet . . .[68]

Following a Christmas recess with the family in Hartford, Clemens rejoined Cable for the second half of the tour, commencing in Pittsburgh on December 29. American publication of *Huckleberry Finn* was only days away. By coincidence, Cable was just then in print with his own take on the Negro's tortured route from bondage to freedom. His essay, "The Freedman's Case in Equity," was gaining wide attention in the January issue of the *Century*—alongside the magazine's second excerpt from *Huckleberry Finn*. It called for white America to "renounce the moral debris of an exploded evil" and to plant "society firmly upon universal justice and equity."[69] This required an end to racial dehumanization and a beginning of racial brotherhood. Failure to take up this task, Cable prophetically warned, will result in "a system of vicious evasions eventually ruinous to public and private morals and liberty."[70] Cable paid a price for this courageous stand; newspapers throughout his native Dixie denounced him as a betrayer of his heritage. But many others applauded him; newspapermen interviewed him at stops along the rest of the tour, and people of color flocked to his appearances to thank him personally.

How Mark Twain felt about Cable's essay and the attention it galvanized is not known. No evidence exists that he saw the piece's sentiments as rebuking his evasion chapters; he may well have seen Cable's work and his own as parallel attacks on the failures of Reconstruction and the rise of Jim Crow. His only known comments on the audience response to his own reading show that he was delighted with the laughter. He continued to chart his own course toward a reckoning with the great mystery of race—a course that his new novel would continue on, long after his death. An entry in his notebook from the previous summer mused,

> I lose my temper over a certain class of business (begging) letters except when they

come from colored (& therefore ignorant) people. Mrs. Clemens suggests that I adopt as a motto "Consider everybody colored till he is proved white."[71]

In the entry just before this, Clemens had returned to the notion that was moving steadily toward the center of his imaginative cosmology: the notion of Man and his world as mere meaningless specks in a larger, unknowable system. "I think the worlds that flow & swing through space are only the microscopic trichinae concealed in the blood of some vast creature's veins, & that it is that vast creature whom God concerns himself, about, & not us," he jotted in his notebook sometime in the spring of 1885; then, crossing out everything from "in some vast creature's veins" on, he substituted the word: "God."[72]

On January 13, the tour brought Samuel Clemens once again to his native ground. He had asked the manager, Major James B. Pond, to schedule stops in Hannibal, and then in Keokuk. He had visited these towns just three years earlier, but he was unprepared for the emotional impact on this occasion. The "fountains of the great deep" that had reopened his childhood upon his marriage to Livy had shifted into something else, as he explained to his wife just days before their fifteenth anniversary.

This visit to Hannibal—you can never imagine the infinite **great deeps** of pathos that have rolled their tides over me. I shall never see another such day. I have carried my heart in my mouth for twenty-four hours.[73]

A spectral figure confronted him, as if to validate his mood: Tom Nash, who as a boy had fallen through the ice on the Mississippi while skating with Sammy some forty years in the past, and lost his hearing and speech in the ensuing illness. Nash approached him, "& hands me this letter, & wrings my hand, & gives me a devouring look or two, & walks shyly away."[74] This letter has never been recovered.

The following night, Mark Twain and Cable dashed off the train at Keokuk and hurried through a snowstorm to the opera house only minutes before their scheduled appearance. Mark Twain was at the top of his form; many in the audience "almost fell from their seats," in the words of one reporter.[75] Afterward, Mark Twain searched the diminishing crowd until he spotted a silver-haired woman sitting at the rear of the auditorium with some relatives and friends. Jane Clemens, eighty-one now, had been living in Keokuk with Orion and Mollie for two years. A local newspaper reporter eavesdropped on the reunion.

"Why, Sam, I didn't know you," was the mother's greeting as he gave her a kiss and a hug.

"That's because I'm getting so good-looking," was the reply as he re-performed the bear act.[76]

"A beautiful evening with ma & she is her old beautiful self; a nature of pure gold," he wrote, "—one of the purest & finest & highest this land has produced . . . What books she could have written!—& now the world has lost them." [77]

Sam Clemens returned to the Hartford house by an afternoon train on Sunday, March 1, to be greeted by Livy and three flustered daughters. The girls had planned to surprise him with a performance of *The Prince and the Pauper,* adapted for the household stage by Livy. They had planned a Monday-evening premiere at the Warner house next door, with Susy, nearly thirteen now, as the Prince and young Margaret Warner as the Pauper. Arriving a day earlier than he'd announced, Sam caught the cast still in the process of sewing plumes and buckles onto the costume. Susy recorded the spur-of-the-moment subterfuge, working in a pun that was either accidental or surreally contrived. After hustling their father into the library,

Clara and I sat with papa a while so as to prevent his being surprised of our seemingly uncalled for disertion of him. But soon we too had to withdraw to the mahogany room . . . Papa was left all alone; Except that one of us every once in a while would slipp in and stay with him a little while. Any one but papa would have wondered at mammas unwonted absence, but papa is to absence minded, he very seldom notices things as accurately as other people do . . .[78]

Opening Night at the Warners' was boffo, and future performances were planned.

THE TOUR behind him at last, Clemens turned his attention briefly to the Concord Library's attack on *Huckleberry Finn,* but agreed with Howells that a direct response would seem like overkill. He resumed his fitful crusade for protection of the printed word by joining Howells and others in an author's reading at Madison Square Theater in late April to benefit the American Copyright League. His overriding preoccupations, however, were his family, the prospects for *The Personal Memoirs of Ulysses S. Grant,* and the rapidly failing health of the former general and president.

All that, plus his ongoing dreams of mental telegraphy. And his daydreams of new Tom and Huck adventures.

And his pipe-dreams of the Paige typesetting machine.

GRANT, GRAY and ravaged under his stocking-cap, toiled at his memoirs in New York, aware that he was in a race with death to finish his book. On April 29, as Grant was dictating the details of the Appomattox campaign,[79] the New York *World* published a cruel article charging that the general was using a ghostwriter: namely his aide and former chronicler, Adam Badeau. The *World* had treated Grant badly in the past. An infuriated Twain launched a campaign to smoke out the source of this libel, calling on all his friends at the newspapers to help him. The trail led directly to Badeau. The ex-officer, as it turned out, was building a clumsy case for a greater share of the riches the book was now certain to bring in. He had gone so far as to write a letter to his employer that demanded a doubling of his salary and hinted that he would denounce Grant as a fraud if he didn't get it.

Badeau, who had served under Grant, and written about Grant's generalship, nonetheless seems to have been the last man in America to miss the point about Grant's tenacity. Grant—what was left of him—faced Badeau down. He blistered the man in a bluff-calling letter of reprimand, reminding Badeau of some shadows in his military past and in essence defying this would-be blackmailer to carry through. Badeau backed off—and soon became the suspected source of a rumor that Grant's memoirs had been written by Mark Twain.[80]

Samuel Clemens visited the general on the day the *World* article was published (neither he nor Grant yet knew of it). He brought Susy with him, and she recorded the visit.

> Papa went up into Gen. Grant's room, and he took me with him, and I felt greatly honored and delighted when papa took me into Gen. Grant's room . . . Gen. Grant is a man I shall be glad all my life that I have seen. Papa and Gen. Grant had a long talk together . . .[81]

It was part of a work-in-progress by Susy, who had just turned thirteen.

A MONTH after that—on May 26—Sam Clemens made a journal entry: "This date, 1858, parted from L, who said 'We shall meet again 30 years from now.' "[82] He could not bring himself, even in the privacy of his journal, to write out the name that "L" stood for—"Laura." Perhaps he wished to protect Livy's feelings.

SUSY'S WRITTEN note about her meeting with Grant was not a random jotting. Earlier that month, she had begun a biography of her father, "—solely of her own motion," Sam noted in his own journal, "—a thing about which I feel proud & gratified."[83] "Joyous" may have been more like it. She wrote it on lined paper, secretly at first until her mother discovered it, in a spiky but legible hand, adding to it for about a year until losing interest, virtually in midsentence ("We have arrived in Keokuk after a very pleasant"[84]) on July 4, 1886. The manuscript, comprising a little over nineteen thousand words,* became a kind of Holy Grail to Clemens after her death; even its "desperate" spelling part of a sacred text—"[I]t was Susy's and it shall stand. I love it and cannot profane it."[85]

---

*In the estimate of the scholar and editor Charles Neider.

He cherished her "unimprovable phrases" as well, such as her account of watching him recite "The Golden Arm" in public for the first time, at Vassar: "He startled the whole room full of people and they jumped as one man."[86]

Clemens doted on each of his daughters, but Susy elicited a kind of reverence from him. She had been a child apart from her earliest years, a whimsical, sometimes meltingly reflective aphorist. She mirrored her mother's dark-eyed beauty, with much of the Clemens strain in her thick hair and brow and wide, shapely mouth. Her fits of passionate temper derived exclusively from Papa. She had caught on, perhaps as early as the European hegira of 1878, that people paid a special kind of attention to her father, and that it had to do with his profession, which was writing. Along with Clara and Jean, she hung on his family readings; unlike them, she hungrily (and critically) explored his books as soon as she was able. She joined the Clemens women consensus in favoring *The Prince and the Pauper*, and considered it her father's best book. After a man wrote to congratulate him on returning to his old style in *Huckleberry Finn*, Susy recorded, "That enoyed me greatly, because it trobles me to have so few people know papa, I mean realy know him . . . I have wanted papa to write a book that would reveal something of his kind sympathetic nature, and the 'Prince and the Pauper' partly does it."[87] Mark Twain incorporated nearly a tenth of Susy's biography into the work that coalesced from his own dictations, conferring a certain refracted timelessness on many of its passages, such as its beginning:

> We are a very happy family! we consist of papa, mamma, Jean Clara and me. It is papa I am writing about . . . He is a very good man, and a very funny one; he *has* got a temper but we all of us have in this family. He is the loveliest man I ever saw, or ever hope to see, and oh *so* absent minded![88]

He loved it that she was "frank" and used no "sandpaper" on him.

> He smokes a great deal almost incessantly. He has the mind of an author exactly, some of the simplest things he can't understand.[89]

> Papa uses very strong language, but I have an idea not nearly so strong as when he first married mamma.[90]

She inventoried endless household details, and captured his mannerisms during the celebrated Clemens dinner parties.

> [The cats] are namely "Stray Kit," "Abner," "Motly," "Freulein," "Lazy," Bufalo Bill" and "Soapy Sal" "Cleveland," "Sour Mash" and "famine."[91]

> He has a peculiar gait we like, it seems just to suit him, but most people do not; he always walks up and down the room while thinking and between each coarse at meals.[92]

While Susy was writing, her younger sister was storing up impressions as well. Clara Clemens waited until adulthood to record hers, but the best of them are indelible.

Once, in the middle of a careful description of a very devout clergyman that Mother was reading aloud, Father sprang to his feet and danced a kind of horn-pipe while he sang, "By the humping, jumping Jesus, what the hell is that to you?"

Never shall I forget the strange sound that burst forth from Mother's lips. It could hardly be called a laugh and yet it certainly was not a sob. It contained mirth and horror . . .[93]

GRANT DETERIORATED through the early summer, but he worked on. Clemens frequently called at the house on 66th Street, talking "cheerful non-sense" to the dying hero. One of the riffs he developed was a comic mythifica-tion of their proximity in Missouri at the Civil War's outset; he noted the contours of it in his journal: "I did not know that this was the future General Grant, or I would have turned & attacked him. I supposed it was just some or-dinary Colonel . . . & so I let him go." Privately, he found this banter "curious and dreadful."[94] It must have amused Grant, though, for Mark Twain began to refine it: "To-day talked with General Grant about his & my first Missouri campaign in 1861 . . . He surprised an empty camp near Florida, Mo., on Salt River, which I had been occupying a day or two before. How near he came to playing the devil with his future publisher!"[95] The murky memory from Sam's Ranger days thus made its inevitable journey from fact to fiction. Mark Twain contemplated inserting Tom, Huck, and Jim into the account—"Union offi-cer accosts Tom & says his name is US Grant," read a notebook entry[96]—but decided against it. By late May, he had completed a draft of "The Private His-tory of a Campaign That Failed," and showed it to Grant, who was its first reader. The finished version ran in the December issue of the *Century*.

By mid-June Grant had effectively completed the two volumes, and hardly a day too soon. He had wasted away to less than 125 pounds now; his distended neck limited his voice to a faint whisper. His family moved him to a summer cottage of a friend at Mount McGregor, New York, a few miles north of Saratoga Springs. The railroad baron Cornelius Vanderbilt provided a pri-vate coach for the journey, perhaps by way of atoning for bankrolling Victoria Woodhull in her 1872 presidential run against Grant. Mark Twain composed a eulogy to the general and sent it to the Hartford *Courant*. (An assistant edi-tor notified him that he could probably use about half of it.) Days passed, and Grant refused to succumb. Once settled inside the wooden cottage, he de-manded page proofs and found the strength to revise them, even to insert im-portant new material. Clemens called on the general toward the end of June. While he was there, Grant composed his Preface: ". . . I present these volumes to the public, asking no favor but hoping they will meet the approval of the reader . . ."[97] Clemens said his farewell to Grant on July 2.

Grant delivered the second volume of his *Memoirs* to Charles Webster at Mount McGregor on Saturday, July 18. Five days later he was dead, of starvation: his cancer had left him unable to swallow.[98] Bells tolled around the world. Clemens traveled to New York, where on August 6 he watched from the Lotos Club as the catafalque, drawn by a line of black horses, passed by, en route from the train station to City Hall. He was not among the hundreds of thousands who lined the route uptown to Riverside Park two days later when the body was interred in its temporary mausoleum, although a letter of his in the New York *Sun* had helped settle a controversy over whether New York or Washington was the appropriate "place of sepulcher" for the general. "We should select a grave which will not merely be in the right place now, but will still be in the right place 500 years from now," Mark Twain maintained. "How does Washington promise as to that? You have only to hit it in one place to kill it . . . But as long as American civilisation lasts New York will last."[99] To the strenuous popular objection that New York was not "national ground," Mark Twain offered a magisterial rejoinder: "Wherever General Grant's body lies, that is national ground."

MARK TWAIN's fiftieth birthday was celebrated in the *Critic* with affectionate essays by many of his literary peers, including Oliver Wendell Holmes and his neighbor Charles Dudley Warner. In *My Mark Twain*, Howells composed a striking word-portrait of his friend at this stage of his life.

[H]e had kept, as he did to the end, the slender figure of his youth, but the ashes of the burnt-out years were beginning to gray the fires of that splendid shock of red hair which . . . tilted to one side in his undulating walk. He glimmered at you from the narrow slits of fine blue-greenish eyes, under branching brows, which with age grew more and more like a sort of plumage, and he was apt to smile into your face with a subtle but amiable perception, and yet with a sort of remote absence; you were all there for him, but he was not all there for you.[100]

Ten days later, Volume 1 of Grant's *Memoirs* was published, consummating the most successful business enterprise of Mark Twain's life, as well as the greatest bequest to American culture outside his own works. Three months later, Webster & Company presented Julia Grant with the largest single royalty payment in the history of publishing to that time: $200,000. Eventually, payments to Grant's widow approached $450,000. Mark Twain netted $200,000, by his own estimate. The memoir became a treasure of American letters, and is recognized as one of the enduring masterpieces of military literature.

Mark Twain's future now belonged to the Paige typesetting machine.

39

Roll Over, Lord Byron

(1886–87)

On February 12, 1886, Susy Clemens recorded some apprehension about her father:

> Mamma and I have both been very much troubled of late because papa, since he has been publishing Gen. Grant's book, has seemed to forget his own books and work entirely, and the other evening as papa and I were promenading up and down the library he told me that he didn't expect to write but one more book, and then he was ready to give up work altogether, die or do anything, he said that he had written more than he had ever expected to, and the only book that he had been pertickularly anxious to write was one locked up in the safe downstairs, not yet published.[1]

The (unfinished) book in the downstairs safe was the long-contemplated "Captain Stormfield's Visit to Heaven." A second work-in-process may have slipped his mind altogether, given that progress on it was so slow. Howells, sensing creative stasis, had tried to cheer Clemens on in January, applauding the rather thin plot-driving idea—time-travel—that his friend had recently shared with him: "That notion of yours about the Hartford man waking up in King Arthur's time is capital. There is a great chance in it."[2] He'd added, his worry palpable beneath the jovial tone, "I wish I had a magazine, to prod you with, and keep you up to all those good literary intentions."[3]

Mark Twain made a brave effort to meet the challenge. He notified Webster that he'd "begun a book, whose scene is laid far back in the twilight of tra-

505

dition."[4] This was the snail's-pace second project. *A Connecticut Yankee in King Arthur's Court,* inspired partly by the Malory romance that Cable had handed him in the Rochester bookstore. On February 22 he calmed Livy's and Susy's apprehension a little by reading them some draft pages from it. But soon afterward he put the manuscript aside again. Susy's entry had got it right: Papa's literary career was grinding to a halt, and Papa didn't seem to care. As the last half of the 1880s began, Samuel Clemens's addiction to speculation (and its discontents) had all but overtaken him. For sheer flamboyance, writing wasn't shucks to a business-world circus. On February 6, 1886, he took another long step into the Paige typesetter quicksand. He signed an agreement to pay the inventor an annual salary of seven thousand dollars that would continue until net yearly profits from Paige's typesetter equaled that salary.[5] The machine was close to perfection, Paige assured his benefactor—but he needed to hire another man, a justifier. ("Justifying" would seem to have been a natural job for Paige.) Clemens also obliged himself to promote the machine when it was finished and raise the capital for manufacture. His business agent, Franklin G. Whitmore, an old Hartford billiards-playing pal, was appalled, and warned Clemens that he was courting bankruptcy. Clemens assured Whitmore that he knew what he was doing. Paige tinkered happily on, with the serenity of one who has secured a lifetime research grant.

On April 22, Vatican officials in Rome signed a contract with Webster & Company to publish a biography of Pope Leo XIII, which Clemens confidently believed would surpass the Grant book in worldwide sales.

His wife and daughters now provided his only source of unalloyed pleasure. When eleven-year-old Clara, recovering from a sprained ankle, took up solitaire, Papa began playing the game, too. Soon Jean and Livy were drawn in, and as Susy described it, "before dinner is at an end, papa has gotten a separate pack of cards . . . mamma and Clara next are made subject to the contagious solatair, and there are four solatairians at the table; while you hear nothing but 'Fill up the place' etc. It is dreadful!"[6]

On April 28, stenographer Fred J. Hall was promoted to a junior partner at Webster & Company. Hall's elevation was clearly at the expense of Charles Webster, but to some extent, Webster had asked for it. Docile, put-upon, and self-sacrificing at the outset of his windfall publishing career, Mark Twain's nephew was growing a little cocky upon the successes of *Huckleberry Finn* and Grant's memoirs. An officious tone crept into his letters from New York; he bombarded Clemens with facts and figures; and he grew ever more independent in his acquisitions of books for the company. He had some reason to strut. The company was flourishing. Clemens himself estimated its sale value at half a million dollars in early 1886. But Webster could not overcome his penchant for ticking off his uncle. In January of that year he asked Clemens to amend his contract (for a second time), raising his salary to three thousand dollars, and giving Webster easier access to his share of the profits, among other things. Clemens complied, but seethed; from then on, he doubted or privately derided virtually every decision his nephew made. Almost immediately afterward, Sam began looking toward Fred Hall.

"SUSIE IS *fourteen* to-day!" Clemens exclaimed to Howells on March 19. "Land, but I do feel old!"[7]

Perhaps it was the burdensome awareness of his slippage away from the literary life that moved him to tears when he met Harriet Beecher Stowe on the sidewalk near Nook Farm and she declared, taking both his hands in hers, "I am reading your 'Prince & Pauper' for the fourth time, & I *know* it's the best book for young folk that was ever written."[8]

His eldest daughter monitored his moods closely—as closely as young Sammy Clemens had monitored the moods of Marshall. "Papa can make exceedingly bright jokes, and he enjoys funny things, and when he is with people he jokes and laughs a great deal," she wrote,

but still he is more interested in earnest . . . subjects to talk upon, than in humorous ones. When we are all alone at home nine times out of ten, he talks about some very earnest subject or not very often about funny things; he doesn't joke as much, tell many more funny stories than most men, when we are all alone.[9]

"IF I come up there, let's be *private* & let nobody know, till the work is finished," he wrote Howells early in May. "Interruptions would be fatal."[10] The "work" was the malingering *Colonel Sellers as a Scientist,* which the two men were trying once again to resuscitate enough to drag onto a stage somewhere in New York. They had been negotiating in Hartford with an "elocutionist" named A. P. Burbank, who'd sought them out to promote himself for the Sellers role. Burbank would fill the hole left by the great John T. Raymond, who'd long since backed out of the role he created, recognizing this latest vehicle as hopeless. Clemens leapt at Burbank's feeler. He was foraging for any new revenue source to offset his tidal flow of investment and expense payouts. He proposed now to join Howells at Auburndale and repair the problematic third act (as distinct from the problematic first and second acts). The two old friends clearly hoped that one more session together would reignite the madcap buoyancy they'd enjoyed two and a half years earlier at Nook Farm: the collaborative hilarity that had inspired the fire extinguisher on the Colonel's back, the angel wings, the claimant-to-peerage idea; and channel it into the semicoherent script.

The prognosis was not hopeful. Clemens, in the throes of his dry period, lacked the inclination to seriously reexamine his popular character—providing this Falstaff with his Prince Hal, for instance. As for Howells, he was a little beaten down from some vitriolic reaction to his first three "Editor's Study" columns in *Harper's,* mostly from newspaper reviewers shocked by his enthusiasm for the Russian realist Tolstoy and his unvarnished contempt for romanticism. Clemens had scissored friendlier reviews out of other papers to salve his friend's bruised feelings, but lost them while searching for Howells's new Auburndale address—an omen for the tragicomedy of errors that ensued.

Howells pronounced what should have been the play's eulogy on May 5. "I've just read over the 3d Act, and reviewed the whole play in my mind," he informed Clemens, "and I must say that I think it will fail. It *is* a lunatic whom we've pictured and while a lunatic in *one* act might amuse, I'm afraid that in three he would simply be a bore . . . and there is nothing in the play but Sellers's character, and a lot of comic situations." [11] He was in no mood for absurdities. News of the previous day's labor rioting (to achieve an eight-hour workday) in Haymarket Square in Chicago, in which a bomb killed seven policemen, and, later, the execution of several labor leaders in response, inflamed Howells's social radicalism. Clemens made the visit anyway; he and Howells tore into the play for a couple of days. As Clemens headed for New York with the revised script, Howells wrote him on May 11 to "[w]ithdraw the play *absolutely*," [12] pending further revisions. The letter failed to reach Sam before he had signed a contract with Burbank in the offices of Webster & Company. Burbank immediately reserved the Lyceum Theater for two weeks. Howells repeated his withdrawal wish in a telegram—sent in care of the "elocutionist." Embarrassed at finding himself undercut by his partner in such an open way, Clemens called on Burbank to give up his production plans, and arranged compensation for the theater owner. The debacle left Clemens frothing with rage—a rage sharpened by his dismay at a lost chance for revenue. Upon receiving an anguished letter from Howells ("I don't know how I've kept alive since you left . . . Every time the bell has rung today my heart has tried to jump out of my mouth . . . Now *I* want to know the damage, so that I may send you my share, for the folly was mine as much as yours . . ." [13]), Clemens rounded on his faithful sponsor, editor, and friend.

"No, no, *sir*—I'm not going to let you shoulder a solitary ounce of the "folly" onto *me!* Observe:" [14] What followed was a blistering, minutely assembled recapitulation of the weeklong spiral into dissolution, laying all the responsibility on Howells.

. . . You let me sit there in Webster's office [with Webster and a number of others present] & go through the profound unwisdom of tying myself to an actor with a gold thread, & tying the actor to a Hebrew manager with a log-chain, by CONTRACTS which you had already, two days before, privately, decided against. *That* was the real mistake . . . [15]

At the end of it, Sam seemed prepared to acknowledge the excessiveness of his tirade:

There—what I'm jumping on top of, & taking by the neck, hair & ears in this schadenfreudig way, is your gentle, & even almost Christlike concession that "the folly was mine as much as yours."

Well, but not exactly:

> No, my boy, I pile it *all* onto you; every ounce of it.[16]

If Clemens's opening blast was intended as a rough sort of joshing with Howells, the humor in it escaped at least one interested party. In a postscript
added a couple of days later, Sam confessed,

> Mrs. Clemens has condemned this letter to the stove—"because it might make Mr.
> Howells feel bad." *Might* make him feel bad! Have I in sweat & travail wrought 12 care-
> fully-contrived pages to make him feel bad, & now there's bloody *doubt* flung about it?
> Let me accept the truth: I am grown old, my literary cunning has departed from me.[17]

SAM CLEMENS enjoyed a hiatus from his troubles beginning on June 21,
when he ushered his wife and daughters and a governess aboard a train for
the first leg of a long journey west. They boarded a Great Lakes steamer at
Erie, Pennsylvania, and, later, a downriver packet from St. Paul—the first Mississippi steamboat ride, and the first glimpse of Sam's home territory, for Livy
and the girls. Their destination was Keokuk, Iowa, and the Orion and Mollie
Clemens household, where Jane now lived. They did not venture farther
south for a look at Hannibal, Missouri. The town had lately depressed Sam,
and was still years away from recognition as literary holy ground. Given his
wife's and daughters' lingering discomfort with Papa's scruffy origins, the
question of "worth a detour" probably never came up. They arrived in Keokuk
on July 2. Sam's notebook is blank as to details of this excursion. (In a letter to
a friend, Clemens did comment on the "days & nights of hell-sweltering
weather.")[18] The visit had the eerie effect of shutting down Susy's biography of
her father, in mid-sentence: "July 4. We have arrived in Keokuk after a very
pleasant"[19]

Perhaps it was nothing more than all the excitement: Sam was a star of the
town's Independence Day ceremonies, arriving at Rand Park in a carriage
with Orion, and dressed modestly in "an entire suit of white duck,"[20] as the
local paper reported, and a tall white hat. Orion, sixty-one now, was given the
honor of reading the Declaration of Independence to the crowd, but Mark
Twain managed to upstage him in his own brief remarks: "When I was here
thirty years ago there were 3,000 people here, and they drank 3,000 barrels of
whisky a day. They drank it in public then."[21] As Philip Ashley Fanning has
noted, this was the first time that Sam and Orion had shared a platform.

BACK AT work on the hilltop in Elmira, Clemens resumed trolling by mail
for prospective book properties for his publishing company—"prospective"
apparently meaning "only if not written by another famous author." The success of Grant's *Personal Memoirs* was attracting dozens of authors' inquiries, but
Clemens was keen mainly on signing up Civil War generals, or such famous

personal friends as Roscoe Conkling, "Orator, Statesman, Advocate." An idea
for a travel book caught his attention (about Palestine, seen through the perspective of Christ's journeys) and an offer by the retired head of the New York
Police and Detective Force. He answered a query about another proposal from
Webster, who was just back from Rome, "[M]ake perfectly conscienceless with
him—terms which will absorb all the profits—and take his book." [22] This referred to a feeler from a retired Wall Street capitalist. (In the end, Webster &
Company landed only the Conkling book.) Clemens's refusal to solicit the
great literary figures of his day, fueled almost certainly by competitive envy,
was to prove a serious drawback.

The late summer and autumn found Clemens deeply absorbed in the
Paige typesetter. While he chased this will-o'-the-wisp, other inventors were
getting rich: a housewife from Shelbyville, Illinois, patented the dishwashing
machine, and Coca-Cola went on sale in an Atlanta drugstore. His notebook
entries reveal his continuing hunger and talent for mastering the minutest details of a new system that he had displayed so often before: fractions of an em;
pay per thousand ems to typesetters; the sizes of matrices; and strategies for
raising capital; and the populations of cities of the world relative to the number of typesetters that might be sold in them. This is not to say that he was all
work and no play. He daydreamed of buying the remains of Christopher
Columbus and placing them in the base of the new Statue of Liberty, scheduled for dedication by President Cleveland at the end of October. Still, the demands of entrepreneurship weighed on him. A notebook entry: "profanity
given up—on account of fatigue." [23] Another entry: "Buy a gun." [24]

The intensity of all this cramming and scheming and strategizing
may have begun to take its toll on Clemens's always-fragile equilibrium, and
to affect his behavior toward those closest to him. In December, he wrote to
Howells,

[Y]esterday a thunder-stroke fell upon me . . . which for a moment ranged me breast to
breast & comraded me as an equal, with all men who have suffered sudden & awful disaster: I found that all their lives my children have been afraid of me! have stood all
their days in uneasy dread of my sharp tongue & uncertain temper. The accusing instances stretch back to their babyhood, & are burnt into their memories: & I never suspected . . .[25]

How and why Clemens discovered this—whether it was Susy who broke it to
him during one of their library promenades, or perhaps Livy in the privacy of
their bedchamber—has never been determined. The evidence of Susy's diary
("We are a very happy family! . . . He *has* got a temper, but we all of us have in
this family. He is the loveliest man I ever saw or ever hope to see") suggests
that he was embellishing at least a little. On the other hand, Clemens could be
a household dragon. Even Clara, protective of her father to a fault, felt compelled to acknowledge this in her memoir of him, while simultaneously trying

to laugh it off. "[T]here was something so overtowering in his personality that my sisters and I often felt positive awe in his presence," she wrote,

It was a feeling so strong that sometimes it seemed as if a voice were saying: "Take care. He may appear to be harmless, but without action or words he can smother you dead . . ."[26]

Clara hastens to add that she meant, "smother you with the mere greatness of his intellect."[27] Perhaps. And perhaps Clara Clemens was being entirely whimsical when she described the escaping of her father's temper "into the open": "Here was the liberation of the caged wild animals of the earth."[28]

HIS AUTOBIOGRAPHY details the consequences of a fit that he threw in his bathroom one morning around 1880, when he discovered that three successive shirts of his were missing buttons. He flung them out the window one after the other, and then "straightened up, gathered my reserves, and let myself go like a cavalry charge."[29] In the midst of his aria, he noticed that the door between the bathroom and the bedroom, where Livy lay, was open. After delaying for as long as he could, he crept sheepishly past his wife, and was frozen by her gaze.

Against the white pillows . . . I saw that young and beautiful face; and I saw the gracious eyes with something else in them which I had never seen there before. They were snapping and flashing with indignation. I felt myself . . . shrinking away to nothing under that accusing gaze . . . Then my wife's lips parted and from them issued—*my latest bathroom remark*. The language perfect, but the expression velvety, unpractical, apprentice-like . . . comically inadequate, absurdly weak and unsuited to the great language.[30]

Clemens recalled that he tried to keep himself from laughing, "for I was a guilty person in deep need of charity and mercy." He succeeded, until his wife followed it up, in her grave voice, with, "There, now you know how it sounds."[31]

Then I exploded; the air was filled with my fragments and you could hear them whiz. I said, "Oh, Livy, if it sounds like that, God forgive me, I will never do it again!"

Then she had to laugh herself. Both of us broke into convulsions and went on laughing until we were physically exhausted and spiritually reconciled.[32]

His children could not have found him quite as dark as he claimed they did to Howells. But then, Samuel Clemens's prodigious guilt seldom needed much priming.

. . .

BACK IN Keokuk, Orion Clemens was doggedly carrying out Sam's latest errand for him: running down historical facts and figures for Mark Twain's "history" game. A month or so earlier, Orion had read a newspaper item to the effect that Mark Twain had read to a military group in New York from a new novel set in the time of King Arthur. Sam had mentioned nothing of this during the summer visit to Keokuk. Orion composed a letter of studied bonhomie to his brother: "I was greatly surprised as well as pleased that you have written another book . . . When will it be published? . . . I imagine you have been at work on it a good while."[33] There is no evidence that Sam replied. After dinner with Mollie a few weeks later, Orion excused himself and trudged upstairs to the bedroom. Almost immediately he came crashing back down. Rushing to him, Mollie found her husband ashen-faced, his mouth gaping. "Oh my God, I have taken poison," he croaked.[34] He had swallowed a cleaning liquid with an ammonia base. Mollie hauled Orion upright and helped him out into the snowy night, hailed a horse and buggy, and got him to a pharmacy. A doctor administered a bromide, and the couple returned home. Orion passed through the critical stage, but remained in excruciating pain from the ammonia's searing effects on his inner mouth, tongue, and palate. Unable to talk or eat, he grew gaunt and susceptible to pneumonia. He suffered through the winter of 1887 and was not fully functional until the following April. Orion told his wife that he had swallowed the ammonia by mistake, thinking that it was cough syrup. "His cough medicin was on our bureau behind the door and he took this bottle off our wash stand," Mollie informed Sam and Livy. "I don't know how or why."[35]

AS 1887 began, Mark Twain's writing consisted mostly of notebook entries: aphorisms and drafts of aphorisms ("Do you know why Balaam's ass spoke Hebrew? Because he was a he-brayist";[36] "My books are water; those of the great geniuses is wine. Everybody drinks water";[37] "What is biography? Unadorned romance. What is romance? Unadorned biography"[38]); shopping lists; lengthy Paige typesetter minutiae; reworkings of the philosophical theme that continued to grip his imagination:

Special providence! That phrase nauseates me—with its implied importance of mankind & triviality of God. In my opinion these myriads of globes are merely the blood-corpuscles ebbing & flowing through the arteries of God, & we but animaculae that infest them, disease them, pollute them: & God does not know we are there, & would not care if he did.[39]

In February, Webster brought up the "Mark Twain Library of Humor," now a seven-year-old white elephant of a project, recommending that it be published in a year, or a year and a half. A few days later, Howells offered to buy the project from Webster & Company and sell it to another publisher under his own name. Webster vetoed the idea: "as you are a partner it would look as though we had had a row, or that you doubted the ability of your own house."[40] It had come to this: Mark Twain could not get his own nephew to either publish or release a book of his. Worse news lay ahead. "The Pope's canvassing-book would sell a Choctaw Bible, it is so handsome," Clemens had exulted to Webster in March 1887, as he looked forward to a deluge of sales revenues from around the world. By August, reality had replaced fantasy. Published in six languages, promoted energetically, *Life of Pope Leo XIII* was selling well below the hundred thousand copies Webster had projected. Its tepid sales marked the beginning of the company's slide into bankruptcy.

Clemens had had impossibly high hopes for the biography of Pope Leo XIII—"which he came to tell me of," Howells remembered, "when he had imagined it, in a sort of delirious exultation."[41] This pope would gain distinction for bringing the Roman Catholic Church somewhat into synch with the modern, secular world (with reservations, including acceptance of democracy). He would rank among the Papacy's first product pitchmen, awarding a gold medal to the hot 19th-century drink "Vin Mariani," with its cocaine base. He would be remembered as the first pope who cut a soundtrack: in 1902, at age ninety, he sat in on a live-at-the-Vatican session headlined by the Italian castrato Alessandro Moreschi; the results are available on CD.*

The thing was that none of this had happened yet. When Webster first approached him on Twain's behalf, in 1885, Leo was in only the seventh of his twenty-five years as pope. The biography was already written, by one Father Bernard O'Reilly. Charles A. Dana, the great editor of the New York *Sun,* had secured rights to it. In December, two days before his fiftieth birthday, Mark Twain dispatched Webster to take over those rights with an offer of $100,000. It was "a book we *must* have. With the priesthood to help, Dana's book is immense."[42]

Webster accomplished his mission—amazingly, perhaps, for one who had trouble negotiating a sofa. Clemens sent him to Rome in the summer of 1886 for an audience with the pope. Webster enjoyed a nice chat with the pontiff, who knighted him even though he was not Catholic, and gave him a knightly uniform.

MARK TWAIN'S initial reaction to the book's failure was remarkably controlled, given his usual tendencies in times of crisis. "I have to confess that to me our outlook is disturbing," he told Webster as the early signs of disaster trickled in. "I suppose the Pope's book and the McClellan book together will not more than pay the expenses of the last year and a half . . ."[43] As time went on, though, his composure gave way to a kind of shock.

Years later, Howells sadly recalled the near-narcotic power of the expectations Clemens had conjured for the book: "It would have a currency bounded

---

* *Alessandro Moreschi: The Last Castrato, Complete Vatican Recordings,* available on Opal. The recordings were recovered from archival cylinder wax by laser technicians at the Belfer Audio Laboratory at Syracuse University. Pope Leo can be heard on the eighteenth cut.

only by the number of Catholics in Christendom . . . it would be circulated literally in every country of the globe, and Clemens's book agents would carry the . . . bound copies of the work to the ends of the whole earth. Not only would every Catholic buy it, but every Catholic must . . . as he hoped to be saved." [44] He recollected how the scheme's "hidden defect" eventually revealed itself: "We did not consider how often Catholics could not read, how often when they could, they did not wish to read . . ." He described the effect of this latest betrayal of faith on its victim: "The failure was incredible to Clemens; his sanguine soul was utterly confounded, and soon a silence fell upon it where it had been so exuberantly jubilant." [45] Mark Twain remained silent on the subject of the pope's book in his autobiographical dictations and in his correspondence. He refrained from scapegoating Charles Webster, but the target on Webster's back grew more conspicuous: every decision, every action of his was a fresh disaster, in the Boss's acutely noticing eye.

In January 1887, Henry Ward Beecher burned anew to write *The Life of Christ*—the project that had inspired him to organize the *Quaker City* expedition twenty years earlier. Webster was keen to sign him up. Beecher offered to write his autobiography (not a tell-all, apparently) for publication in tandem with *The Life of Christ*. Clemens approved a $5,000 advance, and predicted that the Christ book would bring in $350,000, if the reverend "heaves in just enough piousness." [46] Instead, Beecher collapsed and died on March 8 of a cerebral hemorrhage, at age seventy-three. The Beecher family repaid the money, and began to negotiate a biography of Beecher based on his notes and papers, but the Boss was not pleased with this turn of events. He stopped short of blaming Beecher's hemorrhage on his nephew, but later claimed that when Webster told him he wanted to resurrect *The Life of Christ*, "I suggested that he ought to have tried for Lazarus, because that had been tried once and we knew it could be done." [47]

A far juicier opportunity for recrimination occurred in March, when it was discovered that a company bookkeeper named F. M. Scott had absquatulated with some $25,000. Clemens was doubly outraged: at the act itself, and at its incursion into his bank account, every penny of which he desperately needed for payments toward the Paige machine. Webster suspected Scott almost at the outset, Sam wrote in his notebook, "& *told* me so." [48] He took to addressing Webster directly in these journal-writings, in lines filled with invective: "When you imagined that Scott had stolen $4,000 from you, albeit you could produce no evidence of it, you handsomely called on me to make up the loss by an advance of wages—which I did; being an ass." [49] After Scott turned himself in and restored some of the money, Clemens castigated his nephew for advocating leniency on the thief out of consideration to Scott's wife and three children—Sam wanted the family house confiscated and sold out from under them. Webster, with Clemens's urging, pressed for Scott's conviction, and expressed approval for the six-year prison sentence that resulted. It wasn't just the Scott case, though; it was everything. The lavishness of Webster's New

York office rankled Clemens (with luxurious appointments and fourteen clerks, the premises were indeed a little over the top). On April Fool's Day, Webster committed another blunder of tact: he demanded that Clemens agree to limit his capital investments in the publishing house to $75,000 ("to save it from destruction in case I ruined myself," Sam explained to Orion[50]); the contract also raised Webster's salary to $3,800 a year. Webster's worries about his boss's capacity for self-ruin were prescient, but his manner, once again, was abrasive—irrecoverably so, this time. ("He made the mistake of his life last April," Clemens seethed to Orion.[51])

Charles Webster, at thirty-six, began to suffer headaches. He had been prey to attacks of nerves ever since his boyhood accident with a gun; but they were nothing like this. The headaches intensified into the excruciating flashes of facial pain known as neuralgia. Annie Moffett's husband, who just a few years earlier had been an eager young small-town businessman, now found himself a hollowed-out publishing mogul, a public figure and a private wreck. In August, Webster solicited the advice of a fellow sufferer, Thomas Kilby Smith, a former Union officer now employed at the New York *Star*. Visiting Webster at the publishing company's offices, Smith was so horrified at Webster's agony that he quickly left, and framed his advice in a quickly jotted letter.

> The evidence of suffering was so apparent in your countenance just now that I could not bear to add to your pain by the sound of my voice and so curtailed my call. You asked me for the suggestion of remedy for neuralgia . . . Its symptom is exacerbation, acute pain of nerve . . . Few have suffered . . . as you are suffering now . . .[52]

Smith suggested a remedy "that may appear silly & irrational": some fresh lemon juice squeezed into "an ordinary goblet" two-thirds full of boiling water. "After a few mornings you will crave it as a drunkard craves his cocktail."[53] Webster's neuralgia persisted, and periods of bed rest at home began to supplant his visits to the company's offices. Fred Hall filled the vacuum.

MARK TWAIN'S literary impulses continued to lie moribund as 1887 began. He'd scarcely touched the novel about the Hartford time-traveler to the Arthurian court for nearly a year. In November, he'd rationalized his paralysis to Mary Fairbanks.

> I expect to write three chapters a year for thirty years; then the book will be done . . . It is to be my holiday amusement for six days every summer the rest of my life. Of course I do not expect to publish it . . .[54]

The wells were pumped dry, and this time they were not filling up. He needed a thunderbolt. It arrived from across the Atlantic Ocean in the form of an essay ridiculing the literary competence of his idol General Grant. The author was the arbiter-priest of British high culture, Matthew Arnold. Arnold reviewed *Personal Memoirs* in the February 1887 *Murray's,* a British periodical, and "found a language all astray in its use of *will* and *shall, should* and *would."* Grant had further disgraced himself by speaking of "having *badly whipped* the enemy." Arnold pronounced Grant's language "without charm and without high breeding,"[55] as if it were some sort of naïve domestic burgundy.* In fact, Arnold respected Grant, preferring him to Lincoln. ("I hardly know anyone so *selbst-standig,"* he purred to his nephew.)[56] The review of *Memoirs* was mostly positive, but it carried a subtext of cultural disdain. When the Boston publisher Cupples, Upham & Co. reprinted it in the same month, that disdain overpowered the praise in the judgment of many American readers, most especially Mark Twain, whose outrage jolted him back to eloquence. On the evidence, his fury may well have reignited his literary energies. It wasn't just Ulysses S. Grant whom Arnold had patronized, it was the nation Grant embodied and had saved from dissolution; the nation whose raw energies and brass-band strut toward Progress resonated with Mark Twain's energies and optimism. The nation whose own voice Mark Twain had done so much to legitimize.

Mark Twain took it upon him*selbst* to restore Grant's *standig.* On April 27, 1887, he lashed back at Arnold in a speech before the Army and Navy Club of New York. He assailed the great Briton on his own ground of high diction and grammatical correctness—a shocking audacity in the America of that time. "Lately a great and honored author, Matthew Arnold, has been finding fault with General Grant's English," Mark Twain began as the audience gleefully stirred. "That would be fair enough, maybe, if the examples of imperfect English averaged more instances to the page in General Grant's book than they do in Arnold's criticism on the book—but they do not." Laughter, cheers, and "tumultous" applause[57] swelled as Mark Twain gave the belletrist a dose of his own medicine, mockingly reciting one of Arnold's own convoluted passages:

"Meade suggested to Grant that he might wish to have immediately under him Sherman, who had been serving with Grant in the West. He begged him not to hesitate if he thought it for the good of the service. Grant assured him that he had not thought of moving him, and in his memoirs, after relating what had passed, he adds," etc.

The hall erupted as Mark Twain sprang his "snapper":

To read that passage a couple of times would make a man dizzy; to read it four times would make him drunk.[58]

Declaring that, "microscopic motes" aside, Grant's book was a literary masterpiece, Mark Twain rolled out a little jackleg eloquence of his own:

* With apologies to the late James Thurber.

[W]hen we think of General Grant our pulses quicken and his grammar vanishes; we only remember that this is the simple soldier who, all untaught of the silken phrase-makers, linked words together with an art surpassing the art of the schools and put into them a something which will still bring to American ears, as long as America shall last, the roll of his vanished drums and the tread of his marching hosts. What do we care for grammar when we think of those thunderous phrases, "Unconditional and immediate surrender," "I propose to move immediately upon your works," "I propose to fight it out on this line if it takes all summer" . . .[59]

QUARRY FARM'S breezes must have seemed especially welcoming when the Clemens family arrived there for their annual hiatus in late June—they had nicknamed the place "Rest-&-Be-Thankful" by now. Mark Twain was writing again, and with his old headlong avidity. Actually, with something more than his old headlong avidity. His pen warmed up by the Arnold attack, he re-opened the *Connecticut Yankee* manuscript. Work consumed him as it had in the old days, and any interruptions were unwelcome. Impelled to New York and Hartford for a week on publishing house matters in July, he lamented to Mollie Clemens, "If I could buy said week & remain at work here, I could afford to pay $3,000 for it."[60] What he had begun three years earlier as a one-note satire on British feudalism—a kind of *Prince and the Pauper* with attitude—he now reconceived as a fantastical sampling of all the personal preoccupations, societal absurdities, national passions, topical themes, technological curios, consumer products, and personalities historical and present that had claimed Mark Twain's overheated consciousness the past several years.

Tolstoyan realism? Jamesian structure? Howellsean fidelity to the nuances of the daily life-as-lived? No; none of it: the Vandal was back, lashing himself this way and that across the stage, laying down licks that nobody had ever dreamed of: a head-conked factory superintendent waking up in medieval England; knights on bicycles; kings in armor playing baseball; King Arthur in peasant drag; a nobleman doing bad stand-up comedy; magical Merlin's tower dynamited; a medieval hermit's cave converted into a telephone office; a sexy offstage fifteen-year-old telephone operator named Puss Flanagan (Mark Twain reserved a special place in Hell, right beside monarchy, for the telephone); a soap factory that befouls the air of Camelot. All leading up to a grand finale that would blow the lid off the place. Yet there was more to this volcanic work in progress than the comic-therapeutic indulgence that these elements suggest. Surging through them, and expressed mostly by the maddening chameleon that was Hank Morgan, ran a high brash laudation of democracy, American style. Ignited by Arnold, the Vandal was finishing the job he'd begun on Old Europe two decades earlier, this time busting up the stage a little, knocking over some amps. Roll over, Lord Byron, and tell Jane Austen the news.

40

"I Have Fed So Full on Sorrows . . ."

(1887–90)

As Mark Twain regained his writerly chops, Charles Webster & Company continued to lose not only money but a sense of direction. Its literary standards had not deteriorated *altogether:* Clemens rejected a memoir by one Paul Boynton that recounted the author's adventures paddling around the world's streams and rivers while wearing a rubber suit. He resisted (though he was tempted) even after Boynton offered to excite the media by swimming a hundred miles at sea on the day of publication. Once again, Clemens turned to that "big, stupid, laborious piece of work," *The Library of Humor.*

In August 1887, Clemens swallowed his pride and begged Webster to put the humor book into the publishing pipeline ahead of other titles, and without waiting for illustrations—a sign of his desperation to get anything out there under his name, and to get cash back from it. "I want relief of mind; the fun, which was abounding in the Yankee at Arthur's Court . . . has slumped into funereal seriousness . . . I work seven hours a day, and am in such a taut strung and excitable condition that everything that *can* worry me, does it; and I get up and spend from 1 o'clock till 3 A.M. pretty regularly ever night, thinking—not pleasantly."[1] Despite his anxieties, Mark Twain kept up this regimen through the summer, and even predicted completion of "the Yankee" by November 15. By autumn, though, his business/financial concerns had overpowered him again, and the wells ran dry. A terse September entry in his notebook signaled that Webster had ignored, or at least argued successfully against his plea: "Lib. Of Humor postponed till next year."[2] Webster's rejection was only one flake in a blizzard of distracting messages: bad financial news from the publishing house, and endless progress reports (if "progress" was the word) from Franklin Whitmore at Paige's shop at Pratt & Whitney in Hartford. Typical of those reports' usefulness was the information that Pratt & Whitney's rental and production bill for August came to $1,567.23.[3]

At the end of December, it was Webster's turn to complain to Clemens about life's burdens. "I am not whining but I have actually ruined my health by the hard work which I did" on Grants *Memoirs,* he wrote to his boss—adding that he was "willing to make some arrangement to retire from the firm."[4] This was the opening that Clemens had longed for. "Webster ill and about ready to resign," he jotted across the letter's envelope.[5] Six weeks later, the mission was accomplished:

Feb. 16, 1888. On the 13th we at last got Webster to retire from business . . . till April 1, 1889, & try to get back his health. How long he has been a lunatic I do not know; but several facts suggest that it began in the summer or very early in the fall of '85 [during preparation of Grant's *Memoirs*].[6]

Webster never returned to the company, although—despite his employer's hostility—he wanted to. When he signaled his readiness to come back the following November, Clemens and Hall maneuvered against him; Hall bought out Webster's share in the company for twelve thousand dollars. Webster, a shell of himself, spent the remaining two years of his life in Fredonia. His son Samuel recalled that he was elected president of the village there, and created a museum of some sort on the top floor of his house, and amused himself in other quiet ways.

He built a cupola on the house, with a revolving top, and installed a telescope. The most exciting thing I ever saw through it was a fire in Canada, across Lake Erie. He also made some wonderful ship models, perfect in every detail.[7]

Testimony to the damage that Samuel Clemens's fearful temperament inflicted on his family and in-laws is rare, and carefully expressed. Livy almost never spoke of it to others. His daughters may or may not have lived in terror of his temper, but they wrote of it with studied humor and philosophical detachment. (Clara, who survived the longest, became a watchful protector of her father's "beloved humorist" legacy.) Orion seems never to have complained to anyone about his brother's abusiveness. To this scant evidence, Samuel Charles Webster adds a sliver of perspective—both conscious and unconscious—and also an insight or two of singular incisiveness. His book, *Mark Twain, Business Man,* traces his father's tortured relationship with Samuel Clemens mostly through letters that passed between the author and his factotum, flavored here and there by the recollections of Annie Moffett Webster, his mother and Clemens's niece. When Samuel Webster speaks with his own voice, he seems to be articulating the unspoken treaties accepted by these others: an irreducible forgiving love, despite the pain endured, in recompense for the ecstasies that Mark Twain's company conferred. "He was always very nice to us," Samuel Webster writes, "and the most entertaining man I ever met. He never scrupled to damn anybody, and I never thought he suppressed anything."[8] A little further on, Sam Webster reached about as deeply into Mark Twain's psyche as anyone ever tried to do.

Uncle Sam liked public approval as well as anyone, but he never let public opinion rule him . . . He knew his faults as well as anyone, but he was used to them and didn't want to lose them. He did have a strong conscience that worried him at times until he had proved to his own satisfaction that other people were to blame for his sins, but as a rule he let his character alone, and it may have been just as well. If he had worked too hard to improve it he probably would have lost his humor. You never read about a saint who had much humor.[9]

SAMUEL WEBSTER'S sister had a different view altogether. Jean Webster, born in 1876, watched her father suffer and decline under Mark Twain's punishing wrath; she was fifteen when Webster died. The wrath she developed toward Mark Twain rivaled his own. After graduating from Vassar, she became a socialist, a suffragette, and writer of great force, a counter-Twain in her themes and intentions. She produced a succession of novels whose female protagonists, daughters of weak and inattentive fathers, forged bold and independent relationships with men. Her most famous, *Daddy Longlegs* (1911), was translated into eighteen languages and adapted three times to the movies, the last a defanged version starring Leslie Caron and Fred Astaire. Jean Webster died in 1916 on the morning after the birth of her daughter, apparently from an infection caused by the male obstetrician's dirty hands.[10]

Among Charles Webster's last executive decisions at the company which bore his name was to put *The Library of Humor* into production. The book was finally issued in February 1888, with "The Celebrated Jumping Frog" as its lead piece. It featured illustrations by E. W. Kemble, and rib-ticklers from Harriet Beecher Stowe, Howells, Joel Chandler Harris, and Bret Harte among others.

The poor boy who'd sensed an "aristocratic taint" in his humble hometown of Hannibal struggled now to preserve the aristocrat status he had built for himself in wealth and letters. His writing energies may have ebbed again, but Mark Twain remained a conspicuously public man. In the early months of 1888 he traveled frequently to New York and Washington—giving speeches and readings, accepting honorary awards, meeting with potential investors, lobbying Congress for copyright protections—and always managing to get his name in the papers, or enjoy an interlude with another lion of the century. He talked to money people about the Paige machine at the Lamb's Club, and hobnobbed with the actress Eileen Terry at Delmonico's.

· · ·

EVEN AS he tipped his hat to the world and promenaded among the elite of the Gilded Age, his democratic instincts tugged him in the opposite direction, as they always had. The roots of this dual allegiance were deep and complex: in Hannibal, the aristocrats (such as they were) coexisted with "people of unclassified family, people of no family." Nobody put on airs; everybody knew everybody and was affable to everybody; yet "the class lines were quite clearly drawn." Yet, "It was a little democracy which was fully of liberty, equality and Fourth of July . . ." Yet "you perceived that the aristocratic taint was there." Yet "nobody found fault with the fact or ever stopped to reflect that its presence was an inconsistency."[11] Samuel Clemens personified that inconsistency. His nineteen-room Hartford house, furnished and ornamented with the treasures of two continents; his compulsive inventing and investments; his international courtship of statesmen, capitalists, and other men of power—all of this flourished alongside his unquenchable thrall to the primal, exposed humanity of Tom Blankenship, Uncle Dan'l, Thomas Paine, the rough poets of Washoe, the educated South Carolina Negro in Venice, Mary Cord at Quarry Farm, Frederick Douglass, the citizen-soldier Grant, and so many others, including the boy Sammy. Howells, the gentleman of letters with the Haymarket rifle fire ringing in his imagination, trod a parallel tightrope. "Theoretical socialists, and practical aristocrats" was his eventual, rueful description of himself and Clemens.

But now the winds of the Industrial Age were blowing strong, and on them was the manly, true scent of the worker, the rising scourge of decadent monarchs. Mark Twain had been honing his new fanfare for the common man over the past couple of years, as the draft pages of *Connecticut Yankee* testified. His ardor welled up from many sources: his esteem for the tinkerer-hero Paige; his exposure to eloquent typographical union speakers during his copyright lobbying in Washington; his contempt for Matthew Arnold's perfumed defamations. His new god, the Machine, cast its politicizing spell: Clemens began to believe in the "Machine Culture's" promise to release the energies and skills of the oppressed. In papers read to the Monday Evening Club, and in his new book manuscript, he portrayed labor as a noble movement; the trained mechanic as cultural hero; the workingman as "the rightful sovereign of this world,"[12] America as the successor to Europe in human enlightenment, and the progress-driven 19th century itself as "the only century worth living in since time itself was invented," thanks to "the creation of men not college-bred."[13] It certainly did not hurt that these new rightful sovereigns were at once creating democracy *and* wealth.

He tried out his new political voice on Howells; and Howells, himself stirred by Tolstoy and by the efforts of the radical "Son of the Steppes," Sergey Mikhaylovich Kravchinsky, to overthrow the czar of Russia, did all he could to ratify that voice. "The thing which has made Labor great & powerful is labor-saving machinery," Sam declared to Howells in March 1888, going on to argue an imperative that the laborer himself shed his Luddite fear of machines and embrace their liberating potential: "Every great invention takes a livelihood away from 50,000 men—& within ten years *creates* a livelihood for *half a million.*"[14] From his new residence on West 9th Street in New York, Howells greeted Clemens's passions "with thrills almost amounting to yells of satisfaction."[15]

Mark Twain's notebooks reveal the development of his ideology.

There are in Conn, at this moment & in all countries, children & disagreeable relatives chained in cellars, all sores, welts, worms & vermin . . . This is to suggest that the thing in man which makes him cruel to a slave is in him permanently & will not be rooted out for a million years. To admit that slavery exists in any country is to admit that you may describe any form of brutal treatment which you can imagine & go there & find it had been imagined & applied before you.[16]

He brooded on the droit du seigneur, the overlord's ancient right to possess a bride on her wedding night, and its relation to absolute power, and also to "loyalty," which to him was almost categorically undemocratic: "The stupid loyalty of to-day is the same sentiment, unaltered, that made le Droit possible, & the degradation is the same in quality & quantity . . ."[17] This new mental energy did not find its way immediately into his literature. In March 1888, Mark Twain gave two effective readings in Washington in support of international copyright reform; but writing copy seemed mostly beyond him. He could not even manage a coherent response to a new attack on American culture from Matthew Arnold, whose screed, "Civilisation in the United States," appeared in the London journal *Nineteenth Century* in April, and was quickly reprinted by the New York *Post.* In effect, the piece argued that its own title was an oxymoron. Expanding on the thesis introduced in "A Word about America," and drawing on observations made during his lecture tours of 1883 and 1886, Arnold fleshed out his excoriation of America as a benighted, vulgar wasteland, noisily braying its greatness while awash in mindless pursuit of the dollar, and uninterested in ideas. Though probably not conceived as such, the essay was in many ways a withering retort to the red-white-and-blue iconoclasm of *The Innocents Abroad,* which Arnold by then had had nearly two decades to chew on.

In truth everything is against distinction in America . . . The glorification of the "average man," who is quite a religion with statesmen and publicists there, is against it. The addiction to "the funny man," who is a national misfortune there, is against it. Above all, the newspapers are against it.[18]

Arnold did not name "the funny man," but he hardly needed to.

Invited to rebut Arnold by the editor of the *Forum,* a New York journal of the arts and opinion, Mark Twain worked for nearly two weeks on drafts, but saw that none of it added up to a comprehensible essay. He pleaded the need to attend to his wife, who was suffering from a new attack of diphtheria, and gave it up. He wrote a speech attacking Arnold, but never delivered it. He considered a book-length rebuttal to Arnold, but never wrote it. "Matthew Arnold's civilization is *superficial polish*,"[19] he scribbled in his notebook— rather banal *mots,* for the American master of invective.

In fact, the only thing Mark Twain accomplished as a result of Arnold's provocation was the completion, with a vengeance, of *A Connecticut Yankee in King Arthur's Court.* "I had a sort of half-way notion that I might possibly finish [the novel] this summer," Clemens wrote to his British publisher in September, "but I . . . don't suppose I shall finish it till next summer."[20] By that time, though, he was tearing along again. The failed *Forum* essay became the seedbed for the manuscript's final blossoming, just as the Briton's earlier condescensions had infused its conception. Did Arnold worry about the vulgar spread of American culture? Mark Twain's time-traveling alter ego Hank Morgan redecorates Camelot with it. As 6th-century England is transformed by guns, telegraphs, advertising, dynamite, railways, the printing press, the telephone, soap, "prophylactic" toothbrushes, and cutting-edge weaponry, Twain/Grant/Morgan asserts himself as King Arthur's right-hand man, leading him on an incognito tour of his own realm. He is now "the Boss," an ancestor of the Vandal with sidearms and a marketing plan. He starts a newspaper and turns a priest into a sportswriter, assigned to cover jousting tournaments. He de-chivalrizes five hundred knights by putting them on bicycles, and then scatters them with a pair of revolvers.

But cartoonish fun was far from the only theme. A teletype printout of Mark Twain's concerns and obsessions at the time he wrote it, *Connecticut Yankee* has as much regard for realist logic as the Book of Revelation. As the novel moves toward its consummation—Armageddon—Mark Twain abandons satire and farce with hardly a backward glance. His predictive intuition for the America to come is at full force: he conjures a grand finale that is the template for pop-cultural novelists and filmmakers a century in the future. (*Connecticut Yankee* is the first American science-fiction novel, among other things.) The Church of England—a proto–Evil Empire here, lacking only its Ming—has at last organized its vast resources to crush the lone hero Morgan and the liberating apostasy he represents. The final reckoning begins. King Arthur (the classic hero's sidekick now) dies heroically in single combat, as classic heroes' sidekicks must. Now it is only Morgan and fifty-two "clean-minded" teenaged sidekicks untainted by churchly superstition who stand between England and—well, Matthew Arnold. The Church gathers its minions, twenty-five thousand mounted mailed knights, and begins its ponderous exterminating slouch. But the Church hasn't reckoned with the righteous power of . . . The Machine! Furthering the cinematic template, Morgan and his crew lovingly assemble their ordnance ("I've grouped a battery of thirteen gatling guns . . ." "Well, and the glass-cylinder dynamite torpedoes?"[21]) and turn Merlin's Cave into a storehouse for weapons of mass destruction. When the regulation-clueless knights come charging forth into the Sand Belt, Morgan touches a button and blows the first wave to smithereens ("Of course we could not *count* the dead, because they did not exist as individuals, but merely as homogeneous protoplasm, with alloys of iron" and buttons . . .[22]). Another button touch activates a maze of electric fences and takes care of several ensuing waves ("*There* was a groan you could *hear!*"[23]). The remaining ten thousand are dispatched the old-fashioned way: thirteen gatling guns "vomit death" into them; the escapees drown in a ditch. Game Over.

Mark Twain finished *A Connecticut Yankee in King Arthur's Court* in April 1889, and revised it slightly on page proofs for the *Century*, which published excerpts in November. A month later, the book was issued by Charles Webster & Company, with illustrations by Daniel Beard, later a founder of the Boy Scouts of America, whose ornately filigreed drawings Mark Twain hoped would offset some of the crudeness and mayhem inside. (Beard was a little too ornate in designing the cover, crowding it so much that he decided to leave the word "Connecticut" out of the title. Mark Twain loved his drawings anyway, and said they were better than the book itself.) Chatto & Windus published the English edition under the more morning-coated title, *A Yankee at the Court of King Arthur.* Consistent with the novel's futuristic instincts, the first *Yankee* movie was released only thirty-two years later. The first sound version, in 1931, starred Will Rogers, a figure often compared to Mark Twain as a cultural satirist. Other movie and TV adaptations featured Bing Crosby, Boris Karloff, Tennessee Ernie Ford, the ventriloquist Edgar Bergen, Bugs Bunny, and the imagineers of Walt Disney, who in 1979 released an adaptation originally titled *Unidentified Flying Oddball.*[24] The novel also provided a future president with the 20th century's most memorable campaign slogan, when, in Chapter 13, Hank Morgan muses that what the subjugated "freemen" of Camelot need is "a new deal."[25]

Matthew Arnold was spared the danger of being struck dead of a seizure while reading this entrée into emerging American aesthetics. He expired on April 15, 1888, at age sixty-six, while running to catch a tram in Liverpool.

Mark Twain finished the manuscript amid a whirlwind of distractions, some old, some new. The rudderless Charles Webster & Company had managed to publish only seven titles in 1888, none of them blockbusters: the Beecher biography prepared by the late minister's son; the Twain-Howells *Library of Humor;* a how-to book on the buying, cooking, and serving of food; a minister's collection of his Yale lectures about preaching; a book about Hawaii by Rollin Daggett of Washoe days; and something called *Yanks and Johnnies; or, Laugh and Grow Fat.*

The seventh title offered some hope—but it eventually delivered financial calamity, and typified Webster & Company's self-destructive futility. The first few volumes of *A Library of American Literature from the Earliest Settlement to the Present Time* began issuing early in 1888. The *Library* was conceived in 1885 by a New York literary critic and stockbroker named Edmund Clarence Stedman, who sought permission to include some of Mark Twain's works. His query attracted the interest of Charles Webster, who invested $8,000 in the plates for the volumes in late 1887 when the original publisher (W. E. Dibble of Cincinnati) bailed out of it. Mark Twain approved the deal, but remained dubious: "I think well of the Stedman book, but I can't somehow bring myself to think *very* well of it."[26] This time, both Webster and Clemens were right: by May 1889, Fred Hall was able to tell Clemens that the books were selling well. The series eventually numbered ten volumes, containing 1,740 selections by 573 authors, and became a popular success and an enduring archival treasure.

The problem was that its expenses gobbled up its sturdy profits. Salesmen allowed customers to buy the series "on installment," meaning deferred payments. This meant printing and storing *ten* volumes per customer, instead of just one, a quantum jump in unreimbursed production and storage costs. The company had to establish $30,000 in credit with the hard-nosed Mount Morris Bank, an outfit that would show no mercy when the time of reckoning came. By 1893 the *Library* had run up more than $62,000 in uncollected installment payments from customers. And that was not all: it turned out that in buying up the printing plates, Webster had neglected to secure *copyright* on the first five volumes. To make good, the company had to provide Dibble with sets of the series equal to $6,000 in manufacturing costs. (Dibble resold these, and kept the profits.) This meant an extra press run of 3,000 sets, or 33,000 individual books. The absence of revenue necessitated another loan, of $15,000, from Mount Morris Bank. Fred Hall realized belatedly that the company should have established a $200,000 fund for manufacture and sale. More belatedly still, Clemens tried to organize a stock company for the purpose.

Small wonder, then, that cash on hand at the company often dipped below $2,000. Mark Twain's dreams of using the profits of his publishing house to finance the Paige were shattered. There *were* no profits—at least none that he could make use of. Extinction loomed. In the early months of 1889, Clemens and Fred Hall tried to reorganize the company, which was still tethered to the outmoded "subscription" method of selling its product. (Hall had daydreamed "a corps of lady canvassers" to flog the cookbook.)[27] Yet the very means by which Mark Twain fast became a bestselling author had now become a liability. Americans no longer wanted door-to-door book salesmen. From 1888 through 1890, Webster & Company stayed alive—barely—on the strength of profits from a few of its books. Most of these profits, some $50,000 a year, were poured into the maw of the *Library of American Literature*, the title of which might more aptly have been, *The Paige Typesetter of Publishing*. At the end of August 1889, Charles Webster & Company had a cash balance of exactly $859.18, and faced a loan repayment of $4,000 to the Mount Morris Bank by September 11.

AND THEN there was the real Paige Typesetter. In November 1888, Samuel Clemens tried to declare the end of his psychic bondage to Paige and his contraption: "Since the spring of '86, the thing has gone straight downhill toward sure destruction. It must be brought to an end Feb. 1 at all hazards. This is final." [28] This followed a New York *Times* story reporting that a working model of a type-justifying and composition machine was on display in the city. Clemens may have communicated his impatience directly to the inventor: something roused Paige from his dreamy reveries; he wrenched his metallic landslide of movable parts into sufficient working order so that at the end of December, a freshly delighted Clemens was able to hand Livy a sheet of paper that bore the typographical message:

> To Mrs. S. L. Clemens.
> Happy New Year!
> The machine is finished, & this is the first work done on it.
> SL Clemens
> Hartford, Dec. 1888. [29]

The cruel illusion kept Clemens exhilarated for several more days.

EUREKA!

Saturday, January 5, 1889—12:20 p.m. At this moment I have seen a line of movable type *spaced & justified* BY MACHINERY! This is the first time in the history of the world that this amazing thing has ever been done . . . This record is made immediately after the prodigious event. [30]

The machine was not *quite* finished, it turned out. It needed more . . . tinkering. Clemens received a feeler about demonstrating the typesetter at a February 13 newspaper convention. Nope, the assistant Franklin Whitmore confessed. It needed another week. Several small matters. Let the oil get to running freely, limber up all the parts, that sort of thing. By March, for sure. Ready to show the world. Clemens once again embraced his role as Paige's useful idiot. He kept the money stream flowing, and invited some newspapermen to the showing. March arrived. Tinkering needed. Show canceled.

A third distraction for Clemens, which reemerged now and would shadow him throughout his remaining years, was that of the graveyard. Death had struck repeatedly at Samuel Clemens's family in his early life, but had not claimed a close relative since the loss of his son Langdon in 1872. But after a sixteen-year reprieve, a new season of bereavement arrived. Around September 6, 1888, as the Clemenses were preparing to disembark Quarry Farm after another late-summer hiatus there, Theodore Crane collapsed under a paralytic stroke. Sam, Livy, and the girls stayed in Elmira for another three weeks, helping Livy's adoptive sister, Susan Crane, attend to her husband. His condition was so grave that Clemens jotted a reminder to himself to have a death notice prepared in New York. He and Livy opened their Hartford house to the Cranes, who stayed through the winter and spring as Theodore sought treatment from doctors in New York. Livy and Susan watched Crane rally several times, only to sink back again. "These two women will get sick if this continues," Clemens wrote to Mary Fairbanks.[31] It continued.

On March 3, 1889, death visited the household of Sam's brother-in-spirit, William Dean Howells. William and Elinor's poet-daughter Winifred died at age twenty-five. Howells never recovered from this loss, a twin of the one that would crush Sam and Livy seven years later. Winifred was a victim as much of Victorian sexual superstition as of the mysterious, debilitating "disease" that had plagued her for a decade. With conventional doctors unable to diagnose her frequent spells of enervation, the Howellses had finally sent her to Dr. S. Weir Mitchell, an originator of the catch-all "neurasthenia" theory for debilitation in women, and of the equally scattershot "Rest Cure" designed to get them up and functioning again. (Livy Langdon's own long bedridden stint after her youthful illness was a form of the "Rest Cure," from which she never regained her full strength.) Weir believed that "neurasthenia" was caused by the inherent weak will and selfishness of women; his famously strict regimen variously involved forced bed rest, forced walks, forced feeding, and a general aura of control. He chose the force-feeding approach with Winifred, and she died soon afterward. Mitchell conducted his own autopsy, and reported to the Howellses that Winifred's condition had been organic, and hopeless. This fraudulence compounded the parents' grief with guilt over an inability to help their daughter find a physical cure.

THE CLEMENSES' annual summer at Quarry Farm became a death-watch in 1889, as Crane, transported back to his home on the hillside, deteriorated. His physical pain produced deep depression and a gathering sense of hopelessness.

At a little after 5 p.m. on Tuesday, July 2, the telephone at the farmhouse rang and Clemens's thirteen-year-old daughter Clara answered it. She relayed to her father the message that someone had read to her: "The machine is finished; come & see it work. J.W.P."[32]

Sam prepared to depart for Hartford, but the next day Theodore Crane died. He was fifty-eight. Clemens remained in Elmira for another week, arranging for the funeral. Then he set out for Connecticut alone. He inspected the "finished" typesetter at the Pratt & Whitney site, and again built fantasies of wealth without limit. In the solitude of the great Nook Farm house, though, alone except for the servants, he fell prey to mortal thoughts. Theodore Crane's death, following on the heels of Howells's bereavement, moved him to reconsider the question of God. In a letter back to Livy, he came as close to an affirmation of belief as he had since his love-intoxicated courtship letters.

We do see & feel the *power* of what we call God; we do see it & feel it in such measureless fulness, that we "ought to infer"—*not* Justice & Goodness from *that;* but . . . from another thing, namely: the fact that there is a large element of Justice & Goodness in His creature, man; & we may also infer that He has in Him Injustice & Ungoodness, because he has put *those* into man, too. Next I am privileged to infer that there is *far* more goodness than ungoodness in man, for if it were not so man would have exterminated himself before this . . . I detest Man, but nevertheless this is true of him.

As for God, Sam assumed that "he is as good & as just as Man is (to place the likelihood at its lowest term). And if that is so . . . I am plenty safe enough in *his* hands." The Deity that did frighten him "is the caricature of him which one finds in the Bible . . . I have met his superior a hundred times—in fact I amount to that myself." [33] In a similarly reflective mood, he wrote to his sister,

I love you, & I am sorry for every time I have ever hurt you; but God Almighty knows I should keep on hurting you just the same, if I were around; for I am built so, being made merely in the image of God, but not otherwise resembling him enough to be mistaken for him by anybody but a very near-sighted person. [34]

HE HURRIED back to Elmira after a week or so, where proofs of *A Connecticut Yankee in King Arthur's Court* were starting to arrive from New York. Here was Mark Twain's first chance to review his wild pastiche of a novel since he'd finished it three months earlier. He found himself exhilarated by the unbuttoned audacity of it, and a little nonplussed. Sticking it to the British monarchy and the Church didn't bother him; hell, that was half the point, and he put Chatto & Windus on notice that a Brit-baiting manuscript was soon to be on its way across the Atlantic, and that it had better be printed in London word for word. His American readership was another matter. He understood that *Connecticut Yankee* far exceeded *The Innocents Abroad* as a manifesto against the tyranny of America's cultural fatherland. Where *The Innocents* had been an impertinent dig, *Connecticut Yankee* was a full Oedipal revolt (and the Dark Twin of *The Prince and the Pauper,* which it resembled in some ways). As he pored over the proofs, Mark Twain tried to judge the more unbridled scenes and passages against the limitations of his public's tolerance. He thought of someone who might be able to help him.

"I've *got* to get you to read the book," he declared to Howells on August 5. "If Mrs. Clemens could have sat down & read the book herself, I could have got you off, maybe, but she has not had an hour's use of her eyes for reading since she had the pink-eye six months ago. So she is afraid I have left coarsenesses which ought to be rooted out, & blasts of opinion which are so strongly worded as to repel instead of persuade." [35]

Howells's reply to Sam, written on August 10, was typical of him:

You know it will be purely a pleasure to me to read your proofs. So far as the service I may be is concerned, that I gladly owe you for many generous acts . . . next time try to ask something of me that I don't want to do. [36]

Two weeks later, Clemens put forth the second stage of his request: "If you should be moved to speak of my book in The Study, I shall be glad & proud—& the sooner it gets in, the better for the book . . ."[37] Then he added a curiously offhanded revelation: "I don't think I'll send out any other press copy . . . I don't care to have them [the critics] paw the book at all. It's my swan-song, my retirement from literature permanently, & I wish to pass the cemetery uncloddcd."[38] If Howells was startled to learn that this was to be Mark Twain's last book, he kept it to himself. Instead, he issued Clemens a series of bulletins describing his delight in reading it: On September 19: "Last night I started on your book, and it sank naturally into my dreams. It's charming, original, wonderful . . . and sound to the core in morals."[39] On October 17: "This last batch, about the King's and the Boss's adventures, is all good; and it's every kind of a delightful book. I suppose the Church will get after you . . ."[40] On October 27: "The book is glorious—simply noble. What masses of virgin truth never touched in print before!"[41] On November 10, publication day: "Last night, I read your last chapter. As Stedman says of the whole book, it's Titanic."[42] (The New York literary figure Edmund C. Stedman had been asked to read the book in manuscript.)

Howells's "Editor's Study" review in the January 1890 *Harper's Monthly*, which set the general tone for American criticism, was more than an endorsement; it was a benediction. The paladin of "realism" gave his blessing to Mark Twain's explosions and gaudy fabulizings; they produced a comic masterpiece of wrath and pathos and human affirmation, on the scale of Cervantes in *Don Quixote*. "[The novel] is always true to human nature, the only truth possible, the only truth essential, to fiction."[43]

Here he is to the full the humorist . . . but he is very much more, and his strong, indignant, often infuriate hate of injustice, and his love of equality, burn hot through the manifold adventures and experiences of this tale . . . At every moment the scene amuses, but it is all the time an object-lesson in democracy. It makes us glad of our republic and our epoch . . .[44]

The British press, unsurprisingly, was for the most part infuriated. And not nearly so respectful of Howells. "Deplorable," pronounced the *Spectator,* and scolded "Mr. Howells" for being "in raptures over this sorry performance."[45] L. F. Austin in the London *New Review* likewise turned his wrath on "Mr. W. D. Howells" for legitimizing this "huge Colossus of a joke," and implying that "we are to crawl respectfully between its legs and acknowledge its monumental services to the human race."[46] The reading public, whose tastes he had been at such pains to avoid offending, did not fall in love with *Connecticut Yankee*. Despite his hand-rubbing hopes that it would be a "100-ton" book,[47] the novel sold only 24,000 copies in its first six months, less than half the figure Clemens regarded as minimally successful. It managed only 32,000 sales by the end of 1890, despite the circulation of four hundred sales prospectuses and thousands of circulars, and then declined into marginal status—though it has remained in print continuously ever since. What profits it did generate were in large part offset by expensive production costs. The novel fell victim to the decline of subscription publishing's effectiveness, but also perhaps to the darkness of its concluding vision. Rapid mass slaughter on a battlefield: who would want to spend time thinking about a preposterous thing like that?

IT DIDN'T matter. Mark Twain was going to retire from literature anyway. The Paige would soon virtually print money for him and all who invested in it. The steady sale to newspapers of rival typesetters (the Mergenthaler was in use by papers in Chicago, New York, and Louisville, and had typeset a book) did not faze him. This faith was about to change. A letter from Franklin Whitmore in Hartford arrived at Quarry Farm in mid-August: the machine was on the blink again, and James Paige had taken it apart again. ". . . [Q]uite a number of things to fix & to apply," Whitmore explained to him. "You will have to take Mr. Paige's word . . ."[48] The new target date was September 1. Clemens demanded daily reports. When Paige alerted him two weeks after the target date that the machine was ready for testing, Sam, who had petitioned the likes of Jay Gould and Andrew Carnegie for stock investments, turned to his own family. He hit up Susan Crane in June 1889 for a five-hundredths share. Facing a bill of $6,000 due to Pratt & Whitney on September 20, he tried to sell Charles Langdon some royalty rights in return for the necessary funds; Langdon turned him down. (A repayment check of $15,000 from J. Langdon & Company—on a loan by Livy—got him out of that jam.) He calculated obsessively in his notebooks: bar graphs, royalty projections, cost comparisons, cents per em, ems per hour, hours per year. He began to record his complaints against Franklin Whitmore, a dangerous storm warning.

Paige's latest blandishments turned him almost pathetically jolly. "After patiently & contentedly spending more than $3,000 a month on it for 44 consecutive months, I've got it done at last, & it's a daisy!" Sam exulted to Howells. "You & I have imagined that *we* knew how to set type—we shabby poor bunglers . . . Come & see this sublime magician of iron & steel work his enchantments . . . Come!"[49] Howells couldn't make it. In November he urged Joe Goodman, now living in Fresno, California, to "run over here," inspect the machine, and then look up some fellows who'd struck it rich in the Comstock mines. Goodman's assignment was to raise $100,000 in investments, on a 10 percent commission. Goodman indeed "ran over" across the continent, and then spent fourteen months hauling himself from California to New York to Washington and back, in a quest that grew incrementally more hopeless, until he exploded in frustration that he was "going round hat in hand and begging pennies!"[50] Goodman's mission was more urgent than he knew. In November 1889, Clemens had signed another reckless contract with Paige: for a fee of

$160,000, plus $25,000 a year until the patents expired, Clemens would own all rights to the typesetter. Clemens had nothing like $160,000. But he was absolutely confident he could raise it, as soon as all those investors saw that wonderful machine in action.

But the machine wasn't . . . ready. Not yet. Not quite. Paige always seemed to have one more improvement in mind, one more modification. Meanwhile, Samuel and Livy Clemens's fortune, which at one time had financed a luxurious house in Hartford with its Tiffany appointments, large staff, and expenditures of $30,000 a year; "birdcage" hotel suites above the Rhine; mirrors and tapestries and carvings from Venice; $4,000 shopping sprees in Paris; generous charity donations at Christmas—this fortune was all but gone. Clemens had sunk $150,000 of it into the Paige quicksand alone. In March 1890, Clemens was reduced to the embarrassment of asking his Paige partner and lawyer, William Hamerslcy, for a loan so that he could meet Paige's latest expense bill. Hamersley sent him $2,500 on April 3, with the warning that this would be his last payout in the venture; moreover, it was a personal loan payable by July 1. Clemens was unable to meet the deadline.

Nothing was going right. The theater had blossomed as a new source of perpetual wealth with the success of *Colonel Sellers,* but since then, nothing bearing Mark Twain's famous name had achieved anything but calamity and litigation: no novel adaptations, no original works. A dramatization of *The Prince and the Pauper* was half-strangled by lawsuits and injunctions before the first curtain, and struggled on with a bad script and a cute child actress for a few weeks before succumbing. Sam commisioned *Connecticut Yankee* to a playwright fricnd, who produced a script so awful that Clemens could barely endure reading it. Nor would there be a respite at Quarry Farm this summer. Susan Crane closed the farmhouse after her husband's death and took up residence in Elmira, where she lived for a few years before returning to the farm. Through the late winter, the Clemenses had contemplated an open-ended sojourn in England and on the Continent—a concession to overwhelming pressures of finance and health. The American dollar's tremendous purchasing power in Europe was no longer an amusing curiosity, but a survival resource: they could no longer afford the upkeep of the Hartford house and the social productions for which the house was designed. This pitch of living had sapped more than money: Livy, after nearly fifteen years as a perpetual hostess for nine of every twelve months, was suffering heart strain. Her doctors believed the European mineral baths would restore her health—and Sam's increasing rheumatism, too, for that matter. (Mineral baths were something like the prescription drugs of the Gilded Age. The Catskills were a popular destination for them, as was a small town near Detroit called Mount Clemens.)

Clemens went so far as to book staterooms for June 4 aboard the *City of New York.* He canceled these, but as late as May was still contemplating a departure in July. Europe ultimately proved impractical in this time of continual business obligation. ("Youth don't let the thought of Europe worry you *one bit* because we will give all that up," an equally worried Livy wrote to him in early May, during one of his frantic trips to recruit investors. "I want to see you happy *much* more than I want any thing else even the childrens lessons. Oh darling it goes to my very heart to see you worried.")[51]

Instead, in July the family rented a cottage in a colony of wealthy friends, the Onteora Club near Tannersville, New York, in the Catskills. It was a light-hearted retreat, on its surface: Sam and his daughters starred in the nightly rounds of charades, Sam served as starter for the "burlesque races" on the Fourth of July, and Sam charmed the assemblage by the fireside at night with renditions of "The Golden Arm." But anxiety was always just a telegram away: Sam had to interrupt his idyll several times for trips back to Hartford, New York, and Washington.

A double barrel of anxiety arrived on August 14, when he and Livy received simultaneous bad news. Both their mothers had fallen seriously ill. Livy and the children boarded a train from Tannersville for Elmira to be at Olivia Langdon's bedside. Sam, in Washington, learned that Jane had suffered a stroke. He set his work agenda aside and made the long rail journey west to Keokuk, hoping to reach his mother before she died. Instead, she rallied enough that Sam felt safe to return east. He rejoined Livy and the girls at Onteora at month's end.

Susy began her college career in early October, and was immediately afflicted with homesickness. "The last time I saw her was a week ago on the platform at Bryn Mawr," Clemens told Pamela in a letter. "Our train was moving away, & she was drifting collegeward afoot, her figure blurred & dim in the rain & fog, & she was crying."[52] There was to be one further leave-taking of Susy on a railroad platform.

On October 27, Jane Clemens died. She was eighty-seven. Her funeral was at Mount Olivet Cemetery in Hannibal, where she was buried under a large tree, beside the graves of John Marshall and Henry Clemens. Sam endured a twenty-four-hour railroad journey, including an eight-hour delay in Chicago, to attend the funeral; he left again for Hartford that evening.

Olivia Langdon survived her August crisis, but in late November, word reached Sam and Livy at Nook Farm that she too was near death. They entrained for Elmira, leaving the younger daughters with the housekeepers. Clemens had scarcely time to recover from the trip before a shocking message arrived from Hartford: Jean, who had recently turned ten, had been stricken with a severe illness. Undiagnosed at the time, it may have been the onset of the epilepsy that began to ravage her at around sixteen, and shortened her life. Caught between two crises, Clemens hurried back home with Susy (who had left Bryn Mawr and rejoined her family) and Clara. On November 27, on the eve of Olivia Langdon's death at age eighty, he unburdened himself to Howells.

I ought to be there [at the Langdon house] . . . but Jean pleads to be not wholly forsaken; so, when the death-telegram falls, I think I shall stay with Jean & send Susy & Clara to their mother.

I have fed so full on sorrows, these last weeks that I seem to have become hardened to them—benumbed.[53]

A month later, Clemens wrote to Fred Hall: "Merry Xmas to you!—and I wish to God I could have one myself before I die."[54]

41

"We Are Skimming Along Like Paupers . . ."

(1891–June 1893)

Huck comes back, 60 years old, from nobody knows where—& crazy. Thinks he is a boy again, & scans always every face for Tom & Becky &c.

Tom comes, at last, 60 from wandering the world & tends Huck, & together they talk the old times; both are desolate, life has been a failure, all that was lovable, all that was beautiful is under the mould. They die together.[1]

These notes for a new novel, probably from February or March 1891, offer as clear a report from the depths of Clemens's soul as the use of language permits. The work—never begun, or at least no fragment of which survives—would render decrepit and then kill off the two characters most closely drawn from his formative self; it would reprise his native ground, the seedbed of his literature, as a rotting wasteland. The fountains of the deep were closing over.

Life had bludgeoned Samuel Clemens, but it had not defeated him. As his debts accumulated beyond control, and his business enterprises careered toward ruin, he fought against oblivion with every tool he could think of. He set himself the goal of raising seventy-five thousand dollars by the end of the year. He resurrected his history game, patented in 1885 and dormant since, and assigned Fred Hall to make a mockup of it so that it could be sold to a merchandiser. Now it was the "Memory-Builder," "A Game For acquiring & retaining all sorts of Facts & Dates."[2] Taking one more squeeze of his onetime cash-cow character, he launched into a novelization of *Colonel Sellers as a Scientist*, writing nine thousand words of satirical farce in February. When writing-arm ailments grew too painful to bear, he sought help from technology.

> My right arm is nearly disabled by rheumatism, but I am bound to write this book & sell 100,000 copies of it—no, I mean a million—next fall. I feel sure I can dictate the book into a phonograph if I don't have to yell. I write 2,000 words a day; I think I can dictate twice as many.[3]

He needed someone to test the procedure for him, and called on—who else?—Howells.

> Won't you drop in at the Boylston Building (New England Phonograph Co.), & talk into a phonograph in an ordinary conversation-voice & see if another person (who didn't hear you do it) can take the words from the thing without difficulty & repeat them to you.[4]

And if the thing worked, would the Dean of American Letters kindly see about rental terms? Oh—including enough cylinders to carry 175,000 words. Howells complied. His report of the experience evokes the dawn of recorded sound.

> I talked your letter into a fonograf in my usual tone, at my usual gait of speech. Then the fonograf man talked his answer at his wonted swing and swell. Then we took the cylinder to a type-setter in the next room, and she put the hooks into her ears, and wrote the whole out . . . I think that if you have the cheek to dictate the story into the fonograf, all the rest is perfectly easy.[5]

Clemens rented one of Mr. Edison's new machines; an agent of the New England Phonograph Company set it up in early March when the Howellses were visiting. Mark Twain filled some four dozen wax cylinders with dictation (as he estimated to Howells), but gradually gave it up: "you can't write literature with it, because it hasn't any ideas & it hasn't any gift for elaboration, or smartness of talk . . . but is just . . . as grave & unsmiling as the devil."[6] None of these cylinders containing his voice or Howells's has been recovered. Embedded in the lost wax grooves are—to say nothing of the voice itself—treasures of Mark Twain's profanity: he found dictation so awkward and irritating that "I not only curse and swear all the time I am dictating, but am impatient and dissatisfied because God has given me only one tongue to curse and swear with."[7]

He steeled himself again to the pain of hand composition, switching to his untrained left hand from time to time, and sprinted to the finish on May 2, at sixty-six thousand words. The story was sold to the McClure syndicate for $12,000 and serialized in several newspapers. Webster & Company published it in hardcover the following year as *The American Claimant*. Sam had written to Orion during its composition that he woke up in the night "laughing at its ridiculous situations."[8] Hardly anyone else saw the humor. The novel, uneven and forced, sold poorly. His notebook jottings continued their wage calculations, and cost calculations, imagined accusations and chewing-outs, dark ruminations in German—interspersed with flashes from the artist's troubled, free-associating mind.

Letters to a Dog.
About Man, & explaining his Ways.[9]

There are really no rational people but the suicides.[10]

So long as an insane patient's hair remains dry & harsh & refuses to relent, his case is not curable. Examine Darwin again about this.[11]

WEBSTER & COMPANY languished in desperate straits. Its four titles published in 1890 included a biography of "the Father of Ovariotomy." In the spring of 1891, despite a loan by Livy of $10,000, the firm owed $25,000 to the Mount Morris Bank alone. Clemens tried and failed to round up some cash. Fred Hall staved off disaster by prevailing on his own friends for $15,000, but Hall estimated that the company would soon have to borrow $100,000 more. The situation at Pratt & Whitney was, if possible, worse. One of Clemens's prime prospects as an investor was the wealthy Nevada senator John P. Jones, a tough Westerner with a beard like a dagger. Sam and Joe Goodman had known Jones in Washoe days, when he was making a small mining fortune at Gold Hill. At Goodman's urging, Jones had come to Hartford and observed the Paige during a rare moment of functionality the previous year, and then made a modest investment. Clemens pounced on that gesture, and began pressuring Jones to join him in forming a stock company for the machine. As the mid-February date for another testing drew near, Paige dove into the machine's workings yet again. Sam, already in a rage, opened a letter from Jones on February 11 and was thunderstruck to read that the senator was backing out. The Paige simply had no credibility in the financial world: every other investor Jones knew was backing the Mergenthaler. Sam exploded. He wrote a savage letter to Jones that went unmailed, and fulminated to Goodman that the man was "a penny-worshipping humbug & shuffler."[12] He began now to look for a way to unload all his interests in the typesetter. From that day, he never paid another bill sent him by Paige.

A notebook entry: "Paige the Microbe."[13]

SUSY CLEMENS, at Bryn Mawr, remained somewhat insulated from her family's anxieties. Freshly nineteen, high-strung, articulate, and temperamental, she was turning into a replica of her father even as she modified her girlhood veneration of him and struggled to attain her own identity as "Olivia" (her given name). This identity was propelling her toward singing and acting—not exactly what her Victorian parents, who'd shelled out quite a bit for piano tutors, had in mind. (Clara was toeing the line, with five-hour practices each day on piano and violin.) Thin and blonde now, Susy held the stage well—like her father. She'd inspired a school production of the Gilbert & Sullivan operetta *Iolanthe,* with herself in the lead role of Phyllis. And she had formed a strong, deeply emotional friendship with a classmate named Louise Sheffield Brownell, an intellectual girl who was the head of the student government. The two women kept up an intense correspondence and occasionally met until Susy's death. Louise Brownell later studied at Oxford and Leipzig, taught English literature at Cornell, eventually married, and bore four children, one of whom—Olivia—became the wife of the writer James Agee.

Sam found that he could hardly bear the estrangement from his favorite daughter; his distress led Livy to dryly remark that he would have delivered her laundry if he'd been able. In late March, he forged a pretext for visiting her: an invitation from the president of Bryn Mawr, which he had promoted, to deliver a lecture. Susy, her parental radar sweeping the horizon, sensed trouble. She felt it arriving in the form of "The Golden Arm." Her thirteen-year-old's delight when the women of Vassar "jumped as one man" at his rendition was supplanted by the dread of how *déclassé* it would surely seem to her sophisticated friends. Upon her father's arrival, she implored him not to tell the story. Sam promised her that he would not. And then he did. Susy sat in disbelief in the college chapel when Mark Twain launched into it as the finishing flourish of his talk. Shocked and humiliated, she ran from the chapel, found an empty classroom across the hall, threw herself into a chair, and wept over her father's betrayal. When Mark Twain traced her to the classroom, he apologized—but offered a curiously tortured excuse. The reigning American master of the platform explained that he had grown tongue-tied on stage by the sound of Susy's voice in his head, asking him not to tell the story. To quiet her voice and clear his head, he told it.

Susy left Bryn Mawr and returned home in April, underweight and overwrought. On the 26th of that same month, Charles Webster died in Fredonia at age thirty-nine. Sam refused to attend the funeral, offering Annie Webster the fig-leaf excuse of rheumatism, and sent Orion in his place. Susy's reasons for leaving school remain unclear—the "Golden Arm" incident may or may not have been a factor—but her life was about to change in any case. Within the month, her mother and father decided to follow through on their impulse of the previous year: close down the Hartford house, suspend their lives in America, and remove to Europe. Less than a month after that decision, the Clemenses were on their way. Sam chose not to announce his plans to his old sponsor, editor, booster, "fonograf" tester, and friend of unflagging loyalty. Perhaps he just couldn't bring himself to do it. Upon reading about Mark Twain's planned exodus, though, Howells suppressed whatever personal affront he might have felt beneath his ingrained civility.

The papers say you are going to Europe for your few remaining years. I hope this is not ill health or ill luck that is taking you, but I am so worried about where to place myself here for the summer, that I almost wish I was sick or sorry enough to go to Europe, too.[14]

Clemens's reply to Howells opened on the impersonal note of one of his form letters to his reading public: "For her health's sake Mrs. Clemens *must* try some baths somewhere, & this it is that has determined us to go to Europe." He tried a wan joke—"Come, get 'sick or sorry enough' & join us"—and then lapsed back into his tone of lifeless resignation.

I don't know how long we shall be in Europe . . . I'm going to do whatever the others desire . . . Travel has no longer any charm for me. I have seen all the foreign countries I want to see except heaven & hell, & I have only a vague curiosity as concerns one of those.[15]

SAM AND Livy would not live in America again for nine years. They would never live in the house on Farmington Avenue again. Both Sam and Livy may have had some inkling of this truth as they set about the chores involved in closing the house down—including dismissing some of the servants, among them the beloved George Griffin and the driver Patrick McAleer. (Katy Leary accompanied the family to Europe, as did Susan Crane.) Paine, who heard it firsthand, writes that on the day of departure, Livy was the last to leave the house. "She was looking into the rooms, bidding a kind of silent good-by to the home she had made and to all its memories."[16] It was true. In her restrained way, Livy hinted at her anguish to a friend: "I am so truly fond of my home and I love so tenderly my Hartford friends that I cannot bear to think of leaving them."[17] Sam's list of house-closing reminders to himself has the cadence of a requiem.

> Stop street sprinkling.
> And electric lights.
> And publications.
> And clubs, 3 yrs.
> And pensions.[18]
>
> Stop the telephone.[19]

And, interspersed within the list: "Hall, geben Sie mir Geld"[20] ("Hall, give me money").

At age seventeen, Clara Clemens was old enough to understand the leave-taking for what it was. She later wrote:

We adored our home and friends. We had to leave so much treasured beauty behind that we could not look forward with any pleasure to life abroad. We all regarded this break in a hitherto smooth flow of harmonious existence as something resembling a tragedy.[21]

On June 6, 1891, the Clemenses embarked across the Atlantic on the French liner *La Gascogne,* a steamship "about the same length as the City of New York."[22] The ocean was calm, the skies above it spectacular. Sam played the epicure to the extent possible: the smoking quarters were good, the breakfasts delicious, and the rooms had an "[e]lectric stateroom light, all night."[23] He noted "[t]he loneliness of a ship at 4 a. m."[24] and Susy, still her father's daughter, remarked of some French passengers, "Their gesticulations are so out of proportion to what they are saying."[25] Arriving at Le Havre eight days later, they decamped in Paris for four days, and moved on to Geneva, where they found lodging for Susan Crane, Katy Leary, and the daughters. Then Sam and Livy, the bon vivants of London eighteen years earlier, hauled their tired and aching bodies to Aix-les-Bains, across the Swiss border at the foot of the French Alps, where they sank into the pungent sulfuric baths every day for five weeks.

It may or may not have helped. Mineral waters held no power to heal Livy's heart condition, but at least she enjoyed some extended rest, and maybe a little relief from the headaches that now plagued her. As for Clemens, he managed to neutralize whatever therapy the waters brought his arm by immediately overworking it again. He'd accepted a contract with the McClure syndicate and the New York *Sun,* brokered by Fred Hall, to write six letters from Europe at a thousand dollars each—a rather poignant echo of his *Alta California* arrangement of twenty-four years earlier. (The *Illustrated London News* eventually got hold of them and printed all but one for free.)

They visited Bayreuth, with its festival opera house built for Richard Wagner, and Livy, who previously had shown no sadistic tendencies toward her husband, reserved seats for nineteen performances of Wagner's works. (Mark Twain struck back with a McClure's sketch, "At the Shrine of St. Wagner's." It seemed to give him even more grim satisfaction than "Aix, the Paradise of the Rheumatics.") On to the waters at Marienbad in August. (The slightly lame "Marienbad—a Health Factory," came of this.) Then, the rails again: Germany, Switzerland, revisiting sites from the *Tramp Abroad* days, recalling the alpine hikes with Joe Twichell as "Harris." At Heidelberg they were able to stay a few nights in their old "birdcage" apartment in the mountainside Schloss Hotel. Heidelberg was interchangeable with Hell now as far as he was concerned; and his sore-armed writing included too many deadly-gray letters back to Fred Hall dealing with debts, royalties, commissions, and printing plans.

He contemplated a new book of travel, and imagined recycling his agreed-on six letters for McClure in a slim volume that would sell for twenty-five cents, but eventually gave those ideas up. In September, he managed one whimsical/sentimental gesture. With the family ensconced in a hotel in Lausanne, on the shores of what is now Lake Geneva, he engaged a flat-bottom raftlike boat, its pilot, and the pilot's friend for a ten-day drift of two hundred-odd miles on the Rhone River from Lake Bourget northward to Arles. He filled 174 pages with notes on the way, in a kind of communion with the notebook itself, conjuring several fictional characters; but he couldn't think of anything for them to do. His mind drifted to old times—old times when he was forty-two. "[A] pedestrian tour in Europe doesn't begin with a raft voyage for hilarity & mild adventure," he wrote to Joe Twichell; ". . . In fact, there's *nothing* that's so lovely." [26] Across the years, a boy's voice from Chapter 19 of *Huckleberry Finn* echoed, "It's lovely to live on a raft." Huck stirred in Mark Twain's mind, and began to awaken.

Susy was thinking of her friend Louise. "If I could only look in on you!" she wrote on October 2. "We would sleep together tonight . . ." A few days later, from Lucerne: "My darling, I do love you so and I feel so separated from you. If you were here I would kiss you <u>hard</u> on that little place that tastes so good just on the right side of your nose." On the last day of October, she concluded a letter to "Louise beloved,"

I love you night and day with all my might. You are so sweet, dear, so lovely lovely! Goodby my darling, Your Olivia.

I have to go out soon and this is hurried. Oh, Louise if I could only see you! I am so afraid—

<u>Don't forget me!</u>[27]

Despite the obvious sexual ardor that radiates from these lines, Susy and Louise Brownell seem to have been suspended, at Bryn Mawr, in an ambiguous adolescent state between physical and emotional love. Two years after this, in response to an apparently needy missive from Louise, Susy would write, ". . . for you know dear love that altho' there is a great *possibility* of intimacy between us, we have never really been *intimate* yet. We will be some day when it comes natural . . ." [28]

Loneliness, as much as erotic need, flavors these letters. Whether that loneliness was traceable to an emotional estrangement from her parents can never be known, yet as Papa's adored little girls matured into women, the Man in the Moon began to reveal a dark side. That dark side surfaced when the Clemens entourage relocated at Marienbad in October, and Livy and Susan Crane traveled on to Berlin to find apartment rooms for the winter, taking Susy with them. Under the sole supervision of her father for a few days, Clara, a striking, dark-haired young woman, but still shy and self-conscious, found herself invited to a military ball. Sam consented to escort her. With Katy in tow, Clara hurriedly shopped for her first gown—a necessarily cheap one. In a small shop, Katy nudged her toward a "most insignificant-looking pink frock, so slightly *décolleté* that I blushed with shame." [29] She bought it anyway. On the night of the ball, Father and Clara arrived "shamefully early," but soon

Clara was whirling around with young men in gaudy uniforms. After a couple of hours, Sam took her back to the hotel. The next morning, one of the officers who'd danced with her announced himself at the Clemens rooms. Flattered and panicked, Clara sent for her father. Sam appeared. He looked the young soldier up and down. A silence ensued.

Oh dear! I was more embarrassed than ever! Even the officer began to wriggle in his chair. Father's gray eyes could take on a lofty expression that would make a mastodon shrink to a mouse. First the officer lost a grip on his tongue, then his smile faded, and at last his proud military bearing wilted—pitifully. Then he departed.[30]

Later, when Sam noticed Clara and the same young man exchanging glances in the hotel dining room, he took her upstairs and locked her in the suite for several days. Katy brought her meals.

When at last Mother arrived she found a lackadaisical daughter in one room and a fiercely irritated Father in another. She brought us together and listened to our vibrating stories . . . I expected Mother to pour out words of indignant condemnation, when to my amazement, she burst with peals of laughter till her cheeks were bathed in tears.[31]

The suitor of long ago whose own references nearly proved ruinous was not about to let his daughters be swayed by any silver-tongued devils.

In the fall of that year, the Clemenses passed near the village of Domrémy-la-Pucelle, where Joan of Arc was born in 1412. Sam had been fascinated with Joan of Arc's story since that fluttering page from a book about her may or may not have caught his eye in 1849 and drew him into his abiding interest in history and medieval literature. More broadly, she was an icon of the century and a repository for its tortuously shifting view of womankind: a virginal innocent devoted to the hearthside and the spinning wheel, she was also a leading figurehead for women in the military as she took command of her nation's armies at age seventeen, led them to a rout of the occupying British, ended the Hundred Years' War, and forged the liberation of France. Later she was burned at the stake as a heretic, a fate that perhaps served to temper male anxiety about her menace as a role model. International interest in the French heroine had been rekindled in the 1840s with the discovery and publication of the manuscripts describing her heresy trial and her nearly superhuman gifts of courage, conviction, modesty, and unschooled wisdom. New histories, biographies, plays, and paintings about her life were circulating or in production. Construction of a basilica had begun only ten years earlier on the spot near the village where the peasant girl had begun to hear her heavenly voices. As had happened when George Cable handed him a copy of Malory's romances, an idea began to consolidate in Mark Twain's mind. He began to devour books about her life.

In Berlin in 1892, ensconced at the luxury Hotel Royal, the Clemenses decided they could afford a new German tutor for Livy, a governess for Jean, and piano lessons at the estimable Mrs. Willard's school for Clara, who attracted a circle of aspiring young musical artists. Susy remained withdrawn, passive. It soon became clear that Mark Twain was a revered author in the great city: the bookstores featured his translated books, and he was recognized on the street (though some people mistook him for a famous historian named Theodor Mommsen). The American legation opened up Berlin society for the family. The new emperor, Kaiser Wilhelm II, invited Clemens for a palace visit in mid-January. When the author returned his regrets (he was bedridden with the flu, and spent his twenty-second wedding anniversary, February 2, flat on his back), the emperor commanded a cousin of Sam's, the former St. Louisan Mollie Clemens von Versen, to arrange a dinner at her home and that of her husband, a general. Mark Twain sat at the right hand of the emperor who would preside over Germany during its defeat in World War I. Wilhelm held forth at great length in English, allowing rejoinders now and then. Sam, accustomed to dominating table talk at the Hartford house, seized on one of these pauses to deliver a lengthy opinion of his own, and the emperor was a little huffy about it afterward. At least that was what it seemed like to Sam. Years later the kaiser wondered why Mark Twain hadn't spoken up more.

The attention Papa received in restaurants fascinated Clara and Susy, especially the oglers who clustered within a couple of yards from the table to watch him eat. "At first we pretended to be indifferent," Clara wrote, ". . . but at last my sister and I confessed to each other that it must be queer to belong to a family in which no one was distinguished or famous."[32] This was the first real exposure for Jean, now eleven, to her father's international celebrity-hood. "[I]f it keeps on like this," she told him, "there won't be anybody for you to get acquainted with but God."[33] Clemens, of course, was far too modest to take such a notion seriously. He did, however, make an entry in his notebook: "I would like to be Emperor awhile."[34]

CLEMENS ADMIRED Berlin; one of his better letters for McClure described it as "The German Chicago." But as spring arrived and his influenza lingered, Clemens fled the chilly, damp city with Livy while the rest of the family stayed on. The two repaired to Menton, in the south of France, for a while, and then meandered through Italy, visiting Pisa, Rome (where the others joined them for a month), and Florence, which brought Susy alive. She found a voice teacher she admired, and Clara resumed piano lessons. Clara grew ever more self-possessed. Frankly, she was turning into the sort of young libertine who might fold her shawl carefully upon entering a room. When reports reached the family that she had been the only female diner in a room (the von Versens') with forty officers, Sam was staggered. "We want you to be a lady,—a lady above reproach," he wrote to her, "—a lady always . . . never hoydenish . . ."[35]

The family rented a hillside house near the city, the Villa Viviani, two centuries old and capacious and cheap, and soon encountered old friends among the many Americans who passed through there—Robert Underwood Johnson among them. Sam met the philosopher William James, and managed to keep quiet on the relative merits of his brother's novels and John Bunyan's heaven. Back in the States, Webster & Company issued a slim collection of Mark Twain sketches in April. Titled *Merry Tales,* it was distinguished mostly by the lead piece, "The Private History of a Campaign That Failed." The book, almost entirely a Fred Hall production—he even thought up its title, which Mark Twain hated—was part of a larger Hall brainstorm: a series of books (branded "Fiction, Fact and Fancy") cheaply printed and sold for seventy-five cents to a mass audience, in hopes of striking a new cash vein in the marketplace. A similar product, *The £ 1,000,000 Bank Note and Other New Stories,* was in the works for 1893. Neither collection received much critical attention, and neither sold well.

After a month in Florence, and a trek through the alpine splendors of Italy and Switzerland, the Clemenses settled in for the summer at a hotel in the spa city of Bad Nauheim, Germany. There, in the hotel dining room, Sam and Oscar Wilde spotted and greeted each other; Clara later remembered the carnation as large as a baby sunflower in Wilde's lapel, and the colored shoes on his feet. In early June, lacking any inspirational book ideas, Sam began noodling around on the theme of twins and their plight that had amused and unsettled him for most of his life. Just months earlier he had caught an exhibition of Giovanni and Giacomo Tocci, Italian brothers conjoined at the rib cage with separate sets of arms but only one set of legs. The original "Siamese twins," Chang and Eng, who shared only a fused liver, had fascinated him years earlier as stars of Barnum's circus. (They had died in 1874, after fathering twenty-two children between them, as it were.) As he lolled in the Bad Nauheim baths, he thought of one twin sober while the other drank; of both twins in love with the same woman; the twins fighting with each other; one's shoes hurt the other's feet—the possibilities for fun were infinite.

SUCH POSSIBILITIES were considerably less than infinite back at Charles Webster & Company in New York. There, the overmatched Hall struggled to keep the moribund firm on life support. Hall had no real expertise with the paleolithic subscription method, which his boss clung to in defiance of all reason. More damaging, Hall continued to list the warehouses that were full of unpaid-for books as assets, instead of writing them off as liabilities. And Mark Twain's Fact and Date Game was turning out to be a turkey.

Samuel Clemens had departed America having invested a cumulative $74,087.35 in Webster & Company. He not only received no revenue from his own books in 1891—all royalties, interest, and other profits being shoveled back into the maw—he and Livy could not pay the interest on their investments into it; by year's end, the company owed Sam $79,341.79. Meanwhile,

Hall had no choice but to keep running up the obligation to Mount Morris Bank. Of the $30,000-plus total, $6,781.99 was payable personally by Clemens. For his part, Clemens foolishly made himself believe that sales of *The American Claimant* at $1 a copy would bring in a new fortune.

With never-say-die bravado, Hall was gearing up Webster & Company to issue more than thirty titles in 1892, but many of these fell under the "Fiction, Fact, and Fancy" rubric, which was going nowhere, not even on the ballast of Alexander Filippi's *One Hundred Ways of Cooking Eggs* and *One Hundred Ways of Cooking Fish*. *Paddles and Politics Down the Danube,* and *A Perplexed Philosopher: Being an Examination of Mr. Herbert Spencer's Various Utterances on the Land Question* similarly failed to walk off the shelves. To its credit, the house also published volumes from Tolstoy, Walt Whitman, and the Boss.

Clemens needed to arrest the drift of the publishing house as best he could. And he'd received a new siren call from James W. Paige. Paige had actually accomplished something: he'd persuaded some Chicago investors to capitalize a factory to produce an initial fifty models of the soon-to-be-perfected typesetter. This news prompted Clemens to suspend plans to sell off his royalties for cash, pending a personal look at this operation. On March 22 he boarded the steamship *Lahn* for a two-week visit to the United States, having alerted Fred Hall to help him avoid reporters on arriving in New York. His arm was better and the adulation of the passengers cheered him up: he reigned as the life of the party on this first of eight Atlantic crossings in the ensuing two years, each more desperate than the last, as he tried to save the entrepreneurial career he never should have begun.

Among the first people he looked up was William Dean Howells. The two men dined at the Hotel Glenham in New York, repairing a friendship that had atrophied even before Clemens's departure for Europe: this was their first encounter in two years, and their correspondence had all but stopped. In that time, Howells had moved to New York, "and brought the literary center of the country" with him, in the words of Edwin Cady. He had assumed the editorship of *Cosmopolitan* in 1891; and, just weeks earlier, had ceased the "Editor's Study" column at *Harper's.* He had published two novels in 1890, the influential *A Hazard of New Fortunes* and *The Shadow of a Dream,* as well as his own long-deferred childhood memoir, *A Boy's Town.* The two meant to connect again before Sam departed for Europe, but somehow it fell through.

Socially, his trip was pleasant. He was the houseguest in New York of Dr. Clarence C. Rice, whom Clemens knew through the Players Club. Rice was a sort of nose-and-throat specialist to the stars; his patients included Enrico Caruso, Edwin Booth, and Lillian Russell. Besides Howells, he dined with Mary Mapes Dodge, the *St. Nicholas Magazine* editor; Rudyard Kipling; and Andrew Carnegie, whose millions he was still trying to tap for his various disasters—now he wanted Carnegie to buy out Webster & Company. Carnegie's response pretty much summed up the business results of Clemens's transatlantic trip. His sole bequest to the author was one smug little aphorism: "Put all your eggs in one basket, *and watch that basket.*" Mark Twain, frugal now, eventually recycled it into Puddn'head Wilson's calendar.

His last chore was the eight hundred-mile trip to Chicago. There, weakened by his cold, he immediately fell into bed at the Great Northern Hotel and remained there for eleven days, missing the World's Columbian Exposition with its unveilings of the Pledge of Allegiance, Aunt Jemimah pancake syrup, Dvořák's *New World Symphony,* ragtime, and Juicy Fruit gum. Paige, again sensing a doomsday moment, hurried to the hotel and delivered a bravura performance at Clemens's bedside: promises, assurances, injured dignity, and

even more tears than usual . . . he could persuade a fish to come out and take a walk with him. When he is present I always believe him; I can't help it. When he is gone away all the belief evaporates. He is a most daring and majestic liar.[36]

The fact was that Paige had put himself mindlessly at loggerheads with both the Connecticut/New York and the Chicago investors in a ploy to control the proposed manufacturing company. His timing could not have been worse: a financial panic was sweeping through America, the ugly hangover of the Gilded Age. Crooked accountants, corrupt stockbrokers, working-class rebellion—all of these fed the hysteria. Businesses closed, workers were laid off; six hundred banks went under. Money was tight everywhere. Sam returned to New York, tried to sell an option on his royalties to the machine, and failed. He sailed back to Bad Nauheim with the Paige tied to him like an anchor. There, he worked. The pain in his rheumatic arm had receded for a while, and he discovered, as on awakening from a bad dream—or bad reality—that Tom and Huck were alive and well in his imagination: not sixty, not dead, but boys still, awaiting, with Jim, their cues for adventure from the old Black Avenger of the Spanish Main. On August 5—soon after he enjoyed a hotel-garden conversation with Queen Victoria's hard-living eldest son, the Prince of Wales, "Edward the Conqueror" (later King Edward VII)—he turned his most famous characters loose in a new novel, with the working title, *The New Adventures of Huckleberry Finn.* He informed Hall on the 10th that he'd written 12,000 words of it, "using the main episode" of a story he'd abandoned,

telling it through the lips of Huck Finn . . . I have started Huck Finn & Tom Sawyer (still 15 years old) & . . . Jim around the world in a stray *balloon,* with Huck as narrator, & somewhere after the end of that great voyage he will work in the said episode and then nobody will suspect that a whole book has been written and the globe circumnavigated merely to get episode in an effective (& at the same time apparently unintentional) way . . .

It is a story for boys, of course, & I think it will interest any boy between 8 years & 80.[37]

He finished a 40,000-word draft less than four weeks later. Now it was *Tom Sawyer Abroad,* and if it sold well, he told Hall, it would be the first of a new line. As he worked, the family flowed and ebbed around him. Susan Crane returned to America in August 1892, Susy accompanying her through Switzerland. Clara went back to her piano tutor in Berlin, and planned to spend the winter there, against her desiccated mother's wishes. Jean seemed at a loss for enthusiasms; she was now a sullen and uncommunicative girl. Sam's muse was on a hot-air balloon ride of its own. He alerted Fred Hall that yet a new novel was swimming along: "It is the howling farce I told you I had begun a while back . . . I have written about 20,000 words on it . . . It is clear out of the common order . . . I don't think it resembles anything in literature."[38] He could say that again.

September arrived, and the Clemenses left chilly Bad Nauheim to reclaim the boxy, fortress-like Villa Viviani near Florence, with its green masonry façades and greener window shutters. En route, they stopped for four days at Frankfurt so that doctors could examine Livy. "I have been driving this pen hard," Sam wrote to Susan Crane during a layover in Lucerne on September 18. He'd finished 280 pages of what he was now calling *Tom Sawyer Abroad,* he told her, "then took up 'Twins' again, destroyed the last half of the manuscript and re-wrote it in another form, and am going to . . . finish it in Florence."[39]

The Gothic house proved conducive to gothic thoughts. In an impulsive gesture he never fully explained, Clemens briefly matched the strange terrain inside his head with strangeness on the outside. Clara was visiting from piano studies in Berlin. On the stormy night before her departure, as thunder boomed and lightning strobe-lit the stairwells and the ancient family portraits on the walls, she sat talking with Susy in one of the bedrooms, when Susy startled her by giving "a little stifled cry."

Turning to look, I observed that she had blushed to the roots of her hair and way down her neck. Following the direction of her eyes, I saw Father standing in the door . . .[40]

It was a "Golden Arm" moment. He had shaved his skull smooth.

MARK TWAIN completed *Tom Sawyer Abroad* with rapid efficiency; the ending, in fact, amounted to a screeching halt. The story, pure pulp, traces the exploits of the three principals as they waft from St. Louis to North Africa in a hot-air balloon piloted by a crazy inventor (Clemens is stealing a book from his own Paige, in this respect) known as the Professor; they encounter spine-tingling crises along the way. Mark Twain quickly sold the 34,000-word work to the children's journal *St. Nicholas Magazine,* through Fred Hall, and it did bring in some quick cash—five thousand dollars for serial rights. Impatient as usual with editing details, and with no Howells handy, he allowed Mary Mapes Dodge, the magazine's editor, to trim and revise the text at her discretion. He never imagined that her discretion would include writing new and sanitized text to replace the slang and naughtiness that she'd removed. He stormed into the editor's office, declaring, "Any editor to whom I submit my manuscripts has an undisputed right to delete anything to which he objects, but God Almighty Himself has no right to put words in my mouth that I never used!"[41] The deletions and changes stood, but the substituted words were evidently removed. Dan Beard reported that he was obliged to put shoes on the drawings of his characters.

Chatto & Windus published the hardcover edition in April 1894 (with Dodge's dodges still intact), and Webster & Company issued it four days later—its last act as a publishing company. Wacky in a forced sort of way, Jules-Verne-ish in its fantastical balloon-centered antics, the book is at once boylike and redolent of desperation. Mark Twain was frankly writing for commerce now, first and foremost; niceties of plot and plausibility mattered even less to him than they had before. The three main characters talk to one another in set-piece dialogue that anticipates situation comedy, as when Jim, confused over time changes in zones around the world, argues that "De Lord" wouldn't "*scriminate* 'twixt"[42] his children by—well, by putting them in different time zones. One can almost sense a laugh-track cue as Jim's dimwitted confusion deepens—and perhaps the quiet snap of a race card played:

Mars Tom talkin' sich talk as dat—Choosday in one place en Monday in t'other, bofe in de same day! . . . How you gwine to got two days inter one day . . . can't git two niggers inter one nigger-skin, kin you?[43]

With this unsuccessful book and a later collection titled, after its lead entry, *Tom Sawyer, Detective,* Mark Twain was trying to cash in on a popular new trend in books for young people: the series, or a string of novels featuring the same hero. Horatio Alger was the reigning master of the form, with Ragged Dick and Tattered Tom returning to action again and again. But these were dime-novel figures, unabashedly commercial at their very inception. Mark Twain sought to recycle characters he had created for specific, stand-alone works, exploiting their popularity among relatively serious reviewers and readers. The results were painful, almost amateurish. Among the few literary gifts Mark Twain lacked was the ability to write good bad literature.

Far more fruitfully, the twins now overtook Mark Twain's imagination, and the more he wrote, the more their tale changed its shape. As autumn deepened at the villa, he threw away more pages, dashed off and discarded revisions and more revisions. What ultimately resulted, and then re-resulted, defies concise description.

For several weeks it progressed as pure farce, cheerfully indifferent to probability, its structure a patchwork of ready-to-hand devices, few of which related to one another. The twins were Italians named Angelo and Luigi Capello, and shared a single lower body, as did Giovanni and Giacomo Tocci, and one day they just sent a letter to Aunt Patsy Cooper in Dawson's Landing, Missouri, an obscure river hamlet not utterly dissimilar from Hannibal, asking for room and board, as conjoined Italian twins are wont to do. After the locals get over the shock of seeing a pair of well-dressed, well-spoken continentals strolling about town on one pair of legs, the tale tends toward the surreal. More accurately, it tends toward a series of twin-jokes. One sings hymns, the other, bawdy songs; one likes to attend prohibition meetings, the other favors horse races and fandangos. To complicate things a little, control of the legs passes from one to the other for a week at a time. The mechanism? A "mysterious law of our being."[44] As if to allay any lingering suspicions of "realism," Luigi announces that he is a few months older than Angelo. Eventually there arrives a plot device—Luigi kicks the rakehell Tom Driscoll at an anti-temperance meeting. A trial for assault and battery is scheduled; Luigi engages a new young lawyer named David Wilson who wins on a technicality (no one can really testify for sure which twin did the kicking); there is a duel, with one of the twins wounded; there is a lynching, with one of the twins hanged; as for the other—but never mind; the story just ends.

Or did it? Out of the corner of his eye, Mark Twain had noticed something about that new young lawyer at the story's margin. Out of that glimpse, a new novel was conceived: the dissimilar twin of the one just finished, and born a few months later. "I finished 'Those Extraordinary Twins' night before last," he wrote to Fred Hall on December 12, estimating some sixty to eighty thousand words. "The last third of it suits me to a dot." And then, almost as an afterthought:

I begin, today, to entirely re-cast and re-write the first two-thirds—new plan, with two minor characters made very prominent, one major character dropped out, and the Twins subordinated to a minor but not insignificant place.

The minor character will now become the chiefest, and I will name the story after him—*"Pudd'nhead Wilson."*[45]

This new arrival rose from a deeper place. It was fed by its author's interest in topical events of the day, but also by what remained of his artist's muse. Its "chiefest character" turned out not to be Pudd'nhead Wilson, but a profound, near-Shakespearean figure who would rank among Mark Twain's greatest creations, but who had no antecedent in his previous novels. Her gestative force was probably Mary Ann Cord, the former slave who mesmerized Clemens at Quarry Farm with her plainsong saga of forced separation from her youngest son and eventual reunion with him. Her name was Roxana.

The American newspapers that reached the Clemenses at Villa Viviani in 1892 were full of reportage about the most significant legal test to arise from the ruins of Reconstruction: the lawsuit filed against the East Louisiana Railroad by a New Orleans man named Homer Plessy, contending that he had been illegally jailed for trying to board a railroad car in that city. The car was for "whites only," and Plessy was one-eighth Negro. The case was making its way toward the Supreme Court, which, in 1892, would decide against Plessy, establishing a hated precedent by declaring the plaintiff had access to "separate but equal" means of transportation. Mark Twain vented his contempt for this genetic bean-counting and the racial injustice it represented in his portrayal of Roxana.

Another current topic, dear to Samuel Clemens's detective-loving soul, was the science of "fingerprinting" for forensic purposes. Sir Francis Galton, a British scientist, published a book that year proposing that every human being's fingerprints were unique to that person, and thus a means for establishing identity. These topical elements, accompanied by a succession of new characters, progressively elbowed their way into Mark Twain's farce. He tried for a while to keep both story lines active, and ultimately failed, in the process doing great formal damage to the finished work. *Pudd'nhead Wilson* is an unfinished jumble of several colliding plots and half-plots, featuring a major character (Tom Driscoll) whose persona shifts unintentionally between Negro and white, because Mark Twain did not revise him consistently with previous drafts. Yet the jumble comprises its own shrewd integrity: it expresses the existentialist doubt that had beset Samuel Clemens for years, and flickered into some of his earlier works. The doubt concerned human identity, the chance that only dreams were "real," and reality the real "dream." With *Pudd'nhead Wilson*, that doubt gained permanent primacy in his work.

The setting remains Dawson's Landing in the antebellum years. *Prince and the Pauper*–like, it opens on June 5, 1853, quite possibly the day that Sam Clemens left Hannibal on the downriver packet, with the births of two unrelated boys: one rich, one poor. In this tale, the poor boy is also a Negro slave, given that he is born to Roxana—a white woman to all appearances, but condemned by her one-sixteenth Negro blood to a lifetime of slavery. The mother of the white baby, Mrs. Driscoll, soon dies, leaving Roxana, her servant, to look after both infants. Determined that her flesh and blood never suffer the bondage that is her lot, Roxana switches the two babies in their cradles.

Roxana's decision becomes her fate: her son Chambers, now being raised as "Tom Driscoll," grows up as the epitome of the spoiled Southern squire, a sadistic monster and wastrel who treats her horribly. The real Tom, known now as "Chambers," turns out to be gentle and unoffending, but is abused with impunity by Tom. Over the plot's twenty-three-year period, Roxana— although absent from the narrative for long stretches, as though her creator did not fully recognize her power on the page—endures her deepening skein of thwarted hope and degradation with spirit, willpower, wisdom, and flights of eloquence, until she is at the end broken by the revelation of her deceit.

Her story is obscured by the author's other frantic plotlines. *Pudd'nhead Wilson* is a narrative traffic jam. The title character appears only at the beginning and at the end, when his use of "fingerprinting"—nonexistent in that time—helps solve the central mystery. There are many stock send-ups of small-town quaintness; and the Italian twins, separated into two people now, take up a lot of space. Yet when Roxana's voice breaks through the confusion, it lifts the novel to a higher purpose, as in the scene in which she finally gathers her outrage and compels the tyrannizing Tom, under threat of damaging disclosure, to kneel before her. "You can't mean it," Tom protests, to which the "heir of two centuries of unatoned insult and outrage"[46] thunders,

I'll let you know mighty quick whether I means it or not! You call me names, en as good as spit on me when I comes here po' en ornery en 'umble, to praise you for bein' growed up so fine en handsome, en tell you how I used to nuss you en tend you en watch you when you 'uz sick en had n't no mother but me in de whole worl' . . . en you call me names—*names,* dad blame you! Yassir, I gives you jes one chance mo', and dat's *now,* en it las' on'y half a second—you hear?[47]

Thus the infinitely layered Mark Twain, who can still indulge himself in throw-away "darky" humor with Jim in the balloon, speaks through a slave woman to rebuke an America in the lingering throes of its racial dilemma. Roxana, his first fully believable female character, was his last character of enduring significance. With one exception ("The Man That Corrupted Hadleyburg") he would never approach literary greatness again.

"My book is type-writered and ready for print," he announced to Fred Hall on February 3, 1893.[48] He sent the 82,500-word manuscript about three weeks later. That proved premature. Obliged to sail again for America in March on financial business, he put the brakes on its publication schedule. It needed more work. It was July 30, 1893, before he was finally able to declare to Hall,

This time "Pudd'nhead Wilson" is a success! . . . I have pulled the twins apart and made two individuals of them . . . they are mere flitting shadows, now . . . The whole story is centered on the murder and the trial . . .[49]

He identified three characters who now "stand up high" as the principals: "Pudd'nhead, 'Tom' Driscoll and his nigger mother Roxana; none of the others are important . . ."[50] With book publication several months away, he sold serial rights to the *Century,* which published it in seven installments beginning in December 1893.

H E M A Y have regarded his new novel as a success, but there was precious little else in his life that remotely qualified as such. Household money was drying up even in dirt-cheap Florence, siphoned across the Atlantic to pay bills. In June he fretted over the delay of the $500 monthly draft from Fred Hall: "We are skimming along like paupers, and a day can embarrass us."[51] At age fifty-seven, having tried to strike it rich for more than thirty years, he finally grasped that he was not a businessman—"I am by nature and disposition un-fitted for it" [52]—and pleaded with Hall to help him get out. He estimated his and Livy's indebtedness at $175,000. Figuring wishfully, he estimated that with stock and cash assets, plus the copyright and engraving-plate value of the *Library of American Literature,* he owned property worth $250,000, and maybe more. Might a publishing firm—say, Harper or Appleton or Putnam—pay him $200,000 for his debts and his two-thirds interest in the firm? To Fred Hall, he pleaded: "Please advise with me and suggest alterations and emen-dations of the above scheme, for I need that sort of help . . .

"Get me out of business!" [53]

But Fred Hall couldn't get him out of business. Nothing under Sam or Fred's control could reverse the free fall. They needed a savior.

42

Savior

(1893–94)

Henry Huttleston Rogers was not your garden-variety Gilded Age cut-throat piratical plutocrat and multi-multi-millionaire; he was larger and more rapacious than that, and more interesting. Oil was his game, and gas, and railroads, and insurance, and copper, and pipelines for transporting oil across the country; he invented the pipeline. He played the inside game of business pretty well, too: as a young oilman back in 1872, he'd boldly stood up to the great John D. Rockefeller, who was collecting refineries in large Eastern cities and moving in on Rogers's own smaller one. Rogers couldn't prevent the takeover, but two years later, when Rockefeller organized the Standard Oil Company, Rogers joined him and quickly rose to vice president and director. By 1893 he'd amassed a hundred million dollars. He was Colonel Sellers without the buffoonery, Tom Sawyer grown to Alpha Malehood, Silas Lapham with talent and vision and a Visigoth's disdain for fair play. He'd come up by the classic route of his century's industry captains: small-town boyhood (he was born in Massachusetts in 1840), grocery clerk, newspaper boy, a fortune-seeker at twenty-one drawn to the newly burgeoning oil business in Pennsylvania. A refinery company executive at twenty-six; then to Standard Oil and a rising reputation as a tycoon to be feared and avoided. "Hell Hound Rogers," he was called (always at a safe distance); a butcher, a shark, a man without remorse.

But there was also the civilized Rogers: brilliant conversationalist, wit, mesmerizing charmer. He sailed yachts and went to the fights with the boys. He liked to hang expensive windowpane suits on his tall frame, over crisp white shirts with wingtip collars. His blue eyes, wavy hair parted in the middle, his double-scythe mustache and strong nose and chin—all these features made him attractive even to some who loathed the predator in him. And there was the civic-minded Rogers, the patron of art and reader of literature, the builder of schools and libraries, benefactor to Booker T. Washington and sponsor of Helen Keller at Radcliffe. And Rogers, the devoted husband and father. This was the Rogers whom Samuel Clemens, no stranger to layered personas, preferred to recognize after Rogers gusted into his life in September 1893, and rescued him from financial catastrophe.

Rogers was a perfect avatar of the 1890s. With Rockefeller, Andrew Carnegie, J. P. Morgan, and a few others, he bestrode a decade that hurled the United States from the populist creativity of raw postwar industrialism—the twenty-odd years in which Everyman might parlay his better mousetrap (or typesetting machine) into a fortune—and toward a brutally efficient top-down organization of capital, and capital assets, and human assets. It was the dawn of imperialism, mass-marketing, and the corporation. It was the dawn of time present.

ROGERS AND Clemens met by chance after Sam returned to the States on September 7, 1893. Clara came along this time, to give him horseshoe-pitching companionship on the voyage, and then to travel on by herself to Elmira. Despite the financial crises that spurred this second crossing and his night-pacing levels of stress, he had managed some productive work during the summer, which included a move from the villa to a drab health spa in Franzensbad, Germany called the Krankenheil. (As Sam and Clara traveled, Livy now closed things down at Franzensbad and, dodging a cholera scare sprinkled about Europe, removed to Paris, which would be the family's European headquarters for the winter.) He'd finished revisions on *Pudd'n head Wilson* in July and August, and added the famous "calendar" of aphorisms. The Joan of Arc story had consumed him for months now, and he read several accounts of her life, pushing himself through the French-language texts, then experimenting with various beginnings—five of them, by his later count. "Papa is progressing finely with his 'Joan of Arc' which promises to be his loveliest book," Susy wrote to Clara in Berlin. "The character of Joan is pure and perfect to a miraculous degree. Hearing the M.S. read aloud is an up-lifting and revealing hour to us all. Many of Joan's words and sayings are historically correct and Papa cries when he reads them."[1] Susy could not know it, but her father was writing this novel for her, and, in certain idealizing ways, about her.

Mark Twain also developed several sketches and essays, the most striking of which was "In Defense of Harriet Shelley," a white-hot excoriation of a biography of Percy Bysshe Shelley's abandoned young wife written by Edward Dowden. In sixteen thousand bristling words, Mark Twain denounced Dowden for tarring the deceased Harriet with implications that her infidelity had spurred Shelley to take up with Mary Godwin. This essay, in the opinion of one present-day editor, "foreshadowed truly modern thinking about trophy wives and displaced homemakers."[2] The *North American Review* published it over three installments in 1894.

All of this, plus about half a million dollars, would get him out of trouble. When he disembarked at New York Harbor, wracked with a severe bronchial cough, he was in a near-panic. Mount Morris Bank no longer accepted Webster & Company's paper. Only Charley Langdon's generosity (he endorsed notes totaling $21,000 in August) averted a foreclosure, and the permanent loss of $110,000 owed to Sam and $60,000 to Livy. The *Library of American Literature*, which the house had effectively stopped trying to sell, remained a money-devouring white elephant.

As Clara headed to Elmira, Sam entrained for Hartford, where he tried to find someone to advance him a few thousand dollars to cover notes that were due in days. No luck. He wrote to Susan Crane, begging for a $5,000 loan— "for the boat was sinking."[3] He dashed back to New York and Dr. Rice's hospitality on 19th Street, sapped by his lingering cold. To cure it and get some sleep that first night, he "went to bed before dark and drank almost a whole bottle of whisky, and got up perfectly well."[4] The wellness wouldn't last: After Sue Crane, scrambling heroically, notified him she had scraped up the money, Fred Hall pierced that balloon: he "said it wouldn't save us for it was $8,000 we wanted, not $5,000."[5] He and Hall called on every Wall Street bank and broker they could think of, but found no one willing to part with a single investment dollar. "When I fell on the bed at 8 that evening," he wrote to Livy, "ruin seemed inevitable, but I was physically so exhausted that mental misery had no chance & I was asleep in a moment."[6]

Clemens and Rogers met on a mid-September evening as Clemens stood with Dr. Rice in the lobby of the Murray Hill Hotel. Rice, acquainted with the Standard Oil man, made the introductions, and the three sat down for drinks. Within minutes the author and the industrial titan had been friends since God knew when. Sam was his witty self, but was delighted to find that Rogers could match him, *mot* for *mot* and story for story. Better than that, Rogers disclosed that he'd been a big fan since catching one of Mark Twain's "Sandwich Islands" lectures a long time ago.

As the laughter subsided and the three got up to leave, Rice mentioned to Rogers that Mark Twain's finances were a little disheveled. Rogers set up a meeting. At 4 p.m. on Saturday, September 16, Clemens and Fred Hall arrived at 26 Broadway, took the elevator to the eleventh floor, and passed through a series of warrens until they stepped into Rogers's inner chamber: a mahogany-trimmed apartment with bronze bulls and bears and yacht models scattered about, its walls festooned with framed letters from the likes of Lincoln and Grant. From this setting the Statue of Liberty, visible from the window, looked like a paperweight.[7] They were shown in by the terrifying Katharine I. Harrison, the mogul's six-foot secretary whose pitiless stare as she shooed away most visitors had earned her the nickname on Wall Street, "the Sphinx." Rogers listened as Clemens and Hall described the cash-eating oppression of the *Library of American Literature,* and then made it disappear with a wave of his hand: he instructed his son-in-law to buy it from Webster & Company for $50,000. At mention of their ravenous creditors, Rogers produced $4,000 with a few pen strokes—not a loan, exactly; an investment in Webster, more or less. Who was counting? "In six minutes," an awestruck Sam reported to Livy, "we had the check & our worries were over till the 28th."[8]

Clemens was transformed; giddy with hope; silly with infatuation for his new friend. He took to showing up at the financier's office, sweeping past the Sphinx without resistance, drinking the great man in as he wheeled and dealt. He rushed pell-mell to Rogers's 57th Street town house early one evening to report a conversation with a royalty holder's spokesman; nearly ran into the mogul and his wife as they left the premises for a dinner; and ended up stuck with two of their teenaged children. Rogers delighted Clemens by treating him with bluff hail-fellow humor, the sort that Howells always reached for but never quite managed to pull off. In late September, Clemens, regaining his savoir faire, moved out of Dr. Rice's house and into a room at the exclusive Players Club on Gramercy Park. The two played billiards and poker and smoked cigars together, and joked about egg-sucking grandmothers, and eventually developed the running joke that Clemens was an incorrigible thief of household objects, and Rogers his perpetually outraged victim. (Clemens at one point 'fessed up to purloining two books, Rogers's brown slippers, and a ham.)

Rogers trained his vision on the Paige typesetter fiasco. In early November Rogers materialized in Paige's Chicago shop to inspect the machine and the people around it. He returned to New York with a good working knowledge of the contraption's design, and its problems. He'd also made a quick, sharp study of the organizational dysfunction, and now he began to kick it back to normal. With Sam looking on, Rogers hammered out a new proposed contract that would organize the feuding factions into a single entity, the Paige Compositor Manufacturing Company, with coherent plans for stock and royalty distribution and a manufacturing plan. It required a concession from the Chicago people that sent money Sam's way, as well as Paige's. It stipulated options for Sam to the tune of $240,000 cash or $500,000 in stock. The "carrot" here was Rogers's personal involvement as an investor. Paige refused to give an inch; he responded with counterproposals. He was playing on fear: the chance that he would walk away entirely might force Clemens and Rogers to cave in. The inventor had met his match in any war of nerves. As telegrams poured in from the Chicago moneymen urging him to accept Paige's terms, Rogers thrilled his new protégé with the tough-guy assurance that "Mr. Paige must accept *our* terms."[9] Rogers made it more fun by letting Clemens in on his strategic schemes, offering inside tips and chuckling with Sam over plans for hardballing the Windy City "braves." To watch Rogers in action "is better than a circus," Sam assured Livy.[10]

He took a connoisseur's interest in the extraordinary intuition, the acute feel for human character and its limits, that were among the capitalist's great-est weapons, along with his coolness and command of detail. He watched as Rogers efficiently vaporized the Connecticut men's pretensions to inflated as-sets: "he stripped away all the rubbish & laid bare the fact that their whole gaudy property consisted of just $276,000 & no more!" Sam wrote to Livy on December 9. "Then he said, 'Now we know where we stand, gentlemen. I am prepared to listen to a proposition from you to furnish capital.' "[11] The spokesman proposed fifty cents on the dollar, and Rogers suggested adjourn-ment until the next morning. "Along the street he said, 'They ask 50, & would be glad to get 12 . . . I know exactly what it is worth, to a farthing.' "[12] Then he unspooled a complicated little scam in which Clemens, by faking a "conspir-acy" against Rogers, could squeeze the Connecticut Company for some more stock. On December 21, Rogers returned to Chicago, this time with Clemens along, lolling in the titan's private railroad car stocked with liquor and cigars. The two schemed on how to bamboozle their adversaries into trading their royalties for stock in the company, thus increasing the value of Sam's royalties. Rogers presented his terms; Paige remained noncommittal. Back in New York, the waiting game resumed, with telegrams bearing proposals and coun-terproposals burning the wires in both directions.

It was a great lark for Mark Twain, and he passed the time as a man about town—the Belle of New York, as Mary Mapes Dodge dubbed him. He could be seen on the lecture stage along with James Whitcomb Riley, and in Delmonico's, dining with the great actor Sir Henry Irving. Henry Rogers in-troduced Clemens to Hellen Keller, and took him to the fights; they saw Gen-tleman Jim Corbett box an exhibition at Madison Square Garden. Afterward, the great architect Stanford White, who happened along, took Sam into Corbett's dressing room. Clemens told the champ that he wanted a match in June. Corbett "ducked out" of it: if Mark Twain hit him with a lucky punch, "then my reputation would be gone & you would have a double one."[13] He was also writing again: ten thousand words on *Tom Sawyer's Mystery* (later *Tom Sawyer, Detective*), he reported to Livy.[14] To Susy, he wrote, "My new book I am writing makes me jolly. I live in it," quickly adding, "But when I think of Joan of Arc, how I long to get at that again!"[15]

The most hopeful symptom of all, perhaps, was that Mark Twain was rais-ing hell. His "fine fury" ignited as he sat reading his *Pudd'nhead Wilson* proofs in the office of the *Century* one afternoon, and discovered that somebody had been mucking with his punctuation—"my punctuation, which I had deeply thought out, & laboriously perfected! Then my volcano turned itself loose, & the exhibition was not suited to any Sunday school."[16] The culprit, he learned, was a "peerless imported proof-reader, from Oxford University," whose word around the magazine was considered "sacred, final, immutable."

I said I didn't care if he was an Archangel imported from Heaven, he couldn't puke his ignorant impudence over *my* punctuation, I wouldn't allow it for a moment. I said I couldn't . . . sit in the *presence* of a proof-sheet where that blatherskite had left his tracks . . . this stuff must be set up again & my punctuation restored . . . I'm to return there tomorrow & read the deodorized proof.[17]

As a general rule, it was not a great idea to mess with Mark Twain's punctu tion.

Paige cracked on January 15, 1894. A telegram from Chicago announced that he would accept Rogers's terms, given certain cash stipulations. Sam dashed off a letter of exultation to Livy.

> I came up to my room and began to undress, and then, suddenly and without warning the realization burst upon me and overwhelmed me: I and mine, who were paupers an hour ago, are rich now and our troubles are over!
>
> I walked the floor for half an hour in a storm of excitement. Once or twice I wanted to sit down and cry . . .[18]

His public resurgence continued. *Cosmopolitan,* with Howells in the editor's chair, published sketches of his in three of its fall 1893 issues. *Tom Sawyer Abroad* was being featured in *St. Nicholas,* and *Pudd'nhead Wilson* was running in the *Century* in the months leading up to its April 1894 publication, and was already generating buzz: a professor lecturing on "Politics from 1781 to 1815" managed to work in his opinion that Mark Twain had "serious deeps," and that " 'Pudd'nhead' was clearly & powerfully drawn & would . . . take his place as one of the great creations of American fiction." [19] His take on the professor's comment reflected the growing primacy of the machine in his reveries. The idea was "unexpected," he told Livy,

> For I have never thought of Pudd'nhead as a *character,* but only as a piece of machinery—a button or a crank or a lever, with a useful function to perform in a machine, but with no dignity above that.[20]

Webster & Company remained anemic, and so Henry Rogers, despite the distraction of a fire that gutted his summer house in his hometown of Fairhaven, took on the role of book agent for *Pudd'nhead Wilson* and scored a dual-publisher deal for an April 1894 launch: Frank Bliss's American Publishing Company would swallow its old resentments and issue the novel by subscription, while Harper would publish for the bookstore trade. At the end of January, the man who only a little more than four years earlier had declared his "retirement from literature permanently" wrote to his wife,

> When the anchor is down, then I shall say:
> "Farewell—a long farewell—to *business!* I will *never* touch it again!"
> I will live in literature, I will wallow in it, revel in it, I will swim in ink! Joan of Arc— but all this is premature; the anchor is not down yet.[21]

On February 1, James Paige signed Rogers's contract. A cable from Sam to Olivia arrived in Paris the following morning, their twenty-fourth anniversary: "Wedding news: Our ship is safe in port. I sail the moment Rogers can spare me." [22] That moment came on March 7, when Clemens, having given Rogers the power of attorney, embarked for France. His stay lasted three weeks. Then Webster & Company received its death wound, and Samuel Clemens crossed the Atlantic once again. Clemens had let himself believe that Rogers could prevent this. Given the Century Company's wish to buy all of Mark Twain's books, the financier had suggested turning the screws and obliging Century to buy out the entire Webster inventory, which would entail a loss, but at least would get Clemens out of his heavy bank debt. But in early April, the Mount Morris Bank installed a new president and board of directors, and these men called in the publishing house's loans. Only an inspired ploy by Rogers saved Clemens from losing control of his own literary properties.

The bank insisted on taking ownership of every asset under Sam's name until the $100,000 debt was paid off. These would include the Hartford house, and the copyrights to everything he'd published. In what must have been a tumultuous confrontation, Henry Rogers preserved the copyrights by declaring that Olivia Clemens, who was owed $60,000 by Webster & Company, had first claim on this property as a preferred creditor. As for the house—she owned it, not her husband. Rogers also pushed through a settlement that would require Clemens to pay just fifty cents on each dollar owed. On April 18, 1894, Charles Webster & Company was liquefied. Fred Hall nearly wept when he signed—and drew Clemens's steely contempt: ". . . I half thought he would go off & drown himself . . . In all my days I have never seen so dull a fool." [23] As the newspapers played the story prominently, Sam himself kept up a defiant façade. He was insouciance itself on a train to Hartford a couple of days later: "As I hadn't done anything to be ashamed of, I wasn't ashamed; so I didn't avoid anybody, but talked with everybody I knew on the train." [24] Livy felt differently. In a letter to Susan Crane, she poured out the humiliation and despair of a worn-out woman whose own family traditions would never permit such a capitulation—and whose father would never have shown the recklessness and ineptitude that brought catastrophe about.

The hideous news of Webster & Co.'s failure reached me by cable on Thursday . . . Of course I knew it was likely to come, but I had great hope that it would be in some way averted . . . I have a perfect *horror* and heart-sickness over it. I cannot get away from the feeling that business failure means disgrace . . .

Sue, if you were to see me you would see that I have grown old very fast during this last year. I have wrinkled.

Most of the time I want to lie down and cry. Everything seems to me so impossible . . . I feel that my life is an absolute and irretrievable failure. Perhaps I am thankless, but I so often feel that I should like to give it up and die . . .[25]

She never directed any such bitterness at her husband; she tried to soothe him and protect him from self-recrimination. She closed her letters with endearments like, "Good night yours in the deepest love of my heart, Livy L.C."[26] Her ruse worked better than she perhaps knew. "Nothing daunts Mrs. Clemens or makes the world look black to her," Sam wrote to Rogers later that year, "—which is the reason I haven't drowned myself."[27] By the time he wrote this letter, in December 1894, it had grown clear to Sam that the Clemenses could never again afford to live in the Hartford house, "though it would break the family's hearts if they could believe it."[28]

Livy recoiled from Henry Rogers's combative stance against the bank, a stance that her husband had gleefully adopted as his own.

Oh my darling we want those debts paid and we want to treat them all not only honestly but we want to help them in every possible way . . . You say Mr Rogers has said some caustic and telling things to the creditors. I should think it was the creditors place to say caustic things to us.[29]

She went on, drawing upon a sense of civility and fair play that she had learned in the Langdon household, and at the Elmira Ladies Seminary:

My darling I cannot have any thing done in my name that I should not approve. I feel that we owe those creditors not only the money but our most sincere apologies that we are not able to pay their bills when they fall due.[30]

And turning the emphasis back to her husband's interests, "You know my darling, *now* is the time for you to add to or mar the good name that you have made. Do not for one moment let your sense of our need of money get advantage of your sense of justice & generosity."[31] Livy's pacific moral clarity led her to insist on a goal that Rogers supported and Sam Clemens readily, and publicly, embraced: he would pay back not just a fraction of the debt as required, but all of it—one hundred cents on every dollar. He was fifty-eight, sick, rheumatic. His body, including the muscles in his writing arm, was rebelling against him. His wife was hardly more than an invalid; his eldest daughter was depressive and possibly anemic; his youngest daughter was now prey to serious epileptic attacks. His ability to write at a sustained level of high coherence, inventiveness, and purpose had atrophied. Repaying this bankruptcy debt in full would require a hellish effort of some sort—one that almost certainly would call forth every bit of physical and psychic strength that he had left. But Livy wanted it, and so, in fact, did he. All right then. He would go to hell.

There was worse to come.

Even in the uproar of negotiating the terms of his bankruptcy, Clemens had found time in New York to renew his dragnet for investors in Paige machine royalties and stocks. Rogers continued to act as his advocate and informal partner, even though he had now suffered a loss infinitely more devastating than that of his Fairhaven home. His wife, Abbie Palmer Gifford Rogers, died on the operating table on May 21, as surgeons tried to remove a tumor that had gone undiagnosed for weeks. ("Let us be spared this, my darling," Clemens wrote to Livy in reference to Rogers's grief. "May we die together.")[32] With reports from the Paige factory that the machine was finally near perfection (but no Paige signature on the necessary patents as yet) he sailed to France on May 9. "I am glad Paige has signed," he dryly wrote to Rogers in June, when that gesture was finally accomplished. "I wish it was his death-warrant. Well, maybe it is."[33] The Chicago *Herald* agreed to install the typesetter for a series of tests that to all appearances were but a formality, a prelude to its long-anticipated debut in the market. Aboard ship, he moved the "Joan" manuscript ahead. He composed his second piece of literary criticism for the *North American Review,* which was just out with an installment of his Harriet Shelley essay. Far from the severity of that screed, "Fenimore Cooper's Literary Offenses" is a masterpiece of playful demolition: it indicts the sonorous author of *The Deerslayer* and *The Pathfinder* for his utter misconceptions of the forest, the ways of Indians, the art of tracking quarry, and the behavior of rifle bullets—and then moves on to a merciless review of Cooper's rhetorical style. "There are nineteen rules governing literary art in the domain of romantic fiction," Mark Twain intones near the outset, "—some say twenty-two. In *Deerslayer* Cooper violated eighteen of them."[34] The normally humorless *Review* published it word for word.

Life within the family was not exactly trouble-free. Susy remained depressive and feverish; on a family hiatus for her sake to the baths at La Bourboule-les-Bains, in the south of France, she lay in bed for two days. A few weeks earlier, an unsuspecting Livy had approved her request to cross the English Channel for a reunion with Louise Brownell, who was studying at Oxford. There, Susy found that Louise's romantic affection for her had cooled— a traumatic discovery, given that thoughts of Louise were all that had sustained Susy during her European exile. A long undated letter of Susy's, probably written at the end of July 1894, expresses her anguish in prose as heartrending as any her father ever used to portray his own or his characters' suffering.

I don't know how to write you. There seems to be nothing to say . . . Your dear letter has come . . . saying you are likely to go to America this year. I was all unforewarned and it made my heart stand still. I would not, *could* not dream this would happen and that I should lose you *now* at the moment of having you again, after all these years of waiting. It is impossible. I cannot believe it. It cannot be true. Oh no. Dear dear Louise, my *darling* it is too dreadful! . . .

. . . Please come in to me and let me lie down in your arms, and forget everything but the joy of being near you—Write me that you will let me see you once, one

<u>little</u> once before you go . . . Forgive whatever there is wrong in this letter. It's my love that's so violent and demanding my poor terrified love that <u>cannot</u> give you up.[35]

Susy's broken spirit did not stop her father from writing rapidly, on the book he was now calling *The Personal Recollections of Joan of Arc, By the Sieur Louis de Conte*—the epic-sized paean to Susy's soaring and immaculate heart that he deemed too pure even to risk contamination by the taint of "Mark Twain."

Sam sailed back to America for a brief visit in mid-July, mostly to comfort Rogers in his bereavement. He briefly examined some samples of Paige's test production at the Chicago *Herald,* where it was on display for sixty days in competition with rival typesetters. He liked what he saw, and he liked even better some pages that Rogers sent him after his return to France: "The Herald has just arrived, and that column is healing for sore eyes. It affects me like Columbus sighting land."[36] This Columbus, unfortunately, was about to drop off the edge of the world.

As he furiously ploughed on through the "Joan" manuscript at the cliffside coastal village of Etretat, back in Chicago the Paige sputtered again. Something in its eighteen thousand moving parts just wasn't . . . quite . . . right. It began to jam again. In mid-November, the consecutive breakdowns began. Rogers hurried to Chicago, and Clemens waited helplessly in Paris for further news. It arrived at 8 a.m. on Thanksgiving Day, a letter with Henry Rogers's return address. Clemens told himself to stand by for a cyclone as he opened it. The cyclone gusted out: Rogers now doubted that the machine would ever work. Panic-stricken, Clemens could only wait some more. Two days later, on his fifty-ninth birthday, Livy handed Sam his birthday presents, which cost two francs, total. "[A]nd we have begun life on a new and not altogether unpromising basis."[37]

The *Herald* suspended the tests, as expected, and passed on the Paige. On December 22, Clemens learned that Rogers had dissolved the Paige Compositor Manufacturing Company. It was over. So was his fortune. Only partial financial records survive, so it is impossible to know how great his total losses were. Estimates range between $170,000 and $300,000, in late 19th-century dollars, or between $3,300,000 and $4,900,000 in today's money.

In the end, the author-businessman who saw Man as a kind of imperfect machine was done in by a machine that was too manlike.

JAMES PAIGE never reestablished his career. He became caught in a scandal involving a tall, blonde, married former actress who claimed he had once breached a promise to marry her. He died in 1917 and was buried in a potter's field in what is now Oak Park, Illinois, probably by an undertaker named Funk.[38] Samuel Clemens and Henry Rogers remained close friends until Rogers's death in 1909, a year before Clemens's own. Much has been written about the moral contradictions inherent in Clemens's warm regard for the ruthless capitalist, given his own tendencies toward populism and reform. Certainly Rogers's reputation was no secret to the author. Clemens, who at times seemed able to spot a business shenanigan from around the curve of the earth, had watched close up as Rogers employed some of his "Hell-Hound" tactics. He'd chortled with Rogers when one of their prearranged ruses worked on some clueless adversary. He had personally turned down a book manuscript submitted to Webster & Company that attacked the ethics of Standard Oil and its executives. Yet as far as Clemens was concerned, Rogers's dark side did not exist. This opinion stood the test of time. As early as February 1894, he was assuring Livy that Rogers was "the only man I would give a *damn* for." [39] Eight years later, at a tribute to the industrialist, he told the guests, "He is not only the best friend I have ever had, but is the best man I have known." [40] If William Dean Howells was listening somewhere, he kept his reaction to himself.

The elements of Samuel Clemens's regard for Rogers are self-evident. Less clear, perhaps, is the question of why Rogers should feel drawn to Sam Clemens. He was probably drawn to Clemens for the same reasons that moved Howells, and Bret Harte, and Jervis Langdon, and Grant, and Matthew Arnold (in person, anyway), and all the other powerful, irrevocably grown-up eminences whose paths crossed Sam's. They recognized in him their boyhood selves—or the selves they wished they could have been. The most ingenious theory for Rogers's "pirate" persona stipulated that he was simply caught up in a fantasy of the sort that boys play on river islands in summertime. It was offered by a fellow player, the Boston stockbroker and writer Thomas W. Lawson, whose own fortune approached $50 million.

> Above all things Henry H. Rogers is a great actor. Had his lot been cast upon the stage, he might easily have eclipsed the fame of Booth or Salvini. He knows the human animal from the soles of his feet to the part in his hair and from his shoulder-blade to his breastbone, and like all great actors is not above getting down to every part he plays. He is likely also so to lose himself in a role that he gives it his own force and identity, and then things happen quite at variance with the lines. [41]

If nothing else, Mark Twain's friendship with Rogers produced what is perhaps the most quoted of all his lightning ripostes. Repetition has given it countless variations; the locale has ranged from Hartford to New York to New Bedford, and probably beyond. The interlocutor's gender and status vary. It most likely occurred during a dinner given for Mark Twain and Rogers at the Princess Hotel in Bermuda in 1906. One of the guests drew the author aside and murmured, "Your friend Rogers is a good fellow. It's a pity his money is tainted."

"It's twice tainted," agreed Mark Twain—"'tain't yours, and 'tain't mine." [42]

43

Thunder-Stroke

(1895 96)

On a chilly day toward the end of March 1895, Samuel Clemens stepped through the doorway of the nineteen-room house at 351 Farmington Avenue in Hartford, where he and Livy had commenced their lives as social royalty nearly twenty-one years earlier. He was back in America, traveling alone, to arrange details of the odyssey he had conceived to repay his creditors. He hadn't wanted to go near the salmon-colored house with its Gothic spires when he arrived in town, he wrote to Livy, or see any of their old friends.

But as soon as I entered this front door I was siezed with a furious desire to have us all in this house again & right away, & never go outside the grounds any more forever—certainly never again to Europe.[1]

The old life swept before him like a panorama; and he ached to come home.

How ugly, tasteless, repulsive, are all the domestic interiors I have ever seen in Europe compared with the perfect taste of this ground floor, with its delicious dream of harmonious color, & its all-pervading spirit of peace & serenity & deep contentment . . . It is the loveliest home that ever was.[2]

He realized that over time, he'd grown oblivious to the house's claims on his soul: claims contained in the furniture and draperies and statuary and appointments that he and Livy had traveled so many countries and spent so many thousands of dollars to assemble.

. . . I had wholly forgotten its olden aspect. And so, when I stepped in at the front door & was suddenly confronted by all its richness & beauty minus wraps & concealments, it almost took my breath away.[3]

Every rug, picture, ornament, and chair was in its place—woundingly so.

[T]he place was bewitchingly bright & splendid & homelike & natural, & it seemed as if I had burst awake out of a hellish dream, & had never been away, & that you would come drifting down out of those dainty upper regions with the little children tagging after you.[4]

But Livy would never again descend those stairs. The house was inhabited now by John Day and his wife Alice, a daughter of Isabella Hooker, who had leased it from the Clemenses for a vitally necessary two hundred dollars a month. The young Sam Clemens had attended their wedding with Olivia Langdon on June 17, 1869. When Alice Hooker Day tried to say something about the rocking chair that had once belonged to Livy's mother, Olivia Lewis Langdon, she broke down and wept.

SAM HAD disclosed the essence of the plan in a letter to Henry Rogers early in February. It was "(take a breath and stand by for a surge)—to go around the world on a lecture trip."[5] Pridefully, he insisted to Rogers that the trip was not for money, "but to get Mrs. Clemens and myself away from the phantoms and out of the heavy nervous strain for a few months."[6]

It most certainly was for money. Why else did he plan to flog himself and his wife westward on a yearlong itinerary that would take them across oceans and unfamiliar land to a hundred cities in Australia, New Zealand, Tasmania, Ceylon, India, South Africa, and the British Isles, and then (as his plans then called for) on a finishing kick around several American cities in the East? He had come to dread "the platform." (He'd appeared at Madison Square Garden with James Whitcomb Riley in February 1894, for the money; and it had not gone well.) He didn't even have a lecture prepared. This was quite an extravagant way of catching a little rest and relaxation. But it was a good way—probably the only way—of recouping that $100,000 debt of honor.

He gave the game away a little further on in the same letter, calculating some of his expenses against some projected revenues (he said his friend Harry M. Stanley thought he would net $15,000 in Australia and Cape Town alone), and remarking that the tour would aid in sales of the anticipated uniform edition of his works. To clear the decks, he had pushed *Tom Sawyer, Detective,* to its conclusion in January, and then, writing in great clusters of copy, sometimes fifteen hundred words in a day, he wrapped up *Joan of Arc.* He read aloud of the heroine's persecution and deepening peril each night to the family, with Susy frequently excusing herself to get a handkerchief for weeping. "To-night Joan of Arc was burned at the stake,"[7] she wrote in her diary after listening to the novel's conclusion. Mark Twain chose a curious way of characterizing his own feelings upon finishing the manuscript: in a note to himself, he evoked the simile of a death-watch that had finally concluded.

> Do you know the shock? I mean when you come at your regular hour into the sickroom where you have watched for months and find the medicine-bottles all gone, the night-table removed, the bed stripped . . . the room cold, stark, vacant—& you catch your breath & realize what has happened.
> Do you know that shock? [8]

As he contemplated the "desolation" of the now-absent manuscript, it occurred to him that if he were to write another book, "I must restore the aids to lingering dissolution to their wonted places & nurse another patient through & send it forth for the last rites, with many or few to assist there, as that may happen; & that I will do." [9] Sailing to New York, he finalized travel details. The agent James B. Pond, who'd put together Mark Twain and George Washington Cable's "Twins of Genius" tour a decade earlier, was arranging the American lecture bookings. Pond and his wife would accompany the Clemenses as far as the West Coast. The respected Australian lecture agent Carlyle Greenwood Smythe, who had booked the remainder of the tour, would join them in Sydney and travel with them the rest of the way. Clara, fearing boredom in the States, had invited herself on the journey. Susy and Jean would stay behind in Elmira, under Katy Leary's care. Susy, who disliked ocean sailing, would pursue voice training. Jean would enroll at the Elmira Ladies Seminary.

Clemens looked up Howells in New York, and the two of them joined a soirée at the writer Laurence Hutton's house on a Sunday afternoon, where Henry Rogers introduced them to the fourteen-year-old Helen Keller. A few days later, the blind and deaf young woman recounted to Mary Mapes Dodge that "Mr. Clemens told us many entertaining stories, & made us laugh till we cried." She decided that "Mark Twain" was an appropriate nom de plume for him, "because it has a funny & quaint sound that goes well with his amusing writings, & its nautical significance suggests the deep & beautiful things he has written." [10] He headed back across the Atlantic on March 27 aboard the SS *Paris,* paused in London to preside as guest of honor at a dinner given him by Sir Henry Stanley, and then went on to Paris to collect his family. There, he finished reading the proofs of *Personal Recollections of Joan of Arc* and sent them to *Harper's.* The magazine had already begun publishing the yearlong serialization in the April number, under the name "Sieur Louis de Conte." The entourage sailed for New York on May 11, and arrived on the 18th. They entrained to Elmira after a few days in the city, to make final preparations for their mid-July departure on the world tour.

The final weeks weren't easy. Livy's health had improved dramatically for the first time in years, but Sam was attacked by gout, and also by the bacterial skin infection known as a boil, or carbuncle. ("I could have done without it," he confided to Rogers, "for I do not care for jewelry.")[11] The swelling on his left leg produced pain that required bandaging and sent him to bed at the Quarry Hill farmhouse, where he remained for forty-four days, as he later claimed. He tried to work three lecture/readings into shape, but was distracted by demands from Webster & Company's creditors; a couple of these missives arrived in the form of subpoenas. The second one, from a bookbinder, terrified Livy by ordering her to appear before the Supreme Court of New York. In mid-June Frank Bliss offered Clemens ten thousand dollars to write a book on his round-the-world trip. Sam made no promises, but decided to write such a book. He was contractually committed to the *Century* to produce a series of magazine articles (as Livy discovered), and railed when the editors insulted him with an astonishing breach of tact.

The Century people actually proposed that I *sign a contract to be funny* in those 12 articles. That was pure insanity. Why, it makes me shudder every time I think of those articles. I don't think I could ever write one of them without being under the solemnizing blight of that disgusting recollection.[12]

As the departure date grew near, he bombarded Rogers with so many queries for bankruptcy details that he acknowledged his intrusions with a rueful joke: "Look here, don't you think you'd better let somebody else run the Standard Oil a week or two till you've finished up these matters of mine?"[13] He decided on his own to travel to New York and settle the bookbinder's claim of $5,046.83. Livy did not have to testify, but she was humiliated by the New York *Times*'s coverage of the hearing on July 11 and 12, which noted that Mr. Clemens, made "ill through worrying over his business affairs," had traveled from Elmira in the care of a nurse.[14] He tried out one of his new lecture readings on seven hundred young inmates at the Randalls Island House of Refuge. The subject was a comic take on the moral regeneration of mankind. The miscreants were not charmed. "Oh, but wasn't it a comical defeat. . . . Delivering a grown-folks' lecture to a sucking-bottle nursery!" he lamented to Rogers.[15] He threw the lecture away and wrote a revision. He tried one last dress rehearsal, this one in Elmira early on the same Sunday evening that he began his epic trek west. Again his audience was boys—inmates at the Elmira reformatory—and these slightly older hoodlums treated him a little better. Afterward, the Clemenses and the Ponds took carriages through the hot night to the railroad station, where, at 10:30 p.m. on July 14, 1895, the five boarded a train for Cleveland, the first leg of a journey that for Sam, Livy, and Clara would cover one year, and fifty-three thousand miles. As the locomotive hissed steam and began its roll down the tracks, Sam gazed through the glass at his receding eldest daughter, luminous on the platform under the electric lights. Susy smiled and waved. "She was brimming with life & the joy of it," Clemens told Howells a year later. "That is what I saw; & it was what her mother saw through her tears."[16]

· · ·

VIEWED IN retrospect, the year 1895 was the true beginning of the 20th century. Motion pictures were invented, and the x-ray. Freud published *The Interpretation of Dreams*. Babe Ruth was born. Scientists in Sweden and America began to warn against what would one day be called global warming. More ominously, the "Jewish question," stirred up in Austria and Germany, was transmigrating to France. Anti-Semitism, one year after the Dreyfus trial, was reinforced by a primitive interpretation of evolutionist theory, "social Darwinism," and its even uglier stepchild, "racial purity." A reckoning beyond Hank Morgan's dreams gathered force.

In South Africa, the discovery of gold in the Transvaal spurred passions toward an outbreak of the second Boer War. In Cuba, revolutionaries arose against the Spanish colonialists. Spain sent a hundred thousand troops to put down the rebellion; the United States sided with the rebels and the USS *Maine* steamed toward Havana. Mark Twain was marching into the path of this gathering hurricane. His global itinerary, and his European residences through the rest of the 1890s, projected him along the most critical fault lines of empire, imperialism, slavery, colonial rule, the tyranny of the landed over the dispossessed. (The very fact that he was able to lecture around the world in his own language and be understood, he owed to the British Empire and its four hundred million subjects.) The assaults on these institutions and the revised view of humanity the assaults represented would hasten the long-delayed maturity of his political voice, and inspire the strongest writing of the rest of his life.

The expedition got off to a sweat-soaked start in Cleveland on the night of July 15. A capacity crowd of 2,600 marinated in 90-degree temperatures inside the Music Hall. Mark Twain sweltered in the wings as a flute-and-violin ensemble labored away for forty minutes, with many encores. When he finally took the stage, he saw to his horror that two hundred newsboys had been seated behind him (he later boosted the number to five hundred). Every one of them had Tom Sawyer's patience for a stuffy grown-up occasion. He exited the stage with a third of his readings undelivered. "Why, with their scufflings and horse-play and noise, it was just a menagerie," [17] he fumed. Imagine! *Boys!*

They departed Cleveland the next evening for a voyage across the Great Lakes on the luxury steamship *Northland*, with its spacious promenade decks, and Clemens's mood improved. He watched the summer cottages slip by as the ship approached Port Huron, linking lakes Erie and Huron, and noted the "summer-dressed young people" waving flags and handkerchiefs. They were waving for Mark Twain. He noted the "rich browns and greens of the rush-grown far-reaching flat lands . . . the sinking sun throwing a crinkled broad carpet of gold on the water." [18] They steamed north on Lake Huron, Sam roughing out a second lecture. Mark Twain made appearances at Sault Ste. Marie on the Canadian border, and then in Mackinac. Westward then on Lake Superior to the Minnesota shore. He spoke in St. Paul and Minneapolis and

Winnipeg. His lecturing prowess was back. The crowds loved him; few in these regions had ever laid eyes on anyone this famous; but even if they had, this was *Mark Twain*. Trains carried people from as far as two hundred miles away to hear him in towns along the northern Great Plains on a line to Vancouver. Clara found herself hypnotized by his effect on audiences.

Father knew the full value of a pause and had the courage to make a long one when required for a big effect. And his inimitable drawling speech, which he often lost in private life, greatly increased the humorous effect on the stage. People in the house, including men, got hysterical. Cries that resembled the cries of pain could often be heard . . .

It always seemed to me the greatest possible achievement to make a house rock with mirth. And I believe that Mark Twain was often elated by it himself. His cheeks and eyes glowed with color that resembled tinted sparks.[19]

Clemens flourished in the adulation; but he had imagined a more personal triumph on this tour: a return to San Francisco, which he'd last seen half his lifetime ago. He'd been disappointed when Pond ruled it out: the gate prospects in the California city were bad, Pond insisted; people in that city took vacations in August.

Clemens set aside his share of the gate money, roughly $200 out of the average $500 a stop, for delivery back to Henry Rogers. It totaled something over $5,000 by the time he reached the West Coast and mailed it off in a lump sum. He and Livy wanted their creditors paid incrementally as the money came in, but Rogers refused; he prudently banked it and let it accumulate interest.

In Butte, Montana, on August 1, expecting miners, Clemens encountered a "Beautiful audience. Compact, intellectual and dressed in perfect taste."[20] He read to them for an hour and a half, throwing in the Frog, the Old Ram, the Watermelon, and the Golden Arm. The house was packed to the roof at Portland, and he found the twenty-five-cent patrons in the gallery "as intelligent and responsive as the others."[21] Overflow crowds turned out in Olympia, Tacoma, and Seattle. Word of Mark Twain's debt-paying mission had spread through the newspapers, heightening the air of drama at each of his appearances. Hardscrabble farmers and grocery clerks pressed their dollars at him; he gently refused most of these, but recorded the figures at every house to the penny. James Pond had one of the new Kodak cameras, and he took pictures of these gaunt, staring strangers, presaging Walker Evans. Bands played Mark Twain into town, and people waved hats and handkerchiefs. At Victoria, British Columbia, the governor-general, his wife, and son came to hear him, the boy in Highland costume. The band played "God Save the Queen," which Sam enjoyed. Reporters flocked to him, and he indulged them. A "young boy" came to interview him and "asked me in strict detail precisely the questions which I have answered so many million times already."[22] These included "First

visit? Where do you go from here? Have you had good houses? Have you enjoyed the trip? Are you going to write a book about the voyage? What will be
the character of it?"[23] To this last, he confessed he was "tempted to say hy-
drophobia, seamanship and agriculture."[24]

Back East, the "Joan of Arc" serialization in *Harper's* had captured wide
attention. Many readers and newsmen, recognizing the distinctive comic
touches in it, figured out who the author was. Clemens directed Harper &
Brothers to put his name on their forthcoming hardcover edition. Later he
changed his mind, but he would change it again. In Elmira, Susy was fighting
depression. She suffered her father's predisposition to guilt and self-blame.
"I am often deeply cast down with the thought of how I have failed to be what
I should have been to you all," she wrote. "But perhaps I shall have a chance
to try again."[25] In her pining for Louise Brownell, Susy had sometimes felt
suffocated within the family circle; but as the summer of 1895 went on, she
ached to rejoin it: *"You* brilliant, experienced, adorable people, to whom I
belong . . ."[26]

The Clemenses arrived at Vancouver on August 10, and bade farewell to
the Ponds, who returned east. Sam and Livy's voyage to Australia was delayed
a week after their ship, a weather-beaten little mail steamer called the RMS
Warramoo, stumbled across a reef on its way into port. ("Fortunately we did not
know until later," Clara recorded, "that the steamer even after repairs was not
seaworthy and would have gone down in a storm.")[27] Mark Twain shoehorned
some local readings onto his schedule. In reaction to rumors, and after prodding from Rogers, he signed a statement declaring that he was *not* lecturing
for his own benefit, but to pay off his creditors—even though, strictly speaking, he didn't have to: "The law recognizes no mortgage on a man's brain . . .
but I am not a business man, and honor is a harder master than the law. It cannot compromise for less than a hundred cents on the dollar, and its debts
never outlaw."[28]

On Friday, August 23, the bandaged-up *Warramoo* carried the Clemens
entourage, along with several hundred rats and uncounted cockroaches, out
from Vancouver into the Pacific, bound southwest for Australia. Sam watched
the great brown gulls scrape the tips of their wings along the ocean surface,
and dreamed at night about appearing before a lecture audience without his
pants. Clara remembered shuffleboard tournaments and evenings spent
studying the stars by telescope, and dancing. Papa remembered the shuffle-
board, too: it "is rather violent exercise for me," he moaned to Rogers. (He let
it slip that he'd persevered enough to reign as sole "Champion of the South
Seas.")[29] He took his card playing equally seriously, Clara recalled: "Continuous bad luck would start those little twitching muscles under his eyes that sig-
nified a growing storm, and then suddenly followed an avalanche of cards on
the table and Father would sing out: 'By the humping jumping—who can play
with a hand like that?' "[30] Then Livy would begin her cooing noises to calm
him down.

At Honolulu, which Clemens had not seen since his *Ajax* adventures twenty-nine years earlier, he missed a lecture when the ship was quarantined outside port: a cholera scare on shore. A young woman on board told him that her mother had made that *Ajax* voyage with him. He glumly stared at Oahu, thinking that if he did go ashore he might never leave. He contemplated "[t]wo sharks playing around, laying for a Christian."[31]

Southward again toward Australia. They crossed the equator at 4 p.m. on September 6. "Clara kodaked it."[32]

By now, Susy Clemens's quest for serenity had led her to the foothills of the paranormal, and a curing system called Mental Science, developed in the 1840s by a former "mesmerist" named Phineas Parkhurst Quimby, of Portland, Maine. Like several parallel theories of self-transcendence then in vogue, Mental Science assumed that certain "hidden powers of the mind," once brought into active use, were capable of curing disease, which was nothing more than "error of mind." Medicine was thus irrelevant. (Quimby seems to have believed that he cured himself of consumption by driving his carriage horse as fast as it would go one day, but remained elusive about the details.)[33] Quimby was visited in 1862 by a sickly forty-one-year-old New Hampshire woman named Mary Baker, who later harnessed his teachings to the assumption that such healing was a manifestation of God; and, as Mary Baker Eddy, developed Christian Science, a system of belief that, among other things, rejected the doctrines of Christianity in favor of an amorphous consciousness that could be thought of as the Divine Mind.

Mental Science was right up the alley of Samuel Clemens, who remained fascinated with "mental telegraphy" and had been intrigued with mesmerism since his Hannibal days. He'd taken Susy to a mesmerist while the family was in France to help her out of her funk. The chronically ailing Livy believed in it as well. "I have no language to say how glad & grateful I am that you are a convert to that rational & noble philosophy," Sam wrote to his daughter, hardly dreaming how inadequate it would soon prove. "Stick to it; don't let anybody talk you out of it."[34]

THE CLEMENSES arrived at Sydney to a tumultuous welcome: "Newspaper reporters, photographers, callers from all circles; and beggars of every description, slovenly and distinguished."[35] Carlyle Smythe was on hand to begin his management duties—hotels, transportation, lecture arrangements, and general safekeeping. He would prove a jolly companion and ardent billiards rival the rest of the way. Heaps of flowers arrived at their hotel, in such volume that to Clara, "they appeared to be symbols of condolence."[36] Newspapermen scribbled down Mark Twain's every utterance. When he vented a little spleen at Bret Harte's expense, calling the man heartless and his work shoddy, it created an uproar that quickly became international, and he later retracted it, sort of.[37] Even Clemens's festering carbuncle made the news: a reporter from the Adelaide *South Australian Register* asked him how he'd managed to smuggle it past customs, a setup for a witticism that Mark Twain pretty much flubbed. "It sits on me like the nation," was about as good as he could manage.[38] Australia was the Clemenses' port of entry into the global supernation that was the British Empire. For Sam, the Empire's salient features were human bondage and subjugation. The northern province of Queensland interested him as the epicenter of "Labor Traffic," the quasi-legal system of raiding the nearby Timor and Coral Sea islands for "recruits" for working the great sugar plantations. Recent laws forbade coercive tactics, but Clemens lost no time locating a ship captain in the trade who railed, in timeless style, against the "cast-iron regulations"[39] that put a crimp in his harvesting. ("They and the missionaries have poisoned his life . . . See him weep; hear him cuss between the lines.")[40]

Mark Twain kept politics out of his public talks. Chapter 13 of *Following the Equator* even recounts an appealing anecdote about the young Cecil Rhodes, just then a diamond mogul and colonial satrap in South Africa. His four readings over nine days in Sydney were a big hit here—as were his spiffy patent-leather shoes and black formal dress. The Australians treated the family like royalty: they were guests at horse races, polo games, dinner parties, and a ball at the Government House; fawned over by elegant hosts and hostesses whose grandparents were criminal convicts dumped onto the prison-island. Clara encountered a "maniac" who told her that three men were planning to assassinate her father on the lecture platform.[41] Sam had another vivid dream; it seemed that the visible universe was "the physical person of God; that the vast world that we see twinkling millions of miles apart in the fields of space are the blood corpuscles in His veins; and that we and the other creatures are the microbes that charge with multitudinous life the corpuscles."[42] In Melbourne, Mark Twain's lecture one night caused a man in a box seat to laugh until his face turned scarlet and he banged his walking stick on the floor. The Melbourne *Argus* kindly identified him as a local archdeacon. Even the Presbyterians were laughing hard, the story noted.[43] He barnstormed through several other Australian cities and towns—Horsham, Stawell, Ballarat, Geelong, among others—and then headed for Tasmania. New Zealand for six weeks after that, sweeping through large towns and small, telling reporters which of his books he liked best, competing for attention with dogfights at Oamaru, and succumbing to another carbuncle at Napier, which forced him to cancel a talk and ruined his sixtieth birthday. He devised a nickname for towns and regions heavily influenced by transplanted British culture: "Junior Englands."

His renderings of this itinerary in *Following the Equator* are mostly genial, diaristic, but punctuated here and there with observations of the country as a speculator's paradise; of tremendous wealth extracted and exported from the silver mines; the displacement of the aboriginals by British settlers amused by their primitive survival skills and oblivious to their intelligence. At Adelaide, he beheld the native Australian dog, the dingo—an ancient species, and a beautiful one. "He has been sentenced to extermination, and the sentence will be carried out. This is all right, and not objectionable. The world was made for man—the white man." [44] The scars of the great gold strike of 1851, on terrain and humanity, were everywhere obvious to him, and freighted. Ruminating on the reduction of native human beings in Australia by 80 percent in the first twenty years of British colonization, sometimes by means that amounted to mass murder (food laced with arsenic, for instance), he summed it up with the ironic contempt that would season much of his anti-imperialist writing.

You observe the combination? It is robbery, humiliation, and slow, slow murder, through poverty and the white man's whisky . . .

There are many humorous things in the world; among them the white man's notion that he is less savage than the other savages. [45]

In mid-December the Clemenses looped back to Sydney, visited at Melbourne and Adelaide again; and on New Year's Day, 1896, they and Smythe boarded the *Oceana* for the long haul through the Indian Ocean for Ceylon, three thousand miles to the northwest. They passed among the offshore islands, prison colonies not many decades earlier, "whence the poor exiled Tasmanian savages used to gaze at their lost homeland and cry; and die of broken hearts." [46] On this voyage Clemens relaxed a little, despite having to put up with some irritating children and a score or so of "Salvationists" who sang hymns in the rain and then begged for contributions. He worked and reworked his reading/lectures, keeping two or three versions alive, committing to memory every line of each one, including the revisions. He memorized his work so thoroughly that on the platform, he was able to switch from one lecture text to another at whim, sometimes virtually in mid-thought, without betraying a trace of discontinuity.

The vastness of the ocean, he commented in his notebook, lessened his belief in Noah's Ark. He read a stack of novels, a genre that rarely interested him; he noted that he'd recently bailed out of Goldsmith's *The Vicar of Wakefield* and some Jane Austen. He promised Livy one morning that he would swear off profanity, shortly before breaking two tumblers while trying to take some medicine—"then I released my voice. Mrs. C. behind me in the door: 'Don't reform any more, it isn't any improvement.' " [47]

Susy was visiting in New York now, stronger and happier than she had felt in years. Mental Science seemed to be working: a "healer" had visited her several times in Elmira during the summer and fall; Katy Leary skeptically peeked in as the woman would pass her hands over Susy's throat, to strengthen it for singing. When Leary overheard the woman talking about being at a concert the previous night with her husband, it gave her the heebie-jeebies; the husband had been dead a quarter-century. In the city, Susy moved easily among artists and the avant-garde (as had her father in San Francisco). She paid calls on William Dean Howells and on Dr. Clarence Rice, and looked up Louise Brownell in Orange, New Jersey, a visit that seems to have been friendly rather than passionate and fraught. Brownell repaid the visit at Elmira in January. Life felt good again, and hopeful.

Arriving at Colombo, in Ceylon, on January 13, Sam (still coughing), Livy, and Clara learned of a minor eruption from the world of the about-to-happen: the failed Jamestown Raid in the diamond-rich Transvaal, which was on their itinerary. A band sponsored by the extractive British South Africa Company had tried to overthrow the strong nationalist government of "Oom" Paul Kruger, and failed, with many of the insurgents thrown into prison. Cecil Rhodes was forced to resign as prime minister of the British-run Cape Colony; a greater war loomed.

Mark Twain mounted an elephant near Colombo, and called Clara a "sassmill" when she giggled.[48]

Seven days after that, steaming up the Arabian Sea, they arrived at a city that had no "Junior England" about it, and swept away Clemens's jaded irony for a while.

> *Bombay!* A bewitching place, a bewildering place, an enchanting place—the Arabian Nights come again! . . . In the great bazar the pack and jam of natives was marvelous, the sea of rich-colored turbans and draperies an inspiring sight, and the quaint and showy Indian architecture was just the right setting for it.[49]

He could not stop exclaiming over this "land of dreams and romance," with its Aladdin lamps, tigers, elephants, cobras, its thousand religions and two million gods.[50] India was the cradle of the human race, birthplace of human speech; yet as the family was being shown to its hotel rooms by a "burly German" and his seventeen native servants, the German, for no obvious reason, belted one of them across the jaw, then chewed him out for some misstep. The white man's imprint on a dark-skinned land, again. Some of the enchantment returned in the person of a new servant, a "frisky little forked black thing," a "shiney-eyed little devil," on whom Clemens hung the name "Satan."[51] "Satan," answering a knock on the hotel room door, informed Clemens that God wanted to see him. This presence turned out to be a local holy man, and the purpose of his visit turned out to be a discussion of the philosophy contained in *Huckleberry Finn.*

His many lectures were dazzling events there, as the elite of the great city turned out, the women in flashing jewelry, the British men in black evening dress, the Indians in white turbans. Mark Twain thanked the heat for giving him an excuse to wear white clothes whenever he wanted. He lectured one night in "a snow-white fulldress, swallow-tail and all," as he later described it, and dubbed this "delightful impudence" his "dontcaradam suit."[52] Livy wrote letters to Susy describing entertainments at the homes of princes and maharajahs. "Father gathered the impression from his royal host that his country was dissatisfied with the English powers and would never be completely happy until it was completely liberated from English influence," Clara recalled.[53]

Livy visited a museum and found herself surrounded by beautifully dressed and bejeweled women who inspected her closely and chased her behind exhibits and into other rooms. The heat eventually threw Clemens into a mild depression, and he told Livy one sweltering night that because of their debt, they could probably never return to America again.

The Indians' seemingly passive subjugation to the British Empire troubled him. Walking at dawn one morning, he encountered a "Hindoo" servant squatting in front of his master's bungalow. The motionless man looked as though he were freezing. He was still in that position an hour later. "He will always remain with me, I suppose," Mark Twain wrote. ". . . Whenever I read of Indian resignation, Indian patience under wrongs, hardships, and misfortunes, he comes before me. He becomes a personification, and stands for India in trouble." [54]

Susy Clemens turned twenty-four in March.

Sam, Livy, Clara, and Smythe remained more than two months in India, ascending the Himalayas, traveling by rail across its continental vastness to Calcutta, then Darjeeling where, Sam reported, after a lecture, the family "came down the mountain (40 miles) at a dizzy toboggan gait on a six-seated hand-car and never enjoyed ourselves so much in all our lives." [55] Backtracking to Ceylon in early April, they then headed for Mauritius, there to change for the last phase of the itinerary—South Africa. They arrived at Durban, Natal, on May 6, intending to stay three months. Sam allowed Livy and Clara to recuperate in the coastal town while he barnstormed through Johannesburg, Pretoria, Queenstown, and several smaller cities. Letters from home awaited them, but none was from Susy. Livy found herself uneasy about this. She needn't have—not exactly, not yet. Susy had relocated from Elmira, where Jean stayed on in school, to Hartford. She lived for a while with John and Alice Day at the Gothic-spired family house on Farmington Avenue. In midsummer the Days moved elsewhere, and the house fell vacant. Susy boarded with Charles and Susan Warner next door, but she could not resist crossing the lawn most days to spend long stretches by herself as the lone inhabitant of the Clemens mansion. She sang there, accompanying herself on the piano, as Sam used to do, and her voice floated through the open windows, diverting the Nook Farm neighbors, who sometimes sat outdoors to listen to it. Her life was quiescent, on the surface. But in June she wrote Louise Brownell a series of letters that darkly rehashed the turbulence of their former relationship.

Mark Twain found his audiences of Dutch-descended farmers—the Boers—a little unresponsive at first, but quick to laugh once they warmed up. He added a glass of water to his platform props, carrying it onstage with him with an air of casualness that presaged generations of nightclub comics holding drinks in their hands. He made a strange detour in Pretoria: he visited the jail that held sixty-four of the Jamestown raiders and conspirators. He was approaching mental and physical exhaustion after nearly a year of constant sailing, overland travel, and readjustment to local food and customs, and the adrenal rush of performance—most of the time nursing one ailment or another. By his own admission, he was bewildered by the gnarly roots of South African politics. Perhaps for these reasons, and the irresistible glamour of the nearby gold and diamond mines, Clemens sympathized with these would-be usurpers of the Transvaal. (It didn't help that he found the typical Boer "a white savage,"[56] grubby and indolent.) Thinking to amuse the imprisoned men with a little gallows humor, he stood before them and launched into an off-the-cuff riff about the bright side of incarceration. "This jail is as good as any other," he assured them,

and, besides, being in jail has its advantages. A lot of great men have been in jail. If Bunyan had not been in jail, he never would have written "Pilgrim's Progress." Then the jail is responsible for "Don Quixote."[57]

Apparently there weren't too many aspiring novelists behind the bars; the prisoners gaped at him, and the joke fell flat. Worse: the Transvaal president, Kruger, was offended enough that he tightened restrictions on visitors to the jail. To Mark Twain's credit, he visited the president, a heavy-faced man with chin whiskers who sat in an armchair smoking a pungent pipe as the author explained that it was all a joke, and the anticolonialist relented. All but four of the sixty-four prisoners were eventually released. But this was only the beginning. Mark Twain could not have comprehended the scope of the conflict that proceeded from the skirmish that drew him to Pretoria. The Kruger government's resistance to British hegemony increased for three years until it erupted into the second Boer War in 1899. The invading British armies shocked even their fellow citizens with their brutal victory, which included extermination of resisting guerrilla bands and blockhouses and concentration camps for civilian Boers. The Empire's legitimacy was fatally tarnished as the 20th century began. Mark Twain never quite pierced through to the anticolonial heart of this conflict; in *Following the Equator,* he described the jailed raiders as "Reformers"[58] and showed more disapproval for their tactics than for their ideas. His ultimate sympathies in this conflict, though, were clear, and they lay with neither the Boers nor the British, but with the indigenous people that each side dispossessed.

Talking of patriotism what humbug it is; it is a word which always commemorates a robbery. There isn't a foot of land in the world which doesn't represent the ousting and re-ousting of a long line of successive "owners," who each in turn, as "patriots" . . . defended it against the next gang of "robbers" who came to steal it and *did*—and became swelling-hearted patriots in *their* turn. And this Transvaal, now, is full of patriots, who by the help of God, who is always interested in these things, stole the land from the feeble blacks . . .[59]

·   ·   ·

"ABOUT THE time this reaches you we shall be cabling Susy and Jean to come over to England," Clemens happily wrote to Rogers from Port Elizabeth, South Africa, in late June.[60] His odyssey was approaching its homeward phase. A visit to the Kimberley diamond mines, some sightseeing in Cape Town, a final round of public appearances and private soirees, and finally, on July 15, the Clemenses (along with the ever-companionable Mr. Smythe) boarded the S.S. *Norman* for the sixteen-day passage northward to Southampton, England. They had set out on the tour from Elmira on July 14 the previous year. Counting the voyage from Southampton to America just before that, the three had been in transit for fourteen months. Utterly fatigued by the "slavery" of the lecture platform, Clemens nonetheless anticipated a round of speaking engagements in London before finding a cottage in some village near the city where he could spend six months writing his book about the tour in peaceful seclusion. His lecture receipts totaled somewhere between $20,000 and $25,000—satisfying, but well short of his $100,000 goal. He felt confident that the book would bring in the remainder. As he relaxed on board, the future seemed hopeful once again. Harper's had released *Personal Recollections of Joan of Arc* in May, with Mark Twain's name on the cover (though not on the title page). *Harper's Magazine* would begin serialization of *Tom Sawyer, Detective* in August, and would feature the novella in a new collection later in the year. Most satisfyingly, though, the five Clemenses would be reunited. The *Norman* docked at Southampton on July 31, and a day or two later, Livy cabled Katy Leary in Hartford to arrange passage to England for Susy and also for Jean, who was still in Elmira. Livy had delayed sending this instruction until the ship was safely in port, just to be sure she and the others would not be "at the bottom of the sea" when the cable reached home. "Susie & Jean sail from New York today, & a week hence we shall all be together again," Sam notified William Dean Howells on August 5.[61]

But on August 3, the eve of her departure for New York, Susy became feverish and begged for a delay. Katy called a doctor despite Susy's protests that she wanted her healer. The doctor pronounced the young woman overworked—though "work" was hardly the center of her life now. Katy Leary helped her from the Warners' to her old bed in the Clemens house, at her request. On August 4 Susan Crane informed the Clemenses by cable that there had been a delay; departure would now be on the 12th. At Southampton, Livy sprained an ankle—the first injury any of them had sustained over the fifty-three thousand miles. This postponed her search for a summer house for the family, but Clara located a temporary lodging in Guildford, a graceful 12th-century farming village southeast of London, where Lewis Carroll was living out his final years, and they moved in. As Livy's ankle healed, another cable from Susan Crane arrived. In this one she admitted that Susy was a little ill. Suddenly frantic with anxiety, the three packed their bags for an emergency departure home, and returned from Guildford to Southampton. Another telegram awaited them there: Susy's recovery (from what, it did not say) would be "long but certain." Sam elected to regard this as news that Susy was not in mortal peril, and decided to stay on in England. Livy and Clara boarded the S.S. *Paris*, bound for New York, on Saturday, August 15. On that same day, the doctor in Hartford reconsidered his diagnosis: the patient was suffering from meningitis. The rare but lethal infection had entered Susy's system as either bacteria or a virus; she may well have contracted it inside her family house. By now it had begun its work of swelling the meninges, the lining of the brain and spinal cord.

Sam waved his wife and middle daughter out of the harbor and returned to Guildford. He tossed and turned for four nights, blaming himself for this latest ambiguous crisis. It was his fault: if he had listened to his sister and helped discourage Annie Moffett from marrying Charles Warner, there would have been no bankruptcy, no need for this trip, no need to leave Susy behind. On the day after Livy's departure he wrote to her,

My heart was wrung yesterday. I could not tell you how deeply I loved you nor . . . how I pitied you in this awful trouble that my mistakes have brought upon you . . . I shall never forgive myself while the life is in me. If you find our poor little Susie in the state I seem to foresee, your dear head will be grayer when I see it next. (Be good and get well, Susy dear, don't break your mother's heart.)[62]

By that time Susy was beyond help. She was probably beyond help from the outset: antibiotics might have killed the infection; but penicillin was yet thirty-two years away. The Twichells hurried home from the Adirondacks to be at her side, and the Cranes arrived from Elmira, along with Jean. She became a wraith, pacing the rooms and halls of the Hartford house, raving and scribbling pages of half-coherent notes across forty-seven pages, in outsized handwriting. The notes are at once demented—she thought she was a Parisian mezzo-soprano named La Malibran, who'd died young more than half a century earlier—and Joycean in their allusiveness:

Say I will try not to doubt and I *will* obey my benefactress Mme. Malibran . . . Now go and *hold* this song. Nothing but indecision Go on Go on Yes does she bow her too white head? She must she must she must Yes my black Princess . . . Tell her to say— God bless the shadows as I bless the light . . . In me darkness must remain from everlasting to everlasting forever sometimes less painful darkness but darkness is the complement of light yes tell her to say she trusts you child of great darkness and light to me who can keep the darkness universal and free from sensual taint . . . The Universe is united *You* may not dissever greatnesses of the earth . . .[63]

When she heard the familiar bell tinkling down on Farmington Avenue, she would float to the window and intone, "Up go the trolley cars for Mark Twain's daughter. Down go the trolley cars for Mark Twain's daughter."[64] As her mother and sister steamed westward toward her, hopelessly out of reach, her father in England lay brooding about how "the calamity that comes is never the one we had prepared ourselves for."[65] On August 16, Susy came upon a gown of her mother's in a closet and kissed it, thinking it was Livy.[66] Then Susy lost her sight. She groped for things to touch; found Katy Leary's face with her hands, and screamed, "Mamma!," her last word.[67] She lapsed into unconsciousness an hour after that and never awoke. Two days later, at 7 p.m. on Tuesday, August 18, 1896, she died.

DR. RICE boarded the *Paris* at the quarantine stop in New York Harbor to tell Livy and Clara the news, but they had learned it the previous day, at sea. Walking to the ship's saloon to pick up the daily mail, Clara learned from a steward that the captain wanted to talk to her.

He handed me a newspaper with great headlines: "Mark Twain's eldest daughter dies of spinal meningitis." . . . [T]he world stood still. All sounds, all movements ceased. Susy was dead. How could I tell Mother? I went to her stateroom. Nothing was said. A deadly pallor spread over her face and then came a bursting cry, "I don't believe it!" And we never did believe it.[68]

Sam was standing in the dining room of the cottage at Guildford, his mind blank of thought, for a blessed interval, when the cable arrived: "Susy was peacefully released to-day."

"It is one of the mysteries of our nature," he observed years later, "that a man, all unprepared, can receive a thunder-stroke like that and live."[69]

With no chance of arriving home in time for the funeral in Elmira, Clemens stayed on alone in the Guildford house, his mind a garden of morbid rage and sorrow. He grieved that he could not say farewell to his daughter in her coffin, but there were coffins enough in Sam's imaginative visions. "I wish there were five of the coffins, side by side," he wrote to Livy; "out of my heart of hearts I wish it . . . How lovely is death; & how niggardly it is doled out . . ."[70]

"I eat—because you wish it; I go on living—because you wish it; I play billiards, and billiards, & billiards, till I am ready to drop—to keep from going mad with grief & with resentful thinkings."[71]

The absence of condolences from friends in America infuriated him; everything infuriated him, or tormented him. "All the circumstances of this death were pathetic," he wrote to long-time Hartford friend Henry C. Robinson: "—my brain is worn to rags rehearsing them."[72] Some of his friends hesitated because the alternative was excruciating. Howells relived the death of Winifred when he heard of it, he told Charles Warner.[73] He managed to reach out in gentle empathy in mid-September.

There is really nothing to say to you, poor souls, and yet I must write . . . to say that we suffer with you. As for the gentle creature who is gone, the universe is all a crazy blunder if she is not some where in conscious blessedness that knows and feels your love . . . You are parted from her a little longer, and that's all, and the joint life will go on when you meet on the old terms, but with the horror and pain gone forever.[74]

Sam answered his old friend with gratitude, but then added,

To me our loss is bitter, bitter, bitter. Then what must it be to my wife. It would bankrupt all vocabularies of all the languages to put it into words . . .[75]

He recalled the parting on the platform of July the previous year, with Susy waving in the glare of the electric lights.

One year, one month, & one week later, Livy & Clara had completed the circuit of the globe, arriving at Elmira at the same hour in the evening, by the same train & *in the same car*—& Susy was there to meet them—lying white & fair in her coffin in the house she was born in . . .

Will healing ever come, or life have value again?

And shall we see Susy? Without doubt! without *shadow* of doubt, if it can furnish opportunity to break our hearts again.[76]

These corrosive lamentations in letters and notebooks began a literature of grief for Susy that would spill from Samuel Clemens for the rest of his life.

44

Exile and Return

(1896–1900)

Susy was buried in Elmira in the Langdon plot. Livy, Clara, and Jean sailed back to England after the funeral along with Katy Leary. Jean regularly suffered from epileptic attacks now. The family found a small four-story brick house in Tedworth Square, a tiny pocket between King's Road and Royal Hospital Road in Chelsea, and there they burrowed in. Clemens kept the address off the envelopes of letters he sent, for fear the press would discover it. "It was a long time before anyone laughed in our household," Clara later wrote.

Father's passionate nature expressed itself in thunderous outbursts of bitterness shading into rugged grief. He walked the floor with quick steps . . .[1]

She added the acute observation, "there was no drawl in his speech now."[2]

Clara Clemens has been reductively remembered in literary history as the chief architect of Mark Twain's politically and emotionally neutered posthumous reputation: the nation's avuncular cracker-barrel sage. This is an accurate legacy, but it overlooks the incisiveness and eloquence that heightened her own observations of her father, as set down in her book. Susy was not the only poet among the daughters. "A Sunday in London looked like an array of misspent hours," Clara wrote of the autumn days in 1896.

Father would take Jean and me for a walk . . . into Regent's Park . . . [E]verywhere we met an atmosphere of world-loneliness. Poor women seated aimlessly and alone on benches . . . A stray cat, a stray leaf, a stray—Oh, everything looked adrift and unattended.[3]

It was on such days, Clara recalled, "that Father created the habit of vituperat-ing the human race."

What started as formless criticism grew into a sinister doctrine. There was no hope for the human race because no appreciable improvement was possible in any individual. Each one was presented with certain qualities which could not be altered.[4]

Man as Machine. As fatally flawed, eternally irreparable Machine.
    The Clemenses' incognito days did not last long, Sam found.

Our address discovered after three weeks of peaceful seclusion. Given to some re-porter by Chelsea librarian? But how did *he* know me?[5]

How would one know Mark Twain? From his ubiquitous photographic image, of course; but one may have had to do a double-take. The famous shock of hair and bushy eyebrows were nearly devoid of shading, now; the mustache wiry, less carefully trimmed. Pouches had formed under his eyes, and lines had etched themselves into his forehead and jawline. ("Wrinkles should merely show where the smiles have been," he'd written with pathetic insou-ciance in his notebook.)[6] He'd become an old man who had forgotten a few things, including the extent of his fame.

HARPER & BROTHERS had published *Personal Recollections of Joan of Arc* on May 1, 1896, some three months before Susy died, and the reviews began appearing almost immediately, allowing the possibility that Susy read some of them. They were generally not kind, except those that were kind to a fault. Lit-erary criticism for decades had lacked the diagnostic tools necessary to fully il-luminate Mark Twain's revisionist genius in such groundbreaking books as *The Innocents Abroad* and *Huckleberry Finn*. In the 1890s younger intellectuals such as Brander Matthews, a professor of dramatic literature at Columbia University, were integrating cultural and political standards in their reviews. Now, as Mark Twain's gifts declined, the critics were at last proficient enough to fully articulate his limitations. The novel's strongest sections, many review-ers agreed, were the fifteen chapters in Book Three that recount Joan's trials for heresy by a French religious court after her string of victories over the En-glish. This was perhaps a bittersweet compliment by Mark Twain's lights: the power of these chapters derives mostly from the translated Latin records of the trials, which the author followed scrupulously. Their very presence in the novel owed to Henry Mills Alden, the editor at *Harper's Weekly* who persuaded Mark Twain to expand his original intention to merely summarize them at the novel's end.
    The Boston *Literary World* scorched the novel for its anachronistic idioms such as the line that a French general "broke Joan all up" by swearing, and having a 15th-century judge tell a colleague to "Shut up in the devil's name,"

and it faulted Mark Twain for his inability "to write with that *naivete* of spirit so characteristic of all writers of the fifteenth century."[7] The Brooklyn *Eagle* similarly complained that "there is about the manner of the story a modern sentiment or feeling that seems entirely out of keeping with the spirit of Joan's time."[8] "Joan is a nice little American girl of the mid-nineteenth century," observed the New York *Bachelor of Arts,* adding that Mark Twain has turned "into a prosy, goody-goody writer of Sunday-school tales in his old age."[9]

Brander Matthews's opinion mattered particularly because of his high esteem for, and friendship with, Mark Twain. He had been among the few who'd plumbed beneath the surface "annoyances" of *Huckleberry Finn* back in 1885, celebrating the novel as a revolutionary triumph in psychological point of view. ("One of the most artistic things in the book . . . is the sober self-restraint with which Mr. Clemens lets Huck Finn set down, without any comment at all, scenes which would have afforded the ordinary writer for endless moral and political and sociological disquisition . . . In *Tom Sawyer* we saw Huckleberry Finn from the outside; in the present volume we see him from the inside.")[10] Clemens in turn respected Matthews despite having argued with him about copyright issues and having lampooned him mercilessly as one of the "professors" who overpraised the works of James Fenimore Cooper. Matthews would write the introductory essay for a collection of Mark Twain's stories and sketches published in 1899; Mark Twain would one day give a speech that consisted almost entirely in tonal variations on the name "Brander Matthews."

In an essay published in the May 28 edition of *Life,* Matthews let Mark Twain down as gently as he knew how. Mark Twain "was once a writer of comic copy," the critic noted, the faint praise nearly successful in covering up the damnation; and he genuflected once again to the "creative power" of *Huckleberry Finn.* But finally "Mark Twain as a historical novelist is not at his best," because by this last decade of the century, "the "historical novel is an outworn anachronism."[11]

Howells, balancing once again between friendship and principle, placed one foot upon each ice floe and tried for dear life to remain upright. His review in the May 1896, edition of *Harper's Weekly* began with a lengthy vaporizing defense of historical fiction in general and Mark Twain's two previous efforts in particular. Turning at last to the book at hand, he grudgingly conceded that *Joan of Arc* contained "a good many faults," including its unevenness, its failed "archaism," and its "outbursts of the nineteenth-century American in the armor of the fifteenth-century Frenchman." Despite all, he summed up, "the book has a vitalizing force."[12]

UNDAUNTED, MARK Twain noted in his journal on October 24, "Wrote the first chapter of the book today,"[13] the chronicle of his recent travels. He continued writing through the damp London winter and early spring of 1897. He wrote rapidly and grimly, often well into the night. Livy kept herself from staring at the walls by editing his pages as they issued—she'd lost interest in people, her own reading, nearly everything. The book that he was producing—its working title was "Round the World"—was to be undistinguished, merely competent. And yet in a certain way, it was the most important work he ever did—simply because it *was* work. Work was all that kept him motivated enough to meet each day, and the only discharge of his terrible, hell-tossed nights.

He roused himself in late November on behalf of the "stone blind and deaf, and formerly dumb"[14] young woman whom he, Howells, and Henry Rogers had met two years earlier in New York. In a letter to Rogers's second wife, Emilie Hart Rogers, he noted that Helen Keller* had recently passed the Harvard examination for admission to Radcliffe College, scoring a 90 as compared with the average of 78. Noting the young woman's limited finances, Clemens wrote, "It won't do for America to allow this marvelous child to retire from her studies because of poverty—If she can go on with them she will make a fame that will endure in history for centuries."[15] He implored Mrs. Rogers to "lay siege to your husband"[16] and encourage him to interest John D. and William Rockefeller to fund Helen's education. Rogers complied; Helen Keller graduated from Radcliffe College cum laude in 1904, en route to a career as one of the 20th century's most inspirational women. She died in 1964. Clemens's gesture was a bright moment in a dark season. He filled his notebook with lingering grief, and with notes for the great dark themes to come.

We are nothing but echoes. We have no thoughts of our own, no opinions of our own, we are but a compost heap made up of the decayed heredities, moral and physical.[17]

She was a poet—a poet whose song died unsung.[18]

Sometimes . . . her speech was rocket-like; I seem to see it go up and up and up, a soaring, streaming, climbing, stem of fire, and finally burst in the zenith and rain colored sparks all around.[19]

Of the demonstrably wise there are but two; those who commit suicide, and those who keep their reasoning faculties atrophied with drink.[20]

On April 13, he was able to enter a happier thought: "I finished my book today."[21] A month later—May 18—he entered a happier thought still: "Finished the book *again*. Addition of 30,000 words."[22] He'd worked almost robotically for six months on it (it was the first book he'd written without putting the manuscript aside for a period), and the finished product reflected his benumbed state—even after he deleted several passages directly commenting on his grief. His flat options for a title further betray his depression: he toyed with "Imitating the Equator," "Another Innocent Abroad," "The Latest," and

* Clemens consistently misspelled the name as "Kellar."

"The Surviving Innocent Abroad"; not until July did he decide on *Following the Equator* and its faintly redundant subtitle, *A Journey Around the World*. The book was largely a series of transpositions from his notebooks (even sometimes literally including pages torn from the notebook itself), laced with helpings of regional history taken from other authors, about thirty in all. Its narrative spine was a straightforward record of his lecture itinerary, mixing political observation and travelogue tidbits with roughly equal emphasis. He sent it to Frank Bliss at the American Publishing Company as soon as he'd finished the May revisions. Bliss cut the conclusions of several chapters, excising passages that bored him—audacities his late father never would have dared. If Mark Twain noticed, he let it go. Bliss packaged the book handsomely, with a colorful African elephant on the cover and several photographs among its nearly two hundred illustrations, a first for a book by Mark Twain. He published it in mid-November, with Chatto & Windus (using a separately revised text) issuing it as *More Tramps Abroad* at around the same time. The reviews were respectful, and the sales went far toward restoring the balance of Mark Twain's bankruptcy debt. At about the same time, Harper & Brothers brought out the collection of short stories and sketches, *Tom Sawyer Abroad; Tom Sawyer, Detective and Other Stories*.

THROUGH THE early months of 1897, Samuel Clemens tried his best to preserve his obscurity in London, but it was a losing battle. Mark Twain may no longer have been interested in the world, but the world was interested in Mark Twain. Rumors about him floated, including the lurid one that he and his family were destitute. The New York *Herald* took this one seriously enough to launch a charity fund in his name; publisher James Gordon Bennett and the capitalist Andrew Carnegie each chipped in a thousand dollars. On the advice of Rogers, who continued as his financial manager and de facto literary agent, Clemens wrote to the newspaper asking it to close the fund, although the idea had its appeal for him. The rumor drew the attention of a cousin of his, a doctor named James Ross Clemens, who was living in London. Dr. Clemens visited his famous relative, whom he'd not met. The two hit it off famously, but when the doctor fell seriously ill while at Tedworth Square, the London papers noted the address and mistook the name for that of Sam. A new rumor arose: Mark Twain was near death. In early June, a young reporter from the New York *Journal*, named Frank Marshall White, knocked on Clemens's door and guilelessly showed Sam a pair of cablegrammed instructions from his editor. The first read:

If Mark Twain dying in poverty, in London, send 500 words.[23]

The second:

If Mark Twain has died in poverty send 1000 words.[24]

Clemens explained the misidentification and assured White, as he recalled it, that his cousin had recovered. "The report of my illness grew out of his illness; the report of my death was an exaggeration."[25] The literal-minded young man handed in the quote exactly as his source had instructed, and within a day or so people around the world were repeating the key line—"the report of my death was an exaggeration"—to one another, and realizing how long it had been since they'd had a jolt of Mark Twain's humor (if "humor" it was). The remark, which in its variations remains one of the two or three most universally associated with him, restored him to international attention.

Not that he was much interested in international attention. He did agree to supply an American newspaper syndicate with coverage of Queen Victoria's Diamond Jubilee on June 22, the great processional ceremony celebrating her sixtieth year on the throne, and attracted as much attention from his special seat in the Strand as the parade. But a few weeks later, in mid-July, after minor eye surgery for Livy, the Clemens family fled London, bound for Vienna after a summer stay in Switzerland. Not even an offer of fifty thousand dollars from Pond to lecture in America that autumn could dissuade them from continuing their exile. A further incentive, besides seclusion, was the renowned tutor Theodor Leschetizky, a central figure in the Viennese piano world, student of a protégé of Beethoven at ten, mentor to Paderewski; Clara longed to study with him.

Joined by Susan Crane, Charley Langdon's daughter Julie, and Ernst Koppe, a former Berlin waiter who had become Mrs. Crane's caretaker, they settled in at Villa Buhlegg, Weggis, on Lake Lucerne—terms, six franks ($1.20) per day per person, "rent and food included, also candles and two lamps."[26] On August 18, the anniversary of Susy's death, "Livy went away to be alone. She took the steamer and spent the day solitary in an inn in an unknown town up the lake."[27] There she reread Susy's letters to her. It is the first known time that Livy chose seclusion in an emotional time over her husband's company. Sam found a spot under some trees on the side of a mountain and composed an allegorical lament for his daughter. Humidly ornate, painfully earnest in the old Thomas Moore–Robert Burns tradition, "In Memoriam" unwittingly echoes the callow "Love Concealed" and "Separation" published by the young "Rambler" forty-four years earlier in the pages of the Hannibal *Daily Journal.*

> In a fair valley—oh, how long ago, how long ago!
> Where all the broad expanse was clothed in vines
> And fruitful fields and meadows starred with flowers . . .
>   Hard by, apart, a temple stood . . .
> [And] in the temple's inmost place a spirit dwelt,
> Made all of light! . . .[28]

THIS GLOOMY interlude aside, the two months at Weggis marked a return of his writing energies. Working nine hours a day, sometimes seven days a week, he produced notes and drafts for the later manuscripts on the theme of Satan's intervention in the world. "Letters to Satan" is a brief, fairly primitive dress rehearsal of the organizing idea: a deputy of Satan's visits Earth and reports back to the boss on a variety of topical phenomena, such as the telephone and organized tours. It was not published until after Sam's death. He quickly moved to the more focused cluster of drafts that, over several years, reworked the device of Satan's return—first as "The Chronicles of Young Satan," written in 1899 and revised (eventually with Paine's meddlesome posthumous help) into what Paine published as *The Mysterious Stranger, a Romance* in 1916.

Satan had fascinated Clemens since his Presbyterian boyhood, when he'd tricked the pious Jane into defending him as a victim of bad luck. Now he reentered the forefront of the author's imagination, as a plausible critic of humanity. "He had but one term for . . . 'the little stinking human race, with its little stinking kings and popes and bishops and prostitutes and peddlers,' " he wrote, sketching out the viewpoint that his newly favorite character would later express. And: "A person (Satan) who for untold centuries has maintained the imposing position of spiritual head of 4/5 of the human race, and political head of the whole of it, must be granted the possession of executive abilities of the highest order."[29] Satan as antihero (or perhaps suprahero), as Christ's dark twin, made an ideal symbol for his favorite metaphysical themes of the divided self and the blurred boundaries between Good and Evil.

The books he was reading now and in the next few years renewed his confidence in exploring these themes. Reconsidering Robert Louis Stevenson's *Dr. Jekyll and Mr. Hyde,* published in 1886, he recognized an extension of his own dwarf-surrogate as alternate conscience from "Facts Concerning the Recent Carnival of Crime in Connecticut." His twenty-one-year-old work "was an attempt to account for our seeming *duality*—the presence in us of another *person;* not a slave of ours, but . . . with a character distinctly its own," he remarked, before conceding that Stevenson's novel got nearer the heart of it: "J. and H. were the dual persons in one body, quite distinct in nature and character and presumably each *with a conscience of his own.*"[30] Recent inquiries conducted in Baltimore and France, he now believed, proved both Stevenson's and his ideas insufficient, in that the cases "show that the two persons in a man have no command over each other . . . [They] do not even *know* each other and . . . have never even suspected one another's existence . . ."[31]

In January 1897 he proposed a further extension, leavened by his reading of William James's massive *Principles of Psychology,* which drew on both philosophical and scientific precepts in its pre-Freudian effort to construct a theory of consciousness. James strengthened Mark Twain's confidence in the idea of mind cure *as* a science; he also took from the book a new conviction in the substantiality of "realities" embodied in hypnosis and dreams. (James's work was "pre-Freudian" only in that Freud had not yet published in that area. In 1897, in Vienna, he was just then immersed in his own dream analysis, excited by the "intellectual beauty" of probing the unconscious and its power.)

Clemens went on:

To this arrangement I wish to add this detail—that we have a spiritualized self which can detach itself and go wandering off upon affairs of its own . . . I am not acquainted with my double, my partner in duality . . . but I *am* acquainted (dimly) with my spiritualized self and I know that it and I are one, because we have common memory . . .[32]

This other "self" was Samuel Clemens's "dream self," the self that gamboled with his Platonic Sweetheart—his ordinary body and mind "freed from clogging flesh and become a spiritualized body and mind," with the powers of both enlarged.

Waking I move slowly; but in my dreams my unhampered spiritualized body flies to the ends of the earth in a millionth of a second. Seems to—and I believe, *does* . . .

I do actually make immense excursions in my spiritualized person. I go into awful dangers . . . I go to unnamable places, I do unprincipled things; and every vision is vivid, every sensation—physical as well as moral—is *real.*[33]

It is impossible not to sense the ecstasy that radiates through these sentences. Science notwithstanding, they signal a regathering in Samuel Clemens. (Justin Kaplan has conjectured, arrestingly, that "by turning his dream life into a literary problem—into *work*—he saved himself from madness."[34]) His mind had always been voracious to absorb *process,* whether it involved the skills of typesetting; the contours of the Mississippi River; women's fashions and household design; the arcana of mining; the technology and financial structure of book publishing; the workings of Kaolatype or the Paige machine; the class system of medieval Europe; the awful German language; a hundred other areas of specialized expertise. Now that voracity began to extricate itself from the suffocating compost of grief that had formed upon the death of Susy. Clemens would never put that grief to rest, but in allowing his curiosity to be drawn toward that ultimate sphere, the human mind and its mysteries, he forestalled creative death. Reinforced by his interest in the new political currents roiling the world, the nation-sized tests of the weak against the strong, the ethnic scapegoat against the ethnic oppressor, this passion fueled his return to purposeful work through the remainder of his life.

MARK TWAIN began three other significant manuscripts in his fertile weeks at Weggis. None of these was published for decades following his death; two were abandoned, and the third remained in the form of extended notes. Yet each represents an important act of memory and imagination. All are rooted in his boyhood hometown. The most striking of these is the stupendous work of tabulated early memory that he called "Villagers 1840–3." "Villagers" is a kind of city directory of Hannibal in those years, culled from forty-four-year-old information stored in the mind of Samuel Clemens. Faintly presaging *Spoon River Anthology* in its survey of characters in a community, but even darker in its preoccupations—the "heavenly" town now seen as a little slice of Hell—it comprises thumbnail sketches of more than a hundred Hannibal people. These include the Clemens family itself, which in a transparent and useless gesture toward privacy (Sam had no intention of publishing the list) he renamed as "Carpenter." The often squalid lives and grim fates of these townsfolk are sometimes rendered in only a few words (*"Jim Wolf.* The practical jokes. Died."[35] *"Clint Levering* drowned. His less fortunate brother lived to have a family and be rich and respected."[36]). Other lives (and calamities) are more fully fleshed. Physical characteristics were noted, and temperaments, and occupations, and styles (Sam Raymond "[a]lways affected fine city language, and said 'Toosday.' "[37]), and destinies (a sleigh overturned and Mary Moss's "thigh was broken; it was badly set. She got well with a terrible limp, and forever after stayed in the house and produced children"[38]).

The longest single sketch in "Villagers" is the last one, covering "Oscar Carpenter" (Orion). Adding credence to the theory that the notes were intended as references to future fiction projects, Mark Twain shifted immediately after this entry (on August 4) to the second related work: the beginning of "Hellfire Hotchkiss." This novel fragment features "Oscar" as a feminized boy of Dawson's Landing, who is saved from certain death on an ice floe in the river by the hard-charging title character, a beautiful Menkenesque tomboy given to riding around on a black horse with a life preserver at her side, and breaking up lethal assaults perpetrated by the "Stover" brothers (Ed and Dick Hyde) with her trusty baseball bat. "Pudd'nhead Wilson says Hellfire Hotchkiss is the only genuwyne male man in this town and [Oscar] Carpenter's the only genuwyne female girl,"[39] Mark Twain has an onlooker remark helpfully. Given this sex-role reversal, and given that the author shifts some of his own boyhood experiences to "Oscar" (the Cadets of Temperance episode, for instance), and given the shadow of Susy at the edges of Hellfire's world-conquering prowess, it seems a pity that Clemens was not able to show this manuscript to Freud when he reached Vienna.

The third and longest fragment is "Tom Sawyer's Conspiracy." Abandoned after ten chapters and nearly thirty thousand words, it is a promising but overheated effort to reanimate Mark Twain's most replenishing trio of characters. Promising, because settling back into Huck's rich narrative vernacular once again released all sorts of instincts in Mark Twain for layered storytelling unavailable in the stiff, self-conscious exposition that permeated "Hellfire." Here is an older, post–Civil War Huck looking back. Huck (to his author's credit) has not transcended his narrowness of time and place and become a mouthpiece for racial enlightenment—he slings the word "nigger" with far more abandon than in the novel under his name. Exactly through his limited prism, the reader is able to see Jim's own stunted sense of self and his unending victimization with heightened clarity and moral force. (Once again,

Jim is at the mercy of an outraged mob, his fate in the hands of his young white friends.) And "overheated," in that Mark Twain once again made Tom Sawyer the emissary of pulp-fiction plot devices that smother the deeper explorations in a riot of detective intrigue, murder solving, and shenanigans. The novel-that-might-have-been, had Mark Twain enjoyed the luxury of another eight-year cycle of pause, revision, and reconsideration, is likely a loss to American literature.

"I WOULD as soon spend my life in Weggis as anywhere in the geography," Clemens jotted in September 1897,[40] but he stuck to the family plan, and by the end of the month the party was ensconced in the Viennese Hotel Metropole, where seclusion proved out of the question. Hapsburg royalty glittered around them. In the hotel dining room on October 3, they observed, at the next table, an entourage that included Princess Charlotte, gossipy daughter of Victoria (the Dowager Empress Frederick) and granddaughter of Queen Victoria, and a few assorted princes. "Good-looking people," Mark Twain noted. "They *all* smoke."[41]

Clara arranged to meet the tutor Leschetizky even before her bags were unpacked. Papa drove his daughter to the appointment across the city in a two-horse victoria; Clara wanted to hide her acute nervousness from him, "so I started him on the human race,"[42] and the miles melted away. At the master's house, Leschetizky, a tiny, bland-looking old man, asked Clara to play a short piece on the piano, and then showered Sam in German with a long list of Clara's technical shortcomings, but agreed to take her on anyway. Clara soon met another of Leschetizky's pupils, the handsome young Russian-Jewish pianist and orchestral conductor Ossip Gabrilowitsch. Ossip was nineteen, four years younger than Clara, but dazzlingly talented and deeply connected to the musical world: among his close friends was the thirty-seven-year-old Gustav Mahler. Clara and Ossip soon commenced a tempestuous romance; ten years later, they would marry.

IN VIENNA, where he and the family stayed for twenty prolific months, Mark Twain had gravitated yet again to a vortex of historic transformation. The Austrian capital in the late 1890s was at once a world center of art, thought, and café-society elegance—and a post-Dreyfus central battlefield on which the "Jewish question" smoldered toward conflagration. Dvořák was in the city; and the teenaged Schoenberg, not yet dreaming his twelve-tone dreams; and Mahler, directing the Vienna Court Opera; and Freud; and such blinding new artists of the Vienna Secession as Gustav Klimt and Maximilian Kurzweil. Also present was the reactionary genius and radical orchestral composer Anton Bruckner, heir to Wagner's anti-Jewish nativism. The anti-Semite Karl Lueger was elected mayor in the year the Clemenses arrived; Christian socialism was noisily ascendant, threatening the 175,000 Jews who lived in the city and supplied much of its cultural elite. Stirring times lay ahead.

None of the turmoil was immediately apparent, as Vienna showed its creamy surface to the world-famous literary artist Mark Twain. The city's elite flowed toward him. Dukes, barons, princes, and newspaperwomen visited the Clemenses' corner suite in the Metropole, politely adhering to the post–5 p.m. schedule the family had set. Clara recalled that the drawing room came to be known as "the second U.S. Embassy."[43] Sam conducted one interview (the reporter was male) while lounging in bed, to Livy's shock. Sam liked it, and the bed soon became his second office. He was photographed and pointed out and banqueted and invited to speak at opulent charity events. His love of attention resurfaced; he preened and hobnobbed and smiled to those who recognized him on the Ringstrasse. He sat at a concert in the box of Johann Strauss at the Waltz King's invitation. Clara was fascinated by "the life-giving quality of ginger" of the glamorous Viennese women, recalling that when one of them entered a room the air seemed full of little broken dishes.[44] Sam was more interested in the fact that these titled ladies smoked pipes. Some of them—Freud may also have noticed this—even puffed on large cigars.

AS PARLIAMENTARY capital of the Austro-Hungarian empire with its nineteen fractious ethnic states, political Vienna trembled with the same pre-revolutionary currents as the trouble spots of the global British Empire, but with the added shock wave of anti-Semitism. Mark Twain found himself attacked by the ultra-right-wing press, which detected something a little fishy in that Old Testament first name of his, "Samuel." He was far from intimidated—he'd cut his teeth on newspaper feuds in Virginia City. In the autumn of 1897, Sam visited the marbled Lower House of the legislature several times. What he saw there, and what he failed to see, echoed his visit to the Senate chamber in Washington in 1854. Back then, the teenaged Sam had sketched vivid word-pictures of the lawmakers as they debated and declaimed, without grasping the full implications of the subject before them: a legislative act that would hasten the onset of the Civil War. Now, forty-three years later, he again composed a brilliantly detailed tragicomic chronicle of legislators in an uproar, again without grasping—as who could?—that he was witness to the chrysalis of a great war. On October 28 and 29, from his perch in the gallery, he watched an astonishing twelve-hour filibuster by the Moravian socialist Otto Lecher, delivered over a stream of wild shouted insults and bangings of desk boards from right-wing German nationalists. Lecher was stumping for a seemingly marginal rule change, to allow Czech civil service workers the right to speak their own language on the job. In fact, as everyone understood, the issue was whether ethnic minorities (read: Jews) deserved tolerance. Lecher's effort temporarily forestalled defeat of the language proposal; but a month later the factions tore into one another again over the same issue, and this time things ended in mass fisticuffs on the floor, a swarming of the chamber by sixty policemen, rioting in the streets, and a collapse of the parliamentary government.

"Stirring Times in Austria" was published in *Harper's New Monthly Magazine* in March 1898, and remains one of Mark Twain's virtuoso feats of eyewitness reportage, despite its understandable absence of prophetic insight. "They are . . . earnest, sincere, devoted [men]," he wrote of the battling ideologues of the House, "and they hate the Jews." [45] Later, describing the violence that spread outward from the chamber into cities and towns, he observed that "in some cases the Germans [were] the rioters, in others the Czechs—and in all cases the Jew had to roast, no matter which side he was on." [46] Mark Twain was virtually alone among journalists in his reportage of Jewish Europeans as caught in the pincers of rising nationalist antagonisms. The larger import of those antagonisms—as paranoia took hold among heads of state and armed mobilization spread through Europe—would not fully reveal itself for another sixteen years.

ON THE morning of December 11, far away from the turmoil and the glitter, Orion Clemens arose at six, his usual time, and descended the stairs of his small Keokuk house to build a fire. Mollie stirred awake upstairs. Orion sat down at the kitchen table and wrote out some notes for a court case. Molly waited for his rap on the ceiling, their signal that the fire had warmed the room enough for her to come down. The rap did not come. She gave the floor a rap of her own. No response. She hurried downstairs and found her husband upright, but with his head slumped forward and his arms dangling. He was seventy-two.

"We all grieve for you; our sympathy goes out to you from experienced hearts; & with it our love," Sam wrote to Mollie, ". . . & for Orion I rejoice. He has received life's best gift." [47] Orion's remains were taken to Hannibal, and he was buried at Mount Olivet Cemetery alongside Marshall, Jane, and Henry Clemens.

AS THE March issue of *Harper's* circulated among its readers—on February 11, 1898—Henry Rogers's secretary Katharine Harrison mailed a letter to Samuel Clemens with some spectacular news. "I wish I could shout it across the water to you," the Sphinx gushed, "so that you would get it ten days ahead of this letter, but I'm afraid my lungs are not strong enough." [48] (A few businessmen in New York no doubt would have been astounded to learn she could speak at all.) The news was that Clemens's bankruptcy debt was all but paid in full. Henry Rogers had managed the Clemens finances masterfully. In addition to facing down the hard-line creditors and rejecting their demands for immediate payments, Rogers had advised Sam well in his dealings with his publishers; his investments of Clemens's money, infrequent but always prudent, had paid well, with one of them netting a $16,000 profit. Most of the old Webster & Company debts had been settled by early in the year, and in February even the Scroogish Mount Morris Bank had agreed to a compromise settlement. Sam and Livy had seen the good news coming since January, as

Rogers and Miss Harrison kept them apprised of the creditor payoffs. "I have abundant peace of mind again," Clemens wrote his benefactor on January 20, "—no sense of burden. Work is become a pleasure again . . ."[49] The continued sale of his collected works had been assured in 1896, when Harper's began issuing volumes for what would become the Uniform Edition. (The bulk of these volumes would be stalled until 1904, when Henry Rogers finally retrieved Mark Twain's remaining copyrights on the books published between 1869 and 1879 from the American Publishing Company.)

In March, Clemens reported that "Mrs. Clemens has been reading the creditors' letters over and over again . . . and says this is the only really happy day she has had since Susy died."[50] At the end of that year, Livy calculated that the family was not only solvent again, but flush: the house and furniture in Hartford had not been sacrificed; Mark Twain's British and American copyrights were good for $200,000, and the Clemens bank account stood at $107,000. Mark Twain's achievement was world news. The press compared him to his old bête noire Sir Walter Scott, who had similarly refused to accept bankruptcy after a depression wiped out his printing firm in 1825, and wrote to pay off his debts until his death in 1832.

Clemens had learned a thing or two about investments. He would never again take leave of his senses on a harebrained scheme like a machine that supposedly set type like a human being. No: the next harebrained scheme involved a machine that would design patterns in textiles automatically. "I've landed a big fish to-day," he exulted to Rogers, once again channeling Colonel Sellers, in a facts-and-figures-laden letter in mid-March that consumed him for three days in the writing.[51] For a mere $1,500,000 investment . . . It took a few weeks, but Rogers eventually managed to talk Clemens down from this particular ledge.

(In this case, though, the inventor, a young Pole named Jan Szczepanik, was no ineffectual dreamer. Szczepanik's companion invention—a machine that stored and disgorged the patterns to be followed by textile looms—contained paradigm elements of the computer. A few years earlier he'd patented a device that had Clemens salivating, but the Paris exhibition had already cornered it. This was the "telelectroscope," the evolutionary ancestor of television.)

Vienna's warm embrace of Mark Twain chilled and slackened in the spring of 1898, when some stirring times in Havana Harbor ignited a recklessly conceived war between America and Spain. The mysterious explosion on February 15 of the battleship *Maine*, symbol of U.S. solidarity with the Cuban rebels, fanned war fever in the Hearst and Pulitzer newspapers and others of the "yellow" press to levels beyond the control of President McKinley. A "Peace Appeal to Labor," signed by William Dean Howells and others, ran in the New York *Post* on April 17; while generally laughed at, it was the genesis of a movement. The Spanish government monitored the hysteria, figured that it might as well get the first lick in, and declared hostilities. Soon

Lieutenant Colonel Theodore Roosevelt was a world media star for his exploits at the head of the Rough Riders (he wrote a best-seller about it the following year); the Spanish army withered under U.S. shock and awe, and Europe had a reason to fear a huge new player in the empire game. The Clemenses found themselves coolly interrogated by Viennese friends who wondered how long it would be before America annexed Cuba and then went shopping for Spain's remaining territories in the far Pacific.

Clemens did not believe anything like that could happen. He saw the war initially as a righteous American mission to liberate the Cuban people from a distant tyrant that had sought to quell dissent by breaking up the population into a latticework of camps, where death estimates ran as high as four hundred thousand. Empire? That was an Old World value, preposterous as a knight on a bicycle. "I have never enjoyed a war . . . as I am enjoying this one," he wrote in June to Joe Twichell, whose son David had enlisted in the army in defense of Cuba. "For this is the worthiest one that was ever fought, so far as my knowledge goes. It is a worthy thing to fight for one's own freedom; it is another sight finer to fight for another man's. And I think this is the first time it has been done." [52]

The war was over in four months, Spain's infantry shot to pieces, her fleet decimated by Commodore Dewey's warships. Under the Treaty of Paris, signed on December 10, Spain agreed to evacuate Cuba and leave the island an American protectorate en route to independence. But America's victory went beyond liberation. Puerto Rico, Guam, and the Philippine archipelago now belonged to the United States. (Hawaii had been quietly annexed during the war.) America was a fledgling empire. Clemens was shocked. "When the United States sent word to Spain that the Cuban atrocities must end she occupied the highest moral position ever taken by a nation since the Almighty made the earth," he told Paine years later. "But when she snatched the Philippines she stained the flag." [53]

IF HOWELLS was right—that Mark Twain "wrote as he thought" [54]—then Mark Twain was thinking very fast these days, and balefully. In April 1898, he commenced "What Is Man?" a Socratic dialogue for expressing the view of Man as a machine, and a self-interested one at that. He revised the manuscript until 1904, adding in an argument for training Man against these impulses. The slim manuscript was not printed until 1906, after Livy's death, and only in a limited private edition without his name, which Paine was kind enough to add in a profitable essay collection seven years after Mark Twain's own demise. He also began "The Great Dark" (the title is Bernard DeVoto's), a self-referencing and truly bleak piece of work never finished but published after his death, which concerns the fate of a man named Jessie Edwards. Edwards playfully shows his wife and two daughters the tiny life in a drop of water through a microscope one day, then falls asleep and finds himself on a ship in a nighttime storm-tossed sea—that very same water drop. He begs the "Superintendent of Dreams" to let him awaken from this nightmare and learns that he *is* awake; this unending voyage is his life, and the pleasant household of his memory is but a dream. Sam's metaphor was doubtless reinforced by the essay he was drafting at the same time: "My Debut as a Literary Person," recounting his meeting in Hawaii with the sea-ridden survivors of the *Hornet*.

In late July he composed "Concerning the Jews," a well-intentioned attempt to clarify his attitudes on that subject that succeeded mainly in revealing his naïveté about Jewish culture and history. The essay includes one of his more famous aphorisms—"I am quite sure that (bar one)* I have no race prejudices, and I think I have no color prejudices nor caste prejudices nor creed prejudices. All that I care to know is that a man is a human being—that is enough for me; he can't be any worse."[55] Yet in his very attempt to extol the race in question, he ratified the most inflammatory pretext for resentment of it: the Jew as money-getter.

I am persuaded that . . . nine-tenths of the hostility to the Jew comes from the average Christian's inability to compete successfully with the average Jew in business—in either straight business or the questionable sort.[56]

Given that the "average Jew" in these times was a desperate refugee from economic hard times, foraging the world for a place to earn sustenance, his point unintentionally reinforced a key pretext for Semitic hatred.

Philosophy, politics, and dreams: these formed the borders of his imaginative consciousness. It was in August 1898 that he wrote "My Platonic Sweetheart," the phantasmic tone poem concerning his unnamed dream angel Laura Wright. A notebook entry, atypical in its erotic frankness, explores the only overtly sexual dream that he ever recorded. Its subject was a "negress," and perhaps represented fantasies that originated in the Quarles farm days.

. . . I was suddenly in the presence of a negro wench who was sitting in grassy open country . . . She was very vivid to me—round black face, shiny black eyes, thick lips . . . She was about 22, and plump . . . and good-natured and not at all bad-looking. She had but one garment on—a coarse tow-linen shirt . . . She made a disgusting proposition to me. Although it was disgusting . . . it seemed quite natural that it should come from her . . . I merely made a chaffing remark, brushing aside the matter . . .

"It was not a dream—it all *happened*," he insisted in his notebook. "I was actually there in person—in my spiritualized condition . . . dead or alive she is a *reality;* she exists and she was *there*."[57]

In his dreams.

IN SEPTEMBER 1898, Empress Elizabeth of Austria was assassinated in Geneva by an Italian anarchist. "I am living in the midst of world-history again," Clemens observed to Twichell.[58] Mark Twain wrote on.

* *The American Indian,* extrapolating from Mark Twain's writings on the subject.

"I have no special regard for Satan," Mark Twain had written in "Concerning the Jews," "but I can at least claim that I have no prejudice against him . . . we never hear *his* side."[59] Mark Twain seemed bent on rectifying that imbalance. As the year passed into autumn, he turned from "The Great Dark" to two more variations on the theme of Satanic visitation. The first of these was "Schoolhouse Hill," a tale of the appearance in "Petersburg" of a "miraculous boy" who turns out to be the son of the Devil. Far from evil, "Forty-four," as he is known, announces that he has come to cleanse the world of sin, his father's legacy. Mark Twain's extensive notes show that he intended to have "Forty-four" establish a new church with the goal of eradicating hypocrisy and the corrupted Moral Sense, and then fall in love, evidently with Hellfire Hotchkiss. But after six chapters, the author thought of a better way to tell his tale and abandoned that one.

"The Man That Corrupted Hadleyburg" is Mark Twain's late-life masterpiece. He wrote it rapidly and compactly in December 1898, and *Harper's* published it a year later, as a novella of 17,500 words. Ingeniously plotted beyond any of his previous fiction, it efficiently unifies the field of his concerns for corrupt, prideful, deceitful, avaricious, deterministic Man. Its narrative is among the most familiar under his name: through the tidy, self-satisfied village of Hadleyburg, "the most honest and upright town in all the region,"[60] passes a stranger—not Satan, in this case; not overtly, at least—whom the town somehow manages to offend. The stranger devises a revenge plan: he will humiliate Hadleyburg by exposing the town's susceptibility to corruption. He returns there with a sack supposedly filled with gold to be given to the man (nonexistent) who, the stranger tells the bank cashier's wife, saved his life by giving him twenty dollars on his last trip through. The test of the claimant's authenticity, the stranger explains to the woman, will be his ability to repeat a remark he made to the stranger while giving him the handout. The stranger sees to it that the "remark" reaches each of the town's nineteen leading citizens in a sealed envelope. The resulting chain of duplicity, opportunism, self-corruption, and dashed hopes (the "gold" in the sack turns out to be lead slugs) consummates a formally perfect fable and a withering summation of mankind.

ONE BY one, the supporting actors in the epic drama of Samuel Clemens's life continued to withdraw from the stage—as they had been withdrawing since his early childhood. In March, word reached him that his old Washoe friend and rival Dan De Quille (William Wright) had died at sixty-eight in West Liberty, Iowa. He'd returned to Virginia City after publication of *The Big Bonanza,* survived a fire that leveled most of the mountainside boomtown and the folding of the *Territorial Enterprise* in 1893, but never fulfilled his early promise or his dreams. A literary collection of his, *The Fighting Horse of the Stanislaus,* finally got published in 1990.

December 8, 1898, saw the passing of Mother Bear. Mary Fairbanks died at seventy in Providence, Rhode Island. Her fortunes had slipped in the years following her protégé's rise to fame: in 1879, her husband Abel declared bankruptcy after a Twainish spell of ill-chosen investments. The couple had moved to Omaha and then to Newton, Massachusetts. Abel had died four years earlier.

The end of the year found Samuel Clemens turning his thoughts back to the old friends who still remained—Howells and Twichell foremost among them—and to the idea of coming back home. He and the family were living splendidly in Vienna, having left the Metropole in May 1898 for a stay at a villa in Vienna Woods before taking apartments in the elegant Hotel Krantz on Neuer Markt. The stream of royalty, intellectuals, and reporters had not diminished, and the reporters who could not get to him in person queried him by mail. Petitioned from London for his opinion on the Russian czar's proposal for world disarmament, Mark Twain did not hesitate: "The Czar is ready to disarm," he answered; "I am ready to disarm. Collect the *others,* it should not be much of a task now." [61] Yet underneath the surface glamour beat the heart of an aging man yearning once more to move.

"Our project is to go home next autumn if we find we can afford to live in New York," [62] he told Howells. A few months later, reading an installment of Howells's new novel, *Their Silver Wedding Journey,* in *Harper's,* Clemens detected a Wordsworthian strain: "I seem to get furtive & fleeting glimpses which I take to be the weariness & indolence of age; indifference to sights & things once brisk with interest; tasteless stale stuff which used to be champagne . . ." [63] He quickly added, "But maybe that is your art," [64] although the unwritten corollary to that thought was, ". . . and maybe not." He could have been describing himself—but then, these two old friends had much to recognize in each other. Both had suffered bereavements of a beloved daughter; both viewed the world with increasing disgust—Howells's Utopian optimism having long since receded before a sense of cultural emptiness and what he called "the subtle fiend of advertising." [65] In the 1890s, Howells joined Mark Twain in reaching back into his boyhood, and in inventorying his dream life (*The Shadow of a Dream,* "True, I Talk of Dreams"). And both were getting old. In February the portly Howells had suffered the indignity of struggling to get a pair of rubbers on his feet after dining with Rudyard Kipling, who dropped to one knee to help.

Like Clemens, Howells had enjoyed a productive decade. In the 1890s, as his biographer Kenneth Lynn notes,[66] he produced ten novels, three novellas, two children's books, four volumes of memoirs, and twelve plays, in addition to a wide array of criticism, sketches, and social essays. At the same time, he quietly endured a drumroll of criticism hostile to his social radicalism that coexisted, infuriatingly, with the growing perception that he was fatally *suburban* in his literary tastes. Henry James, who had benefited from Howells's esteem and championing, emitted a large groan at his sponsor's new magazine position:

But what, my dear Howells, is the *Cosmopolitan*—and why—oh, why (let me be not odious!) are you hanging again round your neck the chain and emblems of bondage? . . .[67]

Helen Gurley Brown herself would never draw that caliber of artillery fire.

As the 19th century approached its close, Clemens and Howells, who together had done so much to define it in letters, began to recognize anew the rare value of their friendship and the lightness it brought to each of them. "You are the greatest man of your sort that ever lived, and there is no use saying anything else," Howells had blurted in a letter several months earlier;[68] and, a year after that, "I want to get a chance somehow to write a paper about you, and set myself before posterity as a friend who valued you aright in your own time."[69] Clemens returned the affection in his inimitable way. ". . . I am glad you have corralled Howells," he wrote to James Pond, on learning that Howells had retained the agent for a lecture tour. "He's a most sinful man, and I always knew God would send him to the platform if he didn't behave."[70]

COMFORT AND celebrityhood aside, reasons for the Clemenses to remain in Vienna were rapidly evaporating. The doctors there were helpless to slow the symptoms of Jean's epilepsy. Clara had given up her piano tutelage under Leschetizky shortly after the family moved into the Krantz. Her hands were simply too small to cover the octaves required for true preeminence in the concert world. She had an exceptional voice, though, and now planned for a career as a concert singer.

An intriguing doctor named Heinrick Kellgren was reputed to produce miracles by a process known as "Swedish Movement Therapy" in Sanna, Sweden. New York could offer many distinguished voice teachers. It was time for the Clemenses' European exile to wind down, and in May 1899, the long meandering homeward trek began. Among Mark Twain's last acts in Vienna was a courtesy visit to Franz Josef, whose long rule as emperor would extend through the opening years of World War I, triggered partly by the assassination of his nephew, the Archduke Ferdinand. The interview apparently went well; Mark Twain proposed to the emperor a plan to eliminate the human race by withdrawing the oxygen from the air for a couple of minutes, and said he thought that Jan Szczepanik could handle the details.

A crowd followed the family to the railroad station. Their itinerary took them through Prague, then Cologne, and then to London, where Mark Twain allowed himself to be lionized for a few days. They arrived at Sanna in early July, where Kellgren's treatments revitalized Jean enough that her parents returned with her to London to check her in at the movement's institute there. The family remained with her in London for another full year. Finally, on October 6, 1900, Samuel Clemens, Olivia, Clara, Jean, and Katy Leary stepped aboard the steamship *Minnehaha* and headed westward across the Atlantic to reenter American life after an absence of nearly a decade. Walking down the gangplank at New York Harbor nine days later, Mark Twain was greeted by a welcoming uproar from his countrymen so adulatory and so sustained that it must have felt to him as if he were awakening from a long, storm-tossed voyage that had in fact been a dream.

45

Sitting in Darkness

(1900–1905)

The horde of reporters and friends who greeted him at the dockside on October 15, 1900, formed the first tendrils of a human cloud that swirled
about him for the rest of his life. The newspapers heralded his return as that
of a prophet, or something larger than a prophet; the soul of the nation personified. MARK TWAIN HOME AGAIN, the newspaper headlines trumpeted the
day after his arrival, and, MARK TWAIN COMES HOME, and MARK TWAIN IN
AMERICA AGAIN, and MARK TWAIN HOME, AN ANTI-IMPERIALIST. The *Herald*
noted the "smile of good-natured fun on his lips . . . as he came down the
gangplank." The *Press* picked up on his joking response to a question about
his citizenship and blared, MARK TWAIN WANTS TO BE PRESIDENT. The *Sun* correspondent pleaded, "Tell us some of the incidents of your tour of the world."
("There aren't any except what I put in my book," Mark Twain deadpanned,
"and there weren't enough of them to go 'round.") The man from the *Mail and
Express* shouted out to him the inevitable comparison to Sir Walter Scott.
("Nice, but purely personal.") The Chicago *Tribune*, noting that his entourage
was among the last to disembark, quoted him as assuring some friends, "No, I
didn't get off on the other side of the boat." [1]

Reporters caressed his presence in New York for days, getting all *verklempt*
over his ruddy cheeks, his pink hands, the bristles on his mustache, his shoe
blacking, his starched linen. The *World* editor ordered his interviewer to "have
him tell what he thinks about the bay, the Statue of Liberty, the policemen, the
manners of the people, the hotels, the cabs, bootblacks, fashions, the theatres
and everything else that has interested him in New York" [2]—creating an "ask

Mark about . . ." shtick for a century's worth of Mark Twain imitators in white suits and white wigs. The resulting scoop was headlined MY IMPRESSIONS OF AMERICA. The *Herald* man, clearly a veteran of the celeb scene, observed that "he has a trick of bending his knees and throwing back his head, as if in preparation for a good story. It is equivalent to one of President Lincoln's 'That reminds me.' "[3]

He went to the Yale-Princeton football game with a party of Princeton professors—and a reporter at his elbow. "He quickly mastered the main principles of the game," the correspondent informed his readers. ". . . [W]hen Mattis . . . dropped a pretty goal from the field Mr. Clemens laughed loudly, clapped his hands, and exclaimed: 'That's good! That's good! Perhaps Princeton will win after all.' " At the ten-minute halftime, "with the figures standing 11 for Yale and 5 for Princeton, Mr. Clemens was one of the most eager of the mathematicians figuring how Princeton might yet pull the game out of the fire." Princeton didn't, but the reporter recorded the author's color commentary on the first pigskin game he'd ever seen.

"I should think they'd break every bone they ever had!"

"Those Yale men must be made of granite, like the rocks of Connecticut!"

"Those young Elis are too beefy and brawny for the Tigers!"

"Well, say, this beats croquet. There's more go about it!"

"The country is safe when its young men show such pluck and determination as are here in evidence today."[4]

AMERICA HAD missed him. America had found something missing in itself when he was away, it almost seemed. What was it that America needed from him so badly?

His round-the-world tour and repayment of his debts had established him as a national hero and moral exemplar; that was part of it. Yet some of the questions shouted to him on October 15 at New York Harbor could not be written off as celebrity byplay. Anxiety seeped out of them. "Mr. Clemens, have you had time to give any thought to the grave question of imperialism?"[5] asked the *Herald* man. Several reporters wondered how he was doing on the rumored autobiography whose revelations were said to be so portentous that they would not be published until a hundred years after his death. A follow-up question to his throwaway "citizenship" joke went, "Then you haven't made up your mind about the Presidency?"[6] These were peculiar concerns to be directed at a "humorist." But then these were peculiar times, times in which all sorts of comfortable assumptions were being suspended or violently overturned. America, that stately brass-eagle-and-bunting leviathan, had just clawed an imperial power (Spain) off the surface of a tiny offshore island (Cuba) in the name of freedom and self-determination; now America was slashing at the overmatched victims of that same power, in a farther-off war in the Philippines—this time in the *role* of imperialist. How did the one action beget the other? The leading voices of the day saw no discontinuity. The editorial pages, most of Congress, the clergy, the captains of industry*—all of these bellowed the necessity and virtue of this war (not to mention the tasty business-growth prospects that flowed from the necessity and the virtue). The relation between words and truth grew difficult to sort out: what seemed self-evidently wrong only years, months, earlier, was suddenly trumpeted as a self-evident right. The language itself, like Hamlet's time, seemed out of joint.

The explosion of the *Maine* in Havana Harbor that was said to justify the American invasion of Cuba—was it really caused by a Spanish torpedo, that 19th-century ballistic missile? Or was it (as many U.S. naval officers insisted) the result of a combustion in the ship's coal bunkers? It was impossible for the average person to tell. But the dominant news outlets had no doubt. MAINE BLOWN UP BY TORPEDO, screamed the banner headlines in the Hearst papers on February 17, 1898. Was the nation's "honor" at stake, as the papers were maintaining? Did it mean something, as the Humboldt *Times* pointed out on April 12, that on this date thirty-seven years ago *to the day* Fort Sumter had been bombarded, starting the Civil War?[7] (The *Times*'s point seemed to be that it would be nice if some bombarding were going on today.)

Strident calls for *more* force, *more* expansion, rose up from the halls and pulpits of American public power. The Republican president McKinley, running for reelection against the anti-imperialist Democrat William Jennings Bryan, was not a rabid expansionist (contrary to the second man on the ticket, Theodore Roosevelt), but he had approved the annexations, bringing a new phrase into popularity: "manifest destiny." McKinley was en route to victory by the largest margin in presidential history.

The real bombast came from congressional firebrands such as Senators "Jingo Jim" Blaine of Maine and Albert J. Beveridge of Indiana, who raved about following the flag and pitching the tents of liberty westward. Beveridge noticed that the hand gripping the Stars and Stripes was God's. The Protestant clergy had noticed the same thing. The Congregationalist minister Josiah Strong, a friend of Roosevelt's, proclaimed the "Anglo-Saxon" race the great race of history, incomparably superior to people in tropical lands—say, the Philippines. God had thus deputized the Anglo-Saxons to share the joys of superior civilization with inferior races, whether the latter liked it or not.

James M. King, a Methodist minister in New York, was less delicate.

Christianized Anglo-Saxon blood, with its love of liberty, its thrift, its intense and persistent energy and personal independence, is the regnant force in this country . . . God is using the Anglo-Saxon to conquer the world for Christ by dispossessing feeble races, and assimilating and molding others.[8]

---

* Henry Rogers did not join the public debate, but he had made his general views clear to Clemens in a letter written in 1896, during McKinley's first presidential campaign, which he supported: "The truth is that politicians have been running the country for a good many years, and it is quite time that some business sense should be exercised, and I have the feeling that we are on the right track" (MTHHR, p. 248).

Adjusted to the heat level of a later time, this thought might read: "We should invade their countries, kill their leaders, and convert them to Christianity."

Something very close to that, of course, took place. Progressive-minded Americans were in shock over the results of their nation's "liberating" invasion of the Spanish-controlled Philippine Islands that lay more than seven thousand miles west of the California coast. After quickly crushing the Spanish navy and land forces, the United States had brushed aside the nationalist First Philippine Republic—in whose interests it had purportedly launched its attacks—and claimed annexation for itself at the Treaty of Paris, signed on December 10, 1898, paying Spain $20 million dollars for all the territories it had "rescued" from foreign dominion. (Among the American "peace" commissioners at Paris was Mark Twain's old friend Whitelaw Reid.) The Filipino revolutionaries, who took a jaundiced view of McKinley's "benevolent assimilation," proceeded to declare war on the United States in February 1899. By the time the benevolence died down in July 1902, Filipino losses would total twenty thousand soldiers and more than two hundred thousand civilians, against 4,200 Americans dead.

DISSENT FROM the war or criticism of its aftermath carried a price. The dissenter was likely to be branded as nothing more than a damned anti-imperialist, and that was the next thing to being a damned traitor. "There is no reasonable doubt about that," Fred C. Chamberlain would fulminate in the afterglow of victory. "Their work cost the lives of hundreds of American soldiers,—stabbed in the back as they stood out there on the firing line, by their own countrymen . . . All up and down this great country the Anti-Imperialists made speeches of sympathy for the men who were shooting at our own soldiers."[9] And who were the Anti-Imperialists? They were the damn Masons, the damn women's assemblies, the damn Democrats, the damn inflammatory magazine *Farm and Home*. Not to mention the damn Anti-Imperialist League. This last was the outgrowth of that "Peace Appeal to Labor," signed in April by William Dean Howells and several of his friends. These activists, who included Andrew Carnegie and William James, founded the League in October 1899. It went approximately nowhere. The League shared the problem of most who dared speak up in opposition to this onslaught of passionate intensity: a lack of—if not conviction, then at least declamatory power.

The progressive *Nation* of March 24, 1899, cleared its throat and sent forth a mighty whisper of opposition to the jingo firestorm: "Have we a course of war so clear, so loftily imperative that all the hideousness of carnage and the fearful blow to civic progress must be hazarded in order to vindicate humanity and righteousness?"[10] This was hardly a match for Rudyard Kipling's heavy-thumping verse screed "The White Man's Burden," in the February 12 *McClure's*. Kipling, who had knelt to help Howells with his rubbers, was kneeling no more. With elephantine condescension toward the "sullen, silent peoples / Half devil and half child" in the crosshairs of Anglo-style enlightenment, he exhorted the long-suffering master race to "[s]end forth the best ye breed" and rescue the disgusting little wogs from their own abysmal stabs at civilization.[11]

MARK TWAIN'S position on the Philippine war, when it finally coalesced, beggared the Democrats' timidity and the Republicans' bombast. It quickly blossomed into *the* representative, and prophetic, voice of principled American dissent. It defined the public work of his last ten years. Yet it did not stand alongside his literary legacy for many decades after his death, and for good reason. When his posthumous protectors (chiefly Clara and Paine) resumed the work that had ultimately defeated Mary Fairbanks, Livy, Susy, and others during his lifetime—the work of de-Vandalizing him, propping him up in the perfumed costume of a polite National Uncle—his social justice essays suffered the same fate as did his more extreme screeds against religion and mankind: deemphasis, obfuscation, and outright suppression.

"I am an anti-imperialist," Mark Twain told the reporters at dockside. "I am opposed to having the eagle put its talons on any other land."[12] He had said exactly the same thing to reporters in London on the day he boarded the *Minnehaha.* His comments were widely published. In their cadences and compressed clarity, they offered a clue as to why America was so glad to see him again. In contrast to the wild sloganeering, fact-twisting, and question-begging of the yellow press, congressmen, and the clergy, his thoughts could not have been more cogently stated. Here was a demonstration of what Howells maintained—at just about this time—was his most liberating literary strength, his "single-minded use of words, which he employs as Grant did to express the plain, straight meaning their common acceptance has given them . . . He writes English as if it were a primitive and not a derivative language, without Gothic or Latin or Greek behind it."[13]

To wit: "We were to relieve them from Spanish tyranny to enable them to set up a government of their own," Mark Twain had pointed out to his interviewer in London, "and we were to stand by and see that it got a fair trial. It was not to be a government according to our ideas, but a government that represented the feeling of the majority of the Filipinos, a government according to Filipino ideas. That would have been a worthy mission for the United States.

"But now—why, we have got into a mess, a quagmire from which each fresh step renders the difficulty of extrication immensely greater. I'm sure I wish I could see what we were getting out of it, and all it means to us as a nation."[14]

That was the only unfamiliar and unsettling word he used in the entire interview—"quagmire."

AFTER A brief stay at a hotel, the Clemenses rented a house at 14 West 10th Street, at Fifth Avenue, while Livy searched for a more permanent residence.

Clemens had routinely been telling reporters that he and his family would eventually return to their house in Hartford. If he ever really believed that, he was soon to change his mind. Five days after his arrival in New York, Charles Dudley Warner, his old Nook Farm neighbor and co-author of *The Gilded Age*, died at seventy-one. Sam went up to Hartford for his funeral, and the shock of reentering the city where Susy had died sealed his understanding that the family could never bear to live there again. Livy would not have been able to endure the trauma. Livy could hardly endure daily life. She was just shy of fifty-five in the autumn of 1900, and looked seventy. A glass-plate photograph made in London the previous summer shows her seated under a tree between Clara, on her right, who gazes down protectively at her, and Sam, on her left, clutching his pipe, completely engaged in the camera under his sharp white Stetson, his slippers fiercely shined. Livy looks dazed. She is staring somewhere else through sunken, heavy-lidded eyes, the lines around her mouth deeply etched.

The family stayed on at West 10th through the winter, though Livy found the rooms drafty and cold. In January she mustered the energy to travel to Washington, where Clara, on the 22nd, made her debut as a concert singer. Sam, as disapproving of her independent ambitions as he had been of Susy's, stayed home. Jean, who counted horsemanship among her few accomplishments, pursued the cause of animals' rights when not recovering from one of her attacks.

THE HOWELLSES lived just on the far side of Union Square, at 115 East 16th Street. This was the first time that Clemens and Howells had ever lived within walking distance of each other, something Sam had wished for since the 1870s. They made the most of this proximity. They rejuvenated their long friendship, shifting their passions from the literary world to the political. Howells swept Clemens up into the Anti-Imperialist crusade, introducing him at a Lotos Club dinner on November 10 as the ascendant satirist laureate of the country. Mark Twain was mostly charming and gently ironic on that occasion ("We elected a President four years ago. We've found fault with him and criticized him, and here a day or two ago we go and elect him for another four years with votes enough to spare to do it over again." [15]); but within two weeks he was mincing no words. "The Boxer is a patriot," he declared to the Berkeley Lyceum on November 23, speaking of the Chinese guerrillas waging bloody resistance against the occupying Russians, Germans and other great powers who were "carving up the Chinese melon" (as the European policymakers liked to phrase it). He added, "I am a Boxer" [16]—an extraordinarily daring reversal in point of view (a famous Caucasian, asserting the identity of a Chinese peasant?!) that anticipated by nearly sixty-three years President Kennedy's anticommunist declaration in West Berlin, "Ich bin ein Berliner!" Sam remained aggressively candid as he introduced the British war correspondent Winston Churchill to his first American audience at the Waldorf-

Astoria on December 12, offering a muted preview of the slashing voice soon to be unleashed in full.

. . . I think that England sinned when she got herself into a war in South Africa which she could have avoided, just as we have sinned in getting into a similar war in the Philippines. Mr. Churchill by his father is an Englishman; by his mother he is an American; no doubt a blend that makes the perfect man. England and America: yes, we are kin. And now that we are also kin in sin, there is nothing more to be desired. The harmony is complete, the blend is perfect—like Mr. Churchill himself, whom I now have the honor to present to you.[17]

Seldom would the 20th century's signature orator be so upstaged. The New York *Evening Post* loved it: "He drew the razor of his satire across several of the most flaunting and destructive humbugs of the age."[18] The razor slash served notice that the Vandal was back in town, and he had some things on his mind.

Mark Twain became as ubiquitous in New York, and sometimes as formidable, as the new automobiles that were haring around scaring the hell out of pedestrians. (A driver "considers his responsibility fully discharged by the ringing of the gong," sputtered an editorial in the *Tribune*.) He was the star attraction at luncheons and banquets given by the Aldine Club, the Nineteenth Century Club, the City Club, the Society of American Authors, the New England Society. Guests at these functions were as likely to be gonged by his emerging political views as amused by his wit. His cachet only increased; people wanted to hear him, look at him, be in the same room with him. The ringing telephone at the 10th Street house had servants constantly running up and down the stairs with messages. Every day there, Clara recalled, was a festive occasion. "One felt that a large party was going on and that by and by the guests would be leaving. But there was no leaving."[19] In his spare time he took ostentatious walks along Fifth Avenue, as if daring the public not to recognize him. He was in fighting trim, thanks perhaps to his intake of Plasmon, the new health food he'd discovered in Germany, and which had now become his latest investment craze. The chalky stuff, extracted from skim milk, was intended to improve digestion and nutrition. It proved to be the Paige typesetter of gastronomy; Clemens lost about fifty thousand dollars in investments before giving it up.

Howells would eventually worry about "so many dinners . . . so few books"[20] in regard to his friend; but literature was not the point for Mark Twain now, and neither were escalloped oysters; the point was polemics, written fast and broadcast faster; and in this pursuit he excelled brilliantly. In a thundering long riff of speeches and essays that reverberated through 1905, the old Vandal showed his new reformer's chops. He kicked off with his splenetic "A salutation-speech from the Nineteenth Century to the Twentieth Century," which ran in the *Herald* on December 30:

I bring you the stately matron named Christendom, returning bedraggled, be-smirched and dishonored from pirate-raids in Kiaochow, Manchuria, South Africa & the Phillipines, with her soul full of meanness, her pocket full of boodle, and her mouth full of pious hypocrisies. Give her soap & a towel, but hide the looking-glass.[21]

He followed this with his masterpiece. "To the Person Sitting in Darkness," in the February 1901 issue of the *North American Review,* stands as a landmark of social-political satire. The piece hit the benevolent assimilators in the soft solar plexus of their hypocrisies. "The Blessings-of-Civilization Trust," he bitterly allows, had done its work

very neatly, and . . . they could not understand it; for we had been so friendly—so affectionate, even—with those simple-minded patriots! . . . We had . . . fought shoulder to shoulder with them against "the common enemy" . . . petted them, lied to them . . . used them until we needed them no longer; then derided the sucked orange and threw it away . . . What we wanted, in the interest of Progress and Civilization, was the Archipelago, unencumbered by patriots struggling for independence . . .[22]

Excoriating each element of the "Trust"—the empire-minded government, market-maddened business, and the Christian missionaries who served to apologize for both—Mark Twain drew uncomfortably explicit comparisons: the American adventure echoed similar aggressions by Germany against China, Russia against Japan and Manchuria, and the British against the Boers in South Africa. As his analogies expanded, his diction soared. Kipling had couched "White Man's Burden" in the lockstep rhythms of a big bass drum. "Sitting in Darkness," by contrast, picked up the throbbing reiterative cadences of the gospel preacher, the calling Clemens had once considered. (He took the essay's title from Matthew 4:16, which chronicles the beginning of Jesus's ministry.) He infused these familiar old cadences with a righteous snarl.

. . . There have been lies; yes, but they were told in a good cause. We have been treacherous; but that was only in order that real good might come out of apparent evil. True, we have crushed a deceived and confiding people; we have turned against the weak and the friendless who trusted us . . . we have debauched America's honor and blackened her face before the world; but each detail was for the best. We know this. The Head of every State and Sovereignty in Christendom . . . including our Congress and our fifty State Legislatures, are members not only of the church, but also of the Blessings-of-Civilization Trust. This world-girdling accumulation of trained morals, high principles, and justice, cannot do an unright thing, an unfair thing, an ungenerous thing, an unclean thing. It knows what it is about. Give yourself no uneasiness; it is all right.[23]

"Sitting in Darkness" dramatically reignited the Philippine debate in the nation's newspapers, by giving the anti-imperialists, at last, the eloquent voice they had lacked. Papers that opposed the war and annexation reprinted it for weeks, while those in support of the government ignored it as long as they could, after which they blistered Mark Twain with invective. Most of these, finding his positions hard to quickly rebut, sneered that as a mere "humorist," he was out of his depth in weighty public issues.

The New York *Times* on February 7 lacerated Mark Twain for "tumbling in among us from the clouds of exile and discarding the grin of the funny man for the sour visage of the austere moralist."[24] The Minneapolis *Journal* denounced his stance as "a very excellent specimen of flippancy, as well as utter disregard for truth and fact."[25] The imperialist-leaning Hartford *Courant,* so reliably an ally for so many years, mostly kept a pained silence; but its rival, the Hartford *Times,* was jubilant. Noting that Mark Twain was "a man whom the whole American people read," the paper saluted him for bringing "the sad and shocking facts of the crime against the Filipinos home to hundreds of thousands of Americans from whom they have been hitherto hidden."[26] An excerpt of it was read into the *Congressional Record* by the Ohio Democrat John J. Lentz.

By now, some of his friends saw career catastrophe in the works: Mark Twain was jeopardizing the genial goodwill he'd built up with America for more than thirty years. The most wounding call for restraint came from Joe Twichell, the clergyman and friend whose manliness Sam Clemens had so admired. "I'm not expecting anything but kicks for scoffing at McKinley, that consciousless thief & traitor," Sam's second paragraph of reply carefully began, "& am expecting a diminution of my bread and butter by it, but if Livy will let me I will have my say." Then, in an *"et tu . . . ?"* burst of dismayed admonishment:

> *I* can't understand it! You are a public guide & teacher, Joe, & are under a heavy responsibility to men, young & old; if you teach your people—as you teach me—to hide their opinions when they believe their flag is being abused & dishonored, lest the utterance do them & a publisher a damage, how do you answer for it to your conscience? You are sorry for me; in the fair way of give & take, I am willing to be a little sorry for you.[27]

Mark Twain continued tramping out this vintage with "To My Missionary Critics" in April 1901; "A Defense of General Funston" in May 1902; "The Czar's Soliloquy" in March 1905 (all of these in the *North American Review*); "King Leopold's Soliloquy" in September of that year; and finally, his great valedictory in the genre, unpublished in his lifetime, "The War Prayer." In this best-known of all his polemical writings (thanks in part to two television adaptations, an oratorio, and a renaissance on the Internet), Mark Twain employs his favorite fictive spokesman, the Stranger, to interrupt a minister's invocations of God's blessings on young soldiers headed for battle, and deliver an anti-prayer that inventories the hideous truths about warfare—truths that remained susceptible to the fog of piety well into the age of electronic transmission of images.

In 1905, at the height of its influence, Mark Twain's hot dissenting voice largely disappeared from the magazines. It was swallowed up by a combination of financial forces generally assumed to have gathered only in the late 20th century: concentrated media ownership; the influence of wealthy businessmen over editors in the flow of ideas; lavish "celebrity" book and magazine deals. Publishing imperialism, in short. The chain of events, largely unexamined in Mark Twain scholarship, are worth tracing as unheeded prophecy.

IN 1899, the august *North American Review,* a publisher of Mark Twain essays for fifteen years, was purchased by the capitalist George B. Harvey, the head of a $15 million syndicate (a little more than $300 million in today's dollars). Harvey had written for town newspapers in Vermont as a boy and had edited the Newark *Journal* and the New York *World* before joining the Metropolitan Street Railroad Company to earn his fortune. He was known by the honorific "Colonel."

At exactly this same time, Harper & Brothers was trying to pull itself out of debt following some misjudgments worthy of Charles Webster himself. These included a weakness for celebrity-author contracts. Philip Harper (who apothcosized the "family house" publisher when he became his own father's brother-in-law) offered Lew Wallace, author of the wildly popular *Ben Hur,* $10,000 a year for ten years to write more hits. Wallace, whose entire literary career could be summed up as "Ben Hur done that," disgorged something called *The Prince of India,* which flopped—owing perhaps to its scarcity of chariot races.

Philip Harper turned, for a bailout, to the corporate world: specifically, the financial firm of J. P. Morgan & Company. Morgan essentially bought the company, ending its long run as a family house. This sort of thing would recur often in the second half of the 20th century. Morgan hired such publishing stars as S. S. McClure, founder of the magazine that bore his name, and Nelson Doubleday, the nephew of the man who did not invent baseball. Nothing worked; McClure and Doubleday were soon out, and the Morgan people brought in Colonel Harvey, who brought the *Review* with him. Among Harvey's first acts was to declare the house bankrupt. This caused the immediate exodus of such stars as Henry James, Joseph Conrad, and Owen Wister. Harvey recruited replacement stars, among them the "cowboy" novelist Zane Grey. His biggest coup was a deal, negotiated through Henry Rogers in 1903, for exclusive rights to another celebrity author, Mark Twain.

This turned out to be good for Harper's and good for Mark Twain, financially, at least. Colonel Harvey liked to boast that he paid the author 30 cents a word for everything he wrote, which (he said) made Mark Twain the highest-paid man in the history of American and European letters. "Mark Twain earns $59,000 a year," he told a Washington *Post* reporter in 1907. "Indeed, I think his income in 1907 will reach $70,000 [nearly $1.5 million in adjusted dollars]."[28] The publisher maintained that the contract was "absolutely without conditions as to subjects, treatment, or anything else. It is unthinkable that Mark Twain should write a story or article and have it rejected."[29]

But it had already happened. Harvey tolerated "The Czar's Soliloquy," but after that, the company found the author's polemics a little too risky for its circulation interests. "The War Prayer" was rejected by *Harper's Bazar* (as it was then titled) in late 1905 by its progressive editor Elizabeth Jordan, who suppressed her suffragist ideals in being persuaded that it would alarm her feminine readership's sensibilities. The company likewise turned down *King Leopold's Soliloquy* a month later. He was eventually able to issue the *Soliloquy* in pamphlet form with his publisher's permission. Paine included excerpts from it in his biography of Mark Twain, and published it in full (as far as is known) in 1923, in the collection *Europe and Elsewhere*. By then—amid the roaring hedonism following a world war that had generally anesthetized romantic ideals—it was disconnected from the passions of the times, and lay ignored for most of the ensuing century.

Europe and Elsewhere is an interesting graveyard for Mark Twain's reformist work. It also includes the altered remains of "The United States of Lyncherdom," a white-hot condemnation of sanctioned murder by whites against blacks. Mark Twain wrote the essay in fury upon learning in 1901 of one more lynching among many in his home state of Missouri. Vigilante hangings of blacks suspected of crimes—or not suspected of crimes—had increased rampantly since the end of Reconstruction. The spirit, if not the scale of ethnic cleansing, was newly abroad in the land, having rested up after the decimation of the native Indian tribes. Like "The War Prayer," "Lyncherdom" went unpublished in the author's lifetime, and was seriously distorted by Paine's edits in 1923, and thus underappreciated until 2000. Mark Twain had opted against offering it for magazine publication when he completed it. That decision opened him to the century-long received wisdom that he cared more about his popularity in the South than about his social ideals. But he hadn't worried about the South when he published *Life on the Mississippi*, with its dismissal of the region's chivalric pretense, and he certainly hadn't worried about it with *Huckleberry Finn*. More likely, the withholding was a factor of his developing belief that the publishing world could not bear his strongest ideas. He made this belief explicit in an unpublished essay written a few years later.

Sometimes my feelings are so hot that I have to take to the pen and pour them out on paper to keep them from setting me afire inside: then all that ink and labor are wasted, because I can't print the result. I have just finished an article of this kind, and it satisfies me entirely ["As Concerns Interpreting the Deity"]. It does my weather-beaten soul good to read it, and admire the trouble it would make for me and the family. I will leave it behind, and utter it from the grave. There is free speech there, and no harm to the family.[30]

IN PRIVATE for Sam, the new 20th century—"a stranger to me," he'd warily jotted in his notebook—promised to be a long, gentle Arcadian dream, if the summer of 1901 was any evidence. In June, Clemens ensconced his family in a "little bijou" of a log cabin at the edge of Lower Saranac Lake in the Adirondacks, where they swam and boated and went for walks in the woods, and watched the "beautiful little tan-colored impudent squirrels . . . take tea at 5 p.m. (not uninvited)" at the outdoors table where Jean sat typing her father's manuscripts.[31] Sam worked on his indulgently silly send-up of the Sherlock Holmes genre, "A Double-Barreled Detective Story," for *Harper's Magazine,* and decided that all the squirrels were named Blennerhasset.[32] In August, Sam broke away to join Henry Rogers's seagoing stag party aboard the tycoon's 227-foot steam yacht the *Kanawha,* said to be the fastest on American waters with a top speed of twenty-two knots an hour. (Clemens always managed to stifle his anti-imperialist sentiments in Rogers's company.) They cruised from port to port in Maine, New Brunswick, and Nova Scotia; playing poker and smoking large cigars and the stroking of large mustaches was the order of most days. Sam's old class anxieties had arisen in the form of suspicions that he snored at nights. When he asked his companions about it at breakfast one morning, the men assured him that it was no problem, he reported to Livy:

[T]hey often lay awake hours to listen, and Mr. Rogers said it infused him so with comfortableness that he tried to keep himself awake by turning over and over in bed so as to get more of it . . . Colonel Payne said he was always sorry when the night was over and he knew he had to wait all day before he could have some more . . . This is very different from the way I am treated at home, where there is no appreciation of what a person does.[33]

The new century gave a little hint of its darkness on September 6, 1901, when a baby-faced anarchist named Leon Czolgosz excused his way past fifty bodyguards at the Pan American Exposition in Buffalo and pumped two bullets into President McKinley, who gasped out, "Be easy with him boys," and died eight days later. Theodore Roosevelt, racing pell-mell to Washington from his own family getaway at Mount Marcy in the Adirondacks, was sworn into the office at age forty-three. Five weeks later, the new president and hero of San Juan Hill attended the bicentennial ceremonies of his alma mater, Yale University, where he heard a great cheer go up—for Mark Twain. The author, who with Howells was awarded an honorary degree—his second—from Yale had just strolled into the hall. Roosevelt clenched his famous imperialistic teeth and muttered, within the author's hearing, that he would like to see the likes of Mark Twain skinned alive.[34] Clemens and Howells enjoyed calling each other "Doc" for a while.

Sam and Livy had been searching for a house that would recapture some of the grandeur of the mansion in Hartford. A month after the Yale ceremonies they moved into a three-story Greek Revival house in Riverdale, a mostly forested city north of Manhattan. Sam had leased it from the owner, William Henry Appleton, for three thousand dollars a year. Called Wave Hill, the house sat on high land above the Hudson River, its spacious back lawn giving a view of the New Jersey palisades to the west. A summer visitor at Wave Hill in 1870 and 1871, with his parents, was Theodore Roosevelt, who later claimed he had learned his love of nature there. Sam relished the strong winds that blew across the Hudson and through the trees; he built an ornate tree parlor in the branches of a chestnut on the lawn. Here, despite Livy's diminished health, they commenced a scaled-down version of the entertaining that had illuminated so many evenings across the years at Nook Farm. The Howellses were among the frequent guests, "on something like the sweet old terms,"[35] and also Henry Huttleston and Emilie Rogers. A few months later, the Clemenses placed the Nook Farm house on the market.

SAM'S PROSPERITY increased in 1902, the year that Bret Harte and Thomas Nast died. He calculated that he earned $60,000 from combined sales of his books, and $100,000 altogether.[36] He became a regular aboard Henry Rogers's yacht, exploring the Caribbean with him in April. In that month, Clara traveled to Paris to reconnect with Ossip Gabrilowitsch. Mark Twain's renown took on surrealistic proportions: Howells noticed that railroad conductors would hold up the scheduled departure of trains if the great man needed to use the gentleman's room at the station. His notebook aphorisms poured forth with Wildean panache: "To create man was a fine and original idea; but to add the sheep was a tautology."[37]

In May of that year Samuel Clemens reentered his boyhood universe of Hannibal, Missouri, for the last time, and in his honor, Hannibal improvised a transformation—to the extent possible, working without advance notification—back to its own antebellum youth; a white town, drowsing in the sunshine of a summer's morning. He arrived by train from St. Louis on Thursday, May 29, 1902, on a journey begun in New York and destined for the University of Missouri at Columbia, where he was to receive an honorary degree. The hundred-mile detour north to Hannibal was an impulsive decision, and a self-conscious one: he invited a young book reviewer from the St. Louis *Post-Dispatch*, named Robertus Love, to accompany him. Love followed the author around the town for parts of four days, and filed several captivating dispatches about the excitement and pageantry that swirled about the visit.

Clemens and Love stepped off the train in the balmy late afternoon to behold what had become a thoroughly modern little city of 12,500 people. Railroads had brought prosperity to Hannibal, a legacy of John Marshall

Clemens's efforts of more than half a century earlier. Its factories sent shoes and cement out across the nation. Right-angled redbrick buildings housed its downtown businesses, buildings that would remain in use a century hence. The streets were filled with scurrying people interested in making money. Few of them had time to think or care much about the silent moving waters of the Mississippi on the far side of the tracks. The two checked in at the Windsor Hotel, a block from the station. Love, alert for "color," didn't have to wait long. The desk clerk, a man named Will Sutton, recognized the famous guest and spoke up: "Mr. Clemens, I was born close to your birthplace at Florida, and have been in the house where you were born, often." "I was not born often—only once," Sam deadpanned back; "but I'm glad to see you, all the same."[38]

Word spread fast that Mark Twain was back in town, as Mark Twain clearly hoped it would. The leading citizens improvised a publicity and welcoming schedule. ("If we had known he was aboard that train," exclaimed one of them, "the Union Depot platform would not have been big enough to hold the chairmen of committees.")[39] The next morning some townsfolk asked him if he could confirm that the small white house at 206 Hill Street was in fact the one where he had lived for a time in the 1840s. He could and did, and posed for a famous photograph in front of it, wearing a pearl-gray suit. He accepted a carriage ride from a wealthy widow, Helen Garth, through the hilly greening woodlands south of town to Mount Olivet Cemetery, where John Marshall and Jane and Orion and Henry lay side by side under the same tree.

Back in town a mob had collected at the Farmers and Merchants Bank, where a reception had been thrown together. Mark Twain scanned the faces of the old men who squeezed through the door to get a look at him; he recognized a few. "How are you doing, Eddie?" he asked a man named Pierce, who replied, "Like yourself, Sam. Like a cow's tail going down."[40] Another fellow identified himself as Lippincott and tried to get Mark Twain to remember how they used to play marbles together, but the author couldn't make that connection. After a while, he went off to visit the First Presbyterian Church on North Fourth Street where he'd first learned about his own sure damnation.

By Friday afternoon, Hannibal had figured out how to turn itself into a Mark Twain theme center, a talent that it retained. "Today Hannibal is full of Huck Finns, Tom Sawyers and Beckys," Love wrote. "There are more 'originals' of [them] than one would expect to meet in a staid old town with 23 respectable Sunday schools and a Salvation Army."[41] That evening, some smart proto-publicists staged a great media event: they sat Mark Twain/Sam Clemens/Tom Sawyer down to dinner at Helen Garth's mansion with the object of his long-ago somersaults, Laura Frazier/Laura Hawkins/Becky Thatcher, now the matron for the Home of the Friendless in Hannibal. Sam improvised decently. "Gee whiz," he cried out, "—it seems like I ain't seen you in 50 years, Laura."[42] He distributed diplomas that night to the high school graduating class of 1902; after a class delegation presented him with a silver spoon, he froze their grins with the tale of how he tried to contract measles from Will Bowen. "I was very near to death," he told them, "and I have never had such a good opportunity to die. Sometimes I think I should have embraced the opportunity, thereby escaping many unpleasant things." [43]

The following night, his last ever in Hannibal, the sorrow escaped completely. As five hundred guests of the Labinnah Club ("Hannibal" spelled backwards) watched in disbelief, he faltered in his comic address and gave way to convulsive sobs. "A moment before," Love wrote, "the scores of beautiful girls and matrons, handsomely gowned, and the clubmen and their friends had been laughing heartily at the flashes of Mark Twain's characteristic wit." [44] Then, just after a remark that "had everyone helpless with mirth," came the deluge. Mark Twain's head dropped and his shoulders heaved. "He mumbled something that was not understood, and at last he looked up into the now tense, sympathetic faces of his auditors."

"I realize that this must be my last visit to Hannibal," he said to the people who were looking at him, "and in bidding you hail I also bid you farewell." [45]

The next morning, a Sunday, he walked with a Baptist minister ahead of a throng to the railroad station, where he posed for photographers in his gray suit and homburg, a spray of flowers in his fist. As he strolled in the sunlight, an ancient specter materialized from the depths of the crowd, sepulchral as the ghost in "The Golden Arm." It was deaf Tom Nash, who shrieked out: "Same damned fools, Sam!" [46] Then the train engine released its ghostly clouds of steam, and by the time the steam had evaporated, Sam Clemens was gone.

AN INFINITELY more heartbreaking farewell soon threatened. On August 12, 1902, in the midst of a summer holiday with Sam and Jean at York Harbor, Maine, Livy found herself unable to breathe. Her heart beat wildly, and she and Sam both believed that she was dying. Sam telephoned a doctor, who arrived in half an hour. Livy survived, but remained weak through September 20, when she suffered a relapse. Henry Rogers had brought the couple to York Harbor aboard his yacht, but a return home via the ocean was unthinkable, and Clemens arranged to transport her by a private railroad car on October 13. Back in Riverdale, doctors diagnosed her condition as heart disease. Her daily care now became an overriding concern. Clara suspended her singing career at twenty-eight, and became her mother's unofficial nurse, to the extent possible—the doctor summoned from Boston insisted that family members stay out of the sick woman's bedroom. The steadfast Katy Leary did what she could. Jean, twenty-two, became the household's second invalid when she was felled by pneumonia in December.

Clemens decided that everyone could use some reinforcement from the outside. In early November he hired a thirty-four-year-old woman named

Isabel Van Kleek Lyon to serve as Livy's secretary and help out as needed. The Clemenses had vaguely known Isabel Lyon for about twelve years—she had worked as a governess for their Nook Farm neighbors the Franklin G. Whitmores. An attractive, dark-haired, mercurial woman, given to self-dramatizing poses and actions, she'd boldly sat in on a hand of whist one night when Sam and Livy were guests at the Whitmores', a gesture that shocked and interested Sam. She was destined to haunt the author's final years as an intriguer in his literary, financial, and personal affairs, and to be seen by Clemens and Clara as a sinister presence in the household; even as a romantic temptress after Livy's death, in the view of some biographers.

To be near his wife, Clemens wound down and at last suspended the glittering social and public appearance schedule he'd enjoyed in New York—near, but not next to her. "When we are serene & happy old married folk," he'd assured her in the innocent bliss of 1869, "we will sit together . . . all the long pleasant evenings, & let the great world toil & struggle & nurse its pet ambitions . . ."[47] It wasn't working out that way. For great stretches in the months between Livy's attack at York Harbor and her death, doctors did their best to keep Sam away from her. They feared that his intense personality would wear her down. The separation only added to the couple's agony. Desperate for contact, Sam began writing short notes to Livy, which he pushed under the door. He described the landscape outside: "Livy, dear . . . the sea has come ashore. Water, blown by the wind in crinkling curves & long lines, is frozen white, & a stretch of it up the slope of the grassy hill gives the aspect of a section of green sea with wimpling white-caps chasing each other over it."[48] He told her small details about Clara and Jean, and reminded her of the emperor's backyard in Vienna. He signed himself "Y," for Youth.

Sam resumed his polemic writing as well. He returned to an assault on Mary Baker Eddy that he'd begun in Vienna, circumstances having made her concept of "healing" even more of a monstrous joke to him. Bit by bit, sentence by sentence, with deconstructive focus as mercilessly charged as any that would be trained on him, he picked apart her use of language, and, through this conduit, the foundation of her claim to intellectual legitimacy. (Fenimore Cooper got off easy, by comparison.) He pointed to her obsessively control-minded bylaws for her church (a thinly disguised trust, in his view), as evidence of her insatiable will to power: "It is odd and strange, to see intelligent and educated people among us worshipping this self-seeking and remorseless tyrant as a God."[49] He inventoried her rhetorical self-contradictions and garbled syntax: "It is evident that whenever, under the inspiration of the Deity, she turns out a book, she is always allowed to do some of the preface. I wonder why that is? It always mars the work."[50] Ultimately, he indicted her promotion of "divine healing" as irresponsible and dangerous, and predicted that Christian Science would grow in spurious influence until it rivaled the papacy: just another form of imperialism.

As with his other imperialist writings, he encountered squeamishness from his publishers. The *North American Review* gamely published a four-part series of these essays beginning in December 1902, but Harper & Brothers, after accepting the assembled writings for publication in book form, withheld it from the market until 1907, by which time it had blended in with other criticisms of the church.

JEAN'S PNEUMONIA, and Sam's efforts to hide that bad news from Livy, increased tensions in the Riverdale household. The under-the-door love letters continued ("Good morning, dear heart, & thank you for your dear greeting. I think of you all the time . . ."[51] Livy remained gravely weak through the first six months of 1903, but in July, the doctors approved her wish to visit Elmira and Quarry Farm. There, she and Sam spent long hours on the farmhouse porch, Livy supine, Sam at her side. Clara, depleted, stayed behind in Riverdale. Late in the summer Livy began to think fondly of Florence, with its sunlit terraces and balmy tranquillity. She remembered the happy winter at the Villa Viviani eleven years earlier. She wanted to go there. Sam began making plans.

There was no longer a central locale, really, to keep the family in America. Clemens had finally sold the Hartford house in May 1903. The buyer represented yet another of Sam Clemens's remarkable interloopings with history. He was Richard M. Bissell, the president of the Hartford Fire Insurance Company and a Yale graduate. His son, Richard M. Bissell Jr., became a friend of Prescott Bush and an aide of Allen Dulles at the CIA; he is said to have managed plans for the next invasion of Cuba after the one in 1898, and the training of would-be Fidel Castro assassins between 1959 and 1961.[52] The Bissell family lived there until 1917, then rented the house to a boys' school for four years before unloading it to a developer who wanted to tear it down and use the property to expand his complex, known as Mark Twain Apartments. The Friends of Hartford prevented this by buying the house in 1927; its first floor later became the Mark Twain Branch of the Hartford Public Library; then the house was partitioned for and rented as private apartments through the 1960s. In 1963 it was designated a National Historic Landmark, and the long restoration of its original furnishings and appearance began. It now stands as a central tourist attraction in Hartford.

Clemens traveled to New York in late September to make arrangements for an October sailing. From the Grosvenor Hotel he sent his wife a tender, reflective letter, apparently unprompted by anything in particular, that addressed their mutual understanding of the onrushing inevitability.

> Dear, dear sweetheart, I have been thinking & examining, & searching & analyzing, for many days, & am vexed to find that I more believe in the immortality of the soul than misbelieve in it.[53]

Surpassingly tender and compassionate, it was almost certainly a white lie. "One of the proofs of the immortality of the soul," he'd scrawled in his note book not long before this, "is that myriads have believed in it. They also believed the world was flat."[54] A truer statement of his feelings probably lay in lines that he had written to her thirty-four years earlier, during his courtship days, from Hartford: "Livy, you are so interwoven with the very fibres of my being that if I were to lose you it seems to me that to lose memory & reason at the same time would be a blessing to me."[55]

His white lie worked. "I am truly thankful that you 'more believe in the immortality of the soul . . . ' " Livy wrote back. "An immortality already begun seems to make it worthwhile to train oneself. However you don't need to 'bother about' it, 'it' will 'take care of itself.' "[56] She added a request for some Buffalo Lythia water.

The Clemenses boarded the steamship *Princess Irene* on October 24 and departed New York for Genoa. In the entourage besides the parents and their two daughters were Katy Leary, a nurse named Margaret Sherry, Isabel Lyon, and Miss Lyon's mother. What awaited them was a grotesque travesty of Livy's fond Florence fantasy. Their residence, which Sam had rented without firsthand knowledge, was a fifty-room Renaissance palace called the Villa di Quarto. The owner, and their on-premises landlady, was a sour Italian-American woman, the Countess Massiglia. Livy's condition was not the countess's problem; she seemed spitefully interested in creating obstacles for her tenants: shutting off all water inside the building, terminating the telephone service, insisting that the gates be kept locked despite the problems this presented for Livy's doctors. Sam lost no time hurling lawsuits at her. Even the weather was inhospitable—a chilly, overcast winter soon set in, deepening the cheerless mood. The new year, 1904, arrived hung in black crepe: word arrived by cablegram in January that Mollie Clemens had died at Keokuk at the age of sixty-nine, having survived Orion by six years.

Livy's pulse fibrillated in late February, "and there was a collapse."[57] In early April, she struggled for breath for more than an hour. "Clara was in there. Jean and I listened at the door."[58] Livy's Italian doctors continued to enforce limitations on Sam's bedside visits: two minutes a day. The couple continued to suffer for it. Livy and Sam, who years ago had called out the pain of separation from each other by letters across continents and oceans, endured the exquisite torture of separation by a wall. Sometimes Sam broke the rules, slipping unnoticed into the room. "She'd put her arms around his neck the first thing," Katy Leary recalled, "and he'd hold her soft, and give her one of them tender kisses . . . It was a love that was more than earthly love—it was heavenly."[59]

The end came at a little after 9 p.m. on Sunday, June 5, 1904. Livy had been sitting propped against the pillows on her bed, supported by Katy Leary, and talking, and then she was gone. She was fifty-seven. Her final illness had lasted twenty-two months.

Sam described it to his oldest friend the next day.

Last night at 9:20 I entered Mrs. Clemens's room to say the usual good-night—& she was dead! tho' no one knew it. She had been cheerfully talking, a moment before. She was sitting up in bed—she had not lain down for months—& Katie & the nurse were supporting her . . . I bent over her & looked in her face, & I think I spoke—I was surprised and troubled that she did not notice me. Then we understood, & our hearts broke . . .

. . . I am tired & old; I wish I were with Livy.[60]

The Clemens party sailed from Naples to America on June 28. Livy's funeral was on July 14 in Elmira, where she was buried in the family plot. Her husband would be required to linger for six more years, as the Great Dark gathered, and Halley's Comet rounded in its orbit toward Earth again.

Chapter the Last

Mark Twain ended his *Adventures of Tom Sawyer* with a

CONCLUSION

So endeth this chronicle. It being strictly a history of a *boy*, it must stop here; the story could not go much further without becoming the history of a *man* . . .

Soon endeth this chronicle. It being strictly a history of a *man*, it must stop here; the story could not go much further without becoming the history of an *old* man. Which is to say, the history of every old man. Which is to say, a history that depends for much of its nourishment to readers on the extract of pathos.

He aged, and he died. Death and loss and the embarrassment of his own failing body haunted his final years, and sometimes "despair," a word that has often been draped over his life after Livy like a shroud. As with many old men of means, he was prey to loneliness and deep brooding, and to conspiracies among the people he'd drawn close to him, and he was witness to the sordid struggles among these same people for the rights to his soul. Unlike most old men, he was the most conspicuous person on the planet[1]—his own estimation, but likely true—and he enjoyed the planet's ongoing adulation of him. Like most old men with a skill, he employed what he had left of it; he wrote a lot, and some of it was pretty good.

After Elmira, Clemens and his daughters took a summer residence at Tyringham, in the Berkshires of western Massachusetts. Sam made several trips to New York, hunting for a winter residence. His temporary residence in the city was a suite of rooms at the Grosvenor Hotel, in an area that Henry James had made famous with his novel, *Washington Square*. He ran into Henry James at Deal Beach, New Jersey, where Clemens was visiting George Harvey in late August.[2] Clara, undone since her mother's death, had briefly entered a sanitarium. Now, disoriented in Massachusetts, she left Jean with Isabel Lyon and came to the city, along with Katy Leary, and stayed at the home of a friend.

Jean had suffered a seizure in Italy after Livy's death, but seemed to be recovering. On July 31, she went on a moonlight horseback ride with some friends near the village of Lee, about five miles down the road from Tyringham. A trolley* frightened her horse, which bolted into its path and was killed. Jean, knocked unconscious, suffered bruises on most of her body. "Jean is at the summer home in Berkshire Hills, crippled," Sam noted in his journal.[3] While he was recovering from this shock, his sister Pamela died on August 31 at Greenwich, Connecticut, two weeks short of her seventy-seventh birthday.

In September 1904, Clemens rented a rather Gothic house at 21 Fifth Avenue, three blocks north of Washington Square. Clara helped decorate the rooms, choosing lavender wallpaper for her music room,[4] and the family—what remained of it—took possession in November. Jean's accident had reactivated Clara's mounting hysteria, and it all boiled over late that month. She checked into a private sanitarium in New York; and, from there, to another in Connecticut. She was estranged from her father for nearly a year. ("Never well since June 5," Clemens wrote of her.)[5] Clemens, bedridden by bronchitis, turned back to his writing. He produced "The Czar's Soliloquy," a sarcasm occasioned by a bloody reprisal of Russian workers, in January 1905, and then turned to *King Leopold's Soliloquy* and "The War Prayer."

It was in early 1906, after his seventieth birthday, that Mark Twain began to organize what he called his "Aquarium," a brainstorm that gave him a good deal of posthumous grief, and a little heat from Clara in his lifetime. The club consisted of young—very young—girls, whom he called his "Angelfish," after a species he had admired in Bermuda. The girls, whom he encountered in various social situations, ranged in age roughly from ten to fourteen, and by the time of his death, he'd "collected" more than a dozen of them. He invited them to visit him at his house, along with their mothers; he corresponded with them—more than three hundred letters were exchanged—and eventually formalized the club with wholesome rules for membership. When Clara returned from Europe in September 1908 and discovered the club's existence, she sensed scandal in the offing and made her father sharply curtail his activities. Despite a number of pokes in the ribs by Mark Twain chroniclers over the years—if you thought he was kinky in Virginia City, wait'll you hear about Bermuda!—the loneliness and the yearning for the lost Man-in-the-Moon

---

* This was what Sam called the vehicle in his notebook.

days with his own little girls seems self-evidently to have been his impetus. Karen Lystra put to rest most of the heavy breathing with her 2004 study, *Dangerous Intimacy: The Untold Story of Mark Twain's Final Years.* (The "intimacy" alluded to is located elsewhere.)

IN MAY 1906 Mark Twain returned to the dark, profound themes that had gnawed at him over the past quarter-century, themes that he had thrashed out in a dozen papers, stories, essays, and fragments: the themes of God's cynical indifference to Man; of Man's own deterministic corruption; and the dual, dreamlike nature of identity. "What Is Man?" published anonymously in 1906, attempts to consummate all these scattered efforts in a Socratic-like dialogue between an Old Man (representing the fatalistic view) and a Young Man (representing doomed idealism). Flawed as philosophy, the work succeeds as the testament of a man hungry for reconciliation with the perpetual Messiah, and oversated with the knowledge that he will never return to Paradise. He launched into the feverish "3,000 Years Among the Microbes," a novel fragment written from the viewpoint of a cholera microbe. His Adam-and-Eve explorations continued with "A Humane Word from Satan," in April; "A Monument to Adam," in July; and *Eve's Diary* in December. *Eve's Diary* was published in book form in June 1906. A fond tribute to William Dean Howells appeared in July. And then there was the monumental discharge of his final self-reckoning: the oracular mass of dictated verbiage that overwhelmed three successive editors, and remains to this day, nearly a hundred years hence, formally insoluble to orderly minds, a Vandal of the genre. This was the autobiography.

The *Autobiography* of course is the essence of Mark Twain's oeuvre; extract it and you are left with a couple of pamphlets and a story about a saint. (Joan of Arc would be canonized in 1920.) Having fictionalized the facts of his life and factualized its fictions for forty-odd years, he now addressed himself to setting the record straight, in the Twainian sense of "straight." Howells's remark that "he was not enslaved to consecutiveness"[6] never had better evidence. Nor has any Lacanian notion that truth is impossible to "say," yet through this very impossibility it holds on to the real.

The activating agent to this outpouring (and the first person to misuse it) was Albert Bigelow Paine. Paine insinuated his way into Mark Twain's life by stages. The photographic-supplies salesman turned children's book writer turned magazine editor turned biographer was forty when he first met the author at a dinner in New York in 1901. He was starstruck, having read Mark Twain as a boy; and he was a little main chance–struck as well. He reintroduced himself at the seventieth-birthday gala thrown for the author by Colonel Harvey at Delmonico's on December 5, 1905; he dropped the name "Joan of Arc" to get Mark Twain's attention. (Paine would publish his own Joan of Arc biography in 1925.)

In January, on hearing from a mutual friend that Mark Twain had liked his biography of Thomas Nast, published in 1904, Paine obtained permission to call at 21 Fifth Avenue. He found the great man lounging in bed. Bed was where Clemens had spent a great deal of time for some years now, but this bed was special: the great bed of carved oak that he and Livy had bought in Venice, and installed in the Hartford house, the bed where they reclined with their pillows at its foot so they could admire the carved cherubs on the posts at its head. Now, after nearly fifteen years, Samuel Clemens had it back again, and he virtually lived in it, the sole tenant. Paine entered the room to find him propped on some pillows, surrounded by cigars and letters and manuscripts. After some small talk, Paine got to the purpose of his visit: he held out the hope that he might someday undertake a book about Mark Twain.

"When would you like to begin?"[7] Clemens asked him. Paine never forgot the moment: he'd caught his reflection in a mirror behind the oaken bed just as Clemens posed the question, and it felt to him as though he were having a dream. He regathered his wits enough to be back a few days later with a stenographer. Thus began the 242 dictating sessions extending through April 1909. Combined with some meandering thoughts he'd spoken to Isabel Lyon in Florence during Livy's illness, the transcripts encompassed 2,500 pages.[8] No one has better encapsulated the author's methodology than Mark Twain himself. It is a design that would have caused the Transcendentalists to pull their hair, but one that would resonate with Sigmund Freud, the Cubists, and other cognitive reshapers of the new century.

Finally, in Florence in 1904, I hit upon the right way to do an Autobiography: start it at no particular time of your life; wander at your free will all over your life; talk only about the thing which interests you for the moment; drop it the moment its interest threatens to pale, and turn your talk upon the new and more interesting thing that has intruded itself into your mind meantime.[9]

Colonel Harvey, who'd read and liked some excerpts that Mark Twain sent him, began running installments of these transcripts in the *North American Review* on September 7, 1906. They totaled twenty-five through December 1907, but represented only a small fraction of the whole. (Harvey's offer of thirty thousand dollars accelerated Mark Twain's "hundred-years-hence" timetable a little bit.)

Paine harvested his exclusive access to this material in two main ways. One was for the agreed-on purpose, his 1,587-page, three-volume *Mark Twain: A Biography,* which he brought out in 1912. The other was a disheveled two-volume edition of the *Autobiography* in 1924, using a fraction of the dictations and throwing in an assortment of notes and fragments dating from 1870. Typically, he left out material that he thought would shock the public or tarnish his subject's image. Bernard De Voto's *Mark Twain in Eruption* in 1940 published large sections of the dictations passed over by Paine. De Voto's organization was superior to his predecessor's, but his choices were also protective, as he tried to save his subject from his own emotional outbursts, and suppressed the feud with Bret Harte. *The Autobiography of Mark Twain,* edited by Charles Neider and published in 1959—obviously with vetting by Clara Clemens Samossoud—is also selective and arbitrary; but it is the least bowdlerized and the most chronologically coherent of the three—in that it rearranged Mark Twain's own impressionistic approach.

Paine attached himself to Mark Twain. From January 1906 on, he was a fixture in the Clemens household. He exploited the enthusiasm that he shared with Sam for billiards, and hung in gamely for the endless sessions that often continued far into the night. The reward was constant access to his subject. During one of these, Clemens confessed a disturbing dream that echoed an obsession he'd shared with Charles Warren Stoddard in London back in 1873: "There is never a month passes . . . that I do not dream of being in reduced circumstances, and obliged to go back to the river to earn a living . . . [U]sually in my dream I am just about to start into a black shadow without being able to tell whether it is Selma bluff, or Hat Island, or only a black wall of night." [10]

As his involvement deepened, Paine expanded his purview. In 1906, he talked Clemens into buying a 248-acre tract in Redding, Connecticut, near land that Paine had purchased for his own retirement house. Clemens engaged John Mead Howells, the son of his old friend and now a leading architect (his firm later designed the Chicago Tribune building) to build him a two-story Italianate villa with eighteen rooms. He financed the house partly with the thirty thousand that Colonel Harvey paid him for the autobiographical chapters, though it ended up costing twice that amount. Clemens called it "Stormfield," after the fictional ship's captain modeled on Edgar Wakeman, who'd raced comets through space for years in Mark Twain's imagination. Wakeman would finally emerge onto the page in the short book, *Extract from Captain Stormfield's Visit to Heaven,* serialized and later published by Harper's beginning in 1909. Clemens moved into the house sight unseen in June 1908, and loved it.

Paine, meanwhile, was waging an internal power struggle with the fiercely protective, and perhaps emotionally involved, Isabel Lyon for possession of Mark Twain's legacy. Lyon gained an ally with the arrival of a young British entrepreneur named Ralph Ashcroft, who'd met Clemens as a treasurer of the Plasmon company in 1903, and who eventually became his business manager. Ashcroft advised Clemens to register "Mark Twain" as a trademark for copyright protection purposes, and in 1908 helped form the Mark Twain Company. Ashcroft and Lyon, who married in 1909, gained power-of-attorney rights from Clemens, but after some ugly behind-the-scenes feuding with Clara Clemens, Sam turned them both out of the household and canceled their legal authority. While all this was going on, Paine formed an alliance of his own with Clara (nonromantic; he was a Victorian husband and father) that led to his appointment as Mark Twain's literary executor, a position that he nearly redefined as "literary executioner": with the approval of Clara, whose acute observations of her father had congealed into sentimental protectiveness, Paine did his best to gentrify the Vandal's posthumous image. He edited passages from Mark Twain manuscripts and added some of his own without scholarly accounting. He published deeply abridged volumes of Mark Twain letters. His biography, while generally accurate and unimpeachably sourced, is ultimately a fawning deification.

MARK TWAIN'S public life continued on its grand scale. He dined at the White House in 1905 with Theodore Roosevelt, all differences forgiven, or ignored. In 1906, he gave memorable testimony before a congressional committee on copyrighting, clad in one of the white serge suits he was now wearing in public almost exclusively. In 1907 he did not receive the Nobel Prize for literature—Rudyard Kipling did—but in June of that year he traveled to England for a tribute that meant even more to him, an honorary degree from Oxford University. He cherished the red Oxford gown he was given, and wore it whenever he felt like it, which was often. He bound up an old wound, sort of, in February 1908, agreeing to speak at a dinner in honor of Whitelaw Reid, now ambassador to Great Britain. He offered a mild, amiable joke—"I knew John Hay when I had no white hairs in my head and more hair than Reid has now"[11]—and allowed as how Reid and Hay (dead two years) "have regulated troubles of nations and conferred peace upon mankind." (He hastened to add that he himself was the "principal moral force" in those international movements.)[12]

His sorrows continued on, as well. Jean Clemens slipped deeper and deeper into the horrors of her epilepsy. She was naturally an agreeable, warmhearted young woman; but her attacks grew so severe that they affected her sanity; twice, in 1905 and 1906, she tried to kill Katy Leary, and was frequently institutionalized. She sought treatment in Germany in 1908, and returned in April 1909 to live at Stormfield.

Jim Gillis and Thomas Bailey Aldrich died in 1907, and Henry Huttleston Rogers suffered the stroke that hastened his death two years later. On August 1, 1908, Clemens's nephew, Pamela's son Samuel, drowned at the age of forty-seven.

HE SETTLED his literary affairs with the devil. In 1908 he finally set aside "The Chronicles of Young Satan," which he'd been tinkering with since 1897: it had given way to a more powerful and technically unified short novel that was not discovered until after his death. Its title character, "No. 44, the Mysterious Stranger," is a boy with miraculous powers who appears in a medieval Austrian village, finds himself an outcast, and forms a friendship with the narrator August Feldner, with whom he shares the secrets of the dream self and the "real" self.

Perhaps he was inspired by the reemergence, after many years, of the feminine force with whom he'd entered into a continuing dream identity. The Platonic Sweetheart called out to him one final time, in August 1906. The letter from her arrived while Mark Twain was dictating a section of his autobiography. The contact stirred him anew, and with Livy now safe from pain, he finally felt free to write his memories of their shipboard romance. Thus he dictated the passage about the young girl in the unfaded bloom of her youth, with her plaited tails dangling from her young head and her white frock puffing about in the wind of that ancient Mississippi time.

Her letter revealed a far different image. She was sixty-two now, and desperate. Divorced from or abandoned by her husband, Dake, a prominent judge in Missouri, she was still teaching school, at poverty-level wages. She needed a thousand dollars to support herself and her thirty-seven-year-old, disabled son. Fuming at Dake's callousness, Mark Twain sent the money.

In her thankful reply—as reported by Mark Twain—Laura Wright disclosed to her old swain what had happened to her after the two had parted in that long-ago May, when the *John J. Roe* carried her upriver. The boat struck a snag in the night and took on water. She was steered toward the shore, where the Leavenworths evacuated the passengers. Someone noticed that Laura was not among them. The pilot and the mate rushed back aboard the dangerously listing *Roe* and knocked on Laura's cabin door, shouting for her to get out of there at once. She called back calmly that she was still repairing her hoopskirt. Ignoring the men's frantic urgings, she remained in her cabin until the skirt was presentable, and only then made her way ashore. Was it a dream? Did Laura Wright really send this account to the aging Sam? No such letter is known to exist. The authoritative Way's Packet Directory, 1848–1994, compiled by Frederick Way Jr., records that the *John J. Roe* was snagged and sunk, all right—but years later, on the Civil War date of September 12, 1864, at New Madrid, Missouri. She was headed downriver, transporting the 2nd Wisconsin Cavalry. One hundred sixty-five horses were lost. There is no mention of hoopskirts. Perhaps the *Roe* had been salvaged from the earlier snagging. As with so much of Mark Twain's dreamlike memory, the truth is hard to tell—unless one includes passionate fantasy in one's definition of "truth."

Laura's own life seems to have grown nearly as exotic as Sam's dreams of her. Myths accrued: some claimed that she became a Confederate spy during the war, hunted by the Yankees, with a price on her head. She was said to have fallen in love with a steamboat captain while escaping downriver to New Orleans: Dake. They married after the war, it was said, and moved to San Francisco, where Laura opened a school for young ladies, and attained sophistication. Then abandonment. Then, to the rescue, the Black Avenger of the Spanish Main.

LAURA WRIGHT Dake emerged out of the mists once more, fifteen years after Clemens's death. A man named C. O. Byrd recorded his encounters with her, writing in 1964. Byrd was a son of A. K. Byrd, a Missourian born in 1851, and a friend of one Marshall P. Wright, Laura's younger brother. C. O. Byrd met Laura herself around 1925—in Tinseltown, of all places. It was on the occasion of her eightieth birthday.

I took her to the swankiest night club in Hollywood for the celebration where she was the life of the party. She was about five feet tall, a cultured refined lady and had a keen sense of humor. We became intimate friends and I saw her frequently . . .[13]

It was on one of these visits that C. O. Byrd held in his hands a collection of treasures unimaginable.

. . . [W]e happened to be talking about Mark Twain. She took me to her bed room, had me open her trunk, and got out several packages of letters from Sam Clemens. For several hours she read me portions of many of the letters. Then she told me that she had offers from several magazines who wanted to buy the letters. I think Lippincotts offered her $20,000.00. I know that some of the letters were written during the war . . .[14]

Laura Wright Dake told C. O. Byrd that her sisters and brother had urged her to sell the letters—she was yet again in need of money—but she refused.

She made me promise, on my honor, that after her death I would destroy the letters and not let anyone read them. She said Sam Clemens wrote them to her and for her and that they were not to be published.[15]

C. O. Byrd, sadly enough, was one of a breed already vanishing in the early 20th century: a gentleman who kept his word.

CLARA CLEMENS and Ossip Gabrilowitsch were married at Stormfield in October 1909. Joseph Twichell presided. The father of the bride wore his red Oxford gown over a white serge suit and under the tasseled Oxford cap. He gave his last public speech that year, at a Baltimore school for girls. And then the final decline began. Clemens had suffered chest pains in the summer of 1909. In the fall of that year, working rapidly against a deadline he must have sensed, he composed *Letters from the Earth,* the eleven dispatches from Satan, again visiting his favorite planet, to friends around the universe. Bitterly satirical, and uproariously funny, the letters picked apart the Bible, the Ten Commandments (especially the commandment about adultery), and Man's self-satisfaction. He read the letters to prim Paine as he finished each, and Paine, who collaborated with Clara in their suppression until her death (they were published in 1962), laughed himself silly. He and Paine traveled to Bermuda in November of that year; they were houseguests of Mr. and Mrs. William H. Allen, and Sam celebrated his seventy-fourth birthday near the great beaches he'd come to love. He made it back to Stormfield a few days before Christmas, in time to peck in on the "surprise" tree that Jean was decorating in the loggia (the small rooftop room) with foil and candles. On the night before Christmas Eve, he walked hand in hand with his daughter from the dining table to the library, where they talked happily until nine. Beside the door to her bedroom, they kissed each other's hand. At 7:30 the next morning Clemens was jolted awake by Katy Leary, who burst into his room to blurt out, from behind his head: "*Miss Jean is dead!*"[16] She had suffered a seizure in the bathtub and slipped under the water, unable to call for help. She was twenty-nine.

A wailing lament for her, coupled with cynical gratitude for her release—tidied up by Paine—formed the final chapter of his autobiography.[17]

Would I bring her back to life if I could do it? I would not . . . In her loss I am almost bankrupt, and my life is a bitterness, but I am content: for she has been enriched with the most precious of all gifts . . . death.[18]

HE RETURNED to Bermuda on January 5, seeing Howells for the last time on the night before his departure. Howells had ten years of life left, but his era of tremendous influence had passed, and he had become a sort of living ghost, "the dean of American letters." The two spoke of labor unions, and said good-bye, not realizing it was forever. Clemens traveled with Joe Twichell, stayed with the Allens, and played miniature golf with the vacationing Woodrow Wilson. On March 25, he booked passage for home, explaining in a letter to Paine that he did not want to die in Bermuda. Within days after that, the chest pains attacked him again. Paine sailed to the island to bring him home; they departed on April 12. Clemens arrived back at Stormfield two nights later. Paine and Claude Joseph Beuchotte, the butler, carried him in a canvas chair from the carriage to his upstairs room and his doctors. There he waited for two days for Clara and Ossip to join him. He wanted morphine, but the doctors refused him.

On Sunday morning Clara arrived, and Mark Twain brightened and spoke of his plans for the summer. Outside, the new century stumbled toward its Sand Belt; in a few weeks the leading crowned heads of Europe, including Archduke Ferdinand, would assemble in London for the funeral of King Edward VI, their last mingling before World War I ignited. Clemens's breathing grew heavier that evening, and his speech began to slur. He took an opiate and began to speak of dual personalities, and he faded some; and a little later he blurted out something about the laws of mentality; and after a while went to sleep, and faded some more. Halley's Comet was inside the orbit of Venus now, traveling at three million miles a day toward its perihelion, its closest point to the sun, which it reached on Tuesday, April 19. On that day Mark Twain sent for Clara to come and sing for him, and she managed some Scottish ballads, which seemed to comfort him. No one in the house took note of the comet, though it burned brightly that night. Soon it would be gone. By Wednesday, his mind was wandering out of control, and he had trouble making himself understood, and faded some more. On Thursday morning, April 21, he rallied faintly and tried to read from a volume of Seutonius at his bedside. The Mexican people prepared for revolution against the tyrant Porfirio Díaz; an uprising of Albanians against the imperial Turks sent cracks through the Ottoman Empire; plans for war and revolution pulsated through the damned human race. A little before noon, he sent Clara to find Paine, and when Paine arrived, Mark Twain indicated a pair of unfinished manuscripts and whispered, "throw away," and pressed Paine's hand, and that was the last moment Paine had with him. He faded some more; tried to write a note, but his fine handwriting had deserted him. Electricity lighted cities now, but the lamps were going out. He dozed into the early afternoon; awoke; took the hand of Clara beside him; faded some more; managed to say, "Good-bye," and then murmured something that might have been, "If we meet—" and then he faded again, and kept on fading, until there was nothing left of him to hold back the Great Dark descending on the world, except his words.

Notes

ABBREVIATIONS

ET&S   *Early Tales & Sketches*. Vol. 1, 1851–1864. Vol. 2, 1864–1865. Edited by Edgar Marquess Branch and Robert H. Hirst. Berkeley: University of California Press, 1979–81.

LLMT   *The Love Letters of Mark Twain*. Edited by Dixon Wecter. New York: Harper & Bros., 1949.

MFMT   *My Father, Mark Twain*. By Clara Clemens. New York: Harper & Bros., 1931.

MMT   *My Mark Twain: Reminiscences and Criticisms*. By William Dean Howells. Edited by Marilyn Austin Baldwin. Baton Rouge: Louisiana State University Press, 1967.

MTA   *The Autobiography of Mark Twain*. Edited by Charles Neider. New York: Harper & Row, 1959.

MTB   *Mark Twain: A Biography*. By Albert Bigelow Paine. 3 vols. New York: Harper & Bros., 1912.

MTBM   *Mark Twain, Business Man*. Edited by Samuel Charles Webster. Boston: Little, Brown & Co., 1946.

MTHHR   *Mark Twain's Correspondence with Henry Huttleston Rogers, 1893–1909*. Edited by Lewis Leary. Berkeley: University of California Press, 1969.

MTHL   *Mark Twain-Howells Letters: The Correspondence of Samuel L. Clemens and William Dean Howells*. Edited by Henry Nash Smith and William M. Gibson. 2 vols. Cambridge: Harvard University Press, 1960.

MTL   *Mark Twain's Letters*. Vol. 1, 1853–1866, edited by Edgar Marquess Branch, Michael B. Frank, and Kenneth Anderson. Vol. 2, 1867–1868, edited by Harriet Elinor Smith and Richard Bucci. Vol. 3, 1869, edited by Victor Fischer and Michael B. Frank. Vol. 4, 1870–1871, edited by Victor Fischer and Michael B. Frank. Vol. 5, 1872–1873, edited by Lin Salamo and Harriet Elinor Smith. Vol. 6, 1874–1875, edited by Michael B. Frank and Harriet Elinor Smith. Berkeley: University of California Press, 1988–2002.

MTLTP   *Mark Twain's Letters to His Publishers, 1867–1894.* Edited by Hamlin Hill. Berkeley: University of California Press, 1967.

MTP   Mark Twain Papers. Bancroft Library. University of California, Berkeley.

N&J   *Mark Twain's Notebooks & Journals.* Vol. 1, 1855–1873, edited by Frederick Anderson, Michael B. Frank, and Kenneth M. Sanderson. Vol. 2, 1877–1883, edited by Frederick Anderson, Lin Salamo, and Bernard L. Stein. Vol. 3, 1883–1891, edited by Robert Pack Browning, Michael B. Frank, and Lin Salamo. Berkeley: University of California Press, 1979.

OMT   *The Oxford Mark Twain.* Edited by Shelley Fisher Fishkin. 29 vols. New York: Oxford University Press, 1996.

PROLOGUE

1. MTA, p. 1. The quotation, like those that follow here, has been corrected against the original manuscript in the Mark Twain Papers (MTP) at the University of California, Berkeley.
2. MMT, p. 6.
3. Ibid., p. 94.

1: "SOMETHING AT ONCE AWFUL AND SUBLIME"

1. MTA, p. 10.
2. Ibid., p. 7.
3. Dixon Wecter, *Sam Clemens of Hannibal* (Boston: Houghton Mifflin, 1952), p. 44.
4. Mark Twain and Charles Dudley Warner, *The Gilded Age: A Tale of Today,* OMT, pp. 29–30.
5. Retold by Annie Moffett Webster in MTBM, p. 44.
6. MTA, p. 6.
7. Ibid.
8. See the Biographical Directory in *Huck Finn and Tom Sawyer Among the Indians: And Other Unfinished Stories,* Mark Twain Library edition (Berkeley: University of California Press, 1989), p. 316.
9. From "Mark Twain's Cousin," *The Twainian* (July–August 1952), pp. 1–2, cited by Shelley Fisher Fishkin in *Was Huck Black? Mark Twain and African-American Voices* (New York: Oxford University Press, 1993), p. 164.
10. MTA, p. 6.
11. See "Jane Lampton Clemens" in *Huck Finn and Tom Sawyer Among the Indians: And Other Unfinished Stories,* p. 89.
12. See "A True Story Just as I Heard It," in *Sketches, New and Old,* OMT, p. 202.
13. Ibid.

2: "THE WHITE TOWN, DROWSING . . ."

1. N&J, vol. 3, p. 39.
2. *The Essential Writings of Ralph Waldo Emerson,* edited by Brooks Atkinson (New York: Modern Library, 2000).

3. William Dean Howells, *Literary Friends and Acquaintance* (New York: Harper & Bros., 1901), pp. 3–4.

4. Ibid.

5. Ibid.

6. George Washington Harris, *Sut Lovingood: Yarns Spun by a "Nat'ral Born Durn'd Fool"* (University of North Carolina at Chapel Hill, 1997), pp. 152–53, electronic edition. "This work is the property of the University of North Carolina at Chapel Hill. It may be used freely by individuals for research, teaching and personal use as long as this statement of availability is included in the text."

7. Twain and Warner, *The Gilded Age.*

8. Ibid.

3: OF WORDS AND THE WORD

1. "Former Florida Neighbor of Clemens Family Head of School Attended Here by Mark Twain," Hannibal Evening *Courier-Post*, March 6, 1935, p. 12B, printed in *Huck Finn and Tom Sawyer Among the Indians: And Other Unfinished Stories*, p. 338.

2. *Huck Finn and Tom Sawyer Among the Indians*, p. 338.

3. "Italian without a Master," in *The $30,000 Bequest and Other Stories*, OMT, pp. 171–72.

4. "The Awful German Language," in *A Tramp Abroad*, OMT, pp. 607, 610.

5. Speech delivered in New York, April 5, 1889, in *Mark Twain Speaking*, edited by Paul Fatout (Ames: University of Iowa Press, 1976), p. 245.

6. *Mark Twain's Autobiography*, edited by Albert Bigelow Paine, vol. 1 (New York: Harper & Bros., 1924), p. 173.

7. *Mark Twain's Notebook*, prepared for publication and with commentary by Albert Bigelow Paine (New York: Harper & Bros., 1935), p. 303.

8. Originally published in the *Californian*, December 23, 1865, as "The Christmas Fireside for Good Little Boys and Girls."

9. Originally published in the *Galaxy*, May 1870.

10. MTA, p. 41.

11. *Letters from the Earth*, edited by Bernard De Voto (New York: Perennial Library, 1974), p. 20.

12. "Villagers of 1840–3," in *Huck Finn and Tom Sawyer Among the Indians: And Other Unfinished Stories*, p. 104.

13. *Letters from the Earth*, p. 40.

14. MTA, p. 123.

15. MTB, vol. 3, p. 1534.

4: THE HANNIBAL DECADE

1. *The Adventures of Tom Sawyer*, OMT, pp. 83–84.

2. Letter to William Bowen, February 6, 1870; MTL, vol. 4, p. 50.

3. MMT, p. 58.

4. MTB, vol. 1, p. 58.

5. *The Innocents Abroad*, OMT, p. 628.

6. Ibid.

7. MTBM, p. 265.

8. MTA, p. 67.

9. *The Adventures of Tom Sawyer*, OMT, p. 63.

10. "Villagers of 1840–3," in *Huck Finn and Tom Sawyer Among the Indians: And Other Unfinished Stories*, p. 99.

11. MTA, p. 58.

12. Ibid., p. 60.
13. Ibid., pp. 58–59.
14. Ibid., pp. 60–61.
15. Ibid., p. 59.
16. MMT, p. 30.
17. "Concerning the Jews," in *The Man that Corrupted Hadleyburg and Other Stories and Essays,* OMT, p. 254.
18. MTA, p. 30.
19. MTA, p. 28.
20. Lewis Leary, *Mark Twain's Correspondence With Henry Huttleston Rogers,* edited and with an introduction by Leary (Berkeley: University of California Press, 1969), p. 5.
21. First quote is from *The $30,000 Bequest,* OMT, p. 33; second from *The American Claimant,* OMT, p. 149.
22. MTA, p. 25, corrected against the 1897–98 manuscript in MTP.
23. As described by Paine in MTB, vol. 1, p. 41.
24. "Villagers of 1840–3," p. 104.
25. "Jane Lampton Clemens," in *Huck Finn and Tom Sawyer Among the Indians: And Other Unfinished Stories,* p. 89.
26. MTA, pp. 5–6.
27. MTA, p. 26.
28. "Jane Lampton Clemens," p. 84.
29. *The Adventures of Tom Sawyer,* p. 36.
30. Biographical Directory in *Huck Finn and Tom Sawyer Among the Indians: And Other Unfinished Stories,* p. 323.
31. Wecter, *Sam Clemens of Hannibal,* p. 112.
32. *The Gilded Age,* OMT, p. 98.
33. MTB, vol. 1, p. 74–75.
34. Ibid., p. 75.
35. Courtesy, Robert Hirst, Mark Twain Project.
36. Wecter, *Sam Clemens of Hannibal.*
37. Philip Ashley Fanning develops this theory in *Mark Twain and Orion Clemens: Brothers, Partners, Stranger* (Tuscaloosa: University of Alabama Press, 2003).
38. Letter to Samuel Clemens, June 14, 1880; MTHL, vol. 1, p. 315.

5: APPRENTICE

1. *Roughing It,* OMT, p. 292.
2. Ibid., p. 292.
3. Ibid.
4. See "Editorial Agility" in the Hannibal *Journal,* September 16, 1852, p. 3. It is signed "W.E.A.B." (W. Epaminondas Adrastus Blab), one of Sam's pen names. It is a highly scornful description of Ament, who is not named, but who behaved similarly to the character described.
5. In her book of that title, published by Johns Hopkins University Press in 1985.
6. As noted in *The Story of Hannibal,* by J. Hurley Hagood and Roberta Hagood (Hannibal, Mo. Standard Printing Co., 1976), p. 37.
7. Wecter, *Sam Clemens of Hannibal,* p. 163.
8. Letter to Olivia Clemens, January 23, 1885; LLMT, p. 233, quoted in *Huck Finn and Tom Sawyer Among the Indians: And Other Unfinished Stories,* p. 334.
9. Ibid.
10. Ibid.

11. MTA, p. 88.
12. Ibid.
13. Ibid., p. 90.
14. N&J, vol. 3, p. 305.
15. MTA, p. 91.
16. Letter to George Bainton, October 15, 1888; www.twainquotes.com.
17. "The Last Words of Great Men," Buffalo *Express*, September 11, 1869, p. 1.
18. From "Cholera," by Terry Hogan, published in the Galesburg, Illinois, *Zephyr*, 2002.

6: RAMBLER

1. ET&S, vol. 1, p. 75
2. Ibid., p. 75.
3. Ibid., p. 72.
4. Letter to William Dean Howells, September 15, 1879; MTHL, vol. 1, p. 269.
5. In *Mark Twain's Satires and Burlesques*, edited by Franklin R. Rogers (Berkeley: University of California Press, 1967), pp. 134–64.
6. "My First Literary Venture," *Galaxy*, vol. 11 (April 1871), pp. 615–16.
7. As recounted in "My First Literary Venture."
8. ET&S, vol. 1, p. 75.
9. Ibid., p. 73.
10. Ibid., p. 77.
11. ET&S, vol. 1, p. 74.
12. ET&S, vol. 1, p. 62.
13. Ibid., pp. 64–65.
14. Ibid., pp. 67–68.
15. Hannibal *Daily Journal*, May 7, 1853, MTP.
16. Ibid., May 5, 1853, MTP.
17. Writing to the editor of the Hannibal *Courier-Post* on December 3, 1907, Mark Twain admitted that "[s]urreptitiously & uninvited, I helped to edit the paper when no one was watching" (MTP).
18. "A Family Muss," ET&S, vol. 1, pp. 70–71.
19. *Life on the Mississippi*, OMT, p. 541.
20. ET&S, vol. 1, pp. 88–95.
21. Ibid., p. 96.
22. Ibid., p. 97.
23. Ibid., p. 98.
24. Ibid., p. 99.
25. See MTL, vol. 1, p. 2.
26. MTB, vol. 1, p. 93.
27. Letter to Pamela Clemens, September 3, 1853; MTL, vol. 1, p. 13.
28. MTA, p. 94.

7: "SO FAR FROM HOME . . ."

1. Letter to the San Francisco *Alta California*, May 26, 1867; www.twainquotes.com.
2. Letter to Mary Fairbanks, 1868; Mark Twain's Letters, vol. 2, p. 252.
3. MTL, vol. 1, p. 20.
4. *Life on the Mississippi*, OMT, p. 253.
5. Anthony Kennedy, " 'Mark Twain,' a Poor Typo," *Inland Printer*, January 1908; quoted in MTL, vol. 1, pp. 2–3.
6. Ibid., p. 5.

7. Letter to Jane Clemens, August 24, 1853; MTL, vol. 1, p. 3.
8. Ibid.
9. Ibid., p. 4.
10. Ibid.
11. Letter to the *Alta California,* March 28, 1867; www.twainquotes.com.
12. As indicated twelve years later in a February 2 letter in the March 1867 *Alta California.*
13. Letter to Jane Clemens, August 31, 1853; MTL, vol. 1, p. 10.
14. Ibid.
15. Letter to Orion and Henry Clemens, October 26–28, 1853; MTL, vol. 1, p. 20.
16. Ibid., pp. 20, 21, 23.
17. Letter to the Muscatine *Journal,* December 4, 1853; MTL, vol. 1, p. 31.
18. "The Poet," in *Emerson's Essays* (New York: Thomas Y. Crowell Co., 1951), p. 267.
19. Ibid., p. 287.
20. Letter to Orion Clemens, November 28, 1853; MTL, vol. 1, p. 29.
21. Ibid.
22. Letter to the *Journal,* December 24, 1853; MTL, vol. 1, p. 34.
23. Ibid., p. 35.
24. Letter to the *Journal,* February 17 and 18, 1854; MTL, vol. 1, p. 40.
25. Ibid., p. 41.
26. See MTL, vol. 1, p. 45.
27. *Life on the Mississippi,* OMT, p. 507.
28. Letter to the Muscatine, *Tri-Weekly Journal,* February 16, 1855; MTL, vol. 1, p. 47.
29. See MTL, vol. 1, p. 58.
30. Letter to Jane Clemens and Pamela Moffett, June 10, 1856; MTL, vol. 1, p. 63.
31. N&J, vol. 1, p. 37.
32. Ibid., p. 32.
33. Ibid., p. 34.
34. See MTL, vol. 1, p. 59.
35. Letter to Ann E. Taylor, May 21 and 25, 1856; MTL, vol. 1, p. 61.
36. Ibid., p. 59.
37. Quoted in MTL, vol. 1, p. 65.
38. "The Turning-Point of My Life," 1910, in *What Is Man? And Other Philosophical Writings;* quoted MTL, vol 1, p. 68, n. 7.
39. Ibid.
40. Ibid.
41. Letter to Henry Clemens, August 5, 1856; MTL, vol. 1, p. 67.
42. MTA, p. 95.
43. Letter to the Keokuk *Daily Post,* November 1, 1856; www.twainquotes.com/keokuk.

8: The Language of Water

1. MTBM, pp. 31–32; original letter is at Vassar College in Poughkeepsie, N.Y.
2. Edgar Marquess Branch, "Bixby vs. Carroll: New Light on Sam Clemens's Early River Career," *Mark Twain Journal* (Fall 1992), pp. 2–22.
3. MTB, vol. 1, pp. 117–18.
4. Ibid., pp. 118–19.
5. *Life on the Mississippi,* OMT, p. 79. This first appeared in "Old Times on the Mississippi," *Atlantic Monthly* (February 1875), p. 217.
6. MTA, p. 98.

7. "The Turning-Point of My Life," in *What is Man? And Other Philosophical Writings*, ed. Paul Baender (Berkeley: University of California Press, 1973), p. 461.

8. *Life on the Mississippi*, p. 87.

9. Ibid., p. 118.

10. Ibid., p. 246.

11. *The Gilded Age*, p. 42.

12. *Life on the Mississippi*, pp. 166–67.

13. Ibid., pp. 163–64.

14. Ibid., p. 217.

15. These proscriptions and others are delineated in *The Lady's Guide to Perfect Gentility, in Manners, Dress, and Conversation, in the Family, in Company, at the Piano Forte, the Table, in the Street, and in Gentlemen's Society. Also a Useful Instructor in Letter Writing, Toilet Preparations, Fancy Needlework, Millinery, Dressmaking, Care of Wardrobe, the Hair, Teeth, Hands, Lips, Complexion, etc.*, by Emily Thornwell (New York: Derby and Jackson, 1856).

16. *Life on the Mississippi*, p. 408.

17. MTL, vol. 1, p. 72.

18. Ibid., p. 72.

19. Ibid., pp. 72–73.

20. Sydney J. Krause has argued, in a generally approving study of Twain's critical capabilities, that the author diminished his potential in this area by neglecting other important writers—for instance, Spenser, Marlowe, Jonson, Donne, Marvell, Dryden, Sheridan, Blake, Keats, and Coleridge—"a majority, in fact, of the major poets and dramatists who had flourished before his time and to whom he would have been introduced through formal schooling" (Krause, *Mark Twain as Critic*, Baltimore: Johns Hopkins University Press, 1967).

21. Minnie Brashear, *Mark Twain, Son of Missouri* (Chapel Hill: University of North Carolina Press, 1934).

22. MTB, vol. 3, p. 1445.

23. *The Age of Reason*, in *Collected Writings*, edited by Eric Foner (New York: Library of America, 1995).

24. MTA, pp. 79–80.

25. Ibid., p. 80.

26. Ibid., p. 80.

27. Ibid., p. 80.

28. Letter to Orion and Mollie Clemens, February 6, 1861; MTL, vol. 1, p. 107.

29. The details of this event are known largely through the scholarship of Edgar Marquess Branch in *Men Call Me Lucky: Mark Twain and the Pennsylvania*, in *Keepsakes*, no. 1 (Oxford, Ohio: Friends of the Library Society, 1985).

30. MTBM, p. 45.

31. *Life on the Mississippi*, p. 221.

32. MTBM, p. 37.

33. MTA, p. 99.

34. Ibid., pp. 99–100. Annie's recollection differs a little from Mark Twain's, but it has a ring of authenticity. "[Uncle Sam] says that my grandmother never knew about [the dream], but she did, and often talked about it," Annie wrote. And: "The story as the family used to tell it was not quite like Uncle Sam's version. They said his dream occurred in the daytime. The family including Henry were in my mother's [i.e., Pamela's] room and Sam was asleep in the next room. He came in and told them what he had dreamed. My grandmother [i.e., Jane] said he went back and

dreamed the same dream a second and third time, but I think that was her embellishment" (MTBM, p. 37).

35. *Life on the Mississippi*, p. 227.

36. Ibid., p. 228.

37. Ibid., p. 231.

38. In a letter to Mollie Clemens a few days later, Sam said that Brown collared Henry, turned him halfway around and struck him in the face. By the time of *Life on the Mississippi*, Brown had found a weapon, a convenient "ten-pound lump of coal."

39. Ibid., p. 233.

40. Ibid., p. 236.

41. Ibid., p. 237.

42. Branch, *Men Call Me Lucky*, p. 13.

43. "A Sad Meeting," St. Louis *News and Intelligencer*, June 19, 1858, reprinting the Memphis *Eagle and Enquirer*, June 16, 1858, clipping in Mark Twain's own scrapbook, as quoted in MTL, vol. 1, p. 82.

44. MTL, vol. 1, p. 81.

45. MTA, pp. 100–101.

46. G. K. Chesterton in *A Handful of Authors: Essays on Books and Writers*, edited by Dorothy Collins (New York: Sheed & Ward, 1953).

47. MTA, p. 101.

48. Howard G. Baetzhold sees her in Laura Hawkins of *The Gilded Age*, in Puss Flanagan of *A Connecticut Yankee in King Arthur's Court*, and even in the Eve of an early draft of "Eve's Diary." He makes his case in "Found: Mark Twain's 'Lost Sweetheart,' " in *American Literature*, vol. 44, no. 3 (November 1972).

49. Twain does not use Laura Wright's name in this essay, but Baetzhold's persuasive scholarship indicates that she was indeed the dream girl's model. The abbreviated, Paine-edited version of "My Platonic Sweetheart" can be found in *Collected Tales, Sketches, Speeches, & Essays, Volume Two: 1891–1910*, edited by Louis J. Budd (New York: Library of America, 1992).

50. "My Platonic Sweetheart," pp. 286–87.

51. Ibid., pp. 285.

52. Ibid., p. 287, 290.

53. Ibid., p. 295.

54. Ibid., pp. 294–96.

9: RANGER

1. Edgar Marquess Branch, "Sam Clemens, Steersman on the *John H. Dickey*," *American Literary Realism*, vol. 15, no. 2 (Autumn 1982), p. 200.

2. Ibid. p. 200.

3. *Mark Twain, Business Man* (MTBM) was published by the Atlantic Monthly Press. The deceptively humdrum title hardly hints at its treasury of anecdotes by and about several members of the family.

4. Annie Moffett in MTBM, p. 39.

5. Ibid., p. 30.

6. Ibid., p. 41.

7. William H. Rideing, quoted in *Mark Twain as a Literary Artist*, by Gladys Carmen Bellamy (Norman: University of Oklahoma Press, 1950), p. 12.

8. MTBM, p. 39.

9. Letter to Pamela Moffett, March 9 and 11, 1859; MTL, vol. 1, p. 88.

10. Letter to Orion Clemens; June 27?, 1860; MTL, vol. 1, p. 98.
11. *Life on the Mississippi,* p. 497.
12. *Roughing It,* Mark Twain Library edition (Berkeley: University of California Press, 1996), p. 272.
13. Letter from Jane Clemens, October 14, 1862; MTBM, p. 73.
14. Letter to Susan (Belle) Stotts, August 11, 1860; MTL, vol. 1, p. 100.
15. MTBM, p. 48.
16. ET&S, vol. 1, pp. 146–51.
17. MTB, vol. 1, p. 162.
18. MTBM, p. 60.
19. Ibid., pp. 61–62.
20. Ibid. p. 62.
21. Grimes gives a detailed account of the militia adventure in his highly readable memoir, *Absalom Grimes: Confederate Mail Runner,* edited by M. M. Quaife (New Haven: Yale University Press, 1926).
22. Ibid., p. 10.
23. Ibid., p. 11.
24. Ibid., p. 11.
25. "The Private History of a Campaign That Failed, in *Merry Tales,* OMT, p. 47.
26. Ibid., pp. 44–45.
27. "Campaign That Failed," p. 48.
28. See John Gerber, "Mark Twain's 'Private Campaign,' *Civil War History,* vol. 1 (March 1955), pp. 37–60.

10: WASHOE

1. *Roughing It,* OMT, p. 33.
2. Ibid., p. 25.
3. Ibid., pp. 70–72.
4. Ibid., p. 79.
5. Ibid., p. 88.
6. Ibid., p. 119.
7. Ibid., p. 157.
8. Ibid., p. 159. See also p. 612 in the University of California Press, edition for more information on "Jack Harris."
9. Letter to Pamela Moffett and Jane Clemens, October 25, 1861; MTL, vol. 1, p. 132.
10. MTBM, p. 63.
11. *Roughing It,* OMT, p. 176.
12. Letter to Pamela Moffett and Jane Clemens, October 25, 1861; MTL, vol. 1, p. 129.
13. *Roughing It,* p. 191.
14. Letter to Mollie Clemens, January 29, 30, and 31, 1862; MTL, vol. 1, p. 145.
15. Letter to Orion Clemens, April 10, 1862; MTL, vol. 1, p. 184.
16. Letter to Orion Clemens, April 13, 1862; MTL, vol. 1, p. 186.
17. Ibid., p. 187.
18. Letter to Orion Clemens, April 17 and 19, 1862; MTL, vol. 1, p. 189.
19. Letter to Orion Clemens, June 2, 1862; MTL, vol. 1, p. 216.
20. Letter to Orion Clemens, June 25, 1862; MTL, vol. 1, p. 223.
21. Letter to Orion Clemens, July 23, 1862; MTL, vol. 1, pp. 228–229.
22. Letter to Orion Clemens, June 22, 1862; MTL, vol. 1, p. 221.
23. Letter to Orion Clemens, July 23, 1862; MTL, vol. 1, p. 229.

11: A JOURNALISTIC COUNTERCULTURE

1. *Roughing It*, OMT, p. 303.
2. *Dan De Quille, the Washoe Giant*, by Richard A. Dwyer and Richard E. Lingenfelter (Reno and Las Vegas: University of Nevada Press, 1990), p. 47.
3. Ibid., p. 4.
4. ET&S, vol. 1, p. 389.
5. ET&S, vol. 1, p. 159.
6. "A Couple of Sad Experiences," in *Galaxy,* June 1870; ET&S, vol. 1, p. 156.
7. Ibid.
8. Dan De Quille, "Sad Fate of an Inventor," in *Dan De Quille, the Washoe Giant,* pp. 185–86.
9. Philadelphia *Evening Bulletin,* December 8, 1869; MTL, vol. 4, p. 2.
10. Letter to Jane Clemens and Pamela Moffett, April 11 and 12, 1863; MTL, vol. 1, p. 246.
11. Paul Fatout, *Mark Twain in Virginia City* (Bloomington: Indiana University Press, 1964), p. 24.
12. ET&S, vol. 1, p. 176.
13. ET&S, vol. 1, p. 178.
14. Ibid., p. 182.
15. Branch, in ET&S, vol. 1, p. 19.
16. ET&S, vol. 1, pp. 195–96.
17. Ibid., p. 194.
18. Ibid., p. 198.

12: "MARK TWAIN—MORE OF HIM"

1. "At the time that the telegraph brought the news of [Sellers's] death, I was on the Pacific coast," Twain wrote in Chapter 50, p. 498, of *Life on the Mississippi* ". . . and needed a *nom de guerre;* so I confiscated the ancient mariner's discarded one, and have done my best to make it remain what it was in his hands—a sign . . . that whatever is found in its company may be gambled on as being the petrified truth." Sellers died in 1864, a year after Sam began using the pen name. His earliest version of this explanation was written in January 1873 (Horst Kruse, "Mark Twain's *Nom de Plume;* some Mysteries Resolved," *Mark Twain Journal,* spring 1992, p. 4). Some scholars still hold out hope of finding examples of the pen name used by Sellers, or by someone else, in the river columns of New Orleans or possibly St. Louis papers long before Clemens adopted it.
2. Bret Harte, *Overland Monthly,* January 4, 1870, pp. 100–101.
3. "A Mystery," Cleveland *Herald,* November 16, 1868, p. 2.
4. ET&S, vol. 1, p. 218, corrected against the original *Enterprise* printing of February 19, 1863.
5. Letter to Jane Clemens and Pamela Moffett, February 16, 1863; MTL, vol. 1, p. 244.
6. Ibid., p. 245.
7. Ibid., p. 247.
8. Charles P. Kimball, "Brief Historical Sketch," *San Francisco Director,* 1853; "The San Francisco History Index," http://www.zpub.com/sf/history.
9. Ibid.
10. ET&S, vol. 1, p. 250.
11. Letter to Jane Clemens and Pamela Moffett, June 1, 1863; MTL, vol. 1, p. 255.
12. Ibid.

13. Ibid.
14. Letter to Jane Clemens and Pamela Moffett, July 18, 1863; MTL, vol. 1, pp. 259–60.
15. Ibid., p. 260.
16. *Inventing Mark Twain: The Lives of Samuel Langhorne Clemens,* by Andrew Hoffman (New York: William Morrow & Co.) 1997.
17. Letter to Jane Clemens and Pamela Moffett, June 1, 1863; MTL, vol. 1, p. 255.
18. See especially David Deitcher, *Dear Friends: American Photographs of Men Together, 1840–1918* (New York: Harry N. Abrams, 2001).
19. ET&S, vol. 1, p. 255.
20. Ibid., p. 258.
21. The Virginia City *Evening Bulletin,* July 9, 1863; MTL, vol. 1, p. 263.
22. Letter to Jane Clemens and Pamela Moffett, August 19, 1863; MTL, vol. 1, pp. 263–64.
23. ET&S, vol. 1, p. 290.
24. *Dan De Quille, the Washoe Giant,* p. 18.
25. ET&S, vol. 1, pp. 310–11.
26. ET&S, vol. 1, pp. 315, 317–18.
27. Ibid., pp. 324–25.
28. Ibid., p. 325.
29. Ibid.
30. C. A. V. Putnam, "Dan De Quille and Mark Twain," Salt Lake City *Tribune,* April 25, 1898; ET&S, vol. 1, pp. 320–21.

13: *CODE DUELLO*

1. Quoted in *Walt Whitman's America: A Cultural Biography,* by David S. Reynolds (New York: Alfred A. Knopf, 1995).
2. "Artemus Ward," Virginia City *Territorial Enterprise,* c. November 27, 1863, as reprinted in the San Francisco *Golden Era,* November 29, 1863, p. 8; also in *Mark Twain in Nevada,* by Effie Mona Mack (New York: Scribner's Sons, 1947), pp. 289–90; www.twainquotes.com.
3. "A Good-bye Article," San Francisco *Golden Era,* November 22, 1863, p. 4. Ludlow was *Vanity Fair* editor before Ward, a bit of a pothead who published *The Hasheesh Eater* in 1857, and a prominent member of New York's bohemian circle.
4. James C. Austin, *Artemus Ward* (New York: Twayne Publishers, 1964).
5. Quoted in *Mark Twain, Man and Legend,* by DeLancey Ferguson (New York: Charter Books, 1943), p. 88.
6. Virginia City *Territorial Enterprise,* December 26 or 27, 1863; quoted in "An Inapt Illustration," Virginia City *Evening Bulletin,* December 28, 1863, p. 3. More of this review is quoted in Mack, *Mark Twain in Nevada,* pp. 296–97, www.twainquotes.com.
7. Letter to Jane Clemens, January 2, 1864; MTL, vol. 1, p. 267.
8. Ibid., p. 268.
9. Dan De Quille, "Artemus Ward in Nevada," in the *California Illustrated Magazine,* August 4, 1890; reprinted in *Dan De Quille, the Washoe Giant.*
10. Ibid.
11. Joseph T. Goodman, "Artemus Ward: His Visit to the Comstock Lode," San Francisco *Chronicle,* January 10, 1892, quoted in MTL, vol. 1, pp. 269–70.
12. Letter to Mark Twain, January 1, 1864, MTP.
13. Ibid.
14. ET&S, vol. 1, p. 355.

15. Letter to Pamela Moffett, March 18, 1864; MTL, vol. 1, p. 275.
16. Information taken from "Adah Isaacs Menken (1835–1868)," by Samuel Dickson; the Museum of San Francisco Web site, www.sfmuseum.org.
17. "Letter from Mark Twain," Virginia City *Territorial Enterprise*, letter dated September 13, 1863, *Mark Twain of the Enterprise: Newspaper Articles and Other Documents 1862–1864*, edited by Henry Nash Smith (Berkeley: University of California Press, 1957), pp. 78–79.
18. Ibid, p. 79.
19. William Wright, "Salad Days of Mark Twain," San Francisco *Examiner*, March 19, 1893; quoted in MTL, vol. 1, p. 278.
20. MTL, vol. 1, p. 289, n. 2.
21. MTL, vol. 1, p. 289.
22. Letter to Mollie Clemens, May 20, 1864; MTL, vol. 1, p. 287.
23. MTL, vol. 1, p. 288.
24. Letter to Mollie Clemens, p. 288.
25. Ibid., p. 288.
26. MTL, vol. 1, p. 290.
27. MTL, vol. 1, p. 292.
28. MTL, vol. 1, p. 294.
29. MTL, vol. 1, p. 296.
30. Ibid., p. 297.
31. Ibid., p. 299.
32. MTA, p. 115.
33. The Gold Hill *Evening News*, May 29, 1864; quoted in MTL, vol. 1, p. 302.

14: A Villainous Backwoods Sketch

1. *Roughing It*, OMT, p. 419.
2. From "Mark Twain in the Metropolis," Virginia City *Territorial Enterprise*, June 17–23, 1864, reprinted in ET&S, vol. 2, p. 10.
3. Ibid., p. 419.
4. "San Francisco Letter," reprinted in the San Francisco *Evening Bulletin*, October 30, 1865, collected in ET&S, vol. 2, p. 319.
5. ET&S, vol. 2, p. 299.
6. Letter to Jane Clemens, August 12, 1864; MTL, vol. 1, pp. 305–6.
7. MTL, vol. 1, p. 306.
8. Letter to Jane Clemens and Pamela Moffett, September 25, 1864; MTL, vol. 1, p. 312.
9. Letter to Orion and Mollie Clemens, September 28, 1864; MTL, vol. 1, p. 315.
10. Letter to Jane Clemens and Pamela Moffett, September 25, 1864; MTL, vol. 1, p. 312.
11. Ibid., p. 313.
12. *Mark Twain in Eruption*, edited by Bernard De Voto (New York: Harper & Bros., 1940), p. 256.
13. Letter to Orion Clemens, September 28, 1864; MTL, vol. 1, p. 315.
14. *Mark Twain in Eruption*, p. 256.
15. Ibid., p. 259.
16. *The Life of Bret Harte*, by T. Edgar Pemberton (New York: Dodd, Mead & Co., 1903), p. 74, quoted in ET&S, vol. 2, p. 265.
17. *Life of Bret Harte*, pp. 73–74.
18. *Mark Twain in Eruption*, corrected against the original dictation of June 14, 1906, p. 264.

19. Letter to Jane Clemens and Pamela Moffett, September 25, 1864; MTL, vol. 1, p. 312.
20. ET&S, vol. 2, p. 68.
21. Ibid., p. 69.
22. Ibid., p. 111.
23. Ibid., pp. 132–33.
24. The poem was originally titled, "Plain Language from Truthful James."
25. *Mark Twain in Eruption,* pp. 360–61, corrected against the original dictation of May 26, 1907.
26. This is Notebook 4, as preserved in MTP. It is the first notebook among the fifty known to survive which Mark Twain used expressly for literary purposes.
27. Ibid., p. 360.
28. N&J, vol. 1, p. 69, corrected against the manuscript.
29. Ibid., p. 75.
30. Letter to James Gillis, January 26, 1870; MTL, vol. 4, p. 36.
31. Ibid., p. 80.
32. ET&S, vol. 2, p. 263.
33. "Private History of the 'Jumping Frog' Story," by Mark Twain, in *How to Tell a Story and Other Essays* (New York: Harper & Bros., 1897); quoted in ET&S, vol. 2, p. 264.
34. N&J, vol. 1, pp. 89–90.
35. "Bret Harte's 'Roaring Camp' Still Producing: Mother Lode Country Rich in Reminiscences of Mark Twain's Youth," by George P. West, the San Francisco *Call and Post,* May 24, 1924; quoted in MTL, vol. 1, p. 321.
36. ET&S, vol. 2, p. 265, quoting MTB, vol. 1, p. 277.
37. Joe Goodman, quoted in "Mark Twain," a subsection of "What California Has Done for Civilization," San Francisco *Evening Bulletin,* December 23, 1900, p. 11.
38. ET&S, vol. 2, p. 155.
39. ET&S, vol. 2, p. 221.
40. Ibid., pp. 242, 244. These were actually published on June 3 and June 24, 1865, contrary to the conjectured dates offered in ET&S, vol. 2.
41. Ibid., p. 266.
42. Letter to Jane Clemens and Pamela Moffett, January 20, 1866; MTL, vol. 1, p. 327.
43. *The Celebrated Jumping Frog of Calaveras County, and Other Sketches,* OMT, p. 17.
44. Ibid., p. 18.
45. Mark Twain, "How to Tell a Story," *Youth's Companion,* October 1895; reprinted in the collection, *How to Tell a Story and Other Essays,* OMT, p. 4.
46. MTL, vol. 1, pp. 322–23.

15: ". . . And I Began to Talk"

1. "A Graceful Compliment," *Territorial Enterprise,* December 10–31, 1865, ET&S, vol. 2, p. 390.
2. Letter to Orion and Mollie Clemens, October 19 and 20, 1865; MTL, vol. 1, p. 324.
3. Letter to Orion and Mollie Clemens, October 19 and 20, 1865; MTL, vol. 1, p. 324.
4. MTL, vol. 1, p. 325
5. San Francisco *Morning Call,* October 29, 1865, quoted in *Roughing It,* in *The Works*

of Mark Twain, edited by Edgar Marquess Branch et al. (Berkeley: University of California Press, 1993), p. 701.

6. Letter to Orion Clemens, December 13, 1865; MTL, vol. 1, p. 326.
7. Ibid.
8. MTA, p. 219.
9. "An Open Letter to the American People," New York *Weekly Review,* February 17, 1866, p. 1.
10. Letter to Jane Clemens and Pamela Moffett, January 20, 1865; MTL, vol. 2, p. 328.
11. Reprinted in MTL, vol. 1, p. 329.
12. Letter to Jane Clemens and Pamela Moffett, January 20, 1866; MTL, vol. 1, p. 329.
13. Ibid.
14. Ibid.
15. Ibid., p. 327.
16. Ibid., pp. 329–30.
17. Letter to Jane Clemens and Pamela Moffett, March 5, 1866; MTL, vol. 1, p. 333.
18. *Roughing It,* OMT, p. 455. The Honolulu *Advertiser* speculated in May that Mark Twain had made the cats up. But an entry in his notebook suggests otherwise: "1000s of cats and nary snake" (quoted in *Roughing It,* in *The Works of Mark Twain* edition, pp. 708–9).
19. Ibid., p. 526.
20. Ibid., p. 519.
21. Ibid., p. 477.
22. Letter to Samuel C. Damon, July 19, 1866; MTL, vol. 1, p. 349.
23. Mark Twain's account of getting the dispatch to the schooner paralleled the drama of his last-second departure from the *John J. Roe* in New Orleans after his idyll with Laura Wright. "The . . . schooner was to sail for San Francisco about nine," he wrote in "My Début as a Literary Person" for the *Century Magazine* in November 1899; "when I reached the dock she was free forward and was just casting off the stern-line. My fat envelop was thrown by a strong hand, and fell on board all right, and my victory was a safe thing" *(Century Magazine,* vol. 59 [November 1899] p. 77).
24. San Francisco *Alta California,* September 28, 1866, p. 2, through October 2, 1866, p. 4.
25. George Barnes recalled in 1887 that when Clemens consulted him about the lecture, he admitted that he had already been advised against it. "I've been to [journalist Jimmy] Bowman, and I've been to Harte and Stoddard, and the rest of the fellows, and they say, 'Don't do it, Mark; it will hurt your literary reputation' " (George E. Barnes, "Mark Twain, as He Was Known During His Stay on the Pacific Slope," San Francisco *Morning Call,* April 17, 1887, p. 1). If true, Bret Harte may already have been launching the mind-gaming digs at Sam that at first cowed, and eventually infuriated him.
26. *Roughing It,* OMT p. 560.
27. Ibid., p. 560.
28. Ibid., p. 562.

16: ON THE ROAD

1. Paul Fatout, *Mark Twain on the Lecture Circuit* (Bloomington: Indiana University Press, 1960), p. 40.
2. Quoted by Fatout, *Mark Twain on the Lecture Circuit,* p. 41.

3. Ibid., p. 41.
4. Fatout, *Mark Twain on the Lecture Circuit*, p. 46.
5. Ibid., p. 54, corrected and expanded from the *Enterprise*, October 30, 1866, p. 3.
6. Ibid., pp. 54–55.
7. Carson City *Daily Appeal*, October 31, 1866, p. 3, clipping in Scrapbook no. 1, pp. 41 and 71, MTP.
8. MTL, vol. 1, p. 366.
9. Ibid.
10. "Card to the Highwaymen," Virginia City *Territorial Enterprise*, November 11, 1866.
11. *Roughing It*, p. 568.
12. Fatout, *Mark Twain on the Lecture Circuit*, p. 159.
13. Letter to Catherine Lampton and Annie and Samuel Moffett, November 2(?), 1866; MTL, vol. 1, p. 367.
14. Letter to Jane Clemens and family, December 4, 1866; MTL, vol. 1, p. 368.
15. Quoted in MTL, vol. 1, p. 370, n. 8.
16. MTL, vol. 1, pp. 373–74.
17. N&J, vol. 1, p. 253.
18. N&J, vol. 1, p. 255.
19. N&J, vol. 1, p. 250.
20. Ibid., p. 261.
21. Ibid., p. 269.
22. N&J, vol. 1, pp. 273–77.
23. Ibid., p. 287.
24. N&J, vol. 1, p. 260

17: BACK EAST

1. Letter to the San Francisco *Alta California*, written May 17, published June 16, 1867, www.twainquotes.com, which is cited throughout these chapters. All quotations have been checked against photocopies of the original newspaper.
2. *Alta*, written February 2, published March 28, 1867.
3. Letter to John McComb, February 2–7, 1867, summarized in "California Authors," *Alta*, March 15, 1867; MTL, vol. 2, p. 12.
4. Autobiographical dictation, May 21, 1906, in *Mark Twain in Eruption*, ed. De Voto, pp. 144–45.
5. MTL, vol. 2, p. 13, n. 1.
6. Ibid.
7. Ibid.
8. *Mark Twain in Eruption*, p. 145.
9. Letter to Charles Warren Stoddard, April 23, 1867; MTL, vol. 2, p. 30.
10. MTL, vol. 2, pp. 11–12.
11. *Alta*, written February 23, published April 5, 1867.
12. *Alta*, written February 2, published March 28, 1867.
13. Ibid.
14. Ibid.
15. *Alta*, written February 18, published March 30, 1867.
16. *Alta*, written February 23, published April 5, 1867.
17. Ibid.
18. *Alta*, written February 18, published March 30, 1867.
19. Ibid.
20. Ibid.

21. Ibid.
22. Ibid.
23. Ibid.
24. Quoted at www.question.com.
25. *Alta*, written March 2, published April 9, 1867.
26. MTL, vol. 2, p. 17. These two sentences are all that survive in secondhand text.
27. *Alta*, written March 2, published April 9, 1867.
28. MTL, vol. 2, p. 16.
29. Ibid. See also Justin Kaplan, *Mr. Clemens and Mark Twain* (New York: Simon & Schuster, 1966), p. 28.
30. Quoted at www.annebot.com/oldlivebythis.html.
31. James C. Austin, Preface to *Artemus Ward* (New York: Twayne Publishers, 1964).

18: "MOVE—MOVE—*MOVE!*"

1. Letter to the San Francisco *Alta California*, written March 25, published May 19, 1867, at www.twainquotes.com. All quotations have been checked against photocopies of the original newspaper letters.
2. Ibid.
3. *Alta*, written April 16, published May 26, 1867.
4. Ibid.
5. Ibid.
6. *Alta*, written March 25, published May 19, 1867.
7. *Alta*, written May 19, published June 30, 1867.
8. Ibid.
9. MTA, p. 103.
10. Letter to Jane Clemens, April 15, 1867; MTL, vol. 2, p. 23.
11. Letter to Clemens from John J. Murphy, April 1867; MTL, vol. 2, p. 24.
12. *Alta*, written April 30, published June 10, 1867.
13. MTL, vol. 2, pp. 39–40.
14. MTL, vol. 2, pp. 38–39, for both letters.
15. Quoted in MTL, vol. 2, p. 41.
16. New York *Stage*, May 4, 1867, MTL, vol. 2, pp. 41–42.
17. Frank Fuller to Albert Bigelow Paine in MTB, vol. 1, p. 316.
18. MTA, p. 173.
19. New York *Times*, May 7, 1867, quoted at www.twainquotes.com.
20. "Mark Twain As a Lecturer," by Edward House, New York *Tribune*, May 11, 1867; quoted in MTL, vol. 2, p. 417.
21. *Alta*, written May 17, published June 16, 1867.
22. *Alta*, written May 18, published June 23, 1867.
23. Ibid.
24. Ibid.
25. Ibid.
26. Letter to Jane Clemens and the family, June 1, 1867; MTL, vol. 2, pp. 49–50.
27. Ibid. p. 50.
28. Letter to Will Bowen, June 7, 1867; MTL, vol. 2., p. 54.
29. Letter to Jane Clemens, June 7, 1867; MTL, vol. 2, pp. 57–58.
30. The exact number of passengers has never been determined, though Appendix C, MTL, vol. 2, pp. 385–87, puts the number at "no greater than seventy," and provides a well-documented list. Mark Twain wrote in the *Alta* of May 28 that 85 had been booked, and provided a passenger list with that number to Albert

Bigelow Paine; it appears both in the Appendix to Paine's biography and in N&J, vol. 1. Twain amended the number to 65 in one of his onboard letters to the paper.

19: PILGRIMS AND SINNERS

1. *The Innocents Abroad*, OMT, p. 31.
2. *The Innocents Abroad*, p. 33.
3. Letter to the Cleveland *Herald* written June 9, published June 13, 1867; quoted in MTL, vol. 2, p. 66.
4. Quoted by Robert H. Hirst in "The Making of *The Innocents Abroad:* 1867–1872" (Ph.D. diss., University of California, Berkeley, 1975), p. 60.
5. Letter to the Janesville, *Gazette,* written June 22, published July 23, 1867, quoted in Hirst, "The Making of *The Innocents Abroad,*" p. 58.
6. N&J, vol. 1, pp. 329–30.
7. Ibid., p. 33.
8. Ibid., p. 340.
9. *The Innocents Abroad,* pp. 26–27.
10. Letter to the Janesville *Gazette,* written June 22, published July 23, 1867, quoted by Hirst, "The Making of *The Innocents Abroad,*" p. 58.
11. Portland *Oregonian,* April 22, 1910, p. 4; quoted by Hirst, "The Making of *The Innocents Abroad,*" p. 61.
12. *The Innocents Abroad,* p. 41.
13. Ibid., p. 43.
14. Letter to Jane Clemens and Pamela Moffett, January 8, 1868; MTL, vol. 2, p. 144.
15. *The Innocents Abroad,* p. 51.
16. N&J, vol. 1, p. 346.
17. *The Innocents Abroad,* p. 63.
18. Ibid., p. 66.
19. Ibid., pp. 69–70.
20. Ibid., pp. 70–71.
21. Ibid., p. 71.
22. Ibid., p. 76.
23. Ibid., p. 92.
24. Ibid., p. 93.
25. Ibid., p. 97.
26. Ibid., p. 94.
27. Ibid., p. 100.
28. Ibid., pp. 123–24.
29. Ibid., p. 136.
30. Ibid., p. 130.
31. Ibid., p. 159.
32. Ibid., p. 165.
33. Ibid., p. 177.
34. MMT, p. 17.
35. *The Innocents Abroad,* p. 190.
36. Ibid., p. 191.
37. Ibid., p. 192.
38. Ibid., p. 209.
39. Ibid., p. 217.
40. Ibid., p. 218.
41. Letter to Jane Clemens, August 24, 1853; MTL, vol. 1, p. 4.
42. *The Innocents Abroad,* p. 241.

43. Ibid., p. 242.
44. Ibid., p. 267.
45. Ibid., pp. 267, 269.
46. Ibid., pp. 282–83.
47. Ibid., p. 287.
48. Ibid., p. 289.
49. Ibid., p. 291.
50. Ibid., p. 295.
51. Ibid., p. 306.
52. Ibid., p. 307.
53. Ibid., p. 307.
54. Letter to Frank Fuller, August 7, 1867; MTL, vol. 2, p. 75.
55. *The Innocents Abroad,* p. 336.
56. MTL, vol. 2, p. 394.
57. *The Innocents Abroad,* p. 345.
58. Ibid., p. 347.
59. Ibid., p. 349.
60. Ibid., p. 361.
61. Ibid., p. 368.
62. Letter to Jane Clemens, August 26, 1867; MTL, vol. 2, p. 81.
63. *The Innocents Abroad,* p. 395.
64. Ibid., p. 394.
65. Ibid.
66. Ibid., p. 410.
67. MTB, vol. 1, p. 339.
68. Robert H. Hirst, " 'Sinners and Pilgrims,' " *Bancroftiana,* no. 113 (Fall 1998), pp. 1, 6–7.
69. *The Innocents Abroad,* p. 433.
70. Ibid., p. 451.
71. Ibid., p. 452.
72. Ibid., pp. 465–66.
73. Ibid., p. 471.
74. Ibid., p. 496.
75. Ibid., pp. 496–97.
76. Ibid., p. 498.
77. MTA, vol. 1, p. 337.
78. Ibid., pp. 566–67.
79. Ibid., p. 600.
80. N&J, vol. 1, p. 452.

20: In the Thrall of Mother Bear

1. New York *Tribune,* September 19, 1867; quoted in MTL, vol. 2, p. 102.
2. Hirst, "The Making of *The Innocents Abroad,*" p. 83.
3. Fragment of an unpublished play sent to Charles Henry Webb, November 25, 1867; MTL, vol. 2, pp. 114–15; quoted in MTL, vol. 2, p. 103; full transcription of the play in MTL, vol. 2, Appendix E, pp. 406–14.
4. N&J, vol. 1, p. 329.
5. Letter to Mrs. Langdon, October 13, 1867, just off Cagliari; Manuscript in MTP.
6. See Susan Gillman's *Dark Twins: Imposture and Identity in Mark Twain's America* (Chicago: University of Chicago Press, 1989).
7. Letter to Joseph T. Goodman, October 24, 1867; MTL, vol. 2, p. 101.

8. An excellent record of these revisions is found in *Traveling with the Innocents Abroad: Mark Twain's Original Reports from Europe and the Holy Land,* edited by Daniel Morley McKeithan (Norman: University of Oklahoma Press, 1958).

9. *The Innocents Abroad,* p. 499.

10. Letter to Mary Fairbanks, January 24, 1868; MTL, vol. 2, pp. 165–66.

11. *Traveling with the Innocents Abroad,* pp. 309–10; letter to the *Alta,* written November 20, 1867, published January 8, 1868.

12. *Traveling with the Innocents Abroad,* pp. 314–15; letter to the *Herald,* written November 19, published November 20, 1867.

13. Letter to the *Herald* in *Traveling with the Innocents Abroad,* pp. 315–16.

14. Letter to the *Alta,* in *Traveling with the Innocents Abroad,* pp. 310–11.

15. *The Innocents Abroad,* pp. 643–44.

16. Letter to Jane Clemens and family, November 20, 1867; MTL, vol. 2, p. 104.

17. New York *Herald,* November 21, 1867; quoted in MTL, vol. 2, p. 107.

18. Letter to Mary Fairbanks, December 2, 1867; MTL, vol. 2, pp. 122–23.

19. Letter to Frank Fuller, November 24, 1867; MTL, vol. 2, p. 111.

20. Letter to the Virginia City *Territorial Enterprise,* written December 4, published December 22, 1867; quoted in N&J, vol. 1, p. 490.

21. William M. Stewart, *Reminiscences of Senator William M. Stewart of Nevada,* edited by George Rathwell Brown (New York: Neale Publishing Co., 1908), quoted in N&J, vol. 1, p. 456.

22. N&J, vol. 1, pp. 492–94.

23. Ibid., pp. 488–89.

24. Ibid., p. 491.

25. Letter to the *Alta California,* written January 16, published February 14, 1868; quoted at www.twainquotes.com.

26. Unpublished letter to Jane Clemens and Pamela Moffett, January 20, 1868; Paine's typed copy of the manuscript, MTP.

27. Letter to Samuel Clemens, November 21, 1867; MTL, vol. 2, p. 120.

28. Letter to Elisha Bliss, December 2, 1867; MTL, vol. 2, p. 119.

29. Ibid.

30. Letter to Frank Fuller, December 13, 1867; MTL, vol. 2, p. 136.

31. Letter to Jane Clemens and family, December 10, 1867; MTL, vol. 2, p. 129.

32. Ibid.

33. Letter to Mary Fairbanks, December 12, 1867; MTL, vol. 2, p. 133.

34. Letter to Emily Severance, December 24, 1867; MTL, vol. 2, p. 138.

35. "My Late Senatorial Secretaryship," in *Sketches, New and Old,* OMT, p. 152.

36. Letter to Jane Clemens and Pamela Moffett, January 8, 1868; MTL, vol. 2, p. 144.

37. Brooklyn *Eagle,* December 24, 1867; quoted in MTL, vol. 2, p. 142.

38. Letter to the Brooklyn *Eagle,* written December 30, published December 31, 1867; MTL, vol. 2, p. 141.

39. Ibid., p. 142.

40. MTA, p. 175.

41. Ibid., p. 174.

42. Ibid., p. 175.

43. Letter to Jane Clemens and Pamela Moffett, January 8, 1868; MTL, vol. 2, p. 144.

21: "A Work *Humorously Inclined* . . ."

1. Letter to Mollie Clemens, February 21, 1868; Paine's transcript in MTP. See Robert H. Hirst, "What Paine Left Out," *Bancroftiana,* no. 125 (Fall 2004), p. 10.

2. Letter to Jane Clemens and Pamela Moffett, January 8, 1868; MTL, vol. 2, p. 144.

3. Letter of Elisha Bliss Jr. to Clemens, December 24, 1867; Paine's typescript of the original letter manuscript; only partly published in MTL, vol. 2, p. 162.

4. Ibid.

5. Letter from Elisha Bliss Jr. to Clemens, January 18, 1868; Paine's typed copy of the original, MTP.

6. Washington *Evening Star,* January 13, 1868, enclosed in letter to Jane Clemens and family, MTL, vol. 2, pp. 155–56.

7. Will M. Clemens [no relation], *Mark Twain: His Life and Work, a Biographical Sketch,* Chicago and New York: F. Tennyson Neely, 1894, p. 87, quoted in Hirst, "The Making of *The Innocents Abroad,*" p. 121.

8. Quoted in a letter to Jane Clemens and Pamela Moffett, January 24, 1868; MTL, vol. 2, p. 160.

9. Letter to the *Alta,* written February 1, published March 3, 1868.

10. January 24, 1868 letter, pp. 160–61.

11. Letter to William Bowen, January 25, 1868; MTL, vol. 2, p. 167.

12. Ibid., p. 168.

13. "How 'Innocents Abroad' Was Written," New York *Evening Post,* January 20, 1883, quoted in Hirst, "The Making of *The Innocents Abroad,*" p. 121.

14. Letter to Jane Clemens and Pamela Moffett, February 6, 1868; MTL, vol. 2, p. 178.

15. Letter to Mary Fairbanks, January 24, 1868; MTL, vol. 2, p. 166.

16. Letter to Emeline Beach, January 31, 1868; MTL, vol. 2, p. 172.

17. Letter to Mary Fairbanks, February 20, 1868; MTL, vol. 2, p. 191.

18. Letter to Jane Clemens and Pamela Moffett, January 24, 1868; MTL, vol. 2, p. 161.

19. Quoted in MTL, vol. 2, p. 174, n. 1.

20. Letter to Elisha Bliss, February 4 and 6, 1868; MTL, vol. 2, p. 176.

21. San Francisco *Bulletin,* April 15, 1868; quoted in MTL, vol. 2, p. 210.

22. San Rafael *Marin County Journal,* April 18, 1868; *California Weekly Mercury,* April 19, 1868; quoted in MTL, vol. 2, p. 210.

23. Letter to Mary Fairbanks, June 17, 1868; MTL, vol. 2, p. 221.

24. "Mark Twain at Church," San Francisco *Morning Call,* May 20, 1868; quoted in MTL, vol. 2, p. 228.

25. Ibid.

26. Letter to Mary Fairbanks, May 1 and 5, 1868; MTL, vol. 2, p. 212.

27. Letter to Elisha Bliss, June 23, 1868; MTL, vol. 2, p. 232.

28. Letter to Charles Henry Webb, November 26, 1870; MTL, vol. 4, p. 248.

29. Letter to Thomas Bailey Aldrich, January 27, 1871; MTL, vol. 4, p. 316.

30. *Dramatic Chronicle,* July 3, 1868; quoted in MTL, vol. 2, p. 235.

31. *Californian,* July 4, 1868; quoted in MTL, vol. 2, p. 235.

22: THE GIRL IN THE MINIATURE

1. Telegram to Elisha Bliss Jr., July 29, 1868; Paine typescript in MTP.

2. New York *Tribune,* August 4, 1868; quoted in MTL, vol. 2, p. 239.

3. Letter to Frank Fuller, August 15, 1868; MTL, vol. 2, p. 240.

4. *Alta California,* October 22, 1868; quoted in MTL, vol. 2, p. 241.

5. Telegram to Charles Langdon, August 21, 1868; MTL, vol. 2, p. 242.

6. Letter to Jane Clemens, August 24 and 25, 1868; MTL, vol. 2, pp. 243–44.

7. Harriet Lewis Paff, "What I Know About Mark Twain," manuscript, Yale University Library, New Haven, Connecticut, 1897; quoted in MTL, vol. 2, p. 249, n. 4.

8. Ibid.

9. Ibid.

10. Letter to Olivia Langdon, September 7 and 8, 1868; MTL, vol. 2, pp. 247–48.

11. Letter to Olivia Langdon, September 21, 1868; MTL, vol. 2, p. 250.

12. Letter to Olivia Langdon, October 4–5, 1868; MTL, vol. 2, p. 255.

13. Letter to Olivia Langdon, October 30, 1868; MTL, vol. 2, p. 273.

14. Ibid., p. 274.

15. Ibid., p. 271.

16. Harriet Elinor Smith and Richard Bucci, editors of MTL, vol. 2, p. xxiv.

17. Letter to Olivia Langdon, September 21, 1868; MTL, vol. 2, p. 251.

18. Letter to Olivia Langdon; MTL, vol. 2, p. 250.

19. Letter to Frank Fuller, September 24, 1868; MTL, vol. 2, p. 254.

20. Letter to Mary Fairbanks, October 5, 1868; MTL, vol. 2, pp. 256–57.

21. Ibid., p. 257.

22. Letter to Mary Fairbanks, October 12, 1868; MTL, vol. 2, p. 263.

23. Letter to Olivia Langdon, October 18, 1868; MTL, vol. 2, p. 266.

24. Ibid., p. 267.

23: AMERICAN VANDAL

1. Letter to Mary Fairbanks, October 12, 1868; MTL, vol. 2, p. 263.

2. Letter to Olivia Langdon, October 30, 1868; MTL, vol. 2, p. 271.

3. Ibid., p. 271.

4. Ibid., p. 272.

5. Ibid., p. 272.

6. Ibid., p. 274.

7. As described in letter from Margaret Wiley to Samuel C. Webster, November 16, 1944; MTL, vol. 2, p. 279.

8. Ibid., p. 279.

9. Ibid., p. 279.

10. "A Mystery," Cleveland Herald, November 16, 1868, p. 2.

11. "The American Vandal Abroad," in The Trouble Begins at Eight: Mark Twain's Lecture Tours, by Fred W. Lorch (Ames: Iowa State University Press, 1968), p. 285, corrected against manuscript p. 1.

12. Ibid., p. 285.

13. Ibid., p. 289, corrected against manuscript p. 27.

14. Mark Twain Speaking, p. 30, corrected against manuscript p. 30.

15. "The American Vandal Abroad," p. 290, corrected against manuscript p. 42.

16. Ibid., p. 294.

17. Ibid., p. 296, corrected against manuscript p. 55.

18. Mark Twain Speaking, p. 35, corrected against manuscript p. 52.

19. "When Mark Twain Read . . . ," New York Evening Post, December 22, 1884; MTL, vol. 2, pp. 280–81.

20. Ibid., p. 281.

21. Letter to Jane Clemens and Pamela Moffett, November 18, 1868; MTL, vol. 2, p. 280.

22. Mary Fairbanks, Cleveland Herald, November 18, 1868; quoted in MTL vol. 2, p. 280.

23. Cleveland Plain Dealer, November 18, 1868; MTL, vol. 2, p. 280.

24. Pittsburgh Gazette, November 20, 1868; MTL, vol. 2, p. 283.

25. MTB, vol. 1, p. 375.

26. Elmira Advertiser, November 25, 1868; quoted in MTL, vol. 2, p. 286.

27. Letter to Mary Fairbanks, November 26 and 27, 1868; MTL, vol. 2, pp. 283–84.

28. Ibid., p. 284.
29. Ibid., p. 284.
30. Letter to Joe Twichell, November 28, 1868; MTL, vol. 2, p. 293.
31. Ibid., p. 293.
32. MTA, p. 189.
33. Letter to Olivia Langdon, November 28, 1868; MTL, vol. 2, pp. 288–92.
34. Letter from Mrs. Langdon to Mary Fairbanks, December 1, 1868; MTL vol. 2, p. 286.
35. MTA, p. 189.
36. Letter to Olivia Langdon, December 4, 1868; MTL vol. 2, p. 303.
37. Letter to Olivia Langdon, December 5 and 7, 1868; MTL, vol. 2, p. 315.
38. Letter to Olivia Langdon, December 9 and 10, 1868; MTL, vol. 2, p. 318.
39. Letter to Olivia Langdon, November 15 and 16, 1869; MTL, vol. 3, p. 395.
40. Ibid., p. 396.
41. Letter to Jervis Langdon, December 29, 1868; MTL, vol. 2, p. 357.
42. Letter to Olivia Langdon, December 30, 1868; MTL, vol. 2, pp. 363–64.
43. Letter to Olivia Langdon, December 31, 1868; MTL, vol. 2, pp. 369–70.

24: "Quite Worthy of the Best"

1. Letter to Olivia Langdon, January 2, 1869; MTL, vol. 3, p. 4.
2. Letter to Susan Crane, March 9 and 31, 1869; MTL, vol. 3, p. 181.
3. Letters to Olivia Langdon, January 26 and 27, 1869; March 2, 1869; February 13 and 14, 1869; January 17, 1869; MTL, vol. 3, pp. 78, 132, 95, and 45.
4. Letter to Olivia Langdon, January 12, 1869; MTL, vol. 3, pp. 25–26.
5. Letter to Mary Fairbanks, January 7, 1869; MTL, vol. 3, p. 8.
6. MTL, vol. 3, p. 9.
7. Letter to Mary Fairbanks, January 15, 1869; MTL, vol. 3, p. 4.
8. Letter to Francis E. Bliss, January 7, 1869; MTL, vol. 3, p. 14.
9. Letter to Olivia Lewis Langdon, February 13, 1869; MTL, vol. 3, p. 91.
10. Letter to Jervis Langdon, December 2, 1868; MTL, vol. 2, p. 298.
11. Letter to Olivia Langdon, January 20 and 21, 1869; MTL, vol. 3, pp. 52–53.
12. Ibid., p. 53.
13. Letter to Olivia Langdon, January 13 and 14, 1869; MTL, vol. 3, p. 31.
14. Iowa City Republican, January 20, 1869; quoted in MTL, vol. 3, p. 48.
15. Ibid., p. 48.
16. Letter to Jane Clemens and family, February 5, 1869; MTL, vol. 3, pp. 84–85.
17. MTL, vol. 3, p. 57.
18. Letter to Charles Warren Stoddard, August 25, 1869; CU MARK NO. 00340.
19. Ibid.
20. MTA, p. 189, corrected against the original typed dictation of February 14, 1906, in MTP.
21. Letter to Stoddard, August 25, 1869.
22. Letter to Olivia Langdon, November 24, 1869; MTL, vol. 3, p. 405.
23. Letter to Clemens, February 10, 1869; quoted in MTL, vol. 3, p. 99.
24. Letter to Elisha Bliss, February 14, 1869; MTL, vol. 3, p. 98.
25. Titusville Morning Herald, February 17, 1869; quoted in MTL, vol. 3, p. 105.
26. Letter to Olivia Langdon, February 26, 1869; MTL, vol. 3, p. 112.
27. MTA, p. 158.
28. Ibid., pp. 158–59.
29. Letter to Olivia Langdon, March 6, 1869; MTL, vol. 3, p. 139.

30. See Barbara Schmidt, "A Closer Look at the Lives of True Williams and Alexander Belford," presented at the Fourth International Conference on Mark Twain Studies, Elmira, New York, August 18, 2001; www.twainquotes.com.

31. See excerpt of Mark Twain letter to the *Alta California,* July 25, 1869; MTL, vol. 3, p. 160.

32. Letter to Olivia Langdon, March 13, 1869; MTL, vol. 3, p. 172.

33. Letter to Mary Fairbanks, March 13, 1869; MTL, vol. 3, p. 169.

34. Letter to Elisha Bliss, March 30, 1869; MTL, vol. 3, p. 179.

35. Letter to Elisha Bliss, April 20, 1869; MTL, vol. 3, p. 197.

36. Letter to Mary Fairbanks, May 10, 1869; MTL, vol. 3, p. 211.

37. Letter to Olivia Langdon, March 6, 1869 (second of two); MTL, vol. 3, p. 146.

38. Letter to Olivia Langdon, May 8, 1869 (second of two); MTL, vol. 3, p. 206.

39. Letter to Olivia Langdon, May 12, 1869; MTL, vol. 3, p. 222.

40. Letter to Olivia Langdon, May 13, 1869; MTL, vol. 3, p. 224.

41. Letter to Olivia Langdon, May 14, 1869; MTL, vol. 3, 228.

42. Letter to Olivia Langdon, May 24, 1869; MTL, vol. 3, p. 252.

43. Letter to Olivia Langdon, May 12, 1869; MTL, vol. 3, p. 221.

44. Letter to Clemens, July 12, 1869; quoted in MTL, vol. 3, p. 286.

45. Letter to Elisha Bliss, July 22, 1869; MTL, vol. 3, pp. 284–85.

46. Letter to Clemens, July 25, 1869; quoted in MTL, vol. 3, p. 277.

47. Earl D. Berry, "Mark Twain As a Newspaper Man," *Illustrated Buffalo Express,* November 11, 1917; quoted in MTL, vol. 3, p. 296.

48. Ibid., p. 296.

49. R. Kent Rasmussen, *Mark Twain A to Z: The Essential Reference to His Life and Writings* (New York: Facts on File, 1995), p. 47.

50. "Only a Nigger," in the Buffalo *Express,* August 26, 1869; at www.boondocksnet.com/twaintexts/onlynigger.html, edited by Jim Zwick.

51. Letter to Whitelaw Reid, August 15, 1869; MTL, vol. 3, p. 303.

52. Letter to Elisha Bliss Jr., August 12, 1869; MTL, vol. 3, p. 292.

53. Letter to Mary and Abel Fairbanks, August 14, 1869; MTL, vol. 3, p. 298.

54. "Mark Twain's Book," New York *Tribune,* August 27, 1869; quoted in MTL, vol. 3, p. 343.

55. Unless otherwise noted, excerpts of newspaper reviews are taken from *Mark Twain in His Times,* a Web site, written and directed by Stephen Railton, Department of English, University of Virginia; produced by the Electronic Text Center, University of Virginia.

56. Bret Harte, *Overland Monthly,* January 1870; quoted in MTL, vol. 3, p. 356.

57. Letter to Clemens, September 26, 1869; MTL, vol. 3, pp. 365–66.

58. William Dean Howells, review of *The Innocents Abroad,* in *Atlantic Monthly,* December 1869.

59. Anonymous critic in the *Nation,* cited by Margaret Duckett in *Mark Twain and Bret Harte* (Norman: University of Oklahoma Press, 1964), p. 58.

60. New York *Herald,* August 31, 1869; quoted in MTL, vol. 3, p. 330.

61. Letter to Olivia Langdon, December 14, 1869; MTL, vol. 3, pp. 423–24.

62. Letter to Pamela Moffett, November 9, 1869; MTL, vol. 3, p. 387.

63. Letter to Olivia Langdon, December 15 and 16, 1869; MTL, vol. 3, p. 426.

64. Ibid., p. 426.

25: FAIRYLAND

1. Letter to Olivia Langdon, January 20, 1870; MTL, vol. 4, p. 32.

2. Letter to Olivia Langdon, January 14, 1870; MTL, vol. 4, p. 25.

3. Letter to Olivia Langdon, January 15, 1870; MTL, vol. 4, p. 28.

4. Ibid., p. 28.

5. See MTL, vol. 4, pp. 42–44, for a detailed compilation of the known guests.

6. MTBM, p. 109.

7. Ibid., p. 109.

8. Buffalo *Courier,* December 11, 1884; quoted in MTL, vol. 4, p. 48.

9. Joseph Twichell, "Mark Twain," *Harper's Magazine,* May 1896; quoted in Justin Kaplan, *Mr. Clemens and Mark Twain* (New York: Simon & Schuster, 1966), p. 114.

10. MTL, vol. 4, p. 45.

11. MTBM, pp. 109–10; quoted in MTL, vol. 4, p. 46.

12. Letter to Will Bowen, February 6, 1870; MTL, vol. 4, pp. 50–51.

13. Letter to Jervis and Olivia Lewis Langdon, February 6, 1870; MTL, vol. 4, p. 54.

14. Letter to Jervis Langdon, March 2 and 3, 1870; MTL, vol. 4, p. 82.

15. Letter to Mary Fairbanks, March 22 and 24, 1870; MTL, vol. 4, p. 95.

16. Letter to Olivia Lewis Langdon, February 20, 1870; MTL, vol. 4, p. 75.

17. Letter to James Redpath, March 22, 1870; MTL, vol. 4, p. 94.

18. Letter to James Redpath, May 10, 1870; MTL, vol. 4, p. 128.

19. Letter to Francis P. Church, February 9, 1870; MTL, vol. 4, p. 65.

20. Letter to Charles Henry Webb, November 26, 1870; MTL, vol. 4, p. 248.

21. MTL, vol. 4, p. 101, n. 6.

22. "The Late Benjamin Franklin," in *Mark Twain's Sketches,* OMT.

23. "About Smells," in *The Curious Republic of Gondour and Other Whimsical Sketches* (New York: Boni & Liveright, 1919). Originally appeared in the *Galaxy,* vol. 9 (May 1870), pp. 721–22. Reprinted in *What Is Man? And Other Philosophical Writings,* edited by Paul Baender (Berkeley: University of California Press, 1973).

24. Letter to Orion Clemens, April 21, 1870; MTL, vol. 4, pp. 114–15.

25. Letter to Jervis Langdon, May 13, 1870; MTL, vol. 4, p. 129.

26. Letter to Orion Clemens, April 21, 1870; MTL, vol. 4, p. 114.

27. Letter to Jervis Langdon, May 22, 1870; MTL, vol. 4, p. 138.

28. Letter to Orion Clemens, August 1, 1870; MTL, vol. 4, pp. 177–78.

29. Written across envelope of letter to Orion Clemens, September 2, 1870; MTL, vol. 4, p. 187.

30. Letter to Mary Fairbanks, June 25, 1870; MTL, vol. 4, p. 157.

31. Dictation, 1885; quoted in MTL, vol. 4, p. 168.

32. Letter to Olivia Clemens, July 8, 1870; MTL, vol. 4, p. 167.

33. Resa Willis, *Mark and Livy: The Love Story of Mark Twain and the Woman Who Almost Tamed Him* (New York: Atheneum, 1992), p. 62.

34. Letter to Josephus N. Larned, August 7, 1870, printed in the Buffalo *Express,* August 8, 1870; MTL, vol. 4, p. 182.

35. Letter to Orion Clemens, July 15, 1870; MTL, vol. 4, p. 171.

36. Letter to Pamela Moffett, August 17 or 24, 1870; MTL, vol. 4, p. 185.

37. Letter to Elisha Bliss, September 4, 1870; MTL, vol. 4, p. 190.

38. Bret Harte, "Plain Language from Truthful James," *Overland Monthly,* September 1870; Electronic Text Center, University of Virginia Library; http://etext.lib.virginia.edu/railton.

39. Letter to Charles Henry Webb, November 26, 1870; MTL, vol. 4, p. 248.

40. Ibid., p. 249.

41. Letter to Mary Fairbanks, September 2, 1870; MTL, vol. 4, p. 189.

42. Letter to Ella Wolcott, September 7, 1870; MTL, vol. 4, p. 191.

43. Conversation reported by Donn Piatt of the Cincinnati *Commercial,* February 1871; quoted in MTL, vol. 4, p. 199.

44. *Mark Twain in Eruption,* edited by Bernard De Voto (New York: Harper & Bros., 1940), p. 251; quoted in MTL, vol. 4, p. 199.
45. Letter to Mary Fairbanks, October 13, 1870; MTL, vol. 4, p. 208.
46. Letter to Eunice Ford, November 11, 1870; MTL, vol. 4, p. 233.
47. Letter to Langdon Clemens, November 11, 1870; MTL, vol. 4, pp. 225–26.
48. Quoted in Philip A. Fanning, *Mark Twain and Orion Clemens: Brothers, Partners, Strangers* (Tuscaloosa: University of Alabama Press, 2003), p. 139.
49. Letter to Orion Clemens, March 15–18, 1871; MTL, vol. 4, p. 363.
50. Letter to Elisha Bliss, November 28, 1870; MTL, vol. 4, p. 251.
51. Ibid., p. 251.
52. Letter to Clemens, November 30, 1870; MTL, vol. 4, p. 253.
53. Letter to John Henry Riley, December 2, 1870; MTL, vol. 4, p. 259.
54. Ibid., p. 261.
55. Ibid., pp. 259, 261.

26: "My Hated Nom de Plume . . ."

1. Letter to Elisha Bliss, January 27, 1871; MTL, vol. 4, p. 319.
2. As suggested by Harriet Elinor Smith in her Foreword to the Mark Twain Library edition of *Roughing It* (Berkeley: University of California Press, 1993).
3. Letter to the editor of *Every Saturday* (Thomas Bailey Aldrich), January 15, 1871; MTL, vol. 4, p. 304.
4. Letter to Olivia Langdon, December 27, 1869; MTL, vol. 4, p. 440.
5. Quoted in MTL, vol. 4, p. 323, n.1.
6. Ibid., p. 323.
7. Letter to James Redpath, January 30, 1871; MTL, vol. 4, p. 322.
8. "Reviews and Literary Notices," *Atlantic* (May 1867), p. 640; in Making of America database, http://cdl.library.cornell.edu/moa.
9. "Literary Boston as I Knew It," in *Literary Friends and Acquaintance* (New York: Harper & Bro., 1901), p. 117.
10. Ibid., p. 118.
11. *Bret Harte: Prince and Pauper,* by Axel Nissen (Oxford: University Press of Mississippi, 2000).
12. Letter to Orion Clemens, March 11 and 13, 1871; MTL, vol. 4, p. 350.
13. Ibid., pp. 349–50.
14. Letter to Elisha Bliss, March 17, 1871; MTL, vol. 4, p. 365.
15. Ibid., pp. 365–66.
16. Letter to James Redpath, March 15, 1871; MTL, vol. 4, p. 362.
17. Letter to Alice Hooker Day, January 25, 1871; MTL, vol. 4, p. 311.
18. Letter to Susan Crane, March 14, 1871; MTL, vol. 4, p. 358.
19. Letter to Elisha Bliss and Orion Clemens, March 20, 1871; MTL, vol. 4, p. 367.
20. Letter to Orion Clemens, with messages for Elisha Bliss, April 8, 9, and 10, 1871; MTL, vol. 4, p. 376.
21. Ibid., p. 377.
22. Letter to Mary Fairbanks, April 26, 1871; MTL, vol. 4, p. 381.
23. MTB, vol. 1, pp. 435–36.
24. Letter to Elisha Bliss, May 3, 1871; MTL, vol. 4, p. 389.
25. Letter to Orion Clemens, April 30, 1871; MTL, vol. 4, p. 386.
26. Letter to Elisha Bliss, May 15, 1871; MTL, vol. 4, p. 391.
27. Letter to Samuel Clemens, May 8, 1871, in MTP; quoted in MTL, vol. 4, p. 395.
28. Photograph sent to Bret Harte, summer 1871 (date unknown); MTL, vol. 4, p. 397.

29. Letter to James Redpath, June 10, 1871; MTL, vol. 4, pp. 398–99.
30. Letter to James Redpath, June 28, 1871; MTL, vol. 4, p. 421.
31. MTL, vol. 4, p. 402.
32. Letter to Mary Fairbanks, March 22 and 24, 1870; MTL, vol. 4, p. 95.
33. Letter to Olivia Langdon, December 27, 1869; MTL, vol. 3, p. 440.
34. Letter to James Redpath, June 15, 1871; MTL, vol. 4, p. 408.
35. Letter to James Redpath, June 27, 1871; MTL, vol. 4, p. 415.
36. Letter to Elisha Bliss, July 10, 1871; MTL, vol. 4, p. 431.
37. Letter to Olivia Clemens, August 10, 1871; MTL, vol. 4, p. 443.
38. Ibid., p. 443.
39. Ibid., p. 444.
40. Letter to Olivia Clemens, August 10, 1871; MTL, vol. 4, p. 443.
41. *Roughing It,* OMT, Chapter 47, pp. 336–37.
42. Letter to Orion Clemens, August 31, 1871; MTL, vol. 4, p. 452.
43. Letter to Ella Trabue Smith, August 30, 1871; MTL, vol. 4, p. 451.
44. Letter to Olivia Clemens, September 8, 1871; MTL, vol. 4, p. 453.

27: SOCIABLE JIMMY

1. Review, October 17, 1871; quoted in MTL, vol. 4, p. 475.
2. Review, October 18, 1871; quoted in MTL, vol. 4, p. 475.
3. Letter to Olivia Clemens, October 17, 1871; MTL, vol. 4, p. 474.
4. Review, October 24, 1871; quoted in MTL, vol. 4, p. 480.
5. Ibid., p. 480.
6. Great Barrington *Berkshire Courier,* November 1, 1871; in Paul Fatout, *Mark Twain on the Lecture Circuit* (Bloomington: Indiana University Press, 1960); quoted in MTL, vol. 4, p. 483.
7. Ibid., p. 483.
8. Letter to Olivia Clemens, November 1, 1871; MTL, vol. 4, p. 484.
9. Boston *Evening Transcript,* November 2, 1871; MTL, vol. 4, p. 485.
10. Howells letter to Thomas Bailey Aldrich, May 7, 1902; quoted in MTL, vol. 4, p. 485.
11. Letter to Elisha Bliss, November 12, 1871; MTL, vol. 4, p. 489.
12. MTA, p. 289, checked against the typed dictation of April 1904, MTP.
13. Lilian W. Aldrich, *Crowding Memories* (Boston: Houghton Mifflin Co., 1920); quoted in MTL, vol. 6, p. 81.
14. Ibid., p. 81.
15. Ibid., p. 81.
16. Letter to Samuel Clemens, November 20, 1871; MTL, vol. 4, p. 499.
17. Letter to Olivia Clemens, November 27, 1871; MTL, vol. 4, p. 499.
18. Letter to Samuel Clemens, November 28, 1871; MTL, vol. 4, pp. 505–6.
19. Letter to Samuel Clemens, December 2, 1871, MTL, vol. 4, pp. 509–11.
20. Letter to Mary Fairbanks, December 10, 1871; MTL, vol. 4, p. 513.
21. Letter to James Redpath, December 11, 1871; MTL, vol. 4, p. 514.
22. Fredonia *Censor,* December 13, 1871; quoted in MTL, vol. 4, p. 513.
23. Letter to James Redpath, December 11, 1871; MTL, vol. 4, p. 514.
24. Letter to Olivia Clemens, December 18, 1871; MTL, vol. 4, p. 517.
25. Letter to Samuel Clemens, December 30 and 31, 1871; MTL, vol. 4, p. 523.
26. Letter to Olivia Clemens, December 31, 1871; MTL, vol. 4, p. 527.
27. Ibid., pp. 528–29.
28. In Paul Fatout's *Mark Twain Speaks for Himself* (West Lafayette, Ind.: Purdue University Press, 1978).

29. "Sociable Jimmy," reprinted by Shelley Fisher Fishkin in *Was Huck Black? Mark Twain and African-American Voices* (New York: Oxford University Press, 1993), p. 249.
30. Ibid., pp. 251–52. Corrected against the first printing in the New York *Times*, November 29, 1874, p. 7.
31. Letter to Olivia Clemens, January 10 and 11, 1872; MTL, vol. 5, p. 18.
32. Letter to Mary Fairbanks, February 13, 1872; MTL, vol. 5, p. 43.
33. Danbury *News*, February 28, 1872; quoted in MTL, vol. 5, p. 46.
34. Amherst *Record*, February 28, 1872; quoted in MTL, vol. 5, p. 49.
35. Columbus *Ohio State Journal*, January 6, 1872; quoted in MTL, vol. 5, p. 11.
36. Wheeling *Intelligencer*, January 2, 1872; quoted in MTL, vol. 5, p. 19.
37. Letter to Samuel Clemens, January 7, 1872; MTL, vol. 5, pp. 16–17.
38. "Mark Twain at Steinway Hall," by John Hay (unsigned); quoted in MTL, vol. 5, p. 34.
39. New York *World*, February 4, 1872; quoted in MTL vol. 5, p. 40.
40. Charles Frederick Wingate in a commemorative pamphlet, published in 1872; quoted in MTL vol. 5, p. 40.
41. Salamo and Smith, editors of MTL, vol. 5, pp. 41–43.
42. Letter to Mary Fairbanks, February 13, 1872; MTL, vol. 5, p. 44.
43. Letter to William Dean Howells, March 18, 1872; MTL, vol. 5, p. 58.
44. Chicago *Tribune*, March 17, 1872; quoted in MTL, vol. 5, p. 70.

28: The Lion of London

1. Letter from Olivia Clemens to Susan Crane, July 27 and August 4, 1872; Paine's typescript, misquoted by him in MTB, vol. 1, p. 457.
2. Lilly Warner, letter to her husband, George H. Warner, June 3, 1872; MTL, vol. 5, p. 98.
3. Autobiography, vol. 1, p. 190, dictation of March 22, 1906.
4. Ibid.
5. From "Villagers of 1840–3," in *Huck Finn and Tom Sawyer Among the Indians: And Other Unfinished Stories* (Berkeley: University of California Press, 1989).
6. Susan Crane, letter to Albert Bigelow Paine, May 25, 1911; MTL, vol. 5, pp. 100–101.
7. Letter to William Dean Howells, June 15, 1872; MTL, vol. 5, p. 103.
8. Ibid., p. 103.
9. Letter to Mollie Clemens, July 20 or 21, 1872; MTL, vol. 5, p. 125.
10. Isabel Lyon, letter to W. T. H. Howe, November 28, 1934; quoted in MTL, vol. 5, p. 114.
11. Letter to Louise Chandler Moulton, June 18, 1872; MTL, vol. 5, p. 108.
12. "Recent Literature," *Atlantic Monthly*, June 1872; quoted in MTL, vol. 5, p. 95.
13. Letter to William Dean Howells, May 22–29?, 1872; MTL, vol. 5, p. 95.
14. *Roughing It* (Berkeley: University of California Press, 1996), pp. 890–91.
15. In *Roughing It*, p. 881, n. 245.
16. James Redpath, letter to Samuel Clemens, July 12, 1872; MTL, vol. 5, p. 122.
17. Letter from Orion Clemens to Mollie Clemens, July 26, 1872; MTL, vol. 5, p. 145.
18. Letter from Olivia and Samuel Clemens to Jane Clemens, December 20, 1872; MTL, vol. 5, p. 254.
19. Letter to Olivia Clemens, August 29, 1872; MTL, vol. 5, pp. 151–52.
20. Dictation, February 19, 1907; MTL, vol. 5, p. 154.
21. South London *Press*, September 14, 1872; quoted in MTL, vol. 5, p. 156.
22. From a speech to the Savage Club in London; quoted in MTL, vol. 5, p. 173.

23. Letter to Olivia Clemens, September 11, 1872; MTL, vol. 5, pp. 154–55.
24. Letter to the London *Spectator,* September 21, 1871; MTL, vol. 5, pp. 163–64.
25. Letter to Olivia Clemens, October 12, 1872; MTL, vol. 5, p. 196.
26. Quoted by Samuel Clemens in a letter to Henry Lee, November 5, 1872; MTL, vol. 5, p. 214.
27. Letter to Jane Clemens and Pamela Moffett, November 26, 1872; MTL, vol. 5, p. 230.
28. Letter to Thomas Nast, December 10, 1872; MTL, vol. 5, p. 249.
29. Letter to Olivia Lewis Langdon, December 3, 1872; MTL, vol. 5, p. 235.
30. Ibid., p. 236.
31. Letter from Thomas Nast to Samuel L. Clemens, December 15, 1872; MTL, vol. 5, p. 252.
32. Letter to Olivia Clemens, July 8, 1870; MTL, vol. 4, p. 167.
33. MTB, as cited in MTL, vol. 5, p. 259.
34. Quoted in E. J. Edwards, "How Mark Twain and Charles Dudley Warner Came to Write 'The Gilded Age,' " New York *Evening Mail,* May 5, 1910; quoted in MTL, vol. 5, p. 259.
35. New York *Tribune,* December 23, 1872; quoted in MTL, vol. 5, p. 262.
36. MTL, vol. 5, p. 260.
37. *The Gilded Age,* OMT, p. 184.
38. Ibid., p. 80.
39. Letter to Mary Fairbanks, April 16, 1873; MTL, vol. 5, p. 339.
40. Ibid., p. 339.
41. *The Gilded Age,* p. 37.
42. *The Adventures of Huckleberry Finn,* OMT, p. 280.
43. *The Gilded Age,* p. 49.
44. Letter to Whitelaw Reid, January 13 and 17, 1873; MTL, vol. 5, p. 270.
45. Autobiographical dictations, April 5, 1906, MTP; MTL, vol. 5, p. 36.
46. Letter to Whitelaw Reid, March 28, 1873; MTL, vol. 5, p. 324.
47. Letter from Olivia and Samuel Clemens to Olivia Lewis Langdon, May 17, 1873; MTL, vol. 5, p. 366.
48. Letter to Charles Warner, May 17, 1873; MTL, vol. 5, pp. 367–68.

29: GILDED

1. Letter to Olivia Lewis Langdon, May 23 and 26, 1873; Mark Twain House, Hartford, Conn.; quoted in MTL, vol. 5, p. 371.
2. Letter to Olivia Lewis Langdon, May 31, 1873.
3. Letter to Whitelaw Reid, April 20, 1873; MTL, vol. 5, p. 347.
4. This was the term Twain used in a reminiscence written in 1890, "Concerning the Scoundrel Edward House," preserved in MTP.
5. Whitelaw Reid, letter to Kate Field, July 17, 1873; quoted in MTL, vol. 5, p. 369.
6. Autobiographical dictations, MTP; quoted in MTL, vol. 5, p. 369.
7. Moncure Daniel Conway, *Autobiography: Memories and Experiences of Moncure Daniel Conway* (Boston: Houghton, Mifflin, 1904); quoted in MTL, vol. 5, p. 416.
8. Letter to Ellen D. Conway, June 25, 1873; MTL, vol. 5, p. 388.
9. George Dolby, quoted by Samuel Thompson in his unpublished reminiscences, MTP; see MTL, vol. 5, p. 446.
10. MTOC, pp. 157–58.
11. Charles Warren Stoddard, *Exits and Entrances: A Book of Essays and Sketches* (Boston: Lothrop Publishing Co., 1903); quoted in MTL, vol. 5, p. 477.

12. Quoted by George Wharton James in "Charles Warren Stoddard," *National Magazine* (August 1911), pp. 659–72; see MTL, vol. 5, pp. 492–93.
13. Stoddard, *Exits and Entrances;* quoted in MTL, vol. 5, p. 477.
14. Ibid.
15. Ibid., pp. 477–78.
16. Letter to Olivia Clemens, November 23, 1873; MTL, vol. 5, p. 482.
17. Letter to Olivia Clemens, December 13 and 15, 1873; MTL, vol. 5, p. 512.
18. Letter to James Redpath, December 17, 1873; MTL, vol. 5, p. 523.
19. Letter to Olivia Clemens, January 2, 1874; MTL, vol. 5, p. 3.
20. MTL, vol. 5, p. 417, n. 1
21. New York *Daily Graphic*, December 23, 1873; quoted in MTL, vol. 5, p. 466.
22. Chicago *Tribune*, February 1, 1874; quoted in MTL, vol. 5, p. 465.
23. William Dean Howells, letter to Samuel Clemens, December 28, 1873; MTL, vol. 5, p. 468.
24. Letter to Joseph Twichell, January 5, 1874; MTL, vol. 6, pp. 11–12.
25. Letter to London *Standard*, March 12, 1874; MTL, vol. 6, pp. 66–67.
26. Letter to Mary Fairbanks, February 25, 1874; MTL, vol. 6, p. 46.
27. MTB, p. 16.
28. Ibid.
29. Letter to Orion Clemens, February 4, 1874; MTL, vol. 6, p. 26.
30. Ibid.
31. Letter to Frank Fuller, January 31, 1874; MTL, vol. 6, p. 23.
32. Letter to Charles Kingsley, February 13, 1874; MTL, vol. 6, p. 31.
33. Letter to Mary Fairbanks, February 25, 1874; MTL, vol. 6, p. 46.
34. Letter to Howells, February 27, 1874; MTL, vol. 6, p. 52.
35. Cable to James Redpath, March 3, 1874; MTL, vol. 6, p. 60.
36. Lilian Aldrich, *Crowding Memories* (Boston: Houghton, Mifflin, 1920); quoted in MTL, vol. 6, p. 93.
37. Ibid.
38. Ibid.
39. MTA, p. 358.
40. William Dean Howells, *Selected Letters*, edited by George Arms et al., vol. 2, *1873–1881* (Boston: Twayne, 1979), p. 56; quoted in MTL, vol. 6, p. 86.
41. Letter to Thomas Bailey Aldrich, March 25, 1874; MTL, vol. 6, p. 94.
42. Letter to William Andrews, March 28, 1874; MTL, vol. 6, p. 95.
43. Edgar Wakeman, letter, February 12, 1874; MTL, vol. 6, p. 82.
44. Letter to Howells, March 20, 1874; MTL, vol. 6, p. 85.

30: QUARRY FARM AND NOOK FARM

1. Letter to Mary Fairbanks, February 25, 1874; MTL, vol. 6, p. 46.
2. Quoted at www.marktwainhouse.org.
3. Mollie Clemens, letter, April 25, 1874; MTL, vol. 6, p. 112.
4. Letter to Jane Clemens, May 10, 1874; MTL, vol. 6, p. 141.
5. Orion Clemens, letter, April 25, 1874; MTL, vol. 6, p. 113.
6. Letter to William Dean Howells, May 10, 1874; MTL, vol. 6, p. 145.
7. Letter to Joseph and Harmony Twichell, June 11, 1874; MTL, vol. 6, p. 158.
8. Letter to John Brown, September 4, 1874; MTL, vol. 6, p. 222.
9. Letter to Mary Fairbanks, November 6–December 10, 1872; MTL, vol. 5, p. 217.
10. Autobiographical dictation, February 1906, CU-MARK, MTL, vol. 4, p. 158.
11. See "Mark Twain's Days in Elmira," in *New York in Literature*, by Rufus Rockwell

Wilson and Otilie Erikson Wilson (Elmira: Primavera Press, 1947), reprinted in "Mark Twain in Elmira," the Mark Twain Society, Inc., 1977, p. 5

12. Wilson, "Mark Twain in Elmira," p. 8
13. Letter to Charles Dudley Warner, May 5, 1874; MTL, vol. 6, p. 127.
14. Letter to Howells, July 22, 1874; MTL, vol. 6, p. 193.
15. Letter to the Twichells, June 11, 1874; MTL, vol. 6, p. 158.
16. Letter to John Brown, April 27, 1874; MTL, vol. 6, p. 121.
17. MTL, vol. 6, pp. 171–72.
18. "Speech on Accident Insurance," in *Mark Twain's Sketches*, OMT.
19. Letter to Jane Clemens; MTL, vol. 6, p. 184.
20. Letter to John Brown, September 4, 1874; MTL, vol. 6, p. 221.
21. Ibid.
22. Notably Hamlin L. Hill in "The Composition and Structure of *Tom Sawyer*," *American Literature*, vol. 32 (1961–62), pp. 379–92, reprinted in *On Mark Twain: The Best from American Literature*, edited by Louis J. Budd and Edwin H. Cady (Durham: Duke University Press, 1987).
23. Quoted in Hill, "The Composition and Structure of *Tom Sawyer.*"
24. Letter to Mary Field, July 29, 1874; MTL, vol. 6, p. 197.
25. Telegram to John Raymond; MTL, vol. 6, p. 215.
26. Rochester *Union and Advertiser*, September 1, 1874; quoted in MTL, vol. 6, p. 216 op. cit.
27. Rochester *Evening Express*, September 1, 1874; quoted in MTL, vol. 6, p. 216 op. cit.
28. Letter to William Dean Howells, September 2, 1874; MTL, vol. 6, p. 217.
29. "A True Story," in *Mark Twain's Sketches*, OMT, p. 204.
30. Ibid., p. 207.
31. Letter to Howells, September 2, 1874; MTL, vol. 6, p. 217.
32. Letter to Howells, September 20, 1874; MTL, vol. 6, p. 233.
33. Howells, "Recollections of an *Atlantic* Editorship," *Atlantic* (November 1907); quoted in MTL, vol. 6, p. 219.
34. Letter to Rachel Gleason, September 12, 1874; MTL, vol. 6, p. 231.
35. Andrew Carpenter Wheeler ("Nym Crinkle"), review in New York *World*, September 17, 1874; quoted in MTL, vol. 6, p. 645.
36. Ibid., pp. 650–51.
37. Ibid., p. 651.
38. Margaret Duckett, *Mark Twain and Bret Harte* (Norman: University of Oklahoma Press, 1964), pp. 121–22.
39. Wheeler, review; quoted in MTL, vol. 6, p. 648.
40. Ibid.
41. Ibid., p. 649.
42. Letter to Robert Watt, January 26, 1875; MTL, vol. 6, p. 359.
43. Letter to Howells, October 3, 1874; MTL, vol. 6, p. 247.
44. Letter from Howells to Clemens, September 30, 1874, Ibid.
45. Letter to Howells, October 24, 1874; MTL, vol. 6, p. 261.
46. Ibid., p. 262.
47. Ibid.
48. Howells, letter, November 23, 1874; MTL, vol. 6, p. 295.
49. Letter to Howells, December 3, 1874; MTL, vol. 6, p. 304.
50. Letter to Olivia Clemens, November 12, 1874; MTL, vol. 6, p. 278.
51. Ibid.
52. Howells, letter, November, 1874; MTL, vol. 6, p. 282.

53. Howells, *Selected Letters,* vol. 2, *1873–1881;* quoted in MTL, vol. 6, p. 282.
54. Letter to Howells, November 14, 1874; MTL, vol. 6, p. 285.
55. Howells, letter, December 11, 1874; MTL, vol. 6, p. 312.
56. Autobiographical dictation, 1907; in MTL, vol. 6, p. 309.
57. Boston *Globe,* December 16, 1874; quoted in MTL, vol. 6, p. 318.
58. Letter from Howells to Clemens, December 11, 1874; MTL, vol. 6, p. 312.
59. Notation on an envelope from Aldrich dated January 1, 1875; MTL, vol. 6, p. 337.
60. William Dean Howells, "Henry James, Jr.," in *The Century,* November 1882, cited in "Henry James, *The Portrait of a Lady,*" the Harvard Classics Shelf of Fiction, 1917, "Great Books Online," www.bartleby.com.
61. Letter to William Dean Howells, July 21,1885, MTHL.

31: THE MAN IN THE MOON

1. Elaine Showalter, *The Female Malady: Women, Madness, and English Culture, 1830–1980* (New York: Pantheon Books, 1985).
2. Letter to James Redpath, November 29, 1874; MTL, vol. 6, p. 298.
3. Letter to William Dean Howells, December 21, 1874; MTL, vol. 6, p. 326.
4. Howells, letter, December 3, 1874; MTL, vol. 6, p. 301.
5. Howells, letter, January 12, 1875; MTL, vol. 6, p. 351.
6. Howells, letter, May 20, 1875; MTL, vol. 6, p. 483.
7. Howells, letter, December 11, 1874; MTL, vol. 6, p. 312.
8. Letter to Howells, December 14, 1874; MTL, vol. 6, p. 316.
9. Letter to Howells, January 15, 1875; MTL, vol. 6, p. 350.
10. Letter to Howells, November 20, 1874; MTL, vol. 6, p. 294.
11. Letter to Howells, November 25, 1874; MTL, vol. 6, p. 295.
12. Letter to Howells, December 8, 1874; MTL, vol. 6, p. 306.
13. Letter from P. T. Barnum to Mark Twain, January 19, 1875; MTL, vol. 6, pp. 369–70.
14. Ibid.
15. "Recollections of an *Atlantic* Editorship," by William Dean Howells, *Atlantic* (November 1907); quoted in MTL, vol. 6, p. 339.
16. June 8, MTL, vol. 6, p. 494. This was William F. Gill, a publisher who was compiling selections for an announced *Treasure Trove* series of famous authors' works.
17. Howells, letter, December 19, 1874; MTL, vol. 6, p. 327.
18. Howells, letter, January 10, 1875; MTL, vol. 6, p. 349.
19. Letter to Howells, January 12, 1875; MTL, vol. 6, p. 348.
20. Letter to Howells, February 10, 1875; MTL, vol. 6, p. 378.
21. Letter to James Osgood, February 12, 1875; MTL, vol. 6, p. 381.
22. Letter to P. T. Barnum, February 19, 1875; MTL, vol. 6, p. 389.
23. Letter to Elinor and William Dean Howells, February 14(?), 1875; MTL, vol. 6, pp. 385–86.
24. Letter to Elisha Bliss, March 1, 1875; MTL, vol. 6, p. 395.
25. Letter to Orion Clemens, March 1, 1875; MTL, vol. 6, p. 396.
26. Letter to Orion Clemens, March 27, 1875; MTL, vol. 6, p. 427.
27. Letter to Howells, March 16, 1875, MTL, vol. 6, p. 414.
28. Letter to Mary Fairbanks, April 23, 1875; MTL, vol. 6, p. 454.
29. Telegram to Dan De Quille, March 29, 1875, MTL, vol. 6, p. 432.
30. Letter to Dan De Quille, March 29 and April 4, 1875; MTL, vol. 6, p. 434.
31. Ibid.
32. Ibid.
33. Ibid., p. 435.

34. Ibid.

35. Ibid., p. 434.

36. Ibid., pp. 435–36.

37. Ibid., p. 436.

38. Ibid.

39. Howells, letter, July 3, 1875; MTL, vol. 6, p. 504.

40. "A Family Sketch," unpublished manuscript, 1906, James S. Copley Library, La Jolla, Calif.; quoted in MTL, vol. 6, pp. 415–16.

41. Autobiographical dictation, April 11, 1907; quoted in MTL, vol. 6, p. 416.

42. "A Family Sketch."

43. MTB, vol. 2, p. 574.

44. New York *Sun,* April 15, 1875; quoted in MTL, vol. 6, p. 448.

45. Joseph Twichell, "Personal Journal," Joseph Twichell Collection, Beinecke Rare Book and Manuscript Library, Yale University, New Haven, Conn.; quoted in MTL, vol. 6, p. 448.

46. Quoted in MTL, vol. 6, p. 488.

47. Letter to Pamela Clemens, July 23, 1875; MTL, vol. 6, p. 515.

48. Letter to Howells, July 5, 1875; MTL, vol. 6, p. 503.

49. Ibid., p. 504.

50. Ibid.

51. Letter to Howells, July 13, 1875; MTL, vol. 6, p. 509.

52. Howells, letter, July 8, 1875; MTL, vol. 6, p. 510.

53. Howells, letter, November 21, 1875; MTL, vol. 6, p. 595.

54. Ibid.

55. Ibid.

56. Letter to Clemens, Ibid.

57. Ibid.

58. "Adventures of Tom Sawyer," OMT, p. 275.

59. For further discussion, see MTL, vol. 6, p. 596, n. 4.

60. Letter from Howells to Clemens, November 5, 1875, MTL vol. 6, p. 584.

61. Letter to Joseph Twichell, December 29 or 30, 1875; MTL, vol. 6, p. 606.

62. MTL, vol. 6, p. 597.

63. Letter to Susy Clemens, December 25, 1875; MTL, vol. 6, pp. 604–6.

32: "It Befell Yt One Did Breake Wind . . ."

1. Letter to William Dean Howells, January 18, 1876; MTHL, vol. 1, p. 121.

2. Letter to Moncure Conway, January 5, 1876; MTP.

3. Letter to Howells, January 18, 1876; MTHL, vol. 1, p. 121.

4. Ibid.

5. Howells, letter, January 19, 1876; MTHL, vol. 1, p. 124.

6. "Adventures of Tom Sawyer," OMT, p. 162.

7. Letter to Elisha Bliss, March 19, 1876, MTP.

8. Letter to Conway, April 9, 1876, MTP.

9. Letter to Howells, April 26, 1876; MTHL, vol. 1, p. 132.

10. Ibid.

11. Ibid.

12. Letter to Howells, April 3, 1876; MTP.

13. Review of *The Adventures of Tom Sawyer,* in the May 1876 edition of the *Atlantic;* MMT, p. 105. (Howells incorrectly dated the review December 1875.)

14. Ibid.

15. Ibid., pp. 106–7.

16. Letter to Elisha Bliss, June 24, 1876; MTP.
17. Letter to Howells, March 13, 1876; MTP.
18. "The Facts Concerning the Recent Carnival of Crime in Connecticut," in *The Stolen White Elephant and Other Detective Stories*, OMT, p. 106.
19. Ibid.
20. Letter to Howells, August 9, 1876; MTHL, vol. 1, p. 144.
21. Letter to Mary Fairbanks, August 4, 1876; MTMF, p. 201.
22. Letter to John Brown, June 22, 1876; 01343, Electronic edition.
23. Letter to Howells, August 9, 1876; MTHL, vol. 1, p. 143.
24. Ibid.
25. Autobiographical dictation, 1906, CU-MARK.
26. As reported by Rufus Rockwell Wilson and Otilie Erikson Wilson in "Mark Twain's Days in Elmira" in the collection, "Mark Twain in Elmira," Elmira: Primavera Press, 1947, p. 5.
27. Ibid., pp. 143–44.
28. Letter to Will Bowen, August 31, 1876; MTP.
29. Ibid.
30. "Letter to John Burrough, November 1, 1876, *Mark Twain's Letters,* vol. 1, edited by Albert Bigelow Paine (New York: Harper & Brothers, 1917), p. 290.
31. Ibid.
32. Letter to Howells, January 10 or 11, 1876; MTHL, vol. 1, p. 119.
33. Howells, letter, November 30, 1876; MTHL, vol. 1, p. 165.
34. Howells, letter, January 27, 1876; MTHL, vol. 1, p. 124.
35. Howells, letter, August 20, 1876; MTHL, vol. 1, p. 145.
36. Letter to Howells, October 11, 1876; MTP.
37. Howells, letter, August 5, 1876; MTHL, vol. 1, p. 142.
38. Letter to Howells, July 15 or 22, 1874; MTL, vol. 6, p. 193.
39. Letter to Howells, December 21, 1874; MTL, vol. 6, p. 326.
40. Howells, letter, August 5, 1876; MTHL, vol. 1, p. 142.
41. Quoted by Gary Scharnhorst in " 'Ways That Are Dark': Appropriations of Bret Harte's 'Plain Language from Truthful James.' " *Nineteenth-Century Literature*, vol. 51 (December 1996); republished at www.ucpress.edu/scan/nel-e/513/articles/scharnhorst.art513.html.
42. Letter to Howells, October 11, 1876; MTHL, vol. 1, p. 157.
43. *1601, and, Is Shakespeare Dead?* OMT, pp. iii–iv.
44. Ibid., p. v.
45. MTB, vol. 2, p. 581.
46. Letter to Howells, August 23, 1876; MTHL, vol. 1, p. 146.
47. Letter to Howells, September 14, 1876; MTP.
48. Boston *Transcript*, quoted in MTHL, vol. 1, p. 156.
49. Paraphrase of letter, Hartford *Courant*, September 24–30, 1876; MTP.
50. Letter to Howells, November 8, 1876; MTHL, vol. 1, p. 162.
51. "Mark Twain's New Book," Hartford *Times*, December 20, 1876; in *Mark Twain: The Contemporary Reviews,* edited by Louis J. Budd (Edinburgh: Cambridge University Press, 1999).
52. Review, New York *Times*, January 13, 1877; in *Mark Twain: The Critical Heritage*, edited by Frederick Anderson, assisted by Kenneth M. Sanderson (London: Routledge & Kegan Paul, 1971), p. 70.
53. Ibid.
54. Moncure D. Conway, review in London *Examiner,* in Anderson, ed., *Mark Twain: The Critical Heritage*, p. 63.

55. London *Examiner* [unsigned; Moncure D. Conway], June 17, 1876, etext.virginia
.edu/railton/tomsawyer/londonex.

33: GOD'S FOOL

1. Printed form letter with facsimile signature, dated "HARTFORD . . . 1877," Electronic Text 1877, 01399.
2. Draft form letter, CU-MARK, written and used between 1877 and 1880, Electronic Text 1877, 00593.
3. Letter from C. P. Sullivan, Lina Creek, Laurens County, South Carolina, March 24, 1880, CU-MARK 32739.
4. Letter from J. L. Goodloe, Memphis, Tennessee, October 8, 1877, CU-MARK, 32579.
5. Letter to Mary Fairbanks, September 23, 1879, 01692, MTMF, p. 233.
6. Letter to Jane Clemens, February 17, 1878, MTL, vol. 1, pp. 319–20, CU MARK 01530.
7. Letter from Ola A. Smith, Haverhill, Massachusetts, April 18, 1880, CU-MARK 32762.
8. Letter from Edson Q. Beebe, Montrose, Pennsylvania, March 30, 1880, CU-MARK 32743.
9. Letter from W. D. Wells, Jesup, Iowa, November 6, 1877, CU-MARK 32597.
10. Letter from John, H. P., C. Mi, and L. W. Napton, Eelkill, Missouri, December 4, 1877, CU-MARK 32606.
11. "Nature," in "Ralph Waldo Emerson: Selected Essays," edited by Larzer Ziff (New York: Penguin Classics, 1985), p. 78.
12. Letter to Howells, October 11, 1876; MTHL, vol. 1, pp. 157–58.
13. Letter to Hjalmar H. Boyesen, January 17, 1877, Electronic Text 1877, 12673.
14. Letter to Francis Bliss, January 24, 1877, Electronic Text 1877, 01163.
15. Letter to Bayard Taylor, January 24, 1867, Electronic Text 1877, 01403.
16. Letter to Pamela Moffett, January 19, 1877, Electronic Text 1877, 02801.
17. Letter from Clemens and Olivia Clemens to Mrs. Langdon, February 2 and 4, 1877, 01405.
18. Letter to Pamela Moffett, February 27, 1877; MTP.
19. MTA, p. 298.
20. Ibid., pp. 298–99.
21. Ibid., p. 304.
22. Margaret Duckett, *Mark Twain and Bret Harte* (Norman: University of Oklahoma Press, 1964).
23. Letter to Olivia Clemens, April 26, 1877; MTL 1876–1880, electronic edition, vol. 2.
24. Notebooks & Journals II, p. 12.
25. Ibid. p. 31.
26. Ibid., p. 21.
27. Ibid., p. 30.
28. Letter to Mary Fairbanks, August 6, 1877; MTP.
29. DeLancey Ferguson, "Mark Twain's Lost Curtain Speeches," *South Atlantic Quarterly*, vol. 42 (July 1943), p. 269; quoted in Duckett, *Mark Twain and Bret Harte*, p. 153.
30. Ibid.
31. Letter to Olivia Clemens, July 15, 1877; MTP.
32. Olivia Clemens, letter, July 29, 1877; LLMT, vol. 1, p. 203.
33. Duckett, p. 153.
34. Ibid.
35. Clara Clemens, *My Father: Mark Twain*, Harper: New York and London, 1931, p. 62.

36. Ibid., p. 62.
37. Ibid.
38. Letter to Dr. John Brown, August 25 and 27, 1877; MTP.
39. Ibid.
40. Ibid.
41. Ibid.
42. Letter to Howells, June 27, 1878; MTP.
43. Howells; MMT, p. 58.
44. Orion Clemens, letter, December 15, 1877; MTP.
45. Letter to Orion Clemens, December 19, 1877; MTP.
46. Letter to Howells, March 23?, 1877; MTP.
47. Boston *Journal,* December 18, 1877; quoted in Henry Nash Smith, "That Hideous Mistake of Poor Clemens's!" *Harvard Library Bulletin,* vol. 9 (Spring 1955), p. 151.
48. "The Story of a Speech," in *Speeches,* OMT, p. 2.
49. Ibid., p. 5.
50. Ibid., p. 7.
51. Ibid., pp. 11–12.
52. Ibid.
53. Ibid., p. 13.
54. Ibid., p. 14.
55. Smith, "That Hideous Mistake," pp. 146–47.
56. Ibid., p. 154.
57. Howells, MMT, p. 50.
58. Ibid., p. 52.
59. Letter to Emerson, Longfellow, and Holmes, December 27, 1877, 01184, Smith, p. 164.
60. Ibid.
61. Smith, p. 165.
62. Letter from Longfellow to Clemens, January 6, 1878, CU-MARK, Smith, p. 167.
63. Letter from Ellen T. Emerson to Olivia Clemens, December 31, 1877, CU-MARK, Smith, p. 166.
64. Edward B. Osborn, writing in the London *Morning Post,* cited in *Literary Digest,* July 12, 1919; quoted in Smith, "That Hideous Mistake," pp. 165–66.

34: ABROAD AGAIN

1. Letter to William Dean Howells, December 28, 1877; MTP.
2. Letter to Mary Fairbanks, February 5, 1878; MTMF, p. 219, 01528.
3. Letter to Jane Clemens, February 17, 1878; MTP.
4. Letter to Mary Fairbanks, March 9, 1878; MTP.
5. See especially Fanning, *Mark Twain and Orion Clemens,* Chapter 4.
6. Letter to Orion Clemens, February 21, 1878; MTP.
7. Letter to Orion Clemens, March 23, 1878; MTL. vol. 1, p. 322.
8. N&J, vol. 2, p. 64.
9. Letter to Howells, May 4, 1878.
10. Letter to Charles Dudley Warner, June 16, 1878; MTP.
11. Letter to Howells, May 4, 1878.
12. Letter to Howells, May 26, 1878; MTP.
13. *A Tramp Abroad,* OMT, p. 31.
14. Letter to Howells, June 27, 1878; MTP.
15. Ibid.
16. N&J, vol. 2, p. 89.

17. Ibid., p. 81.
18. Ibid., p. 80.
19. Ibid., p. 67.
20. Ibid., p. 140.
21. Ibid., p. 74.
22. Ibid., p. 146.
23. Ibid., p. 147.
24. Ibid., p. 80.
25. Ibid., p. 149.
26. Ibid., p. 92.
27. Ibid., p. 93.
28. Ibid., p. 139.
29. *A Tramp Abroad,* p. 83.
30. N&J, vol. 2, p. 123.
31. Letter to Howells, January 30, 1879; MTP.
32. N&J, vol. 2, p. 145.
33. *A Tramp Abroad,* p. 103.
34. N&J, vol. 2, p. 118.
35. Ibid., p. 132.
36. Ibid., p. 134.
37. *A Tramp Abroad,* p. 124.
38. Ibid., p. 126.
39. Ibid., p. 156.
40. Ibid., pp. 182–83.
41. *Adventures of Huckleberry Finn,* OMT, p. 130.
42. Justin Kaplan, *Mr. Clemens and Mark Twain* (New York: Simon & Schuster, 1966), p. 219.
43. N&J, vol. 1, p. 160.
44. Joseph Twichell, letter, cited in MTB, vol. 2, p. 629.
45. Ibid.
46. Letter to Jane and Pamela Clemens, December 1, 1878; MTP.
47. Letter to Olivia Lewis Langdon, December 2, 1878; MTP.
48. Letter to Bayard Taylor, September 8, 1878; MTP.
49. Ibid., December 14, 1878; MTP.
50. *A Tramp Abroad,* p. 37.
51. Ibid.
52. Ibid., p. 38.
53. Letter to Howells, January 30, 1879; MTP.
54. Letter to Howells, January 21, 1879; MTP.
55. Ibid.
56. N&J, vol. 2, p. 304.
57. Letter to Howells, February 9, 1879; MTP.
58. Ibid.
59. Ibid.
60. Letter to Mary Fairbanks, March 6, 1879; MTP.
61. Ibid.
62. Letter to the New York *Evening Post,* May 20–25, 1879.
63. Ibid.
64. N&J, vol. 2, p. 306–7.
65. Ibid., p. 336.
66. Ibid., p. 310.

67. Ibid., p. 309.
68. Letter to Mary Fairbanks, March 6, 1879; MTP.
69. Letter to Twichell, June 10, 1879; MTP.
70. Letter to Orion Clemens, May 29, 1879; MTP.
71. N&J, vol. 2, p. 318.
72. Ibid., p. 323.
73. Letter to Twichell, June 10, 1879; MTP.
74. Fatout, *Mark Twain Speaking*, p. 126.
75. N&J, vol. 2, p. 320.
76. Ibid., p. 318.
77. Ibid., p. 300.
78. Letter to Frank Bliss, September 8, 1879; MTP.
79. Letter to Olivia Clemens, November 12, 1879; MTP.
80. Ibid.
81. Ibid.
82. Ibid.
83. The author acknowledges Shelley Fisher Fishkin, president of the Mark Twain Circle of America, who assembled these details.
84. "The Babies," Electronic Text Center, University of Virginia Library, http://etext .lib.virginia.edu/railton.
85. "The Babies," *Speeches*, OMT, p. 64.
86. Ibid., pp. 64–65.
87. Ibid., p. 65.
88. Ibid., p. 66.
89. MTA, p. 245.
90. Ibid.
91. "The Babies," in *Speeches*, pp. 67–68.
92. Letter to Olivia Clemens, November 14, 1879; MTP.
93. Ibid.

35: "A Personal Hatred for Humbug"

1. Clara Clemens, *My Father, Mark Twain,* (New York: Harper & Bros., 1931), p. 35.
2. Olivia Clemens to Olivia Lewis Langdon, November 30, 1879, Mark Twain House, 01730.
3. Letter to Susan Crane and Olivia Lewis Langdon, probably January 1880, E-text 1880, 08711.
4. Letter to Howells, January 8, 1880, MTHL, vol. 1, p. 286, 02538.
5. Letter to Elisha Bliss, March 20, 1880, MTLP, p. 121, 02540.
6. Ibid.
7. William Dean Howells, "A Tramp Abroad," *The Atlantic,* May 1880, reprinted in MMT, p. 111.
8. Ibid.
9. Howells review, p. 108.
10. Howells review, p. 109.
11. Letter to Pamela Clemens, February 28, 1880, E-text 1880, 01765.
12. Letter to Orion Clemens, February 26, 1880, E-text 1880, 01763.
13. N&J, vol. II, p. 391.
14. MTB, vol. II, p. 904.
15. Ibid.
16. N&J vol. II., p. 360.
17. Ibid., p. 361.

18. Ibid., p. 377.
19. Letter to Howells, March 11, 1880, MTHL, vol. 1, p. 291, 12539.
20. Ibid.
21. Ibid.
22. Letter from Mary Fairbanks to Samuel Clemens, July 26, 1880.
23. "Dear Master Wattie: the Mark Twain–David Watt Bowser Letters," edited and annotated by Pascal Covici, Jr., in the *Southwest Review,* Spring 1960, p. 106. Covici obtained permission to publish the letters from Bowser's niece, Mrs. E. C. Stradley, of Dallas, and the trustees of the Mark Twain Estate.
24. Ibid., p. 106, n. 2.
25. Ibid., p. 106.
26. Ibid.
27. Ibid., p. 107.
28. Ibid., p. 108.
29. Ibid.
30. Ibid., pp. 110, 111, 112, 114.
31. Ibid., p. 109.
32. Ibid., pp. 110–11.
33. Letter from Thomas H. Murray to Clemens, May 8, 1880, CU-MARK, 32782.
34. Letter to Thomas H. Murray, May 13, 1880, E-text 1880, CU-MARK, 01803.
35. Mark Twain's Notebooks and Journals, vol. 3, p. 153.
36. Letter to Samuel Clemens, November 18, 1879, quoted by Fanning, p. 181.
37. Letter to Orion Clemens, February 26, 1880, E-text 1880, 01763.
38. Ibid.
39. Letter to Orion Clemens, April 4, 1880, 01782.
40. Letter to Orion Clemens, May 6, 1880, 01799.
41. Letter to Howells, June 9, 1880, 2nd of 2, MTHL, vol. 1, p. 313, 02812.
42. Letter to Howells, August 1, 1880, MTHL, vol. 1, p. 319, 01820.
43. N&J vol. II, p. 355.
44. Letter to Howells, October 19, 1880, MTHL, vol. 1, p. 332, 01843.
45. Letter to Orion Clemens, October 24, 1880, MTLTP, p. 125, 08145.
46. Letter from Howells to Clemens, December 13, 1880, MTHL, vol. I, p. 338, 32889.
47. Ibid.
48. Letter to James Osgood, October 19, 1880, E-text 1880, 10668.
49. Letter to Orion Clemens, November 27, 1880; Electronic edition, 08157.

36: "A POWERFUL GOOD TIME"

1. These figures are listed in *Mark Twain's Letters to His Publishers,* Hamlin Hill, ed. (Berkeley: University of California Press, 1967), p. 128.
2. Letter to Pamela Moffett, November 14?, 1880, MTB, vol. 2, p. 696.
3. Letter to Howells, February 15, 1887, MTHL, vol. II, p. 586, 02655.
4. N&J, vol. 2, p. 400.
5. Letter to Horace Scudder, February 8, 1881, *Life in Letters of William Dean Howells,* Mildred Howells, ed. (Garden City, N.Y.: Doubleday, Doran & Company, 1928), MTHL, vol. I, p. 350.
6. Ibid.
7. Letter to Howells, February 15, 1881, MTHL, p. 350, 01908.
8. Ibid., p. 350.
9. *My Father Mark Twain,* p. 43.
10. MTB, p. 125.

11. Letter to Olivia Lewis Langdon, quoted in MTB, vol. II, p. 730.
12. Letter to Annie E. Lucas, January 31, 1881, E-text 1881, 01899.
13. Letter to Daniel Slote, March 31, 1881, MTBM, p. 152, 01934.
14. Samuel Charles Webster, MTBM, p. 153.
15. Letter to Charles Webster, April 29, 1881, MTBM, p. 152, 01940.
16. MMT, pp. 60–61.
17. Letter from Howells to Clemens, September 11, 1881, MTHL, vol. I, p. 373, 40858.
18. Letter from Howells to John Hay, October 16, 1881, *Life in Letters of William Dean Howells*, vol. 1, Mildred Howells, ed. (Garden City, N.Y.: Doubleday, Doran & Company, 1928, p. 303.
19. Letter to Clemens, October 12, 1881, MTHL, p. 375, 40879.
20. Ibid.
21. Letter to Howells, October 15, 1881, MTHL, vol. I, p. 376, 02053.
22. Letter from Winifred Howells to Samuel Clemens, January 18, 1882, MTHL, vol. I, p. 383, 40989.
23. H. H. Boyesen, "Mark Twain's New Departure," *The Atlantic*, December 1881, MTCR, p. 199.
24. Ibid., p. 200.
25. "P&P," OMT, p. 327.
26. Ibid., p. 135.
27. Letter from Roswell Phelps to Clemens, March 14, 1882, N&J II, p. 517., citing transcript in MTP, 41075.
28. Letter from Howells to Clemens, April 18, 1882, MTHL, vol. I, p. 403, 41256.
29. Letter to James Osgood, March 23?, 1882, MTHL, vol. I, p. 397, 02183.
30. As noted in MTHL, vol. I, p. 400.
31. N&J, vol. II, pp. 355–56.
32. Letter to Howells, January 28, 1882, MTHL, vol. I, p. 386, 02560.
33. N&J, vol. II, pp. 420–24.
34. Ibid., pp. 440–41.
35. Letter to Howells, January 28, 1882, MTHL, vol. I, p. 387, 02560.
36. Ibid., p. 389.
37. Letter to Howells, April 16, 1882, MTHI, pp. 400–401.
38. Letter to Olivia Clemens, April 21, 1882, and April 22, 1882, *The Love Letters of Mark Twain*, Dixon Wecter, ed. (New York: Harper & Brothers, 1949), pp. 207, 208.
39. N&J, vol. II, p. 526.
40. "Life on the Mississippi," chapter 22, OMT, p. 249.
41. N&J, vol. II, p. 472.
42. Ibid., p. 531.
43. "Life on the Mississippi," OMT, p. 263.
44. Ibid., p. 272.
45. N&J, V II, p. 458.
46. Ibid., p. 454.
47. Ibid.
48. Ibid.
49. Ibid., p. 530.
50. Ibid., p. 466.
51. Ibid., p. 490.
52. Ibid., p. 501.
53. Ibid., p. 469.
54. Ibid., pp. 541–42.
55. Letter to Olivia Clemens, April 25, 1882, LLMT, p. 210, 02205.

56. "Modern Critical Views: Mark Twain," edited and with an introduction by Harold Bloom, p. 5, New York and Philadelphia, 1986.
57. N&J vol. II, p. 478.
58. Ibid., pp. 489–90.
59. Ibid., p. 479.
60. Ibid., p. 480.
61. Letter to Howells, November 4, 1882, MTHL, vol. I, p. 418, 02568. Corrected against the original typescript.

37: "ALL RIGHT, THEN . . ."

1. William Dean Howells, "Mark Twain," *Century* magazine (September 1882), reprinted in MMT; p. 118.
2. Ibid., p. 122.
3. Ibid., p. 120.
4. Letter to Howells, November 4, 1882; MTHL, vol. I, p. 418.
5. Letter to James R. Osgood, June 11, 1882, E-text 1882, 08975.
6. *Life on the Mississippi*, OMT, p. 300.
7. Ibid., p. 303.
8. James M. Cox, "*Life on the Mississippi* Revisited," in Bloom, ed., *Modern Critical Views: Mark Twain* (New York: Chelsea House, 1986).
9. Letter to James Osgood, October 18, 1882; MTLTP, p. 158.
10. Letter to Howells, October 30, 1882; MTHL, vol. 1, p. 417.
11. Ibid.
12. Ibid.
13. Letter to Howells, November 4, 1882; MTHL, vol. 1, p. 418.
14. MTLTP, p. 161.
15. Ibid.
16. Letter to Howells, July 20, 1883; MTHL, vol. 1, p. 435.
17. *Life on the Mississippi*, OMT, p. 42.
18. Ibid., p. 246.
19. Chicago *Tribune*, "Mark Twain Produces Another Compound of Fiction, Humor, and Fact," May 19, 1883; in Budd, ed., *Mark Twain: The Contemporary Reviews*, p. 235.
20. Ibid., p. 144.
21. Letter to Clemens, December 8, 1883; MTLTP, p. 165.
22. Letter to Osgood, December 21, 1883; MTLTP, p. 164.
23. Ibid.
24. Letter to James R. Osgood, May 24, 1884; MTLTP, p. 168.
25. Ibid.
26. Letter to Howells, March 1, 1883; MTHL, vol. 1, p. 427.
27. N&J, vol. 3, p. 13.
28. Letter to Clemens, September 18, 1883; MTHL, vol. 1, p. 442.
29. N&J, vol. 3, p. 24.
30. Letter to Jane Clemens, July 21, 1883; quoted in N&J, vol. 3, p. 3.
31. Letter to Howells, July 20, 1883; MTHL, vol. 1, p. 435.
32. Letter to Howells, August 9, 1876; MTHL, vol. 1, p. 144.
33. *Adventures of Huckleberry Finn*, OMT, p. 1.
34. Ibid., p. 137.
35. Ibid.
36. Ibid., p. 138.
37. Ibid., p. 139.
38. Ibid., p. 141.

39. See Clemens's letter to Pamela Moffett of November 14(?), 1880, as quoted in the Introduction to *Adventures of Huckleberry Finn* edited by Victor Fischer and Lin Salamo (Berkeley: University of California Press, 2003), p. 684.

40. See the monograph, *The Grangerford-Shepherdson Feud by Mark Twain*, by Edgar Marquess Branch and Robert H. Hirst (Berkeley: Friends of the Bancroft Library, 1985).

41. *Adventures of Huckleberry Finn*, OMT, p. 188.

42. *Adventures of Huckleberry Finn*, ed. Fischer and Salamo (Berkeley: University of California Press, 2003), Appendix D, p. 574.

43. Ibid.

44. *Adventures of Huckleberry Finn*, OMT, p. 270.

45. Ibid., p. 271.

46. Ibid., p. 272.

47. Norman Podhoretz, "The Literary Adventures of Huck Finn," New York *Times*, December 6, 1959.

48. *Adventures of Huckleberry Finn*, OMT, p. 296.

49. Ibid., p. 337.

50. Ibid., p. 361.

51. Ibid., p. 366.

52. As researched and demonstrated by Victor Fischer and Lin Salamo in their Introduction to *Huckleberry Finn*, p. 691.

53. CU-MARK, quoted in Fischer and Salamo, eds., *Huckleberry Finn*, p. 691.

54. Ibid.

55. Letter to an unidentified recipient, April 24, 1883; quoted in Introduction to *Adventures of Huckleberry Finn*, cd. Fischer and Salamo, p. 689.

56. Letter to Howells, June 22, 1882; MTHL, vol. 1, pp. 407–8.

57. Letter to Clemens, October 12, 1883: MTHL, vol. 1, p. 444.

58. Letter to Clemens, October 17, 1883: MTHL, vol. 1, p. 446.

59. MTB, vol. 2, p. 756.

60. MMT, p. 25.

61. Ibid.

62. Ibid.

38: *THE* AMERICAN NOVEL

1. Letter to Clemens.

2. Merle Johnson, *A Bibliography of the Works of Mark Twain* (New York: Harper Bros., 1935), p. 155, quoted at www.twainquotes.com.

3. See Barbara Schmidt, "A Closer Look at the Lives of True Williams and Alexander Belford," paper presented at the Fourth International Conference on Mark Twain Studies, Elmira, N.Y., August 18, 2001; www.twainquotes.com.

4. Letter to Charles Webster, April 12, 1884; quoted in Introduction to *Huckleberry Finn*, ed. Fischer and Salamo, p. 701.

5. Letter to Webster, April 22, 1884, MTBM, pp. 249–50; quoted in Introduction to *Huckleberry Finn*, p. 706.

6. Letter to William Dean Howells, April 8, 1884; MTHL, vol. 2, pp. 482–83.

7. Howells, letter, April 10, 1884; MTHL, vol. 2, p. 484.

8. Letter to Webster, May 7, 1884; MTLTP, p. 174.

9. Letter to Webster, May 24, 1884, MTBM; quoted in Introduction to *Huckleberry Finn*, p. 717.

10. Ibid., p. 716.

11. Letter to Webster, May 24, 1884; MTBM, pp. 255–56.

12. Ibid., p. 260.

13. R. Kent Rasmussen, *Mark Twain A to Z: The Essential Reference to His Life and Writings* (New York: Facts on File, 1995), p. 269.

14. Letter to Webster, May 23, 1884; MTLTP, p. 175.

15. Letter to Howells, October 18, 1885; MTHL, p. 539.

16. As reported by Paine in MTB, vol. 2, p. 767.

17. Ibid.

18. Letter to Howells, August 7, 1884; MTHL, vol. 2, p. 497.

19. Letter to Webster, August 7, 1884, MTBM, p. 271; quoted in Introduction to *Huckleberry Finn,* p. 731.

20. Howells, letter, August 10, 1884; MTHL, vol. 2, p. 499.

21. Richard Watson Gilder, letter, October 10, 1884; quoted in Introduction to *Huckleberry Finn,* p. 748.

22. Ibid.

23. Susy Clemens, *Papa: An Intimate Biography of Mark Twain,* edited by Charles Neider (Garden City, N.Y.: Doubleday, 1985), pp. 188–89.

24. The illustration ran on page 283 of the first edition, and on 281 of later editions.

25. "Novels of the Week," London *Athenaeum,* December 27, 1884; quoted in Introduction to *Huckleberry Finn,* p. 759.

26. Brander Matthews, "Huckleberry Finn," London *Saturday Review,* January 1885; quoted in Introduction to *Huckleberry Finn,* p. 760.

27. "Huckleberry Finn," Hartford *Courant,* February 20, 1885; quoted in Introduction to *Huckleberry Finn,* pp. 760–61.

28. Letter to Webster, January 27, 1885, MTBM, p. 298; quoted in Introduction to *Huckleberry Finn,* p. 758.

29. Letter to Webster, February 10, 1885, MTBM, p. 300; quoted in Introduction to *Huckleberry Finn,* p. 759.

30. Ibid.

31. Webster, letter, February 14, 1885, MTBM, p. 303; quoted in Introduction to *Huckleberry Finn,* p. 759.

32. "Mark Twain's Bad Boy," New York *World,* March 2, 1885; quoted in Introduction to *Huckleberry Finn,* pp. 761–62.

33. Boston *Advertiser,* March 12, 1885; quoted in Introduction to *Huckleberry Finn,* p. 762.

34. "Current Literature," San Francisco *Bulletin,* March 14, 1885; quoted in Introduction to *Huckleberry Finn,* p. 762.

35. "Literature," San Francisco *Chronicle,* March 15, 1885; quoted in Introduction to *Huckleberry Finn,* p. 763.

36. St. Louis *Globe-Democrat,* March 17, 1885; quoted in Introduction to *Huckleberry Finn,* p. 763.

37. Letter to Charles Webster, March 18, 1885, MTL, vol. 2, pp. 452–53; quoted in Introduction to *Huckleberry Finn,* p. 763.

38. Letter to Webster, July 28, 1885, MTBM, p. 331.

39. Charles G. Van Schuyver, in *Typographical Printing-Surfaces,* by Lucien A. Legros and John C. Grant (London: Longmans, Green and Co., 1916); quoted in N&J, vol. 3, p. 246.

40. N&J, vol. 3, p. 147.

41. Mark Perry, *Grant and Twain: The Story of a Friendship That Changed America* (New York: Random House, 2004), p. 63.

42. "Interviews With Grant's Doctor," *Saturday Evening Post,* September 9, 1901, cited in Perry, *Grant and Twain,* p. 81.

43. MTA, p. 236.

44. Ibid., p. 237; see also Perry, *Grant and Twain*, p. 85.

45. Ibid.

46. MTA, p. 240; Perry, *Grant and Twain*, p. 89.

47. N&J, vol. 3, p. 96.

48. H. L. Mencken, "The Smart Set," February 1913.

49. Waldo Frank, *Our America* (New York: Boni & Liveright, 1919).

50. Bernard DeVoto, *Mark Twain's America* (Cambridge: Houghton Mifflin, 1932), p. 312.

51. Ernest Hemingway, *Green Hills of Africa* (New York: Scribner's, 1935), p. 22.

52. T. S. Eliot, Introduction to *Adventures of Huckleberry Finn* (London: Cresset, 1950); reprinted in Norton Critical Edition of *Adventures of Huckleberry Finn*, edited by Sculley Bradley et al. (New York: Norton, 1977), p. 328.

53. Lionel Trilling, Introduction to *Adventures of Huckleberry Finn* (New York: Rinehart, 1948); reprinted in Norton Critical Edition, p. 318.

54. Leo Marx, "Mr. Eliot, Mr. Trilling, and *Huckleberry Finn*," *American Scholar*, vol. 22 (Autumn 1953); reprinted in Norton Critical Edition, p. 343.

55. Stephen Railton, "Jim and Mark Twain: What Do Dey Stan' For?" *Virginia Quarterly Review*, vol. 63 (Summer 1987), pp. 393–408.

56. Charles H. Nilon, "The End of *Huckleberry Finn* Freeing the Free Negro," in *Satire or Evasion? Black Perspectives on Huckleberry Finn*, edited by James S. Leonard et al. (Durham: Duke University Press, 1992), p. 62; essay originally published in *Mark Twain Journal*, vol. 22 (Fall 1984), pp. 21–27.

57. Bruce Michelson, *Mark Twain on the Loose: A Comic Writer and the American Self* (Amherst: University of Massachusetts Press, 1995), p. 136.

58. Conversation with Robert Hirst.

59. Toni Morrison, Introduction to *Adventures of Huckleberry Finn*, OMT.

60. Thomas Quirk, "Is *Huckleberry Finn* Politically Correct?" in *Coming to Grips with Huckleberry Finn: Essays on a Book, a Boy, and a Man* (Columbia: University of Missouri Press, 1993).

61. Conversation with Robert Hirst.

62. *Adventures of Huckleberry Finn*, OMT, p. 121.

63. Brooklyn *Daily Eagle*, November 21, 1884; quoted in N&J, vol. 3.

64. Letter to Olivia Clemens, January 18, 1885; LLMT, pp. 230–31.

65. N&J, vol. 3, p. 81.

66. Ibid.

67. Chapter 7, "Chapters from My Autobiogaphy," in *The North American Review*, p. 1094, OMT.

68. N&J, vol. 3, p. 86.

69. George Washington Cable, "The Freedman's Case in Equity," *Century* (January 1885); see Stephen Railton, "Mark Twain in His Times," Electronic Text Center, University of Virginia, http://etext.lib.virginia.edu/railton.

70. Ibid.

71. N&J, vol. 3, p. 57.

72. N&J, vol. 3, p. 73.

73. Letter to Olivia Clemens, January 14, 1885; LLMT, p. 229.

74. Ibid.

75. Keokuk *Daily Gate City*, January 16, 1885; see Railton, "Mark Twain in His Times."

76. Ibid.

77. LLMT, p. 229.

78. Susy Clemens, *Papa*, pp. 135–36.

79. See Perry, *Grant and Twain*, p. 197.

80. Ibid., pp. 199–202.
81. Susy Clemens, *Papa,* pp. 121–22.
82. N&J, vol. 3, p. 153.
83. N&J, vol. 3, p. 112.
84. Susy Clemens, *Papa,* p. 000.
85. MTA, p. 202.
86. Ibid., pp. 130–31.
87. Susy Clemens, *Papa,* pp. 106–7.
88. Ibid. pp. 83–84.
89. Ibid., p. 91.
90. Ibid.
91. Ibid., p. 100.
92. Ibid., p. 99.
93. MFMT, p. 26.
94. N&J, vol. 3, p. 152.
95. Ibid., p. 105.
96. Ibid., p. 105.
97. Ulysses S. Grant, *The Personal Memoirs of U.S. Grant: Two Volumes in One* (New York: Konecky & Konecky, 1992).
98. Perry, *Grant and Twain,* p. 228.
99. Letter to New York *Sun.*
100. MMT, p. 29.

39: ROLL OVER, LORD BYRON

1. Susy Clemens, *Papa,* p. 187.
2. Howells letter, January 18, 1886, MTHL; vol. 2, p. 550.
3. Ibid.
4. Letter to Charles Webster, February 13, 1886, MTBM, p. 355.
5. N&J, vol. 3, p. 241.
6. Susy Clemens, *Papa,* p. 205.
7. Letter to Howells, March 19, 1886; MTHL, vol. 2, p. 552.
8. As quoted in N&J, vol. 3, p. 287.
9. Ibid., p. 207.
10. Letter to Howells, May 3, 1886; MTHL, vol. 2, p. 554.
11. Howells, letter, May 5, 1886; MTHL, vol. 2, p. 556.
12. Howells, letter, May 11, 1886; MTHL, vol. 2, p. 558.
13. Howells, letter, May 12, 1886; MTHL, vol. 2, pp. 558–59.
14. Letter to Howells, May 13, 1886; MTHL, vol. 2, pp. 559–60.
15. Ibid., p. 560.
16. Ibid.
17. Ibid., p. 562.
18. Letter to Franklin G. Whitmore, July 12, 1886; quoted in N&J, vol. 3, p. 242.
19. Susy Clemens, *Papa,* p. 225.
20. Keokuk *Weekly Constitution,* July 7, 1886; quoted in Fanning, *Mark Twain and Orion Clemens,* p. 203.
21. Ibid., p. 204.
22. Letter to Webster, November 17, 1886; MTLTP, p. 208.
23. N&J, vol. 3, p. 254.
24. Ibid., p. 258.
25. Letter to Howells, December 12, 1886; MTHL, vol. 2, p. 575.
26. MFMT, p. 74.

27. Ibid.

28. Ibid., p. 24.

29. MTA, p. 211.

30. Ibid., p. 212.

31. Ibid.

32. Ibid.

33. Orion Clemens, letter, November 24, 1886; MTP, quoted in Fanning, *Mark Twain and Orion Clemens*, p. 205.

34. Quoted in Fanning, *Mark Twain and Orion Clemens*, p. 205.

35. Ibid.

36. N&J, vol. 3, p. 235.

37. Ibid., p. 238.

38. Ibid., p. 239.

39. N&J, vol. 3, pp. 246–47.

40. Webster, letter, February 17, 1887; quoted in MTHL, vol. 2, p. 587.

41. MMT, p. 62.

42. Letter to Charles Webster, December 28, 1885; MTBM, p. 348.

43. Letter to Webster, August 3, 1887; MTLTP, p. 22.

44. MMT, p. 62.

45. Ibid.

46. Letter to Webster, February, 1887; quoted in MTBM, p. 376.

47. MTA, p. 255.

48. N&J, vol. 3, p. 312.

49. Ibid., p. 315.

50. Letter to Orion Clemens, September 7, 1887; MTLTP, p. 229.

51. Ibid., p. 230.

52. Thomas Kilby Smith, letter to Webster, August 9, 1887; quoted in MTBM, p. 385.

53. Ibid.

54. Letter to Mary Fairbanks, November 16, 1886; MTP, quoted in N&J, vol. 3, p. 225.

55. Matthew Arnold, *General Grant: With a Rejoinder by Mark Twain*, edited by John Y. Simon (Kent, Ohio: Kent State University Press, 1995), p. 13.

56. Ibid., p. 3.

57. Ibid., p. 55.

58. Ibid., p. 56.

59. Ibid., p. 57.

60. Letter to Mollie Clemens, July 24, 1887; quoted in LLMT, p. 249.

40: "I HAVE FED SO FULL ON SORROWS . . ."

1. Letter to Charles Webster, August 3, 1887; MTLTP, p. 222.

2. N&J, vol. 3, p. 305.

3. Ibid., p. 311.

4. Charles Webster, letter, December 29, 1887; quoted in N&J, vol. 3, p. 374.

5. MTLTP, p. 241.

6. N&J, vol. 3, p. 374.

7. MTBM, p. 390.

8. Ibid.

9. Ibid., p. 394.

10. C. Karen Alkalay-Gut, "Jean Webster," www.karenalkalay-gut.com/web.html.

11. MTA, p. 28.

12. From "Knights of Labor—The New Dynasty," paper read to the Monday Evening Club in Hartford, March 22, 1886; quoted in MTHL, vol. 2, p. 598.

13. Thought to be from a paper read to the Monday Evening Club on February 26, 1887, and later used in *An American Claimant,* OMT, p. 101.
14. Letter to William Dean Howells, March 31, 1888; MTHL, vol. 2, p. 597.
15. Howells, letter, April 5, 1888; MTHL, vol. 2, p. 599.
16. N&J, vol. 3, p. 414.
17. Ibid.
18. Ibid.
19. Ibid., p. 383.
20. Letter to Andrew Chatto, September 17, 1888; quoted in N&J, vol. 3, p. 394.
21. *A Connecticut Yankee in King Arthur's Court,* OMT, p. 542.
22. Ibid., pp. 554–56.
23. Ibid., p. 564.
24. Cf. *Mark Twain A to Z,* by Kent Rasmussen (New York: Facts on File, 1995) p. 98.
25. *Connecticut Yankee,* p. 160.
26. Letter to Webster, March 1, 1887; MTLTP, p. 214.
27. Cf. MTLTP, p. 252.
28. Ibid., p. 431.
29. N&J, vol. 3, p. 439.
30. Ibid., p. 441.
31. Letter to Mary Fairbanks, December 30, 1888, MTMF, pp. 262–63.
32. N&J, vol. 3, p. 498.
33. LLMT, pp. 253–54.
34. Letter to Pamela Moffett, July 15, 1886, 10893. Text is a combination of Paine typescript and MS at Vassar.
35. Letter to Howells, August 5, 1889; MTHL, vol. 2, p. 608.
36. Howells, letter, August 10, 1889; MTHL, vol. 2, pp. 609–10.
37. Letter to Howells, August 24, 1889; MTHL, vol. 2, pp. 610–11.
38. Ibid.
39. Ibid., September 19, 1889, p. 612.
40. Ibid., October 17, 1889, p. 614.
41. Ibid., October 27, 1889, p. 617.
42. Ibid., November 10, 1889, p. 619.
43. MMT, p. 128.
44. Ibid., p. 124.
45. "Mark Twain's Camelot," *Spectator,* April 5, 1890; in *Mark Twain: The Contemporary Reviews,* p. 316.
46. L. F. Austin, "Folios and Footlights," London *New Review* (February 1890), in *Mark Twain: The Contemporary Reviews,* p. 306.
47. Letter to Charles Webster and Fred Hall, September 5, 1887; MTLTP, p. 228.
48. Franklin Whitmore, letter, August 16, 1889; quoted in N&J, vol. 3, p. 500.
49. Letter to Howells, October 21, 1889; MTHL, vol. 2, p. 615.
50. Joseph Goodman, letter, July 26, 1890; quoted in N&J, vol. 3, p. 481.
51. Olivia Clemens, letter, around May 2, 1890; quoted in LLMT, pp. 255–56.
52. Letter to Pamela Moffett, October 12, 1890; quoted in LLMT, p. 258.
53. Letter to Howells, November 27, 1890; MTHL, vol. 2, p. 633.
54. Letter to Fred Hall, December 27, 1890; MTLTP, p. 266.

41: "WE ARE SKIMMING ALONG LIKE PAUPERS . . ."

1. N&J, vol. 3, p. 606.
2. Ibid.
3. Letter to William Dean Howells, February 28, 1891; MTHL, vol. 2, p. 637.

4. Ibid.
5. Howells, letter, March 3, 1891; MTHL, vol. 2, pp. 638–39.
6. Ibid., p. 641.
7. Letter to Mary Fairbanks, May 29, 1891; quoted in N&J, vol. 3, p. 574.
8. Letter to Orion Clemens, February 25, 1891; quoted in N&J, vol. 3, p. 573.
9. N&J, vol. 3, p. 600.
10. Ibid., p. 601.
11. Ibid., p. 606.
12. Letter to Joe Goodman, February 22, 1891; quoted in N&J, vol. 3, p. 573.
13. N&J, vol. 3, p. 619.
14. Howells, letter, May 19, 1891; MTHL, vol. 2, p. 643–44.
15. Letter to Howells, May 20, 1891; MTHL, vol. 2, p. 645.
16. MTB, vol. 2, p. 920.
17. Letter from Olivia Clemens to Mrs. James Trumbull, May 31, 1891, 11039 at the University of Virginia, Charlottesville.
18. N&J, vol. 3, p. 621.
19. Ibid., p. 623.
20. Ibid., p. 621.
21. MFMT, p. 87.
22. N&J, vol. 3, p. 640.
23. Ibid., p. 638.
24. Ibid., p. 642.
25. Ibid., p. 643.
26. Letter to Joe Twichell, September 1891; quoted by Paine in MTB, vol. 2, p. 928.
27. Introduction to Susy Clemens, *Papa,* p. 15.
28. Ibid., p. 17.
29. MFMT, p. 91.
30. Ibid., p. 92.
31. Ibid , p. 93.
32. MFMT, p. 96.
33. Quoted in MTB, vol. 2, p. 936.
34. *Mark Twain's Notebooks,* edited by Albert Bigelow Paine (New York: Harper & Bros., 1935), p. 222.
35. Samuel Clemens to Clara Clemens, January 21, 1893, CU-MARK, record number 04328.
36. *Mark Twain's Notebook,* p. 232.
37. Letter to Fred Hall, August 10, 1892; MTLTP, pp. 313–14.
38. Letter to Fred Hall, September 4, 1892; MTLTP, p. 319.
39. Letter to Susan Crane, September 18, 1892; MTLP, vol. 2, p. 568.
40. MFMT, p. 120.
41. Quoted by Dan Beard, *Tom Sawyer Abroad/Tom Sawyer, Detective,* ed. John C. Gerber, et al., Mark Twain Library, UC Press, 1982, "Note on the Texts," pp. 189–90.
42. *Tom Sawyer Abroad,* OMT, p. 51.
43. Ibid., p. 53.
44. *The Tragedy of Pudd'nhead Wilson and the Comedy of Those Extraordinary Twins,* OMT, p. 357.
45. Letter to Fred Hall, December 12, 1892; MTLTP, p. 328.
46. *The Tragedy of Pudd'nhead Wilson and the Comedy of Those Extraordinary Twins,* OMT, p. 109.
47. Ibid.
48. Letter to Fred Hall, February 3, 1893; MTLTP, p. 337.

49. Letter to Fred Hall, July 30, 1893; MTLTP, p. 354.
50. Ibid.
51. Letter to Fred Hall, June 2, 1893; MTLTP, p. 343.
52. Ibid.
53. Ibid., p. 344.

42: SAVIOR

1. Letter to Clara Clemens, date unknown, MFMT, pp. 126–27.
2. Marjorie Williams, *Slate,* July 15, 1998.
3. Letter to Olivia Clemens, September 17, 1893; LLMT, p. 270.
4. Letter to Clara Clemens, September 10, 1893, MTP; quoted in MTHHR, p. 10.
5. Letter to Olivia Clemens, September 17, 1893; LLMT, p. 270.
6. Ibid., p. 270.
7. See Thomas W. Lawson, *Frenzied Finance,* vol. 1, *The Crime of Amalgamated* (New York: Ridgway-Thayer Co., 1905), excerpt at www.millicentlibrary.org/lawson.htm.
8. Letter to Olivia Clemens, September 17, 1893; LLMT, p. 270.
9. Quoted in MTHHR, p. 16.
10. Letter to Olivia Clemens, December 9, 1893; quoted in MTHHR, p. 17.
11. Ibid., p. 17.
12. Ibid., p. 17.
13. MTB, vol. 2, pp. 973–74.
14. Letter to Olivia Clemens, November 10, 1893; LLMT, p. 277.
15. Letter to Susy Clemens, November 6, 1893; LLMT, p. 276.
16. Letter to Olivia Clemens, September 21, 1893; LLMT, p. 273.
17. Ibid., p. 273.
18. Letter to Olivia Clemens, January 15, 1894, MTP; quoted in MTHHR, p. 20.
19. Letter to Olivia Clemens, January 12, 1894; LLMT, p. 291.
20. Ibid., p. 291.
21. Letter to Livy Clemens, January 27–30, 1894, MTP; quoted in MTHHR, p. 20.
22. Cablegram to Olivia Clemens, February 2, 1894, MS copy in CU-MARK, E-edition 1894, #04685.
23. Letter to Olivia Clemens, April 20, 1894; LLMT, p. 299.
24. Ibid., p. 299.
25. Letter from Olivia Clemens to Susan Crane, April 22?; MTB, vol. 2, p. 986–87, op. cit.
26. Letter from Olivia Clemens to Samuel Clemens, July 31, 1894; LLMT, p. 310.
27. Letter to Henry Huttleston Rogers, December 27, 1894; MTHHR, p. 114.
28. Ibid., p. 114.
29. Letter to Samuel Clemens, July 31, 1894; LLMT, pp. 308–9.
30. Ibid., p. 309.
31. Ibid., p. 309.
32. Letter to Olivia Clemens, July 17, 1894; quoted in MTHHR, p. 58.
33. Letter to Rogers, June 16, 1894; MTHHR, p. 66.
34. "Fenimore Cooper's Literary Offenses," in *How to Tell a Story, and Other Essays,* OMT, p. 94.
35. Letter to Louise Brownell, undated, in *Papa,* pp. 23–28.
36. Letter to Rogers, October 7, 1894; MTHHR, p. 83.
37. Letter to Rogers, November 30, 1894; MTHHR, p. 100.
38. See "Whatever Happened to James Paige," by Barbara Schmidt, www.twain quotes.com/paige.
39. Letter to Livy Clemens, February 15, 1894; MTHHR, p. 6.

40. "A Tribute to Henry H. Rogers (1902) by Samuel L. Clemens," Appendix G, MTHHR, p. 711.

41. Lawson, *Frenzied Finance*, excerpt at www.millicentlibrary.org/lawson.htm.

42. The source here is *Francis Wilson's Life of Himself* (Boston: Houghton Mifflin, 1924), p. 299.

43: THUNDER-STROKE

1. Letter to Olivia Clemens, March 20, 1895; LLMT, p. 312.

2. Ibid., p. 312.

3. Ibid., p. 312.

4. Ibid., p. 312.

5. Letter to Henry Huttleston Rogers, February 3, 1895; MTHHR, p. 126.

6. Ibid., p. 126.

7. MTB, vol. 2, p. 997.

8. MTB, vol. 2, p. 998.

9. Ibid.

10. Letter from Helen Keller to Mary Mapes Dodge, March 29, 1895; quoted in LLMT, p. 314.

11. Letter to Henry Rogers, June 14, 1895; MTHHR, p. 150.

12. Letter to Henry Rogers, June 15, 1895; MTHHR, p. 152.

13. Letter to Henry Rogers, June 30, 1895; MTHHR, p. 161.

14. New York *Times,* July 12, 1895; quoted in MTHHR, p. 168.

15. Letter to Henry Rogers, July 14, 1895; MTHHR, p. 167.

16. Letter to William Dean Howells, September 24, 1896; MTHL, vol. 2, p. 663.

17. Letter to Henry Rogers, July 16, 1895; MTHHR, p. 171.

18. *Mark Twain's Notebook*, p. 244.

19. MFMT, pp. 139–40.

20. *Mark Twain's Notebook*, p. 246.

21. Ibid., p. 247.

22. Ibid., pp. 247–48.

23. Ibid., p. 248.

24. Ibid., p. 248.

25. Letter from Susy Clemens to Clara Clemens, August 10, 1895, typescript in CU-MARK, E-edition 1895, #04941.

26. Letter from Susy Clemens to Clara Clemens, September 16, 1895, typescript copy in CU-MARK, E-edition 1895, #04962.

27. MFMT, p. 141.

28. Statement given to a correspondent for the New York *Times,* and reported on August 17, 1895; quoted in MTHHR, p. 182.

29. Letter to Rogers, September 13–15, 1895; MTHHR, p. 187.

30. MFMT, p. 142.

31. *Mark Twain's Notebook*, p. 250.

32. Ibid., p. 251.

33. Julius A. Dresser, "The True History of Mental Science," lecture delivered at the Church of the Divine Unity, Boston, Mass., February 6, 1887 (Boston: Alfred Mudge & Son, 1887); republished at http://ppquimby.com/jdresser/jdresser.htm.

34. Letter to Susy Clemens, February 7, 1896, E-edition 1896, #05018.

35. MFMT, p. 143.

36. Ibid., p. 143.

37. Adelaide *South Australian Register,* October 14, 1895; reprinted in *Mark Twain*

Speaks for Himself, edited by Paul Fatout (West Lafayette, Ind.: Purdue University Press, 1978), p. 153.

38. Ibid., p. 151.
39. *Following the Equator,* OMT, chapter 6, p. 87.
40. Ibid., chapter 6, p. 87.
41. MFMT, pp. 145–46.
42. *Following the Equator,* chapter 12, p. 132.
43. Melbourne *Argus,* quoted in *Mark Twain on the Lecture Circuit,* edited by Paul Fatout (Bloomington: Indiana University Press, 1960), p. 255.
44. *Following the Equator,* chapter 19, p. 186.
45. Ibid., chapter 21, p. 213.
46. Ibid., chapter 27, p. 256.
47. *Mark Twain's Notebook,* p. 268.
48. MFMT, p. 154.
49. *Following the Equator,* OMT, chapter 38, pp. 345–46.
50. Ibid., chapter 38, pp. 347–48.
51. Ibid., chapter 39, pp. 365–66.
52. MFMT, p. 153.
53. Ibid., p. 160.
54. *Following the Equator,* chapter 49, p. 468.
55. Letter to Rogers, February 17, 1896; MTHHR, p. 195.
56. *Mark Twain's Notebook,* p. 298.
57. New York *Times,* October 16, 1900; quoted in Fatout, ed., *Mark Twain on the Lecture Circuit,* p. 264.
58. *Following the Equator,* chapter 66, p. 657; see also chapters 66 & 67, pp. 654–85.
59. *Mark Twain's Notebook,* pp. 295–96.
60. Letter to Rogers, June 22, 1896; MTHHR, p. 223.
61. Letter to Howells, August 5, 1896; MTHL, vol. 2, p. 660.
62. Letter to Olivia Clemens, August 16, 1896; LLMT, p. 317.
63. As quoted in the Introduction to Susy Clemens, *Papa,* pp. 44–46.
64. *Mark Twain's Notebook,* p. 319.
65. Letter to Olivia Clemens, August 16, 1896; LLMT, p. 317.
66. *Mark Twain's Notebook,* p. 321; Autobiography, p. 324.
67. MTA, p. 324; also, *Mark Twain's Notebook,* p. 315.
68. MFMT, p. 171.
69. MTA, p. 323.
70. Letter to Olivia Clemens, August 19, 1896; LLMT, p. 322.
71. Letter to Olivia Clemens, August 21, 1896; MTHL, vol. 2, p. 323.
72. Letter to Henry C. Robinson, September 28, 1896, author's copy in "Mark Twain's Notebook," p. 318.
73. Letter from Howells to Charles Warner, September 27, 1896; quoted in MTHL, vol. 2, p. 662.
74. Letter from Howells to Samuel Clemens, September 13, 1896; MTHL, vol. 2, p. 662.
75. Letter to Howells, September 24, 1896; MTHL, vol. 2, p. 663.
76. Ibid.

44: EXILE AND RETURN

1. MFMT, p. 179.
2. Ibid.
3. Ibid., pp. 180–81.

4. Ibid.
5. *Mark Twain's Notebook,* p. 306.
6. Ibid., p. 310.
7. "Joan of Arc," Boston *Literary World,* May 30, 1896; in Louis J. Budd, ed., *Mark Twain: The Contemporary Reviews* (Edinburgh: Cambridge University Press, 1999), p. 394.
8. "New Books," Brooklyn *Eagle,* May 31, 1896; in *Mark Twain: The Contemporary Reviews,* p. 395.
9. "Book Notices," *Bachelor of Arts* (New York), July 1896; in *Mark Twain: The Contemporary Reviews,* p. 403.
10. Brander Matthews, unsigned review of *Huckleberry Finn,* London *Saturday Review,* January 31, 1885; in *Mark Twain: The Contemporary Reviews,* p. 261.
11. Brander Matthews, "Concerning the Seven Circles of Humor," *Life,* May 28, 1896; in *Mark Twain: The Contemporary Reviews,* p. 393.
12. Review of *Personal Recollections of Joan of Arc* by William Dean Howells in *Harper's Weekly,* May 1896.
13. *Mark Twain's Notebook,* p. 306.
14. Letter to Emilie Hart Rogers, November 26, 1896; in MTHHR, p. 25.
15. Ibid., p. 253.
16. Ibid., p. 254.
17. *Mark Twain's Notebook,* p. 312.
18. Ibid., p. 315.
19. Ibid., p. 319.
20. Ibid., p. 344.
21. Ibid., p. 327.
22. Ibid.
23. Ibid., p. 328.
24. Ibid.
25. Ibid.
26. Ibid., p. 331.
27. Ibid., p. 336.
28. First published in *Harper's* (November 1897); included in *The $30,000 Bequest and Other Stories,* OMT, p. 350.
29. *Mark Twain's Notebook,* p. 343.
30. Ibid., p. 348.
31. Ibid., p. 349.
32. Ibid., pp. 349–50.
33. Ibid., pp. 350–51.
34. MCMT, p. 343.
35. "Villagers: 1840–3," in *Mark Twain: Huck Finn and Tom Sawyer Among the Indians and Other Unfinished Stories,* texts established by Dahlia Armon, Paul Baender, Walter Blair, William M. Gibson, and Franklin R. Rogers (Berkeley: University of California Press, 1989), p. 98.
36. Ibid., p. 101.
37. Ibid., p. 96.
38. Ibid., p. 94.
39. "Hellfire Hotchkiss," *Indians,* p. 121.
40. *Mark Twain's Notebook,* p. 338.
41. Ibid., p. 339.
42. MFMT, p. 190.
43. Ibid., p. 193.

44. Ibid., p. 194.
45. "Stirring Times in Austria," in *The Man That Corrupted Hadleyburg and Other Stories and Essays*, OMT, p. 316.
46. Ibid., p. 340.
47. Letter to Mollie Clemens, December 11, 1897, E-edition 1897, #05320.
48. Katherine Harrison, letter, February 11, 1898; MTHHR, p. 322.
49. Letter to Henry Huttleston Rogers, January 20, 1898; MTHHR, p. 316.
50. Ibid., p. 325.
51. Letter to Rogers, March 17–20, 1898; MTHHR, p. 327.
52. Letter to Joseph Twichell, June 17, 1898; MTL, vol. 2, p. 663, corrected against Paine's own typed copy.
53. MTB, vol. 2, p. 1064.
54. MMT, p. 17.
55. "Concerning the Jews," in *The Man That Corrupted Hadleyburg*, OMT, p. 253.
56. Ibid., pp. 266–67.
57. *Mark Twain's Notebook*, pp. 351–52.
58. Letter to Twichell, quoted by Paine in MTL, vol. 2, p. 667.
59. "Concerning the Jews," *The Man That Corrupted Hadleyburg*, OMT, p. 254.
60. "The Man That Corrupted Hadleyburg," *The Man That Corrupted Hadleyburg*, OMT, p. 1.
61. Letter to William T. Stead of the London *Review of Reviews*, January 9, 1899, MTL, vol. 2, p. 672.
62. Letter to Howells, December 30, 1898; MTHL, vol. 2, p. 685.
63. Letter to Howells, April 2–13, 1899; MTHL, pp. 689–90.
64. Ibid., p. 690.
65. MMT, p. 49.
66. In *William Dean Howells: An American Life* (New York: Harcourt, Brace Jovanovich, 1971), p. 4.
67. Quoted by Lynn in *William Dean Howells*, p. 7.
68. Howells, letter, October 23, 1898; MTHL, vol. 2, p. 679.
69. Howells, letter, October 19, 1899; MTHL, vol. 2, p. 707.
70. Clemens, quoted in James B. Pond, *Eccentricities of Genius* (New York: G. W. Dillingham Co., 1900), p. 227; MTHL, vol. 2, p. 704–5.

45: SITTING IN DARKNESS

1. All newspaper quotations courtesy of Gary Scharnhorst, in *Interviews with Mark Twain, 1871–1910,* scheduled for publication by the University of Alabama Press, fall, 2005.
2. New York *World*, October 21, 1900, courtesy of Scharnhorst.
3. New York *Herald*, October 16, 1900, courtesy of Scharnhorst.
4. New York *World*, November 18, 1900, courtesy of Scharnhorst.
5. New York *Herald*, October 16, 1900, courtesy of Scharnhorst.
6. New York *Times*, October 16, 1900, courtesy of Scharnhorst.
7. John Baker, "Effects of the Press on Spanish-American Relations in 1898," www.humboldt.edu/njcb10/spanwar.shtml.
8. Quoted by Terry Matthews in his lecture series, "The Social Gospel, Part II: The Social Crusades," www.wfu.edu/matthetl/perspectives/twenty.htm.
9. Fred C. Chamberlain, *The Blow from Behind: A Defense of the Flag in the Philippines* (Boston: Lee & Shepard, 1903); Chapter 9, republished in "Anti-Imperialism in the United States, 1898–1935," edited by Jim Zwick, www.boondocksnet.com/ai/reaction/bfb_09.html.

10. *Nation,* March 24, 1899, cited by William H. Berge in "Voices for Imperialism: Josiah Strong and the Protestant Clergy," in *Border States* no. 1 (1973); http:// spider.georgetowncollege.edu/htallant/border/bs1/berge.htm.

11. *Rudyard Kipling: Complete Verse* (New York: Anchor Books, 1989), p. 321.

12. New York *Herald,* October 16, 1900, courtesy of Scharnhorst.

13. William Dean Howells, "Mark Twain: An Inquiry," *North American Review* (February 1901); republished in Zwick, ed., "Anti-Imperialism; www.boondocksnet.com/ twaintexts/mmt/mmt_inquiry.html.

14. "Mark Twain, the Lotos Club Dinner," New York *Times,* November 17, 1900; quoted at www.twainquotes.com.

15. Mark Twain's "I Am a Boxer" speech to the Berkeley Lyceum, New York, November 23, 1900; cited by Jim Zwick in "Chinese and American Boxers"; www.boon docksnet.com/twainwww/essays/american_boxers0009.html.

16. Quoted in William H. Gibson, "Mark Twain and Howells: Anti-Imperialists," *New England Quarterly,* vol. 20 (December 1947), p. 449, n. 1; William R. Macnaughton, *Mark Twain's Last Years as a Writer* (Columbia: University of Missouri Press, 1979), p. 147.

17. Editorial, New York *Evening Post,* December 13, 1900; in Zwick, ed., "Anti-Imperialism," wwwboondocksnet.com/ai/twain/ed/ed_nyep1213.html.

18. MFMT, p. 217.

19. Letter to Thomas Bailey Aldrich.

20. "Salutation to the Twentieth Century," New York *Herald,* December 30, 1900; in *Mark Twain's Weapons of Satire: Anti-Imperialist Writings on the Philippine-American War,* edited by Jim Zwick (Syracuse: Syracuse University Press, 1992); www.boon docksnet.com/ai/twain/salutate.html.

21. "To the Person Sitting in Darkness," in "Following the Equator and Anti-Imperialist Essays," from *North American Review,* February 1901, OMT, p. 14.

22. Ibid., p. 14.

23. "Certainly False, but Probably Funny," New York *Times* editorial, February 7, 1901, in Zwick, ed., "Anti-Imperialism," www.boondocksnet.com/ai/twain/ed/ed_nyt 207.html.

24. "Scurrilous 'Humor,'" Minneapolis *Journal* editorial, February 6, 1901; in Zwick, ed., "Anti-Imperialism," www.boondocksnet.com/ai/twain/ed/ed_mj010205.html.

25. "Chastising Mark Twain," Hartford *Times* editorial, February 6, 1901; in Zwick, ed., "Anti-Imperialism," www.boondocksnet.com/ai/twain/ed/ed_ht206.html.

26. Letter to Joe Twichell, January 29, 1901, *Mark Twain's Letters,* vol. 2 (New York: Harper & Brothers, 1917), pp. 704–5.

27. "Mark Twain's Exclusive Publisher Tells What the Humorist Is Paid," the Washington *Post,* March 3, 1907, *www.twainquotes.com.*

28. Ibid.

29. "The Privilege of the Grave," in "22 Easy Pieces," 1905, CU-MARK.

30. Letter to Joe Twichell, July 28, 1901; MTL, vol. 2, p. 711, corrected against the manuscript at Yale.

31. Ibid.

32. Letter to Olivia Clemens, August 9, 1901; quoted in MTHHR, p. 468.

33. MTHL, vol. 2, p. 743.

34. MMT, pp. 68–69.

35. *Mark Twain's Notebook,* p. 380.

36. Ibid., p. 379.

37. St. Louis *Post-Dispatch,* May 30, 1902.

38. Ibid.

39. Ibid.
40. Ibid.
41. Ibid.
42. Ibid.
43. Ibid.
44. Ibid.
45. Ibid.
46. Letter to Olivia Langdon, January 12, 1869; MTL, vol. 3, pp. 25–26.
47. Note to Olivia Clemens, January 14, 1903; LLMT, p. 341.
48. "Christian Science," OMT, p. 186.
49. Ibid., p. 131.
50. Note to Olivia Clemens, possibly March 1903; LLMT, p. 342.
51. As reported in *George Bush: The Unauthorized Biography,* by Webster Griffin Tarpley, Marianna Wertz, and Anton Chaitkin, *Executive Intelligence Review,* 1991, Chapter 7.
52. Letter to Olivia Clemens, September 20, 1903; LLMT, p. 344.
53. Notebook entry, quoted in LLMT, p. 344.
54. Letter to Olivia Langdon, May 8, 1869 (2d of 2); MTL, vol. 3, p. 206.
55. Olivia Clemens, letter, September 23, 1903; LLMT, p. 345–46.
56. *Mark Twain's Notebook,* p. 386.
57. Ibid.
58. Resa Willis, *Mark and Livy: the Love Story of Mark Twain and the Woman Who Almost Tamed Him* (New York: Atheneum, 1992), p. 6.
59. Letter to Howells, June 6, 1904; MTHL, p. 785.

Chapter the Last

1. Notebook 48, TS p. 2, CU-MARK.
2. *Mark Twain's Notebook,* p. 391.
3. See *Dangerous Intimacy: the Untold Story of Mark Twain's Final Years,* Karen Lystra (Berkeley: University of California Press, 2004), p. 43.
4. *Mark Twain's Notebook,* p. 391.
5. MMT, p. 17.
6. MTB, vol. 3, p. 1264.
7. Michael J. Kiskis, p. 5 of the Afterword to "Chapters from My Autobiography," OMT.
8. "Author's Note," MTB, vol. 1, p. 193.
9. MTB, vol. 3, p. 1368.
10. "Dinner to Whitelaw Reid," in *Speeches,* OMT, p. 173.
11. Ibid., p. 174.
12. Letter from C. O. Byrd to Charles H. Gold, February 25, 1964, CU-MARK.
13. Ibid.
14. As quoted in the *Autobiography,* p. 371.
15. "The Death of Jean," published in edited form in *Harper's* in 1911, is printed in full for the first time in *Dangerous Intimacy: the Untold Story of Mark Twain's Final Years,* Karen Lystra (University of California Press, 2004). Lystra's work is a comprehensive examination of Samuel Clemens's last decade that corrects many earlier false impressions and importantly illuminates the dynamics among Isabel Lyon, Ralph Ashcroft, Paine, Clara, and Jean, as they bore on Clemens's life.
16. *Autobiography,* p. 375.

Bibliography

WRITINGS BY MARK TWAIN

Adventures of Huckleberry Finn. Edited by Victor Fischer and Lin Salamo. Berkeley: University of California Press, 2003.

The Adventures of Huckleberry Finn. Norton Critical Edition. Edited by Sculley Bradley et al. New York: Norton, 1977.

The Autobiography of Mark Twain. Edited by Charles Neider. New York: Harper & Row, 1959.

"The Babies." Electronic Text Center, University of Virginia Library. http://etext.lib.virginia.edu/railton.

The Bible According to Mark Twain: Irreverent Writings on Eden, Heaven, and the Flood by America's Master Satirist. Edited by Howard G. Baetzhold and Joseph B. McCullough. New York: Simon & Schuster, 1995.

Clemens of the "Call": Mark Twain in San Francisco. Edited by Edgar Marquess Branch. Berkeley: University of California Press, 1969.

Collected Tales, Sketches, Speeches, & Essays, 1891–1910. Edited by Louis J. Budd. New York: Library of America, 1992.

A Connecticut Yankee in King Arthur's Court. Edited by Bernard L. Stein. Berkeley: University of California Press, 1979.

The Curious Republic of Gondour and Other Whimsical Sketches. New York: Boni & Liveright, 1919.

" 'Dear Master Wattie': The Mark Twain–David Watt Bowser Letters." Edited and annotated by Pascal Covici Jr. *Southwest Review,* vol. 45 (Spring 1960).

Early Tales & Sketches. Vol. 1, 1851–1864. Vol. 2, 1864–1865. Edited by Edgar Marquess Branch and Robert H. Hirst. Berkeley: University of California Press, 1979–81.

Huck Finn and Tom Sawyer Among the Indians: And Other Unfinished Stories. Berkeley: University of California Press, 1989.

The Literary Apprenticeship of Mark Twain. Edited by Edgar Marquess Branch. Iowa City: University of Iowa Press, 1950.

The Love Letters of Mark Twain. Edited by Dixon Wecter. New York: Harper & Bros., 1949.

Letters from the Earth. Edited by Bernard De Voto. New York: Perennial Library, 1974.

Mark Twain-Howells Letters: The Correspondence of Samuel L. Clemens and William Dean Howells. Edited by Henry Nash Smith and William M. Gibson. 2 vols. Cambridge: Harvard University Press, 1960.

Mark Twain in Eruption. Edited by Bernard De Voto. New York: Harper & Bros., 1940.

Mark Twain in Virginia City. Edited by Paul Fatout. Bloomington: Indiana University Press, 1964.

Mark Twain of the Enterprise: Newspaper Articles and Other Documents, 1862–1864. Edited by Henry Nash Smith. Berkeley: University of California Press, 1957.

Mark Twain on the Damned Human Race. Edited by Janet Smith. New York: Hill & Wang, 1962.

Mark Twain on the Lecture Circuit. Edited by Paul Fatout. Bloomington: Indiana University Press, 1960.

Mark Twain's Correspondence with Henry Huttleston Rogers, 1893–1909. Edited by Lewis Leary. Berkeley: University of California Press, 1969.

Mark Twain's Letters. Edited by Albert Bigelow Paine. 2 vols. New York: Harper & Bros., 1917.

Mark Twain's Letters. Vol. 1, 1853–1866, edited by Edgar Marquess Branch, Michael B. Frank, and Kenneth Anderson. Vol. 2, 1867–1868, edited by Harriet Elinor Smith and Richard Bucci. Vol. 3, 1869, edited by Victor Fischer and Michael B. Frank. Vol. 4, 1870–1871, edited by Victor Fischer and Michael B. Frank. Vol. 5, 1872–1873, edited by Lin Salamo and Harriet Elinor Smith. Vol. 6, 1874–1875, edited by Michael B. Frank and Harriet Elinor Smith. Berkeley: University of California Press, 1988–2002.

Mark Twain's Letters to His Publishers, 1867–1894. Edited by Hamlin Hill. Berkeley: University of California Press, 1967.

Mark Twain's Notebook. Edited by Albert Bigelow Paine. New York: Harper & Bros., 1935.

Mark Twain's Notebooks & Journals. Vol. 1, 1855–1873, edited by Frederick Anderson, Michael B. Frank, and Kenneth M. Sanderson. Vol. 2, 1877–1883, edited by Frederick Anderson, Lin Salamo, and Bernard L. Stein. Vol. 3, 1883–1891, edited by Robert Pack Browning, Michael B. Frank, and Lin Salamo. Berkeley: University of California Press, 1979.

Mark Twain Speaking. Edited by Paul Fatout. Iowa City: University of Iowa Press, 1976.

Mark Twain Speaks for Himself. Edited by Paul Fatout. West Lafayette, Ind.: Purdue University Press, 1978.

Mark Twain's Satires and Burlesques. Edited by Franklin R. Rogers. Berkeley: University of California Press, 1967.

Mark Twain's Weapons of Satire: Anti-Imperialist Writings on the Philippine-American War. Edited by Jim Zwick. Syracuse: Syracuse University Press, 1992.

The Oxford Mark Twain. Edited by Shelley Fisher Fishkin. 29 vols. New York: Oxford University Press, 1996.

The Portable Mark Twain. Edited by Thomas Quirk. New York: Penguin, 2004.

The Prince and the Pauper. Edited by Victor Fischer and Lin Salamo. Berkeley: University of California Press, 1979.

Roughing It: The Authoritative Text. Berkeley: University of California Press, 1995.

Traveling with the Innocents Abroad: Mark Twain's Original Reports from Europe and the Holy Land. Edited by Daniel Morley McKeithan. Norman: University of Oklahoma Press, 1958.

What Is Man? And Other Philosophical Writings. Edited by Paul Baender. Berkeley: University of California Press, 1973.

OTHER PRIMARY AND SECONDARY SOURCES

Aldrich, Lilian W. *Crowding Memories.* Boston: Houghton Mifflin, 1920.

Alkalay-Gut, Karen. "Jean Webster." www.karenalkalay-gut.com/web.html.

Anderson, Frederick, ed. *Mark Twain: The Critical Heritage*. London: Routledge & Kegan Paul, 1971.

Andrews, Kenneth. *Nook Farm: Mark Twain's Hartford Circle*. Cambridge: Harvard University Press, 1950.

Arnold, Matthew. *General Grant: With a Rejoinder by Mark Twain*. Edited by John Y. Simon. Kent, Ohio: Kent State University Press, 1995.

Austin, James. C. *Artemus Ward*. New York: Twayne, 1964.

Baetzhold, Howard G. "Found: Mark Twain's 'Lost Sweetheart.'" *American Literature*, vol. 44, no. 3 (November 1972).

Baker, John. "Effects of the Press on Spanish-American Relations in 1898." www.humboldt.edu/~jcb10/spanwar.shtml.

Bellamy, Gladys C. *Mark Twain as a Literary Artist*. Norman: University of Oklahoma Press, 1950.

Berge, William H. "Voices for Imperialism: Josiah Strong and the Protestant Clergy." *Border States*, no. 1 (1973). http://spider.georgetowncollege.edu/htallant/border/bs1/berge.htm.

Berry, Wendell. *What Are People For?* San Francisco: North Point Press, 1990.

Blair, Walter. *Native American Humor (1800–1900)*. Boston: American Book Co., 1937.

Bloom, Harold, ed. *Mark Twain's Adventures of Huckleberry Finn*. New York: Chelsea House, 1986.

———, ed. *Modern Critical Views: Mark Twain*. New York: Chelsea House, 1986.

Branch, Edgar Marquess. "Bixby vs. Carroll: New Light on Sam Clemens's Early River Career." *Mark Twain Journal* (Fall 1992).

———. *Men Call Me Lucky: Mark Twain and the Pennsylvania*. In *Keepsakes*, no. 1. Oxford, Ohio: Friends of the Library Society, 1985.

———. "Sam Clemens, Steersman on the *John H. Dickey*." *American Literary Realism*, vol. 15, no. 2 (Autumn 1982).

Branch, Edgar Marquess, and Robert H. Hirst. *The Grangerford-Shepherdson Feud by Mark Twain*. Berkeley: Friends of the Bancroft Library, 1985.

Brashear, Minnie. *Mark Twain, Son of Missouri*. Chapel Hill: University of North Carolina Press, 1934.

Broaddus, Dorothy C. *Genteel Rhetoric: Writing High Culture in Nineteenth-Century Boston*. Columbia: University of South Carolina Press, 1999.

Brooks, Van Wyck. *The Ordeal of Mark Twain*. New York: Dutton, 1920.

Budd, Louis J. *Mark Twain, Social Philosopher*. Bloomington: Indiana University Press, 1962.

———, ed. *Mark Twain: The Contemporary Reviews*. Edinburgh: Cambridge University Press, 1999.

Budd, Louis J., and Edwin H. Cady, eds. *On Mark Twain: The Best from American Literature*. Durham: Duke University Press, 1987.

Cardwell, Guy. *The Man Who Was Mark Twain: Images and Ideologies*. New Haven: Yale University Press, 1991.

Chamberlain, Fred C. *The Blow from Behind: A Defense of the Flag in the Philippines*. Boston: Lee & Shepard, 1903. Chapter 9 republished in "Anti-Imperialism in the United States, 1898–1935," edited by Jim Zwick. www.boondocksnet.com/ai/reaction/bfb_09.html.

Clemens, Clara. *My Father, Mark Twain*. New York: Harper & Bros., 1931.

Clemens, Susy. *Papa: An Intimate Biography of Mark Twain*. Edited by Charles Neider. Garden City, N.Y.: Doubleday, 1985.

Collins, Dorothy, ed. *A Handful of Authors: Essays on Books and Writers*. London: Sheed & Ward, 1953.

Conway, Moncure Daniel. *Autobiography: Memories and Experiences of Moncure Daniel Conway*. Boston: Houghton Mifflin, 1904.

Cox, James M. *Mark Twain: The Fate of Humor*. Princeton: Princeton University Press, 1966.

Crews, Frederick. *The Critics Bear It Away: American Fiction and the Academy*. New York: Random House, 1992.

Deitcher, David. *Dear Friends: American Photographs of Men Together, 1840–1918*. New York: Harry N. Abrams, 2001.

Dempsey, Terrell. *Searching for Jim: Slavery in Sam Clemens's World*. Columbia: University of Missouri Press, 2003.

DeVoto, Bernard. *Mark Twain's America*. Cambridge: Houghton Mifflin, 1932.

Dolmetsch, Carl. *Our Famous Guest: Mark Twain in Vienna*. Athens: University of Georgia Press, 1992.

Dresser, Julius A. "A True History of Mental Science." Lecture delivered at the Church of the Divine Unity, Boston, Mass., February 6, 1887. Boston: Alfred Mudge & Son, 1887. http://ppquimby.com/jdresser/jdresser.htm.

Duckett, Margaret. *Mark Twain and Bret Harte*. Norman: University of Oklahoma Press, 1964.

Dwyer, Richard A., and Richard E. Lingenfelter, eds. *Dan De Quille, the Washoe Giant: A Biography and Anthology*. Reno and Las Vegas: University of Nevada Press, 1990.

Eble, Kenneth E. *Old Clemens and W. D. H.: The Story of a Remarkable Friendship*. Baton Rouge: Louisiana State University Press, 1985.

Emerson, Everett. *The Authentic Mark Twain: A Literary Biography of Samuel L. Clemens*. Philadelphia: University of Pennsylvania Press, 1985.

Emerson, Ralph Waldo. *Emerson's Essays*. New York: Thomas Y. Crowell Co., 1951.

———. *The Essential Writings of Ralph Waldo Emerson*. Edited by Brooks Atkinson. Princeton: Princeton Review, 2000.

———. *Ralph Waldo Emerson: Selected Essays*. Edited by Larzer Ziff. New York: Penguin, 1985.

Fanning, Philip Ashley. *Mark Twain and Orion Clemens: Brothers, Partners, Strangers*. Tuscaloosa: University of Alabama Press, 2003.

Ferguson, DeLancey. *Mark Twain, Man and Legend*. New York: Charter Books, 1943.

———. "Mark Twain's Lost Curtain Speeches." *South Atlantic Quarterly*, vol. 42 (July 1943).

Fishkin, Shelley Fisher. *Lighting Out for the Territory: Reflections on Mark Twain and American Culture*. Oxford: Oxford University Press, 1997.

———. *Was Huck Black? Mark Twain and African-American Voices*. Oxford: Oxford University Press, 1993.

Foner, Philip S. *Mark Twain, Social Critic*. New York: International Publishers, 1958.

Frazier, Ian. *Great Plains*. New York: Farrar, Straus Giroux, 1989.

Gerber, John. "Mark Twain's 'Private Campaign.'" *Civil War History*, vol. 1 (March 1955).

Gibson, William H. "Mark Twain and Howells: Anti-Imperialists." *New England Quarterly*, vol. 20 (December 1947).

Gillman, Susan. *Dark Twins: Imposture and Identity in Mark Twain's America*. Chicago: University of Chicago Press, 1989.

Graff, Gerald, and James Phelan, eds. *Adventures of Huckleberry Finn: A Case Study in Critical Controversy*. Boston: Bedford Books, 1995.

Grant, Ulysses S. *The Personal Memoirs of U. S. Grant*. New York: Konecky & Konecky, 1992.

Gribben, Alan. *Mark Twain's Library: A Reconstruction*. 2 vols. Boston: G. K. Hall, 1980.

Grimes, Absalom. *Absalom Grimes: Confederate Mail Runner.* Edited by M. M. Quaife. New Haven: Yale University Press, 1926.

Hagood, J. Hurley, and Roberta Hagood. *The Story of Hannibal.* Hannibal, Mo.: Standard Printing Co., 1976.

Harris, George Washington. *Sut Lovingood: Yarns Spun by a Nat'ral Born Durn'd Fool.* Electronic edition. University of North Carolina at Chapel Hill, 1997.

Harte, Bret. "Plain Language from Truthful James." *Overland Monthly* (September 1870). http://etext.lib.virginia.edu/railton.

Hemingway, Ernest. *Green Hills of Africa.* New York: Scribner's, 1935.

Hill, Hamlin. *Mark Twain: God's Fool.* New York: Harper & Row, 1973.

Hill, Richard, and Jim McWilliams, eds. *Mark Twain Among the Scholars: Reconsidering Contemporary Twain Criticism.* Albany: Whitston Publishing Co., 2002.

Hirst, Robert H. "The Making of *The Innocents Abroad.*" Ph.D. dissertation, University of California, Berkeley, 1975.

———. " 'Sinners and Pilgrims.' " *Bancroftiana,* no. 113 (Fall 1998).

———. "What Paine Left Out." *Bancroftiana,* no. 125 (Fall 2004).

Hoffman, Andrew. *Inventing Mark Twain: The Lives of Samuel Langhorne Clemens.* New York: William Morrow & Co., 1997.

Howells, William Dean. *Literary Friends and Acquaintance.* New York: Harper & Bros., 1901.

———. *My Mark Twain: Reminiscences and Criticisms.* Edited by Marilyn Austin Baldwin. Baton Rouge: Louisiana State University Press, 1967.

———. *Selected Letters, Volume II: 1873–1881.* Edited and annotated by George Arms et al. Boston: Twayne, 1979.

Johnson, Merle. *A Bibliography of the Works of Mark Twain.* New York: Harper Bros., 1935.

Kaplan, Fred. *The Singular Mark Twain.* New York: Doubleday, 2003.

Kaplan, Justin. *Mr. Clemens and Mark Twain.* New York: Simon & Schuster, 1966.

Kipling, Rudyard. *Complete Verse.* New York: Anchor Books, 1989.

Krause, Sydney J. *Mark Twain as Critic.* Baltimore: Johns Hopkins University Press, 1967.

Lauber, John. *The Making of Mark Twain: A Biography.* New York: Noonday Press, 1985.

Lawson, Thomas W. "Thomas Lawson's Description of Henry Rogers." Excerpt from *Frenzied Finance,* vol. 1, *The Crime of Amalgamated.* New York: Ridgway-Thayer Co., 1905. www.millicentlibrary.org/lawson.

Leonard, James S., et al., eds. *Satire or Evasion? Black Perspectives on Huckleberry Finn.* Durham: Duke University Press, 1992.

Lorch, Fred W. "The American Vandal Abroad." In *The Trouble Begins at Eight: Mark Twain's Lecture Tours.* Ames: Iowa State University Press, 1966.

Lynn, Kenneth S. *Mark Twain and Southwestern Humor.* Boston: Little, Brown, 1959.

———. *William Dean Howells: An American Life.* New York: Harcourt, Brace Jovanovich, 1971.

Lystra, Karen. *Dangerous Intimacy: The Untold Story of Mark Twain's Final Years.* Berkeley: University of California Press, 2004.

Mack, Effie Mona. *Mark Twain in Nevada.* New York: Charles Scribner's Sons, 1947.

Macnaughton, William R. *Mark Twain's Last Years as a Writer.* Columbia: University of Missouri Press, 1979.

Masters, Edgar Lee. *Mark Twain: A Portrait.* New York: Charles Scribner's Sons, 1938.

Matthews, Terry. "The Social Gospel, Part II: The Social Crusades." www.wfu.edu/~matthetl/perspectives/twenty.html.

Michelson, Bruce. *Mark Twain on the Loose: A Comic Writer and the American Self.* Amherst: University of Massachusetts Press, 1995.

Nissen, Axel. *Bret Harte: Prince and Pauper.* Oxford: University Press of Mississippi, 2000.

Paine, Albert Bigelow. *Mark Twain: A Biography.* 3 vols. New York: Harper & Bros., 1912.

Paine, Thomas. *Collected Writings.* Edited by Eric Foner. New York: Library of America, 1995.

Pemberton, T. Edgar. *The Life of Bret Harte.* New York: Dodd, Mead & Co., 1903.

Perry, Mark. *Grant and Twain: The Story of a Friendship That Changed America.* New York: Random House, 2004.

Pettit, Arthur G. *Mark Twain & the South.* Lexington: University Press of Kentucky, 1974.

Phipps, William E. *Mark Twain's Religion.* Macon, Ga.: Mercer University Press, 2003.

Powers, Ron. *Dangerous Water: A Biography of the Boy Who Became Mark Twain.* New York: Basic Books, 1999.

Quirk, Thomas. *Coming to Grips with Huckleberry Finn: Essays on a Book, a Boy, and a Man.* Columbia: University of Missouri Press, 1993.

Railton, Stephen. "Jim and Mark Twain: What Do Dey Stan' For?" *Virginia Quarterly Review,* vol. 63 (Summer 1987).

Rasmussen, R. Kent. *Mark Twain A to Z: The Essential Reference to His Life and Writings.* New York: Facts on File, 1995.

Reynolds, David S. *Walt Whitman's America: A Cultural Biography.* New York: Alfred A. Knopf, 1995.

Richardson, Robert D., Jr. *Emerson: The Mind on Fire.* Berkeley: University of California Press, 1995.

Sanborn, Margaret. *Mark Twain: The Bachelor Years.* New York: Doubleday, 1990.

Scharnhorst, Gary. *Interviews with Mark Twain, 1871–1910.* Tuscaloosa: University of Alabama Press, forthcoming.

———. " 'Ways That Are Dark': Appropriations of Bret Harte's 'Plain Language from Truthful James,' " *Nineteenth-Century Literature,* vol. 51 (December 1996). www.ucpress.edu/scan/ncl-e/513/articles/scharnhorst.ar t513.html.

———, ed. *Critical Essays on The Adventures of Tom Sawyer.* New York: G. K. Hall, 1993.

Schmidt, Barbara. "A Closer Look at the Lives of True Williams and Alexander Belford." Paper presented at the Fourth International Conference on Mark Twain Studies, Elmira, New York, August 18, 2001. www.twainquotes.com.

———. "Mark Twain Quotations, Newspaper Collections, & Related Sources." www.twainquotes.com.

Sedgwick, Ellery. *A History of the Atlantic Monthly, 1857–1909: Yankee Humanism at High Tide and Ebb.* Amherst: University of Massachusetts Press, 1994.

Sentilles, Renee. *Performing Menken: Adah Isaacs Menken and the Birth of American Celebrity.* Cambridge: Cambridge University Press, 2003.

Showalter, Elaine. *The Female Malady: Women, Madness, and English Culture, 1830–1980.* New York: Pantheon Books, 1985.

Skandera-Trombley, Laura. *Mark Twain in the Company of Women.* Philadelphia: University of Pennsylvania Press, 1994.

Smith, Henry Nash. "That Hideous Mistake of Poor Clemens's!" *Harvard Library Bulletin,* vol. 9 (Spring 1955).

Stewart, William. *Reminiscences of Senator William M. Stewart of Nevada.* Edited by George Rathwell Brown. New York: Neale Publishing Co., 1908.

Stoddard, Charles Warren. *Exits and Entrances: A Book of Essays and Sketches.* Boston: Lothrop Publishing Co., 1903.

Tarpley, Webster Griffin, and Anton Chaitkin. *George Bush: The Unauthorized Biography.* www.tarpley.net/bushb.htm.

Twichell, Joseph. *Personal Journal.* Joseph Twichell Collection, Beinecke Rare Book and Manuscript Library, Yale University, New Haven, Connecticut.

Ward, Artemus. *The Complete Works of Artemus Ward.* Edited by Charles Farrar Browne. Whitefish, Mont.: Kessinger Publishing Co., 2004.

Ward, Geoffrey C., et al. *Mark Twain: An Illustrated Biography.* New York: Alfred A. Knopf, 2001.

Webster, Samuel Charles, ed. *Mark Twain, Business Man.* Boston: Little, Brown & Co., 1946.

Wecter, Dixon. *Sam Clemens of Hannibal.* Cambridge: Riverside Press, 1952.

Willis, Resa. *Mark and Livy: The Love Story of Mark Twain and the Woman Who Almost Tamed Him.* New York: Atheneum, 1992.

Wilson, Francis. *Francis Wilson's Life of Himself.* Boston: Houghton Mifflin, 1924.

Ziff, Larzer. *Return Passages: Great American Travel Writing, 1780–1910.* New Haven: Yale University Press, 2000.

Zwick, Jim. "Chinese and American Boxers." www.boondocksnet.com/twainwww/essays/american_boxers0009.html.

———, ed. "Anti-Imperialism in the United States, 1898–1935." www.boondocksnet.com/ai.

Acknowledgments

The Mark Twain Project at the University of California, Berkeley, is one of the world's great archives of literary scholarship, and a national treasure. Growing exponentially out of a small curatorial mission that originated with a bequest to the University in 1949 by Clara Clemens Samossoud of all her father's manuscripts and papers (Mrs. Samossoud died in 1962), the Project has assembled a magisterial and still-growing inventory of Mark Twain's work, and has illuminated that work with decades of painstaking editorial research and annotation. Among its resources, in original or photocopied form, are 11,000 letters written by Samuel Langhorne Clemens or members of his family and 17,000 letters to them; 50-odd of Clemens's notebooks; all the published literary manuscripts known to survive; 600 unpublished and/or unfinished manuscripts; a dozen scrapbooks, and uncounted photographs, newspaper clippings, business records, typescripts, and other documents related to his life and work. More valuable still has been the exhaustive scholarship that the Project has conferred on this material: annotated editions of Mark Twain's letters and notebooks; scholarly editions of his most enduring literature.

Like hundreds of Mark Twain scholars, critics, and biographers before me, I found the bounties of the Mark Twain Project to be of indispensable value, and I extend my unlimited gratitude and admiration for these. My book has also benefited from the inexhaustible personal generosity of Robert Hirst, the Project's general editor since 1980. Mr. Hirst put aside his demanding schedule for many interpretive conversations regarding Samuel Clemens's life and literature; he led me to a great number of original textual citations that otherwise would have been unavailable or unknown to me; and his exemplary standard of accuracy is one that I can only hope to have approximated.

I received many helpful responses and useful guidance, as well, from Mr. Hirst's editorial colleagues at the Mark Twain Project, including Harriet

Smith, Victor Fischer, Lin Salamo, and Michael B. Frank. The wizards of electronic access Anh Bui and Andrea Laue kept information flowing freely, and office manager Neda Salem provided files and archival documents with unfailing efficiency and good cheer.

I have found a similar spirit of magnanimity in the larger community of Mark Twain scholars, many of whom might plausibly have wished to remain protective of work that has consumed much of their professional lives. Their willingness to share ideas and, in some cases, the fruit of specialized inquiry, at once humbled me and inspired a wish for emulation. Among the many who made themselves available to me over the past several years, I am especially grateful to the following: Tom Quirk of the University of Missouri; Gary F. Scharnhorst of the University of New Mexico; Terry Oggel of Virginia Commonwealth University; Shelley Fisher Fishkin of Stanford University; Michael Kiskis of Elmira College; Barbara Snedecor and Gretchen Sharlow of the Mark Twain Center at Elmira; Henry Sweets, curator of the Mark Twain Museum in Hannibal, and Terrell Dempsey, Esq., of Hannibal, Missouri. My good friend Jay Parini of Middlebury College, whose graceful biographies have memorably cast many preeminent novelists and poets from Robert Frost to William Faulkner, has enriched my understanding of American literature through conversations over many years, and his work has provided me with working models of clarity, interpretation, narrative scope, and an abiding respect for his subjects' humanity.

My literary agent Jim Hornfischer of Hornfischer Literary Management recognized the suitability of a new Mark Twain biography long before I did; he advocated for it for many months until I overcame my reluctance to take on a subject of Samuel Clemens's galactic complexity, significance, and centrality to the American experience. Jim's superb instincts for matching author and publisher led us to Bruce Nichols and Free Press. Bruce proved himself not only an editor of exceptional professional skills (such as trimming back the author's fatal attraction to wordiness); he became an ally in my wish to incorporate the historical and cultural permutations of the 19th and early 20th centuries that are so indispensable to a portrayal of Mark Twain in the context of his American-ness. By turns demanding and accommodating, an advocate and a critical interrogator, and always an unflappable friend in times of crisis, Bruce Nichols enlarged both the book and the writer. His assistant Kadzi Mutizwa proved her great value as a copy reader by exasperating the author on many occasions with her gimlet-eyed demands for rhetorical tightening and heightening, and always proving herself correct. Any surviving puns, ironic asides, and belabored analogies are the author's responsibility alone. I am grateful to Tom Pitoniak for his scrupulous copyediting.

I also wish to thank Ken Burns and Dayton Duncan for their encouragement and moral support; William Kostura for architectural information concerning San Francisco hotels in the 1860s; Karen Alkalay-Gut for sharing her scholarship on Jean Webster; my longtime Hannibal friends Dulany Winkler and Joan Hibbard Ryan for conversations that stimulated ideas about elements of Mark Twain's life; my son Dean Powers for sharing his critical essay on "Puddn'head Wilson," for providing scholarly resources I hadn't thought to pursue and for taking my jacket-cover photograph; my son Kevin Powers for lending his musician's expertise to discussions about the affinities between jazz and spoken language; and my wife, Honoree, for her acute comments on the manuscript-in-progress and for her abiding, loving support of the incorrigible Tom Sawyer in her household.

Index

A. B. Chambers, 95
abolitionism, 2, 30, 40, 64, 68, 81, 82,
  231, 243, 316, 383
Academy of Music, 163, 164, 165, 185,
  258
Academy of Sciences, 263
Adams, John, 46
Adventures of Huckleberry Finn, The
  (Twain), 22, 32*n*, 37, 164, 354, 363,
  379, 389, 471–78, 493, 502, 573,
  581, 582, 609
  banning of, 490, 495, 500
  in *Century,* 487–88
  criticism of, 494–97
  dialect in, 155
  Huckleberry Finn in, 34, 82, 117,
    313*n*, 314, 489
  illustrations of, 482–84, 488–89
  Jim in, 12, 13, 82
  Jim's early speeches in, 13
  manuscript of, 477–78
  model for Huckleberry Finn in, 34
  model for Jim in, 12
  model for Miss Watson in, 26
  publication of, 482–84, 485–89, 497,
    498
  race and racism in, 332, 475–76,
    495
  raft accident in, 420
  raft chapter of, 468
  reviews of, 489–90
  sales of, 489, 490, 506
  song in, 282
  sunrise passage in, 460, 540
  Tom Sawyer and, 396, 481
  typing of, 477
  writing of, 471–73, 477

Adventures of Tom Sawyer, The (Twain), 5,
  33, 44, 389, 392, 417, 582, 618
  dramatic version of, 481
  grave-robbing scene in, 89
  Huckleberry Finn and, 396, 481
  Huckleberry Finn in, 34–35
  model for Becky Thatcher in, 41
  model for Joe Harper in, 32
  model for Judge Thatcher in, 14
  model for Sid in, 90
  publication of, 395
  reviews of, 385–86, 395–96
  sales of, 396, 450*n*
  writing of, 348, 351–52, 354–55, 372,
    374–75, 377, 378, 382
Agassiz, Louis, 270, 296
Agee, James, 390*n*, 537
Agee, Olivia, 537
Age of Reason, The (Paine), 81
Ah Sin: A Drama (Twain and Harte),
  391–92, 396, 397, 401–2, 405, 406,
  407
"Aix, The Paradise of the Rheumatics"
  (Twain), 539
Ajax, 160, 183, 197
Alabama, secession of, 95
Alcott, Louisa May, 26, 294
Alden, Henry Mills, 581
Aldrich, Lilian, 308–9, 344–46, 364
Aldrich, Thomas Bailey, 239, 294, 307–9,
  344–45, 347, 385, 387, 450, 459,
  485, 623
Alessandro Moreschi: The Last Castrato,
  Complete Vatican Recordings, 513*n*
Alexander II, Czar of Russia, 212
Alfred T. Lacy, 86, 92
Alger, Horatio, 294

Alger, William Rounseville, 296
"All About the Fashions" (Twain), 125
Allen, William H., 625
Allen, Woody, 125, 380
Allentown *Chronicle*, 306, 339, 490
Alonzo Child, 95, 96
Alta California, 145, 154, 170, 176, 177, 179, 184–85, 190, 194, 200, 210, 232, 237, 482
    SLC's letters to, 4, 176, 177, 184, 186, 187, 189, 194, 200, 210, 220, 222, 226, 233, 234, 235–36, 237–38, 241
Ament, Joseph P., 46, 47, 48, 49, 51, 56
America, 171–72, 197
American Claimant, The, 172n, 536, 544
American Copyright League, 500
American Courier, 56
American Literary Bureau, 241
American Publisher, 291, 297, 298, 333
American Publishing Company, 4, 227, 232, 233, 240, 268, 302–3, 323, 341, 350, 371, 386, 396, 415, 434, 445, 446, 447, 448, 462, 469, 493, 557, 584, 592
American Revolution, 81
"American Scholar, The" (Emerson), 17
Amnesty Act (1872), 394
Andrews, Edward, 202
Andrews, William, 346
Anthony, Susan B., 301
Antietam, Battle of, 194
Anti-Imperialist League, 602, 604
"Appeal in Behalf of Extending the Suffrage to Boys, An" (Twain), 300, 301
Appleton, William Henry, 611
Appomattox campaign, 500
Aquarium club, 619–20
Argus, 571
Arnold, Matthew, 69, 264, 480, 516, 521, 522–23, 524, 562
Arthur, Chester A., 444
"As Concerns Interpreting the Deity" (Twain), 609
Ashcroft, Ralph, 622
Astaire, Fred, 520
Asylum Hill Congregational Church, 252
"Atalanta in Calydon" (Swinburne), 289
Athenaeum, 489
Atheneum, 457
Athens, Greece, 210–11
Atlantic Monthly, 2, 3, 18, 239, 270, 276, 289, 295–96, 307, 321, 325, 346, 356, 361, 363–65, 367, 368, 369, 377, 378, 423, 434, 454, 468, 487
    "Carnival of Crime" in, 387

Howells's departure from, 450
    and SLC's "skeleton novelette," 387
    "Some Rambling Notes of an Idle Excursion" in, 405
"At the Shrine of St. Wagner's" (Twain), 539
Aunt Hannah (slave), 12
Austen, Jane, 572
Austin, L. F., 529
Australia, 569, 570–72
Austria, 589–96
"Autobiography of a Damned Fool, The" (Twain), 53, 414
    model for Mrs. Bangs in, 25–26
Autobiography of Mark Twain, The (Twain), 90, 141, 147, 320, 410, 492, 511, 600, 620, 621
Autocrat of the Breakfast Table (Holmes), 270, 271
Azores, 197, 201

"Babes in the Wood" (Ward), 132
"Babies" (Twain), 429–31
Bachelor of Arts, 582
Badeau, Adam, 492, 500–501
Baetzhold, Howard G., 636n
Bailey, John A., 369
Banks, Nathaniel Prentiss, 183
Barnes, George E., 146, 163, 642n
Barnum, P. T., 64, 317, 368–69, 371, 372, 543
Barstow, Bill, 109
Batavia, 326, 334, 338
Bates, Edward, 95, 101
"Battles and Leaders of the Civil War," 487
Beach, Emma, 198, 223, 230–31, 235
Beach, Moses Sperry, 181, 183, 198, 218, 252
Beard, Daniel, 524
Beats, 144
Beebe, William, 38–39, 41, 42
Beecher, Henry Ward, 81, 170, 176, 181–82, 189, 192, 228, 229, 230–31, 233, 237, 243, 248, 280, 301, 400, 514, 524
    and *Quaker City* cruise, 3, 183, 185, 190, 195, 197
    scandal of, 182, 327–28, 329, 376
Beecher, Julia Jones, 281, 400
Beecher, Lyman, 182
Beecher, Thomas K., 243, 281, 282, 287
Beethoven, Ludwig van, 585
Belford, Alexander, 482
Belford Brothers, 385, 401
Belknap, William W., 394

Bell, Alexander Graham, 452
Ben (slave), 51
Ben Hur (Wallace), 444
Bennett, James Gordon, 222, 584
Bergen, Edgar, 524
Berkeley, University of California at, 254n
Bermingham, Nellie, 334
Berne Convention, 323n
"Best Friend of Charleston, The" (train), 11
Bethlehem *Times*, 306
Beuchotte, Claude Joseph, 626
Beveridge, Albert J., 601
Beyond the Mississippi (Richardson), 232, 273
Bible, 26–27, 28, 29, 80, 93, 210, 240, 246, 252, 261, 262, 421, 438, 466, 528, 625
Bierce, Ambrose, 325
Big Bertha, 135
Big Bonanza, The (De Quille), 377, 595
Bigler, John, 124
Billings, Josh, 177, 464
Birch, George Bright, 199, 210, 213
Bissell, Richard M., 615
Bissell, Richard M., Jr., 615
Bixby, Horace, 75–76, 78, 94, 95, 172, 461
Black Crook, The, 191
Black Friday, 394
Black Warrior Gold and Silver Mining Company, 106
Blackwell, Elizabeth, 353
Blaine, James, 601
Blaisdel, H. G., 262
Blankenship, Bence, 37
Blankenship, Mahala, 35
Blankenship, Tom, 34–35, 521
Blankenship, Woodson, 35
Bleak House (Dickens), 57
Bliss, Amelia, 252
Bliss, Elisha, 4, 238, 241, 292, 297, 338, 348, 353, 372, 377, 415, 446, 448n, 481
  advance to SLC from, 236
  Gilded Age and, 333, 338, 341
  Innocents Abroad and, 227, 231–32, 240, 252, 268–71, 273, 308
  Orion and, 291
  Roughing It and, 288, 298, 300, 302–3, 317–18, 323
  Tom Sawyer and, 382, 384–86
  Tramp Abroad and, 433–34
Bliss, Frank, 265, 379, 401, 415, 424, 425, 427, 433–34, 445, 482, 493, 557, 566, 584

"Bloody Massacre near Carson, A" (Twain), 126, 127
Bloom, Harold, 460
Boer War, 567, 575
Boggs & Grant, 99
bohemians, 129–30, 148
Booth, Edwin, 180, 343, 544
Borneo, dwarfish twins of, 64, 65
Boston, Mass., 1, 362–63, 432, 456, 458
Boston *Advertiser*, 307, 409, 411, 490
Boston *Daily Globe*, 411
Boston *Evening Transcript*, 307, 321, 411
Bostonians, The (James), 365, 487
Boston Lyceum Bureau, 241
Boston *Sun*, 290
Boston *Transcript*, 391n, 394
Bowen, Bart, 92
Bowen, Mattie, 234
Bowen, Samuel, 32, 94, 97, 99
Bowen, William, 32–34, 95, 115, 195, 233–34, 250, 282–83, 344, 346, 388, 408, 613
Bowles, Samuel, 268
Bowman, Jimmy, 642n
Bowser, David Watt "Wattie," 439–42, 460
Boxer rebellion, 604
Boyesen, H. H., 454
Boynton, Paul, 518
Boy's Town Described, A (Howells), 5, 544
Bradley & Rulofson, 236
Brady, Mathew, 279–80, 286–87, 297
Branch, Edgar Marquess, 55n, 76n, 117
Brazil, 72–73
Briggs, John, 346
Brittingham, L. T., 46
Broadway, 323
Brooklyn *Eagle*, 190, 218, 228–29, 497, 582
Brooks, Fidele, 255
Brown, John, 353, 354, 407
Brown, Walter F., 425
Brown, William, 84, 85, 87, 107
Browne, Charles Farrar, *see* Ward, Artemus
Browne, Junius Henri, 273
Brownell, Ed, 70
Brownell, Louise Sheffield, 537, 540, 560–61, 569, 572–73, 574
Browning, Elizabeth Barrett, 264
Browning, Robert, 337
Bruckner, Anton, 589
Bryan, William Jennings, 601
Bryant, William Cullen, 180
Buchanan, James, 67, 81
Buchanan, Joseph, 51

Buchanan, Robert (nephew), 51
Buchanan, Robert (uncle), 51
Budd, Louis, 145
Buddha, 17
Buell, Dwight, 436
Buffalo *Express*, 275, 284, 290, 293–94, 297, 326
  SLC's purchase of, 274, 316
Bugs Bunny, 524
Bulette, Julie, 111
Bulletin, 236–37
Bull Run, Battle of, 98
Bunyan, John, 240, 269, 365
Burbank, A. P., 507, 508
Burlingame, Anson, 162, 170, 236, 240–41
Burns, Robert, 59
Burr, James, 40
Burrough, Jacob, 389
Butler, Ben, 225
Byng, Carl, 294
Byrd, A. K., 624
Byrd, C. O., 624–25
Byron, George Gordon, Lord, 18, 135

Cable, George Washington, 461, 485, 492, 497–99, 506, 541, 565
Cady, Edwin, 544
Calaveras County, 150
California, 100
  skirmish with Nevada of, 120
Californian, 146–49, 154
California Steam Navigation Company, 160–61
California Weekly Mercury, 237
Call, 163
Calvin, John, 29*n*
Calvinism, 17
Camp, Herman, 158
Campbell, Alexander, 49
Campbell, John, 114
Campbell, Thomas, 49
Campbellites, 49
Canada, 567–69
"Cannibalism in the Cars" (Twain), 323
Cap'n Simon Wheeler; The Amateur Detective (Twain), 405, 415
"Captain Stormfield's Visit to Heaven" (Twain), 172, 414–15, 505
Carleton, George W., 154, 177–79
Carlyle, Thomas, 80
Carnegie, Andrew, 366, 530, 537, 544, 584, 602
Caron, Leslie, 520
Carpenter, Judge, 39
Carpet-Bag, 55, 131

Carroll, Lewis, 125, 576
Carson, Kit, 103
Carson City, Nev., 103–4, 105–6, 107, 127, 135, 138, 166, 237
Carson Theater, 166
Caruso, Enrico, 544
Cass, Lewis, 67
Castro, Fidel, 615
Celebrated Jumping Frog of Calaveras County, and Other Sketches, The (Twain), 190, 199, 262, 264, 323–24
"Celebrated Jumping Frog of Calaveras County, The" (Twain), 150–55, 158, 176, 184, 188, 189
Century, 162, 464, 486–89, 497, 498, 503, 524, 550, 556, 557
Century Club, 180
Century Company, 492–93, 558
Cervantes, Miguel de, 80, 529
Ceylon, 572–73
Chamberlain, Fred C., 602
Chamberlin, Franklin, 333
Chancellorsville, Battle of, 120
Chandler, Zachariah, 395
Chang and Eng, 543
Charles L. Webster & Company, 481, 487, 503, 506, 508, 518, 524, 525, 535, 536, 543, 544, 554, 557, 558, 562, 566, 591
Charlotte, Princess, 589
Chatto, Andrew, 471
Chatto & Windus, 384–85, 401, 489, 524, 528, 584
Cheever, John, 279
Chesterton, G. K., 89, 396
Chicago, Ill.:
  Grant banquet in, 427–31
  Great Fire in, 312
Chicago *Herald*, 560, 561
Chicago *Inter-Ocean*, 42
Chicago *Tribune*, 318, 342, 411, 457, 469, 599, 622
Child's History of England (Dickens), 309
China, 240–41, 317
Christian Science, 570
"Chronicles of Young Satan, The" (Twain), 586, 623
Church, Francis P., 284
Church, William Conant, 284
Church, William F., 213
Churchill, Winston, 353, 604–5
Cincinnati, Ohio, 73, 74
Cincinnati *Commercial*, 411
City of Baton Rouge, 461
City of Memphis, 94

City of New York, 531
"Civilisation in the United States"
    (Arnold), 522
Civil Rights Act (1874), 394
Civil War, U.S., 4, 68, 79, 95–100, 103,
    113, 137, 143, 146, 192, 224, 242,
    251, 280, 466, 590, 601
    see also specific battles
Clagett, Billy, 106, 115
Clapp, Henry, Jr., 154, 177
Clare, Ada, 136
Clarke, Harry M., 478
Clemens, Benjamin (SLC's brother), 15,
    28–29, 320, 350, 409
Clemens, Clara, *see* Samossoud, Clara
    Clemens Gabrilowitsch
Clemens, Henry (SLC's brother), 15, 34,
    45, 57, 69, 70, 71, 72, 73, 409, 425,
    459, 466, 468
    attacked by Brown, 85, 107, 636*n*
    death and burial of, 86–89, 90, 262,
      320, 458, 532, 591
    letter to SLC by, 74–75
    as "mud-clerk," 83
    SLC's dream about, 84–85, 635*n*–36*n*
    in SLC's fiction, 90
    SLC's relationship with, 83–84
Clemens, James, Jr., 34, 40, 45, 69
Clemens, James Ross, 584
Clemens, Jane Lampton (SLC's mother),
    8, 9, 12, 14, 20–21, 24, 38, 41, 51,
    57, 60, 69, 75, 95, 107, 187, 188,
    273–74, 302, 310, 338, 499–500,
    506, 613
    death and burial of, 89, 532, 591
    and death of children, 21, 28
    and death of husband, 42–43
    in England, 580
    in mourning for husband, 45
    religion and, 29, 34
    sale of SLC's letters by, 145
    SLC's education and, 39
    SLC's employment and, 46
    SLC's Indian prejudice and, 23,
      127
    SLC's letters to, 62, 63, 64, 70, 71–72,
      101, 105, 106, 107, 119, 121, 124,
      132–33, 144–45, 154, 159, 191,
      195–96, 210, 223, 230–31, 233, 267,
      343, 349, 371, 421, 471
    in SLC's psychology, 220
    SLC's relationship with, 40
    SLC's wedding and, 281
    as target of SLC's satire, 159
    on visit to SLC, 285
    wit of, 25

Clemens, Jane Lampton "Jean" (SLC's
    daughter), 474, 542, 565, 574, 576,
    577, 610
    animals' rights and, 604
    birth of, 444–45
    death of, 626
    epilepsy of, 532, 597, 619, 623
    fire in crib of, 449
    in Germany, 542
    pneumonia of, 613–14, 615
    scarlet fever of, 462
    sullenness of, 546
Clemens, Jennie (Orion's daughter), 70,
    95, 102, 115, 127, 135, 138
Clemens, John Marshall (SLC's father),
    9, 11, 13–14, 22, 27, 34, 37, 50, 192,
    409, 444, 462, 611–12
    aloofness of, 14
    burial of, 44, 89, 532, 591
    contradictions of, 39–40
    death of, 41–42
    and death of children, 20, 28
    land deals of, 9, 20, 21, 40
    lawsuits of, 41
    money problems of, 9, 10, 15, 20, 23,
      38, 39, 40, 41, 101, 104
    personality of, 25
    religion of, 23, 29
    in SLC's fiction, 14–15
Clemens, Langdon (SLC's son), 291,
    297–98, 300, 303–4, 309, 312, 319,
    353
Clemens, Margaret (SLC's sister), 10, 15,
    20–21
Clemens, Mollie (Orion's wife), 69, 70,
    88, 89, 95, 102, 107, 115, 123, 127,
    135, 137, 138, 140, 145, 227, 230,
    236, 288, 291, 300, 302, 321, 333,
    343, 349–50, 424, 499, 509, 512,
    517, 591, 616, 636*n*
Clemens, Olivia Langdon "Livy" (SLC's
    wife), 213, 323, 339, 350, 500, 526,
    539, 553, 561, 562, 603
    Ah Sin and, 403
    anniversary of Susy's death and, 585
    "Autobiography of a Damned Fool"
      and, 414
    background of, 242–43
    birthday of, 245*n*
    birth of, 242
    and birth of Langdon, 291
    breathing trouble of, 613–14
    childhood illness of, 244–45, 527
    Clara's birth and, 353
    Colonel Sellers debacle and, 509
    Connecticut Yankee and, 506

Clemens, Olivia Langdon "Livy" (SLC's
    wife) (cont.)
  dark moods of, 406
  death of, 616–17
  and death of mother, 532
  department stores and, 279
  at Dickens reading, 229, 446
  diphtheria of, 402, 468, 523
  end of bankruptcy of, 591–92
  engagement of, 266–67
  in England, 335, 337–38, 580
  father's death and, 287, 290
  first house of, 282
  in Germany, 415–18, 539–42
  Gilded Age and, 329
  heart strain of, 531
  Huckleberry Finn and, 488
  income of, 417
  inheritance of, 287
  Innocents Abroad proofs and, 270–71
  Jane's birth and, 444–45
  Langdon's death and, 319
  Langdon's illness and, 303–4, 433
  letters of, 309–11, 312, 316, 321, 451,
    532
  in move to Europe, 538–51
  New York illness of, 358
  New York trip of, 482
  at Nook Farm, 304, 327, 332–33,
    360–61, 432–33, 449–50, 563–64
  nurse for, 375
  in Paris, 424, 426
  pregnancy troubles of, 291, 346
  Prince and the Pauper and, 438
  rheumatism of, 388, 402
  science studies of, 263
  on SLC's around the world tour, 566,
    568–69, 573–74
  SLC's English trip and, 324
  at SLC's lecture, 259
  SLC's letters to, 249, 251, 260, 262,
    266, 268, 269, 307, 309, 312–13,
    315, 324–25, 326, 341, 427, 431,
    458, 460, 527–28, 555, 556, 557,
    558, 560, 563, 578, 610, 614
  SLC's love letters to, 245–47, 250, 254,
    260, 261, 267, 272, 280
  as SLC's nurse, 250
  SLC's profanity and, 368
  SLC's proposal to, 244–45
  in SLC's psychology, 220
  and SLC's religion, 254
  SLC's temper and, 405, 519
  solitaire and, 506
  sprained ankle of, 576
  Susy's birth and, 318

  Susy's death and, 578
  trip west of, 509
  typhoid fever of, 297–300
  at Wave Hill, 611
  on Webster & Co.'s collapse, 558–59
  Webster loan made by, 536
  wedding of, 280, 281–82
  women's suffrage and, 301
Clemens, Olivia Susan "Susy" (SLC's
    daughter), 304, 323, 328, 333, 339,
    350, 388, 426, 449, 451, 471, 485,
    486, 500, 501, 539, 565, 573, 576
  aphoristic skills of, 388
  appearance of, 342–43
  biography of SLC by, 501–3, 505, 507
  birth of, 318
  birth weight of, 353
  at Bryn Mawr, 532, 536–37
  burial of, 580
  Connecticut Yankee and, 506
  depression of, 559, 560, 569
  in Germany, 415–18
  Harte's affection for, 402
  Huckleberry Finn and, 488
  illness and death of, 576–78
  in Italy, 542
  on Joan of Arc, 553, 564–65
  Louise Brownell and, 537, 540,
    560–61, 569, 572–73, 574
  Prince and the Pauper and, 438
  scarlet fever of, 462
  SLC's temper and, 510
  on trip to England, 335
  twenty-fourth birthday of, 574
Clemens, Orion (SLC's brother), 14, 20,
    22, 34, 43, 45, 51, 63, 65, 66, 70–71,
    75, 84, 88, 94, 124, 135, 146,
    227–28, 233, 236, 302–3, 324,
    346–47, 372, 436, 466, 467, 499,
    536, 537
  accusations against Bliss, 317–18, 322
  American dream of, 349
  American Publisher and, 291
  autobiography of, 442–44
  book ideas of, 408–9, 415
  burial of, 89
  Cap'n Simon Wheeler and, 415
  death of, 591
  and death of daughter, 127
  editorials of, 57–58
  electric light investment and, 467
  imagined lecture series of, 423–24
  inventions of, 288, 300, 339
  Journal and, 52–54, 56–58, 59–61, 69
  law practice attempted by, 95
  in Lincoln campaign, 95

money troubles of, 210, 285–86
as Nevada governor, 119–20
as Nevada secretary, 101–4, 106–9, 115
as Nevada secretary of state, 127
in New York, 338–39, 343
poison incident of, 512
printing trade learned by, 38, 39
Roughing It manuscript and, 298
Roughing It notes of, 288–89, 293
on Rutland *Globe*, 333
in SLC's fiction, 53
SLC's letters to, 108, 141, 145, 146, 155–56, 157, 276, 288, 299, 304, 343–44, 425–26, 435, 442–43, 445, 515
SLC's ridicule of, 350, 423–24
SLC's visit to, 509
temperance supported by, 149, 158–59
Clemens, Pamela, *see* Moffett, Pamela Clemens
Clemens, Pleasant Hannibal, 10, 15
Clemens, Samuel, 15, 44
abstinence of, 266, 340
alcohol and, 63, 107, 114, 133, 159, 340
Aldrich as viewed by, 308–9
alleged homosexuality of, 122
on Americans, 16
anglophilia of, 325
Annie Moffett's relationship with, 93–94
anti-French feelings of, 426
anti-imperialism of, 82, 571, 603, 604–8, 615
Aquarium Club of, 619–20
Arnold and, 480
at *Atlantic* dinner, 363–65, 367
attack on Arnold by, 516–17
autobiography of, 90, 141, 147, 320, 410, 492, 511, 600, 620, 621
as autodidact, 82
automated house and, 403–4
in Azores, 197, 201
bandit hoax on, 167
bawdy jokes of, 122
at Beecher's trial, 376
Benjamin's death and, 28–29, 320, 350
Bermuda trip of, 404–5
Bible and, 26–27, 28, 29, 30, 36, 80, 93, 246, 261, 262, 421, 438, 528
biographers and, 6
birth of, 8
Bixby's hoax on, 78

Bliss contract of, 288
at Bliss house, 250–51
boarding-house fire and, 123
as Bohemian, 130
boils of, 565–66, 571
book sales of, 350
at Boston luncheon, 308
Boston trip of, 362–63
Bowen's fight with, 95
boyhood pranks of, 33–34
Brazil trip planned by, 72–73, 75
British reviews of, 325
Brown's abuse toward, 84, 85
Brown's fight with, 85–86, 636*n*
Buffalo *Express* purchase of, 274
California arrest of, 159
Carleton's relationship with, 177–79
on Charley Langdon, 249–50
childhood games of, 32
church epiphany of, 312–13
Churchill speech of, 604–5
church reading by, 188
Clara's suitor and, 540–41
clothing of, 80, 115, 147
Colonel Sellers debacle and, 508–9
on communism, 417*n*
conscripted into Union Army, 97–98
Cooper Union lecture of, 190–93
Corbett and, 556
cottage workspace of, 351
covering Nevada state convention, 127
cowboy outfit of, 105
Crane's illness and, 526–27
in D.C., 67–68
death in writings of, 89
death of, 627
and death of mother, 532
in departure from Nevada, 141–42
descriptions of Mississippi by, 22
and diamond rush book idea, 291–92
at Dickens reading, 229, 446
dinner behavior of, 372
on drama, 397
dream notebooks of, 90
and dream of Henry's death, 84–85, 635*n*–36*n*
on dreams, 587, 594
on duality, 586–87
duel challenge of, 139–41
dysentery of, 424
early employment of, 45, 46
early love of steamboats, 22–23
on earthquakes, 144
education of, 25–28, 39, 45
end of bankruptcy of, 591–92
eulogy for Langdon by, 287

Clemens, Samuel (*cont.*)
European fame of, 542
fake map made by, 290
fan letters to, 398–400
father's business troubles and, 23
fifty-ninth birthday of, 561
fight for authors' rights by, 323–24,
   326, 623
first gunfight seen by, 104
first house of, 282
first romance of, 82–83, 90
first trip to England of, 323–27
foreign languages and, 27
form letters of, 398
in France, 202, 204–5, 542
and Freudian psychoanalysis, 6,
   219–20
gambling of, 144
on "Genius," 172
on German language, 418
in Germany, 415–24
at *Gilded Age*'s opening night, 358–59
in Gillis's cabin, 150–52
Goodman's relationship with, 116
gout of, 565
at Grant banquet, 427–31
Grant's friendship with, 46, 225–26,
   286, 492–93, 500–501, 503–4
Grant visited by, 452
in Greece, 210–11
at Greeley reception, 316–17
in Guard during Civil War, 98–100
guilt of, 28–29, 43–44
Halley's Comet boast of, 9*n*
handwriting of, 50
Hannibal trips of, 456, 499, 611–13
Harper's deal of, 608–9
Harte's arguments with, 390–91, 396,
   402–3, 404–8
Harte's collaboration with, 159, 401,
   402–3, 404–8
Harte's competition with, 377, 386,
   390
Harte's popularity and, 289–90,
   293–94, 297
Hartford house of, 332–33, 361
Hawaiian trip of, 160
health of, 23
Henry's death and, 86–89, 635*n*–36*n*
Henry's relationship with, 71, 83–84
Hinton satire of, 53–54
Holmes toast of, 432
in Holy Land, 212–16
honorary Oxford degree of, 623
household fires of, 449
Howells's advice to, 367–68

Howells's appreciation of, 464–65
Howells's first meeting with, 2–6
Ida's runaway carriage and, 406–7
income of, 295
Indian prejudice of, 23–24, 127
influence of women on, 219–20
Innocents Abroad royalty of, 277, 284,
   318, 322
inventions of, 304, 322, 324, 435, 481,
   485, 521
investments of, 353–54, 448–49, 450,
   452, 466, 490–91, 507, 521, 543,
   555, 559–60, 592, 605; *see also* Paige
   Typesetter
in Iowa, 69–73
in Italy, 205–11
James compared with, 364–65
Jane's birth and, 444–45
on Jefferson Davis, 193
in Jerusalem, 4
on Jews, 594
joining ministry considered by, 89
lampoons McGuffey, 27–28
Langdon house visited by, 241–47
Langdon's death and, 319–20
Langdon's illness and, 303–5
learning French, 80
on leave-taking from mother, 60–61
Livy's death and, 616–17
as Livy's suitor, 244, 245–46, 249–50,
   259–60, 265
Livy's typhoid fever and, 297–300
loan to Orion by, 349
lumbago of, 465
Margaret's death and, 20–21
and "Mark Twain" pseudonym,
   117–19
"Mark Twain's Voyage Around the
   World by Proxy" idea of, 284, 291
Mary Baker Eddy attack by, 614–15
mediums and, 317, 425
Memory Builder game of, 534, 543
memory of, 9, 28, 51
mining attempts of, 106–9
minstrel show's appeal to, 35–36, 131
Mississippi River and, 58–59, 73
Mississippi River notebooks of, 76
on Mississippi River period, 82
money troubles of, 9, 38, 340, 530–31,
   550–51, 553–55, 559–60, 561, 564,
   574
on Mormonism, 103
on mother, 40–41
in move to Europe, 538–51
Mrs. Fairbanks's influence on, 220
music and, 35, 93

Nevada fire and, 101, 105–6
in New York, 63–65, 68, 189–96,
    482–83, 599, 604–5, 619
New York arrest of, 193
New York printing job of, 65
Nicaraguan voyage of, 171
nicknames of, 176
nightmares of, 23
at Nook Farm, 304
notebooks of, 29, 69, 70, 93, 172–74,
    201, 225, 425, 437, 457, 460, 471,
    498–99, 512, 522, 536, 540, 572,
    582, 584, 594
on Open Door treaty, 241
Orion's relationship with, 70, 210,
    285–86, 408–9, 423–24, 467
Orion visited by, 509
Osgood and, 446–47
Osgood deal of, 448
Paine and, 620–21
in Paris, 424–26
pen names of, 1
in Philadelphia, 65–66, 68
phonograph of, 535
photographs of, 286–87
physical appearance of, 1, 8, 11, 93,
    147, 198, 287, 426–27
physical world in prose of, 417
pilot's license earned by, 94
poetry of, 59, 73
on police, 194
political views of, 187–88
on politicians, 225
possible origin of name of, 94, 94n,
    118, 638n
profanity of, 368
on proof-readers, 271
proposal to Livy by, 244–45
prospecting attempts of, 151–52
prostitution and, 79–80, 83
on *Prudence Palfrey*, 346
psychic abilities and, 373–74, 421
psychoanalysis of, 8, 387
and publication of books, 466–67,
    481–83
on *Quaker City* cruise, 3–4, 197–221
on Quarry Farm, 388
at quartz mill, 108
race and, 57, 332
racism and, 35–37, 146, 405, 594
raft accident of, 420
rapprochement with Hart by, 308
reading of, 24, 26–27, 80–81, 264, 572
redecorations and, 449–50
reformist passion of, 330
on relics, 206

religion and, 21, 29, 30–31, 81, 82, 89,
    157, 172, 246–47, 249, 254, 259,
    261–62, 406, 421, 499, 527–28, 586,
    615–16, 625
rheumatism of, 419, 424, 465, 531,
    535, 537, 559
Rice's relationship with, 115–16
ridicule of Orion by, 350
as riverboat pilot, 75–80, 92
Rogers and, 552–62
Roosevelt dinner of, 623
Roughing It publication and, 317–18,
    322, 333
rumors about, 584–85
in Russia, 212
in St. Louis, 62–63, 73
in St. Louis militia, 68–69
Samuel Webster on, 520
Sandwich Island lectures of, 163–64,
    188, 190–93
Sanitary Fair hoax, 137–40
satire of, 53
second trip to England by, 334–35
sectional division and, 82, 188
self-editing of, 179
sensitive ear of, 418
seventy-fourth birthday of, 625
in showdowns with Bliss, 318
Slade seen by, 103
slavery and, 8, 11–13, 30, 36, 39, 82
SLC's first use of, 117
sleepwalking of, 9, 23
on Southern speech, 459–60
spoken language and, 8
Stanley's friendship with, 189
steamboat characters and, 79
steamboat crashes of, 94–95
Such lawsuit of, 337
superstitions of, 21
support for Douglas by, 92–93
Susy's death and, 577–79
Susy's relationship with, 501–2
on Tahoe, 124–25
telephone of, 408
temper of, 70, 114–15, 405, 408, 423,
    510–11, 519
Tennessee land deal and, 158–59
theater as enthusiasm of, 145–46
Thomas Paine's influence on, 81
thoughts on secession by, 95n, 96–97
and "Three Aces," 294
on Tilden, 394–95
toast on women by, 232–33, 248
total financial losses of, 561
tribute to Howells of, 620
in trip to San Francisco, 120–23

Clemens, Samuel (*cont.*)
  in Turkey, 211
  twin theme in work of, 39–40, 118
  typesetting and, 46, 47–48, 49–50, 51, 74
  typewriter purchase of, 363, 379
  in Vienna, 589–90, 592–96
  vindictiveness of, 112, 456–57
  voice of, 93–94, 147
  wagon accident of, 250
  Ward compared to, 131
  Ward's friendship with, 128, 130–31, 133–34
  Ward's hoax on, 133
  Ward's influence on, 135
  Warner compared with, 331
  on "waterfall" hairstyle, 143
  at Wave Hill, 611
  wedding of, 280, 281–82
  at Whittier's birthday party, 409–13
  Wilde's meeting with, 543
  at Wiley house, 255
  on women lecturing, 301
  women's suffrage and, 342
  work drive of, 401–2
  writing style of, 27, 142, 184
  at Yale Princeton game, 600
  see also specific works
  JOURNALIST:
  Ajax interview of, 160
  as *Alta California* "Travelling
    Correspondent," 170
  ambition of, 56
  on Andrew Johnson, 224
  on Beecher, 181–82
  Californian pieces of, 148–49, 152
  dispatches to *Morning Call* by, 123
  on Duncan's drinking, 228–29
  early *Enterprise* reports of, 112
  early pseudonyms of, 1, 58, 59, 73, 92, 94, 109
  engagement of, 266–67
  at *Enterprise*, 109–42, 153, 157, 159
  Enterprise piece of, 126–27
  Enterprise spoofs of, 116
  for *Express*, 274–75
  first appearance in print of, 55–56
  as first time editor, 53
  for *Galaxy*, 285–86
  Golden Era pieces of, 125
  for *Harper's*, 162–63
  Hawaiian reports of, 160–62
  Herald piece of, 222
  hired by *Morning Call*, 144
  Hornet fire report of, 161–62, 176
  as Insider, 92

"Josh's letters" written by, 109
at *Journal*, 52–58, 59–61
on Menken, 136
misidentified as "Mark Swain," 162, 176
on New York police, 180–81
parody of Ward by, 130
Sabine's castigation by, 294–95
start at *Enterprise* of, 111–12
Unreliable and, 117, 121, 124, 140, 142, 363
for *Weekly Review*, 159
on women's fashion, 180
see also specific works
LECTURER:
around the world tour of, 564
in Australia, 569, 570–72
Bryn Mawr lecture of, 537
with Cable, 485, 492, 493, 497–99, 565
in Canada, 567–69
as celebrity, 164, 167–69
in Ceylon, 572–73
1868–69 tour of, 241, 247–48, 252–53, 256–59, 262, 264–66, 267–69, 277–78, 280–81, 450
in England, 338, 339, 340–41
first tour of, 164–70
"Frozen Truth" lecture of, 236
in India, 573–74
lecturing stopped by, 284
on mental telegraphy, 458
oratorical style of, 13, 50
pay of, 165, 248, 311, 316, 497, 576
reviews of, 165, 166, 236–37, 258–59, 266, 268, 306–7, 311–12, 315–16
Roughing It anecdotes used by, 311–12, 344
in South Africa, 574–76
temper of, 266
as Vandal, 252–54, 256–59, 264–65, 485
Ward lecture of, 306–7, 309
LETTERS:
for *Alta California*, 4, 176, 177, 184, 186, 187, 189, 194, 200, 210, 220, 222–23, 226, 233, 234, 235–36, 237–38, 241
to Ann Taylor, 80
to Bliss, 273
to Bowen, 233–34, 282–83, 389
on death of Jervis Langdon, 286
for *Enterprise*, 116–17, 121, 177
for *Evening Post*, 424–25
for *Herald*, 336, 337
to Howells, 344, 347, 350, 361, 363, 372, 377–78, 390, 394, 407, 408,

409, 414, 416, 417, 422, 423, 437,
449, 457, 462, 470, 471, 486, 508–9,
521–22, 528–29, 530, 532–33, 535,
538, 579
for *Journal*, 66–67
to Laura Wright, 107
to Livy, 249, 251, 260, 262, 265, 266,
268, 269, 307, 309, 312–13, 315,
324–25, 326, 341, 427, 431, 458,
460, 527–28, 555, 556, 557, 558,
560, 563, 578, 610, 614
for London *Standard*, 342
love letters to Livy, 245–47, 250, 254,
260, 261, 267, 272, 280
"Pauline" mentioned in, 230*n*
to Mary Field, 355–56
to Mollie, 230
for *Morning Call*, 121, 123
to mother, 62, 63, 64, 70, 71–72, 101,
105, 106, 107, 119, 121, 124,
132–33, 144–45, 154, 155, 191,
195–96, 210, 223, 230–31, 233, 267,
343, 349, 371, 421, 471
to Murray, 441
to Olivia Langdon, 327–28
to Orion, 108, 141, 145, 146, 155–56,
157, 276, 299, 304, 425–26, 435,
442–43, 445, 515
to Pamela, 119, 121, 145, 159, 233,
278, 288, 435
to river-town newspapers, 92
to Rogers, 564
to Susy, 380–81, 411
for *Tribune*, 217–18
to Warner, 352
to Wattie, 440–41
Clermont, 11
Cleveland, Grover, 498, 510
Cleveland, Ohio, SLC's lectures in, 247,
255–58, 267, 566–67
Cleveland *Herald*, 198, 235, 238, 255,
265, 273, 281
Cold Harbor, Battle of, 146, 428
Colfax, Schuyler, 191, 233, 329
Coliseum, 209
Colonel Crossman, 75
Colonel Sellers (Twain), 450
Colonel Sellers as a Scientist (Twain and
Howells), 471, 479–80, 481, 485,
507, 508, 531, 534
Colt, Samuel, 433
Columbus, Christopher, 209, 510
Comic Annual for 1873, 141
Common Sense (Paine), 81
Comstock, Henry, 104
Comstock Lode, 104, 105, 111, 373, 530

"Concerning the Jews" (Twain), 594, 595
Concord, Mass., Public Library, 490, 500
Condensed Novels (Harte), 178
Confederate States of America, 79, 95,
123, 146
Confucius, 17
Congressional Record, 607
Conkling, Roscoe, 510
Connecticut Company, 556
Connecticut Yankee in King Arthur's Court, A
(Twain), 221, 512, 528
dramatization of, 531
England in, 528
film versions of, 524
Hank Morgan in, 90
Howells on, 505
reviews of, 529
sales of, 529–30
slavery in, 36
writing of, 506, 517, 521, 523–24
Conrad, Joseph, 608
Conrad, Lou, 230
Conway, Moncure, 337, 382–84, 396,
397, 401
Coon, Ben, III, 151
Cooper, James Fenimore, 24, 26, 28, 32,
150, 203, 296, 582, 614
Cooper, Peter, 181, 189
Cooper, Sarah, 189
Cooper Union, *see* Peter Cooper Institute
Corbett, Jim, 556
Cord, Henry, 357
Cord, Mary Ann, 13, 356–57, 406, 521,
548
Cosmopolitan, 544, 557, 597
Cox, James, 466, 468*n*
Crane, Stephen, 5
Crane, Susan Langdon, 242, 249, 281,
287, 297–99, 320, 349, 350–51, 356,
388, 404, 466, 526, 530, 531, 538,
539, 546, 554, 558, 576, 577
Crane, Theodore W., 243, 298–99, 349,
350–51, 356, 388, 406–7, 466,
526–27
Crédit Mobilier scandal, 329, 394
Crescent City, 76, 80
Crimean War, 205
Crinkle, Nym, 359–60
Critic, 504
Crosby, Bing, 524
Cross, Sam, 27
Crown Point Iron Co., 448
Cuba, 567, 592–93, 600, 601, 615
Cupples, Upham & Co., 516
"Curious Republic of Gondour, The"
(Twain), 378

Currier, Nathaniel, 436
Cutler, William K., 140, 166
"Czar's Soliloquy, The" (Twain), 607, 609, 619
Czolgosz, Leon, 610

Daddy Longlegs (Webster), 520
Daggett, Rollin Mallory, 111, 113, 114, 141, 142, 148, 524
Daisy Miller (James), 364, 423
Dake, Laura M. Wright, 82–83, 90, 107, 122, 145, 211, 439–42, 501, 594, 624–25, 636n, 642n
Damascus, Syria, 213–14
Dana, Charles A., 513
Dana, Richard Henry, Jr., 270, 296, 351
"Dandy Frightening the Squatter, The" (Twain), 55–56
Dangerous Intimacy: The Untold Story of Mark Twain's Final Years (Lystra), 620, 682n
Daniel Slote & Company, 436
Dante Alighieri, 18
Darnell-Watson feud, 473–74
Darwin, Charles, 80, 400
David Copperfield (Dickens), 229
Davis, Jefferson, 95, 96, 193, 394
Davis, Joshua William, 213
Dawson, John D., 27
Dawson Brothers, 489
Day, Alice Hooker, 229, 298, 304, 564, 574
Day, John C., 298, 564, 574
"Death of Jean, The" (Twain), 682n
Declaration of Independence, 66, 509
Deerslayer, The (Cooper), 560
"Defense of General Funston, A" (Twain), 607
Defoe, Daniel, 26
de Kay, Helena, 486
Delinquent Tax, 394
Demosthenes, 211
Dempsey, Terrell, 11n
Denny, William R., 200, 210, 213
Densmore, Gilbert, 352
Dent, L. Holden, 281
De Quille, Dan, 111, 113, 122, 125, 133, 136, 137, 138, 142, 147, 150, 373–74, 377, 378, 595
Derby, George Horatio, 113
Desatir, 17
DeVoto, Bernard, 494, 593, 621
Dewey, George, 593
Díaz, Porfirio, 627
Dibble, W. E., 525

Dickens, Charles, 14, 26, 57, 65, 70, 135, 223, 229, 263, 289, 295, 309, 321, 323, 353, 390, 446, 469
Dickinson, Anna, 181, 248, 301
Dickinson, Emily, 5
Dilberry, Lady Alice, 392
Disciples of Christ, 49
Disraeli, Benjamin, 335
Dodge, "Buffalo Joe," 111
Dodge, Mary Mapes, 544, 546–47, 556, 565
Dolby, George, 338
Donelson, Fort, 430
Don Quixote (Cervantes), 301, 529
Dostoyevsky, Fyodor, 370
"Double-Barreled Detective Story, A," 610
Doubleday, Nelson, 608
Douglas, Stephen, 67, 92–93, 97, 224
Douglass, Frederick, 36, 243, 278, 300, 327, 521
Douglass, Rosetta, 278
Dowden, Edward, 553
Drake, Sidney, 269, 270, 277
Dramatic Chronicle, 157
Dred Scott case, 40, 81–82
Dreyfus trial, 567
Dr. Jekyll and Mr. Hyde (Stevenson), 586
Drummer Boy of the Rappahannock, see Hendershot, Robert Henry
Duckett, Margaret, 359, 403
dueling, code of, 139
Dulles, Allen, 615
Dumas, Alexandre, fils, 135
Dumas, Alexandre, père, 135, 204
Duncan, Charles C., 3, 185, 195, 197, 199, 217, 218, 228–29
Dvořák, Antonín, 545, 589

Ealer, George, 87, 92
East Louisiana Railroad, 548
Eclectic Readers (McGuffey), 26–28, 234
Eddy, Mary Baker, 570, 614–15
Edison, Thomas, 535
Edward VI, King of England, 626
Eliot, T. S., 77, 119, 494
Elizabeth, Empress of Austria, 594
Elizabeth I, Queen of England, 392
Elmira, N.Y., 243, 249, 287, 299, 444, 477, 509, 528, 565, 569, 580, 615
Elmira Advertiser, 259, 275
Elmira Ladies Seminary, 559, 565
Elmira Water Cure sanitarium, 388
Emancipation Proclamation, 138
Emerson, Everett, 467

Emerson, Ralph Waldo, 2, 17–18, 57, 66, 130, 132, 150, 167, 170, 183, 188, 203, 245, 270, 296, 364, 378, 400, 401, 409–11, 413, 432, 446, 458, 469
England, 323–27, 335–38, 576–78, 581–85
Euripedes, 450
Europe and Elsewhere (Twain), 609
Evans, Albert S., 145, 159
Evans, Walker, 568
Evans, William, 314
Every Saturday, 293, 294
Eve's Diary (Twain), 620
Extract from Captain Stormfield's Visit to Heaven (Twain), 622
Eye Openers, 324

"Fable for Old Boys & Girls" (Twain), 950
Fackler, St. Michael, 174
"Facts Concerning the Recent Carnival of Crime in Connecticut, The" (Twain), 386–87, 455, 586
Fair, Laura, 329
Fairbanks, Abel, 198, 248, 256, 273, 275, 281, 318, 596
Fairbanks, Alice, 281
Fairbanks, Charlie, 328
Fairbanks, Mary Mason, 179, 198, 199, 219–20, 222–23, 228, 235, 237, 239, 241, 248–49, 253, 254n, 256, 259, 261, 264, 265, 267–68, 270, 271, 275, 281–82, 286, 291, 298, 311, 317, 318, 328, 332, 334, 343, 344, 348, 372–73, 399, 409, 424, 452, 515, 527, 595–96, 603
"Family Muss, A" (Twain), 58
Fanchon the Cricket, 195, 197
Fanning, Philip Ashley, 509
Farm and Home, 602
Farragut, David, 430
Fatout, Paul, 256n
Fay & Cox, 270
"Fenimore Cooper's Literary Offenses" (Twain), 560
Ferguson, Henry, 162–63
Ferguson, Samuel, 162
Ferlinghetti, Lawrence, 144
Field, Kate, 336–37
Field, Mary M., 355–56
Field, Stephen Johnson, 227, 235
Fields, James T., 2, 3, 18, 289, 307, 391
Fields, W. C., 135
Fifteenth Amendment, 4, 225, 300, 366
Finn, Jimmy, 35, 283
Finney, James "Ole Virginny," 110–11

First Independent Congregational Church, 243
Fishkin, Shelley Fisher, 47, 313, 496
Fiske, John, 363
Fitch, Thomas, 124, 140, 166n, 167
Five Points, 180
Flaubert, Gustave, 370
Fletcher, Thomas C., 429
Florida, Mo., 10, 11, 15, 21, 100
Florida, secession of, 95
Florida Academy, 14
Florida & Paris Railroad, 14
Following the Equator (Twain), 571, 575, 582–84
Ford, Darius, 281, 284, 291
Ford, Eunice, 281
Ford, Tennessee Ernie, 524
Forrest, Edwin, 65, 68
"Forty-Three Days in an Open Boat" (Twain), 162
Forum, 522
Fourteenth Amendment, 366
France, 202, 204–5, 542, 567
Franco-Prussian War, 290
Frank, Michael, 356
Frank, Waldo, 494
Franklin, Benjamin, 47, 50, 66, 71, 284, 337, 436
Franz Ferdinand, Archduke of Austria, 597, 626
Franz Josef I, Emperor of Austria, 597
Fredericksburg, Battle of, 183
Fredonia *Censor*, 312
Fredonia Watch Company, *see* Independent Watch Company
"Freedman's Case in Equity, The" (Cable), 498
Freeman, Mary E. Wilkins, 387n
French Spy (Haines), 136
Freud, Sigmund, 90, 567, 589, 621
Frost, Robert, 353
Froude, J. A., 438
Fuller, Frank, 179, 191, 210, 224, 227, 241, 249, 344
Fullerton, William, 376
Fulton, Robert, 11

Gabriel Conroy (Harte), 377, 396
Gabrilowitsch, Clara Clemens, *see* Samossoud, Clara Clemens Gabrilowitsch
Gabrilowitsch, Nina, 445, 589
Gabrilowitsch, Ossip, 589, 611, 625, 626–27
Gaines, General, 283
Galaxy, 284, 290, 294

"Gallant Fireman, A" (Twain), 55
Gallia, S.S., 426
Galton, Francis, 549
Garfield, James A., 444, 445, 452
Gargantua and Pantagruel (Rabelais), 165
Garibaldi, Giuseppe, 208
Garrett, Henry, 470
Garrison, William Lloyd, 40, 409
Garth, Helen, 612
Gebbie, George, 445, 450
Genoa, Italy, 205–6
George Routledge & Sons, 303, 323, 325, 326
Georgia, secession of, 95
Gerhardt, Karl, 485
Germany, 415–24, 539–42
Gettysburg, Battle of, 123, 251–52, 407, 486
"Ghost Life on the Mississippi" (Twain), 96
Gilbert & Sullivan, 537
Gil Blas (LeSage), 301, 377
Gilded Age, 174, 279, 367, 394, 521, 545, 552
Gilded Age, The (Twain and Warner), 328, 351, 400, 417, 604
  British edition of, 338
  critique of, 330–32
  model for "Colonel" Eschol Sellers in, 10
  models for Hawkins family in, 14, 42, 53
  pirating of, 352, 369
  publication of, 333, 341
  Reid's advertisement for, 336
  reviews of, 341–42
  sales of, 342, 434
  SLC's stage adaptation of, 352–53, 354, 358–60, 378, 397
  steamboat explosion in, 87
  steamboats in, 77
  writing of, 328–29, 351
Gilder, Richard Watson, 486–89, 491–92
Gillespie, William, 113, 115, 123
Gillette, Francis, 231, 304
Gillette, William, 231
Gillis, Angus, 150
Gillis, Billy, 150
Gillis, Jim, 150–51, 623
Gillis, Steve, 113, 140, 141, 143, 145, 149, 166, 170
Gleason, Rachel Brooks, 353, 358, 388
Gluck, James Frazer, 477*n*
Godey's Lady's Book, 392
Godwin, Mary, 553
Goethe, Johann Wolfgang von, 18

Goldberg, Whoopi, 393
Gold Dust, 458, 468
"Golden Arm, The," 13, 532, 537, 613
Golden Era, 114, 125, 144, 147–48, 151, 307, 352
Gold Hill, 106
Gold Hill *Evening News,* 141–42
Gold Hill News, 159
Gold Rush, 50–51, 103–4, 120–21, 143, 150, 289
Goldsmith, Oliver, 572
Goodman, Joe, 111, 113, 115, 116, 119, 124, 133–34, 137, 138, 139, 142, 149, 157, 167, 221, 237, 262, 274, 298–99, 353, 373, 377, 536
Goodwin, C. C., 111–12, 113
Gould, Jay, 329, 491, 530
Gould & Curry, 123
Grant, Fred, 492
Grant, Jesse, 416
Grant, Julia, 226, 416, 444, 485, 493, 504
Grant, Orville, 41
Grant, Ulysses S., 68–69, 95, 99, 120, 123, 137, 146, 182, 316, 366, 393–94, 444, 445, 457, 466, 485, 521
  administration scandals of, 329
  Arnold on, 515–16
  elections of, 254–55, 327
  in England, 416
  Gilded Age and, 360
  inauguration of, 269
  memoirs of, 452, 481, 484, 492, 497, 500–501, 503–4, 505, 506, 509, 515–16, 519
  at reunion banquet, 427, 428–31
  Shiloh essay of, 487–88, 491–92
  SLC's friendship with, 46, 225–26, 286, 492–93, 500–501, 503–4
  SLC's "historical note" on, 210
Grass Valley, Nev., SLC's lecture in, 165–66
Gray, John A., 65
Gray, Lem, 468*n*
"Great Dark, The" (DeVoto), 593, 595
Great Dark, The (Twain), 172*n*
Great Metropolis, The (Browne), 273
Greece, 210–11
Greeley, Horace, 68*n*, 160, 169, 181, 248, 265, 316, 327, 329, 338, 368
Greer, Frederick H., 200
Grey, Zane, 608
Gridley, Reuel Colt, 137, 139
Griffin, George, 13, 376, 538
Grimes, Absalom, 97–99

Griswold, Anna, 148, 228–29
Guam, 593
Guiteau, Charles J., 452, 471

Haines, John Thomas, 136
Hale & Norcross, 150
Hall, Fred J., 506, 515, 519, 525, 533,
    536, 539, 543, 544, 546, 550–51,
    554–55, 558
Halley, Edmund, 9
Halley's Comet, 9n, 617, 626
Hamersley, William, 491, 531
Hamlet (Shakespeare), 343, 453
Hannibal, Mo., 20, 21–22, 32–44,
    461–62
  cholera epidemic in, 50–51
  fashion in, 35
  first murder in, 37
  Gold Rushers in, 50–51
  growth of, 57
  measles epidemic in, 34
  music in, 35
  newspapers in, 47
  SLC's returns to, 456, 499, 611–13
  tourism in, 205
  Union troops in, 97–98
Hannibal & St. Joseph Railroad, 42, 462
Hannibal City, 89
Hannibal *Commercial Advertiser*, 47
Hannibal *Courier*, 46, 48, 49, 50
Hannibal *Gazette*, 45, 46
Hannibal *Journal*, 38, 46, 47, 50, 51,
    52–54, 56–58, 59–61, 66, 69, 585
Hannibal Journal and Native American, 47
Hannibal Library Institute, 40
Hannibal *Tri-Weekly Messenger*, 52, 54–55
Hardy, Thomas, 470
Harley, John J., 470
Harper, Philip, 608
Harper & Brothers, 569, 581, 608, 615
Harper's, 565, 569, 576, 682n
Harper's Bazaar, 387n, 609
Harper's Monthly, 90, 162, 507, 529, 544
Harper's New Monthly Magazine, 591, 610
Harper's Weekly, 280, 327, 368, 369,
    581–82
Harris, Jack, 104
Harris, Joel Chandler, 13, 422, 461,
    520
Harris, Thomas H., 98, 100
Harrison, Katharine I., 554, 591–92
Harte, Anna, 295, 403
Harte, Bernard, 408n
Harte, Francis Bret, 114, 146–47, 149,
    150, 154, 159, 163, 177, 178, 191,
    289, 293, 295–97, 300, 305, 307,

317, 320–21, 322, 324, 352, 364,
    387, 405, 446, 520, 562, 570, 642n
  death of, 611
  Innocents Abroad edited by, 239
  rapprochement with SLC, 308
  SLC reviewed by, 119, 165, 276
  SLC's arguments with, 390–91, 396,
    402–3, 404–8
  SLC's competition with, 377, 386, 390
Harte, Frankie, 295
Harte, Wodie, 295
Hartford, Conn., 250–51, 271–72, 300,
    302, 309, 310, 327, 344, 353, 382,
    427, 433, 436, 465, 532
  American Publishing in, 4, 249
  Arnold in, 480
  first phone in, 408
  intellectuals of, 386
  SLC landmarks in, 615
  SLC's house in, 360–61, 531, 538, 558,
    559, 563–64, 604, 615
  SLC's move to, 356
  SLC's plan to live in, 267–68, 350
  Taylor's talk in, 401
Hartford Accident Insurance Company,
    353–54
Hartford *Courant*, 268, 273, 275, 321,
    328, 395, 408, 471, 489, 503, 607
Hartford *Daily Times*, 349
Hartford *Evening Post*, 324, 329
Hartford Fire Insurance Company, 615
Hartford Public Library, 615
Hartford *Times*, 469, 607
Harvard College, 17
Harvey, George B., 608–9, 621, 622
Hawaii, 160–62, 177, 197, 593
Hawkins, Anna Laura, 41, 283
Hawley, Joseph R., 268, 328
Hawthorne, Nathaniel, 2, 150, 203, 296,
    363
Hawthorne, Rose, 363
Hay, John, 317, 324, 329, 393, 453, 623
Hay, Rosina, 415, 416, 449
Hayes, Rutherford B., 390, 393–95, 408,
    473
Haymarket Square riots, 508
Hazard of New Fortunes, A (Howells), 544
Hearst, William Randolph, 592, 601
"Hearts Lament, The" (Twain), 59
"Heathen Chinee, The" (Harte), 289,
    293, 391
"Hellfire Hotchkiss" (Twain), 53, 595
Hemingway, Ernest, 476–77, 494
Hendershot, Robert Henry, 183, 195,
    197
Henley, William Ernest, 489

Henry Chauncey, 236, 239
Henry IV (Shakespeare), 74
Herodotus, 211
Hesse, Fanny, 400
Higginson, Thomas Wentworth, 378
Hill, Hamlin, 355
Hinton, Josiah T., 52–54, 55, 58
hippies, 144
Hirst, Robert, 226n, 254n, 496–97
"Historical Exhibition—A No. 1 Ruse"
    (Twain), 58
History of the Hawaiian Islands, 161
Hitchcock, Lillie, 144
Hitchcock, Martha, 144
Holland, George, 294–95
Holmes, Oliver Wendell, 2, 18, 57, 130,
    264, 270, 276, 296, 308, 364, 378,
    386, 387, 409–12, 432, 437, 446,
    469, 504
Holsatia, 415
Homer, 426
Homer, Winslow, 486
Hood, Tom, 141
Hooker, Alice, *see* Day, Alice Hooker
Hooker, Eliza, 231
Hooker, Isabella Beecher, 231, 233, 251,
    284, 327, 342, 349, 564
Hooker, John, 231, 233, 251, 304, 333,
    342, 349
Hooker, Thomas, 231
Hopkins, Philip, 126
Hoppin, Augustus, 341
Hornet, 161–62, 176, 594
Hotten, John Camden, 324, 326,
    352
Houdini, Harry, 353
Houghton, Henry O., 358, 363, 368
Houghton, Mifflin, 446
Houghton, Oscar, 446
Houghton, Osgood & Co., 446
House, Edward H., 3, 177, 185, 193,
    334, 336–37
House of Representatives, U.S., 366
Howe, Julia Ward, 378
Howells, Elinor, 296, 346, 350, 368,
    370–71, 393, 451, 478–79, 527
Howells, John Mead, 346, 622
Howells, Mildred, 346
Howells, W. C., 452
Howells, William Dean, 5–6, 18–19, 33,
    36–37, 43–44, 179, 203, 206, 278,
    284, 318, 320, 324, 347, 350, 361,
    371, 387, 469, 478–79, 485, 487,
    500, 507, 538, 544, 562, 572, 576,
    583, 596, 610–11
  advice to SLC by, 367–68

American literature and, 5, 19, 367,
    370
  Anti-Imperialist League and, 602, 604
  Atlantic Monthly and, 2–3, 18–19, 295,
    362, 363, 423, 450
  at Boston luncheon, 307–8
  Clara on, 450–51
  Colonel Sellers as a Scientist and,
    479–80
  Connecticut Yankee and, 528–29
  critical reviews of, 507–8
  Gilded Age and, 342
  Hayes biography of, 394
  Huckleberry Finn proofs and, 483, 486,
    488
  illness of, 456
  Library of Humor and, 445, 452, 484,
    512, 520, 524
  on *Life of Pope Leo XIII,* 513–14
  Lowell's first meeting with, 18
  "Old Times on the Mississippi" and,
    362
  Orion's autobiography and, 442–44
  physical appearance of, 3, 370
  Prince and the Pauper and, 445
  Prince and the Pauper review by, 453,
    454
  realism and, 296
  Roughing It reviewed by, 321
  SLC "appreciation" by, 464–65
  SLC's first meeting with, 2–6, 278
  SLC's last visit to, 626
  SLC's letters to, 344, 347, 350, 361,
    363, 372, 377–78, 390, 394, 407,
    408, 409, 414, 416, 417, 422, 423,
    437, 449, 457, 462, 470, 471, 486,
    508–9, 521–22, 528–29, 530,
    532–33, 535, 538, 579
  SLC's Mississippi reminiscences and,
    369–70
  SLC's profanity and, 368
  on SLC's style, 603
  SLC's tribute to, 620
  and SLC's typewriter, 363, 379
  as suburban novelist, 279
  Tom Sawyer and, 379, 383–86
  Tom Sawyer drama and, 378–79
  on *A Tramp Abroad,* 434–35
  "True Story" and, 356–58
  as typesetter, 436
  in visit to Emerson, 458
  visit to Grant by, 452
  visit to Nook Farm by, 344–46
  at Whittier's birthday party, 409–13
  Winifred's death and, 527, 578
  see also specific works

Howells, Winifred, 346, 450, 454, 456, 527, 578
"How I Escaped Being Killed in a Duel" (Twain), 141
Hubbard, Stephen A., 329, 331
Huck Finn and Tom Sawyer Among the Indians (Twain), 485
Hugo, Victor, 264, 426
"Humane Word from Satan, A" (Twain), 620
Humboldt *Times,* 601
Hume, David, 438
Hundred Year's War, 541
Hutton, Laurence, 565

Ibsen, Henrik, 5
Illustrated London News, 539
"In Defense of Harriet Shelley" (Twain), 553–54, 560
Independent Watch Company, 451, 456, 466
India, 573–75
Indians, 23–24, 127, 594n
Ingersoll, Robert Green, 426
"In Memoriam" (Twain), 585
Innocents Abroad (Twain), 2, 5, 33n, 189, 199n, 200–216, 268, 323, 325, 354, 400, 415, 417, 422, 432, 436, 455, 522, 581
  British edition of, 324
  Coliseum in, 209
  early title for, 240, 270–71
  England in, 528
  as grab bag, 206
  Harte's review of, 119
  illustrations of, 269–70, 302
  passengers' reactions to, 217–18
  pirated editions of, 324
  production of, 249, 252
  proofs of, 270
  publication of, 273
  reviews of, 275–77, 321, 453
  revisions of, 221, 238–39
  sales of, 277, 284, 288, 336, 450n, 469
  in SLC's lecture, 306
  style of, 234
  tour guides in, 204
  writing of, 3–4, 232–33, 235, 238
Insider, 92
Interpretation of Dreams, The (Freud), 90, 567
"Interview with Gen. Grant" (Twain), 226n
Iolanthe (Gilbert & Sullivan), 537
Iowa, 69
Iowa City *Republican,* 266

Irving, Henry, 556
Irving, Washington, 150, 203, 296
Irving Hall, 193
Isaac Newton, 64
Isbell, Oliver C., 71
Italy, 205–11, 542–43, 616
Ives, Charles, 353
Ives, Frederic, 436
Ives, James, 436

Jackson, Abraham Reeves, 200, 203, 208, 210, 219, 223
Jackson, Andrew, 46, 224
Jackson, Thomas "Stonewall," 183
James, Henry, 5, 284, 296, 364–65, 370, 387n, 423, 450, 479, 487, 596–97, 608, 619
James, Henry, Sr., 364
James, William, 364, 543, 586, 602
James R. Osgood and Company, 446
Jamestown Raid, 573
Jarves, James, 161
Jefferson, Joseph, 295
Jefferson, Thomas, 46
Jell-O, 189
Jennie (slave), 12, 38–39, 41
Jerusalem, 4, 213
Jewett, Sarah Orne, 5, 370
Jim Crow (minstrel show character), 17, 35
Jim Crow laws, 498
"Jim Smiley and His Jumping Frog," *see* "Celebrated Jumping Frog of Calaveras County, The"
J.J. Little and Company, 482
J. Langdon, Miner & Dealer, 243
J. Langdon & Company, 530
Joan of Arc, 154, 186, 541, 553
John H. Dickey, 92
John J. Roe, 82–83, 96, 441, 624, 642n
Johnny Appleseed, 253
Johnson, Andrew, 224–25, 226, 233, 235
Johnson, J. Neely, 117, 262
Johnson, Robert Underwood, 487, 491, 543
Jolliet, Louis, 468
Jones, John P., 536
Jonson, Ben, 392
Jordan, Elizabeth, 387n, 609
Jordan, Octavius, 304
Josh (pseudonym), 1, 109, 119
"Josh's letters" (Twain), 109
J. P. Morgan & Company, 608
Julius Caesar, 426
Julius Caesar (Shakespeare), 73

Kanawha (yacht), 610
Kansas-Nebraska Act (1854), 67, 81, 224
Kaolatype, 435, 448, 449, 451, 474, 587
Kaplan, Justin, 118, 186, 420, 587
Karloff, Boris, 524
Kate Frisbee, 87
Keeler, Ralph, 307–8
Keller, Hellen, 553, 556, 565, 583
Kellgren, Heinrick, 597
Kemble, Edward Windsor, 482, 483, 488, 520
Kemble, Fanny, 258
Kennedy, John F., 604
Keokuk, Iowa, 69–70, 71–73, 74, 426, 442, 467, 499, 509, 512, 616
Keokuk City Directory, 72, 532, 591
Keokuk *Daily Post,* 73, 74
Keokuk *Gate City,* 105
Kerouac, Jack, 144
Kerr, Orpheus C., 135–36
Key, Francis Scott, 251
Kilauea volcano, 161, 169
Kilby, Thomas, 515
King, James M., 601
King, Samuel D., 166
King Lear, 418–19
King Leopold's Soliloquy (Twain), 607, 609, 619
Kinney, John D., 105
Kipling, Rudyard, 544, 596, 602, 606
Kleinfelter, John S., 85–86, 87
Klimt, Gustav, 589
Know-Nothings, 68–69
Knox, John, 29n
Koppe, Ernst, 585
Krause, Sydney J., 635n
Kravchinsky, Sergey Mikhaylovich, 521
Kruger, Paul, 573, 575
Ku Klux Klan, 366, 394
Kurzweil, Maximilian, 589

Labinnah Club, 613
La Cossitt, Henry, 46
Lady of the Aroostok, The (Howells), 423, 446, 450
La Gascogne, 539
Lahn, 544
Laird, James, 139, 141
Lampton, Benjamin, 14
Lampton, James, 288, 353
Langdon, Charles Jervis, 200, 213, 218–19, 221, 222, 241, 242, 247, 249–50, 259, 271, 281, 282, 283, 284, 287, 310, 317, 338, 406, 417, 530, 554, 562
Langdon, Eunice, 242

Langdon, Ida, 406, 407
Langdon, Jervis, 242–43, 249, 259, 260, 261–62, 265, 267, 282, 286, 290, 297, 298, 351, 409
Langdon, Olivia, *see* Clemens, Olivia Langdon "Livy"
Langdon, Olivia Lewis (Olivia's mother), 242, 259, 261, 265, 271, 282, 283, 297, 304, 323, 327–28, 338, 349, 415, 421, 433, 532, 564
Lardner, Ring, 135
Larrowe, Nina, 200
La Salle, Antoine de, 468
Last Supper, The (Leonardo), 206, 256
Lawson, Thomas, 562
Leary, Katy, 61, 445, 538, 539, 540, 565, 572, 576, 578, 580, 597, 613, 616, 626
Leary, Lewis, 38
Leavenworth, Zeb, 83, 96
Leaves of Grass (Whitman), 66, 193
Lecher, Otto, 590
Lecky, William E. H., 438
Lee, Gypsy Rose, 135
Lee, Robert E., 146, 394, 486
Lentz, John J., 607
Leonardo da Vinci, 206, 256
Leo XIII, Pope, 506, 513
Leschetizky, Theodor, 585, 589, 597
Letters from the Earth (Twain), 625
"Letters to Satan" (Twain), 586
Levering, Clint, 283
Lewis, Harriet, 264, 281
Lewis, John, 407
Liberator, 40
Library of American Literature from the Earliest Settlement to the Present Time, A, 55, 524, 525, 551, 554
"Lick House Ball, The" (Twain), 125, 392, 472
Life of Christ, The (Beecher), 514
Life on the Mississippi (Twain), 5, 85, 354, 407, 455n, 459, 461n, 467–68, 482, 609
   as first typed manuscript, 363
   Henry Clemens in, 90
   Henry Clemens's death in, 89
   illustrations of, 470
   model for John Stavely in, 59
   origin of "Twain" pseudonym in, 118
   reviews of, 468–69
   sales of, 469, 470
   typing of, 477
   writing of, 462, 465–66, 467
Life of Pope Leo XIII, 513
"Lightning Express," 64

Lincoln, Abraham, 63, 67, 92, 95, 101–2, 103, 122, 129, 137, 149, 183, 192, 224, 287, 317, 390, 452
Lippincott (Hannibal resident), 612
Literary World, 581
Little Duke, The (Yonge), 438
Little Women (Alcott), 294
Livermore, Mary, 301
Livingstone, David, 189, 325
Loan of a Lover, The, 387
Locke, David Ross, *see* Nasby, Petroleum V.
Logan, Olive, 248
London *Examiner,* 396
London *Graphic,* 325, 326, 482
Longfellow, Henry Wadsworth, 2, 203, 296, 314, 363, 386, 409–12, 432, 430, 446, 469
Longstreet, James, 252
Lorch, Fred W., 256n
Louis C. Tiffany & Co., 449
Louisiana, secession of, 95
Love, Robertus, 611, 613
"Love Concealed" (Twain), 59, 585
Lowell, Amy, 353
Lowell, James Russell, 2, 18, 26, 130, 165, 203, 270, 289, 296, 378, 408n
"Luck of Roaring Camp, The" (Harte), 147
Luck of the Roaring Camp and Other Sketches, The (Harte), 289
"Lucretia Smith's Soldier" (Twain), 149
Ludlow, Fitz Hugh, 131, 133, 136
Lueger, Karl, 589
Luncheon of the Boating Party (Renoir), 444
Lustful Turk, The, 392
Lyceum Magazine, 301
Lynn, Kenneth, 596
Lyon, Isabel Van Kleek, 321, 614, 616, 619, 621, 622
Lystra, Karen, 620, 682n

McAleer, Patrick, 538
Macaulay, Thomas, 80
McCarthy, Denis E., 113, 165, 166
McClellan, George B., 100, 513
McClure, S. S., 608
McClure's, 602
McClure syndicate, 539, 542
McComb, John, 177
McCormick, Wales, 48–49
McCullers, Carson, 312
McGuffey, William H., 26n
McGuffey's Reader, 26–28, 234
McIntyre Coal, 417, 426

McKinley, William, 592, 601n, 607, 610
McLaughlin, Mara, 375–76
McLaughlin, Pat, 103–4, 110
McMurry, T. P. "Pet," 48
Madonna, 135
Maguire, Thomas, 163, 164
Mahler, Gustav, 589
Mail and Express, 599
Maine, USS, 567, 592, 601
Malory, Thomas, 80, 498, 506, 541
Mansfield, James Vincent, 317, 425
"Man That Corrupted Hadleyburg, The" (Twain), 595
"Man the Architect of Our Religion" (Orion Clemens), 426
Marchioness's Amorous Pastimes, The (Ashbee), 392
Marconi, Guglielmo, 353
"Marienbad—a Health Factory" (Twain), 539
Marin County Journal, 237
Mark Twain, Business Man (Webster), 519
Mark Twain: A Biography (Paine), 621
Mark Twain Company, 622
Mark Twain in Eruption (DeVoto), 621
Mark Twain Project, 76n, 254n, 256, 371, 496
Mark Twain's (Burlesque) Autobiography and First Romance (Twain), 298
Mark Twain's Library of Humor, 445, 452, 484, 512, 518, 520, 524
Mark Twain Speaking, 256n
Mark Twain's Self-Pasting Scrapbook, 324, 435, 436
Mark Twain's Sketches, New and Old (Twain), 371, 378, 446, 450n
Marseilles, France, 204–5
Martin, Joseph S., 72
Martin, Steve, 125
Martin Chuzzlewit (Dickens), 14
Marx, Leo, 494–95
Mary (slave), 12
Marysville, Calif., SLC's lecture in, 165
Masters, Edgar Lee, 312
Matthews, Brander, 489, 581, 582
Maupassant, Guy de, 370
Mazeppa (Byron), 135, 136
Medea (Euripedes), 450, 478
Melville, Herman, 65, 150
Mencken, H. L., 494
Menken, Adah Isaacs, 135–36, 142, 144, 167, 301
Menken, Alexander Isaac, 135
Meredith, Hugh, 41, 43, 50
Mergenthaler, Ottmar, 491, 530, 536
Meridian *Republican,* 275

Merry Tales (Twain), 543
Metropolitan Street Railroad Car
    Company, 608
Mexican War, 45–46
Michelangelo, 209
Michelson, Bruce, 495
Mifflin, George H., 363–64
Milan, Italy, 206
Millennial Harbinger, 49n
Miller, Arthur, 349
Miller, Joaquin, 377, 444
£1,000,000 Bank Note and Other New
    Stories, The, 543
Milton, John, 18, 264
Minister's Charge, A, 479
Minister's Charge, The (Howells), 479
Minneapolis, 462
Minneapolis *Journal,* 607
minstrel shows, 17, 35–36, 131
Mission School, 30
Mississippi, secession of, 95
Mississippi River, 21–22, 24, 73,
    76, 78–79, 82, 94, 362, 369, 372,
    388, 417, 455, 456, 459, 461, 465,
    473
Missouri, 9, 10
    secession and, 97
    slavery in, 40
    whimsical town names in, 10
Missouri Compromise (1820), 67, 81
Missouri Courier, 59n
Missouri-Democrat, 188
Missouri *Republican,* 92
Mitchell, Josiah A., 162
Mitchell, Maggie, 183
Mitchell, S. Weir, 527
Mitre Tavern, 325
"Model Artists, The," 65, 180
Modern Instance, A (Howells), 450, 456,
    478
Moffett, Annie, *see* Webster, Annie
    Moffett
Moffett, Pamela Clemens (SLC's sister),
    10, 15, 34, 40, 41, 42, 45, 57, 60, 70,
    95, 137, 187, 188, 281, 285, 310,
    327, 338, 401–2, 451, 466
    death of, 619
    SLC's letters to, 61, 65, 94, 119, 121,
        145, 159, 233, 278, 288, 435
    work on SLC's notebooks by, 189
Moffett, Sammy, 187, 285, 302, 310, 327,
    401–2, 623
Moffett, Stillwell and Company, 57
Moffett, William Anderson, 57, 62, 70,
    76, 88, 95, 106
Mommsen, Theodor, 542

Monday Evening Club, 386–87, 390n,
    521
Monet, Claude, 444
Monroe, Marilyn, 135
Montana, 239
"Monument to Adam, A" (Twain), 620
Moreschi, Alessandro, 513
Morgan, J. P., 553
Mormonism, 103
Morrison, Toni, 496
Morte D'Arthur, Le (Malory), 498
Mosley, Walter, 496
Mouland, John Elsey, 334, 335
Moulton, Julius, 200, 213, 219
Mount Morris Bank, 525, 536, 544, 554,
    558, 591
Mullen, Edward F., 302
Munson, Alma Hutchison, 281n
Murray, Thomas H., 441
Murray's, 516
Muscatine *Journal,* 65, 66–67
"My Début as a Literary Person" (Twain),
    162, 594, 642n
My Mark Twain (Howells), 5n, 504
"My Platonic Sweetheart" (Twain),
    90–91, 594
Mysterious Stranger, The, a Romance
    (Twain), 586
"Mystery, A" (Twain), 255–56

NAACP (National Association for the
    Advancement of Colored People),
    495
Napoleon III, Emperor of the French,
    205
Nasby, Petroleum V., 270, 300, 301
Nash, Tom, 613
Nast, Thomas, 193, 327, 328, 341, 414,
    457, 611, 621
Natchez-Under-the-Hill, 80
Nation, 276, 301, 602
National Association for the
    Advancement of Colored People
    (NAACP), 495
National Home for Disabled Volunteer
    Soldiers, 399
National Museum, 68
National Theatre, 68
Nebraska, 96
Neider, Charles, 501n, 622
Nellie (nursemaid), 321
Nelson, David, 30
Nevada, 100
    skirmish with California of, 120
    statehood of, 149
Nevada City, Nev., SLC's lecture in, 166

New Adventures of Huckleberry Finn, The,
   see *Tom Sayer Abroad*
Newark *Journal,* 608
Newark *Register,* 275
Newcomb, Mary Ann, 25
Newell, Julie, 198, 199, 219
New England, literature in, 5–6, 17, 19,
   20
New England Tragedies (Longfellow), 314
New Jersey *National Standard,* 275
New Orleans, La., 94–96, 458–61
New Orleans *Crescent,* 94
*New Pilgrims Progress, The, see Innocents
   Abroad,*
New Review, 529
New World Symphony (Dvořák), 545
New York, Newfoundland & Telegraph
   Co., 189
New York, N.Y., 63–65, 554, 565–66,
   572, 604–5, 619
   Grant's home in, 492
   in post-war years, 175–76
   SLC's return to, 173–86
New York *Citizen,* 191
New York *Daily Graphic,* 341–42
New York *Dispatch,* 191
New York *Evening Post,* 424–25, 605
New York *Express,* 179, 191, 275
New York *Herald,* 193, 221, 222, 224,
   248, 258, 259, 264, 277, 336, 481,
   584, 599–600, 605
New York *Journal,* 584
New York Post, 522, 592
New York *Press,* 599
New York *Star,* 515
New York *Sun,* 218–19, 376, 504, 513,
   539, 599
New York Sunday Mercury, 133, 134,
   179
New York Times, 191, 313, 353, 396, 406,
   526, 566, 607
New York *Tribune,* 191, 193, 210,
   217–19, 222–23, 224, 227, 231, 238,
   241, 275, 316–17, 329, 333, 336,
   337, 376, 453, 457
New York Weekly, 179
New York *World,* 11n, 290, 317, 359, 406,
   489, 500, 608
Nicaragua, SLC's trip to, 171–74
Nicholas I, Czar of Russia, 403n
Nicholas II, Czar of Russia, 212
Nicolay, John, 317
Niles, Hezekiah, 46
Niles' Register, 46
Nilon, Charles H., 495
Nineteenth Century, 522

Nobel Prize, 623
Nolan, Andrew, 173
Nook Barn, 316, 317, 328, 336, 339,
   349
Nook Farm, 35, 231, 251, 267, 279, 304,
   327, 332, 336, 342, 343, 348,
   360–61, 372, 386, 388, 392, 432,
   441, 450, 467, 604, 611
Norman, S.S., 576
Norris, Frank, 5, 370
North American Review, 554, 560, 606,
   607, 608, 615, 621
Northland, 567
Nye, Emma, 287, 290, 291, 297
Nye, James W., 101, 104, 107, 119–20,
   189–92

Ober, Louis P., 307
Observer, 40
Oceana, 572
O'Hara, John, 279
"Old Times on the Mississippi" (Twain),
   362, 364, 366, 468
Oliver, Gus, 106
Olmsted, Frederick Law, 137, 180
"Only a Nigger," (Twain), 274–75
O'Reilly, Bernard, 513
O'Reilly, Peter, 103–4, 110
Osgood, Edward, 446
Osgood, James, 293, 344–45, 371,
   446–49, 450, 453, 456, 458, 466,
   467, 469–70, 473, 481
Ottoman Empire, 627
Our American Cousin (Taylor), 344
"Our Assistant's Column" (Twain), 60
"Our Fellow Savages of the Sandwich
   Islands" (Twain), 163, 338
"Outcasts of Poker Flat, The" (Harte),
   147
Overland Monthly, 239, 289
Owsley, William Perry, 37, 40, 283
Oxford University, 623

Pacific Monitor, 47
Paderewski, Ignacy Jan, 585
Paff, Harriet Lewis, 244
Paige, James William, 365, 436, 437,
   474, 490–91, 521, 525–26, 527,
   530–31, 544, 545, 546, 555–57, 558,
   561
Paige Compositor Manufacturing
   Company, 555, 561
Paige Typesetter, 365, 436, 474, 490–91,
   493, 504, 506, 510, 512, 514, 519,
   520, 525–26, 527, 530–31, 536, 555,
   559–60, 561, 587

Paine, Albert Bigelow, 33*n*, 42, 43*n*, 75, 76, 213, 230, 259, 288, 299, 320, 359, 376, 393, 421, 444, 465, 538, 593, 603, 609, 620–21, 622, 623, 625–27

Paine, Thomas, 36, 81, 521

Paint Brush (mule), 98

Panic of 1837, 20

Paradise Lost (Milton), 424

Paris, France, 424–26

Paris, Mo., 15, 69

Paris, S.S., 565, 577

Parsloe, Charles Thomas, 391, 403, 404

Parsons, Marc, 49*n*

Parthia, 341

Patent Office Building, 68

Pathfinder, The (Cooper), 560

Paul, Saint, 211

Paul Bunyan, 253

Paul Jones, 75

Payne, Colonel, 610

"Peace Appeal to Labor," 592, 602

Peake's Commercial Advertiser, 20

Pennsylvania, 82–86, 442*n*
  explosion on, 86–88, 92, 458, 468

Pepys, Samuel, 80, 351, 392

Perelman, S. J., 125

Pérez Galdós, Benito, 5, 370

Perkins, Charles, 448

Perkins, Mary Beecher, 434

Perkins, W. Epaminondas Adrastus, 1, 58

Perry, Mark, 491

Persia, Shah of, 336, 337

Personal History of Ulysses S. Grant (Richardson), 240, 273

Personal Memoirs of Ulysses S. Grant, The (Grant), 452, 481, 484, 492, 497, 500–501, 503–4, 505, 506, 509, 515–16, 519

Personal Recollections of Joan of Arc, 220, 227, 561, 564–65, 569, 576, 581–82

Peter Cooper Institute, 181, 189, 190

"Petrified Man" (Twain), 112

Pfaff's Beer Hall, 129, 130

Phelps, Roswell, 456, 458, 460, 461, 462

Philadelphia, Pa., 65–66

Philadelphia *Evening Bulletin*, 113, 123

Philadelphia *Inquirer*, 65

Philippines, 593, 600–602

Phoenix, John, 113

Pierce, Eddie, 612

Pittsburgh *Gazette*, 259

Plain Dealer, Cleveland, 129, 131, 132, 258

"Plain Language from Truthful Jane," *see* "Heathen Chinee, The" (Harte)

Plato, 211

Players Club, 544, 555

Plessy, Homer, 548–49

Plutarch, 80

Plymouth Congregational Church, 3, 170, 183, 192, 228

Podhoretz, Norman, 475

Poe, Edgar Allen, 70

Pomeroy, Samuel, 329

Pompeii, 210

Pond, James B., 499, 565, 566, 568, 597

Pony Express, 102, 298

Pope, John, 428

Porter, Naomi, 191

Portrait of a Lady (James), 450

Postal Act of 1792, 56

Potter, Edward Tuckerman, 333, 360

Pratt & Whitney, 519, 527, 530, 536

Presbyterianism, 29, 30–31, 34

Prince and the Pauper, The (Twain), 184, 220, 299*n*, 405, 414, 447, 449, 451, 457, 500, 502
  dramatization of, 531
  England in, 528
  publication of, 453
  reviews of, 453–54, 455
  sales of, 456, 466, 470
  song in, 282
  Stowe on, 507
  writing of, 437–38, 445, 446, 473, 474

Prince of India, The (Wallace), 608

Princess Irene, 616

Principles of Psychology (James), 586

"Private History of a Campaign That Failed, The" (Twain), 98, 99, 100, 503, 543

prostitution, 79–80

Prudence Palfrey (Aldrich), 346

Pudd'nhead Wilson (Twain), 36, 39, 51, 407, 548, 549–51, 553
  calendar in, 545
  father as model for Driscoll in, 14
  publishing of, 550, 556–57
  slavery in, 36

Puerto Rico, 593

Pulitzer, Joseph, 592

Puritans, 29*n*

Quaker City, 3–4, 160, 183, 185, 192–221
  passengers of, 198–200, 202

Quaker's Temptations, The, 191

Quarles, John, 11–12, 15, 41, 69, 151, 298
  as model for Sellers in *The Gilded Age*, 10

Quarles, Tabitha, 12

Quarry Farms, 287, 298, 299, 356, 388, 405, 460, 462, 466, 472, 488, 517, 521, 526, 527, 530, 548, 566, 594, 615
Quartz, Tom, 151
Quimby, Phineas Parkhurst, 570
Quirk, Thomas, 496

Rabelais, François, 165*n*
Ragged Dick (Alger), 294
railroads, 11, 77, 279*n*
Railton, Stephen, 495
Raleigh, Walter, 392–93
Ralls, John, 98
Ralls County Rangers, 98–99
Ramage, Adam, 48
Rambler, 1, 59*n*
Randalls Island House of Refuge, 566
Raymond, John T., 352, 354, 356, 359–60, 485, 507
Raymond, Samuel R., 51
Reconstruction, 224, 225, 366, 393–94, 395, 495, 498, 548, 609
Red Badge of Courage, The (Crane), 100
Red Cross, American, 137
Red Dog, Nev., SLC's lecture in, 166
Redpath, James, 241, 275, 277, 291, 295, 297, 300, 301, 316, 322, 324, 341, 344, 367
Reformation, 29
Refuge of the Derelict, The (Twain), 172*n*
Reid, Whitelaw, 275, 301, 329, 332, 333–34, 336–37, 401, 408, 453, 457–58, 471, 491, 602, 623
"Reminiscences of Some un-Commonplace Characters I Have Chanced to Meet" (Twain), 301, 305, 306
Renan, Ernest, 426
Renoir, Pierre-Auguste, 444
Republican Party, 67, 192
Rhodes, Cecil, 571, 573
Rice, Clarence, 544, 554, 555, 575, 578
Rice, Clement T., 115–16, 120–23, 124
Rice, H. F., 166
Rice, Thomas "Daddy," 17, 35
Richardson, A. D., 232, 233, 240, 273
Riley, James Whitcomb, 556, 564
Riley, John Henry, 292, 323
Rise of Silas Lapham, The (Howells), 479, 487
Ristori, Adelaide, 191, 193
riverboats, *see* steamboats
Robertson, T. W., 132, 186
Robin Hood, 32, 283
Robinson, Henry C., 578

Rockefeller, John D., 279, 366, 552, 583
Rockefeller, William, 583
Roderick Hudson (James), 364
Rodin, Auguste, 444
Rogers, Abbie Palmer Gifford, 560
Rogers, Emilie Hart, 583, 611
Rogers, Henry Huttleston, 552–62, 565–66, 568, 569, 576, 583, 584, 591–92, 601*n*, 608, 610, 611, 613, 623
Rogers, Will, 368, 524
Roman, Anton, 239
Rome, Italy, 208–9
Roop, Nev., 120
Roosevelt, Theodore, 593, 601, 610–11, 623
Rosencrantz and Guildenstern Are Dead (Stoppard), 343
Rossetti, Dante Gabriel, 135
Roughing It, 5*n*, 102, 109, 164, 166*n*, 172, 391, 400, 417
  aborted duel left out of, 141
  early titles of, 303
  Hawaiian trip in, 161
  in lectures, 311–12, 344
  model for Ballou in, 106
  model for Oliphant in, 106
  model for Secretary in, 53
  parody of Nevada legislature in, 106
  publication of, 317–18
  reviews of, 321–22, 325
  sales of, 318, 396, 434, 450*n*, 469
  Sandwich Island lecture in, 163
  Slade in, 103
  writing of, 288, 289–90, 298–99
Rough Riders, 593
Routledge, Edmund, 325
Routledge, George, 325
Royal Humane Society, 334
Ruffner, Ann Virginia, 73
Russell, Lillian, 544
Russia, 212
Russian Revolution, 212
Ruth, Babe, 393, 567
Rutland *Globe*, 338, 363
Rutland *Herald*, 324, 338
Rutledge, Robert, 325
Rutledge, William, 325

Sabine, William T., 294–95
Sacher-Masoch, Leo, 392
Sacramento, 236
Sacramento, Calif., SLC's lecture in, 165
Sacramento *Union*, 109, 160–62, 177, 179, 236

St. Louis, Mo., 62–63, 68, 73
    Sanitary Fair in, 137
St. Louis Apprentice Association, 39
St. Louis *Evening News*, 62, 68
St. Louis *Globe-Democrat*, 490
St. Louis *Post-Dispatch*, 611
St. Louis *Republican*, 188
St. Nicholas Magazine, 544, 546
Salamo, Lin, 317
Salisbury Cathedral, 341
Salt River Navigation Company, 14
"salutation-speech from the Nineteenth
    Century to the Twentieth Century,
    A" (Twain), 605–6
Samossoud, Clara Clemens
    Gabrilowitsch (SLC's daughter),
    388, 406, 426, 433, 451, 471, 486,
    503, 506, 538–39, 543, 553, 574,
    576, 596, 605, 623, 626–27
    Aquarium Club and, 619–20
    birth of, 353
    in England, 580
    father's literary legacy and, 580–81,
        603
    father's temper and, 510–11, 519
    fire in bed of, 449
    Gabrilowitsch's marriage to, 625
    in Germany, 415–18, 539–42
    Harte's affection for, 402
    on Howells, 450–51
    in Italy, 542
    music and, 537, 546, 585, 597, 604,
        613
    nurse for, 375
    on SLC's around the world tour, 565,
        566, 569, 571, 573
    suitor of, 540–41
    Susy's death and, 578
    in Vienna, 590
San Diego *Herald*, 113
Sandwich Islands, *see* Hawaii
Sandy (slave), 12
San Francisco, 173, 174
San Francisco, Calif., 120–23, 143–49
San Francisco *Examiner*, 159
San Francisco *Morning Call*, 121, 123,
    144, 145–46, 148, 158
Sanitary Commission, U.S., 137, 140,
    166, 301
Saroyan, William, 399
Saturday Evening Post, 18
Saturday Morning Club, 438
Saturday Press, 154, 176, 177
Saturday Review, 489
Saviolo, Vincentio, 139
Scaturro, Frank, 394

Scharnhorst, Gary, 391*n*
Schoenberg, Arnold, 353, 589
Schofield, John, 428
"Schoolhouse Hill" (Twain), 41, 595
Schrady, George Frederick, 492
Scotia, 323, 324
Scott, F. M., 514
Scott, Walter, 28, 32, 139, 337, 341, 592,
    599
Screamers, 324
Scribner's, 368, 377, 486
Second Great Awakening, 17
Selkirk, George, 297
Sellers, Isaiah, 78, 94, 118
Senate, U.S., 366
"Separation," 59*n*, 585
Seutonius, 80, 627
Severance, Emily, 198, 218, 223, 228
Severance, Solon Long, 218, 223, 228,
    258
Sewall, G. T., 112
Seward, William H., 67, 101, 104, 190,
    224
Shadow of a Dream, The (Howells), 544,
    596
Shakespeare, William, 69, 80, 148, 242,
    264, 301, 352, 383, 392, 438, 453
Sharon *Herald*, 271
Shelley, Mary, 553
Shelley, Percy Bysshe, 553
Sheridan, Philip, 428
Sherman, William Tecumseh, 3, 146,
    183, 190, 195, 197–98, 225, 270,
    428, 452
Sherry, Margaret, 616
Shurtleff, Roswell, 302
Shute, A. B., 470
Sickles, Dan, 251–52, 395
Simon Wheeler, Detective (Twain), 14, 415,
    474
    father as model for Judge Griswold in,
    14
"1601" (Twain), 122, 392–93, 426, 470
Slade, Joseph Alfred, 102–3, 290
Slason, William, 164
slaves, slavery, 4, 11–13, 37, 40, 67, 68,
    81–82, 231, 270
Slote, Daniel, 195, 200, 203, 208, 213,
    219, 223, 228, 435–36, 449, 451,
    452
Slote, Woodman & Company, 436
Smarr, Sam, 37, 40, 41, 283
Smith, Harriet Elinor, 317, 322, 356
Smith, Henry Nash, 411, 413
Smith, Roswell, 492
Smith, Thomas Kilby, 515

Smithsonian Institute, 68
Smyrniote, 162
Smythe, Carlyle Greenwood, 565, 570, 574
Sneider (metallurgist), 449, 452
Snodgrass, Thomas Jefferson (pseudonym), 1, 73, 118, 131*n*
"Sociable Jimmy" (Twain), 13, 28, 314–15, 332, 353, 356–57, 496
Social Darwinism, 400
"Some Rambling Notes of an Idle Excursion" (Twain), 172, 405
"Some Thoughts on the Science of Onanism" (Twain), 426
Songs in Many Keys (Holmes), 432
Sonora *Herald,* 151
Soto, Hernando de, 468
South, literature in, 19–20
South Africa, 574–76
South Africa Company, 573
South Australian Register, 570
South Carolina, secession of, 95
Southern Famine Relief Commission, 191
Southern Michigan, 64
Spanish-American War, 592–93
Spanish Sketchbook (Irving), 203
Spaulding, Allie, 263
Spaulding, Clara, 263, 334, 335, 353, 358, 415
Spectator, 326, 529
Spencer, Herbert, 337
Spoon River Anthology (Masters), 588
Springfield (Mass.) *Daily Republican,* 268
Springfield (Mass.) *Republican,* 411
Spring Valley Water Company, 127
Stabler, John W., 59
Stage, 191
Standard, 342
Standard Oil, 279, 552, 562, 566
Stanley, Henry Morton, 189, 325, 423, 564, 565
Stanton, Edwin, 226
Stanton, Elizabeth Cady, 301
steamboats, 22–23, 47, 77, 78
Stebbins, Horatio, 260, 267
Stedman, Edmund Clarence, 524–25, 525, 529
Stein, Gertrude, 353
Stephens, Henry Louis, 341
Sterne, Lawrence, 264
Stevens, Thaddeus, 225
Stevenson, Robert Louis, 444, 586
Stewart, William M., 210, 224, 225, 233, 286
"Stirring Times in Austria" (Twain), 591

Stoddard, Charles Warren, 163, 267, 339, 394, 401, 622, 642*n*
Stoddard, Richard Henry, 180, 317
Stoker, Dick, 150–51
Stolen White Elephant, The (Twain), 456, 466, 470
Stomach Club, 426
Stonehenge, 341
Stoppard, Tom, 343
Story of a Bad Boy, The (Aldrich), 294, 307–8, 385
"Story of the Bad Little Boy, The" (Twain), 28
"Story of the Good Little Boy, The" (Twain), 28
Stotts, Susan, 95
Stout, Big Ira, 20, 21, 23, 39
Stowe, Harriet Beecher, 2, 63, 176, 230–31, 243, 251, 347, 360, 507, 520
Strauss, Johann, 590
Strong, Josiah, 601
"Struggles of a Conservative with the Woman Question" (Nasby), 301
Such, Benjamin J., 337
Sunset on the Seine in Winter (Monet), 444
"Superintendent of Dreams" (Twain), 593–94
Supreme Court, U.S., 40, 549
Sut Lovingood, 253
Sutter's Mill, 120
Swain, R. B., 147
Swedish Movement Therapy, 597
Swift, Jonathan, 264
Swinburne, Algernon Charles, 135, 289
Szczepanik, Jan, 592, 597

Talmage, Thomas DeWitt, 285
Tammany Hall, 104
Tangier, 202
Taylor, Ann Elizabeth, 71–73, 80
Taylor, Bayard, 18, 203, 296, 401, 421–22
Taylor, Mary Jane, 71, 72
Tennyson, Alfred, Lord, 264
Terry, Eileen, 520
Tess of the D'Urbervilles (Hardy), 470
Testa, Barbara Gluck, 477*n*
Texas, secession of, 95
Thackeray, William Makepeace, 446
Theater of the Absurd, 343
Their Silver Wedding Journey (Howells), 596
Their Wedding Journey (Howells), 318
"The Killing of Julius Caesar 'Localized'" (Twain), 148

Thinker, The (Rodin), 444
Third House, 135
Thompson, George, 40
Thompson, Samuel, 334, 335
Thoreau, Henry David, 2, 150, 446
Those Extraordinary Twins (Twain), 172n, 548
"1002nd Arabian Night" (Twain), 471
"Three Aces, The" (Byng), 294
"3,000 Years Among the Microbes" (Twain), 620
Thurber, James, 290, 516n
Tichborne, Roger Charles, 438
Ticknor, Benjamin, 446
Ticknor, William D., 2
Ticknor & Fields, 1–2, 446, 469
Tiffany, Louis Comfort, 361
Tilden, Samuel J., 393, 394
Tillou, Combury, 106, 107
Tilton, Elizabeth, 327
Tilton, Thomas, 327, 376
Titanic, 324
Titusville *Morning Herald*, 268
Tocci, Giacomo, 543
Tocci, Giovanni, 543
Todd, Neriam, 37, 38
Tolstoy, Leo, 5, 370, 507, 521, 544
Tom Sawyer, Detective, 556, 564, 576
Tom Sawyer Abroad, 545–47, 557
Tom Sawyer Abroad; Tom Sawyer, Detective and Other Stories, 584
Tom Sawyer's Conspiracy (Twain), 32n
   model for Bat Brandish in, 41
"To My Missionary Critics" (Twain), 607
Torbert, G. L., 241, 247
"To the Person Sitting in Darkness" (Twain), 606–7
Townshend, James W. E., 151
Tramp Abroad, A (Twain), 299n, 354, 418, 419, 420, 422, 433, 439, 465, 473
   reviews of, 434–35, 446
   rough drafts of, 416–17, 427, 466
   sales of, 434, 450, 450n, 469
Transcendentalism, 17, 29, 130, 182, 276, 487, 621
travel literature, 203, 220, 238, 296
Treasure Island (Stevenson), 444
Treaty of Paris, 593, 602
Trilling, Lionel, 494
Trollope, Anthony, 284, 337
Trollope, Francis, 74
Trotsky, Leon, 95
Trouble Begins at Eight, The: Mark Twain's Lecture Tours, 256n
Troy *Times*, 280

"True, I Talk of Dreams" (Howells), 596
True Story, and the Recent Carnival of Crime, A (Twain), 446
"True Story Just as I Heard It, A" (Twain), 28, 36, 356–58
Trumbull, James Hammond, 341
Tucker, Joshua, 30
Turgenev, Ivan, 284, 337, 370
Turkey, 211
Twain, Mark, *see* Clemens, Samuel
Twainian, 313
" 'Twas the Night Before Christmas" (Moore), 433
Tweed, William Marcy, 175, 193, 327, 329, 393
Twelfth Night (Shakespeare), 242
Twichell, Harmony, 270, 281
Twichell, Joe H., 254, 260, 267, 270, 272, 284, 300, 342, 376, 380, 386, 400, 425, 426, 471, 479, 485, 539, 593, 594, 596, 607, 626
   background of, 251–52
   on Bermuda cruise, 405–6
   at Clara's wedding, 625
   in Germany, 415–16, 419–22
   1606 and, 392–93
   SLC's hikes with, 362–63
   SLC's prayer sessions with, 261
   at SLC's wedding, 281
   Susy's death and, 577
Twichell, Julia Curtis, 270, 284
"Twins of Genius" tour, 493, 497–99, 565
Two Men of Sandy Bar (Harte), 391
Two Years Before the Mast (Dana), 351
T. Wrightson and Company, 74

Uncle Dan'l (slave), 12, 13, 95, 132, 151, 278, 521
   in *Gilded Age*, 332, 353
Uncle Remus, 461
Uncle Tom's Cabin (Stowe), 65, 176
Underground Railroad, 243
Ungar Publishing Company, 387n
Unidentified Flying Oddball (film), 524
Union Pacific railroad, 329
Unionville *Northern Californian*, 147
United States:
   "American Nervousness" in, 366–67
   centennial of, 382
   China's Open Door treaty with, 240–41, 317
   culture of, 16–17, 207, 253
   education in, 26
   in 1870, 279
   Gilded Age avarice in, 329
   lecture circuit in, 168

literature of, 17, 19, 130, 150, 176, 220, 234, 276, 296, 367, 370
newspapers in, 46–47
psychic loneliness of, 400
racism in, 224, 366, 498, 548–49
religion in, 17
science vogue in, 263
sophistication of, 435
in Spanish-American War, 592–93
sports in, 279
United States Gazette, 18
"United States of Lyncherdom, The" (Twain), 609
Updike, John, 279
Utopia (Miller), 444

Vanderbilt, Cornelius, 327, 366, 503
Van Gogh, Vincent, 444
Vanity Fair, 131
Van Nostrand, John A., 200, 213, 215, 219
Vatican, 506
Venice, Italy, 207–8
Verga, Giovanni, 5
Verne, Jules, 339, 387, 415
Vesuvius, Mount, 210
Vicar of Wakefield, The (Goldsmith), 572
Vicksburg, campaign of, 120, 123, 430
Victoria, Queen of England, 235, 416, 444, 585
Vidal, Gore, 331
Vietnam, 205
Views A-Foot (Taylor), 18
"Villagers of 1840–3" (Twain), 29, 39, 42, 43, 587–89
    model for Carpenter family in, 29*n*
    model for Carpenter in, 53
Virginia City, Nev., 104–5, 110–11, 119, 123–24, 135
    Menken's act in, 136
    Ward's lectures in, 132
Virginia City *Territorial Enterprise,* 109–14, 125, 129, 130, 132, 149, 151, 157, 166, 298, 373
    fire at, 123
    SLC offered job by, 109
    SLC's leave from, 120
    SLC's letters to, 116–17, 119
    SLC's Sanitary Fair hoax in, 137–40
    SLC's start at, 111–12, 114
    staff imagination at, 112–13
Virginia City *Union,* 115, 124, 139, 167
Virginia *Daily Union,* 138
Virginia House, 21–22, 34, 38, 39
Vishnu Sarma, 17
von Versen, Mollie Clemens, 542

Wadsworth, Charles, 260
Wagner, Honus, 353
Wagner, Richard, 418, 539, 589
Wakeman, Edgar, 171–74, 197, 347, 422, 622
Walker, William, 150
Wallace, Lewis, 444, 608
Walt Disney, 524
Ward, Artemus, 122, 130, 136, 142, 147, 154, 163, 164, 165, 169, 176, 183, 193, 258, 464
    death of, 131–32, 186
    oratorical style of, 132
    SLC compared with, 131
    SLC hoaxed by, 133
    SLC's friendship with, 128, 130–31, 133–34
    SLC's lecture on, 306–7
Warner, Charles Dudley, 268, 334, 344–46, 489, 504, 574, 578, 604
    death of, 604
    Gilded Age and, 328, 331–32
    Roughing It reviewed by, 321
    SLC compared with, 331
Warner, George, 333, 457
Warner, Margaret, 500
Warner, Susan, 328, 574
    Gilded Age and, 329
"War Prayer, The" (Twain), 607, 609, 619
Warramoo, RMS, 569
Washington, Booker T., 553
Washington, D.C., 67–68
Washington, George, 66
Washington *Evening Star,* 307
Washington *Morning Chronicle,* 307
Washington Newspaper Correspondents' Club, 232
Washington *Post,* 609
Washington Square (James), 619
Washoe City, Nev., 103–9, 521
    SLC's lecture in, 166
Was Huck Black? Mark Twain and African-American Voices (Fishkin), 313*n,* 496
Watch and Ward (James), 364
Watson, Thomas, 353
Wave Hill, 611
Way, Frederick, Jr., 624
"Ways That Are Dark" (Scharnhorst), 391*n*
Webb, Charles Henry, 146, 177, 179, 184–85, 189, 230*n,* 239, 290, 520, 608
Webster, Annie Moffett, 83–84, 93, 95, 96–97, 105, 187, 281–82, 285, 302, 310, 326, 451, 515, 519, 577, 635*n*–36*n*

Webster, Charles, 451, 452, 457, 462, 466, 467, 469, 482, 483, 485, 486, 488–91, 504, 505, 506–7, 510, 512–13, 514–15, 518, 519, 525, 537, 577
Webster, Jean, 520
Webster, Samuel Charles, 93, 451, 519–20
Weekly Review, 159, 176
West:
   literature of, 113
   SLC's embrace of, 105
Western Union, 51, 55
Western Whig, 50
Wharton, Edith, 370
"What a Sky-Rocket Did" (Twain), 145
"What is Man?" (Twain), 593, 620
Wheeler, Andrew Carpenter, *see* Crinkle, Nym
Whiskey Ring, 394
Whistler, George Washington, 403*n*
Whistler, James McNeill, 403*n*
White, Frank Marshall, 584–85
White, Stanford, 556
Whitefriars Club, 325
"White Man's Burden, The" (Kipling), 602, 606
Whitman, Walt, 66, 113, 130, 135, 137, 190, 193, 245, 544
Whitmore, Franklin G., 506, 519, 526, 530, 614
Whittier, John Greenleaf, 196, 289, 386, 409–13, 432, 439, 446
Wilde, Oscar, 131, 186, 543
Wilder, Thornton, 312
Wilderness, Battle of the, 428
Wiley, George, 255
Wiley, Margaret, 255
Wilhelm II, Kaiser, 542

Williams, True, 269–70, 302, 341, 378, 383, 482
Willis, Resa, 244
Wilmington, J. W., 140
Wilson, Woodrow, 626
Winans, Thomas DeKay, 403
Wingate, Charles, 317
Wister, Owen, 608
Wodehouse, P. G., 340
Wolf, Jim, 55
Wolfe, Thomas, 65, 312
Wolfe, Tom, 331
"Woman: The Pride of the Professions, and the Jewel of Ours" (Twain), 232–33
Woman of Reason, A (Howells), 479
Woodhull, Victoria, 327, 503
Work, Alanson, 40
Works of Mark Twain, The: Early Tales & Sketches, 55*n*, 59*n*
World War I, 542, 597
Wright, Laura, *see* Dake, Laura M. Wright
Wright, Marshall P., 625
Wright, William, *see* De Quille, Dan

Xenophon, 211

Yanks and Johnnies; or, Laugh and Grow Fat, 524
"Ye Sentimental Law Student" (Twain), 119
Yonge, Charlotte, 438
You Bet, Nev., 166
Young, Dave, 99
Young, Reed, 87
Youngblood, William, 82
Young Men's Christian Association, 477*n*

Zola, Emile, 5, 370

About the Author

Ron Powers is a Pulitzer Prize– and Emmy Award–winning writer and critic. He is the author of ten books and co-author of two, including the *New York Times* No. 1 best-seller *Flags of Our Fathers*.

Powers has written for several periodicals, including, most recently, the *Atlantic Monthly*. He wrote the introduction to *The Tragedy of Pudd'nhead Wilson* and *Those Extraordinary Twins* for a new Modern Library anthology of Twain's works, as well as the profile on Mark Twain for the 2004 edition of the *Oxford Encyclopedia of American Literature*.

He lives in Middlebury, Vermont.